D0000665

BAJA

JOE CUMMINGS & NIKKI GOTH ITOI

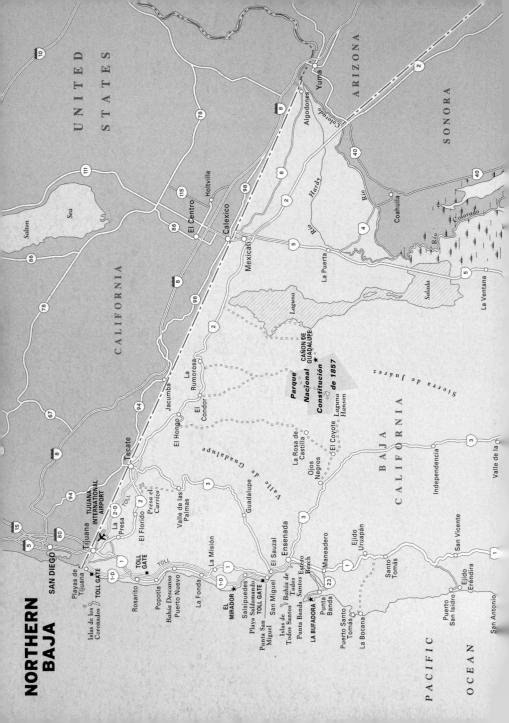

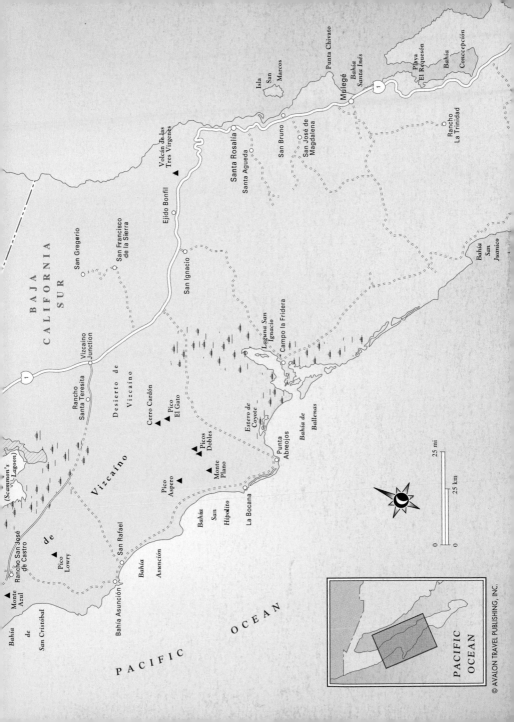

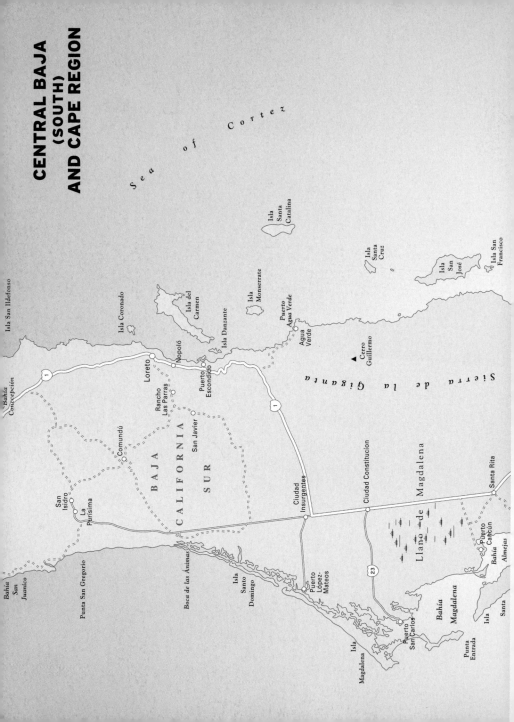

CENTRAL BAJA (SOUTH) AND CAPE REGION

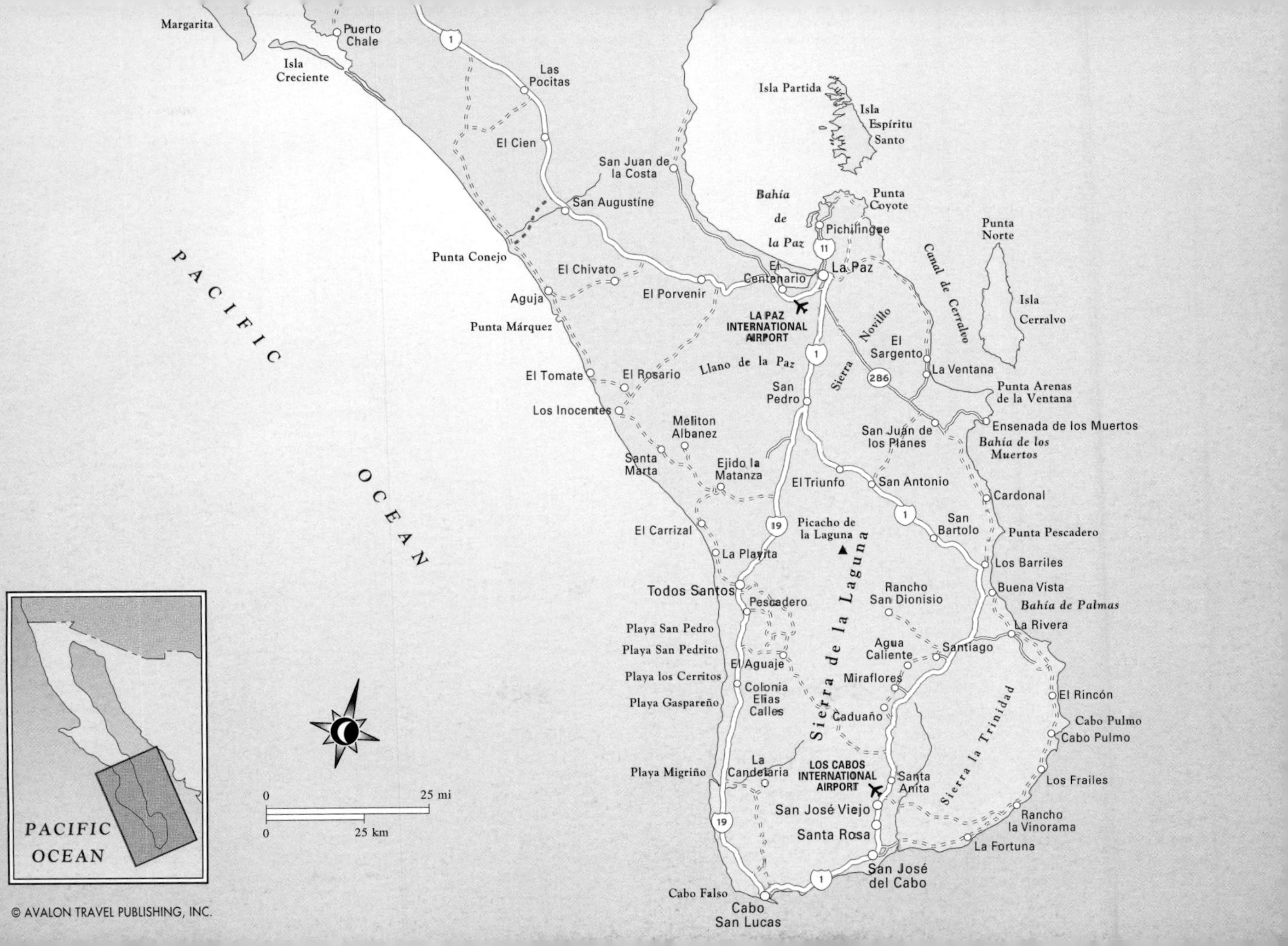
Margarita
Puerto Chale
Isla Creciente
Las Pocitas
El Cien
San Juan de la Costa
San Augustíne
Punta Conejo
PACIFIC OCEAN
El Chivato
Aguja
Punta Márquez
El Porvenir
El Tomate
El Rosario
Los Inocentes
Meliton Albanez
Santa Marta
Ejido la Matanza
El Carrizal
La Playita
Todos Santos
Pescadero
Playa San Pedro
Playa San Pedrito
El Aguaje
Playa los Cerritos
Colonia Elías Calles
Playa Gaspareño
Playa Migriño
La Candelaria
Cabo Falso
Cabo San Lucas
Isla Partida
Isla Espíritu Santo
Bahía de la Paz
Punta Coyote
Pichilingue
El Centenario
La Paz
LA PAZ INTERNATIONAL AIRPORT
Llano de la Paz
Sierra Novillo
El Sargento
La Ventana
Canal de Cerralvo
Punta Norte
Isla Cerralvo
San Pedro
Punta Arenas de la Ventana
Ensenada de los Muertos
Bahía de los Muertos
San Juan de los Planes
El Triunfo
San Antonio
Cardonal
Picacho de la Laguna
San Bartolo
Punta Pescadero
Los Barriles
Buena Vista
Bahía de Palmas
Rancho San Dionisio
Sierra de la Laguna
La Rivera
Agua Caliente
Santiago
Miraflores
Caduaño
El Rincón
Cabo Pulmo
Cabo Pulmo
Sierra la Trinidad
LOS CABOS INTERNATIONAL AIRPORT
Santa Anita
Los Frailes
San José Viejo
Rancho la Vinorama
Santa Rosa
La Fortuna
San José del Cabo
1
11
19
286
0
25 mi
0
25 km
PACIFIC OCEAN

DISCOVER BAJA

All travelers who make the journey to the tip
of the Baja Peninsula remember their first taste of the "real" Baja.
Maybe they chanced upon a baby turtle release and sipped beers
with the conservation guide while watching the little ones tumble
into the sea. Maybe they encountered kindred spirits at a surf break
on the Pacific and decided to caravan around the Cape together.
Or perhaps their 10-year-old pickup truck would no longer shift into
reverse the moment they crossed the border.

The typical pattern goes something like this: Fly to a coastal
destination for a short trip to see what the fuss is all about. Return
for a longer vacation a year later with family or friends in tow. Then
plan a sabbatical, take a leave of absence, retire early, or volunteer to
shuttle supplies to a local charity – any excuse to spend a season exploring every beach and town from Ensenada to Cabo San Lucas.

The first maps of Baja California, drawn by 16th-century Spanish
explorers, depicted it not as a peninsula but as an island. Lured by

a burro looking for lunch

tales of gold cities and a kingdom of warrior women, the conquistadors were among the first in a long line of seekers who have approached Baja's shores with a sense of mystery. Though the maps have long since been corrected, explorers continue to tramp the peninsula with dreams of finding Shangri-La in a hidden canyon or secluded cove.

Scattered along Baja's natural and artificial borders are outward concessions to the modern world – including Mexico's fifth-largest city – as well as sufficient recreational opportunities to satisfy the most hedonistic refugees from that same world. This is one Baja: a peninsula wedged between one of the world's wealthiest and most technologically advanced countries and one struggling to develop with dignity.

But another Baja remains an island, in spite of 21st-century mapping. For four centuries, this Baja has stubbornly resisted the efforts of conquistadors, missionaries, miners, developers, and tourist boards to bring "civilization" into its rugged interior. The fortunate few who make it to the cultural and geographic heart of

pangas **in a harbor on the central Sea of Cortez**

the peninsula will find that it belongs to an era lost long ago to most of North America.

Between these seeming polar opposites, the visitor can pick and choose from a broad spectrum of travel experiences. Whether it's stretching out on a beach towel, margarita in hand, at the edge of the Sea of Cortez, or hoisting a backpack and hiking deep into the sierras – whether it's perusing the art galleries of Todos Santos or wandering the neon-bathed bars of Tijuana – Baja offers something for just about every proclivity.

Standing physically and culturally apart from the rest of Mexico – the former territories achieved Mexican statehood only during the last half century – Baja California (Norte) and Baja California Sur represent a side of the country largely unfamiliar to foreigners and mainland Mexicans alike. Often dubbed "the other Mexico," the 1,000-kilometer peninsula is in some ways more sophisticated, in other ways more untamed, than the mainland. If your mental picture of Mexico conjures up Aztec temple ruins and grand Spanish baroque cathedrals, you're in for a surprise – you won't find these anywhere

Casa Lereé, San Ignacio

in Baja. Most of the architecture visible today in Baja was created only within the last 200 years.

Bajacaliforniano culture likewise stands apart from that of mainland Mexico. Although the cuisine, regional literature, and social patterns of the peninsula share much in common with Mexico as a whole, the visitor will notice myriad small differences. Whether it's the way they fashion rustic furniture from *palo de arco* or the way they fillet halibut for a fish taco, *bajacalifornianos* are proud of the many ways in which they don't conform to the rest of Mexico.

Being the two least-populated states in Mexico, Baja California (Norte) and Baja California Sur have largely escaped the relatively heavier pressures on the natural environment that occur in more densely populated regions of the mainland. Thus opportunities for the enjoyment of one's natural surroundings and for outdoor recreation are, by comparison, greatly enhanced. Baja tends to attract more of a physically active, nature- and sports-loving crowd than the mainland. Fishing, surfing, scuba diving, hiking, camping, birding, whale-watching, and off-highway exploration top the list.

riding the waves

Although this "forgotten peninsula" every year gains more development and better facilities, the farther and deeper you explore, the farther you get from Baja's border cities and main highways, the closer you'll come to the "real" Baja of remote villages, fish camps, empty beaches, and rugged islands. Much of the peninsula remains a true frontier with an attendant frontier ethos. If you run out of gas or need help fixing a tire, don't be surprised to find a seemingly impoverished fisherman or rancher coming to your aid and then politely refusing a fistful of pesos in return, declaring sincerely, "Out here we are all brothers."

Baja has a way of etching itself onto the brain. That plunge into a sparkling freshwater pool high in the mountains. The first night you slept in a hammock under a *palapa* by the sea. The time you hooked a *pargo* from a line cast into the surf. A warm sea breeze, an icy *michelada*... You get the idea. Traveling here is about collecting moments — and forming friendships — that will stay with you forever.

front-row seats at a whale watch

Contents

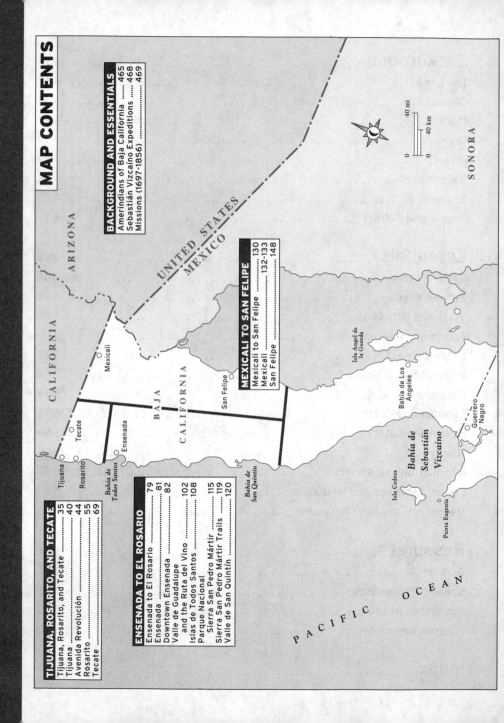

MAP CONTENTS

ARIZONA

CALIFORNIA

UNITED STATES

MEXICO

Mexicali

Tijuana

Rosarito

Tecate

BAJA CALIFORNIA

Ensenada

Bahía de Todos Santos

San Felipe

Bahía de San Quintín

Isla Cedros

Bahía de Sebastián Vizcaíno

Isla Ángel de la Guarda

Bahía de Los Ángeles

Punta Eugenia

Guerrero Negro

SONORA

PACIFIC OCEAN

0   40 mi
0   40 km

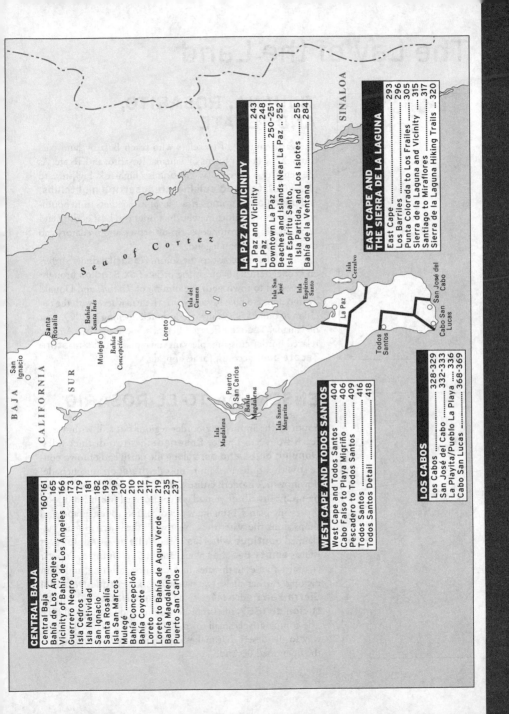

The Lay of the Land

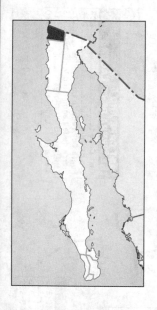

TIJUANA, ROSARITO, AND TECATE

The vast majority of travelers who reach Baja by land pass through the border towns of Tijuana, Rosarito, and Tecate. As the peninsula's largest city, **Tijuana** is a high-risk, high-reward place. **Outstanding cuisine, trendsetting nightclubs,** and **upscale shopping** attract loyal weekenders from Southern California. Unfortunately, the stories you hear of drug and sex trafficking, corrupt cops, rip-off artists, and predatory cab drivers are not urban legend.

On the Pacific coast to the south, **Rosarito** draws surfers and college students on spring break. **Fox Studios** brought Hollywood to town with the filming of *Titanic,* and Donald Trump hopes to take Rosarito to a whole new level with the decision to build a 500-suite condo-hotel, opening in 2009. East of Tijuana, **Tecate** offers a different scene altogether. A more relaxed border crossing, pleasant town plaza, and **signature Tecate beer** account for its appeal.

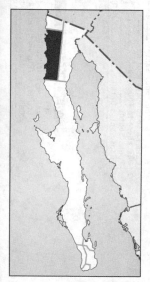

ENSENADA TO EL ROSARIO

South of the immediate border region, but still within easy reach from San Diego, **Ensenada** has two distinct sides: **Hopping clubs and bars** along the north end of town contrast with a quiet and more upscale *malecón* (promenade) downtown. A modern cruise ship port has replaced some (but by no means all) of yesterday's commercial fishing and food processing plants, bringing waves of visitors to restaurants and shops along the waterfront. Nearby are the internationally acclaimed **boutique wineries** of the **Valle de Guadalupe,** as well as **empty beaches** along **Bahía San Quintín.** Popular coastal activities in this area include surfing, fishing, and clam digging. Farther afield, two national parks, **Parque Nacional Sierra San Pedro Mártir** and **Parque Nacional Constitución de 1857,** offer trails for hiking and viewing wildlife. The comparatively small town of **El Rosario** marks the gateway to the desert that makes up the peninsula's interior and the open road beyond.

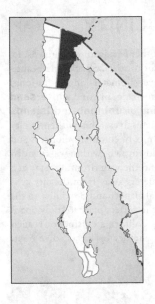

MEXICALI TO SAN FELIPE

Baja California's "other border town" functions as an economic and government center more than as a tourist destination. Second only to Tijuana in population, **Mexicali** is also the state capital. Its palm-lined boulevards lead to quiet suburban neighborhoods, and the **Chinesca** district offers a Mexican twist on Chinese cuisine. Travelers headed to points south will find all manner of supplies here.

Nearby, take a dip in the hot springs in the **Cañon de Guadalupe.** Or head south to **San Felipe** on the Sea of Cortez, where a sizable gringo community has taken hold. Extreme coastal tides, fully occupied RV parks, and a vibrant spring-break scene define the experience along this northern edge of the sea. To the south, hike among towering *cardones* (cacti) in the **Valle de los Cardones Gigantes** or camp on secluded beaches near **Puertecitos** and **Bahía San Luis Gonzaga.**

CENTRAL BAJA

Roughly defined as a 700-mile stretch from El Rosario to La Paz, the Central Baja region is for many travelers the quintessential Baja. Vast stretches of undeveloped coastline present opportunities to view **gray whales** up close, and a unique ecosystem of **desert flora** entertains naturalists and hikers, as well as those who are simply passing through. On the Sea of Cortez, an international airport, **national marine park,** and designation as a government-funded tourist corridor have turned **Loreto** into the largest and best-known destination in this region. Connecting the larger towns of **Guerrero Negro, Santa Rosalía,** and Loreto are historic mission towns like **San Ignacio** and **Mulegé** and the pristine beaches along **Bahía Concepción.** In the **Sierra de San Francisco,** several preserved **rock-art sites** offer a glimpse into Amerindian culture.

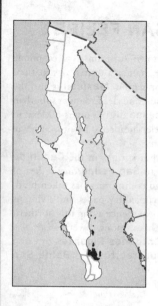

LA PAZ AND VICINITY

Unlike Cabo San Lucas and other Mexican resort towns, La Paz has little need to preen for tourists. Shockingly beautiful sunsets viewed from its five-kilometer-long (3-mi-long) **malecón,** or waterfront promenade, pristine **white-sand beaches** nearby, and a string of **uninhabited islands** just offshore all speak for themselves. This authentic city of 200,000 residents offers a mix of colonial influences and modern conveniences. Stay downtown, within walking distance to shops, restaurants, and the waterfront. Or stay at a beachfront resort a few kilometers away from the city center. With its own international airport and proximity to the peninsula's interior, La Paz is the perfect place to study Spanish, enjoy the emerging Baja California cuisine, or launch an **outdoor expedition**—whether by kayak, dive boat, yacht, or bicycle.

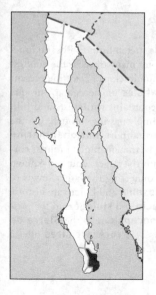

EAST CAPE AND THE SIERRA DE LA LAGUNA

Travelers with a passion for water sports and a willingness to forgo the conveniences of a fully developed tourist infrastructure will find paradise along the eastern shores of the lower Baja peninsula. Here, the Sea of Cortez serves up secluded beaches, steady winds, abundant game fish, a **living coral reef,** and days of 100-foot visibility underwater. For **fishing, diving, kayaking,** and **windsurfing,** conditions don't get much better than this. Development at the northern and southern edges of the region is changing access to some beaches and inviting a less adventurous set to enjoy the views; overall, however, the East Cape remains a place of solar power, dirt roads, *panga* boats, and *palapa* restaurants.

Inland, the **Sierra de la Laguna** attracts hikers, mountain bikers, and horseback riders with cascading **waterfalls,** 7,000-foot peaks, and a chance to experience the rancho way of life.

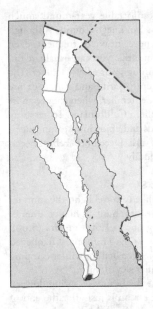

LOS CABOS

It's with good reason that the majority of first-time visitors to Baja plant themselves along the southernmost tip of the peninsula: The contrast of rock cliffs, white-sand beaches, and turquoise water produces **scenery** unlike any other in the world; plentiful **five-star resorts** pamper guests with luxury amenities; and the weather defines perfection.

Once a pair of quiet fishing villages, today's Cabo is a town, resort, and region all wrapped up into one. Los Cabos, as the tourist corridor is now known, refers to the twin cape towns of **San José del Cabo** and **Cabo San Lucas.** San Lucas entertains the young and young at heart with **beach clubs,** bars, and discos, while quieter San José offers a growing number of gourmet restaurants serving *alta cocina mexicana.* Many come to fish and dive, but **world-class golf** and luxurious spa treatments can also be part of the experience.

WEST CAPE AND TODOS SANTOS

North of Cabo San Lucas, strong winds and heavy swell from the Pacific Ocean have sculpted a **rugged shoreline** that extends to the modern-day artist community of Todos Santos and beyond. Experienced surfers camp out here for weeks on end hoping to catch the perfect wave, and a few pioneers have built vacation homes near the water's edge, but for the most part, the West Cape remains the least developed stretch of coastline on either side of the peninsula south of La Paz.

A well-maintained paved road makes **Todos Santos** and neighboring **El Pescadero** easily accessible from La Paz or Los Cabos. Set back from the ocean in a lush oasis environment, Todos Santos has become a crossroads where artists, yoga students, surfers, and retirees all mingle in pursuit of their activities. There is no shortage of **art galleries** to browse, beaches to comb, or interesting people to meet.

Planning Your Trip

Baja offers a world of adventure to many different kinds of visitors. Foodies can delve into a broad range of eating experiences, from roadside *tacos de carne asada* stands to upscale Pacific Rim fusion emporiums. History and culture buffs can busy themselves with Baja's mission churches, festivals, historical museums, and local customs. Active travelers find their choices especially challenging, with world-class sea kayaking, scuba diving, deep-sea fishing, hiking and camping, and mountain climbing all competing for attention.

Travel in Baja can be magical or frustrating depending on your expectations and how well you plan to meet them. If you intend to navigate the entire length and breadth of the peninsula in your own vehicle, you'll want to acquire maps, check road conditions, and assemble an auto repair kit before you go. By contrast, a quick fly-in trip to Los Cabos, La Paz, or Loreto requires less forethought. Once you've arrived in Baja, you can get around most easily by car. Public transportation is a less convenient but more affordable option. With a few exceptions, you can get around the peninsula by bus. Organized tours for whale-watching, kayaking, mountain biking, and other activities typically include transportation by van or bus within the region.

Rosarito, Ensenada, Tecate, and the Valle de Guadalupe are all reachable in a day trip from San Diego, while San Felipe and San Quintín are within striking distance for a weekend getaway. If you plan to fly to destinations farther south, such as Loreto, La Paz, or Los Cabos, allow a minimum of four days; three weeks is ideal for driving the entire peninsula round-trip.

WHEN TO GO
Northwestern Baja

The area encompassing Tijuana, Tecate, Rosarito, and Ensenada lies within the Californian Region and is affected by the mild Pacific climate. It's comfortable year-round, much like California's San Diego County. Although rain is almost never heavy or frequent, even in the winter months, you can usually avoid all rain by planning visits May–October. The beaches between Rosarito and Ensenada are warmest July–September, when they're most visited by Southern Californians. To get away from the crowds and enjoy low-season prices, visit October–April. December–February can be chilly and cloudy.

High Sierras

For those who like to travel light, the summer months are best for mountain hiking; even in July everything above 1,500 meters (5,000 ft) will feel like spring. From mid-October to mid-April, come prepared for winter camping for hikes at similar elevations.

To appreciate the beauty of spring flowers, the best hiking season is just after the end of the rainy seasons: April–May in the north, October–November in the Sierra de la Laguna near Los Cabos.

Deserts

Avoid inland desert explorations May–October, when daytime temperatures are fierce. The remaining cooler months are usually fine, although in the Central Desert, January daytime temperatures may be cool in areas exposed to high coastal winds or at higher elevations. The San Felipe and Gulf Coast Deserts are usually warm and comfortable throughout the winter; however, desert nights can be cold at any time of year.

Sea of Cortez Coast

Along Baja's Sea of Cortez coast, temperatures are moderate October–mid-June. High tourist season is November–March, even though for most people, the north coast is too cool for swimming during these months. Water sports are enjoyable from Loreto south, even in the winter.

From mid-June through September, the entire coast can be uncomfortably hot, and many businesses close for the summer or at least the month of September; the fishing, however, is usually good during these months, as is the diving. And out on the sea it's usually breezy. One of the best times to visit the Sea of Cortez coast is April–mid-June, when the weather is balmy and few tourists are about.

Cape Region

The flat end of the peninsula from San José del Cabo to Cabo San Lucas is warm year-round. Pacific influences generally moderate the heat July–September, while the tropic waters of the Gulf Current make this stretch the warmest coastal zone on the peninsula during winter months. Except for the occasional *chubasco* in late summer, the climate seems darn near perfect here, which is why Los Cabos has become such a popular vacation destination. Cabo San Lucas receives about 45 percent of its measurable annual rainfall—a total of 15–18 centimeters (6–7 in) a year—in September.

August and September tend to be extremely hot. Todos Santos, on the West Cape's Pacific coastline, is considerably cooler than Cabo San Lucas in the summer, and Cabo San Lucas is usually cooler than San José del Cabo or La Paz.

The two months when you're least likely to have Los Cabos beaches to yourself are December and January, when large numbers of North Americans come here seeking respite from rainstorms and blizzards. Crowds dwindle in summer and early fall due to the heat, although anglers and divers keep at least some hotels fully booked during these months as well.

WHAT TO TAKE

Seasoned Baja travelers pride themselves on the detailed nature of their packing lists. Spreadsheets with multiple tabs for each kind of gear are not unheard of. Below are some items to consider. See the *Essentials* chapter for lists of driving, camping, diving, fishing, and surfing supplies.

Documents: Passports are now required for U.S. citizens. Print out confirmations and contact information for your flight, rental car, hotel, and any prebooked activities.

Auto: If you are driving your own vehicle, bring two copies of your Mexican auto liability insurance policy, plus roadmaps and at least a basic auto repair kit.

Gadgets: A camera is a must-have for any trip to Baja. A GPS, laptop, cell phone, and portable music player may also come in handy while on the road, but the more electronics you pack, the heavier your bags will be, and the more you'll have to keep track of your belongings. Even if you don't plan to camp, a headlamp is useful in remote places where there are no streetlights for getting around at night.

Toiletries and First Aid: You can buy just about anything you need in major cities and larger towns, but bring any favorite specialty items from home, just in case. Tums and Pepto come in handy when you OD on the hot sauce. Bug repellent and anti-itch lotion help prevent and soothe insect bites. Hand sanitizer is always a good idea.

Shoes, Clothes, and Accessories: Bring sturdy footwear for walks and hikes, and Tevas or other water-friendly footwear for the beach. Sunhat, sunglasses, and sunscreen are essential. Layers come in handy. Also pack your reading material of choice—English-language books and magazines are hard to find and more expensive here.

Sports Equipment: Consider the size of your vehicle when packing up the sports closet. Camping equipment, fishing rods, scuba gear, and surfboards take up lots of room. Bring straps for securing gear on the roof and repair kits for fixing dings and leaks. Renting equipment is an option in the more developed towns. Even out of the way places sometimes have kayaks and scuba gear available for rent.

Explore Baja

BEST OF BAJA ROAD TRIP

The road may be paved and fuel much easier to come by than in the early days of peninsular travel, but Baja California remains a classic route for travelers who enjoy the thrill of a long road trip. All you need is ample time, a reliable vehicle, and an ability to cope with unpredictable situations. This itinerary follows Mexico 1 from the border crossing in Tijuana to the Los Cabos tourist corridor at the southern tip of the peninsula, 1,000 miles, away, with a few options for sidetrips and off-highway scenic drives along the way.

Day 1

Cross the U.S.–Mexico border at San Ysidro early in the day and head south through **Tijuana** with an optional sightseeing stop to tour the **Foxploration Studios.** Try a lobster roll in **Puerto Nuevo** (30 km from TJ). Make your way to **Ensenada** by afternoon (116 km from TJ). Walk the downtown promenade and spend the night at one of the modest hotels in town.

Day 2

Spend the day tasting **boutique wines** in the rural **Valle de Guadalupe,** a half-hour drive from downtown Ensenada, then pack the car and return to Mexico 1 to continue the drive south. Before Maneadero, take the turnoff to **La Bufadora** to watch seawater explode out of a blowhole in the rocks.

Reach **San Quintín** (190 km from Ensenada) or **El Rosario** (374 km/3 hours) by nightfall. At low tide, dig for clams along **Playa Santa María** near San Quintín.

Alternate Route: If you're in a hurry to reach destinations farther south and have the stamina for a long day of driving, you can skip some of these northern attractions and overnight at **Guerrero Negro** instead.

Day 3

Buy fresh tortillas and stock up on water and groceries in San Quintín or El Rosario, then prepare to make the four-hour trip across the desert. A smorgasbord of cacti—some of them 40 feet tall and hundreds of years old—extends from highway to horizon in all directions. Giant boulder piles, roadside shrines, and jagged peaks of the Sierra de la Asamblea complete the picture. Fill up on gas in **Cataviña** if the station is open, and stay overnight if daylight is waning; otherwise, continue to **Guerrero Negro.**

Sidetrip: After Cataviña, take the paved road east to **Bahía de los Ángeles** on the Sea of Cortez (68 km one-way; add 1–2 days).

Day 4

Back on Mexico 1, a 145-kilometer drive from Guerrero Negro leads to the palm oasis of **San Ignacio.** With more time, you can tour the historic mission, arrange a guided trip to nearby cave paintings, or in winter head west to the Ignacio Lagoon to see the whales.

Sidetrip: South of Guerrero Negro at Vizcaíno Junction, take the 166-kilometer road (paved the first half of the drive) west to the Vizcaíno Peninsula and the sleepy coastal towns of **Bahía Asunción** and **Bahía Tortugas** (6 hours one-way; add 2–3 days).

Days 5-6

Today's journey brings the first glimpse of the shimmering **Sea of Cortez** as you

descend into the former silver mining town of **Santa Rosalía** (74 km). Walk the busy streets of town and note the French influence that lingers long after the mines closed. In the afternoon, follow Mexico 1 to **Mulegé,** 134 kilometers farther south. Spend a couple nights at a B&B along the river in this tropical seaside town, or camp on a remote beach along **Bahía Concepción.** Spend the next two days wandering the town; book a day of diving through Cortez Explorers; snorkel the beaches along Bahía Concepción just south of town; or arrange a guided tour of the nearby cave paintings.

Days 7-9

Pack up for the 135-kilometer (2.5-hr) drive south to **Loreto.** Settle in for a few days to enjoy the wealth of outdoor recreation at your doorstep. A **national marine park,** historic mission, and pleasant *malecón* await exploration.

Excursion: Visit one of the best-preserved **Jesuit missions** on the peninsula in the tiny village of **San Javier,** a 36-kilometer (22-mi) drive southwest of Loreto.

Day 10

Day 10 is a travel day to **La Paz,** 367 kilometers south on Mexico 1. Allow about six hours for the trip, including a brief stop for gas and food in the agricultural supply center of Ciudad Constitución. Book a room near the *malecón* in La Paz in time to catch the sunset.

Sidetrip: During **whale-watching** season (Nov.–Mar.), **Puerto San Carlos** on Bahía Magdalena is worth a drive west from Ciudad Insurgentes (57 km).

Day 11

Spend at least one day at the beach or in the water. Explore the pristine beaches along Bahía La Paz, finishing the day at breezy **Playa Tecolote,** 30 minutes from downtown. Or book a day of diving or kayaking and snorkeling at **Isla Espíritu Santo.**

Day 12

Shop for souvenirs, supplies, and gifts in the morning. Stock up on groceries, and prepare to begin the Cape loop. Next up: the East Cape. It's a 90-minute drive through the mountains and mining-turned-farming towns of **El Triunfo, San Antonio,** and **San Bartolo.** Your particular destination depends on the activities you wish to pursue, the type of accommodations you prefer, and the amount of off-road driving you are willing to do. **Los Barriles** (paved roads only) has several modest hotels, RV campgrounds, a windsurfing camp, and some private vacation rentals; a half-hour farther south, **Cabo Pulmo** has more primitive lodging in solar-powered *casitas* and three dive operators. In between are a handful of fishing lodges and private vacation rentals.

Sidetrip: During the windy season (Nov.–Mar.), drive 40 kilometers southeast from La Paz along BCS 286 to Bahía de La Ventana and the neighboring villages of **La Ventana** and **El Sargento.** Watch the colorful sails of kiteboarders and windsurfers gliding through the chop; or pile in a *panga* for a day of diving at **Isla Cerralvo** across the channel. Return to Mexico 1 via the newly paved road that connects San Juan de los Planes to San Antonio. (Add one day.)

Day 13

Spend today playing on, in, or near the Sea of Cortez, then pack wet gear in the car and continue the Cape loop to the southernmost tip of the peninsula. Prepare for culture shock as you enter the scenic Los Cabos Corridor. After two weeks of relative isolation, the mega-resorts and developed tourist infrastructure of **San José del Cabo** and **Cabo San Lucas** may come as a surprise. Wander the streets surrounding the plaza and Boulevard Mijares to get a feel for San José. Browse the art galleries and Mexican fire opal stores downtown and splurge on a late lunch or early dinner at a restaurant that specializes in *alta cocina mexicana.* Continue along the Transpeninsular Highway to Cabo San Lucas if you're in the mood for a more vibrant nightlife.

Day 14

Snorkel at **Playa Chileno** or **Playa Santa María** on the Corridor. Book a massage at one of the five-star resorts if the mood strikes and budget allows. Tour the marina and downtown area of Cabo San Lucas, and take a water taxi to **Playa del Amor** and El Arco at **Land's End.** Stay the night to enjoy the lively bar and disco scene around town.

Day 15

Now it's time to point the GPS north and explore the West Cape and Todos Santos. Follow Mexico 19 out of Cabo San Lucas. Look for surf, or just have a picnic at one of the rugged beaches west of the highway. Continue north to Km 64 and **Playa Los Cerritos.** Swim, boogie board, or surf at one of the only protected beaches along the West Cape. Then make your way to accommodations on the beach in **El Pescadero** (Km 62) or in the town **Todos Santos,** a few miles farther north.

Day 16

Head northwest across the *huerta* to *el otro lado,* the other side of town, where you can catch waves, cast a fishing line in the surf, or simply stroll the beach at **Playa La Pastora.** In winter, watch for flying mantas and whales breaching just offshore. Around 3 P.M., drive south to **Punta Lobos** to watch local fishermen unload their fresh catch, and buy some dorado or *huachinango* (red snapper) for dinner.

Days 17-18

Complete the Cape loop along Mexico 19 by returning to **La Paz,** where you'll pick up Mexico 1 again. Now it's time to begin retracing your steps, filling in any missed sights or optional side trips along the way. Spend the first night in **Loreto,** after a seven-hour drive, and the next in **San Ignacio** (5 hours) or **Guerrero Negro** (7 hours).

Days 19-20
Leave the state of Baja California Sur early in the morning, and head back across the desert to **El Rosario** (5 hours) or **San Quintín** (6 hours).

Day 21
Today, it's back to civilization. Follow Mexico 1 north to the last military checkpoint at **Maneadero.** At **El Sauzal,** north of Ensenada, choose between the toll road north to **Tijuana,** or Mexico 3, which heads northeast to **Tecate** (105 km). Savor one last meal of tacos and Tecate beer. Then cross the border and leave Baja behind, for now.

FOUR-DAY GETAWAYS

Winter blues got you down? Looking to escape muggy summer days at home? A long weekend in the dry Baja sun may be just the answer. Travelers based in the western United States can reach San Diego, Ensenada, Loreto, La Paz, or Los Cabos by air in a matter of hours. From these international airports, a variety of weekend itineraries are possible. Here are just two of the possibilities.

WINE COUNTRY ESCAPE

Day 1
Cross the U.S.–Mexico border at San Ysidro after the morning rush hour and head south through **Tijuana** and onto the toll road. Stop in **Rosarito** for lunch at **El Nido.** Sit in the shaded back patio if it's not too hot and try the locally raised quail and venison dishes. Walk off lunch by cutting through the Rosarito Beach Hotel and onto the pier that runs 600 yards out over the Pacific. If you have extra time, take the *libre* south out of Rosarito and stop in the housewares stores along the roadside in **Popotla.** If walking and shopping are too tame, keep an eye out between Km 34 and 35 for the **Inner Reef Surf Shop.** Rent a board and ask the staff for the best break to visit for the conditions that day.

The total driving time from Tijuana to **Ensenada** will be less than two hours on the *cuota* and around 2.5 hours on the *libre,* depending on traffic. When you arrive in Ensenada, check into the **Corona Hotel.** Hit the downtown area for dinner, and then head north to **Hussong's Cantina** for a beer. If the spirit moves you, walk to the corner and join the party at **Papas and Beer** until the wee hours of the morning.

Day 2
If you weren't out too late and you've called ahead, hop on a chartered fishing boat with **Sergio's Sportfishing Center.** The rock fishing nearby can be excellent; during the winter months there are **whale-watching** tours.

Back on the docks, take your catch to a vendor in the **Mercado de Mariscos** to have them cook up a custom batch of fish tacos.

Spend the afternoon strolling the shops along López Mateos and visit **La Esquina de Bodegas** for some preliminary wine tasting.

In the late afternoon make your way north out of Ensenada to Route 3. A green overhead sign will welcome you to the **Ruta del Vino.** Check into the Tuscan-style **La Villa del Valle** for the next two nights, and grab a casual dinner at **La Casa Vieja.**

Day 3
After breakfast at the Villa, hang out by the pool

until Steve Dryden, your personal guide to the wine country, arrives in a custom motor coach. He'll take you on a tour of some of the leading Baja wineries, including **L. A. Cetto, Monte Xanic,** and **Chateau Camou.** Remember to carefully choose the single bottle you're allowed to take back home.

You'll appreciate the designated driver on your way to a truly unique dining experience at **Restaurant Laja.** Gourmands flock to this restaurant, calling it a "south of the border Chez Panisse."

Retreat to the Villa del Valle for some much-earned rest.

Day 4

An after-breakfast massage at the hotel will prepare you for the drive home. If you have time, goof off at **Foxploration** and grab a lobster roll in **Puerto Nuevo** on your way north. Get to the border crossing before 3 P.M. on a weekday if you can. If you're crossing on a Sunday, you'll have plenty of time to reflect on your trip as you crawl through traffic back into the United States.

A LONG WEEKEND IN LORETO

Day 1

Arrive mid-day at Loreto International Airport and transfer to a hotel, bed-and-breakfast, or vacation rental in downtown Loreto. Some good choices include **Coco Cabañas, Las Cabañas de Loreto,** or the upscale **Hotel Posada de las Flores.** Stroll the *malecón* and plaza at sunset. Mingle with local expats over dinner at the **Los Cuatros Altos Sports Bar,** or sample the legendary fish tacos at **El Rey del Taco.**

Day 2

Rise early to spend the day fishing, kayaking, diving, or touring the islands in the **Loreto Bay National Marine Park** directly offshore. Then reward yourself with a meal of hearty Argentinian fare at **Pachamama** and drinks at the second-story, open-air **Bar Eclipse.**

Day 3

Sleep in, then visit one of the best-preserved Jesuit missions on the peninsula in the tiny village of **San Javier,** a 36-kilometer (22-mi) drive southwest of Loreto. You can drive yourself, hire a van and driver, or join a guided ATV tour. Finish the excursion with a meal at **Del Borracho Saloon and Grill.** Add an optional 15-minute drive south to tour the FONATUR development at **Nopoló** and have a drink at the seaside **Inn at Loreto Bay.**

Day 4

Take an early morning walk along the waterfront. Enjoy the views over breakfast and an "energy juice" at the **Santa Lucia** café. Browse the shops near the plaza for souvenirs. Take one last dip in the pool, and off you go.

SCUBA DIVING AND SNORKELING

Certified divers with limited time to travel have some difficult choices to make when planning a trip to the inviting waters of the Sea of Cortez. The good news is that wherever you go, you'll encounter one of the world's richest marine ecosystems, with sea lions, numerous whale and dolphin varieties, manta rays, amberjacks, and schooling hammerhead sharks all living amid the more than 100 islands and islets that dot the sea. Larger species native to temperate northern waters mix with colorful, smaller species of tropical origin that have found their way north from Central and South American waters, providing underwater scenery that is especially vivid and varied. Water temperatures are comfortable most of the year; visibility rarely falls below 20 feet and can exceed 100 feet on the best of days.

WHERE TO GO
Cabo San Lucas
One option is to stay close to the lively scene in Cabo San Lucas, where the diving consists of wall dives and boulder fields along a vast **underwater canyon,** plus a one-of-a-kind dive around the point at **Land's End,** during which you descend in the Sea of Cortez and surface in the Pacific Ocean. Short boat rides are an advantage to diving here; crowds and noise from harbor traffic are the main deterrents. Snorkeling near **Playa del Amor** is surprisingly good, despite the crowds. More snorkeling opportunities await at **Playas Chileno and Santa María** on the Corridor.

Cabo Pulmo
Alternatively, you can sacrifice nightlife and amenities to explore the **living coral reef** and national marine park offshore from Cabo Pulmo in the East Cape region. Drift dives are common here, and boat rides are short. Several sites, including a sea lion colony, are ideal for novices. Guides tend to have smaller groups and visit more advanced sites during the week. On Saturday mornings, tour vans from Cabo San Lucas bring mostly novice divers to Cabo Pulmo to see the reef. Snorkelers can access the reef in waist-deep water directly in front of the **Cabo Pulmo Beach Resort.**

La Paz
The **islands** and **seamounts** offshore from La Paz harbor some of the most exciting underwater topography and the largest marine creatures in the sea. Boat rides are long—an hour or more—and currents tend to be strong at these sites. The reward is the chance to experience the deep blue and to spot schooling hammerhead sharks, giant mantas, and the majestic whale shark. In addition, the snorkeling in the bays around **Espíritu Santo** and neighboring islands is as good as it gets.

Loreto and Bahía Concepción
Loreto offers access to **Isla Coronado,** among other islands, and the wreck of a 120-foot **sunken freighter.** Wall dives and underwater caves are additional highlights of the diving in this location. Proximity to historic missions and rock-art sites are another reason to choose the Central Baja region. To the north, the protected inlets of **Bahía Concepción** offer opportunities for snorkeling calm and clear waters.

Pacific Coast
Heavy swells and surging along the Pacific coast mean that Pacific diving should be tackled only by experienced scuba divers or with an experienced underwater guide.

Dive Operators
Dive operators in all of these locations provide expert guiding and instruction services. For those who are seriously dedicated to the sport,

liveaboard trips are another option. Plan on a five-day trip to allow for multiple dive days and at least one rest day. A full week allows time for an excursion to one of the other dive areas.

WHEN TO GO

From La Paz south, onshore water temperatures usually hover between 21°C (70°F) and 29°C (85°F) year-round, making the southern Cortez the most popular diving destination on this side of Baja. Water visibility is best July–October, when it exceeds 30 meters (100 ft); this is also when the air temperature is warmest, often reaching well over 32°C (90°F).

ISLAND HOPPING

Whether you are already a pro or are picking up a paddle for the very first time, kayaks are a perfect way to experience Sea of Cortez marinelife up close. Whales, flying mantas, and sea turtles are just some of the creatures you might see from the surface. Throw on a mask and fins, and an entire world becomes visible below. Beach camping on uninhabited islands completes the experience. Overnight trips can take a couple of days, a full week, or more; organized trips are an appealing option, especially for novices.

WHERE TO GO
Mulegé to Loreto

Many kayakers begin their Baja expedition paddling the islands of **Carmen** and **Danzante,** offshore from Loreto, for a week or more. Protected by land on three sides, 14-mile-long **Bahía Concepción** between Mulegé and Loreto is a good choice for novice kayakers who want to try a multiday paddle. It takes 5–7 days to complete the coastal trip from Mulegé to Loreto.

Loreto to La Paz

A more ambitious coastal route begins in Loreto and ends in La Paz, taking in the island of **Espíritu Santo** at the finish. This 65-mile paddle usually takes 8–10 days. For a shorter trip, make La Paz your home base and spend two or three days camping on the islands offshore.

Bahía de los Ángeles

With its many islets and islands, Bahía de los Ángeles appeals to kayakers of all levels, though the strong channel currents require some caution.

Pacific Coast

Conditions are much rougher on the Pacific, even in the most protected parts of the coast. Experienced kayakers head to **Punta Banda,** an inlet-scalloped cape near Ensenada. **Bahía Magdalena,** a large, protected bay in southern Baja, attracts many kayakers during the winter whale-watching season.

WHEN TO GO

Temperatures are hottest July–September, and winds are strongest November–February, making March–May the best months for a long-distance paddle. Whale-watching trips take place on the Pacific coast November–March.

AROUND THE CAPE IN SEVEN DAYS

Travelers with a week or more can experience the many dimensions of the lower Baja peninsula by making a circular route around the Cape Region via paved highways Mexico 1 and Mexico 19. Extending a total distance of approximately 564 kilometers (350 mi), this route takes visitors along the lower slopes of the Sierra de la Laguna, through the sierra's former mining towns, across the plains of La Paz, and along the coastlines of the East and West Capes as well as the Corridor between San José del Cabo and Cabo San Lucas.

It's possible to complete the loop by bus, but expect to do a fair amount of walking to get from the stops along the highway to the scenic coastal areas. A rental car affords more flexibility and convenience, and you can park easily in all of the towns along the route.

This loop can be comfortably driven in two or three days, but since there are many towns worth exploring and activities to enjoy at each stop, most travelers prefer to allow a week or longer. For more of an adventure, consider widening the loop by taking the sandy Camino Rural Costero, or Rural Coastal Road.

Day 1

Arrive at Los Cabos International Airport (SJD); transfer to a hotel in downtown **San José del Cabo** and spend the evening around town. Browse the art galleries and Mexican fire opal stores downtown before sitting down to a leisurely dinner at a restaurant serving *alta cocina mexicana*.

Day 2

Drive to **Cabo Pulmo** via Mexico 1 (1–1.5 hrs), exiting at La Ribera and heading east to pick up the coastal road. The last few miles will be on dirt road. Head straight for the beach and spend the rest of the day **snorkeling** the live coral reef that comes all the way into shore. Order fish tacos and an icy *michelada* for dinner at the *palapa* restaurant on the beach, or stop by Nancy's Restaurant and Bar for a more upscale experience. Book your activity of choice for the next morning: Fishing, kayaking, and diving top the list.

Sidetrip: At Santiago, head west to reach the **Cañon de la Zorra** and a 30-foot waterfall, just a 10-minute walk from the parking lot.

Alternate Route: To avoid the off-road driving and relatively primitive accommodations, skip Cabo Pulmo and stay on Mexico 1 until **Los Barriles,** popular with anglers, windsurfers, and kiteboarders.

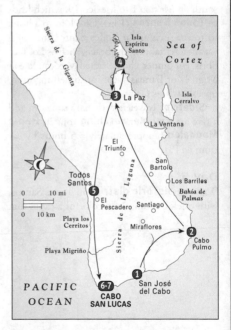

Day 3

Spend the morning out at sea, and in the afternoon continue north along Mexico 1 to **La Paz** (1.5–2 hrs). Check in to a downtown hotel and walk the *malecón* at sunset. Seek out seafood at Mariscos Moyeyo's or *arranchera* at Rancho Viejo, then head to

Casa de Villa or Las Varitas for drinks and live music.

Day 4

Take a *panga* shuttle to **Isla Espíritu Santo** for a day of kayaking and snorkeling, or book a day of diving. Alternatively, paddle or drive to a few of the beaches along the Pichilingue Peninsula. Enjoy the views from one of the waterfront seafood restaurants at **Playa Tecolote.** Spend the remaining time this morning exploring the **Museo Regional de Antropología e Historia** in downtown La Paz, and shopping for pottery and other crafts.

Depart La Paz in the afternoon, heading south on Mexico 1 to Mexico 19, which leads to **Todos Santos** (1 hr). Check in to a hotel in town, such as the Todos Santos Inn, or a vacation rental near the beach, such as Los Colibrís. For dinner, choose casual Mexican fare at Miguel's or Barajas Tacos, or something more upscale at Tres Gallines.

Sidetrip: Travelers with extra time can add a day for a **whale-watching** tour in **Bahía Magdalena,** approximately 3.5 hours by car from La Paz.

Day 5

Walk the **historic district** in Todos Santos, with brick buildings and colorful facades that date back to the town's status as Baja's sugarcane capital in the late 19th century. Admire the artwork in a few of the town's dozen **galleries.** Drive north along the coast to **Playa La Pastora** or south along Mexico 19 to **Playa Los Cerritos,** at Km 64, to stroll the beach in the afternoon. Continue south along Mexico 19 to reach **Cabo San Lucas** before dark (1 hr). Check in to a hotel in downtown Cabo San Lucas or a resort along the Corridor, such as the Sheraton Hacienda del Mar. Make a reservation at Nick-San Restaurant for outstanding sushi, and later taste Baja California's best wines at Sancho Panza Wine Bistro and Jazz Club Restaurant.

Day 6

Hire a water taxi, paddle a kayak, or rent a WaveRunner to visit **Playa del Amor,** or plan a day of fishing or diving out of Cabo San Lucas. Wander the shops and enjoy afternoon cocktails at The Nowhere Bar or the Giggling Marlin along the marina. Take a nap so you can rally for the nightlife at Cabo Wabo or El Squid Roe after dark.

Day 7

Schedule a massage for your last morning in paradise. Take a dip in the pool, hit the shops, and return to the airport with sand in your shoes.

TIJUANA, ROSARITO, AND TECATE

The northwestern corner of Baja California holds two contrasting border towns: At one extreme is metropolitan Tijuana, one of the youngest cities in Mexico, with its upscale dance clubs and trendy restaurants. Less than 50 miles away, laid back Tecate is the oldest border town in Baja and maintains the feel of an authentic Mexican community. South along the coast, Rosarito has become a favored weekend getaway for San Diego and Los Angeles residents, except during March and April, when spring breakers from across the western United States come to town.

PLANNING YOUR TIME

Many travelers try to minimize time spent hanging around the border in order to have more time at their eventual Baja destination; however, Tijuana, Rosarito, and Tecate each has its ap-peal. You might spend a day, a weekend, or, in the case of Rosarito, a whole week enjoying the culture and adjusting to the change of pace.

A popular weekend itinerary involves crossing from San Diego into Tijuana, heading south to Rosarito and Ensenada, then northeast via Mexico 3 and the Ruta del Vino (Wine Route) to exit at Tecate.

If you're heading all the way to Baja California Sur, you can cover the length of Baja California (Norte) from Tijuana to Guerrero Negro in one long day, or, more comfortably, with a stopover in San Quintín or El Rosario.

Climate

Northwestern Baja lies within the Californian Region and is affected by the mild Pacific climate. Hence it's fairly comfortable year-round,

© PAUL ITOI

TIJUANA

HIGHLIGHTS

◖ **Zona Río Dance Clubs:** The trendsetting clubs in Tijuana's upscale Zona Río pack thousands of people onto their dance floors every night (page 42).

◖ **Rosarito Beach:** A string of mega-clubs along Rosarito Beach provide 24/7 entertainment for American college students during the annual spring break holiday (page 56).

◖ **Estudios de la Playa (Fox Studios Baja):** One of the more unusual attractions in Baja is the Hollywood theme park Foxploration, where visitors go behind the scenes of a working movie house to learn about the process of producing a blockbuster film (page 63).

◖ **Parque Hidalgo:** Food and festivities center on Tecate's shady plaza, making it a fitting starting point for many northern Baja tours (page 70).

◖ **Tecate Brewery:** While in Tecate, tour the plant that produces Baja's most popular brew. Located on the site of the original keg brewery, today's operation uses modern, high-tech equipment to produce 40 million liters per month (page 70).

LOOK FOR ◖ TO FIND RECOMMENDED SIGHTS, ACTIVITIES, DINING, AND LODGING.

much like California's San Diego County. Although rain is almost never heavy or frequent, even in the winter months, you can usually avoid rain altogether by planning visits anytime from May to October. The beaches between Rosarito and Ensenada are warmest July–September, when they're most visited by Southern Californians. To get away from the crowds and enjoy low-season prices, visit between October and April. December to February can be a bit chilly and cloudy, so if maximum sunshine is your objective, head farther south.

Tijuana and Vicinity

With a population approaching 1.5 million, Tijuana is the seventh-largest city in Mexico. It's also one of Mexico's youngest cities, established as a line of defense against American freebooters like William Walker following the Treaty of Guadalupe Hidalgo in 1848. During the U.S. Prohibition era, when Americans flocked south to the city's casinos, cantinas, and bordellos, Tijuana developed a bawdy, rough-and-tumble reputation. That image persists in the minds of many gringos, though the city has long since changed.

Today's Tijuana is a rapidly modernizing, bicultural city, where skyscrapers and shopping malls have replaced yesterday's shantytowns, and discos outnumber cantinas. A nearby industrial zone supports more than 500 maquiladoras, or in-bond plants, where international companies such as Sony, Kodak, and Mattel manufacture export products. Tijuana's colleges and universities (Colegio de la Frontera Norte, Iberoamericana University, Universidad Autónoma de Baja California) attract students from all over the peninsula as well as northwestern Mexico.

For some visitors, "TJ" is merely a gateway to Baja, while for others—especially San Diegans—it's a destination in its own right. Like the rest of Baja, Tijuana enjoys duty-free status; hence one of its main attractions is

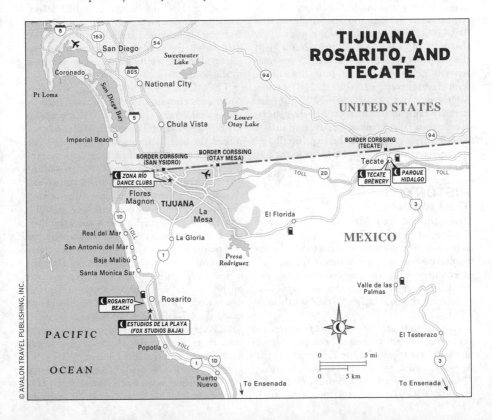

TIJUANA, ROSARITO, AND TECATE

shopping—everything from Casas Grandes pottery to Tequila Sauza to Louis Vuitton luggage is available at discount prices. Avenida Revolución, once the city's booze-and-gambling center, is now lined with restaurants, cafés, and boutiques. Bullfights are no longer the only cultural attraction; the Tijuana Cultural Center and other city venues host symphonies, theater, art exhibits, and other events, thus firmly establishing Tijuana as the cultural heart of northern Baja.

And yes, you can still don a glittering sombrero and have your photo taken sitting atop a zebra-striped burro, in front of a cloth canvas painted with famous Aztec royals.

CLIMATE
As in nearby San Diego, the climate in Tijuana is moderate year-round. November–March, temperatures average 16°C (60°F) during the day, 12°C (53°F) at night. Rain is more likely this time of year but shouldn't deter a visit; the city generally receives less than 25 centimeters (10 inches) per annum. June–September, temperatures average 22–29°C (72–85°F) during the day and 18–21°C (65–70°F) at night. It rarely rains in summer; on still days, however, a thin layer of smog (originating in Los Angeles) may collect over the city. In fall and spring, daytime temperatures hover in the low 20s C (70s F).

HISTORY
The Frontier
Before the end of the Mexican-American War in 1848, when the Río Tijuana was designated as the westernmost portion of the U.S.–Mexico border, no town as such existed in the shallow river valley. Until the postwar border agreement, the border between Alta and Baja California lay about 20 miles farther south near El Descanso.

San Dieguito and Yumano Amerindian cultures intermittently occupied the area before the Spanish came in the late 17th century; the Yumano called the valley Ti-wan, meaning "Near the Sea." Early 19th-century maps refer to today's Río Tijuana as Arroyo de Tijuan,

obviously a Spanish rendering of the Yumano name. A local Mexican ranch in existence as early as 1809 was called Rancho Tia Juana— "Tijuan" had no Spanish meaning and "Tia Juana" (Aunt Jane) was easier to pronounce. Anglo settlers in California somehow latched onto this name, and today many Americans persist in calling the city "Tia-wana." The pronunciation might have remained a Southern California colloquialism if it hadn't been for the Kingston Trio's 1959 international hit "The Tia Juana Jail."

In the 1870s the Mexican government established a small customs house at the border, but Tijuana would probably have remained nothing more than a ranching area if it hadn't been for the development of San Diego across the border. In 1887 a savvy developer built the sprawling Hotel del Coronado, which advertised the locale's favorable year-round climate and quickly became a famous resort. A minor gold rush in the El Alamo area of northern Baja in 1888 brought additional American attention to the border area.

The Mexicans, knowing that wherever Americans congregated there was a danger of losing real estate, created the "Pueblo de Tijuana," or Town of Tijuana, in 1889 and promoted the local hot mineral springs, Pozo de Agua Caliente. A small bathing resort established at the springs extolled the virtues of the water for treatment of rheumatism and arthritis, attracting visitors from across the border. During the Spanish-American War in 1898, San Diego grew further with the establishment of a U.S. naval base, and following the war many Navy men and their families chose to remain in the San Diego area. By the turn of the 20th century, local entrepreneurs had opened several small resort hotels in Tijuana to compete with those in San Diego. Visitors made the 64-kilometer (40-mi) trip between San Diego and Tijuana by horse or stagecoach; since there was no bridge in those days it was necessary to ford the Río Tijuana.

U.S. attention focused on Tijuana during a local revolution in the early 20th century. Following the 1910 Mexican Revolution, a group of Industrial Workers of the World (Wobblies), affiliated with the Mexican Liberal Party and under the leadership of Ricardo Magón, briefly took control of the town. Hundreds of San Diegans watched from the U.S. side of the border as Mexican federal troops entered Tijuana on June 22, 1911, to rout the Magonistas, killing 31 rebels. This was the first time many Americans had heard of Tijuana.

Prohibition and Tourism

The town's frontier image was further enhanced in 1915 when the Tijuana Fair proffered bullfights, horse racing, boxing, cockfighting, and casino gambling. Curious San Diegans came in droves for the event, but Tijuana returned to its sleepy state once the fair was over. The city boomed practically overnight, however, when the San Diego city government banned cabaret dancing in 1917; as Tijuana's casinos and cabarets multiplied, the city began drawing visitors from Hollywood—only a three-hour drive away.

The 1920 grand opening of Tijuana's magnificent El Casino de Agua Caliente coincided with the announcement of the 18th Amendment to the U.S. Constitution, which prohibited the sale, manufacture, and consumption of alcoholic beverages. Well-heeled U.S. residents flocked to the plush new casino, which had no peer anywhere in the Americas. The lavish interior blended art deco, Spanish colonial, Moorish, and French provincial designs; Hollywood glitterati such as Douglas Fairbanks, Jean Harlow, Rita Hayworth, Clark Gable, Dolores del Rio, and the Aga Khan danced on its Italian marble floors beneath Louis XV chandeliers.

As the Tijuana highlife boomed, rich American and Mexican investors poured millions of dollars into developing more racetracks, casinos, hotels, restaurants, and high-class bordellos. Mexicans from the interior of Mexico, hearing that the gutters of Tijuana ran with money (literally true inasmuch as drunk Americans were notorious for dropping change and greenbacks as they stumbled in and out of taxis), rushed to Tijuana as well.

Post-World War II Tijuana

Tijuana's golden days of sin lasted until the repeal of Prohibition in 1933. The ensuing slump became a crash when President Lázaro Cárdenas outlawed casino gambling in 1938 and expropriated all the resorts and lands around Agua Caliente, including those owned by Mexicans. Baja—and the rest of Mexico—was able to reverse its precipitous economic decline only after the outbreak of World War II. To alleviate unemployment in the border area, and to provide needed labor for the wartime U.S. economy, the United States and Mexico created the Bracero Program in 1942; this program gave Mexican workers the temporary right to work for American agricultural concerns in California. Another action that prevented Tijuana from becoming a ghost town was the declaration of Baja California as a duty-free zone.

The expansion of San Diego's military presence during World War II brought a new prosperity to the San Diego–Tijuana area, and shopping gradually replaced boozing and gambling as the main Tijuana attraction. Many Californians crossed the border regularly to purchase items rationed in the United States during the war—stockings, butter, meat, gasoline. Eventually, Tijuana began to grow even faster than San Diego; between 1950 and 1970 the city's population grew 600 percent. This growth severely taxed the city's infrastructure as Tijuana became ringed by shantytowns practically overnight.

The situation of too many people and too few jobs created problems on both sides of the border. Although the United States discontinued the Bracero Program in the early 1960s, the flow of migrant labor to California continued. Improper sewage and garbage disposal on both sides of the border threatened to turn the San Diego–Tijuana area into an environmental disaster. Periodic flooding of the Río Tijuana was a bane to communities on either side as unchecked development came ever closer to the river.

Because there was simply no alternative, U.S.–Mexico cooperation over the last 25 years has begun to deal successfully with these problems. The arrival of the maquiladoras in the 1970s and

LA FRONTERA

We often think of international borders as thin lines separating entirely different worlds – geopolitical reference points that symbolize a great gulf between cultures. But the reality along the United States–Mexico border is that this jagged line – extending 3,326 kilometers (2,062 mi) from the Gulf of Mexico in the east to the Pacific Ocean in the west – acts more as a glue binding cultures together.

Here First World meets Third World, and northern-European Protestant capitalism meets southern-European Catholic feudalism, forming a third, hybrid culture that's neither American nor Mexican. This newer world has its own name, "La Frontera" – the frontier – and its own culture, *fronteriza*. White Anglo-Saxons dine on fish tacos and breakfast burritos regularly and celebrate the availability of inexpensive, handmade leather boots, while mestizos (Mexicans of mixed Spanish and Amerindian ancestry) patronize Pizza Hut and use installment plans to purchase Japanese-made washing machines at Wal-Mart – all without ever crossing the border.

MAQUILADORA

As a cultural region, La Frontera extends as far as 100 miles north and south of the border. Despite the fact that Mexico ranks as America's second-largest trading partner, this wide swath contains some of the poorest areas in either country. The burgeoning twin-plant *(maquila* or *maquiladora)* industry along the Mexican side of the border, in which American – and, increasingly, Canadian, European, and Japanese – technology and management exploits cheap Mexican labor, was supposed to be the hope of the future for the borderland. Goods produced at these plants are granted special trade status because they're established in "export processing zones" using U.S. capital. But the *maquilas* have been heavily criticized in recent years for their contribution to regional air and water pollution as well as worker exploitation.

As the number of *maquilas* increases, more unemployed Mexicans migrate to Northern Mexico in hopes of landing steady though low-paying jobs. Once on the border there's the attraction of higher-paying work just over the river, so labor tends to flow back and forth according to supply-and-demand forces in the border labor market. Many Mexicans work on the U.S. side during the day and sleep at home in Mexico at night.

HUMAN SMUGGLING

The westernmost 27 kilometers of the border – between the Otay Mountains and the Pacific Ocean – is commonly called *la tierra de nadie* (no man's land) and is the busiest area of illegal human traffic in the world. Ninety percent of all illegal entries into the U.S. state of California occur here. Visitors driving south just north of the Tijuana international gateway often see Mexicans running alongside the freeway as they make their way into or out of Mexico – part of the daily commute. Made from surplus Gulf War materials, the corrugated metal fence running along the border has had an arguable effect on migration patterns but has not stopped the flow. The fence has become a canvas for graffiti artists on the Mexico side. Slogans scrawled on the metal compare the fence to the Berlin Wall; whether to call it a "fence" or a "wall" has become very much a political choice on both sides of the line.

For more permanent immigration, and to better avoid the U.S. Border Patrol, "coyotes," or *polleros*, regularly smuggle groups of 7-10 *pollos* ("chickens," undocumented immigrants) across the border, delivering them to Los Angeles for fees of US$300-400 per Mexican, US$400-500 per Central American. Portions of these fees are used to pay safe houses and drivers along the way. Once they've arrived, the immigrants easily blend into the huge, ever-growing Latino population in Southern California.

1980s alleviated unemployment to some degree, and stricter law enforcement is halting much of the environmental damage caused by uncontrolled waste disposal. Channelization of the Río Tijuana at the border, under the auspices of the International Boundaries and Water Commission (IBWC), solved the flood problem.

More recent economic reform at the national level allowed Tijuana a wider selection of resources, including foreign investment, with which to develop a livable city. Visitors who haven't been to Tijuana for some time may be surprised to find the city has made great strides during the last decade or so and now enjoys one of the highest standards of living of any city in Mexico. Conditions have improved to such a degree that many U.S. citizens who work in San Diego now reside in Tijuana, where living costs are at least a third lower than those north of the border.

SIGHTS
Centro Cultural Tijuana
One of the city's most distinctive monuments, this huge, government-built complex (tel. 664/684-1111, www.cecut.gob.mx), at the intersection of Paseo de los Héroes and Avenida Independencia, was designed by Pedro Ramírez Vásquez—the same architect responsible for Mexico City's Museum of Anthropology. Its centerpiece is the spherical **Space Theater,** meant to resemble the Earth emerging from a broken shell.

The center's **Museum of Mexican Identities** features historical, anthropological, and archaeological displays focusing on various Mexican ethnic groups. The exhibits pack a lot of information into a relatively compact area negotiated by an ascending ramp—a pleasant change from the angular stairways found in most museums. The museum is open weekdays 9 A.M.–7 P.M., weekends 10 A.M.–7 P.M.; guided English-language tours are offered at 1 P.M. Museum admission is US$2.

Other cultural center facilities include a 1,000-seat performing-arts theater where the National Symphony and Ballet Folklórico perform regularly, exhibit halls with rotating art exhibits, a cafeteria serving *platillos típicos,* a

bookstore specializing in materials on Baja California, a shopping arcade with shops selling Mexican arts and crafts, and an outdoor area where cultural performances take place in summer. The cafeteria, bookstore, shops, and ticket windows are open daily 10 A.M.–7 P.M.

Tijuana Wax Museum
Located in the former chamber of commerce building, the wax museum (Calle 1 8281 at Av. Madero, tel. 664/688-2478) presents more than 80 Mexican and international celebrities (Marilyn Monroe, Elvis, John Lennon, Lola Beltrán), horror faves (Jack the Ripper, the Wolfman), and Mexican historical figures (Pancho Villa, Miguel Hidalgo y Costilla). This is a good place to kill time if you're waiting for a bus at the nearby downtown terminal. Admission is less than US$2 and pictures are allowed; open daily 10 A.M.–7 P.M.

Tijuana Arch and Monumental Clock
This controversial addition to the skyline is located at Avenida Revolución and Primera, but it is visible from most of the city. To its backers, it's the symbolic gateway to Baja, but to most locals it's a visual hangover from the Y2K celebration. Either way, it's a good landmark to meet your friends after a long night in TJ.

Catedral Nuestra Señora de Guadalupe
At Calle 2 and Avenida Constitución, this large, urban cathedral is worth a visit only if you're Catholic or you've never seen a Mexican cathedral. The interior is perhaps more impressive than the exterior. Vendors on the adjacent sidewalks sell Catholic ritual objects. Once your spiritual needs are sated, there are also several vendors selling churros and *elotes* out front.

Parque Teniente Vicente Guerrero
Tijuana doesn't have a *zócalo,* or public square, but four blocks west of Avenida Revolución off Calle 3 is a park where late-afternoon strollers may tarry for a few minutes or hours. It's dedicated to the heroes of the 1911 Tijuana battle

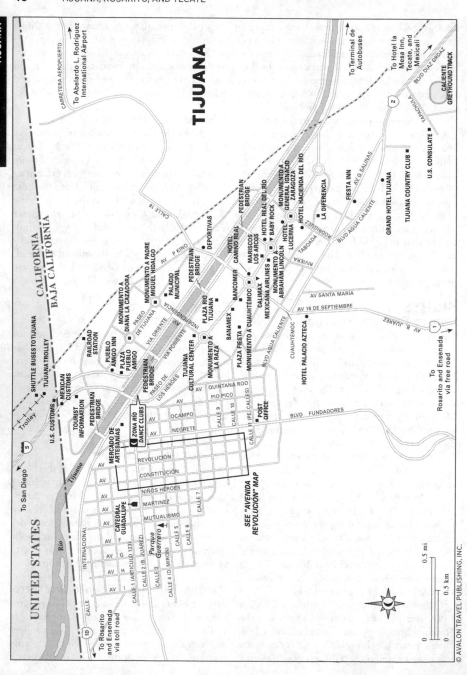

TIJUANA

© AVALON TRAVEL PUBLISHING, INC.

against the Magonistas; the park's namesake, Lieutenant Guerrero, led the federal troops who quashed the rebellion.

SPORTS AND RECREATION
Galgódromo Caliente
(Caliente Greyhound Track)

Tijuana's first racetrack opened in 1916 just 400 meters south of the current border crossing, in response to a 1909 ban on pari-mutuel betting in California. Business was good right from the start, and when Prohibition sent even greater numbers of Californians south of the border, a larger track was needed. The Hipódromo Agua Caliente (Agua Caliente Horse-Racing Track) was constructed in 1929 following the highly successful 1928 opening of Tijuana's El Casino del Agua Caliente.

Caliente is 12 kilometers (8 mi) south of the international border on Boulevard Agua Caliente, just east of the Plaza Agua Caliente twin towers. Red-and-black route taxis marked La Mesa pass in front of the entrance, as do green-and-cream city buses.

Horses no longer pound the turf at Caliente—thoroughbred racing has been discontinued—but greyhounds run nightly at 8 P.M., with 2 P.M. matinees on Saturday and Sunday. Grandstand seating is free.

Race and Sports Book

Sporting folk don't have to go all the way out to Caliente Greyhound Track to make a wager, as Tijuana offers several venues for sports and off-track betting closer to the border. These legal betting lounges feature plush bars and restaurants, plus banks of closed-circuit TV monitors, so you can keep up with your wagers or just watch for fun. Sports bets are based on line odds direct from Las Vegas, and all wagers and payoffs are in U.S dollars. Taxes are paid by the booking establishments, so what you see on the tote board represents your take-home winnings.

Caliente Race and Sports Book occupies locations at the Plaza Pueblo Amigo (Paseo de Tijuana, Zona Río), the Grand Hotel Tijuana, the Caliente Greyhound Track, and at Avenida Revolución and Calle 8. All book lounges keep the same hours: Monday–Friday 9 A.M.–1 A.M., Saturday and Sunday 8 A.M.–1 A.M.

Caliente operates a free minivan shuttle between the border and each of its racing and sports-book locations. The shuttle runs daily every half hour 9 A.M.–1 A.M.

Bullfights

The bullfight season in Tijuana runs May–November—usually two *corridas* in May, one in June, and twice monthly thereafter through October. The city supports two permanent bullrings. El Toreo de Tijuana was the oldest and most atmospheric location, but it was torn down in early 2007. The **Plaza Monumental** (Paseo Monumental, tel. 664/680-1808) is approximately 10 kilometers (6 mi) west of the city, in the Playas district next to the Pacific Ocean. Dubbed the "Bullring-by-the-Sea," this huge, stadiumlike edifice is reportedly the world's second-largest bullring; when the world's top matadors visit Tijuana, they always perform at the Plaza Monumental.

During the bullfight season, tickets are sold Wednesday–Sunday 10 A.M.–2 P.M. and 4–6 P.M. Tickets usually go on sale the Thursday before the scheduled event. You can purchase tickets at Ticketron (Ticketmaster) outlets in San Diego (tel. 619/220-8497) and Los Angeles (tel. 213/480-3232), San Diego's Santa Fe Depot (tel. 619/239-9021), Mexicoach (tel. 619/428-9517) in San Diego or Tijuana, the bullfight information booth on Avenida Revolución, in front of the Hotel Lafayette between Calles 3 and 4, or at the bullrings themselves.

Baseball

Tijuana claims its own pro baseball team, Los Potros (The Colts, www.potrosdetijuana.com), who play other ball clubs in the Mexican-Pacific League as well as the occasional visiting team from the United States or Central America. Games are played at the exemplary 15,000-seat **Estadio de los Potros** (tel. 664/625-1056) off Blvd. Los Insurgentes near the Otay border crossing. The Mexican baseball season runs approximately from the end of the American World Series through late January. The games are popular and parking is tough. Game admission costs around US$10.

Golf

The **Club Campestre Tijuana,** or Tijuana Country Club (tel. 664/681-7855, www.tijuanacountryclub.com), off Boulevard Agua Caliente near the Caliente Greyhound Track, offers a decent 6,800-yard, par-72, 18-hole course. The Mexican Open is played here on occasion. Greens fees from US$18–45. Driving range, pro shop, and golf instruction are available.

ENTERTAINMENT

Although Tijuana is considerably tamer now than during Prohibition, it still has some nightlife—albeit of a more polished sort. For the most part, the entertainment center has shifted from the La Reforma district around Avenida Revolución to the Zona Río along Paseo de los Héroes.

⟨ Zona Río Dance Clubs

The Zona Río boasts some of the largest and liveliest clubs in the world. Plaza Pueblo Amigo is one of the most happening dance spots in Tijuana on weekends. Any night of the week, don't expect any action before midnight. Dance clubs tend to stay open till around 5 A.M.

Tangaloo (Monterrey 3215, tel. 664/681-8091, www.tangaloo.com) has taken over from Baby Rock as the latest place to see and be seen.

Club Balak (Plaza Pueblo Amigo, Vía Oriente, tel. 664/682-9222, www.balakdisco.com) is the latest and greatest, with US$35 million worth of sound and lighting gear designed by the impresarios who created the famous Paladium Acapulco. Ricky Martin showed up for the dance club's 2003 inauguration. The cover charge runs a stiff US$18 during the week, US$20 on weekends. This is the one dance stop in Tijuana where you're most likely to hear the latest homegrown DJ form, Nortec (a blend of electronica/techno and *norteña* music).

Baby Rock (Diego Rivera 1482, tel. 664/684-9438) looks like it escaped from the set of *The Flintstones,* but it is a long-time favorite with

a good house mix. Expect a cover charge and dress code prohibiting jeans or sneakers.

Oriented toward young San Diegans, more-casual dance clubs along Avenida Revolución—known locally as "La Revo"—include **Animale** (the most popular when we last visited), **Iguanas Ranas, Tilly's,** and **Margarita Village.**

Mike's Disco, on the east side of Revolución at Calle 6, is a long-running gay and lesbian dance club that features drag shows on weekends. On nearby Calle 7, **Los Equipales** is another G&L-oriented disco.

Bars

For those who prefer sitting and drinking to dancing, Avenida Revolución offers a string of bars and dance halls, from sleazy to posh, attracting an eclectic mix of cholos, punks, tourists, and the occasional American sailor. What was once the longest bar in the world, the Mexicali Beer Bar (also known as La Ballena) ran the entire length of the block between Calles 2 and 3 under a tent until the early 20th century. Beer cost $0.05 a glass. Now the strip consists of a succession of similar-looking discos and a few curtained go-go bars; in the cheaper places beer costs US$1 a bottle.

Locals patronize a boisterous collection of small bars along a diagonal pedestrian alley that cuts between the southwest corner of Calle 1 and Avenida Revolución and the northeast corner of Calle 2 and Avenida Constitución. Guitar-bass-accordion ensembles wander from bar to bar playing a repertoire of *norteña* and Mexican standards. Drinks in these bars cost around US$1, while a song from one of the *trovadores* typically costs US$3–5. **Bar Ballena,** one of the oldest of the half dozen on this alley, is a pretty safe bet.

Bar San Marcos (tel. 664/688-2794), attached to Caesar's, is a classic leftover from Tijuana's pre–World War II boom. In the old days, a 10-piece mariachi band performed on a semicircular platform over a glistening bar done up in 1940s–1950s decor, like a set from a Ricky Ricardo show. The mariachi stand has since shrunk and is dwarfed by all the paraphernalia for sale around it. The clientele consists of day tourists from San Diego and local businesspeople. The sign on the outside of the building reads Le Drugstore Tijuana.

Exercise caution if you decide to visit the notorious **Zona Norte** (also known as "La Coahuila"), a district of around 10 square blocks that extends from Calle 1 downtown to the north, not far from the border. Drug dealing and prostitution (which is legal in Tijuana) are two of the main income-generating activities in this area, and the local bars can be on the rough side. On the tamer side, several of the bars offer "taxi dancing," where customers pay to dance with female staff. If you must venture into the "zone," it's best to do so in a group.

Cultural Performances

Highbrow evening entertainment takes place at the **Centro Cultural Tijuana** (see *Sights*). Mexico's National Symphony performs at the center on a regular basis, as do the Ballet Folklórico and other performing-arts groups from around the country.

SHOPPING

For most visitors, shopping is perhaps Tijuana's number-one attraction. Although both Baja California states are designated duty-free zones, Tijuana offers the widest variety of merchandise—everything from Mexican-Amerindian handicrafts to pharmaceuticals to top-of-the-line European clothing.

Nearly everything is cheaper in Tijuana than it is north of the border. Some of the better bargains are found in leather goods, cosmetics, drugs (prescriptions aren't usually required, even for drugs dispensed by prescription in the United States), high-tag import items (e.g., designer fashions), cooking spices (vanilla costs a fraction of the U.S. price), handicrafts (especially blankets, rugs, basketry, and ceramics), and liquor.

Except at department stores, pharmacies, and liquor stores, bargaining for a lower price than marked or quoted is acceptable. U.S. currency is accepted anywhere in the city; some shops take credit cards. Most of the sales staffs in Avenida Revolución stores employ at least one person who can speak some English.

Avenida Revolución

For individual shops and boutiques, Avenida Revolución between Calle 2 and Calle 9 is one of the best window-shopping areas. **Sanborns,** at the corner of Avenida Revolución and Calle 8, is a favorite department store among day-tripping San Diegans. Although not large, it's divided into book, arts-and-crafts, pharmacy, liquor, and restaurant sections.

For high-quality Mexican handicrafts, **Tolan** (Av. Revolución 1111, tel. 664/688-3637) has one of the best reputations in the city, but is a bit pricey. In the same vicinity, **Casa Uribe** (Av. Revolución 1309, tel. 664/685-8332) has a tasteful selection of Mexican interior-design accessories, including colorful tablecloths and napkins, charming children's furniture, *alebrijes,* perforated tin mirror frames, and woodcarvings—all at reasonable prices. **La Fuente** (Av. Revolución 921-10) offers arts and crafts of similar quality, including masks, woodcarvings, *retablos* (altarpieces), and life-size papier-mâché Day of the Dead skeletons. **Irene's** (Av. Revolución 921) is a good spot for embroidered dresses at moderate prices.

Farther north along Avenida Revolución, at Calle 2, is **Plaza Revolución,** a two-story mall with around 65 shops purveying arts and crafts, leather goods, jewelry, and other items. At the **Old Curio Market,** on the east side of Revolución, quality isn't usually very high, but then neither are the prices. The huge hangarlike structure brings together a large number of different *artesanías* proffering everything from hammocks and blankets to black-velvet paintings.

Avenida Constitución

Few visitors seem to know it, but one block west of Avenida Revolución is the town's major downtown shopping area. This is where the locals go. Especially for shoes and boots, liquor, and pharmaceuticals, shops on Avenida Constitución almost always beat the prices of their counterparts on Avenida Revolución. And, unlike at some shops on Revolución, bargaining—or Spanish language mastery—isn't necessary because prices are always marked and fixed.

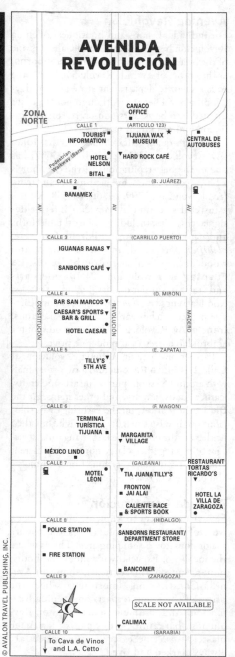

Shopping Centers

Tijuana was the first city in Mexico to erect American-style shopping malls; at last count, the city boasted more than a dozen major *centros comerciales* (shopping centers), with more undoubtedly on the way.

The most praised is **Plaza Río Tijuana,** on Paseo de los Héroes between Via Poniente and Boulevard Cuauhtémoc in the Zona Río. Here you'll find more than one hundred businesses, including department stores, pharmacies, optometrists, banks, jewelry and gift stores, music shops, clothing stores, a bakery, a florist, a cinema, photo shops, travel agencies, bookstores, sporting-goods stores, and even a chapel, all surrounded by a large parking lot.

Other Tijuana shopping centers of note include **Plaza Patria** (Blvd. Díaz Ordaz, east of Caliente Greyhound Track), Plaza Pueblo Amigo (Av. Vía Oriente, near the border crossing), and Plaza Agua Caliente (Av. Agua Caliente, adjacent to the Grand Hotel Tijuana).

Californians who don't want to venture far from home can shop at **Viva Tijuana,** a big indoor-outdoor mall about 150 meters from the border gate. In fact, all pedestrians entering or exiting the country are forced to walk through this mall. Neither the restaurants nor the shops at Viva Tijuana offer anything special—it's strictly a place to pick up last-minute souvenirs.

Markets

For a more Mexican shopping experience, seek out Tijuana's public markets. The large **Mercado de Artesanías,** at the intersection of Avenida Ocampo and Calle 2, offers thousands of pottery items at low prices. Much of what's stacked up in row after row is junk, but you can uncover worthwhile pieces with some diligent searching.

Opposite the Tijuana Cultural Center at Paseo de los Héroes and Avenida Independencia is the more atmospheric **Mercado Hidalgo.** This outdoor municipal market features dozens of vendor stalls arranged in a large square. Items for sale vary from year to year but generally include fresh fruits and vegetables, spices, and various other grocery items. A couple of *loncherías* and crafts shops make the market more than just a grocery stop.

The **Mercado de Todos** (Market of Everything) is on the 1800 block of Boulevard Agua Caliente/Díaz Ordaz, about four kilometers east of the racetrack. Vendors here offer bargains on clothing, housewares, electronics, and just about anything else you might need to set up house on the peninsula. This market doesn't really get rolling until around 10 A.M. on weekdays, or 9 A.M. on weekends; it stays open until dark.

Books

Sanborns, on Avenida Revolución at Calle 8, is the place to go for English-language books and magazines. For Spanish-language media, especially anything with a cultural bent, try **Librería El Día,** which has two storefronts: Boulevard Sánchez Toboada 10050-A, Zona Río, and Calle 6 1908, next to Cine Roble.

Furniture and Tile

Mexican-made furniture—of wood or wrought iron—and tile are considerably less expensive in Tijuana than in the United States or Canada. Most of the larger tile and furniture stores are on Boulevard Agua Caliente between Avenida Revolución and the Caliente Greyhound Track. A few stores specialize in high-quality, handmade wood furniture, but generally the wrought-iron pieces are a better bargain.

For a welcome break from the same tourist kitsch, visit the **Bazar de México,** at the end of Tia Juana Tilly's, at the corner of Avenida Revolución and Calle 7, which displays a quality selection of Mexican housewares and furniture, including wrought-iron furniture (one of Mexico's best bargains). Another commendable aspect of this *artesanía* center is that, so far, the salespeople aren't as aggressive as in many shops along this street. Validated parking for three hours is available in the Frontón Jai Alai lot.

One of the widest wall and floor tile selections,

including imported tiles from Europe, Brazil, and Japan, is at **Tile Express** (Av. Salinas at Aviación, tel. 664/681-8287 or 664/681-8305).

Be sure to check the latest U.S. Customs regulations before buying huge amounts of furniture or tile for U.S. import.

ACCOMMODATIONS

Since most leisure visitors to Tijuana are coming only for the day—or are passing through on their way south—not many foreign tourists spend the night in the city. Most hotels and motels cater either to foreign and domestic business travelers or to impecunious transients.

Under US$50

Hostal Barnes (Calle Relampago 1230, Seccion Dorado, no tel.), located outside of the downtown area at Playas Tijuana, offers safe accommodations for US$15 per person. Private one- or two-bed rooms instead of dorm-style makes it a steal, but you'd have to bus or cab to La Revolución. If you can hold out for Ensenada, you can get nicer accommodations for a few bucks more.

La Reforma district, in the vicinity of Avenida Revolución, boasts several decent hotels around US$25. One of the best deals is **Hotel Lafayette** (Av. Revolución 926 btw Calles 3/4, tel. 664/685-3940), a surprisingly quiet and clean place offering simple rooms with private baths, phone, and TV.

The pink, five-story **Hotel Nelson** (Av. Revolución 151, tel. 664/685-4302, fax 664/685-4304, US$50) is a historic place that imparts some of the flavor of early Tijuana at reasonable rates (though some rooms now cost as much as US$60). The hotel features 92 worn but clean and comfortable rooms, all with heat, satellite TV, and telephone. A popular, inexpensive coffee shop and a barbershop are attached to the hotel. Pack your earplugs.

Modern, four-story **Motel León** (Calle 7/Galeana 1939, just west of Revolución, tel. 664/685-6320) has a friendly staff and clean rooms. There are secure parking spots beneath the building, but not enough to guarantee a spot.

US$50-100

Northwest of El Toreo del Tijuana, off Boulevard Agua Caliente, **Hotel Palacio Azteca** (Av. 16 de Septiembre/Blvd. Cuauhtémoc Sur 213, tel. 664/681-8100, www.hotelpalacioazteca.com, US$80) has above-average rooms with large TVs, heat and air conditioning; amenities include a laundry room, coffee shop, pool, parking lot, and car rental. In the Zona Río, **Hotel Real del Río** (Calle J. M. Velazco 1409, tel. 664/634-3100, fax 664/634-5053, US$75) features nice but plain rooms with heat and air conditioning; amenities include a business center, bar, coffee shop, snack bar, parking, and car rental agency. Suites available.

Hotel Hacienda del Río (Blvd. Sánchez Taboada 10606, tel. 664/684-8644, U.S. tel. 800/303-2684, www.bajainn.com, US$69) caters to business travelers with a restaurant/bar, heated pool, parking, gym, copier and fax service, and courtesy coffee and newspaper. The 131 large, clean rooms and suites come with satellite TV, Internet access, air conditioning, and heat. Ask for rooms at the back of the hotel facing the pool, since the front rooms are at ground level and face the road.

If you're driving and want to stay within walking distance of La Revolución, try the **Hotel La Villa de Zaragoza** (Av. Madero 1120 btw Calles 7/8, tel. 664/685-1832, www.hotellavilla.biz, US$60). Rooms are hit or miss, but your best bet is to ask for one of the garden rooms. They have heat and air conditioning, TV, and telephone. A parking lot and laundry room are also on the premises. The hotel offers nonsmoking and handicapped-accessible rooms. Kitchenette suites are available. The security guards do a good job, but the front desk staff can be surly.

US$100-150

Your best choice in this price range is located in the Zona Río. **Hotel Lucerna** (Av. Paseo de los Héroes 10902, tel. 664/633-3900, U.S./Canada tel. 800/582-3762, www.hotel-lucerna.com.mx, US$120) is a large, modern place with a laundry room, restaurants,

a piano bar, two pools, gardens, a car rental desk, and a gym. The 168 rooms and suites come with all the amenities expected of an international-class hotel. Ask for a room in the annex if one is available.

The landmark **Grand Hotel Tijuana** (Blvd. Agua Caliente 4500, tel. 664/681-7000, U.S./Canada tel. 800/472-6385, www.grandhoteltijuana.com, US$120) was completed in 1986 as one of Plaza Agua Caliente's glittering glass-and-steel twin towers—the city's first skyscrapers. The 22-floor, 422-room, five-star hotel features several restaurants and discos, a race-and-sports betting lounge, and penthouse suites accommodating visiting celebrities and politicos. The walls are very thin and you can easily hear what your neighbor is watching on TV. The shopping area has a ghost-town feel. Facilities include a pool, tennis courts, a fitness center with sauna and hot tub, a car rental office, shopping gallery, and cinema. Complimentary airport transportation is available.

US$150-250

Hotel Pueblo Amigo Inn (Vía Oriente 9211, tel. 664/683-5030 or 800/026-6386, U.S. tel. 800/386-6985, www.hotelpuebloamigo.com, US$170) stands next to Plaza Pueblo Amigo shopping/entertainment center near the border and offers 108 rooms with posh standard amenities, plus a swimming pool. Because of its proximity to the Pueblo Amigo night scene, the hotel is popular with business travelers and conventioneers.

In the heart of the Zona Río, the grand **Hotel Camino Real** (Paseo de los Héroes 10305 and Cuauhtémoc, tel. 664/633-4000, U.S. tel. 800/722-6466, www.caminoreal.com, US$150) offers 250 deluxe rooms and suites in a branch of one of the nicer Mexican-owned hotel chains. If you stay at the club floor or above, you have access to a business center and breakfast dining room with views. The rooms are underwhelming, but the staff makes up for it with top-tier service. A new restaurant specializing in *alta cocina mexicana,* Maria Bonita, was in the works at press time.

Camping and RV Parks

The nearest camping/RV facilities are on the coast between San Antonio del Mar and Rosarito, some 20–25 kilometers south of Tijuana via Mexico 1-D (see *Rosarito*).

FOOD

Some of Baja's best food is found in Tijuana; it's worth a stopover just for a meal or two. Menus in the La Reforma (Avenida Revolución) district list prices in both pesos and dollars, but if you pay in pesos you'll almost always save a little money. Virtually all the restaurants described below serve at least beer; most offer full bars as well.

Avenida Revolución and Vicinity

Caesar's Sports Bar & Grill (Calle 5 at Avenida Revolución, tel. 664/685-1664, daily for lunch and dinner), in front of the Hotel Caesar, is a wood-paneled bar/restaurant famous for Caesar salad, invented here by Alex and Caesar Cardini in 1924. The original Caesar's recipe is prepared tableside, using coddled eggs—eggs boiled for one minute—in the dressing rather than the customary raw egg yolks used in America. Shrimp cocktail, which comes with huge grilled shrimp, spicy salsa, avocado, and lime, is among the best in Tijuana. Prices are moderate.

Sanborns (Av. Revolución at Calle 8, tel. 664/668-1462, daily for breakfast, lunch, and dinner, mains US$10–15) is one block south of the Frontón Jai Alai. Not related to Sanborns insurance or any other American company, this is part of a Mexican department-store chain well known in Mexico for its *cafeterías*. The food is of high quality, prices are reasonable, and the menu runs the gamut from original-recipe Mexican standards to steaks, seafood, salads, sandwiches, and soups. If you're tired of huevos rancheros for breakfast, the large hotcakes are a welcome change of pace. Other branches are on Avenida Revolución between Calles 3 and 4, Avenida Revolución 737, and at Plaza Río.

Tia Juana Tilly's (Calle 7 at Av. Revolución, tel. 664/685-6024, noon–midnight, Fri. and Sat. until 3 A.M., mains US$15 and up) is part of the Frontón Jai Alai. Although basically a tourist scene, the food at Tilly's—Mexican, steak, and seafood—is good, especially the *caldos*, served with chipotle salsa. The service is fine, too.

Zona Río

If you only have time for one "nice" dinner in Tijuana, call **La Diferencia** (Blvd. Sanchez Taboada 10611, Rio Tijuana, tel. 664/634-3346, www.ladiferencia.com.mx, Mon.–Thurs. noon–10:30 P.M., Fri.–Sat. noon–midnight, Sun. noon–8 P.M., US$10–23) for a reservation. The seasonally available Chile en Nogada or the duck with hibiscus flower *(jamaica)* sauce are standouts on an all-around excellent menu. Attentive service and a contemporary setting make the meal.

La Casa de Mole Poblano (Blvd. Paseo de los Héroes 1501, tel. 664/634-6920, daily 10 A.M.–11 P.M., mains under US$10) serves delicious and authentic Mexican dishes and is one of the best values found in Tijuana. The *mixiote de pollo* (chicken baked in maguey leaves) is particularly good, as is the house mole. There's live mariachi music. A second (actually the original) branch can be found at Calle Serdán 543, Col. Libertad (tel. 664/682-9074).

The popular and reasonably priced **Mariscos Los Arcos** (Blvd. Sánchez Taboada at Diego Rivera intersection, tel. 664/686-4757, daily 8 A.M.–10 P.M., Thurs.–Sat. till midnight) dishes up Mazatlán-style *pescado zarandeado*—whole fish spread with a secret blend of spices, slashed to let the flavors in, and broiled to perfection. Other recommended menu items include ceviche, *sopa de mariscos* (seafood soup), and smoked marlin tacos.

Vips Restaurant Cafetería (Blvd. Sánchez Taboada 10750, tel. 664/634-6196, daily 7 A.M.–10 P.M., mains under US$10) is a well-managed branch of one of Mexico's largest coffee-shop chains, with a long menu of breakfasts, Mexican standards, sandwiches, salads, and soups. It's popular with locals, and it's inexpensive.

Agua Caliente

Check the specials menu on the blackboard on your way in at **La Querencia** (Escuadron

201 No. 3110 Sanchez Taboada at Blvd. Salinas, tel. 664/972-9940). It's easy to get distracted by the strange combination of safari decor and industrial chic. The lamb chops are well prepared and not oversauced. Just make sure your cab driver doesn't mistake it for the well-known La Diferencia.

Carnitas Uruapán (Blvd. Díaz Ordaz 550 opposite Plaza Patria, tel. 664/681-6181, daily 7 A.M.–5 A.M., mains US$10–15) is a classic *carnitas* joint where the pig is cooked onsite and sold by the kilo along with rice, beans, salsa, and guacamole. There's family-style seating.

Groceries

Calimax and Gigante stores are easily found throughout Tijuana. There is a Super Gigante on Boulevard Aqua Caliente directly across from the racetrack. Food prices at Calimax are often lower than at smaller stores and the selection is huge. Probably the most accessible Calimax for those driving through the city is the one on the south side of Paseo de los Héroes just east of Boulevard Cuauhtémoc. The huge **Ley** supermarket/department store at Plaza Pueblo Amigo shopping center near the border has a tremendous selection, including lots of takeout Mexican food. A good supermarket within walking distance of the Avenida Revolución tourist strip is **Gigante** on Juárez between Calles 2 and 3.

INFORMATION AND SERVICES

Tourist Assistance

The **Tourist Information Booth** (Av. Revolución at (Calle 1, tel. 664/688-0555, Mon.–Fri. 8 A.M.–8 P.M., Sat.–Sun. 10 A.M.–3 P.M.) distributes maps and useful informational brochures on Tijuana and northern Baja; the bilingual staff also handle simple inquiries about where to go and what to see. Similar booths can be found at the Tijuana border crossing and Tijuana International Airport. Any questions about Tijuana these people can't answer should be referred to the **Tijuana Tourism and Convention Bureau,** at the intersection of Calle Mina and Paseo de los Héroes in the Zona Río (tel. 664/684-0537 or 664/684-

0538, Mon.–Fri. 9 A.M.–2 P.M. and 4–7 P.M.). A private consortium also operates the friendly **Tijuana Tourism Board** (Blvd. Agua Caliente 4558-1108, tel. 664/686-1103, U.S./Canada tel. 888/775-2417, www.seetijuana.com).

The **Cámara Nacional de Comercio, Servicios y Turismo de Tijuana** (CANACO), opposite the State Secretary of Tourism (SECTUR) booth on Avenida Revolución at Calle 1 (tel. 664/684-0537, www.seetijuana.com, weekdays 9 A.M.–7 P.M.) dispenses tourist information, stamps, and envelopes; it also offers restrooms and a public telephone.

For more tourist information on Baja California Norte, contact the **State Secretary of Tourism** (Plaza Patria, 3rd floor, Blvd. Díaz Ordaz, tel. 664/688-0555). Legal problems should also be referred to this office.

Money

The Banamex just southeast of Plaza Fiesta and Plaza Zapato on Paseo de los Héroes has an ATM. The best place to exchange foreign currency for pesos is at one of the many *casas de cambio* along the pedestrian route from the border to about halfway down Avenida Revolución. You'll also find a couple of *casas de cambio* next to the Calimax supermarket on Paseo de los Héroes in the Zona Río.

The banks in Tijuana aren't accustomed to changing small amounts of foreign currency, since just about everyone uses *casas de cambio* exclusively. If you want to cash travelers checks, the banks will give you dollars, not pesos. As usual in Mexico, hotels offer low exchange rates but fast service.

Public buses and government offices excepted, every business and service in Tijuana accepts U.S. currency.

Post and Telephone

The main post office is on Calle 11 (P.E. Calles) at Avenida Negrete (Mon.–Fri. 8 A.M.–7 P.M.). The CANACO office (Calle 1 at Av. Revolución) sells stamps and envelopes. The long-distance telephone and telegraph office is on Calle 10 at Av. Pío Pico (Mon.–Fri. 8 A.M.–2 P.M. and 4–7 P.M.).

Internet Access

As with most of the larger towns in Mexico, Tijuana has no shortage of Internet cafés, far too many to list. The highest concentration can be found along the northern end of Avenida Revolución, usually off of the main road.

Immigration and Customs

Immigration and customs matters are handled at the Tijuana/San Ysidro border crossing. These offices are open 24 hours a day (see *Visas and Officialdom* in *Essentials*).

Foreign Consulates

The **U.S.** consulate (Calle Tapachula 96, Col. Hipódromo, tel. 664/622-7400, Mon.–Fri. 8 A.M.–4 P.M., closed American and Mexican holidays) can assist with lost or expired U.S. passports or American visa problems. The **Canadian** consulate (Calle Germán Gedovius 10411-101, Condominio del Parque, Zona Río, tel. 664/684-0461, Mon.–Fri. 9 A.M.–1 P.M.) offers similar services for Canadians.

The **French** consulate is located at Av. Revolución 1651, 3rd floor (tel. 664/685-7172, btdmex@telnor.net). The **German** consulate is at Avenida Mérida 221, Col. Hipódromo (tel. 664/680-2515). The **United Kingdom** consulate (Blvd. Salinas 1500, Col. Aviación, La Mesa, tel. 664/686-5320, fax 664/681-8402) serves citizens of Australia and Belize.

Green Angels

The Green Angels automotive assistance service is headquartered in the Garita Federal Building (Edificio Federal Garita) at the Otay Mesa border crossing. For assistance or information in Tijuana, call 664/624-3479.

GETTING THERE
By Air
Abelardo L. Rodríguez International Airport (TIJ, tel. 664/607-8200) is in Mesa de Otay, about 10 kilometers northeast of Tijuana's city center. The following airlines fly to and from Tijuana:

> # TIJUANA PHONE NUMBERS
>
> Tijuana area code: 664
> Fire Department: 068
> General Hospital: 684-0922
> Green Angels: 624-3479
> Highway Patrol: 682-5285
> Immigration: 682-3439
> Police: 060
> Red Cross: 066
> State Police: 685-4444
> State Tourism Office: 688-0555
> Tourist Assistance: 078

- **Aeroméxico** (Plaza Río Tijuana 12-A1, Paseo de los Héroes, tel. 664/638-8444 or 800/021-4010, U.S. tel. 800/237-6639)

- **Mexicana** (Edificio Fontana, Diego Rivera 1511 at Av. Paseo de los Héroes, tel. 664/634-6566, airport tel. 664/682-4184 or 800/509-8960, U.S./Canada tel. 800/531-7921)

- **Aero California** (Plaza Río Tijuana C-20, Paseo de los Héroes, tel. 664/684-2876, U.S. tel. 800/237-6225)

- Monterrey-based **Aviacsa** (Blvd. Sánchez Taboada 4499, Plaza Guadalupe 6, tel. 664/622-5024, airport tel. 664/683-8202 or 800/711-6733, U.S. tel. 888/528-4227)

The airport has plenty of little gift shops, a restaurant/bar, snack bar, bookstore, taxis, a Serfín ATM, and a three-story parking garage with no elevator.

Foreign pilots may use this airport as an official port of entry. Check with Baja Bush Pilots for current information (www.bajabushpilots.com).

Airport Transportation: The airport is about eight kilometers east of the city; taxis to and from anywhere in the city cost a flat US$12 for up to five passengers. A taxi between the airport and the Central de Autobuses costs US$10. Public buses to downtown Tijuana are marked Centro and leave regularly from in front of the airport; fare is about US$0.60 per passenger.

By Bus

Several intercity bus lines operate out of Tijuana. The main terminal for Mexico-based lines is the **Central de Autobuses de Tijuana** (also known as the Central Camionera), about five kilometers east of the city on Lázaro Cárdenas at Blvd. Arroyo Alamar (tel. 664/621-2982). The modern structure contains a restaurant, *lonchería,* telephone office, immigration office, and money changer. **Transportes Norte de Sonora** (TNS) and **Autotransportes de Baja California** (ABC) run buses eastward to Mexicali (US$9–12, nine times daily) and to various points on the Mexican mainland. **Transportes de Pacífico** and **Chihuahuenses** offer more extensive services to the mainland.

ABC (tel. 664/621-2668) runs a deluxe *ejecutivo* bus with air conditioning, movies, and beverage service to Ensenada every half hour 6 A.M.–midnight from the second Central de Autobuses, at the intersection of Avenida Madero and Calle 1 downtown. ABC also offers regular non-air-conditioned buses departing for Ensenada from the small **Plaza Viva** bus station at the border, near the U.S. Customs/immigration post. Another ABC *ejecutivo* goes to San Felipe. There are also regular non-air-conditioned ABC buses to San Felipe.

Southward, **Autotransportes Águila** runs buses to El Rosario, Santa Rosalía, and La Paz.

The U.S.-based **Greyhound** buses from San Diego and Los Angeles terminate at the downtown Tres Estrellas de Oro terminal (Av. México and Av. Madero, tel. 664/688-0082). Call 800/231-2222 in the United States for more information. This same terminal also serves Mexican ABC buses running every 20 minutes between Tijuana and Tecate.

Mexicoach (from San Ysidro) occupies its own depot called Terminal Turística Tijuana on Avenida Revolución between Calles 6 and 7 (see *Getting There* in *Essentials*).

By Taxi

A taxi from the U.S.–Mexico border crossing to anywhere in central Tijuana costs a flat US$5. You can charter a Tijuana taxi all the way to Rosarito for US$35 (one-way) or to Ensenada for US$100.

By Car

See *Driving into Baja* in *Essentials* for specifics on driving to Tijuana.

On Foot

A large number of tourists who visit Tijuana reach the city on foot from San Ysidro, the small California town on the immediate U.S. side of the border, after having parked their vehicles in one of the San Ysidro lots or after taking the Tijuana Trolley (daily 5 A.M.–12:40 A.M., US$2.50) from San Diego.

The sidewalks that lead to the border crossing, then through Mexican immigration and customs and all the way to Avenida Revolución, are clearly marked. Along the way, you'll pass rows of handicraft booths and money changers. A leisurely stroll from the border crossing to Avenida Revolución in the heart of downtown Tijuana takes 15–20 minutes.

GETTING AROUND

You can see much of downtown Tijuana on foot—Avenidas Revolución and Constitución, the cathedral, the jai alai palace, the Mercado Artesanías. You can reach outlying attractions like the Zona Río and the racetrack by city bus, taxi, or your own car.

By Bus

Tijuana's city buses, or *urbanos,* come in several colors, shapes, and sizes. The route destination—usually the name of a district (e.g., Centro or La Mesa)—is displayed on a sign over the windshield or whitewashed directly on it. Fares are around US$0.50, payable only in pesos. Most *urbanos* in and out of the downtown area *(centro)* can be caught along Avenida Constitución.

Two of the most useful bus lines are the "green and cream" *(verde y crema),* which operates between the city center and La Mesa district, east of Caliente Greyhound Track, and the "blue and white" *(azul y blanco)*, running between the city center and the Playas district (Plaza Monumental). The "Baja P" is the bus to take for jaunts to Zona Río attractions, including the Tijuana Cultural Center, Plaza Fiesta, and Plaza Río Tijuana.

By Taxi

Most trips by hired taxi within the *centro* cost US$4–5. From the city center to the Grand Hotel Tijuana/racetrack area costs as much as US$10; to the airport or Central de Autobuses expect to pay up to US$15 (although in the reverse direction it's only US$12). Taxis hired from hotels generally cost more than taxis hired on the street; rates are usually posted. If in doubt about a fare, inquire at the tourist information booths at the border or on Avenida Revolución at Calle 1. Drivers are happy to accept U.S. currency.

Bargaining usually isn't necessary—drivers generally quote the standard price immediately, with the exception of the yellow border taxis. You shouldn't have to pay more than US$8 from the border taxi stand to Avenida Revolución, but drivers often ask gringos for more. A better deal involves taking one of the several shuttle bus services that run from the Tijuana Trolley terminal in San Ysidro on the U.S. side of the border directly to Avenida Revolución; each costs only US$1 per person.

Route taxis *(taxis de ruta)* in Tijuana are large American-made station wagons holding up to 12 passengers. These taxis operate along set routes, much like city buses, but stop wherever they're flagged down. Fares are US$0.60 per person, only a tad higher than city bus fares; as on buses, only pesos are accepted. Route taxis are one of the best ways to get around Tijuana cheaply, since you can tell the drivers exactly where you want off along their route—better than waiting for a bus stop to come along.

Like the city buses, route taxis are painted according to their routes. Red-and-black taxis operate between Calle 2 (between Avenidas

Revolución and Constitución) and La Mesa, along Boulevard Agua Caliente; brown-and-white route taxis run to the Zona Río and Otay Mesa.

By Car

Rental Cars: Tijuana has several different car rental operations, such as Avis, Budget, Central, Dollar, Hertz, and National. (See the sidebar *Where to Rent a Car in Baja* in the *Essentials* chapter.) All offer day, weekend, and weekly deals either with per-kilometer charges added in (best rates for local driving only) or as flat rates only (most economical if you plan to drive long distances in Baja). Car rentals are less expensive in Tijuana than anywhere else on the peninsula. Especially for auto tours of northern Baja, you'll enjoy considerable savings if you rent a car here rather than in Ensenada or Mexicali.

Advance reservations are a good idea, as most agencies don't maintain large fleets of cars. With or without reservations, a credit card is a prerequisite for car rental.

Driving: The traffic in Tijuana is fairly stiff all day long, so it's not one of the most pleasant cities in Baja to drive in. On the other hand, lots of visitors do manage to drive themselves around the city—all it takes is a good map and plenty of patience. During morning rush hour, Revolución and the adjacent avenues that run North to South are closed to traffic to allow for the backup from the border that runs through town.

Another problem is parking, although the situation is not nearly as bad as in most larger cities in the United States. In the Avenida Revolución area, street parking is hard to come by; it's best to choose one of the fee parking lots. One of the less expensive ones is a parking garage called **Estacionamiento Leyva** (Av. Revolución 1026 between Calles 6 and 7). The 24-hour open lot behind the Frontón Jai Alai costs US$5–6 a day, but if you patronize any of the restaurants or shops in the *frontón* complex, including the Bazar de México, you receive three hours free parking with validation of the parking ticket.

LEAVING TIJUANA
To the United States

To get back across the border, simply drive north on Avenida Revolución and follow signs to San Diego. When traffic is stiff, especially on Sunday, you can avoid much of it by circling around to Avenida Padre Kino on the north side of town to approach the border crossing from the east lanes. The west lanes are almost always busiest. A carpool lane for vehicles with three or more occupants has been added on the far right side.

South to Rosarito and Ensenada

The drive from Tijuana to Ensenada or any points between is fairly straightforward, even for drivers who would never consider navigating the Transpeninsular all the way to the Cape. You can choose between two roadways: a modern, four-lane toll expressway (Mexico 1-D, also called the Carretera Cuota, or "Toll Highway") and a slightly more challenging two-lane highway (the original Mexico 1, called along this stretch the Carretera Libre, or "Free Highway"). Both are scenic drives of around 100 kilometers (60 mi).

Mexico 1-D, the toll highway, parallels the coast the entire distance from Tijuana to Ensenada and offers generally better coastal views than the free road. On the negative side, there are limited opportunities for stopovers since highway exits can be as far as 18 kilometers apart. To get on the toll road, take Calle 3 west and follow the signs for Ensenada; traffic is often very slow until you reach the toll-road entrance near Playas. Tolls are collected at three tollgates (casetas de cobro) along Mexico 1-D: at Playas de Tijuana, Rosarito, and San Miguel. At each gate, the toll is less than US$3 for passenger cars, a bit more for cars with trailers, motor homes, or large trucks. From Tijuana to Ensenada the total runs US$6, or US$10–15 for larger vehicles. Both U.S. and Mexican currencies are accepted at the tollgates; change is given in pesos, dollars, or a mixture of the two.

Mexico 1, the free road, begins just south of Tijuana and winds through a mountainous area for 18 kilometers before reaching the coast at Rosarito. From Rosarito it hugs the narrow coastal plain for the next 50 kilometers—providing plenty of opportunities for beach stopovers—then turns inland again at La Misión. The final 31 kilometers threads through the mountains before joining Mexico 1-D just north of Ensenada at San Miguel. Getting onto the free road in Tijuana is a challenge; some visitors say they gave up looking for it and settled for the toll road. There's only one sign indicating the way; if you drive south along Avenida Revolución until it curves east into Boulevard Agua Caliente, you'll soon see a sign reading A Rosarito (To Rosarito) with an arrow pointing to the right; watch for a large Calimax store on the right. The next right-hand turn, Boulevard Cuauhtémoc, is the correct turnoff. You can also connect with Boulevard Cuauhtémoc by driving east on Paseo de los Héroes; look for the statue of an Aztec—that's Cuauhtémoc. Once on Boulevard Cuauhtémoc, make no other turns, wade through a seemingly endless succession of stoplights and stop signs, and eventually you'll find yourself on Mexico 1.

East to Tecate and Mexicali

For Tecate, Mexicali, and other points east via the free road, simply follow Boulevard Agua Caliente southeast out of town until it turns into Boulevard Díaz Ordaz and, finally, Mexico 2. If you want to take the toll road to Tecate, follow the signs for the airport rather than signs for Tecate, which are misleading.

ISLAS LOS CORONADOS

The four Los Coronados islands lie only 11 kilometers west of San Antonio del Mar, a mostly American residential area 12 kilometers south of Tijuana. The Spanish explorer Juan Cabrillo passed by in 1542 and called them Las Islas Desiertas (Desert Islands) because of the apparent lack of vegetation; in 1602 Vizcaíno renamed them Los Cuatros Coronados (The Four Coronados) after four brothers who died as Christian martyrs during the era of the Roman Empire.

Too steep and rugged for permanent habitation, the islands were briefly used as a pirate hideaway and later as a rendezvous for smugglers bringing rum and Chinese immigrants into the United States. In 1931, a short-lived hotel and casino called the Coronado Islands Yacht Club rose at the edge of a cove on the largest island, Coronado del Sur. The establishment closed in 1933 with the repeal of Prohibition, and little remains of the decaying three-story building. A few Mexican navy personnel live on the island to protect it from intruders.

Geography and Natural History

All four of Los Coronados are the tips of undersea mountain ridges. The largest island, Coronado del Sur, is about three kilometers long and reaches an elevation of 204 meters at its highest point; California sea lions and northern elephant seals reside in a cliff-lined cove on the island's windward side. The second largest, Coronado del Norte, is about a kilometer long and a steep 142 meters high. The remaining two, Roca Media (Middle Rock) and Coronado del Medio (Middle Coronado), lie between the larger islands and are little more than rock outcroppings. Seagoing birds favor the middle islands as nesting grounds.

The islands and the surrounding immediate area are protected by the Mexican government; commercial fishing, with the exception of a few lobster and sea urchin concessions, isn't permitted, nor can visitors land on any of the islands without government permission. As a result, the islands have become one of the most important brown pelican rookeries on the Pacific coast; more than 160 other bird species have been identified as well. Along the west side of Coronado del Norte is a large sea lion colony; harbor seals are common along the same shoreline, with elephant seals occasionally seen. Island plant varieties number around 100, mostly cacti, mimosas, and other species suited to arid climates.

Fishing

Yellowtail fishing is usually excellent in the vicinity of the Coronados, with peak season running April–October. Rock cod, bonito, halibut, barracuda, calico bass, and white sea bass are also frequently taken. Favorite fishing spots lie just north of Roca Media, at the southeast tip of Coronado del Sur, and inshore along the western side of the same island.

Diving

Los Coronados is the most heavily dived area in Baja waters. Many San Diego novices make their first open-water dives here, and spearfishers have long extolled the abundance of underwater game (but remember that spearfishing is illegal if you're wearing anything more than mask, snorkel, and fins). In some places the moray eels are so accustomed to handouts they immediately approach any diver who happens along.

Good sites for divers of all levels include "The Slot," an area of rich marinelife between the two middle islands; a rocky cove on the northeastern coast of Coronado del Norte called the "Lobster Shack" for an old shack onshore used by lobstermen; the large kelp bed just south of the southern tip of Coronado del Sur; and the rock reef at the northern end of Coronado del Sur. Advanced, open-ocean divers can tackle "Eighty-five-foot Reef," named for the depth at which much of the reef begins. The shallowest portion is about 18 meters (60 ft) below the ocean's surface.

Transportation and Tours

No regular boat service to Islas Los Coronados exists—most visitors navigate their own craft—although you might find charters in San Antonio del Mar if you ask around.

Several San Diego fishing outfitters offer fishing tours of the islands. And **Horizon Charters** (tel. 858/277-7823, www.horizoncharters.com) operates liveaboard diving trips to various islands in northern and central Baja. Boats depart from San Diego.

Rosarito

Rosarito's multiple personalities—ranchtown, beachtown, and boomtown rolled into one—reflect a short but varied history. During the mission era, the area was virtually uninhabited—out of the reach of Dominican missions to the south and Franciscan missions to the north. Although the Camino Real (Royal Road) passed nearby, it wasn't until a parallel road began snaking southward along the coast from Tijuana that anyone but ranchers developed an interest in the area. Early Baja travelers discovered the huge beach at Rosarito (one of the widest and longest on Baja's Pacific coast) in the 1920s, and it has become more popular with each passing decade.

A new side to Rosarito development arrived with the establishment of a massive American film set at nearby Popotla for the production of *Titanic* in 1996. Before the film had completed shooting, the city council granted permission for Fox Studios Baja to become a permanent production facility. The intermittent Hollywood presence is bringing a new style to the town, one that some residents and visitors love while others abhor.

Summer months see the highest tourist numbers in Rosarito, both Mexicans and foreigners. Winter—except Thanksgiving and Christmas/New Year's—is slow, and room rates hit their lowest. Between Semana Santa and U.S. college/university spring break, March and April can be busy—avoid Rosarito during those times unless you like crowds. May, September, and October are splendid months for enjoying the town at its best, when the weather is still warm but crowds are few.

HISTORY

In 1827, as Mexico was gaining its independence from Spain, Juan Machado received a land grant of 407,000 acres in the Rosarito area, then called El Rosario. The Machado family raised cattle and sheep on the property and leased land to other ranchers. In 1914 the family sold 14,000 coastal acres to a land development corporation, which in turn sold them to a New York attorney in 1920.

In 1924 the attorney opened El Rosario Resort and Country Club next to the beach. Initially the resort was little more than a rustic hunting cabin. A dirt road between Tijuana and Ensenada passed El Rosario, however, and it became a popular stopover for Americans sampling the casinos at either end of the road. The free camping allowed on the property probably didn't hurt its success.

Manuel Barbachano bought the property around 1930 and built the Rosarito Beach Hotel, a 10-room hotel with a small lobby, one bathroom, and a casino to take advantage of the Prohibition boom in gambling. Apparently no record exists as to why Barbachano changed the name from El Rosario to Rosarito—perhaps because "Rosarito" is easier for gringos to pronounce. Another theory claims that he named the hotel after Lee J. Rose, developer of one of Tijuana's first racetracks.

For most of the next 40 years, all development in Rosarito focused around the Rosarito Beach Hotel. After Prohibition ended and the Mexican government banned casino gambling, Barbachano closed the casino but enlarged the hotel, employing a Belgian architect and Mexican muralist to turn it into a major attraction. During the 1940s and 1950s, Rosarito became a favorite haunt of Hollywood celebrities, Latin American presidents, and well-heeled international travelers.

The completion of a four-lane toll road to Rosarito in 1967 brought many more Californians into town and modified the exclusive nature of the resort. Other hotels were built and, although the Rosarito Beach Hotel remained the beach centerpiece for some time, the town expanded from a weekend resort to a large residential community of retirees and self-employed expatriates.

Today a four-lane roadway with bike lanes and lighted traffic islands passes through the center of Rosarito, lined with shopping plazas,

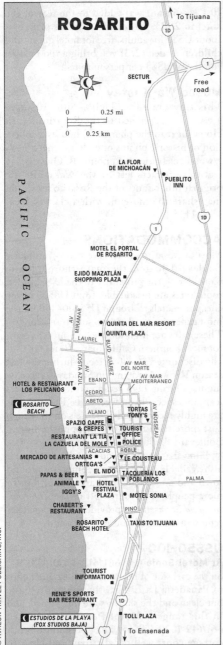

ROSARITO

To Tijuana

1D

SECTUR

Free road

1

0   0.25 mi

0   0.25 km

PACIFIC OCEAN

LA FLOR DE MICHOACÁN

PUEBLITO INN

1D

1

MOTEL EL PORTAL DE ROSARITO

EJIDO MAZATLÁN SHOPPING PLAZA

AV MIRAMAR

QUINTA DEL MAR RESORT
QUINTA PLAZA

LAUREL

BLVD JUÁREZ

AV COSTA AZUL

AV MAR DEL NORTE

AV MAR MEDITERRANEO

EBANO

HOTEL & RESTAURANT LOS PELICANOS

CEDRO

ABETO

ROSARITO BEACH

ALAMO

TORTAS TONY'S

AV MOSSEAU

SPAZIO OAFFE & CREPES

TOURIST OFFICE

RESTAURANT LA TIA

POLICE

LA CAZUELA DEL MOLE

ACACIAS

ROBLE

MERCADO DE ARTESANIAS

LE COUSTEAU

ORTEGA'S

EL NIDO

PAPAS & BEER

TACQUERIA LOS POBLANOS

PALMA

ANIMALE

IGGY'S

HOTEL FESTIVAL PLAZA

MOTEL SONIA

CHABERT'S RESTAURANT

PINO

ROSARITO BEACH HOTEL

TAXIS TO TIJUANA

TOURIST INFORMATION

RENE'S SPORTS BAR RESTAURANT

1D

ESTUDIOS DE LA PLAYA (FOX STUDIOS BAJA)

TOLL PLAZA

1

To Ensenada

TIJUANA

neon-lit restaurants, high-rise hotels, and condominiums. Vacation and retirement homes, an estimated 10,000 owned by Americans and Canadians, stretch along the ocean for miles in either direction. During the last few years, city officials have given some 40,000 trees to local citizens for planting throughout the city. Yet only about half the town's residents have running water.

Rosarito was once part of the *municipio* of Tijuana, and its relative prosperity provided a large portion of Tijuana's annual budget. Rosarito residents argued that if the town could secede from municipal Tijuana, more money could go toward local urban improvements. A 15-year battle to separate from Tijuana ended in June 1995, when Rosarito became BCN's fifth *municipio*. INEGI counted the population at just over 73,000 as of 2005.

One outcome of Rosarito's new independence from Tijuana was the quick decision to allow the movie *Titanic* to set up production facilities nearby in 1996. As a result, Rosarito was the only *municipio* in the state to post a budget surplus that year. Several more blockbusters have been made here, including the Russel Crowe heroism-at-sea vehicle, *Master and Commander*.

Many residents voice the hope that zoning restrictions will come with increased wealth. However, high-rise buildings continue to race toward the Rosarito skyline, crowding the once-peaceful beach town closer and closer toward a Miami Beach fate. The controversial Hotel Festival Plaza, a bright yellow-and-green high-rise on the main drag, is meant to look like an amusement park with its roller-coaster facade and working Ferris wheel—a Coney Island touch hated by some, loved by others. The latest addition has been a 500-meter cruise ship and sportfishing pier attached to the Rosarito Beach Hotel. So far the cruises haven't been scheduled because the city needs to build a breakwater first. Slow-growth advocates maintain that cruise-ship traffic will spoil Rosarito's central attraction, the beach, while local merchants are delighted that cruise passengers may one day wander the town boulevard, their pockets bulging with dollars.

SIGHTS

Rosarito Beach

Rosarito's main draw is its eight-kilometer-long sandy beach. Several beachwear and surf shops in town offer swimming, snorkeling, floating, and surfing equipment for rent or purchase. But the real entertainment happens on the sand and not in the water. The section of the beach north of the pier houses several mega-clubs that provide beach chairs and drinks by day and rave-like atmosphere at night. During the annual spring break holiday, American college students invade the town and take full advantage of the 18-year-old drinking age. Horseback riding used to be another popular pastime, but it was banned in 2006. You can rent ATVs, fish from the pier, or just people-watch as you sunbathe.

Rosarito Beach Hotel

An attraction in itself, this hotel was the only place to stay in Rosarito for nearly 75 years; for many repeat visitors it's still the first choice. Originally built in 1926 with only 12 rooms, during its heyday in the 1940s and 1950s the hotel gained a reputation among the Hollywood set as a romantic retreat. Frequent guests included Victor Mature, Mickey Rooney, Joan Bennett, Lana Turner, and Orson Welles. International playboy Ali Khan and actress Gene Tierney, along with an entourage of 24, took over the entire hotel for several weeks in 1955; Kim Novak and Dominican Republic president Rafael Leonidas Trujillo trysted here during the same era.

The original owner's nephew, Hugo Torres, acquired the property in 1974. Following his uncle's example, Torres continues to expand the facilities and currently offers 280 rooms. Although no longer a celebrity hideaway, a tour of the Belgian-designed architecture, the Matía Santoyo murals, and the seaward-facing Beachcomber Bar is on the itinerary of nearly every Rosarito visitor.

A 500-meter sportfishing pier (daily 10 A.M.–6 P.M.) was added to the rear of the hotel in 2003. Admission onto the pier costs about US$1 for adults, free for hotel guests and children under 12. If you bring a rod or line, you'll pay US$5 per person to fish.

Museo Wa-Kuatay

This tiny museum (Thurs.–Sun. 10 A.M.–4 P.M., free) attached to the Rosarito Beach Hotel (next to the pharmacy) houses a collection of historic photos of early ranchers, Hollywood celebrities, and politicos. One display features artifacts left by the Wakutais, the original inhabitants of the Rosarito area. You may share the museum with a class of local school kids.

ACCOMMODATIONS

Most of Rosarito's hotels are strung out along Boulevard Juárez, the main thoroughfare. Considering the proximity to the U.S. border, room rates are reasonable: from US$35 at the cheapest motels to around US$100–150 for the most expensive hotel rooms, suites, and condos. These rates are high for Mexico but a bargain for most Southern Californians. Rates are usually discounted 30–50 percent during the low season (Nov.–Apr.) and on Sunday–Thursday nights. During high season (Jul.–Aug.), rates leap up, especially on weekends. Reservations are highly recommended. Hotels on the beach cost more than those on the opposite side of Boulevard Benito Juárez.

Time-share condos and vacation homes are also available at the various complexes around town and are often good bargains for four or more people. The tourist office (see *Information and Services*) can provide a list of agencies representing rental houses and condos.

US$50-100

At **Motel Sonia** (tel. 661/612-1260, US$50), on the east side of Boulevard Juárez, next door to Panadería La Espiga, the rooms are basic but clean and the showers are hot. A real find in this range is **Motel Paraíso Ortiz** (tel. 661/612-1020, US$65), an old-fashioned beach cottage court well off the road and close to

© PAUL ITOI

Rosarito Beach Hotel

the beach at Rosarito's south end. To find the place, proceed south along Boulevard Juárez past the Rosarito Beach Hotel and associated beach home development, and look for Rene's Sports Bar Restaurant; Paraíso Ortiz is right next door. The tidy rooms all have wall heaters, and some face the ocean. The staff is friendly and parking seems secure.

In the same general vicinity but on the east (non-beach) side of the road, **Motel Quinta Chica** (Km 25 Rosarito–Ensenada Hwy., tel. 661/612-2991, US$75) offers decent rooms in a modern, three-story brick building.

Motel Villa de Lis (Calle Alamo at Av. Costa Azul, tel. 661/612-2320, US$75) occupies a modest building in a quiet downtown location with Rosarito Beach frontage. Although it's nothing special in terms of atmosphere or amenities, the motel appears to be clean and well run.

In the north-central part of town, on the west side of the main drag but not on the beach, 24-room **Motel El Portal de Rosarito** (Blvd. Juárez at Via de las Olas, tel. 661/612-0050, US$50) offers clean rooms with TV

in a two-story pink building with offstreet parking. In the same vicinity but on the other side of the street, the older **Motel Don Luis de Rosarito** (Blvd. Juárez 272, tel. 661/612-1166) offers good-sized rooms in a motel court at similar rates.

Hotel Los Pelicanos (Calle Ebano 113, tel. 661/612-0445, US$65) is well off the main drag, quiet, and on the beach. The place doesn't look like much on the outside, but the 39 rooms are spacious and well kept, and all contain heaters and TVs.

At the north end of town on the west side of the main avenue (right next to the towering Quinta del Mar Resort condo complex), **Hotel Quinta Terranova** (Blvd. Juárez 25500, tel./fax 661/612-1650, www.hotelquintaterranova. iwarp.com, US$65–109) features 84 fresh, clean rooms, each with coffeemaker and TV. Well-behaved dogs are welcome here.

At the north end of town the **Pueblito Inn** (Blvd. Juárez 286, tel. 661/612-2516, www.sdro.com/pacifico, US$80–110), features 47 air-conditioned rooms with cable TV and phone; most rooms contain two double beds.

The hotel is clean and comfortable but a bit sterile feeling. Amenities include a restaurant, pool, and ATM.

US$100-150

The venerable **Rosarito Beach Hotel, Pier & Spa** (south end of Blvd. Juárez, tel. 661/612-1111, U.S. tel. 800/343-8582, www.rosaritobeachhotel.com, US$129) has grown into a sprawling complex with several different varieties of rooms. Rooms in the oldest wing are atmospheric but in need of refurbishing, rooms in the tower are modern. The piano bar has great atmosphere, but the drinks are absurdly priced. Facilities include restaurants, pools, tennis, and hot tub. The gym and racquetball courts are closed during the construction of a new condotel. On the adjacent hotel grounds, Casa La Playa offers European-style spa treatments. The new condotel will feature 250 new condos, some of which will be available for rent.

The **Hotel Festival Plaza** (Blvd. Juárez north of the Rosarito Beach Hotel, tel. 661/612-2950, U.S. tel. 888/295-9669, www .festivalplazahotel.com, US$130–160) is still the party epicenter in Rosarito for summer and spring break. It's proximity to the beach clubs keeps drawing the crowds, but in recent years readers have reported thefts and incidences of bedbugs at the hotel. The valet parking system is of particular concern, since you have to leave your keys with the staff. The unique all-in-one complex surrounds a plaza loaded with a Ferris wheel, tequila museum/bar, café, two restaurants, two dance clubs, a heated freeform pool, and a hot tub. The 114-room hotel section has very basic rooms that have been frat-partied nearly to death. Suites and more expensive "villas," each with two bedrooms and a fully equipped kitchen, are available. And on the hotel's back side toward the beach are even more expensive townhouse-like *casitas*. Wrist bands are required to enter the hotel, so you won't be able to invite that special someone back to your room unless they are staying at the hotel already.

Out of Town

Las Rocas Resort and Spa (tel. 661/614-0354, U.S./Canada tel. 888/527-7622, www .lasrocas.com, US$160) is an isolated resort hotel 9.5 kilometers south of Rosarito at Km 37.5 on the free road. The cubelike concrete structures aren't particularly attractive on the outside, but cozy Mexican rustic interiors feature ocean views, fireplaces, and kitchenettes. The rooms can be hit and miss, so ask to see one before you commit. Other facilities include secured parking, cable TV, restaurant, pool, and hot tub. The hotel also has a spa featuring massages, facials, hydrotherapy, full salon treatments, and a steam room.

Camping and RV Parks

Chuy's Trailer Park (Av. Costa Azul 175 downtown, tel. 661/612-1608, US$22) features around 30 beachfront sites with full hookups; it's often full. Also on Costa Azul, near the Motel Villa de Lis, **Alamo Trailer Park** (opposite Alamo Hostel, tel. 661/613-1179, US$25) has a few basic spaces with electricity and water.

The **Century Resort** (formerly the Oasis Beach Resort) has 55 full-hookup RV spots, each with individual barbecue pits, satellite cable TV connections, and the use of all resort facilities. Beachfront sites for up to four adults cost US$45 and up. The resort also offers 22 mobile homes for rent for US$100 per day and up.

Most of the slots at **Popotla Trailer Park** (tel. 661/612-1502) are occupied by long-term residents; when vacant, a space costs US$45 a night, while tent sites are US$20. Permanently sited trailers are sometimes available for rent for US$25–30 a night.

FOOD

Rosarito's Boulevard Juárez is jammed with restaurants of every description. Every block seems to contain at least one taco stand and one seafood restaurant. Some of the better choices are listed below.

Mexican

El Nido (Juárez 67, tel. 661/612-1430, daily

8 A.M.–midnight, US$6–23) has great atmosphere and the food to back it up. The beef is grilled over an open fire. For breakfast, try the quail eggs and venison *machaca*. The restaurant's owner raises his own quail and red deer.

High marks go to **La Cazuela del Mole** (Wed.–Mon. noon–8 P.M.), on the west side of Blvd. Juárez, just south of Banamex and Calle René Ortiz, more or less opposite the police station. As the name suggests, the house specialty is mole, an extremely rich sauce made with chocolate, chilies, ground sesame seeds, and many other ingredients and usually served over chicken or turkey. Especially recommended are the *pollo en mole poblano* (Puebla-style chicken mole), *molotes* (chicken and cheese wrapped in corn-flour dough and fried, somewhat like piroshkis), *pollo en mixiote* (roast chicken in a spicy, orange-colored sauce reminiscent of some curries), *sopes* (thick fried cornmeal cakes topped with chopped meat, onions, and chilies), and *tamales de dulce* (sweet tamales, here made with pineapple). The food and service are good, and prices are low—the average entrée costs just US$3.

At **La Flor de Michoacán** (Blvd. Juárez 291, tel. 661/612-1858, daily 8 A.M.–10 P.M.), the Ochoa family has been making the best *carnitas* in town since 1950. Besides *carnitas* by the half kilo (US$14) or kilo (US$23–25—beans, guacamole, salsa, and tortillas are included in the price), the menu offers tacos, *tortas, burritos de carnitas* (US$4), and quesadillas (US$2), all served with bowls of fiery salsa, lime sections, and pickled chilies and vegetables. Breakfast is served till noon. All breakfasts cost US$4 (except *bistek ranchero* and *machaca con huevo*, which cost about US$6). Menudo is available on Saturday and Sunday. The service is excellent; some nights a roving group of *músicos* performs *norteña* music on request.

Seafood

The Ortega family, owner of **Ortega's Place** (Blvd. Juárez 200, tel. 661/612-0022, daily for breakfast, lunch, and dinner), started out serving lobster dinners to tourists at their home in nearby Puerto Nuevo in 1945. The house specialty is Puerto Nuevo–style lobster, but the massive buffet of other dishes has overtaken lobster as the favorite among most of the clientele. Their champagne brunch draws a hungry crowd every Sunday.

Portofino (tel. 661/612-2950, daily 1–11 P.M., Fri.–Sat. till midnight), formerly Puerto Langosta, on the second floor of the Hotel Festival Plaza, most matches the overall sense of whimsy of Rosarito's most unique hotel. Reached via an "underwater" staircase, the darkened restaurant is lit by neon stars, the floor is thickly covered in sand, and the tables are set beneath individual palapa roofs. The menu focuses on seafood, of course, and it's not bad, if a little on the pricey side. Tailor-made fun for spring breakers.

Los Pelicanos (Calle Ebano at Av. Costa Azul, tel. 661/612-1737, daily noon–midnight), part of the hotel of the same name, is one of the few restaurants in town that's on the beach, offering a full ocean view. Good seafood and quail; upscale ambience.

French

Chabert's (Fri.–Sun. 5 P.M.–midnight in the low season, daily in high season), housed in the restored Barbachano mansion next to the Rosarito Beach Hotel (and under the same ownership), is an upscale French restaurant serving French and Continental cuisine. The elegant decor includes a Tiffany chandelier, Italian baroque tables, Louis XIV chairs, and mirrors framed in expensive dragon-carved teak. The pricey international menu covers all the bases, from chateaubriand to chicken Kiev. An attached ballroom hosts live music on occasion.

Bistro le Cuestau on Juárez just north of the intersection of Calle del Encino, serves French and continental food daily 1–10:30 P.M., and savory crepes 10 P.M.–midnight. A filet mignon entrée costs US$20.

Antojitos, Tacos, and Tortas

Tacquería Los Poblanos (daily 11 A.M.–1 A.M.), on Boulevard Juárez across from the Festival Plaza, serves up spicy but good *tacos al pastor* for US$1. **Restaurant La Tía** (daily

8 A.M.–3:30 P.M.) sits across from the Pemex on the southwest side of Calle Ciprés, packed with locals and not a tourist in sight. It serves *birria*, chicken, or beef in chipotle sauce. Plates start at US$5.

Ice Cream, Pastries, and Cafés

El Canaveral Frutería, next to the Banamex on Boulevard Juárez, sells fresh fruit *licuados* (smoothies). For Mexican pastries, your best bet is **Panaficadora La Espiga,** across Boulevard Juárez from Hotel Festival Plaza. Espiga also occupies two other locations: one at the north end of town opposite Ejido Mazatlán shopping plaza and a *tortillería,* and one opposite Ortega's Place.

For a superb cappuccino, try **Cappuchino's Coffee and Pastry House,** diagonally across the street from Hotel Festival Plaza. Internet access is available. **Spazio Caffe & Crepes,** across from the Banamex behind the Extra market on the southwest side of Juárez (8–10 P.M., US$4–6) serves espresso drinks, bagels, sandwiches, and crepes. There is an Internet café next door.

SPORTS AND RECREATION

Surfing

During the winter, intermittent surf—usually nothing huge, but still surfable—may appear at either end of the beach. Better breaks are usually found south of Rosarito, starting at Km 33, from Punta Descanso to Punta Mesquite. **Inner Reef Surf Shop** (Km 34.5 on the free road, tel. 661/615-0841) sells and rents surfboards and other surf gear. Inner Reef recently opened a new location in the string of stores just south of the Rosarito Beach Hotel (daily 9 A.M.–5 P.M.) where they sell a line of boards shaped by the owner, as well as clothing and accessories.

BAJA SURFING TOP 40

More than 80 named surf breaks dot the Pacific and lower Sea of Cortez coasts of the Baja Peninsula, and there are probably at least that many unnamed breaks. Here are some of the best, arranged from north to south down the Pacific side of the peninsula, then back north up the Sea of Cortez side.

- Playa Rosarito – long beach break, NW
- Baja Malibu – beach break, NW
- Rene's – beach break, NW
- Popotla – left reef break, SH
- "Mushroom" – right reef break, NW
- Calafia – right reef break, NW
- Km 36.5 – reef break, left or right, NW/SH
- Km 39 – right point, NW
- Km 42 – reef break, NW
- Playa La Fonda – long beach break, NW
- Salsipuedes – reef break, right or left, NW/SH

- San Miguel – right point, NW
- Punta San José – right point break and reef break, NW/SH
- Eréndira – reef break, right or left, NW/SH
- Cabo Colonet – reef break, NW
- Camalú – right point and reef break, NW/SH
- Cabo San Quintín – beach, reef, and point breaks, NW/S/SH
- Playa Santa María – beach break, SH
- Punta Baja – reef break, NW/SH
- Bahía Asunción – reef break, beach break, NW/SH
- Punta Abreojos – right point, reef break, NW/SH
- Isla Natividad – four right point breaks, two left point breaks, NW/S/SH
- San Juanico – right point break, NW/S/SH

Horseback Riding and ATV Rental

As of 2006, riding on the beach is no longer allowed. The local wranglers have been moved off the beach to the north and south end of Juárez. ATVs can be rented at Iggy's Club, right next to the Rosarito Beach Hotel.

Charreadas

Small *charro* rings near town occasionally host *charreadas* (Mexican-style rodeos)—check with the tourist office on Boulevard Juárez for the latest schedule. Once a year, during the summer, a *gran charreada* takes place at Lienzo Charro Ejido Mazatlán—this is the one to see.

ENTERTAINMENT AND EVENTS

Bars and Nightclubs

On weekend nights and any night in July or August, Rosarito throbs with a disco beat.

Several clubs are concentrated just north of the Rosarito Beach Hotel, on the beach side of Boulevard Juárez. **Papas and Beer,** at the beach end of Calle Nogal, features multilevel indoor and outdoor bar areas, plus a sand volleyball court; the low cover charge keeps it packed on warm summer nights, but it's all but deserted in winter. The open bar policy at **Iggy's,** next to the Rosarito Beach Hotel, for the price of the cover (negotiable), can seem like a deal, but the drinks are often watered down. You can overcome that problem by working with the same bartender and tipping well. The crowds seem to pass by Señor Frogs located on Juáez and head straight for the beachside clubs.

The Hotel Festival Plaza features four bars/dance clubs designed to attract night owls young and old. **Rock and Roll Taco** has a Boulevard Juárez entrance as well as a poolside area. The

- Punta Conejo – right and left point breaks, NW/S/SH

- Punta Márquez – reef break, beach break, S/SH

- La Bocana – beach break, S/SH

- La Pastora – right sand point break, beach break, NW/SH

- Punta Pescadero – reef break, S/SH

- Playa Los Cerritos – beach break, reef break, NW/S/SH

- Punta Gaspareño – right sand point break, NW

- Bahía Migriño – beach break, NW/S/SH

- Bahía Chileno – right reef break, S/SH

- Playa Palmilla – right point break, reef break, S/SH

- Zippers (Playa Costa Azul) – reef break, S/SH

- Punta Gorda – right point break, reef break, S/SH

- Boca del Salado (north of Gorda) – beach break, S/SH

- Bahía Los Frailes – reef break, S/SH

- Cabo Pulmo – reef break, SH

- Punta Arena – right point break, SH

- Punta Colorado – reef break, SH

  Owing to ongoing natural climatic and geographic changes, surf locations and conditions may change from year to year. For further details on these and other surfing locations in Baja and the rest of Mexico, visit www.surfline .com, or pick up a copy of the *Surfer's Guide to Baja* by Mike Parise.

NW =	northwest windswell and/or west-northwest groundswell
S =	southeast-southwest groundswell
SH =	southeast-southwest hurricane swell

hotel's **El Museo Sal y Limón Cantina** also opens onto Juárez and claims the world's largest tequila collection. Other pluses are its semi-authentic Mexican cantina feel, good jukebox, and pool table. On the hotel's second floor, **Cha Cha Cha Barefoot Bar** attempts to imitate a Latin Caribbean beach club, including the appropriate music—canned during the week, live on Friday and Saturday nights.

Rene's Sports Bar, right next to Paraíso Ortiz at the southern outskirts of town, maintains a few pool tables and a bank of TVs tuned to sports channels. It's very much a gringo hangout, but a comfortable one. The attached dining room, which serves seafood, steak, and quail, is mostly empty except in the highest of high seasons, when strolling *trovadores* offer *música romántica.*

Events

Twice yearly in April and September, Rosarito kicks off the **Rosarito-Ensenada 50-Mile Bicycle Ride.** It is reportedly the third-largest biking event in the world, with close to 10,000 cyclists. For more information, call Bicycling West in San Diego (tel. 619/424-6084), or register online (www.rosaritoensenada.com). Even if you can't beat the course record of 2 hours and 13 minutes, you'll still have a great time.

Bajacaliforniano food fans won't want to miss the **Festival del Vino y la Langosta** (Festival of Wine and Lobster), held mid- to late-October; call Cámara Nacional de la Industria Restaurantera (CANIRAC; tel. 661/612-0700), a restaurant-industry consortium, for information.

SHOPPING

Rosarito offers a representative sampling of the same kinds of retail outlets found in Tijuana—liquor stores, pharmacies, curio shops, furniture outlets, leather shops, art galleries, and boutiques—most catering to American tastes. **Tile Express** (Blvd. Juárez 54A, tel. 661/612-1913), for example, is a branch of the larger Tijuana store. An even larger selection of handmade tiles is available at **Artesanías Hacienda** (Blvd. Juárez 2500-C, tel. 661/612-2435).

For high-end, hacienda-style Mexican furniture, have a look at **Fausto Polanco** (Blvd. Juárez 2400, tel. 661/612 2271, www .faustopolanco.com.mx). You'll find a second branch just out of town at Km 35 on the toll road to Ensenada.

On the west side of Boulevard Juárez, about midway between the Quinta del Mar and Rosarito Beach hotels, is the **Mercado de Artesanías,** a crafts market with around 200 vendors selling ceramics, textiles, wood carvings, sculptures, and other handmade items. Just south of town is a string of vendor stalls where handicraft prices tend to be a bit lower. Bargaining is expected; most vendors are open 9 A.M.–6 P.M.

Many shops are grouped in shopping plazas, e.g., Plaza Ejido Mazatlán, Quinta Plaza, and the arcade attached to the Rosarito Beach Hotel.

INFORMATION AND SERVICES
Tourist Assistance

SECTUR (tel./fax 661/612-0200, Mon.–Fri. 9 A.M.–7 P.M., weekends 10 A.M.–4 P.M.) is at the north end of town, north of the Tecate beer dealer and across from a Pemex station on Boulevard Benito Juárez. The helpful staff distributes Rosarito area and Baja California tourist information; English is spoken.

Money

Banamex and Serfín, both on the west side of Boulevard Juárez north of Hotel Festival Plaza, offer ATMs and can cash travelers checks.

GETTING THERE AND AROUND

No regular buses run between Tijuana and Rosarito. Instead, yellow-and-white station wagons called *taxis de ruta* ply the half-hour stretch between Tijuana and Rosarito from early in the morning until late at night for US$2 per person. These taxis can take you as far as La Mesa in Tijuana, depending on the route (five in all). The trip takes about 40 minutes or less, depending on traffic. You can catch these taxis anywhere along Boulevard Juárez, though the main *sitio* (taxi stand) seems to be at the southern end of the avenue near the Hotel Festival Plaza and Rosarito Beach Hotel. The white-and-red taxis offer only local service.

Route taxis also go to La Misión and Puerto Nuevo, both coastal towns south of Rosarito, for US$2. The main *sitio* for the latter is along Calle Villa Alamo, just south of Hotel Brisas del Mar and east of Boulevard Juárez.

Mexicoach (see bus information for *San Diego to Tijuana,* under *Getting There* in the *Essentials* chapter) operates between Tijuana and Rosarito for US$14 per person during regular operating hours.

From Tijuana to Rosarito, it's 31 kilometers via the toll road or 27 kilometers via the free road. Mexico 1-D, the toll road, is much faster, with four lanes in each direction, no traffic lights, and a maximum speed limit of 110 kilometers per hour (about 65 mph). The toll-road entrance in Tijuana is just south of the Río Tijuana.

To take the free road (Mexico 1) from Tijuana, you'll need to find Boulevard Cuauhtémoc by driving east on either Paseo de los Héroes or Boulevard Agua Caliente, then turn south on Cuauhtémoc. Coming from San Diego, you can avoid Tijuana altogether by crossing the border at Otay Mesa east of Tijuana, then following signs for Tecate. Instead of taking the turnoff for Mexico 2 to Tecate, continue straight on Boulevard Lázaro Cárdenas—which becomes Boulevard Independencia or "Libramiento-Oriente"—until the road intersects with Mexico 1. Follow signs reading Ensenada Libre.

If you're driving north out of Rosarito, note that the highway signs are misleading—the sign for Tijuana actually puts you onto the highway south to Ensenada. For Tijuana, follow the sign reading San Diego.

Small buses called *calafias* transport people up and down Boulevard Juárez for a few pesos.

South from Rosarito

The coast south of Rosarito holds a string of beaches, *ejidos* (collectively owned agricultural lands), and residential communities: Popotla, Las Gaviotas, Puerto Nuevo, Cantamar, El Descanso, La Fonda, La Misión, La Salina, Bajamar, and San Miguel. Real estate developers call this the Gold Coast, but only the coves and beaches are particularly attractive.

From Bahía Descanso (especially Km 33–38, Km 48, and Km 56 on the free road) to as far south as La Misión, several surfing spots offer decent reef or beach breaks. An area of sand dunes near Km 54 south of Cantamar is frequented by hang-gliding enthusiasts.

POPOTLA

Roughly 6.5 kilometers (4 mi) south of Rosarito via the free road, near Km 33, is a turnoff leading through a large cement arch to Popotla. The village attracts a strong following of seafood aficionados.

Around 30 seafood stands and rustic cafés crowd onto a point at one end of a small bay. Each draws its menu choices from the catch of the day, hauled directly from local boats and stuffed into plastic coolers. The food is delicious and inexpensive relative to prices in Rosarito and Puerto Nuevo, but not necessarily as cheap as places farther south, such as the seafood market in Ensenada or fish camps along the Baja California Sur coast. Popotla's vendors open around 11 A.M.

Estudios de la Playa (Fox Studios Baja)

Twentieth Century Fox built this huge indoor/outdoor studio complex for the 1996 filming of the Academy Award–winning blockbuster *Titanic.* A 95 percent scale replica of the original ship was constructed on the lot and floated in a giant seawater tank near the beach, allowing camera angles that blended the tank's water surface with that of the Pacific Ocean. After production on *Titanic* ended, Fox decided to maintain the US$25 million studios as a permanent production facility and to lease it out to other filmmakers.

The latest addition to the complex, **Foxploration,** gives movie buffs an inside look at a working studio in a theme park–style experience. Some of the attractions include: "Canal Street, New York," an actual movie set re-creating a vintage Manhattan street; "Cinemágico," interactive exhibits involving sound effects, optical illusions, and animatronics; and "Titanic Expo," a guided tour through the actual sets, costumes, and props from the movie of the same name, including a replica of the White Star Southampton Pier and sets from the ship's interior, including first-class smoking room, dining salon, and corridor; Palm Court Cafe; boiler room; and stateroom. Also on display are various pieces of furniture, suitcases, teacups, mailbags, signs, posters, toys, lifeboats, lifesavers, lifejackets, oars, and miscellaneous ship parts used in the movie.

Foxploration is open Wednesday–Friday 9 A.M.–5:30 P.M., Saturday–Sunday 10 A.M.–6:30 P.M. Admission is adult US$12, seniors and children 3–11 US$9, children under three free. Visa and MasterCard are accepted. Call 661/614-9444, U.S. tel. 866/369-2252, or visit www.foxploration.com for more information.

Fox Studios Baja, known locally as Estudios de la Playa (Beach Studios), is about five kilometers (3 mi) south of Rosarito, just off the free road between Mexico 1-D and the ocean. Exit the toll road at the La Paloma, Popotla, Calafia exit, and look for the studio complex entrance at Km 32.8 on the free road, just before the big white arch advertising Popotla.

Along the dirt road that leads to Popotla, a cement wall separating the village from Fox Studios Baja is adorned with multimedia art created by local children.

PUERTO NUEVO

The tiny seaside town of Puerto Nuevo, 19 kilometers (12 mi) south of Rosarito via Mexico 1, is known as Baja's lobster capital. Although the actual lobster harvest in the area isn't what it once was—the lobster served in Puerto Nuevo is mostly harvested in areas off the coast of Baja California Sur and distributed through San Diego—lobster restaurants are more plentiful than ever. When Baja travelers first discovered Puerto Nuevo in the 1950s, they dined in the houses of two or three local families. Now the village offers nearly 30 side-by-side seafood restaurants, some quite modern. It's an entire village devoted to eating.

The **Festival del Vino y la Langosta** (Festival of Wine and Lobster) occurs in Puerto Nuevo's restaurant zone in mid-October. For around US$25 per person, participants are welcome to sample all the Baja lobster and wine they can consume.

Accommodations

The **Grand Baja Resort** (tel. 661/614-1493, U.S. tel. 877/315-1002, www.grandbaja.com, US$79–275), just south of Puerto Nuevo at Km 44.5 on the free road, features one-, two-, and three-bedroom condos on a bluff overlooking the Pacific. The rooms can be hit or miss and the lack of air conditioning can be a real problem depending on the season.

A good option for a group of four or more are the condos at Las Gaviotas (www.las-gaviotas.com). Condos range from one to six bedrooms for US$100–350 per night. The gated community also has a rare combination of beginner and expert surf.

Just south of Puerto Nuevo at Km 38 on the free road, a small RV park called **Surfpoint Camping** is sandwiched between a couple of moldy-looking condo developments—it's easy to miss. Rates are US$7 per night for tent sites, US$15 for RVs. Look also for **Cantamar** (US$10/night per site) at Cantamar Beach.

Food

The typical Puerto Nuevo–style lobster platter includes lobster, beans, rice, and tortillas. The lobster is usually lightly fried in spiced oil and then briefly grilled before serving, but in some restaurants it is also prepared in

BAJA CALIFORNIA LOBSTERS

Of the several species of lobster scooting about in Baja seas, the most numerous are *Panulirus interruptus* (known as "red lobster," or *langosta roja*), found as far south as the 25th parallel on both the Pacific and Sea of Cortez sides, and *P. inflatus* ("blue lobster," or *langosta azul*), found in the Pacific and lower Cortez as far south as Tehuantepec, Oaxaca. None of the lobsters found in Baja waters are related to the cold-water type (genus *Homarus*) found off the coast of the northeastern United States and southeastern Canada. Baja's warm-water lobsters are sometimes referred to as "spiny lobsters" because their shells bear spiny projections (the *Homarus* shell is smooth). Spiny lobsters also feature smaller pincers than the cold-water varieties.

Adult spiny lobsters reach up to 61 centimeters (24 In) in length and weigh as much as six kilograms (13 lbs). Most varieties are nocturnal and tend to frequent depths of 5-30 meters. During the day they stay beneath or between rocks, hiding from natural enemies like sharks, octopuses, rays, and a few larger finfish. Their diet consists mostly of crustaceans, mollusks, and other small sea organisms.

Lobstering is a major part of the fishing industry in Mexico, the world's eighth-largest harvester of lobster. The official lobstering seasons are March 16–September 30 for red lobster and June 1–September 15 for blue lobster. Most of the lobsters taken in Baja come from coastal waters off Baja California Sur, which now accounts for 55 percent of the total Mexican harvest.

It's illegal for foreigners to capture *any* lobster; only Mexican members of registered *cooperativas de pesca* (fishing cooperatives) may take lobsters.

© PAUL ITOI

Puerto Nuevo, home of the lobster roll

a *ranchera* (tomato and chili) sauce or boiled New England–style.

The very first true restaurant to serve lobster here was **Restaurant Puerto Nuevo,** and judging from the crowds this is still the local favorite. The original Restaurant Puerto Nuevo serves only lobster, shrimp, and fish-fillet platters, and only cash is accepted. The fancier **Restaurant Puerto Nuevo II** next door features a more extensive menu and accepts credit cards; most of the clientele are visiting gringos. Other family-run favorites include **Miramar, Chela's, La Escondida, El Galeón,** and **La Perlita.** All of these restaurants are clustered around the Puerto Nuevo exit on the west side of the toll road. Smaller lobsters with rice, beans, and tortillas cost US$12, medium-sized crustaceans run US$14–16, and a half-kilo (1.5-pound) lobster costs US$16–18 or more. A few places offer weekday specials as low as US$9 including a complimentary beer or margarita. As you walk or drive through town, men in front of the restaurants hold up hand-lettered signs advertising their restaurant's lobster dinners and prices; just remember, cheaper doesn't always mean better!

Getting There

Red-and-white route taxis operate between Rosarito and Puerto Nuevo for US$2 per person. In Rosarito, they leave from in front of the Hotel Festival Plaza. In Puerto Nuevo, you must stand at the side of the highway opposite the village entrance and flag one down; these taxis actually ply a Rosarito–La Misión route. For evening excursions, it's safer to hire a *taxi de ruta* to Puerto Nuevo from Rosarito than to drive it yourself—these drivers know the road very well.

LA FONDA AND LA MISIÓN

To reach this area, approximately 60 kilometers (37 mi) south of the border, take the La Misión–Alisitos exit from the toll road at Km 59. Here you'll find the best beaches between Tijuana and south of Ensenada. At one time, the valley surrounding La Misión sheltered Misión San Miguel Arcángel de la Frontera, founded

by Dominican Padre Luis Salles in 1788 and secularized in 1833. The only remains of the mission are two adobe walls standing in a schoolyard on the east side of the free road as it passes through the village.

Beaches

Playa La Misión is the better of the two gently curving beaches. A large public parking lot just off the highway makes it more accessible than most. Also here are rental horses, bathrooms, cement picnic tables, and trash barrels. **La Salina,** a few kilometers south of La Misión, is an up-and-coming beach area as well. A small marina has recently been constructed.

Near Km 55, a local surf spot known as Campo López features a consistent beach break that comes up best during a southwest swell.

Accommodations

Overlooking the broad beach at La Misión, **Hotel La Misión** (tel. 615/155-0205, US$50) has 10 clean and large rooms, all with ocean view and fireplace. Suites with private hot tub and refrigerator are available, and the hotel has a decent restaurant and small grocery store. Noise from the downstairs lobby can be a problem in this small hotel.

La Salina Restaurant Bar and Hotel (US$75–95), six kilometers south of La Misión, follows the example of the Hotel La Fonda and Hotel La Misión in providing good food and comfortable rooms near the beach at reasonable rates.

Beach condos are available at **Plaza del Mar** (tel. 664/685-9152, U.S. tel. 800/868-0248), at Km 58, about three kilometers (2 mi) north of La Misión. The property has a pool, hot tub, basketball and tennis courts, gardens, and a small archaeological museum. Rates start at US$125 for a one-bedroom.

In addition to its standard rooms, **Hotel La Fonda** (tel. 615/628-7352, US$85) offers oceanfront apartments—each with kitchen and fireplace—that accommodate up to four persons. La Fonda's restaurant serves good seafood with an ocean view.

Baja Seasons (Km 72, tel. 646/155-4015,

© PAUL ITOI

La Fonda

U.S. tel. 800/754-4190, www.bajaseasons.com) offers 20 motel rooms from US$80–120. They also offer several types of well-appointed villas that can accommodate four to six people for US$140–250. The park is accessible only from southbound Mexico 1-D, so if you're coming from Ensenada you'll have to make a U-turn at some point farther north. If you notice the powered hang gliders buzzing along the beaches and want to get involved, check out www.volareaircraft.com, which offers lessons from the resort.

Camping and RV Parks

Alisitos Trailer Park Ejidal, a little north of Hotel La Misión, charges just US$7 per 24 hours whether you have a tent or a motor home. There are no facilities as such, so you must be self-contained, but given the quality of the beach this is a steal.

Baja Seasons (Km 72, tel. 646/155-4015, U.S. tel. 800/754-4190, www.bajaseasons.com) has RV sites for US$72 oceanfront or US$48 interior.

Food

La Palapa de San José, just north of Hotel La Fonda on the west side of the free road at Km 58, is a simple café with indoor-outdoor seating for breakfast, lunch, and dinner. On weekends the café usually hosts live music.

SAN MIGUEL AND EL SAUZAL

A unique cross between retirement-oriented trailer park and surf camp, San Miguel is the legacy of a Polish-Mexican-American family, the Robertsons, who've lived in northern Mexico and southern California for most of this century. The late Tomás Robertson, who founded the Villa de San Miguel residential community in the 1950s, was a mission historian and an active member of the Comité por Conservación de Misiónes de Baja California. His family now manages the trailer park, bar, and restaurant. Technically San Miguel belongs to the pueblo of El Sauzal.

The bay formed by Punta San Miguel is the most popular surfing locale in Baja. Mexico's first surfboard manufacturer—San Miguel—is named after the point. A few hardcore surfers live in San Miguel on a semipermanent basis, and during the winter a small legion takes up residence on the beach or in rented trailers to ride the bay's fast right point break. On winter evenings, those who aren't partying in Ensenada or exhausted by the day's surfing hang out in the San Miguel Restaurant bar swapping war stories about the three-story waves at Islas de Todos Santos.

Accommodations

In El Sauzal, **Hostel Sauzal** (Av. L 344, tel. 646/174-6381, http://hostelsauzal.tripod.com, $15 pp) offers dormitory-style accommodations—four beds to a dorm—all with an ocean view. Amenities include pillows and blankets, storage lockers for backpacks, hot showers with an ocean view, free continental breakfast, storage for bikes and surfboards, writing desks, and a library of Baja books, maps, and magazines. If you're driving south, El Sauzal begins about two miles after the San Miguel tollbooth. To find the hostel, pass under the footbridge, then turn left after the Pemex station. Go two blocks, turn right, then go one block, turn left up a dirt road, and the hostel is in the third house on the right.

Camping

Camping is permitted on the beach at San Miguel for US$4–10 per night; full-hookup trailer sites are US$12–15. Facilities include a dump station, bar, restaurant, reasonably well-kept bathrooms, and hot showers. Trailers on the hill above the beach can sometimes be rented for US$25–30 a night. Inquire at the restaurant (tel. 646/174-6225). Check to see if the water supply is working before accepting an offer; water pressure in the trailers near the top of the hill is sometimes low or even absent. For permanent trailers with their own water storage tanks, this isn't a problem. Occasionally a trailer slot on the hill opens up.

Ramona Beach RV (Km 104, tel. 646/174-6045, US$15), opposite the big Pemex facility, offers 50 simple RV spaces with full hookups near the beach—many are permanently occupied but we've seen a few open ones. RV storage is available. **Motel Puesta del Sol** (Km 100, Mexico 1, US$20) also offers RV spaces.

Getting There

San Miguel can be difficult to locate, especially if you're driving south from Rosarito or Tijuana, because the exit is poorly marked. Driving south on the toll road, take the Tijuana Libre exit just past the tollgate at Km 99, then follow the road west across the toll road until it curves south and begins to merge with the toll road a half kilometer farther. Instead of returning to the highway, follow the short, paved loop to the right and you'll come to San Miguel Village. If you're arriving via the free road, remember to take this road almost immediately before merging with the four-lane highway.

From Ensenada, take the exit marked San Miguel just before the first tollgate heading north. To get there by public transportation from Ensenada, take the yellow-and-white Brisa minibus.

Tecate and Vicinity

During his 1964 presidential campaign, Gustavo Díaz Ordaz referred to Tecate (pop. 91,000) as *la ventana mas limpia de México,* "the cleanest window of Mexico." He may have been fishing for the Tecate vote (which he didn't get; Díaz was unpopular in northern Baja), but as Mexican border towns go, this one is easily the most inviting.

Set in a bowl-shaped valley in the lower Sierra Juárez—known as the Laguna Mountains on the California side—Tecate is insulated from industrial Tijuana and Mexicali to the west and east. The fresh, unpolluted air in the valley lured the developers of North America's first and longest-running health spa, Rancho La Puerta. Tecate's other claim to fame is its namesake cerveza, brewed here from spring water since the 1940s.

Though it has become busier in recent years, the border crossing, four blocks north of town at the end of Calle Lázaro Cárdenas, remains one of Baja's most relaxed. Savvy Californians use this crossing instead of Tijuana's when returning from an Ensenada holiday; the wait is much shorter, and the drive along Mexico 3 between Ensenada and Tecate provides an alternative to Mexico 1's coastal scenery. The town on the U.S. side of the border is also called Tecate.

Tecate is famous for its mild summers, thanks to an elevation of 514 meters (1,690 ft) and distance from both cold Pacific breezes and the high temperatures of the San Felipe Desert. The city's general ambience is more that of a provincial Mexican town than a border town.

Note: Sights along Mexico 3 between Tecate and Ensenada are covered at the end of this *Tecate* section. Sights along Mexico 2 between Tecate and Mexicali are covered in the *Vicinity of Mexicali* section in the chapter *Mexicali to San Felipe.* Sights along Mexico 2 between Tecate and Tijuana are covered under *Leaving Tijuana* in the *Tijuana and Vicinity* section in this chapter.

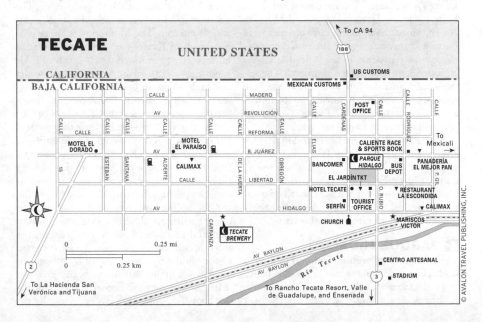

HISTORY

Tecate is the oldest border town in Baja, though in terms of peninsular history it's still relatively young. In the early 19th century, a few mestizo farmers began working the valley lands. As word got around that the valley was fertile and water—supplied by the Tecate and Las Palmas Rivers—was abundant, more followed. In 1831, Peruvian Juan Bandini received a land grant of 4,500 hectares from the Mexican government, and two years later laid out a town to serve the budding farming community.

Long before Bandini's arrival, the valley surrounding Tecate had been sporadically inhabited by Yuma Amerindians, who called it Zacate. The Yumas revered 1,520-meter (5,000-ft) Monte Cuchumá, the valley's most outstanding geographic feature, which today straddles the U.S.–Mexico border. Surviving Kumyais, a subtribe of the Yumas, still revere the mountain, and in 1982 they successfully obtained a U.S. agreement to dismantle radio towers on Cuchumá's California side.

Most likely the name Tecate developed from a Spanish corruption of the Amerindian name for the valley, Zacate. Another theory, rather unlikely, has it that Tecate comes from the English "to cut," since Anglos to the north often came to the valley to cut wood in the late 19th century—though the vegetation in the valley has always consisted mostly of treeless chaparral. The settlement became the capital of a new Mexican municipality in 1892, following completion of a railroad built to connect Tijuana, Tecate, and Mexicali with the national rail system.

Tecate became a household word in Mexico after the founding of the Tecate Brewery in 1943. Aside from the brewery and a growing number of *maquiladoras* east of the city on Mexico 2, the town remains primarily dependent on agriculture. Tourism, though relatively limited, is also a source of local revenue.

◖ PARQUE HIDALGO

Town life centers around Parque Hidalgo, a shady plaza at the intersection of Avenida Juárez and Calle Lázaro Cárdenas, Tecate's main thoroughfares. At the southeast corner of the park

stands a statue of Miguel Hidalgo, the Dolores priest who issued the call for Mexican independence in 1810. In the vicinity of the small plaza are a number of restaurants, taco stands, *paleterías y neverías* (popsicle and ice-cream stands), crafts shops, and the tourist office.

◖ TECATE BREWERY

Tecate beer, the only beer in Mexico named for a town, was first brewed by Tecate entrepreneur Alberto Aldrete in 1943. Aldrete started the brewery as a sideline to his *maltería* (malt factory). The first bottles distributed to the public carried a label that read "Rubio Tecate" over a silhouette of Monte Cuchumá. Although the beer sold well locally and was even exported to San Diego, Los Angeles, and San Francisco via train, Aldrete went bankrupt after 10 years. In 1954, Eugenio Garza Sada from Monterrey bought the brewery and added it to Cervecería Cuauhtémoc (later called Cervecería Cuauhtémoc Moctezuma), brewers of Carta Blanca and Bohemia, two other well-known Mexican beers.

Today, Cuauhtémoc Moctezuma operates breweries in five other Mexican cities and produces 10 different labels, including Tecate. The Tecate brand, however, is brewed only in Tecate and Monterrey. The Monterrey brewery produces canned Tecate—in the red-and-silver can familiar to many Americans—much of it for export; the Tecate plant produces only bottles and kegs. Mexican beer drinkers mostly consume Tecate in long-necked deposit bottles or liter-size *caguamas* ("sea turtles"). On both cans and bottles, every label still carries the profile of Cuchumá, the Kumyais' sacred mountain.

Beer aficionados claim the best Tecate comes from Tecate; the water used at the brewery there, tapped directly from local springs, is considered the purest in Mexico. According to Cuauhtémoc brewers, Tecate is brewed as a lager, with an alcohol content of 3.6 percent and sufficient hops to rate a 20 on the international bitterness scale. Tecate exported to the United States is reduced to 3.2 percent alcohol—a major reason the brand tastes so different north of the border (along with the fact that U.S.-consumed Tecate is usually the

© JIMCLNE.COM

Tecate Brewery

canned product from Monterrey). The hops level for export Tecate is also reduced to produce the smoother, blander beer taste preferred by mainstream America.

Carta Blanca, the only other label produced at the Tecate brewery, is a lighter pilsner with a bitterness grade of 16 and an alcohol content of 3.5 percent. *Bajacalifornianos* overwhelmingly prefer Tecate to Carta Blanca, partially out of loyalty to Baja California—Carta Blanca originated in Monterrey—but also because they believe the latter a bland brew. Incidentally, the custom of drinking Tecate with salt and a squeeze of lime, now part of Cuauhtémoc's Tecate advertising campaign, was probably introduced by gringo Baja hands—who squeeze lime over everything they consume in Mexico—concerned with killing bacteria on the top of the can. Lime juice also tends to neutralize the "can" taste. Follow the *mexicano* example and drink bottled Tecate; it's cheaper (if you return the bottles for a deposit refund), better tasting, and more ecologically responsible.

The present brewery complex (Dr. Arturo Guerra 70, tel. 665/654-9478, www.ccm.com.mx, Mon.–Fri. 10 A.M.–noon, 3–4:30 P.M., Sat. 9–10:30 A.M.) stands on the same site as Aldrete's original keg brewery; high-tech German equipment is used to produce 40 million liters per month and ship to 100 countries around the world. Call ahead to book a free tour, or plan your visit during the times above.

RAIL TOUR

Once or twice a month, the **Pacific Southwest Railway Museum** (State Hwy 94 and Forest Gate Rd., Campo, CA, U.S. weekend tel. 619/478-9937, U.S. weekday tel. 619/465-7776, www.sdrm.org, US$43) organizes Saturday rail excursions from its Campo Depot (80 minutes by car from downtown San Diego) to Tecate, an hour and fifteen minute ride. Trains typically depart Campo at 10:30 A.M. and return at 4:30 P.M. In summer, twilight trips depart Campo at 3 P.M. and return at 9 P.M. Reservations required. Credit cards and PayPal are accepted.

strumming while waiting for the rest of the band

© JIMCLINE.COM

ENTERTAINMENT AND EVENTS

Tecate is not big on nightlife; the main source of evening entertainment seems to be promenading back and forth along Avenida Juárez until around 9 P.M., when the streets become practically deserted.

Although it almost seems out of place in this low-key town, **Caliente Race and Sports Book** (www.caliente.com.mx, Wed.–Sun. 9 A.M.–11 P.M., Tues. 9 A.M.–8:30 P.M.), at the northeast corner of Calle Rodríguez and Avenida Juárez, offers the usual betting lounge, restaurant, and bar.

The Santa Veronica Offroad Park and Roadway, a series of dirt racetracks at Hacienda Santa Veronica, 30 kilometers (19 mi) east of Tecate off Mexico 2, hosts several racing events throughout the year. The biggest is the three-day **Gran Carrera de Tecate,** held in late May. More popular among *bajacalifornianos* is Santa Veronica's **Gran Carrera de Caballos,** which takes place the last weekend in March.

The **SCORE Tecate Baja 500** occurs in June and early November (U.S. tel. 818/225-8402). (See *Events* under *Ensenada and Vicinity* in the *Ensenada to El Rosario* chapter for information on SCORE activities.)

During the second week of October, local residents celebrate the **Fiesta de la Fundación de Tecate,** honoring the founding of the city with parades, music, dancing, and fireworks.

SHOPPING

A few *alfarerías* (pottery and tile works) and *vidrierías* (glassworks) sell products in local stores. Visitors crossing into Baja at Tecate can't miss the highly visible **Patio del Sol** on the east side of Calle Lázaro Cárdenas, two blocks south of the gateway. The outdoor display features a large selection of unglazed pottery, plus a smaller number of decorative sculptures.

The government-sponsored **Centro Artesanal,** south of the railway and Río Tecate on Mexico 3 (about 1.5 km south of Av. Juárez), houses two shops: **Tecate Handicraft Center** and **Artesanías Mexicanas.** Besides glasswork and pottery, the vendors offer blankets, rugs, folk art, and other crafts from elsewhere in Northern Mexico.

ACCOMMODATIONS
Hotels and Motels

Under US$50: On the south side of the plaza, around the corner and upstairs from El Jardín restaurant, **Hotel Tecate** (Cardenas y Callejón Libertad No. 20, tel. 665/654-1116, US$35) features 12 basic rooms, some with TV. Ask for a room overlooking the plaza—the rooms without a view are rather dark.

Close to the center of town, **El Paraíso** (Calle Aldrete 83 at Av. Juárez, tel. 665/654-1716, US$40) offers basic but clean rooms with air conditioning (old window units) and attached hot showers. In winter, if necessary, you can ask for a space heater *(calentador)*. Guests can park in the garage beneath the hotel.

Just west of town on the north side of Mexico 2, the two-story, pink **La Hacienda** (Av. Juárez 861, tel. 665/654-1250, US$45) offers clean rooms with TV and air conditioning. The interior courtyard is decorated with potted tropical plants and features offstreet parking.

US$50-100: Two blocks west of the Paraíso, **El Dorado** (Av. Juárez 160, tel. 665/654-1333, eldorado@yahoo.com.mx, US$57) is a two-story wood-and-stucco motel court near the western entrance to Tecate at Av. Juárez and Calle Esteban. Spacious, well-kept rooms come with air conditioning, heat, TV, and phones. Offstreet parking is available.

Ranch Resorts

ATV- and motorcycle-friendly **Hacienda Santa Verónica** (tel. 665/681-7428, US$70) is a ranch resort off Mexico 2, about 30 kilometers east of Tecate near Km 106 on the free road or Km 94 on the toll road. You must exit from the free road as there is no exit from the toll road. Guestrooms, in mission-style condos, come with fireplaces and patios. Meal plans are available. On the premises are six tennis courts, off-road racetracks for motorcycles and four-wheelers, equestrian trails, a swimming pool, volleyball court, and basketball court. Originally a *ganadería,* or breeding ranch for fight-

ing bulls *(ganados bravos),* the Hacienda also offers elementary bullfighting lessons for ranch guests. Other facilities include a restaurant/bar decorated with bullfighting memorabilia and a campground/RV park open to the public.

Rancho La Puerta

One of the most famous spas in North America, Rancho La Puerta (tel. 760/744-4222 or 800/443-7565, www.rancholapuerta.com) counts Madonna, Steven Seagal, Jodie Foster, Oprah Winfrey, and Monaco's Princess Stephanie among its celebrity guests. Enrollees participate in an all-inclusive, weeklong health regime designed for physical and spiritual rejuvenation. The regimen includes hiking, yoga and tai chi, swimming, weight training, and organic cuisine. The site was chosen for its location in one of the Californias' last "safe zones" for the environmentally sensitive and for its proximity to Monte Cuchumá, viewed by the spa's founders as a source of spiritual power.

Hacienda-style architecture includes cottages and suites for a maximum of 150 guests. Most units have fireplaces, and each has its own garden. A dining hall serves organic fruits and vegetables, along with occasional fresh fish.

All-inclusive prices for the daily health program, meals, and accommodations range from US$2,780 per week for a studio with bath to US$4,205 for a two-bedroom villa suite. Summer rates—late June–early September—are lower.

Camping and RV Parks

Rancho Ojai RV Park (tel. 665/655-3014, www.tecatekoa.com) lies 21 kilometers (13 mi) east of Tecate on Mexico 2. If you're on the toll road, exit at El Hongo and drive west on Mexico 2 for eight kilometers (5 mi) until you see the Rancho Ojai gates. Part of a working ranch, the campground offers 41 oak-shaded sites with full hookups, surrounded by 16 hectares of boulder-studded rolling hills and chaparral. Tent sites for up to four people cost US$11 a night, RV sites with full hookups go for US$30. On the premises are a swimming pool, gender-separated restrooms and showers, a restaurant, camp store, clubhouse, dump station, laundry, and open-air grills. Available activities include horseback riding and wagon and hay rides. Cabins with shared bath are US$68, US$90 with private bath, and US$135 with private bath and kitchenette. **Rancho Santa Verónica** (30 km east of Tecate at Km 98, Mexico 2, US$20) also has full-hookup slots and tent spaces. Guests have access to all the ranch recreational facilities.

FOOD

Among Tecate's most renowned culinary attractions are the long-established taquerías surrounding Parque Hidalgo, which serve better-than-average tacos, burritos, and tostadas. Each taquería has its unique way of assembling the basic ingredients. The taquerías are typically open from late morning till late evening.

La Escondida (daily 7 A.M.–5 P.M.), on Callejón Libertad east of the plaza near Hotel Colonial, has a more complete menu of *antojitos* and Mexican breakfasts.

For quick, inexpensive, sit-down meals, try **🍴 El Jardín** (daily 6 A.M.–noon, mains under US$10). This tiny diner on the south side of the plaza, a few doors west of the tourist office, offers Mexican standards at reasonable prices for lunch and dinner, plus a large variety of breakfasts. During warm weather, the Jardín places a few tables outside and instantly becomes the only sidewalk café in Tecate, complete with wandering *trovadores.*

Mariscos Victor (Hidalgo 284) serves reasonably priced Mexican-style seafood, including ceviche tostadas, fish tacos, seafood cocktail, and shrimp, as well as ranchero standards like *burritos de machaca, gorditas,* quesadillas, and *bistek* (steak). A choice of nine different full breakfasts is available, starting at 7 A.M., for about US$5. It's open for breakfast, lunch, and dinner.

El Passeto (Callejón Libertad 200) offers Italian fare and seafood dishes for lunch or dinner.

Groceries

Tiendas on Avenida Juárez and Avenida Hidalgo sell basic foodstuffs; there's also a medium-size **Calimax** supermarket on Avenida Juárez near the Calle Carranza intersection. For excellent *pan dulce, bolillos,* and other Mexican bakery items, grab tray and tongs at **🍴 Panadería El Mejor Pan** (Juárez 331 btw Rodríguez/Portes Gil). Some folks claim it's the best Mexican bakery in all of Baja; it's certainly a contender, and it's open 24 hours. Coffee is dispensed free.

INFORMATION AND SERVICES
Tourist Assistance

The state tourist office (tel. 665/654-1095, www.tecatemexico.com.mx, Mon.–Fri. 9 A.M.–7 P.M., Sat. 9 A.M.–3 P.M., Sun. 10 A.M.–2 P.M.) faces the south side of Parque Hidalgo. The police station is next door. There is also a tourist information booth near the border crossing at Calle Lázaro Cárdenas and Calle Madero.

Money

U.S. dollars are accepted at most shops, hotels, and restaurants. If you want to change to pesos before crossing into Mexico, you'll find a money-changing service in Tecate, California, in the same strip center as a U.S. post office and Western Union office.

A Banamex on Avenida Juárez and a Serfín on Calle Cárdenas each offers foreign exchange services and ATMs. There's also a private *casa de cambio* opposite the northwest corner of the plaza.

Post and Telephone

Tecate's post office is on the corner of Calles Madero and Ortiz Rubio. Probably the best place to make a long-distance call is from the staffed *caseta* at the bus depot.

Immigration and Customs

Immigration and customs offices at the border gateway in Tecate are open daily 6 A.M.–midnight.

GETTING THERE
By Bus

Tecate's bus depot is on Avenida Juárez at Calle Rodríguez; on the premises are a snack bar and long-distance telephone service. Frequent departures include **ABC** buses to Mexicali, Tijuana, and Ensenada.

By Car

To drive to Tecate from San Diego, take U.S. 805 to U.S. 94 east 66 kilometers (41 mi) to the Tecate turnoff near the border. From Arizona and points east, take I-8 west to the U.S. 94 junction at Jacumba, then follow U.S. 94 west to the Tecate turnoff. The Tecate border gate is open 5 A.M.–11 P.M.

A branch of **Oscar Padilla's Mexican Insurance** (825 Imperial Ave., Calexico, tel. 800/258-8600) can be found in a small shopping center on the American side, located inside Checkmate.

If you're on your way to mainland Mexico and need a temporary vehicle import permit, note that permits are issued only Monday–Saturday 8 A.M.–4 P.M. at the customs office. If you're planning to drive in Baja only, you don't need an import permit and can cross any day of the week.

Tecate lies at the intersection of Mexico 2 (to Tijuana or Mexicali) and Mexico 3 (to Ensenada). The toll road between Tijuana and Tecate, Mexico 2-D, parallels the border closely; tolls come to about US$11.

By Rail

The **Pacific Southwest Railway Museum** (State Hwy 94 and Forest Gate Rd., Campo, CA, U.S. weekend tel. 619/478-9937, U.S. weekday tel. 619/465-7776, www.sdrm.org, US$43) runs the only passenger rail service to Tecate. Daylong and twilight tours run only a few times each month. See *Rail Tour* earlier in this section.

By Foot

For a day trip, you can park in any number of lots on the American side of the border and walk over to Tecate.

MEXICO 3 TO ENSENADA

The two-lane highway between Tecate and Ensenada (Mexico 3) winds through the rolling, boulder-studded western slopes of the Sierra Juárez to historic Guadalupe (Km 77), centered in a large valley created by the Río Guadalupe. A Russian colony and valley of vineyards are the primary attractions (see *Valle de Guadalupe and the Ruta del Vino* in the *Ensenada to El Rosario* chapter).

ENSENADA TO EL ROSARIO

Whether they are on a cruise from Los Angeles, driving from San Diego, or passing through on the way to points south, many travelers find themselves in Ensenada for an afternoon or longer. Those who venture away from the commercial port into the town center find that a surprisingly pleasant Mexican town awaits.

Many of Ensenada's visual attractions lie out of town—at Estero Beach, Punta Banda, and La Bufadora—but a number of places of interest in the city are accessible by foot.

South of Ensenada, Mexico 1 meanders through a series of farming communities, including the vineyards of Valle de Santo Tomás.

For an inland adventure, explore the 170,000-acre national park at Sierra San Pedro Mártir, the highest mountain range on the Baja Peninsula. Then return to the coast to make your way along three interconnected bays on the Pacific Ocean, which offer numerous surf breaks, good fishing, and solitary beach camping.

PLANNING YOUR TIME

Half a day is plenty of time to get a feel for Ensenada. If you have a car, you might spend a few hours or an entire day visiting wineries along the Ruta del Vino. Anglers will be content to spend a week or more plying the waters of Bahía San Quintín.

For sierra-bound visitors, the best hiking seasons are mid-April–mid-June (good for wildflowers) and late September–early November (when quaking aspens put on a show). For backpackers, the April–June season is optimal because water sources from the snowmelt are most abundant. Late summer rains can cause hazardous flash floods in the arroyos.

HIGHLIGHTS

◖ Riviera del Pacífico: For a slice of Ensenada history, walk the grounds of the former Playa Ensenada Hotel and Casino, once run by American boxer Jack Dempsey, and now the city's cultural center (page 80).

◖ Valle de Guadalupe and the Ruta del Vino: Taste Mexico's finest vintages at the growing number of boutique wineries in the rural Valle de Guadalupe along Mexico 3 between Ensenada and Tecate (page 101).

◖ La Bufadora: One of the more touristy attractions in northern Baja, this blowhole is an easy excursion from Ensenada. Visitors congregate around the top of a cavern to watch spumes shoot 100 feet in the air (page 106).

◖ Islas de Todos Santos: In winter, take a boat from Ensenada or San Miguel out to Islas de Todos Santos to watch surfers tackle waves that can measure three stories high (page 108).

◖ Clamming Along Bahía San Quintín: Digging for giant pismo clams is a popular pastime among locals who live along this Pacific Ocean bay. Use your hands, or bring a pitchfork to harvest your catch of the day (page 122).

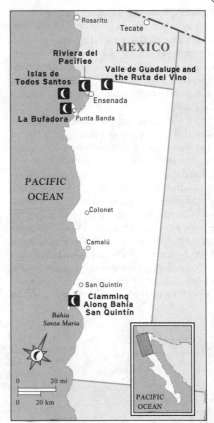

LOOK FOR ◖ TO FIND RECOMMENDED SIGHTS, ACTIVITIES, DINING, AND LODGING.

ENSENADA TO EL ROSARIO

Ensenada and Vicinity

Ensenada (pop. 413,000) sees far more visitors than any other nonborder town on the peninsula. Every summer an estimated four million people—most of them Americans—pass through. Yet as a busy trade center for northern peninsula fishing and agriculture, the city retains a *bajacaliforniano* identity in spite of the tourists.

Baja California's third-largest city is also the peninsula's largest seaport due to its position on the wide Bahía de Todos Santos. The main industries in the area, aside from tourism, are fishing, fish processing, and agriculture, all relying on the bay as a shipping point for sending products to mainland Mexico, the United States, Canada, and Asia. Olives and grapes are the principal crops produced in the Ensenada area; the huge Oliveres Mexicanos plantation (48 km northeast of Ensenada, near Guadalupe) is the world's largest single olive producer, with over 120,000 trees under cultivation.

A portion of the grape harvest is used by a half dozen wineries based in Ensenada to produce wines for both domestic and international markets. Yellowtail and halibut are the top fish harvests, followed by various bottom fishes, lobster and other shellfish, and anchovies. Light manufacturing has also taken root in a warehouse area in the southern part of the city, where Fender Musical Instruments has a small plant.

During recent years Ensenada has expanded efforts to attract visitors. Cruise ships from Los Angeles and San Diego bring large groups of day-trippers who are gone at night. A first-class sailing facility, Marina Coral, can be found at the north end of the bay. The revenue generated from cruise ship and yacht tourism has been used to beautify the waterfront. A *malecón,* or waterfront promenade, has been added, along with Ensenada Cruiseport Village, a cruise-ship facility boasting three state-of-the-art cruise ship berths, a 200-slip marina, retail shops, restaurants, crafts market, and small businesses

© PAUL ITOI

A huge Mexican flag waves from the Parque Ventana al Mar.

ENSENADA TO EL ROSARIO

Guadalupe

VALLE DE GUADALUPE AND THE RUTA DEL VINO

RIVIERA DEL PACÍFICO

ISLAS DE TODOS SANTOS

Bahía Todos Santos

Ensenada

To San Felipe

Cabo Punta Banda

LA BUFADORA

Maneadero

IMMIGRATION CHECKPOINT

Cabo Santo Tomás

SANTO TOMÁS DE AQUINO

Punta San José

SAN VICENTE FERRER

San Vicente

To San Felipe

Colonet

Punta Colonet

To San Pedro Mártir National Park

PACIFIC

OCEAN

Camalú

SANTO DOMINGO

Isla San Martín

San Quintín

Lázaro Cárdenas

CLAMMING ALONG BAHÍA SAN QUINTÍN

Bahía San Quintín

Playa de Oeste Médano

Cabo San Quintín

Bahía Santa María

Santa María

0   10 mi

0   10 km

Bahía Rosario

El Rosario

To Rosarito

© AVALON TRAVEL PUBLISHING, INC.

offering sportfishing, diving, and sightseeing tours. A long section of Avenida López Mateos between Calles Ryerson and Castillo, a traditional focus of tourist shopping and dining, has received a face-lift comprising brick paving, wider sidewalks, wrought-iron street signs, street lighting, and the underground relocation of power and telephone lines. This section is now called Paseo Calle Primera.

Although some old Baja hands buzz right past Ensenada in a rush to get to the "real Baja" farther south, for many repeat visitors a Baja trip simply doesn't get off to a good start without a ritual *cerveza* at Hussong's or a couple of *tacos de pescado* from the harbor fish market. Is Ensenada Americanized? Though it's undeniably a hybrid culture, Mexican tourists prefer the town to San Felipe or Cabo San Lucas; once you escape the waterfront area, you'll find neighborhood *panaderías,* quiet residential streets, and few tourists of any nationality.

CLIMATE AND TOURIST SEASONS

Ensenada's climate is similar to San Diego's. Yearly rainfall amounts to about 25 centimeters (10 in), most of which falls October–May. Temperatures are mild year-round, averaging 7–18°C (45–64°F) in January and 17–24°C (63–75°F) in August.

The high tourist season is June–August, when the weather is warm and rain is rare. The Christmas/New Year's holidays and spring break in March through early April are also peak periods. To avoid the crowds, consider visiting Ensenada October–November or April–May.

HISTORY

In pre-Hispanic times, nomadic Yumano Amerindian tribes occasionally stopped at Bahía de Todos Santos to fish and gather clams, but no permanent Amerindian settlements existed in the area when the Spanish missionaries arrived in the 18th century. The first Spaniard to lay eyes on the bay was explorer Juan Cabrillo, who in 1542 named it San Mateo. Sebastián Vizcaíno's voyage of 1602 lent a different name to this piece of California coastal geography—Ensenada de Todos Santos, or "All Saint's Cove." Most likely this referred to a smaller cross-section of the bay (possibly the estuary where the Río San Carlos empties into the bay's south end), but eventually the entire bay came to be known as Bahía de Todos Santos.

Following a Spanish land grant to José Manuel Ruiz in 1804, several small farms and ranches were established in the hills east of the bay, including Ruiz's own Rancho Ensenada. A Spanish sergeant, Francisco Gastelum, bought and expanded the ranch in 1824. Following Mexican independence, the discovery of gold at nearby Real del Castillo in 1870 brought miners to the area; the miners needed supplies, and Ensenada, named for Gastelum's ranch, bloomed into a port practically overnight.

In 1882, Ensenada became the capital of the Territory of Baja California. The town continued to attract miners, farmers, and entrepreneurs who came to take advantage of the town's increasing prosperity. The boom lasted until the early 20th century, when few significant gold deposits remained and the political situation in the border area was becoming increasingly unstable. To counter growing Anglo-American influence along the border, the territorial capital was moved to Mexicali in 1915.

Ensenada faded into a farming and fishing village until U.S. Prohibition revived the economy. In the late 1920s, heavyweight boxer Jack Dempsey and a number of other Americans opened the Playa Ensenada Hotel and Casino, a grand Spanish-style structure overlooking the bay. Along with Tijuana and Mexicali, Ensenada became a favorite destination for the American drinking-and-gambling set until Prohibition's repeal in 1933 and Mexico's casino closure of 1938. The Playa Ensenada casino-hotel was converted to a resort hotel under a new name, the Riviera del Pacífico, but, unable to attract guests in sufficient numbers, it soon closed. About this time, following the government's agrarian reforms, Valle de Mexicali agriculture expanded rapidly, and Ensenada's port facilities were steadily upgraded.

Throughout the 1940s and 1950s, the Ensenada area became a favorite destination for sportfishers and earned its title as "Yellowtail Capital of the World." Although increased commercial fishing and shipping decreased the bay's value as a sportfishing destination, overall economic development has fostered a cosmopolitan atmosphere, and Ensenada continues to cultivate its split personality as both tourist center and seaport.

SIGHTS

Ensenada's dual character—half resort, half commercial center—is split into two grids by Avenida Juárez in the center of the city. The portion of the city south of Juárez, toward the bay, is mostly given over to tourist-oriented businesses, while the portion to the north consists of local businesses like those found in any Mexican city. Most of the city's hotels, restaurants, and gift shops are found along Boulevard Costero and Avenida López Mateos, two parallel streets close to the waterfront.

◖ Riviera del Pacífico

Ensenada's most impressive edifice opened in 1929 as the Playa Ensenada Hotel and Casino, owned and operated by Jack Dempsey and his financial backers; Al Capone was allegedly a silent partner. The opening act in the hotel ballroom was Bing Crosby, backed by the Xavier Cugat Orchestra. The orchestra included a singer named Margarita Carmen Cansino, a Baja native later known as Rita Hayworth. Facing the bay, the hotel's massive white-walled, red-roofed, palm-encircled exterior became a prime symbol of the city's prosperity.

Like Tijuana's El Casino del Agua Caliente and Rosarito's Rosarito Beach Hotel, Playa Ensenada was a big hit with the Hollywood crowd until the U.S. repeal of Prohibition in 1933. Casino management converted it into the Hotel Riviera del Pacífico, but, deprived of its gambling clientele and suffering the effects of the 1930s Depression, the hotel closed and fell into disrepair shortly thereafter.

In 1977, the city decided to restore the structure and turn it into the **Centro Social Cívico**

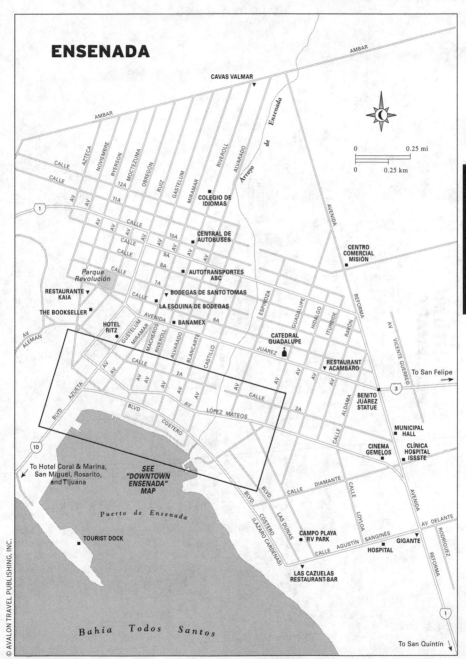

ENSENADA

AMBAR

CAVAS VALMAR

Arroyo de Ensenada

0   0.25 mi
0   0.25 km

AMBAR

CALLE
CALLE

AZTECA
NOVIEMBRE
RYERSON
MOCTEZUMA
OBREGÓN
RUIZ
GASTELUM
MIRAMAR
RIVEROLL
ALVARADO

12A
11A

AV
AV

AV
AV
AV
AV
AV

CALLE
CALLE
CALLE

10A
8A
8A
7A

COLEGIO DE
IDIOMAS

CENTRAL DE
AUTOBUSES

AVENIDA

CENTRO
COMERCIAL
MISIÓN

AUTOTRANSPORTES
ABC

Parque
Revolución

CALLE

BODEGAS DE SANTO TOMAS

RESTAURANTE
KAIA

LA ESQUINA DE BODEGAS

THE BOOKSELLER

AVENIDA   6A   BANAMEX

HOTEL
RITZ

GUSTELUM
MIRAMAR
MACHEROS
RIVEROLL
ALVARADO
BLANCARTE
CASTILLO

ESPINOZA
GUADALUPE
HIDALGO
ITURBIDE
RAYÓN

REFORMA

AV
ALEMAN

CALLE

2A

CATEDRAL
GUADALUPE

JUÁREZ

RESTAURANT
ACAMBARO

AV
VICENTE GUERRERO

To San Felipe

AV
AZUETA

AV
AV
AV
AV

AV

AV
AV

CALLE

3

BENITO
JUAREZ
STATUE

ALDAMA

BLVD
BLVD

COSTERO

LÓPEZ MATEOS

2A

CALLE

MUNICIPAL
HALL

1D

CINEMA
GEMELOS

CLÍNICA
HOSPITAL
ISSSTE

To Hotel Coral & Marina,
San Miguel, Rosarito,
and Tijuana

SEE
"DOWNTOWN
ENSENADA"
MAP

Puerto de Ensenada

BLVD
COSTERO
(LÁZARO CARDENAS)

LAS DUNAS

CALLE   DIAMANTE

CALLE
LOYLOA

AVENIDA
DELANTE

RODRÍGUEZ

TOURIST DOCK

CAMPO PLAYA
RV PARK

CALLE   AGUSTÍN   SANGINÉS

GIGANTE

HOSPITAL

AV DELANTE

REFORMA

LAS CAZUELAS
RESTAURANT-BAR

Bahía Todos Santos

To San Quintín

1

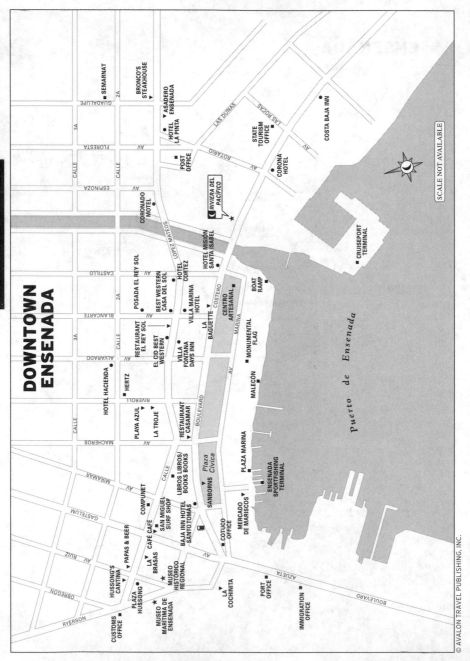

DOWNTOWN ENSENADA

SCALE NOT AVAILABLE

Puerto de Ensenada

© AVALON TRAVEL PUBLISHING, INC.

© PAUL ITOI

Bodegas de Santo Tomás, Mexico's largest winery

y Cultural Riviera (Social, Civic, and Cultural Center of Ensenada). The various ballrooms and halls of the former hotel are now hired out for civic events, conventions, weddings, art exhibits, and other public and private occasions. One wing houses several municipal agencies; another contains a small Casa de la Cultura with a public library (Mon.–Fri. 8 A.M.–7:30 P.M.).

On one of the upper floors at the northwest end of the building is the **Museo de Historia de Ensenada** (tel. 646/177-0594, Mon.–Sat. 9:30 A.M.–2 P.M. and 3–5 P.M., Sun. 10 A.M.–5 P.M., US$1), a small historical museum with six permanent exhibition rooms dedicated to different historical periods, plus a gallery for traveling exhibits and a gift shop. One of the permanent exhibits focuses on Baja California's Amerindian heritage with displays of artifacts, pottery, weaponry and photographs (most captioned in Spanish and English), which are further enhanced by recordings of native chants. A unique "rupestrian pathway" reveals the four styles of rock art found in northern Baja while

winding upward to the next exhibition level. Another exhibit examines early European seafarers and their routes, and the role of Catholic missionaries on the peninsula.

Much of the Riviera del Pacífico's original interior tile work, murals, and painted ceilings remain intact. The **Bar Andaluz,** on the ground floor of the rear portion of the building, near the large parking lot, features a long, polished wooden bar and a mural by Alfredo Ramos Martínez (1871–1946), one of the original Mexican muralists and founder of Las Escuelas de Pintura al Aire Libre (Schools of Painting in the Open Air) in Mexico City. Visitors are welcome to tour the premises daily 9 A.M.–5 P.M. The bar is an excellent place for a quiet drink during these hours. The Riviera del Pacífico is at the corner of Avenidas Costero and Riviera—hard to miss since it's the largest structure along Boulevard Costero.

Museo Histórico Regional

Ensenada's Museum of Regional History (Av. Gastelum near Av. López Mateos downtown, tel. 646/178-2531, Tues.–Sun. 10 A.M.–5 P.M., by donation) is housed in a former military garrison dating to 1886 (and thus probably the oldest building in Ensenada) and contains a permanent display of artifacts pertaining to Amerindian culture in northern Baja, as well as temporary exhibits on various historical themes.

Museo Ex-Aduana Marítima de Ensenada

American-owned International Land Company of Mexico constructed this building in 1887, and for a while it was used by the British-owned Mexican Land and Colonization Company. Mexico's Aduana Marítima (Maritime Customs) gained control of the warehouselike structure in 1922, and in 1992 the Instituto Nacional de Antropología e Historia (INAH) renovated the building at Avenida Ryerson and Calle Uribe downtown and turned it into a museum (tel. 646/178-2531, Tues.–Sun. 10 A.M.–5 P.M., by donation). INAH manages the rotating exhibits, most of which focus on Mexican cultural themes.

Malecón

A *malecón* or waterfront promenade, inaugurated by President Ernesto Zedillo in 1997, affords views of the Bahía de Todos Santos from the **Parque Ventana al Mar** (Window to the Sea Park). A huge Mexican flag waves from the park's 106-meter (350-foot) flagpole. On clear days you should be able to see as far as Punta Banda and Islas de Todos Santos.

Along Boulevard Costero, near Plaza Marina and the cruise ship pier, the elliptical **Plaza Cívica** contains three huge busts of national heroes Benito Juárez (Mexico's first president), Miguel Hidalgo (the Catholic priest who initiated the Mexican Revolution), and Venustiano Carranza (Mexico's first post-Revolution president). Locally the plaza is more commonly called Plaza de las Tres Cabezas (Plaza of the Three Heads). The sportfishing piers and **Mercado de Mariscos** (Seafood Market) toward the north end of the waterfront continue to be the focus of most activity.

Catedral Nuestra Señora de Guadalupe

This cathedral at Avenida Floresta and Calle 6 exhibits standard-issue, Mexican colonial–style architecture, though the stained-glass windows are well executed. The best times to visit the cathedral are during the Fiesta Guadalupano (Día de Nuestra Señora de Guadalupe, December 12 and 13) or Las Posadas (December 16–25), when the interior is filled with candles and worshippers.

El Mirador

The Chapultepec Hills rise along the city's west side and afford a city and bay view. To find El Mirador (The Viewpoint), follow Calle 2 west until it terminates at Avenida Alemán, then turn right and follow the road to the top.

Wineries

Ensenada's wine legacy continues to grow, and seven wineries now maintain offices in the city. Only one winery in town is open to the public on a regularly scheduled basis. **Bodegas de Santo Tomás** (Av. Miramar 666, tel. 646/178-3333, bstwines@hotmail .com) is Mexico's largest winery, the oldest winery on the peninsula, and a direct descendant of the Dominicans' first Valle de Santo Tomás harvest of 1791. The winery sold its first wine to the public, by the barrel, in 1888. In 1934, Bodegas moved its winemaking operation to Ensenada, although most operations have recently been transferred back to Santo Tomás. The grapes are still grown in the Santo Tomás area as well as in other northern Baja valleys.

The facilities in downtown Ensenada cover one and a half city blocks and produce more than a half million cases of wine annually. Master vintners employ around 30 different varietals to produce wine, sherry, port, brandy, and champagne-style sparkling wine. Public tours of the winery, in English, are offered. The tours last about 15 minutes and are free. Bread and cheese are served along with the wines. You can purchase bottles of Santo Tomás wine in the tasting room.

BAJA CALIFORNIA'S WINE TIMELINE

Though it's a relatively new phenomenon to many foreign wine connoisseurs, Baja California's wine history dates back several centuries.

* Early 16th century: Hernán Cortés brings vinifera cuttings from Spain to Mexico.

* 1597: Jesuit padres establish the first winery in the Western Hemisphere outside Parras de la Fuente (in today's Mexican state of Coahuila).

* 1697: Padre Juan Ugarte transplants vinifera at Misión San Javier.

* 1791: Dominican Padre José Lorieto establishes Misión Santo Tomás de Aquino, planting the first Spanish vinifera in the Valle de Santo Tomás, 45 kilometers south of Ensenada.

* 1888: Following the secularization of Misión Santo Tomás, an Italian miner named Francisco Andronequi takes over the mission vineyards and founds Baja's first commercial winery, Bodegas de Santo Tomás. Andronequi enjoys some success selling wine by the barrel in booming late-19th-century Ensenada.

* 1906: Some 500 Russian immigrants settle the Valle de Guadalupe and cultivate extensive vineyards. Wine grapes thrive in the sandy soil and Mediterranean climate of northern Baja, and other winemakers,

including the Italian family of oenologist Angel Cetto, follow the success of the Santo Tomás and Guadalupe operations with viticulture in valleys near Tecate, San Vicente, Guadalupe, Mexicali, and Ensenada.

* 1939: Former Mexican Revolution general Abelardo Lujan Rodríguez buys Bodegas de Santo Tomás and moves the winery to Ensenada.

* Early 1960s: Rodríguez hires an American oenologist from the school for viticulture and oenology at the University of California at Davis. This wine expert ushers in a new era for wine culture in Mexico, introducing grape varieties such as chenin blanc, chardonnay, and reisling, as well as cold fermentation and other modern techniques.

* 1972: Spanish brandy-maker Pedro Domecq establishes a winery in Valle de Guadalupe, attracting international attention to the wine-producing valleys of northern Baja for the first time.

* 1990s: Boutique labels like Monte Xanic and Chateau de Camou (Viñas de Camou) raise the quality of Baja wines to a world-class level.

* 2007: Approximately 90 percent of all wine produced in Mexico comes from Baja California.

SPORTS AND RECREATION
Fishing

Although commercial fishing (both local and foreign) has depleted the overall supply of game fish in the Ensenada area, sportfishing here can still be rewarding, especially June–mid-September when several species make coastal runs from the south. Bahía de Todos Santos catches include lingcod, rockfish, calico bass, sand bass, barracuda, bonito, and occasional yellowtail. Though this was once known as the "yellowtail capital of the world,"

yellowtail catches now are generally rare and rather puny.

Long-range fishing trips from Ensenada—to Punta Colonet, Isla San Gerónimo, or Isla San Martín—yield bluefin, yellowfin, and albacore tuna; skipjack; white sea bass; salmon grouper; and the occasional dorado.

Several companies operate sportfishing trips from the Ensenada Sportfishing Terminal, off Boulevard Costero near the end of Avenida Macheros. **Sergio's Sportfishing Center** (tel./fax 646/178-2185, U.S. tel. 800/336-5454,

sand dunes near Ensenada

© PAUL ITOI

www.sergio-sportfishing.com) runs day trips for US$50 per person, or overnights and multiday, long-range trips by charter. Rates for local trips (day and overnight) include license, tackle, and live bait when available; added services, like fish cleaning and filleting, cost extra. On the same pier, **Gordo's Sportfishing** (tel. 646/178-3515 or 646/178-2377, fax 646/174-04810) and **Juanito's Boats** (tel. 646/174-0953 or 800/569-1254) offer similar services, and are also recommended. Gordo's also operates its own smokehouse.

See *Punta Banda and La Bufadora* later in this chapter for information on fishing trips arranged by Dale's La Bufadora Dive Shop.

Sergio's, Juanito's, and Gordo's all offer **tackle rental and sales** at the sportfishing pier.

Boating

A concrete launch ramp off the *malecón* accommodates boats up to 10 meters (32 ft) in length. Ensenada's **Marina Coral** (radio VHF 71), the first marina along northern Baja's west coast, has 373 slips available up to 150 feet in length;

eventually, says marina management, there will be 600 slips. Services include electricity, water, restrooms, showers, lockers, telephones, cable TV, fuel, ramp, tennis court, two pools, a hot tub, spa, restaurant, and nightclub. Short-term slip rates for boats are US$1.25 per foot per day, with discounts for long-term stays. This includes electricity (110–220 V), cable TV, and use of facilities at the adjacent Hotel Coral. For further information or slip reservations, contact the Hotel Coral and Marina (tel. 646/175-0000, U.S./Canada tel. 800/862-9020, www.hotelcoral.com).

Ensenada Cruiseport Village Marina (tel. 646/173-4141 or 800/027-3678, U.S. tel. 877/219-5822, www.ecpvmarina.com) offers similar facilities and similar rates.

Juanito's Boats (tel. 646/174-0953 or 800/569-1254), a boatyard at the old marina in back of Plaza Marina, offers a few slips and accepts foreign boats for servicing or repair, as does **Baja Naval** in the same area. Service rates are lower than for comparable work done in the United States. Fuel is also available here.

As Ensenada is an official Mexican port of entry, arriving boaters must check in with the COTP on Boulevard Azueta. (See *Sports and Recreation* in *Essentials*.)

For outboard-motor repairs, inquire at **Motores de Baja California Norte** (Calle 6 1990, tel. 646/176-3025), which specializes in sales and service of American-made motors.

Surfing

The nearest consistent surfing areas are at Punta San Miguel, several kilometers north of Ensenada off Mexico 1, and Islas de Todos Santos, 20 kilometers (12 mi) west by boat (see *San Miguel and El Sauzal* in the *Tijuana, Rosarito, and Tecate* chapter, and *Islas de Todos Santos* later in this chapter). Playa La Jolla, approximately 16 kilometers (10 mi) south of town via Mexico 1 and BCN 23, occasionally benefits from the winter northwest swell.

Diving

The best local diving spots are the rocky shorelines and sandy coves around Punta Banda and Islas de Todos Santos, and the seamount of El Bajo de San Miguel, about midway between San Miguel and Islas de Todos Santos.

Ensenada's only dive shop is **Almar** (Av. Macheros 149, tel. 646/178-3013). See *Punta Banda and La Bufadora* for information on dive trips arranged by Dale's La Bufadora Dive Shop.

Whale-Watching

Sergio's Sportfishing Center (see *Fishing*) offers four- to five-hour whale-watching trips late December–late March for US$25 per person (US$15 for ages 11 and under). Sergio's needs a minimum of 15 people to run a trip—usually not a problem on weekends. **Gordo's** (next door) offers similar trips at similar rates.

Spa Services

Spa Cirse at the Hotel Coral & Marina (tel. 646/175-0000, U.S./Canada tel. 800/862-9020, www.hotelcoral.com, Mon.–Thurs. 7 A.M.–6 P.M., Fri.–Sat. 7 A.M.–8 P.M., Sun. 8 A.M.–4 P.M.) offers a full line of spa treatments, including facials and massage as well

as a hot tub, sauna, steam room, weight-lifting equipment, heated indoor pool, and two lighted tennis courts.

Race and Sports Book

Caliente Race and Sports Book maintains an outlet at the Hotel San Nicolás, Avenida López Mateos at Blancarte, as well as one in Plaza Marina.

Cruises

As part of a four-day cruise along Mexico's Pacific coast from Los Angeles, Royal Caribbean's *Monarch of the Seas* (U.S. tel. 800/327-6700, www.royalcarribean.com, US$430–630) stops over in Ensenada. Carnival offers a similar trip aboard the *Paradise* at slightly higher prices.

As the name suggests, **We Hook 'Em** (tel. 949/650-4735, U.S. tel. 866/934-6653, wehookem@aol.com) specializes in sportfishing charters, but the company also offers a wide range of professional boating services, including whale-watching tours and sunset cruises. We Hook 'Em operates out of the Hotel Coral & Marina.

ENTERTAINMENT AND EVENTS
Bars and Discos

Many of the hotels and motels in the main tourist district—along Avenida López Mateos and Boulevard Costero between Calle Sanginés and Avenida Macheros—feature bars or lounges with occasional live music, usually *trovadores* (troubadours) or mariachis playing Mexican standards. **Ibis** (Blvd. Costero at Av. Alvarado, tel. 646/176-1440) offers dancing to recorded music and light shows—not on a par with Tijuana's high-tech discos, but good enough.

West of Avenida Macheros, the city leaves behind the middle-class tourist zone and revels in cheap seafood joints, bars, and dance halls with a slightly seedy air. In this area is one of Baja's most famous landmarks, **Hussong's Cantina** (Av. Ruiz 113, tel. 646/178-3210, daily 10 A.M.–1 A.M.), quite justifiably advertised as "the bar that built a town." This could be amended to "the bar that built a shopping center" now that the neighborhood is studded with Hussong's souvenir shops.

At the same location since Johan Hussong, a German immigrant, opened shop in 1892, and still owned by his grandson, the clapboard structure has hardly changed in a hundred years but for the addition of electricity. A massive eland head mounted high on the wall at the back surveys the one-room cantina from above, while the resident shoeshine man takes in the view from the sawdust-covered floor. Hussong's carries three only kinds of beer—Tecate, Bohemia, and XX, plus its own brand of tequila (quite good). On any given night, tourists are outnumbered two to one by regulars (a mixture of expats and *bajacalifornianos*). Unamplified *norteña* ensembles sometimes play polkas and *rancheras* as *gritos* (shouts) pierce the smoky air. Come in the late afternoon if you hope to claim a table, as it's always crowded.

Across the street from Hussong's is **Papas and Beer,** a slightly more sedate two-story bar with recorded music and a collegiate atmosphere. It lacks character but is a reasonable alternative for folks who find Hussong's too rowdy. Next door to Papas is **Oxidos,** a bar/restaurant that has the flavor of Soho hightech, with lounge chairs and tables, long bar, and dance floor.

A wander north along Avenida Ruiz or especially Avenida Gastelum will turn up a number of Mexican-oriented bars and cantinas, many of the red-light sort. Out on Boulevard Costero at Avenida Miramar, **Anthony's** is a classic in this category, with a large bar/dance hall and a bawdy, boy's-town reputation. Look for the big gorilla head over the door. Beyond the curtained entrance revolves a merry-go-round of ranchers, surfers, painted ladies, and other lost—at least for the night—souls. **Coyote Club** (Blvd. Costero 1000, tel. 646/177-7369) is a predominantly gay video disco playing both Latin and Anglo-American pop.

El Gran Chaparral, a dance hall on the east side of Avenida Reforma just north of Avenida Delante, is occasionally open for live *norteña* music and dancing.

El Patio (López Mateos 1088) is a tastefully designed bar set in a charming garden patio—a nice change from the raucous sports bar, stuffy hotel lounge, or trendy club.

Events

Partly as a result of its mild climate, Ensenada hosts more events—many of them sports-oriented—than any other city in Baja.

FEBRUARY

Ensenada has observed the pre-Lenten festival of **Carnaval** since 1918, and the celebration seems to get bigger every year—more than 300,000 visitors in an average season. Usually held for six days before Ash Wednesday, the second week in February, festivities start with the Quema de Mal Humor (Burning of Bad Humor), in which an effigy is hanged and burned. The victim is usually modeled after an unpopular politician.

Throughout the week, a nightly street fair stretches for 12 downtown blocks, offering food vendors, carnival rides, live music, and a steady flow of Mexican beer, brandy, and tequila. Carnaval parades, consisting of flowered floats and legions of costumed dancers, wind through the streets every afternoon amid clouds of confetti. The best streets for viewing the three main parades—held from around 2:30 P.M. until around 4:30 P.M. on Saturday, Sunday, and Tuesday—are Boulevard Costero, Avenida López Mateos, and Avenida Ruiz.

Carnaval's grand finale is a masquerade ball held on the Tuesday night before Ash Wednesday. Prizes are awarded for best costumes as well as for other attainments over the course of the week—best float, best dance troupe, etc.

So many leather-clad motorcyclists—including show-biz celebs like Peter Fonda and Jay Leno—come down from Southern California for Carnaval nowadays that city officials allow them to participate in at least one of the parades.

For specific information on Carnaval scheduling and venues for individual events, pick up a copy of the *California Sun* or contact the tourist office on Boulevard Costero.

APRIL

The **Rosarito-Ensenada 50-Mile Fun Bicycle Ride** (tel. 619/424-6084, www.rosarito ensenada.com) takes place on a Saturday in April and attracts as many as 10,000 participants, making it one of the world's largest cycling events. The route follows the coast, with an elevation differential of around 300 meters (1,000 ft). You can register online (US$35) or on the day of the event (US$40).

Tommy Bahama Newport-Ensenada Race (www.nosa.org) is the mother of all west coast regattas, in which more than 600 sailors leave Newport Beach at noon on the last Friday in April and see who reaches Ensenada first.

MAY

The mid-May **Lifeguard Triathlon** based at the Hotel Coral & Marina consists of two events: a sprint event (750-meter swim, 20-km cycle, 5-km run) and an Olympic-distance triathlon (1.4-km swim, 40-km cycle, 10-km run).

JUNE

The **Baja 500,** a 500-mile off-road race out of Ensenada, is held in early June and sponsored by SCORE International and Tecate beer. See the November entry for the **Baja 1000.**

The **Ensenada Grand Prix** is the only race of its kind in Mexico, a NASCAR-style rally through the streets of Ensenada. Held in mid-June.

JULY

In the **Baja Volleyball Open,** held in late July at Playa El Faro, local teams compete against teams from the United States for cash trophies. Call Ensenada Sports Promotions (tel. 646/177-6688) for details. Another Baja Open is held in August.

AUGUST

At **Fiesta de la Vendimia Bajacaliforniana** (Bajacalifornian Wine Harvest Festival, tel. 646/174-0170), wineries in Ensenada, Tijuana, and Valle de Guadalupe cosponsor 10 days of wine-tasting, music, vineyard tours,

and gourmet cooking at various venues; usually commences the second or third week of the month. Most events have admission prices; a wine-tasting at the Riviera del Pacífico, for example, costs US$20 for all the hors d'oeuvres and wines you can sample. On the final Saturday of the festival, a panel of judges conducts a blind tasting of wines from Mexico and abroad during the Concurso Internacional.

The **Corona Cup Regatta** is a multi-lap yacht race held in the bay. For information, contact the state or city tourist offices.

SEPTEMBER

Feria Internacional del Pescado y el Marisco (International Seafood Fair, tel. 646/174-0448 or 646/174-0435, canirac@infosel.net.mx), usually held the first weekend of the month, is one of the city's best-attended fiestas. Many local restaurants participate, as well as chefs from Tijuana, Rosarito, and Southern California. A ticket entitles the holder to four dishes and four beverages. Sponsored by the restaurant association CANIRAC.

J. D. Hussong Baja International Chili Cookoff & Salsa Contest, a cookoff sanctioned by the International Chili Society (ICS) and one of Ensenada's biggest events, is usually held the third weekend in September at Quintas Papagayo Resort. The cookoff winner is eligible to compete in the annual ICS World Championship Chili Cookoff in Nevada. In addition to chili-cooking competitions for individuals, clubs, and local restaurants, the day's activities typically include chili-pepper-eating and tequila "shoot-and-holler" contests, live music and dancing, and the selection of Ms. Chile Pepper and Mr. Hot Sauce. You can extinguish the fire with beverages provided by Cervecería Cuauhtémoc Moctezuma, brewers of Tecate, Carta Blanca, Dos Equis (XX), and several other popular Mexican beers; tequila purveyors Viuda de Romero; and winemakers Bodegas de Santo Tomás. A US$10 admission fee is charged; part of the proceeds go to charity. For current information on scheduling and venue, contact Juan Hussong at tel. 646/174-4575 or visit www.hussongs.com.

BAJA 1000

Every November, desert rats from around the globe gather in Ensenada for the grueling Baja 1000 (Baja Mil), the world's most prestigious off-road race. The first organized contest took place in October 1967, though dirt bikers had informally raced from Ensenada to La Paz since the 1950s. In 1962, Dave Ekins and Bill Robertson Jr. were the first to record their efforts when they raced two Honda 250 motorcycles the length of the peninsula, establishing their times by stamping sheets of paper at telegraph offices in Tijuana and La Paz. Ekins pulled into La Paz after 39 hours, 54 minutes; Robertson made it an hour later.

From 1967 to the present, the event has occurred yearly except in 1974, when the National Off Road Racing Association lost Mexican permission to operate the race. Since 1975, SCORE International has organized the race, most recently with the sponsorship of Tecate beer. Participants can enter in one of 24 categories – 16 car-and-truck, six motorcycle, and two ATV classes. The course alternates year to year between a straight 1,000-mile Ensenada–La Paz run and a shorter 1,000-kilometer loop beginning and ending in Ensenada; the latter course offers more spectator opportunities and pit stops.

SCORE also sponsors a separate Baja 1000 Endurance Safari on a course parallel to, but rougher than, the usual 1,000-mile Ensenada–La Paz route. A rally rather than a race, this event rates contestants not on their time achievements but rather on endurance – a quality of obvious interest to automotive manufacturers and marketers seeking the imprimatur "Baja-proven." Shorter races include the Baja 500 (out of Ensenada, in June) and the San Felipe 250 (from San Felipe, in February or March). For further information, check www.score-international.com.

OCTOBER

Watch top surfers from the Pacific coast of Mexico and California ride the waves at the two-day **Mexican Surf Fiesta** at Playa de San Miguel (tel. 858/586-9173, surfiesta@ yahoo.com).

NOVEMBER

SCORE-Tecate Baja 1000, the granddaddy of all off-road races, takes place over a four-day period during the first or second week of the month. Call SCORE International in the United States (tel. 818/225-8402) for complete information. On even-numbered years, the race is run as far south as La Paz. For a race schedule, consult the Ensenada tourist office, pick up a current issue of the *California Sun,* or visit SCORE's website at www.score-international.com.

SHOPPING

You'll find the usual assortment of tourist-oriented souvenir and beachwear shops along Avenida López Mateos and Boulevard Costero. The **Centro Artesanal,** on Boulevard Costero, caters mostly to cruise-ship passengers in town for a few hours, but is worth a look for Oaxacan folk art and neo–Casas Grandes pottery from Chihuahua's Valle de Casas Grandes. **Plaza Marina** and the adjacent **Plaza Palmira** were developed as shopping venues for cruise passengers, but so far they offer little in the way of unique purchases—just the usual gift and clothing shops you'd find along Avenida López Mateos.

Possibly the most interesting *artesanías* shop in town, **Galería de Pérez Meillon,** in the Centro Artesanal, carries a high-quality selection of Paipai and Casas Grandes pottery, Kumyai basketry, and contemporary art by up-and-coming Latin American artists. **Bazar Pa'todos** (Av. López Mateos between Miramar and Gastelum) also sells high-quality, unique pieces, including Mexican colonial-style paintings and wood carvings.

Another interesting find is **Bazar Casa**

Ramírez (Av. López Mateos 496-3), a family-owned *artesanías* shop with two floors of arts and crafts from all parts of Mexico. Upscale items include good-quality *alebrijes* (carved animal sculptures), a vast collection of handmade Mexican crosses with religious icons attached, black clay pottery from Oaxaca, and hand-carved and -painted mirrors from the state of Michoacán.

A large flea market called **Los Globos** (Calle 9 three blocks east of Av. Reforma, daily 9 A.M.–6 P.M.) features vendor stalls selling everything from housewares to sandals. A similar market at Calle 6 and Avenida Riveroll is open only on weekends.

The best bargains for everyday items are found deeper in the downtown area, away from Boulevard Costero and Avenida López Mateos. The locals do much of their shopping in the vicinity of the Avenidas Juárez and Ruiz intersection, where bookstores, record shops, and *zapaterías* are particularly numerous. Ensenada's *zapaterías* specialize in boots made from "exotic" skins, such as lizard or ostrich—don't buy anything prohibited by U.S. Customs if you plan on taking it across the U.S.–Mexico border.

Nuevo México Lindo (Av. López Mateos 688, tel. 646/178-1381) is a *talabartería* where you can buy handcrafted saddles, riding tack, handbags, and other leather goods.

Wine

The wine shop within **La Esquina de Bodegas** (Av. Miramar 666 btw Calles 6/7, tel. 646/178-3557) carries a good assortment of California and Baja California labels, plus wine accessories and assorted wine-associated gifts. Santo Tomás wines can be purchased by the case across the street at **Bodegas de Santo Tomás;** however, U.S. customs only allows you to return with one bottle.

Books

Libros Libros/Books Books (López Mateos 690, tel. 646/178-8448, daily 9 A.M.–5 P.M.) sells videos, CDs, magazines, cards, and books. The selection is impressive—from classic literature to children's stories, art history to science journals. Some of the titles are in English. Another good source for material in English is **The Bookseller** (Calle 4 240, tel. 646/178-8964, Mon.–Sat. 10 A.M.–5 P.M.), which sells and trades used books and magazines.

Shopping Centers

Ensenada has several large *centros comerciales,* or shopping centers, the largest of which is **Centro Comercial Misión** on the northeast corner of Calle 11 and Av. Reforma. Among the businesses are Gigante supermarket, Banamex (with an ATM), Lavamática Express, Smart and Final, and Cinema Gemelos.

ACCOMMODATIONS
Downtown

Most of Ensenada's hotels are on or just off Avenida López Mateos and Boulevard Costero. For most of the year except July and August, Carnaval, and U.S. college spring break, the supply of hotel rooms surpasses the demand; hence room rates are often negotiable. At any given moment several hotels may stock one or both tourist offices with promotional flyers advertising room specials.

Rates are highest May–September. Any time of year weekday rates may be lower than weekend and holiday rates. Add 12 percent hotel tax to all rates (some hotels may charge an additional 10 percent service charge).

UNDER US$50

Hotel Hacienda (211 Calle 2 at Alvarado, tel. 646/178-2344, US$40) has a good location just one full block from the main drag. Traffic noise is an issue for the rooms that face Calle 2, but all of the rooms are well maintained and clean.

One of our favorite Ensenada hotels in this price range is the three-story **Hotel Ritz** (Av. Ruiz at Calle 4, tel. 646/174-0501, fax 646/178-3262, US$32). If you don't need a parking lot (the Ritz has none) and would like to stay off the Avenida López Mateos tourist strip—but only three blocks north of Hussong's Cantina—you may find this hotel to

Posada El Rey Sol

your liking. Rooms are spacious and clean; the staff is friendly. Ask for a corner room if you want a view of bustling Avenida Ruiz below.

US$50-100

Bahía Resort Hotel (Av. López Mateos btw Riveroll/Alvarado, tel. 646/178-2101, U.S. tel. 888/308-9048, www.hotelbahia.com .mx, US$59) is a rambling, 64-room, two-story wooden hotel in the center of the tourist zone. The clean, comfortable rooms and suites all have tiled bathrooms, queen-size beds, spacious closets, cable TV, and direct-dial phones. Some rooms on the upper floor have bay views. On the premises are a restaurant, bar, pool, and secure parking lot. Both bar and hotel are favorites with Southern California motorcycle clubs. Continental breakfast is included in the rate.

The **El Cid Best Western** (Av. López Mateos 993, tel. 646/178-2401, www.hotelelcid.com. mx, US$92) is built in the mission style and offers 52 comfortable rooms, a Spanish tapas restaurant, coffee shop, pool, and parking.

Rooms come with one or two beds, and a suite with a hot tub is available for US$100. Weekend prices are at least 30 percent higher than weekday rates.

The **Desert Inn/La Pinta Hotel** (Av. Floresta at Bucaneros, tel. 646/176-2601, U.S./Canada tel. 800/346-3942, www.lapintahotels.com, US$65–75) features 52 rooms with air conditioning, heat, TV, and phone in a three-story, semimodern, Spanish-style building. Amenities include a restaurant and pool. This is the headquarters for Baja's La Pinta chain, and is relatively friendly and atmospheric. Although the hotel has no parking lot as such, a guard keeps an eye on the small street-side parking area out front. Midweek rates usually drop below US$50.

Days Inn Villa Fontana (Av. López Mateos 1050, tel. 646/178-3434, U.S. tel. 800/DAYS-INN, www.villafontana.com.mx, US$60) is a rambling wooden place opposite El Cid. Each of the hotel's 66 rooms and suites has air conditioning, heat, phone, satellite TV, and bay-view balcony. Amenities include a coffee shop, bar, liquor store, courtyard parking, pool, hot tub, and sundeck. Complimentary coffee and Mexican pastries are available every morning in the tidy lobby. Midday rates occasionally drop below US$50.

Hotel Misión Santa Isabel (Blvd. Costero 1119, tel. 646/178-3616, fax 646/178-3345, US$55 and up) takes up an entire block along Avenida Castillo stretching from Avenida López Mateos south to Costero. One of the more impressive mission-style Ensenada hotels—with its big arched gate, tall domed tower, and tiled roof—the Santa Isabel features 57 small- to medium-size rooms with Spanish-inspired furnishings, air conditioning, heat, TVs, and phones. On the grounds are a restaurant and bar, parking lot, gift shop, and a small but well-designed courtyard pool. Rates go up Friday and Saturday nights and holidays.

Villa Marina Hotel (Av. López Mateos 1094, tel. 646/178-3321, fax 646/178-3351, U.S. fax 619/454-2703, US$90) is a high-rise with 130 rooms and suites, all with air conditioning, heat, TVs, and phones. Other features include a coffee shop, pool, and parking lot.

Best Western Casa del Sol (Av. López Mateos 1001, tel. 646/178-1570, U.S. tel. 877/316-1684, www.motelcasadelsol.com, US$55) is another place that capitalizes on Spanish mission–style architecture, with plenty of arched windows, white stucco, and a terra-cotta tile roof. Each of the 48 well-worn but good-sized rooms comes with air conditioning, cable TV, phone, carpet, and Mexican-tiled bathroom. The Casa del Sol also boasts a well-maintained swimming pool—the only hotel pool in Ensenada suitable for lap swimming. Other amenities include a restaurant, secure parking lot, and courtesy coffee every morning.

Costa Baja Inn (Blvd. Costero 1536, tel. 646/177-2255 or 800/025-5215, U.S. tel. 877/666-0706, fax 646/177-2257, US$95) is a charmless, cinder-block highway hotel featuring 51 rooms with air conditioning, heat, phone, and satellite TV; other amenities include a swimming pool and covered parking lot. This one's overpriced in our opinion.

US$100-150

The well-run **Hotel Cortez** (Av. López Mateos 1089, tel. 646/178-2307 or 800/026-6999, U.S. tel. 800/303-2684, www.bajainn.com, US$110) is housed in a two-story mission-style building with a nice lobby. All 75 rooms and suites come with air conditioning, heat, direct-dial phones, carpet, cable TV, courtesy newspaper, and coffee. Nonsmoking rooms are available. On the premises are a heated pool, restaurant/bar, and parking lot.

Baja Inn Hotel Santo Tomás (Blvd. Costero 609, tel. 646/178-1503 or 800/026-6999, U.S. tel. 800/303-2684, www.bajainn.com, US$110) is a modern three-story place dominating the corner of Costero and Avenida Miramar. The staff seems exceptionally friendly and efficient, and the hotel's 80 well-maintained and comfortable rooms come with air conditioning, heat, and satellite TV. Nonsmoking rooms are available. Other amenities include a coffee shop, restaurant, and secure parking lot. A large suite with three beds is available for US$100—a bargain.

US$150-250

The best choice in this price range is the newly renovated, five-story, 93-room **(Corona Hotel** (Blvd. Costero 1442, tel. 646/176-0901, www.hotelcorona.com.mx, US$159). It's the closest hotel to the bay and offers rooms with bay views, balconies, satellite TV, air conditioning, and heat. The spa is well appointed and clean. The bar has the feel of a hip ski bar in Switzerland. The secure parking out front can handle any size rig. You can even back your car up to the ground floor rooms at the front of the hotel.

Just northwest of town off Mexico 1 at Km 103 is one of Ensenada's top hotels, the **Hotel Coral & Marina** (Km 103, tel. 646/175-0000, U.S./Canada tel. 800/862-9020, www.hotelcoral.com, US$150–600). Take the Ensenada Centro exit off the highway to get there. The Coral combines modern, international-class accommodations with a full-service marina and European-style spa. Large, nicely decorated suites of various configurations with separate sitting areas feature satellite TVs, international direct-dial phones, coffeemakers, refrigerators, and balconies overlooking the marina. Other facilities include an *alta cocina* restaurant, lobby bar, nightclub, heated indoor and outdoor pools, a hot tub, sauna, lighted tennis courts, and parking garage. It's kid friendly, to boot.

Posada El Rey Sol (Av. Blancarte 130, tel. 646/178-1601, U.S. tel. 888/315-2378, www.posadaelreysol.com, US$190) is as charming and elegant as its celebrated restaurant across the street. The recently refurbished hotel offers a heated pool, spa, restaurant, bar, and enclosed parking. The 52 spacious, meticulously decorated rooms come with climate control, direct-dial phone, in-room Internet connection, satellite TV, safe, and service bar. Each suite features a private hot tub. Children under 18 stay free.

Out of Town
UNDER US$50
About eight kilometers south of town, on Mexico 1 at Km 12.5 opposite Ciprés airfield in Ejido Chapultepec, **Joker Hotel and Trailer Park** (tel. 646/176-7201, fax 646/177-4460, U.S./Canada tel. 800/256-5372, US$45) looks like a pseudo-Bavarian castle that could have come from Disneyland, with a few Aztec statues thrown in for full incongruence. Its 40 rooms are spread out around landscaped grounds and feature satellite TV, direct-dial phones, air conditioning, and private balconies. Facilities include a hot tub, restaurant, bar, pool, and several features oriented toward RVers staying at the adjacent trailer park. The trailer park isn't meant for the big rigs, but they have eight full hookups available for US$15/night.

US$100-150
Five kilometers north of town at Km 106 off Mexico 1, on a point jutting into the Pacific, **Punta Morro Hotel and Suites** (tel. 646/178-3507, fax 646/174-4490, U.S./Canada tel. 800/526-6676, www.punta-morro.com, US$150) offers studios and one-, two-, and three-bedroom apartments. All units come with kitchens (with utensils) and terraces overlooking the ocean and pool area. This location is quiet and next door to a branch of the Universidad Autónoma de Baja California. The food and spa aren't at the same level as the accommodations.

Las Rosas Hotel and Spa (6 km north of town on Mexico 1, tel. 646/174-4310, www.lasrosas.com, US$150) offers 48 deluxe suites with ocean view. On the premises are a restaurant, seaside pool, hot tub, sauna, exercise center, and tennis court.

OVER US$250
At the high end, check into **(Casa Natalie** (Km 103, tel. 646/174-7373, U.S./Canada tel. 800/562-8254, www.casanatalie.com, US$250), located near the Hotel Coral & Marina. The five suites are furnished to a level rarely seen in Baja. And three more rooms opened in 2007. If you can drag yourself away from the infinity pool, this would be the ideal home base for a weekend of wine tasting in Guadalupe Valley.

Camping and RV Parks
The only RV park within the Ensenada city limits is **Campo Playa RV Park,** at Calles Las Dunas and Sanginés (tel. 646/176-2918). Shady spots with hookups are available for US$20, campsites without hookups go for US$18. Hot showers are available.

Joker Hotel and Trailer Park, across the highway from Ciprés airfield in Ejido Chapultepec (tel. 646/176-7201, fax 646/177-4460, U.S./Canada tel. 800/256-5372), has a dozen full-hookup sites shaded by olive trees entwined with bougainvillea for US$15 a night. Cable TV hookups are available at extra cost. Other facilities include hot showers, flush toilets, a restaurant, brick barbecue grills, and a ping-pong table; RVers are permitted to use the hotel's pool and hot tub.

See *San Miguel and El Sauzal* in the *Tijuana, Rosarito, and Tecate* chapter for details on campgrounds in these areas just a few kilometers north of Ensenada. See also *Vicinity of*

Ensenada later in this chapter for information on campgrounds and trailer parks at Estero Beach, La Jolla, and Punta Banda.

FOOD

Ensenada features just about every kind of restaurant imaginable, but seafood and northern Mexican ranchero-style food are the city's culinary strong suits. *Tacos de pescado* (fish tacos) are an Ensenada specialty, usually made from fresh yellowtail or halibut fillets cut in strips, deep-fried in a light batter, and served in folded corn tortillas with salsa, guacamole, and a touch of mayonnaise or *crema* (a less sour Mexican version of sour cream).

Seafood stands are scattered throughout the city, many of them selling *cocteles* (spicy shellfish cocktail) and ceviche (a lime-marinated seafood salad). Clams *(almejas)*, abalone *(abulón)*, shrimp *(camarones)*, and oysters *(ostiones)* make the most popular cocktail. The healthiest stands use purified water—usually clearly displayed in large bottles—to wash ingredients and utensils before preparing each dish. One of the best places to sample fish tacos and seafood cocktails is the (**Mercado de Mariscos,** next to and a little bit behind the huge Plaza Marina on the waterfront. You can also buy fresh fish to take away and cook elsewhere.

Speaking of cocktails, the *clamato,* a beverage made from clam, tomato and lime juices, Mexican spices, and vodka, was probably invented in Ensenada. *Clamatos* here are nothing like the pale imitations served north of the border—a good one comes half-filled with fresh clams.

If you don't like seafood on your plate or in your glass, try other Ensenada specialties like *tacos de carne asada* (grilled-beef tacos), Sinaloa-style grilled or roasted chicken, or one of the many varieties of burritos available. Several restaurants also specialize in American and Continental cuisines.

Mexican

Rinconcito Oaxaqueño (daily 9 A.M.–5 P.M.), off Diamante and a block south of Reforma, serves authentic Oaxacan cuisine. You can order nopales, *chicharron,* or carne asada in a

taco or plate from US$1–5. If they are in season, and you're an adventurous eater, try the grasshoppers *(chapulines)* washed down with an ice cold Dos Equis.

Acambaro (El Refugio Ensenadense) (Av. Iturbide 528 off Av. Juárez btw Calles 5/6, tel. 646/176-5235, daily for breakfast, lunch, and dinner, mains US$10–15) offers traditional Mexican dishes—*pozole, mole, birria, chilaquiles,* chiles rellenos, enchiladas, and nopales (prickly-pear cactus)—freshly prepared and served with bowls of limes, oregano, and salsa. Also try the delicious breakfasts and the Mexican *postres* (desserts), which include homemade flan, *arroz con leche* (rice pudding), *capirotada* (Mexican-style bread pudding), and *pay de manzana* (apple pie). *Champurrado* (thick hot chocolate) is served in winter. The wood-and-brick decor is rustic but tasteful.

Las Brasas (Av. López Mateos 486 btw Av. Gastelum/Ruiz, tel. 646/178-1195, Wed.–Mon. for lunch and dinner, mains under US$10) specializes in Sinaloa-style, marinated, and mesquite-grilled chicken, and also serves steak, seafood, and Mexican platters, all at reasonable prices.

Popular with locals and tourists alike, **Hacienda del Charro** (Av. López Mateos 454, tel. 646/178-2114, daily for lunch and dinner till 11:30 P.M.) serves tasty roast chicken, homemade chicken tamales, *pollo pipián* (chicken cooked in a pumpkin-seed mole), grilled seafood, burritos, tacos (three large ones for US$4 with rice and beans), chicken *pozole,* and *botanas* of all kinds. Fresh tortillas are handmade on the spot. Beverages include *jamaica,* a refreshing Mexican drink made from crushed hibiscus seeds.

Pollo Feliz (Av. Macheros at Calle 2, tel. 646/178-3111, daily 10 A.M.–10 P.M., mains under US$10) is a fast-food place that cranks out Sinaloa-style roast chickens—whole or half—for eating on the premises or *para llevar* (to go). Served with tortillas, beans, and salsa.

A local favorite is **La Troje** (Riveroll 143-8R, tel. 646/178-8747, daily 8 A.M.–10 P.M., mains US$10–15), which offers traditional Mexican dishes such as *nopalitos navegantes* (delicate cactus strips with eggs).

Las Cazuelas Restaurant Bar (Calle Sanginés 6 near Blvd. Costero, tel. 646/176-104, daily 7 A.M.–11 P.M., mains US$10–15) is an old standby serving border-style cuisine, including *codorniz* (quail), seafood, steaks, ribs, and hearty Mexican breakfasts.

Our favorite *tacos de carne asada* come from **Asadero Ensenada** (daily 9 A.M.–2:30 P.M.), a small and humble shop on the south side of López Mateos right around the corner from the Desert Inn/La Pinta Hotel (heading toward the San Nicolas Resort). Whatever they do to the beef there, it stands head and shoulders above the rest.

About a mile from the center of town is **❰ El Taco de Huitzilopochtli** (Av. de las Rosas 5, Col. Valle Verde, tel. 646/174-2381, Sat.–Sun. 9 A.M.–5 P.M., mains under US$10). The hard-to-find, hard-to-pronounce spot is open only on weekends but is well worth the trouble it takes to plan a visit. Food preparation begins five days in advance; many of the ingredients are grown behind the restaurant by the family owner-operators who moved to Ensenada about 25 years ago from Texcoco in the state of Mexico. Quite simply, no other restaurant in Ensenada serves more authentic central Mexican food. House specialties include *mixiote* (lamb wrapped in maguey leaves and baked in a mesquite-fired oven), *barbacoa chancla* (thick corn tortillas with beef fillet and grilled nopal), *romeritos* (nopal, potato, and shrimp fritters in mole), *huauzontle* (a green pepper–like vegetable filled with cheese and cooked like a chile relleno, *tlacoyos* (thick corn tortillas filled with beans and served with grated cheese and *chile verde*), and *huitlacoche* (corn fungus) cooked with *rajas poblanas* (chili strips). It's a good place for lacto-vegetarians because many dishes feature solely vegetable (and dairy) ingredients. Unique beverages include *licuado de nopal* (a prickly-pear-cactus smoothie) and *pulque* (slightly fermented maguey juice); the latter is rather difficult to find outside central Mexico, so it's a real treat for the many Mexico fans who have read about *pulque* but have never tasted it. An English-language menu is available. At least four or five salsas are brought to the table, along with sliced limes, chopped onions, and cilantro. The modest decor consists of little more than a few Mexican calendars, ceramics, and serapes. Tapes of *música tropical* from Texcoco, including tunes by the well-known *cumbia* group Ángeles Azules, are played in the background.

To find the restaurant, follow Avenida Reforma north from the Benito Juárez statue about 2.5 kilometers (1.6 mi) to the second small bridge, and turn right (east) onto Calle Ambar just before the bridge. This intersection is six traffic lights from the traffic circle with the statue of Benito Juárez. Look for Farmacia San Marín de Porres on the northeast corner of the intersection. Follow Ambar to its end, then turn left and continue two blocks; make another left and you'll see the brightly painted restaurant on the left side of the street.

Despite its cowboy name, **Bronco's Steakhouse** (Av. López Mateos and Av. Guadalupe, tel. 646/176-4900, daily 8 A.M.–10:30 P.M.), near the Hotel Colón, serves a large variety of traditional Mexican platters. Hearty breakfasts cost US$4–7 and include *crepas de huitlacoche* (crepes made with a mushroomlike corn fungus), *cazuela de huevos puntas de filete al chipotle* (terra-cotta dish filled with eggs and beef tips in a spicy chipotle sauce), *nopal asado* (grilled prickly pear cactus), *chilaquiles toluqueños* (Toluca-style *chilaquiles*), and *enchihuevos* (egg enchiladas). Weekend breakfast buffets (Sat.–Sun. 9 A.M.–1 P.M.) cost US$10 per adult or half that for children and offer a wide range of fresh fruit, Mexican breakfast dishes, and made-to-order omelets. Lunch and dinner offerings are equally large: USDA rib-eye steaks and ribs, *parilladas* (grill platters), *tripitas asadas* (grilled tripe), chile rellenos, and more, for prices ranging US$6–20 per entrée.

Seafood

Las Conchas Oyster Bar and Restaurant (tel. 646/175-7375, daily for lunch and dinner, mains US$15 and up), in Plaza Hussong, serves perfectly prepared oysters, along with other seafood selections. This chic little restaurant is very popular; be prepared to wait (at the bar if you like) for a table.

€ Mercado de Mariscos (Seafood Market, daily late morning–early evening), on the harbor at Boulevard Costero at Avenida Miramar, is a real fish market, not a restaurant; vendors serve fresh shrimp, octopus, squid, clams, lobster, tuna, abalone, halibut, and yellowtail. This is the best and cheapest place in town for fish tacos. **Tacos el Fenix** (Av. Espinosa at Av. Juárez, daily 8 A.M.–8 P.M.) serves excellent fish and prawn tacos for US$1.

American and Pizza

Alfonso's (Av. Macheros 4-5 at Blvd. Costero, tel. 646/174-0570, daily for breakfast, lunch, and dinner), offers good pizza, seafood, and Mexican breakfasts at reasonable prices.

Asian

La Cochinita (Paseo Hidalgo next to Maritime Customs, tel. 646/178-3443), is an indoor-outdoor place popular with local residents for its low prices, fast service, and Mexican-style Japanese food. The seafood can be overcooked, at least by Japanese standards; better are the chicken, tofu, or vegetable dishes. In addition to teriyaki, sushi, sukiyaki, and soups, the menu features such Mexican dishes as *cochinita pibil* (Yucatán-style marinated pork) and *tortas de pollo asado* (barbecued chicken sandwiches). A few vegetarian dishes are available, too. This is the original La Cochinita; there are now 12 more locations in Ensenada. Other links in this popular chain can be found in Mexicali, Tijuana, and La Paz.

Cafés

El Faro Café (mains under US$10), next to Gordo's Sportfishing, behind Plaza Marina on the waterfront, offers breakfast only, from 4:30 A.M. It's oriented toward early-rising anglers, both sporting and commercial.

Pueblo Café Deli (Av. Ruiz 96, tel. 646/178-8055, daily 8 A.M.–midnight) claims to be Ensenada's first full espresso bar. It also serves breakfast, traditional Mexican foods, salads, pastries, wine, and beer. Service is friendly.

Sanborns Café (Plaza Marina, Blvd. Costero, tel. 646/174-0971, daily 7:30 A.M.– 10 P.M., mains US$10–15) is the Old Faithful choice when you're looking for a low-risk meal. This location offers a reliable range of soups, salads, sandwiches, breakfasts, and Mexican dishes.

Café Café (Av. López Mateos 496, tel. 646/178-8209, daily from 9 A.M.) provides a relaxed environment where you can sip espresso while admiring an array of artwork, some of which the owner has created, and all of which is for sale. On some nights the café doubles as a venue for cultural and artistic events, such as performances of acid jazz, poetry, Latino rock, experimental performance art, and avant-garde cinema.

European

For fine French cuisine, head to **El Rey Sol** (Av. López Mateos 1000 at Av. Blancarte, tel. 646/178-1733, daily 7:30 A.M.–10:30 P.M., mains US$20 and up). The renowned Doña Pepita, a native of southern Baja's French-influenced town of Santa Rosalía, opened this elegant French restaurant in 1947 after spending 16 years in France (where she studied at the famous Cordon Bleu cooking school). The kitchen prepares seafood, poultry, and meat dishes served with herbs and vegetables grown on the family's farm in Santo Tomás. One of the house specialties is a rabbit-quail-chicken pâté. The menu also includes a few Mexican dishes. In front of the restaurant is a sidewalk seating area where morning coffee and pastry can be enjoyed.

La Embotelladora Vieja (Av. Miramar at Calle 7, tel. 646/174-0807, Mon. and Wed. noon–10 P.M., Thurs.–Sat. noon–11 P.M., Sun. noon–5 P.M., mains US$20 and up), in the Bodegas de Santo Tomás building, offers gourmet Mediterranean cuisine with a Mexican flair, served in a wine-cellar ambience. At least 20 different wines from Mexico, the United States, France, and Italy are available each month by the glass. This was the first phase of the expanding Centro Cultural Santo Tomás.

La Esquina de Bodegas (Av. Miramar

666 btw Calles 6/7, tel. 646/178-3557, Mon.–
Thurs. 8 A.M.–10 P.M., Fri.–Sat. 8 A.M.–midnight, mains US$15 and up) is a bistro and
wine bar in the back of a Soho-style renovated
warehouse decorated in industrial chic. It's also
part of the Centro Cultural Santo Tomás but
is considerably more casual than La Embotelladora. The menu offers changing entrées and
fixed-price meals, usually very good. On your
way in you can browse the wine shop, bookstore, and art gallery.

Restaurante Kaia (Calle Moctezuma 479,
tel. 646/178-2238, Tues.–Sun. 1–11 P.M.)
serves Basque cuisine, including paella, in a
small house.

Groceries

The **Gigante** at Avenidas Reforma and Delante
is a huge supermarket with just about anything
you might need for picnics, camping, or an
epic transpeninsular road trip. There are eight
other Gigantes in town.

Scattered along Avenida Diamante are inexpensive *panaderías, tortillerías,* and *dulcerías.*
For European-style baked items, investigate
La Baguette (on Blvd. Costero near Av. Blancarte, tel. 646/178-2814). Prices at La Baguette
are about double what you'd pay in an Avenida
Diamante bakery; if you're pinching pesos,
stick with the latter.

On Mexico 1, a few kilometers south of
town between Estero Beach and La Bufadora,
is a row of vendors selling fresh tamales stuffed
with pineapple *(piña),* corn *(elote),* olives *(acei-
tunas),* chicken, beef, or red chilies. Vendors
along this road also sell jars of olives, chilies,
and honey.

La Milpa (Calle Espinoza 246, tel. 646/177-
2092) is a health-oriented store carrying natural
foods, nonalcoholic wine and beer, herbs, dried
fruits, baked goods, and natural remedies.

INFORMATION AND SERVICES
Tourist Assistance

The Delegación de Turismo del Estado (State
Tourism Delegation) office (Blvd. Costero
and Calle Las Rocas, tel. 646/172-3022, fax
646/172-3081, Mon.–Fri. 8 A.M.–5 P.M., Sat.–

Sun. 10 A.M.–3 P.M.) dispenses information on
Ensenada events, dining, and hotels, as well as
on BCN travel. The English-speaking staff is
competent and helpful.

The Mexicali Tourism and Convention
Bureau, COTUCO (Blvd. Costero 540, tel.
646/178-2411, cotucoe@telnor.net, Mon.–
Fri. 9 A.M.–7 P.M., Sat. 10 A.M.–6 P.M., Sun.
11 A.M.–3 P.M.), is opposite the Pemex station at the north entrance to town. It distributes much of the same information as the state
tourist office.

The Tourism Trust, or Fondo Mixto (tel.
800/025-3991, U.S. tel. 800/310-9687,
info@enjoyensenada.com) offers information
about hotels, restaurants, and attractions in
Ensenada.

Ensenada has an active chamber of commerce (CANACO, Av. López Mateos 693, tel.
646/178-2322, canaco@telnor.net), and a restaurant association (CANIRAC, Calle 3 451,
tel. 646/174-0448, fax 646/174-0435, cani-
rac2@infosel.net.mx) with many American
members.

Money

ATMs are available at several Banamex
branches, including one at Avenida Juárez and
Riveroll, and at Banca Serfín, Avenida Ruiz
290. Most banks in Ensenada refer visitors to
a *casa de cambio* for foreign-exchange services.
Several shopping centers along Avenida Juárez
and Avenida Reforma feature money-changing
booths or storefronts.

Post and Telephone

The most convenient post office for visitors
staying near the waterfront sits at the corner
of Avenidas López Mateos and Rotario (Riviera), opposite the Desert Inn/La Pinta Hotel.
It's open Monday–Friday 8 A.M.–6 P.M., Saturday 9 A.M.–1 P.M.

Ensenada has a number of public telephones in the downtown area. For both local
and long-distance calls, these are less expensive
than hotel phones. If you need a phone line installed, pay a visit to the municipal telephone
office at the intersection of Boulevard Ramírez

ENSENADA PHONE NUMBERS

Ensenada area code: 646
Customs: 174-0897
Fire Department: 068
Green Angels: 176-4675
Highway Patrol: 176-1311
Immigration: 174-0164
IMSS Hospital: 172-4500
ISSSTE Hospital: 176-5276
Police: 060
Red Cross: 066
State Police: 061
State Tourism Office: 172-3022
Tourist Assistance: 078

Mendez and Avenida Reforma, near the Limón Bahía shopping center.

Immigration

The Ensenada immigration office (tel. 646/174-0164, daily 9 A.M.–5 P.M.) is next to the port captain's office (COTP) on Avenida Azueta near the waterfront at the northern entrance into town. If you plan to travel farther south than Maneadero and haven't validated your tourist card yet, this is the place to do it. Parking in the vicinity can be problematic—the office has no public lot, and most of the curbs nearby are painted red. You may have to park elsewhere in town and walk to the office.

Note: We once stopped here to have our Mexican visas validated, and the officer on duty refused to do the job, saying we had to return to Tijuana and have them validated at the border immigration office. We also heard from other foreigners who had similar experiences, although this unofficial "moratorium" lasted only a short while. If you have any trouble with your paperwork at the immigration office in Ensenada, go straight to the state tourism office (Blvd. Costero and Calle Las Rocas, tel. 646/172-3022); ask for the SECTUR *delegado*, who should be able to straighten things out.

Language Schools

Colegio de Idiomas de Baja California (Baja California Language College), Av. Riveroll 1287, tel. 646/174-1741, U.S. tel. 619/758-9711 or 877/444-2252, www.bajacal.com) offers 30-hour small-group week-long Spanish classes at a cost of US$245. Private classes run US$495. Homestays with Mexican families can be arranged.

The **Center of Languages and Latin American Studies** (Calle San Carlos 242, Fracc. Buenaventura near Av. Reforma and Calle Diamante, tel. 646/178-7600, U.S. tel./fax 760/476-9730 or 800/834-2256, www.mexonline.com/cllas.htm), operates a similar program but offers one hour less of classroom instruction per day. Tuition is US$270–295 per week depending on the time of year (US$180–210 per week for four or more weeks), plus additional costs for materials, private homestay and meals, and registration.

UCSD Extension Travel Study Programs (U.S. tel. 858/964-1050, fax 858/964-1099, travelstudy@ucsd.edu) arranges weekend and week-long Spanish study courses in Ensenada most of the year.

Real Estate

Bienes Raíces Roca (Av. Riveroll 143, tel. 646/174-0053, www.ensenada.net/roca) offers various real estate services, including sale and purchase of existing houses, vacation rentals, and property management. **Century 21** (Calle 9 1701, tel. 646/177-2777) can also provide information on houses, condos, and lots for sale in the Ensenada area.

Media

The *Ensenada Baja News-Gazette* is an informative Web magazine at www.baja-web.com/ensenada/gazette. Although the listings reach far beyond Ensenada, the Ensenada info is the most complete and up to date. The gazette aims to update the site monthly.

Mini Detalles Liquor Store in the Limón Bahía shopping center (Av. Delante at Av. Reforma) carries the *San Diego Union-Tribune* and the *Los Angeles Times* on a regular basis.

Emergencies

The **Clínica Hospital ISSSTE** (Calle Sanginés and Av. Pedro Loyola, tel. 646/176-5276) has 24-hour emergency services. For ambulance service, call **Cruz Roja** (tel. 066). For medical problems requiring emergency treatment at San Diego medical facilities, contact **Transmedic** (Av. Obregón at Calle 11, tel. 646/178-1400), a 24-hour ambulance service providing either air or surface transportation to San Diego.

GETTING THERE

By Air

No regularly scheduled flights currently serve Ensenada. **Aeropuerto El Ciprés** (tel. 646/177-4503), just south of town off Mexico 1, is an official Mexican airport of entry with a paved airstrip suitable for small-plane arrivals and departures. An air service operated by the **Sociedad Cooperativa de Producción Pesquera** (tel. 646/176-6076)—nicknamed Cannery Airlines by resident Americans—flies small planes between this airfield and Isla Cedros near the tip of the Vizcaíno Peninsula farther south. (See *Isla Cedros* in the *Central Baja* chapter.)

Baja Helicopters (Obregón 527-6 at Calle 4, tel./fax 646/178-8266) offers chopper charters in the region or to just about anywhere in Baja California.

By Bus

Intercity bus services to and from Ensenada are operated by **Autotransportes de Baja California** (ABC). Most air-conditioned buses use the Central de Autobuses terminal at Avenida Riveroll and Calle 11 (tel. 646/178-6680), while non-air-conditioned departures use a smaller terminal at Avenida Riveroll and Calle 8 (tel. 646/177-0909). The Central de Autobuses has a snack bar and a telephone office. ABC's *servicio plus* offers frequent, deluxe buses to Tijuana and Mexicali. ABC's regular non-air-conditioned buses leave for Tijuana every hour. Buses to/from San Felipe also use this terminal.

From the larger ABC terminal, you'll also find twice-daily departures for points south, including San Quintín (4 hours), Guerrero Negro (8 hours), Santa Rosalía (12 hours), Loreto (15 hours), and La Paz (20 hours).

Transportes Norte de Sonora (TNS), Elite, and **Estrellas de Oro** operate services to Guaymas, Los Mochis, Mazatlán, Guadalajara, and Mexico City on the Mexican mainland.

By Car

Ensenada is the southern terminus of Mexico 1-D, the four-lane toll road from Tijuana. Beyond Ensenada, Mexico 1 is, for the most part, a two-lane highway with road conditions varying from kilometer to kilometer.

Mexico 3 from Tecate also terminates in Ensenada, then reappears east of town winding across the Sierra Juárez to join Mexico 5 for San Felipe. Finding Mexico 3 east out of Ensenada can be difficult, as the route is not well signposted in the city. The simplest way to get there is to follow Avenida Juárez until it meets Avenida Reforma at the Benito Juárez statue. The street directly across Avenida Reforma is Calzada Cortés; after crossing Avenida Reforma, follow Calzada Cortés until it curves to the left and feeds into Mexico 3.

GETTING AROUND

By Bus

Several varieties of buses and vans ply the city's main avenues (e.g., López Mateos, Juárez, Ruiz, Diamante, Delante, Reforma, and Calle 9). The route—designated by street name—is usually whitewashed on the vehicle's windshield or printed on a marquee over it. Fares are roughly US$0.50, depending on the size of the vehicle; bigger is cheaper. Buses to outlying districts like Ejido Chapultepec leave from Avenida Juárez.

Cali-Baja Tours (Plaza Marina, Local G-3, tel./fax 646/178-1045) offers reasonably priced Ensenada city tours.

By Taxi

Most of the city's taxis park along López Mateos or Juárez, or near the bus depot at Calle 11 and Avenida Riveroll. Fares are negotiable; most trips in the city cost around US$3–7. A taxi to La Bufadora costs US$8–12.

By Car and Motor Scooter

Rental Cars and Motor Scooters: Ensenada is an expensive place to rent a car compared to Tijuana or Los Cabos. The most reasonable rates are charged by **Fiesta Rent-A-Car** (Blvd. Costero 1442, in the lobby of Hotel Corona, tel. 646/176-3344). Rates at this agency for a Nissan Sentra or something similar run around US$50 per 24 hours, including 100 free kilometers; there is a US$0.10 charge for each additional kilometer. Two- to four-day rentals come down less than 10 percent.

Hertz (in the Bahía shopping center at Calle 2 and Av. Riveroll, tel. 646/178-3776, U.S. tel. 800/654-3001) has considerably higher rates.

See the sidebar *Where to Rent a Car in Baja* in the *Essentials* chapter for other options.

A vendor at the south end of the Plaza Cívica (Plaza de las Tres Cabezas on Blvd. Costero), **Chavo's Sport Rentals,** rents Yamaha motor scooters for US$18 per hour.

Driving: Driving in Ensenada is fairly straightforward as long as you're prepared to stop at *every* intersection. Even when you don't see a stop sign, chances are a stop is required. The Ensenada traffic police don't go out of their way to hassle visitors, but fines are stiff for speeding, running stop signs, and drinking while driving. Fines must be paid in cash at the municipal police station (Calle 9 at Av. Espinoza).

Vicinity of Ensenada

◖ VALLE DE GUADALUPE AND THE RUTA DEL VINO

Dominican padres established the last and shortest-lived of the Baja California missionary efforts, **Misión Guadalupe,** west of the current village in 1834. In 1836, the mission was successfully defended against an attack by 400 Yumanos; four years later a much smaller force, led by a Neji Amerindian baptized at the mission, chased away the last Dominican padre. The remains of the mission were incorporated into other buildings and are now difficult to identify.

The Russian Colony

A small Russian cemetery and around 25 Russian-style homes occupy a part of Guadalupe known as Colonia Rusa. The original Russian immigrants were Molokans (the word means "milk-drinkers," presumably in reference to the sect's abstinence from alcohol), a straitlaced Christian sect that broke from the Russian Orthodox Church. Around 105 Russian families (approximately 500 individuals) migrated to Guadalupe in 1905, fleeing religious persecution in czarist Russia.

The group purchased 13,000 acres of valley land from the Mexican government. There they planted grapes and wheat, raised geese, kept honeybees, and built whitewashed adobe and wood homes, complete with thatched roofs and glass windows. As in their Russian homeland, the Molokans built their houses along a main street with the front doors facing away from the street. The simple chapel contained no religious decorations or icons, but the Molokans worshipped with such fervor that to the local Mexicans they were known as the Spirit Jumpers.

In 1938, following President Cárdenas's seizure of all foreign-owned lands, the community was engulfed by 3,000 Mexican squatters and renamed Francisco Zarco. Many of the Russians left the valley. Of those who stayed on, most ended up marrying Mexicans; today only four families of pure Russian lineage remain. In almost every respect they've become ordinary Mexican citizens; Russian is the first language only among a few elders.

Physical, if not cultural, evidence of the Russian colony remains. Around 25 of the original Molokan houses are intact. In the cemetery, the older tombstones at the back are engraved in Russian, while later stones toward the front show a combination of Russian and Mexican names—e.g., Juan Samarin, Pedro Pavloff.

VALLE DE GUADALUPE AND THE RUTA DEL VINO

Two small museums about 25 meters apart— **Museo Comunitario del Valle de Guadalupe** (646/174-0170, Tues.–Sun. 10 A.M.–6 P.M., by donation) and **Museo Histórico del Valle de Guadalupe** (Tues.–Sun. 10 A.M.–5 P.M., by donation)—contain exhibits of Russian memorabilia from the former colony, including clothing, old photos, and tools. The exhibits in the latter are better labeled, and the curator there emphasizes the overall history of the valley, with some emphasis on Spanish and Amerindian influences, while the former focuses only on Russian history in the valley. To find the cemetery and museums, take the turnoff for Francisco Zarco (near Km 77 on Mexico 3) and follow the paved road to its end, then turn right and drive about 150 meters; the cemetery should appear on your left, opposite Monte Xanic.

Vineyards and Wineries

Ensenada is the unofficial capital of Mexico's finest winemaking region, northwestern Baja California. Most Canadians and Americans are unaware of the quality of Mexican wines and assume beer and tequila are all the country has to offer. On the contrary, *bajacaliforniano* wines are shipped all over Mexico and western Europe, but because of U.S. and Canadian trade policies, they weren't exported north of the border until recent years. They're still difficult to find in Canada and the United States, but this may change as NAFTA reaches full implementation in 2009.

The highest concentration of wineries— more than two dozen at last count—are located in the 14-mile-long Valle de Guadalupe, located off Mexico 3, northeast of Ensenada. The introduction of stainless steel tanks and temperature-controlled barrels at many of these vineyards have helped put Baja wines on the world map. But you can still enjoy personal service and, often, time with the winemakers themselves as you make your way through the valley. Spring and summer are the most popular time to visit, though Mexican holiday weekends also draw a crowd.

You might start your tour at the west end of Guadalupe Valley in the village of San Antonio de las Minas. At **Vinisterra** (Km 94.5, tel. 646/178-3350, www.vinisterra.com, Sat. 11 A.M.–4:30 P.M., Sun. 11 A.M.–3 P.M.), Abelardo and Patricia Macouzet Rodriguez offer a cabernet sauvignon–merlot blend, tempranillo, and other award-winning wines.

Inquire about the award-winning merlot at family-owned **Viña de Liceaga** (Km 93.5, tel. 646/155-3093, www.vinosliceaga.com, Mon.–Fri. 8 A.M.–3 P.M., Sat.–Sun. 11 A.M.–3 P.M.). Choose from several tasting options for US$3–5. Reservations recommended. Nearby, contemporary **Casa de Piedra** (Km 93.5, tel. 646/155-3097, www.vinoscasadepiedra.com) offers tastings in a farmhouse setting. Reservations required. Once a year, it offers a four-weekend wine-making seminar. **La Casa Vieja** (Km 93.5, tel. 646/155-3153, lacasavieja.baja@hotmail.com) opens daily at 9 A.M. and closes at sunset, or whenever the crowd disperses. In addition to tastings, this winery has a deli, arts and crafts store, and information center onsite.

Chateau Camou (tel. 646/177-2221, www.chateau-camou.com.mx, Mon.–Sat. 10 A.M.–4 P.M., Sun. 10 A.M.–2 P.M.) specializes in expensive Bordeaux-style reds. It offers three tasting/tour options: Try four wines and a tour for US$5, six tastings and a tour for US$10, or a tour with the winemaker and a complete tasting including a barrel sample for US$40.

Next up, **Mogor Badán** (Km 86.5, tel. 646/177-1484, abadan@cicese.mx) is a combination organic produce farm; vineyard; and winery with tours, tastings, and shopping. Reservations required. Baja's most acclaimed winery, **Monte Xanic** (tel. 646/174-6769, www.montexanic.com, Mon.–Fri. 9 A.M.–4 P.M., Sat. 8 A.M.–noon), produces 50,000 cases of wine per year, and many of its labels have won awards in the United States, Canada, and Mexico. The winery charges US$4 for tasting whites and an additional US$4 for reds. Reservations required.

Housed in an adobe brick building, **Barón Balché** (El Porvenir, tel. 646/183-9501, www.baronbalche.com, daily 10 A.M.–4 P.M.)

is another winery using the latest technology to make boutique wines—10,000 cases a year. The largest winery in the region—and in all of Latin America—Italian-owned **L. A. Cetto** (Km 73.5, tel. 646/155-2264, www.cettowine.com or www.lacetto.com, daily 10 A.M.–3 P.M.) has gardens and a picnic area, as well as an inviting tasting room. You can tour the winery without reservations, and there are no tasting or tour fees. Past L. A. Cetto, **La Casa de Doña Lupe** (Rancho La Gotita, Francisco Zarco, www.donalupe.com, daily 9 A.M.–sunset) tempts visitors with home-baked goods, as well as farm-fresh cheese, honey, and produce and organically grown wines. In the same vicinity, you'll pay US$2.50 to taste the tempranillo, graciano, and mazuelo varietals at **Casa Pedro Domecq** (Km 73.5, tel. 646/155-2333, www.vinosdomecq.com.mx, Mon.–Fri. 10 A.M.–4 P.M., Sat. 10 A.M.–5 P.M.). The fee includes a cellar tour, plus use of a picnic area on the grounds.

Baja Wine Country Tours

Local resident Steve Dryden (U.S. tel. 619/300-4976, www.mexicowinetours.com) offers wine-tasting tours by private van or motor coach. Daylong bus tours depart from San Diego and include tastings at three wineries and lunch at Mustafa's Moroccan Restaurant. Steve is a former Napa Valley winery manager with extensive knowledge of the Mexican wine industry, as well as the native Kumiai people, Russian (Molokan) history, and the culture and history of Baja California. To follow the action in Baja's wine country, read his *Baja Times* column online (www.bajatimes.com).

Fiesta de la Vendimia Bajacaliforniana

Every year in August or September, Baja wineries collaborate on a 10-day winemaking festival in Ensenada and the Valle de Guadalupe that includes wine-tasting, paella cookoffs, culinary exhibitions, fireworks, music, dancing, and other bacchanalian activities. Sponsored by the Asociación de Vinicultores de Ensenada (Ensenada Viniculturists Association), the fes-

tival offers a wonderful opportunity to taste wines not easily found in Baja restaurants and to sample dishes not normally seen in Ensenada restaurants (e.g., tuna chateaubriand and wonton stuffed with crab). On Saturday a panel of judges gathers for the Concurso Internacional, a blind tasting of wines from Mexico and abroad. For information on upcoming festivals, contact Bodegas de Santo Tomás in Ensenada (tel. 646/178-3333).

Accommodations

Under US$50: Budget travelers can rent a cottage for US$35 a night at **Viños Sueños** (tel. 646/179-4763) winery in Francisco Zarco.

US$50-100: Warm colors set the tone in affordable rooms at **El Mezon del Vino** (tel. 664/162-9010, www.elmezondelvino.com, US$60 weekdays, US$80 weekends, suites US$150). Book an in-room massage for US$45. The hotel has a restaurant (weekends 8 A.M.–7 P.M.), for wine-tasting as well as breakfast and lunch.

US$100-250: Tuscan-style **La Villa del Valle** (tel. 646/183-9249, U.S. tel. 818/207-7130, www.lavilladelvalle.com, US$175) stands atop a hill on 70 acres with sweeping views of surrounding vineyards, orchards, and gardens. Four of its six rooms have private balconies; all have luxury linens and many more elegant touches. In between tastings, guests relax by the pool or soak in the hot tub, book a massage onsite, or play a game of bocce ball. Rates include full breakfast, afternoon glass of wine and *botanas,* and Wi-Fi access. There is a two-night minimum on weekends.

Near the Monte Xanic and Chateau Camou wineries, the **Adobe Guadalupe B&B** (Francisco Zarco, tel. 646/155-2094, www.adobeguadalupe.com, US$168) was the first winery to offer accommodations in the valley. The 60-acre winery offers six guestrooms in a rambling adobe-walled, hacienda-style complex. Rates include a complete breakfast served at a common table in the huge kitchen. Other meals may be arranged per cost. Recently, some guests have complained of overly protective dogs roaming common areas of the inn (reportedly, they do bite) and less-than-attentive service. Also note that double beds are twins pushed together. If these issues are a concern, you can try the La Villa del Valle or El Mezon del Vino.

Camping: You can camp on an 80-acre farm at **Bibayoff-Bodegas Valle de Guadalupe** (tel. 646/177-2722, bibayoff@telnor.net), run by a Russian family in San Antonio de las Minas. Exit Mexico 3 at El Tigre and follow the dirt road to Rancho Bibayoff. The Kumiai have opened a campground just north of L. A. Cetto Winery. Some say it resembles a California State Park at the turn of the 20th century. Sites cost US$5, and services include firewood, water, showers, and a general store. Guided hikes, horseback riding, cultural displays, and crafts are also available. Reservations required. Contact Horacio Moncada at tel. 646/178-8093 or 646/118-9113.

Food

The valley now has a few well-known restaurants to go with its boutique wineries: Around 22 kilometers (14 mi) northeast of Ensenada, perched on a hill just north of the small community of San Antonio de las Minas, **Restaurant Mustafa** (Km 93, tel. 646/155-3185, Wed.–Mon. 8 A.M.–7 P.M., mains US$7–12) serves Moroccan-influenced dishes, including lamb shish-kebab and chicken breast stuffed with spinach and cheese, along with a menu of Mexican specialties. In San Antonio itself, **El Mesón** is popular for breakfast and lunch; it's closed on Thursday. The owner is an admirer of British aviation artist Robert Taylor and displays Taylor's work on the restaurant walls.

Visiting gourmands praise **Restaurant Laja** (Km 83, tel. 646/155-2556, www.laja mexico.com, prix fixe menu US$52 or US$69) for farm-fresh cuisine on par with California's celebrated Chez Panisse and French Laundry restaurants. The brainchild of former Four Seasons chef Jair Téllez, the restaurant is located about 50 meters off Mexico 3 via a washboard road, in a private home with white walls and a red tile roof.

Francisco Zarco itself has a couple of small eateries worth trying. **Doña Chuy's** (mains under US$10) offers an economical Mexican alternative to the other restaurants in the valley, which tend to be a bit on the expensive side, while small, clean **Restaurante La Cabaña de las Lomas** (Km 92.5, Cajeme St., tel. 646/155-3033, Fri.–Sun. 8 A.M.–5 P.M.) specializes in northern Mexican food, including fresh quail.

You can pick up travel supplies at **Mercado La Chica** or **Abarrotes C. R.**, both in Francisco Zarco. Abarrotes C. R. has its own *panadería* and *tortillería*.

Getting There

The Valle de Guadalupe is less than a two hour drive (70 mi) south of San Diego on the toll road from Tijuana to Ensenada. After paying the last toll, watch for a sign to Tecate via Mexico 3 and the Ruta del Vino. Travel east on Mexico 3 for seven miles until you drop down into the Baja wine country at San Antonio de las Minas. This is the western end of the Guadalupe Valley wine region, which extends 14 miles east toward Tecate, ending near Km 73.5 at L. A. Cetto and Domecq wineries.

ESTERO BEACH

This huge, estuarial beach at the junction of Bahía de Todos Santos and Río San Carlos lies about 12 kilometers south of the center of Ensenada via Mexico 1, behind Ejido Chapultepec. Not everyone will find the beach—which tends toward mudflats at low tide—to their tastes, but the area is quiet and nice for beach-walking, surf-casting, and bird-watching. Opinions differ as to just how clean the water is, but plenty of folks swim here without any complaints.

The turnoff from Mexico 1 is 7.5 kilometers (4.7 mi) south of the Gigante at Avenidas Reforma and Delante. Except during July and August, the beach is surprisingly uncrowded. Ejido Chapultepec itself is a mostly uninspiring neighborhood of unfinished concrete-block houses and graffiti-covered walls, with a few nicer houses mixed in.

The **Estero Beach Museum** (daily 9 A.M.–5 P.M., US$5), part of the Estero Beach Resort complex, offers natural-history exhibits and a display of Mexican folk art.

Accommodations

Under US$50: Motel Costa Mar (Calle Veracruz 319, 1.5 km south of town, tel. 646/176-6425) is small and cheap. **Motel Hacienda Don Juan,** on the road to Estero Beach and within walking distance of the beach, offers rooms with kitchenettes and TVs.

Three-story **Hotel Joya Mar** (Calle Veracruz 360, tel./fax 646/176-7430) stands about a block away from Cueva de los Tigres, still a few blocks from Playa Hermosa, and offers 61 standard rooms. Facilities include a restaurant, small pool, and enclosed parking.

Along Playa Hermosa itself are several motels attached to trailer parks. **El Faro Beach Motel and Trailer Park** (tel. 646/177-4625, fax 646/177-4620) offers 23 basic rooms with kitchens in a two-story brick-and-stucco motel. To find El Faro, follow signs for Estero Beach off Mexico 1 at around Km 14, then continue straight ahead on this road (ignoring further signs for Estero Beach) until it dead-ends at El Faro. **La Villa Real Motel** features larger *palapas* and grills. A rustic but atmospheric restaurant overlooks the bay.

US$50-100: Estero Beach Resort Hotel (Km 14, Carretera Transpeninsular, tel. 646/176-6225 or 646/176-6230, www.hotelesterobeach.com) is a Spanish mission–style complex scattered over much acreage landscaped with palms and grass. The 104 rooms and suites all enjoy beach views. Amenities include tennis courts, a boat ramp, boat rentals, horseback riding, pool, playground, clubhouse, restaurant, bar, store, and museum. An adjacent RV park offers 60 RV spaces with full hookups and grassy camping areas.

Camping and RV Parks

The deluxe **Estero Beach Trailer Park** (tel. 646/176-6265) is adjacent to the Estero Beach Resort Hotel. RVers can use all the hotel facilities, including boat ramp, tennis courts, and clubhouse. Full-hookup sites are US$25.

On Playa Hermosa, **El Faro Beach Motel and Trailer Park** (tel. 646/177-4625, fax 646/177-4620) maintains 20 full-hookup sites, many of them permanently rented, plus bathrooms and hot water showers, right on the beach. Rates are US$8–12 a night. You may park for the day (7 A.M.–7 P.M.) at El Faro for just US$3, a fee that includes use of showers and restrooms.

Several other motel/trailer parks at Playa Hermosa offer similar setups. **Corona Beach Hotel** (no tel.) has 60 pull-through RV sites with electricity and water in a big open sand area for US$10 a night. Facilities include flush toilets and cold showers; tent camping is permitted. **La Villa Real Motel,** in the same vicinity, has better RV sites (US$10), although all of the beachfront sites appear to be permanently occupied. Some sites have *palapa* tables.

Frequent buses, marked Chapultepec, ply between downtown Ensenada and this neighborhood.

PUNTA BANDA AND LA BUFADORA

The rocky Punta Banda peninsula juts into the Pacific at the south end of Bahía de Todos Santos and is largely undeveloped except for a few campgrounds and small residential communities. Hikers can explore the peninsula's windswept spine on unmarked trails leading from turnouts along the only paved road, BCN 23. From lookout points on Punta Banda, you can often see spouting gray whales as they pass by during their annual January–March migration.

◖ La Bufadora

One of the Ensenada area's prime tourist sites, the scenic La Bufadora blowhole at the tip of Punta Banda is about 25 kilometers (16 mi) from the city via Mexico 1 and BCN 23. During incoming tides, waves rush into an underground cavern and force spumes as high as 25–30 meters (80–100 ft) through a hole in the top of the cavern. "La Bufadora" means

"The Snorter," referring to the sound created as water spews from the blowhole. A visitor center contains toilets and an interpretive display. Outside the center is a small desert garden in which the plants are accurately labeled.

A favorite weekend excursion among local Ensenadenses as well as foreign visitors, La Bufadora has taken on a look of prosperity. Vendors selling snacks and souvenirs still line the road from the parking lot to the blowhole, but the storefront shacks have been replaced with more substantial buildings, all connected with wooden and red-tile roofs that arch over the walkway. This spot could be nicknamed "Baja's *churro* capital," since there are probably more *churro* vendors here than anywhere else on the peninsula. Besides the vendor stalls, there are a few restaurants to choose from. One of the more popular seafood places is **Mariscos Alicia**. Also good are **Celia's Restaurante Bar** and **Restaurant Bar Los Gordos**. For the best bay view there is also **Los Panchos**.

A couple of pay lots at La Bufadora offer parking for US$5 per vehicle. Below the blowhole is Bahía Papalote (a bay) and the small residential/recreational community Rancho La Bufadora.

Fishing

Dale's La Bufadora Dive Shop (tel. 646/154-2092, www.labufadoradive.com) arranges half-day fishing trips for about US$35–50 per person, depending on the number of signups (two minimum). Dale's overlooks Bahía Papalote at Rancho La Bufadora and is open on weekends or by appointment.

Scuba Diving

Detached rocks, underwater pinnacles, sea caves, and kelp beds below the cliffs on Punta Banda's south shore are popular among scuba divers, and accessible by boat or from the shore. Giant green anemones are another underwater attraction. Easiest access is at Bahía Papalote, the bay below La Bufadora; it's sheltered enough for intermediate divers or supervised novices; an underwater hot springs at a depth of 25–30 meters warms the bottom of the bay.

Note, due to water currents, dive conditions here are often colder than in San Diego. You'll need lots of neoprene or, preferably, a dry suit to be comfortable.

Off the northwest tip of Punta Banda lies an underwater ridge—accessible by boat only—topped by a 2.4-kilometer chain of small islands. The ridge is dotted with underwater cliffs, caves, rock reefs, and kelp beds. Cold-water upwellings along the ridge stimulate marinelife and help maintain good visibility. Because of swells and currents in the area, only divers with open-ocean experience should consider diving here unless accompanied by someone who knows local diving conditions well.

At Bahía Papalote, **Dale's La Bufadora Dive Shop** (see *Fishing*) offers half-day guided dive trips for US$35–50 per person, depending on the number of signups (two minimum). Dale's also rents diving and snorkeling gear. The Almar dive shop in Ensenada can also arrange guided trips to any Punta Banda dive spot.

Kayaking

Challenging sea kayak routes include following the peninsular shore from La Jolla around to La Bufadora, or crossing over to the Isla Sur of the Islas Todos Santos. The latter is a fairly straightforward 6.4-kilometer (4-mi) paddle from Punta Banda. At Rancho La Bufadora near the blowhole, **Dale's La Bufadora Dive Shop** (see *Fishing*) rents kayaks for US$20 per half day, US$30 per full day.

Camping and RV Parks

A short distance along the road to La Bufadora (BCN 23), in the American retirement enclave of La Jolla, is the large, secure, and well-kept **La Jolla Beach Camp** (tel. 646/154-2005, fax 646/154-2004), facing Bahía de Todos Santos. It has 200 sites with the option to pull-through or backup, 25 of which have electric only. Sites cost US$10 for two people. Other facilities include hot showers, a boat ramp, tennis court, disposal station, market, and restaurant.

The adjacent **Villarino RV Park (Campamento Turístico Villarino)** (tel. 646/176-4246, Ensenada tel. 646/154-2045, fax

646/154-2044) offers 35 tent/camper sites with electricity for US$10, full hookups for US$15. Other facilities include clean bathrooms, hot showers, picnic tables, a boat ramp, boat rentals, restaurant, and market. The office is open daily 9 A.M.–noon and 1–5 P.M.

A couple of *ejido*-operated campgrounds with minimal facilities (toilets and water only) are available farther up on Punta Banda. **Ejido Coronel Esteban Cantú,** on the west side of Punta Banda about a half mile off the dirt road that forms the final approach to La Bufadora, is a quiet spot ideal for self-contained campers with an interest in nearby fishing or diving (US$5).

Rancho La Bufadora, overlooking Bahía Papalote (tel. 646/178-7172) offers oceanview dry campsites (flush toilets available) with 24-hour security and is within walking distance of La Bufadora, Dale's La Bufadora Dive Shop, a boat ramp, restaurants and bars, and a minimarket. Rates run US$5–10, depending on the number of campers. **Dale's La Bufadora Dive Shop** also offers beds in a bunkhouse sleeping up to 15 persons for US$10 per person; there's a US$200 minimum per weekend for use of the bunkhouse. On weekdays you may be able to get a discount.

Getting There

To drive to Punta Banda from Ensenada, take Mexico 1 south to BCN 23 (just north of Maneadero), then follow this road west through olive orchards and the La Jolla community onto the peninsula. After La Jolla, the road begins to climb, winding its way toward La Bufadora and ending at a parking lot for the blowhole. You can hire a taxi from the city to La Bufadora for US$15–20.

◖ ISLAS DE TODOS SANTOS

These twin islands about 20 kilometers (12 mi) west of Ensenada—or southwest of San Miguel the same distance—offer a variety of recreational opportunities. Fishing is good along the western shores of both islands, especially for yellowtail, halibut, and sea bass. For longer visits, boats can safely anchor in three coves

along the eastern shore of the southern island; the middle cove offers the best shelter overall. Local anglers stay at seasonal fish camps at the southern ends of both islands.

For hikers, the southern island offers the most interesting terrain, with cliffs along the perimeter and a hilly interior. The highest elevation, just below the island's midpoint, is approximately 100 meters. Near the northern end of this island are several caves; at the southern tip are a few tidal pools worth exploring. The northern island is mostly flat, with a radio tower and two lighthouses—one abandoned, one in use. Both islands are nesting grounds for brown pelicans, cormorants, blue herons, ospreys, and various other bird species.

Surfing

Islas de Todos Santos is perhaps best known as the site of the Pacific coast's biggest, baddest surf. As *Surf Guide* magazine wrote, "The waves here laugh at your 8'2"." November through February, a deep-water northwest swell sweeps the skinny northwestern point (partially submerged at high tide) of Isla Norte to produce powerful, 8- to 10-meter (25–30 foot) waves. Dubbed Killer's, this is a break best attempted only by experienced gunners—unless it's running small. Todos surfers estimate that whatever height the surf at San Miguel is running, waves at Isla Norte will be double plus 2.5 meters (8 ft).

The northwest corner of the southern island also offers an excellent winter break. When the northwest swell is rolling hard, the channel between the two islands conjures up a monumental, long-riding right called Thor's Hammer, formed by the confluence of direct swell movement toward this point and refracted swell as it wraps eastward around the north island, then bounces off the south island and into the channel. This same channel pumps a grinding left break during the summer southwest swell, making the islands a year-round surf destination. Surfers sometimes camp on the flat northern island, but most boat in for the day from Ensenada or San Miguel.

Getting There

All-day *panga rápida* (fast *panga*—an open, motorized fiberglass skiff) charters to the islands can be arranged for US$150 at **Juanito's Boats,** in Ensenada behind the Plaza Marina on the waterfront (tel. 646/174-0953, U.S. tel. 800/569-1254). The trip takes around 30 minutes each way; one boat can take up to six surfers. You can also charter boats at fish camps in Punta Banda south of Ensenada, or sometimes in San Miguel. San Miguel surfers with their own boats will usually take along a passenger or two if the guests agree to buy gas for the trip and beer for the survivors.

East from Ensenada

Mexico 3 stretches southeast 198 kilometers (123 mi) from Ensenada to San Felipe on the Sea of Cortez. The first two-thirds of the highway traverses high chaparral along the gradually ascending western slopes of the Sierra Juárez. Just past Km 39 is a short paved road leading north into **Ojos Negros,** a small farming center with a Pemex station (which more often than not pumps gas from a can), as well as several markets, an auto parts dealer, and a pharmacy.

A natural spring flows from a steep hillside on the east side of the highway between Km 73 and 74—a good place to stock up on drinking water.

PARQUE NACIONAL CONSTITUCIÓN DE 1857

The most commonly used road to this national park branches northeast off Mexico 3 at Km 55 near Ojos Negros. Most of the road to the park was recently paved, but it hasn't exactly flooded the park with visitors. As the road climbs, passing a number of ranchos, the chaparral gradually gives way to conifer forests and the temperature drops.

Most of the 5,000-hectare park encompasses a subalpine plateau at the center of the Sierra Juárez with an average elevation of around 1,200 meters (3,950 ft); several granite peaks reach over 1,500 meters (5,000 ft). Containing several different species of pines, some exclusive to the region, the forests here form one of the most important woodland areas in Baja California—a virtual oasis surrounded by the rest of the state's aridity.

Two natural lakes, Laguna La Chica and Laguna Juárez, surrounded by granite boulders, low hills, and Ponderosa pines, add to the oasis effect and generate scenes of great beauty during occasional winter snowfalls. Laguna Juárez—more commonly known as Laguna Hanson after an American settler who disappeared here in 1880 (legend has it he was cooked in a cauldron by a friend)—is for all intents the center of the park.

In years when rainfall is plentiful, the scenic lake is filled with bass and catfish; in the fall, ducks are common. Fishing is permitted; hunting is not. A campground at the lake features raked grounds and neat fire pits, some furnished with firewood and grills. Except for a 10-kilometer path around the lake, there are no established hiking trails in the park. Smaller Laguna La Chica is less visited; in dry years it may not contain any water at all.

After you have chosen a campsite, a ranger or the park caretaker will drop by, place a trash container at the spot, and collect US$5 per night per vehicle. A fine for littering will be imposed if garbage is discarded anywhere but in the trash can. Most of the year the park receives few visitors. This changes at Easter, when enough jeepsters arrive to dispel all peace and quiet. If you visit in winter, come prepared for cold weather and possible snow. The latter may make park roads temporarily impassable.

The road from Mexico 3 continues northeastward through the park and ends at Mexico 2—60 kilometers (36 mi) from Laguna Hanson—near La Rumorosa. See *Vicinity of Mexicali* in the *Mexicali to San Felipe* chapter for details on the northern approach to Laguna Hanson.

VALLE DE LA TRINIDAD AND MIKE'S SKY RANCH

A paved road to Valle de la Trinidad branches south from Mexico 5 at Km 121. This farming community of around 5,000 offers a Pemex station, a bank, several markets, cafés, and auto shops. Southwest of Valle de la Trinidad, a dirt road suitable only for sturdy, high-clearance vehicles continues southward some 48 kilometers (30 mi) past a few ranchos to the northern boundary of Parque Nacional Sierra San Pedro Mártir.

Just beyond Km 138, a dirt road leads 35.5 kilometers (22 mi) south to Mike's Sky Ranch, a remote resort at the northwestern edge of Parque Nacional Sierra San Pedro Mártir (elevation 1,200 m/3,950 ft). Named for its late founder, Mike Leon, the ranch has long served as a checkpoint for the Baja 500 and Baja 1000 off-road races; nearby are hiking trails to year-round waterfalls and Río San Rafael. Ranch accommodations include 27 cabins for US$50 per person per night (includes all meals and swimming pool access) and campsites for US$5 per vehicle per night (water and shower privileges only). Guests eat family-style meals together (campers pay US$12 for dinner and US$7 for breakfast and lunch). For information or reservations write Mike's Sky Ranch, 607 Twining Ave., San Diego, CA 92154, or call Mike's number in Mexico (664/681-5514).

The road to Mike's is rough in spots and can change drastically with recent rains. Beyond the ranch, this road continues southwestward to join the newly paved road between Mexico 1 and the national park. For more information on this route and Parque Nacional Sierra San Pedro Mártir, see *South from Ensenada*.

South from Ensenada

MANEADERO TO COLONIA VICENTE GUERRERO

Maneadero

This farming community 20 kilometers (12 mi) south of Ensenada is unremarkable except for the fact that it's the southernmost limit of Baja's "free zones." Beyond Km 23, every visitor is supposed to possess a valid tourist permit or visa. The immigration checkpoint at Km 23 has been closed for several years now, so be sure to validate your tourist card in Ensenada. A military *puesto de control* may be in operation to check for drugs and weapons.

Restaurants, small grocery stores, auto parts shops, and other small businesses line Mexico 1 in the middle of Maneadero. Locally grown olives—along with tamales—are sold in great abundance at roadside stands. A car wash on the east side of the highway performs an excellent exterior and interior cleaning for around US$5, something to consider if you're on the way north after extensive off-highway driving in the interior.

Las Canadas Campamiento (Km 31–32, tel. 646/153-1055, U.S. tel. 800/027-3828, www.lascanadas.com, US$12 pp) is a popular swimming resort that offers water activities in the summer and camping year-round. A half dozen pull-through sites with full hookups are available.

The highway through Maneadero is famous for its prodigious *topes,* or speed bumps. Drive slowly.

La Bocana and Puerto Santo Tomás

Off Mexico 1 at Km 48, an unpaved graded road follows the Río Santo Tomás 29 kilometers (18 mi) west to the seaside fishing villages of La Bocana and Puerto Santo Tomás, both on the south side of Punta Santo Tomás. The Río Santo Tomás drains into the Pacific at La Bocana (The Mouth); during the Dominican era, Puerto Santo Tomás served as a supply port for nearby Misión Santo Tomás.

The scenic coastal topography along Punta Santo Tomás and the coves to the south have attracted a small gringo settlement, but for the most part you'll have the beach all to yourself. Camping is free; you can rent rustic cabins at either village. The villagers also rent fishing *pangas.*

The shoreline in front of La Bocana offers occasional beach and reef breaks. Determined surfers can brave an ungraded dirt road that runs south off the graded road from Mexico 1—the turnoff is approximately 20.5 kilometers (12.7 mi) west of the highway—and straggles 11 kilometers (7 mi) southwest to Punta San José, where there are often good reef and point breaks.

Santo Tomás

The Valle de Santo Tomás, left by the Río Santo Tomás, is one of Baja's prime agricultural regions and a visual highlight of any transpeninsular journey. Winding up, down, and around olive-green hills, the highway repeatedly suspends drivers over vignettes of tidy olive groves, vineyards, fields of flowers, and the occasional herd of goats. For some visitors, a day's stopover turns into weeks, perhaps because Santo Tomás offers the ambience of California's Sonoma or Napa valleys without the

tourists and high prices. The valley community of around 1,500 is friendly and welcoming.

The valley was originally settled in 1790 by Dominican missionaries as an intermediate point between Misión San Miguel to the north and San Vicente to the south. In 1791, the Dominican padres established **Misión Santo Tomás de Aquino,** which by 1800 boasted more than 3,000 cattle, sheep, and goats, plus an estimated 200 acres of grapes, corn, and wheat. The mission wine produced at Santo Tomás was famous throughout the California mission system and is now one of several wines produced by Ensenada's Bodegas de Santo Tomás. The Santo Tomás mission was secularized in 1849.

The **Mission Ruins** lie in two locations. The original site is on a low mesa off the unpaved road to La Bocana and Puerto Santo Tomás; the second site, where the mission was moved in 1794, is just off the east side of Mexico 1 in the village of Santo Tomás, north of El Palomar Trailer Park. At both sites, the only remains are a few ruined adobe walls and a foundation.

Although grapes grown in this region may end up squeezed into the wines of several *bajacaliforniano* wineries, **Bodegas de Santo Tomás,** a descendant of the original Santo Tomás mission winery, still presides over the valley. For much of the 20th century, the winery's main operations took place in Ensenada, but in recent years the owners have been moving the company back to the valley. Wine-tasting tours for groups of 12 or more are now available at the bodega's new eco-tech, gravity-fed winery overlooking the valley (by appointment only, tel. 646/177-0836, bstwines@hotmail.com).

The inexpensive family-owned **El Palomar,** at Km 154 on Mexico 1 in Santo Tomás (tel. 646/178-2355) began as a restaurant in 1948 but now includes a motel, trailer park with 101 spaces, Pemex station, and even a small zoo. Rooms at the motel are comfortable and heated, and fall into the US$25–50 range. Full-hookup RV sites in the trailer park cost US$12 a night for two people. El Palomar's dining room offers a full list of *bajacaliforniano* wines and home-cooked meals starting at US$7. The two swimming pools at El Palomar are a treat during the summer months, though the place is much less popular now that Las Canadas has opened to the north.

Ejido Eréndira and Puerto San Isidro

At Km 78, a paved road leads west off Mexico 1 to the fishing and farming community of Ejido Eréndira. Although the village is far from attractive, the beaches north of town offer plenty of opportunities for camping and surf or boat fishing. The road to Puerto Isidro (2 km north of Ejido Eréndira) and beyond is unpaved, ungraded, sandy, and potholed—a passenger car can manage it, but very slowly. Surfers will find six different point and reef breaks in the vicinity of Puerto Isidro. River's Mouth and Barny's Cove are closest to the *ejido,* while Half Moon Bay, Sunset Beach, Lighthouse, and Cuatro Casas are a bit farther away.

Twenty-four kilometers from Mexico 1, **Hostel Coyote Cal's** (www.coyotecals.com) is a gringo-run surf camp with shared rooms for US$15 per person, private rooms for US$45 per couple, and tent/RV sites for US$10 per person. If you can swing it, the Crow's Nest room has a great view for US$60. Room (but not camping) rates include breakfast. For enjoying the surrounding coast and hills, Cal's rents out mountain bikes, mask/snorkel/fins, surfboards, and boogie boards.

Castro's Place, near Puerto Isidro (tel. 646/176-2897), is one of the classic Baja fish camps, with simple cabins that sleep up to six people in bunk beds for around US$25–30 a night. Camping is permitted at Castro's for a nominal fee. The owner, Fernando Castro Ríos, leads guided fishing trips in the vicinity from US$140 per day for four persons, plus US$30 for each additional person. Reservations may be necessary on weekends.

San Vicente

The scenic Valle de San Vicente and adjacent Llano Colorado (Reddish Plain), like the Río Santo Tomás valley, are heavily cultivated with olives, grapes, wheat, and corn.

Just south of the Km 88 marker, a dirt road leads west off Mexico 1 to the ruins of **Misión San Vicente Ferrer,** a Dominican mission in use 1780–1833. During its half-century tenure, the mission came under repeated attacks by Yumano warriors living in the Sierra Juárez. On a small mesa near the adobe walls of the mission is a mission-established cemetery—still in use—and the remains of a Spanish presidio. The mission area is fenced off and appears to be under private control at the moment. To enter, you must pay a US$5 admission fee at a new visitors center out front.

Along Mexico 1 in the small town of San Vicente sit a sprinkling of cafés, markets, an ABC bus terminal, a Pemex station, and several hotels with basic accommodations for under US$25.

San Antonio del Mar

At Km 126, just north of Colonet, an unpaved graded road leads 12.5 kilometers (8 mi) northwest to this seaside settlement, little more than a collection of trailers, rustic beach houses, and a couple of beach camps that charge US$5–10 a night for tents or campers. The beach at San Antonio del Mar, wedged into a large gap between high cliffs created by a tidal estuary, is wide, windy, and backed by sand dunes. If you can stand the wind, you can camp for free on the beach. Surfcasting and clamming are usually excellent here; the estuary is an added attraction.

The main road in from Mexico 1 becomes softer as it gets closer to the beach. Unless you have four-wheel drive, stick to the most well-worn, hardened tracks.

Colonet

Like San Vicente, Colonet is a small farming center with a Pemex station and a couple of cafés and markets. Travelers spending time at San Antonio del Mar, Rancho Meling, or Parque Nacional Sierra San Pedro Mártir often use the town as a supply depot. There are plans under discussion to build a large port in Colonet, but it is currently mired in political debate.

A graded dirt road leads southwest out of town 14 kilometers to a fish camp on Bahía

Colonet. Cabo Colonet, at the north end of the bay, offers a point break during winter northwest swells. The town, bay, and cape are reputedly named for Captain James Colnett, a British sea captain who explored this section of the Pacific coast in the late 18th century. At **Cuatro Casas,** about 4.5 kilometers south of Cabo Colonet on the bay, campsites are available for US$4–5 a day. Surfcasters will find plenty of barred surfperch, halibut, and bass.

San Telmo and Rancho Meling

Between Km 140 and 141, a newly paved road branches east to San Telmo, Rancho Meling, and **Parque Nacional Sierra San Pedro Mártir.** San Telmo, six kilometers (3.5 mi) east of Mexico 1, is a small farming and ranching settlement with little of interest to the traveler; supplies for extended trips into the interior should be procured in Colonet or Camalú on Mexico 1. There's a Pemex station with Premium fuel just north of San Telmo.

Rancho Meling (tel. 646/179-4106, www.melingguestranch.com, US$145), also known as Rancho San José, lies 42 kilometers (26 mi) farther southeast along the road, at an elevation of 670 meters (2,200 ft). Founded in 1893 by Danish immigrant and Texas miner Harry Johnson as a base for his gold-mining operations in the western Sierra de San Pedro Mártir, the ranch was destroyed by Magonistas during the 1911 border rebellion. A Norwegian family, the Melings, helped rebuild the ranch shortly thereafter, turning it into a 10,000-acre cattle ranch.

After being closed for a few years around 2000, the ranch is open again to guests who want to experience Baja's high country. Visitors are accommodated in a comfortable one-story, 12-room stone lodge. Optional activities include swimming in a spring-fed pool, horseback riding, quail and dove hunting, and excursions into the Sierra de San Pedro Mártir—an excellent opportunity to see the national park with experienced guides. Guests with their own planes may use the rancho's airstrip. Rates include three family-style meals.

Heading to the coast from San Telmo,

take the dirt road turnoff just past Abarrotes Ormart right before you leave town and you'll find a longboarding spot called Quatro Casas and a hostel by the same name. It is a fickle spot that doesn't break consistently. The hostel provides basic but clean rooms (US$10–15) in a large house with fenced parking. You can camp out front along the point for US$5. There were some short-sighted fishermen out front using bleach to ferret out octopuses from their holes in the tidepools.

Punta San Jacinto and Camalú

Between Km 149 and 150, a dirt track suitable in good weather for ordinary passenger vehicles proceeds west nine kilometers (5.5 mi) to a sandy beach at Punta San Jacinto. There is a surf spot at the site of a huge freighter, *Isla del Carmen,* that is beached on the sand. It's a soft wave, but it's a good choice for days when the northwest swell is huge. Baja Surf Adventures (www.bajasurfadventures.com) runs a surf resort here providing lessons and basic accommodations. You can camp for free among the dunes behind the beach, but it's not recommended since crime in this area is a real concern.

Camalú, beginning at Km 157, offers markets, pharmacies, and cafés, a mechanic's shop, and a Pemex station (diesel fuel is available). Punta Camalú is a worthwhile right point break.

Misión Santo Domingo and Colonia Vicente Guerrero

Colonia Vicente Guerrero is a growing agricultural center with a post office, market, motel, two banks (including a Banamex with ATM), restaurants, a police station, *panadería,* 24-hour Pemex station, *butano* (butane/propane) plant, clinic, ABC bus terminal, and two trailer parks. The surrounding fields produce a variety of vegetables and fruit.

The ruins of Misión Santo Domingo (named for the founder of the Dominican Order) lie north of town, eight kilometers (5 mi) east of Mexico 1, in a canyon formed by Arroyo de Santo Domingo. An earlier mission, established in 1775, lay eight kilometers farther east along the arroyo. Moved to the current site in 1782, the mission closed in 1839 after most of the Amerindians in the area either died in battle or succumbed to smallpox. The meter-thick adobe walls at Santo Domingo are more extensive than those at Santo Tomás or San Vicente; the outline of the mission quadrangle and several rooms are clearly visible.

The mission road parallels Arroyo de Santo Domingo for several kilometers beyond the ruins, offering a scenic, if rough, drive past two ranchos. Originating in the high reaches of the Sierra de San Pedro Mártir, this arroyo is said to carry the largest volume of water of any stream on the peninsula and is stocked with an abundance of trout in season.

Motel Sánchez, in the middle of town on the west side of Mexico 1, offers basic rooms for under US$25. At the south end of town, on the west side of the highway next to the butane facility, is the nicely landscaped **Mesón de Don Pepe RV Park** (tel. 616/166-2216). Tent sites, on green grass—a Baja rarity—are US$6 a night; full-hookup sites cost US$10 for two people (US$2 for each additional person); rates may vary according to the time of year. Don Pepe's restaurant serves Mexican standards and seafood.

Follow the same turnoff to Don Pepe's farther west, toward the beach, and you'll come to the quiet **Posada Don Diego Trailer Park** (tel. 616/166-2181, www.posadadondiego.com). Full hookups are US$10–15 a night, tent space US$6–9. The 100-site park is popular with caravans and also has a few small trailers for rent (US$25), in case you didn't bring your own. A restaurant in the park specializes in Mexican seafood dishes. If you dig up your own pismo clams on the beach, ask Señora Martínez, who operates the park with her husband José, to steam them for you. The park also features laundry facilities, clean bathrooms, a fully stocked bar, and a playground.

Camping on the beach among the dunes is a possibility, but the sandy track gets a bit dodgy once you pass Posada Don Diego. Passenger cars can make it, but RVs—except those with four-wheel drive—risk getting stuck.

PARQUE NACIONAL SIERRA SAN PEDRO MÁRTIR

Founded in 1947, this 170,000-acre national park is centered on the Sierra de San Pedro Mártir—the highest mountain range in the peninsular cordillera. Like other northern Baja sierras, the San Pedro Mártir tips toward the west, with its highest peaks thrusting out along the precipitous eastern escarpment. The peninsula's highest peak, Picacho del Diablo (Devil's Peak)—also known as Cerro de la Encantada (Enchanted Mountain) and La Providencia (Providence)—looms over the San Felipe Desert at 3,095 meters (10,154 ft). It's a challenging Class 3–5 climb.

Three prominent canyons radiate eastward from the base of the mountain—Cañon del Diablo, Cañon Providencia, and Cañon Tel-edo, providing magnificent bouldering and scrambling opportunities, sheer cliffs, water-falls, fan palms, Amerindian petroglyphs, and several approaches to Diablo's twin granitic summits. Hikers interested in these eastern canyons, which lie just outside the park boundaries, usually approach them from Mexico 3 to the northeast.

Within the park, hikers and backpackers can choose from a network of trails and campsites on a pine- and juniper-forested plateau—approximately 70 kilometers by 15 kilometers—at the heart of the range. Because much of the park exceeds 1,800 meters (6,000 ft) in elevation, annual precipitation averages 60 centimeters (24 in); thus water sources are abundant and shady conifers predominate. Only a few hundred people visit San Pedro Mártir each year, making it one of the most undervisited national parks in Mexico and an extraordinary opportunity for wilderness solitude. The mountain hiking conditions enjoyed here are similar to those in California's Sierra Nevada, but the park attracts far fewer people.

National Observatory

Because the air is exceptionally clear and potential sources of light pollution are remote, the Mexican government selected the San

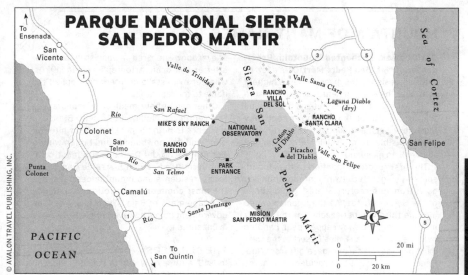

Pedro Mártir Plateau in 1967 as the site for its Observatorio Astronómico Nacional. The observatory facilities are at the end of the park access road (20 km past the park entrance), atop Cerro de la Cúpula at an elevation of 2,830 meters (9,286 ft). A locked gate just before the observatory means visitors must park and walk two kilometers to reach the domed buildings. Several telescopes are in use at the observatory, including Mexico's largest, a 2.11-meter (83-inch) reflector.

Schedules for observatory tours vary greatly depending on time of year. For more information contact the Observatorio Astronómico Nacional in Ensenada (tel. 646/174-4580, contacto@astrosen.unam.mx). A viewpoint nearby offers an inspiring glimpse of the eastern escarpment and canyons. At night, stars appear over the plateau like a sea of diamonds—who needs a telescope?

Climate

Temperatures on the plateau, 1,800 meters above sea level, average 26°C (80°F) in July and August during the daytime, down to 4.5°C (40°F) at night. From December through March, temperatures run from 4.5°C (40°F) down to -12°C (10°F). Freezing nights sometimes occur in the spring and fall, with daytime temperatures in the 15–21°C (60–70°F) range.

Snowfall is common above 2,000 meters during the winter; Picacho del Diablo is often snowcapped November–April While occasional heavy rains fall in late summer, it's usually dry in spring, early summer, and fall.

The best hiking seasons are mid-April–mid-June (good for wildflowers) and late September–early November (when quaking aspens put on a show). For backpackers, the April–June season is optimal because water sources from the snowmelt are most abundant. Late summer rains can cause hazardous flash floods in the arroyos.

Flora and Fauna

About 53 kilometers east of Rancho Meling the San Telmo road begins ascending rapidly, the terrain changing from arid coastal plains to scrubby high chaparral. At 900–1,500 meters (3,000–5,000 ft), stands of pine, oak, and juniper appear, mixed with a dwindling number of desert and chaparral species—sagebrush, verbena, yucca, and fan palm. Above

MOUNTAIN OF MANY NAMES

Devil's Peak, Enchanted Mountain, Providence, and **Mt. San Pedro Mártir** are a few of the map designations given to Baja's highest peak over the last four centuries. Whether the Yumano or Cochimí Amerindians had a name for the soaring peak isn't known, but they must have been acquainted with its serrated profile, visible from 160 kilometers away on the Mexican mainland.

The first recorded mention of the jagged, sparsely vegetated, twin-summit mountain dates from 16th-century Spanish explorations of the Sea of Cortez. As the Spanish sailed into the thirsty upper reaches of the Cortez in late spring, the snowcapped peak hanging over the searing San Felipe Desert to the west must have seemed a mirage, a gift from God. Hence they called it La Providencia, a name sustained through the early 20th century.

DEVIL'S PEAK

La Providencia's semantically opposite name, El Picacho del Diablo (Devil's Peak), surfaced during the missionary period, probably in reference to the peak's formidable appearance when viewed from the west; Misión San Pedro Mártir, perhaps the most remote mission on the peninsula, was established some 25 kilometers to the southwest. Another possible semantic explanation suggests that the mountain was revered by local Amerindians; to divert spiritual attention from the peak and toward the mission, the San Pedro Mártir padres may have consigned it to the Devil.

The padres called a large, open meadow between the mission and the mountain La Encantada (The Enchanted), perhaps because it appears in the midst of heavy pine and juniper forests as if cleared by supernatural forces.

The meadow appeared on Spanish maps thereafter, and Mexican cartographers in the 1920s, whether by mistake or intention, applied the name to the mountain.

Other names have made brief appearances this century, including El Picacho Blanco, a reference to both the peak's mostly white coloring and its snowbound condition in winter. But El Picacho del Diablo is the most common term used among Sierra de San Pedro Mártir residents and mountaineers; it's also the most common name found on English-language maps of Baja. The official Mexican government name, however, remains Cerro de la Encantada.

THE CLIMBERS

In 1910, author A. W. North called El Picacho del Diablo "the unchallenged retreat of lions and mountain sheep, the unscaled lookout of eagles and mighty condors." The following year, American cartographer Donald McLain successfully attained the summit. The next recorded climb was made in 1932 by a U.S. Sierra Club group, which was forced to spend the night in Cañon del Diablo after struggling with the mountain's west face.

The peak was ascended by another American climber (Randall Henderson, editor of *Desert* magazine) in 1937, and by several more in the 1950s. By the early 1970s, more than 50 people a year (both Mexicans and foreigners) were scaling the heights – with as many attempting the climb but turning back short of the summit. Today the Class 3 Slot Wash approach is a straightforward but challenging ascent for experienced climbers, while the other six proven approaches encompass some of the toughest climbing in Mexico.

1,500 meters, thickly forested glens leave the Baja desert mythos behind. Here you'll find piñon and Jeffrey pine, incense cedar, white fir, sugar pine, and at least three species not found elsewhere in Baja—quaking aspen, lodgepole pine, and the endemic San Pedro Mártir cypress.

Streams in the sierra's western canyons carry an endemic trout species, the Nelson rainbow trout (*Salmo nelsonii*, named for E. W. Nelson, who discovered the fish in 1905). In the early 1980s, a group of Mexico City naturalists transplanted Nelson rainbows to several other canyon streams in the park.

Today, fishing without a license is permitted. Mule deer, mountain lions, wildcats, coyotes, and the rare *borregón* (bighorn sheep) inhabit some of the canyons.

Domestic animals—cattle and sheep—are often seen in the park, especially along the east side where two ranches lie within park boundaries. Unfortunately, overgrazing is destroying much of the vegetation in this portion of the park, with the full consent of the Mexican government. On the positive side, the Mexican park service forbids logging in all national parks.

Park Facilities and Regulations

The park entrance is 78 kilometers (47 mi) from Mexico 1 via an unpaved but graded roadway; follow signs marked Observatorio. In winter, the occasional snowstorm may force temporary road closure, but during most of the year the road is passable by passenger car. The entrance station, at a forested meadow called La Corona de Abajo (Lower Crown), is open daily 7 A.M.– 7 P.M.; the entry fee is US$7.50 per vehicle.

Established campsites and trails are minimally maintained by park staff. Overall, the park is most suited to wilderness hiking and camping. Although no facilities exist for car or trailer camping, it's safe to leave a vehicle parked anywhere within the park boundaries.

Neither hunting nor the possession of firearms (even with a Mexican permit) is permitted within park boundaries. When the occasional sanctioned deer hunt is held in adjacent Cañon del Diablo, the canyon may be closed to hiking and backpacking. Off-road driving is banned at all times. Fires, using fallen deadwood, are permitted only within established fire rings at a few campsites on the plateau; backpackers should carry portable camp stoves. Before leaving on an overnight hike, let park rangers know where you're going and how long you intend to be gone.

Preparations and Precautions

Park trails are not well marked; don't consider even a day hike without carrying a compass or GPS. The observatory road bisects the park east to west and makes a useful mental landmark. When embarking on a hike, note whether you're heading north or south of the road. If you get lost anywhere west of the eastern escarpment, simply head directly north (or south) from your current location and you should intercept the roadway.

Canyon hiking along the eastern escarpment is rugged and should be attempted only by experienced climbers or those in the company of someone who knows the terrain. You may be able to arrange for a guide through Rancho Meling (tel. 646/179-4106, www.melingguestranch.com).

The Mexican government publishes two topographic **maps** (20-m contour)—*San Rafael H11B45* and *Santa Cruz H11B55*—that cover an area that includes the park. They're available by mail from **Map Centre** (U.S. tel. 619/291-3830 or 888/849-6277, www.mapcentre.com), or at the offices of the Instituto Nacional de Estadística, Geografía e Informática (INEGI) in Tijuana and Mexicali (see *Hiking and Backpacking* in *Essentials*).

More up-to-date and easier to use is a 1988 topo map published by San Diego–based Centra Publications and titled *Parque Nacional San Pedro Mártir: Topographic Map and Visitor's Guide to Baja's Highest Mountains*. This well-designed, readable map is based on the Mexican topos but adds many physical features never mapped before. Also printed on the map are brief descriptions of 17 different hiking trails, including seven Picacho del Diablo climbing routes. This map/guide may be available through Map Center, at the INEGI offices, or at bookstores in Ensenada.

Except during midsummer, streams are abundant on the plateau and are generally considered clean enough to drink from. In the eastern arroyos and canyons, **water** is usually available year-round, though it may be contaminated by livestock. Whether on the plateau or in the canyonlands, always treat local water, just to be sure. Wherever you go in the San Pedro Mártir, carry extra water and a water-purification system—filter, iodine, or halazone.

Trails

The park is honeycombed with footpaths and hiking trails, particularly in the vicinity of Picacho del Diablo at the edge of the eastern escarpment. Longer, more isolated trails connect the large meadow areas of Vallecitos, Los Llanitos, La Encantada, La Grulla, and Rancho Viejo in a 50-kilometer (31-mi) loop. The three trails described in this section, on the park's scenic northeastern edge, are well traveled and thus relatively easy to follow. For a more complete inventory, obtain Centra Publications' detailed topo map of the park.

Vallecitos-Blue Bottle Peak (9.5 km/5.9 mi): Vallecitos (Little Valleys) is the name given to a complex of little flats southeast of the observatory road, reached via a dirt track that begins 16.5 kilometers (10 mi) from the park entrance. About 3.5 kilometers (2 mi) from the observatory road, a footpath branches left (east) up an arroyo for 1.7 kilometers (1 mi), then into an aspen-studded meadow. A smaller path leads north from the meadow to an excellent escarpment-edge view of Cañon del Diablo.

Two kilometers (1.2 mi) farther southeast on the main trail is a north-branching path that leads to Scout Peak (2,850 m, 9,350 ft), where you'll find primitive campsites and an unobstructed view of Picacho del Diablo's western face. From this point, climbers can scramble down the side of the Cañon del Diablo to Campo Noche below and continue on to Cerro Botella Azul (Blue Bottle Peak) via the arroyos at the southern end of the canyon.

Meanwhile, the main trail below Scout Peak continues south and then east a couple of kilometers to a point just northwest of Blue Bottle Peak; a smaller trail ascends the peak itself. At 2,950 meters (9,680 ft), Blue Bottle is the highest point on the plateau and a reasonable alternative to Picacho del Diablo for the less adventurous. On a clear day—perhaps 85 percent of the time—you can see both the Pacific and the Sea of Cortez.

Observatory-Cañon del Diablo (5.3 km/3.3 mi): Just below the observatory gate, a trail branches east from the main road and leads into Cañon del Diablo, the deepest and longest canyon in the Sierra de San Pedro Mártir. Along

the way, this trail passes through a scenic aspen meadow where a short path branches north to a rocky viewpoint over the canyon. Beyond the meadow, the trail becomes a demanding Class 3–4 descent that requires hikers to negotiate brush and boulders along an arroyo intersecting with the larger canyon. Water is available at several streams and waterfalls in the canyon.

Near the bottom of the canyon this trail joins the Cañon del Diablo–Campo Noche Trail, the beginning of one of the eastern approaches to Picacho del Diablo. This latter trail, though rated Class 2–3, involves a four-day hike in desert conditions and is best undertaken with a guide who knows the terrain.

The **Slot Wash Ascent of Picacho del Diablo** is the easiest—Class 3—of the seven routes used to climb Baja's highest mountain. To reach Slot Wash, an arroyo that descends Diablo's west face, follow the Vallecitos–Blue Bottle Peak Trail until you've passed the saddle northwest of Blue Bottle, then continue along the peak's north flank until the trail narrows and descends into Cañon del Diablo.

Near the bottom of the canyon, on the east side, is Campo Noche, a large campsite with a fire ring and nearby pools. The ascent to Slot Wash begins at a shallow arroyo, next to Campo Noche, called Arroyo Noche, or "Night Wash," which segues into Slot Wash at an elevation of 2,240 meters (7,350 ft). The way is well marked with ducks (stone trail markers). At about 2,500 meters (9,840 ft) the route forks. The little-used southern branch leads out of Slot Wash, through a brushy side ravine, to the lower of Diablo's twin peaks (3,094 m, 10,150 ft). The northern route, which most climbers take, continues through Slot Wash and over large stone slabs, until ducks point out a sharp left (north) up a rocky slope. This leads to a steep-walled arroyo nicknamed Wall Street, which in turn proceeds directly to the higher of the peaks (3,095 m, 10,154 ft). If you continue straight up Slot Wash instead of taking the north branch, you'll come to a saddle between the two summits.

Starting at Blue Bottle Peak on the plateau, the trip to Picacho del Diablo and back usually takes three days—one night at Campo Noche

SIERRA SAN PEDRO MÁRTIR TRAILS

VIEWPOINT

NATIONAL OBSERVATORY

GATE

VIEWPOINT

RESIDENCES

Aspen Groves

Cañon del Diablo

Cañon Diablito

Vehicle Track
Established Trail
Obscure Cross-Country Trail or Climbing Route

Vallecitos

Cañon Providencia

3,095m/ 10,154ft

Picacho del Diablo

VIEWPOINT

Aspen Groves

Scout Peak

CAMPO NOCHE

3,094m/10,152ft

Slot Wash

Night Wash

Cerro Botello Azul

Cañon Teledo

0   1 mi

0   1 km

Los Llanitos

VIEWPOINT

© AVALON TRAVEL PUBLISHING, INC.

in each direction, plus one night in the vicinity of the summit. Fit hikers with good orienteering skills can make it to Campo Noche in less than a day, but you really should spend the night for a fresh morning start on the peak.

Approaching Picacho del Diablo from Mexico 3

You can approach the network of trails below Picacho del Diablo from Mexico 3 (the section between Ensenada and Crucero La Trinidad), to the northeast of the park, via Cañon del Diablo. The road to the canyon area is 164 kilometers (102 mi) southeast of Ensenada (or 34 km/21 mi

northwest of Crucero La Trinidad, if you're driving from Mexicali or San Felipe), south off Mexico 3. The road is graded as far as Rancho Villa del Sol, about eight kilometers (5 mi) south of the Mexico 3 junction, then joins vehicle tracks southeast across the salt flat Laguna Diablo.

Approximately 24 kilometers (15 mi) south of Mexico 3, another set of tracks branches straight west toward Rancho Santa Clara. At Rancho Santa Clara, a dirt track passes just south of the ranch and leads nine kilometers (5.5 mi) west until it ends at Cañon Diablito. You can park here, but don't leave valuables in the vehicle.

From Diablito, a three-kilometer (1.9-mi) trail heads northeast to the mouth of Cañon del Diablo. Perhaps the greatest obstacle in the canyon is only about 800 meters into the mouth—a sizable waterfall tumbling down smooth granite walls. A cable bolted to the wall allows hikers to scramble up one side; sometimes accumulated sand creates a temporary platform high enough for you to surmount the wall without the assistance of the cable. The canyon itself is mostly a Class 2 hike with a few Class 3 bouldering exercises along the way; there are plenty of year-round pools and waterfalls to cool off in along the way.

Campo Noche lies 11 kilometers (7 mi) into the canyon, at an elevation of 1,915 meters (6,300 ft). A round-trip hike at a comfortable pace from the end of the vehicle track to Picacho del Diablo usually takes four days, including stops at Campo Noche each way. See Slot Wash Ascent of Picacho del Diablo under *Trails* for a description of the usual route from Campo Noche.

VALLE DE SAN QUINTÍN AND BAHÍA DE SAN QUINTÍN

The Valle de San Quintín, actually more a coastal plain than a valley, is a broad flat between a row of seven extinct volcano cones to

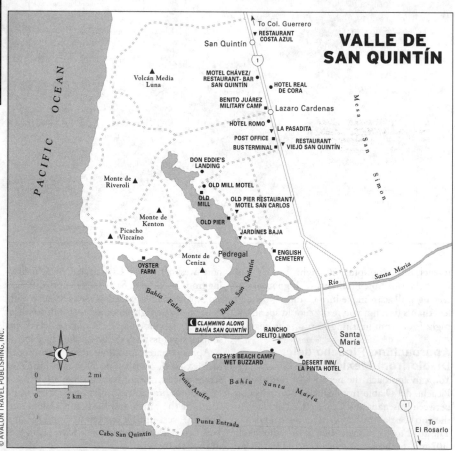

the west—six on the peninsula, one on Isla San Martín just offshore—and the Sierra San Miguel to the east. Two small rivers, Río San Miguel and Río Santa María, bisect the flat east to west and feed an irrigation system that makes the valley an important vegetable-farming center. Many Amerindians from the interior of Mexico, especially Oaxaca and Chiapas, work on the farms and live in shacks on the outskirts of San Quintín.

For visitors, San Quintín's main attraction is a complex coastal environment, the chief features of which are three large, interconnecting bays: Bahía San Quintín, Bahía Falsa, and Bahía Santa María. The innermost bay, surrounded by tidal flats and salt marshes, is referred to as both Bahía San Quintín and Puerto San Quintín. The outermost bay, facing the Pacific, is called Bahía Santa María as far south as the tip of Cabo San Quintín; beyond, it's usually referred to as Bahía San Quintín.

The town of **San Quintín** itself is little more than a collection of shops, motels, restaurants, and other businesses clustered along Mexico 1. Useful services include a long-distance telephone booth, 24-hour medical clinic, travel agency, a couple of Internet cafés, and a couple of banks. Five kilometers (3 mi) south of San Quintín is another town of similar size, **Lázaro Cárdenas**, consisting of Mexico's 67th Infantry battalion camp, the intercity bus terminal, a few shops and restaurants, and two motels.

Many people pass by San Quintín simply because the twin towns—as seen from the highway—don't appear to be very engaging. Traditionally most visitors staying more than one night in the area are sportfishers or hunters. But the pristine beaches and year-round mild climate also attract a number of folks content with long beach walks, bird-watching, and less active pursuits.

Climate

While most of northwestern coastal Baja features a climate similar to San Diego's, San Francisco is a better comparison for Valle de San Quintín. As in the San Francisco area, Pacific influences combine with the insulating effect of a large bay—in this case, three bays—to keep average temperatures within a narrow range year-round: from 12°C (54°F) December–January to 20°C (68°F) August–September.

Annual precipitation averages 31 centimeters (12 in); December usually records the most rainfall (average six cm), with February–March coming in second (4–5 cm); summer months are usually rain free, with occasional coastal fog.

History

In the 1880s, British-owned Mexican Land and Colonization Company purchased much of the San Quintín area from the U.S.-based International Land Company (ILC), with plans to create a wheat empire. At the time, the ILC owned most of northern Baja. In response to promises of agricultural wealth, around a hundred English colonists purchased subdivided land tracts from the parent company, planted wheat, and constructed a gristmill. For flour transportation, the English built a pier on inner Bahía San Quintín and began constructing a railway to link up with the Southern Pacific tracks in California. Thirty kilometers of track were laid—including a rail causeway from the west bank of inner Bahía San Quintín—before the colony failed. A 17-ton, six-wheeled locomotive still lies underwater at the mouth of the bay, the remains of a loading accident for the aborted railway.

A drought devastated one of the first wheat harvests, and by 1900 all colonists had abandoned San Quintín. Although individual farmers were economically ruined, the U.S. and British land companies walked away all the richer, a pattern that would recur several times in northern Baja. Remains of the gristmill, railroad causeway, pier, and English cemetery still stand along the perimeter of the inner bay. The English names on the cemetery's heavily weathered wooden crosses have faded from sight, and more-recent Mexican graves are crowding out their neglected English counterparts.

In recent decades a small community of gringo retirees has moved into the area, leasing bay-front property and building homes. The most concentrated area is Pedregal, where some houses are built of volcanic rock. Around San

ENSENADA TO EL ROSARIO

Quintín, you'll see many lots posted "for sale"; actually these are available only through lease or *fideicomiso* (bank trust) arrangements.

Beach and Bay Access

Several dirt roads south of Lázaro Cárdenas lead directly west from Mexico 1 to the inner bay; follow signs to the Old Mill Motel and Old Pier Restaurant. You can launch car-topped or trailered boats either here or from a boat launch on the bay's west shore. To reach the latter site, drive west out of Lázaro Cárdenas on a gravel road that leaves Mexico 1 between the Pemex station and a military camp; a sign here reads Bahía Falsa. This is a long, rough ride. Fourteen kilometers (8.5 mi) from Mexico 1, just past Monte de Kenton, with a cinder cone immediately to the west, a lesser dirt road forks left and leads to Pedregal, a bayside settlement suitable for boat launching. The marshes and tidal flats at the north end of Bahía Falsa make an excellent birding venue.

If, instead of turning south to Pedregal, you continue west along the road from Lázaro Cárdenas, you'll pass an oyster farm on Bahía Falsa (about 14.5 km, 9 mi from the Bahía Falsa highway turnoff), where fresh oysters may be purchased by the dozen, then you'll reach the road's end at a fish camp on the Pacific.

To reach Bahía Santa María or the larger, Pacific-facing Bahía San Quintín, drive 16 kilometers (10 mi) south of Lázaro Cárdenas and turn right (west) on the paved road to Santa María. The turn is marked by signs advertising the Desert Inn/La Pinta Hotel and Rancho Cielito Lindo. Follow the signs along this pine-tree-lined road to the La Pinta; Playa Santa María, the area's largest, longest, and most beautiful beach, lies behind the hotel. Sunsets can be superb at this beach.

Fishing

The unusually varied marine environment, created by the intersection of the Pacific and the three bays, makes the San Quintín coast an excellent area for surf casting and inshore fishing. Because the entrance to the two inner bays, Bahía Falsa and Bahía San Quintín (Puerto San Quintín), is blocked by steady surf year-round, the bays are inaccessible to commercial fishing fleets. This means more game fish is available for casual anglers, who can launch small boats from inside or from the Pacific shore.

In general, San Quintín attracts the same fish species found north to Ensenada—except they're more highly concentrated. Flatfish are common in the shallows of the inner bays, bottom fish in the deeper sections. The channel near the bay entrance is reportedly good for large halibut; live mackerel is the recommended bait. Perch and croaker run along the Pacific beaches. According to several sources, nowhere in their range are croakers as large as the ones typically caught along San Quintín's beaches. **El Socorro,** 27 kilometers (17 mi) south of Lázaro Cárdenas, is known for surf fishing and has attracted a small group of devoted gringo anglers who maintain homes there.

Farther out in the Pacific, particularly near the south end of volcanic Isla San Martín and at the tip of Cabo San Quintín, yellowtail, yellowfin, white and black sea bass, rock cod, and lingcod are common—in season, of course, and to properly equipped anglers. Tuna and dorado are occasionally caught. Isla San Martín features a fish camp and mussel farm; sheltered anchorages are possible in two coves, one at either side of a rocky cape at the southeast end of the island. If you plan to camp on the island, bring all the supplies and fresh water needed for your stay. Sturdy hiking shoes are necessary if you plan to explore San Martín; volcanic rock and cactus thorns will destroy the average pair of sneakers.

San Quintín Sportfishing (Rancho Cielito Lindo, tel. 616/165-9229), **Pedro's Pangas** (tel. 888/568-2252), **Tiburon's Pangas Sportfishing** (near The Old Mill, U.S. tel. 619/428-2779), **The Old Pier, Don Eddie's Landing,** or **Campo Lorenzo** can arrange guided fishing trips for around US$150–250 per *panga*, depending on the season. You can rent light fishing tackle at the La Pinta Hotel.

Clamming

All three bays are teeming with clams and mussels. The easiest and most scenic spot for digging up large pismo clams is Playa Santa María, behind La Pinta Hotel. If you come at low tide, you'll most likely join a legion of local clam diggers. A turnoff at Km 182 leads to Playa San Ramón (four-wheel drive recommended), another excellent clamming and surf-fishing spot. You can use your fingers to dig the huge clams out of the sand, or bring along a mesh bag and pitchfork—available in Lázaro Cárdenas—as the locals do. A pro threshes the sand at the surf line with a pitchfork, tossing the clams into a bag tied around the waist. A mesh bag works best because it holds the clams but allows water and sand to drain away. Remember not to take more clams than you can eat that day, and don't take clams smaller than your hand.

Boat Rentals

San Quintín Sportfishing (tel. 616/165-9229, book4fish@aol.com), rents boats for bay fishing and offers guided sportfishing trips. Aluminum *pangas* go for US$20–28 a day and carry 3–5 people, depending on the length. You can charter a 22-foot, outfitted fishing cruiser for around US$225 a day. Special packages that include three nights lodging at Rancho Cielito Lindo, two days guided fishing, and lunches cost US$114–150 per person per day, depending on the size of the boat. Anglers can purchase ice to preserve their catch at the **ice factory** next to Bloques y Maderas hardware store, Km 194 in Lázaro Cárdenas.

Hunting

The tidal flats and marshlands around the inner bays attract migrating ducks and Pacific brant (a small, black goose) during the winter and quail most of the year. The Old Mill and Cielito Lindo hotels organize local hunting trips.

Scuba Diving

Johnston's Seamount, 9 kilometers (5.5 mi) southwest of Cabo San Quintín, is a renowned site for underwater photography and spearfishing. Sixteen kilometers northwest of Cabo San Quintín, Isla San Martín is surrounded by kelp beds, several rock reefs, and underwater pinnacles. Roca Ben, five kilometers south of the island, rises within three meters of the surface,

with intermediate depths of 30 meters (100 feet). Encrusted with hydrocoral formations, the rock is a habitat for abundant abalone, scallops, lobsters, and other shellfish. Due to cold-water upwellings, visibility ranges 15–25 meters (50–80 feet).

Surfing

Valle de San Quintín's Pacific coast offers at least two decent surfing spots. Both require tackling the long and bumpy coastal road from Lázaro Cárdenas to Bahía Falsa, then continuing to the coast on a lesser road. Follow the main road around Bahía San Quintín as far as Chapalita and the oyster farm, then continue west to the coast until the road forks south toward Cabo San Quintín. At the top of the cape a strong northwest swell produces a good beach break, while at the tip of the cape a couple of *puntas* catch both northwest and southern swells for long-riding point breaks. The beach along the west side of the cape, known as Playa Médano (or Playa Oeste Médano), is suitable for camping. Just be sure you're well supplied, as it's a relatively long haul back to civilization.

Accommodations

Under US$50: In Lázaro Cárdenas, near the military camp, **Motel Las Hadas** (US$20) and **Hotel Romo** both offer basic, nondescript rooms. The Romo is the better of the two.

In San Quintín, **Motel Chávez** (tel. 616/165-2005, US$30), next to a highway bridge toward the south end of town, offers clean, well-maintained rooms, some with kitchenettes; weekly and monthly rates available. The relatively new **Hotel Real de Cora** (tel. 616/166-8576, US$32) has secure parking.

Southwest of Lázaro Cárdenas, on the inner bay next to the Old Pier Restaurant, is **Motel San Carlos** (tel. 616/163-4206, US$30), where simple, quiet rooms have bay views.

At the northeast end of the inner bay, **Don Eddie's Landing** (formerly Ernesto's Motel, tel. 616/162-2722, www.doneddies.com, US$45), has older rooms with lots of beds and sagging mattresses. Fishing packages are available and include lodging, boat, and food.

Just south of Don Eddie's Landing, **Old Mill Motel** (tel. 616/165-3376 or 800/025-5141, U.S. tel. 619/428-2779 or 800/479-7962, US$30) lies on the site of a former gristmill and next to the main public boat launch. It's a longtime favorite among hunters and anglers, and nights here are anything but tranquil. Accommodations at the Old Mill—including some newly renovated brick cottages—are comfortable and well maintained. An RV park and campground are attached. The electricity is usually turned off midnight–5:30 A.M. The wide range of accommodations here includes basic rooms with private bath, rooms with kitchenette or full kitchen, a rustic "sleeping room" with four twin beds and private bath, rooms with fireplaces, and a two-bedroom suite.

Next to Bahía Santa María, **Rancho Cielito Lindo** (U.S. reservations 619/593-2252, cielitolindo@bajasi.com, US$10) is mainly a restaurant and bar, but large, plain rooms are also available for rent.

US$50-100: On Bahía Santa María, the **Desert Inn/La Pinta Hotel** (tel. 616/165-9008, U.S./Canada tel. 800/800-9632, www.lapintahotels.com, US$80) was remodeled in 2004 in cool blue tones with floral spreads and drapes. Spacious rooms have remote-control heat and air-conditioning units, plus sea views and terraces. Modern tiled baths have glass shower doors; full-size bath towels are a treat. A palm-lined walkway leads to the beach. If you find yourself in the area at sundown and you don't want to shack up in a sportfishing lodge, this hotel is a good bet for a quiet night's sleep.

Camping and RV Parks

Primitive beach camping is available at a number of spots in the San Quintín area, including Playa Santa María south of La Pinta Hotel—probably not the safest spot—and out at Bahía Falsa. More secluded cobble beaches are south of Santa María from Km 18 onward—a good number of dirt tracks lead west from the highway almost all the way to El Rosario.

If you're planning to stay a while, you can check the west side of inner Bahía San Quintín at Pedregal or the Pacific shore (Playa Médano)

Rancho Cielito Lindo

© PAUL ITOI

below the cinder cone Picacho Vizcaíno. The latter area can be cold and damp, and the road there is long and rough; this is a place best enjoyed by hardcore Robinson Crusoes. The clams here are huge and plentiful.

Gypsy's Beach Camp offers shaded sites for self-contained tent or trailer camping for US$5 per night. Also on the premises are clean restrooms, a restaurant called Wet Buzzard, and an RV dump. A night watchman patrols the area 9 P.M.–5 A.M. **Rancho Cielito Lindo** (U.S. reservations 619/593-2252, cielitolindo@bajasi.com) offers tent camping for US$10.

At the **Old Pier/Motel San Carlos** (tel. 616/163-4206), self-contained camping costs only US$5 per person. Facilities include fire rings, toilet, and showers. RVs can park nearby for no charge. Farther north along this same shore, beyond the Old Mill, Campo Lorenzo has sites with full hookups, but they all seem to be permanently occupied by retirees. Tent/camper sites on the beach, with no hookups, may be available for US$5 a night.

A more remote choice, **El Pabellón RV**

Campground, lies on a secluded beach 15 kilometers (9 mi) south of Lázaro Cárdenas and 1.6 kilometers (1 mi) west of Mexico 1 (the turnoff is near Km 16). Sites with water and sewage, but no electricity, cost US$5 per night for tents or RVs. Other facilities include hot showers and flush toilets. The road to El Pabellón—two rutted tracks—could be a bit much for some rigs.

Food

Although at first glance it may seem that the San Quintín area doesn't offer much in the way of places to chow down, in fact the choices are numerous and varied. The highway through Lázaro Cárdenas and San Quintín is lined with taco and *mariscos* stands. Clam cocktails are usually superb. One of the best spots for *tacos de pescado* is **La Pasadita** (8 or 9 A.M.–around 4 P.M.), a modest stand on the plaza in Lázaro Cárdenas.

Pollos Lalos (daily 10 A.M.–10 P.M.), on the west side of the highway in San Quintín, offers good *pollos al carbon*. Nearby **Tuco's Pizza** (daily 3–10 P.M.) will take care of pizza cravings.

The clean, efficient, and friendly **Restaurant Viejo San Quintín** (daily for breakfast, lunch, and dinner), between two pharmacies (Farmacia del Parque and Super Farmacia San Diego), directly opposite the post office in Lázaro Cárdenas, is still the area's best Mexican eatery. Menu offerings include *machaca,* chiles rellenos, carne asada, enchiladas, flautas, fish fillets, steak, burritos, quesadillas, *sincronizadas,* and beer served in frosted mugs. Most entrées cost US$5–7.

The tourist-oriented **Restaurant-Bar Quintín** (tel. 616/165-2005), next door to Motel Chávez, serves good Mexican dishes and seafood for US$9–14 per meal. The hearty breakfasts served here are tasty and reasonably priced at US$3–5.

Also in the town of San Quintín is **Costa Azul,** which offers fresh seafood in Continental and Mexican styles. Credit cards are accepted, and it's open for breakfast, lunch, and dinner, except on Sunday evenings when the restaurant becomes a disco. Like the Restaurant-Bar Quintín, Costa Azul is a little pricier than average.

Restaurant Misión Santa Isabel (tel.

616/165-2309), at Km 190 toward the north end of San Quintín, specializes in *carne tampiqueña* and *machaca*. This is also a popular breakfast stop. Major credit cards are accepted. Nearby **Palapa de Mariscos El Paraíso** (daily for lunch and dinner) is often touted as the best spot in town for fresh seafood.

The Old Mill has a large restaurant and bar called **Gaston's Cannery** (daily 5:30 A.M.–9:30 P.M., mains US$10–28) that serves good seafood and Mexican meals, including home-raised chicken and goat. Prices are relatively high, but portions are large.

The well-known **Old Pier (Muelle Viejo),** next to Motel San Carlos on the inner bay, offers pricey—for Mexico—seafood, from clam dinners for around US$15 to abalone or lobster for US$20–22.

If you're driving to either the Old Mill Motel or the Old Pier Restaurant/Motel San Carlos in the afternoon with plans for an evening meal, be sure to note each turn along the way so you can find your way back. At night, it's easy to become lost in the maze of sandy roads.

For long, leisurely meals in a quiet garden setting, brave the washboard road out to **Jardínes Baja** (Tues.–Sun., noon–10 P.M.). An oasis seemingly plunked down in the middle of nowhere, this family-owned restaurant offers a long menu of Mexican and American dishes. The bar stays open till midnight, and there's usually live music on Friday and Saturday. To reach Jardínes Baja, look for the sign on Mexico 1, then drive around 900 meters along a dirt road till you see the cluster of trees surrounding the restaurant, which stands a little south of the second turnoff for Old Mill. This place was closed for renovations in 2006.

The seafood at the **Rancho Cielito Lindo** restaurant can be as good as any in San Quintín, and prices are reasonable. Fish burgers and tasty crab claws in paprika are house specialties. They have been known to serve complimentary meals on Mexican or American holidays. It's open for dinner only. **Wet Buzzard,** at adjacent Gypsy's Beach Camp, does big breakfasts plus tacos and burritos for lunch.

You'll find a number of *tiendas de abarrotes* in

ENSENADA TO EL ROSARIO

San Quintín, but the best are in Lázaro Cárdenas, including **Avigal, Alejandra,** and **Adelita.** San Quintín features a couple of *panaderías,* while Lázaro Cárdenas has a *tortillería.*

Information and Services

The nearest state tourist office is between Colonia Vicente Guerrero and San Quintín at Km 178. The office is officially open weekdays 8 A.M.–5 P.M., and weekends 10 A.M.–3 P.M., but hours vary.

For medical emergencies there is one 24-hour clinic in San Quintín, Clínica Santa María (tel. 616/165-2653).

Getting There

Two Pemex stations—one each in San Quintín and Lázaro Cárdenas—offer Magna Sin and Premium gas. Diesel is available at the San Quintín station only. Intercity buses arrive and depart from a bus depot in Lázaro Cárdenas, on the west side of Mexico 1. The San Quintín area is not a suitable destination for travelers arriving without their own vehicles, however, since everything is spread out and there is virtually no public transportation to the bayshores and beaches. **ABC** runs a *servicio plus* bus, with air conditioning and toilets, between Tijuana and Lázaro Cárdenas for US$18.

EL ROSARIO AND VICINITY

Near the mouth of a deep valley formed by Río del Rosario lies the town of El Rosario, a market center for valley farms and ranches as well as fish camps along the nearby Pacific coast. Although the valley has been continuously inhabited for at least 300 years, El Rosario today is little more than a cluster of modest homes, a rustic baseball field, a hospital, a school, a town hall, several markets, two motels, two Pemex stations, and a few taquerías and cafés. It is, however, the largest town for 356 kilometers (221 mi) southward, and as such it's an important supply point for anyone exploring north-central Baja.

El Rosario actually consists of two communities: the larger El Rosario de Arriba, along the highway in the upper part of the valley, and the smaller El Rosario de Abajo, south of the highway and the Río del Rosario, toward the coast.

History

Little is known about the Cochimí who lived here when the Spanish arrived except that they subsisted mostly on Pacific shellfish and wild desert plants and called their valley community Viñadaco. In 1774, the Dominican Order established its first and southernmost California mission, **Nuestra Señora del Rosario,** on the east side of the valley facing the Pacific; the mission was moved downstream in 1802 to take advantage of a better water supply. The adobe ruins of the newer mission site can be found by turning right—west—at the supermarket, where Mexico 1 curves east, then left at the first road. After crossing the riverbed to El Rosario de Abajo, the minimal ruins lie on the right.

The valley was perfectly suited for agriculture, and at first the mission community thrived, producing the most abundant crops of any northern Baja mission. As elsewhere in the Californias, the Amerindians eventually succumbed to diseases brought by the missionaries, and, left without converts or laborers, the mission closed in 1832.

A Spanish land grant in the 1840s brought Carlos Espinosa to the valley, where he and his family became successful ranchers and farmers. Italian copper miner Eduardo Grosso arrived at the end of the 19th century. The union of the two families has been a prime source of El Rosario history ever since.

In the 1960s, El Rosario became a checkpoint for the Baja 1000 off-road race and the first landing for the Flying Samaritans, a group of American doctors who provide volunteer medical service by plane to several northern Baja settlements. El Rosario's Doña Anita Grosso de Espinosa, proprietor of Espinosa's Place café, helped assure the initial success of both endeavors by acting as a liaison between Americans and the local community.

In its disfavor, El Rosario has straddled its roads with an annoying number of speed bumps in recent years.

Punta Baja and Agua Blanca

Sixteen kilometers (10 mi) southwest of El Rosario de Arriba, via an unpaved but all-vehicle road, is Punta Baja, a fish camp and headland at the north end of Bahía del Rosario. You can rent *pangas* here, or launch your own; the perch and rock cod fishing is good year-round. Farther offshore, tuna, croaker, bonito, and yellowtail are abundant. During northwest swells, the surfing off Punta Baja is excellent.

Agua Blanca is another fish camp, eight kilometers (5 mi) south of Punta Baja toward the middle of the bay. Between Punta Baja and Agua Blanca you may notice piles of sea urchin shells at the roadside. The harvesting of sea urchins constitutes the bulk of the local fishing industry; 90 percent of the catch is exported to Japan, mostly for sushi. The orange-colored "roe" consumed by the Japanese isn't the sea urchin's eggs, as is commonly believed, but the sex organs.

Accommodations and Food

Between the Pemex station and Mama Espinosa's restaurant, the recently renovated **Baja Cactus Motel** (Km 55, tel. 616/165-8850, www.bajacactus.com) has caused quite a stir among Transpeninsular insiders. Where else in the world can you enjoy all the amenities of a four-star establishment—immaculate tiled baths, granite counters, four-poster king-size beds, luxury linens, gorgeous woodwork, 29-inch satellite TVs, purified water, air conditioning—for US$35 a night? The story goes that the son of the motel owners wanted to help his parents fix the place up. All 22 rooms are wired with Ethernet cables, so that when high speed Internet comes to El Rosario, Baja Cactus patrons will be among the first to enjoy it. You probably won't escape

the sound of trucks decelerating through town, but you'll enjoy some of the finest accommodations anywhere on the peninsula.

The legendary **Espinosa's Place (Mama Espinosa's Lobster Burritos)** has hosted Baja 1000 drivers, Flying Samaritans, and thousands of other Baja travelers since before the completion of the Transpeninsular. The burritos—from beans to lobster—are as tasty as ever. A plate of lobster burritos along with rice, beans, potatoes, tortillas, and salad—enough food for two—costs US$13. Profits from the restaurant help support a local orphanage. Doña Espinosa is also happy to accept donations of food staples and clothing for distribution among the community's poor.

Around the bend is **Restaurant Yiyo's** (mains US$4–8) a popular local hangout serving a variety of egg dishes, fish, lobster, beef *machaca,* breaded shrimp, and steak.

At the southern edge of town, a house converted into **Baja's Best Café** (daily 7 A.M.–7 P.M., mains US$7–15) serves light meals, real sausage, and fresh-brewed coffee, allegedly made with beans from the U.S.–based Starbucks chain. Baja's Best also runs a B&B on the premises. Rooms have comfortable beds and rain showers (US$50).

Beach camping is free along Bahía del Rosario.

Supplies

Several *tiendas* offer fresh vegetables, baked goods, and a variety of automotive and household items. **Mercado Hermanos Jaramillo,** a supermarket at the first bend in the highway, near Espinosa's Place, has the largest selection, including vaquero hats. The Pemex station at the town's northern entrance stays open 24 hours.

MEXICALI TO SAN FELIPE

Among Baja's border towns, agricultural Mexicali strikes a balance between bustling Tijuana and quiet Tecate. Its palm-lined boulevards are cleaner and less touristy than other Baja California cities of its size. In addition to farming, state government drives much of the local economy, as Mexicali is the capital of Baja California (Norte).

Given it's location in the northeastern part of the state, Mexicali serves as a gateway to mainland Mexico, as well as the northern Sea of Cortez area.

Southwest of Mexicali are plenty of opportunities for desert hiking, soaking in natural hot springs, and off-road racing. A sizable gringo community has developed at San Felipe on the Sea of Cortez, where visitors enjoy beach and boating activities.

PLANNING YOUR TIME

In a long weekend of aggressive driving, you could make it from Mexicali to Ensenada and as far south as Bahía Los Angeles, returning via San Felipe (assuming you're comfortable driving off-road). But you wouldn't have time for more than a quick look around at each stopover. A more popular weekend itinerary is the easier one from Mexicali to San Felipe and back. Spring breakers tend to stay a week, while snowbirds happily spend the entire winter in or near San Felipe.

THE NET-SAN FELIPE HTTP://WWW.SANFELIPE.COM.MX

HIGHLIGHTS

◖ La Chinesca: The only true Chinatown in all of Mexico, this Mexicali neighborhood reflects Prohibition-era history, when Chinese laborers and farmers opened businesses in Mexicali. With restaurants on every block, the district offers a great opportunity to taste Chinese cuisine that has been adapted to suite the Mexican palate (page 136).

◖ Cañon de Guadalupe: A collection of turquoise-hued hot springs perched above the desert plains of northeastern Baja rewards those willing to tackle washboard roads from Mexicali (page 144).

◖ San Felipe *Malecón:* At night, the action in San Felipe takes place in discos and clubs along the waterfront. Start the evening off right with a seafood dinner in one of the town's open air restaurants (page 149).

◖ Valle de los Cardones Gigantes: Between San Felipe and Puertecitos, the Valle de los Cardones Gigantes is an ideal place to snap postcard-perfect images of the world's tallest cactus species, some of which live to be hundreds of years old (page 155).

◖ Bahía San Luis Gonzaga: Popular with pilots and seasoned Baja travelers, this remote, gray-sand beach on the Sea of Cortez is worth the white-knuckle drive. An overnight stay here will transport you back in time (page 156).

LOOK FOR ◖ TO FIND RECOMMENDED SIGHTS, ACTIVITIES, DINING, AND LODGING.

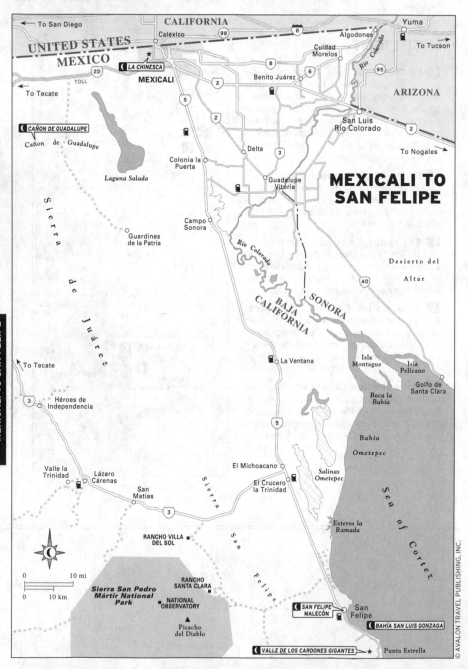

To San Diego

CALIFORNIA

Yuma

UNITED STATES

Calexico

98

8

Algodones

To Tucson

MEXICO

2D

LA CHINESCA

TOLL

MEXICALI

Cuidad
Morelos

Río Colorado

95

To Tecate

2

8

Benito Juárez

6

5

ARIZONA

CAÑON DE GUADALUPE

2

San Luis
Río Colorado

2

Cañon de Guadalupe

Delta

3

To Nogales

Laguna Salada

Colonia la
Puerta

Guadalupe
Vitoria

**MEXICALI TO
SAN FELIPE**

S i e r r a

Campo
Sonora

Río Colorado

Guardines
de la Patria

BAJA
CALIFORNIA

SONORA

Desierto del

Altar

d e

40

J u á r e z

La Ventana

Isla
Montague

Isla
Pelicano

To Tecate

5

Boca la
Bahía

Golfo de
Santa Clara

Héroes de
Independencia

3

Bahía
Ometepec

Valle la
Trinidad

Lázaro
Cárenas

El Michoacano

Salinas
Ometepec

S e a

San
Matías

El Crucero
la Trinidad

o f

S i e r r a

3

RANCHO VILLA
DEL SOL

S a n

Esteros la
Ramada

C o r t e z

0   10 mi

0   10 km

Sierra San Pedro
Mártir National
Park

RANCHO
SANTA CLARA

NATIONAL
OBSERVATORY

F e l i p e

SAN FELIPE
MALECÓN

San
Felipe

Picacho
del Diablo

BAHÍA SAN LUIS GONZAGA

VALLE DE LOS CARDONES GIGANTES

Punta Estrella

© AVALON TRAVEL PUBLISHING, INC.

Mexicali

Like other large Mexican border districts, downtown Mexicali is chockablock with street vendors, souvenir shops, and *casas de cambio* (money changers). But a few blocks away from the border in any direction are broad, palm-lined boulevards and tidy residential areas reminiscent of San Diego or Phoenix.

The only Mexican border town that's also a state capital, Mexicali boasts Baja's second-largest population: 856,000. You won't find any zebra-painted burros on Mexicali street corners, or any place resembling Tijuana's Avenida Revolución. Mexicali is much cleaner and more orderly city than either Ensenada or Tijuana.

The best months for a Mexicali visit are September and October, when the temperature averages 23°C (73°F) and desert plants are usually in bloom. Spring is also pleasant. The peak period for visitors from the north is November–February, especially for those on

their way to San Felipe. July and August are the least hospitable months, as soaring temperatures bring the city to a standstill.

THE LAND

The nearly flat Valle de Mexicali extends westward from the Río Colorado delta to the Sierra de Cucapá. Millennia ago the entire area was covered by a northern extension of the Sea of Cortez; California's Salton Sea and Baja California Norte's Laguna Salada are vestiges of the Cortez trapped by the gradual silting of the Colorado delta. The city of Mexicali, in fact, is a foot below sea level.

South of the valley lies the San Felipe Desert, an extension of the Sonora Desert. The valley itself can be classified as desert since it averages less than 25 centimeters (10 in) of rainfall a year. Unlike many deserts, centuries of river silting have made the soil here nutrient-rich; earth that once filled the Grand Canyon

© PAUL ITOI

cactus farm

was carried into the delta at a rate of 160 million tons per year. Yet the region's overall lack of water sources meant that agriculture outside the Colorado floodplain was almost impossible before U.S. land companies established a canal system in the early part of the 20th century to irrigate California's Imperial Valley and the Valle de Mexicali.

Before the damming of the Colorado River in the United States, the floodplain was enormous. The tidal bore at the mouth of the river, where it fed into the Cortez, was strong enough to sink ships. The outflow slowed with the U.S. dams and was then reduced to a trickle by the 1950 construction of Mexico's Morelos Dam near Los Algodones, which diverts water into the Valle de Mexicali to supplement the American-built canal system.

With irrigation, a 2.5-kilometer-thick layer of river silt, and an abundance of sunshine, most of the valley today is under intensive cultivation, producing cotton, wheat, grapefruit, lemons, oranges, carrots, corn, asparagus, onions, broccoli, potatoes, lettuce, cauliflower, and grapes.

HISTORY
Pre-Hispanic Amerindian Cultures

In pre-Cortesian times, the Río Colorado delta—which, at the time, included the Valle de Mexicali—was inhabited by a centuries-long succession of Yumano tribes. When the Spanish first stumbled upon the delta after traversing, with great difficulty, the Sonora Desert's Camino del Diablo (Devil's Road), a sophisticated Río Colorado culture was cultivating squash, melons, peas, and five colors of corn: yellow, blue, white, red, and blue-white. The Amerindians also possessed an impressive knowledge of medicinal herbs and employed desert plants like mesquite and agave in a wide variety of uses.

Among the major Yumano groups in the region were the Cucapá, who navigated the difficult Río Colorado on reed rafts. Like their neighbors the Kiliwa, the Cucapá's numbers were greatly reduced by Spanish missionization

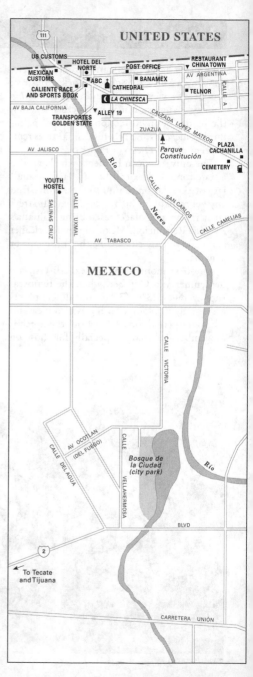

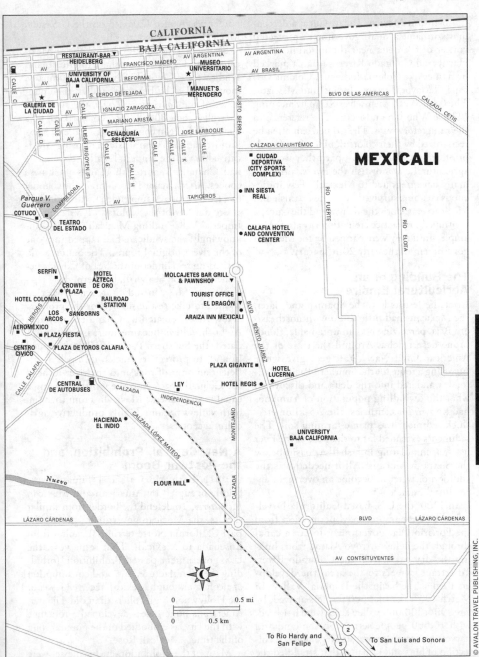

CALIFORNIA
BAJA CALIFORNIA

RESTAURANT-BAR
HEIDELBERG
AV ARGENTINA
AV ARGENTINA
FRANCISCO MADERO
AV
UNIVERSITY OF
BAJA CALIFORNIA
REFORMA
AV BRASIL
MUSEO
UNIVERSITARIO
AV
S. LERDO DE TEJADA
MANUET'S
MERENDERO
GALERÍA DE
LA CIUDAD
IGNACIO ZARAGOZA
MARIANO ARISTA
CENADURÍA
SELECTA
JOSE LARROQUE
BLVD DE LAS AMERICAS
CALZADA CETIS

AV
AV
CALLE C
CALLE D
CALLE E
ULISES IRIGOYEN (F)
COMPRESORA
CALLE G
CALLE H
CALLE I
CALLE J
CALLE K
CALLE L

AV JUSTO SIERRA
CALZADA CUAUHTÉMOC

CIUDAD
DEPORTIVA
(CITY SPORTS
COMPLEX)

MEXICALI

Parque V.
Guerrero
COTUCO
TEATRO
DEL ESTADO
AV
TAPICEROS
INN SIESTA
REAL

CALAFIA HOTEL
AND CONVENTION
CENTER

RIO FUERTE
C. RIO ELOTA

SERFÍN
MOTEL
AZTECA
DE ORO
MOLCAJETES BAR GRILL
& PAWNSHOP
CROWNE
PLAZA
RAILROAD
STATION
TOURIST OFFICE
EL DRAGÓN
HOTEL COLONIAL
HÉROES
LOS
ARCOS
SANBORNS
ARAIZA INN MEXICALI
AEROMÉXICO
PLAZA FIESTA
CENTRO
CÍVICO
PLAZA DE TOROS CALAFIA
PLAZA GIGANTE
HOTEL
LUCERNA

BLVD BENITO JUÁREZ

CALLE CALAFIA
CENTRAL
DE AUTOBUSES
CALZADA
LEY
INDEPENDENCIA
HOTEL REGIS

HACIENDA
EL INDIO
CALZADA LÓPEZ MATEOS
UNIVERSITY
BAJA CALIFORNIA

MONTEJANO
CALZADA

Nuevo
FLOUR MILL

LÁZARO CÁRDENAS
BLVD
LÁZARO CÁRDENAS

AV CONTSITUYENTES

0   0.5 mi
0   0.5 km

To Río Hardy and
San Felipe
To San Luis and Sonora

2
5

in northwest Mexico. Today, Cucapá descendants inhabit a small government-protected corner of the delta near the junction of the Hardy and Colorado Rivers, an area marked by names like Colonia Indígena, Colonia Cucapá El Mayor, Terrenos Indios, and Mestizos. The Cucapá call themselves Ko Ipat, meaning "Those Who Go and Return," a reference to their migratory ways. The women can often be recognized by their colorful, billowing, floral-print dresses. For the most part, they work on agricultural *ejidos* or fish the rivers, although many have migrated to Mexicali. Few indigenous customs survived both the Spanish and Mexican eras; both the Kiliwa and the Cucapá continued to practice cremation rituals, for example, until they were banned by the Mexican government in the early 20th century.

The Building of an Agricultural Empire

After the Jesuits left, the Spanish and, later, the Mexicans had little to do with northeastern Baja, perceiving it as an untamable, flood-prone desert delta. Around the time of the American Civil War, a Yale geologist, while surveying a route for the Southern Pacific Railroad, wandered into the delta and discovered what the dwindling population of Yumanos had known for centuries: the 2.5-kilometer-thick sediment was prime farming soil. The sediments extended far to the west of the river itself, accumulating in a shallow basin below the Sierra de Cucapá. All it needed was the addition of water to become an overnight agricultural miracle.

In 1900, the U.S.-based California Development Company received permission from the Porfirio Díaz government to cut a canal through the delta's Arroyo Alamo, thus linking the dry basin with the Colorado River. To attract farmers to the area, the developers named the basin the Imperial Valley. In March 1903, the first 500 farmers arrived; by late 1904, 100,000 valley acres were irrigated, with 10,000 people settled on the land and harvesting cotton, fruits, and vegetables. A collection of huts and ramadas that straddled the

border was named Calexico on the U.S. side, Mexicali on the Mexican side.

Seeing that the equally fertile Valle de Mexicali lay undeveloped, another American land syndicate, the Colorado River Land Company, moved in. Led by Harry Chandler, then publisher of the *Los Angeles Times,* the syndicate controlled some 800,000 acres of northern Baja and in 1905 began constructing a Valle de Mexicali irrigation system. Instead of using Mexican labor, as the Imperial Valley developers had, Chandler imported thousands of Chinese coolies. After a major 1905 rainfall, the channel dug from Arroyo Alamo ended up diverting the entire outflow of the Colorado River into the Imperial Valley, taking Mexicali with it—unknowingly, the syndicate had tapped into one of the river's original routes. The Salton Sink, a dried-up remainder of the Sea of Cortez, became the Salton Sea virtually overnight.

Neither the United States nor Mexico wanted to take responsibility for the growing "New River" created by Chandler's mistake. As both valleys became increasingly inundated, the Southern Pacific Railroad stepped in and, to protect its tracks, dumped a sufficient amount of rock into the river to head the Colorado back into the Cortez, leaving a canal to the Valle de Mexicali. From then on, both valleys became highly productive agricultural centers.

A New Capital, Prohibition, and the Postwar Boom

In 1911, both Mexicali and Tijuana were briefly occupied by American and Mexican *filibusteros.* To defend the border from similar threats, the Mexican government moved the Baja California Norte territorial capital from Ensenada to Mexicali. That same year, the U.S. government passed Prohibition, forbidding the manufacture, sale, and consumption of alcohol; although Mexicali received fewer of the Hollywood high-rollers than did Tijuana, Americans nonetheless developed a romance with the city, as embodied in the popular song of the time, "Mexicali Rose."

Many of the Prohibition-era businesses were

operated by *chinos,* Chinese laborers and farmers who moved into the city and spent their hard-earned savings to open bars, restaurants, and hotels. With people from both sides of the border drawn to the burgeoning town, Mexicali's urbanization accelerated. In the 1920s, Mexicali experienced an influx of Punjabis from India, who in many cases took over Chinese farming enterprises.

Like Tijuana, Mexicali suffered an economic recession with the repeal of Prohibition in 1933 and the Mexican ban on casino gambling in 1938. But with a flourishing agricultural base and a federal presence, Mexicali bounced back sooner than Tijuana did. The 1947 establishment of the Ferrocarril Sonora–Baja California, a railroad link between Mexicali and the main Nogales–Mexico City trunk line, further boosted the local economy. After Baja California Norte attained statehood in 1952, the capital began receiving a steady rotation of *chilangos* (Mexico City residents), some of whom stayed on and started new businesses after completing their terms of office. Although local residents might hesitate to admit it, part of Mexicali's postwar success in shedding its border-town image should probably be credited to the influx of outsiders—from the coming of the Chinese in the early 20th century to the postwar arrival of the *chilangos.*

Mexicali Today

Today, the main source of Mexicali income remains agriculture, primarily cotton, wheat, alfalfa, and vegetables. Another moneymaker is geothermal power; the string of geothermal plants at nearby Cerro Prieto constitutes the world's third-largest producer of such power. The electricity it generates powers most of northeastern Baja and is even sold north of the border. A third major industry is the growing complex of in-bond plants, or *maquiladoras,* which currently number more than 200 in 11 different industrial parks. Major multinational firms with Mexicali in-bond plants include Rockwell International, Daewoo, Hughes Aircraft, Emerson Electric, ITT, Goldstar, Nestle's, and Sony. From all appearances, Mexicali's *maquilas* seem to be among the cleanest and best managed along the entire U.S.–Mexico border.

The economic symbiosis evident all along the U.S.–Mexico border is especially visible in the Mexicali–Los Algodones area. Laborers work alternately at Imperial Valley or Valle de Mexicali farms on either side of the border. And, like Tijuana, Mexicali is a free-trade zone. Television and radio stations in El Centro (California) and Yuma (Arizona) broadcast ads for pharmacies in Mexicali and Los Algodones, where generic equivalents for American drugs are available without prescription at prices several times lower than those in the United States. In return, the small California town of Calexico (pop. 15,000) serves as a convenience mart for Mexicalienses shopping for discounted American-made apparel and housewares.

Mexicali serves as an important educational center for all of Baja. Reflecting the city's international orientation, the Universidad Autónoma de Baja California administers a reputable foreign-languages department offering instruction in teaching, translating, and interpreting English, French, German, and Japanese (see *Sights*).

Tourism is important to Mexicali but is for the most part limited to short American shopping trips or brief stopovers by San Felipe–bound visitors. Most visitors—international and domestic—spending the night in Mexicali are business travelers. Less than a third of overnight hotel guests hail from the United States; about 70 percent come from Mexico, with the rest a mix of visitors from Japan, Central and South America, and Europe.

SIGHTS

Mexicali has few tourist attractions; rather, the city seems to focus on creating an amenable environment for government- and business-oriented activities, while trying to make the community as comfortable a place to live as possible. There are, however, a few modern cultural venues of interest.

The city has two hearts. First is the old

downtown area, pushed up against the border and featuring early-20th-century architecture. A prime example is the Hotel Del Norte, almost Texan or New Mexican in appearance. The newer **Centro Cívico-Comercial de Mexicali** (Mexicali Civic-Commercial Center), is located southeast of downtown along Calzada Independencia. Ambitiously dubbed the Zona Rosa after Mexico City's chic business-entertainment district, the center is a renovated warehouse district containing offices, restaurants, bars, and utilitarian shops selling paint, furniture, stationery, and office supplies. Although it's near the bullring and the bus and train stations, the Centro Cívico has become more of an attraction for Mexicali residents than for foreign visitors.

Linking the various city sectors is a system of wide avenues and *glorietas* (traffic circles), many encircling statues of Mexican national heroes.

Museo Universitario

This Universidad Autónoma de Baja California–sponsored museum of anthropology and natural history (away from main UABC campus, at Av. Reforma and Calle L, tel. 686/554-1977, Mon.–Fri. 9 A.M.–6 P.M., Sat.–Sun. 9 A.M.–2 P.M., US$1) is unequaled on the peninsula. In spite of the museum's compact size, the exhibits manage to pack in a wealth of information on northern Baja's pre- and post-Cortesian history as well as the flora and fauna unique to the region. Exhibits are labeled in Spanish only; if you're familiar with the language, you can learn much about northern Baja ethnology, especially regarding the Yumano and San Dieguito cultures.

Temporary exhibitions are of equally high quality, such as the recent hosting of an exquisite and well-curated collection of indigenous textiles from the region, from the woven grass garments of the early Cucapá to the colorful silk saris of more recent Indian immigrants to Mexicali.

Museo Sol del Niño

This museum (on Blvd. López Mateos near the Hotel Crowne Plaza, tel. 686/554-9494 or 686/554-5579, Mon.–Fri. 9 A.M.–7 P.M., Sat.–Sun. 10 A.M.–2 P.M., free) is oriented toward children, with an emphasis on science and technology.

Galería de la Ciudad (City Gallery)

This privately owned gallery (Av. Obregón 1209 btw Calles D/E, tel. 686/553-5044, ext. 23, Mon.–Fri. 9 A.M.–8 P.M., Sat.–Sun. 9 A.M.–1 P.M., free) exhibits works by painters, sculptors, photographers, and other artists from the region and around Mexico.

La Chinesca

Mexicali's Chinatown, known locally as Chinesca, is the only identifiably Chinese urban district anywhere in Mexico—unless you count one short street in Mexico City. It centers around the intersection of Calle Benito Juárez (don't confuse this street with the much larger and newer Boulevard Benito Juárez in the southeast sector of town) and Calle Altamirano. This intersection is just southwest of the traffic circle nearest the border crossing; if you're coming across the border by car or on foot, turn right immediately on Altamirano, which leads into Chinesca.

Although the neighborhood is anything but fancy, the first thing you may notice is the lineup of gold shops *(casas de oro)* selling gold chains and other jewelry—very much like Chinatowns throughout the world. Also obvious are the unusually numerous Chinese restaurants; in fact, every block in this area features at least three Chinese eateries. Even the Mexican restaurants here may bear Chinese names, as at Taquería de Chungui. Several Chinese associations and clan houses can be found tucked away in the neighborhood, including the Asociación Chung Shan de Baja California and Asociación China, both on Calle Juárez.

Another hallmark of the city's Chinese heritage is a Chinese pavilion standing on Plaza de Amistad near the border crossing (not in Chinesca, but nearby). Made entirely with Chinese materials by Chinese artisans, and inaugurated during Chinese New Year 1994, the pavilion is one of only two such structures in the Americas. A couple of downtown shopping centers nearby, such as Plaza Mandarín, feature modern architecture adorned with curving tile roofs and other Chinese motifs.

Parks

Bosque de la Ciudad (in southwest Mexicali at Av. Ocotlán and Calle Alvarado, Tues.–Sun. 9 A.M.–5 P.M.), an oasis of green in a dry city, offers picnic areas, a playground, a botanical museum, and a zoo. The smaller **Parque Vicente Guerrero,** wedged between Calzada López Mateos and Calle Compresora southeast of downtown Mexicali, is similar except that it's always open.

ENTERTAINMENT AND EVENTS

Bullfights

In Baja, Mexicali's **Plaza de Toros Calafía** (at Blvd. de los Héroes and Calle Calafía near the Centro Cívico, tel. 686/557-3864) is second in size only to the Plaza Monumental in Playas de Tijuana. The stadium hosts *corridas* two or three Sundays a month, September–November (especially during Fiesta del Sol in October). Current schedule information is available from the city tourist office. Ticket prices range from US$6 general admission to US$26 for a first-row seat on the shady side *(sombra);* most tickets cost US$14–20. This is considerably less expensive than in Tijuana.

Charreadas

Mexicali has two *charro* rings: **Lienzo Charro de Mexicali** (tel. 686/566-5545), six kilometers east of Calzada Justo Sierra on Calle Compuertas (the airport highway), and **Lienzo Charro Zaragoza,** west of Mexicali on Mexico 2. Regular *charreadas* are scheduled about once a month September–April, but may also be held during a fiesta any time of year. Contact the city tourist office for the latest *charreada* schedules.

Baseball

Mexicali has its own baseball team, Las Águilas (The Eagles), and its local stadium is known as El Nido de las Águilas (Eagles' Nest). The stadium, in the **Ciudad Deportiva** (City Sports Complex, on Calz. Cuauhtémoc east of Calz. Justo Sierra), periodically hosts other teams in the Mexican Pacific League, as well as the occasional visiting team from the United States or Central America. The season lasts from the end of the American World Series in November through late January. Seats cost around US$6–10; to find out when home games are played during the season, contact the city tourist office or call the stadium (tel. 686/567-5129, www.aguilasdemexicali.com.mx).

Live Music

Bars at the Lucerna, Hotel Crowne Plaza, Araiza Inn Mexicali, and Araiza Inn Calafía (see *Accommodations*) are popular local meeting spots where you can usually count on a *botanas* layout most weekdays around 6 P.M., with live music—*norteña,* Latin pop, international—later in the evening.

Every Sunday afternoon during warmer weather, mariachi groups play outdoors at **Parque Constitución,** a small downtown park bordered by Avenida Zuazua, Avenida Hidalgo, Calle Mina, and Calle México.

Also see Molcajetes Bar-Grill & Pawnshop, under *Food.*

Bars and Discos

Nightlife is in short supply in Mexicali. Try **Forum** (Av. Reforma and Calz. Justo Sierra, tel. 686/552-4091), open Thursday–Sunday nights. Expect to pay a cover charge of US$6–7.

El Taurino (Calle Zuazua 480 at Calle José María Morelos) is a popular gay and lesbian bar.

Teatro del Estado (State Theater)

A variety of local and visiting theatrical, dance, and musical performances are held year-round at this modern, 1,100-seat building at Calzado López Mateos and Avenida Castellanos. Ticket prices vary according to the performance but are usually quite reasonable. For information on the latest theater schedule, call 686/554-6418 or contact the city tourist office at 888/268-8262.

Radio

Mexicali broadcast media receive a wide variety of transmissions from Mexican, Arizonan, and Californian stations. Two of the better local radio stations are XED (1050 AM), which mostly broadcasts Mexican folk music, and Pulsar (90.7 FM), a bilingual station that broadcasts everything from jazz to techno to banda to rock.

Events

In early February, the three-day **Salada 200** rally brings off-road racers to nearby Laguna Salada. For information, call Cachanillas Off-Road Promotions (tel. 686/552-5928).

Centered at Parque Vicente Guerrero in October, **Fiesta del Sol** celebrates the 1904 founding of Mexicali with the crowning of a festival queen, industrial/agricultural expositions, various cultural performances around town, art shows, horse races, and cockfights.

In mid-November the Chamber of Restaurants (CANIRAC) sponsors the **Muestra Gastronómica,** a food fair featuring Mexican, seafood, and Chinese cuisines. Call CANIRAC at 686/554-2666 for scheduling and venues.

SHOPPING

Mexicali features the usual border-town assortment of souvenir shops, many clustered along Calle Melgar in the downtown area, near the border crossing. **El Sarape** and **Mario's Curios,** both in the 100 block of Calle Melgar, carry a broad selection of Mexican handicrafts. As the name suggests, **Curiosidades Taxco,** also on Calle Melgar, offers silverwork from the Valle de Mexico.

El Armario (Calz. Justo Sierra 1700, Plaza Azteca, at the junction with Blvd. Juárez, tel. 686/568-1906) stocks a selection of rustic furniture, glassware, ceramics, sculpture, and other handicrafts.

Something you might not expect to find in Mexicali is a shop specializing in guayaberas, the pleated men's shirt characteristic of Mexico's Yucatán Peninsula. **Guayaberas Yucatecas,** in the 700 block of Avenida Madero near the post office, does a good business selling these shirts to locals and visitors during Mexicali's furnacelike summers. In Mexico, the light, short-sleeved guayabera is considered appropriate apparel for any occasion, even in place of coat and tie.

A bit farther from downtown, **Arte Mexicano** (Calz. Independencia 3301) carries a higher quality selection of Mexican arts and crafts than most of the downtown places.

Mexicali's main *mercado municipal* is housed in a large green building on the west side of Calle Ramírez between Obregón and Lerdo de Tejada. As Mexican markets go, however, it's not a particularly interesting one.

Department Stores

Plaza Cachanilla (on Calz. López Mateos northwest of Parque Vicente Guerrero) contains more than 300 stores of all types, including **Dorian's** and **Coppel,** both middle-class department stores. **Plaza Fiesta** (at the intersection of Calz. Independencia and Av. de los Héroes) has more than 190 stores, including **Sanborns Department Store.** As usual, Sanborns carries a decent selection of books, magazines, and handicrafts.

ACCOMMODATIONS

Room rates for Mexicali hotels and motels are reasonable, and overall it's less expensive to spend the night here than in Tijuana, Ensenada, or San Felipe. Most of the higher-end places are business hotels with large conference rooms and meeting services. Add 12 percent tax to all rates quoted here unless otherwise noted.

Under US$50

Diagonally opposite the train station, 57-room **Motel Azteca de Oro** (Calle de la Industria 600, tel. 686/557-1433, www.hotelaztecadeoro.com, US$42–60) is a two-story place with rooms surrounding a courtyard. The main bus station is only 10 minutes away by foot. On Calzada López Mateos, near the Civic Center and main intercity bus terminal, is a cluster of inexpensive places to overnight. **Hotel Hacienda del Indio** (Calz. López Mateos 101 at Av. Fresnillo, almost opposite Las Fuentes, tel. 686/557-2277, www.hotelelindio.com, US$45) features two stories with 50 decent rooms around a totally enclosed courtyard. **Hotel Regis** (Calz. Juárez 2150, tel. 686/566-8801, www.hotel-regis.com, US$45) also has clean and comfortable rooms.

US$50-100

Out in the eastern part of the city and more convenient for people driving their own vehicles onward to Mexico 2 or Mexico 5, the friendly and efficient **Hotel Siesta Real** (Calz. Justo Sierra 899, tel. 686/568-2001, U.S. tel. 800/426-5093, www.hotelsiestareal.com, US$48–80) offers 90 well-maintained rooms with air conditioning, TV, and phone. On the premises are a swimming pool, restaurant, and parking lot.

In the industrial zone, **Hotel Posada Inn** (López Mateos 939 at Calle Torneros, tel. 686/558-6100, www.hotelposadainn.com, US$63) opened with wireless Internet.

Hotel Del Norte (Calle Melgar at Av. Madero, tel. 686/554-0024, www.hoteldelnorte .com, US$54) is a downtown Mex-Deco classic within easy walking distance of the border gate. Rooms come in three sizes; all have air conditioning, phone, and TV. Facilities include an inexpensive coffee shop, a bar, and parking.

The **Calafía Hotel and Convention Center** (Calz. Justo Sierra 1495, tel. 686/568-3311 or 800/026-5444, U.S. tel. 877/727-2492, www.araizainn.com.mx, US$87) is a well-managed four-story motel with 170 rooms containing all the usual amenities. Facilities include a swimming pool, Calafía Steakhouse restaurant, 24-hour coffee shop, bar, and security parking.

Hotel Colonial (Blvd. López Mateos and Calle Calafía, tel. 686/556-1312, U.S./Canada tel. 800/437-2438, www.hotelescolonial.com, US$68) is a well-run, two-story American-style hotel with 145 rooms next to Sanborns restaurant.

US$100-150

South of Araiza Inn Calafía along the same boulevard (which changes names en route) is the 170-room **Araiza Inn Mexicali** (Calz. Juárez 2220, tel. 686/564-1100 or 800/686-5444, U.S. tel. 877/727-2492, www.araizainn.com. mx, US$120). On the premises are a pool, restaurant, coffee shop, bar, and disco.

Hotel Lucerna (Calz. Juárez 2151, tel. 686/564-7000, www.hotel-lucerna.com.mx, US$106) is a multistory Mexicali original. Its 176 well-appointed rooms feature climate control, mini-bars, satellite TV, and direct-dial phones. Facilities include two pools, a fitness center, the Restaurant Mezzosole, a coffee shop, piano bar, and disco.

US$150-250

The **Crowne Plaza** (Blvd. López Mateos at Av. de los Héroes, tel. 686/557-3600, U.S./Canada tel. 800/227-6963, www.crowneplaza.com, US$104–209) has all the features you'd expect of the chain, including a pool, spa, restaurant, business center, and travel agency. A sports bar contains pool tables and a widescreen TV for sporting events. The hotel's 158 rooms come with climate control, satellite TV, high speed Internet, and direct-dial phones. Nonsmoking rooms are available.

FOOD

Although not ordinarily thought of as a tourist town, Mexicali has more restaurants in the state-proclaimed *turística* category—125 out of more than 550 total—than any other city in Baja. The older downtown area near the border offers the least expensive, most authentic northern Mexican food, with vendors and cafés every other block or so. Another good area for cheap eats is opposite the bus station on Calzada Independencia, where taco and *torta* stands vie for the patronage of arriving and departing passengers.

Chinese

Mexicali has more Chinese restaurants per capita than any other city in Mexico—well over a hundred at last count. Chinese food is so much a part of the scene that the Baja California state tourist office recognizes Chinese cuisine as the city's most typical food.

TEN TO TRY IN BAJA

For those who like to travel from one meal to the next, Baja presents a lot more than Tecate beer and fresh fish tacos (although both of these are must-taste delights). Use the list below as a culinary guide to the peninsula.

1. Ceviche – many different styles; often served as a seafood cocktail in a martini glass with red sauce
2. Lobster roll – in Puerto Nuevo
3. Fish tacos – made everywhere, but especially tasty at the Mercado de Mariscos in Ensenada
4. Chinese food with a Mexican twist – in Mexicali
5. The best *bolillos* – at El Mejor Pan in Tecate
6. Freshly made tortillas – corn or flour, buy them hot off the press at any *tortillería* for about US$1 per dozen
7. Abalone sausage – from Isla Cedros
8. Clamato cocktail – a meal in a cup that is nothing like its American counterpart
9. Award-winning red wines – made in the Valle de Guadalupe
10. *Alta cocina mexicana* – served at upscale restaurants in San José del Cabo, La Paz, and Tijuana

Cantonese cooking predominates, but with few exceptions it's not the sort you'd recognize from Canton or Hong Kong—or Vancouver or San Francisco, for that matter. As in many Chinese restaurants outside of China, Hong Kong, Singapore, and Taiwan, immigrant cooks have adapted their native cuisine to local tastes. Almost every Chinese restaurant in Mexicali, for example, serves each dish with a small bowl of what tastes like generic steak sauce or ketchup, a distinctly *norteño* touch. Still, the city's Chinese restaurants are among the most economical places to eat and are worth visiting for their interior decor alone—some represent the ultimate in Chinese restaurant kitsch.

In Chinesca itself, most of the Chinese places fall into the "hole in the wall" category. **China Town** (Av. Madero 701, tel. 686/554-0212, daily for lunch and dinner, mains under US$10) is a good, inexpensive choice.

In a small shopping center just north of the Araiza Inn Mexicali, **Restaurant El Dragón** (Blvd. Juárez 1830, tel. 686/566-2020, mains US$10–15) features one of the most elaborate Chinese interiors in town. Large portions and fresh ingredients make it one of Mexicali's most popular restaurants; the huge menu features several regional styles.

Other International

Restaurant-Bar Heidelberg (Av. Madero at Calle H close to downtown, tel. 686/554-2022, Mon.–Sat. noon–1 A.M., mains US$10–15) offers German and Continental dishes. **Restaurant Italiano Mandolino** (Av. Reforma 1070, tel. 686/552-9544, daily for lunch and dinner, mains US$10–15) is the place to go for Italian food in Mexicali. A piano bar is attached. **Sakura Restaurant Bar Japonés** (Blvd. Lázaro Cárdenas 2004 at Calz. Montejano, tel. 686/566-4848, daily for lunch and dinner, mains US$10–15) offers teppanyaki, tempura, sushi, and the like.

Mexican

Cenaduría Selecta (Calle G 1510 at Av. Arista, tel. 686/552-4047, daily 8 A.M.–11 P.M., mains US$10–15) lies in a slightly less congested downtown area. The renowned Selecta has crowded them in since 1945 for some of the best tacos and burritos in town.

Popular with UABC staff, **Merendero Manuet's** (Calle L at Av. Pino Suárez, tel. 686/552-5694, daily 10 A.M.–1 A.M.) occupies a large, semicircular pink building resembling a 1950s American drive-in. The moderately priced menu focuses on *antojitos*. There's also a full bar.

Molcajetes Bar-Grill & Pawnshop (Calz. Montejano across from the state tourism office, tel. 686/557-0600, Mon.–Sat. 1 P.M.–2 A.M.) specializes in fajitas, including chicken, shrimp, and fish versions or a combination of all three. "Pawnshop" refers to a business that previously occupied the space. On Friday and Saturday after 11 P.M. the tables are moved to create a dance floor, and a live band rocks until 4 A.M.

Sara's Restaurant (Blvd. Benito Juárez, Centro Comercial 19 across from UABC, tel. 686/566-2455, daily 7 A.M.–10:30 P.M.) offers good basic *comida mexicana*, including inexpensive breakfasts and *comida corrida*.

Seafood

In the Centro Cívico district, decorated with fishnets and vibrant Mexican colors, **Los Arcos Restaurant/Bar** (Calafía 454, tel. 686/556-0886, Mon.–Thurs. 11 A.M.–10 P.M., Fri.–Sun. 11 A.M.–11 P.M., mains US$10–15) is the best place in town for fresh seafood. Its "seafood fiesta"—a stew consisting of fresh squid, octopus, shredded fish, marlin, and shrimp in a tomato-basil sauce—is the local favorite. A trio of Mexican singers provides entertainment on weekends.

Groceries

The city's best supermarkets include a **Gigante** at Plaza Gigante on Boulevard Juárez, almost opposite the Hotel Lucerna, and a 24-hour **Ley** on Independencia. Plaza Fiesta on Calzada López Mateos also features Ley.

INFORMATION AND SERVICES
Tourist Assistance

The Mexicali Tourism and Convention Bureau (COTUCO) maintains an office on Boulevard López Mateos at Calle Camelias (tel. 686/557-2561 or 888/268-8262, www.mexicaliturismo.com, Mon.–Fri. 8 A.M.–7 P.M.). The information counter has a a helpful, English-speaking staff.

The SECTUR office is at Boulevard Benito Juárez 1 and Calzada Montejano (tel. 686/566-1161 or 686/558-1000, Mon.–Fri. 8 A.M.–5 P.M., Sat.–Sun. 10 A.M.–3 P.M.). SECTUR's legal assistance department (Attorney for Tourist Protection) is headquartered here (tel./fax 686/566-1116).

Money

Banamex, Bancomer, Banco Internacional, Serfín, and several other large Mexican banks maintain branches in Mexicali; most have ATMs. As in most Mexican cities, the foreign-currency exchange service closes around noon each day. For better hours, shorter lines, and competitive rates, use any of the several *casas de cambio* in the vicinity of the Hotel Del Norte downtown, particularly along Madero near Azueta. The Bancomer on the northwest corner of Madero and Azueta features a 24-hour ATM.

South of downtown, Servi Cambios Mexicali in Plaza Cachanilla offers good exchange rates. As in most border towns, the best rates are given for cash rather than travelers checks.

Downtown Calexico, near the border crossing, also features several small money changers. The dollar-to-peso rate is sometimes a bit higher here than in Mexicali, but check to see whether there's a commission before exchanging currencies.

Post and Telephone

Mexicali's main post office, at the corner of Calzada Independencia and Calle Pioneros downtown, is open Monday–Friday 8 A.M.–3 P.M., Saturday 9 A.M.–1 P.M. Mail to the United States will move more quickly if deposited at a post office in Calexico; the main post office there is at Birch Street and George Avenue, four blocks west of Imperial Avenue. A Western Union office can be found in the Mexicali post office, and is open Monday–Friday 8 A.M.–4 P.M., Saturday 8 A.M.–1 P.M. Long-distance Ladatel phones can be found throughout Mexicali; however, be sure you know the rate before making any international call.

Mexican Consulate in Calexico

The Mexican government maintains a conveniently located consular office (331 W. 2nd St., tel. 760/357-3863, fax 760/357-6284, Mon.–Fri. 8 A.M.–3 P.M.) in Calexico, just across the border. If you're entering Mexico via Mexicali, you can save a stop in San Diego for information on tourist cards, visas, and other Mexican immigration or customs information.

Border Crossing

The Mexicali border gateway is open 24 hours. Although the crossing here is less congested than Tijuana's, it's still wise to avoid morning and afternoon commute hours. If you're planning to drive east into the state of Sonora or to other points east of Baja and don't already possess a temporary vehicle import permit, obtain one from the Mexican customs office at the border. The permits can be issued any time of day Sunday–Friday, but issuance on Saturday is restricted to the hours of 10 A.M.–2 P.M.

A second crossing east of the city links Calexico East with Mexicali's main industrial park and is open daily 6 A.M.–10 P.M.

GETTING THERE
By Air

Mexicali's **Aeropuerto Internacional General Rodolfo Sánchez Taboada** (MXL) lies 20 kilometers (12 mi) east of the city via Boulevard de las Américas. **Aeroméxico** (Pasaje Alamos 1008-D, Centro Cívico Comercial, tel. 686/557-2551), and **Mexicana** (Av. Obregón, tel. 686/553-5401) each serve Mexicali from Hermosillo, Sonora, on the mainland. Mexicana also fields flights to/from Guadalajara, Monterrey, and Mexico City. The Aeroméxico flights connect with service to/from Tucson and Phoenix.

Taxi service between Mexicali and the airport costs US$15 per vehicle.

By Bus

Mexicali's intercity bus depot, Central de Autobuses (on the south side of Calz. Independencia, btw Calz. López Mateos/Centro Cívico, tel. 686/557-2410 or 686/557-2450) contains a snack bar, money changer, and left-luggage service. Buses bound for northern Baja destinations are operated by **Autotransportes de Baja California** (ABC) and leave at least once a day for Tijuana, Ensenada, Tecate, and San Felipe. Southbound buses go at least once a day to La Paz via Santa Rosalía, Mulegé, and Loreto. **Transportes Norte de Sonora** (TNS), **Transportes del Pacífico**, and **Elite** handle services to these mainland destinations: Hermosillo, Guaymas, Mazatlán, Chihuahua, and

Mexico City. To reach the bus terminal, board a bus marked Calle 6 from anywhere along Calzada López Mateos.

ABC also has a small downtown terminal on López Mateos between Azueta and Madero, where you can catch frequent buses to Tijuana, Ensenada, or Tecate.

The Greyhound station in **Calexico** (tel. 760/357-1895), a few steps from the pedestrian border crossing on 1st Street, offers direct buses into Mexicali from Los Angeles for US$30 one-way.

GETTING AROUND
By Bus

Mexicali's city buses are large converted school buses; the final destination is marked on the bus marquee (e.g., Centro Cívico for the civic center/zona rosa area, Justo Sierra for Calzada Justo Sierra). Many city buses start from Calle Altamirano downtown, just two blocks from the border crossing. Fares are less than US$1.

By Taxi

Large *taxis de ruta* (route taxis) compete with city buses along popular routes and cost just a few pesos more. A private hired taxi costs US$3–5 within the downtown area, US$6–8 to the Centro Cívico area or the Boulevard Juárez hotel strip from the border crossing. Taxis are most concentrated near the pedestrian border crossing and at the Lucerna, Calafía, and Crowne Plaza hotels.

Radio Taxis Cervantes (tel. 686/568-3718) and **Ecotaxi** (tel. 686/562-6565) offer radio-dispatched, 24-hour taxi service.

By Car

Except for the congested downtown area near the border, the traffic in Mexicali moves fairly easily. Parking is sometimes a problem near the border but elsewhere in the city it is plentiful. The *glorietas* (traffic circles) are a bane for timid visiting drivers; lanes within the circles aren't generally marked, and drivers jockey for position according to where they plan to exit the circle. It's important to stay alert while maneuvering around the circle, always counterclockwise, so that when the desired spoke approaches you're in a position to take it.

To get onto Mexico 5 south for San Felipe, drive southeast on Calzada López Mateos until it meets Boulevard Juárez; follow the signs to the right (south). Just south of this intersection, Mexico 5 crosses Mexico 2, the highway west for Tecate and Tijuana or east to Sonora.

The city has plenty of Pemex stations, and most stock Premium. The Pemex opposite Plaza Cachanilla sells Premium and is open 24 hours.

Oscar Padilla Mexican Insurance (747 Imperial Ave. in Calexico, tel. 760/357-4883) is a reliable source for auto and boat policies (see *Getting There by Car* in *Essentials*).

Vicinity of Mexicali

MEXICO 2 TO TECATE

West of Mexicali, Mexico 2 skirts the northern edge of the Sierra de los Cucapá and flattens out along the top of **Laguna Salada,** a huge dry salt lake extending southward nearly 100 kilometers (60 mi). At Km 24, an unpaved, ungraded road leads south to the northern shore of the lake, where a small fish camp survives on accumulated runoff from the Río Colorado delta; visitors are permitted to camp overnight. A Pemex station near this junction offers a chance to gas up before proceeding farther along Mexico 2 or south along Laguna Salada. The next gas station is 53 kilometers (33 mi) west, in La Rumorosa.

Between Mexicali and Tecate on Mexico 2-D there are two tolls of US$2.50.

Palm Canyons

Several steep-walled palm canyons cutting deeply into the eastern escarpment of the Sierra Juárez have become prime destinations for a generation of adventurous visitors to northeastern Baja's desert extremes. The larger Tajo, El Carrizo, Guadalupe, and El Palomar canyons contain year-round streams and *tinajas* (springs) and are highly desirable hiking and backpacking destinations November–mid-April. Late April–October, temperatures often exceed 37°C (100°F)—not the best of conditions for desert hiking. For all overnight hikes, come prepared for wilderness camping.

At Km 28 off Mexico 2-D, a graded and unpaved road to the south threads between the western edge of Laguna Salada and the east-

ern escarpment of the Sierra Juárez. Because of the way the toll highway (Mexico 2-D) is constructed—there is no free road along this stretch—you cannot take this turnoff directly if you're coming from Mexicali; a concrete barrier along the highway blocks access from the highway's north lanes, so you have to continue toward Tecate until you find a place to make a U-turn.

Although washboard surfaces much of the way mean progress is slow, the road to the canyon areas is adequate for ordinary passenger vehicles as far south as the turnoff for Cañon de Guadalupe; beyond that a four-wheel-drive vehicle is usually necessary.

Cañon Tajo, the most spectacular of the palm canyons, is reached by an unmarked sand road that branches west off the Laguna Salada road 34.5 kilometers (21.5 mi) south of Mexico 2. From this point, most vehicles can only make it 2.5 kilometers (1.5 mi) or so before the track contours become too extreme and the sand too deep; after that it's 5.5 kilometers (3.5 mi) of hard slogging across sand flats to the mouth of the canyon. If you're concerned about security, you might be able to leave your vehicle at tiny **Rancho los Laureles del Desierto,** about a mile west of the Tajo turnoff, before hiking in.

Your hike will be rewarded with a wide canyon studded with thousands of fan palms and adorned with freshwater pools below 450-meter (1,500-foot) granite walls. It's 6.5 kilometers (4 mi) to the head of the canyon, where an old Amerindian trail leads north; you can see—but not touch—a number of petroglyphs and Amerindian relics along the way. *Borregón* (desert bighorn sheep) and deer occasionally wander into the canyon.

Cañon de Guadalupe

The signed turnoff west to Cañon de Guadalupe comes along nine kilometers (5.6 mi) south of the Tajo turnoff, or about 44 kilometers (27.5 mi) south of Mexico 2. Unlike the approach to Tajo, this side road is passable by car or truck all the way to the mouth of the canyon (12 km/7.5 mi), where you'll find a public campground and hot mineral springs. Average driving time is 45 minutes. About five kilometers (3.2 mi) from the main road, the road to Guadalupe jogs left—ignore the lesser fork that goes straight. Shortly thereafter the road narrows considerably, and at 9.6 kilometers (6 mi) the road surface contains many exposed boulders and large rocks that could pose problems for vehicles with lower-than-normal clearance. This is a pretty road, with lots of paloverde, cholla, ocotillo, and other Baja desert flora along the way.

Although not as large as Tajo, Cañon de Guadalupe is impressive, with tiered waterfalls, pools, and plenty of blue fan palms. The main stream through the canyon leads to the "Pool of the Virgin," surrounded by white granite walls and fringed with ferns, cottonwoods, and willows. As in Cañon Tajo, there are signs of an earlier Amerindian presence. Both canyons were used by the Cucapá and Paipai during seasonal pilgrimages to collect piñon nuts on the Sierra Juárez plateau.

At around 12 kilometers (7.5 mi) from the main road a fence marks off **Guadalupe Canyon Hot Springs and Campground** (U.S. tel. 949/673-2670, www.guadalupe-canyon.com), divided into two separate campgrounds: Arturo's Campo and Los Manantiales (Mario's Campo). Campsites start at US$50/night for one auto on weekdays. There's a two-night minimum on weekends (US$75–90 for two nights, one car), and a three-night minimum on holidays (US$200 for three nights, one car); rates depend on the campsite and number of vehicles (some sites hold up to six vehicles). Each of 20 campsites comes with its own cement hot tub linked to the main hot springs, which pump out 120,000 gallons a day at temperatures of 41.5°C (107°F). Some sites are better than others, so take your time making a choice.

Outhouses and showers are available, and a small market sells burritos, tacos, egg dishes, and soft drinks. Firewood is also available. The campgrounds are open year-round but are most popular during the cooler winter months. Weekends and holidays can be crowded—you'll do much better to visit during the week.

An alternate route to reach the Cañon de Guadalupe turnoff from Mexico 2-D is usually quicker and smoother than the more well-known road described at the top of this section. Leaving the highway between Km 23 and 24 (accessible only when driving east from Tecate), opposite a Pemex station, this track goes right through the middle of Laguna Salada. It's only one lane wide, so you may have to pull over for other vehicles along the way, but the road is usually considerably smoother and less washboard-prone. Along the expansive salt flats in the middle, you can often drive much faster than on the main road. Some sections of the road feature soft sand, so you must be adept at sand driving—during the odd rain the road may be temporarily impassable.

The main problem with this road is that at its southern end, near the turnoff for Cañon de Guadalupe, it intersects a maze of connecting roads running in all directions, making it rather difficult to find the canyon access road. For this reason, we recommend using the main road coming south, then returning to the highway via the Laguna Salada road—you can ask for directions from the campground proprietors and at the same time inquire about road conditions.

La Rumorosa

At around Km 44, Mexico 2-D begins climbing the Juárez escarpment along the steep Cantú grade (also called Cuesta de la Rumorosa). The town of La Rumorosa, topping the grade at Km 68, is named for the constant murmuring of winds through the 1,275-meter (4,200-ft) mountain pass. Many Tijuana and Mexicali residents own summer homes in the vicinity, and the town holds a couple of cafés (**Restaurant Sonorita** is recommended), bakeries, grocery stores, a Red Cross, and a self-serve Pemex station.

Descending along the more gradual western slope of the Sierra Juárez, the environment changes rapidly from the arid, scrubby vegetation east of the mountains to piñon stands and chaparral. The toll between Mexicali and Rumorosa is US$0.65; there is no longer a free road along this stretch.

La Rumorosa to Laguna Hanson

West of La Rumorosa at Km 73 is a dirt road that leads 63 kilometers (39 mi) south to Laguna Hanson (also known as Laguna Juárez), part of the Parque Nacional Constitución de 1857. The road is graded for the first 37 kilometers (23 mi) or so but rapidly deteriorates as it approaches the national park's northern boundary. High-clearance vehicles, preferably with four-wheel drive, are recommended for this route.

The more popular and easier route into the national park is via Mexico 3, southeast of Ensenada. For information on this road, and on the national park itself, see *East from Ensenada* in the *Ensenada to El Rosario* chapter.

El Condor to Tecate

At El Condor (Km 83), 14.5 kilometers (9 mi) west of La Rumorosa, another unpaved road heads south to Laguna Hanson, passing the ranchos of Cisneros, Jacaranda, El Encanto, Tres Pozos, and others. Although this route proves slower going than the La Rumorosa road, there's more to see, including several abandoned mines. Just beyond Rancho Jesayo and Mina Margarita (Margarita Mine), about 30 kilometers (19 mi) from Mexico 2, the road joins the La Rumorosa–Laguna Hanson road. Basic services—food and gas—are available in El Condor.

The *ejido* settlement of **El Hongo** appears off Mexico 2 at Km 99, where a paved road leads southwest toward Hacienda Santa Veronica and a network of unpaved roads and vehicle tracks in the western foothills of the Sierra Juárez. The largest is an 83.5-kilometer (52-mi) road, mostly ungraded, that winds southward to join the Mexico 3–Laguna Hanson road near Rancho El Coyote. Along the way are several ranchos and abandoned mines, including **La Rosa de Castilla,** a former gold-mining center that served as the territorial capital (1870–1882) before Ensenada. This road is suitable for high-clearance vehicles only.

Beyond El Hongo, Mexico 2 dips through rolling dairy farms and olive groves, a relatively uneventful ride until you arrive in Tecate at Km 130. You may be able to camp at one of the *ejidos* between El Hongo and Tecate for US$5–10 a night.

MEXICO 5 TO SAN FELIPE

Mexico 5, the paved, mostly two-lane highway (some parts have four lanes) between Mexicali and San Felipe, is flat all the way and features one of the more durable roadbeds in Baja. The first 45 kilometers (27 mi) of the highway is flanked by *ejido* lands with irrigated vegetable farms and dairy farms. You'll find several nopal (prickly pear cactus) farms along the highway around Km 15; fresh and pickled cactus is sold from roadside stands.

Just south of the town of **La Puerta,** at Km 38, BCN 4 branches east to the town of Coahuila and the Sonoran state border. La Puerta offers a Pemex station, a market, and a café. At about Km 48, the pastureland gives way abruptly to desert as you reach the southern limit of the delta irrigation system.

Río Hardy

Beginning at around Km 50 off Mexico 5, the marshy Río Hardy is easily accessed by a number of dirt tracks heading east off the highway. Several rustic *campos,* mostly catering to hunters and anglers, lie along the river to its junction with the Río Colorado (about 15 km southeast).

The Río Hardy attracts migrating bird

species, including pintails, green-wing teals, egrets, pelicans, coots, cranes, and a dozen or more duck species. The main quarry for visiting hunters are quail and white-wing and mourning doves. Dove-hunting season generally runs September–December.

Local Cucapá Amerindians fish the river for carp, flathead catfish, largemouth and striped bass, and, more recently, *mojarra* (tilapia), a prolific African species that has come down into the Río Hardy through locks in Colorado River dams. Reportedly, the best fishing is at the junction of the Hardy and Colorado Rivers, near Campo Los Amigos. This area is accessible by vehicle track from Río El Mayor (Km 55) or San Miguel, about 12 kilometers farther south, just before the causeway over Laguna Salada.

Just south of **Cucapá el Mayor** (also called El Mayor Indígena), around Km 57, the tiny **Museo Cucapá** (tel. 686/552-3591, daily 9 A.M.–2 P.M.) stands alongside a police station. Exhibits inside include historical photographs and artifacts, while outside the center are models of traditional willow-and-arrow weed thatched homes. An area is also set aside for the display and sale of traditional handmade Cucapá crafts, such as beaded collars and willow-and-cottonwood bark skirts.

Camps in the Río Hardy area open and close from year to year depending on river conditions. They include Sonora, Las Cabañas, Mosqueda, Río Hardy, Club BBB, El Mayor, Muñoz, and Los Amigos. **Sonora, Las Cabañas, Mosqueda, Río Hardy,** and **El Mayor** are usually open and can accommodate RVs; rates are around US$10–12 a night. Las Cabañas also offers rustic cabins for rent.

La Ventana to San Felipe

Kilometer 105 marks the one-café town of La Ventana—sneeze and you'll miss it. The Pemex station at La Ventana is no longer open for business, so if you need to gas up you'd best stop earlier in Ejido Nayarit, at Km 31—coming from Mexicali, this is the last Pemex station before San Felipe. Farther south at Km 122 is an unpaved, graded road leading west to the Sierra Las Pintas and three abandoned mines: La Fortuna, Buena Vista, and La Escondida. A fourth, Jueves Santo, is still a working gold mine.

South of this turnoff, the highway crosses the **Llano El Chinero** (Chinese Plain), where a large group of Chinese immigrants died of heat and thirst while trying to reach Mexicali on foot in the early 20th century. The lone peak east of the highway is 200-meter **Cerro El Chinero.**

Mexico 5 intersects with Mexico 3, the highway to Ensenada, at **Crucero La Trinidad** (Km 140). Just south of the junction is a Pemex station. A string of signs for beach camps on the east side of the highway, beginning at around Km 172, marks the final approach to San Felipe, reached at Km 189.

San Felipe

This unlikely beach community (pop. 25,000) squeezed between the San Felipe Desert and the Sea of Cortez received its name from Jesuit Padre Fernando Consag, who briefly landed four canoes here in 1746 and named the gently curving bay San Felipe de Jesús. In 1797, a padre from Misión San Pedro Mártir de Verona established a supply port at Bahía San Felipe; both the port and mission failed in 1806. In the late 19th and early 20th centuries, virtually the only people who knew of San Felipe's existence were nomadic fishermen working the Sea of Cortez coast.

The post–World War II construction of a paved road to a radar station at the south end of the bay finally linked San Felipe with the outside world. In the late 1940s and 1950s, American anglers came in droves to land *totuava*, a strong-fighting, copper-silver-gray croaker with a weight range of 16–115 kilograms (35–254 lbs). Old-timers say it's one of the tastiest fish in the Cortez, but since they

fished the species onto the endangered species list, most of us will never get a taste. Mexican law now forbids the taking of *totuava*.

The bay is protected from north-northeast winds by Punta San Felipe, a jutting headland topped by 240-meter Cerro El Machorro at the bay's north end. The summit offers a good view of the bay and bears a shrine dedicated to the Virgin of Guadalupe. Below the headland are an estuary and boatyard. At the bay's south end, an artificial harbor shelters the local commercial shrimp fleet—one of five such fleets licensed to net shrimp along Mexico's entire west coast. The tidal range in the northern Cortez is extreme, so only the harbor's outer section is suitable for larger craft.

San Felipe today is a beach playground for Californians and Arizonans—some 250,000 visitors annually—who camp or park their RVs on the many golden-hued beaches extending north and south of the bay. The nearby dunes

THE NET-SAN FELIPE HTTP://WWW.SANFELIPE.COM.MX

San Felipe lighthouse

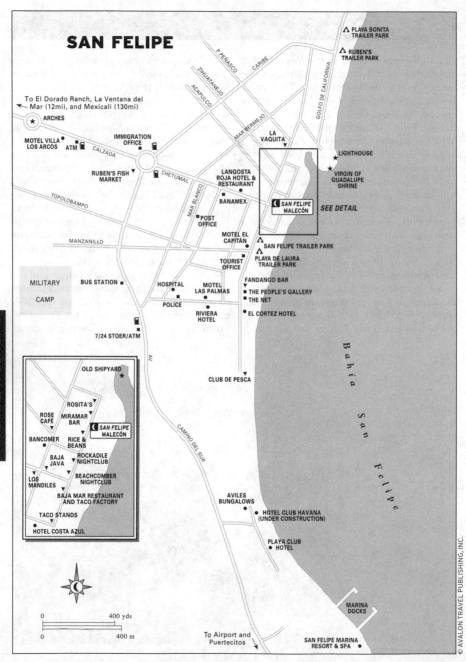

SAN FELIPE

To El Dorado Ranch, La Ventana del
Mar (12mi), and Mexicali (130mi)

P. PEÑASCO

CARIBE

ZIHUATANEJO

ACAPULCO

MAR BERMEJO

GOLFO DE CALIFORNIA

PLAYA BONITA
TRAILER PARK

RUBEN'S
TRAILER PARK

ARCHES

MOTEL VILLA
LOS ARCOS   ATM

IMMIGRATION
OFFICE

CALZADA

LA
VAQUITA

LIGHTHOUSE

RUBEN'S FISH
MARKET

CHETUMAL

LANGOSTA
ROJA HOTEL &
RESTAURANT

VIRGIN OF
GUADALUPE
SHRINE

TOPOLOBAMPO

MAR BLANCO

BANAMEX

SAN FELIPE
MALECÓN

SEE DETAIL

MANZANILLO

POST
OFFICE

MOTEL EL
CAPITÁN

SAN FELIPE TRAILER PARK

TOURIST
OFFICE

PLAYA DE LAURA
TRAILER PARK

MILITARY

CAMP

BUS STATION

HOSPITAL

MOTEL
LAS PALMAS

FANDANGO BAR

THE PEOPLE'S GALLERY

THE NET

POLICE

RIVIERA
HOTEL

EL CORTEZ HOTEL

7/24 STOER/ATM

AV

B a h í a

S a n

F e l i p e

OLD SHIPYARD

ROSITA'S

ROSE
CAFÉ

MIRAMAR
BAR

SAN FELIPE
MALECÓN

BANCOMER

RICE &
BEANS

BAJA
JAVA

ROCKADILE
NIGHTCLUB

LOS
MANDILES

BEACHCOMBER
NIGHTCLUB

BAJA MAR RESTAURANT
AND TACO FACTORY

TACO STANDS

HOTEL COSTA AZUL

CAMINO DEL SUR

CLUB DE PESCA

AVILES
BUNGALOWS

HOTEL CLUB HAVANA
(UNDER CONSTRUCTION)

PLAYA CLUB
HOTEL

MARINA
DOCKS

0   400 yds

0   400 m

To Airport and
Puertecitos

SAN FELIPE MARINA
RESORT & SPA

attract dune-buggy and ATV enthusiasts who scream up and down the sloping sands with Cerro Juan (1,025 m/3,369 ft) and Cerro Kino (1,304 m/4,290 ft) to the west as a backdrop. A number of Americans have retired in San Felipe, but most gringos come for a cheap beach or fishing vacation within two to three hours' drive of the U.S. border.

Visitors going no farther than San Felipe are not required to pay the US$15 tourist fee if staying less than 72 hours.

CLIMATE AND TOURIST SEASON

Peak tourist season in the San Felipe area is November–April, when temperatures are mild. Note, though, that December–February the northern Cortez may be a bit chilly for most swimmers. May–October, daytime air temperatures frequently break 38°C (100°F), but it doesn't get quite as hot as Mexicali. In summer, many gringos residing in San Felipe go elsewhere—usually to the Pacific coast—to cool off. Rainfall at any time of year is virtually nil.

◖ MALECÓN

Whether it's day or night, the action in San Felipe takes place along the waterfront promenade of Avenida Mar de Cortez. Lined with casual restaurants, outdoor cafés, and dance clubs, the *malecón* is steps away from Playa San Felipe, where visiting college students set up sunbathing stations, and *panga* boats stand ready to transport anglers to destinations offshore.

SPORTS AND RECREATION
Fishing

Although the San Felipe fishery is not what it used to be, with the magnificent *totuava* now a protected species and many other varieties in the northern Cortez also becoming scarce, sportfishing is still one of the primary local tourist activities. The high fishing season is March–June, when white sea bass runs are common. Croakers are available year-round, corvinas late March–November. Cabrilla, yellowtail, sierra, and grouper are plentiful May–October; in the fall you can catch pompano.

Generally, the best onshore fishing area runs from Punta San Felipe north, while inshore fishing is good from Punta Estrella south. The best offshore fishing and the best overall fishing is found around Roca Consag, 27 kilometers (17 mi) east of Punta San Felipe. This is a particularly good area for croaker and white sea bass. For those with time to spare, multiday liveaboard trips reach the Midriff Islands 400 kilometers (250 mi) to the south, where sportfishing is excellent.

A sportfishing service at the north end of the *malecón*, **Tommy Sport Fishing** (tel. 686/577-0446), offers guided fishing trips aboard eight-meter (24-ft) *pangas*. A 7 A.M.–noon bay fishing trip costs US$40 per person or US$35 per person for three or more people; bay angling usually nets calico bass, small croaker, sierra, or triggerfish. An all-day island fishing trip costs US$250 for two anglers.

Down at the new marina, **Tony Reyes Fishing Tours** (Av. Mar Bermejo 130, tel. 686/577-1120, www.tonyreyes.com) operates two vessels: The 86-foot liveaboard sportfishing cruiser called *José Andres* holds 18 anglers. The craft features a large walk-in freezer and ice hold, two live bait tanks, a modern galley, three heads, two showers, and staterooms with open-air bunks for those who want to enjoy the beautiful evenings at sea. Six *pangas* ride piggyback on the back deck so that anglers can go out three at a time from the Midriff Islands. The 107-foot *Tony Reyes* holds 27 anglers. The boats sail from San Felipe to the Midriff Islands March–November for six days at a time. (In March only, you can book a three-day trip aboard the *Tony Reyes*.) Typical catches include giant black sea bass, white sea bass, cabrilla, giant squid, red snapper, pargo, yellowtail, grouper, and, later in the season, roosterfish, sailfish, marlin, amberjack, and more yellowtail. The company can also be reached c/o the Orange, CA–based Longfin Tackle Store (tel. 714/538-9300).

You can purchase fishing tackle at **Proveedora de Equipos de Pesca,** on Avenida Mar de Cortés near the commercial marina south of town. Minimarket Las Americas also sells hooks and sinkers, and you can buy live bait from the shrimpers at the marina. As elsewhere in Mexico, every person in every boat that carries fishing tackle needs a valid fishing license. You can legally fish from shore without a license.

If you have your own small boat, you can launch at ramps at the Motel El Cortez, Ruben's Trailer Park, and the San Felipe Marina. All charge fees of around US$4 per launch.

Boating

Experienced, self-sufficient small-boaters and kayakers can put in at San Felipe for the 258-kilometer (160-mi) coastal cruise to Bahía de los Ángeles. Although there are plenty of coves along the way, only a few places—Puertecitos, Punta Bufeo, and Bahía San Luis Gonzaga—offer limited supplies. It's best to do this route with someone who's done it before.

The *capitanía del puerto,* or captain of the port (COTP), can be found at the marina.

Golf

The developer of the El Dorado Ranch and La Ventana del Mar resorts has opened **Las Caras de Mexico Golf Course** (tel. 686/576-0517, www.lascarasdemexico.com), a seaside 18-hole, 7,202-yard course designed with salt-tolerant turf and plants to allow seawater irrigation. Though open to the public now, the course will become private when a separate 18-hole mountain course is complete on the west side of Mexico 5. Greens fees are US$70–85 for 18 holes. Taylor-made clubs rent for US$30.

ENTERTAINMENT AND EVENTS
Entertainment

At night, the young and not-so-young shake it at **Rockodile** or **Beachcomber,** both large dance clubs on the *malecón.* Weekdays are usually on the dead side, while the weekends are packed. Rockodile has a sand volleyball court, while Beachcomber features a state-of-the-art laser light system. Both places offer happy hours from noon till around 5 P.M.

La Iguana, with entrances on both the *malecón* and Avenida Mar de Cortés, just north of Acapulco, is a lively sports bar and night-club. Pool tables here are only US$0.50 a game, beers US$2. On the hill just below Guadalupe's watchful eye, the three-story **Boom Boom Room** dwarfs all other clubs in town (and the lighthouse itself, for that matter) and boasts multitiered, indoor/outdoor dance floors, a giant sound system, and impressive balcony views. It's open evenings from 9 P.M. on.

For something more local in flavor, check out the **Club Miramar** toward the north end of the *malecón.* Open since 1948, it's basically just a bar with pool tables, though on occasion it may host wandering *trovadores.*

Events

Most of San Felipe's yearly events calendar revolves around desert or Sea of Cortez racing. The **Tecate SCORE San Felipe 250** off-road race, is held in March, while late February or March winds bring the **Hobie Cat Midwinters West Regatta,** a catamaran race on Bahía de San Felipe.

Late February or early March is also time for **Carnaval,** which in San Felipe is celebrated in a much more macho fashion than in Mazatlán or La Paz, with amateur boxing, *palenque* (cockfighting), chili-eating contests, and greased-pole climbing.

California and Arizona college students invade the town the third week of March for their annual **spring break,** while Oregon and Washington students tend to arrive the fourth week of March. Either way, the last two weeks of March can be considered a total write-off (unless, of course, you're one of the spring-breakers).

Navy Day (Día de la Marina), observed on June 1, is celebrated in San Felipe with a street festival, music, and dancing. Also in June is an all-terrain cycling race between San Felipe and Puertecitos; contact the tourist office in San Felipe or Mexicali for information on this new sporting event.

SHOPPING

If you're looking for fine art, you won't find it at **The People's Gallery** (Av. Mar de Cortés Sur 381, tel, 686/577-2898, daily 10 A.M.–5 P.M.), but you will find a unique and fun collection

© PAUL ITOI

roadside antiques

of paintings, jewelry, and crafts made by locals and local expatriates.

ACCOMMODATIONS

Because San Felipe is so popular and so close to the U.S. border, hotel and motel rates tend to be a bit on the high side, at least for Baja. Rate categories below correspond to peak-season (Nov.–Apr.) prices. Off-season rates drop as much as 30 percent. Add 12 percent hotel tax to all rates unless otherwise specified; some hotels may charge an additional 10 percent service charge.

During the last two weeks of March, San Felipe is filled with hundreds of Arizona and California college and university students celebrating spring break. Needless to say, this is a bad time to look for a room.

Under US$50

Near the marina at the south edge of town, **Terraza Motel** (Av. Misión de Loreto 103, tel./fax 686/577-1844, US$30) offers a cluster of 12 separate, prefabricated cabins built on a hillside near the marina and beach. Each cabin has TV and a hot-water shower. Out by the entrance to town coming from Mexicali, near the arches monument, **Motel Villa Los Arcos** (Calz. Chetumal s/n, tel. 686/577-1588, US$35) contains 11 comfortable rooms in duplex whitewashed, red-tiled cabins, each with its own parking spaces. All units come with air conditioning, TV, and kitchenettes. A small pool area in back offers palapa-shaded chairs. Villa Los Arcos is not within easy walking distance of the beach.

US$50-100

Near the waterfront in the center of town, aging **Motel Chapala** (Av. Mar de Cortés, tel. 686/577-1240, US$50) is one of the cheapest sleeps in town. Despite its worn look, it's clean and safe. On the opposite side of the street, farther south, **Motel El Capitán** (Av. Mar de Cortés 298, tel./fax 686/577-1303, bsf@telnor. net, US$75) is a well-run, two-story place with 45 rooms built around a large parking lot and small pool. Rooms are clean and each has air conditioning, TV, and a large private bathroom. The waterfront is a short walk away. El Capitán is popular with Mexican business travelers. Weekend rates are considerably higher than midweek rates.

Two blocks from the beach, **La Hacienda de la Langosta Roja** (Calz. Chetumal 125, tel. 686/577-0483 or 800/967-0005, www.sanfelipelodging.com, US$85) has re-opened under new management with 39 newly furnished rooms in a pink two-story building. Amenities include air conditioning and satellite TV with 15 channels.

El Cortez (east of the Palmas on Av. Mar de Cortés, tel. 686/577-1055 or 686/577-1056, cortezno@telnor.net, US$85) is a long building right on the beach with a pool, boat launch, laundry, beach *palapas,* and a restaurant. The 109 rustic rooms have air conditioning, TV, and phone.

US$100-150

San Felipe Marina Resort and Spa (Km 4.5, tel. 686/577-1455 or 800/025-6925, U.S. tel. 800/291-5397, www.sanfelipemarina.net, US$144), farther south off Avenida Camino del Sur, offers nicely furnished rooms and villas. Rates vary according to the day of the week and the size of the unit. Rooms have fully equipped kitchens, satellite TV, and phones. The property includes a pool, tennis courts, a restaurant and bar, snack bar, indoor heated pool, outdoor pool with panoramic view, lighted tennis courts, a clubhouse, gym, sauna, massage room, minimarket, and laundry. Construction of a 243-slip marina recently resumed, with the first floating dock installed in early 2007. The beach, a short walk away, is not San Felipe's best because of its proximity to the marina.

Overlooking the sea on the road to Puertecitos, **Las Casitas Beach and Tennis Resort** (Km 1.6, U.S. tel. 888/700-0369, www.micasadelmar.com/las_casitas, US$110–130) has air-conditioned bungalows and studios with king-size beds and private decks.

Condominiums

The San Felipe area has a rising number of "condotels" and resort villas—often part time-share, part hotel, and part year-round condo complex. Ask at the tourist office about renting local condos or apartments by the night; in some cases they're a better deal than the local hotels and motels. A typical place with two bedrooms and two bathrooms goes for US$100 per day Sunday–Thursday, US$125 per day Friday and Saturday, or US$600 per week. **Condominiums Playa Bonita** (tel. 686/577-1215, U.S. tel. 626/967-8977, www.sanfelipebeachcondos.com, US$100–125) has eight one-bedroom units on the beach and an adjoining RV park.

El Dorado Ranch (tel. 686/576-0402, U.S./Canada tel. 303/790-1749 or 800/404-2599, www.eldoradoranch.com) is a large gated community north of town with vacation and retirement homes for rent and for sale. Facilities include a tennis club, restaurant, bar, campground, car rental, recreational equipment rentals, *palapas,* heated pool, and whirlpool tub. Rates vary; call for information. The new **La Ventana del Mar** complex has several two- and three-bedroom units complete and available for rent (U.S. tel. 877/787-2624, www.laventanadelmar.com, two-bedroom units US$260–310 per night).

Camping and RV Parks

Condo developments have taken over some of San Felipe's largest campgrounds in recent years. Of the ones that remain, few, if any, are designed with big rigs in mind. Some—mostly those out of town—offer few facilities beyond a graded road between the highway and beach. Others come with full RV hookups, restaurants, bars, hot showers, and flush toilets.

Those in town generally cost US$20–30 nightly per site for two people. Long-term stays generally cost US$100 per week or US$350 per month. The beach camps farther north and south of town typically run US$5–10 for two per site, depending on the facilities; long-term stays of seven days or more earn 10–20 percent discounts.

The most popular campgrounds among the RV crowd are those along the beach just north of Punta San Felipe, on the outskirts of town. This area generally receives a good sea breeze and is thus cooler than parks on the bay itself. **Playa Bonita RV Park** (tel. 686/577-1215, U.S. tel. 626/967-8977, www.sanfelipebeachcondos.com, US$25 for full hookups), and **Ruben's RV Trailer Park** (Av. Golfo de California 703, tel. 686/577-1442, US$15, full hookups only) are particularly popular for their large deck-topped *palapas*. Ruben's caters to a younger crowd these days, and some people might complain about the sound level of the music emanating from the Coco Loco House Restaurant and Bar. Playa Bonita takes phone reservations; Ruben's does not.

Cheaper spots in this area include **Marco's** (tel. 686/577-1872) and **Vista del Mar** (tel. 686/577-1252), both back from the beach with rates of US$10–14 per vehicle.

On the beach toward the south end of town, but still within easy walking distance of shopping and restaurants, is a cluster of places that have been around a long time. All offer hot showers and flush toilets. **Campo San Felipe** (Av. Mar de Cortés, tel. 686/577-1012, US$15–20 for RVs depending on proximity to the beach). Next south along this stretch is **Playa de Laura RV Park** (tel. 686/577-1128), where simple spots with picnic tables and ramadas cost US$10 for tents, US$16–30 for RVs, depending on proximity to the beach. **Club de Pesca RV and Trailer Park** (tel. 686/577-1180, fax 686/577-1888) sits at the southern end of Avenida Mar de Cortés; many of the sites are permanent, but a few places are usually available toward the beachfront—for US$25 a night—if you call in advance.

FOOD
Seafood
Seafood is what San Felipe restaurants do best. Vendors sell fresh seafood cocktails and fish tacos along the *malecón* (waterfront) toward the south end of Paseo de Cortés. **Mariscos La Vaquita** (Puerta Peñasco and Av. Mar de Cortez North) serves breakfast, lunch, and dinner in an open-air setting. A block and a half west of the *malecón*, **(La Hacienda de la Langosta Roja** (Calz. Chetumal 121, tel.

686/577-1571) is the only restaurant in town with a patio receiving full sun all day during the winter. Seafood entrées are moderately priced; the ceviche tostadas are delicious, and beer is served in chilled mugs. It's also open for breakfast, lunch, and dinner.

Mexican
On the *malecón*, **Rice and Beans** (Mon.–Fri. 7 A.M.–11 P.M.) serves breakfast, lunch, and dinner with tables inside (air-conditioned) or on a street-side terrace. Fresh fish and carne asada anchor a menu of Mexican fare.

Good, moderately priced Mexican breakfasts can be found at **Las Chabelas** (daily 8 A.M.–noon), on Mar Jónico Sur just off Chetumal. Look for a vintage 1928 Ford truck out front. Seating is on an outdoor patio that resembles a museum with antique artifacts, such as an old cast-iron stove and a horse-drawn buggy.

New Greenhouse (132 Av. Mar de Cortés, daily 7 A.M.–10 P.M., closed Sept.) is one of the only places to enjoy a not-too-greasy breakfast. For lunch and dinner, it serves tasty seafood entrées. The fish tacos are especially good, and inexpensive.

Restaurant Bar Los Mandiles (also known as La Esquina de Luis), diagonally opposite Baja Java, is one of the oldest restaurants in town. With its bar and pool table it's more of a local hangout, but the Mexican menu, mostly *antojitos,* is fine, and the sidewalk tables are a plus.

Rockodile Patio and Grill (on the *malecón*, tel. 686/577-1219) serves tasty fish tacos along with a tray of six different condiments. It also has burgers, fries, and huge beef tacos called "tacodiles." Food is served from around noon till midnight. **International Rosita** (daily 9 A.M.–10 P.M.), at the north end of the *malecón*, is a friendly, nautical-kitsch-decorated spot with good Mexican standards and seafood.

Cafés
You can also enjoy café latte and fresh baked goods, sandwiches, bagels, or a light breakfast at **Baja Java**, upstairs on the corner of Avenida Mar de Cortés and Calzada Chetumal. It has a sunny patio with a view of Bahía de San Felipe.

To the north of Calzada Chetumal on Avenida Mar de Cortés are several small, inexpensive cafés, including **Petunia's Café** at the corner of Calle Puerto de Acapulco and Avenida Mar de Cortés. The main draw: tacos and burritos, along with Mexican and American breakfasts. **Lonchería El Club,** near Rockodile on the *malecón,* is popular for Mexican breakfasts, including *chilaquiles,* one of Mexico's best hangover remedies.

International

At the golf course of La Ventana del Mar Resort, **Pavilion** (Mon.–Fri. 8 A.M.–7 P.M., Sat.–Sun. 8 A.M.–10 P.M., mains US$10–18) offers a gourmet menu with entrees such as fricassee of veal, walnut encrusted rack of lamb, and champagne poached scallops.

Groceries

Several *tiendas* along Calzada Chetumal on the way into San Felipe sell fresh vegetables, ice, canned goods, and camping and household supplies. **Mercado Baja** (Mar de Cortez and Calle del Telegrafo, tel. 686/577-1132) stocks a variety of meat, fruits, and vegetables. At least three bakeries are located along Avenida Mar Caribe: Las Flores, at Avenida Mar Caribe 210; Cornejo Brothers at Calle Ensenada; and Especial at Mar Caribe Norte 560.

To buy fresh, locally harvested finfish and shellfish, pay a visit to one of the *pescaderías* off Avenida Mar de Cortés just north of Punta Santa Felipe. Run by local fishing co-ops, they are usually open daily 7 A.M.–7 P.M. Look for **Pescadería Pepito** and **Pescadería San Felo,** or, on Calzada Chetumal at the traffic circle as you enter town, **Pescadería Rubén.**

INFORMATION AND SERVICES
Tourist Assistance

The state tourist office (Av. Mar de Cortés at Calle Manzanillo, tel. 686/577-1155) is open Monday–Friday 8 A.M.–7 P.M., Saturday 9 A.M.–3 P.M., Sunday 10 A.M.–1 P.M.

Money

There are half a dozen ATMs around town, including a machine at the 7-Eleven/Pemex station as you enter town, a Bancomer on Mar de Cortez, and a Banamex on Calzada Chetumal. There are also several *casas de cambio,* one at the end of Calzada Chetumal, across the street from the Beachcomber disco.

Post and Telephone

San Felipe's post office (Mon.–Fri. 8 A.M.–1 P.M. and 2–6 P.M.) is on Mar Blanco, a block south of Calzada Chetumal. Yet Mail Etc. (Av. Mar de Cortés 75, tel. 686/577-1255) offers P.O. boxes for U.S. mail delivery, as well as photocopy, fax, and message services.

Internet Access

The Net (Mar de Cortés, Plaza Canela 1, tel. 686/577-1600, www.sanfelipe.com.mx, Mon.–Fri. 8 A.M.–4 P.M., Sat. 9 A.M.–1 P.M., closed Sat. in summer), next to the El Cortez motel, charges US$4 per hour for high speed, wired or wireless access. Centrally located, less expensive (US$3 an hour), and bigger, is **Conexiones** (on Av. Mar de Cortés, daily 10 A.M.–9 P.M.).

Emergencies

The **St. James Infirmary** (tel. 686/577-0117) and the **police station** (tel. 686/577-1134 or dial 060) are located next to each other on the south side of town.

GETTING THERE AND AROUND
By Air

Currently there are no commercial airline flights to San Felipe.

Aeropuerto Internacional de San Felipe (tel. 686/577-1368) lies 9.2 kilometers (5.7 mi) southeast of the town center. For pilots flying private planes to Baja, San Felipe is a good place to clear customs and fill up on aviation fuel.

By Bus

San Felipe's bus depot is on Avenida Mar Caribe, south of Calzada Chetumal. **ABC** operates buses to and from Mexicali, Ensenada, and Tijuana. Bus tickets go on sale an hour before departure.

By Taxi

Local taxis wait for the occasional fare on Calzada Chetumal just west of Restaurant Bar Los Mandiles. You can order a taxi by dialing 686/577-1293. Fares in central San Felipe should run US$3–5.

By Car

Thrifty (Av. Mar de Cortez 75B, tel. 686/577-1277, www.thriftysanfelipe.com) has an office on the *malecón*. Rates range US$66–75 including insurance.

SOUTH TO MEXICO 1

This route offers hardy drivers the opportunity to see a side of Baja that can't be experienced from Mexico 1—a world of unpaved roads, subsistence ranches, fish camps, and desert coast wilderness.

◖ Valle de los Cardones Gigantes

Fifteen kilometers south of San Felipe, on the way to Puertecitos, photographers and naturalists will enjoy the chance to view the world's tallest cactus species up close in the Valle de los Cardones Gigantes. These towering cacti grow to heights of more than 60 feet and can weigh up to 12 tons. Many live to be hundreds of years old (see *Flora* in the *Background* chapter). Look for a turnoff near Km 14 on the east side of the highway, and follow the unpaved road about 200 meters to the park entrance. Bring your own water for hiking the trails.

To Puertecitos

The road from San Felipe to Puertecitos (85 km/53 mi), though paved, is in a fairly constant state of disrepair, especially south of the turnoff for Residence Faro Beach Trailer Park. In many places, a sand track parallels the paved road and provides a smoother ride for vehicles that can handle sandy surfaces. In some places, giant chunks of the road are missing, or there's heavy washboarding. Still, the road is passable by ordinary passenger vehicles—slowly. The *vados,* or places where dry culverts intersect the road, bear mention as they're some of the most treacherous in all of Baja. Road signs are mostly in English, as only Anglos seem interested in driving this desert road.

Indications of human habitation grow increasingly sparse the farther south you proceed. Three kilometers south of San Felipe lie a handful of condo developments. Just past the Residence Faro turnoff is a huge, unsightly trash dump right off the highway, used by Faro and other beach-camp owners. Around this point begins an enchanting desert landscape of mesquite, ocotillo, cholla, elephant trees, cenizo, and sage. **Punta Estrella,** a good beach for clamming, is 6–7 kilometers south of El Faro.

All the way to Puertecitos, every so often a beach camp is signed on the left. The going rate to park on the beach is around US$5, with facilities usually limited to drinking water and outdoor toilets. Numbers are multiplying year by year, and there's hardly a stretch of beach left that isn't affiliated with one camp or another. **Chelo's Café** (daily 7 A.M.–8 P.M.), at Km 35, makes a nice breakfast stop if you've started early. There's an adjacent curios shop, **El Toro,** and resident Dr. José López offers medical assistance to travelers at the **Clinica San Pablo.**

Campo García, 37.5 kilometers (23.3 mi) north of Puertecitos, is one of the better beach camps toward the north end. Between Km 38 and 40 is **Playa Mexico,** a more elaborate one with restaurant and lots for sale. At around Km 42, you'll start seeing isolated beach homes, some of them loosely associated with Mexican property management companies. At the same time, beach camps in this middle stretch tend to be primitive—perfect for self-contained rigs, not so good if you need hookups of any kind.

Closer to Puertecitos—beginning at around Km 54—the camps become more elaborate again. **Campo Playa Cristina, Campo Alejandra, Campo Turisto Vallarta,** and **Campo Los Pulpos** all appear to be fairly well run.

Just north of Puertecitos, **Playa Escondida RV Trailer Park** fronts a broad, north-facing cove with white sand, brick grills, *palapas,* picnic tables, and two-way hookups for US$10 a day. Around a small headland toward San Felipe, the smaller **Campo Las Chivas** charges US$5 a day for *palapa*-shaded sites ensconced between a rocky hill and some sand dunes.

Puertecitos is a large cluster of small wooden, stone, or cinder-block homes built around a shallow cove with a small beach at one end. Probably a beautiful spot at one time, today it's a jumble of mismatched shelters, rusting trailers, and discarded auto parts only a dune-buggy or fishing fanatic could love. An unnamed gated **tourist complex** offers a boat ramp, restaurant, airstrip, *tienda de abarrotes,* hot springs, camping (US$7), and beach *palapas.* The restaurant is open only Thursday–Sunday 8 A.M.–2 P.M. Gasoline is available from a Pemex station with inoperative pumps; fuel is dispensed from large plastic bottles next to the pumps. A mechanic's shop called Taller Panama can help with vehicle repair.

South of Puertecitos

South of Puertecitos the road is appropriate only for vehicles with sturdy tires and shocks. **Bahía Cristina,** roughly five kilometers (3 mi) south of Puertecitos, offers a few *palapas* on a large, reddish sand beach; you can camp here or at other tiny rock coves nearby for a fee of around US$2 a night, collected by local *ejidos.* Just south of Bahía Cristina, **Campo La Costilla** is a small gated trailer community where most sites are permanently occupied. The coastline around Cristina and La Costilla is rocky but suitable for hiking and fishing.

About 29 kilometers (18 mi) south along the coast are two small beach camp/retirement communities—**El Huerfanito** and **Nacho's Camp**—with minimal facilities for nonresidents. **San Juan del Mar,** another kilometer or so south, is a cluster of retirement/vacation homes similar to those farther south at Bahía San Luis Gonzaga. **Campo Tavo's,** just south of San Juan del Mar, offers primitive camping along a pretty bay. **Isla Miramar,** a few kilometers offshore, is a prime fishing destination for El Huerfanito, San Juan del Mar, and Campo Tavo's.

After another 30 kilometers (19 mi) several more fish camps appear, with cabins for rent, at **Punta Bufeo.** The onshore fishing here and at the nearby **Islas Encantadas**—five islands and several islets close to shore—is reputedly good for yellowtail, croaker, corvina, and sierra. Several of the Encantadas—San Luis, Pomo, Encantada, Lobos—are of volcanic origin, displaying pumice and lava deposits. The islands make a good kayaking destination, although offshore winds can blow forcefully in winter. **Campo Punta Bufeo** charges US$3 to camp on the beach; the premises hold a restaurant, outhouses, showers, an airstrip, and a long rock motel with basic rooms for US$18. It's a better deal than Alfonsina's farther south. Other reputable camps along the coast on or just north of Punta Bufeo include **Campo Los Delfines, Campo Islas,** and **Campo Las Encantadas.** Each offers campgrounds (typically US$5 a night) as well as boat transport out to the islands.

Punta Willard

About 12 kilometers (7 mi) south of Punta Bufeo is Punta Willard, home of **Papa Fernández Resort,** a campground with secluded *palapa* beach sites (US$5), outhouses (but no showers), gas, meals, and fishing *pangas* for rent. Just north of the Papa Fernández Resort, **Campo El Faro** offers similar facilities. Just a few kilometers below Punta Willard, at the south end of Bahía Willard on a sandspit connected to Isla San Luis Gonzaga during low tide, is **Alfonsina's** (Tijuana tel. 664/648-1951), the main supply point for visitors and residents enjoying large, pristine Bahía San Luis Gonzaga, the next bay south.

◖ Bahía San Luis Gonzaga

Popular with old Baja hands, the flat, gray-sand beach along remote Bahía San Luis Gonzaga reminds one of an earlier time. Lining the shore are a few dozen clapboard beach houses, some of which are elaborate two-story affairs while others are little more than small trailer shelters. Many are prefab structures that have been trailered down from the United States. Airplanes, boats, and dune buggies are parked alongside. Many visitors and residents are pilots; along the main unpaved road, airplanes have the right of way over cars and trucks. Next to Alfonsina's is an unpaved 700-meter (2,300-ft) airstrip; during monthly high tides it may be partially submerged, so if you plan to stay overnight, taxi your plane up onto one of the inclined ramps just above the high tide line. Nearby, next to Rancho Grande, are two newer 1,220-meter (4,000-ft) runways that don't receive tidal inundation.

Climb Punta Final (actually a small cape with five points and a small lagoon) at the south end of Gonzaga for a good bay view. Fishing *pangas* are available for rent at Alfonsina's. Rooms cost US$40. Alfonsina's restaurant is also rather upmarket, with the cheapest dinner for two with one beer each costing around US$15. Alfonsina's was once famous for its annual Memorial Day bash, which drew visitors from all over the peninsula.

Rancho Grande, a campground facing Bahía San Luis Gonzaga just south of the main strip of beach homes, offers *palapas* on the beach for US$5 a night. Facilities include showers, a minimarket, and several outhouses.

The entire 72.5-kilometer (45-mi) trip from Puertecitos to Alfonsina's takes 5–6 hours by car.

Bahía San Luis Gonzaga to Mexico 1 (Chapala)

From Bahía San Luis Gonzaga, a mostly graded but unpaved road leads southwest 64.5 kilometers (40 mi) to meet Mexico 1 at Km 229–230; the drive generally takes about 90 minutes— this stretch is usually in much better condition than the road north to Puertecitos. About 38 kilometers (24 mi) from Bahía San Luis Gonzaga, near Rancho Las Arrastras, the same road intersects an unpaved, partially graded road east to **Bahía de Calamajué,** another nearly untouched bay. You must pass through gated *ejido* property to reach the bay—you may have to search for someone to unlock the gate (ask at Coco's Corner). Rancho Las Arrastras offers some mechanical services and sells cold beer and sodas.

Coco's Corner, roughly halfway between Gonzaga and Mexico 1, consists of a small open-air café creatively decorated with beer cans and other discarded junk as well as desert plants. Owner Coco sells cold beer, soft drinks, and burritos. You can also camp here for US$5 a night—a primitive toilet and shower are available. A former Ensenada resident, Coco has lived alone in the middle of the desert here since 1990, following a 1989 accident in which he lost one leg. He speaks some English and is happy to dispense information on the area, including Calamajué, Gonzaga, and the road to San Felipe. Sign his guestbook, to which he will add a color sketch of your vehicle.

Reportedly, the Mexican government has plans to extend the paved road from San Felipe all the way to Bahía San Luis Gonzaga and eventually to Mexico 1. This would provide an alternative route to Baja California Sur, along the east coast via Mexicali, for drivers of ordinary, low-clearance vehicles.

CENTRAL BAJA

The Central Baja region, from El Rosario near the Pacific coast east to Bahía Los Angeles on the Sea of Cortez and south to La Paz, presents some of the most dramatic desert and coastal scenery on the entire Baja Peninsula, as well as a variety of inviting Mexican and gringo communities, from the saltworks town of Guerrero Negro and the palm oasis of San Ignacio to the river town of Mulegé, remote beaches of Bahía Concepción, and national marine park offshore from Loreto. Visitors come to watch whales in winter and catch fish in spring and summer. Deep in the interior, the region offers opportunities to view historic missions and Amerindian cave paintings.

PLANNING YOUR TIME

It takes about 15 hours to drive the 1,124 kilometers (693 mi) from El Rosario to La Paz, the beginning of the Cape region. If you're in a hurry, you can make it from Guerrero Negro to Cabo San Lucas (990 km/613 mi) in one long day of driving, with a stop for lunch in Loreto. But if your goal is to experience a little more of the peninsula (and to have a safer drive), you'll want to take more time. Allow 3–4 days to see the major towns along Mexico 1; longer for an excursion off Mexico 1 to a place like Bahía Los Angeles, Bahía Magdalena, or San Javier.

Mulegé and Loreto each offer enough activities to occupy visitors for at least a couple of

©JIMCLINE.COM

HIGHLIGHTS

◖ Misión San Ignacio Kadakaamán: At one time, this mission was the largest and most successful in Baja California, with a parish of more than 5,000 Amerindians. The church's elaborate facade, with its engraved stone plaques and plaster ornamentation, makes it one of the most impressive of all Baja's mission churches (page 182).

◖ Sierra de San Francisco Rock Art: Some of Baja's greatest historical treasures are hidden in the caves and arroyos of the Sierra de San Francisco, near San Ignacio (page 186).

◖ Playa Santispac: Sheltered from northerly winds, the largest and most popular beach along Bahía Concepción provides *palapa*-shaded beach camping and a safe launching point for kayaks (page 211).

◖ Loreto Bay National Marine Park: More than a decade ago, the Mexican federal government declared the entire marine system offshore from Loreto a national marine park, forbidding trawlers and commercial netters in a 60-kilometer zone from **Isla Coronado** in the north to **Isla Catalán** in the south. The result? A greater volume and variety of fish under the sea (page 220).

◖ San Javier: This tiny village southwest of Loreto contains one of the peninsula's best-preserved Jesuit mission churches (page 230).

◖ Bahía Magdalena: During the winter gray whale migration, outdoor enthusiasts head to shallow Magdalena Bay to see – and even pet – friendly mothers and calves (page 235).

LOOK FOR **◖** TO FIND RECOMMENDED SIGHTS, ACTIVITIES, DINING, AND LODGING.

weeks, including hikes to nearby Amerindian cave paintings, snorkeling, scuba diving, fishing, clamming, birding, and kayaking.

Weather conditions along the coast from Mulegé to Loreto are subtropical. December–March, daytime temperatures average 15–21°C (60–70°F); April–July, daytime temperatures run 26–35°C (80–95°F); and August–November the thermometer ranges 32–43°C (90–110°F). Annual rainfall averages 10 centimeters (four in), with much of the precipitation occurring in late summer and early fall. These weather patterns mean that, for most prospective visitors (divers and anglers excepted), August–November is low tourist season.

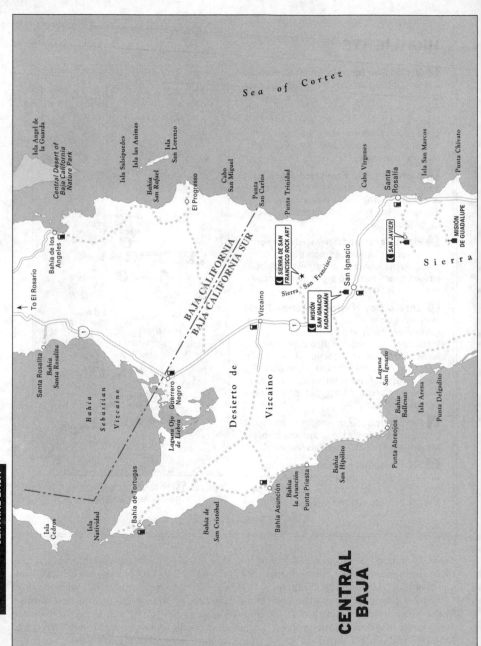

Sea of Cortez

Isla Angel de la Guarda

Central Desert of Baja California Nature Park

Isla Salsipuedes

Isla las Ánimas

Isla San Lorenzo

Bahía San Rafael

El Progresso

Cabo San Miguel

Punta San Carlos

Punta Trinidad

Cabo Vírgenes

Santa Rosalía

Isla San Marcos

Punta Chivato

BAJA CALIFORNIA
BAJA CALIFORNIA SUR

SIERRA DE SAN FRANCISCO ROCK ART

★

Sierra San Francisco

San Ignacio

SAN JAVIER

MISIÓN DE GUADALUPE

Sierra

Bahía de los Angeles

To El Rosario

Vizcaíno

MISIÓN SAN IGNACIO KADAKAAMÁN

1

1

Santa Rosalita

Bahía Santa Rosalita

Bahía Sebastián Vizcaíno

Guerrero Negro

Laguna Ojo de Liebre

Desierto de Vizcaíno

Laguna San Ignacio

Bahía Ballenas

Isla Arena

Punta Delgadito

Punta Abreojos

Bahía de Tortugas

Bahía de San Cristóbal

Bahía la Asunción

Punta Priesta

Bahía San Hipólito

Bahía Asunción

Isla Cedros

Isla Natividad

**CENTRAL
BAJA**

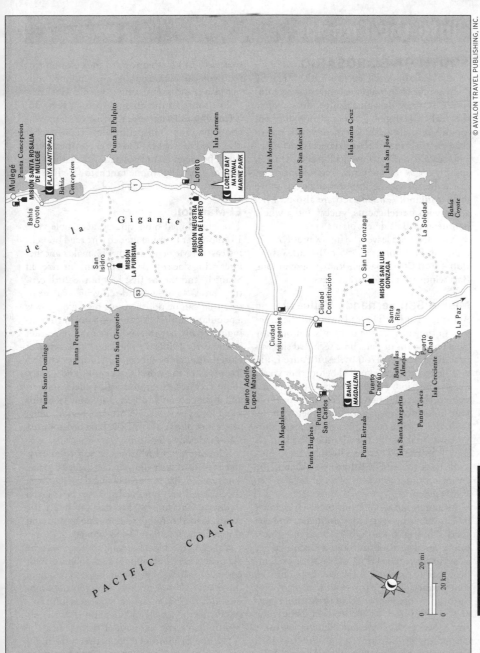

Into the Interior

SOUTH OF EL ROSARIO

After El Rosario, the Transpeninsular Highway drifts southeast, toward the center of the peninsula. For many Baja aficionados, this is where the "real" Baja begins. The population thins out rapidly, revealing 200 kilometers (120 mi) of the peninsula's most classic desert scenery.

Once across the Arroyo del Rosario (Km 62), spindly *cirios*, or boojums, begin appearing, gradually increasing in number as you move farther inland. *Cardón* cacti are also prolific, along with barrel cactus, yucca, and a whole pantheon of Baja desert plants.

A graded road leaves the highway at Km 78, traveling 56 kilometers (35 mi) southwest to **Bahía San Carlos,** a well-known spot among Baja windsurfers and surf anglers.

Misión San Fernando Velicatá

A dirt road at Km 114 leads west off the highway to the ruins of the only mission built by the Franciscans in Baja. The secluded site was first discovered in 1766 by Jesuit Padre Link, but the Jesuits were expelled before they could found a mission. Father Junípero Serra, on his way north, established San Fernando in 1769. Due to its location at a midpoint between the Gulf and Pacific coasts, it became an important way station on the Camino Real; at its peak 1,500 native devotees lived here. Dominicans took over the mission in 1772, but the entire community was wiped out by a 1777–1780 epidemic.

Although the adobe ruins themselves aren't much, the arroyo setting is dramatic, and the short side trip (8 km/5 mi) affords an opportunity for desert solitude and a chance to get closer to the regional flora and fauna. Two families operate *ranchitos* at the site, living off the slim bounty of the arroyo and making use of the original Spanish *acequias* (irrigation channels) built of stone block. Rock cliffs near the arroyo bear petroglyphs and pictographs, some created by the Cochimí in the 17th and 18th centuries, others possibly older. About 8 kilo-

meters (5 mi) farther toward the coast on this road you can view a couple of abandoned copper mines and the rusting ruins of a smelter.

Just south of the mission road, at Km 116, is **Rancho El Progreso,** the first of many ranchos along the Transpeninsular Highway that offer food to truckers and other passing motorists. The menu includes whatever's on the stove that day, usually simple ranchero fare like enchiladas, chiles rellenos, frijoles, and rice.

El Mármol

This abandoned onyx quarry, accessible via a 15-kilometer (9-mile) graded dirt road branching east off Mexico 1 at Km 143, makes another interesting side trip. *Mármol* means "marble" in Spanish, and for the first half of the 20th century, onyx—a brown-and-red-veined calcite or tufa that can be polished to a high gloss—was a popular marble substitute. A San Diego mining company began the El Mármol operation in the early 1900s; by the late 1950s, when it closed due to the advent of cheaper synthetics, many of the world's onyx inkstands, bathroom fixtures, floor and wall panels, statues, and other decorative objects had come from this site. Onyx's peak was the art deco period, when celebrities like actress Theda Bara ordered custom-made onyx bathtubs.

The onyx at El Mármol is easy to quarry, since layers of it sit right on the desert surface. The problem lies in transporting the stone from this isolated site; onyx slabs had to be trucked to Puerto Catarina (80 km west on the Pacific coast), loaded through the surf one by one, and shipped north to San Diego by boat.

Banded onyx blocks remain strewn about the old quarry site. The ruins of a schoolhouse built entirely of thick onyx blocks sit to one side of the quarry. About midway between the highway and the old quarry a huge mesquite tree stands next to a well and an antique Aermotor windmill, a scene right out of West Texas.

Off the El Mármol road, between the highway and the quarry, **Rancho Tres Enriques** offers meals and rustic accommodations. **Rancho (Lonchería) Sonora,** between Km 144 and 145 on Mexico 1, also serves food.

CATAVIÑA

This Mexico 1 way station at Km 174 lies in the middle of possibly the most spectacular desert scenery on the peninsula. Protected by **Parque Natural del Desierto Central,** it's a vast area of car-sized boulders, *cardón* cacti, elephant trees, *cirios,* and a hundred other desert oddities. Look for a new museum in a yurt a half mile north of town on the east side of the highway, which displays natural and cultural history exhibits and has interpretive trails for identifying desert plants. Several campsites are nestled among the boulders.

Cataviña Boulder Field

At the north end of the Desierto Central is an excellent area for hiking—except in summer when the heat is deadly.

Cueva Pintada

Just a short hike from the highway, a rock-art cave lies above Arroyo Cataviña (also known as Arroyo El Palmarito because of the fan palms growing here). From the Desert Inn/La Pinta Hotel, walk or drive three kilometers (2 mi) north along the highway to the second dirt track past a prominent *vado* where the arroyo crosses the highway, near the Km 171 marker. Proceed down the dirt road to the edge of the arroyo, which is usually dry at this point. If driving, park here. Before hiking across the arroyo, look for a white wooden sign on the other side, high up on a bouldered bluff a bit south of your position at the edge of the arroyo. This marks the way to the nearby cave. If you can't locate the sign, start hiking in the described direction and *maybe* you'll stumble on it. It's much easier to spot from the west side of the arroyo.

No one knows who painted the geometric patterns and humanoid figures on the rock face, though the Cochimí have been suggested, due to the presence of equestrian images.

During times of rain, you might find enough water in the arroyo for a refreshing swim.

Mission Ruins

A tough vehicle track—experienced dirt bikers or four-wheelers only—leads 23 kilometers (14 mi) east of Rancho Santa Inés, just south of Cataviña, to the adobe ruins of **Misión Santa María de los Ángeles,** the last New World mission (1767–1769) founded by the Jesuits. The site was known among the Cochimí as Cabujakamaang, "Place Where Spirits Dwell," when the Franciscans arrived in Baja. Though Father Junípero Serra refused to close the nonproductive mission simply because he found himself "addicted to the place," the mission was totally depopulated by 1800. The original roofs were palm thatch, so only portions of the adobe walls still stand. (Though touted today as a building aesthetic, the truth is adobe melts when exposed to rain.) A *palma azul* oasis near the ruins is almost worth the ordeal of negotiating steep grades, switchbacks, and melon-sized rocks—definitely a destination best reserved for obsessed historians or off-roaders.

Pacific-Coast Detour

Just north of Cataviña, a dirt road signed Faro San José 90 km leads to a lighthouse on the Pacific coast. From that point, you can head north to **Punta Canoas** or south to **Punta Blanca,** both renowned surf spots.

Accommodations

Cabañas Linda, a pink low-rise motel on the east side of Mexico 1, offers plainly furnished rooms for US$35. The proprietor, Lucy, also serves lunch or dinner daily for US$5 and coffee for US$1. She also allows camping in front of her place for US$5 in screened *palapa*-roof cabañas. A kilometer south of Cataviña, Lucy's mother offers ranchero food, hot showers, and bunkhouse accommodations at **Rancho Santa Inés.** Self-contained campers/RVers can also park here for US$6 a night, although the dirt lot is exposed to the wind. The ranch was originally founded by a Spanish mission soldier stationed at the now-ruined Misión Santa María farther inland.

One of the most recently renovated properties, the **Desert Inn/La Pinta Hotel** (tel.

200/124-9123, U.S. tel. 800/800-9632, www.lapintahotels.com, US$79) has large, clean guestrooms around a small pool.

Criolo cacti dot the grounds of the new **Parque Natural Desierto Central de BC RV Park,** which has 65 spaces with full hookups for US$6. Look for the sign on the west side of Mexico 1 before the Desert Inn/La Pinta Hotel. Several campsites are nestled among the boulders at the new museum.

Food

Antojitos Mexicanos, a tiny café at the north end of Cataviña on the east side of the highway, serves Mexican food and coffee. **Café La Enramada,** in front of the defunct highway Pemex station opposite Desert Inn/La Pinta Hotel, is similar but also stocks a few groceries.

Driving

The stretch of highway between El Rosario and either Bahía de los Ángeles or Villa Jesús María presents the most challenging fuel situation along the entire length of Mexico 1. It's best to top off your tank in El Rosario before heading south toward Cataviña. If you know your tank won't bring you as far as Cataviña, be sure to carry a spare can of fuel.

Opposite Desert Inn/La Pinta Hotel is a de-

funct Pemex station. The fuel tanks at the hotel station were replaced in late 2006, but the pump often opens only late in the afternoon, from 4 P.M. till dark. Even if you have plenty of fuel left when you reach Cataviña, top off again here before heading farther south. Occasionally the pump here runs dry. If that happens, you'll be stuck in Cataviña till more gas is delivered the next day.

SOUTH TO PARADOR PUNTA PRIETA

About 30 kilometers (19 mi) south of Cataviña, off the west side of the highway between Km 207 and 208, is **El Pedregoso,** a massive natural rock formation 610 meters (2,000 ft) high that looks as if it were constructed from a pile of boulders.

Between Km 229 and 230, a graded road heads northeast to Bahía San Luis Gonzaga and Bahía de Calamajué on the Sea of Cortez coast (see *San Felipe* in the *Mexicali to San Felipe* chapter). The *cirio, cardón,* yucca, and cholla in the area are often exemplary specimens.

Parador Punta Prieta is a defunct rest stop at Km 280. Mexico 1 splits here, with the east fork leading southeast 68 kilometers (42 mi) to Bahía de los Ángeles. Opposite the old *parador,* **Restaurant Los Dos Hermanos** serves inexpensive Mexican dishes daily 6 A.M.–10 P.M.

Bahía de los Ángeles

The highway to Bahía de los Ángeles passes thick stands of *copalquín* (elephant tree) as it winds through the Sierra de la Asamblea. The road was repaved in 2005, but drivers should always watch for large potholes. At Km 44, a four-wheel-drive-only track leads southwest 35 kilometers (21 mi) to the restored Misión San Borja; you can also access a better road of similar distance from Rosarito, off the west branch of Mexico 1. The final descent to the bay from the sierra affords an inspiring view of island-studded blue waters. The bay probably got its name because the white islands resembled someone's vision of angels floating in heaven.

Beginning in the late 1940s, American sportfishing enthusiasts began flying private planes into Bahía de los Ángeles; a few hardy souls even drove down here from San Diego and points north. Today, a new sailboat monument on the main boulevard through town harbors the arrival of visiting yachters, although so far the majority of Bahía de los Ángeles guests still come to fish, kayak, kiteboard, or windsurf. In 2007, power lines were to make their way to the bay, ending decades of reliance on a generator that shut down at night.

Behind the town park is the small but well-curated **Museo de Naturaleza y Cultura** (daily 9 A.M.–noon and 2–4 P.M.), displaying gold- and silver-mining exhibits, shells and fossils, two whale skeletons, ranch life re-creations, and a collection of Seri and Cochimí artifacts. The toylike locomotive in front of the museum once ran on the San Juan mine railway, 17.5 kilometers (11 mi) south of the current town. Volunteers staff the museum. Postcards, books, and monographs on Baja are for sale.

MARINELIFE
Mammals
A variety of whales—including Bryde's, minke, gray, finback, blue, sperm, humpback, orca, and pilot—as well as common and bottlenose dolphins ply the **Canal de Ballenas** between Isla Ángel de la Guarda and the peninsula. Bryde's (summer) and finback (winter) are the most common whales here, although every one of the aforementioned species is spotted year after year by visiting marine biologists. Dolphins are most numerous in summer and early fall.

Along island shores, the California sea lion is common year-round; during spring, northern elephant seals occasionally make an appearance.

Sea Turtles
The Sea of Cortez and lower Pacific coast are prime breeding areas for sea turtles, specifically the Pacific varieties of the green, loggerhead, hawksbill, and leatherback. At one time, Bahía de los Ángeles was one of Mexico's principal turtle fisheries, but overharvesting in the 1960s and 1970s placed every species under threat of extinction.

Programa Tortuga Marina, a sea turtle conservation and research station in operation since 1979, lies along the north shore of the bay behind Brisa Marina; cooperative local fishermen bring in sea turtles in hopes their chances of survival will increase and that someday there will again be a viable turtle fishery.

A loggerhead released from here in 1994 after several years in captivity was found in Japanese waters in 1995. Loggerheads nest in Japan, Australia, and Baja only, swimming with

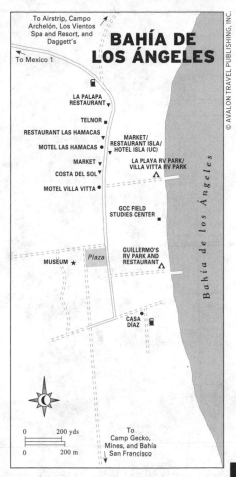

the Northern Pacific and Northern Equatorial currents. You can view sea turtles—both loggerheads and greens—in tanks at the facility.

SPORTS AND RECREATION
Hiking
Arroyos west of the bay lead into the Sierra San Borja; for a good day hike, pick out a dry wash and follow it. As long as you keep the bay in sight, it's impossible to get lost.

Mina Santa Marta, a nearby abandoned mine, makes an interesting hike. Along with the more successful Mina San Juan farther south,

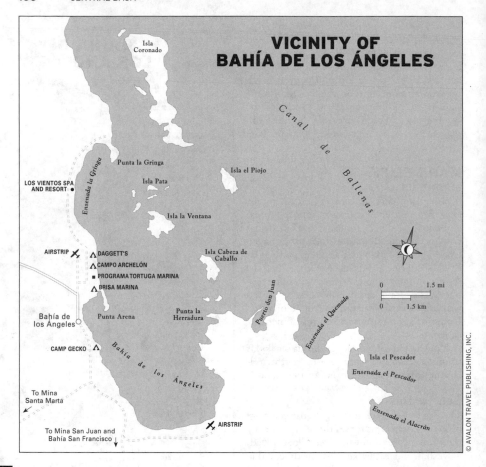

VICINITY OF
BAHÍA DE LOS ÁNGELES

Isla Coronado

Canal de Ballenas

Punta la Gringa

Isla el Piojo

Ensenada la Gringa

LOS VIENTOS SPA
AND RESORT

Isla Pata

Isla la Ventana

AIRSTRIP

DAGGETT'S

CAMPO ARCHELÓN

PROGRAMA TORTUGA MARINA

BRISA MARINA

Isla Cabeza de
Caballo

Puerto don Juan

Ensenada el Quemado

0   1.5 mi

0   1.5 km

Bahía de
los Angeles

Punta Arena

Punta la
Herradura

CAMP GECKO

Bahía de los Ángeles

Isla el Pescador

Ensenada el Pescador

To Mina
Santa Marta

To Mina San Juan and
Bahía San Francisco

AIRSTRIP

Ensenada el Alacrán

© AVALON TRAVEL PUBLISHING, INC.

Santa Marta operated during the 1890s using a cable-and-bucket system to transfer gold and silver ore (mostly the latter) from steep hillsides to a miniature railway below. Access to Mina Santa Marta begins about 3.5 kilometers (2 mi) south of Casa Díaz next to the town dump. Once you've located the dump alongside the graded road south, walk west until you come across the remains of the railway grade, then follow the grade west to the remains of the mine itself. The round-trip hike can be completed in one day, though many hikers spend a night at the mine.

The San Juan (also known as Las Flores) mine is reached by following the same road 17.5 kilometers (11 mi) southwest of the bay to Valle Las Flores. You'll see the remains of a smelter and boiler along the west side of the road. This road can be followed farther south into the Sierra San Borja, where there are several major Amerindian rock-art sites; inquire at local ranches for trail guides. The graded road continues southward through the sierra all the way to **Bahía San Francisquito,** approximately 132 kilometers (81 mi) south of Bahía de los Ángeles.

Fishing

Due to heavy local gillnetting, Bahía de los

Ángeles fishing is not what it once was, although recent years have seen improved catches compared with a decade ago. The best bets are onshore angling for sand bass, guitarfish, and triggerfish, or spring fishing at Punta La Gringa for croaker and halibut. Farther out at nearby islands—especially near **Isla La Ventana, Isla Cabeza de Caballo,** and **Isla Coronado**—you can try for yellowtail, white and black sea bass, dorado, tuna, and grouper. Most of the offshore fish run in the summer months, though yellowtail runs are sometimes seen January–March.

Any of the hotels or campgrounds in town can arrange rental *pangas* for either sportfishing or scuba diving trips. Daggett's, Guillermo's, Camp Gecko, and Casa Díaz can arrange guided fishing trips to the islands for around US$100–120 a day. Bring your own tackle; it's scarce in Bahía de los Ángeles.

Boating and Kayaking

Guillermo's, La Playa, Villa Vitta, and Casa Díaz each maintain boat launches; they also rent *pangas*. The bay is protected by the 68-kilometer-long (42-mile-long) **Isla Ángel de la Guarda,** but strong northeasterlies set up a nasty chop on occasion. Make local weather inquiries before venturing any considerable distance from shore.

Bahía de los Ángeles is popular among kayakers, who paddle to the nearby coves and islands. **Isla Coronado** (also known as Isla Smith) is three kilometers (2 mi) northeast of Punta La Gringa, while the southern tip of Isla Ángel de la Guarda is 19 kilometers (12 mi) away. Landings for day-trippers are usually easiest on the west side of the islands.

Most anchorages on Isla Ángel de la Guarda, the second-largest island in the Sea of Cortez after Tiburón, are a day's sail from Bahía de los Ángeles. **Puerto Refugio,** at the island's northern tip (64 km/40 mi from Bahía de los Ángeles), provides all-weather protection along with several coves and beaches, hence it's the most popular landing. Also good are **Caleta Pulpito** on the mideastern shore and **Este Ton** on the southwestern shore. The latter is the closest safe anchorage from the mainland. Explorations on Ángel de la Guarda can take in *cirio* stands, 1,200-meter (4,000-ft) peaks, and beaches with basking sea lions. The best sand beaches are along the island's southeastern reach. The common rorqual, or fin whale, occasionally visits the island's coastal waters, especially Canal de Ballenas to the west. This cetacean measures up to 24 meters (78 ft) long—only the blue whale is larger—and can be recognized by its small dorsal fin and long, flat, V-shaped head.

An easier two- to three-day kayaking circuit involves paddling from the bay to Isla Coronado and back, stopping at smaller islands Ventana, Pata, and Cabeza de Caballo along the way.

East and south of Bahía de los Ángeles, several coves have beaches and camping areas: **Puerto Don Juan, Ensenada del Quemado,** and **Ensenada del Pescador.**

It's possible to complete a "stepping stones" kayak route from Bahía de los Ángeles (or from farther south at Bahía San Francisquito) to Isla Tiburón and Bahía Kino on the Mexican mainland. The usual route, once followed by Seri Amerindians in reed canoes, is Partida–San Lorenzo–San Esteban–Tiburón–Kino, but navigating the currents requires advanced kayaking abilities and knowledge of local geography.

Kiteboarding and Windsurfing

Bahía de los Ángeles is a good bay for novice windsurfers and kiteboarders because of the lack of large swells. Prevailing northeasterlies are strongest in the northern parts of the bay. Try the 10- to 12-kilometer (6- to 7-mi) downwind run from Punta La Gringa through the small islands west of Isla La Ventana, then all the way to the town waterfront.

Diving

Daggett's campground (see *Camping and RV Parks*) can arrange dive trips in the bay through local resident Francisco, who maintains an air compressor and rents scuba equipment. For US$85 a day he will take a small group out on a 17-foot aluminum skiff to a rock reef at

La Ventana; price includes unlimited airfills. If you're going out on your own, you can buy air from Francisco.

Bird-Watching

The shores of Bahía de los Ángeles and the bay islands host a wide variety of bird life, including terns, pelicans, gulls, egrets, herons, cormorants, petrels, boobies, and ospreys. The most renowned local marine bird rookeries are **Isla Partida** and **Isla Raza.** The latter, a tiny, guano-covered, sparsely vegetated island of 250 acres, is the site for annual territorial wars between approximately 100,000 Heermann's gulls and 200,000 elegant terns, who battle for nesting grounds on the small island. The conflict—including "war formations" and egg-smashing—takes place in April; Casa Díaz can arrange special boat trips to view the annual event.

A number of rare royal terns and tropic birds also inhabit Isla Raza, declared a national wildlife sanctuary in 1964 to stop egg-hunters from destroying the bird populations. It's possible the gull-tern wars are related to the elimination of egg-hunting, which local Amerindians had practiced—albeit at a slower pace than their Mexican successors—for centuries.

ACCOMMODATIONS
Hotels and Motels

Presently, the local power plant still shuts down at 10 P.M. each night, plunging most hotels and motels into darkness until 9 A.M. the next morning; however, at press time, plans were in place to put the town on the grid.

Under US$50: Las Hamacas (no tel.), just south of the restaurant of the same name, offers 10 good-sized rooms with drinking water supplied and attached hot-water showers.

At the south end of town, the long-established **Casa Díaz** (no tel.) offers large, funky, bayfront rooms. The Díaz family operates a fishing and bird-watching guide service to the bay islands, as well as a small market and a Pemex pump.

The 40-room **Villa Vitta** (tel. 200/124-9103, U.S. tel. 619/454-6108, www.villavitta.com)

is a modern low-rise motel in the center of town. Facilities include a swimming pool, restaurant/bar, boat ramp, and ample parking. Room rates vary widely according to the occupancy rate and season—sometimes a fine value, other times overpriced. Water heaters are electric, so there's no hot water after 10 P.M.; the same applies to air conditioning. Fishing packages are available. An adjoining RV park and campground has 30 spaces with electrical hookups and 20 without, a dump station, and bathrooms/showers. Caravans are welcome.

US$50-100: Costa del Sol (U.S./Canada tel. 562/803-8873 or Mexico City tel. 555/151-4195, US$65), just north of motel Villa Vitta, has half a dozen rooms. Somewhat out of place in this rustic fishing village, the small hotel resembles a Mexican-style Holiday Inn with peach-colored stucco and a red-tile roof. Rooms are spacious and clean with hot showers, air conditioning, and 24-hour electricity. The hotel's small restaurant/bar serves breakfast, lunch, and dinner. It also rents kayaks.

The rooms at **Guillermo's RV Park and Restaurant** (tel. 200/124-9104) each have two king-size beds and one double bed, as well as air conditioning 24/7. Its restaurant serves seafood entrees for US$12–24 and fish tacos US$6. You can camp on the beach here for about US$5.

US$100-150: Three miles north of town, on the way to Punta la Gringa, **Los Vientos Spa and Resort** (Ensenada tel. 646/178-2614, U.S. tel. 619/308-7099, www.losvientos spaandresort.com, US$106–175) has a large stone fireplace in the lobby and 13 rooms and suites with air conditioning and power 24/7. On windy days, you can stroll to the pool or the beach in the robe that comes in your room.

Camping and RV Parks

Across the street from Motel Villa Vitta on the bay, 30 unshaded tent/RV sites with morning and evening electricity (plus 20 spaces without hookups), showers, flush toilets, dump station, and a boat launch are available at **Villa Vitta**

RV Park and Campgrounds for US$12. Adjacent **La Playa RV Park** offers 30 sites with full hookups, flush toilets, and a boat ramp for US$10.

Just south of Villa Vitta and La Playa is **Guillermo's,** a fairly well-run trailer park, motel, and restaurant operation with *palapas,* tent sites, and full hookups for US$12 per night. Facilities include a boat launch (fee for nonguests), showers, toilets (sometimes they flush, sometimes they don't; no seats), and a small market/gift shop.

Nine RV sites with full hookups are available at **Casa Díaz** for US$5 a night.

North of the sea turtle project, rustic and ecologically oriented **Campo Archelón** offers semicircular rock shelters with *palapa* roofs (some with old chairs in them), three outhouses, and a wood-fired *baño,* all within a few feet of the bay. The shelters cost US$10 for up to four people.

Daggett's, a well kept campground about a half mile north of Archelón, boasts wooden ramadas with grills alongside sizable campsites, plus separate showers and outhouses, for US$10. Daggett's also offers fishing trips and diving trips, as well as lots for lease.

A graded road continues along the bayshore as far as **Punta La Gringa,** the end of the bay and a fish camp/retirement community. Along the way are a number of open campsites where camping is free.

In the opposite direction, about eight kilometers (5 mi) south of town, lies secluded **Camp Gecko,** a unique spot featuring huts with rock walls and *palapa* roofs as well as simple open-sided *palapas.* The huts cost US$15, tent/camper sites are US$5. Larger, more substantial cabins with kitchens go for US$25. During the summer, you can probably negotiate rates of US$10 and US$3, respectively. The offshore breeze is refreshing, and the beach is kept exceptionally clean. Ramón, the man who runs the camp, leads fishing and whale/porpoise-watching trips aboard *pangas.*

Farther southeast of Camp Gecko you can find a number of bay-shore areas suitable for camping.

FOOD

Ostensibly because of Bahía de los Ángeles's relative isolation, food—whether bought in local markets or at restaurants—is pricier here than in many places in Baja. If pinching pennies, stock up in Guerrero Negro before coming.

Guillermo's well appointed restaurant/bar offers breakfasts for around US$4, dinner US$8, beer US$2. Specialties include fresh fish, shrimp, and lobster; the *palapas* out front are a nice spot for a margarita.

Restaurant Las Hamacas serves seafood and ranchero dishes for breakfast, lunch, and dinner (mains US$5–15). The restaurant also sells used paperbacks; proceeds reportedly go to the town museum.

The inexpensive **La Palapa Restaurant,** toward the north end of town on the west side of the main road, specializes in Mexican seafood, including fish tacos. **Tacos La Reyna,** in front of the town plaza, has cheap and filling tacos.

A couple of small *tiendas* in town sell canned food, beer, and staples. On Thursday, you can buy fresh vegetables from a vendor at the north end of the main road through town on the east side.

INFORMATION AND SERVICES

Telephones are still a relatively new phenomenon in town. A **TelNor** office on the main road offers long-distance phone service and Internet 9 A.M.–7 P.M. daily. **Isla Market** has high-speed Internet, stamps, and a mailbox.

Credit cards are not widely accepted; bring cash.

GETTING THERE AND AROUND

Bus service to Bahía de los Ángeles is nonexistent; to get here you need your own wheels, boat, or plane, or you must hitch from the Parador Punta Prieta junction. Once you've arrived, all of Bahía de los Ángeles is accessible on foot. For trips to the Punta La Gringa airfield, you can hire a taxi at Restaurant Las Hamacas.

The road from Mexico 1 was repaved in 2005, and paving had begun on the road out to Punta la Gringa. Look for a new Pemex station at the turnoff to Punta La Gringa, and a second one under construction just across the street.

Behind Casa Díaz is an auto mechanic's shop offering minor repair services and air for tires. The Pemex station at the Parador Punta Prieta highway junction has been closed for more than a decade.

A busy, paved airstrip serves small planes; buzz the town once for taxi service. Visit www.bajabushpilots for information.

South of Punta Prieta

Southwest of the Bahía de los Ángeles junction, the main section of Mexico 1 is marked by a new kilometer sequence beginning at Km 0. The ranch community of **Punta Prieta** is at Km 13; between Km 38 and 39 a graded gravel road heads west 13 kilometers (8 mi) to **Santa Rosalillita,** a fish camp below Punta Santa Rosalillita. Designated as the site of one of 28 nautical "steps" in the Mexican government's Sea of Cortez Project, the port at Santa Rosalillita will undergo considerable expansion as the project moves into its second phase in 2007–2012.

SURFING AND WINDSURFING

The Santa Rosalillita area is a well-known surfing destination; in a northwest swell, the point break at the north end of the bay reportedly offers Baja's longest ride (much depends on current bottom conditions). Windsurfers also enjoy the breaks and the bay's steady breeze. At the bay's south end, **Punta Rosarito** produces decent reef breaks in swells from any direction. If the waves aren't tipping right at either of these spots, follow the dirt road north out of Santa Rosalillita for 24–30 kilometers (14–18 mi) to breaks at **Punta Negra, Punta María,** and **Punta Cono**—all positioned perfectly to catch winter swells.

The wreck of the double-masted schooner *Jennie Thelin* (built in 1869, stranded in 1912) lies buried in the sand dunes along Bahía Santa María. The schooner and her captain, Alexander McLean, were the inspiration for the infamous ship *Ghost* and skipper Wolf Larson in Jack London's novel *The Sea Wolf.* The ship was reputedly often used to transport illegal immigrants and untaxed merchandise between the United States and Mexico.

SAN BORJA

This small ex-mission farm settlement in the foothills of the Sierra San Borja is well worth visiting if you have the time and if you and your vehicle are capable of driving rough roads. **Misión San Francisco Borja de Adác** was founded here by Jesuit padres in 1759 (or 1762 according to some chronicles), then handed over to the Franciscans in 1767 along with large numbers of sheep, goats, cattle, horses, and mules. In 1773, the Dominicans took charge of the mission property and the 1,600 Amerindian parishioners in the Adác (the original Cochimí name for the site) community. Although the mission was officially secularized in 1818, it is undergoing restoration and offers occasional services for local residents. Ruined adobe walls of the original Jesuit mission—the last to have been built anywhere on the peninsula—have been preserved. A stone spiral staircase in the *campanario,* or bell tower, of the later Dominican mission is impressive.

The fig, pomegranate, olive, guava, mango, and date orchards planted by the missionaries continue to provide a livelihood for mission caretaker José Ángel Gerardo Monteón, a fourth-generation Cochimí, and his family of seven. The mission is open daily 8 A.M.–6 P.M. José's children are happy to take visitors on a half-hour walk through the orchards to a small, clean hot springs. A longer, 1.5-hour tour to see local rock art—using your own vehicle—can also be arranged. The family doesn't ask any set fee for such tours, although a donation is much appreciated.

Two unpaved roads, each about 36 kilometers (22 mi) long, lead to San Borja. The faster and better-signed road, suitable for any sturdy, high-clearance vehicle, heads east from Rosarito on Mexico 1. Count on reaching the mission in about 45 minutes, an hour tops.

A considerably rougher track provides access from Km 44 on the road that links Bahía de los Ángeles with Mexico 1. Although this road is graded, there are still two or three spots where four-wheel drive is advisable due to the steep, slippery grades, deep *vados,* and stretches where you must drive 10 meters or more over basketball-size boulders. Coming from Bahía de los Ángeles, take the first fork to the left, then stay right. Just before reaching the mission area, roughly 34 kilometers (21 mi) from the road entry, you'll come to a three-way fork; the leftmost tong leads to San Borja. Along the way, you'll pass thick stands of *cirio* and elephant trees. Coming in this way takes about an hour and half. Assuming your vehicle is suitable, you could make a partial loop by entering via one road and leaving via the other.

ROCK ART

Northeast of San Borja are at least two major Amerindian rock-art sites: **Las Tinajitas** and **Montevideo** are well known. Las Tinajitas can be difficult to find—inquire in San Borja for a guide. Montevideo can be reached by high-clearance vehicle, preferably four-wheel drive for safe traverse across sections of deep sand.

The road between the Transpeninsular Highway and Bahía de los Ángeles provides the quickest access for Montevideo, a rock-art site of interest mainly because the journey there traverses superb desert scenery. Take the turn-off signed for Misión San Borja at Km 44 and head west into the desert. This graded gravel road is in fair condition for several miles. Turn left (south) after 3.5 kilometers (2.2 mi) onto a less-traveled road. After another 3.2 kilometers (2 mi) you should pass a small corral on your right. At this point the desert flora becomes thick and beautiful, with lush stands of *cardón,* ocotillo, and *cirio.* After another 6.4 kilometers (4 mi) you'll come to a large tree almost in the middle of the road, with a canyon wall on your right. Park here; you'll find the rock paintings—several *monos* (stylized human figures) and many more geometric designs—along the canyon wall. This spot would make a good campsite. As always, bring plenty of drinking water; assistance is scarce in this area.

PARALELO 28

The northern border of Baja California Sur, at 28° N latitude, is reached at Km 128. A giant Mexican flag and a 43-meter-high (140-ft-high) steel monument—a stylized eagle that looks more like a giant tuning fork—mark the border and the change from Pacific to Mountain time. South of the 28th parallel, kilometer markers on the Transpeninsular Highway begin at Km 220 and descend toward Km 0 (at Santa Rosalía). Mexico's First Cavalry maintains a military base around the perimeter of the eagle monument; a *puesto de control* often stops vehicles in either direction for a quick check. Be prepared to show your tourist card or visa.

Between the border and the town of **Guerrero Negro** (7 km south of the state border) is an immigration checkpoint and agricultural inspection station. Stops are now mandatory for all vehicles. In addition to checking your immigration papers, officials will spray insecticide under your vehicle (for which you may be charged about US$1).

Guerrero Negro and Vicinity

This town of around 10,000 took its name from the *Black Warrior,* a Hawaii-ported whaling barque that foundered in Laguna Guerrero Negro in 1858. Too overloaded with whale oil to leave the lagoon under its own power, the barque sank while being towed out to sea. This was just a year after Charles Melville Scammon "discovered" the Baja lagoons where migrating gray whales came to calve.

Within 20 years, tens of thousands of gray whales had been slaughtered and the whalers moved on to other Pacific hunting areas. But the gray made a remarkable comeback from the brink of extinction and currently numbers more than 20,000. Once again, the whales of Laguna Ojo de Liebre are attracting visitors, only this time the visitors are shooting photos instead of harpoons.

Today, a huge sea-salt-extraction facility, jointly owned by the Mexican government (51 percent) and Japan's Mitsubishi Corporation (49 percent), is Guerrero Negro's largest employer—see *Saltworks and Sand Dunes* later in this chapter for a description.

Note: After you cross the state line into Baja California Sur, don't forget to move your timepieces forward one hour; BCS follows the United States' Mountain Time.

CLIMATE

Temperatures in Guerrero Negro remain fairly steady year-round, due to the overall Pacific influence and the insulating effect of bays and lagoons to the west. Daytime highs are 21–24°C (70–75°F) in summer, 15–18°C (59–65°F) in winter. Rainfall is scarce, but an almost constant fog keeps the air moist in summer.

WHALE-WATCHING AT LAGUNA OJO DE LIEBRE

During the season, January–March, Laguna Ojo de Liebre (also known as **Scammon's Lagoon**) offers several whale-watching options. Local tour operators take small groups of up to 10 people for US$40 per person, which often includes a box lunch. One of the most popular tour organizers is **Malarrimo Eco-Tours** (tel./fax 615/157-0100, www.malarrimo.com). Prospective participants should book at the tour office next to Malarrimo Restaurant at least a day in advance. During the height of the season, vans leave daily from the restaurant at 8 A.M. and 11 A.M. and drive, via salt-company roads, to a shore of the lagoon, where a *panga* takes participants out on the water for about two hours. Passengers must arrive at the patio of the restaurant a half hour before departure time to sign the passenger list. Lunch, included in the tour fee, is served on Isla Arena, a large sandbar island covered in dunes.

You can book a similar tour at the same price through **Mario's Tours,** at Restaurant Mario's (no tel.; see *Food*) or **Laguna Tours** (tel. 615/157-0050) on Boulevard Zapata next to Motel San Ignacio.

A less expensive alternative is to drive on your own to the shore of the lagoon and deal directly with the *pangeros*. To do this, take Mexico 1 south of town 9 kilometers (5.5 mi) to the turnoff marked **Parque Natural de la Ballena Gris** and turn right (southwest). This 24-kilometer (15-mile) road alternates between washboard and sandy surfaces that sometimes require slow driving. After about six kilometers (3.5 mi), the road reaches a salt company checkpoint where you usually must wait for an attendant to open the gate. After the checkpoint, the road runs between two salt-evaporation flats; the drying salt looks like packed snow. The road ends at the edge of the lagoon, where a small parking fee is collected. If you don't have your own wheels, hire a cab from in front of the bus depot in Guerrero Negro out to the *panga* piers at Laguna Ojo de Liebre for about US$5; one cab can take up to five passengers.

Once you're at the shore, you can watch the whales from land or sign on with a boat tour. With a good pair of binoculars, you can see the whales from shore, but you get close enough to hear them blowing when you're on the water.

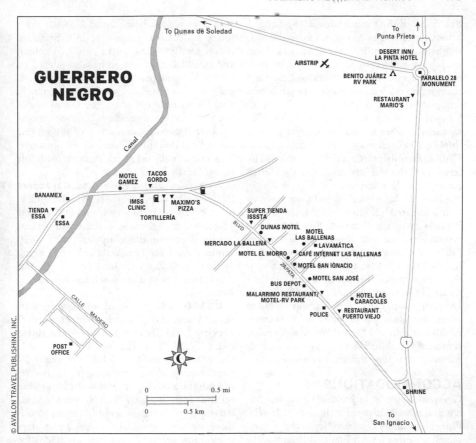

To Dunas de Soledad

GUERRERO NEGRO

To Punta Prieta

DESERT INN/
LA PINTA HOTEL

AIRSTRIP

BENITO JUÁREZ
RV PARK

PARALELO 28
MONUMENT

RESTAURANT
MARIO'S

Canal

MOTEL GAMEZ

TACOS GORDO

BANAMEX

IMSS CLINIC

MAXIMO'S PIZZA

TIENDA ESSA

ESSA

TORTILLERÍA

SUPER TIENDA ISSSTA

BLVD

DUNAS MOTEL

MOTEL LAS BALLENAS

MERCADO LA BALLENA

LAVAMÁTICA

MOTEL EL MORRO

CAFÉ INTERNET LAS BALLENAS

MOTEL SAN IGNACIO

ZAPATA

MOTEL SAN JOSÉ

BUS DEPOT

MALARRIMO RESTAURANT/
MOTEL-RV PARK

HOTEL LAS CARACOLES

POLICE

RESTAURANT
PUERTO VIEJO

CALLE MADERO

POST OFFICE

0   0.5 mi

0   0.5 km

SHRINE

To San Ignacio

© AVALON TRAVEL PUBLISHING, INC.

January–March, two or three boats are usually on hand at the park for charters. The going rate is US$25 per adult; boats leave 9 A.M.–3 P.M. only and stay out about an hour and a half. After 3 P.M., the wind comes up, fog comes in, and whale-watching conditions are poor.

Private boats, kayaks, inflatable rafts, and other floatables aren't permitted anywhere in Laguna Ojo de Liebre during the whale season. The *pangeros* who take tourists out to see the whales are granted seasonal permits to do so. They're also very skilled at running the *pangas* so as not to frighten or threaten the whales, most of whom are mothers and babies. The

males, for the most part, cavort near the entrance of the lagoon, farther from shore.

Once a year in March, travel photographer Jim Cline leads a **Baja Gray Whales** photo tour (U.S. tel. 877/350-1314, www.jimcline.com) from San Diego to the Ojo de Liebre lagoon. Tours include visits to Cataviña and San Ignacio, plus accommodations and seafood dinners.

SALTWORKS AND SAND DUNES

More important to the local economy than whale-watching tourists is the local saltworks, a large solar-evaporative operation producing around six million tons of salt a year. Exportadora

Sal, S.A. (ESSA) maintains a 182-square-kilometer (70-sq-mi) system of diked ponds southwest of town that take in seawater from the lagoons and impound it, at a depth of about one meter, until the fierce Vizcaíno Desert sun turns it into thick layers of salt. The salt is then scooped into trucks and driven to Puerto El Chaparrito at the north end of Laguna Ojo de Liebre, where it's loaded onto barges and shipped 80 kilometers (50 mi) northwest to Isla Cedros. From Isla Cedros the salt is shipped by freighter to the Mexican mainland, the United States, Canada, and Japan.

About 9.5 kilometers (6 mi) from town or four kilometers (2.5 mi) from Mexico 1 near Paralelo 28 are the **Dunas de Soledad,** a large system of coastal sand dunes up to eight meters (26 ft) tall. Along the other side of the dunes facing the Pacific is **Playa Don Miguelito,** a pristine beach named for the man considered the father of Guerrero Negro. In 1926, fisherman Don Miguelito came to the lagoon by burro all the way from Sonora and stayed in the area till his death in 1992 at age 96. You can reach the dunes by taking the wide sand/salt road off Mexico 1 near the Paralelo 28 monument.

ACCOMMODATIONS

Guerrero Negro has a handful of modest hotels and motels. Except for the Desert Inn/La Pinta Hotel, all of Guerrero Negro's hotels and motels are on or just off Boulevard Zapata, the main street through town, west of Mexico 1.

Hotels and Motels

Under US$50: Behind Motel El Morro on Calle Victoria, the quiet **Motel Las Ballenas** (tel. 615/157-0116, US$27) offers 14 carpeted rooms with TV and private bath. **Motel San José** (tel. 615/157-1420, US$31), across from the bus station, has simple, clean rooms with hot showers and color TV.

Near Malarrimo Restaurant, the two-story **Motel San Ignacio** (tel. 615/157-0270, US$27) offers 24 simple but cozy rooms with a relatively late checkout time (1 P.M.).

Adjoining the Malarrimo Restaurant, **Cabañas Don Miguelito** (tel./fax 615/157-

0100, www.malarrimo.com, US$40) rents rooms in detached trailer-style units. Standard rooms are furnished with a small TV, chair, and two beds that rest on hard wooden platforms. A sloped, beamed ceiling; yellow stucco walls; and cactus decor add a cheerful touch. Bathrooms have old plumbing but plenty of hot water and good pressure. Threadbare towels, bare lightbulbs, and a few empty sockets remind you that this is Baja. Four family rooms are done in colorful Mexican decor with loft bunks for the kids.

New as of 2006, **Hotel Los Caracoles** (Calz. de la República, tel. 615/157-1088, www.hotelloscaracoles.com.mx, US$43) has 13 rooms, with 5 more in the works. Access the Internet from the lobby only; the first 20 minutes are free. This hotel is located north of Boulevard Zapata, along one of the first cross streets as you approach the town from Mexico 1.

US$50-100: Just south of the state border and west of the Paralelo 28 monument off Mexico 1, the **Desert Inn/La Pinta Hotel** (tel. 615/157-1304, U.S. tel. 800/800-9632, www.lapintahotels.com, US$79) offers 27 large, comfortable rooms at higher-than-average rates. It's conveniently situated for getting on and off the highway but a bit overpriced for what you get. It's also a seven-kilometer (4-mi) drive into town; if you plan to spend a few days exploring Guerrero Negro, you might look for something in the town itself.

Camping and RV Parks

Coastal areas around Guerrero Negro offer plenty of free camping spots, but few are accessible by ordinary passenger vehicle. Camping is permitted along the lagoon in the Parque Natural de la Ballena Gris; a daily parking fee of US$5 is usually collected during whale-watching season, January–March. A few RVers have set up camp at a dirt lot near the old salt wharf, about 10 kilometers (6 mi) northwest of town via a graded road that meets Boulevard Zapata just past the Banamex.

In town next to Malarrimo Restaurant, **Cabañas Don Miguelito RV Park** (tel./fax

615/157-0100) offers 45 sites with electricity/ water hookups and dump stations for US$12 up to 35 feet, US$15 over 35 feet, or US$10 for campers and vans. Tent camping costs US$5 per person. Use of restrooms with hot showers is included in the rates.

Benito Juárez RV Park (formerly The Dunes), just south of the Desert Inn/La Pinta Hotel next to the state border off Mexico 1, has 18 electricity/water hookups (no shade) plus toilet and shower facilities for US$7–9.

FOOD

Guerrero Negro has several places to eat and a couple of supermarkets that supply residents as far away as Bahía de los Ángeles and San Francisquito. Like the hotels and motels, most are spread out along Guerrero Negro's main avenue, Boulevard Zapata.

The most popular restaurant in town, especially for gringos, is **Malarrimo Restaurant** (tel. 615/157-0100, daily 7 A.M.–11 P.M., mains US$10–20), on the north side of Boulevard Zapata as you enter Guerrero Negro. The pismo clams, deep-sea scallops, lobster, and other fresh seafood are always good. Breakfasts are another highlight, and include lobster omelets, homemade chorizo and eggs, and other diet-busters, served with beans, *chilaquiles,* and tortillas. Near the edge of town, **Puerto Viejo** (daily 7 A.M.–11 P.M., mains US$10–20) offers a similar menu.

Close to the Pemex on the north side of Zapata, **Carnitas Michoacán** (daily 9 A.M.–8 P.M., tacos US$1) serves shredded pork in tacos, *tortas,* and *desebrada* styles. Across from the hospital on the north side of Zapata, toward the saltworks plant, **Tacos El Gordo** (Mon.–Sat. 8 A.M.–3 P.M. and 6 P.M.–midnight, Sun. only in morning, tacos US$1–2) draws a crowd for carne asada.

On the south side of Boulevard Zapata, roughly across from the first Pemex and Tacos Gordo, **Maximo's Pizza** (Tues.–Sun. 11 A.M.–10 P.M., mains US$3–6) prepares a menu of burgers, *tortas,* pizza, and pasta. Dine in air-conditioned comfort inside.

At the edge of town, across from the Hotel San José, **Paris Café** (tel. 615/157-1510, daily 7 A.M.–10 P.M.) brews espresso drinks to go with burgers, salads, and yogurt.

Groceries

Guerrero Negro has the only supermarkets south of Ensenada and north of Santa Rosalía. **La Ballena** is the largest and most popular of the pair on Boulevard Zapata and is the only store in town that accepts travelers checks. It stocks an amazing variety of things, including full picnic supplies.

The government-subsidized **Tienda ISSSTE** carries basic grocery items at discounted prices. **Tienda ESSA,** across from the main entrance to the salt plant, around the corner from Banamex, is similar.

INFORMATION AND SERVICES
Tourist Assistance

The tourist office (tel. 615/157-0100, daily 10 A.M.–2 P.M. and 4–7 P.M.) in front of Malarrimo Restaurant has information on Guerrero Negro and the surrounding areas.

Money

A **Banamex** (Mon.–Fri. 8:30 A.M.–3 P.M.) near the ESSA buildings, near the end of Boulevard Zapata, offers an ATM, as well as a currency exchange service.

Telephone and Internet Access

Except for the **TelNor** office in Bahía de los Ángeles, Guerrero Negro has the only public telephone service in a 200-kilometer (120-mi) radius. Several privately operated phone offices in town add service charges to the cost of any call. Collect calls can be made at the public phone booth in front of Malarrimo Restaurant for no charge.

Next to Motel Las Ballenas, **Café Internet Las Ballenas** (Mon.–Sat. 10 A.M.–1 P.M. and 4–9 P.M.) offers high-speed Internet access.

Laundry

Opposite Motel Las Ballenas, **Lavamática Express** (daily 8 A.M.–9 P.M.) offers coin-operated washers and dryers.

GETTING THERE
By Air to/from Isla Cedros
Aero Cedros (tel. 615/157-1626) operates flights to and from Isla Cedros daily at 10 A.M. The flight lasts about 40 minutes, and one-way tickets cost US$55; the airline office, next to the police station on Boulevard Zapata, is open Monday–Saturday 9 A.M.–4 P.M.

Guerrero Negro's airfield is north of town near Paralelo 28, a few hundred meters off Mexico 1; the turnoff occurs between Km 125 and 126.

By Bus
Transportes de Águila and **ABC** use a small depot on the west side of Boulevard Zapata (btw Malarrimo Restaurant/Motel San Ignacio). Five first-class buses head north daily to Punta Prieta, San Quintín, Ensenada, and Tijuana, and south to Vizcaíno (US$5), San Ignacio, Santa Rosalía, Mulegé, Loreto, Ciudad Constitución, and La Paz (US$70).

GETTING AROUND
Yellow *urbanos,* or city buses, marked **Infonavit-Centro,** run frequently between the Paralelo 28 monument and the old town via Boulevard Zapata and Calle Madero; the fare is less than US$1. You can hire taxis at the bus depot; a cab ride to anywhere in town costs about US$5. The Pemex stations in town often seem to run out of premium grade fuel.

SIDE TRIP TO SAN FRANCISQUITO
A side trip east out to the Sea of Cortez passes through good desert mountain scenery and terminates in the small, secluded fish camp of San Francisquito on Bahía Santa Teresa. The turnoff for San Francisquito (signed for El Arco) occurs about 27 kilometers (16.5 mi) south of the Guerrero Negro junction. From the highway, the 121-kilometer (75-mi) road to the bay takes 3–4 hours, including the steep downgrade known as Cuesta de la Ley (Slope of the Law), which comes along approximately 29 kilometers (18 mi) before San Francisquito. The grade has been lessened and is not quite as challenging as it once was. Modest supplies may be available along the way in El Arco, 34 kilometers (21 mi) east of Mexico 1. Many roads join the main one east of El Arco, and you may have to ask directions along the way to ensure you're on a direct course for San Francisquito.

You can also reach San Francisquito by road from Bahía de los Ángeles in about the same amount of time. Count on lots of washboard along either road; be sure to gas up first in Bahía de los Ángeles, Guerrero Negro, or Vizcaíno. Both roads meet near Rancho El Progresso, approximately 21 kilometers (13 mi) east of Bahía San Francisquito. The network of roads surrounding the ranch can be a trifle confusing; take the branch heading due east to reach the bay (a southeasterly branch goes to the fish camp of El Barril).

Accommodations and Camping
San Francisquito Resort (U.S. tel. 619/690-1000) maintains five simple, thatched-roof cabañas right on the beach. The resort charges US$15 per person for accommodations only, or US$30 with breakfast and dinner. *Pangas* are available for hire starting at US$80/day. Dive trips out to Isla San Lorenzo, Isla San Esteban, and other nearby islands can also be arranged. Rental tanks are available, but you must bring your own regulators. Camping on the grounds is permitted for US$5 per person, which includes use of hot-water showers and restrooms.

Vizcaíno Peninsula

Jutting northwest into the Pacific, the coast of this huge desert peninsula is renowned among outdoor adventurers for the abundant opportunities to participate in their favorite recreational activities far from "civilization." The isolation and long distances involved in navigating the peninsula's interior deter the casual visitor, despite the fact that the roads aren't really all that bad. The greatest distance between Pemex stations on the Vizcaíno Peninsula is 166 kilometers (100 mi). More critical is the lack of automotive and medical assistance along lengthy stretches of road.

Although most visitors head straight for the peninsular shores, a leisurely drive through the interior affords close, uninterrupted views of the Vizcaíno Desert. Rainfall is scant, and the desert vegetation mostly survives on Pacific fog; yucca trees *(datilillos)* are particularly abundant. Several of the cactus and succulent species chosen for Biosphere II—an experimental dome environment in Arizona—were borrowed from this desert.

Fuel, food, and other supplies are available at four cannery towns along the southwest coast of the peninsula and, to a much lesser extent, from a handful of fish camps and ranchos between these settlements. A comprehensive loop trip involves driving west from Vizcaíno (Mexico 1, Km 144) to Bahía Tortugas or Bahía Asunción, then southeast to Punta Abreojos and back to Mexico 1 at Km 98. Beach camping is possible at numerous spots between Bahía Asunción and Punta Abreojos, and rustic rooms are available in Bahía Tortugas.

The best onshore/inshore fishing areas are generally between Bahía Asunción and Punta Abreojos. Typical catches include halibut, corvina, croaker, and sand, calico, and pinto bass.

Reserva de la Biósfera del Vizcaíno

Since 1988, much of the peninsula has belonged to the Reserva de la Biósfera del Vizcaíno, the largest such reserve in Mexico and one of the largest in the world at more than 2.5 million hectares (77 percent of the Mulegé *municipio*). In 1993, Vizcaíno was added to UNESCO's list of "Man and the Biosphere" reserves. Sixteen different core zones, where human activity is heavily restricted, comprise 363,438 hectares; the remainder are buffer zones where limited activity is permitted. In addition to peninsular areas, the reserve boundaries take in all or parts of the islands of Isla Delgadito, Islotes Delgadito, Isla Pelican, Isla Malcob, Isla San Ignacio, Isla San Roque, Isla Asunción, and Isla Natividad. Coastal waters along the peninsula harbor at least 66 percent of all marine mammal species in Mexico, including eight dolphin and 15 whale varieties.

Aerial surveys have confirmed that around 200 rare *berrendo* (desert pronghorn) survive on the peninsula. The only antelope in the world that doesn't need to drink water, the *berrendo* satisfies all its moisture needs through the ingestion of plants, which are in turn nourished on Pacific fog. Other rare fauna include the *borrego cimarrón* (desert bighorn sheep), fishing eagle, white pelican, peregrine falcon, loggerhead sea turtle, and elephant seal.

Vizcaíno

Also known as Fundolegal and on American maps as Vizcaíno Junction, this small town on Mexico 1 is the easiest starting point for any peninsula trip, not least because supplies are available here. The bulk of the pueblo (pop. 2,500) lies west of the highway on the road leading into the peninsula interior, but several services lie along Mexico 1 itself. A huge packing plant processes local produce, so the junction is often lined with parked 18-wheelers.

Driving the Vizcaíno Road

The first 35 kilometers (22 mi) of the 166-kilometer (103-mi) Vizcaíno road are paved, after which, depending on how recently it has been graded, the unpaved surface tends toward heavy washboard. At some points along the way, parallel sand roads may provide smoother passage.

In other places, salt flats offer several hundred meters of flat surfaces. About eight kilometers (5 mi) south of the Bahía Asunción junction is an attractive area of *bolsones* or salt-flat wetlands. Those with four-wheel-drive vehicles can make a side journey to **Playa Malarrimo** via a challenging track that branches north off the Vizcaíno–Bahía Tortugas road 116 kilometers (72 mi) from Mexico 1, near Rancho San José de Castro. It then winds through arroyos and around mesas for 44 kilometers (27 mi) before fading out at the dunes behind the beach. Malarrimo receives the brunt of northwest Pacific currents and is therefore a beachcomber's paradise. It takes a hardened beachcomber to appreciate the beach, however, since much of the flotsam washed ashore consists of the dregs of civilization—Styrofoam, plastic, and garbage jettisoned from ships throughout the North Pacific.

In 2006, local construction crews began to pave a four-mile stretch of road connecting Vizcaíno to Asunción Bay and Tortugas Bay, as well as a three-mile stretch from Fisher Camp to Punta Abreojos and another three miles from Punta Eugenia to Vizcaíno and Tortugas Bay.

BAHÍA ASUNCIÓN AND PUNTA ABREOJOS
Bahía Asunción

Bahía Asunción (pop. 1,200) lies 42 kilometers (26 mi) southwest of the Vizcaíno–Bahía Tortugas road via a fair, unpaved branch road. You can also reach Asunción via a second, longer road that leaves the Vizcaíno road farther northwest near Rancho San José del Castro. The latter makes a perfect approach for motorcyclists, as it's a sand road with lots of mogul-like hills; the northern section of this road passes through a low mountain range as well.

The town consists of clusters of ramshackle homes, trailers, small businesses, and sand streets around a pretty, sharply curving bay. Services include an unsigned Pemex station, SEMARNAT office (government entity responsible for issuing permits for island visits), airstrip, marine products processing plant, clinic, and a few markets and cafés. Just north of town is a small beach.

Restaurant El Mayico, on the main strip through town, is a clean and friendly spot serving seafood, eggs, quesadillas, coffee, and cold beer.

Estero de Coyote

South of Bahía Asunción, this complex of lagoons and salt marshes a few kilometers east of Punta Abreojos is well known as fishing grounds for bass (spotted bay and barred), corvina, and halibut. Anglers also take grouper and sierra at the mouth of the estuary, where it drains into the Bahía de Ballenas. You can camp on the beach near the mouth of the estuary.

Services are minimal in La Bocana and Punta Abreojos—the two nearest towns—though barrel gas is usually available in both.

BAHÍA TORTUGAS

The largest Vizcaíno town (pop. 2,640) lies 166 kilometers (100 mi) from Vizcaíno junction on Mexico 1. Aside from a cannery and Pemex station, the town offers several markets and cafés, a clinic, post office, modest motels, and an airfield. Most of the buildings—brightly painted in pinks, blues, and oranges—are constructed of wood that arrived by boat from the American Northwest. The dry hills around Tortugas bear almost no vegetation, and the little town swirls with dust and sand.

A gray sand beach not far from the town's long wooden pier looks inviting, but with all the shipping and boating in the area it's doubtful the water is clean. Toward the southeast end of the bay are some longer sand beaches. Bahía Tortugas's harbor is the best between Ensenada and Bahía Magdalena in terms of all-weather protection.

North of Bahía Tortugas, 26.5 kilometers (16.5 mi) by graded dirt road, is **Punta Eugenia,** a small fishing village and jumping-off place for boat trips to Islas Natividad, Cedros, and San Benito.

Accommodations and Food

Motel Nancy (tel. 615/158-0100, US$15–20), housed in a bright blue, U-shaped building around a small parking lot, offers modest rooms with private hot-water showers. The motel office is in Novedades Lupita, next door. On the southwest side of town, **Motel Rendón** is a two-story cinder-block place with similarly priced rooms.

Near the entrance to town via the Vizcaíno road, **Taquería El Muro** sells tacos and *antojitos*. **Restaurant El Moroco,** near Motel Rendón, has a more complete menu that includes fresh seafood.

Information and Services

You can cash travelers checks at a **Banamex** just up the street from Motel Nancy. A *farmacia* on the same street (Juárez) offers long-distance phone and fax services. You can also make calls from a **Telecomm** office in town and from the Motel Vera Cruz.

ISLA CEDROS

Baja's largest Pacific coast island not of oceanic origin is 20 kilometers (12 mi) north of the tip of the Vizcaíno Peninsula, or about 72 kilometers (43 mi) northwest of Guerrero Negro. The two main industries on the 24-kilometer-long (14.5-mi-long) island are fishing and off-loading salt from Guerrero Negro's saltworks for long-distance shipping. Because of the salt business, Cedros ranks as Mexico's third-largest port after Veracruz and Tampico, carrying more than 9 percent of all offshore cargo. It is also the sixth most populated island in Mexico (pop. 3,000).

Note: Isla Cedros lies in the same time zone as Baja California Norte; i.e., an hour behind Guerrero Negro.

Flora and Fauna

Among naturalists, Isla Cedros is known for its small stands of scrub juniper and pine in the center of the island between its tallest peaks, Pico Gill (1,063 m/3,488 ft) toward the north end and Cerro de Cedros (1,200 m/3,950 ft) toward the south. Like cedars, the island's mistaken namesake, junipers belong to the cypress family. Even more impressive are the Cedros Island oak *(Quercus cedrosensis)* and Cedros Island pine *(Pinus radiata* var. *cedrosensis),* both endemic to this island. A rare variety of mule deer reportedly inhabits the island's center. Date palms stand along the northeast coast; no one remembers who planted them.

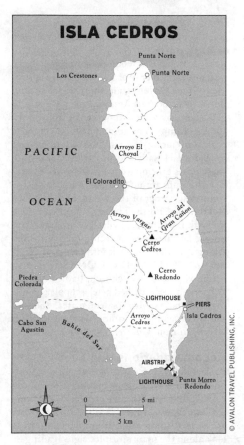

Cerro de Cedros

A three-hour hike from town to the island's high point leads to good views. To reach Cerro de Cedros, follow the road northwest out of town till it ends at a trail that follows a water pipe most of the way up the hill. Keep an eye on the summit's radio towers and you'll have no problem following the trail.

Around the Island

From the town and airport, the nearest good beach is at **Punta Prieta,** at the southwest end of the island; locally this beach is referred to as Playón. Taxis cost a standard US$10 for the 10-kilometer (6-mi) trip from town. After

Punta Prieta, the vehicle road ends, but a rough track continues along the coast. You can also reach Playón by traversing the island via Cerro de Cedros, but this requires an overnight at the beach—carry plenty of water. Surfing is possible at **Playa Elefante,** an empty stretch of sand north of Cabo San Agustín; the only way to get there is by *panga* from town or from one of the fish camps. The going rate for a complete coastal circuit by *panga* is US$80–100. A *panga* to nearby Isla Natividad also costs US$80–100; these boats take up to five passengers.

Fish camps are at **Cabo San Agustín,** on the southwest corner of the island, and at **Punta Norte** to the north. The largest settlement on the island, **Cedros,** is a village of around 2,500 on the southeast coast facing the peninsula. Along the main street leading from the harbor are a COTP office, CONASUPO, fish cannery, post office, church, bank (travelers checks cannot be cashed here), school, a couple of cafés, and a sizable residential area. South of the village along the same coast are the docks where salt from Guerrero Negro is off-loaded.

Accommodations and Food

Basic lodgings in *casas de huéspedes* (guesthouses) in town can be arranged for under US$25; the best of the two or three in operation is **Casa Elsa García** (US$15–20). If it's full, ask a taxi driver for other recommendations or look along the main street for signs reading Se Rentan Cuartos. Primitive camping on a rocky beach north of town is also an option.

La Pacenita (daily 6 A.M.–8 P.M.), a block south of the main drag and two blocks inland from the harbor, offers a basic menu of Mexican fish, chicken, and beef dishes. The nearby **Restaurant El Marino,** on the north side of the main street three blocks from the harbor, has more expensive—though not necessarily tastier—Mexican dishes and seafood.

Getting There

Aside from sailing over in your own boat, the easiest way to reach the island is by plane. Aero Cedros flies from Guerrero Negro daily at 10 A.M. for US$55 each way; the flight takes

around 40 minutes. The return trip leaves straightaway, and you need to be at the airfield early in the morning to be sure of securing a seat. Sociedad Cooperativa de Producción Pesquera (Cannery Airlines) also flies periodically from Ensenada. The island's paved airstrip lies south of Cedros village at Punta Morro Redondo. It's sometimes possible to charter a boat to the island from either Bahía Tortugas or Punta Eugenia.

A taxi from the airfield into town costs US$5 per car. Up to five passengers can split the fare.

OTHER ISLANDS
Isla Natividad

During the Spanish missionary period, a Cochimí subtribe lived on this arid island 10 kilometers (6 mi) northwest of Punta Eugenia, calling it Afegua, or Island of Birds. Eventually a Jesuit padre from Misión San Ignacio convinced them to leave the island and live at the mission. Renamed Christmas Island, today it's one of the most famous **surfing** destinations along the Pacific coast of the Americas.

Most of the island's surf action can be found at the southern end of the island. The most popular Natividad break, Open Doors, is off the southwest tip; it catches summer swells from the southwest—peak time is generally July–September. Waves here typically run 4–6 feet, with occasional sets up to 15 feet. Frijole Bowl, off the southeastern tip (Punta Arenas), also catches southern or southwestern swells. In winter, large breaks—for pros only—are found at the northwest and southwest tips; the former break can be reached only by boat. The small village of Isla Natividad, on the southeast shore of the 22.5-square-kilometer (14-sq-mi) island, houses around 200 fishermen during the summer. In winter many visit relatives on the peninsula or work on farms in the Ensenada area. Thus boats out to the northwest shore break should be arranged in Punta Eugenia. Or bring your own.

In Punta Eugenia you can charter a boat to Isla Natividad for US$15 one-way; the best time to find a boat is the early morning, when local fishermen are heading out to sea. Like-

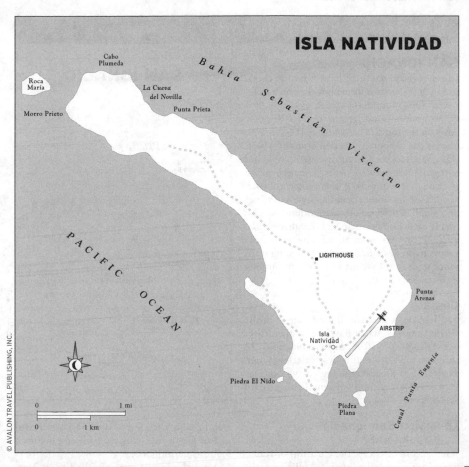

ISLA NATIVIDAD

Cabo Plumeda

Roca María

La Cueva del Novilla

Morro Prieto

Punta Prieta

Bahía Sebastián Vizcaíno

PACIFIC OCEAN

LIGHTHOUSE

Punta Arenas

Isla Natividad

AIRSTRIP

Piedra El Nido

Piedra Plana

Canal Punta Eugenia

0   1 mi

0   1 km

© AVALON TRAVEL PUBLISHING, INC.

wise, afternoons 2–3 P.M. are best for boat rides back to Punta Eugenia. Boat transportation to and from Isla Natividad can be difficult in the winter, when the island is mostly deserted.

In summer, and when there are enough passengers, Sociedad Cooperativa de Producción Pesquera flies to the island from Ensenada via Isla Cedros. The airstrip is less than a half kilometer from the village of Isla Natividad. The island has a clinic to handle small injuries.

Islas San Benito

This group of three small islands (Isla Benito del Este, Centro, and Oeste), about 25 kilo-meters northwest of Isla Cedros, has the best yellowtail fishing on the Pacific coast. Boats usually anchor along the leeward (southeastern) shore of Isla Benito del Oeste, opposite the tiny village of Benito del Oeste. Elephant seals, the world's largest pinnipeds, often sun themselves along the coves north of the village.

Rock reefs along the western shores of all three islands provide the best diving and fishing opportunities. Divers may be interested in the wreck of the U.S. tanker *Swift Eagle,* which went aground in 1934 off the north shore of Isla Benito del Oeste; parts of the wreck lie within two meters of the ocean surface.

San Ignacio and Vicinity

SAN IGNACIO

In pre-mission days, the local Cochimí called the sheltered arroyo formed by the Río San Ignacio Kadakaamán, or Creek of Reeds. Fed by an underground stream, this fertile palm oasis on the southeastern edge of the Vizcaíno Desert has supported mission crops of wheat, figs, grapes, pomegranates, oranges, corn, and dates for more than 200 years. The sleepy town of San Ignacio (pop. 4,000) is a cluster of stuccoed, pastel-colored, colonial-style buildings and small *rancherías* centered around Misión San Ignacio Kadakaamán and the adjacent *plazuela.* Hemmed in on all sides by mesas, the town's palm-oasis ambience and ongoing resistance to change have made it a favorite among Baja travelers for decades.

Climate

San Ignacio is pleasant, if a bit buggy, in the winter months, when daytime temperatures are 18–21°C (65–70°F), nights a bit cooler. In summer, the surrounding desert sizzles as high as 40°C (105°F), although the valley floor may be a few degrees cooler. Rainfall is nearly nil year-round.

◖ Misión San Ignacio Kadakaamán

Jesuit records indicate the Cochimí of Kadakaamán sent several requests for mission assistance to Italian Jesuit Padre Píccolo of Misión Santa Rosalía de Mulegé in the early 18th century. Píccolo first visited the area in 1716 and stayed in a brush cabaña for a month, apparently converting and baptizing a willing Amerindian population. In 1728, Jesuit Padre Juan Bautista Loyando constructed a church and mission house on the present site, then proceeded to build a number of visiting chapels at nearby *rancherías.* He was succeeded by Padre Sigismundo Taraval, who brought Amerindians from the Pacific islands off the tip of the Vizcaíno Peninsula into the mission community. Eventually, the San Ignacio mission became the largest and most successful in Baja California, with a parish of more than 5,000 Amerindians.

After the Jesuits were expelled from New Spain, Dominican Friar Juan Crisóstomo Gómez took charge of the mission, building a grander church on the original site in 1786. The walls, 1.2 meters (4 ft) thick, were constructed of local volcanic stone without the use of mortar. The lumber for the wooden beams was transported from Misión Guadalupe in the high sierra; the carved doors at the front of the church were brought from the Mexican mainland. According to Jesuit records, the queen of Spain paid 1.5 million pesos for the church's construction.

Today, the venerable church stands largely in its original condition, thanks to a 1976 res-

THE *DÁTILES* OF SAN IGNACIO

The lush, feathery date palm of Arroyo de San Ignacio, a welcome sight to those who've driven the Transpeninsular Highway south across Baja's Central and Vizcaíno Deserts, has multiplied considerably since its introduction to the valley by Spanish missionaries more than 200 years ago. At last count, Baja has some 100,000 of them.

First cultivated in Mesopotamia around 1000 B.C., *dátiles* (dates) were originally brought to Spain during the Moorish occupation of the Iberian peninsula. The Middle East is the second-greatest date producer after the United States; Mexico is a distant third.

Although mature date palms are easy to maintain, palm shoots must be planted near the mother tree for several years before they can be separated. If moved too soon, they'll perish. From germination, it takes an average of 12 years for a date palm to mature and begin to produce commercially. It can then yield fruit for 85 years. Dates are rich in potassium and protein – the protein content of two dates equals that of one egg.

The annual date harvest is celebrated in San Ignacio on July 31, which also happens to be the feast day for the town's patron saint, San Ignacio Loyola. During the fiesta, all manner of date products are displayed in the town plaza, La Reina del Dátil (The Date Queen) is crowned, and music and dancing keep things lively well into the night.

toration, and is used by the local community for masses, weddings, funerals, and daily worship. The church's elaborate facade, with its engraved stone plaques and plaster ornamentation, makes it one of the most impressive of all Baja's mission churches. The plaque to the left of the main doors, above the lower left window, is emblazoned with two crowned lions (symbol of the Kingdom of León in Spain), two castles (for the Kingdom of Castile), and the crown of Spain. To the right of the portal, over the corresponding lower window, is a simpler plaque with two overlapping globes (representing the Old and New Worlds), flanked by the twin Hercules pillars of Spain and North Africa; the pillars are topped by the crowns of Spain and Portugal, while the globe motif features a hybrid crown combining aspects of both the Portuguese and Spanish crowns.

Inside the church, the statue at the center of the main viceregal-style altar is of the mission's patron saint, St. Ignacius Loyola. Surrounding the statue are paintings of St. Joseph and the infant Jesus (upper left), St. Bernard (lower left), Vírgen de Pilar (above the statue), St. John the Baptist (upper right), and St. Dominic (lower right). The two side altars, while not as impressive, also date from the mission period.

Museo Local de San Ignacio

Next to the church, a small museum (Mon.–Sat. 8 A.M.–6 P.M., free) operated by the Instituto Nacional de Antropología e História (INAH) contains color photos and mock mural exhibits dedicated to regional history, with a primary focus on the rock art of the nearby Sierra de San Francisco. The displays are heavily captioned in Spanish only.

Next to the museum, a small **Unidad de Información y Manejo** (tel. 615/154-0222) serves as an INAH office that handles information about and registration for visits to Sierra de San Francisco rock-art sites. You're required to register here and obtain an INAH permit before visiting any of the sites.

Organized Tours

Servicios Ecoturísticos Kuyimá (Ecoturismo Kuyimá, tel. 615/154-0070, kuyima@prodigy.net.mx, www.kuyima.com) has an office facing the plaza in the old Bancomer building. Kuyimá specializes in whale-watching tours at nearby Laguna San Ignacio, but can also arrange guided trips into the Sierra de San Francisco to view prehistoric rock-art sites. Kuyimá guides can speak Spanish, English, and French.

a river runs through it: Río San Ignacio Kadakaamán

Entertainment

Discoteque La Pila, next to Rene's, is a small but well-equipped dance club open Friday and Saturday nights only. Count on a steady bill of *norteña* and *banda.*

Accommodations

Under US$50: Baja Oasis Motel (US$35), less than one kilometer south of San Ignacio on the west side of Mexico 1, is an orange stucco building with 10 clean rooms, some with king beds, others with queen and single beds, all with portable fans, pure drinking water, and hot showers.

Under new ownership, **Casa Leree** (tel. 615/154-0158, www.prodigyweb.net.mx/janebames) is housed in a historic one-story building with thick adobe walls and a shady garden patio. Built around 1880 as a family home, the house became the first guesthouse in San Ignacio around 1900 and has served many generations of travelers in the years since. In its latest incarnation, the guesthouse offers two small patio rooms (US$35) with shared bath

plus a larger suite (US$65) in the main house with private bath and anteroom. Gated parking is available.

US$50–100: Next to the oasis coming into town, Canadian expats Terry and Gary have expanded ❰ **Ignacio Springs Bed & Breakfast** (tel. 615/154-0333, www.ignaciosprings.com, US$62–93) little by little during the six years since they opened. Their accommodations now include five yurts, some with private baths (US$87–93), others with shared facilities (US$62); one small *palapa casita* next to the river (US$80); two block-style buildings with a shared shower facility; and a backpackers' tent (US$28). Prices include tax and a hearty home-cooked breakfast; credit cards are accepted. Kayaks and skiffs are available for guest use. Ignacio Springs has Internet access, but it's not yet high speed. Terry and her staff prepare home-cooked dinner for guests and nonguests (reservations required by 2 P.M. same day). Her prix fixe menu changes according to what's fresh and in season, but she'll take special dietary needs and allergies into consideration when planning the meal. The price of US$14–16 includes homemade pie or cake for dessert, and Terry usually has Starbucks coffee on hand to satisfy your espresso craving.

About 3.5 kilometers (2 mi) off Mexico 1 on the edge of town, the **Desert Inn/La Pinta Hotel** (tel./fax 615/154-0300, U.S. tel. 800/800-9632, www.lapintahotels.com, US$84) got a much-needed facelift in late 2006. It offers 28 clean, spacious, air-conditioned rooms, a restaurant, pool, and a billiards room. Rates are highest during the whale-watching season.

Camping and RV Parks: Several small campgrounds on the outskirts of town lie in palm groves on the Río de San Ignacio. **Camping La Muralla,** near the entrance to town between the highway and the river, has rustic, shaded sites for US$3 a day. No hookups, although the campground now has bathrooms and a barbecue pit.

Almost opposite the Desert Inn/La Pinta Hotel, **El Padrino RV Park** (tel./fax 615/154-0089) has much more in the way of facilities, beginning with close to 100 well-kept camper sites, about 20 of which have full hookups. These sites go for US$15 a night. Tent camping is US$8 per night. Also on the premises are a dump station, bar, and restaurant. El Padrino can arrange whale-watching and rock-art tours.

At all of San Ignacio's campgrounds, mosquitoes and/or *jejenes* (no-see-ums) are sometimes a problem.

Rice and Beans (see *Food*) offers 30 RV spaces with full hookups and hot showers for US$15; US$5 without hookups. Tent sites are also available for US$10, including the use of toilets and hot showers.

Food

Rene's (Mon.–Sat. around 8 A.M.–9 or 10 P.M., Sun. dinner only), a *palapa* hut just east of the plaza next to an irrigation pond built by the Spanish, has tasty and reasonably priced seafood and *antojitos* served in a congenial atmosphere. An outside seating area under brick arches is a pleasant spot to dine. Victor,

who usually works as a waiter in the evenings, speaks good English.

Restaurant La Muralla (daily 7 A.M.–10 P.M.), on the grounds of Camping La Muralla, serves straightforward Mexican and seafood meals in a clean, outdoor setting.

Rice and Beans Restaurant Bar (daily 7 A.M.–11 P.M., dinners US$5–15, breakfasts US$5–15) sits at the edge of an arroyo northwest of town, off the highway; to find it, make a U-turn at the Pemex station and follow the road parallel to the highway four bocks. Traditional Mexican and seafood dishes are cooked using vegetable oil only.

Out on Mexico 1, about three kilometers (2 mi) northwest of town, **Restaurant Quichule** (daily 8 A.M.–11 P.M.) has a good menu of breakfasts, *antojitos,* and seafood. The meat, milk, and cheese served at Quichule comes from the owners' Rancho El Carricito. Locally, Quichule is well known for its seafood cocktails and for the house specialty *tortas de almejas,* delicious clam cakes made with egg and chilies and served with lettuce, tomatoes, mayonnaise, and french fries.

A couple of small *tiendas* and *miscelanéas* in town supply the basics. **Mercados Mayoral López** has the best selection of groceries. **Tortillería La Misión,** just up from Rene's on the way toward the lagoon, makes and sells flour tortillas. Dates are plentiful, typically costing around US$2 per kilogram. Vendors near the plaza sell ripe dates as well as tasty *pay de dátil* or "date pie" (actually more of a cake).

Mercadito Rovi, on Mexico 1 next to the turnoff for Rice and Beans, is small but has a decent selection of groceries, as does the **Diconsa** next to the Pemex.

Getting There

Águila and **ABC** buses traveling north and south stop in front of the *tienda* next to the Pemex station on the highway. Because there is no bus depot or ticket office in town, you can't make reservations or buy tickets in advance; when the bus arrives (usually twice daily), you buy your ticket inside the *tienda.*

CENTRAL BAJA

Seats are usually available except during Holy Week in April.

If you're driving south, it's a good idea to fill up at Guerrero Negro as the Pemex station on the highway opposite the turnoff for San Ignacio often runs out of fuel.

SIERRA DE SAN FRANCISCO ROCK ART

San Ignacio sits in the middle of what Amerindian cave painting expert Harry Crosby has termed the Great Mural Region of Baja California. The most extensive and numerous pictograph and petroglyph sites are found in caves and arroyos north of San Ignacio in the Sierra de San Francisco, an area added to UNESCO's prestigious World Heritage list in 1993. Among the prehistoric archaeological sites found in this sierra are iron and stone tool workshops, camps, sleeping circles, petroglyphs (carved rock art), pictographs (painted rock art), ceremonial sites, cremation sites, and funeral caves. Only the pictograph sites are expressly open to visitors, although many of the other sites are associated with major pictograph areas and hence may be visited en route—guides usually point them out along the way.

Viewing these rock-art sites requires the services of a guide, not only because of the difficulties involved in finding the sites, but because the Mexican government requires it to prevent potential vandalism or pilfering. Registration with the Instituto de Antropología e História (INAH) is also required; arrangements can be made in San Ignacio or La Paz. This means traveling to one or the other *before* you head into the sierra; San Ignacio is obviously the most convenient stop if you're coming from the north (see *Registration and Guides* later in this section).

Each site is classified into one of four different levels *(niveles)* of permissible access according to its perceived importance or sensitivity to human visitation. The most accessible sites are those found in the canyons of San Pablo (also known as Santa Teresa), San Gregorio, El Batequí, and Santa Marta. The Arroyo de San Pablo offers first-time visitors the most thorough introduction to the Great Mural Region, with five different painted caves: Cueva del Ratón, Cueva La Pintada, Cueva de las Flechas, Cueva de la Música (Los Músicos), and Boca de San Julio. All of these sites fall into Level 2, which means anyone may visit them with the proper permit and in the company of a guide. Cueva del Ratón lies only 20 minutes by foot from the village of San Francisco de la Sierra. The other four sites are all deep in Arroyo de San Pablo (which our guide called Cañon de Santa Teresa; we have heard it called other names as well), requiring a good six-hour hike or mule ride from San Francisco de la Sierra and an overnight stay.

Cueva del Ratón

Cave of the Rat is the easiest of the sites to access. Visitors with campers or small RVs can park in a wide space in the road near the stairs that lead up to the cave, but take care not to block the road, and be sure to register and engage the services of a guide at the village first.

Follow the path up the stone stairs, across a wooden bridge, and through a cleft in a lower ridge of Cerro de la Laguna to reach the rock overhang that served as a minor canvas for the Painters. Game animals form the main theme, along with a few *mono*, or humanlike figures, and the namesake rat, which may actually be a representation of a mountain lion.

Cueva de las Flechas

A large rock overhang high up the canyon wall, Cave of the Arrows is most notable for a cluster of three red-and-black *monos,* or human figures, wearing prominent headdresses. Two of the figures are pierced with multiple arrows and lances; projectile points depicted in the central figure are similar to types found in the area. The meaning of the arrows invites much conjecture, the most common theory being that the scene represents some sort of intertribal war. Such conflicts have been documented among the Cochimí, and it may be that the pictographs in this cave marked territorial limits between rival clans. Another hypothesis suggests that the human figures represent Amerindian shamans and the arrows serve as a metaphor for death and dying, thus symbolizing a shamanic passage into the supernatural realm.

Cueva La Pintada

Across the canyon from Las Flechas and north a few hundred meters is the Painted Cave, also known as Gardner's Cave because of its associations with the late mystery writer Erle Stanley Gardner (creator of Perry Mason and a Baja rock-art fanatic who "discovered" this cave in 1962).

In his unparalleled book *The Cave Paintings of Baja California,* Harry Crosby wrote that Cueva La Pintada "may be considered the focus of the Great Murals" and that "it is the most painted place in the most painted part of the entire range in which these giant realistic artworks are found." The 150-meter (500-ft) rock overhang "cave" is jammed with figures of all kinds, many of them superimposed on one another in ways that imply they were executed in feverish bouts of artistic creativity; over three times as many clearly visible figures can be seen here as in any other comparable cave site in Baja. La Pintada is also unique because the paintings here are unusually well preserved compared to those of other caves in the region, in large part as a result of the intrinsic durability—the geological "freshness"—of these particular rock faces.

Various shades of black and red are the only colors employed, but the sheer number of figures and homogeneity of style suggest a highly systematic output. Whales, deer, *monos,* fish, rabbits, and an unusually numerous and impressive-looking collection of birds—they're all here, dancing to the rhythm of a long-gone muse who inspired the mysterious group of tribal artists we now call the Painters.

Planning Your Trip

On a one-night, two-day trip you can take in Cueva de las Flechas and Cueva La Pintada. The usual itinerary involves descending to the canyon floor by midday, making camp, spending the remainder of the day visiting the caves, and then ascending the canyon trail the following morning. As you descend more than 365 meters (1,200 ft) to the canyon bottom, you'll enjoy unparalleled canyon vistas, passing startling red rock pillars and sheer rock walls. On the floor of the canyon, you'll find profuse stands of sky-high palms, clear-running streams, large boulders, and cool *tinajas.* Camping is permitted in the canyon at selected sites.

By adding more days to your itinerary, you can take in Cueva La Soledad (in a branch canyon off Arroyo de San Pablo, not far from Cueva La Pintada), Cueva La Música (a small site farther down Arroyo de San Pablo), and Boca de San Julio (a beautiful site in a branch canyon almost opposite La Música).

Visits to other pictograph sites in the arroyos of San Gregorio, El Batequí, and Santa Marta can also be staged out of San Francisco de la Sierra. The Santa Marta sites can also be reached via **Rancho Santa Marta,** from a turnoff 40 kilometers south of San Ignacio via Mexico 1. As always, check with the INAH office in San Ignacio first—it may regulate this choice.

Registration and Guides

All prospective visitors to Sierra de San Francisco rock-art sites must first register with the INAH in either San Ignacio (INAH Unidad de Información y Manejo, next to the mission church, tel./fax 615/154-0222) or La Paz (Centro Regional INAH, Calle Aquiles Serdán 1070, tel. 612/123-0399, fax 612/122-7389). Upon registration and payment of a nominal registration fee, the INAH office will contact the appropriate INAH custodian in the area you want to visit (either San Francisco de la Sierra or Santa Marta) and give you a copy of the *Rules of the Archaeological Zone of Sierra de San Francisco* with the name of the custodian handwritten on the front, along with the number of days, number of people, and destinations approved.

Your next stop is the house of the local INAH custodian *(costudio de bienes patrimoniales)* in the appropriate town; in San Francisco de la Sierra, visitors check in with custodian Enrique Arce. Señor Arce will register your arrival, obtain your signature on a waiver (saying INAH isn't responsible for any accidents,

CENTRAL BAJA

THE PREHISTORIC MURALS OF BAJA CALIFORNIA

In hidden palm oases and remote canyons throughout the sierras of Baja California, far from the Transpeninsular Highway and most of the peninsula's larger towns, the artistic heritage of a lost Amerindian culture arcs across rock walls. Dubbed the Painters by Baja rock-art expert Harry Crosby, these anonymous artists painted thousands of figures in hundreds of murals that rival the cave paintings of Lascaux and Altamira in Europe. Most are concentrated in the central peninsular sierras of San Francisco, San Borja, San Juan, and Guadalupe. Paleolithic paintings are also found in northern Baja at San José de Tecate, Palmas de Cantú, Pilitas, and Arroyo Grande, and in the south at Sierra de Cacachillas and Miraflores.

THE PAINTINGS

Though largely unknown outside Mexico, central Baja's prehistoric murals are actually larger and more numerous than those found at Lascaux, France, and Altamira, Spain. Between Bahía de los Ángeles and Comondú alone are more than 400 mural sites. Most paintings are placed high – as high as 10 meters (33 ft) – on the walls or ceilings of arroyos, canyons, and rock overhangs. Scaffolds, probably made of *cardón* ribs or palm trunks, were used to reach these heights. Styles were codified to such an extent that all human figures feature arms extended upwards, all four-legged animals are depicted running or leaping, fish are always shown from a dorsal view, and birds are in flight as seen from below, with their heads turned in profile.

Ritual purposes are implied by the fact that only the outlines of painted figures are representational, while interiors contain conventionalized abstractions. In some areas of the sierras, human figures are occasionally bicol-ored, with the left half of the body painted red and the right half painted black. Figures may also wear headdresses or top-knotted hair. Rock-art experts have discerned several different schools within the Great Mural Region of central Baja: In the Sierra San Borja, *monos* are painted in red; Sierra de San Francisco paintings show red-black bicolors; the Sierra de Guadalupe features monochrome, bicolor, and checkerboard color schemes, along with *monos* filled in with vertical lines.

One of the more awe-inspiring examples of prehistoric rock art is a 166-meter (500-ft) by 10-meter (33-ft) mural at Cueva Pintada in the Cañon de Santa Teresa (Sierra de San Francisco); the mural holds overlapping images of men and women, deer, bighorn sheep, rabbits, and birds. At Arroyo de San Gregorio a four-meter (12-ft) whale is painted onto a rock overhang.

THE PAINTERS

Little is known about the Painters except that they belonged to the only culture, in a succession of central peninsula cultures, to leave behind artifacts borne not of economic necessity but from the realms of art and ritual. Ancillary evidence discovered at the rock-art sites – *metates* (grinding plates), *manos* (grindstones), bows and arrows, choppers, scrapers, carved bone, woven fibers, and fire pits – identify the Painters as Paleolithic. The artwork itself, ritualistic paintings of human and animal figures, correlates with art styles found in Paleolithic sites the world over.

Eighteenth-century missionary documents from Baja refer to a few mural sites, but the Cochimí living in the central peninsula at the coming of the Spanish padres had no knowledge of the significance of the symbols or motifs in the paintings, nor of the techniques of painting; they themselves didn't paint. Cochimí legends said the paintings were the work of a race of giants who inhabited the region well before the time of their ancestors. The Painters must have been giants, according to the Cochimí, because many of the paintings appear on rock walls up to 10 meters above the ground.

Because archaeological and anthropological research in Baja has been so scant, scholars haven't a clue whether the Painters were a separate cultural group that migrated from the north or an early phase of the Cochimí culture. That the Painters were migratory – like all early Amerindian cultures in Baja – is certain since they left behind no permanent dwellings or pottery. The desert conditions of central Baja meant they had to move with the migrations of game and the seasonal changes in surface water. Such a culture required highly portable materials made mostly of wood, hide, and fibers. The minerals used for painting, as well as materials for building the scaffolds, could be gathered on-site.

ROCK-ART RESEARCH

Although the Spanish missionaries of the 18th and 19th centuries were aware of the murals, the first systematic study of the paintings was conducted by Leon Diguet, a French naturalist working at El Boleo copper-mining company in Santa Rosalía. Diguet visited several mural sites in 1893-1894 and published his findings in a few French journals; he missed the Painters' most extensive sites in San Francisco.

The next person to delve into the mysteries of the murals was American mystery writer Erle Stanley Gardner, of Perry Mason fame. Gardner began traveling to Baja in the 1940s

and was first led to El Batequí and other Sierra de San Francisco sites in 1962 by local ranchers. Realizing he'd viewed sites of great archaeological significance, Gardner devoted a considerable part of his income to the study of the murals and wrote about them for *Life* magazine and in his book *The Hidden Heart of Baja*.

In 1972, Baja historian Harry Crosby succeeded Gardner in the search for undiscovered sites, making extensive forays into the San Borja, San Francisco, San Juan, and Guadalupe mountain ranges. Crosby printed the results of his explorations in *National Geographic*, as well as in his excellent 1984 book, *The Cave Paintings of Baja California*, the most authoritative general reference work on Baja rock art.

Based on an assortment of facts and artifacts – including what appears to be a mural rendering of the supernova birth of the Crab Nebula in A.D. 1054 – Crosby speculates that the Painters' artistic output extended over a thousand-year period around A.D. 500-1500. More recent studies by Mexico's Instituto de Antropología e Historia (INAH) have expanded the mural era considerably, finding evidence of Great Mural Region rock art dating from 3000 B.C. to A.D. 1650. If the latter date is correct, it means the Cochimí must have contributed to at least some of the paintings; it's very possible they denied involvement when queried by the Spanish to avoid persecution for their belief systems. To verify or refute these datings, more research is needed in the fields of archaeology, anthropology, geology, and meteorology.

UNESCO has designated Baja's Great Mural Region a World-Class Rock Art Site, an honor that allows mural researchers to apply for UNESCO grants.

LEVELS OF ACCESS TO ROCK ART IN THE SIERRA DE SAN FRANCISCO

Level 1: All may enter with permit and guide; accessible by road. Examples: Cueva del Ratón, Cuesta Palmarito.

Level 2: All may enter with permit and guide; accessible only by foot or on saddle stock, and pack animals are required. Examples: Arroyo de San Pablo (Cañon de Santa Teresa), Arroyo del Parral.

Level 3: Only for those who have already visited Level 2 sites, with guide and permit, and in the company of an INAH custodian; must apply for permits at least three months in advance. Examples: Cañon de San Gregorio, Arroyo de San Gregorito, Arroyo del Batequi.

Level 4: Only for academic purposes; all research must be approved well in advance by INAH or SEMARNAT. Site names and locations not available to the general public.

injuries, or delays), assign you a local guide, and, if necessary, arrange pack animals and riding stock.

All visits must be conducted by an authorized INAH guide, to whom you will pay daily guide fees set by INAH; these currently run around US$10 per day. Arce and his Santa Marta counterpart coordinate each visit and call up each guide according to a rotation schedule.

You are responsible for your own food, plus food for the guide "in accordance with regional customs and preferences." In everyday practice, guides will bring a thick stack of tortillas, cans of tuna, instant noodles, and other food because they fear relying solely on your food selection. They will, however, eat just about anything you have to offer. You can also substitute money for food, at a mutually agreed upon rate.

For overnight treks, you are also required to hire one pack animal—usually a burro or mule—for every 60 kilograms (132 lbs) of luggage and equipment. The standard rate as of this writing is US$10 per animal. Riding animals—usually mules—are optional and cost the same. Note that there is a maximum weight limit of 110 kilograms (242 lbs) per person, regardless of whether you ride a mule or not. Anyone weighing more won't be accepted to participate in a trek, ostensibly because pack animals can't carry weights greater than this on canyon ascents. Guides must guarantee they can pack someone out by mule in case of emergency.

All trip fees are to be paid after completion of the trip, not before.

If you arrive too late in the day to set out for the caves, Señor Arce has a small campsite (with an outhouse toilet) near his house where you may camp. The village itself also has some primitive campsites; if you're taking a canyon trip the following day, there's no charge.

Once out on the trail, visitors and guides are supposed to stick to established campsites in the canyons; in reality, guides sometimes bend the rules in favor of common sense owing to weather and other considerations. All trash must be packed out, no open fires are permitted, and you're not supposed to bathe in canyon streams. Water may be taken from the streams for drinking and cooking only.

Tours

You need to speak Spanish to negotiate all of this on your own. If your Spanish skills aren't up to it, you may want to book a tour out of San Ignacio through **Motel La Posada** (tel. 615/154-0313) or **Servicios Ecoturísticos Kuyimá** (tel. 615/154-0070, www.kuyima.com), either of which can provide—for an extra charge—an English-speaking guide along with the local guide required by law.

Getting There

The well-signed turnoff for San Francisco lies 36 kilometers (22 mi) northwest of San Ignacio. This road ascends gradually into the sierra and winds its way along mesa ridges into the interior of the range, passing splendid scenery along the way. A rocky road surface, prone to heavy washboard, ensures slow vehicle speeds—all the better for enjoying the view. Sand tracks paralleling the road much of the way can be much smoother and faster.

Around 10.5 kilometers (6.5 mi) from the highway the road begins climbing and soon provides views of the Valle del Vizcaíno below. At about 14.5 kilometers (9 mi) from the highway, much of the cacti are draped with moss, proof that moist Pacific air travels far and high. Los Crestones, a goat ranch, appears after 21.4 kilometers (13.3 mi), and at about 26 kilometers (16 mi) you'll begin seeing *cirios*, or boojum trees, an unusual sight this far south. After another two kilometers or so you'll come to a fork; don't take the left branch, which goes to Rancho Santa Ana. Another small rancho appears on the left 31.5 kilometers (19.5 mi) from the highway, and after another couple of kilometers the road starts winding along the edge of a deep canyon. The steps to Cueva del Ratón appear on the right at 35.5 kilometers (22.1 mi). You'll reach the settlement of San Francisco de la Sierra at 37.8 kilometers (23.5 mi).

LAGUNA SAN IGNACIO

Southeast of San Ignacio on the Pacific coast lies a large bay used by calving gray whales January–March every year. The grays are closer to shore here than at Laguna Ojo de Liebre to the north or Bahía de Magdalena to the south and seem to exhibit friendlier behavior here than at other calving lagoons. Many mothers and calves at Laguna San Ignacio actively seek out tactile encounters, i.e., petting and scratching. They also like to play hide-and-seek with the boats, sometimes blowing bursts of bubbles into the bow, then spyhopping (extending the head vertically above the sea surface) to see the effect their shenanigans may have had on the passengers.

During the calving season, only boats with whale-watching permits are allowed on the bay. Around a half-dozen camps along the sand road that parallels the bay offer the services of licensed *pangeros*, who will take visitors out to meet the whales for US$40 per person, gener-

ally with a minimum of four persons. **Campo La Fridera** is particularly friendly and efficient. The typical tour lasts 3–4 hours; you should be at the camp by around 9 A.M. to get on one of the boats. Since the 59-kilometer (35-mi) drive from San Ignacio takes 90 minutes to two hours due to road conditions (most passenger vehicles can make it—slowly), you must leave town early in the morning or spend the previous night at one of the camps. If you don't have your own vehicle, taxi transportation to the bay can be arranged in San Ignacio for around US$50—inquire at the taxi stand on the main plaza in front of the church.

The farther south you go along the bayshore by car, the less time you'll spend on boat transit to the prime whale-watching area near the mouth of the bay. One of the last camps on the bay, **Ecoturismo Kuyimá** (Morelos 23, San Ignacio, tel. 615/154-0070, www.kuyima.com) has a fully equipped campground with hot-water showers, ecologically sound outhouses, and a tented dining room. Along with the 20 tent sites there are also 10 rustic cabins. It costs US$10 a night to pitch your own four-person tent, or for US$40, Kuyimá will provide a two-person tent, sleeping bags, and flashlights. Food, depending on the menu of the day, runs US$7–10 per meal. A four day/three night adventure package costs US$165 per person per day, and includes lodging in a cabin, all meals, and daily whale-watching tours, as well as the use of bicycles, kayaks, a library and video services, a trip to the salt fields, and access to naturalist guides. Travel from San Ignacio to the camp is not included in the package rate, but van transportation is available to/from San Ignacio for US$130 for up to 10 people. Kuyimá charges a little more for whale-watching *panga* tours than other camps on the bay—US$40 per person with a minimum of four. Kuyimá is far enough south that you can see whales spouting and spyhopping from shore in season.

Punta Piedra

Farther south toward the mouth of the bay lies Punta Piedra, also known as Punta Peñasco, a peninsula jutting out into the bay near the main calving grounds. **Baja Discovery** (U.S. tel. 619/262-0700 or 800/829-2252, www.bajadiscovery.com) maintains a well-equipped camp on Rocky Point where whales can be seen just yards offshore, but you must book a tour package (US$1,825 pp for five days) to make use of it. The package is all-inclusive and covers round-trip charter airfare out of San Diego. **Baja Expeditions** (2625 Garnet Ave., San Diego, CA 92109, tel. 858/581-3311 or 800/843-6967, www.bajaex.com) also has a camp here; five-day packages cost US$1,925 per person, including round-trip air from San Diego. Both companies run their tours late January–late March.

You should be able to camp elsewhere on the point on your own; no one can legally block access to the tide line, which is a federal zone. High-clearance vehicles can reach Punta Piedra by road—a stream must be crossed along the way—or you can arrange to be dropped off by boat from one of the camps farther north. The road to Punta Piedra continues south all the way to Bahía San Juanico but is recommended only for four-wheel-drive vehicles.

Isla de Pelicanos

This island in the northern section of the bay serves as nesting grounds for a large number of ospreys and a variety of other birds. Also known as Isla Garza and Isla de Ballenas, the island is closed to visitors during the whale season, but you can visit by boat the remainder of the year. Inquire at the fish camps along the bay's eastern shore for *panga* hire. In the case of Isla de Pelicanos, those camps farthest north along the bayshore—such as **Chema's** or **Maldo's**—provide the quickest access to the island. Figure on US$30 per person for a group of four.

Santa Rosalía

At Santa Rosalía (pop. 10,400), the Transpeninsular Highway completes its 215-kilometer (129-mi) journey from Pacific coast to Cortez coast. As in San Ignacio, the town is wedged into a deep arroyo between mesas, but the similarity between the two towns ends there. Whereas San Ignacio's architecture is strongly Spanish-flavored due to the mission influence, the buildings along Santa Rosalía's narrow streets—many of them wood-frame houses fronted by long verandas in the French colonial style—were designed by a French mining company in the 19th century.

Other Gallic touches include a French bakery and the only Eiffel-designed church in Mexico (see *Iglesia Santa Bárbara de Santa Rosalía*). One of the most impressive French-built structures in town, the Palacio Municipal, was once a school. Although many of the town's current residents certainly appear as if they could be of French or part-French ancestry, the locals claim most French citizens left town when the mines closed in 1954.

A *malecón* (waterfront promenade) with benches, cement sidewalk, and street lamps runs along the bayfront near the Pemex station and bus depot, south of the ferry pier. Though not particularly scenic, this is a good spot to catch a refreshing offshore breeze.

Santa Rosalía is the capital of the Municipio de Mulegé, and a terminus for the ferry to Guaymas, seven hours across the Sea of Cortez. The weather can be stiflingly hot June–October.

HISTORY

Copper-bearing deposits, in blue-green globules called *boleos*, were discovered near here in 1868, and in 1885 a French mining company calling itself El Boleo acquired mineral rights to the area for 99 years. To help build more than 600 kilometers (375 mi) of mine tunnels, a large copper-smelting foundry (imported by ship from Europe), a pier, and a 30-kilometer (18-mi) mine railway, the French brought in Yaqui Amerindians from Sonora; fresh water

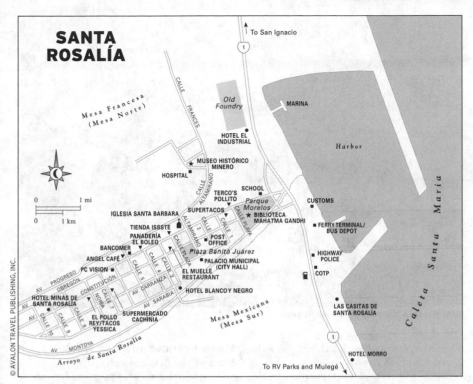

SANTA ROSALÍA

To San Ignacio

Mesa Francesa
(Mesa Norte)

CALLE FRANCES

Old Foundry

MARINA

HOTEL EL INDUSTRIAL

Harbor

MUSEO HISTÓRICO MINERO

HOSPITAL

CALLE ALTAMIRANO

TERCO'S POLLITO   SCHOOL

Parque Morelos

CUSTOMS

IGLESIA SANTA BARBARA   SUPERTACOS

BIBLIOTECA MAHATMA GANDHI

TIENDA ISSSTE

CALLE PLAYA

FERRY TERMINAL/ BUS DEPOT

PANADERÍA EL BOLEO

POST OFFICE

BANCOMER

CALLE ALTAMIRANO

CALLE 2

Plaza Benito Juárez

ANGEL CAFÉ

PALACIO MUNICIPAL (CITY HALL)

HIGHWAY POLICE

PC VISION

CALLE 3

CALLE 4

EL MUELLE RESTAURANT

COTP

AV PROGRESO OBREGÓN

CALLE 5

AV CARRANZA

HOTEL MINAS DE SANTA ROSALÍA

AV CONSTITUCIÓN

CALLE NORIA

AV SARABIA

HOTEL BLANCO Y NEGRO

LAS CASITAS DE SANTA ROSALÍA

AV CALLE 10   CALLE 9

EL POLLO REY/TACOS YESSICA

CALLE 8

SUPERMERCADO CACHINIA

Mesa Mexicana (Mesa Sur)

AV MONTOYA

Arroyo de Santa Rosalía

To RV Parks and Mulegé

HOTEL MORRO

Santa Maria

Caleta Santa Maria

0   1 mi
0   1 km

© AVALON TRAVEL PUBLISHING, INC.

was piped in from the Santa Agueda oasis, 16 kilometers (10 mi) west. Two thousand Chinese and Japanese laborers, told they would be able to plant rice, also came to work at El Boleo. When they found that rice wouldn't grow in central Baja, almost all of them left; many ended up in Sinaloa across the Cortez.

After smelting, the copper ore was shipped to Tacoma, Washington, for refining. Instead of returning empty, copper-transport ships brought lumber from the Pacific Northwest to Santa Rosalía, and, as the town grew, the French filled the arroyo and mesas on either side with wooden buildings to house workers, company officials, and Mexican soldiers. During El Boleo's heyday in the 1940s, a sooty cloud issued constantly from the foundry's smokestack, hanging over the town. Eventually the ore began to run out, and in 1954 the French company sold its mining facilities back to the

Mexican government. Copper ore from the Mexican mainland is smelted in Santa Rosalía on occasion, but the mines closed in 1985.

Without the mines in operation, Santa Rosalía is probably a far more pleasant place to live than ever before. Today it serves as a government, transportation, and market center for central Baja. It's also an important tourist crossroads for visitors stocking up on supplies for further peninsular explorations.

The **Mahatma Gandhi Public Library** in Parque Morelos, at the east end of town near the harbor, features an exhibit of historic photos from Santa Rosalía's mining days.

SIGHTS
Iglesia Santa Bárbara de Santa Rosalía

A novelty in Baja—or anywhere, for that matter—is this prefabricated, iron-walled church

CENTRAL BAJA

© PAUL ITOI

Iglesia Santa Bárbara de Santa Rosalía

designed by famous French architect Alexandre Gustave Eiffel in 1884.

Eiffel, who earned his reputation by designing locks for the Panama Canal and the frame for the United States's Statue of Liberty, originally constructed this church in France in 1887; it was intended as a prototype for missionary churches built to withstand the climate in France's equatorial colonies. Two years later it was exhibited in Paris, together with the Eiffel Tower, at the 1889 Paris World Exposition. Eiffel took first prize for the church's modular, tropics-proof design.

When a French official at Compañía El Boleo later heard the church had been warehoused in Brussels, he purchased it and had it shipped in sections to Santa Rosalía, where it was reassembled in 1897. The exterior is modern, even minimalist, in tone, while the interior resembles that of any Catholic church. Except for two side wings added locally, the entire structure is made of galvanized iron. The church is still very much in use, with an Italian priest in residence.

Mesa Francesa (Mesa Norte)

Some of the best examples of French colonial-style architecture in town can be seen on the mesa along the north side of town, known locally as Mesa Francesa (French Mesa). Several of the homes in this neighborhood—large wooden affairs with wraparound verandas and pitched roofs—are being restored with help from INAH.

The **Hotel Frances** is one of the best preserved of the old French structures on the mesa (see *Accommodations*). Various examples of rolling stock and locomotives from El Boleo's short-line railway are displayed in front of the hotel.

Another of the French buildings on the mesa houses the **Museo Histórico Minero de Santa Rosalía** (Mon.–Sat. 8 A.M.–2 P.M. and 5–7 P.M., US$1.30), which focuses on the town's mining history. Exhibits on display include miniature models of historic buildings in the area; historical photos; handwritten accounting ledgers used by El Boleo; old office furniture; a walk-in bank vault; various minerals of local provenance; miners' equipment; and a ship's wheel from the *Argyle,* an English barque originally launched in 1892. A small snack bar in the back of the building is occasionally open, as is a counter selling books on Mexican history.

You can reach Mesa Francesa via a steep and decrepit set of stairs that starts near the Iglesia Santa Bárbara, or by following curving Calle Altamirano.

EVENTS

Santa Rosalía's biggest festival is **Carnaval,** a pre-Lenten celebration held six days before Ash Wednesday, usually in mid-February. The **Fiesta de Santa Rosalía,** held annually around September 4, brings concerts, food fairs, and fishing tournaments to town, all in honor of patron saint Santa Rosalía. A **founder's day celebration** takes place the second week of October.

ACCOMMODATIONS
Hotels

Under US$50: In an old wooden French building, the **Hotel Blanco y Negro** (Av. Sarabia at Calle 3, tel. 615/152-0080, US$15) offers relatively clean if ramshackle rooms, some with private baths, and friendly proprietors. The most expensive room has a TV, and they offer one single room with private bath upstairs. To reach this hotel through the town's one-way street system, head southwest on Avenida Obregón, turn left at Calle 4 (in front of Panadería El Boleo), and follow Calle 4 until it ends at Avenida Sarabia; turn left at Avenida Sarabia, and after two short blocks you'll find the Hotel Blanco y Negro on your right.

Located above a video arcade, the two-story **Hotel Minas de Santa Rosalía** (on Av. Constitución btw Calles 9/10, tel. 615/152-1060, US$30) has large rooms, each with two double beds with soft and sagging mattresses, an older air conditioning unit, ceiling fan, cable TV, and private bath.

The business-oriented **El Moro Hotel** (tel./fax 615/152-0414, US$35–52), overlooking the Sea of Cortez about 1.5 kilometers (1 mi) south of town on Mexico 1 (between Km 194 and 195), features 39 large air-conditioned rooms with ocean views, plus secure parking, a restaurant, bar, and swimming pool.

US$50-100: Perched on a cliff overlooking the bay, and conveniently located just off Mexico 1, **Las Casitas de Santa Rosalía** (tel. 615/152-3023, mariahsantarosalia@hotmail.com, US$50–70) has a number of clean, comfortable cottages built in modern Mexican style. On the premises are a whirlpool tub and a terrace where guests may relax and enjoy a drink while watching boats come in and out of the harbor.

Overlooking the copper smelter on Mesa Norte is the venerable **Hotel Frances** (Calle Jean M. Cousteau 15, tel./fax 615/152-2052, US$50). The restored 1886 French colonial–style building features 17 rooms with high ceilings, TV, and air conditioning. The hotel courtyard holds a small pool and the Museo Pierre Escalle—a small outdoor display of historical objects pertaining to the town's French mining era.

Camping and RV Parks

Just south of Santa Rosalía off Mexico 1, **Las Palmas RV Park** offers 30 spaces (some with full hookups), hot showers, and a dump station; US$12 per vehicle per night. Tent sites rent for US$6 per site.

Fifteen kilometers (9 mi) south of town off Mexico 1, on the pretty bay of Caleta San Lucas and accessible via a bumpy sand road, is the secluded and well-kept **San Lucas Cove RV Park.** Tent/camper sites (no hookups) cost US$6 per vehicle. Facilities include hot showers, disposal station, and boat ramp. Caleta San Lucas is somewhat protected from winter northerlies, so it's generally a calm, warm place to camp. Only small boats can moor here since the *caleta* entrance is very shallow. Nearby, the newer **Camacho RV Park** is similar, with hot showers and flush toilets for US$5.

FOOD

Most of the town's restaurants and cafés are spread out along Avenida Obregón.

taquería in downtown Santa Rosalía

Restaurant Terco's Pollito (Av. Obregón at Calle Playa opposite Parque Morelos, tel. 615/152-0075, daily 8 A.M.–10 P.M.) specializes in mouthwatering barbecued chicken as well as a wide variety of moderately priced breakfasts, seafood, soups, and Mexican standards. You'll find a pleasant *palapa* eating area off the main air-conditioned dining room.

Several vendors sell tacos from carts around town: **Pepe's,** usually parked along the north side of Parque Morelos on Avenida Obregón, makes delicious fish and shrimp tacos, triggerfish ceviche, and shrimp cocktail. **Supertacos,** on the south side of Obregón right before Calle 1, is a popular spot for beef tacos.

El Muelle Restaurant Bar (Calle 9 and the plaza, tel. 615/152-0931, daily 8 A.M.–11 P.M.), housed in an old wooden building, serves breakfasts, seafood, and pizza. Its outdoor patio is a pleasant dining spot during the cooler months.

Angel Café (Calle 5, off Obregón) prepares tasty tortas, plus burgers and breakfasts for US$3–5. **Café Combate** (Obregón btw Calles 5–6, Mon.–Fri. 8 A.M.–1 P.M. and 3–6 P.M., Sat. 8 A.M.–2 P.M.) has espresso drinks.

Groceries

The **Super ISSSTE Tienda** (Obregón at Calle 3), purveys a wide selection of foodstuffs and household supplies at government-subsidized prices. Just west of this store, on the same side of the street, is the famous **Panadería El Boleo** (Mon.–Sat. 8 A.M.–9 P.M.), which typically draws a long line out front when it opens each morning. The baguettes, or *pan birote,* here are legendary. The bakery also offers a good variety of other Mexican- and French-style baked goods, including delicious *kakita de zanahoria*—carrot muffins.

For fresh flour tortillas, visit the **Tortillería Santa Agueda** (Av. Obregón near Calle 6, just west of the Bancomer). If corn tortillas are your preference, try the **Tortillería Ranchería** toward the west end of Obregón where it merges with a two-way street.

© PAUL ITOI

CEVICHE

Ceviche (sometimes spelled "cebiche" or "sibiche") is a seafood appetizer in which fish or shellfish is marinated in lime juice until "cooked." It's very popular throughout Baja, and there are as many recipes as there are cooks — it can be a wonderful experience in one restaurant and a bad excuse for getting rid of fish scraps in another.

Since it's easy to make even while camping on the beach (no fire necessary), ceviche offers an excellent alternative to the usual fried, baked, or grilled fish dishes. One of the best types of fish to use for ceviche is sierra, a common type of mackerel usually caught inshore/offshore; John Steinbeck, during his 1941 Sea of Cortez expedition, pronounced it "the most delicious fish of all." Other great candidates for ceviche are halibut, shark, shrimp, lobster, or just about any other fish whose flesh is not too dry. The oilier the better, since the lime juice counteracts the oil. Always use the freshest fish available.

CEVICHE DE SIERRA
serves four
1 pound fresh sierra fillets, thinly sliced
$1/2$ cup fresh lime juice
1 ripe avocado, peeled and cut into half-inch cubes
8 ripe, red cherry tomatoes cut in half (or one large ripe tomato, cut into sixteenths)
1 serrano chili, minced (or more if you want it *really* hot)
2 tablespoons fresh cilantro leaves, minced
2 tablespoons olive oil
1 teaspoon salt, or to taste (optional)

Put the sliced sierra in a large bowl, mix with the lime juice, and marinate in a cooler for a half hour. Drain, then gently toss the remaining ingredients. Best served with fresh tortilla chips and cold *cerveza*.

INFORMATION AND SERVICES

You can exchange foreign travelers checks or cash for pesos at the Bancomer and Banamex branches, both on Av. Obregón and both with ATMs (Mon.–Fri. 8:30 A.M.–3 P.M.).

The post office is east of the plaza at Calle 2 and Avenida Constitución. On the south side of the plaza is a public telephone available for local and long-distance calls. Plenty of TelMex Ladatel card phones are scattered around town, especially on Avenida Obregón. The bus depot contains a *caseta de larga distancia*.

PC Vision (on the corner of Avenida Obregón and Calle 6, daily 10 A.M.–10 P.M.) has a few relatively fast Internet connections. Air-conditioned **Mas Internet Café** (Mon.–Sat. 9 A.M.–6 P.M.), next to the Hotel Minas, has a half dozen computers with flatscreen LCD monitors and webcams for US$2/hour. You can connect your own laptop too.

For repairs and supplies, there is a hardware store on the east side of the plaza (tel. 615/152-1234) and a **Go4Value** (Calle 5 and Constitución) discount store with food, cleaning supplies, and paper goods.

GETTING THERE

Santa Rosalía has an **airfield** outside of town, but so far no regularly scheduled commercial flights are offered. **Taxis Aereos Santa María** (no tel.) offers chartered flights out of Santa Rosalía and maintains an office a little southwest of Terco's Pollito on Avenida Obregón.

Santa Rosalía's **intercity bus depot** has moved to the ferry terminal. Two or three first-class buses a day travel north to San Ignacio, Guerrero Negro, San Quintín, Ensenada, Mexicali, and Tijuana, as well as south to Mulegé, Loreto, and La Paz. Less expensive second-class buses are also sometimes available to San Ignacio, Guerrero Negro, Mulegé, and La Paz.

The Pemex station, near the ferry terminal on Mexico 1, is infamous for overcharging and or short-changing tourists. Most locals recommend you not fill up in Santa Rosalía if you can help it. Instead get gas in San Ignacio to the north or Mulegé to the south.

Marina Santa Rosalía (tel./fax 615/152-0011), in the breakwater-protected harbor, has 20 moorings for rent with fuel available. Because Santa Rosalía is an official port of entry, the harbor boasts COTP, immigration, and customs offices.

The Santa Rosalia ferry (tel. 615/152-0013, www.ferrysantarosalia.com) is now running several times a week, leaving Santa Rosalía in the evening and returning from Guaymas in the morning.

VICINITY OF SANTA ROSALÍA

South of Santa Rosalía, on the way to Mulegé via Mexico 1, two side roads suitable for high-clearance vehicles lead into the Sierra de Guadalupe. At Km 188, just beyond the state prison, a graded road branches 12 kilometers (7.5 mi) west to **Santa Agueda** and beyond to several ranchos. Local ranchers may be willing to act as guides to Amerindian murals at La Candelaria, San Antonio, or Los Gatos. The Guadalupe "school" of Amerindian rock art shows more variation than the paintings found farther north in the Sierra de San Francisco, and known sites are more numerous. According to author Harry Crosby, more sites are found in the Guadalupe than in any of Baja's other sierras. Murals here are typically smaller than those in the San Francisco area, however.

An even more scenic side road leaves Mexico 1 at Km 169, about 20 kilometers (12 mi) south of the Santa Agueda turnoff, and heads 14 kilometers (8.5 mi) west to the isolated farming community of **San José de Magdalena.** The winding, rocky road climbs several steep grades with inspiring views of palm-studded canyons, healthy stands of *cardón,* mesquite, and ocotillo, and picturesque rock outcroppings—you almost expect to see the Lone Ranger and Tonto around the next bend. San José de Magdalena is known as Baja's garlic capital, and many visitors purchase long *ristras* (strands) of linked garlic bulbs here.

Beyond San José, the road continues another 48 kilometers (30 mi) to several ranchos. A number of Amerindian mural sites are accessible in this area, assuming you can find a guide at one of the ranchos. You can also reach the adobe ruins of **Misión Señora de**

© PAUL ITOI

view from Mexico 1 north of Santa Rosalía

Guadalupe de Guasinapi (1720–1795), one of the peninsula's most remote mission sites, a hard three hours' drive from San José. Only parts of the stone-block foundation and adobe walls remain, so this side trip is best reserved for hard-core mission buffs.

San Bruno

The small fishing community of San Bruno, located near Km 173, before the turnoff to San José de Magdalena, has more *pangas* than residents, and more than half of the boats seem to be named Lupita. A brand new harbor and paved boat ramp were completed in 2006 with state government funding.

With prior experience at the Hotel Serenidad in Mulege and Punta Chivato, Alberto Carrillo runs the first and only hotel in town. The new **Hotel Costa Serena** (tel. 615/153-9022, US$35) has half a dozen air-conditioned rooms in a single story building facing the sandy beach. Each room is individually appointed with antique furnishings and named for one of Alberto's uncles. White bathrobes are a plus. Alberto was also building the first restaurant in town, and his nephew offers *panga* tours to Isla San Marcos.

San Bruno celebrates its town festival in early October.

Services include a Pemex station, bus stop, and *aborrotes* store on Mexico 1.

Isla San Marcos

A few kilometers off the coast of San Bruno, 32-square-kilometer (12-sq-mi) Isla San Marcos holds a settlement of 600–700 people at its southwestern tip and is the only permanently inhabited island in the Sea of Cortez—all other contenders have seasonal populations. A gypsum mine near the main village supports the population. The island even has its own baseball team, the San Marcos Stars, who host games at a stadium complete with bleachers and outfield wall.

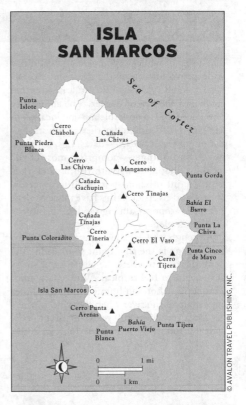

ISLA SAN MARCOS

© AVALON TRAVEL PUBLISHING, INC.

Hiking the interior of the dry, hilly, and relatively barren island might be interesting; there is one main cross-island trail about a third of the way up from the south and several minor ones elsewhere. Diving and snorkeling are best at Punta Piedra Blanca (at the northwest end of the island) and at two points—Punta Gorda and Punta La Chiva—at either end of Bahía El Burro along the eastern shore.

Boats to San Marcos can be chartered from the fishing community in San Bruno on the mainland. You may also be able to hitch a ride on one of the infrequent supply boats from Santa Rosalía.

CENTRAL BAJA

Mulegé

The town of Mulegé (pop. 4,000) straddles a wide arroyo formed by the Río Santa Rosalía (also called Río Mulegé), an estuarial river that feeds into the Sea of Cortez. The abundance of water made it a desirable mission location in the early 1700s, and today the agricultural legacy of the Jesuit padres—dates, figs, bananas, olives, and oranges—comprises most of the local livelihood, along with fishing and tourism. Quaint mission-style buildings, narrow streets, and riverside palms have made Mulegé a favorite stopover among modern Transpeninsular travelers.

Although it's well above the Tropic of Cancer, Mulegé is the first point south along the peninsular coast where the climate and ambience begin to feel tropical. Winters are mild, summers are hot and humid, and mosquitoes appear along the river when the wind is still.

Once every 50 or 100 years, the river floods, as it did following Hurricane John in 2006,

pushing trees, cars, and homes toward the sea. Floodwaters rose in a matter of minutes and nearly reached the first story ceilings of properties along the water's edge. Two local residents drowned, and property damage was severe. All but the hardest hit businesses had reopened by year-end, though power was still going out for long stretches most days.

Local facilities include a dive shop, laundry, auto mechanics, auto parts stores, markets, restaurants, hotels, and campgrounds. And Mulegé offers enough activities to occupy visitors for at least a couple of weeks, including hikes to nearby Amerindian cave paintings, snorkeling, scuba diving, fishing, clamming, birding, and kayaking.

SIGHTS

Misión Santa Rosalía de Mulegé

Mulegé's original mission was founded on the riverbanks in 1705. In 1770, a flood destroyed

Río Santa Rosalía, also known as Río Mulegé

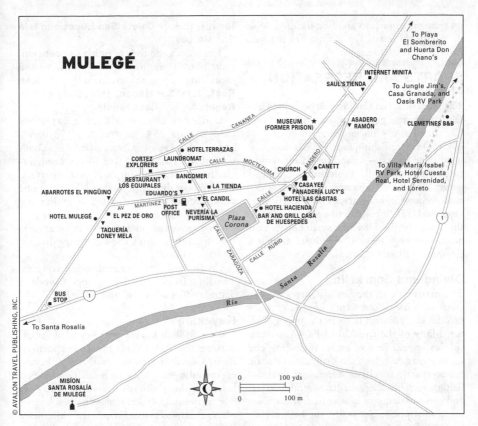

MULEGÉ

To Playa
El Sombrerito
and Huerta Don
Chano's

INTERNET MINITA

SAUL'S TIENDA

To Jungle Jim's,
Casa Granada, and
Oasis RV Park

CANANEA

MUSEUM ★
(FORMER PRISON)

ASADERO
RAMÓN

CLEMETINES B&B

CALLE

HOTEL TERRAZAS

CORTEZ
EXPLORERS

LAUNDROMAT

CALLE

MOCTEZUMA

MADERO

CHURCH

CANETT

To Villa María Isabel
RV Park, Hotel Cuesta
Real, Hotel Serenidad,
and Loreto

RESTAURANT
LOS EQUIPALES

BANCOMER

ABARROTES EL PINGÜINO

EDUARDO'S

LA TIENDA

CASA YEE
PANADERÍA LUCY'S
HOTEL LAS CASITAS

AV MARTINEZ

EL CANDIL

CALLE

POST
OFFICE

HOTEL MULEGÉ

EL PEZ DE ORO

NEVERÍA LA
PURÍSIMA

Plaza
Corona

HOTEL HACIENDA
BAR AND GRILL CASA
DE HUESPEDES

TAQUERÍA
DONEY MELA

CALLE ZARAGOZA

CALLE RUBIO

Santa Rosalía

BUS
STOP

1

Río

To Santa Rosalía

MISIÓN
SANTA ROSALÍA
DE MULEGÉ

0   100 yds
0   100 m

© AVALON TRAVEL PUBLISHING, INC.

CENTRAL BAJA

most community structures, and shortly thereafter the church was rebuilt at its current site, on a bluff overlooking the river. Although not one of Baja's most striking mission churches (compared to the missions at San Ignacio and San Javier), it's worth a visit just for the unobstructed views of the town and palm-lined river below. The church is usually locked except when services are held.

The church is best approached by following Calle Zaragoza southwest beneath the highway bridge, then west (right) until the road climbs the bluff by the church, about three kilometers (2 mi) from the bridge.

Museo Regional de Historia

The prison on the hill overlooking town func-tioned as a criminal detention facility 1907–1975. During much of that time the prison operated on an honor system; trustee prisoners were permitted to walk into town from 6 A.M. each day as long as they returned when the conch shell blew at 6 P.M.

The walled facility stood empty until a few years ago, when a local historian and a group of volunteers established a small museum inside. In addition to the old cells, visitors can view a collection of local historical artifacts—many marine-related—and a desk used by mystery writer Erle Stanley Gardner while researching central Baja's prehistoric murals.

Although hours are supposed to be Monday–Friday 9 A.M.–1 P.M., in reality the museum is open only sporadically. If you're intent on seeing the museum and find it closed, look up curator Homero Yee at Casa Yee market. Admission is by donation.

SPORTS AND RECREATION
Fishing

The Hacienda, Las Casitas, and Serenidad hotels can arrange guided fishing trips to Punta Chivato, Bahía Concepción, and nearby islands. Onshore fishing near the estuary—the south side is best—sometimes lands winter catches of yellowtail, roosterfish, sierra, and pargo; farther offshore are summer runs of dorado, yellowfin, and various billfish. Typical rates are US$120 per day in a *panga* for up to three persons, US$180 in a small cruiser that holds four anglers, or US$200 per day for a five-person diesel cruiser.

Diving and Snorkeling

The marinelife in the Sea of Cortez off the coast of Mulegé and Santa Rosalía is more prolific and colorful than in the upper Cortez. Many of the tropical or Pan-American species appear in reef areas, including the green moray eel (much less shy than its Pacific counterpart), angelfish, damselfish, parrotfish, triggerfish, flag cabrilla, several wrasses, and three varieties of lobster (red, spiny Cortez, and slipper). Generally, the best diving season is June–November, when visibility extends up to 30 meters (100 ft) and water temperatures near the surface are in the mid-20s C (mid-80s F). Full wetsuits are necessary in winter; in summer a Lycra skin is good protection against jellyfish.

Islas Santa Inés, three small islands in the northern part of Bahía Santa Inés, offer good snorkeling along their eastern shores, where rock reefs with soft corals lie at depths of around 4.5–12 meters (15–39 ft). There's also a sea lion colony here. Reefs and rock pinnacles extending from the north end of these islands are excellent scuba diving spots, with depths of 6–25 meters (20–85 ft). Scuba diving is also good at a reef at the north end of the bay, about a kilometer northeast of **Punta Chivato.** Other possibilities, farther north toward Santa Rosalía, include **Caleta San Lucas** and **Isla San Marcos.**

The islands and reefs of **Bahía Concepción,** south of Mulegé, provide plenty of diving and snorkeling opportunities, including **Pelican Reef, Isla Santispac, Isla Guapa, Isla Requesón,** and **Roca Frijole.**

Under new ownership, **Cortez Explorers** (Moctezuma 75A, tel./fax 615/153-0500, www.cortez-explorers.com) offers just about everything scuba and free divers need, including air, equipment, and boat charters. Guided boat dive trips start at US$70 for one tank, US$110 for two. Guided shore dives are US$50/90. You can rent all the basic gear, including a dive computer. Snorkeling gear rents for US$21/day. Check the website for dive instruction courses.

Credit cards are accepted for all services. The shop front in Mulegé is open Monday–Saturday 10 A.M.–1 P.M. and 4–7 P.M.

Kayaking

You can launch kayaks at the estuary for excursions into Bahía Santa Inés to the north or Bahía Concepción to the south. Most kayakers intending to paddle in Bahía Concepción launch farther south (see *Vicinity of Mulegé*).

Experienced kayakers enjoy the well known Mulegé–Loreto coastal trip, a 135-kilometer (84-mi), five- to seven-day paddle. Because shore campsites are few and far between, you should attempt this route only in the company of someone who's made the trip before.

Bird-Watching

The small lagoon where the river meets the sea is a good bird-watching site. For a view of the lagoon, river, fishing marina, and town, climb to the top of **El Sombrerito,** the hat-shaped hill topped with a cross at the south end of Mulegé's beach. Mornings are best for photography.

Baja Adventure Tours (Calle Rubio 27, tel./fax 615/153-0481, cirocuesta@yahoo.com) leads small-group tours of the Mulegé area for visitors interested in cave paintings, bird-watching, petroglyphs, or fishing.

Organized Tours

Salvador Castro Drew (tel. 615/153-0232, cell 615/103-5081, mulegetours@hotmail.com) offers guided cave painting tours delivered in flawless English for US$40 per person. He'll pick you up in his air conditioned van and share his knowledge of local natural and cultural history during the day. The standard tour includes stops at a local orchard, Rancho Las Tinajitas, then the cave sites in La Trinidad. Participants need to bring photo ID to register at the INAH office. Good walking shoes, a hat, sunblock, camera, and water are good things to pack.

Salvador also leads walking tours through the towns of Mulegé, Santa Roasalía, and San Ignacio. And he can arrange bird-watching, clamming, snorkeling, and sportfishing outings. Overnight trips include cave paintings in the Sierra Guadalupe and whale-watching at Laguna San Ignacio. Airport transportation is also available. If you don't reach Salvador by phone, inquire at the Hotel Las Casitas.

ENTERTAINMENT

The plainly named **Disco Bar,** an upstairs place at the southwest corner of Calle Moctezuma and Zaragoza, packs a crowd on the weekends. Usually the music is live *norteña* or *banda,* though occasionally the management resorts to recorded sounds in true disco fashion. Sometimes the whole place will be hired for a private function.

Scott's Pelicano Bar and Grill (on the plaza by the baseball stadium, Tues.–Sat. 9 A.M.–around 10 P.M., Sun. 11 A.M.–around 10 P.M., Mon. 3 P.M.–around 10 P.M.) is the place to watch NFL football games, NASCAR races, golf tournaments, and other sports on a big-screen TV. Breakfast mains are US$4–7.

Las Casitas hosts live *norteña* music on Fridays and mariachis on Saturdays. The Serenidad puts on a pig roast with mariachis every Saturday night (see *Accommodations*).

SHOPPING

A general store in the truest sense, **La Tienda** (Martínez and Zaragoza, Mon.–Sat. 9 A.M.– 1 P.M. and 3–6 P.M.) stocks fishing tackle and charts, books about Baja, gifts, swimsuits, wetsuits, and more. The Ladetel phone inside is a good place for a relatively quiet conversation. Credit cards are accepted as long as the power is on.

ACCOMMODATIONS

Mulegé offers several choices in modest and budget hotels, plus a few bed-and-breakfast inns and places to camp, as well.

Hotels

Under US$50: Popular **Hotel Las Casitas** (Madero 50 on the town's main east–west street, tel. 615/153-0019, fax 615/153-0190, US$39) was once the home of Mexican poet Vicente Gorosave. The eight-room establishment features modest air-conditioned accommodations and a nice patio restaurant and bar. Like most hotels in town, Las Casitas offers no offstreet parking.

Hotel Terrazas (tel. 615/153-0009, US$35), at the north end of Calle Zaragoza, has seen better days but is one of the quietest places to stay in town. Each of the good-sized, clean rooms has two double beds, a fan, TV, air conditioning, and private bath. Hot-water showers are on-again, off-again, but the rooms are still a bargain. Free coffee and toast with jam are provided every morning; take it on the *palapa* terrace on the second floor with pastries purchased in town and you'll have breakfast with a view for pennies. Guests also have free use of a small kitchen. The hotel has a small parking lot across the street plus three offstreet spaces in front of the hotel itself.

Two kilometers east of town off Mexico 1 is the well maintained **Hotel Cuesta Real** (tel./ fax 615/153-0321), with 12 air-conditioned rooms. Look for the archway that marks the hotel's entrance off Mexico 1 at Km 132. The hotel has a tiny swimming pool, restaurant/ bar, and laundry. The hotel also offers mountain bike rentals for the short ride into town via the old road along the river.

US$50-100: Four kilometers (2.5 mi) east of town off Mexico 1 is Mulegé's largest inn, the 50-room **Hotel Serenidad** (tel. 615/153-0530, www.serenidad.com, US$70–125), a favorite among *yanqui* pilots, many of whom fly in for the Saturday night all-you-can-eat pig roast. Spacious hotel grounds include a pool, tennis court, boat ramp, restaurant, and bar. Each year the kitchen closes for the month of September, while the bar and hotel remain open. Besides the standard rooms, the Serenidad offers two-bedroom air-conditioned cottages with a fireplace and parking space.

Bed-and-Breakfasts

Near the Oasis Rio RV Park on the south side of the river, newcomer **◖ Clementine's Inn** (www.clementinesbaja.com, US$450/week) has the most comfortable beds in Baja in this price range. Owners Cliff and Judith, who also run a top-rated B&B on the Oregon Coast—made a speedy recovery after the flood of September 2006 and bought all new beds, linens, appliances, and artwork for their guest accommodations. Four rooms and three bungalows achieve a unique balance between upscale B&B (luxurious sheets, tiled baths, stylish light fixtures, extra towels, tea lights) and authentic Baja (wood-paneled ceilings, basic faucets, abalone shells for soap dishes). Rooms are decorated in warm colors and set around a large, well-equipped open-air kitchen, thoughtfully designed with the culinary enthusiast in mind. Appliances include a large refrigerator, double toaster, coffee maker, and ice machine. A Weber gas grill, bottled water, and bug screens for covering prepared food are also provided. Bungalows range in size from a studio to three bedrooms, and the owners were building additional units on the property. Free wireless Internet is another plus.

Our only minor complaints about this property: Line-dried towels were scratchy, mist-style shower head made for a colder than desired shower, even though the water temp was hot; and we could have used a mosquito net over the bed.

Closer to the sea, **Casa Granada** (Estero de Mulegé 1, tel. 615/153-0688, www.casagranada.net, US$75) has four rooms with high ceilings, tiled baths, Talavera sinks, and remote-control air conditioning.

Casas de Huéspedes

Mulegé supports several *casas de huéspedes,* or guesthouses, generally with accommodations under US$25. **Casa de Huéspedes Cannett** (tel. 615/153-0272, US$10–15), on Calle Madero opposite a church, is the most livable of the group; the rooms are clean, and some have a private bath. A drawback is that the church bells across the street ring most mornings at around 6 A.M.

Camping and RV Parks

Properties along the river were among the worst hit areas during the flood of September 2006, and while some were already rebuilding by year-end, others are closed for good. Much loved **Orchard Vacation Village** was among the hardest hit and did not appear to be opening for some time, if ever again.

East of Mexico 1, south of town, **Villa María Isabel RV Park** (tel. 615/153-0246) features 30 pull-through RV spaces with full hookups for US$15, shaded tent camping sites for US$6.50 per person, hot showers, a swimming pool, boat ramps, a good bakery, and a laundry.

On the opposite side of the river off the dirt road to Playa El Sombrerito, **Huerta Don Chano's** offers RV and tent sites at similar rates. The Hotel Serenidad has 15 full hookup RV spaces next to the hotel for US$15.

Many camping visitors to Mulegé end up camping south of town at Bahía Concepción (see *Vicinity of Mulegé*) because of the shortage of places on the river—and because of the mosquitoes.

Free Camping: Playa El Sombrerito, the beach between the estuary and the Sea of Cortez, is a fine place to spend a few nights. Just take care not to pitch a tent too far toward the lagoon side, which cars and trucks use as a road to the fishing marina.

FOOD

Mulegé boasts several good restaurants; like the town's hotels, they're generally less expensive than those in most other Baja resort towns. During the off-season (anytime outside November–February), they look rather empty, but this doesn't mean they're not good—it's typical outside "the season."

The tastefully decorated **Los Equipales** (Calle Moctezuma, tel. 615/153-0330, mains US$10–15), named for the style of leather-and-wood chair featured prominently in the restaurant's decor, has a second-floor dining room overlooking Calle Moctezuma. Though a bit on the pricey side, this restaurant features the best Mexican specialties and seafood in town; it's worth every peso.

The service at **El Candil** (Zaragoza 8 opposite Plaza Corona, tel. 615/153-0185, mains US$6–10) is slow, as everything is made from scratch. But the food is generally worth the wait and prices are reasonable. House specialties include fresh seafood and the *combinación mexicana,* a huge plate of *taquitos,* enchiladas, chiles rellenos, beans, rice, and tortillas.

On the south side of the river, past Clementines B&B, **Jungle Jim** (mains US$6–12) feels a bit like an eating club, with regulars helping themselves to drinks at the bar. Decent burgers and seafood are the mainstays of the changing menu.

Antojitos, Tacos, and Fast Food

Mulegé has several good taco stands. On Calle Romero Rubio, **Asadero Ramon** (Mon.–Sat. 8 A.M.–8 P.M.) specializes in *tacos de carne asada* and quesadillas. This is also a good spot for brewed coffee in the mornings. On Saturdays, the cook whips up a batch of mouthwatering *carnitas,* which can be purchased as tacos or by the kilo.

Great fish tacos are available from **Taquitos Mulegé,** a taco vendor on Plaza Corona, usually open 9 A.M.–1 P.M. or until the fish supply runs out.

Eduardo's on Calle Moctezuma bakes pizza from 7 P.M.–10 P.M. during the week but on Sunday makes a total departure to serve family-style Chinese food. Corona beer is available on tap.

MULEGÉ PHONE NUMBERS

Mulegé area code: 615
Fire Department: 153-0079
Highway Patrol (Santa Rosalía): 152-0839
Hospital: 153-0298
Immigration (Santa Rosalía): 152-0313
Police: 153-0049
Red Cross: 153-0110 or 153-0380
State Tourism Office: 124-0199
Taxi Service: 153-0420
Tourist Assistance: 078

Excellent *nieve* (Mexican-style, no-milk ice cream) is available from **Nevería La Purísima** near El Candil.

The restaurants at the **Las Casitas** (breakfast mains US$3–6, dinner mains US$9–17) and **Serenidad** hotels are popular among the tourist crowd and serve decent, moderately priced Mexican fare. The garden patio at Las Casitas offers the best all-around ambience in town, and the delicious daiquiris—especially the "bango" (banana/mango) concoction—are legendary.

Groceries

Several *tiendas* stock fresh, locally produced meats, poultry, fruits, and vegetables, along with smaller supplies of canned goods. Generally the best stocked are **Casa Yee** (Calle Madero 46 near Las Casitas), **Abarrotes El Pingüino** (on the road in from the highway, near Hotel Mulegé), and **Saul's Tienda** (on Calle Madero where it becomes Calle Playa). Saul's caters to the gringo market; owner Saul Davis speaks English and can get just about anything grocery-related—Thanksgiving turkeys, for example—if given enough advance notice.

Block ice and purified water are available from the **Hielera Mulegé** on "Ice House Road," the road signed San Estanislao just north of town west off the highway. It's open 24 hours. You can also get free drinking water from the spigot at the small plaza opposite Las Casitas. Purified water is available in gallon jugs from local grocery stores.

Villa María Isabel RV Park on the river operates a small bakery with reasonably priced *bolillos* and cookies.

INFORMATION AND SERVICES
Money
The Bancomer is located on Zaragoza, between Madero and Moctezuma. You can cash travelers checks at **El Pez de Oro** (Moctezuma 17), a *casa de cambio* (money changer) just about opposite the Hotel Mulegé (open 9 A.M.–1 P.M. and 3–7 P.M.), and also at Hotel Las Casitas. Neither place will change pesos back to dollars, only dollars to pesos.

Communications
The post office (tel. 615/153-0205, Mon.–Fri. 8 A.M.–1 P.M.) is on Avenida Martínez, just before the Pemex station. A public phone with local and long-distance service can be found on the plaza off Calle Zaragoza. More reliable is a small, private long-distance telephone office in the Minisuper Padilla (at the corner of Calle Zaragoza and Av. Martínez, tel./fax 615/153-0190). As usual, a service charge is added to the phone charges. **Internet Minita** (Mon.–Sat. 9 A.M.–9 P.M.) at the end of Calle Madero has eight desktop computers for rent for US$2/hour.

Laundry
Lavamática Claudia (Zaragoza and Moctezuma, tel. 615/153-0057, Mon.–Sat. 8 A.M.– 6 P.M.) is one of the cleanest public laundries you'll ever see in Mexico.

GETTING THERE AND AROUND
The nearest commercial **airport** is Loreto. **ABC** and **Águila buses** stop at the town entrance on Mexico 1 on the way north and south. Although they follow no strict schedules, two southbound buses usually arrive every day, one in the late morning and one in mid-afternoon, while northbound buses arrive one in the mid-afternoon and one each in the early and late evening. The schedule is highly variable from year to year. Because there is no bus depot or ticket office in town, you can't make reservations or buy tickets in advance. When the bus arrives, buy your ticket on board.

You can easily reach every point in town on foot, even from the riverfront RV parks. For a bit more reach, rent a **mountain bike** at Cortez Explorers.

Downtown Mulegé's system of narrow one-way streets might seem a bit confusing at first but is pretty easy to figure out. Some streets are marked with arrows; some aren't. A policeman usually stands at the main intersection of Avenida Gral. Martínez and Calle Zaragoza to make sure motorists drive in the correct direction.

The Pemex station in town, on Avenida Martínez, sometimes has vehicles waiting for gas backed up all the way to the end of the block. A quicker alternative—in spite of the drive— is the **Mulegé Pemex Centro** on Mexico 1, about 15 minutes south of Mulegé by car. This station offers several self-service pumps, and there's rarely a long wait. The locals all claim the pumps at this highway station are rigged to give you 10 percent less fuel than what the pumps read out. A small café and a minimarket with ice are attached to the station.

Vicinity of Mulegé

SIERRA DE GUADALUPE CAVE PAINTINGS

The Sierra de Guadalupe, west of Mulegé, contains the largest number of known prehistoric mural sites in Baja California. Several hotels in Mulegé can arrange excursions to the more accessible sites for US$25–35 per person.

La Trinidad

One of the best rock-art hikes is to a canyon near Rancho La Trinidad, about 29 kilometers (18 mi) west of Mulegé. As with other sites encompassed by central Baja's Great Mural tradition, those at La Trinidad are federally protected, and you must visit with a licensed guide. Viewing the major sites at La Trinidad means a challenging canyon hike of around 6.5 kilometers (4 mi) that includes several river crossings—at least two and sometimes three usually require swimming. Although the hike isn't particularly difficult or dangerous, it requires good overall fitness, the ability to swim up to a hundred meters (300 ft) through calm waters, the strength to hoist oneself out of the water onto stone riverbanks up to a meter high, and a fair sense of balance for walking along narrow paths.

You should also carry at least two liters (roughly a half gallon) of drinking water per person, preferably in canteens or other containers slung over the shoulder. You can float a limited amount of camera gear up the river on small, impromptu rafts made of inflated inner tubes and any flat, sturdy material used as a platform over the tube. Everything else you bring along, including shoes (Teva-style sports sandals are the perfect footwear for this trip), should be submersible. Count on a half day to complete the canyon hike itself, although some visitors prefer to spend an entire day in the canyon. Others may want to spend some time at the various ranchos along the way.

The trip begins with a scenic desert drive to Rancho La Trinidad, a large goat and cattle ranch at the foot of the mountains. Some guides stop at other ranches along the way to allow visitors to observe leather tanning, cheese-making, and other ranch crafts. After you arrive at Rancho La Trinidad, you hike about 800 meters (a half mile) to a four-meter (12-foot) stone dam. These are reportedly the headwaters of the Río Mulegé, though the river drops underground before resurfacing near town. Once inside the mouth of the canyon, you make one river crossing before reaching the first and largest group of murals. Among the many red and black animal representations on the canyon walls is a large ocher deer silhouette, considered one of the best prehistoric deer paintings in Baja; others throughout the peninsula are often compared to the "Trinidad deer." Among humanoid representations in this group is a shamanistic figure sometimes referred to as a "*cardón* man," though there's no real evidence to suggest the image is linked to local legends about *cardón* cacti coming to life at night. Arrows pierce the figure's neck, chest, and groin. There are also a couple of vulva drawings and a painting of a fish skeleton, thought to be the only such work in Baja; other fish paintings in Baja appear to represent whole fish.

To reach the second group of murals you must ford the river several more times. Depending on river height, at least one crossing requires a swim of up to 100 meters through a narrow stone gorge. For many people this is the high point of the trip. The water is safe to swim in but should be boiled or treated before drinking. Some years a swim isn't necessary, but hurricanes in some years fill the canyon. The canyon scenery is spectacular, with cactus and wild fig trees clinging to the sides of high tuff (volcanic ash) cliffs.

The final site is reached by ascending a sloped canyon wall affording long views of the canyon, which splits in two here. The paintings at this site are neither as numerous nor as impressive as the first, but the hike/swim through the canyon makes it a worthwhile objective.

Two of the most experienced guides in

Mulegé authorized by INAH to lead this trip are Salvador Castro (tel. 615/153-0232) and Ciro Cuesta (tel. 615/153-0021). Any hotel in town can arrange for one of the guides. The usual price is US$35 per person, less if there are four or more persons or you drive your own vehicle rather than using those belonging to the guides. High road clearance is required, and a cache of spare parts is suggested. The fee usually includes a simple burrito lunch at the ranch, sodas, and beer. Overnight Trinidad trips cost US$50 per person if a guide is available. Most tours include an interesting stop in the desert to learn about medicinal plants. At the ranch itself you'll be required to sign an INAH register.

You can also drive to Rancho La Trinidad and arrange for someone at the ranch to take you to see the murals. Although this is much less expensive—no more than US$10 per person—the drive to the ranch involves several unsigned turns. Ask at one of the hotels for detailed directions. The turnoff for the main road from Mexico 1, known locally as Ice House Road for the ice factory alongside it, is just a few miles north of Mulegé; it's signed San Estanislao. Continue following signs to San Estanislao until you see a sign for La Trinidad.

San Borjitas

Another area of prehistoric rock art, the San Borjitas site has been known to local residents since mission times; Leon Diguet visited San Borjitas in the 1890s, Erle Stanley Gardner in the 1960s, and Harry Crosby in the 1970s. To get there from Mulegé, drive north on Mexico 1 to the Km 157 marker near Palo Verde at the turnoff for Punta Chivato, then take the dirt road west into the sierra. This route is appropriate for high-clearance vehicles only and takes around two hours each way. Be sure to bring plenty of drinking water, as this area tends to be warm even in winter.

Keep left at all forks, pass two abandoned ranchos (when you reach a gate, go through it and close it behind you), and continue until you arrive at Rancho Las Tinajas (also known as Rancho Cerro Gordo, approximately

27 km/17 mi from the highway), where you should be able to hire a guide. Until recently you had to arrange a two-hour mule ride and hike to reach Cueva San Borjitas from here. A new road allows you to drive to within just a mile of the cave. At Rancho Las Tinajas you must register and obtain keys for two locked gates that must be entered between here and the cave; a fee of around US$4 in pesos is collected. With the first key, unlock the gate next to the ranch and continue driving northwest 2.1 kilometers (1.3 mi) till you reach yet another fork (this will be the third fork coming from the highway), then pass through an unlocked metal gate and drive another mile till you reach a T-intersection. Turn left and pass through another locked gate (using your second key), continue another mile, pass through an unlocked gate, and at 35.7 kilometers (22.2 mi) from the highway you can park at **Rancho San Baltasar.** From here it's a one-mile walk to the cave along a trail that begins at the far end of a small corral, follows the left (south) side of an arroyo, then cuts into the canyon wall and leads to the main cave.

The paintings at San Borjitas are unique among Baja rock-art schools in several respects: At least a dozen of the more than 50 large *monos* (human figures) in the rock shelter are apparently transfixed with arrows; some exhibit male genitalia; and about a dozen are filled in with longitudinal stripes. Colors employed at San Borjitas include black, red, ocher, gray, white, and combinations of all five, painted in monocolor, bicolor, and checkerboard patterns. Along the tuff side walls of the cave is a collection of petroglyphs (rock carvings) depicting female genitalia; the fire-blackened back wall shows fish and deer.

BAHÍA SANTA INÉS AND PUNTA CHIVATO

Large, gently curving Bahía Santa Inés, just north of Mulegé, bears very little coastal development and is a great site for beachcombing and beach walking. The bay is rimmed almost its entire length by sandy **Playa Santa Inés,** which can be reached via a long sand road that turns off Mexico 1 near Km 151. This road branches frequently, but if you always take the trunk most traveled and ignore any small branches you'll eventually come to the beach. The road is soft and hilly in places. At five kilometers (3 mi) from the highway you'll come to a relatively major fork; take the right fork to run parallel to the shoreline and then choose any of several very sandy turnoffs to the left leading directly to the beach.

The wide, white-sand beach is backed by low dunes topped with cholla and other thorny plants. Driving beyond the crest of the dune line isn't recommended as you're likely to become mired in deep, soft sand unless you're driving on sand tires or using chains. Self-contained camping is certainly possible anywhere along the beach. Toward the center of the beach are a couple of trash barrels; whoever collects the trash may want to collect a couple of dollars from campers for hauling garbage away.

Accommodations

At the north end of Bahía Santa Inés, 44 kilometers (30 mi) northeast of Mulegé (24 km north via Mexico 1, then another 20 km/13 mi east on a graded, unpaved road), is the secluded **Posada de las Flores** (formerly Hotel Punta Chivato, tel./fax 615/153-0188, U.S. tel. 877/245-2860, www.posadadelasflores.com, US$300–800/night) with its own boat ramp, small desert golf course, pool, sea kayaks, and lovely nearby beaches. The hotel sits on Punta Mezquitito, part of the larger cape known as Punta Chivato. Large, attractive rooms feature air conditioning, private baths, fireplaces, and semiprivate garden patios. Rates include breakfast, snacks, and dinner, but not tax or a US$18/day service fee.

BAHÍA CONCEPCIÓN

From this point south to the Cape Region, the Sea of Cortez and its many bays begin matching the tourist-brochure description of a "desert Polynesia." This huge bay, open to the north and sheltered on the east, has a string of sandy beaches along its west side and a number of small islands anchored in the middle—a perfect

© PAUL ITOI

on the beach at Bahía Concepción

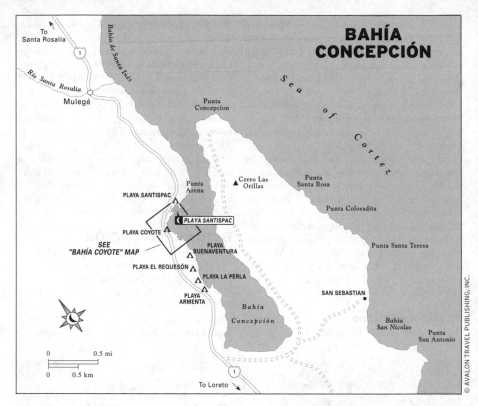

setting for anglers, small-boaters, kiteboarders, windsurfers, divers, and especially kayakers.

The entire bay, now a national marine preserve, is reportedly one of the cleanest marine bay systems in the world. It's home to an amazing variety of marinelife, from blue-footed boobies and magnificent frigates to whales, porpoises, and abundant shellfish. Commercial fishing is prohibited within the bay—if you spot any fishing boats working in Concepción and feel like doing something about it, report your sighting to Mulegé authorities immediately. If you plan to sail a yacht into the bay, please refrain from dumping the head until north of Punta Concepción.

Mexico 1 parallels the west bayshore, providing inspiring views of the blue-green bay and conical, flat-topped islands to the east and Sierra Coyote peaks to the west, as well as access to several beaches and coves along the way. Most of the beaches are *ejido* lands where the local *ejidatarios* collect camping fees of US$6, regardless of whether you're parking a motor home or sleeping on the sand.

Bahía Concepción attracts a loyal following of Canadians, Mexicans, Americans, and Europeans who return year after year to the beaches—staying in tents, *palapa* huts, and motor homes—for intervals ranging from two weeks to six months. So far only one permanent settlement, Posada Concepción, has developed along the bayshore.

In late 2006, local authorities asked semipermanent residents at Playa Santispac and other beaches in the area to remove all structures from the beach, restoring it to its undeveloped state; according to local sources, a large Mexican real estate company had purchased land from the *ejido* and planned to commence resort development soon.

For the most part, Concepción's sandiest beaches are concentrated along the northwest shore in a bay subsystem sometimes called Bahía Coyote (not to be confused with Playa Coyote, near Bahía Coyote's south end).

Punta Arena
At the top of the bay's western shore, a signed, four-kilometer (2.5-mi) road leads to Punta Arena, a sandy, windy point with a string of *palapas* and *palapa* huts—many of them permanent homes—for US$8 a night. This area offers the best windsurfing along the bay's west shore; the winds also make this one of the more comfortable camping beaches in the summertime. The turnoff for Punta Arena is 13.2 kilometers (8.2 mi) from the Motel Serenidad turnoff from Mexico 1.

◖ Playa Santispac
Farther south (entrance btw Km 114–115) is the largest and most popular beach, Playa Santispac, where tent and trailer camping next to shade *palapas* is available. The fee here is about US$6 per vehicle whether you camp or not. In recent years, this beach had become the most developed camping beach along the bay; however, the government required semipermanent residents to remove all structures in 2007, ostensibly to restore the beach to its former state, and perhaps to make it more appealing to future developers. **Ana's Restaurant Bar** (daily 7 A.M.–10 P.M., mains US$6–15) is a full-service operation that serves fresh seafood and a full bar especially known for its Bloody Mary cocktails. Ana's has firewood, groceries, sundries, and propane, as well as tools for repairing cars and boats. The owner, Russ, rents kayaks (US$25–35/day), *pangas* (US$20/hr), and snorkeling gear (US$10/day). He can also arrange guided tours. Next to the restaurant, four basic rooms share a hot shower and toilet facility (US$20). Nonguests can use the showers for US$2. Public Internet access was in the plans.

This is a popular put-in point for kayakers. You can reach several nearby islands by small boat or kayak, including **San Ramón, Liebre, Pitahaya** (Luz), and **Blanca.** Between Liebre and Pitahaya is a reef known as **Arrecife Pelicanos,** or Pelican Reef. On the point at the south end of Santispac are a couple of thermal springs.

Posada Concepción
Accessed at Km 113, this congested development of houses and trailer homes along Playa Concepción offers a market and tennis courts. Full-hookup slots, when vacant, cost US$10 for two persons, including flush toilets and showers. Electricity is available 10 A.M.–10 P.M. You can sometimes rent houses on **Punta Tordillo,** a steep, rocky point southeast of the beach community; inquire at Posada Concepción.

Playa Escondida
About 50 meters south of the Posada Concepción entrance, at Km 111, an 800-meter (half-mile) bumpy, narrow road unsuitable for larger RVs parallels the highway and provides access to other beaches. Follow the road over some hills to Playa Escondida, a scenic, uncrowded beach with a few *palapa* campsites for US$5 a day. The beach is rather shelly, confirming the fact that the clamming is very good here.

Playa Los Cocos
Slightly north of Km 111 lies Playa Los Cocos, one of the prettiest beaches along this section of Bahía Concepción; the limestone in the surrounding cliffs lends a turquoise hue to the bay. Camping is permitted here for US$5; the only facilities are a few two- and three-sided, well-spaced *palapas* and pit toilets. Behind the beach is a small, pristine lagoon lined with mangrove.

Playa El Burro and Playa Coyote
Two kilometers farther along the shore is Playa El Burro, a public beach with *palapas* and trash barrels next to a scrappy-looking residential section; it costs US$6 per day to camp there. Separated by Punta Cola de Ballena (Whale's Tail Point) is the adjacent Playa Coyote, with a

BAHÍA COYOTE

To Mulegé

Playa Santispac

PLAYA SANTISPAC

HOT SPRINGS

Isla San Ramón

Playa Concepción

Punta Piedrita

Arrecife Pelicanos

Punta Tordillo

Isla Pitahaya

Playa Escondida

Isla Liebre

Playa los Cocos

Isla Blanca

PETROGLYPHS/ BELL ROCK

Bahía   Coyote

Playa el Burro

Punta Cola de Ballena

Isla Bargo

Isla Guapa

Playa Coyote

Punta Santa Bárbara

Playa Santa Bárbara

0   1 mi

0   1 km

To Loreto

To Playa Requesón

© AVALON TRAVEL PUBLISHING, INC.

campground/RV park (pit toilets, well-spaced *palapas,* showers, drinking water) that charges US$6 per vehicle for camping, RV, or day use with a *palapa.* Semi-permanent structures at both of these beaches were expected to be torn down in 2007.

The **Restaurant Estrella del Mar,** opposite Playa Coyote, serves breakfast, lunch, and dinner. **Restaurant Bertha's** serves good, simple Mexican meals at Playa Coyote itself.

On the opposite (north) side of the high-

way from Playa El Burro is an arroyo containing hundreds of prehistoric **petroglyphs.** This site may have been sacred to Amerindians in the area because of a large, horizontal "bell rock" lying in the arroyo; when struck with a stone or hard stick, the rock resonates with a bell-like tone. A few hundred meters east of Playa Coyote is **Isla Bargo** (Coyote Island), an elbow-shaped island with a sandy beach suitable for camping in the "elbow." It is reachable by kayak.

Playa Santa Bárbara

Around 2.4 nautical kilometers (1.5 nautical mi) southeast of Playa Coyote is the idyllic **Playa Santa Bárbara,** also known as Honeymoon Cove. This sandy, palm-fringed inlet is accessible only by boat and makes an excellent kayak camp for those paddling the bay circuit.

Playa Buenaventura

After El Coyote, Mexico 1 veers away from the coast for a short distance, returning at Km 94.5 to Playa Buenaventura.

This half-sand, half-rock beach holds **Hotel San Buenaventura** (Km 94.5, tel. 615/155-5616, www.hotelsanbuenaventura.com, US$79), a small resort with a modern motel, campground, market, and restaurant/sports bar. The motel features well-maintained rooms with air conditioning and ceiling fans surrounding a courtyard. *Palapa*-shaded campsites go for US$20; toilets and hot showers are available (US$2 for nonguests). The beach at Buenaventura has coarse sand but is kept clean. **George's Olé Sports Bar and Grill** (daily 8 A.M.–10 P.M.) serves food and drinks; chessboards and a paperback library are available.

Playa El Requesón and Playa La Perla

A kilometer or so farther south is the nicer Playa El Requesón. Tent and RV camping (pit toilets, *palapas,* no drinking water) is permitted along the broad, sandy beach here for US$6 per vehicle. At the north end a sandbar connects the shore with Isla El Requesón, forming sheltered coves on either side.

South of Requesón the bayshore becomes a bit rocky and swampy. Accessible by the same road that leads to Playa Requesón, Playa La Perla lies just 400 meters south and offers several *palapa* campsites at similar rates.

Playa Armenta

The last road-accessible beach on Bahía Concepción, Playa Armenta can be reached via a signed dirt/sand road off Mexico 1 between Km 90 and 91. This road cuts south and runs parallel to the highway, passing a little *ranchito*

sandbar at Playa El Requesón

before hitting the beach after about 800 meters. It's a pretty beach facing northwest, so it can get pretty breezy in the winter on some days. A few substantial *palapa* campsites and a couple of outhouses are available; when anyone bothers to collect, camping costs US$5 a day.

Península Concepción

The peninsula forming the east side of the bay is visited less than the western shore because access requires a sturdy, high-clearance vehicle, preferably with four-wheel drive. None of the numerous camping areas along the peninsula's usually deserted bayshore have toilet or water facilities. Branching off Mexico 1 at the south end of the bay, the 60-kilometer (37-mi) road north along the far bayshore ends just southeast of Punta Concepción at an abandoned manganese mine. The road follows the left (west) side of the peninsula most of the way, then just before it reaches the end, it cuts across the mountains and terminates near the northeastern tip. At some points the road bisects the high-tide line, so during high-tide periods you must time it right to traverse the road all the way. The beaches and coves of Península Concepción are best visited by boat from Punta Arena, west across the bay.

Kayaking

Scalloped with sandy beaches, dotted with islands, and protected from winds on three sides, Concepción is the perfect Sea of Cortez kayaking destination. While many other Baja kayaking spots may be blown out several months per year, kayakers in Concepción typically lose less than a cumulative two weeks—spread out over a year—to high winds.

SOUTHWEST OF MULEGÉ

Southwest of Mulegé lies a series of volcanic valleys, isolated from the rest of Baja California Sur by the rugged Sierra de la Gigante, that support the historic farm/ranch communities of San Isidro, La Purísima, and Comondú. Although a journey to this region is easiest via the paved and gravel roads heading north from Ciudad Insurgentes, the rugged trip from Mexico

1, from a point south of Bahía Concepción, is shorter and more scenic.

The turnoff for this rough byway into Old Baja branches west from Mexico 1 just below the Km 60 marker, 75 kilometers (46 mi) south of Mulegé. The first 18 kilometers (11 mi) is graded, threading through a series of steep-walled arroyos before meeting a four-way junction.

Left is an unpaved, ungraded, 40-kilometer (25-mi) road southwest to San José de Comondú, the larger of the two villages comprising Comondú. The second half of the Comondú road is rough and features steep grades; except for four-wheel-drive vehicles, a better approach would be from San Isidro to the northwest or La Poza Grande to the southwest.

The road to the right at the four-way junction is abandoned. Take the unpaved, ungraded road straight ahead to arrive, via a series of switchbacks, in Valle de la Purísima, at San Isidro (37 km/23 mi west of the junction).

San Isidro

San Isidro (pop. 1,000) offers a church, a rustic café, clinic, market, *télefono rural,* barrel gas, and drinking water, but most visitors continue another five kilometers (3 mi) west—past stands of date palm, *higuera,* mango, and citrus—to the slightly larger and more historic La Purísima.

La Purísima

Amid ponds and orchards (date, citrus, and mango), surrounded by high volcanic cliffs, and backed by a sloped butte—Cerro El Pilón, considered an emblem of the region—La Purísima represents a fairly typical early Baja settlement of the interior. Originally established by Padre Nicolás Tamaral as a mission community in 1717, the village was abandoned in 1822 and revived in the late 19th century by Mexican farmers. Splendid examples of purple bougainvillea cascade over crumbling walls here and there around town. The ruined foundation of Misión de la Purísima Concepción, incorporated into a private residence, lies several kilometers north of the village.

If a proposed second highway along the peninsula's east side becomes a reality, it will most likely pass just west of here. A small Mexican army post sits at the east end of town.

Facilities in La Purísima include barrel gasoline (look for a small sign reading Gasolina off the main road near the northeast end of town), a post office, market (with ice), auto parts store, drinking water, and medical clinic. **Abarrotes Neferik,** near the airstrip, offers cheap, simple fare such as burritos, *tortas,* hamburgers, and quesadillas. You can camp at a primitive campground—really no more than a cleared spot— just off the main road through town.

Following the late-summer rains, it's possible to canoe or kayak—with a few portages— all the way west down Arroyo de la Purísima to the Pacific Ocean at Punta San Gregorio. A 48-kilometer (30-mi) graded road leads west and then north to Bahía San Juanico, a little-known surfing destination; from San Juanico another graded road heads northwest to Laguna San Ignacio.

Comondú

To reach the twin communities of **San José de Comondú** and **San Miguel de Comondú** (known collectively as Comondú), take the road east out of San Isidro, following an old stone acequia (irrigation canal). You'll pass a picturesque lagoon and the tiny village of **Caramuche** before the road splits at 3.7 kilometers (2.3 mi); bear right to continue on to Comondú. From San Isidro to San José de Comondú it's 36 kilometers (22 mi)—not 24.8 kilometers (15.4 mi) as the AAA map says—of unpaved, ungraded, and often stony road surfaces.

The descent from the desert plains into steep-sided, 11-kilometer-long (7-mi-long) Arroyo de Comondú is dramatic. Wedged between barren volcanic mesas, well-watered Comondú produces dates, figs, mangoes, bananas, citrus, corn, grapes, sugarcane, and vegetables; in fact there appear to be more date palms here than in either Mulegé or San Ignacio. A small plaza in San José is surrounded by stone and adobe buildings, including a surviving Jesuit missionary house from Misión San José de Co-

mondú (1737–1827); the boxy stone structure is now used as a church. A church bell dating to 1708 is on display next to the edifice. A restoration of sorts is proceeding slowly.

San Miguel de Comondú, about three kilometers (2 mi) west of San José, was originally the site of a *capilla de visita* (visiting chapel). Architecturally it's the most impressive of the two towns; before the completion of Mexico 1, Todos Santos and San Ignacio must have resembled this place. Locally grown sugarcane is still processed in San Miguel using traditional donkey-powered presses. Although smaller than San José, the village offers more local services because it's on the road southwest to Ciudad Insurgentes. San Miguel has a post office, a restaurant, and a *tienda rural;* drinking water is available at either village. **Restaurant Oasis** is open all year 8 A.M.–8 P.M. It serves regional dishes for US$5– 10. The owner, Martina, is happy to give out help and information to any tourists who might happen by. She sells finely woven palm-leaf baskets, as well. Along the 2.4-kilometer (1.5-mi) road between San José and San Miguel, mango trees are abundant, and rock walls have been used to build terraced gardens.

One of the best times of year for a Comondú visit is on the feast day for San Miguel (29 September), when tiny San Miguel de Comondú bursts with music and dancing.

You can complete a loop drive back to Mexico 1 by continuing southeast from San José to Loreto via the charming mission village of **San Javier.** Although the road was scheduled for paving, it was suitable only for sturdy, high-clearance vehicles at press time (see *Loreto and Vicinity*).

Alternate Route

Another way—in fact the easy way—to reach La Purísima, San Isidro, and Comondú is to use the paved road that runs north from Ciudad Insurgentes to within a few kilometers of La Purísima, joining the network of unpaved roads that link all three communities. If you don't have your own vehicle, catch one of the Águila buses traveling once a day between Ciudad Insurgentes and La Purísima.

San Isidro lies within easy walking distance of La Purísima, and you may be able to hitch rides onward to Comondú, San Javier, and Loreto.

Bahía San Juanico

From La Purísima, an ungraded road leads northwest 48 kilometers (30 mi) to Bahía San Juanico on the Pacific coast. Gas, a public phone, and limited supplies are available there. Punta Pequeña (Little Point) at the north end of the bay protects sailors from the predominant northwest winds and provides a good launching point for local fisherfolk. Fishing is in fact the main local livelihood, with low-key tourism a distant second.

Surfers, who know San Juanico as Scorpion Bay, can choose from six different point breaks here during summer swells, some of which reportedly hook up on occasion to provide epic two-point rides. Winter surfing isn't too shabby, either. Counting from the north, the first point is often too weak to ride, the second point is usually best for beginning surfers, and the third point puts out perfect 100-meter peelers in a southern swell. Pack your guns for the remaining breaks.

A few expat Americans and Canadians have begun building rustic homes and *palapa* trailer shelters along a low bluff over the ocean near the village.

Scorpion Bay, Destination Surf Resort

(tel. 613/138-2850, U.S. tel. 619/239-1335, ruben@scorpionbay.net or scorpionbay2002@ hotmail.com, www.scorpionbay.net) offers a quiet campground for tents, campers, and self-contained RVs. Two sites include three *palapa* shelters. Tent and camper sites near the beach cost US$5 per person (children under 8 free) per day, including the use of hot shower facilities. *Palapa* shelters with four padded cots and sleeping bags are US$30 per day for one or two persons, including hot showers and a private bath. The spacious shelters can accommodate up to eight people. Self-contained trailers and RVs may park for a bargain US$5 a night or US$50 a month, plus the camp fee. Scorpion Bay Resort boasts a restaurant-cantina (daily 7:30 A.M.–10 P.M.). Grilled seafood is a specialty.

In addition to the resort restaurant, **Restaurant Gloria's** (Calle Rosalía, 8 A.M.– 8 P.M.), on the road to San Ignacio, serves the usual seafood and Mexican dishes under a *palapa* roof.

The road continues north from San Juanico all the way to San Ignacio via Laguna San Ignacio. Portions of the road between San Juanico and Laguna San Ignacio require four-wheel-drive vehicles and skilled driving—it's best to drive the road with someone who knows the way well because of the many intersecting turnoffs.

Loreto and Vicinity

For outdoor enthusiasts who would like to experience a little bit of history and culture too, Loreto makes an ideal home base. Fishing, kayaking, and diving here are all world-class; on land, a restored cobblestone plaza adjoins the historic mission church and museum, and a *malecón* has transformed the old seawall into a picturesque promenade. You won't have white sand beaches, but with the National Marine Park offshore and the Sierra de la Giganta in the background to the west, the scenery is plenty dramatic.

Loreto became the first European settle-

ment in the Californias more than 300 years ago and served as the Californias' secular and religious capital for 132 years. Superseded by La Paz following an 1829 hurricane, Loreto all but vanished for three-quarters of a century, until Mexican fishermen again began frequenting the area. As word of the prolific fisheries spread, a handful of American anglers started flying to Loreto fish camps in private planes.

Although Loreto never regained its former glory, the 1973 completion of the Transpeninsular Highway brought the area within

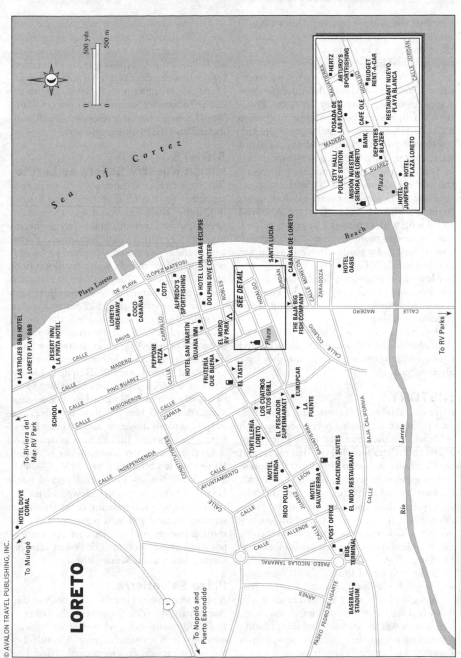

LORETO

Sea of Cortez

Beach

To Mulegé

To Nopoló and Puerto Escondido

To Riviera del Mar RV Park

To RV Parks

© AVALON TRAVEL PUBLISHING, INC.

CENTRAL BAJA

Detail map:

POSADA DE SALVATIERRA
LAS FLORES
ARTURO'S SPORTFISHING
HERTZ
BUDGET RENT-A-CAR
CAFÉ OLÉ
RESTAURANT NUEVO PLAYA BLANCA
CALLE JORDAN
HIDALGO
MADERO
CITY HALL/ POLICE STATION
BANK
DEPORTES BLAZER
HOTEL PLAZA LORETO
MISIÓN NUESTRA SEÑORA DE LORETO
P. SUAREZ
Plaza
HOTEL JUNIPERO

Main map labels:

Playa Loreto
DE PLAYA
(LÓPEZ MATEOS)
COTP
ALFREDO'S SPORTFISHING
HOTEL LUNA/BAR ECLIPSE
DOLPHIN DIVE CENTER
SANTA LUCIA
CABAÑAS DE LORETO
HOTEL OASIS
LAS TROJES B&B HOTEL
LORETO PLAY B&B
DESERT INN/ LA PINTA HOTEL
LORETO HIDEAWAY
COCO CABAÑAS
CARRILLO
DAVIS
CALLE
MADERO
PINO SUAREZ
MISIONEROS
CALLE
ZAPATA
PEPPONE PIZZA
HOTEL SAN MARTIN
IGUANA INN
FRUTERIA QUE BUENA
EL MORO RV PARK
EL TASTE
LOS CUATROS ALTOS GRILL
EUROPCAR
LA FUENTE
EL PESCADOR SUPERMARKET
TORTILLERIA LORETO
THE BAJA BIG FISH COMPANY
SEE DETAIL
Plaza
ROBLES
HIDALGO
JORDAN
CALLE MORELOS
ZARAGOZA
CALLE COLEGIO
MADERO
CALLE
BAJA CALIFORNIA
Loreto
Río
SCHOOL
CALLE
CALLE
CALLE
INDEPENDENCIA
CONSTITUYENTES
CALLE
AYUNTAMIENTO
MOTEL BRENDA
RICO POLLO
MOTEL SALVATIERRA
HACIENDA SUITES
EL NIDO RESTAURANT
LEON
JUAREZ
SALVATIERRA
CALLE
POST OFFICE
ALLENDE
CALLE
CALLE
BUS TERMINAL
PASEO NICOLAS TAMARAL
BASEBALL STADIUM
ARNES
PASEO PEDRO DE UGARTE
HOTEL DUVE CORAL

range of the average tourist. About 60,000 visitors each year find their way to Loreto these days, most of them American and Canadian snowbirds.

Today, once-sleepy Loreto is a town in transition. Through a deal with the American- and Canadian-owned Loreto Bay Company, Fonatur is finally making good on a plan to develop a 27-kilometer (17-mi) coastal segment, including **Nopoló** and **Puerto Escondido,** as a major tourist resort. Some 5,000 new residents settled in Loreto between 2004 and 2006, bringing the total population to 15,000. With construction underway on nearly every block in town, builders are hiring workers from the mainland to keep up with demand. The influx of visitors has caused more traffic and less parking, and the price of a modest home in town has climbed to US$350,000.

Most of the large-scale development is centered outside Loreto proper, in the Fonatur-sponsored Nopoló zone—and that suits local residents just fine.

Beyond the town and Fonatur zones, more than a hundred small ranching settlements and fishing communities remain much as they have always been.

HISTORY

After several unsuccessful attempts over a 167-year period to establish a permanent Spanish settlement on the peninsula, Jesuit Padre Juan María Salvatierra founded the first mission in the Californias at Loreto in 1697. As the Loreto colony grew, it served as a base for California exploration and for the expansion of the mission system throughout the peninsula. Franciscan Padre Junípero Serra started his journey north to California from here in 1769, eventually founding Alta California's first mission at San Diego Bay.

As the "mother of the California missions" and Spanish California capital, Loreto prospered until a hurricane destroyed much of the town in 1829. The mission church survived, but damage was so extensive, and fear of future hurricanes so high, the capital was moved from Loreto to La Paz the following year.

The town remained virtually deserted until the 1850s and '60s, when a small group of intrepid immigrants—some from England—resettled the area. A surprising number of Loreto residents today bear surnames such as Green, Davis, Cunningham, and Drew. Loreto remained a frontier backwater until after World War II, when it began developing a small commercial and sportfishing industry.

SIGHTS
Misión Nuestra Señora de Loreto

The first chapel at Loreto was a large tent erected at the mouth of Arroyo San Dionísio in October 1697. The building of the mission church proper proceeded in three stages, beginning in 1699 with a simple rectangular chapel with presidio near the current site. The foundations for a larger church, with a cruciform floor plan, were laid in 1704, and the church as it now appears attained its basic form in 1752.

After weathering the 1829 hurricane and several subsequent earthquakes, the church was restored in 1976 and is currently in use as a place of worship. A sign over the massive front doors reads Head and Mother of the Missions of Lower and Upper California. Despite its history, however, it's not a particularly impressive Spanish mission church. Nonetheless, the original Virgen de Loreto, brought ashore by Padre Kino in 1697, is nicely displayed, and the church contains a well-restored 18th-century gilded altar.

Of equal or greater interest is the adjoining **Museo de los Misiónes** (tel. 613/135-0441, Tues.–Sun. 9 A.M.–1 P.M. and 1:45–6 P.M., US$4), a small but well-endowed historical and anthropological museum with exhibits on regional history and culture, Baja California mission history, and religious art. An anthropological library and small bookstore offer literature on Baja and Mexico history.

Plaza Salvatierra

A plaza southwest of the church is dedicated to Padre Juan María de Salvatierra, the father of all California missions, whose likeness appears on a bust in the square's center. A handful of shops, businesses, and municipal offices line

LORETO TO BAHÍA AGUA VERDE

To Mulegé

Isla Coronado

Puerto de la Lancha

LORETO BAY NATIONAL MARINE PARK

Salt Pond

Loreto

Puerto Balandra

Bahía Salinas

Nopoló

INN AT LORETO BAY

To San Javier

Playa Juncalito

Bahía Chuenque

Isla del Carmen

Sea of Cortez

Puerto Escondido

TRIPUI RESORT

Punta Baja

Isla Danzante

ENSENADA BLANCA/ DANZANTE ADVENTURE RESORT

EL SANTUARIO

Los Candeleros

Ligüi

Punta Candeleros

Isla Monserrate

Isla Santa Catalina

Isla San Cosme

Playa San Cosme

Playa San Pasquel

To Ciudad Constitución

Bahía Agua Verde

Punta San Marcial

0   0.5 mi

0   0.5 km

© AVALON TRAVEL PUBLISHING, INC.

the streets enclosing the plaza, including city hall and the tourism office.

Nopoló and Puerto Escondido

Loreto—along with Cancún, Huatulco, Ixtapa, and Los Cabos—was slated for tourist development on the recommendation of a computer study carried out by the Mexican government during the oil-rich 1970s. The prime criterion in Loreto's selection was the fact the area enjoys an average of 360 sunny days per year. Most of the completed and ongoing projects in the Loreto area have been entirely or partially funded by Fonatur, which has invited investors from around the world to participate in the area's future.

The focus of most ongoing local development is Nopoló, eight kilometers (5 mi) south of Loreto. Nopoló consists of a hotel zone, a recreation zone (tennis center and golf course), and a residential zone, linked by wide, palm-lined boulevards.

After years of little development, Fonatur has entered a deal with American- and Canadian-owned Loreto Bay Company for a 15-year, US$3 billion effort to build 6,000 homes on 3,200 hectares, stretching across both sides of Mexico 1. Development on this scale will likely be a mixed blessing. The developer is contributing 1 percent of proceeds from the sale of homes back into the community, which

© PAUL ITOI

harbor at Puerto Escondido

has already resulted in a US$800,000 upgrade for the local hospital. Yet, it remains to be seen whether the stated goal of creating a sustainable community can be met. And with prices starting at US$750,000 for a townhouse near the beach, the development is sure to change the demographic makeup of the town.

In the first phase of development, a wide-reaching direct-mail campaign had piqued the interest of many a near-retiree. And in late 2006, the first hundred homes had been delivered.

The same streetlamps and curbs at Nopoló line the road to Puerto Escondido, where a few older boats are moored in the protected harbor. Here, as in La Paz, Fonatur has completed a three-story gray/green building to house the marina operations. The boat launch fee was around US$13, but changes frequently.

◖ Loreto Bay National Marine Park

In 1997, President Zedillo declared Loreto's entire offshore marine system, from **Isla Coronado** in the north to **Isla Catalán** in the south, a preserve called **Parque Marítimo Nacional Bahía de Loreto** (Loreto Bay National Marine Park). Part of the federal Sistema Nacional de Areas Protegidas (SINAP), the park forbids trawlers and commercial netters for a distance of 35–47 kilometers (22–29 mi) offshore along the park's entire 60-kilometer (37-mi) length. This decree has been a major boost to tourism in the Loreto area.

Primer Agua

The graded, unpaved road to Primer Agua, a Fonatur-owned palm oasis, begins near the San Javier turnoff at Km 114 on Mexico 1. Look for a road sign posted just south of a highly visible electric transformer station next to the highway. The Primer Agua road reaches the oasis after 6.5 kilometers (4 mi); ordinary passenger vehicles can make it in dry weather. This fenced-off section of arroyo, a branch of Arroyo de San Javier, serves as a nursery for propagating plants to be used at nearby Fonatur projects. A picnic area, complete with tables and barbecue grills, is near a natural pool at the bottom of the arroyo. If the gate to the facility is locked—and it sometimes is, even in the middle of the day—a hike into nonfenced sections of the arroyo, west of the orchards, is still worthwhile. The Fonatur office in Nopoló (tel. 613/135-0650) says that, if given a day's notice, it will provide a visit permit and ensure that the park is open.

SPORTS AND RECREATION

Most visitors to Loreto come to enjoy the desert, the sea, the mountains—or all three. If you feel like taking an organized trip into any of these worlds, making arrangements is easy, and costs tend to be reasonable.

Fishing

Offshore fishing is best east of Isla del Carmen, where you'll find yellowtail and sierra in winter, dorado, snapper, cabrilla, grouper, tuna, sailfish, and marlin in summer. Inshore fishing, between Loreto and Isla del Carmen (particularly at the north end of Carmen), nets smaller yellowtail, snapper, white sea bass, and, in spring, roosterfish. Boats typically leave the marina at 6 A.M. and return around 1–2 P.M.

Many hotels in town arrange fishing trips and activity packages that include accommodations. **Arturo's Sportfishing Fleet** (tel. 613/135-0766, www.arturosport.com), near restaurant Nuevo Playa Blanca on Calle Hidalgo, and **Alfredo's Sportfishing** (tel. 613/135-0132, fax 613/135-0590), on the *malecón,* are two of the oldest sportfishing fleets. The going rate for a day of fishing in a standard *panga* is US$170–190 for up to two anglers. Super *pangas* run US$195–270 for three, and fishing cruisers run US$340 and up for four. The Hotel Oasis also has its own fleet, and serves an early breakfast at 5 A.M. Its prices include fish filleting, vacuum packing, freezing, and taxes.

Record-setters bring their catch to **The Baja Big Fish Company** (Corner of Madero and Jordan, tel. 613/135-1603, www.bajabigfish.com), Loreto's official IGFA weighing station. Baja Big Fish leads conventional and fly fishing trips in small groups. *Panga* fishing costs US$240

for up to two anglers, US$270–300 for up to three in a super or deluxe super *panga*. Half-day rates are US$150/standard *panga* and US$170/ super *panga*. This outfit also rents fly-fishing gear for US$30. Credit cards are accepted.

Based at the Tripui Trailer Park, **Jose Torres Fishing Charters** (tel. 613/104-4030, www.loreto.com/josetorres) is run by a local fisherman who takes anglers, divers, and snorkelers out in a fleet of three *pangas*.

Boating

You can launch small boats at the north end of the *malecón,* at the Loreto Shores Villa and RV Park, or farther south at Playa Juncalito and Puerto Escondido. The *municipio* of Loreto boasts the highest percentage of Cortez islands of any *municipio* in Mexico. Jaunts to Isla del Carmen (18 km from Loreto, 8 km from Puerto Escondido) are popular; the island has several good beaches, with the best anchorages at Puerto Balandra and Bahía Marquer on the island's west shore or at Bahía Salinas on the east.

Any of the hotels that organize fishing trips can arrange *pangas* by the day. You can also rent *pangas* at the harbor at the north end of Loreto's waterfront.

Sea cruisers generally anchor at the sheltered, deep-water marina at Puerto Escondido. Both Loreto and Puerto Escondido have COTP offices. Loreto's COTP (tel. 613/133-0656, fax 613/133-0465) issues launch ramp permits for US$3. For safety reasons the Loreto COTP requests that kayakers file float plans in advance of any overnight paddling expedition. The COTP monitors VHF radio channel 16.

Kayaking

Put in at Loreto for excursions to Isla Coronado or the north end of Isla Carmen. For the southern or eastern shores of Isla Carmen, as well as for Isla Danzante and Los Candeleros, start at Puerto Escondido. Setting out from Puerto Escondido, the ambitious, experienced sea kayaker can paddle out to Isla Monserrate or even Isla Santa Catalina. A logical run begins at Puerto Escondido, then continues south with the currents to Bahía Agua Verde (see *South*

COURTESY OF LORETO BAY COMPANY

tennis courts at Nopoló

toward Ciudad Constitución) by way of Danzante (13 km/8 mi) and Monserrate (24 km/15 mi). **Paddling South** (U.S. tel. 707/942-4550 or 800/398-6200, www.tourbaja.com) offers highly regarded multiday kayak trips. Cofounders Trudi Angell and Douglas Knapp have been leading trips since 1983. Trudi graduated from the National Outdoor Leadership School (NOLS) Baja course, while Doug has sailed the Gulf of California in a catamaran. They also organize mountain biking, horseback riding, and sailing trips.

Diving

About 1,000 divers a year make their way to Loreto to explore rock reefs, seamounts, and underwater caves along the islands offshore. The best local diving areas include the north end of Isla Coronado; the north and east shores of Isla del Carmen; the 120-foot sunken freighter near del Carmen's Bahía Salinas; Playa Juncalito, with its wreckage of a small, twin-engine plane; and the smaller islands of Monserrate, Santa Catalina, and Danzante (northern and eastern shores). South of

Isla Danzante is a string of granite islets called Los Candeleros; the vertical walls make an awesome underwater sight.

Several shops lead guided dive trips and offer equipment rentals and instruction. Conveniently located a half block from the marina, **Dolphin Dive Center** (Juárez btw Davis/Mateos, tel. 613/135-1914, www .dolphindivebaja.com) is a PADI shop that leads dive tours and courses. Rinse stations for gear and cameras and a secure room for overnight drying minimize the number of times you'll have to lug your gear across town.

Arturo's Sportfishing (tel. 613/135-0766, www.arturosport.com) runs dive trips aboard a fleet of 12 *pangas* equipped with oxygen, radios, first aid, cell phone, shade, and fish finders. Boats leave at 9 A.M. Dive-and-stay packages are available at the La Pinta, Sukasa, and El Dorado hotels. Located in the Hotel Junipero, **Cormorant Dive Center** (Hidalgo at Misoneros, tel. 613/135-2140, www.loretours.com) runs dive trips to Coronado Island (US$79), as well as SSI Discover Scuba classes and whale-watching tours.

HOW MUCH DOES IT COST?

GUIDED DIVE AND SNORKEL TOURS

Snorkel trip	US$55
Two-tank dive to Coronado Island	US$80-90
Carmen Island	US$100
Danzante Island	US$110
Las Ánimas	US$200 (5 divers min.)
Extra tank	US$45
Night dive	US$65
Discover scuba course	US$110-150
Open water certification	US$400
Advanced certification	US$250
Scuba rental package	US$30

OTHER GUIDED TOURS

San Javier Mission	US$120
Cave paintings	US$115
Whale-watching	US$120

Horseback Riding

In March, **Saddling South** (U.S. tel. 707/942-4450 or 800/398-6200, www.tourbaja.com), the equestrian branch of Paddling South, leads a seven-day Ranch Gardens trip (US$995) into the peninsular interior. At the end of November, a mixed group of riders heads for the annual San Javier festival. Saddling South provides two nights' hotel, ground transportation, meals on tour days, end-of-tour fiesta dinner, guides, mules, pack animals and related equipment, camping gear, tents, repair and first aid kits, saddlebags, and informational books.

Mountain Biking

Pedaling South (U.S. tel. 707/942-4450 or 800/398-6200, www.tourbaja.com) runs the following multiday cycling tours: Sierra Ridge Ride (9 days for US$795 pp), San Javier Singletrack (8 days, US$795), Oasis Bases (7–8 days, US$695), and Cross Baja/Whale Watch (9 days, US$995). Combo sea kayak/mountain bike trips are also available at US$795 for seven days. If you bring your own bike, Pedaling South deducts US$95 from the tour rates. Included in the price are accommodations, ground transport, meals on tour days, camping gear, tents, guides, tracking vehicles, and first aid.

Cormorant Dive Center/Loretours (Hidalgo at Misoneros, tel. 613/135-2140, www.loretours.com) has Mongoose bikes for guided trips to San Javier (US$123) and Primer Agua (US$55).

Golf

Neglected for years, the 18-hole **Campo de Golf Loreto** at Nopoló is probably the least crowded coastal golf course in North America. Greens had dried out and the driving range was only marked out 200 yards at last check; however, the Loreto Bay Resort Company recently negotiated to take over the course from Fonatur and had plans to revive the course, beginning with new Nike rental clubs (US$30). Greens fees were US$58 for 18 holes/US$40 for 9 holes. An electric cart cost US$36, pull cart US$15.

Tennis

The **Nopoló Tennis Center** (Centro Tenístico de Nopoló, tel. 613/133-0129) has nine lighted courts, a clubhouse, bar, and pro shop. Resort guests may use the courts at no charge; nonguests pay very reasonable court fees.

Guided Tours

Most of the outfitters that specialize in one activity also dabble in the others, so if you like your boat crew, you can probably go with the same shop to see the cave paintings or the gray whales. Most trips require a minimum of two or three people.

You can see San Javier by ATV tour through **Cormorant Dive Center/Loretours** (Hidalgo at Misoneros, tel. 613/135-2140, www.loretours.com, US$90).

Desert and Sea Expeditions (Paseo Hidalgo btw Colegio/Suarez, tel. 613/135-1979, www.desertandsea.com) leads trips to San Javier, local cave paintings sites, Pacific and gulf-side whale-watching, and Coronado Island.

Once a year in April, May, or November, travel photographer Jim Cline leads a **Wonders of Baja** photo tour (U.S. tel. 877/350-1314, www.jimcline.com) of La Paz, Loreto, Mulege, Todos Santos, and Cabo San Lucas, including three boat trips to islands on the Sea of Cortez. Participants get to try their hand at capturing the seascapes, cacti, historic missions, and wildlife through the lens of their camera. Tours include accommodations and seafood dinners.

SHOPPING

A handful of shops line the streets surrounding the plaza, with handicrafts, silver jewelry, home furnishings, and Mexican-style apparel for sale. Note: In many of these stores, prices for crafts are about 2–3 times higher than for the same items elsewhere in Baja.

In front of the mission, **La Casa de la Abuela** sells an assortment of handicrafts in a building as old as the mission itself (1744). **Artesanias Colibrí** (Salvatierra at Independencia) carries a nice selection of ceramics, jewelry, maps, and handicrafts.

Following in the footsteps of Todos Santos, Loreto now hosts its first art gallery, **Galería de Loreto** (Juárez btw Madero/Suarez, Tues.–Sat.), with a small collection of oil paintings and watercolors by local artists.

A retired school teacher from New Mexico, Jeannine Perez opened **El Caballo Blanco** (Paseo Hidalgo 19 at Madero, jeannine1220@

yahoo.com, Mon.–Sat. 9 A.M.–7 P.M.) in 2005 with thousands of used books, plus new Baja titles and art supplies for sale. Jeannine contributes regular dispatches to the *Gringo Gazette* and has published a personal account of Loreto history, sights, and attractions, including her own sketches.

The Baja Big Fish Company (Corner of Madero and Jordan, tel. 613/135-1603, www.bajabigfish.com, Mon.–Sat. 9 A.M.–5 P.M.) carries a wide selection of flies, plus leaders and lines. Credit cards are accepted.

ENTERTAINMENT

The majority of nightlife spots in Loreto are sports bars, where expats and Mexicans alike gather to watch American football and international soccer games. An open *palapa* bar on the second story of the Hotel Luna, **Bar Eclipse** (Vizcaíno btw Davis/Mateos, tel. 613/135-2288, www.hotellunaloreto.com, Wed.–Sun. 7 P.M.–midnight, Fri.–Sat. till 1 A.M.) has a 42-inch plasma screen for viewing sports events. Enjoy cocktails and espresso drinks while taking in sea and mountain views. On the same block, next to the Dolphin Dive Center, **Giggling Dolphin** is one of the newer establishments in town, with a bar made out of a converted boat.

You can play a round of pool over drinks at **Jarros & Tarros** (Paseo Hidalgo near Madero, daily 6 P.M.–2 A.M.). Also on Hidalgo near Madero, **Mike's Bar** (tel. 613/135-1126) plays live music most nights 11 P.M.–3 A.M.

EVENTS

The Loreto Dorado International Fishing Tournament takes place each June. On the first weekend of every September, the church and town cosponsor a Virgin of Loreto festival with plenty of feasting, music, and dancing. Loreto celebrates another big fiesta during the last week of October to commemorate the city's founding. Activities for both events center around the plaza.

ACCOMMODATIONS

Most visitors choose downtown Loreto for their home base in this area for access to a wide variety of travel services; however, there are a few options south of town if you don't mind the drive.

Loreto offers budget travelers several convenient options, and for those who seek a few more amenities, a number of moderately priced hotels and B&Bs are scattered throughout the area. Some have seaviews, and almost all are within walking distance of the marina, shops, and restaurants. Vacation rentals are another option as more homes come on the market.

Hotels

Under US$50: **Hotel San Martín** (Juárez 14 btw Madero/Davis near the plaza, tel. 613/135-0442, US$25) offers eight spartan rooms with either two or three beds, plus floor fans and private bathrooms.

Centrally located **Hotel Junípero** (on Calle Hidalgo near the mission, tel. 613/135-0122, US$40) has 12 clean rooms with ceiling fans, hot showers, and double beds; some rooms have TV.

One block from the *malecón*, **El Moro RV Park** (Rosinda Robles 8, tel. 613/135-0542, www.loreto.com/elmoro, US$40) offers eight basic rooms with air conditioning, offstreet parking, and cable TV (see *Camping and RV Parks*).

North of town, Mexican-owned **Duve Coral Hotel** (Independencia at Arcoiris, Col. El Jaral, tel. 613/135-1037, www.duvecoral.com, US$39) has 16 doubles and 14 singles in a two-story building with satellite TV and secure parking.

US$50-100: Next door to the Hotel San Martín, the small and charming **Iguana Inn** (Juárez btw Madero/Davis, tel. 613/135-1627, www.iguanainn.com, US$48–59) has four spacious, spotless bungalows, with a well-equipped kitchenette, two queen beds, and a fabulously oversized tile shower. Rates include tax.

The two-story, neocolonial-style **Hotel Plaza Loreto** (Paseo Hidalgo 2, tel. 613/135-0280, www.loreto.com/hotelplaza, US$62) is a block from the mission church. It offers 29 clean, well-furnished rooms with hot water, air conditioning, Internet, and cable TV; a small restaurant/bar is attached.

Hotel Luna (Vizcaíno btw Davis/Mateos, tel. 613/135-2288, www.hotellunaloreto.com, US$65) has three minimally furnished rooms with queen beds, cable TV, and Wi-Fi in a convenient location.

Sukasa (on the corner of Paseo López Mateos and Calle Jordán, tel. 613/135-0490, www.loreto.com/sukasa, US$75), on the *malecón*, has two bungalows in a brick duplex and a main house with one bedroom and two baths. Units are furnished with king-size beds, air conditioning, TV/VCR (Spanish channels only) and basic cooking equipment. No pool, satellite, phone, or Internet. Daily maid service is a plus.

American-owned **(Coco Cabañas** (Davis 71, tel. 613/135-1729, www.coco-cabanas.com, US$70) is a relatively new collection of well-constructed cottages that are perfect for travelers who want privacy and a place to cook their own meals. Thick walls and airtight windows block the sound of wind, dogs, and roosters in the residential surroundings. Cottages come with air conditioning, hot water, small TV, and the best kitchenettes we've seen anywhere in Baja: new and spotless appliances including a blender, matching dishware, and ice cubes already made from purified water. Bathrooms are tiny but clean and functional. Beds on metal frames are a little squishy. Hand-painted vines over doorways add a nice touch. Inside the gated compound are a small swimming pool and barbecue area. It's a five-minute walk to the waterfront. Rates include tax.

Hacienda Suites (Salvatierra 152, Mexico tel. 800/224-3632, U.S. tel. 866/207-8732, www.haciendasuites.com, US$79) is among the newest properties in town. Faux-hacienda courtyard rooms come with air conditioning, direct-dial phone, cable TV, minibar, safety deposit box, and coffeemaker kit. There's also a large pool, secure parking, wireless Internet, and a minimarket. Rates include full breakfast. Every Saturday night, the hotel hosts a "Mexican fiesta," replete with huge platters of Mexican food and live music.

North along the waterfront, on Calle Davis, the **Desert Inn/La Pinta Hotel** (tel. 613/135-0025 or 800/026-3605, U.S. tel. 800/800-9632, www.lapintahotels.com, US$79) offers spacious, air-conditioned rooms with seaviews and terraces. Facilities include a restaurant, bar, and pool. For longer stays, the fourth and seventh nights are free; the hotel also offers fishing packages.

One row back from the waterfront at the southern edge of town, **(Las Cabañas de Loreto** (Morelos off the *malecón,* tel. 613/135-1105, U.S. tel. 707/933-0764, www.lascabanas deloreto.com, US$85/night) has four modern studios set around a small pool with comfy chaise lounges and hammocks. Prepare simple meals in the kitchenette inside, or use the outdoor kitchen and barbecue to grill your fresh catch. The main house, also available for rent, has an ocean view from the upstairs deck; studios have garden views.

This place fills up well in advance; check availability online and make reservations. Studios have TV/VCR, air conditioning, free Wi-Fi, and secure offstreet parking, but no satellite or phones. There's a three-night minimum.

Loreto Hideaway, across from Playa Loreto (tel. 613/135-0212), offers well-furnished bungalows with barbecue grills, TV, VCRs, and air conditioning. **Loreto Shores Villas and RV Park** (see *Camping and RV Parks*) also has bungalows available in this price range.

US$100-150: A longtime favorite among anglers, the **Hotel Oasis** (at the south end of Calle de la Playa/Blvd. López Mateos, tel. 613/135-0211, U.S. tel. 800/497-3923, www.hoteloasis.com, US$115–144) is the only hotel in town that has its own brown sand beach. For anglers, the best part about a stay here is the fact that breakfast service begins at 5 A.M. Its 39 air-conditioned rooms are large but minimally furnished and not well lighted. Some rooms were freshly painted with older bath fixtures. Bright orange cotton bedspreads cover sagging mattresses. Other properties in town offer more modern accommodations at a lower price. Naturally, the Oasis has its own fishing fleet (see *Fishing*),

as well as a pool, tennis court, free Wi-Fi, and a swing set for kids.

US$150-250: One of the most elegant hotels in all of Baja, the **Hotel Posada de las Flores** (tel. 613/135-1162, U.S./Canada tel. 877/245-2860, www.posadadelasflores.com, US$150–180) occupies a heavily renovated colonial-style building adjacent to Plaza Salvatierra. A rooftop pool features a glass-block bottom through which sunlight shines into the antique-decorated lobby below. Handcrafted furniture, pottery, tile, and wrought iron from the mainland decorate all 15 rooms and suites— each named for a flower. Amenities include air conditioning, satellite TV, and wireless Internet. Guests enjoy continental breakfast in a rooftop garden. This hotel has equally charming locations in La Paz and Punta Chivato.

Bed-and-Breakfasts

Six long blocks north of the town plaza, **Las Trojes Bed & Breakfast Hotel** (Davis Norte, tel. 613/135-0277, www.loreto.com/costa2. htm, US$50) is a unique collection of eight cottages cobbled together from remodeled wooden Tarascan granaries *(trojes)* brought in from the Michoacán highlands. Each room is different, but all come with air conditioning, ceiling fans, and private showers. A beach bar and pebbly beach are a short walk away through a cactus garden. Free use of bicycles and Internet access. Rates include continental breakfast.

At the north end of the *malecón,* **Loreto Playa Bed and Breakfast** (tel. 613/135-1129, www.loretoplaya.com, US$145–195) has two suites and a beach house for rent. Accommodations come with king-size beds, bubble bath, and robes, plus the use of mountain bikes and kayaks and a full breakfast.

Vacation Rentals

As new homes are constructed, a few have come on the market as vacation rentals. For example, **Stay in Loreto** (tel. 613/135-0791, www.stayinloreto.com, US$800–900/wk) manages a beachfront condo, house, and suite for weekly or monthly rentals. The newly constructed properties are located 100 feet from the water, with granite counters, seaview decks, satellite TV, and air conditioning. **La Giganta Real Estate** (Madero 22-C, tel. 613/135-0802, www.lagiganta.com) manages a few vacation rentals in the area.

Nopoló and Puerto Escondido Accommodations

For some longtime Loreto expats, poking fun at the real estate development underway in Nopoló is serious sport. But though they may have mixed feelings about the building of a 6,000-unit community, many would gladly trade beaches with the **Inn at Loreto Bay** (formerly the Camino Real, tel. 613/133-0010 or 800/507-6979, U.S. tel. 866/850-0333, www.innatloretobay.com, US$135–330). Now owned by the same Canadian developer that has partnered with Fonatur to build townhouses and restore the golf course, this expansive hotel also handles owner check-in for the hundred or so townhomes that have been delivered to date.

Choose from 150 oceanfront and oceanview rooms set around a lawn and pool. New curtains and modern bathrooms make for cheerful decor, but beds are sagging; this remains a 20-year-old hotel in need of a more complete makeover. The pool was first in line for renovation in 2007. Wi-Fi is available in the lobby area only. You can book trips and rent gear for the water sport of your choice from the hotel. The **Loreto Bay Restaurant** serves breakfast 7–11 A.M., snacks, and dinner 7–10:30 P.M. Bordering the grounds are an 18-hole golf course and the Centro Tenístico de Loreto, both free for guests.

The trailer park at **Tripui Resort** (tel. 613/133-0818, U.S. tel. 512/749-6070, www.tripui.com), in Puerto Escondido, contains 120 "permanent" yearly spaces and only 31 overnight slots. A full-hookup slot costs US$17 a night for two people. Facilities include a boat launch, boat storage, pool, restaurant, laundry service, bar, and grocery store.

Beware the "Call the USA" pay phone at Tripui. Although rates listed on the phone claim that a call to the United States will cost US$1/minute, the real charges are more like US$7 per minute; thus a 15-minute call to the United States on this phone will cost more than US$100.

Camping and RV Parks

One block from the *malecón,* **El Moro RV Park** (Rosinda Robles 8, tel. 613/135-0542) offers full hookups for US$12/day (US$220/month). You'll receive one night free for each week of your stay. Outsiders may use the hot showers for US$2. El Moro also offers fishing packages that include three nights' hotel accommodation and two days of fishing on a 22-foot *panga* with airport transfer, continental breakfast, box lunch, captain-guide, and fishing gear.

In Colonia Zaragoza, just across the arroyo at the south edge of town, **Loreto Shores Villas and RV Park** (tel. 613/135-0629, fax 613/135-0711) offers 36 RV spaces with full hookups for US$15 per day; tent spaces cost US$5 per person, showers are US$3 per person. Every seventh day is free. Facilities include hot showers, laundry service, a boat launch, and *palapas* along the waterfront. Bungalows are also available (see *Hotels*).

Rivera del Mar RV Park and Camping (Madero Norte 100, 613/135-0718, www.riveradelmar.com, US$15–18) has 25 spaces with full hookups and some shade, two blocks from the beach and five blocks from the center of town. Amenities include showers, hot water, laundry, and barbecue. Tent camping costs US$5.

Although officially prohibited, many folks still camp at the south end of Playa Juncalito, 22.5 kilometers (14 mi) south of town, at a small, brown-sand cove backed by date and Washington palms. The north end is private, but some foreigners are able to rent spaces on a semipermanent basis. North of Juncalito, toward Nopoló, you should be able to camp on the beach for free.

FOOD

Loreto's restaurants are mostly casual places that serve a variety of Mexican specialties. Seafood and steak find their way onto just about every menu.

Mexican

El Nido (Salvatierra 154, tel. 613/104-4016, daily for breakfast, lunch, and dinner) features the usual menu of mesquite-grilled steaks and seafood, but this restaurant is generally considered one of the better links in the small Baja chain. Rib eye is the house specialty at **El Taste** (Juárez at Zapata, tel. 613/135-1489), across from the Pemex on Juárez.

La Terraza (tel. 613/135-0496, daily 1–10 P.M.), above Café Olé, has an open-air terrace overlooking the plaza. Grilled steaks made with fresh Sonoran beef (US$10) are a house specialty.

Los Cuatro Altos Grill Sports Bar (Fri.–Wed. 1 P.M.–midnight, mains US$7–15)—named in reference to the four stop signs at the intersection of Juárez and Independencia—is on the second floor of a brick building with a minimarket on the bottom floor. Decorated in a desert/nautical theme, the cozy pub has a flatscreen TV and two other sets for showing American and Mexican football games. (When two important games are broadcast simultaneously, management switches at commercial breaks to serve both American and Mexican patrons.) Against one wall is a full bar, and on the next floor up is a rooftop garden terrace. The restaurant is air-conditioned in hot weather. The menu includes juicy hamburgers, *carne tampiqueña* (on the grill), and rib eye steak, as well as seafood and simple *botanas*.

Seafood

Nuevo Playa Blanca (Hidalgo at Madero, tel. 613/135-1126, opens at noon) is an old Loreto standby with an upstairs, open-air dining area decorated with whale vertebrae, lacquered turtle shells, and other marine memorabilia. You can order food in the downstairs Bar Playa Blanca as well.

La Palapa (tel. 613/135-0284, daily 1–11 P.M.), on Paseo Hidalgo about a half block up from the *malecón*, serves moderately priced—and very good—seafood and Mexican dishes in an informal palm-roofed ambience.

International

Pachamama (Zapata 3, tel. 613/135-2219, daily 5–10 P.M.) is a cozy, rustic restaurant/bar that specializes in traditional Argentine fare such as empanadas, grilled sweet peppers, thick grilled steaks, and caramel-gilded desserts.

Two restaurants in town have adopted a Spanish theme: **1697** (Davis 13, tel. 613/135-2538) does Spanish cuisine with an Italian twist, and **Bar de Tapas** (Madero at Salvatierra) specializes in small plates.

Peppone Pizza (at the northwest corner of Calle Camarillo and Calle Madero, daily 2 P.M.–midnight) is dedicated to the flat round stuff, and they do a good job of it.

Antojitos, Tacos, and Fast Food

When it comes to fish tacos, the efficient husband-wife team who now run ◖ **El Rey del Taco** have won the hearts of many a Loreto regular—some of whom place their orders before they fly into town, in case the place is closed when they arrive. Located on the south side of Juárez near the Pemex, El Rey gets high marks for *tacos de cabeza* as well as *pescado*. Those in the know say the fastest way to get your tacos is to sit down at a table, not wait at the window. Another longtime favorite for quick, inexpensive snacks, **McLulu's** (Salvatierra west of Colegio, daily 10 A.M.–6 P.M.) prepares *tacos de carne asada, tacos de guisado*, homemade chorizo, and *picadillo* (spicy meat-and-chili salad). The once-legendary fish tacos were on the soggy side last time we tried them. Three tacos and a soda cost US$5. Lulu doesn't mind if you buy beer at the nearby supermarket to drink while eating at her tables.

Next to McLulu's, **Lupita's** serves mesquite-broiled pork tacos. It usually opens midmorning then closes midday and reopens toward late afternoon. **La Fuente**, a small, thatched-roof eatery on Calle Salvatierra southwest of El Pescador supermarket, serves *antojitos* and breakfasts.

Rico Pollo (just west of Márquez de León on the north side of Juárez, daily 8 A.M.–9 P.M.) serves good mesquite-grilled chicken at a few indoor tables. **Taquería la Esquina** (on Calle Davis next to the fish market, 11 A.M.–1 P.M. and 4–8 P.M.) is a local favorite for *tacos de carne asada*. Near El Pescador market, **Win's** does hamburgers right.

Cafés

Café Olé (Madero 14 on the plaza, tel. 613/135-0495, Mon.–Sat. 8 A.M.–10 P.M., mains US$3–6) serves inexpensive breakfasts and lunches, including seafood omelets, *huevos con nopales* (eggs with cactus), tacos and other *antojitos,* plus burgers, ice cream, and milkshakes. Indoor and outdoor tables. Check the community bulletin board for rentals, sales, and other local information.

Sweet crepes draw a crowd at **Las Crepas** (Juárez near the Hotel San Martín, tel. 613/113-4846, Tues.–Sun. 9 A.M.–9 P.M., mains US$3–4), but you can also order sandwiches, salads, and pizzas.

At the south end of the *malecón,* with views of the sea, ◖ **Santa Lucia** (Mateos at Jordón, tel. 613/100-1332, congoher@hotmail.com, Thurs.–Tues 6 A.M.–4 P.M., breakfast mains US$3–5, antojitos, tortas, and box lunches US$5–10) is popular among expats for breakfasts of pancakes, yogurt, eggs, and delicious homemade breads. Refreshing "energy juices" are squeezed fresh and blended.

Groceries

El Pescador, on Calle Salvatierra, is the largest supermarket in town, and a reference point for many other businesses. **Tortillería Loreto,** on Calle Juárez between Ayuntamiento and Independencia, sells fresh tortillas as well as *bolillos* and Mexican pastries. **Panadería Kiz,** just east of Restaurant La Fuente on Calle Salvatierra, sells *pan dulce* and other Mexican pastries and breads. For fresh fruit and vegetables, amble down to the friendly, open-air **Frutería Que Buena** on Calle Juárez. Small *tiendas* and *ultramarinos* are scattered around town. A government-subsidized **Tienda ISSSTE** (Mon.–Sat. 8 A.M.–8 P.M., Sun. 8 A.M.–2 P.M.) is located on Madero, north of the plaza.

South of Loreto

Despite the name, **Del Borracho Saloon and Grill** (daily 8 A.M.–sunset) is a family place run by Americans and located a half mile from the highway on the road to San Javier. Burgers, fries, and corndogs tempt the expat crowd. In Nopoló, the **Loreto Bay Restaurant** (mains US$12–24), on the premises of the Inn at Loreto Bay, serves breakfast 7–11 A.M., snacks, and dinner 7–10:30 P.M.

INFORMATION AND SERVICES

Tourist Assistance

A SEMARNAT office (tel. 613/135-0477, Mon.–Fri. 8 A.M.–3 P.M.) is at the marina. Along with its many other functions, government agency SEMARNAT is responsible for issuing permits for island visits.

The tourist office, Departamento de Turismo Municipal (tel. 613/135-0411, Mon.–Fri. 8 A.M.–8 P.M.), is in the Palacio de Gobierno on the plaza at Calles Salvatierra and Madero. Fonatur (tel. 613/135-0650) runs an office in Nopoló, where you can pick up tourist information on the area.

Money

The **Bancomer** on the plaza offers exchange services Monday–Friday 8:30–11:30 A.M. only. The bank changes dollars to pesos but not pesos to dollars. It has an ATM. Hotels will exchange dollars for pesos at a low rate.

Post and Telephone

Loreto's post office (Allende btw Salvatierra/Juárez) is open Monday–Saturday 8 A.M.–4 P.M. You'll also find a public phone with long-distance service inside Mercado El Pescador and a couple of private telephone offices toward the west end of Calle Salvatierra. There are several Movistar and Telcel stores in town for mobile phone needs.

Internet Access

Many hotels now have wireless Internet for guests traveling with their own laptops, and a desktop machine or two for those who are traveling sans electronics. Internet cafés/business centers are located on Calle Madero, Calle Vizcaíno near Independencia, and next to Café Ole.

Bike Repair

Bicitaller Manny is a bike repair shop on Calle Allende north of Juarez.

Emergencies

A new hospital was under construction near the highway, with a target opening date of summer 2008.

GETTING THERE AND AROUND

By Air

Four major airlines now service Loreto's small international airport (LTO). **Aero California** (tel. 613/135-0500 or 613/135-0555, U.S. 800/237-6225, www.aerocalifornia.com) schedules daily nonstop flights from Los Angeles and La Paz. The airline has an office in town at Calle Juárez and Zapata. AeroMexico subsidiary **Aerolitoral** (tel. 613/135-0999) has nonstop flights to Los Angeles and La Paz.

Thanks in part to the Loreto Bay Company, **Delta** has initiated a new route connecting Los Angeles, Loreto, and La Paz (LAP). Alaska Airlines also flies LAX to LTO several times a week. Fares on these airlines started around US$300 at last check.

By Bus

Loreto's bus terminal, one of the nicest and cleanest in Baja, is at the junction of Paseo Ugarte, Calle Juárez, and Calle Salvatierra. Departures change frequently, but there are usually six ABC buses per day in either direction. Fare to La Paz is US$32, and about US$100 to Tijuana.

By Taxi

The main taxi stand sits at Madero and Hidalgo. Taxis between Loreto and Nopoló or the airport cost US$12 (US$5.50 *colectivo*). Loreto to Puerto Escondido costs about US$25, and a trip to the airport from Puerto Escondido is US$15. In town, you shouldn't pay more than US$3–4. Call 613/135-0047 for pickups.

By Car

Loreto had three rental car agencies at last check: **Budget Rent-A-Car** (tel. 613/135-1090, www.budgetbaja.com), on Hidalgo near the *malecón;* **Hertz** (tel. 613/135-0800), on an alley between Hidalgo and Salvatierra, just

off the *malecón;* and **Europcar** (tel. 613/135-2260), at the intersection of Independencia and Salvatierra, across from Win's Restaurant. These companies also have desks at the Loreto airport. See the sidebar *Where to Rent a Car in Baja* in the *Essentials* chapter for contact information.

(SAN JAVIER

This village of thatched-roof stone or adobe houses, 36 kilometers (22 mi) southwest of Loreto, contains one of the peninsula's best-preserved Jesuit mission churches. In a deep arroyo paralleling the road west of town, a small dam impounds water to irrigate the area's many farms via traditional acequias, narrow irrigation canals fashioned by the Spanish. The cultivation of citrus, onions, guavas, figs, papayas, grapes, corn, chilies, and dates supports a local farm population of around 150 people. Onions are the major crop; San Javier produces around 400 tons of onions per year.

A good time to visit is during the week leading to December 3, San Javier's patron-saint day. Pilgrims sometimes number in the hundreds. Another occasion for much *alegría* arrives on August 15, when an onion harvest dance is held at the large village community center.

Misión San Francisco Xavier de Viggé-Biaundó

This mission, nowadays simply called Misión San Javier, was originally founded by Italian padre Francisco Píccolo in 1699, two years after the establishment of the peninsula's first mission in Loreto. In 1701, Padre Juan de Ugarte arrived at Arroyo de San Javier from Mexico City, bringing with him seeds and seedlings for the Californias' first cultivated fruit orchards. Many of the mission varieties of grapes, olives, figs, oranges, and lemons now grown throughout the Californias are descended from Ugarte's original San Javier plantings.

To make room for the orchards, the mission church was moved to its current site in 1720 and rebuilt by Padre Miguel del Barco between 1744 and 1758. Del Barco was a writer of some talent who brought an organ to the mission and, after his return to Italy, produced two notable books: *The Natural History of Baja California* and *Ethnology and Linguistics of Baja California*, both published in English by Dawson's Book Shop, Los Angeles (in 1980 and 1981, respectively).

The entire building, from the foundation to the fine vaulted roofs, was constructed using stone blocks quarried from nearby Arroyo de Santo Domingo. Although the church facade is not as ornate as that of Misión San Ignacio to the north, the side windows are splendid—no two are alike. The statuary and three gilded *retablos* inside the church were probably transported from Mexico City by boat and burro in the mid-18th century. The center altar bears a statue of San Javier, while the two side altars are devoted to San Ignacio and the Virgen de los Dolores. Two of the bells in the single church tower are dated 1761, the third 1803. A glass cabinet in the sacristy contains imported silk vestments worn by resident padres more than 200 years ago.

A priest from Loreto says mass on the second Wednesday of every month. On other days the church is usually open 7 A.M.–6 P.M.; caretaker Francisca Arce de Bastida will gladly lead visitors on a short tour of the church in return for a small donation. If the church is closed, ask around the village for Señora Arce.

Accommodations

If you're on a budget and need to spend the night in San Javier, follow the footpath behind the church through the *huertas* (orchards) and ask at the farmhouse for Ramón. He rents a *palapa*-roofed, A-frame *casita* (US$10–15) with three beds (one double, two twins). The *casita* has its own bathroom, but the toilet must be flushed with a bucket of water and there is no electricity; a lantern is provided. The cabin is surrounded by a menagerie of peacocks, chickens, donkeys, dogs, and fighting cocks. **Casa Ana,** at the east end of the cobblestone road that leads to the church entrance, offers nice little *palapa*-roofed cabañas, each with its own bathroom (US$35). For more information, contact Ana Gloria at Hotel Oasis in Loreto (tel. 613/135-0112, fax 613/135-0795).

Food

Ramón's brother runs the only restaurant in the village, **La Palapa San Javier Guillermos** (8 A.M.–8 P.M.), near the church. The limited but tasty menu includes simple quesadillas, beans, and fried potatoes. A couple of small *tiendas* sell beverages and limited foodstuffs.

Getting There

The road to San Javier, beginning at Km 118, is a section of the old Camino Real (Royal Road) used by Spanish missionaries and explorers—and one of Baja's most scenic interior drives. In 2007, government funds available for connecting Mexico 1 to communities in the interior of the peninsula were to be applied to pave the road to San Javier. But until pavement is complete, only drivers with sturdy, high-clearance vehicles should attempt the trip, as surfaces are stony, and, except in the driest years, it's necessary to ford a winding stream in several places. Following heavy rains, this road shouldn't be driven at all for a few days, unless you have a four-wheel-drive vehicle and are skilled at driving through mud. Grades approach 15 percent in places; the average driving time is 90 minutes.

Along the way, the road winds around Cerro La Gigántica (1,490 m/4,885 ft), passing several palm oases hidden away in narrow arroyos, *zalates* (wild fig trees) clinging to cliffs, and other rewarding vignettes. **Rancho Las Parras**—an oasis settlement consisting of a stone chapel; small dam; and orchards of dates, mangos, grapes, olives, figs, and citrus—appears about midway to the mission (20 km/12 mi from Mexico 1) in the Arroyo de las Parras. This arroyo provided water and a way into the Sierra de la Giganta for Amerindians and later missionaries; the vicinity holds old Amerindian trails and rock art.

About 9.2 kilometers (6 mi) beyond Las Parras, the San Javier road meets a lesser branch road leading 34 kilometers (21 mi) northwest to San José de Comondú (not 26 mi as indicated on the AAA map). This route to Comondú is in poor condition, although it has been regraded in recent years so that road inclines aren't as steep as they once were. Any sturdy vehicle can make the trip nowadays, though high clearance helps, and if it rains all bets are off.

For those without their own vehicles, or without the right kind of vehicle, it's possible to arrange a car and driver or guided ATV or mountain biking tour from Loreto to San Javier. (See *Sports and Recreation* earlier in the *Loreto and Vicinity* section.)

SOUTH TOWARD CIUDAD CONSTITUCIÓN
Ensenada Blanca

Around 40 kilometers (25 mi) south of Loreto, behind the fishing village of Ligüi, lies an area of white-sand beaches, dunes and estuaries known as Ensenada Blanca. Near the latter is **El Santuario** (tel. 613/100-1206, www.el-santuario.com, US$120), a collection of six environmentally friendly *casitas* designed to appeal to those seeking a quiet place to reflect and interact with the natural surroundings. Lights are solar powered and showers are solar heated, so don't bother bringing a hair dryer or boom box. At times, meditation- or yoga-oriented groups book all of the *casitas* for retreat purposes, so it's best to call ahead to make sure space is available.

To find Ensenada Blanca, keep an eye out for the Ligüi turnoff between Km 83 and 84 (about 10 km/6 mi south of the Tripui turnoff). Coming from Loreto, the Mini Super Ligüi will be on your left and you'll see a sign announcing the Parque Marino Nacional. Just after the market, turn into the first dirt road heading east. If you take a bus from Loreto or La Paz, ask to be let off in Ligüi, and you'll end up at this same spot.

From this point it's around four kilometers (2.5 mi) to Ensenada Blanca and El Santuario. Follow the dirt road toward the coast, and ignore lesser roads branching off. When the road forks, stay to the right. You'll cross a large *arroyo* (usually dry, unless there's been a tropical storm) and the road will extend another kilometer or so before reaching the village of Ensenada Blanca. Drive or hike through Ensenada Blanca, past a collapsed church.

Keep to the right of the church and follow the road behind the bay. On the left, you'll see a small sign reading El Santuario Retreat.

Above Ensenada Blanca, the ringing of a bell signals the start of happy hour every afternoon at the eco-friendly **Danzante Adventure Resort** (U.S. tel. 408/354-0042, www.danzante.com, US$185–205 pp all-inclusive). Guests climb stairs from the beach or roll out of their hammocks and descend to the communal dining room as the blender springs into action. Sculpted into a hillside with views of Isla Danzante, this small resort runs on solar power and local talent. Construction features French doors, slate terraces, and *palapa* roofs. Inside, local artisans have designed custom ironwork and furnishings for nine junior suites that afford views of Isla Danzante in the distance. Enjoy meals cooked with organic produce from a garden on the premises. The owners, Michael and Lauren Farley, are experienced divers who led trips in the Sea of Cortez for many years before opening their own resort. They organize marine safaris, picnic lunches, and whale-watching tours on the Pacific (90 minutes away). Rates include all meals, drinks, and snacks. The only downside for some travelers is the 25-mile drive to town. Bird-watch by day; star-gaze by night. It's remote, but not rustic. No air conditioning. Horseback riding, massage, and guided hikes, fishing, and dive trips cost extra.

There are no signs along the 6.5-kilometer (4-mi) road from Mexico 1 to Danzante; reservations are required (three-night minimum) and you'll get directions when you book. There's no phone, Internet, or TV. Children eight and older are welcome.

A taxi from Loreto airport to Ensenada Blanca costs US$60 *colectivo* (up to five people).

Bahía Agua Verde (Puerto Agua Verde)

Between Km 64 and 63, where Mexico 1 veers inland from the Cortez coast, a part-graded, part-ungraded, gravel-and-dirt road heads southeast for 41 kilometers (26 mi) to the fish camp of Agua Verde. The roadbed is steep and winding in places, not at all suitable for trailers or motor homes. As the road approaches Agua Verde, it flattens out and divides into several tracks running to five small coves scalloped into the bayshore. The turquoise waters are framed by Islas Monserrate and Santa Catalina to the north and east, and hillsides of paloverde, palo blanco, *cardón,* palm, and mesquite to the west—very picturesque.

Local residents make a living herding goats, fishing for small shark *(cazón),* or servicing a steady trickle of outside visitors who brave the road in from Mexico 1. Near the first coastal contact the road makes, **Rancho El Carricalito,** a goat ranch 24 kilometers (15 mi) from the highway, boards visitors for a few dollars a night and can also provide meals. As for groceries, you can buy tortillas and goat cheese from the restaurant, but that's about it. Rocky bayshore campsites with *palapas* cost about US$5. Ask directions to the local hot springs. *Panga* fishing trips and mule trips into the sierra can also be arranged. **Isla San Cosme** and **Isla Damian,** opposite this bay, feature good snorkeling along their south shores.

A graded gravel-and-sand road continues parallel to the shoreline from this point. At a few places along the way you can drive down to the taupe-colored sand beaches. Self-contained camping is possible in several places.

About 34 kilometers (21 mi) from the highway the road begins climbing into the hills again, and at 38 kilometers (23 mi) you'll have a splendid view of rock formations, sandbars, and coves below. The steepest grade along the entire road comes upon the final approach to Bahía Agua Verde, more commonly known in these parts as Puerto Agua Verde. As the cove becomes visible you'll see how it got its name—reflections off the white-sand bottom give off a brilliant emerald-green hue similar to that seen at Bahía Concepción and many other places in the southern coastal reach of the Sea of Cortez. Puerto Agua Verde is a popular anchorage for pleasure boats as well as the occa-

sional shrimp trawler. The road ends next to a beach at Puerto Agua Verde's west bight, which curves around to face south and thus provides some protection from north winds. This end of the bay is formed by a narrow neck of Punta San Pasquel; on the opposite side of the neck is another beach. You can camp on either side; someone from the local *ejido* will probably come along and collect a few dollars a day.

Limited supplies—including drinking water—are available at a little green-and-white *tienda* in the nearby settlement of Agua Verde.

Isla Montserrate and Isla Santa Catalina

Uninhabited Isla Montserrate lies around 13 kilometers (8 mi) north of Puerto Agua Verde and is ringed by rock reefs with excellent snorkeling. The north end of the island features a long and pretty beach known to gringo yachties as Yellowstone Beach, considered a good summer anchorage.

Larger Isla Santa Catalina, 18 kilometers (11 mi) east of Isla Monserrate, is known for its endemic "rattleless rattlesnake" *(Crotalus catalinensis)* and for the largest barrel cactus species in Baja, *Ferocactus diguettii,* named for French naturalist Leon Diguet. Individuals of this variety may reach four meters (13 ft) in height and a meter (more than 3 ft) in diameter. *Ferocactus diguettii* is also found on Islas Cerralvo, Monserrate, Danzante, and Del Carmen.

Ciudad Insurgentes

At Ciudad Insurgentes (pop. 10,000), the kilometer marker countdown from Santa Rosalía reaches Km 0 and starts over again at Km 236. The town itself has little to recommend it except as a fuel and food stop or as a transit point for the "easy" road north to La Purísima (102 km/61 mi) and Comondú (101 km/60.5 mi). The road is now paved to within a few kilometers of La Purísima, after which it is graded to San Isidro and San Miguel de Comondú.

Ciudad Constitución to La Paz

CIUDAD CONSTITUCIÓN

Even though it boasts more hotels than any other town between Santa Rosalía and La Paz, few Baja travelers stop over in Ciudad Constitución (pop. 45,000), the capital of Municipio de Comondú and one of the largest population centers in Baja California Sur. Founded in the 1960s to serve as a market center for the irrigated Llano Magdalena (Magdalena Plain) agricultural basin, the town features several Pemex stations (the ones at each end of town stay open on Sundays, and the one just north of town at Km 213 offers the use of bathrooms with hot showers), as well as banks, bicycle shops, supermarkets, pharmacies, a *mercado,* hospital, Aero California office, *panaderías, tortillerías,* auto shops, and more.

Boulevard Olachea, the main thoroughfare through town, is divided into two lanes in each direction, along with one-way frontage roads on either side, with stoplights every other block or so. None of the lights ever seem to work, and negotiating back and forth between the central lanes and frontage roads can be a daunting experience on one's first driving visit.

Accommodations

There are a dozen or so hotels in town, and you won't need to spend more than US$35 for a top-notch place to sleep.

Our current top pick would be the (**Hotel Oasis** (Guerrero 284 btw Prieto/Farias, tel. 613/132-3919, hoasis01@prodigy.net.mx, US$35), located three blocks off the main drag. Modern, clean rooms come with air conditioning, phone, TV, parking, a pool, and wireless Internet throughout. Another good choice is the **Posada del Ryal Hotel** (Victoria btw Olochea/Lerdo de Tejada, tel. 613/132-4800, US$35), where clean rooms have new bath fixtures. This hotel has secure parking and a pleasant courtyard, and there is a laundry next door. Wireless Internet works in the lobby.

Camping and RV Parks

Manfred's Pull Thru RV Trailer Park (Km 213, just north of the John Deere dealership, tel. 613/132-1103), right on the east side of Boulevard Olachea at the north edge of town, has hookups that run US$17–20 a night and a swimming pool.

Spacious, palm-surrounded **Campestre La Pila RV Park** (tel. 613/132-0562), well off the highway south of town, has full hookups, a pool, hot showers, a picnic area, and dump station. There is limited shade, but the grounds are quiet. Rates are US$10 for two people. The turnoff is on the west side of the highway next to a textile *maquiladora* called California Connection de México, near a power substation.

Mike's Palapa RV Park (tel. 613/132-3463, fax 613/132-5128), at the south edge of town, looks a bit nicer although many of the spots are unshaded. Full hookups are US$12, water and electric US$10, dry camping US$6. Like La Pila, it's well off the highway. RV storage is available.

Food

The main boulevard—part of Mexico 1—through Ciudad Constitución is dotted with restaurants, *asaderos* (grills), and taquerías. On Sunday afternoons, lines form at **Taquería Karen** (corner Hidalgo/Olochea) for cabeza, pescado, and other tacos. **Tortas and Tacos Las Tortugas** (corner Olochea/Bravo) makes tortas, carne asada, and Cuban sandwiches for US$2–3. At **Brismar** (Olochea at Zapata, tel. 613/137-0270, daily 8 A.M.–9 P.M., Sun. till 8 P.M., mains US$6–10), a friendly staff serves *mariscos* and *carnes* in a pleasant, clean, and air-conditioned space.

At the southwest corner of Mexico 1 and the highway to San Carlos, **El Taste** (daily for lunch and dinner) is a branch of a La Paz restaurant of the same name. The menu is oriented toward tourists and wealthy Mexicans, with heavy Mexican *platillos* and steak. At the northwest corner of the same intersection (and in a second location at the south end of town), **Gran Pollo** outdoes Super Pollo for barbecued chicken.

Lonchería La Laguna (Mon.–Sat. 8 A.M.– 5 P.M.), north of the plaza on the main boulevard just north of Calle Olachea, serves reliable *tortas,* tacos, *chilaquiles,* carne asada, mole, and a decent cup of *café de olla.*

The best supermarkets, both on Boulevard Olachea, are **Super Ley** and **La Americana** (behind the Pemex at the south end of town). The town also offers several *tiendas de abarrotes* and *ultramarinos.*

Misión San Luis Gonzaga

Ciudad Constitución is a convenient departure point for an excursion to this surviving mission settlement 42 kilometers (26 mi) southeast of Mexico 1. The best of two secondary roads leading from Mexico 1 starts at Km 195, where a sign reads La Presa Iguajil. Founded in 1737 and rebuilt in 1751, the simple mission church is well maintained by local ranchers and farmers. The surrounding arroyo is planted in figs, dates, pomegranates, citrus, grapes, and olives.

◖ BAHÍA MAGDALENA

During the annual gray whale migration, January–March, the canals, bays, and *bocas* of the Bahía Magdalena complex are practically filled with undulating forms of friendly adult and juvenile whales. This unique marine environment is only a 45-minute drive from Ciudad Constitución, yet many Transpeninsular voyagers pass it by. Where the flat Llano Magdalena has sunk lower than the Pacific, the ocean has intruded and created a string of barrier islands more than 209 kilometers (130 mi) long, separated from the peninsula by a series of shallow bays with an average depth of less than 18 meters (60 ft). Arroyos that sank under the Pacific have become *bocas,* or "mouths," that let the sea in; these *bocas* now form channels between the barrier islands.

Starting at Boca de las Ánimas in the north, the most prominent barrier islands are **Isla Santo Domingo, Isla Magdalena, Isla Santa Margarita,** and **Isla Creciente.**

The largest of the bays between the islands and peninsula, Bahía Magdalena and Bahía Almejas, are linked by Canal Gaviota to form a vast, protected waterway—the best on Baja's Pacific coast for kayaking and windsurfing. Naturalists could spend a lifetime exploring the mangroves and estuaries along the eastern bayshores, which support an astounding variety of marinelife and bird life.

Because of the proximity of Bahía Magdalena's natural harbor to the fertile Llano Magdalena, several groups of colonists attempted to settle the coastal plains here. In 1879, the Chartered Company of Lower California, an

WHALE-WATCHING

The gray whale is the most common subject of whale-watching expeditions. While other whales tend to frequent deeper parts of the ocean, the gray swims mostly in coastal shallows and seeks out lagoons for calving. Also, because it's a bottom feeder, the gray tolerates areas so shallow its abdomen rests on the sea bottom, a position no other large whale can accomplish; most whales would suffocate in such a position. This means large grays are often seen very close to shore.

A visit to a gray calving lagoon can be exciting. Sometimes whales seem to be everywhere you look – "spouting" (clearing their blowholes with pneumatic blasts that send vapor spumes high into the air), "breaching" (leaping out of the sea and arching through the air), "spyhopping" (poking their heads, eyes, and mouths vertically out of the water, possibly to peek at the nonaquatic world), "tail lobbing" (slapping their flukes on the water surface), or just floating by, sleeping on the tide. At other times the whales are relatively inactive. Choppy water seems to occasion more activity.

You can spot grays almost anywhere along Baja's peninsular coast, from Punta Banda near Ensenada right around to the Sea of Cortez. However, the best places to see them up close and in large numbers are three protected bays in Baja California Sur: Laguna Ojo de Liebre (Scammon's Lagoon) near Guerrero Negro; Laguna San Ignacio, southwest of San Ignacio; and Bahía Magdalena or adjacent Bahía Almejas, southwest of Ciudad Constitución. Of these three areas, Laguna San Ignacio seems to attract the greatest number of "friendlies," gray whales that actively approach whale-watching boats for human contact.

Although whales can be seen in Baja waters from the beginning of January through the end of March, February is when they're generally present in greatest numbers. At any given lagoon, you can view whales from three vantage points: shore, air, and water. Viewing from shore is sometimes frustrating, since even the closest whales frolic at least 100 meters away; also, since the closest whales usually lie in the shallowest water, they're less likely to perform their more exciting maneuvers, like spyhop-

ping or breaching. Distance is also a problem from the air, since you can't approach too closely without endangering the whale's life as well as the lives of those in the plane. And, of course, to consider whale-watching from the air you must either own a small plane, know someone who does, or charter one.

The optimum way to experience the gray whale, then, is from the water. Any boat entering an area where whales are protected – including all three of the bays mentioned above – during calving season must possess a special whale-watching permit issued by the Mexican government on a year-to-year basis. Ordinarily permits are issued only to boat owners with registered whale-watching concessions and academic researchers from approved institutions.

The least expensive whale-watching trips are those you arrange on your own from the shores of the lagoons. During the season, licensed Mexican boatmen linger with their *pangas* (skiffs) at approved launching points in each lagoon. All you have to do is drive out there, park your vehicle, and pay the going price, which varies with the distance the boats must travel to reach the whales and the number of hours you stay out.

In Guerrero Negro and San Ignacio, a couple of local hotels arrange excursions that include round-trip ground transportation to the lagoons. Prices are usually reasonable; the per-person rate usually goes down the more people you have in your party. Next up in price are trips arranged in major tourist towns like Ensenada, Mulegé, Loreto, La Paz, and Cabo San Lucas. The problem with locally hired whale-watching tours is that the guides are often not very knowledgeable about the whales or can't speak enough English to communicate the knowledge they do possess to non-Spanish-speakers.

Some whale-watchers prefer the convenience and expertise of whale-watching cruises sponsored by scientific or environmental organizations. This sort of trip costs a great deal more than arranging one on your own, but you'll enjoy the advantage of having every contingency planned in advance and will receive the commentary of experienced naturalists.

American land syndicate, settled 5,000 Americans along the bayshore. For a time, the colony made money harvesting orchilla, a lichen used in commercial dye. The introduction of synthetic dyes killed the orchilla industry and the colony along with it.

The shore remained unpopulated throughout the first half of the 20th century except for the occasional visit by *bajacaliforniano* anglers and a few unplanned visits by passing mariners. Several ships foundered on the barrier islands, including the famous steamer *Independence* in 1853. Of the 400 passengers aboard, 150 perished in fires on the ship or by drowning after jumping into the breakers.

In 1920, the U.S. submarine *H-1* ran aground on Isla Santa Margarita. What the sub was doing in Mexican waters—at a time when relations between the two countries were tense—has never come to light. Although all but four of the crew were rescued by a passing ship, the sub was mysteriously looted of all logs and other classified material before U.S. Navy rescue ships could approach it; the Navy scut-tled the sub at a depth of nine fathoms just off the island coast and erased virtually all records of its existence. More submarine lore: During World War II, Japanese submarines used Bahía Magdalena as a hiding place. Max Miller, author of *Land Where Time Stands Still*, spotted a Japanese sub in the bay when he made an overland journey to the edge of the Llano Magdalena in 1941.

In the 1960s, after Mexico recovered full ownership of the Llano Magdalena basin from foreign investors, the valley was irrigated and farmers began moving in. The harbor settlement of **Puerto San Carlos** soon developed as a relay point for the shipping of agricultural products, principally cotton and alfalfa, from the plains to mainland Mexico and abroad.

PUERTO SAN CARLOS AND VICINITY

From Ciudad Constitución, paved highway Mexico 22 leads west 57 kilometers (34 mi), then crosses a causeway onto a small hooked peninsula. Mangroves fringe the peninsula; a

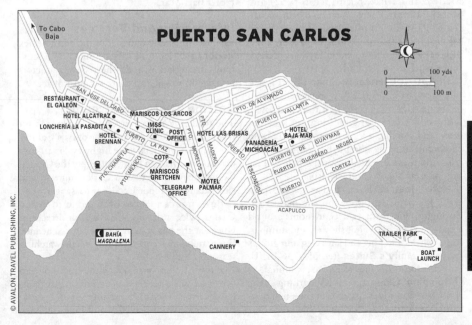

PUERTO SAN CARLOS

To Cabo Baja

0   100 yds
0   100 m

RESTAURANT EL GALEÓN
HOTEL ALCATRAZ
LONCHERÍA LA PASADITA
HOTEL BRENNAN
SAN JOSE DEL CABO
MARISCOS LOS ARCOS
IMSS CLINIC   POST OFFICE
PTO. LA PAZ
COTP
MARISCOS GRETCHEN
PTO. CHAMETLA
PTO. MEXICO
TELEGRAPH OFFICE
PTO. DE ALVARADO
PUERTO VALLARTA
PTO. MADERO
HOTEL LAS BRISAS
PTO. MORELOS
PUERTO ESCONDIDO
MOTEL PALMAR
HOTEL BAJA MAR
PANADERÍA MICHOACÁN
PUERTO DE GUAYMAS
PUERTO GUERRERO NEGRO
PUERTO CORTEZ
PUERTO
PUERTO ACAPULCO
BAHÍA MAGDALENA
CANNERY
TRAILER PARK
BOAT LAUNCH

CENTRAL BAJA

long wharf stretches from the western shore to the only other deepwater port besides Ensenada on the Pacific coast. Often simply called San Carlos, this small port town of 3,200 residents comprises a motley collection of prefab or cinder-block buildings lining sandy roads. The smell of the cannery wafts through town at times, particularly toward the southwest end of the peninsula.

Events

The **Festival de Ballena Gris** (Gray Whale Festival) takes place at the embarcadero in the west end of town every weekend from mid-February to the end of March. It's like the usual small-town festival in Mexico—food vendors, music, *artesanías,* and balloon vendors. In mid-February they have a big one-day celebration with entertainment, disco music, regional dance performances, and singers, all topped off with a 30-minute fireworks display.

Accommodations and Camping

Under US$50: Hotel Las Brisas (Puerto Madero at La Paz, tel. 613/136-0152) and **Motel Palmar** (Puerto Acapulco at Morelos, tel. 613/136-0035) offer basic rooms. A better deal is the friendly **Hotel Baja Mar,** a few blocks east on Puerto de Guaymas, a clean motel with hot-water bathrooms.

US$50-100: Hotel Brennan (Puerto Acapulco, tel. 613/136-0288, www.hotelbrennan .com.mx, US$60) has the best rooms in town, with ceiling fans, air conditioning, kitchenettes, and satellite TV. A restaurant/bar is on the premises. The hotel can arrange fishing trips and tours oriented toward whale-watching, natural history, and kayaking.

Hotel Alcatraz (Puerto La Paz, tel. 613/136-0017, fax 613/136-0086), on the main road through town, features decent rooms around a courtyard with TV, hot shower, and minibar. Many whale-watching and kayaking tour groups stay here. **Molly's Suites** (tel. 613/136-0131), next door on Calle Puerto La Paz, is similar.

Camping: Camping and RV parking at the northwest and southeast ends of the small peninsula costs around US$5 per vehicle.

Food

Restaurant El Galeón, a seafood place not far from Hotel Alcatraz, Molly's Suites, Motel Palmar, and Hotel Brennan, features the largest dining room in town. In addition to lots of fresh seafood, such as a delicious clam dip served free with *totopos,* the restaurant offers *carnes* and chicken.

On Calle Juan Padrín (formerly Calle La Paz), the main dirt road in town, **Mariscos Los Arcos** serves delicious seafood, *antojitos,* and hearty Mexican breakfasts. The *ceviche de callos* (scallops ceviche) is excellent.

Near the plaza is **Lonchería La Pasadita,** a small seafood restaurant with tasty, cheap Mexican food. They serve some delicious *pozole* here, and the coffee is quite good. It opens around 7 A.M.

About 20 meters from the plaza you'll find **Mariscos Gretchen,** which features tacos filled with shrimp, fish, or *machaca.* Open early in the morning. You'll also find **taco stands** on Calle Puerto La Paz.

Panadería Michoacán is a bakery near Hotel Baja Mar.

Information and Services

Facilities in Puerto San Carlos include a Pemex station, *tiendas,* and offices for COTP, customs, immigration, and fishery. Several doctors practice in town, and there is a post office.

Getting There and Around

The road to Puerto San Carlos (57 km/35 mi from Ciudad Constitución), one of Baja California Sur's only official state highways, is an easy drive of less than an hour. Buses ply the Ciudad Constitución–Puerto San Carlos route several times daily for about US$1 per passenger.

Buses from La Paz go back and forth to San Carlos twice a day for US$10 each direction. Check at the bus station for the latest schedule. Buses are more frequent during whale-watching season.

Puerto López Mateos, to the north of San Carlos, can be reached via Ciudad Insurgentes; Puerto Cancún, to the south, is accessible from Mexico 1 at Km 173; and Puerto Chale, farther south, can be reached via Santa Rita, Km 157, Mexico 1.

For finding roads along the coast of Bahía Magdalena and Bahía Almejas, the 1:250,000-scale INEGI La Paz map (G12-10-11) is invaluable.

Puerto López Mateos

Puerto López Mateos is a small town with a cannery, post office, barrel gas, *tiendas,* a *farmacia,* three hotels, and a few seafood restaurants.

Hotel Posada La Pasadita (tel. 613/131-5032) has four rooms—only one of which has a private bath. **Hotel Posada Tornavuelta** (Abelardo L. Rodríguez, tel. 613/131-5106) offers basic rooms with private bath. Check in at the *farmacia* next door. It's open year-round.

Posada La Belleza López (Abelardo L. Rodríguez 219, no tel.) features one room with private bath and three others with shared bath. Showers are available for nonguests.

The town boasts a few seafood restaurants. **El Camarón Feliz** (Abelardo L. Rodríguez, tel. 613/131-5032) serves good fish tacos. **Restaurant Ballena Gris,** on the right as you come into town, features fish, shrimp, and lobster dishes in the US$6.50–11 range. Restaurant **Cabaña Briza,** one block west of the church, is similar. Most of the restaurants in town are open only January–April, during the whale-watching season.

Puerto Chale

Puerto Chale—basically a fish camp on a beautiful bay system—is marked on some Mexican maps as Puerto Charley. The settlement offers a minisuper with all the basics, a church, a school, and several clean outhouses. There are good camping spots here along the inland waterway. Hotel Brennan in San Carlos rents kayaking equipment. Bay destinations of interest include the populated islands of Isla Santa Margarita (pop. 549) and Isla Magdalena (pop. 275).

During the peak January–March whale-watching season, kayaking and other boating is restricted to areas north or south of Boca de Soledad, and even for these areas you must first obtain a permit from SEMARNAT in La Paz.

Boating

Trailered or cartopped boats can be launched from a concrete boat ramp in San Carlos; you can easily launch *pangas* from the beach. Other launching points for small boats or kayaks are Puerto López Mateos to the north, Puerto Cancún to the south, and Puerto Chale, farther south.

Fishing

The bay fisheries provide steady sportfishing due to the relative lack of commercial fishing interests. Onshore catches, near the mangroves, include halibut, occasional yellowtail, red bass (mangrove snapper), corvina, and snook. Farther out in the bay, anglers take grouper, black bass, and yellowtail; offshore, beyond the 100-fathom line, are sailfish, marlin, dorado, wahoo, and giant sea bass. Although most of these game fish frequent the area year-round, July–November is generally the most productive fishing season. The best places to get live bait are the mackerel holes off Punta Entrada.

You can gather clams in the shallows of both bays, although Bahía Almejas lives up to its name with the most extensive clam grounds.

Windsurfing

Mag Bay, as gringos usually call it, offers the best windsurfing on Baja California's Pacific coast. A strong year-round breeze, together with the relatively calm bay surface, creates perfect conditions for novice and intermediate windsurfers; experienced wave-sailors can experiment at or near the *bocas,* where breakers and stronger winds increase the challenge.

A protected run of 88 kilometers (52 mi) begins at Puerto López Mateos and ends at Puerto Cancún; you can lengthen this run to 113 kilometers (70 mi) by staying in until Puerto Chale.

Whale-Watching

Puerto López Mateos and San Carlos are the usual centers for whale-watching activities. Often you can spot grays from shore at Puerto López Mateos as they come and go via Boca de Soledad to the north; a public parking and

CENTRAL BAJA

viewing area lies north of the port's fish-processing plant. *Pangeros* offer two-hour *panga* tours from this area for US$50 per person if you can find six people; four people can go for US$55 per person. Ask at any hotel in San Carlos, or go talk to the *pangeros* directly at the embarcadero on the west side of town near the lighthouse. Local operators officially authorized to lead whale-watching tours include: **Viajes Mar y Arena** (tel. 613/136-0076, fax 613/136-0232); **Brennan's y Asociados** (tel. 613/136-0288, fax 613/136-0019, turismo@balandra.uabcs.mx); and **Unión de Lancheros y Servicios Turísticos de Puerto San Carlos (ULYSTOURS)** (tel. 613/136-0310). Although limited numbers of *pangas* are allowed in the bay at any one time, early morning and late afternoon are best for avoiding crowds. Because the waters of San Carlos are deeper, you can usually see more whale acrobatics in this area than off López Mateos.

While pregnant female grays venture into shallower parts of the bay for calving, males tend to loiter near bay entrances, where they cavort with other males and nonpregnant females, often breaching and spyhopping—but not "mating," as myth would have it. One of the best viewing spots is **Punta Entrada,** at the southern tip of Isla Magdalena, which forms the north end of the wide channel between Bahía Magdalena and the Pacific. The island is accessible only by boat, with the best anchorage on the southeast side of the point, or by small plane (a landing strip lies just north of Punta Entrada). You can camp at the fish camp near the tip or farther north near the village of **Puerto Magdalena.** A San Carlos *pangero* will drop you off on the island and pick you up the following day; the usual hourly rates apply.

You can book Bahía Magdalena whale-watching tours in La Paz, Loreto, or Todos Santos through many hotels and tours operators.

Late January–early March, **Baja Expeditions** (U.S. tel. 858/581-3311 or 800/843-6967, www.bajaex.com) offers frequent seven-day kayaking and whale-watching trips in Bahía Magdalena for US$1,275–1,350 per person. Trips originate in La Paz.

EL CIEN AND PUNTA EL CONEJO

At Km 100, about midway between Ciudad Constitución and La Paz, lies the tiny roadside settlement of El Cien (One Hundred). As a pit stop, El Cien offers the **Lonchería El 100** (*machaca* and carne asada are the mainstays; open daily), a CONASUPO, and barrel gas, the only place for gas between Ciudad Constitución and La Paz. A nearby fossil reef reportedly contains whale vertebrae and other marine skeletons; inquire at the *lonchería* for a guide.

At Km 80, a good dirt road branches west 19 kilometers (12 mi) to Punta El Conejo. El Conejo (The Rabbit) is well known among surfers for steady point breaks in both northwest and southwest swells. Near the coast, the road to El Conejo intersects a lesser dirt road heading south 17 kilometers (12.5 mi) to another surfing spot, **Punta Márquez.** This road continues southward along the coast all the way to Todos Santos (124 km/77 mi from El Conejo), passing a number of good beach breaks. Recommended for four-wheel-drive vehicles only.

Just south of a cobblestone road to Las Pocitas at Km 112, **Restaurant Don Manuel** is a clean family-style setup with a giftshop called Dolores. The shop sells pottery, baskets made of palm fronds, antique sewing machines, and other handcrafted items.

LA PAZ AND VICINITY

Ensconced along the largest bay on Baja's Sea of Cortez coast, La Paz is a city of more than 200,000 noted for its attractive *malecón* (waterfront walkway) backed by swaying palms and pastel-colored buildings, its splendid sunsets, easygoing pace, sunny climate, and its proximity to uncrowded beaches and pristine islands. Many Baja travelers—Mexicans and gringos alike—cite La Paz (Peace) as their favorite city on the Baja California peninsula; a few even go so far as to pronounce it their favorite in all of Mexico. La Paz is ideal for the traveler who wants more than a beach and booze vacation; here, you'll get some history, eco-adventure, and a taste of the real Mexico mixed in.

Cabo San Lucas, 221 kilometers (137 mi) farther south, still receives more attention than

La Paz in the American press, which suits La Paz fans fine since it means fewer tourists—around 4,500 gringos in all spend the winter season here; and some stay year-round. But the Baja Sur state government is investing heavily in tourism in the area around La Paz, and new direct flights from California to the city's international airport may herald a new wave of visitors in coming years.

Indeed, as the real estate market becomes saturated in Los Cabos, developers are looking northward. Three large-scale resort developments are already underway: Like Cabo San Lucas, La Paz now has its own hilltop Pedregal neighborhood in the making, at the northeastern edge of town on the way to Pichilingue. Cobblestone roads and utilities are the first step in the creation of a

HIGHLIGHTS

◖ **Malecón:** You haven't experienced La Paz until you've strolled the waterfront promenade at sunset. Visitors and residents alike pause to watch the dramatic display of color. Stop for a cocktail or an ice cream, and enjoy the evening breeze (page 247).

◖ **Museo Regional de Antropología e Historia:** Think you know your Baja history? Save time for a tour of the fossils, minerals, and maps of rock-painting sites in this well-run museum. Exhibits depict Amerindian and colonial life throughout central and southern Baja (page 247).

◖ **Playa El Tecolote:** A drive to the end of the road along Bahía de La Paz leads to this wide, sandy beach. Wade into clear, shallow waters and enjoy views of Isla Espíritu Santo across the channel. A steady breeze keeps the bugs away if you decide to spend the night (page 251).

◖ **Isla Espíritu Santo:** The best-known of the islands offshore from La Paz entertains paddlers, divers, and boaters with white-sand beaches and rock reefs. You can camp in several places on the island and enjoy endless opportunities for outdoor adventure (page 254).

◖ **Bahía de la Ventana:** A short drive south of La Paz, this L-shaped bay offers steady winds for kiteboarders and windsurfers, plus easy access to Isla Cerralvo for scuba diving adventures. Enjoy the remote feel while it lasts (page 284).

LOOK FOR ◖ TO FIND RECOMMENDED SIGHTS, ACTIVITIES, DINING, AND LODGING.

128-acre (52 hectare) private, gated community of 370 lots, a 200-room hotel, condos, and a shopping plaza. Nearby, a second beach development, the 500-acre CostaBaja Resort & Marina (www.costabajaresort.com) already has an operational 280-slip marina and Fiesta Inn resort. When complete, the development will include 50 villas, plus shops and restaurants. The real estate fever has spread to the south as well, with five hotels, a residential neighborhood, and airport planned for the Bay of Dreams.

The most controversial development is taking shape on the Mogote Peninsula, a spit of land that juts out in the bay. Environmentalists are concerned that the future site of the Paraíso del Mar (www.paradiseofthesea.com) project, consisting of two golf courses, a 535-slip marina, 2,000 hotel rooms, and 2,000 private homes, will permanently destroy hundreds of acres of mangrove essential to the health of the marine ecosystem.

Despite the feverish pace of real estate activity, La Paz remains steeped most profoundly

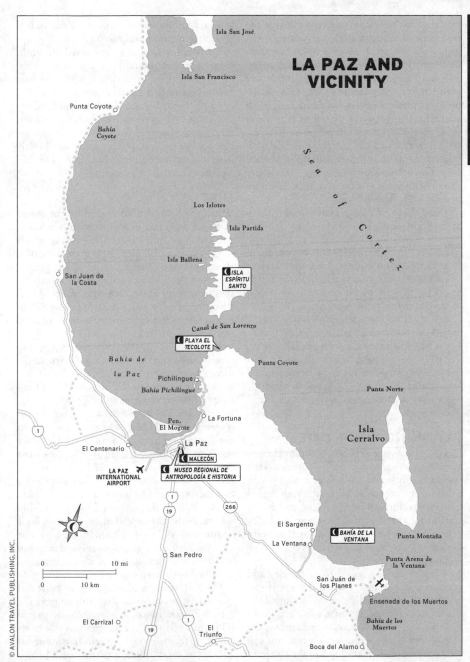

LA PAZ AND VICINITY

LA PAZ AND
VICINITY

Isla San José

Isla San Francisco

Punta Coyote

*Bahía
Coyote*

S e a   o f   C o r t e z

Los Islotes

Isla Partida

Isla Ballena

San Juan de
la Costa

(ISLA
ESPÍRITU
SANTO

Canal de San Lorenzo

(PLAYA EL
TECOLOTE

*Bahía de
la Paz*

Pichilingue

Punta Coyote

Bahía Pichilingue

Punta Norte

Pen.
El Mogote

La Fortuna

Isla
Cerralvo

El Centenario

La Paz

1

(MALECÓN

LA PAZ
INTERNATIONAL
AIRPORT

(MUSEO REGIONAL DE
ANTROPOLOGÍA E HISTORIA

1

19

266

El Sargento

(BAHÍA DE LA
VENTANA

Punta Montaña

La Ventana

Punta Arena de
la Ventana

San Pedro

0   10 mi

San Juán de
los Planes

0   10 km

Ensenada de los Muertos

El Carrizal

19

1

El
Triunfo

*Bahía de los
Muertos*

Boca del Alamo

© AVALON TRAVEL PUBLISHING, INC.

in mainland Mexico's traditions; it was the first major European settlement on the peninsula and has long been a haven for Mexicans dissatisfied with life on the mainland. Many *Paceños* (La Paz residents) are descendants of mainlanders who sailed to La Paz to avoid the political turmoil of the 19th and early 20th centuries. And it's not uncommon to meet more recent Mexican émigrés who have re-settled in La Paz after becoming fed up with modern-day political machinations in Mexico City, Guadalajara, or Monterrey. *Paceños* are proud of the many ways in which their city lives up to its name.

Along the bay, La Paz remains much as John Steinbeck described it in 1941:

La Paz grew in fascination as we approached. The square, iron-shuttered colonial houses stood up right in back of the beach with rows of beautiful trees in front of them. It is a lovely place. There is a broad promenade along the water lined with benches, named for dead residents of the city, where one may rest oneself.... [A] cloud of delight hangs over the distant city from the time when it was the great pearl center of the world.... Guaymas is busier, they say, and Mazatlán gayer, but La Paz is antigua.

PLANNING YOUR TIME

La Paz offers a wide variety of accommodations and dining venues, well-stocked supermarkets, marine supply stores, and a ferry terminal with a daily departure for Mazatlán across the Sea of Cortez. Parking can be a bit tight, and minor traffic snarls are common in *el centro,* the city center, but can be avoided by using Boulevard Forjadores, a wide avenue skirting the southern section of the city.

Allow several days to explore the city and surrounding beaches; a week or more if you plan to fish, snorkel, dive, or kayak around the islands just offshore. If you're coming to learn Spanish, local schools recommend a minimum stay of two weeks, up to a month if you can swing it. Travelers planning to take the ferry

to Mazatlán should allow an extra day or two to arrange permits and reservations.

February is La Paz's peak tourist month. Even then, you should be able to find a hotel room easily. One exception is when the Baja 1000 off-road race comes to town in mid-November. With the race finish just outside the city limits, every room, condo, and vacation rental books up months in advance. If you roll into La Paz without reservations, you'll likely have to continue south to Los Barriles to find a place to crash for the night.

HISTORY

When the Spanish first landed on the shores of Bahía de la Paz in the early 16th century, the area was inhabited by migrating bands of Guaicura and Pericú, who allegedly called their homeland "Airapi." Hunters and gatherers, these Amerindian groups lived mostly on shellfish, small game, and wild plants. As artifacts on display at La Paz's Museum of Anthropology demonstrate, they were also skilled weavers and potters.

Into this peaceful scene entered the first European, a Basque mutineer named Fortún Jiménez, who commandeered the Spanish ship *Concepción* on the Sea of Cortez in 1533. Originally under the command of Captain Diego Becerra, the *Concepción* had been sent to explore the sea on behalf of Spain's most famous conquistador, Hernán Cortés. After executing the captain, Jiménez landed at Bahía de La Paz in early 1534, where he and 22 of his crew were killed by Amerindians while filling their water casks at a spring. The survivors sailed the *Concepción* back to the mainland, where the ship was immediately captured by Cortés's New Spain rival, Nuño de Guzmán. At least one crew member managed to escape and returned to Cortés with descriptions of a huge, beautiful bay filled with pearl-oyster beds.

Cortés himself landed at the northeast end of the bay, probably at Pichilingue near the present ferry terminal, in May 1535 and named it Puerto de Santa Cruz. Cortés was able to effect a truce with local Amerindians, but his attempt at establishing a permanent Spanish

ENGLISH PIRATES ON THE SEA OF CORTEZ

Sir Francis Drake, Thomas Cavendish, William Dampier, Woodes Rogers, Thomas Dover, and other English privateers left behind a colorful Baja legacy. In spite of Spain's repeated attempts to colonize the peninsula, throughout the Spanish colonial period the pirates probably gained more wealth in the Californias than the Spanish themselves. For 250 years they plagued the Manila galleons off the coast of the Californias, finding the bays and lagoons of Baja's Cape Region perfect hiding places from which to launch attacks on treasure-laden ships.

In La Paz, using their knowledge of the strong breeze that blows into the harbor every summer afternoon, the pirates attacked Spanish galleons while the vessels were effectively trapped in the bay. Four centuries after the first Manila-Acapulco voyages, this afternoon wind is still known as *el coromuel*, named for the Puritan Cromwells – father and son – who ruled successively as Lord Protectors of England.

THE DISAPPEARANCE OF THE *DESIRE*

The most notorious of the Pacific privateers was Sir Thomas Cavendish, whose greatest feat of plunder occurred at Cabo San Lucas in 1587. There is two English vessels, *Desire* and *Content*, commandeered the Spanish galleon *Santa Ana* after a protracted sea battle.

Cavendish set fire to the *Santa Ana* after looting its cargo holds and setting its crew and passengers ashore. The Spanish crew later retrieved the burned hulk and restored it for a return to Acapulco.

The plundered treasure, meanwhile, was divided between the *Desire* and the *Content*. The ships set sail for England immediately, but during the first night of their triumphant voyage the *Desire* disappeared. Cavendish reported in England that the captain and crew of the *Desire* must have scuttled the ship on a nearby island and disappeared with the loot. Neither the wreckage of the vessel nor the treasure was ever discovered; some historians speculate that at least part of the missing wealth remains buried near the Cape.

A VISIT BY ROBINSON CRUSOE

In 1709, famed corsair Woodes Rogers landed in La Paz after rescuing a seaman who'd been marooned five years on a deserted island off Chile's coast. The rescued man was Alexander Selkirk, whose island sojourn became the inspiration for Daniel Defoe's *Robinson Crusoe*, published in 1719. Selkirk was aboard Rogers's *Dover* when the crew captured the Spanish galleon *Encarnación* off Cabo San Lucas in 1709; he served as sailing master on the ship's return voyage to England the following year.

colony lasted only through 1538, when the colonists were forced to abandon the peninsula because of supply problems.

The next Spaniard to visit the bay was famed explorer Sebastián Vizcaíno, who landed here in 1596 during his long voyage around the peninsula's perimeter and north to California. Because he and his crew were treated so well by the Pericú, Vizcaíno named the bay Bahía de La Paz (Bay of Peace).

Pirates and Colonization

Baja California remained free of Spaniards another 100 years before the successful establishment of a mission colony at Loreto to the north. By this time, English and Dutch pirates were plundering New Spain's Manila galleons as they returned from the Orient weighted down with gold, silks, and spices. One of the freebooters' favorite staging areas was Bahía de La Paz, which contained numerous *ensenadas* (coves) and inlets perfect for concealing their swift corsairs. When Spanish crews put in for water, the pirates raided the galleons, often using their knowledge of strong afternoon winds to attack the ships when they were effectively pinned down.

Increased pirate activity in the late 17th and early 18th centuries created the need for a Spanish presence in the Cape Region. In 1719,

Padre Juan de Ugarte, then president of the missions, contracted a master shipbuilder to construct a ship for the specific purpose of exploring the Sea of Cortez coast and improving supply lines with the mainland. The barque *El Triunfo de la Cruz*, assembled of native Baja hardwood at the Mulegé estuary, made its first sailing to Bahía de La Paz in 1720 with Ugarte and Padre Jaime Bravo as passengers.

Ugarte and Bravo founded the mission community of Nuestra Señora del Pilar de la Paz at the current city site. The padres didn't find the Pericú to be as friendly this time around; the mission lasted only until 1749, when it was abandoned after a series of Amerindian rebellions. By this time, another mission and a presidio had been founded farther south at San José del Cabo—a better location for monitoring pirate activity.

La Paz Reborn

Left with European diseases and without the support of the mission system, the local Pericú population dwindled quickly. By 1811, Mexican ranchers and *pescadores* who had settled along the Bahía de La Paz started their own town, which they named La Paz after the bay. After Loreto was severely damaged during a hurricane in 1829, the capital of Baja California Sur was moved to burgeoning La Paz, where it has remained ever since.

During the Mexican-American War (1846–1848), U.S. troops occupied the city; the soldiers left when the Californias were split by the 1848 Treaty of Hidalgo. But American general William Walker, dissatisfied with the treaty and hoping to add another slaveholder state to

counter the growing U.S. abolitionist movement, formed his own army of "New York Volunteers" and retook La Paz in November 1853. Proclaiming himself "president of the Republic of Sonora," Walker lasted only six months; he and his mercenaries fled upon hearing that the United States wouldn't back their claims, and that the Mexican army was on its way to La Paz from the mainland. Walker was tried in the United States for violation of neutrality laws, fined, and two years later was executed by the Nicaraguan army for attempting a similar takeover of Nicaragua.

La Paz remained a sleepy tropic seaport, known only for pearl harvesting, until it was declared a duty-free port after World War II. After an epizootic disease killed off the entire pearl-oyster population, the city's economic focus turned to farming and trade with the mainland. During Mexico's postwar economic boom, mainland Mexicans crossed the Sea of Cortez in droves to buy imported merchandise; enchanted by La Paz itself, many stayed on.

In the 1950s, La Paz became well-known as a fishing resort and was visited by a succession of North American literati and Hollywood celebrities, thus initiating the city's reputation as an international vacation spot. But until the Transpeninsular Highway was completed in 1973, the city remained for the most part a tourist destination for mainland Mexicans.

Statehood was bestowed on the Territory of Baja California Sur in 1974, and La Paz was made state capital. Linked by air, ferry, and highway to mainland Mexico and the United States, the city has grown considerably in the decades since; yet it manages to maintain its tropic port ambience.

Sights

◖ Malecón

The pleasant five-kilometer *malecón,* a seawall promenade along the northwest side of Paseo Alvaro Obregón extending from Calle 5 de Febrero (Mexico 1 south) to the northeastern city limits, is looking better than ever these days. Decorative paving, newly painted crosswalks, and wrought-iron benches invite visitors and residents alike to take a walk along the bay. Water quality has improved too, making it possible to swim once again (though most people continue northeast to the beaches along the Pichilingue Peninsula).

The best time of day for people-watching is around sunset, when the city begins cooling off, the sun dyes the waterfront orange, and *Paceños* take to the *malecón* for an evening stroll or jog. Snacks and cold beverages are available at several *palapa* bars along the way. Restaurants, shops, real estate offices, car rental agencies—and a brand new Applebees chain—line the opposite side of Obregón.

© PAUL ITOI
cucumbers for sale

An archway marks the entry to the Muelle Turístico (Tourist Pier), with cobblestone paving, potted plants, and well-lighted wrought-iron seating areas. With locals strolling and hanging out on the pier on warm evenings, it has taken on the feel of a traditional Mexican plaza.

◖ Museo Regional de Antropología e Historia

Baja California history buffs shouldn't miss this well-designed museum (5 de Mayo and Altamirano, tel. 612/125-6424, daily 9 A.M.–6 P.M., admission free). Three floors of exhibits cover Cape Region anthropology from prehistoric to colonial and modern times. On display are fossils, minerals, Amerindian artifacts, dioramas of Amerindian and colonial life, and maps of rock-painting sites throughout central and southern Baja. Labels are in Spanish only.

Plaza Constitución (Jardín Velazco)

La Paz's tidy downtown *zócalo* is enclosed by Avenida Independencia and Calles 5 de Mayo, Revolución de 1910, and Madero. At the southwest side of the plaza is the post-missionary-style **Catedral de Nuestra Señora de La Paz,** which replaced La Paz's original mission church in 1861. Although the twin-towered brick edifice looms over the plaza, it lacks the charm of earlier Jesuit missions. Inside, only an image of Nuestra Señora del Pilar and a few theological books survive from the earlier 1720 mission. A couple of blocks southwest of the plaza, on Calle Zaragoza between Arrival and Lerdo de Tejada, a plaque commemorates the original mission site.

At the northwest side of Plaza Constitución, opposite the cathedral, is the **Biblioteca de História de las Californias** (Library of Californias' History). Housed in the 1880s-era former Casa de Gobierno (Government House), the library is filled with Spanish- and English-language volumes on Alta and Baja California history. The

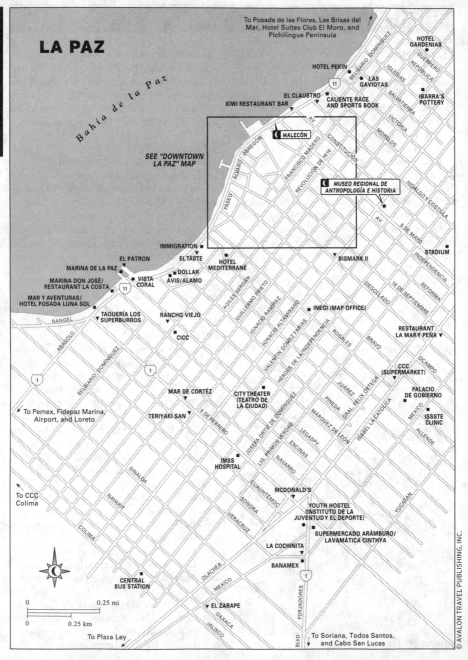

LA PAZ

To Posada de las Flores, Las Brisas del Mar, Hotel Suites Club El Moro, and Pichilingue Peninsula

Bahía de la Paz

HOTEL GARDENIAS

HOTEL PEKIN

LAS GAVIOTAS

EL CLAUSTRO

KIWI RESTAURANT BAR

CALIENTE RACE AND SPORTS BOOK

IBARRA'S POTTERY

MALECÓN

SEE "DOWNTOWN LA PAZ" MAP

MUSEO REGIONAL DE ANTROPOLOGÍA E HISTORIA

IMMIGRATION

EL PATRON

EL TASTE

STADIUM

MARINA DE LA PAZ

HOTEL MEDITERRANÉ

BISMARK II

MARINA DON JOSÉ/ RESTAURANT LA COSTA

DOLLAR AVIS/ALAMO

VISTA CORAL

MAR Y AVENTURAS/ HOTEL POSADA LUNA SOL

RANGEL

TAQUERÍA LOS SUPERBURROS

RANCHO VIEJO

INEGI (MAP OFFICE)

CICC

RESTAURANT LA MARY PEÑA

To Pemex, Fidepaz Marina, Airport, and Loreto

CCC (SUPERMARKET)

MAR DE CORTÉZ

CITY THEATER (TEATRO DE LA CIUDAD)

PALACIO DE GOBIERNO

TERIYAKI SAN

ISSSTE CLINIC

IMSS HOSPITAL

To CCC Colima

MCDONALD'S

YOUTH HOSTEL (INSTITUTO DE LA JUVENTUD Y EL DEPORTE)

SUPERMERCADO ARÁMBURO/ LAVAMÁTICA CINTHYA

LA COCHINITA

BANAMEX

To Plaza Ley

CENTRAL BUS STATION

0   0.25 mi
0   0.25 km

EL ZARAPE

To Soriana, Todos Santos, and Cabo San Lucas

© AVALON TRAVEL PUBLISHING, INC.

general public is welcome to use the library for research. Officially, the library hours are Monday–Friday 9 A.M.–6 P.M., Saturday 9 A.M.–3 P.M., though these are not always strictly adhered to. For library information, call 612/122-0162.

La Unidad Cultural Profesor Jesús Castro Aqúndez

This cultural center (Navarro btw Altamirano/Independencia, tel. 612/125-0207, Mon.–Fri. 8 A.M.–3 P.M.) includes an art gallery, community art school, city archives, and the **Teatro de la Ciudad** (City Theater), a 1,500-seat performing-arts facility that hosts musical, the-atrical, and dance performances throughout the year.

Universities

As Baja California Sur's educational center, La Paz supports a large number of schools at the primary, secondary, and tertiary levels. The prominent **Universidad Autonomía de Baja California Sur** (University of Baja California South), on Boulevard Forjadores, has reputable programs in agriculture, engineering, and business. The **Instituto Tecnológico de La Paz** (Technological Institute of La Paz), also on Boulevard Forjadores, is primarily known for its commercial-fishing department.

Beaches

BAHÍA DE LA PAZ

Bahía de La Paz is scalloped with 10 signed, public beaches. Most inviting are the seven beaches strung out northeast of La Paz along Península de Pichilingue—they get better the farther you get from the city.

Playa Palmira and Playa el Coromuel

Playa Palmira, around four kilometers (2.5 mi) east of downtown La Paz via the La Paz–Pich-ilingue Road, has been taken over by the Araiza Inn Palmira and Club de Yates Palmira, leaving little remaining beachfront. A kilometer farther, the small but pleasant Playa el Coromuel is pop-ular with local residents and offers restaurant/bar service, a waterslide, *palapas*, and toilets.

Playa Caimancito

In front of La Concha Beach Resort near Km 5, Playa Caimancito (named for an offshore rock formation that resembles a small gator) features a rock reef within swimming distance of the grayish beach. Although it's close to the city and resort developments, you can see a surpris-ing number of tropical fish here; incoming tide is the best time for swimming and snorkeling.

Playa del Tesoro and Playa Punta Colorada

Playa del Tesoro, 14 kilometers (8.5 mi) from the city, is another casual, semiurban beach with *palapas* and a sometimes-open, often-closed restaurant. The beach was purportedly named for a cache of silver coins unearthed by crews building a road to the Pichilingue ferry terminal near the beach. Just southwest of El Tesoro, a dirt road leads to hidden Playa Punta Colorada, a small, quiet cove surrounded by red-hued hills that protect it from the sights and sounds of the La Paz–Pichilingue Road.

Playa Pichilingue

At Km 17, just beyond the SEMATUR ferry terminal, is Playa Pichilingue, the only public beach in the La Paz vicinity with restrooms available 24 hours for campers. The beach also has a modest *palapa* restaurant (tel. 612/122-4565, mains US$5–10). A taxi from the *malecón* to the ferry terminal will run US$20.

Playa Balandra

After Pichilingue, the once-sandy track has been replaced by pavement as far as Playa El Tecolote. An unsigned left turnoff for Playa

DOWNTOWN LA PAZ

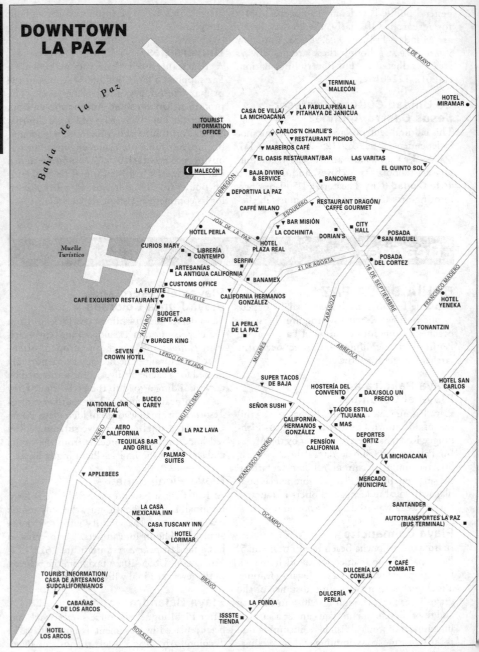

Bahía de la Paz

Muelle Turístico

MALECÓN

TOURIST INFORMATION OFFICE

TERMINAL MALECÓN

HOTEL MIRAMAR

CASA DE VILLA/ LA MICHOACANA

LA FABULA/PEÑA LA PITAHAYA DE JANICUA

CARLOS'N CHARLIE'S

RESTAURANT PICHOS

MAREIROS CAFÉ

EL OASIS RESTAURANT/BAR

LAS VARITAS

EL QUINTO SOL

BAJA DIVING & SERVICE

BANCOMER

DEPORTIVA LA PAZ

OBREGÓN

CAFFÉ MILANO

RESTAURANT DRAGÓN/ CAFFÉ GOURMET

ESQUERRO

BAR MISIÓN

CITY HALL

POSADA SAN MIGUEL

JON. DE LA PAZ

HOTEL PERLA

LA COCHINITA

DORIAN'S

CURIOS MARY

LIBRERÍA CONTEMPO

HOTEL PLAZA REAL

POSADA DEL CORTEZ

16 DE SEPTIEMBRE

FRANCISCO MADERO

SERFIN

21 DE AGOSTA

ARTESANÍAS LA ANTIGUA CALIFORNIA

BANAMEX

CUSTOMS OFFICE

CAFÉ EXQUISITO RESTAURANT

LA FUENTE

MUELLE

CALIFORNIA HERMANOS GONZÁLEZ

HOTEL YENEKA

BUDGET RENT-A-CAR

ÁLVARO

ZARAGOZA

ARREOLA

TONANTZIN

LA PERLA DE LA PAZ

BURGER KING

SEVEN CROWN HOTEL

LERDO DE TEJADA

MIJARES

ARTESANÍAS

SUPER TACOS DE BAJA

HOSTERÍA DEL CONVENTO

DAX/SOLO UN PRECIO

HOTEL SAN CARLOS

BUCEO CAREY

NATIONAL CAR RENTAL

MUTUALISMO

SEÑOR SUSHI

TACOS ESTILO TIJUANA

AERO CALIFORNIA

LA PAZ LAVA

CALIFORNIA HERMANOS GONZÁLEZ

MAS

DEPORTES ORTIZ

TEQUILAS BAR AND GRILL

PENSIÓN CALIFORNIA

LA MICHOACANA

PALMAS SUITES

PASEO

APPLEBEES

MERCADO MUNICIPAL

FRANCISCO MADERO

SANTANDER

LA CASA MEXICANA INN

AUTOTRANSPORTES LA PAZ (BUS TERMINAL)

CASA TUSCANY INN

OCAMPO

HOTEL LORIMAR

CAFÉ COMBATE

DULCERÍA LA CONEJA

TOURIST INFORMATION/ CASA DE ARTESANOS SUDCALIFORNIANOS

BRAVO

DULCERÍA PERLA

CABAÑAS DE LOS ARCOS

LA FONDA

ISSSTE TIENDA

HOTEL LOS ARCOS

ROSALES

E DE MAYO

Balandra appears five kilometers (3 mi) beyond Pichilingue, and then it's another 800 meters (0.5 mi) to the parking area and beach, which has several *palapas* and brick barbecue pits. Depending on the tide, the large, shallow bay of Puerto Balandra actually forms several beaches, some of them long sandbars. Ringed by cliffs and steep hills, the bay is a beautiful and usually secluded spot, perfect for wading in the clear, warm waters. Clams are abundant, and a coral reef at the south end of the bay offers decent snorkeling. Climb the rock cliffs—carefully—for sweeping bay views. Camping is permitted at Balandra, but oftentimes a lack of breeze brings out the *jejenes* (no-see-ums), especially in the late summer and early fall. The beaches sometimes draw crowds on weekends.

Playa El Tecolote

About three kilometers (1.5 mi) beyond the Playa Balandra turnoff is Playa El Tecolote, a wide, long beach backed by vegetated dunes. Because El Tecolote is open to the stiff breezes of Canal de San Lorenzo, the camping here is usually insect-free. Two *palapa* restaurants, **El Tecolote** (tel. 612/127-9494, mains US$8–15) and **Palapa Azul** (tel. 612/122-1801, mains US$8–15), sell seafood and cold beverages and rent *pangas,* beach chairs and umbrellas, fishing gear, and plastic canoes. Both restaurants have pay showers. Free municipal *palapas,* barbecue grills, and trash barrels dot the beach north and south of the restaurants.

Isla Espíritu Santo, 6.5 kilometers (4 mi) away, is clearly visible in the distance; for around US$40–50 you can hire a *panga* to cross the channel (see *Islands*).

FARTHER AFIELD

From El Tecolote, the road returns to sand as it winds across the peninsula for about 13 kilometers (8 mi) before ending at remote **Playa Coyote.** Along the way, shorter roads branch off to rocky coves suitable for camping. Don't tackle this road expecting to find the perfect white-sand beach; the farther northeast from El Tecolote you go, the stonier and browner the beaches become.

South of Playa Coyote, you can navigate a network of sand roads to Puerto Mejia and **Las Cruces.** Named for three crosses topping a bluff near the cove where Cortés supposedly landed, Las Cruces served as a supply port for Isla Cerralvo pearl beds during the pearl era. It was abandoned in the 1930s after the pearl-bearing oysters died out. In 1949, Abelardo L. Rodríguez III, grandson of a former Mexican president, designed and built at Las Cruces a fly-in getaway resort for Hollywood celebrities, including Desi Arnaz and Bing Crosby. The 20,000-acre resort was incorporated as Club de Caza y Pesca Las Cruces (Las Cruces Hunting and Fishing Club) in 1961 and today remains a private association counting around 225 members. Although the resort's popularity peaked in the 1950s and 1960s, some of the fabulous beach villas are still occupied on occasion. The road's final approach is so difficult (intentionally so, according to rumors) that few people arrive by road; instead, guests use the resort's private airstrip or arrive by yacht. Membership is conferred by invitation and sponsorship only.

PENÍNSULA EL MOGOTE

This 11-kilometer (7-mi) thumb of land juts across the top of Ensenada de la Paz directly opposite the city. The southern shore of the peninsula is rimmed by mangroves, while the north side facing the open bay offers clean water and a long beach sullied only by everyday flotsam. It's not uncommon to see dolphins swimming by. Local myth says that if you eat the wild plums of the *ciruelo (Cryptocarpa edulis)* growing on El Mogote's sand dunes, you'll never want to leave La Paz.

Access to El Mogote is changing rapidly as a new US$240 million real estate project takes shape. The Paraíso del Mar plans call for two golf courses, a club house, hundreds of homes, a shopping mall, church, hotels, marina, and park. Necessary infrastructure will include desal plants, water and sewage treatment plants, and a ferry terminal. (Although there is a dirt road leading out to the peninsula from El Comitá, north of La Paz, primary access for

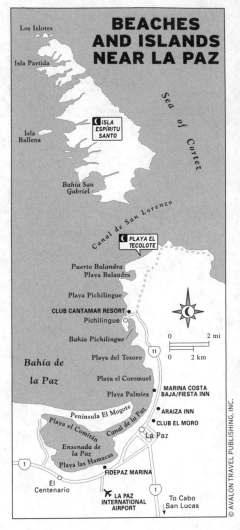

visitors will be by ferryboat, since the distance is only one-half mile from the *malecón*.) The project has come under criticism from environmentalists, including Greenpeace, for endangering hundreds of acres of mangroves, which provide a habitat and nutrients for thousands of marine species in the Sea of Cortez.

Unless you're interested in touring the de-

© AVALON TRAVEL PUBLISHING, INC.

THE PEARLS OF LA PAZ

Pearls develop from sand grains or other small particles that manage to get between an oyster's mantle and its shell. The oyster secretes a substance that cushions it from the irritation of the particle – if the grain moves freely during the secretion buildup, the pearl is more or less spherical; if it stays in one place or is embedded in the shell, it becomes a "baroque" pearl. Even when an oyster doesn't contain a pearl, the interior of the shell is valued for its rainbow luster, known as mother-of-pearl. Only particular mollusk varieties within the family Pteridae, found only in certain coastal areas off East Asia, Panama, and Baja California, can form pearls.

Pearl gathering in the New World goes back at least 7,000 years. When the Spanish found Amerindians along the Sea of Cortez coast wearing pearls and pearl shells as hair ornaments in the early 16th century, they quickly added pearls to the list of exploitable resources in Mexico. Finding the source of the luminescent, milky-white spheres – oyster beds – became a priority of marine expeditions off Mexico's west coast.

After a Spanish mutineer reported the presence of pearls in Bahía de la Paz in 1533, harvesting them became one of Cortés's primary interests in exploring Baja's lower Sea of Cortez coast. Between 1535, when Cortés finally managed to establish a temporary settlement at Bahía de la Paz, and 1697, when Jesuit padres began missionizing the Baja peninsula,

untold thousands of pearls were harvested. The Jesuits, however, strongly objected to any secular exploitation of the peninsula, preferring to keep Baja within the domain of the church. Hence during the mission period (1697-1768), pearling was restricted to sporadic illegal harvests; still, many pearls found their way to Europe, where they encrusted the robes of bishops and Spanish royalty.

In the mid-19th century, after the secularization of Baja missions, the Baja pearl industry was revived by *armadores* (entrepreneurs), who hired Yaqui divers from Sonora to scour the shallow bays, coves, and island shores between Mulegé and La Paz. The invention of diving suits in 1874 revolutionized pearling by allowing divers access to deeper waters. By 1889 the world pearling industry was dominated by Compañía Perlífera de Baja California, based in La Paz.

Intensive harvesting rapidly depleted the oyster beds, and between 1936 and 1941 most of the remaining pearl oysters were wiped out by an unknown disease. Many La Paz residents today believe the disease was somehow introduced by the Japanese to eliminate Mexican competition in the pearl industry, but it's more likely the disease simply took advantage of an already weakened population.

The mystique of La Paz pearls continued long after the industry's demise. John Steinbeck based his novella *The Pearl* on a famous pearl story he heard while visiting La Paz in 1941.

velopment, the easiest way to reach the peninsula is by kayak from the Marina de La Paz area (see *Kayaking* under *Sports and Recreation* later in this chapter for more information).

Most kayakers land on the mangrove side facing Ensenada de la Paz and then walk across the peninsula's narrow isthmus to reach the bay/ocean side.

Islands

The large and small islands clustered just north of Península de Pichilingue offer an amazing variety of recreational possibilities both in and out of the water. The 22.5-kilometer-long (14-mi-long) Isla Espíritu Santo and its smaller immediate neighbor to the north, Isla Partida, are excellent destinations for all manner of watercraft from sea kayaks to yachts. Sandy beaches and large coves along the western shores of both islands provide numerous opportunities for small-craft landings and camping. In full sun, the sand-bottom reflections of these bays create such a bright, translucent color that white seagulls flying over them are transformed into glowing blue-green UFOs.

Isla Espíritu Santo

Formerly owned by a local *ejido,* this island was "sold" to the Mexican government in 2003, through the cooperative efforts of several nonprofits, which raised US$3.3 million to compensate *ejido* members for the land. For the traveler in search of outdoor adventure, this means the island has a good chance of remaining undeveloped, even as large real estate projects take shape on the peninsula.

Around Isla Espíritu Santo, rock reefs provide good **snorkeling** at Punta Prieta, at the north end of Bahía San Gabriel toward the island's southwestern tip; at the west end of Isla Ballena, an islet off the northwest coast of Espíritu Santo; at three islets in Caleta El Candelero, toward the island's northern end; and off Punta Bonanza on Espíritu Santo's southeast side.

Even if you don't snorkel, picturesque, sand-bottom **Bahía San Gabriel** is worth a visit to see the ruined walls of a pearley dating to the early 20th century. The low walls form an inner lagoon that fills and empties with the tides, creating little waterfalls along the edges of the bay.

Just north of Ensenada La Ballena (directly opposite Isla Ballena), near a spot where the Guaicura found year-round water, several small rock shelters known as **Las Cuevitas** bear petroglyphs. More caves formerly used by the Guaicura can be found in the dry arroyo behind Ensenada La Ballena.

Espíritu Santo's most interesting **hike** starts from the beach at Caleta El Candelero and follows a deep, rocky arroyo inland into the 200-meter-high (650-ft-high) volcanic bluffs. The trail passes wild fig and plum trees clinging to the arroyo's rock sides; if you're lucky you might even spot a rare, endemic black jackrabbit.

Isla Partida

On the northern tip of Isla Partida you can hike to the top of a bluff called **El Embudo** for sweeping sea and island views. At the north and south ends of Isla Partida a couple of fish camps may have drinking water and food, but don't count on it. Plenty of yachts frequent the area. A narrow sandbar almost bridges Partida and Espíritu Santo, leaving a tight channel for small boat movement between the two islands.

Los Islotes

Just north of Isla Partida lie Los Islotes, a cluster of guano-covered volcanic rock islands popular among divers, anglers, birds, and sea lions. The sea lions and their pups often join divers and snorkelers for a swim. However, be cautious around lone adult male elephant seals. While these animals may appear friendly, their great size, strength, and large teeth have the potential to inflict serious injury; local dive operators advise that you not approach lone males or attempt to swim with them (see *Diving* under *Sports and Recreation*).

Camping

Caleta El Candelero and El Cardonalcito, on the west sides of Isla Espíritu Santo and Isla Partida, respectively, are generally considered the best camping beaches because each has a freshwater well suitable for bathing. To be certain of hauling some water out, you should

ISLA ESPÍRITU SANTO, ISLA PARTIDA, AND LOS ISLOTES

Los Islotes

El Embudo

Arroyos

Isla Partida

Punta Tintorera

Ensenada Grande

Punta Tijeretas

Las Cuevitas

El Cardonal

FRESHWATER WELL

Sand Spit

El Cardonalcito

Caleta Partida

Arroyo

Bahía el Mesteño

Isla Espíritu Santo

FRESHWATER WELL

Arroyos

Caleta el Candelero

ISLA ESPÍRITU SANTO

Bahía la Salinita

Isla Ballena

Playa Ballena

Arroyos

Punta Lobos

HOT SPRINGS

Isla Gallo

Playa Gallina

Isla Gallina

Arroyo

LIGHTHOUSE

Puerto Ballena

Arroyo

Punta Bonanza

Sea of Cortez

Bahía de la Paz

Playa Coralito

Punta Prieta

Bahía San Gabriel

Bahía Bonanza

Punta Morito

Punta Colorada

Playa Dispensa

Punta Lupona

Punta Dispensa

0   1 mi

0   1 km

To La Paz

© AVALON TRAVEL PUBLISHING, INC.

LEAVE NO TRACE

Visitors intent on setting foot on the delicate islands of the Sea of Cortez should heed the recommendations proffered by Conservation International, as follows:

- Check your equipment and provisions thoroughly before landing to avoid the introduction of rats, mice, insects, or seeds from other islands or from the mainland. Check your shoes and cuffs.

- Don't bring cats, dogs, or any other animals to the islands.

- Don't take plants, flowers, shells, rocks, or animals from the islands.

- The animals and plants that live on the islands are not used to human presence. Keep this in mind during your visit.

- Keep a minimum distance of 45 meters (150 ft) from all sea bird and sea lion colonies, and keep at least 300 meters (1,000 ft) away from pelicans during their nesting period (Apr.-May).

- Don't cut cacti or shrubs. Don't gather wood; plants take a long time to grow on these arid islands. Dry trunks are the home of many small animals. If you need to cook, take your own stove, and avoid making fires.

- Don't make new walking paths. Don't remove stones or dig holes; you will cause erosion.

- Don't camp on the islands unless you are familiar with low-impact techniques. Conservation International México can provide you with that information.

- Help keep the islands clean. Don't throw or leave garbage on the islands or in the sea. Help even more by bringing back any garbage you find.

- To camp or even land for any activity on the islands of the Sea of Cortez you need a permit from the Secretaría de Medio Ambiente y Recursos Naturales (SEMARNAT). To obtain a permit, contact Instituto Nacional de Ecología, Dirección de Aprovechamiento Ecológico, Periferico 5000, Col. Insurgentes Cuicuilco, C.P. 04530, Delegación Coyoacán México D.F. 01049, México, www.ine.gob.mx.

For more information, contact Conservation International, Calle Banamichi Lote 18 Manzana 1, Lomas de Cortés, Guaymas, Son. 85450, México, tel./fax 622/221-1594, 622/221-2030, m.carvajal@conservation.org, www.conservacion.org.mx, or its main U.S. office at 1919 M St., NW Suite 600, Washington, DC 20036, tel. 202/912-1000 or 800/406-2306, www.conservation.org.

bring your own bucket and five meters (15 ft) of rope. For drinking, bring enough purified water for the duration of your stay. If you must drink from the well, treat the water with purification tablets/iodine or boil it for at least 10 minutes.

Because these islands are part of an ecological preserve, you must obtain permission from the La Paz SEMARNAT office (2nd floor, Ocampo 1045 btw Rubio/Verdad, tel. 612/128-4171, Mon.–Fri. 8 A.M.–3 P.M.) before setting up camp. Camping is not allowed on Ensenada Grande or Playa Ballena. No pets or harvesting wood for campfires.

Getting to the Islands

Punta Lupona, on the southern tip of Espíritu Santo, lies within kayaking range—just 6.5 kilometers (4 mi)—from Península de Pichilingue. Once at Espíritu Santo, it's easy to explore Isla Partida by kayak; the shallow channel between the two islands is only a few hundred meters across. Playa El Tecolote or the smaller beaches just to its east are good put-in points for kayak trips to the island. Because of winds and tidal currents, this isn't a trip for the novice paddler. Even experienced sea kayakers on a first voyage to the island should follow someone who knows the tricky interplay of currents, shoals, tides, and winds. Outfitters in La Paz lead kayak trips to the islands with experienced guides (see *Kayaking* under *Sports and Recreation*).

Several companies in La Paz arrange two-hour powerboat jaunts to Isla Espíritu Santo and Isla Partida for around US$140 per boat including lunch. At Palapa Azul (tel. 612/122-1801), on Playa El Tecolote, you can arrange a four-hour trip around the west side of Espíritu Santo to a large island bay (Ensenada Grande) on Isla Partida and to the sea lion colony at Los Islotes; the cost for this trip, US$100 for up to six people, includes lunch. A one-way shuttle out to the island costs US$60.

Whether booking with an agency in town or at the beach, remember to inquire about the quality and contents of the lunch. If the lunch situation sounds iffy or awful (a prominent La Paz company at one time was serving a single lousy sandwich of white bread glued to two slices of processed American cheese), demand more food or carry your own lunch. Life preservers are another variable worth inquiring about; some boats don't carry them.

Sports and Recreation

FISHING

Outer bay and offshore fishing in the La Paz area are very good; a boat is mandatory since onshore and surf-fishing opportunities are limited. The bay and canals west of the islands hold roosterfish, *pargo,* cabrilla, needlefish, bonito, amberjack, jack crevalle, yellowtail, sierra, and pompano. Beyond Isla Espíritu Santo are the larger game fish, including dorado, grouper, marlin, tuna, and sailfish. Yellowtail usually run in the area January–March, while most other game fish reach peak numbers April–November. Canal de Cerralvo, around the east side of Península de Pichilingue, provides excellent fishing for roosterfish and *pargo colorado* January–July.

Any of the major La Paz hotels will arrange fishing trips. One of the oldest operations is **Jack Velez Sport Fishing Charters** (tel. 612/128-7518, jackvelez@hotmail.com). Another established outfit is **Fisherman's Fleet** (tel. 612/122-2744 ext. 628), also with a desk at Los Arcos. Both offer fully equipped boats with guides, tackle, ice, and fish-cleaning and -filleting service at daily rates ranging from US$200 (for a 22-foot *panga*) to US$375 (for a 30-foot cabin cruiser).

You can also arrange guides and boats at the pier just east of the Pichilingue ferry terminal. From here, *panga* fishing trips in the bay generally cost US$100 a day for two people, while trips beyond Isla Espíritu Santo or to Canal de Cerralvo cost around US$200. Long-range fishing cruises run US$275–380 a day and usually accommodate up to four anglers.

Anglers with a sturdy set of wheels and their own tackle can drive the desolate road north from El Centenario (west of La Paz on the way to Ciudad Constitución) to **Punta El Mechudo** and **San Evaristo** at the northernmost end of Bahía de la Paz, where the onshore and inshore fishing—for grouper, snapper, *pargo,* cabrilla, sierra, dorado, and yellowfin—is almost as good as in the Canal de Cerralvo. Most visiting anglers camp on either side of Punta El Mechudo. The road is paved for the first 40 kilometers (25 mi) as far as the phosphate-mining town of San Juan de la Costa, then it becomes graded gravel interspersed with ungraded sand for the final 53 kilometers (33 mi) to San Evaristo. This road is best traversed by high-clearance vehicles only.

Buy fishing tackle at **Deportiva La Paz** (Mutualismo, tel. 612/122-7333), one block in from the Applebees on the *malecón*.

DIVING AND SNORKELING

The islands offshore from La Paz present divers of all skill levels with some of the

HOW MUCH DOES IT COST?

GUIDED DIVE/SNORKEL TOURS
Discounts apply for multiday dives (overnight in La Paz hotel, typically the Los Arcos).
Hotel/dive packages are available.

Snorkel tour (equipment included)	US$50-65
Two- or three-tank boat dive	US$85-135
Night dive	US$60
Package of two days/three nights, with accommodations and meals	US$300-400
Package of six days/seven nights, with accommodations and meals	US$700-800
Nondiver passenger	US$10-15

LIVEABOARD DIVE TRIPS
Types of liveaboard trips: Socorro Island, Whale Shark Expedition, Island Tour

Six days/seven nights	US$1,565
Eight days/nine nights	US$1,495-2,500
Night dive on liveaboard trip	US$30

DIVE INSTRUCTION

Open water certification (classroom and dives)	US$420
Discover Scuba/resort course (Introduction to scuba)	US$110-140
Advanced certification	US$390
Nitrox certification	US$220

GUIDED KAYAK TOURS

Day trips	US$35-95
Two-day trip	US$250-300
Four-day trip	US$400-500
Six-day trip	US$1,100
Ten-day trip	US$2,000

DIVE AND KAYAK EQUIPMENT RENTAL

Snorkel gear (usually included with tour)	US$6-15
Scuba package with dives (discounts for multiday dives)	US$20-30/day
Rebreather	US$65
Airfills	US$5
Nitrox refills	US$8-12
Panga shuttle to Espíritu Santo (round-trip from Playa Tecolote)	US$200-400
Double kayak	US$60/day
Single kayak	US$40/day
Truck shuttle to Playa Tecolote	US$25
Island camping fee	US$4

most interesting underwater topography in the Sea of Cortez, as well as opportunities to spot some of the largest pelagics in the sea. Sea lions frolic at Los Islotes, while hammerhead sharks school around the El Bajo seamount and giant mantas cruise against the current. From the surface, you may see flying mantas, schools of dolphins, and giant bait balls. But unlike the reef and wall diving in Cabo Pulmo and Cabo San Lucas, where dive sites are a 5- to 15-minute boat ride from shore, long, choppy boat rides are the norm here (45–60 minutes)—hence the higher rates. Remember to take your seasickness medicine the night before. (Many divers swear by Bonine, found over the counter in the United States and Mexico.) A day of diving typically begins around 7–8 A.M. and finishes in the late afternoon. Lunch is usually included at no extra cost. *Note:* Most operators require a minimum of at least two divers to send a boat out to the islands. Some require four divers to visit the more remote sites. See the sidebar *How Much Does It Cost?* for standard prices.

Dive Sites

Most boats frequent about a dozen different sites around the islands offshore from La Paz. A sea lion colony at Los Islotes (25–50 ft) provides loads of underwater entertainment. Also suitable for beginners, the *Salvatierra* wreck (60 ft) presents an opportunity to explore the remains of a cargo ferry that sank in 1976. If conditions permit, advanced divers might request a trip to the El Bajo seamount (60–100+ ft) in hopes of encountering a school of hammerhead sharks, as well as giant mantas, whale sharks, and towers of schooling amber jacks and tuna. (See the sidebar *Diving and Snorkeling Around La Paz.*)

Day Trips

In business since 1992, **Buceo Carey** (Legaspy and Topete, tel. 612/128-4048, U.S. tel. 877/239-4057, www.carey.com.mx) is one of the more respected dive centers in town. A staff of local captains and international dive guides leads one-day and multiday dive trips to Espíritu Santo sites for US$85 a day, and to El Bajo and Isla Cerralvo for US$95. The cost includes guide, transportation, lunch, unlimited sodas and beer, weight belt, and two tanks. Rental equipment includes regulators, BCDs, wetsuits, masks, snorkels, fins, tanks, weight belts, booties, and portable air compressors. Carey prides itself in the fact that it offers its clients a choice of 15 different lunch menus. The company maintains a second office at Marina de La Paz. Inquire about accommodations packages: Two days/three nights at the Los Arcos runs US$317; six days/seven nights is US$773.

The granddaddy of all dive outfits in La Paz is Fernando Águilar's **Baja Diving and Service** (B.C.S. 11/Carr. a Pichilingue, past the ferry terminal, tel. 612/122-7010, www. clubcantamar.com). Based at the Club Cantamar Resort and Sports Centre on the Peninsula Pichilingue, the company operates a fleet of eight vessels, including some of the largest dive boats on the Sea of Cortez, holding more than 20 divers. Its custom-built 53-foot *Liberación* is the newest dive boat in La Paz, with air conditioning and hot water, two heads, and a pleasant sundeck for warming up after each dive. The boat accommodates 30 divers for day trips and 10 divers as a liveaboard (see *Liveaboard Trips*). The company was putting the finishing touches on a new 70-foot catamaran in 2007. They also run *pangas* for divers who consider the larger boats to be too much like cattle cars. Besides the sheer scale of the operation, shorter boat rides are a significant advantage of diving with the Cantamar staff. Boats typically depart at 8:30 A.M. and return by 5 P.M. For divers who aren't staying at the resort, a shuttle service is provided at no additional cost.

Dive rates are US$95 per person per day for two or three tanks, depending on conditions. Day trips include transportation, boat ride, lunch, and drinks. The resort has an ultralight plane used for spotting whale sharks (extra charge of US$20 pp). Shorter boat rides also make the more

DIVING AND SNORKELING AROUND LA PAZ

Some of Baja's best dive sites lie in the vicinity of La Paz, but most are accessible only by boat. Along the western shores of **Isla Espíritu Santo** and **Isla Partida** lie several good diving reefs. Bahía San Gabriel, a large cove along Espíritu Santo's southwest shore, features a shallow boulder reef (San Rafaelito) at its northern end suitable for both scuba diving and snorkeling. Similar rock reefs – along with submarine caves – can be found farther north off Espíritu Santo's western shore near Caleta El Candelero, extending from the west side of **Isla Ballena.** The latter islet also features a black coral forest and is protected from strong prevailing winds. All of these sites lie 1–2 hours from La Paz by boat.

LOS ISLOTES

One of the most colorful dive sites in the vicinity is Los Islotes, the tiny islet group off the north end of Isla Partida. Boulder reefs and underwater pinnacles off the north and northeast shores draw large marine species, including schools of hammerhead sharks, manta rays, and other pelagic (open-ocean) fish. A nearby cove is home to around 300 sea lions, who seem to enjoy swimming alongside divers and performing tricks for the camera. Late in the breeding season (Jan.-May) is the best time to visit the colony, since this is when the adolescent pups are most playful. The south side of Los Islotes is well protected from prevailing winds virtually year-round.

EL BAJITO

To the southwest of Los Islotes lies El Bajito, a large rock reef that extends to within six meters (20 ft) of the sea's surface; the base of the reef meets a sandy bottom at about 24-28 meters (80-90 ft). The diverse marinelife frequenting the reef includes grouper, cabrilla, and an unusually large number of morays living among the many cracks and crevices in the reef; attached to the rocks are gorgonians, sea fans, and other invertebrates. Wind protection here is scant.

EL BAJO

A group of three sea pinnacles called El Bajo (also known as Marisla Seamount), about 13 kilometers (8.2 mi) northeast of Los Islotes, is renowned for the presence of large pelagics such as marlin, sharks (hammerhead, blacktip, tiger, and silvertip), dorado, corvina, and

distant dive sites like Las Animas and the San Diegito Reef more accessible for day-trippers (extra charge of US$25 per diver for trips to these sites).

Dive packages for 3–14 nights with half- or full-board cost US$370–1,522 and US$402–1,692; nitrox and rebreather dive packages are also available at additional cost. Included are round-trip airport transfers and lunch on dive days.

Rental gear is available (snorkel set US$6/day, dive gear US$21/day). Certified divers can also get nitrox refills for US$8–12 and rent rebreathers for US$65. New divers can get certified in the resort's own pool (US$420, includes two days open-water dives) or try an introductory Discover Scuba course (US$140). Advanced certification costs

US$390. Nitrox certification is US$220. In case of a dive emergency, the Cantamar has the only recompression chamber in La Paz. For more information or to make a reservation, drop in to the Cantamar's downtown sales office (Obregón 1665-2, Plaza Cerralvo, near the Hotel Perla, tel. 612/122-1826, daily 9 A.M.–8 P.M.).

Another multiboat operation is based at the La Concha Beach Resort. **The Cortez Club Dive Center** (Km 5 Carr. a Pichilingue, tel. 612/121-6120, www.cortezclub.com) has 12 dive boats, its own classroom for dive instruction, and a private jetty and ramp. Rates are a little higher than other shops for day trips, but lower for scuba courses.

Day excursions aboard Baja Expeditions' 45-foot *Don Cano* or 48-foot *Pez Sapo* cost

manta rays. Mantas frequent El Bajo July–mid-October and here seem unusually friendly. Whale sharks, the largest fish in the world, are occasionally seen near El Bajo during the same months, as are pilot whales. Depths range 18-43 meters (60-140 ft). Boats typically take 2-3 hours to reach El Baja from La Paz.

Because of strong tidal currents and lack of wind protection, El Bajito and El Bajo are best left to experienced open-ocean divers.

SALVATIERRA
The wreck of the *Salvatierra,* a 91-meter (300-ft) La Paz-Topolobampo ferry that went down in the Canal de San Lorenzo in 1976, presents one of the more challenging dives. The hull lies about 2.5 kilometers (1.5 mi) southeast of the southern tip of Isla Espíritu Santo at a depth of approximately 10 fathoms (18 m/60 ft). Encrusted with sponges, sea fans, mollusks, and gorgonians, the wreck attracts numerous varieties of tropical fish, including groupers, barracuda, angelfish, goatfish, parrotfish, moray eels, and rays.

ISLA CERRALVO
Southeast of Península de Pichilingue, the somewhat more remote Isla Cerralvo offers several additional diving opportunities. **La Reinita,** a rock reef off the island's northern shore, attracts large pelagic fish. Even more remote – generally reached by liveaboard boat trips – are **Isla Santa Cruz** and **Islas Las Animas** to the north. The former is known for rock reefs at depths of around 17 meters (35 ft) with a profusion of sea horses, while the latter reportedly offers the greatest variety of diving experiences – caves, hammerheads, whale sharks, sea lions – of any site in the Sea of Cortez. Only Baja Expeditions leads Santa Cruz and Animas dives.

WHEN TO GO
Optimum diving months are May–August, when visibility reaches 30 meters (100 ft) or more and water temperatures run around 27°C (80°F). In September, tropical storms can be an obstacle. October conditions are often spectacular, but during the late fall and winter high winds and changing currents reduce visibility to 10-15 meters (35-50 ft). A light wetsuit is necessary any time except June-August.

US$125 per day (Mar.–Dec.), which covers three dives, breakfast, lunch, snacks, and happy hour (tel. 612/125-3828, U.S. 800/843-6967, www.bajaex.com).

Liveaboard Trips
If viewing underwater marinelife is the focus of your trip to La Paz, consider a multiday trip aboard one of these custom-designed dive boats. Packages typically include the first and last nights in a La Paz hotel, usually the Los Arcos. Rates below are for double occupancy. An additional fee often applies for single occupancy.

Baja Diving and Service (see *Day Trips*) runs several liveaboard trips through the summer and fall months. A nine-night trip to Socorro Island (eight days of diving) costs US$2,500. A seven-night (six days of diving) whale shark expedition is US$1,565. **Buceo Carey** (see *Day Trips*) runs multiday trips on two boats: *Marco Polo* holds 6–8 divers, six days/five nights for US$1,399; first and last night at the Los Arcos. **Baja Expeditions** (tel. 612/125-3828, U.S. 800/843-6967, www.bajaex.com) offers liveaboard trips on the air-conditioned, 80-foot *Don José.* Trips are booked out of the U.S. office, but it's occasionally possible to sign up in La Paz when space is available. The company runs eight-day expeditions aboard the *Don José* May 28–November 30, from US$1,445 per person for standard rooms to US$1,645 per person for superior rooms (double occupancy). Three eight-day excursions specifically dedicated to viewing the magnificent whale shark are offered in May and June from US$1,495 per person for standard rooms to US$1,695 per person for superior rooms (double occupancy). The boat holds 16 divers. The *Don José* has a loyal following since the staff allows divers to go on their own schedule by running constant shuttles to many different sites.

Operated by a Mexican-Japanese couple, **Baja Quest** (Rangel 10 btw Sonora/Sinaloa, tel. 612/123-5320, www.bajaquest.com.mx) offers two-night/three-day dive-trip packages May–December, for US$850 including hotel and airport transfers, and longer trips for US$1,040–1,190. Luxury accommodations aboard *The Sandman* cost US$993–1,395. Baja Quest also organizes dive/cruise/camping combinations (Apr.–Nov. only). Whale-watching and camping tours include campsite with large kitchen, tents, cots, sleeping bags, sun showers, toilets, round-trip transportation, kayaking equipment and instruction, and *pangas,* but not airfare, hotel, airport to hotel transfers, meals on arrival and departure dates, airport taxes, or crew tips.

Another dive operator in town is **Toto's Dive Shop and Service** (Guerrero btw Revolución de 1910/Serdán, tel. 612/122-7154, fax 612/123-4521). **Deportiva La Paz** (Mutualismo, tel./fax 612/122-7333) sells diving equipment and air-fills but doesn't organize dive trips.

Snorkel Tours

Most dive and kayak outfitters also run snorkel tours. Less expensive trips visit the beaches along Peninsula Pichilingue; the more expensive ones go to the islands for the day. For example, **Buceo Carey** (see *Day Trips*) offers snorkeling trips for US$65 to Playa Encantada and the sea lion colony. **Baja Diving and Service** (see *Day Trips*) at the Cantamar does local snorkel trips for US$50. And **Azul Tours** (Obregón 774, tel. 612/122-4427, azultours@gmail.com) brings snorkelers to Espíritu Santo for US$55 per person.

El Tecolote Rest/Bar/Playa (tel. 612/127-9494, www.eltecolote.net) transports snorkelers to Espíritu Santo in *pangas* for US$40. The price includes gear and lunch. Boats depart between 10–11 A.M. for a four-hour tour. Stop by the booking office, just off the plaza next to the Hotel Miramar, for more information. Other water activities include: WaveRunners, kayaks, banana boat, and water skiing.

WHALE-WATCHING

There are several ways to see gray and blue whales in action: Dive and kayak outfitters offer special whale-watching tours. Some tours go to the Sea of Cortez, while others go to the San Ignacio Lagoon on the Pacific side of the Baja Peninsula. Some trips involve snorkeling and paddling; others are just boat cruises. You can go for one day or eight, depending on your budget and how much time you want to spend with the mammals.

Baja Outdoor Activities (tel. 612/125-5636, U.S. tel. 888/217-6659, www.kayakinbaja.com) offers a package with two three-hour boat trips plus an overnight stay and all meals for US$250 per person.

Johnny Friday and Maldo Ficher lead ecotours in the area through **Baja Adventure Company** (tel. 612/124-6629, U.S. tel. 877/650-2252, www.bajaecotours.com), a division of Mar de Cortez sports. Its marine biologists, zoologists, and other professionally trained guides lead whale-watching trips.

KAYAKING

Several local outfits operate excellent guided kayak trips in the region. Packages usually include the first and last nights in hotel accommodation, with camping on the nights in between. Meals, transportation to the islands, and airport transfers are also typically covered by the price. Some trips return to a base camp every night, while others move to a new place each day. Some supply camping gear, others ask that you bring your own.

Baja Expeditions (tel. 612/125-3828, U.S. tel. 800/843-6967, www.bajaex.com) has been running seven-day trips to Espíritu Santo (US$1,045) since 1985. Other destinations include the Loreto to La Paz coast (10 days) and Magdalena Bay (8 days). An adventurous

10-day, open-water kayak trip hops among the islands of Espíritu Santo, Los Islotes, San José, Santa Cruz, and Santa Catalina (Oct.–Apr. only).

Owned by a La Paz native, **Mar y Aventuras** (Topete 564 btw 5 de Febrero/Navarro, tel. 612/123-0559, U.S. tel. 800/355-7140, www.kayakbaja.com), near La Marina Don José and Marina de La Paz, leads one-day and multiday trips and rents kayaks and gear to experienced paddlers. Its boats are a mix of doubles and singles made of fiberglass and some plastic. All have rudders. Day trips range US$35–95 per person, depending on the destination and size of the group. Two- to four-day tours cost US$250–495. Magdalena Bay whale-watching trips cost US$300–795 for two to five days. Longer trips to Espíritu Santo are available as well.

Experienced kayakers can also rent kayaks from Mar y Aventuras for paddling to El Mogote or to the islands on their own. The company rents single kayaks for US$40 a day, including PFD (personal flotation device), paddle, bilge pump, and spray deck. Double kayaks go for US$60/day. You can also rent snorkeling gear, wetsuits, dry bags, tents, small stoves, and sleeping bags. Boat shuttles out to Isla Espíritu Santo (US$200–400 round-trip for 1–2 people) as well as truck shuttles to Playa El Tecolote for beach launches to Espíritu Santo (US$25 one-way for 1–2 people), can be arranged. There is a camping fee of US$4/day for the island camping, which can be paid at the Mar y Aventura office.

Several other outfitters lead paddling trips to Isla Espíritu Santo. **Baja Quest** (Rangel 10 btw Sonora/Sinaloa, tel. 612/123-5320, www.bajaquest.com.mx) organizes three- to six-day kayaking/hiking/camping trips (Mar.–May and Oct.–Dec., US$540–1,080 pp). **Baja Outdoor Activities (BOA)** (tel. 612/125-5636, www.kayakinbaja.com) offers two different styles of kayak trips: "Cooperatively catered" trip participants carry their own gear each day and help guides prepare meals, making for a more self-sufficient experience, but with heavier boats to paddle. Others prefer a fully catered trip, in which guides prepare all meals

and camping supplies are transported by motorboat. Four-day island tours range US$420–490. Daily dolphin sightings are common on the 10-day Loreto to La Paz trip (US$1,090). Participants should expect to paddle about four hours per day on this trip.

The half-day tour for US$35 is a nice way for beginners to get a feel for the sport without committing to a full-day adventure. BOA also offers a one-day tour of Balandra Bay for US$60. BOA rents sit-on-top kayaks and sea kayaks by the day or week (US$35–60/day and US$110–220/week).

BOATING

With a huge, protected bay, several public and private marinas, and several boatyards and marine supply stores, La Paz is Baja California's largest and best-equipped boating center.

At the west end of the *malecón*, the **Marina de La Paz** (Topete 3040 at Legaspy, tel. 612/122-1646, www.marinadelapaz.com) has completed numerous upgrades in recent years: New docks and a new layout came in 2004, followed by a fixed breakwater system in 2005, and an additional 120 feet of fixed breakwater plus a new 160-foot dock for accommodating large vessels in 2006. Facilities at this floating marina now include a launch ramp, fuel dock (diesel), market with groceries and marine supplies, café, water and electricity outlets, cable TV, laundry, showers, restrooms, wireless Internet, a chandlery, and boat and vehicle maintenance and storage. **Club Cruceros de La Paz** (www.clubcruceros.org, Mon.–Sat. 9 A.M.–6 P.M.) is a local nonprofit association that maintains a clubhouse at the marina and offers incoming mail service, as well as a book exchange library.

Rates for one of the marina's 150 slips range from US$19/day and US$350/month for a 30-foot craft to US$88/day and US$1,650/month for a 100-foot craft. Discounts also apply for stays of 4–21 days, if paid in advance. Showers cost US$1.30 daily. Cable TV is US$1 per day or US$15 per month. Parking for slip clients is US$1 daily or US$22 per month. Prices include tax.

Marina de La Paz is the most popular marina in the bay and is often full November–May; check for vacancies before sailing in. A US$200 deposit will hold your space on the waiting list. Reserve online, or by mailing a personal check.

Northeast of town, on the Canal de La Paz at Km 2.5, the well-planned **Marina Palmira** (tel. 612/123-7000 or 877/217-1513, www.marinapalmira.com) offers 186 full-service slips accommodating yachts up to 130 feet long and 12 feet deep. The marina recently reinforced its breakwater and launching ramp. There is free wireless Internet, and a free shuttle to downtown is available at various times each day. Other services include dry-storage facilities, a market, laundry, water, showers, bathrooms, a pool, hot tub, tennis court, two restaurants, a bar, 24-hour security, parking for one car per registered guest, a public phone, marine supplies, a fuel dock (diesel as well as gas), and boat launch. Crewed and bareboat yacht charters are available. Daily slip rates range US$15.75–60 depending on the size of the boat; monthly rates are US$10–21 per foot for slips of 30–100 feet. Electrical service costs extra. Condos and hotel rooms adjacent to the marina available for rent by the day, week, or month.

Based at the Club Cantamar Resort and Sports Centre, **Marina Pichilingue** (tel. 612/122-7010, www.clubcantamar.com) has 35 slips for boats up to 75 feet long (US$8.10/ft/month). Water, electricity, and dry storage are available.

La Marina Don José (Encinas 15, tel./fax 612/122-0848), at the end of Calle Encinas, one street south of Marina de La Paz, offers mooring facilities but is often full. Rates run US$8.80 per foot per month. The marina office is open Monday–Friday 8 A.M.–noon and 2–6 P.M., Saturday 8 A.M.–1 P.M.

A newcomer on the Peninsula Pichilingue, **Marina CostaBaja** (tel. 612/121-6225, www.costabajaresort.com) can accommodate megayachts up to 200 feet in 250 slips. Rates start at US$11.50/foot up to 39 feet for one month, up to US$22/foot for a 150- to 200-foot boat.

Daily rates are subject to availability (US$1.10/ft/day up to 99 feet and US$1.65/ft/day for 100–200 ft boats). Liveaboards require special permission from the marina. Amenities include Internet, TV, and phone; at-slip pumpout service, dry storage, restrooms and showers, parking, pool, and shuttle to La Paz. Some travelers who have used this marina report problems with black soot from the nearby oil refinery damaging canvas on their boats. A reservation form is available online.

The new Marina Fidepaz (Mexico 1/Constituyentes, near Km 4.5, tel. 612/124-2206), part of the Mexican government's Sea of Cortez Project, is being constructed near the airport, with 40 boat slips.

You can launch trailered and cartopped boats at Marina de La Paz, Marina Palmira, La Marina Don José, Aquamarina RV Park, and Pichilingue. Smaller boats and kayaks can put in at any of the public beaches.

Parts and Repairs: Marina de La Paz is the best local source of information about boating needs; **Ferretería Marina SeaMar** (SeaMar Marine Chandlery, Topete and Legaspy, tel. 612/122-9696, Mon.–Fri. 8:30 A.M.–1:30 P.M. and 3–6 P.M., Sat. 8:30 A.M.–1:30 P.M.), opposite the marina entrance, stocks many everyday nautical items. **López Marine Supply** (Vista Coral Plaza, tel. 612/125-4160, Mon.–Sat. 8 A.M.–5 P.M.) accepts Visa and MasterCard. Club Cruceros keeps a list of local marine service providers at www.clubcruceros.org/services.

Buying a *Panga:* La Paz is the *panga* capital of Mexico. Until 1968, when American Mac Shroyer designed and built the first molded fiberglass *pangas,* many Sea of Cortez fishermen still used dugout canoes of Amerindian design; glass *pangas* made in La Paz are now sold all over Mexico. **Embarcaciones Arca** (tel. 612/122-0874, fax 612/122-0823) makes and sells *pangas* at a factory on Calle Guillermo Prieto between Juárez and Allende. The standard *panga* is sold in 16- to 26-foot lengths, but the factory can accommodate special orders as long as 36 feet. The standard *panga* outboard motor is a *cinco-cinco caballos,* 55 horsepower.

Boat Charters

Baja Coast SeaFaris (Dock B, Marina de La Paz, tel. 612/125-9765, www.bajaseafaris.com) can organize customized charters aboard its *Irish Mist* 50-foot sailing yacht and *Tesoro del Mar*, a Beneteau 50 sailboat. Multiday trips (3–5 days or longer) include visits to Espíritu Santo, Isla Partida, and Los Islotes, with stops along the way for swimming with sea lions, scuba diving, kayaking, tubing (for kids), sailing, beachcombing, whale-watching, bird-watching, snorkeling, or fishing. Rates start at US$695–865 per person per day, based on a group of two, with substantial discounts for larger groups (US$145–165 additional pp per day). Rates include all onboard meals, snacks, and cocktails, lodging at Los Arcos Hotel on the last evening, and airport transfers. Scuba diving and rental gear are also available. Reservations should be made at least four months in advance for trips during the spring, fall, or major holidays. A 10 percent discount is offered for families and special occasions like honeymoons and anniversaries.

ATVS

ATV tours have become a popular way to explore the Baja Peninsula, and La Paz now has its first tour operator: **La Paz ATV's Adventures** (cell 612/131-0784, www.lapaza-tvs.com, US$75/90 s/d) runs three-hour tours on Honda Rancher 350 ATVs. The ride includes safety equipment, instruction, and bottled water, and the route goes from the village of El Comitán, a half hour north of La Paz, through El Mogote sand dunes, to the end of the peninsula and back. Shuttle service is provided from La Paz to the departure site.

MOUNTAIN BIKING

Colocated in the Baja Outdoor Activities (BOA) office next to the El Moro hotel, Mexican-owned **Katún** (tel. 612/348-7758, www.katuntours.com) runs guided tours of the Sierra de La Laguna (US$1,980/two weeks, US$1,299/one week, US$50–75/day). Combination kayak/bike trips cover travel from the Sea of Cortez to the Sierra de la Laguna in

10 or 14 days (US$1,350/US$1,980). And the weeklong Jesuits trail tour traces historic routes through the Sierra la Giganta, from the Sea of Cortez to the Pacific (US$1,199).

Katún also rents 2006 Giant Yukon bikes with front suspension for US$10 an hour, US$15 for four hours, or US$20 per day. **Azul Tours** (Obregón 774, tel. 612/122-4427, azultours@gmail.com) rents mountain bikes for US$15/day.

HIKING AND HORSEBACK RIDING

Antonio Moller (tel. 612/123-1370, t_moller@hotmail.com) leads one-day and overnight trips into the Sierra de La Laguna from La Paz. Day trips (US$120 for one person, US$70 pp for two people, US$60 pp for a group of 3–6) include transportation from La Paz to the biosphere, lunch at a local ranch, and a one-hour horseback ride. Student discounts available.

SPA SERVICES

The Hotel Los Arcos offers spa services at reasonable rates: A 45-minute massage is US$45, and a 50-minute sports massage is US$55. Hacienda del Cortez was adding a full-service spa in 2007.

ORGANIZED TOURS

Travel companies and outfitters offer a variety of guided tours and organized activities, from island kayak trips and whale-watching to language immersion and cooking classes. Here are a few additional options:

Readers have reported pleasant outings with **Eduardo's Tours** (044-612/105-2609, eduardoviajes@hotmail.com). Eduardo Gomez provides ground transportation and leads guided trips to Los Cabos (US$99 pp), Todos Santos (US$77 pp), and El Triunfo (US$77 pp). A La Paz city tour costs US$27.50 per person. Whale-watching (US$120) and snorkeling (US$77 pp) tours are also possible. **Azul Tours** (Obregón 774, tel. 612/122-4427, azultours@gmail.com) offers a La Paz city tour for US$30 per person, as well as island trips (see *Diving and Snorkeling* and *Kayaking*).

Mar y Aventura (Topete 564 btw 5 de Febrero/Navarro, tel. 612/123-0559, U.S. tel. 800/355-7140, www.kayakbaja.com) offers a Spanish language immersion and cooking class package, in partnership with Se Habla La Paz. Packages include seven nights/eight days accommodations in the Posada Luna Sol, 25 hours of Spanish classes, and three nights of cooking classes (US$495 pp, double occupancy).

Once a year in April, May, or November, travel photographer Jim Cline leads a **Wonders of Baja** photo tour (U.S. tel. 877/350-1314, www.jimcline.com) of La Paz, Loreto, Mulege, Todos Santos, and Cabo San Lucas, including three boat trips to islands on the Sea of Cortez. Participants get to try their hand at capturing the seascapes, cacti, historic missions, and wildlife through the lens of their camera. Tours include accommodations and seafood dinners.

Entertainment and Events

BARS AND MUSIC

Bar Pelícanos (Paseo Obregón 498, tel. 612/122-2744, www.losarcos.com, daily 10 A.M.–1 A.M.), in Hotel Los Arcos, overlooking the *malecón*, is a large, sedate watering hole popular among tourists and old hands. It's worth at least one visit to peruse the old photos along the back wall; subjects include a motley array of unnamed vaqueros and revolutionaries, as well as Pancho Villa, General Blackjack Pershing, President Dwight Eisenhower, Emiliano Zapata, and Clark Gable (posed with a marlin).

On Calle Esquerro near the Hotel Perla, the slightly seedy **Bar Misión** features live *norteña* bands nightly.

Tequilas Bar and Grill, in a rustic house next to El Palmar Suites on Calle Mutualismo near Bravo, is an intimate bar with pool tables and a small private room popular with local politicians.

The rather interesting-looking **El Claustro** (Obregón btw Hidalgo/Costilla, tel. 612/122-1609, Tues.–Sun.) is a rock 'n' roll bar ensconced in a two-story pseudo-Italianate structure, complete with heavy faux-painted "marble" pilasters around the doors and stained-glass windows, plus lots of ironwork. It's decorated inside and out with an angel motif.

Caliente Race and Sports Book (Paseo Obregón at Morelos, tel. 800/027-3354, www.caliente.com.mx, Mon.–Fri. 10 A.M.–midnight, Sat.–Sun. 9 A.M.–midnight) has the usual array of satellite-linked TV monitors for viewing international sports events—and betting on them if the mood strikes you.

Living up to its laid-back reputation, La Paz isn't big on discos. A slightly older crowd frequents **Las Varitas** (Independencia 111, tel. 612/125-2025, www.lasvaritas.com), downtown near El Quinto Sol natural foods store and Plaza Constitución. The club offers dancing to recorded and live music. It also has a second location in Cabo San Lucas.

Carlos'n Charlie's, on Paseo Obregón, has an attached dance club, **La Paz Lapa** (Obregón and 16 de Septiembre, tel. 612/122-9290), that experiences occasional waves of popularity, especially on Thursday evenings when women are admitted without having to pay the usual cover charge. Above Pizza Fabula and La Pitahaya, **Casa de Villa** (Obregón and 16 de Septiembre, tel. 612/122-5799) is a rooftop bar and nightclub that's popular with locals.

Nightclub La Cabaña (Paseo Obregón 1570, tel. 612/122-0777, daily 9 P.M.–3 A.M.) at the Hotel Perla, usually offers live *norteña* music and attracts a local crowd. There's live music on Thursday and Sunday, and no cover charge on Wednesday.

In a courtyard behind La Fabula Pizza on Obregón, **Peña La Pitahaya de Janicua** (Obregón 15, tel. 612/126-2234) is an almost hidden spot with a bohemian ambience and live Latin folk music nightly.

BULLFIGHTS AND CHARREADAS

The municipal stadium at Constitución and Verdad occasionally hosts *corridas de toros* in the late winter, usually February–March.

Paceños are more active in *charrería* than in bullfighting, and you can attend *charreadas* (Mexican-style rodeos) at **Lienzo Charro Guadalupano,** just south of the city on the west side of Mexico 1 south (heading toward San Pedro). For information on the latest schedules for *charreadas* and *corridas de toros,* contact the state tourism office (tel. 612/124-0199), between Km 6 and 5 on Mexico 1 (Avenida Abasolo), opposite the Fidepaz marina. A *gran charreada* is usually held to celebrate Cinco de Mayo (May 5).

CINEMAS

In the city center, **Cinema Versalles Plus** (Revolución de 1910, tel. 612/122-9555) shows first-run movies on four screens. The largest and most popular cinema in town is the 14-screen **Cine Gemelos** in the new Soriana shopping complex out on Boulevard Forjadores at the corner of Avenida Luis Donaldo Colosio.

EVENTS

Carnaval

La Paz's biggest annual celebration is Carnaval, held for six days before Ash Wednesday in mid-February. Carnaval is also held in the Mexican cities of Mazatlán, Ensenada, and Veracruz, but Carnaval connoisseurs claim La Paz's is the best—perhaps because the city's *malecón* makes a perfect parade route.

As at all Mexican Carnavals, the festival begins with the Quema de Mal Humor, or "Burning of Bad Humor," in which an effigy representing an unpopular public figure is burned. Other events include the crowning of La Reina del Carnaval (Carnaval Queen) and El Rey Feo (Ugly King), colorful costumed parades, music, dancing, feasting,

costumed Carnaval celebrant in La Paz

© JOE CUMMINGS

cockfights, and fireworks. The festival culminates in El Día del Marido Oprimido, or "Day of the Oppressed Husband" (23.5 hours of symbolic freedom for married men to do whatever they wish), followed by a masquerade ball on the Tuesday evening before Ash Wednesday.

Fiesta de La Paz

Also prominent on the city's yearly events calendar is the Fiesta de La Paz (officially known as "Fiesta de la Fundación de la Ciudad de La Paz"), held May 3, the anniversary of the city's founding. The state tourist office (tel. 612/124-0100, turismo@correro.gbcs.gob.mx), between Km 6 and 5 on Mexico 1 (Avenida Abasolo), opposite the Grand Plaza Resort, can provide up-to-date details on festival scheduling and venues.

Baja 1000

The Baja 1000 off-road race comes to town in mid-November. Produced by SCORE International (U.S. tel. 818/225-8402, www.score-international.com), the event is the sixth and last in a series of desert races that take place in the southwestern United States and Mexico each year. The Baja 1000 attracts more than 400 pro contestants who drive trucks, motorcycles, ATVs, and every imaginable variation of off-road vehicle. They start in Ensenada and cruise at breakneck speeds through the desert to the outskirts of La Paz. Only about half of the race entrants complete the challenging 1,000-mile course.

In its 40th year in 2007, the race draws thousands of support crew and spectators to the most remote parts of the peninsula. The course opens for pre-running approximately three weeks before the race start. Travelers on Mexico 1 during this time will often see vehicles kicking up a cloud of dust in the distance, moving at speeds faster than highway drivers go. *Note:* This is one of the only times a year you may encounter traffic on the more remote stretches of Mexico 1.

Shopping

Before the city's duty-free status was recalled in 1989, imported merchandise could be purchased in La Paz free of import duties and sales tax. Nowadays, sales tax is commensurate with the rest of Mexico's. But the city still offers some of Baja's best shopping in terms of value and variety.

DEPARTMENT STORES

La Paz's main department stores are **Dorian's** (16 de Septiembre at Esquerro) and **La Perla de La Paz** (Arrival at Mutualismo), which was temporarily closed in late 2006 due to a fire. A newer Dorian's can be found in the Soriana shopping complex on Boulevard Forjadores, at the southwestern edge of town.

MAS (Madero at Degollado, daily 9 A.M.–9 P.M.) is a three-story discount department store that stocks everything from clothing to luggage to housewares. Next door on Madero between Tejada and Arreola, opposite Hostería del Convento, **DAX** (Mon.–Thurs. 8 A.M.–9 P.M., Fri.–Sat. 8 A.M.–10 P.M.) is an American-style pharmacy with many hard-to-find cosmetic and toiletry items. And next to DAX is the popular **Solo Un Precio** ("Only One Price," Madero btw Tejada/Arreola, daily 8 A.M.–9 P.M.), where everything in the store is only 10 pesos (US$1). You can find some great deals here.

ARTS AND CRAFTS

Along Paseo Obregón in the vicinity of the Hotel Perla and Hotel Los Arcos are a number of souvenir and handicraft shops of varying quality. One of the better ones is **La Antigua California** (Paseo Obregón 220, tel. 612/125-5230), which sells quality folk arts and crafts from the mainland. There are a few similar shops on Obregón between Degollado and Ocampo. **México Lindo** (Paseo Obregón at 16 de Septiembre), next to Carlos'n Charlie's, is also good for *artesanías*. **Curios Mary** (Arreola 25 at Obregón, tel. 612/122-0815) specializes in Majorcan pearls.

Casa de Artesanos Sudcalifornianos, a government-supported shop next door to the Tourist Information/Tourist Police office on Paseo Obregón between Allende and Rosales, focuses on *artesanías* from Baja California Sur.

Away from the city center, the **Centro de Arte Regional** (Calle Chiapas at Encinas) produces and sells pottery, as does **Ibarra's Pottery** (Prieto 625 btw Iglesias/República, tel. 612/122-0404, Mon.–Fri. 9 A.M.–3 P.M., Sat. 9 A.M.–2 P.M.), where you can watch pottery being made. **Artesanía Cuauhtémoc** (Av. Abasolo btw Jalisco/Nayarit) weaves rugs, blankets, wall hangings, tablecloths, and other cotton and wool items. Custom orders are possible, and customers are welcome to watch the weavers at their looms in the back of the shop. **Artesanías Colibri** (Paseo Obregón btw Muelle/Arreola, tel. 612/128-5833, Mon.–Sat. 10 A.M.–1 P.M. and 3–8:30 P.M.) carries a good selection of *artesanías*, rustic furniture, and decorating accessories, plus cute clothes for babies and kids.

For bottom-dollar bargains on clothing, housewares, and leather, browse the **Mercado Municipal Francisco E. Madero** (Revolución de 1910 at Degollado). Inexpensive electronics, watches, and jewelry are available at a string of shops along Calles Domínguez and Madero between Avenida Independencia and Calle 16 de Septiembre, and along a pedestrian alley off Calle 16 de Septiembre near Dorian's department store. **Santander** (tel. 612/125-5962), a large store

at the corner of Serdán and Degollado, stocks a wide variety of useful *artesanías*, including saddles, guitars, and huaraches.

SPORTING GOODS

Deportes Ortiz (Degollado 260, almost opposite Pensión California, tel. 612/122-1209) carries a modest selection of camping, diving, and other sports equipment.

BOOKSTORES

Librería Contempo (Calle Arrival at Paseo Obregón) carries Mexican newspapers as well as a few American magazines.

The La Paz branch of **Libros Libros/Books Books** (Constitución at Madero, tel./fax 612/122-1410, Mon.–Sun. 9 A.M.–8:45 P.M.) has a limited selection of American newspapers, magazines, and books.

Accommodations

La Paz offers the most varied and least expensive selection of places to stay of any city in Baja, and new options are opening all the time. There are hotels in all budget categories, many with kitchenettes, plus bed and breakfast inns, condo complexes, and private vacation rental homes. Rates do not include tax or service fees. And many places offer discounts for stays of a week or longer.

Beach camping is available in several places outside the city limits.

HOTELS

Despite the planned construction of several large luxury hotels, most rooms in La Paz still fall in the US$50–125 range. Some of the older establishments could use a makeover, but the time warp is also part of their charm. You'll pay a bit more to stay right on the water rather than along the *malecón*. And none of the bayfront hotels are within easy walking distance of the *malecón* or downtown La Paz, although taxis are always available.

Most times of year, you can wing it and find

a room when you arrive. But if you plan to visit during mid-November, check the Baja 1000 event schedule and make reservations well in advance. The tourist information office on the *malecón* is a good place to stop for updated information on most local hotels.

Under US$50

Budget accommodations often come without air conditioning—a significant inconvenience July–October. And since most of them are in the central commercial zone, they can be a bit noisy.

As old as the city itself, **Pensión California** (Degollado 209, tel. 612/123-3508, fax 612/122-2896, US$20) is housed in a former 18th-century convent between Revolución de 1910 and Madero. The interior courtyard of this rambling Moorish-style building contains a tropical garden of sorts and a display of old and new paintings that lend a distinctly Bohemian feel to the atmosphere. Rooms are basic—little more than a few worn sticks of furniture, fan, and hot shower—but reasonably comfortable. Practically every backpacker on the Baja circuit turns up at the Pensión California at one time or another. Discounts are possible for long-term stays, and there is Internet at the front desk. The same family operates **Hostería del Convento** (Madero Sur 85, tel. 612/122-3508, fax 612/123-3525, misioner@prodigy.net.mx, US$20) in another former convent right around the corner. It has a similarly funky and faded feel, with a bit more greenery in the courtyard.

Seemingly undiscovered by visiting budget travelers is the family-run **Hotel Señorial** (Domínguez 254, no tel., US$16), which offers a cozy front balcony sitting area and 10 clean rooms with attached bath. The public areas aren't too charming, but the beds are comfortable. TV costs US$2 extra. The **Hotel San Carlos** (16 de Septiembre btw Serdán/ Revolución de 1910, tel. 612/122-0444, fax 612/122-3991, US$20, US$25 with a/c) has 30 basic rooms.

La Paz has a youth hostel at the **Instituto de la Juventud y el Deporte** (Villa Juventil La Paz, tel. 612/122-4615, US$20), a sports complex on Boulevard Forjadores (Km 3) near Calzada 5 de Febrero. Facilities include a pool, gym, cafeteria, and volleyball and basketball courts. Beds are single bunks in gender-segregated, four-person dorm rooms. The hostel is distant from the town center and about the same cost for two people as some of the more centrally located hotels, considering the cost per bed. But it's closer to the main bus terminal than the downtown lodgings. All ages are welcome.

Posada Hotel Yeneka (Madero 1520 btw 16 de Septiembre/Av. Independencia, tel./fax 612/125-4688, ynkmacias@prodigy.net.mx, US$39) looks and operates much like a guesthouse. Long known on the backpacker circuit, the Yeneka is built around a courtyard filled with tropical vegetation, a rusting Model T, and an amazing collection of other items giving the appearance of an ongoing garage sale. The proprietors can arrange snorkeling, diving, fishing, boating, and horseback-riding excursions. A *lavandería* and car rental agency are also on the premises. Rooms are basic, dark, and a bit scruffy. You can find

nicer accommodations for just a few dollars more per night.

Around the corner from Hotel Los Arcos, the friendly **Hotel Lorimar** (Bravo 110 btw Madero/Mutualisimo, tel. 612/125-3822, fax 612/125-3822, US$27–39) is a longtime budget favorite with European, Canadian, and U.S. visitors. Its 20 air-conditioned rooms are clean and well maintained. The proprietors speak English but are happy to let you practice your Spanish; they can also arrange kayaking and diving trips through local outfitters. The Lorimar is just a block off the *malecón;* guests often meet in the cozy upstairs dining area to exchange travel tips. Groups of three or four people can also be accommodated in some rooms.

The **Hotel Plaza Real** (Callejón de La Paz and Esquerro, tel. 612/122-9333, fax 612/122-4424, US$40), a block off the *malecón* and right around the corner from the Hotel Perla, is a three-story, modern hotel popular with middle-class Mexican businesspeople. Rooms have air conditioning and TV, and the downstairs coffee shop is a popular local spot for breakfast and Mexican food.

Hotel Restaurant Nuevo Pekin (Paseo Obregón 875 at Victoria, tel. 612/125-5335, www.nuevopekin.com.mx, US$47) occupies a pagoda-like building facing the *malecón*. It offers 30 clean rooms with TV and air conditioning (some with bay views). Credit cards are accepted.

Swimming pools and secure parking are hard to find in this price range, but you'll find both at the friendly **Hotel Gardenias** (Serdán Norte 520, tel. 612/122-3088, www.hotelgardenias.com.mx, US$45). Located in a residential neighborhood in the northwest part of the city, the hotel is a large, modern, two-story building set around a pleasant courtyard and pool. Popular among Mexicans, the Gardenias offers 56 clean rooms with TV and air conditioning. The attached restaurant is open for breakfast and lunch. *Note:* Although the hotel's street address reads Calle Serdán, the entrance is on Guerrero between Serdán and Guillermo Prieto.

If you're blazing through town on your way south to Los Cabos, well-kept **Hotel Calafía** (Km 4, tel. 612/122-5811, hotelcalafia@gmail. com, US$35) is a budget hotel along the highway that makes a convenient stop. It has 35 rooms, secure parking, and a pool. Rates include tax.

US$50-100

A block off Paseo Obregón, the three-story, apartment-style **Hotel Miramar** (5 de Mayo at Domínguez, tel. 612/122-8885, fax 612/122-0672, hmiramar@prodigy.net.mx, US$57) features clean but darkish rooms with air conditioning, minibar, and small TV with VCR. Beds rest on concrete platforms and slope a bit. Some rooms come with balconies and bay views at no extra charge, so be sure to ask what's available. The parking lot is a plus. Credit cards are accepted.

Hotel Posada Luna Sol (Topete 564 btw 5 de Febrero/Navarro, tel. 612/123-0559, U.S. tel. 800/355-7140, www.posadalunasol.com, US$60–130), located a half block from the bay and on the premises of Mar y Aventura, has 14 spacious, clean rooms decorated in Mexican kitsch. Enjoy a sunset cocktail under the rooftop *palapa*. In recent years, the property has added a new top-floor suite and a room with a small kitchen. Posada Luna also is one of the few hotels in this price range where rooms have satellite TV. Rates include tax. Credit cards are accepted.

The venerable **Hotel Perla** (Paseo Obregón 1570, tel. 612/122-0777 or 800/716-8799, U.S. tel. 888/242-3757, www.hotelperlabaja. com, US$75–100) has long been one of the city's most popular hotels, but unfortunately improvements haven't kept pace with rate increases. The two-story, tile-roofed hotel enjoys a prime location right at the center of the *malecón* and just a few steps away from the main shopping district. La Terraza, the hotel's downstairs, open-air restaurant, remains a favorite gathering place for power business lunches, while the upstairs nightclub draws a mostly local crowd. The mezzanine floor features a small pool. Clean, but

plain and small, rooms have high ceilings, air conditioning, TVs, and telephones. Stay here if a central, waterfront location and secure indoor parking are important and the price is right. *Note:* There was no Internet service at last check.

Another *malecón* standby around since the dawn of La Paz's tourist industry is **Cabañas de los Arcos** (Paseo Obregón 498, tel. 612/122-2744 or 800/716-8644, U.S. tel. 800/347-2252, www.losarcos.com, US$75–100). Built in 1954, during La Paz's heyday as an exotic playground for Hollywood celebrities, *paceño*-owned Los Arcos became the city's first center for sportfishing trips. Today you can choose from among 52 air-conditioned rooms in the original cabaña section (fireplaces), junior suites behind the cabaña section (no fireplaces), and rooms and suites in the much larger **Hotel Los Arcos** section less than 100 meters down the street. Some rooms have bay views, others overlook the interior courtyard and pool. Both the new and original sections have swimming pools; the new one also offers a coffee shop, restaurant, bar, gift shop, sauna rooms, massage service, and whale-watching, diving, and sportfishing tours. Rooms at the Arcos are a bit nicer than the Perla for the same price, but still retain a 1970s feel. Friendly service and wireless Internet are two additional features.

Seven Crown Hotel (corner of Obregón and Lerdo de Tejada, tel. 612/128-9090, sevencrown@prodigy.net.mx, US$95), facing the *malecón,* looks like an office building from the outside, with a lobby one might mistake for an airlines office. Nonetheless, the rooms are quiet, clean, and well equipped. Amenities include a gym, parking, and wireless Internet.

Under Swiss ownership, the three-story, blue-and-white stucco **(Hotel Mediterrané** (Allende 36, tel./fax 612/125-1195, www.hotelmed.com, US$72–83) enjoys a great location, just a half block from the *malecón.* The small, well-managed hotel features large, airy, sparkling-clean rooms with air conditioning, refrigerator, and TV/VCR; each room is named for a different Greek island. Rooms with views are also the closest to the street and pick up a little more noise than those at the back of the hotel. There's also a rooftop sundeck with lounge chairs and a view of the bay. Kayaks and canoes are on hand for guests who would like to paddle in the bay. Bicycles are available for land-lovers. La Pazta restaurant and café are downstairs; the café has wireless Internet.

North of downtown, the **Hotel Suites Club El Moro** (Km 2 Carr. a Pichilingue, tel./fax 612/122-4084, www.clubelmoro.com, US$74–146) is a whitewashed, Moorish-style place on landscaped grounds. All rooms and kitchenette-equipped suites come with air conditioning, satellite TV with HBO, reliable wireless Internet, and private terrace. Standard rooms are a little small for the price (US$74 including tax), but at US$110, large junior suites are a great value. Other amenities include a pool, hot tub, offstreet and gated parking, and newly remodeled bar. The adjoining **Café Gourmet** serves great espresso, as well as breakfast and lunch every day. Hotel guests receive free coffee and a coupon for US$2.50 per day. Friendly staff and an attractive frequent-guest program bring repeat visitors back year after year. Buses heading downtown pass the hotel frequently during daylight hours; otherwise it's a two-kilometer (1.2-mi) walk to the town center.

Open since 1975, **Hotel La Concha Beach Club Resort and Condominiums** (Km 5 Carr. a Pichilingue, tel. 612/121-6161 or 800/726-8603, U.S. tel. 800/999-2252, www.laconcha.com, US$85) sits on Playa Caimancito, the city's closest swimming beach. All of the 94 well-kept rooms and suites have bay views. On the premises are two pools, tennis courts, an aquatic sports center, restaurant, bar, spa, and gift shop. The swimming pool in La Concha's newer condo section (see *Apartments, Condos, and Long-Term Rentals*) is nicer than the original hotel pool; both pools are open to hotel guests. The resort has equipment and services onsite for fishing, snorkeling, diving, sailing, and water skiing.

Next to the Baja Ferries terminal in Bahía Pichilingue, **Club Cantamar Resort and Sports Centre** (B.C.S. 11/Carr. a Pichilingue, tel. 612/122-7010, www.clubcantamar.com, US$80–102) caters to serious scuba divers and

other water enthusiasts. This family business has grown steadily since it opened in 1994 with one 22-foot *panga* and an old 40-horsepower outboard engine. A boat ramp and tank-filling station paved the way to a full-scale resort.

Today, guests sleep in a four-story lodge with 45 standard rooms (11 of which were new in 2006), eight double condos, and two junior suites; a separate building contains four apartments, each with two bedrooms, two bathrooms, kitchenette, dining room, living room, and private balcony. Rooms are decorated in desert colors and stucco walls with rustic furnishings. Air conditioning and satellite TV are included, and most rooms have phones too. Other resort amenities include a 35-slip marina, swimming pool overlooking the ocean (deep enough for scuba training), bar, dockside restaurant, and swim-up bar. There are also a boat ramp, kayak rentals, private beach, fishing fleet, dive shop, scuba shop, and recompression chamber. Proximity to the industrial ferry terminal, with semi-trucks coming and going, is one disadvantage of the location. Night owls will find the Cantamar much to remote, but for those who want to maximize their time on the water, this resort is a fine home base. Rates include breakfast and taxes.

US$100-150

At Km 2.5 on the La Paz–Pichilingue Road, almost opposite Club de Yates Palmira, the palm-encircled **Hotel Palmira La Paz** (Km 2.5 Carr. a Pichilingue, tel. 612/121-6200 or 800/026-5444, U.S. tel. 877/727-2492, www.araizahoteles.com, US$135) caters to conventioneers as well as vacationers with its large meeting rooms, banquet halls, and quiet garden rooms. Other facilities include a pool, tennis court in good shape, restaurant, bar, and disco.

South of the *malecón* and Marina de La Paz is **Hacienda del Cortez** (formerly the Hotel La Posada de Engelbert, Nuevo Reforma and Playa Sur, tel. 612/129-9999, www.haciendadelcortez.com, US$106–244). Originally built by pop crooner Engelbert Humperdinck for the Hollywood set, the recently renovated property offers 25 large suites and fireplace-equipped *casitas.* All rooms have satellite TV, phone, Internet, and air conditioning. A pool, tennis court, activities center, restaurant, and *palapa* bar fill out the compound. The quiet waterfront atmosphere is a plus. A full service spa was in the works at last check.

Opposite the Hotel Palmira La Paz (adjacent to the plush Club de Yates Palmira) is the **Hotel Marina** (Km 2.5 Carr. a Pichilingue, tel. 612/121-6254 or 800/685-8800, U.S. tel. 800/250-3186 or 800/826-1138, www.hotel-marina.com.mx, US$100–180) with 150 clean suites and master suites, somewhat saggy beds, and older furnishings. Facilities include tennis courts, a large pool, and an outdoor bar; boat slips are available nearby for visiting yachties.

At the center of the new 500-acre CostaBaja Resort & Marina (www.costabajaresort.com), the **Fiesta Inn La Paz** (Km 5.5 Carr. a Pichilingue, tel. 612/123-6000, www.fiestainn.com, US$95–163) is popular with families as well as boaters, who can anchor at the onsite marina. The resort has 120 guestrooms, including accessible rooms for handicapped guests; amenities include wireless Internet and a separate lap-swimming lane in addition to the main pool. To find the hotel, look for a signed entrance on a rise on the seaside of the road to Pichilingue.

US$150-250

Some of the nicest accommodations in town are found at the coral-hued ◖ **Posada de las Flores** (Obregón 440 btw Militar/Guerrero, tel./fax 612/125-5871, www.posadadelasflores.com, US$150–250). Well-tended landscaping and a small pool grace the entry, which faces the *malecón.* Rustic Mexican furniture and tile are used throughout, and the all-marble bathrooms feature a large bathtub and extra-thick towels. Rooms are outfitted with air conditioning, wireless Internet, cable TV, and a small refrigerator. A larger *casa* is next door. Bikes and kayaks for guest use at no extra charge. Rates include breakfast. Posada de las Flores also has sister properties in Loreto and Punta Chivato.

Southwest of town, at Km 5.5 on northbound Mexico 1 (it turns north eventually),

the three-story **Grand Plaza Resort** (Lte. A, Marina Fidepaz, tel. 612/124-0830, U.S. tel. 866/357-9711, www.grandplazalapaz.com, US$150–200) is a typical airport business hotel with 50 bayside suites. Rooms are on the dark side, and beds sag a bit, but the pool is large, and bay views are a plus (no swimming). Notable amenities include free wireless Internet in the lobby and restaurant area, plus a sauna, pool tables, gym, hot tub, tennis court, massage room, and restaurant/bar. Rooms come with air conditioning and refrigerators. The hotel stands opposite the state tourism office and next to the nearly complete Marina Fidepaz.

BED-AND-BREAKFASTS

If you like cozier accommodations and the opportunity to socialize with your host, bed-and-breakfast-style accommodations can be a wonderful way to meet Mexican or expat families.

Under US$50

A branch of the same family that runs the popular Club El Moro hotel has opened ◖ **Baja Bed and Breakfast** (Madero 354, tel. 612/123-1370, www.bajabedandbreakfast.com, US$45–60) in a centrally located home just off the plaza. Two street-level rooms share a bath and a patio with a small swimming pool and barbecue. Above, a spacious first-floor apartment for rent by the night or week has a kitchen, separate bedroom, and living room. Rates include tax and wireless Internet.

Cecilia Moller serves a multicourse breakfast each morning on the third-floor terrace. You'll start your day filled with fresh breads, fruit, juice, coffee or tea, and eggs, quesadillas, *chilaquiles,* or other Mexican specialties. Some of La Paz's hottest new restaurants are less than a block away, and the *malecón* is a two-block walk. The inn is especially popular with kayakers preparing for a multiday paddle to Isla Espíritu Santo. Next door, the Mollers were building an additional four rooms with private baths, and there were plans to upgrade the existing rooms as well.

US$50-100

A half block off the *malecón,* **La Casa Mexicana Inn** (Bravo 106 btw Madero/Mutualismo, tel./fax 612/125-2748, www.casamex.com, US$65–95) offers five tastefully decorated rooms in a Moorish/art deco–style inn. All rooms come with remote-control air conditioning, fans, VCRs, and private baths. Rates include a breakfast of home-baked pastries, as well as tax. The property was up for sale and undergoing renovations in 2007.

Next door, a charming couple from down under, Patricia Lowe and Ken Bonner, have channeled their love for all things Italian into **Casa Tuscany Inn** (Bravo 110A, tel. 612/128-8103, www.tuscanybaja.com, US$90–125). Four colorful guestrooms overlook a garden courtyard behind the main house. Each has a comfortable queen bed, private bath, ceiling fan, and remote-control air conditioning. Prices include tax and breakfast.

US$100-150

El Ángel Azul (Independencia 518, tel./fax 612/125-5130, www.elangelazul.com, US$80–145) is housed in a historic building that once served as the La Paz courthouse. Carefully restored with INAH guidance, the hotel offers nine guestrooms and one suite around a large, landscaped courtyard. All rooms are air-conditioned and nonsmoking. The work of local artists is showcased throughout. Secure parking.

APARTMENTS, CONDOS, AND LONG-TERM RENTALS
US$50-100

Operated by La Concha Beach Resort, **Las Gaviotas** (Domínguez at Salvatierra, tel. 612/123-5298, US$135) is a five-story apartment-style complex in a residential neighborhood downtown. Each huge, two-bedroom apartment features a bay view, air conditioning, TV, phone, kitchen, two bathrooms, and private patio. There is Wi-Fi in the lobby and secure parking. Rates vary depending on whether or not the kitchen is used. You can also rent by the week. Electricity is billed separately.

US$150-250

On Playa Caimancito near Km 5 on La Paz–Pichilingue Road. **La Concha Beach Resort and Condos** (Km 5 Carr. a Pichilingue, tel. 612/121-6161 or 800/726-8603, U.S. tel. 800/999-2252, www.laconcha.com, US$85) rents large one- to three-bedroom condos with air conditioning, TV, and kitchenette. Condo residents have full use of hotel facilities, including two pools, a beach, restaurant/bar, and water-sports center.

CAMPING AND RV PARKS

Free beach camping is available north of the Pichilingue ferry terminal at Playas Pichilingue, Balandra (Puerto Balandra), El Tecolote, and El Coyote. Except for El Tecolote, none of these beaches has freshwater; all supplies must be brought from La Paz. Two restaurants at El Tecolote supply food and beverages. Though not common, theft unfortunately does occur at these beaches. A couple reported a pair of mountain bikes stolen from the locked bike rack on their car, just steps away from where they slept in December 2006. Keep valuables out of sight if at all possible.

Several trailer parks spread west from the city's edge out onto Mexico 1. Starting from the farthest away, just before Km 15 in El Centenario comes **Los Aripez (Oasis de Aripez) RV Park** (tel. 612/124-6090 or 612/125-6202), popular among Transpeninsular voyagers making short La Paz stopovers; 26 full-hookup slots here cost US$12–16. Facilities include hot showers, flush toilets, laundry, restaurant, bar, and boat access to Ensenada de la Paz. Tents are permitted. It's open year-round.

Five kilometers (3 mi) west of the city on Mexico 1, across from Motel Villa del Sol, is the well-maintained **Casa Blanca RV Park** (tel. 612/124-0009, fax 612/125-1142, open Nov.–May), where more than 46 full-hookup sites are US$16/night. The facility includes showers, flush toilets, a pool, tennis courts, spa, laundry, restaurant, and a small market.

A kilometer closer to the city center and surrounded by a high wall, **El Cardón Trailer Park** (Km 4, tel./fax 612/124-0078, elcardon@starmedia.com) features 80 shaded, well-tended *palapa* sites with full hookups for US$12–15 for two, depending on the size of your vehicle, plus US$2 for each additional person. Tent camping is permitted, and fees vary from US$3 for people on foot to US$4 for those arriving on bicycles, and a little bit more for those coming in on motorcycles. El Cardón offers a pool, groceries, bathrooms with flush toilets and hot showers, a children's play area, a dump station, and laundry. An Internet café in the park offers good rates and is open daily 6 A.M.–8 P.M. The park is open year-round.

Off Avenida Abasolo (Mexico 1) not far from the bayshore is the upscale, 96-slot **La Paz RV Park** (tel. 612/122-4480 or 612/122-8787, fax 612/122-9938). Full hookups alongside concrete pads cost US$17. Tent sites on the ground go for US$14. Facilities include showers, flush toilets, potable tap water, a small but clean pool, hot tub, tennis court, laundry, restaurant, and bar. Cash only. To find this well-kept RV park, go east on Avenida Abasolo and turn left (toward the bay) just before the VW dealer, then turn left on Calle Brecha California just before Posada Engelbert and continue three or four blocks. Open year-round.

A bit farther east toward the city center, off Calle Nayarit on the bay, is the smallish, palm-planted **Aquamarina RV Park** (Nayarit 10, tel. 612/122-3761, open Nov.–May). Though a bit run-down compared to La Paz RV Park, its shady spots are a favorite among boaters and divers. Aquamarina features its own marina, complete with boat ramp, storage facilities, and air for scuba tanks, plus showers, flush toilets, potable tap water, a pool, and laundry facilities. Nineteen full-hookup sites cost US$19. The Aquamarina also offers three apartments for rent.

Food

La Paz offers dining venues for all tastes and budgets, and, as might be expected in a coastal city, the seafood selection is particularly good.

ALTA COCINA MEXICANA

A new generation of chefs up and down the peninsula are working hard to create a more distinct identity for Baja regional cuisine. La Paz enjoyed its first such restaurant debut with the opening of **Las Tres Virgenes** (Madero at Constitución) in December 2006. The restaurant name refers to three mountains, one of which is a dormant volcano, visible in the distance on the drive from San Ignacio to Santa Rosalía. On the menu are innovative entrées like mesquite grilled baby octopus and *cabrillo* over garlic mint mashed potatoes. The restaurant gets rave reviews for the high quality of its food and a reasonably priced wine list. Indeed, local expats are calling it the best meal they've had in La Paz, period.

MEXICAN

A popular coffee shop–style place, **Restaurant Plaza Real** (Hotel Plaza Real, Esquerro at Callejón de la Paz, tel. 612/122-9333, daily 7 A.M.–3 P.M.) offers moderate prices, efficient service, and good Mexican food. The fresh orange juice is quite refreshing on a hot day.

Carlos'n Charlie's (Obregón at 16 de Septiembre, tel. 612/123-4547, daily noon–1 A.M., mains US$6–17) is part of the same chain as Squid Roe and Señor Frog's, but the atmosphere is much more low-key than the typical Grupo Anderson enterprise. The interior decor features old Mexican movie posters, while the menu emphasizes good Mexican fare, seafood (try the *ceviche paceño*), and steak dishes. Much of the clientele is Mexican. The terrace tables usually catch a breeze. Credit cards are accepted.

In a courtyard behind La Fabula Pizza on Obregón, **Peña La Pitahaya de Janicua** (Obregón 15, tel. 612/126-2234) is an almost hidden spot with a bohemian ambience and a Mexican menu. Artwork and Mexican crafts

LA PAZ AND VICINITY

food vendor stall in La Paz

© JOE CUMMINGS

are on display throughout, and there's live Latin folk music nightly.

The simple but pretty restaurant/bar **€ El Zarape** (Av. México 3450 btw Oaxaca/Nayarit, tel. 612/122-2520, daily 7:30 A.M.–midnight, mains US$10–15) features a tiled entryway and a menu of traditional Mexican dishes. On Saturday evenings, El Zarape hosts a *cazuelada,* i.e., a buffet of *cazuelas* (large, open clay pans) filled with moles and other specialties of central and southern Mexico. A popular breakfast buffet is offered Tuesday–Sunday; a more modern Mexican buffet on Sunday noon–6 P.M. brings together recipes from all over the republic.

SEAFOOD

Restaurant La Costa (Navarro and Topete near La Marina Don José, daily 2 P.M.–2 A.M., mains US$10–15) is a simple *palapa*-roofed restaurant with some of the freshest seafood in La Paz. Operated by local seafood wholesalers Mar y Peña, **Restaurant La Mar y Peña** (16 de Septiembre btw Isabel la Católica/Albáñez, tel. 612/122-9949, daily 9 A.M.–10 P.M.) is a small,

air-conditioned place with a terrific menu that features practically everything that swims, including several *machaca* (dried and shredded) versions. The *sangría preparada* (homemade sangria) is also good. Prices are moderate to expensive. Credit cards are accepted.

Once a best-kept secret, **Bismark II** (Degollado at Altamirano, tel. 612/122-4854, daily 8 A.M.–10 P.M., mains US$10–20), has become one of the most popular tourist restaurants in La Paz in recent years, and locals no longer recommend it with as much enthusiasm. It specializes in lobster, abalone, and carne asada. The ceviche is also good. On the *malecón,* **Bismarkcito** (Paseo Obregón near Constitución, tel. 612/128-9900, mains US$10–15) is a waterfront offshoot of its parent restaurant. This casual eatery draws a crowd for weekday business lunches; however, when the exceptionally loud marching band starts playing on the sidewalk, conversation of any sort becomes impossible. The menu includes all manner of seafood cocktails, and fish and shellfish entrées; Peñafiel brand Mexican sodas are a treat.

One of the better hotel restaurants, **Restaurant Bermejo** (Hotel Los Arcos, Paseo Obregón, tel. 612/122-2744, Mon.–Sat. 7 A.M.–11 P.M., Sun. 8 A.M.–11 P.M., US$13–20) overlooks the *malecón*—ask for a window table. The Italian chef prepares a varied menu of seafood, steaks, and pastas. If you've had a successful day fishing, the restaurant will prepare your catch.

The popular **Mariscos Moyeyo's** (corner of Obregón and Calle Héores de 47, mains US$4–11), just past El Moro hotel, packs a crowd on weekend afternoons, when locals stop in for towering seafood cocktails. The floor is sand, and the tables and chairs are plastic. It takes a dozen wait staff to keep the fresh catch flowing. The restaurant has occasional live music.

Near the Posada las Flores on Obregón, **Las Brisas del Mar** (Obregón at Militar, tel. 612/123-5055, lasbrisasdelmbcs@hotmail.com, daily for dinner, mains US$13–27) serves seafood cocktails, fish *a la parilla, empanizado,* shrimp, lobster, and red meat from Sonora.

ITALIAN

Owned by a friendly Chinese/Italian couple, **Caffé Milano** (Esquerro 15, btw Callejón de la Paz/16 de Septiembre, tel. 612/125-9981, www.caffemilano.com.mx, Mon.–Sat. 4–11 P.M., mains US$6–18) prepares traditional Italian fare. Start with an order of fried oysters with caviar and move on to a homemade pasta or a hearty main dish like osso buco and *frutti di mare.* The restaurant received a AAA diamond rating in 2006. Look for the tall, light blue wooden doors.

La Pazta (Allende, adjacent to Hotel Mediterrané, tel. 612/125-1195, Wed.–Mon. 7 A.M.–11 P.M., Tues. 7 A.M.–3 P.M., mains US$10–15) is simply decorated with works of art, pastel stucco, and exposed brick. The light and airy restaurant offers breakfast, lunch, and dinner. The evening menu features a long list of pastas, pizzas, fondues, and other Swiss and Italian specialties. An extensive wine list includes Italian, U.S., Chilean, and *bajacaliforniano* labels. Marine biologist Christian Liñan took time

away from his studies to open **Toscana Pizza Gourmet** (Dominguez and Constitución, Mon.–Sat. 3–11 P.M., mains US$5–10)in 2006. This Italian pizzeria makes European-style pies for eating in or takeout; salads pasta, and drinks complete the menu. Dine at six pine picnic tables outside, or window counter seating inside.

ECLECTIC MENUS

Kiwi Restaurant Bar (on the *malecón* btw 5 de Mayo/Constitución, tel. 612/123-3282, daily 8 A.M.–midnight, mains US$6–15) offers a scenic bay view and varied menu of seafood, Mexican, and international recipes. The people-watching is better than the food, but this is not a bad choice for lobster. On weekends, the restaurant occasionally features live music.

The venerable **El Taste** (Paseo Obregón at Juárez, tel. 612/122-8121, daily 8 A.M.–midnight, mains US$10–20), while known for its breakfast, features steaks, Mexican food, and seafood. It's patronized by a mostly tourist and expat clientele.

Outdoors beneath the Hotel Perla, **La Terraza** (Paseo Obregón 1570, tel. 612/122-0777, mains US$10–20) features an extensive menu of seafood, Mexican, steak, and Italian dishes. A steady crowd of both tourists and locals comes for the best people-watching in town, as well as for the reasonably tasty, reasonably priced food.

Friendly **El Oasis Restaurant and Bar** (Paseo Obregón 115 btw 16 de Septiembre/Callejón de la Paz, tel. 612/125-7666, daily noon–midnight, mains US$6–17) is a sidewalk patio restaurant with great service and a large menu of well-prepared seafood, steaks, and Mexican dishes. Live music plays in the evening. Credit cards are accepted.

AMERICAN AND PIZZA

Near the plaza and across from Baja Bed and Breakfast, **Buffalo BAR-B-Q** (Madero 1240, tel. 612/128-8755, Mon.–Fri. 6 P.M.–midnight, Sat.–Sun. 2–10 P.M., mains US$10–20) gets high marks from locals for its steaks and burgers.

An upscale newcomer to the waterfront near the Marina de La Paz, **El Patrón Bar & Grill** (Plaza Vista Coral, tel. 612/125-9977, www.elpatronbarandgrill.com, Sun.–Wed. 2–11 P.M., Thurs.–Sat. 2 P.M.–midnight, mains US$12–24) serves lamb, Sonora beef, grilled fish, tequila shrimp, and Cornish game hens in a casual indoor/outdoor setting. Some say the quality of the food doesn't match the prices.

Visiting and resident yachties crowd **The Dock Café** (Marina de La Paz, corner Topete/ Legaspy, tel. 612/125-6626, daily 8 A.M.– 10 P.M., mains US$10–15), a small, casual diner serving fried chicken, hamburgers, fish-and-chips, bagels, salads, steaks, American breakfasts, some Mexican dishes, and homemade apple pie. A blues trio occasionally performs in the evening. (It's usually closed for two weeks at the end of August/beginning of September.)

Restaurant Grill Campestre (tel. 612/124-0454, daily for lunch and dinner, mains US$10–15), opposite the Fidepaz building on Mexico 1 north near Km 5.5, is popular with gringos and Mexicans alike for barbecued ribs, Cobb salad, and other American specialties.

ASIAN

La Cochinita (Forjadores and Veracruz, tel. 612/122-1600, daily 10 A.M.–10 P.M., mains US$5–10) is an extremely clean fast-food spot serving generous portions of Mexicanized Japanese dishes. It's a very popular lunch spot with the locals. A newer, smaller branch has opened on Calle Mutualismo, next to Bar El Misión.

ANTOJITOS

It's easy to find ((**Rancho Viejo** (Legaspy, half a block from the Marina de La Paz, tel. 612/128-4647, daily 24 hrs, dinner mains US$12–17) from the smell of the grill wafting up the street. Sit at a picnic table on the sidewalk, or in either of two dining rooms inside, to get away from the smoke. *Tacos de arranchera,* carne asada, or *pastor* arrive with the usual tray of fresh condiments. You can also order by the kilo. Service is prompt and friendly, and you can't beat the prices.

A half block from the *malecón* on 16 de Sep-tiembre, **Restaurant Pichos** (tel. 612/128-9109, Tues.–Sun. 8 A.M.–11 P.M., mains US$3–6) serves delicious *tortas, licuados,* tacos, burgers, and *chilaquiles.* The *Hamburguesa Mexicana* comes with carne asada instead of ground beef, bacon bits, cheese, sliced avocado, tomato, and shredded lettuce, all on a lightly toasted bun. Two people can easily have lunch here for less than US$10, including sodas.

In the afternoons, the downtown area centered around the *malecón* and Calle 16 de Septiembre features street vendors serving fish tacos and *cocteles.* One of the best stands for fish, shrimp, and clam tacos, and *aguas frescas* is the extremely popular **Super Tacos de Baja California Hermanos González.** On Calle Esquerro beneath a big tree, opposite the side entrance of La Perla department store, this famous stand is still packed around lunchtime. Fish tacos and condiments are outstanding, and the *horchata* is delicious. Look for a second location on Degollado at Madero, next to Pensión California, and a larger restaurant location on Degollado at Mijares.

Taquería Los Superburros (Abasolo btw 5 de Febrero/Navarro) serves hamburgers, tacos (US$0.95), quesadillas (US$0.89), *huaraches* (US$3.50), and *papas rellenas.*

During the daytime, the cluster of *loncherías* in the **Mercado Municipal Francisco E. Madero** (Revolución and Degollado) serves as a very inexpensive grazing spot for *antojitos* and *comidas corridas.*

CAFÉS

The espresso business is booming in La Paz. Several chains now have multiple locations, and new ones seem to open every month. Starbucks look-a-like **5th Avenida Coffee** has wireless Internet in various locations, including 5 de Mayo on the plaza and Abasolo near the Marina de La Paz. **Café Exquisito** has a *malecón* location with sidewalk tables (Obregón south of La Fuente, Mon.–Sat. 6 A.M.–10:30 P.M., Sun. 8 A.M.–10:30 P.M., drinks US$1–3), plus two drive-through espresso stands north and south of town on Mexico 1, and one more at the airport. **Café Combate** has at least two locations in town: Serdán between Ocampo and Degollado, and on Bravo at the southeast entrance to Mercado Bravo.

Aside from these chains, a good place to enjoy coffee drinks and pastries in air-conditioned comfort is **Caffé Gourmet** (Esquerro and 16 de Septiembre, tel. 612/122-6037, Mon.–Sat. 8 A.M.–10 P.M.). The menu offers a long list of hot and cold coffee drinks, chai, smoothies, Italian sodas, pies, cookies, and pastries along with cigars and liquors. A cozy nonsmoking section can be found in the back. A second location was opening on the *malecón* in 2007.

Mareiros Café (Obregón north of Oasis, tel. 612/123-5439, Mon.–Sat. 8 A.M.–11 P.M., Sunday 9 A.M.–5 P.M.) is also air-conditioned, and the menu contains a whole page of coffee drinks, hot and cold, plus deli sandwiches, salads, snacks, and pastries. Mareiros has a few tables outside as well, and it is attached an Internet cafe. Air-conditioned **La Pazta Café** (daily 7 A.M.–11 P.M.), next to La Pazta Restaurant and Hotel Mediterrané serves excellent espresso drinks made from imported Italian Illy brand coffee, as well as cocktails, beer, and wine. Wireless Internet is free, and a desktop computer is available.

A café attached to the El Moro hotel (Km 2 Carr. a Pichilingue, tel./fax 612/122-4084, www.clubelmoro.com, daily 7 A.M.–4 P.M., mains US$5–15) is a good place to stop for breakfast on the way to Pichilingue.

El Quinto Sol (Domínguez and Independencia, tel. 612/122-1692) is a natural food/vegetarian store with a café section serving *tortas, comida corrida,* pastries, salads, granola, fruit and vegetable juices, and yogurt. The healthful breakfasts are particularly nice after extended travel. Readers also recommend **La Virtud** (Ramirez btw Bravo/Rosales, tel. 612/128-6940) for sandwiches, pastries, and healthy snacks.

GROCERIES

The **Mercado Municipal Francisco E. Madero** (Revolución de 1910 at Degollado) houses a collection of vendor stalls purveying fresh fish, meats, fruit, vegetables, and baked goods at non-subsidized free-market prices. Since prices are usually posted, no bargaining is necessary. At the corner of Revolución and Bravo is a *tortillería.* Other traditional markets include **Mercado Bravo** (Bravo at Guillermo Prieto) and **Mercado Abastos** (on Boulevard Las Garzas).

The government-subsidized **ISSSTE Tienda** (Revolución de 1910 at Bravo) has the city's best grocery prices, although the selection varies according to what ISSSTE bought cheaply that week. The **Tienda Militar** (Military Store, 5 de Mayo at Padre Kino) offers a larger selection than ISSSTE Tienda and is almost as inexpensive.

La Paz supermarkets include two large **CCC** (Centro Comercial California) outlets—one on Avenida Abasolo at Colima, the other on Isabel La Católica at Bravo. These carry American-brand packaged foods as well as Mexican products, but prices are about a third higher than what you'd usually pay elsewhere in town. Another good supermarket chain is **Supermercado Arámburo,** with three branches: 16 de Septiembre at Altamirano, Madero at Hidalgo y Costilla, and Durango 130 Sur (btw Ocampo/Degollado).

Plaza Ley, on the eastern outskirts of town on Las Garzas at Teotihuacán, carries a huge selection of groceries—at lower prices than CCC—as well as clothing, gardening supplies, small appliances, books, videos, housewares, and more. For buying in bulk, visit Walmart- and Costco-like **Soriana** (tel. 612/121-4771) and **City Club** (tel. 612/165-4990), owned by the same company, in a new shopping plaza on Boulevard Forjadores at the corner of Luis Donaldo Colosio.

NATURAL FOODS

El Quinto Sol (Domínguez at Av. Independencia) offers natural juices, wheat gluten, soybean meat substitutes (including soybean *chorizo*), whole-wheat flour, herbs, yogurt, and ice cream, as well as a few ready-to-eat items such as *tortas* and salads. More herbal medicines can be found at **Tonantzin** (Madero and 16 de Septiembre, Mon.–Sat. 10 A.M.–8 P.M.).

SWEETS

Downtown La Paz is packed with *tiendas* selling *nieves* (Mexican-style ice cream) and *paletas* (popsicles). **Paletería y Nevería La**

Michoacana is a big one, with branches on Paseo Obregón and Calle Madero. A personal favorite is tiny ◖ La Fuente (Paseo Obregón btw Degollado/Muelle); though small, this place offers an amazing variety of flavors (including *capirotada*, a Mexican bread pudding), as well as *licuados, aguas frescas,* and all-fruit *paletas*. (The ones made from *pitahaya* are delicious.) Look for a polka dot tree in front of the entrance.

Two *dulcerías* (sweet shops) lie on two corners of the intersection of Calles Ocampo and Serdán. On a third corner is a large school, the obvious target market for these sweet shops. Dulcería Perla has a complete selection of traditional and modern Mexican sweets, while Dulcería La Coneja on the opposite corner specializes in candy-filled piñatas.

Information and Services

TOURIST ASSISTANCE

Baja California Sur's Coordinación Estatal de Turismo office (tel. 612/124-0100, turismo@correro.gbcs.gob.mx) lies between Km 6 and 5 on Mexico 1 (Avenida Abasolo), opposite the Grand Plaza Resort. The friendly staff can assist with most tourist inquiries; the Attorney for the Protection of Tourists is also stationed here. The office maintains an information booth on the *malecón* near the Los Arcos hotel, where you can pick up maps and brochures. The office on the highway is open Monday–Friday 8 A.M.–8 P.M., while the information booth on Obregón is open the same hours Monday–Saturday.

MONEY-CHANGING

Pesos are a must for everyday purchases in La Paz; city merchants are not as receptive to U.S.-dollar transactions as their counterparts in Cabo San Lucas, simply because they're not as used to them. Three banks with ATMs are clustered near the intersection of Calle 16 de Septiembre and the *malecón*. As elsewhere in Baja, the banks provide currency-exchange service only before noon Monday–Friday. The two branches of Tony Money Exchange (Mutualismo near La Perla, and nearby on 16 de Septiembre near the *malecón*, Mon.–Sat. 9 A.M.–9 P.M.) have decent rates. On Sundays, your only alternative is to change money at a hotel at lower rates.

The local American Express representative is Viajes Perla (Obregón, tel. 612/122-8666, Mon.–Fri. 9 A.M.–5 P.M.), on the ground floor of Seven Crown Hotel.

POST AND TELEPHONE

The main post and telegraph office is at Revolución and Constitución, a block northeast of the cathedral; open Monday–Friday 8 A.M.–3 P.M., Saturday 9 A.M.–1 P.M.

DHL (Abasolo at Nayarit, tel. 612/122-8282) is the most reliable courier service in the city. The company picks up packages at no extra charge. If you are sending goods out of the country via DHL, you must first stop at the nearby Mexican customs office to have the parcel opened and inspected. Your parcel will then be sealed, and you'll receive an official customs form, which you must subsequently show to DHL before it can accept the parcel for shipping.

INTERNET ACCESS

Internet cafés can be found all over town, especially in the real estate offices along the stretch of waterfront between Hotel Los Arcos and Posada de las Flores. For example, Omni Services (Obregón 460-C, tel. 612/123-4888 or 877/805-7372) has Internet, PCs, copies, and fax services. Rates in La Paz are generally a reasonable US$2/hour. And many hotels and cafés now offer high-speed wireless Internet access for free. The 5th Avenida and Café Exquisito chains offer wireless access,

LA PAZ PHONE NUMBERS

La Paz area code: 612
Baja Ferries Office (Pichilingue): 123-0208
COTP (Captain of the Port): 122-0243 or 122-4364
Green Angels: 124-0100, 124-0199
Highway Patrol/Federal Police: 122-0369
Immigration: 125-3493, 124-6349
IMSS Hospital: 122-7377
Police, Fire Department, Red Cross (emergency): 066
SEMATUR Ferry Office (Pichilingue): 122-5005
State Tourism Department: 124-0100, 122-0199

as do most of the marinas. Hotels with wireless connections include the Los Arcos, Mediterrané, Fiesta Inn, Seven Crown, El Moro, and Posada de las Flores. Air-conditioned **La Pazta Café** (daily 7 A.M.–11 P.M.), next to La Pazta Restaurant and Hotel Mediterrané, has a desktop computer set up for customer use; wireless access if free if you bring your own computer.

PEMEX

The most central Pemex to downtown is located on 5 de Mayo between Serdán and Prieto. A second is 10 blocks away at the intersection of Isabel la Católica, and a third is on Avenida Abasolo as you leave La Paz headed toward the airport.

LAUNDRY

If you need to do some laundry, **La Paz Lava** (Ocampo at Mutualismo, tel. 612/122-3112, daily 8 A.M.–9:30 P.M.) is a good choice. This clean, modern, self-service launderette is within walking distance of the *malecón*, so you can stroll along the waterfront while waiting for your clothes. La Paz Lava also provides delivery service to home or hotel.

On Boulevard Forjadores adjacent to Supermercado Arámburo (opposite the youth hostel) is the enormous **Lavamática Cinthya;** you're sure to get a machine here. The marinas in town have their own laundry services as well.

LANGUAGE COURSES

If you'd like to study Spanish while you're in La Paz, Swiss-run **Centro de Idiomas, Cultura y Comunicación (CICC)** (Madero 2460 at Legaspy tel. 612/125-7554, www.cicclapaz.com, Mon.–Fri. 8:30 A.M.–1 P.M., Sat. 9:30 A.M.–1 P.M.) offers classes at all levels, from beginner to advanced. The standard course costs US$780 and includes four weeks of intensive classes (25 hours per week); book a homestay with a Mexican family at additional cost. Longer or shorter courses are available; a one-week travel Spanish course, for example, costs US$99. Business-Spanish and medical-Spanish courses are also offered.

Se Habla La Paz (Madero 540, tel./fax 612/122-7763, www.sehablalapaz.com) also offers more expensive classes and homestays for travelers and medical or legal professionals. Fees include a US$75 registration fee that covers student/family matching for homestays and airport pickup. Lessons run US$22/hour for a private session, US$16.50 for couples, and US$11 for group lessons. A one-week course is US$220 (20 hours), and a four-week program costs US$880 (80 hours). Payment is accepted via PayPal online.

NEWSPAPERS AND MAGAZINES

Two Spanish-language dailies are published in La Paz: *Diario Peninsular* and *El Sudcaliforniano*. **Librería Contempo** (Arrival at Paseo Obregón) carries Mexican newspapers, as well as a few American magazines. The La Paz branch of **Libros Libros/Books Books** (Constitución at Madero, tel./fax 612/122-1410, Mon.–Sun. 9 A.M.–8:45 P.M.) has a limited selection of American newspapers, magazines, and books.

IMMIGRATION

If you're planning to cross the Sea of Cortez by ferry and haven't yet validated your tourist card (see *Getting There*), stop by the immigration office on Paseo Obregón between Allende and Juárez, tel. 612/124-6349. It's usually open daily 8 A.M.–8:30 P.M. The immigration office at the airport is open seven days a week, while the one at the Pichilingue ferry terminal is open only an hour or so before each ferry departure.

Getting There and Around

GETTING THERE

By Air

Márquez de León International Airport (LAP) is 12 kilometers south of the city; the airport access road leaves Mexico 1 at Km 9. Although it's a small airport, facilities include a couple of gift shops, two snack bars, rental car booths, Ladatel phones (purchase cards from the snack bar), and an ATM machine. Although direct flights from the United States came to a halt for a number of years, Aero California, Aero Mexico, and Delta recently reinstated or added connections, making it easier and more affordable for travelers to reach La Paz without having to drive from Los Cabos. See the sidebar *Airlines Serving the Cape Region* in the *Essentials* chapter for specific connections and contact information.

Airport Transportation: Transporte Terrestre (tel. 612/125-3274) operates yellow-and-white vans between the city and the airport. The standard fare is US$15 *colectivo* (shared), US$30 for private service *(especial),* and US$56 for a larger van. To Todos Santos the prices run US$200 *especial,* US$278 for a large van; to Los Cabos US$245/333; to San Carlos and López Mateos US$311/556. A regular taxi to the airport should cost around US$15. Some hotels operate airport vans that charge about US$5–10 per person.

By Bus

From the **Central Camionera** (Jalisco at Av. Independencia), **Águila** (tel. 612/122-3063 or 612/122-4270) runs northbound buses at least once a day to Ciudad Constitución, Puerto San Carlos, Puerto López Mateos, Loreto (US$32, twice daily), Mulegé, Santa Rosalía, San Ignacio, Vizcaíno Junction, Guerrero Negro (US$70, several times daily), San Quintín, Ensenada (US$85, four times daily), Tijuana (US$134, four times daily), Tecate, and Mexicali. These buses also stop at the much more convenient, centrally located terminal on the *malecón.*

Southbound, Águila buses depart from the **Terminal Malecón** (tel. 612/122-7898). Only one bus (5 P.M.) runs through the central Cape Region towns of El Triunfo, San Antonio, San Bartolo, Los Barriles (US$9), Santiago, and Miraflores, terminating in La Ribera/Las Cuevas. Most run via Mexico 19 through Todos Santos (nine buses per day, beginning at 7 A.M., US$7), continuing to Cabo San Lucas (US$14) and San José del Cabo (US$17); the 3 P.M. bus continues all the way to La Ribera.

If you're traveling southbound, you may find it more convenient to head to the centrally located terminal of **Autotransportes La Paz** (Degollado at Guillermo Prieto, tel. 612/122-2157), which has eight departures to Los Cabos via the West Cape. Fares are the same as listed above.

By Boat

The ferry port at Pichilingue, 16 kilometers (9.5 mi) northeast of downtown La Paz via Mexico 11, serves vehicle and passenger ferries between La Paz and Mazatlán or Topolobampo. Currently, the main passenger service is run by **Baja Ferries** (Pichilinque Terminal, tel. 612/123-0208, La Paz city office: Calle Isabel la Católica and Navarro, tel. 612/125-7443 or 800/122-1414, www.bajaferries.com). You can book tickets in advance online, in downtown La Paz, or at the ferry terminal. (See *By Ferry from Mainland Mexico* in the *Essentials* chapter for details.)

A temporary **vehicle import permit** is necessary for vehicular travel on the Mexican mainland. These permits aren't needed for Baja California travel, but if you've driven down to La Paz and decide you'd like to take your wheels on a mainland-bound ferry, you need to get one before buying a ticket. The whole process operates more smoothly in Tijuana, so if you anticipate using the ferry service, doing the paperwork in advance will save time and hassle.

If for whatever reason you decide to take the ferry and haven't done the paperwork in advance, you can obtain the proper permit in La Paz from the **Aduana Maritima** office (Mon.–Sat. 9 A.M.–1 P.M. and 5–7 P.M.), at the north end of the Pichilingue ferry terminal. To receive the permit, you need the original and three copies of your vehicle title or registration, a major credit card (in the vehicle owner's name), your driver's license, and your passport with valid Mexican visa. The permit can usually be processed on the spot (after a long wait in several lines), but budget a couple of days anyway, just in case all the right bureaucrats aren't in.

La Paz is an official Mexican port of entry, so the COTP office near Marina Palmira has authority to clear yachts for movement throughout Mexican waters. Unless you plan to anchor outside, the easiest way to arrange this is to check in at Marina de La Paz or Marina Palmira, and let the marina staff process all port clearance papers. Only one clearance in and out is required for entering and exiting the country; between Mexican ports the same papers can be presented. (See *Sports and Recreation* for information on La Paz marinas.)

GETTING AROUND

You can reach most points of interest downtown on foot. For outlying areas, you can choose city buses or taxis, or rent a car. *Note:* If you are driving into La Paz from the south and want to head directly to Peninsula Pichilingue

and the ferry terminal, you can take a shortcut just after the university on Boulevard Forjadores. Look for a sign for Libramiento Norte heading off to the right. If you get to Soriana and Office Depot, you've missed the turn. Best to continue on into the city and make your way to the waterfront.

By Bus

Regular city buses and *colectivos* radiate in all directions from the *zona comercial* surrounding the Mercado Municipal on Calle Degollado. Each bears the name of either the principal street along its run or the district where the route begins and ends. Any bus marked "El Centro," for example, will end up near the Mercado Municipal at Revolución and Degollado. For a few pesos, you can catch a bus out to the new Soriana shopping complex. These buses have signs in the windshield that say Soriana. Look on 16 de Septiembre, a few blocks in from the *malecón*.

From Terminal Malecón (Paseo Obregón 125), **Águila** (tel. 612/122-7898) runs seven buses daily between La Paz and various points along Península de Pichilingue. Buses to Playa Balandra and Playa El Tecolote operate at noon and 2 P.M., on weekends only.

By Taxi

Taxis can be found throughout El Centro, the downtown area between Calles 5 de Mayo and Degollado (especially along the west end of Calle 16 de Septiembre in the shopping district), and in front of the tourist hotels. On the *malecón* (Paseo Obregón), the main taxi stands are in front of Hotel Los Arcos and Hotel Perla. The average taxi hire downtown costs around US$2–3, a bit more after dark, and US$5 to Soriana. Trips to the airport are US$15, and to the ferry terminal, US$20. La Paz taxis don't have meters, so it's sometimes necessary to haggle to arrive at the correct fare. Longer trips are more economical if you use a shared taxi van, or *colectivo*.

By Car

A handful of international car rental agencies have airport and downtown locations in La

Paz. Rates start around US$25/day for unlimited miles, not including tax and insurance. See the sidebar *Where to Rent a Car in Baja* in the *Essentials* chapter for specific locations.

La Paz has plenty of Pemex stations, all offering Magna Sin (unleaded), Premium, and diesel.

Construction has been underway to widen Mexico 19 to a four-lane highway connecting La Paz and Cabo San Lucas. To date, about 20 miles have been widened near La Paz. There was talk at press time of a private corporation completing the expansion and then charging a toll.

Southeast of La Paz

State highway BCS 286 begins south of La Paz off Mexico 1 (at Km 211) and leads southeast 43 kilometers (26 mi) to the agricultural center of San Juan de los Planes. Along the way, this paved road climbs over the northeastern escarpment of the Sierra de la Laguna (here sometimes given its own name, Sierra de las Cacachilas), then descends toward the coastal plains, offering a panoramic view of aquamarine Bahía de la Ventana and Isla Cerralvo in the distance. At the crest of the ridge, you'll pass stands of live oak, several ranches, and the village of **La Huerta** (Km 17 on BCS 286). When the weather in La Paz seems intolerably hot, a drive up into the Sierra de las Cacachilas is a good way to cool off.

◖ BAHÍA DE LA VENTANA
At Km 38, a paved road branches northeast off BCS 286 and leads eight kilometers (5 mi) and 11 kilometers (6.8 mi), respectively, to the neighboring fishing villages of La Ventana and El Sargento on Bahía de la Ventana. About 1,000 people live here year-round, but the towns fill with American and Canadian windsurfers—and more recently, kiteboarders—during winter months. Wind sports are exceptionally good at La Ventana because of the strong *El Norte* northeasterlies channeled through Canal de Cerralvo to the north.

When the winds aren't blowing, onshore and inshore fishing is good all the way along the L-shaped bay; farther offshore in the Canal de Cerralvo, catches of marlin, skipjack, and dorado are common in the summer. The gently sloped beach offers easy small-boat launching. If you don't fish, the bayshore still makes

a worthwhile destination for camping, swimming, diving, and snorkeling, especially in the spring and fall (summers are hot). Isla Cerralvo lies about 16 kilometers (10 mi) offshore. Boats can easily be launched from the beach here.

The word is out on La Ventana, and the area is experiencing the beginnings of a real estate boom, with dozens of properties for sale, and many new buildings taking shape each year.

Windsurfing and Kiteboarding
Windsurfers discovered the ideal conditions at La Ventana a decade or two ago, but in recent years, the rising popularity of kiteboarding has brought many more adventure-seeking travelers to the area. Kiteboarders say La Ventana is

© STEPHANIE HARGRAVE

the view from Mokie's *casitas*

one of the best places in the world to learn the sport, because the shoreline of the bay curves around to catch those who drift downwind on white sand beaches. Experienced windsurfers say the wind at La Ventana isn't as strong as at Los Barriles, but it tends to be more consistent. The wind typically picks up around 11 A.M. and holds steady until just before sunset.

Several shops along the bay rent gear and offer lessons for windsurfing and kiteboarding. (They'll also come get you up if you have trouble staying upwind.) One of the first to set up shop in the early nineties was **Captain Kirk's Windsurfing** (U.S. tel. 310/833-3397, www.captainkirks.com), with headquarters in Los Angeles. The shop also rents a two-bedroom home with kitchen (US$275/day) and a *casita* with two double beds and bath (US$149/day). Rentals come with free use of mountain bikes, sea kayaks, and snorkeling equipment. A windsurfing or kiteboarding gear package is US$50.

With headquarters in Hood River, Oregon, the **New Wind Kite School** (U.S. tel. 541/387-2440, www.newwindkiteboarding.com, Nov.

15–Mar. 15) offers lessons for new and experienced kiteboarders (US$195–280/day, depending on the number of students). Custom instruction runs US$101 for one person for two hours. Board rentals cost US$40, but the school doesn't typically rent kites. This school also has a beach house next door. An upstairs room has its own bath and balcony, with access to a kitchen downstairs (US$89). Store your gear and use the air compressor to inflate your kite for free.

British Columbia–based **Elevation Kiteboarding School** (Canada tel. 604/848-5197, www.elevationkiteboarding.com) offers private lessons for CDN$100/hour and multiday kiteboarding camp packages. **Sheldon Kiteboarding** (U.S. tel. 707/374-3053, www.sheldonkiteboarding.com) provides beds and mattresses, a shared kitchen, and bath with a hot water shower. Bring your own sleeping bag.

Baja Adventures at Ventana Bay Resort replaces its rental gear each season, selling the previous year's equipment at reduced prices. In 2007, the shop had stocked up on 2007 North sails (3.7–6.7), 2007 Mistral Explosion, Syncros, and Screamers for boards, and custom boards by Open Ocean. Kiteboarding equipment includes North Rhino, Vegas, and Rebel kites and North Jamie Pros kiteboards. You can also rent K2 full suspension mountain bikes from the shop.

Scuba Diving

Palapas Ventana (tel. 612/114-0198, www. palapasventana.com) has opened a certified PADI dive shop onsite, for leading guided trips to Isla Cerralvo. The 26-foot super-*panga* has a four-stroke engine and takes up to six divers per trip. Scuba certification packages are available. Captain Tavo is a shark fisherman and dive instructor. Several of the windsurfing and kiteboarding resorts dabble in scuba trips, as well (see *Isla Cerralvo*).

Accommodations

Located about a half mile past El Sargento, the **Ventana Bay Resort** (tel. 612/128-4333, U.S. tel. 800/533-8452, www.ventanabay.com, US$110–140) completed its second phase of construction in late 2006 and now counts a few new rooms, plus an office, shop, and bar. Its bungalow-style guestrooms are set around a clubhouse, along with about a dozen private homes, a restaurant, bar, and full-service windsurfing, kiteboarding, and dive shop operated by Baja Adventures. The eco resort also offers kayaking, Hobie Cat sailing, mountain biking, sportfishing, and snorkeling. Room rates include breakfast and lunch. A seven-day package includes accommodations, two meals per day, and unlimited use of recreation equipment. Rates run US$695 for a "sports package," US$725 for a windsurfing package, and US$850 for a kiteboarding package. Wireless Internet is available at additional cost. The resort also manages a few of the private homes as vacation rentals.

Between La Ventana and El Sargento, **Palapas Ventana** (tel. 612/114-0198, www .palapasventana.com) has two types of newly constructed *palapa*-roof casitas. Regular ones sleep two in a king or two twin beds with shared shower and bath and no air conditioning (US$55 pp double occupancy). Specialty *casitas* sleep four

(in one room) with private tiled bath and air conditioning (US$77.50 pp double occupancy). Extra touches include high ceilings (with fans), Mission-style furnishings, hammocks, purified water dispensers, and rain showers. Also onsite are a dive shop, gated parking area, Internet café, and restaurant. Stay-and-dive packages include five days/four nights of accommodations; three days of diving (two tanks per day); breakfast everyday and lunch on dive days; and free use of kayak, snorkeling gear, and sailboat.

Mokie's (www.mokies.com) rents studio and one-bedroom (US$550/wk or US$1,500/mo) *casitas* on 3.5 fenced acres fronting the beach. Both *casitas* come with full-size bed, kitchen (including margarita glasses), two full-size futons, bath with large shower, mountain and sea views, and an outdoor terrace. Guests store their gear in a beachfront loft just 30 feet from the water's edge, or walk to shops that rent gear and offer lessons. When not on the water, enjoy a partially shaded beachfront terrace has a glass wall for shelter from the wind. Pay by credit card via PayPal.

Kurt-n-Marina (tel. 612/114-0010, U.S. tel. 509/590-1409, www.ventanakiteboarding. com) offer several *casitas* with *palapa* roofs and tiled baths, as well as camping and a shared outdoor kitchen.

Comfortable beds are a plus in relatively new and very clean rooms at **❰ Casa Verde** (tel. 612/114-0214, U.S. tel. 509/590-4595, www. bahmahal.com, US$90). Enjoy natural light, private baths, small refrigerators, and seaviews in each one. Three Native American Lodges are set up for camping (US$30/40 s/d); guests may use a main kitchen or garden kitchen and shared bath with hot showers. Bikes, kayaks, and wireless Internet are included as well.

Steps from the sea, **Baja Joe's** (tel. 612/114-0001, www.bajajoe.com) has several *palapa*-roof cabins for rent (US$70–100). Some share a bath; others have their own. All have air conditioning and a small refrigerator. RV cabanas have private kitchens, and economical bunkhouse rooms go for US$30/40 s/d, with use of a shared outdoor kitchen and one of six baths on the property. Rates include mountain bikes, sea kayaks, snorkel equipment, and a storage area for gear. Baja

casita for rent

Joe's also manages a few private beach houses (US$600–1,200/week). No children under four. Discounts for long-term stays. Baja Joe's rents windsurfing (US$25/hour or US$40/day) and kiteboarding equipment as well.

La Ventana Campground, along the beach just north of the village of La Ventana, offers simple tent/camper sites, trash barrels, toilets, and showers for US$5 a night. Playas Miramar also offers sites for US$5, with no hookups but flush toilets.

Food

Each winter season brings a new wave of eateries to these sleepy bayside towns. Expect to find several small grocery stores (no supermarkets), a few traditional Mexican restaurants, several newer gringo establishments, a number of taquerías, and a *tortillería* (on the paved part of the road in El Sargento). Prices are generally low, and the atmosphere is casual. Mango margaritas at the Ventana Bay Resort clubhouse get especially high marks. If you plan to cook most of your own meals, stock up on supplies in La Paz.

Two hundred yards south of the trailer park, **Rincon del Bahia** (mains US$7–13) serves tasty seafood and Mexican fare on the beach. Owner Joaquin will serenade you while you dine. Fifty yards south of Palapas Ventana, **Tacos Rafa** grills fish tacos for US$6–13. The restaurant at **Palapas Ventana** (Fri.–Sat., mains US$8–13) prepares lasagna, steaks, BBQ ribs, fresh grilled fish, and you can enjoy local wines or an icy margarita. Reservations are recommended. **Ventanas del Sol** (mains US$6–12) is the place for ceviche and chicken mole, with a pool table and bar. Look for **Tacos en la Torre** (mains US$4–7) at the base of the radio tower in El Sargento, with a menu of *chilaquiles, tortas cubanas,* and flautas. On the west side of the road in El Sargento, **Tacos Leon** has hot dogs, *papas rellenas,* and enchiladas for US$4–10. Popular with RV park residents, **Viento del Norte** (mains US$4–9) serves hearty breakfasts, enchiladas, and jumbo margaritas.

Information and Services

Many local resorts and campgrounds now

have wireless Internet; some offer it for free, while others charge for access. Across from the main beachfront campground, **El Norte Restaurant** has satellite Internet for US$3/30 minutes. Use the restaurant's computers or bring your own. Mobile phones work here but get spotty signals. There are public pay phones here as well; pick up a Ladatel card at one of the mini-supers. **Palapas Ventana** has long-distance service.

Near the end of the pavement in El Sargento are a hardware store, mechanic, pharmacy, and Internet café, as well as **Miscelania Lupita.** A couple of launderettes offer drop-off or self service. El Sargento also has a Centro de Salud (Public Health Clinic) and a place where you can buy barrel gas.

ISLA CERRALVO

Across Bahía de la Ventana and Canal de Cerralvo lies Isla Cerralvo, one of the largest islands in the Sea of Cortez. At the time of early Spanish exploration, the island held large pearl-oyster beds and was inhabited by a small group of Pericú. Later, the rugged island reportedly became a favored final resting place for the *vagabundos del mar,* Amerindians who roamed the Sea of Cortez in dugout canoes until well into the 20th century.

Today Cerralvo remains one of the least visited of Baja's large coastal islands, simply because of its location on the far side of the Península de Pichilingue. Coral-encrusted **Roca Montaña,** off the southeastern tip of the island, is an excellent diving and fishing location, as is **Piedras Gordas,** marked by a navigation light at the southwestern tip. Depths at these sites range 3–15 meters (10–50 ft). Other good dive sites include the rock reefs off the northern end (average depth 18–21 m/60–70 ft), which feature a good variety of reef fishes, sea turtles, and shipwrecks. One of the reefs, **Arrecife de la Foca,** features an unidentified shipwreck with "Mazatlán" marked on the hull. **La Reina,** another reef at the north end of the island, is the site of a large steel-hulled freighter that sank a half century ago. Barely a hundred meters off the

island's west shore are two adjacent rock reefs known as **La Reinita.**

Access to Isla Cerralvo is easiest from Bahía de la Ventana or Punta Arenas, where beach launches are possible. From La Paz, it's a long haul around the Península de Pichilingue via Canal de San Lorenzo.

SAN JUAN DE LOS PLANES

Los Planes, as it's usually called, has several markets, a café, *dulcería, tortillería,* taxi stand, and around 1,500 inhabitants supported by farming (cotton, tomatoes, beans, and corn) or by fishing at nearby bays. There is a Pemex station where the road from San Antonio joins Mexico 286. During the windy season, dust blowing from cultivated fields on either side of the highway can cause a complete whiteout. Once you leave the main drag in Los Planes, there is little in the way of commercial businesses until you reach the Giggling Marlin on Bahía de los Muertos.

BAHÍA DE LOS MUERTOS

A graded road running east 21 kilometers (13 mi) from San Juan de los Planes leads to a pretty, curved bay. Historians don't know why a 1777 Spanish map named this shore "Bay of the Dead," but the name gained substance when a Chinese ship beached here in 1885. The ship had been refused entry at La Paz harbor because the crew was suffering from yellow fever; after putting in at this bay, all 18 crewmen died. Mexican fishermen buried the bodies above the tideline and marked their graves with wooden crosses, a few of which still stand. In the early 20th century, a community of American farmers tried unsuccessfully to cultivate the desert surrounding the bay; some died of thirst or hunger, adding to the bay's list of *muertos.*

Ensenada de los Muertos, an abandoned port at the north end of the bay, was built in the 1920s for the shipping of ore from El Triunfo mines in the Sierra de la Laguna.

Panga boats still line the shore, but the bay is changing little by little each year, as a 4,000-acre luxury real estate development takes shape to the south.

Bahía de los Sueños (Bay of Dreams)

When complete, the American-owned Bay of Dreams project will encompass an 18-hole golf course designed by Tom Doak, 432 homes, and 192 villas and condos. Inside the Bay of Dreams development, **Villas of Casa de los Sueños** sits on 25 landscaped acres with tennis courts, nine-hole golf course, multiple swimming pools, fitness facility, and a long list of luxury amenities including an onsite chef service and concierge. Its seven villas have king-size beds, rain showers, barbecues, satellite TV, wireless internet, and complimentary Internet calling to the United States. One-bedroom villas range US$450–700; two-bedrooms are US$650–1,200/night.

The crowd at the **Giggling Marlin Beach Club at Bay of Dreams** is much more sedate than at its parent bar and restaurant in Cabo San Lucas, though, should the mood strike, you can still get tangled upside down in its signature marlin hanging contraption.

PUNTA ARENAS DE LA VENTANA

A lesser road branches northeast about four kilometers before Los Muertos and leads eight kilometers (5 mi) to beautiful Punta Arenas de la Ventana and the abandoned **Las Arenas Resort.** The waters off Punta Arenas reputedly offer Baja's best roosterfish angling; wahoo, amberjack, grouper, dorado, and billfish are also in abundant supply. Guided *panga* trips may be available from the beach next to the resort, where local *pangeros* moor their boats, for US$60–85 per day. A bit south of the resort, off **Punta Perico** (Parakeet Point), is a lively reef with varied depths of 3–25 meters (10–82 ft).

The private **Aeromar las Arenas** airfield

offers tie down service and 24-hour security for guests of the Bay of Dreams resort.

GETTING THERE

Most travelers reach La Ventana by rental car or private vehicle (35–40 minutes from downtown La Paz, and about 45 minutes from the airport), but shuttles and bus service are available. A one-way shuttle from the La Paz airport to La Ventana runs US$120 (US$350 from Los Cabos). Pubic transportation is less expensive, but more complicated: First, you must get from the airport to the La Ventana bus stop (a US$15 cab ride). From there, you can catch a US$5 bus that leaves daily at 2 P.M.

Bahía de los Muertos can be reached from the south via a 47-kilometer (30-mi) dirt road between Los Barriles and San Juan de los Planes. The road is wide and flat from Los Barriles as far as Punta Pescadero and El Cardonal—13 kilometers (8 mi) and 22 kilometers (14 mi), respectively. North of El Cardonal, the road begins to rise along the Mesa Boca Alamo, eventually cutting inland and ascending steeply into the jagged, red Sierra El Carrizalito. Several kilometers of the road here wind around narrow, adrenaline-pumping curves with steep dropoffs. Contrary to popular belief, four-wheel drive is not a necessity for this section of road, but careful driving and good road clearance are. Twenty-four kilometers (15 mi) from El Cardonal, the road leaves the mountains and meets the paved end of BCS 286.

San Juan de los Planes, La Ventana, Punta Arenas de la Ventana, and Bahía de los Muertos can also be reached from Mexico 1 via a graded, unpaved road from San Antonio. (Construction was underway in 2007 to pave this stretch of road.) The road's east end begins on BCS 286 about 3.5 kilometers (2.2 mi) south of the turnoff for La Ventana and El Sargento.

EAST CAPE AND THE SIERRA DE LA LAGUNA

The promise of calm seas, steady winds, and abundant game fish lures many adventure-seekers away from the resorts of Los Cabos to the remote beaches and rocky points of the Cabo del Este, or East Cape. Indeed, the opportunities for deep-sea fishing, windsurfing, kayaking, and scuba diving here are among the best in the world. And when you've had your fill of white-sand beach and salty air, the Sierra de la Laguna beckons, with 7,000-foot peaks, freshwater springs, and waterfalls.

In September 2006, Hurricane John made landfall at Bahía de Los Frailes, causing severe wind and flood damage. Although roofs and roads took a beating, the towns in its path had mostly recovered by year-end.

PLANNING YOUR TIME

Towns along the East Cape are small and don't take much time to explore; you could easily take in a little of each in a four- to five-day trip. However, if you've come to the East Cape for a specific activity, such as fishing, diving, or windsurfing, you'll likely want to stay in one place for a while. If fishing is your top priority, then it makes sense to stay in Los Barriles or Buena Vista and add a day of diving. But if diving is the draw, best to head north or south to be closer to the dive sites. And if you plan to drive along the coastal road, as opposed to Highway 1, note that the unpaved 77-kilometer (48-mi) stretch between El Rincón and San José del Cabo can take up

© PAUL ITOI

HIGHLIGHTS

◖ Bahía de Palmas: Anglers, kiteboarders, and windsurfers all find paradise in the Sea of Cortez near Los Barriles and Buena Vista (page 292).

◖ Cabo Pulmo: Reef-building corals, crystal waters, and white-sand beaches attract divers, snorkelers, and kayakers to Bahía Pulmo and Playa La Sirenita (page 306).

◖ Gorda Banks: Six miles from shore, this pair of seamounts draws anglers from across the world for unrivaled marlin and wahoo fishing (page 313).

◖ San Bartolo: A pleasant central Cape Region settlement overlooking a lush arroyo makes a perfect stopover on the drive from La Paz to Los Barriles (page 316).

◖ Cañon de la Zorra: At the edge of the Sierra de la Laguna, near Santiago, a 30-foot waterfall plunges over smooth granite rock into a swimmable lagoon below (page 321).

LOOK FOR ◖ TO FIND RECOMMENDED SIGHTS, ACTIVITIES, DINING, AND LODGING.

EAST CAPE

to four hours, depending on your vehicle and its ability to handle washboard roads.

Santiago, at the foothills of the Sierra de la Laguna, is an easy day trip from San José del Cabo, or a good place to stretch your legs during the drive between San José and La Paz. Allow 3–5 nights if you want to explore the backcountry of the Sierra de la Laguna.

East Cape

Consisting of a succession of scenic arid-tropical coves and beaches along the Sea of Cortez, the East Cape extends from the northern end of Bahía de Palmas south to San José del Cabo, at the tip of the Cape. Below La Ribera, several tiny seaside communities remain off the grid—though mainstream power and phone service loom in the not-too-distant future. Coastal development is ongoing from Buena Vista to Cabo San Lucas, with land prices skyrocketing in recent years. Most of these developments resemble Southern California–style subdivisions, complete with signed gate, paved entrance, and concrete curbs. But few, if any, of the developments are fully built yet. So aside from the gates and model homes, many parts of the coast still look pretty secluded; the challenge is finding access to the sea.

There are a few remaining spots where the fishing and camping are free. The coastline north of El Cardonal as far as Bahía de los Muertos (also called Bahía de los Sueños, or Bay of Dreams, by optimistic developers) remains relatively untouched. But although beaches are officially public, access is increasingly limited.

◖ BAHÍA DE PALMAS

The gently curving shore of Bahía de Palmas, stretching 32 kilometers (20 mi) from Punta Pescadero south to Punta Arenas, began its commercial life in the 1960s as a fishing resort accessible only by yacht or private plane. Now that the Transpeninsular Highway swerves to within a couple miles of the bay, it has become a full-fledged fishing and windsurfing mecca.

In many places along the bay, anglers can reach the 100-fathom line less than a mile from shore, especially toward Punta Pescadero (Fisherman's Point) at the north end. (See *Fishing* in the *Essentials* chapter for details on common catches.) The world-famous "Tuna Canyon," about 6.5 kilometers (4 mi) directly south of Punta Pescadero, reaches depths of 50 fathoms and has a year-round population of sizable yellowfin tuna; rocks along Tuna Canyon's submerged walls tend to cut the lines of all but the most skilled sportfishers. Guided fishing trips, arranged at any of the hotels along the bay, cost US$200–260 a day for a *panga*, US$200–325 a day aboard a fishing cruiser. Launch trailered or cartopped boats off sandy beaches or at the boat ramp just north of the Hotel Buena Vista Beach Resort (see *Buena Vista*).

Windsurfers and kiteboarders flock to Los Barriles November–April when sideshore winds—collectively called *El Norte* and aided by thermals from the Sierra de la Laguna—blow 18–30 knots for weeks at a time. The rest of the year, you'll have to settle for around 12–14 knots—not too shabby. During the high-wind season, inshore water temperatures average 22–24°C (72–75°F), with air temperatures in the 25–29°C (78–85°F) range. The same basic conditions can be found all the way north to El Cardonal. Several hotels on the bay rent equipment and provide basic instruction.

With such favorable recreational conditions, it's little wonder that legions of *norteamericano* anglers, boaters, and windsurfers are buying up property along the bay to build vacation and retirement homes. The Barriles–Buena Vista area is starting to look like a San Diego suburb. Several roads branch east off Mexico 1 between Km 110 and 105 to hotels and trailer parks—most owned by foreigners—scattered along the central section of Bahía de Palmas. Because zoning regulations are virtually nonexistent, construction varies from flimsy *palapa* extensions to impressive beach homes. Those seeking more solitude and less development can head north of Los Barriles to Punta Pescadero at the northern end of Bahía de Palmas, or farther north to El Cardonal.

PUNTA PESCADERO AND EL CARDONAL

There are now two ways to reach the northern end of Bahía de Palmas and the southern end of Bahía de los Muertos: A sandy, washboard

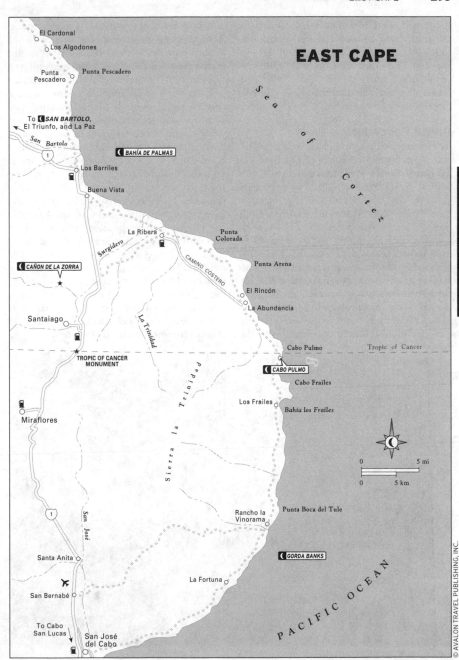

EAST CAPE

El Cardonal
Los Algodones
Punta Pescadero
Punta Pescadero

Sea of Cortez

To (SAN BARTOLO,
El Triunfo, and La Paz

San Bartolo
1
(BAHÍA DE PALMAS
Los Barriles
Buena Vista

La Ribera
Surgidero
Punta Colorada

CAMINO COSTERO
Punta Arena

(CAÑON DE LA ZORRA
★
El Rincón
La Abundancia

Santaiago
La Trinidad

Cabo Pulmo
Tropic of Cancer

TROPIC OF CANCER
MONUMENT
(CABO PULMO
Cabo Frailes

Los Frailes
Bahía los Frailes

Miraflores
Sierra la Trinidad

0   5 mi
0   5 km

San José

Punta Boca del Tule

Rancho la Vinorama

(GORDA BANKS

Santa Anita
San José

La Fortuna

San Bernabé
PACIFIC OCEAN

To Cabo San Lucas
San José del Cabo

EAST CAPE

road heads north from Los Barriles—look for a turnoff from Mexico 1 signed Punta Pescadero. The road crosses a couple of arroyos that could be problematic in heavy rains. Alternatively, a relatively new, paved road continues along an inland route from Los Barriles directly to El Cardonal.

Punta Pescadero

At the extreme north end of Bahía de Palmas (13.6 km/8.5 mi north of Los Barriles), **Hotel Punta Pescadero** (tel. 612/141-0101, U.S. tel. 800/426-2252, www.puntapescadero.com, US$150) is a small fishing resort on 125 palm-studded acres overlooking a sandy beach. The resort is popular with private pilots, since it has a paved landing strip (1,065 m/3,500 ft, Unicom 122.8, US$25 landing fee), and you'll likely hear regular fly-in guests trading stories at the bar. (As at other Baja airfields, plane theft is a very real concern here; throttle locks and prop chains are essential. Contact Baja Bush Pilots, www.bajabushpilots.com, for more information. Baja Bush Pilot

and AAA discounts available.) A small housing development is growing up next to the airstrip, so the Punta Pescadero's once-secluded nature is changing, but compared to the congestion of Los Barriles, it remains off the beaten track.

Each of 21 spacious rooms comes with a seaview, private veranda, air conditioning, satellite TV, and refrigerator; some have cathedral ceilings and fireplaces (quite nice on winter evenings), and all were renovated in 2005. King-size beds are made in crisp white linens with fluffy pillows and down comforters. During the windy season, ask for a room that faces southwest for a terrace that's sheltered from the El Norte gusts. A gracious staff speaks excellent English, and public areas include a restaurant with large picture windows, outdoor patio dining, dive shop with compressor, small pool, lighted tennis court, and rental equipment for scuba and free diving, boating, and fishing. Petroglyphs are visible in nearby rock caves that once served as Amerindian burial sites. The unpaved side road out to the actual point is not recommended for RVs or trailers.

view from Punta Pescadero

© PAUL ITOI

El Cardonal

A new, paved highway makes it much easier and faster to reach El Cardonal, located past Punta Pescadero and technically at the south end of Bahía de los Muertos (23 km/14 mi from Los Barriles). Inshore coral heads here provide worthwhile underwater scenery, while nearby prehistoric cave paintings reportedly depict marlin, turtles, and human figures.

The Canadian-owned **El Cardonal's Hide-A-Way** (tel./fax 612/141-0040, www.elcardonal.net) offers six sparsely furnished suites for US$72/482 per night/week as well as spaces for RV and tent camping. Each of the large beachfront studios comes with two full-size beds, a sofa, kitchen, and ceiling fan. Small campers and tent camping on large campsites costs US$10 per day; sites with electricity and water only are US$12; full hookups cost US$13. A dump station is available, as are fishing boats (*pangas* and a 32-foot cruiser), hot-water showers, a 24-hour restaurant, launderette, public telephone, horseshoe pit, badminton court, picnic tables, ice, and rental shop with equipment for fishing, windsurfing, diving, kayaking, and snorkeling.

Beyond El Cardonal, the road continues northward along the coast, then west across the Sierra El Carrizalito to San Juan de los Planes (see *Southeast of La Paz*).

LOS BARRILES

The defining image of day-to-day life in Los Barriles these days is that of early retirees happily speeding along dirt roads on ATVs, which they ride to the supermarket, the hardware store, the beach, and everywhere in between. No longer the sole domain of sports fishermen and windsurfers, the town has broadened its appeal with more guest accommodations, restaurants, and services—and a vibe that is friendly and relaxed.

A strip mall on the main access road from Mexico 1 is the defacto town center, with another row of commercial businesses along Calle 20 de Noviembre, heading north to Punta Pescadero. A row of gringo McMansions front the beach behind a stone retaining wall, and several

© PAUL ITOI

rolling dock at Los Barriles

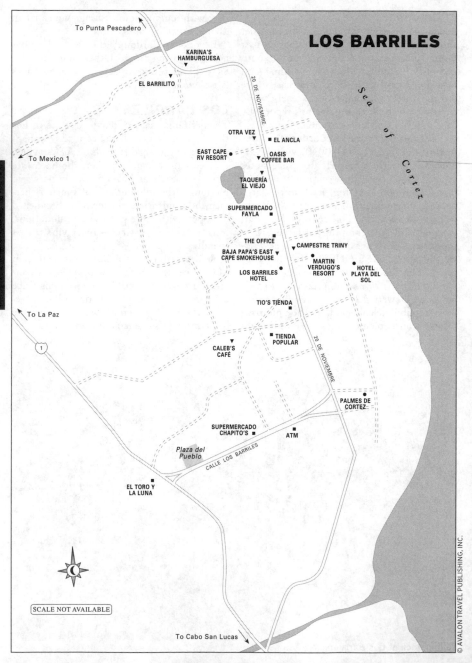

LOS BARRILES

To Punta Pescadero

KARINA'S
HAMBURGUESA

EL BARRILITO

20 DE NOVIEMBRE

Sea of Cortez

OTRA VEZ

EL ANCLA

To Mexico 1

EAST CAPE
RV RESORT

OASIS
COFFEE BAR

TAQUERÍA
EL VIEJO

SUPERMERCADO
FAYLA

THE OFFICE

CAMPESTRE TRINY

BAJA PAPA'S EAST
CAPE SMOKEHOUSE

MARTIN
VERDUGO'S
RESORT

HOTEL
PLAYA DEL
SOL

LOS BARRILES
HOTEL

To La Paz

TIO'S TIENDA

1

TIENDA
POPULAR

20 DE NOVIEMBRE

CALEB'S
CAFÉ

PALMES DE
CORTEZ

SUPERMERCADO
CHAPITO'S

ATM

Plaza del
Pueblo

CALLE LOS BARRILES

EL TORO Y
LA LUNA

SCALE NOT AVAILABLE

To Cabo San Lucas

developments are in varying stages of completion in the hills above and to the north of town. However, those in search of the "real" Baja should not despair; Los Barriles retains an authentic *tortillería,* plus roosters that roam the streets, a cement factory where blocks are still made by hand, numerous taco stands, and countless other family-owned businesses. Local Mexicans know each other by their *sobrenombres* (nicknames), and the untamed backcountry is just minutes away.

Windsurfing

During the high-wind season, November–March, hotels in Los Barriles can arrange package deals that include windsurfing seminars, use of state-of-the-art equipment, air transportation, and accommodations. Keep in mind that although lessons are typically geared to your level, wind and surf conditions at Los Barriles are best enjoyed by experienced boardsailors rather than novices.

Vela Windsurf Resort

Fishing

Martin Verdugo's Resort and the Hotel Palmas de Cortez offer fishing packages; the concierge at the Hotel Palmas de Cortez can arrange fishing trips for guests and nonguests. In addition, **Congo's Awesome Sportfishing** (tel. 624/141-0231, U.S. tel. 208/726-1955, www. awesome-fishing.com), headquartered at the East Cape RV Resort and run by Jeronimo "Congo" Casio, operates two cruisers, a 30-foot island hopper (US$450 for 1–4 anglers) and a 32-foot Blackfin sportfisher (US$600 for 1–4 anglers). A popular day trip when the conditions aren't too windy is to travel north by boat to Bahía de los Muertos, fish on the way, and stop for lunch at the Giggling Marlin.

East Cape Tackle (Plaza del Pueblo, www. eastcapetackle.com, Mon.–Fri. 9 A.M.–5 P.M., Sat. 9 A.M.–2 P.M.) sells bait and tackle and also rents surf rods, pole spears, and snorkeling gear; plus, you can pay with plastic.

Guided Tours

ATVs are a popular mode of transportation in Los Barriles. Inquire about rentals and tours at **Amigos ATV Tours** on the main access road (Calle Los Barriles near Plaza del Pueblo, tel. 624/141-0430, www.amigosactivities .com). Tours cost US$60–70 for a single rider, and US$75–90 for a double. Rental rates are US$20/100 per hour/day. Amigos also rents Wave-Runners and leads horseback rides and snorkeling tours. Other possibilities include hikes, bird-watching, mountain biking, and snorkeling. You can book any of these activities through the concierge at the Hotel Palmas de Cortez, whether or not you are staying at the resort.

Quadman, across from the Amerimed clinic, on the north side of Calle Los Barriles near the T intersection at 20 de Noviembre, also rents ATVs (US$50/4 hrs) and Rhinos (US$150/day and US$1,000 deposit). Rhinos seat four people and you must be 35 or older to drive. ATVs have racks for fishing poles, though riders must stay at least 60 feet from the high tide line to protect turtle nests.

Spa Services

Above the gym in the Hotel Palmas de Cortez, at the end of Calle Los Barriles, **Spa de Cortez** (tel. 624/141-0050 ext. 616, massagewithchristene@hotmail.com) offers Swedish, therapeutic, and sports massage, plus aromatherapy, body scrubs, facials, and waxing services. A one-hour massage is US$80, and a 90-minute treatment is US$115.

Shopping

Tío's Tienda (20 de Noviembre, approximately one block north of Calle Los Barriles, daily 7:30 A.M.–10 P.M.), next door to Tío Pablo's, carries everything from fishing tackle and souvenirs to apparel, gift wrap, and office supplies. It also stocks one of the most impressive collections of books about Baja California found on either side of the border. Many of the titles are self-published memoirs written by gringo transplants; others are field guides, travel books, and novels that take place in Mexico. **Baja Beach Company** (Plaza del Pueblo, Mon.–Fri. 9 A.M.–5 P.M., Sat. till 3 P.M., Sun. till 1 P.M.), in the strip mall near Buzzard Bay, has ceramics, textiles, gifts, and a few books and maps. Back on the highway, across from the main entrance to town, **El Toro y La Luna** (Mexico 1 Entrada a Los Barriles, tel. 624/141-0696, www.eltoroylaluna.net, daily 8 A.M.–5 P.M.) carries ceramic sinks, tiles, and other home furnishings.

Accommodations

Choices of accommodations in Los Barriles include two all-inclusive hotels, several hotels and RV parks, and private vacation homes available for rent either by the owner or through a property manager.

US$50-100: Martin Verdugo's Beach Resort (20 de Noviembre, approximately one block north of Calle Los Barriles, tel. 612/141-0054, www.verdugosbeachresort.com, US$60–70) has updated air-conditioning units in each of its 29 well-kept rooms, located in a two-story hotel next to the beach. Facilities include a small pool, boat launch, and restaurant. Kitchenettes are a plus here (though not in every room), but when the wind is blowing hard, the pool at the Los Barriles Hotel offers more shelter.

Off the beach but within walking distance to restaurants and shops, the exceptionally clean **⊂ Los Barriles Hotel** (20 de Noviembre, approximately one block north of Calle Los Barriles, tel. 624/141-0024, www.losbarrileshotel.com, US$53) looks unremarkable from the outside, but feels something like a well-kept Swiss chalet inside. It has 20 spacious rooms set around a swimming pool, each with high ceilings, two firm but comfortable queen-size beds, large tiled showers, and remote-controlled air conditioning. Minimal but quality furnishings include rustic wooden dressers, tables, and headboards. A cedar hot tub is the latest addition to the pool area. Popular with families, this hotel is a great value for the price.

All-Inclusive: The Van Wormer family runs two all-inclusive resorts in Los Barriles: **Hotel Playa del Sol** (tel. 624/141-0050, U.S. tel. 877/777-8862, www.vanwormerresorts.com, US$120–130), on the beach off 20 de Noviembre north of Calle Los Barriles, has 26 air-conditioned rooms, an oceanfront pool, tennis and volleyball courts, an outdoor terrace restaurant, bar with satellite TV, rental gear (for fishing, kayaking, mountain biking, and windsurfing), charter boats for sportfishing (US$220–300 per day, not including fishing permits), and a full-service Vela windsurfing center. The hotel is closed in September.

On the beach at the end of Calle Los Barriles, about 300 meters south of Hotel Playa del Sol and just a half mile off the highway, the all-inclusive **Hotel Palmas de Cortez** (tel. 624/141-0050, U.S. tel. 877/777-8862, www.vanwormerresorts.com, US$190–220) offers 50 poolside, oceanfront, and garden-view rooms, plus several cabanas and condos that sleep up to six guests. Facilities include a restaurant and bar, ping pong tables, driving range, infinity pool, tennis and racquetball courts, an 868-meter (2,850-ft) landing strip (Unicom 122.8), windsurfing gear, charter boats (US$250–660, not including fishing permits), and equipment for fishing. The Van Wormer family also runs the Hotel Punta Colorada farther south along the East Cape.

Vela Windsurf Resort (U.S./Canada tel. 831/461-0820 or 800/223-5443, www.velawindsurf.com) is based at the Hotel Playa del

TO BUY OR NOT TO BUY: TIPS FOR PURCHASING REAL ESTATE IN BAJA

It started as a trickle, and by 2003 had progressed into a full-scale land rush. As Mexican law and real estate services make it easier for foreigners to own property, many Baja-bound Americans and Canadians are answering the call.

1. THE TERMS

Foreigners can only purchase coastal property (within 31 miles of the coast) in Mexico through a limited real estate trust *(fideicomisos)*. Trusts are renewable every 50 years, with no limit on the number of renewals. In most cases, you will need a Mexican real estate attorney to complete a transaction.

2. FINANCING

You can finance the purchase through several lenders: Mortgages are now available for financing up to 70 percent of appraised property values with terms of 15-20 years. Lending rates run around 3 percent higher than in the United States, and closing costs for a mortgage deal are high.

Some sellers ask that the full purchase price be paid up front. Because a large number of gringos buy land in Mexico with cash, some Mexicans assume this is customary for all Americans and Canadians. Paying up front is not the typical procedure for Mexicans themselves, who usually make down payments and send in monthly time payments; mortgage terms similar to those found in Canada and the United States are available in Mexico, though they are difficult for nonresidents to obtain. Even if you have the cash, don't hand over more than half the full amount until you have the *fideicomiso* papers in hand.

3. TITLE INSURANCE

You can purchase title insurance, previously unavailable, from several providers.

4. PRICES

Prospective buyers can find small plots in subdivisions near the beach from US$20,000. Completed small vacation homes range US$200,000-500,000, and full-scale mansions are in the millions.

5. REAL ESTATE AGENTS

Choose a reputable agent: A lot of people get burned in Mexican real estate deals. It's best to deal through an established, reputable agent. Mexican tourist offices in Baja often carry information on residential property. Talk to current owner-residents about which real estate companies have the best and worst reputations.

6. CONDOS AND SUBDIVISIONS

In condominium and subdivision situations, a master *fideicomiso* is created. Only as the units are sold does the trust pass to the buyer, and then only if proper procedures are followed – which they often aren't. If you buy a condo or subdivision unit, you should receive a document naming you as beneficiary, thus transferring property from the master trust holder to the buyer. If you don't, you'll have to get the master trust holder's signature before you can sell or otherwise transfer the property to someone else.

7. DO YOUR HOMEWORK

Mexico doesn't require salespeople or brokers to obtain any sort of real estate license. Investigate agents and properties thoroughly before signing on the dotted line.

Sol. Seven-night packages start at US$945–1,280 and include all windsurfing equipment, instruction at every level except novice, accommodations, meals, tax, and service. Guests also have free use of kayaks and mountain bikes; the staff provides good maps and descriptions of nearby kayaking and biking routes. Snorkeling, tennis, and volleyball are also available through the center at no cost to package guests. Scuba diving, kiteboarding lessons, and horseback riding can be arranged at additional cost.

Vela opens just before Thanksgiving and closes the first week in March. Outside the center's peak period (Dec. 20–Jan. 20), nonpackage guests at Hotel Playa del Sol may be able to rent windsurfing boards, kayaks, and bikes.

Camping and RV Parks

A trendsetter among parks in Mexico, the **East Cape RV Resort** (tel. 624/141-0231, U.S. tel. 208/726-1955, www.eastcaperv.com) designed its property with big rigs in mind. Located a short walk from the beach, at the intersection of 20 de Noviembre and Ocean Drive (unmarked at last check), the resort has 51 spaces with full hookups for US$25/150/525 per night/week/month. Another dozen spaces with limited hookups are located in an adjacent palm garden that sometimes floods during the rainy season (US$18/105 per night/week). Bathrooms are modern and clean, and the wall around a new pool and hot tub got its first coat of paint in late 2006. High-speed wireless Internet costs US$4/15/40 per day/week/month. Washing machines and dryers require U.S. quarters. Owner Theresa Comber is the closest thing Los Barriles has to a chamber of commerce. Ask her for advice on day trips and activities in the area.

North of Hotel Playa del Sol, **Martin Verdugo's Beach Resort** (20 de Noviembre, approximately one block north of Calle Los Barriles, tel. 612/141-0054, www.verdugosbeachresort.com) caters to families and retirees with lower rates and a beachfront location. This well-run and well-maintained park has dump stations, flush toilets, showers, boat ramps, laundry facilities, and full hookups for

US$15 for two people, plus US$3.50 for each additional person. Weekly/monthly rates are US$100/345 (credit cards are accepted). Tent sites cost US$12 per night. Kids play Marco Polo in the beachfront swimming pool, and locals gather for breakfast in the third-story restaurant. Fishing rates are US$380 for a 28-foot cruiser and US$240 for a 23-foot super-*panga*. Inquire about fishing packages that include accommodations and meals, and be sure to make reservations well in advance during the peak windsurfing season, January–March.

Another big-rig-friendly park, **Playa Norte RV Haven** (harnecker@gmail.com, US$18–22), on the beach off Calle 20 de Noviembre, past the wide arroyo, has upgraded its infrastructure in recent years to include hot showers, electricity, a dump station, and Wi-Fi. Caravans are welcome.

Free primitive camping is available in the area north of these parks, usually referred to by gringos as Playa Norte.

Vacation Rentals

Many American owners rent their Baja vacation homes by the night, week, or month. **East Cape Property Management and Vacation Rentals** (Plaza del Pueblo, tel./fax 612/141-0381, www.abajavacation.com, Mon.–Sat. 10 A.M.–2 P.M.) handles rental properties in Los Barriles, Buena Vista, Punta Pescadero, Rancho Leonero, and Los Frailes. **Sunset Rentals** (20 de Noviembre, just past the Hotel Los Barriles, tel. 624/141-0416) offers short- and long-term rentals in studios as well as one- and two-bedroom condos. All have kitchens, garages, balconies, wireless Internet, and air conditioning. **Vacation Rentals by Owner** (www.vrbo.com) also has a few dozen East Cape listings. Rates range US$75–195 a night for one-bedroom homes.

Food

The number and variety of restaurants in Los Barriles is multiplying by the day. Today's menus feature grilled fish and meats, traditional Mexican *platos,* pasta, sushi, pizza, sandwiches, soups, espresso, and, of course, mouthwatering tacos.

© PAUL ITOI

fiesta in Los Barriles

Restaurants: In a strip mall just off Mexico 1 on the access road to Los Barriles, **Buzzard Bay Sports Cantina** (Plaza del Pueblo 21, daily for lunch and dinner, mains US$7–15) offers a menu of burgers, sandwiches, appetizers, and Mexican food, and has both outdoor and indoor seating. Next door, **Baja Pizza Kitchen** (Plaza del Pueblo 19, tel. 624/150-8372, Mon.–Fri. 4 P.M.–8 P.M.) makes pizzas during limited hours. A small pizza costs US$7 and a large is US$15.

Tío Pablo's (20 de Noviembre, tel. 612/142-1214, daily 11 A.M.–10 P.M., mains US$7–20), on the main north–south road through Los Barriles, is a large, smartly designed *palapa*-style structure with ceiling fans, a well-stocked bar, sports TV, and a menu of salads, sandwiches, and burgers. In the same complex, Tío's takeout window offers pizzas to go.

Martin Verdugo's Restaurant (20 de Noviembre, approximately one block north of Calle Los Barriles, tel. 612/141-0054, daily 6 A.M.–noon, mains US$4–7) is a third-story restaurant that serves Americanized breakfast fare. *Chilaquiles* arrive smothered in melted cheese but without the signature *queso fresco* on top. Omelets come with seasoned hash browns and a choice of toast or tortillas. Seaviews and air conditioning are the main draw. Service is friendly, though slow even by Mexican standards.

Run by the same owners as the once-famous Restaurant Balandra in Cabo San Lucas, which closed more than 30 years ago, **Campestre Triny** (20 de Noviembre across from the East Cape Smokehouse, daily noon–10 P.M., mains US$9–20) offers freshly prepared traditional Mexican fare, including specialties of *huachinango frito* (whole fried red snapper), paella, and imperial shrimp. High-quality ingredients and a somewhat upscale presentation are reflected in menu prices. This is also one of the few places in town that serves Negro Modelo beer. Dine family-style under a canopy of trees behind the main house or at your own table on the porch. Check out the collection of arrowheads hanging on the wall while you're there.

About a quarter mile farther on 20 de Noviembre, **Otra Vez** (20 de Noviembre, tel. 612/141-0249, Mon.–Sat. 5–10 P.M., mains US$8–20) occupies a long, low, whitewashed building with a colorful arch out front. Popular with local gringos, the menu includes freshly prepared parrot fish, burgers, steaks, fresh salads, and pasta dishes.

Another favorite among locals for dinner, **(El Barrilito** (20 de Noviembre, daily for lunch and dinner, mains US$6–15) serves large portions of fresh seafood under a large *palapa* at the bend in the road heading out toward Pescadero. Ceviche is a standout. In a smaller *palapa* next door, the same owners have opened **Kenichi Sushi & Bar,** with all-you-can-eat specials for US$20. More sushi can be found at **Yako's Sushi-Bar** (tel. 624/141-0050) in the Hotel Palmas de Cortez, on the beach at the end of Calle Los Barriles.

Antojitos **and Fast Food:** During American football season, you're likely to find a number of tourists watching the game at **Taquería El Viejo** (20 de Noviembre near El Oasis Coffee and Baja Land Deals, daily for breakfast and lunch). The restaurant has about a dozen shaded outdoor tables where you can enjoy a breakfast of eggs, omelets, or *chilaquiles* for US$5–6, tacos for US$1–2, and burgers for US$5. Lunch specials vary daily (US$7–8). **Taquería Los Barriles,** at the junction with the beach road, is packed all afternoon and evening for the great seafood and carne asada tacos; the breakfasts are cheap. The enormous super burros at **La Palma Taquería** are a great value, too. Look for the sign on a surfboard just off 20 de Noviembre near Tio Pablo's.

Across the street from El Barrilito, on the inside of the bend that turns to Pescadero, **Karina's Hamburguesas** serves carne asada, *papas rellenos,* and other quick meals from a restaurant cart.

Cafés: Oasis Coffee Bar (20 de Noviembre, past The Office) serves a US$2-cup of coffee, as well as hot and cold espresso drinks and smoothies for US$2–4. It shares the space with Baja Land Deals, so you can browse pictures of real estate for sale while you wait for your drink. High-speed wireless Internet service is free, and there are a few shaded tables outside.

Groceries: Closer to Los Barriles on the main Los Barriles access road, between Plaza del Pueblo and 20 de Noviembre, **Supermercado Chapito's** is the largest grocery store in town, with a pharmacy. A new market, **Tienda Popular** (daily 7 A.M.–10 P.M.), west of 20 de Noviembre, about one block north of the intersection with Calle Los Barriles, recently opened just up the hill from Tio Pablo's. **Supermercado Fayla,** on 20 de Noviembre just past the Hotel Los Barriles, is more gringo-oriented, stocking basic food supplies as well as souvenirs, videos, and U.S. newspapers on Fridays. During the peak winter season, a bakery truck from La Paz visits town on Fridays and a fresh produce vendor comes on Saturday mornings.

Buy frozen or smoked fish or have yours prepared and vacuum-packed at the **Baja Papa's East Cape Smokehouse** (20 de Noviembre at Calle Don Pepe, tel. 624/141-0294, www.bajapapas.com, daily 9 A.M.–6 P.M.). Allow 48 hours turnaround time.

Information and Services

East Cape RV Resort owner Theresa Comber is the closest thing Los Barriles has to a chamber of commerce. Stop by to ask for advice on restaurants, day trips, and activities in the area.

La Plaza del Pueblo shopping center, near the highway on the main access road, has clean public restrooms and public telephones. The post office recently closed. Near the end of the main access road to Los Barriles, an **Amerimed Clinic** is open Monday–Saturday 8 A.M.–2 P.M. and 4 P.M.–6 P.M. for medical needs. Call 624/141-0797 for emergencies.

If you don't already have a car, **National Car Rental** maintains an outpost at the Oasis Coffee Bar, but in most cases an ATV would be a better vehicle for getting around town. The closest PEMEX is just south of town on Mexico 1. **El Lavadero/The Washroom** (20 de Noviembre near the Los Barriles Hotel, Mon.–Sat., hours vary), is the only place to have your clothes washed, unless you're staying at one of the full-service RV parks.

For high speed Internet, head to **The Office** (20 de Noviembre across from Sunset Rentals, tel. 624/141 0142, fax 624/141 0259, theoffice@prodigy.net, Mon.–Sat. 8 A.M.–8 P.M., Sun. 10 A.M.–6 P.M.). Work on one of 10 Samsung desktop machines, or bring your laptop, for US$0.10/minute. Fax, phone, and copy services are also available. Better yet, enjoy free wireless Internet while you sip a latte at Oasis Coffee Bar, just a few doors away. East Cape RV Park, Sunset Rentals, and many private home owners have wireless Internet, too.

Several businesses in town accept credit cards, but you'll still need cash (dollars or pesos) for tacos and the like. **Baja Money Exchange** (Mon.–Sat. 9 A.M.–5 P.M.), near the Oasis Coffee Bar, can trade your dollars or travelers checks for pesos. At last check, the ATM that had been located near The Office had been removed. The only ATM in town is next to the Amerimed clinic on Calle Los Barriles.

BUENA VISTA

Smaller and quieter than its neighbor to the north, Buena Vista attracts a similar crowd of families, fishermen, and retirees—many of them reportedly former law enforcement professionals from Southern California. It won't be long before the two towns are connected by the homes and businesses that are spreading out between them. Southbound travelers may have difficulty finding the unsigned entrance to town: Look for the turn on a curve between Km 104 and 105.

Scuba Diving

Buena Vista has a reputable dive center located on the beach, next to the Vista del Mar trailer park. **Vista Sea Sport** (tel. 624/141-0031, www.vistaseasport.com) is run by two PADI-certified dive instructors from Southern California who own three super-*pangas* and one cruiser. However, boat rides to the major sites—Cabo Pulmo, Los Frailes, Punta Pescadero, and Isla Cerralvo—are long and costs are higher (US$110–120 for a two-tank dive) than at shops based in La Paz or Cabo Pulmo. Scuba gear rental is US$20 with a tour. Airfills

cost US$8; snorkeling gear US$10. Look for a giant earthmover that serves as the boat launch. To find the shop from Mexico 1, take the turn across from the Calafia Hotel, then turn left at the T in the dirt road and follow the signs.

Ecotours

Ángel Ortiz and Paul Ortiz Meza offer guided ecotours and adventure tours through **Ángel Eco Tours** (tel. 624/141-0838). Options include snorkeling and kayaking in the Cabo Pulmo Marine Sanctuary, whale-watching in Magdalena Bay on the Pacific coast, tours of ceremonial rock-art sites near Santiago, and visits to an inland oasis, canyon, and rancho, also near Santiago. Tours last 7–8 hours and include refreshments.

Accommodations

US$100-150: Old-timer **Rancho Buena Vista** (Km 106, U.S. tel. 805/928-1719 or 800/258-8200, www.ranchobuenavista.com, US$105 pp) features a nice restaurant and bar facing the sea, as well as a pool, whirlpool, tennis and volleyball courts, a weight room, fitness programs, fishing tackle (including fly-fishing equipment), cruisers, windsurfing gear, a boat ramp, boat storage, unpaved airstrip, and 57 air-conditioned cottages. All meals are included. It's easy to miss the entrance to Rancho Buena Vista if you're coming south on Mexico 1. The left turn comes just after a small mountain pass that obscures it; watch for a blue highway sign on the right that says Hotel.

US$150-250: Popular with families and retirees, the **Hotel Buena Vista Beach Resort** (Km 105, tel. 624/141-0033 or 800/623-0710, U.S. tel. 619/429-8079 or 800/752-3555, www.hotelbuenavista.com, US$150–180) offers 60 air-conditioned Mediterranean-style bungalows with private baths, sitting areas, and private terraces. Buildings are arranged close together against a hillside, and the resort feels somewhat dated, but the location just across from the beach is ideal. Facilities include a garden, two pools, a swim-up bar, cocktail lounge, beachfront dining, water aerobics center, tennis courts, two whirlpool tub–powered hot springs mineral spas, spa services, kayaks, horseback riding, and equipment for diving, snorkeling, fishing, and hunting. The resort organizes various outings, such as tours of cave paintings and waterfalls, as well as bird-watching, hiking, and snorkeling tours. All meals, snacks, nonalcoholic beverages, beer, and domestic well drinks are included. Lower European plan rates are available. Fishing and diving packages are also offered.

The sportfishing fleet at the resort features a 23-foot *panga* (US$240), a 28-foot cruiser (US$350), a luxury 29-foot twin-engine cruiser (US$410), and a 31-foot twin-engine cruiser (US$450). Tax, tips, tackle, bait and fishing licenses are extra.

Round-trip or one-way transportation from the airport can be arranged by the U.S. reservations office.

Food

Restaurant Calafia (mains US$7–17), on Mexico 1 near the Buena Vista police station, offers good shrimp tacos, chiles rellenos, and tables with views of Bahía de Palmas. It's usually open for lunch and early dinner only. Popular **Flag's Sports Bar,** on Mexico 1 opposite the Pemex, isn't really a sports bar, but it has lots of libation options. A **Tienda Popular** minimarket is located north of the main entrance to town.

LA RIBERA

To reach the Coastal Road from the north, take the paved road signed La Ribera east at Km 93 off Mexico 1 (at Las Cuevas), and watch for potholes. This 20-kilometer (12-mi) road passes through La Ribera (La Rivera), a small town of around 2,000 with a Pemex station, church, *tortillería,* cemetery, banana and mango trees, trailer shelters, and simple homes lined up along a network of sandy roads overlooking a sand beach. Worn *palapa* shelters at the south end of the beach can be used for camping when not occupied by fishermen. Several *mercaditos* in the village offer local produce and other supplies for long-term visitors.

A sandy road just south of La Ribera Trailer Park leads 0.6 kilometer (0.4 mi) to a casuarina-shaded beach where you can camp for free. A point at the north end of the small bay (also accessible from La Ribera) creates a surf break during heavy southwest swells.

Food

A new restaurant has opened at the Y in La Ribera, where the road turns south to Cabo Pulmo (9 A.M.–10 P.M., breakfast mains US$6–8, dinner mains US$9–25). It serves steak, lobster, fish, shrimp, Caesar salad, and chiles rellenos. **Mercado Rey,** on El Camino Rural Costero, just past the Y and across from the Pemex, carries tools, propane tank parts, chains, and beer, plus basic groceries and a good selection of American liquors.

Shopping

A branch of the Los Barriles home decor store, **El Toro y La Luna** (tel. 624/141-0698, www. eltoroylaluna.net, daily 8 A.M.–5 P.M.), on Avenida Santa Maria at the turn for the road to Cabo Pulmo, has ceramic sinks, tiles, and other home furnishings at the Y.

Information and Services

A medical clinic and pharmacy are collocated next to the athletic fields on the way into town, on the south side of Avenida Santa Maria past the turnoff to Cabo Pulmo. An Internet café on Calle 29 de Enero is open daily 8 A.M.– 3 P.M. and 5–8 P.M. (tel. 624/130-0302).

AROUND PUNTA COLORADA

Punta Colorada lies at the south end of the bay, 16 kilometers (10 mi) east of Mexico 1 via the La Ribera road.

Accommodations

US$100-150: Perched on a seaside cliff near La Ribera, the **◖ Hotel Punta Colorada** (tel. 612/121-0044, U.S. tel. 818/222-5066 or 800/368-4334, www.vanwormerresorts.com, US$110–160) is a longtime favorite of roosterfish fanatics; the roosterfishing off nearby Punta Arena is usually the best in Baja, as evidenced

PUNTA COLORADA TO LOS FRAILES

Laguna Salina

PACIFIC OCEAN

La Ribera

Salinas Punta Colorada

La Trinidad

Punta Colorada

Punta Colorada

Matanza

Punta Arena

Tropic of Cancer

Miramar

Los Mangles

Parque Marina Nacional Cabo Pulmo

Cabo Pulmo

CABO PULMO

La Boquita

San Miguel

Los Frailes

Cabo Frailes

0   2 mi

0   2 km

© AVALON TRAVEL PUBLISHING, INC.

cruisers. The hotel is closed September and the first week of October.

US$150-250 (All-Inclusive): South of Buena Vista lies the secluded **Rancho Leonero Resort** (tel./fax 612/141-0216, U.S. tel. 760/634-4336 or 800/646-2252, www.rancholeonero.com, US$150–250). Perched on a low promontory overlooking the sea, this comfortable, quiet, and rustic resort features 30 spacious, rock-walled, *palapa*-roofed rooms, suites, and bungalows. All have seaviews, but none contains a phone or TV. As at Punta Pescadero, a small development now adjoins the resort, with new homes built on land sold by the owner of Rancho Leonero.

The expansive grounds hold a restaurant and bar, pool, hot tub, fully equipped dive center, sportfishing fleet, and 20 miles of running/hiking trails. A rock reef in front of the hotel is suitable for snorkeling. Three meals a day are included in the room price. Fishing charters start at US$250 for a super-*panga,* US$385 and up for cruisers. Snorkeling equipment costs US$10 per day. Horseback riding, kayaking, scuba, and hiking trips can also be arranged. US$25 discount August–September and November–March, excluding December 20–January 1.

Surfing

One of Baja's least-known surfing spots—simply because no one expects surf this far up the Sea of Cortez—can be found at **Punta Arena,** just below Punta Colorada. A left point break can crop up here anytime during the March–November southwest swell, but the peak surf usually comes in late summer or early fall—*chubasco* season.

EL CAMINO RURAL COSTERO

La Ribera is the northern end of the notorious El Camino Rural Costero (The Rural Coastal Road), which runs all the way to Pueblo La Playa. About halfway along the route stands a brass plaque commemorating the road's May 1984 grading. For first-time drivers who have braved washouts and sandpits to read it, the sign never fails to elicit a few chuckles.

In general, driving conditions along the

by the photo of a record-setting 93-pound catch on the wall in the bar. The hotel offers 40 large rooms, all but eight of which have ocean views. About half of its rooms were renovated in 2006. Three meals daily are included in the price, and the restaurant serves a buffet dinner open to the public on Wednesdays and Saturdays. Call by noon for reservations. The hotel also has an indoor/outdoor bar and its own airstrip (1,000 m/3,300 ft, Unicom 122.8). All tap water at the resort comes from a mountain well. Guided fishing trips are available starting at US$220 a day for a super-*panga* and US$330–385 for

DRIVING WASHBOARD ROADS

Whether you rent a car or drive your own, exploring Baja's back roads takes a toll on vehicle and driver alike. Follow the tips below to enjoy a safe and smooth ride:

Less is more: Lower the air pressure in your tires for driving on softer sand.

Stay to the side: You can often find a smoother track on the far left or right side of the road.

Pick up the pace: Faster speeds often smooth out the bumps, but be sure to slow down when approaching turns to avoid skids and unexpected obstacles.

Know your clearance: Watch for large rocks and deep potholes that can wreak havoc on low-hanging oil pans.

Travel with tools: At a minimum, a spare tire and jack are essential. Old carpet remnants work well for getting traction on soft sand.

Ask around: For less traveled routes, inquire when the road was last graded and what kind of vehicle you need to pass through safely.

Coastal Road are suitable for passenger cars of average road clearance; even smaller RVs sometimes manage to make it all the way. Sand can be a problem in places, and shoulders are invariably soft. Weather plays an important role in day-to-day conditions; after late-summer or early-fall storms, parts of the Coastal Road can be impassable. Make inquiries before embarking on the trip and be prepared to turn back if necessary.

Eventually the Coastal Road is supposed to be paved all the way to San José del Cabo. In early 2006, local government officials staged a press event to commemorate the beginning of work on a five-mile-long paved road to Los Frailes; however, the earthmover that was to be the star of the show reportedly got a flat tire and the event was canceled. The machine stayed by the side of the road for weeks after, but no dirt was ever moved. Plans to pave the road have been repeatedly delayed in recent years, to the relief of local residents, who fear the arrival of mainstream power and phone service will change their towns forever.

In spite of the rough access, certain areas along the route—including Cabo Pulmo and Los Frailes—are filling up with small-scale housing and resort developments. Open space for beach camping is still available, but access is becoming increasingly limited as new developments lay cinder blocks and finish their first few homes. Several ranchos along the central and southern sections still raise cattle, goats, pigs, and sheep—mostly without fencing. If you substitute fiberglass *pangas* for dugout canoes, the ranchos today appear much as they must have in 1941, when John Steinbeck described Cabo Pulmo:

On the shore behind the white beach was one of those lonely little rancherías we came to know later. Usually a palm or two are planted nearby, and by these trees sticking up out of the brush one can locate the houses. There is usually a small corral, a burro or two, a few pigs, and some scrawny chickens. The cattle range wide for food. A dugout canoe lies on the beach, for a good part of the food comes from the sea. Rarely do you see a light from the sea, for the people go to sleep at dusk and awaken with the first light.

◖ CABO PULMO

Heading south from La Ribera, the Coastal Road is paved for a short way, then turns to dirt. The unpaved part of the 26.5-kilometer (16.5-mi) stretch between La Ribera and Cabo Pulmo is usually in fair condition.

Bahía Pulmo

Noted for its reef-building corals, this shallow bay is bounded by Cabo Pulmo to the north and Corral de los Frailes to the south. Coarse white-sand beaches ring the bay, most of them readily accessible from the parallel Coastal Road. Baja California pearling once reached its southernmost point here.

Playa La Sirenita

A pristine, fine-sand beach known as Playa La Sirenita (Mermaid Beach, named for a rock formation whose silhouette resembles the head and bust of a female figure) lies against the north escarpment of Corral de los Frailes at the bay's southeastern tip. Best reached by small boat or kayak from the village of Cabo Pulmo, the beach's crystal waters are protected from southerly winds in the summer and early fall; rock reefs close by offer snorkeling opportunities. There's just enough room above the tideline for undisturbed overnight camping.

Farther south around the wide headland of **Corral de los Frailes** (named for a rock formation with a resemblance to hooded friars), a colony of sea lions lives among geometric boulder piles.

Take the first sand road north of Corral de los Frailes that isn't barbwired to reach **Playa**

Corral de los Frailes, a secluded beach sheltered from most onshore winds.

Pulmo Reef System

The bay's reef system, the northernmost of only three coastal reefs in North America and the only coral reef in the Sea of Cortez, is rich with tropical marine life and hence a favorite snorkeling and scuba diving destination. Its accessibility from shore adds to the attraction. You can watch a wide variety of tropical fish, eels, and rays—as well as the occasional nurse shark—in waist-deep water.

The reef consists of eight hard coral fingers scattered throughout the bay, from Cabo Pulmo at the north end to Corral de los Frailes at the southern end. Four finger reefs extend from the center of the bayshore: two solid lengths called **Las Navajas;** an unnamed broken length used by (harmless) nurse sharks as a breeding zone; and a solid, kilometer-long finger known as **El Cantil.** Water depths along these four reefs range 4.5–10.5 meters (15–35 ft).

Farther offshore (up to 3.2 km/2 mi), running

© NIKKI GOTH ITOI

a *panga* bound for the reef at Cabo Pulmo

ENDANGERED SEA

In 2005, the United Nations Educational, Scientific and Cultural Organization (UNESCO) added the Gulf of California to its World Heritage List of close to 200 areas of outstanding natural and cultural value around the globe. Citing its striking beauty and critical role as a natural laboratory for the study of thousands of marine species, UNESCO identified a site of 244 islands, islets, and coastal areas within the Gulf of California, or Sea of Cortez. Also important was the fact that all major oceanographic processes occurring in the planet's oceans take place in this body of water.

Environmental conservation groups heralded the designation as a critical step forward in curbing severe damage wrought by commercial fishing and bottom trawling, which destroy eelgrass beds and shellfish that sustain many other species in the sea. But World Heritage status is only the beginning of a long and costly battle. Two international organizations, Conservation International (www.conservation.org) and the World Wildlife Fund (www.worldwildlife.org) are funding projects in the area in an effort to protect the fragile ecosystem for generations to come. Meanwhile, the Mexican government is stepping up its commitment to fund marine parks and conservation activities throughout the region.

more or less parallel to the bayshore, are the reef fingers of **La Esperanza** (at depths of around 18 m/60 ft), **El Bajo de los Meros** (15 m/50 ft), and **Outer Pulmo** (30 m/100 ft).

Soft coral heads can be found at **El Islote**— a rock island near La Esperanza—and at **Las Casitas,** rock caves just off Corral de los Frailes at a depth of 13 meters (45 ft).

The reef system here is very delicate; reef corals can't tolerate temperatures lower than 21°C (70°F) and must have clear water since debris settling on their disks and tentacles will kill them. The reefs are important breeding grounds for several marine species, so if the corals die it will negatively affect all manner of fish in the area.

The Mexican government established the Cabo Pulmo National Marine Park in 1995, and no fishing or anchoring at the reef (or anywhere in Bahía Pulmo) is permitted. Shore development remains among the reef's biggest ecological challenges, because the corals rely on unpolluted and unimpeded runoff. If resorts or housing developments further expand along Bahía Pulmo, the reef will probably perish.

Diving

Optimum visibility in the waters around Pulmo Reef occurs March–October. Aside from the natural reefs cited above, directly off Cabo Pulmo (the cape itself) lies the wreck of *El Vencedor,* a tuna boat that sank in 1981 and now forms an excellent artificial reef. Pilot whales are commonly seen in the vicinity in April, large jack crevalles August–September.

Three dive centers run guided tours from Cabo Pulmo. All are located within 100 yards of each other. In the village center, the **Cabo Pulmo Beach Resort** (El Camino Rural Costero, tel. 612/141-0244, U.S. tel./fax 208/726-1306 or 888/997-8566, www.cabopulmo.com) operates a PADI-certified dive center with two boats, well-maintained gear, and experienced, professional dive guides. A two-tank boat dive costs US$75 and an equipment rental package is US$20 with a boat dive. You do not need to be a guest of the resort to snorkel or dive with the shop. On weekends, the dive center often hosts groups of day-trippers from resorts in the Cabo San Lucas area. These dives tend to be more crowded with novice divers. Plan to dive midweek if you want to do more advanced dives. Snorkeling tours are US$35 with gear, and single kayaks rent for US$35 a day. Experienced divers can rent tanks and a kayak for self-guided beach diving.

Pepe's Dive Center (tel. 877/733-2252, www.cabopulmo.com.mx), across from El Ca-

© PAUL ITOI

dive center at Cabo Pulmo Beach Resort

ballero restaurant, also offers a complete diving service, as does **Cabo Pulmo Divers** (www.cabopulmodivers.com)—located in the Castro family complex, next to the Miscellanea Market. Rates at both are comparable to those at the Cabo Pulmo Beach Resort, although readers have reported higher rates (up to US$72 pp) for tours of only one or two people. It pays to shop around.

The dive operators are also happy to arrange boat trips for nondivers interested in touring the bay, Playa La Sirenita, and the Corral de los Frailes seal colony.

Fishing
Neither sport nor commercial fishing is permitted in Bahía Pulmo, but inshore north of Cabo Pulmo, anglers can find giant sea bass, snapper, *pargo,* ladyfish, and roosterfish. Offshore are grouper, sierra, skipjack, dorado, marlin, and tuna. The tuna are found closer in at Bahía de los Frailes farther south, but anywhere along this coastal stretch the heavyweights can come within three kilometers (2 mi) of the shoreline.

Tuna season begins most years in late March or early April, and peak months for most varieties are May–June and October–November. Kiki and Paco Castro offer half-day (US$160) and full-day (US$260) tours in their super-*pangas,* including gear and bait. Inquire at the dive center behind the El Palapa beachfront restaurant.

Accommodations and Camping
As new owners build and acquire properties in Cabo Pulmo, the number of rental options has increased. Expect most high-season rates to climb even higher during the peak season around Christmas and New Year's.

US$50-100: In the midst of Cabo Pulmo village, **〖 Cabo Pulmo Beach Resort** (El Camino Rural Costero, tel. 612/141-0244, U.S. tel./fax 208/726-1306 or 888/997-8566, www.cabopulmo.com, US$60–125) offers 25 *palapa*-roofed, solar-powered units by the day, week, or month. The bay is just a short walk from each. The choice of accommodations here includes a beach house that accommodates 4–6 people, *casitas,* and basic and deluxe bungalows;

all come with kitchenettes or full kitchens, plus bed and bath linens. Some feature patios, roof decks, and barbecue grills. Marly Rickers and Clint Fultz, a friendly young American couple with longtime ties to Cabo Pulmo, also manage a handful of rentals in the same group of *casitas* for US$65–125 per night. Contact **Cabo Pulmo Casas** (tel. 877/754-5251, www.cabo-pulmocasas.com).

Across the dirt road from the Cabo Pulmo Beach Resort, Kent Ryan rents **Baja Bungalows** (www.bajabungalows.com, US$45–125), with a main house that has spectacular views from the upstairs master suite, plus a two-bedroom unit on the lower level and an additional bungalow and *palapa* suite with shared bath and full outdoor kitchen. The beach is a three-minute walk away. **Nancy's Restaurant and Bar,** adjacent to the Cabo Pulmo Beach Resort, also has a few basic rooms for US$40–50.

Over US$250: Just north of Cabo Pulmo Beach Resort stands **Villa and Casa del Mar** (U.S. tel. 208/726-4455 or 888/225-2786, www.bajaparadise.com, US$170–375), a large, deluxe beachfront house with a full kitchen, spacious living areas, shaded terraces, and a rooftop sundeck. All rooms come with fan and air conditioning, which must be run sparingly since the house is solar-powered. The main part of the house rents for US$375 a night or US$2,500 per week for two guests in peak season. The smaller attached studio apartment costs US$170/night or US$1,150/week. A newer, self-contained cottage called El Nido goes for US$215/night or US$1,400/week and includes a fully equipped kitchen.

Camping: At the other extreme, you can camp for free on the beach at the south end of Bahía Pulmo, or for US$2 per night at the north end.

Food

Adjacent to the Cabo Pulmo Beach Resort, **Nancy's Restaurant and Bar** (Thurs.–Tues., mains US$16–20) began as a trailer and two tables 12 years ago, and has evolved into a charming venue with a rustic collection of tables beneath a *palapa* shelter. Fresh guacamole

sushi for supper

© PAUL ITOI

with homemade chips is a delightful way to begin the meal. Lobster enchiladas, crab cakes, and fresh catch (yours or Nancy's) are accompanied by crisp side salads. Popular with divers during the dive season, the simple restaurant has an especially cozy ambience at night when illuminated by hurricane lamps. Nancy also offers occasional cooking classes. The **Coral Reef Bar and Grill** (Wed.–Mon., mains US$10–20) is a cozy restaurant with a TV and bar located above the blue building that serves as the resort dive center. Enjoy a cocktail at sunset and then choose from a limited menu of the day.

At last check, **Restaurant El Caballero** (Mon.–Sat. 7 A.M.–10 P.M., Sun. 7 A.M.–12 P.M., mains US$6–14), on the opposite side of the road near Nancy's, had the best menu in town, thanks to a professional chef who came from San José del Cabo initially to work at the Coral Reef and then moved next door. Caballero also has a bar and small assortment of groceries, drinks, and snacks for sale. **El Palapa** (formerly called Restaurant Lupita, Tues.–Sun., lunch plates US$4–10, dinner mains US$8–18) offers casual beachfront dining from a menu of fish tacos, carne asada, and other traditional fare. Cabo Pulmo's restaurants are notoriously understaffed even during peak season. It can take up to 45 minutes or longer to be served, even at lunch.

For groceries, several vendors make the rounds through town during the week. A bakery truck comes from La Paz on Wednesdays; Polo brings fresh fruit, vegetables, and meats in his pickup truck on Wednesdays and Sundays; Ysidro delivers fish, scallops, and shrimp on Tuesdays. Strawberries and ice cream come intermittently as well. You can buy fresh tortillas (10 for less than US$2), homemade tamales (US$1), and empanadas (US$1) for takeout at **Elvira's Kitchen,** near the Cabo Pulmo Divers shop. The **Miscellanea Market** (daily 9 A.M.–7 P.M., limited summer hours), with colorful snails painted on the side of the building, is located next to the Cabo Pulmo Divers shop and stocks basic supplies, including dairy, juice, produce, bread, toiletries, candy, and canned goods. For a long stay, it's best to load up on groceries at Soriana or one of the other supermarkets in San José del Cabo or at Supermercado Chapitos in Los Barriles. Mexican food brands generally cost less than their U.S. counterparts. It's a good idea to buy ice, as the propane refrigerators in most Cabo Pulmo rentals cool very slowly, and a car full of groceries will take a long time to chill.

Information and Services

Internet access via satellite is possible in Cabo Pulmo, but service is by no means reliable, and it will cost you. Inquire at Pepe's Dive Center. At last check, rates were US$5 for 10 minutes, and US$1 per additional minute. In an emergency, the owners of the Cabo Pulmo Beach Resort or Cabo Pulmo Casas can usually get a message out. For casual correspondence, plan to connect in San José or Los Barriles.

There are no banks or ATMs in Cabo Pulmo or Los Frailes, and few places except the largest resorts accept credit cards. U.S. or Mexican currency is accepted, and you can load up on cash at an ATM machine in San José or Los Barriles. Be sure to get plenty of small bills, as many businesses cannot change larger bills.

Basic medical services are available in La Ribera and Los Barriles, and the closest hospital is in San José.

Getting There

Most visitors drive themselves to Cabo Pulmo via El Camino Rural Costero. From San José del Cabo, follow Highway 1 north 50.6 kilometers (31.5 mi) to an overpass at Las Cuevas, and bear right (east) onto the single lane road to La Ribera. From La Paz, pass Buena Vista heading south, and take the exit for La Ribera. As you approach La Ribera (9.6 km/6 mi), turn right before the soccer field. Follow the coastal road 26 kilometers (16 mi) south to Cabo Pulmo. The drive should take about 40 minutes from the time you leave Highway 1.

If you are flying into San José and plan to drive the same day to Cabo Pulmo, aim to arrive no later than noon. By the time you get through passport control, retrieve your luggage, rent a car, and buy your groceries, several hours will have passed, and it is not advisable to drive the highway or coastal road after dark. If you arrive in the afternoon, consider staying overnight in San José before departing for Cabo Pulmo the next day.

The closest gas to Cabo Pulmo is at La Ribera to the north. Be sure to fill up before heading south along the coastal road.

Aguila bus service from San José will get you as far as Las Cuevas for about US$11 one-way, but from there, you'll have to hitch a ride or arrange in advance for someone to pick you up. Another option for traveling sans auto is to contact one of the companies that transport divers from the Los Cabos area to Cabo Pulmo for the day. For example, **Impala Transportation** (tel. 624/141-0726 or cell 122-0141) has a van that holds 14 passengers. With notice, Cabo Pulmo Resort can arrange round-trip transportation from Los Cabos airport for a fee; a stop at a grocery store near the airport on the way up can be included.

BAHÍA DE LOS FRAILES

About eight kilometers (5 mi) south of Cabo Pulmo village is a sandy spur road east to gently curving, white-sand Bahía de los Frailes. With Bahía Pulmo just to the north serving as a protected nursery, onshore and inshore fishing is unusually good here. Surfcasters can land roosterfish, while boating anglers can hook yellowfin tuna, leopard grouper, skipjack, dorado, and marlin, all within a couple miles of shore.

The north end of the bay is protected from November–April northern winds by Cabo Los Frailes, but windsurfers will find a steady crossshore breeze at the bay's south end. The bay plummets here as deep as 210 meters (688 ft).

Accommodations and Camping

Villa Los Frailes (El Camino Rural Costero, U.S. tel. 206/984-3483, www.bajavilla.com, US$550) is an oceanfront home that sleeps 10 people in four bedrooms and five baths with a hot tub and pool deck. Cabo Villa Rentals manages a few vacation properties along the East Cape, including Casita Luna Azul at Estancia (U.S. tel. 877/473-1946 or 310/943-7614, www.cabovillarentals.com). This one-bedroom *casita* is set on a point overlooking the sea and costs US$225 per night.

Beach camping is permitted along the north end of the bay—a nominal fee of US$2–3 per site may be collected to pay for trash collection.

Information and Services

Los Frailes has little commercial infrastructure of its own, but a new "mini-super" market named **Quitos** has opened across the street from the Villa Los Frailes on El Camino Rural Costero. The airstrip was closed in 2007 but scheduled to reopen in the near future.

SOUTH TO SAN JOSÉ DEL CABO

South of Los Frailes the Coastal Road deteriorates rapidly, but those with sturdy vehicles and steady nerves will be rewarded by secluded arroyo campsites and vignettes of disappearing ranch life.

a burro looking for lunch

© NIKKI GOTH ITOI

La Vinorama

About 12.5 kilometers (7.5 mi) south of Los Frailes is **Rancho Tule,** followed after 5.5 kilometers (3.5 mi) by **Rancho Boca de la Vinorama.** The coastal desert scenery along this stretch can be particularly impressive, with lots of green cacti and *torotes* (elephant trees). A late-summer beach break sometimes hits at Boca del Tule, sending a few clued-in surfers scurrying across the landscape in this direction. Near La Vinorama, the **Crossroads Country Club Beachfront Playa** isn't really a country club in the traditional sense, but it has a bar and restaurant with Internet service, public phone, and even a book exchange. For breakfast, choose eggs any style for US$3 or a cheese omelet for US$4. For lunch or dinner, there are fish tacos (US$6), quesadillas, and ham and cheese sandwiches. Jesse Ventura, of Montana governorship fame, lives in a new beachfront mansion just up the road. **Villa del Faro** (www.villadelfaro.net, US$125–450) consists of four deluxe *casitas* and a primitive stone cottage on the beach.

Palo Escopeta

Just south of Vinorama, a graded dirt road heads west across the lower Sierra La Trinidad to the ranching settlement of **Palo Escopeta.** From there it continues on to meet Mexico 1 near San José Viejo, a distance of 34 kilometers (22 mi). Although roughly the same distance as the remainder of the Coastal Road to San José, the Palo Escopeta road often rides more smoothly and quickly. Hence, unless you're heading for a specific spot along the coast between Pueblo La Playa and La Vinorama, it's normally faster to cut across the hills here to Mexico 1 rather than follow the coast.

From La Vinorama along the coast, it's another five kilometers (3 mi) and 1.5 kilometers (one mile) southwest, respectively, to **Rancho San Luis** and **Rancho Santa Elena.** This section of road is often the most rugged along El Camino Rural Costero, with lots of soft spots and washouts. Beyond another 5.5-kilometer (3.5-mi) section is the small dairy farm of

La Fortuna. Nearby, Oregonians Lloyd and Marti Miesen host a small bed and breakfast, **Boca de Los Palmas** (U.S. tel. 503/922-0465 or 866/781-8159, www.martimiesen.com, US$225). Accommodations are in a one-bedroom guesthouse with a king-size bed, private bath, and luxury linens; an additional guestroom is available in their home on the same property for US$85 (only with rental of the guesthouse).

After La Fortuna, the road improves a bit for 24 kilometers (15 mi) before terminating at **Pueblo La Playa,** a fishing village on the eastern outskirts of San José del Cabo.

Jutting from the coast about 10.3 kilometers (6.4 mi) before Pueblo La Playa is **Punta Gorda,** known for good onshore/inshore fishing and, in a south or southwest swell, surfing. Surfers know the breaks here as "Santa Cruz," the name of a small *ranchería* nearby (actually Santa Cruz de los Zacatitos). Beach campsites are free and plentiful in this area.

After 15 years in business, Sharon and Robert Ruyg, the owners of the once-loved Casa Terra Cotta B&B in San José, have moved on to a more upscale and remote location: **Hacienda Soleada del Mar** (Manzana A-Lote 7, tel. 624/113-6386, www.haciendasoleada.com) is available as a B&B with seven rooms for US$100–230 a night, or as a 9,200-square-foot vacation rental that sleeps 14 for US$1,000/night. There is a small pool on the property, and kayaks, snorkeling gear, and beach umbrellas and chairs are provided.

◖ Gorda Banks

Around 10 kilometers (6 mi) offshore lie the world-famous Gorda Banks, a pair of seamounts that are a hot spot for marlin and wahoo fishing. *Pangeros* are sometimes available for guided fishing trips out to the banks, but it's easiest to hire someone at La Playita, the beach behind Pueblo La Playa farther on. If you have your own boat, beach launching is generally easier at La Playita. Guided scuba trips to the Gorda Banks can be arranged through dive outfitters in Cabo San Lucas.

Sierra de la Laguna and Vicinity

Along Mexico 1 between La Paz and San José del Cabo, a number of mining-turned-farming towns sport cobblestone streets and 19th-century stone-and-stucco architecture. Nestled among well-watered arroyos in the Sierra de la Laguna, these neglected settlements now support themselves growing citrus, avocados, mangoes, corn, and sugarcane, and, to a lesser extent, serving the needs of passing travelers. Many of the families living in the central Cape Region are descended from Spanish settlers of the 18th and early 19th centuries. Others are newcomers—including a few Americans and Canadians—drawn by the area's solitude and simplicity.

SAN PEDRO TO SAN BARTOLO

San Pedro

This town of only a few hundred inhabitants appears—and quickly disappears—just before the junction of Mexico 1 and Mexico 19. *Carnitas* connoisseurs swear by **El Paraíso** and **El Pin** (featuring *carnitas, chicharones,* and hot dogs), two unassuming roadside cafés on the west side of Mexico 1. The junction itself is reached at Km 185; if Cabo San Lucas is your destination, you must decide whether to take Mexico 19 via Todos Santos or the Transpeninsular Highway (Mexico 1) via El Triunfo, San Antonio, San Bartolo, Santiago, and Miraflores.

Unless you're in a hurry to reach Cabo San Lucas, Mexico 1 is the most scenic choice for drivers of autos and light trucks. South of San Pedro, Mexico 1 winds through the Sierra de la Laguna and features a succession of dizzying curves and steep grades. Hence for trailers, RVs, and other wide or lengthy vehicles, Mexico 19 is the better choice since it runs along relatively flat terrain (see the *West Cape and Todos Santos* chapter).

El Triunfo and San Antonio

During the Jesuit missionary period, this section along the lower northern slopes of the sierra was earmarked for cattle ranching. But mining concessions moved in after the discovery of silver in 1748, and San Antonio quickly grew into a town of 10,000 people, many of them Yaqui laborers. Then known as Real de Minas de Santa Ana, it was the first nonmission town founded in Baja. The Spanish crown took over the mines in 1769 and struggled to turn a profit from a relatively low quality of ore. When Loreto was heavily damaged by a hurricane in 1829, San Antonio briefly served as capital of the Californias before the capital was transferred to La Paz in 1830.

In 1862, better gold and silver deposits were uncovered at El Triunfo (Triumph), seven kilometers (4.5 mi) north of San Antonio. By 1878 the large Progreso mining concern had established seven gold and silver mines around the village, attracting a number of Mexican, French, English, Italian, German, and American immigrants. The company paid for the region's first post office and installed the first electrical and phone lines to La Paz.

Both San Antonio and El Triunfo bustled with frontier commerce through the end of the 19th century, when the ore began running out. Then a hurricane flooded the mines in 1918 and sounded the death knell; by 1925, both towns were virtually abandoned. Today El Triunfo has only around 400 residents, most of them involved in small-scale mining (extracting ore from leftover tailings) or the weaving of palm baskets. A few *artesanías* can be found on the main road through town. San Antonio, in a lushly planted valley that descends eastward all the way to the Sea of Cortez, has developed into a farming community with around 800 residents, a Pemex station, a post office, and a few markets.

A number of historic adobe buildings in both towns have been restored, including El Triunfo's Casa Municipal and San Antonio's unusual 1825 church exhibiting train and paddle-wheeler motifs. A fun time to visit San Antonio is June 13, the feast day of St. Anthony, when everyone from both San Antonio and El Triunfo turns out for music and dancing.

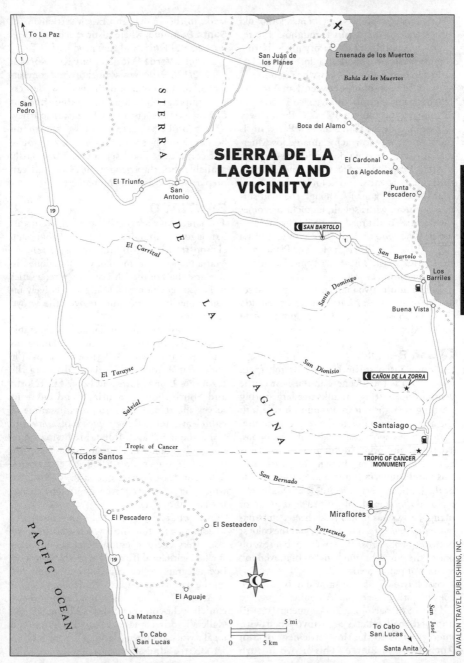

To La Paz

San Juán de los Planes

Ensenada de los Muertos

Bahía de los Muertos

San Pedro

Boca del Alamo

SIERRA DE LA LAGUNA AND VICINITY

El Cardonal

Los Algodones

El Triunfo

San Antonio

Punta Pescadero

SAN BARTOLO

El Carrizal

San Bartolo

Los Barriles

Santo Domingo

Buena Vista

El Tarayse

San Dionisio

CAÑON DE LA ZORRA

Salsial

L A G U N A

Santaiago

Tropic of Cancer

Todos Santos

TROPIC OF CANCER MONUMENT

San Bernado

El Pescadero

El Sesteadero

Miraflores

Portezuelo

PACIFIC OCEAN

El Aguaje

La Matanza

To Cabo San Lucas

0   5 mi

0   5 km

To Cabo San Lucas

San José

Santa Anita

Baja travelers have also mentioned lots of old mines and mining paths throughout the region, often good for exploratory hikes. Hiring a guide is always a good idea; locals in El Triunfo and San Antonio know who's good.

Near San Antonio, between Km 158 and 159, a road heads north off Mexico 1 and leads 22 kilometers (14 mi) to BCS 286, the highway to San Juan de los Planes and La Paz. This is the shortest way to reach Bahía de los Muertos (also called Bahía de los Sueños) and La Ventana from the Central Cape. The unsigned road is easy to miss. (Look for an intersection near the school zone.) Although the road surface starts out with asphalt, it quickly becomes a wide, graded dirt road traversable by most vehicles. Once you hit BCS 286, turn left for La Paz and La Ventana, right for Los Planes and the Cortez coast. There is a Pemex station at this intersection as well.

In El Triunfo, two markets have a modest selection of groceries: **Abarrotes La Escondida** (on Mexico 1) and the **Tienda Comunitaria** (off Mexico 1 in the center of town).

☾ San Bartolo

Beginning just past Km 128, San Bartolo (pop. about 550) is the greenest and lushest of the central Cape settings, thanks to a large spring gushing straight out of a mountainside into the arroyo. To complete the tropical picture, many homes sport thatched roofs. Mangoes, avocados, and other fresh fruits are available at roadside stands or in town. **Restaurant El Paso** and **Dulcería Daniela's,** on the east side of the highway, serve meals. ☾ **El Oasis** sells regional *dulces* made of fruit such as guava or mango, as well as homemade cheese, empanadas, *bistec ranchero,* quesadillas, and the coldest beer in town. Across the street, grab a seat on one of the wrought iron benches that overlook a valley of palms below.

San Bartolo's patron saint day is June 19, conveniently close to San Antonio's.

From San Bartolo, a 26-kilometer (16-mi) unpaved road follows an arroyo lined with huge *güeribos* to the tiny settlement of **San Antonio de la Sierra.** This arroyo in turn leads to the arroyo and ranch settlement of **Santo Domingo,** where rustic ranch furniture, leather, and fruit candy are produced.

Rancho Verde (Mexico 1 btw Km 143/142, tel. 612/126-9103, www.rancho-verde.com) offers 3,400 acres of mountain desert wilderness for camping, biking, or just taking time out during a Transpeninsular Highway journey. Spaces cost US$11/day (US$66/week) with full hookups and hot showers, or US$7 if you're self-contained. Food service isn't ordinarily available, but the friendly Mexican staff can prepare simple *antojitos* on request.

SANTIAGO

The largest of the central Cape Region towns, Santiago was founded as Misión de Santiago el Apóstol in 1723 by Italian padre Ignacio María Nápoli. The mission was abandoned in the latter half of the 18th century after a series of Pericú rebellions, and only in relatively recent times has agriculture revived the arroyo community.

A two-kilometer road flanked by vegetable plots, leafy fruit orchards, and blue fan palms leads west from Mexico 1 (Km 85) across the wide, flat Arroyo de Santiago, dividing the town into Loma Norte and Loma Sur (North and South Slopes). Santiago and environs serves the region as an important source of palm leaves for making *palapa* roofs. *Palmeros* claim the fan-shaped fronds are best cut during a full moon, as rising sap makes the palm leaves last longer. Properly dried and stored, 250 palm leaves equals one *carga,* or load, for which the *palmeros* receive US$30–50, depending on leaf quality.

A newly paved road circles the town, and various *tiendas* line the town plaza; the town also offers a Pemex station, hotel, supermarket stocked with local fruit and vegetables, post office, telegraph office, church, and the only zoo on the peninsula south of Mexicali.

A small, rustic museum adjacent to the church at the corner of Calzada Misioneros and Calle Victoria contains colonial artifacts and local fossils. It's open Monday–Friday 8 A.M.– 1 P.M.; free admission.

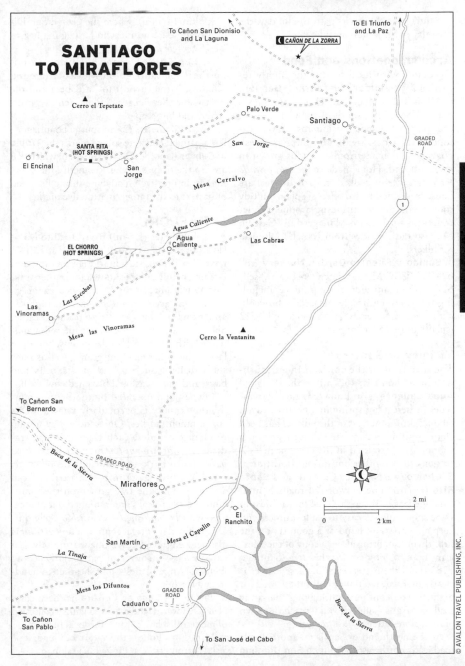

SANTIAGO TO MIRAFLORES

To Cañon San Dionisio
and La Laguna

To El Triunfo
and La Paz

CAÑON DE LA ZORRA

▲ Cerro el Tepetate

Palo Verde

Santiago

GRADED ROAD

San Jorge

SANTA RITA (HOT SPRINGS)

El Encinal

San Jorge

1

Mesa Cerralvo

Agua Caliente

Agua Caliente

Las Cabras

EL CHORRO (HOT SPRINGS)

Las Vinoramas

Las Escobas

Mesa las Vinoramas

▲ Cerro la Ventanita

To Cañon San Bernardo

Boca de la Sierra

GRADED ROAD

Miraflores

El Ranchito

San Martín

Mesa el Capulín

La Tinaja

Mesa los Difuntos

1

Caduaño

GRADED ROAD

To Cañon San Pablo

Boca de la Sierra

To San José del Cabo

| 0 | | | 2 mi |
| 0 | | 2 km | |

Santiago celebrates its patron saint day, the feast day of St. James, on July 25.

Accommodations and Food

Decorated with local fossils, the highly regarded **Palomar Restaurant-Bar** (tel. 612/130-2126, Mon.–Sat. 11:30 A.M.–8 P.M., mains US$11–15), south of the plaza on the east side of Calzada Misioneros, serves seafood, enchiladas, steak, and burgers. Fresh guacamole is made from avocados grown in the courtyard. Homemade soups and *pescado mojo de ajo* (fish cooked in garlic butter) are house specialties. It also offers six plain but tidy rooms with air conditioning around a quiet courtyard for US$40. Manager Luis Castillo can also radio guides from Rancho Dionisio for hikers.

Sonido y Silencio Garden Nursery (tel. 624/113-5362, Mon.–Fri. 9 A.M.–11 A.M.) sells baskets of organically grown produce, including tomatoes, chilies, lettuce, kale, broccoli, herbs, and whatever else is in season, for US$12 (small) and US$20 (large).

Vicinity of Santiago

The dirt road to the zoo continues southwest nine kilometers (5.5 mi) to the village of **Agua Caliente** (also known as Los Manantiales), where a hot spring in a nearby canyon (about 7 km/4 mi west of the village) has been channeled into a concrete tub for recreation. Camping is permitted in the canyon. Ask directions to two other hot springs in the area: **El Chorro** (west of Agua Caliente) and **Santa Rita** (north). The network of roads behind Santiago passes through dense thorn forest in some spots, and it's easy to get lost unless you keep a compass on hand or a good fix on the sun. If you can bring along a copy of the Mexican topographic map for this area (Santiago 12B34), all the better; each of these locales is clearly marked. Do not attempt these roads at night. If you continue south along the sandy road past Agua Caliente, you'll reach the town of Miraflores after 8.7 kilometers (5.4 mi).

At the north end of Santiago, another dirt road leads northwest to **Rancho San Dionísio**

(23.5 km/14.5 mi), where the Cañon San Dionísio approach to Picacho La Laguna begins (see *Sierra de la Laguna*).

At **Las Cuevas,** eight kilometers (5 mi) northeast of Santiago on Mexico 1 (around Km 93), is the turnoff to La Ribera and the East Cape. Services include a Pemex, minisuper, and bus stop.

Three kilometers (2 mi) south of Santiago, a large painted concrete sphere marks the **Tropic of Cancer** (latitude 23.5° N), south of which you are "in the tropics." As if to sanctify the crossing, an impressive Guadalupe shrine has been built next to the rather unattractive marker.

MIRAFLORES

A 2.5-kilometer (1.5-mi) paved road to Miraflores branches west off Mexico 1 at Km 71 next to a Pemex station. This ranching and farming community is known for leatherwork; **Curtiduría Miraflores** (Miraflores Tannery), just off the access road between the highway and town (look for a small sign reading Leather Shop on the north side of the road), sells handmade leather saddles, bridles, whips, horsehair lariats, and other ranching gear, as well as a few souvenir items such as leather hats, belts, and bags, and the occasional bleached cow skull.

Owned and operated by the Beltrán family, the tannery is particularly known for its rustic ranch saddles. One saddle may use up to eight cowhides, each tanned in the traditional *sudcaliforniano* manner with local *palo blanco* bark and powdered *quebrache,* a reddish-brown, tannin-rich extract from a type of dogbane tree grown on the mainland. Saddle frames are fashioned out of local woods—*ciruelo, copal*—or *cardón* skeletons. Custom orders are accepted. The *curtiduría* also sells engraved knives made from salvaged car springs—a source of particularly strong metal for knife blades—and sheathed in hand-tooled leather.

The town's **Casa de Cultura** has been completely renovated, and it now contains a collection of modest displays chronicling local history.

Miraflores honors the Virgin of Guadalupe as its patron saint, so Fiesta Guadalupana (December 12), celebrated throughout Mexico, is especially fervent here.

Well past the tannery, after you've crossed an arroyo and are just getting into the center of Miraflores, a large hedge of bougainvillea nearly obscures the open-air, *palapa*-roofed **Restaurant Las Bugambilias,** to the left on a small side street off the main road. All manner of inexpensive, *bajacaliforniano*-style *antojitos* are available here from morning till evening. **Restaurant Miraflores,** next to Mini Super El Nidito near the market and plaza, makes good tacos with shrimp, fish, or beef. Several *mercaditos* in town provide local produce and *machaca*.

Vicinity of Miraflores

A dirt road northwest of Miraflores leads to **Boca de la Sierra** (Mouth of the Sierra), a settlement at the mouth of Cañon San Bernardo—the second of the three canyons providing access deep into the Sierra de la Laguna. *Ejido* farms in the Boca de la Sierra area cultivate vegetables and herbs—especially sweet basil—for Cape Region supermarkets and restaurants as well as for export to the United States.

Another dirt road southwest of town leads to the mouth of Cañon San Pablo, a third Laguna hiking route. Inquire at the tannery about guided trips into the sierra to view Amerindian rock-art sites.

SIERRA DE LA LAGUNA

The mountainous heart of the Cape Region extends southward from the Llano de la Paz (the plains just south of La Paz) to Cabo San Lucas, a distance of around 135 kilometers (81 mi). Originally called Sierra de la Victoria by the Spanish, the interior mountains were renamed Sierra de la Laguna in the early Mexican era. These peaks are unique among sierras in the southern half of Baja California in that they're granitic rather than volcanic. And unlike the sierras to the north, the entire Laguna range is tilted eastward instead of westward; i.e., its steepest slopes are on the west side of the escarpment rather than the east.

Picacho de la Laguna (elevation 2,161 m/7,090 ft), roughly in the sierra's center, is usually cited as the highest peak in the range, although according to some sources **Cerro las Casitas**—approximately 6.5 kilometers (4 mi) southeast of Picacho de la Laguna and measuring 2,083 meters (6,835 ft) by most accounts—may be higher. Between these two peaks is a large, flat meadow called **La Laguna** (elevation 1,707 m/5,600 ft). This depression held a mountain lake until around 1870, when Cañon San Dionísio became sufficiently eroded to drain away accumulated water.

The sierra flora has been little researched; the most recent detailed studies were undertaken in the 1890s by botanist T. S. Brandegee for the California Academy of Sciences. The foothills and mesas below 500 meters are covered with dry *matorral*—low-growing cacti, succulents, thornscrub, and abundant herbs. Common species include barrel cactus, cholla, *palo verde,* ironwood, damiana, and oregano. Canyon walls may be draped with *zalate* (wild fig). At elevations of 500–750 meters (1,640–2,460 ft), tropical-subtropical deciduous forest and columnar cacti are the dominant flora (e.g., *mauto, palo blanco,* prickly pear, *cardón, palo adán*). At 750–1,200 meters (2,460–3,940 ft), live-oak woodlands (*encino,* madrone) dominate, and above 1,200 meters a mix of live oak and piñon pine prevails. At its highest elevations, La Laguna qualifies as a cloud forest during the moist summer months, when the peaks are consistently shrouded in mist or rain.

Islands in the Sky

The range's highlands receive more annual precipitation—up to 89 centimeters (35 in) per year in some microclimates—than any other place in Baja California. As a result, the meadow of La Laguna and other flats and high canyons in the sierra contain a number of "relic environments" preserving flora and fauna long ago lost on the arid plains below.

These "islands in the sky" support a sensational mix of desert, tropical, and subalpine

SIERRA DE LA LAGUNA
HIKING TRAILS

To La Paz
To San Bartolo and La Paz
Sea of Cortez
Los Barriles
Picacho de la Laguna 2,155m/7,090ft
Buena Vista
Cañon San Dionisio
Rancho San Dionisio
Todos Santos
La Burrera (San Juan del Aserradero)
Cerro las Casitas 2,078m/6,818ft
Las Cuevas
Santiago
CAÑON DE LA ZORRA
El Pescadero
Rancho Santo Domingo
Cañon San Bernardo
PACIFIC OCEAN
El Refugio
El Güerigo
Cañon San Pablo
Miraflores
Punta Gaspareño
Rancho el Salto
Caduaño
0   5 mi
0   5 km
Colonia P.E. Calles
El Aguaje
To Cabo San Lucas
To San José del Cabo and Cabo San Lucas

© AVALON TRAVEL PUBLISHING, INC.

plant species that are found together nowhere else in North America. Among the unlikely combinations seen growing side by side: mosses and cacti, madrone and monkey flower, palm and willow. Of the 447 plant species known to grow in the sierra, at least 70 are reportedly indigenous. Undisturbed by human progress, deer, coyote, mountain lion, Pacific tree frog, and dozens of hummingbird species also thrive in the highland areas of the sierra.

For many years, naturalists and outdoor enthusiasts clamored for the upper sierra to be declared a national park or preserve, and in June 1994 the Mexican government finally granted the Sierra de la Laguna official recognition as a "biosphere reserve." Such status prohibits development within the reserve's 32,519-hectare core zone; local ranchers are permitted to graze livestock in a buffer zone surrounding the protected core.

Hiking and Backpacking

The Sierra de la Laguna is a popular hiking area for Cape residents, as it offers the op-portunity to leave behind the fig trees and palms of the arid-tropical environment for a walk among cottonwoods and subalpine meadows. Three lengthy east–west canyons—Cañon San Dionísio, Cañon San Bernardo, and Cañon San Pablo—provide the principal access into the sierra. All three routes enable hikers to cross the sierra's spine from east to west or vice versa. Primitive campsites are available along each of the three routes.

The northernmost and most popular route, via Cañon San Dionísio, leads directly to La Laguna, the range's largest and highest meadow. La Laguna lies at an altitude of just under 1,800 meters (6,000 ft), between Picacho de la Laguna and Cerro las Casitas, the sierra's tallest peaks. The scenery on this hike is impressive. A straight traverse of this route, starting from either side, is possible in three days, although this would allow little time for taking it easy. Add at least another day to allow some time to enjoy La Laguna once you've reached it.

© PAUL ITOI

Sierra de la Laguna entrance

◖ Cañon de la Zorra

Freshwater is a sight to behold in the Baja desert landscape. For those travelers who would like to venture into the Sierra but do not have time for a multiday hike, there is a 30-foot waterfall just six miles beyond Santiago that has a swimmable lagoon and is reachable by foot. At the far end of the divided avenue that leads into Santiago (as you approach the plaza), turn right and set your trip odometer to zero. At 0.48 kilometer (0.3 mi), go straight through the dirt road intersection and head up the hill, past a sign for San Dionísio. At 1.29 kilometers (0.8 mi) and the crest of the hill, turn left. At 1.77 kilometers (1.1 mi), turn right across a small arroyo and follow this road to 4.02 kilometers (2.5 mi), where the road forks and there is a sign pointing to the right fork marked Cañon de la Zorra. Follow this fork to the end of the road at 9.66 kilometers (6.0 mi) and park at the trailhead. Small wooden outhouses are popping up in remote areas of the Cape, and you'll find one of them here. Go through the gate and follow

the trail for 10 minutes down to the river bottom and the falls.

Cañon San Dionísio: Western (Todos Santos) Approach

Most hikers ascend to La Laguna from the west side, which is a steeper but more straightforward hike (and about 2 km shorter) than from Rancho San Dionísio. Unlike the network of cattle trails on the east side—which are best negotiated with local guides—the western ascent can be easily accomplished without a guide. From the west side a round-trip can be completed in two days.

Near Todos Santos, the sandy road to La Burrera leaves Mexico 19 about 100 meters south of the Punta Lobos turnoff. Past an old water tower, take the first left and continue straight through several intersections till the road ends at a gate and parking area. From the gate, follow the dirt road till you reach La Burrera (about 25 minutes away), where a sign in English advises hikers to follow marked trails (ironic since we've never seen any marked trails in the sierra). Also known as San Juan del Aserradero, this village on the sierra's western slopes lies around 17.5 kilometers (11 mi) northeast of Todos Santos. Continue along this road another 20 minutes or so till you see a clearing on the right that has been used for camping; look for a sign reading No Tire Basura (Don't Throw Trash). Just past this sign, the road ascends to a small rise, at the top of which the main trail begins. After 30 meters or so of easy grade, the trail begins its long, steady climb straight up the mountain. Following this wide, established (rutted in places), 11-kilometer (7-mi) trail, you should reach La Laguna in 5–8 hours, depending on your pace. Along the way the vegetation changes quickly from desert and thorn forest into lush piñon-oak woodlands; about 20 minutes before you reach La Laguna the forest canopy opens to magnificent views of the sierra and Pacific Ocean.

Follow the arroyo that drains La Laguna at its southeast corner, near where the trail comes in from Rancho San Dionísio, to reach

EAST CAPE

a 20-meter (66-ft) cascade with deep pools suitable for swimming.

The return descent along the same trail takes about four hours to reach La Burrera.

If you need a ride to La Burrera from Todos Santos, your best bet is to inquire at Siempre Vive (at the corner of Calles Juárez and Márquez de León) in the late morning, when ranchers from the western sierra sometimes turn up for supplies and gossip. Fees for such a ride are negotiable—some ranchers will give you a lift for gas money and a six-pack of Tecate, others ask up to US$30. You might also inquire at the Todos Santos taxi stand next to the town park.

Cañon San Dionísio: Eastern (Santiago) Approach

From the east side of the sierra, count on 3–4 days to La Laguna and back with time to explore the area. The eastern mouth of the main canyon is reached via a dirt road to Rancho San Dionísio from Santiago (19 km/12 mi). From there it's a 13-kilometer (8-mi) hike west through the canyon mouth, then into a side arroyo and finally along the southern rim of the canyon to La Laguna. Piñon pine and cape live oak began appearing about two-thirds of the way up. This trail is relatively difficult to follow and is intersected by potentially confusing animal paths; a guide, available at Rancho San Dionísio or in Santiago, is highly recommended. If you decide to go it alone, be sure to carry a topo map and compass, and watch out for cattle trails branching off the main trail in every direction. Scout ahead at questionable junctions, even if it means going slower. Once you're up on the ridgeline you should be able to spot La Laguna in the distance and then confidently follow any trail heading in that direction.

Those wishing to explore a bit can follow the canyon four kilometers (2.5 mi) straight west of the ranch into a steep area of boulders; where the arroyo forks there's a 20-meter (66-ft) waterfall and deep pools suitable for swimming. Don't attempt to follow the canyon all the way to the meadow un-

less you're into some very serious bouldering and scrambling.

Near the northwest edge of the meadow itself are a couple of herder's shacks. Just past these the trail cuts into the forest and divides; the southern branch descends to La Burrera, while the north branch ascends Picacho de la Laguna, a 90-minute hike away. (A lesser third trail leads to an arroyo with freshwater.) Easy to climb, the peak is bare of trees and provides splendid views of the surrounding terrain. Closer to the meadow, a hill surmounted by radio towers also makes a good vantage point.

Those wishing to traverse the sierra can descend westward from La Laguna another 11 kilometers (7 mi) to La Burrera; see *Cañon San Dionísio: Western (Todos Santos) Approach.* About 20 minutes into the descent from the meadow, you'll come upon terrific views all the way to the Pacific Ocean. Roads from La Burrera meet Mexico 19 south and north of Todos Santos; the area east of these junctions is honeycombed with other dirt roads, but if you continue in a westerly direction you'll eventually come to the highway.

Cañon San Bernardo

The next route to the south, via Cañon San Bernardo, is a relatively easy (from east to west) hike that crests at around 900 meters (3,000 ft). The canyon trailhead is accessible via an eight-kilometer (5-mi) dirt road from Miraflores to Boca de la Sierra, where the trail skirts a dam and follows the canyon to the crest, 16 kilometers (10 mi) northwest. Several pools along the way provide freshwater year-round. From the 900-meter crest, the trail continues over the sierra to the village of Santo Domingo on the western side, for a total traverse of 22.5 kilometers (14 mi). The Cañon San Bernardo crossing makes a good four- to five-day hike, although it's possible to make a quick overnight to the crest and back from the eastern approach.

Cañon San Pablo

Cañon San Pablo provides the southernmost route into the sierra, reaching an elevation of around 1,000 meters (3,300 ft). The canyon mouth is best approached by taking a 6.5-kilometer (4-mi) dirt road west from Caduaño, a village four kilometers (2.5 mi) south of Miraflores, to Rancho El Salto. From Rancho El Salto, it's approximately 10.5 kilometers (6.5 mi) to the crest; the trail continues over the ridge and along a steeper 4.8-kilometer (3-mi) westward descent to the village of El Güerigo on the other side, where a network of dirt roads leads west to Mexico 19. A leisurely El Salto–El Güerigo hike takes 4–5 days.

Seasons

The best backpacking season here is late fall, after the rainy season has passed and sierra streams and *tinajas* are full. Temperatures above 1,500 meters (5,000 ft) typically measure 12–22°C (54–72°F) during the day, 5–12°C (41–54°F) at night. In January and February, temperatures can dip below freezing at night, while daytime temps run around 10–20°C (50–68°F).

The warmest temperatures are usually encountered in May and June, when the mercury reaches around 25°C (77°F) during the day, 10–15°C (50–60°F) at night. Although the scenery isn't as spectacularly green this time of year, it's a fine time to beat the heat down on the coastal plains.

July–October rains may wash out trails and flood the canyons. Rainfall peaks in August, averaging 7.5 centimeters (3 in) but sometimes reaching a drenching 20 centimeters (7.8 in) for the month.

Supplies

A compass and good topographic map are musts for any trip into the Sierra de la Laguna. To cover all three routes, you should possess copies of Mexico's relevant 1:50,000-scale topos: El Rosario F12B23; Las Cuevas F12B24; Todos Santos F12B33; and Santiago F12B34 (see *Hiking and Backpacking* in the *Essentials* chapter). Bring warm clothing and sleeping bags for the summit; morning frost isn't uncommon even in fall and spring. Long pants and sturdy hiking shoes are rec-

ommended as a defense against the abundant cactus and nettles.

On the Cañon San Dionísio trail, bring all the water you'll need to reach La Laguna, as there are no dependable sources on the way up, even in wet weather. An arroyo at La Laguna itself carries water year-round. On the Cañon San Bernardo trail, pools of water can be found along the way year-round. Water may be available from ranchos along the Cañon San Pablo trail, but bring your own to be safe. Be sure to use a water-purification system of some kind on all water sources in the mountains; although the water is generally uncontaminated, the presence of livestock precludes absolute safety.

Guides

For eastern ascents into the sierra, those unsure of their backpacking and orientation skills should consider hiring a local guide, since trails across the eastern escarpment are often obscured and junctions not always obvious. A guide can also prepare simple camp meals and point out items of natural interest—Amerindian rock art, flora and fauna—that first-timers might otherwise miss. Ask around for guides in Santiago or Miraflores. For the Cañon San Dionísio route, you can sometimes arrange a guide at Rancho San Dionísio, just before the eastern trailhead.

The going rate for guides in Santiago is US$30–35 per day per person, plus an extra US$15 per day per pack animal. Rancho San Dionísio charges US$30 for a guide without mules, no matter how many people are hiking.

Many hikers make the western approach to Cañon San Dionísio from Todos Santos without a guide; the main difficulty is finding your way (or arranging a ride) to the trailhead. If you decide to hire a guide, there are a couple of options in Todos Santos. Fernando Arteche (sierradelalaguna@hotmail.com) is fluent in English and knowledgeable about the Sierra de la Laguna. His guided trips usually take three days, and you can go on foot or by mule. Another local guide, Juan Sebastián López (onejohnone@hotmail.com), offers three-day trips on horseback, with packhorses to carry the gear. He also leads two-day trips to the hot springs.

Information and Services

Services are few and far between in this part of the Cape Region. San Antonio (Km 157) and Miraflores (Km 71) have Pemex stations. Buses stop at Santiago, for access to the Sierra de la Laguna, and at La Ribera/Las Cuevas, Km 93, for access to Cabo Pulmo (no connecting service).

Driving Across the Sierra

Visitors with sturdy, high-clearance vehicles may be able to traverse the Sierra de la Laguna in dry weather via a road that leaves Mexico 1 about 16 kilometers (10 mi) south of Miraflores (about 8 km/5 mi north of Santa Anita) near Km 55. Among gringo road hogs this route is often called the "Naranjos road"; the correct name is Ramal Los Naranjos (*naranjo* means "orange tree," a probable reference to the many small citrus farms in the area). Because parts of it may suffer from washouts, this is not a road to tackle during the rainy season (July–Sept.), and you should make inquiries at

any time of year to determine whether the road is clear all the way.

From the Mexico 1 turnoff the road leads west-northwest 42 kilometers (26 mi) to the village of **El Aguaje,** past the *ranchitos* of San Miguelito, Cieneguita, San Pedro de la Soledad, and El Remudadero. The ungraded road passes a couple of 1,500- to 1,800-meter (5,000- to 6,000-ft) peaks before cresting at around 1,035 meters (3,400 ft) and descending into a challenging set of sharp curves and grades approaching 30 percent. At 27 kilometers (17 mi) from Mexico 1 you get your first view of the Pacific Ocean, by which point the road begins hugging the edge of a rock mountain. Shortly thereafter the road may be washed out or blocked by rock slides and you may not be able to continue. The track eventually widens to a graded, gravel road near El Aguaje, then continues another 12.8 kilometers (8 mi) before terminating at Mexico 19 near Playa Los Cerritos south of Todos Santos. Two INEGI topo maps, San José del Cabo F12B44 and La Candelaria F12B43, would make helpful—though not required—companions on this cross-sierra road trip.

LOS CABOS

Something magical happens at the point where the cool green Pacific Ocean crashes into the blue sapphire Sea of Cortez at Land's End. The fish that inhabit these waters drew the original visitors 30 years ago. Then the anglers began to bring their golf clubs, dive gear, and college-age kids. Today, stunning geography, perfect weather, endless opportunities for outdoor recreation, and federal funding from the Mexican government have transformed the area from a cluster of fishing villages into a full-scale tourist corridor.

From Cabo San Lucas to San José del Cabo, and everywhere in between, highway exit ramps are replacing dirt-road turnoffs, new resorts and condo buildings are under construction, golf courses are opening, and restaurant menu prices are reaching for the stars.

Some say Los Cabos is well on its way (if not already there) to becoming Mexico's most expensive destination.

Adventure travelers, fear not: Los Cabos offers much more than nine-bedroom villas and 110-foot yachts. Beneath the upscale veneer, quaint B&Bs, modest hotels, free snorkeling beaches, authentic taquerías, and affordable *panga* boat tours invite exploration.

Cabo San Lucas and San José del Cabo enjoy equal access to a string of beautiful beaches along the Corridor between the two towns, but because the San Lucas harbor provides shelter for a sizable sportfishing and recreational fleet, the preponderance of yearly Los Cabos visitors station themselves here rather than in San José or along the Corridor.

Although it's located closer to Los Cabos

HIGHLIGHTS

◖ **Plaza Mijares:** A shady plaza at the intersection of San José's two main streets features the twin-towered **Iglesia San José,** built in 1940 on the site of the original 1730 Misión San José del Cabo (page 335).

◖ **Estero San José:** The freshwater Río San José meets the Pacific Ocean at a 50-hectare (125-acre) estuary that hosts more than 200 species of birds (page 336).

◖ **Playas Chileno and Santa María:** Two of the Corridor's most popular and accessible beaches offer safe swimming and good snorkeling (page 356).

◖ **Land's End:** A large cluster of granitic batholiths, carved by wind and sea into fantastic shapes, tumbles into the sea at the Cape's southernmost point (page 371).

◖ **Playa del Amor:** The Sea of Cortez meets the Pacific Ocean at this two-sided beach just outside the Cabo San Lucas harbor. Calm waters on Bahía San Lucas invite underwater exploration, while pounding surf on the Pacific side warns sunbathers to keep their distance (page 372).

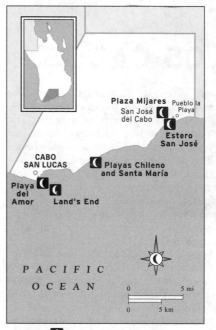

LOOK FOR ◖ TO FIND RECOMMENDED SIGHTS, ACTIVITIES, DINING, AND LODGING.

International Airport, San José del Cabo is a quieter, more traditional resort town than neighboring Cabo San Lucas. A somewhat older tourist crowd frequents San José (pop. 25,000), leaving Cabo San Lucas to partying college students, bachelor parties, and young couples. That said, San José is experiencing some growth pains of its own—in the form of heavier traffic and noise pollution from pervasive construction. And there is concern that the town is becoming unaffordable for local residents.

The Transpeninsular Highway's 29-kilometer (18-mi), four-lane stretch between San José del Cabo and Cabo San Lucas—known as the Corridor—provides access to numerous beaches, coves, points, and tidal pools along the Pacific Ocean and Sea of Cortez.

PLANNING YOUR TIME

In a couple of days, you can easily explore the main sections of downtown San José and sample a few restaurants, plus have time for the beach. Add extra days for any special activities, such as scuba diving, fishing, or mountain biking. The drive from San José del Cabo to Cabo San Lucas along the Corridor takes about 30–45 minutes. Surfers and beachcombers will happily spend a full week at a resort along the Corridor. But aside from the beaches (which are spectacular) and associated activities, there is little else to see—meaning, you don't need a lot of time to cover the area if you're just passing through.

For some travelers, a half day in Cabo San Lucas will be more than enough time; others will be content to spend a week. It all depends on whether you prefer nightlife or a more remote setting for your vacation.

CHOOSING AN ACCOMMODATION

Whether you are a first-time or veteran Los Cabos visitor, finding a place to stay involves an overwhelming variety of choices. There are all-inclusive resorts, boutique hotels, basic motels, bed-and-breakfast inns, condominiums, timeshares, and villas of all sizes. (And some resorts mix and match, to give even more choice.) You can be at the beach, on a golf course, or in town. You can book directly with a resort or private owner, or use a booking service or property management company. And you can spend US$50 to US$950 a night, depending on your budget and the level of comfort you seek.

If you'd like a quieter location where you can look at the beach but swim in a pool, the Corridor or hotel zone of San José would be good choices. If you want to surf, consider Playa Costa Azul, just outside of San José. For swimming and nightlife within walking distance of your hotel, head to Cabo San Lucas.

High-end resorts feature a full list of amenities, usually including air conditioning, direct-dial phones, satellite TV, multiple swimming pools, swim-up bars, tennis courts, hot tubs, fitness centers, kids' club, and beach *palapas,* plus onsite restaurants and bars. Some resorts also have their own dive centers, spa services, horseback riding, and ATV rental services. High-speed wireless Internet, voice-over-IP phones (free long distance), and flatscreen TVs are some of the newest amenities that hotels and condo owners are adding to differentiate themselves.

Vacation rental condos or villas, or condo-style hotels, afford the most flexibility, as you can cook some of your own meals and venture out for others. Many of the newest condo complexes are concentrated near Playa Costa Azul, between San José and the Corridor. Most are on or near the beach and many have tennis courts,

swimming pools, and laundry facilities; however, the persistent sound of traffic on Mexico 1 is a drawback to this location. You can rent units directly from private owners by searching for listings online (on www .craigslist.com and www.vrbo.com, for example), or by contacting a property management service. (Many of these services also advertise on the private-owner sites.)

Planning Ahead

If you are thinking about a year-end holiday vacation, book as far in advance as possible. Repeat visitors reserve many of the most popular rooms and rentals as much as a year in advance for the weeks around Christmas and New Year's. February and March are popular too, and despite the number of choices for accommodations, there are a handful of resorts—including the One&Only Palmilla, Dreams, and Riu Palace—that seem to be full almost all the time. Flexible travelers need not plan so far ahead, and they are often rewarded with better deals.

Booking Services and Property Management Companies

If you haven't yet decided on a specific location within Los Cabos, or you have a very specific set of criteria for choosing a place to stay, contact a booking service agent, who can give you an overview of several different properties that meet your criteria and your budget. The following companies specialize in Los Cabos area bookings: **Delfin Hotels & Resorts,** also called **Cabo Hotels** (U.S. tel. 800/524-5104) lists a wide variety of villas, condos (Terrasol, Las Manañitas, Mira Vista, Mykonos) all-inclusive resorts, and bed-and-breakfast inns. It also publishes several Cabo accommodations websites, including www.cabohotels.com, www.cabocondos.com, and www.allinclusivescabo. com. **Baja Properties** (Doblado and Morelos, San José tel. 624/142-0988, Cabo San Lucas tel. 624/143-2560, U.S. tel. 877/462-2226, www.bajaproperties.com) has 20 years of experience in Los Cabos real estate

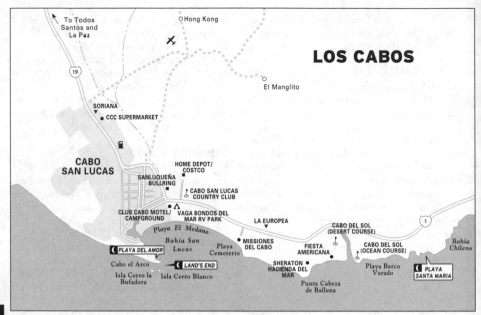

marketing, eight office locations, and a team of 25 agents.

Watsonville, California–based **Earth, Sea, and Sky Vacations** (ESSV, U.S. tel. 800/745-2226, www.cabovillas.com) specializes in luxury vacation packages to the Los Cabos area. It represents 90 villa rentals, ranging from two- to nine-bedroom units, with a starting pricepoint of US$1,500 per night, as well as 30 resorts. For an extra fee, ESSV staff will stock your villa prior to your arrival with the foods and supplies you request. Guests can also opt for in-villa services, such as pilates or yoga classes, spa treatments, and chef services (for one special meal or three meals daily). Since ESSV also handles activity bookings for whale-watching, fishing, and snorkeling, many travelers work with the company to coordinate group trips, such as large family vacations or small weddings.

Companies that focus exclusively on Cabo San Lucas or San José del Cabo (as opposed to the entire region), are listed in the accommodations section for those towns.

GETTING THERE

The majority of Los Cabos visitors arrive by air, but you'll meet many who have traveled by car, boat, bicycle, or even on foot. Public transportation by bus is also a possibility. Once you've arrived, you can do without a car if you plan to stay at an all-inclusive resort or at a hotel in town. Rent a car if you want to take a day trip to the East Cape or Todos Santos.

By Air

Los Cabos International Airport (SJD), located about eight miles north of San José del Cabo via a speedy four-lane section of Mexico 1 (Km 44, tel. 624/142-5111), serves both San José and Cabo San Lucas. The airport does not have Jetways, so have your shades at the ready as you exit the plane and climb down the stairs to the tarmac.

The process of going through customs can take more than an hour, depending on how many people are working and if other flights have arrived at the same time. After you go

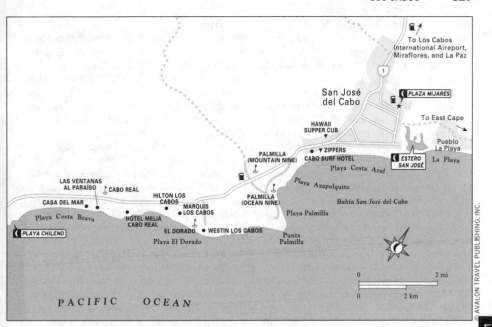

LOS CABOS

through passport control, you'll proceed to the baggage claim area. Claim your bags and have your paperwork ready to show the customs official. You'll be asked to run your bags through a scanner and to press a button that determines whether your bags will be randomly searched.

The airport has three terminals served by several major airlines, including:

- Terminal 1: American, Aeromexico, US Airways, Continental, Mexicana

- Terminal 2: General aviation and cargo

- Terminal 3: Alaska, Delta, Frontier, United

Terminal 1 holds a few food kiosks (Domino's Express, Subway Sandwiches, Dunkin' Donuts), two snack bars, souvenir shops, a money-exchange service, and an upstairs restaurant, but has no seats in the waiting area for arriving flights—a minor inconvenience for those meeting incoming passengers.

There are no seats in the waiting area for arriving flights at the new terminal either, except at the small bar. The second level (inside security) has a bar in the center and a cafeteria at one end.

A *colectivo* (shared) van into the San José area runs US$12 per person and US$15 to the Cabo San Lucas area. A private taxi from the airport to any destination in San José del Cabo costs US$35; US$70 to Cabo San Lucas.

BY PRIVATE AIRCRAFT

Private pilots will find a 1,550-meter (5,100-ft) paved airstrip just north of Cabo San Lucas. Contact Baja Bush Pilots (www.bajabushpilots.com) for up-to-date information about making the trip to Los Cabos.

By Car

Most of the big auto rental agencies have desks at Los Cabos International Airport, as well as offices in or near town. (See the sidebar *Where to Rent a Car in Baja* in the *Essentials* chapter.) Rates will be similar across most companies, and since car rentals don't require a deposit up front, it doesn't hurt to make a reservation in advance. You can always cancel if you change your mind. When you reserve or prepay for a car online, the price typically will not include Mexican liability insurance. Be sure to factor this cost (around US$25 per day for the minimum required coverage of US$50,000) into your travel planning. Vehicles range from standard transmission subcompact sedans to SUVs, wagons, jeeps, pickup trucks, and vans. Independent agencies sometimes include insurance in the rates (see *Insuring Your Rental Car* in the *Essentials* chapter).

If you don't reserve a car before you arrive in Los Cabos, you can look at price lists at the airport. By comparing rates across the various desks, you can sometimes negotiate the price downward. It's usually cheaper to rent a car at Los Cabos International Airport than in Cabo San Lucas or San José, but it's always worth shopping around.

If you're driving yourself, there are two ways to reach the towns along the Los Cabos Corridor from the airport: Follow signs for Mexico 1 south through town, passing through several stoplights before you reach the town of San José. Continue on Mexico 1 another 10–20 minutes for destinations along the Corridor, or about 30 minutes to Cabo San Lucas. Alternatively, if you don't mind paying a toll of US$2, you can exit the airport onto the *quota,* a fast four-lane road with no exits until you enter San José at the junction of Paseo Los Cabos and the Mega grocery store plaza. If you pick up a rental car offsite, you'll have to return to the terminal to get to the toll road.

By Bus

Buses to/from La Paz: Autotransportes Águila
(tel. 624/143-7880) operates 17 buses a day to La Paz (US$14 from Cabo San Lucas and US$17 from San José), a dozen via Todos Santos. This is the quickest route at 3.5 hours total; the rest go via San José del Cabo, Los Barriles, and the East Cape, totaling 4–4.5 hours. The first bus leaves Cabo San Lucas at 5:45 A.M.; the last leaves at 8:30 P.M. Buses that depart at 7:40 A.M., 9:40 A.M., and 12:30 P.M. continue to Pichilingue for the ferry; if you miss these, take any La Paz bus and transfer to one of the hourly buses to Pichilingue from the La Paz bus station. Cabo's main intercity bus terminal is on Mexico 19, just north of the Mexico 1 junction, opposite the Pemex station.

Autotransportes La Paz also has buses to La Paz, usually slightly cheaper than the competition. The bus stop is on the opposite side of the road, just south of the same junction. Buses depart at 6, 7, 8:30, and 9:30 A.M., then roughly every 90 minutes thereafter.

Buses Farther North: Each day at 4 P.M. a first-class bus also leaves for the 24-hour trip to Tijuana (US$125), with stops in Ciudad Constitución (US$25), Loreto (US$33), Mulegé (US$35), Guerrero Negro (US$57), and Ensenada (US$90).

By Sea
The nearest ferry service to the mainland operates between La Paz and Mazatlán (see *Getting There and Around* in the *La Paz and Vicinity* chapter).

Marina Cabo San Lucas is the main docking facility for transient recreational boats; bow-stern anchorages are also permitted in the outer bay (see *Boating* in the *Cabo San Lucas* section).

San José del Cabo

The Jesuit padres who founded a mission community here in the 18th century situated San José on a mesa a couple of kilometers north of the beach. Century-old brick and adobe buildings, many of them proudly restored, line the main streets radiating from the plaza and church. These are interspersed with Indian laurel trees and other greenery, making San José one of the most pleasant pedestrian towns in the Cape Region.

The architecture thins out and becomes more modern as you descend toward the beach, culminating in a golf course, condos, resort homes, and the *zona hotelera*. Because of the town's mesa geography, the beachfront hotels don't obscure the view from town. Areas to the north and east of town are dotted with irrigated orchards producing mangoes, avocados, bananas, and citrus.

As the *cabecera* (roughly equivalent to "county seat") of the Municipio de San José del Cabo, the town enjoys well-maintained streets and city services. Employment in the public as well as private sector has lured a variety of talented *bajacalifornianos* to establish residence here. A number of foreigners also have retirement or vacation homes in the area, although the overall gringo presence, whether resident or visiting, is much smaller than in Cabo San Lucas.

HISTORY

The Pericú who frequented the San José area before the Spanish *entrada* called the area "Añuiti," a name whose meaning has been lost. Spanish galleons first visited Estero San José—the mouth of the Río San José—to obtain freshwater near the end of their lengthy voyages from the Philippines to Acapulco in the late 17th and early 18th centuries. During this period the estuary was known among seamen as Aguada Segura (Sure Waters) and, less commonly, San Bernabe, a name left behind by Sebastián Vizcaíno

LOS CABOS

Playa California

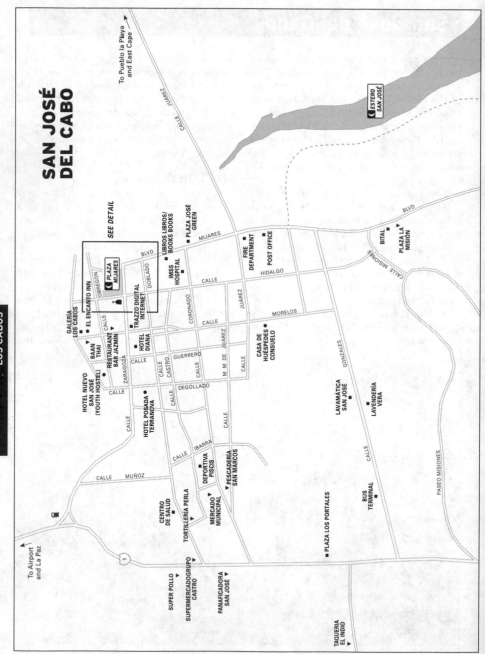

SAN JOSÉ DEL CABO

To Pueblo la Playa and East Cape

CALLE JUAREZ

ESTERO SAN JOSÉ

SEE DETAIL

BLVD

BLVD

LIBROS LIBROS/BOOKS BOOKS

PLAZA JOSÉ GREEN

MIJARES

PLAZA MIJARES

OBREGÓN

EL ENCANTO INN

GALERIA LOS CABOS

BLVD

IMSS HOSPITAL

DOBLADO

FIRE DEPARTMENT

POST OFFICE

BITAL

PLAZA LA MISIÓN

TRAZZO DIGITAL INTERNET

CALLE

HIDALGO

CALLE MISIONES

CALLE

CORONADO

JUAREZ

BAAN THAI

RESTAURANT BAR JAZMIN

CALLE

HOTEL DIANA

CALLE

MORELOS

ZARAGOZA

CALLE CASTRO

GUERRERO

CASA DE HUÉSPEDES CONSUELO

HOTEL NUEVO SAN JOSÉ (YOUTH HOSTEL)

CALLE

CALLE

M M DE JUAREZ

CALLE

GONZALES

LAVAMÁTICA SAN JOSÉ

DEGOLLADO

HOTEL POSADA TERRANOVA

CALLE

LAVENDERÍA VERA

CALLE

IBARRA

CALLE

CALLE

DEPORTIVA PISCIS

PASEO MISIONES

CALLE   MUÑOZ

PESCADERÍA SAN MARCOS

PLAZA LOS PORTALES

To Airport and La Paz

CENTRO DE SALUD

TORTILLERÍA PERLA

MERCADO MUNICIPAL

BUS TERMINAL

1

SUPER POLLO

SUPERMERCADOGRUPO CASTRO

PANAFICADORA SAN JOSÉ

TAQUERIA EL INDIO

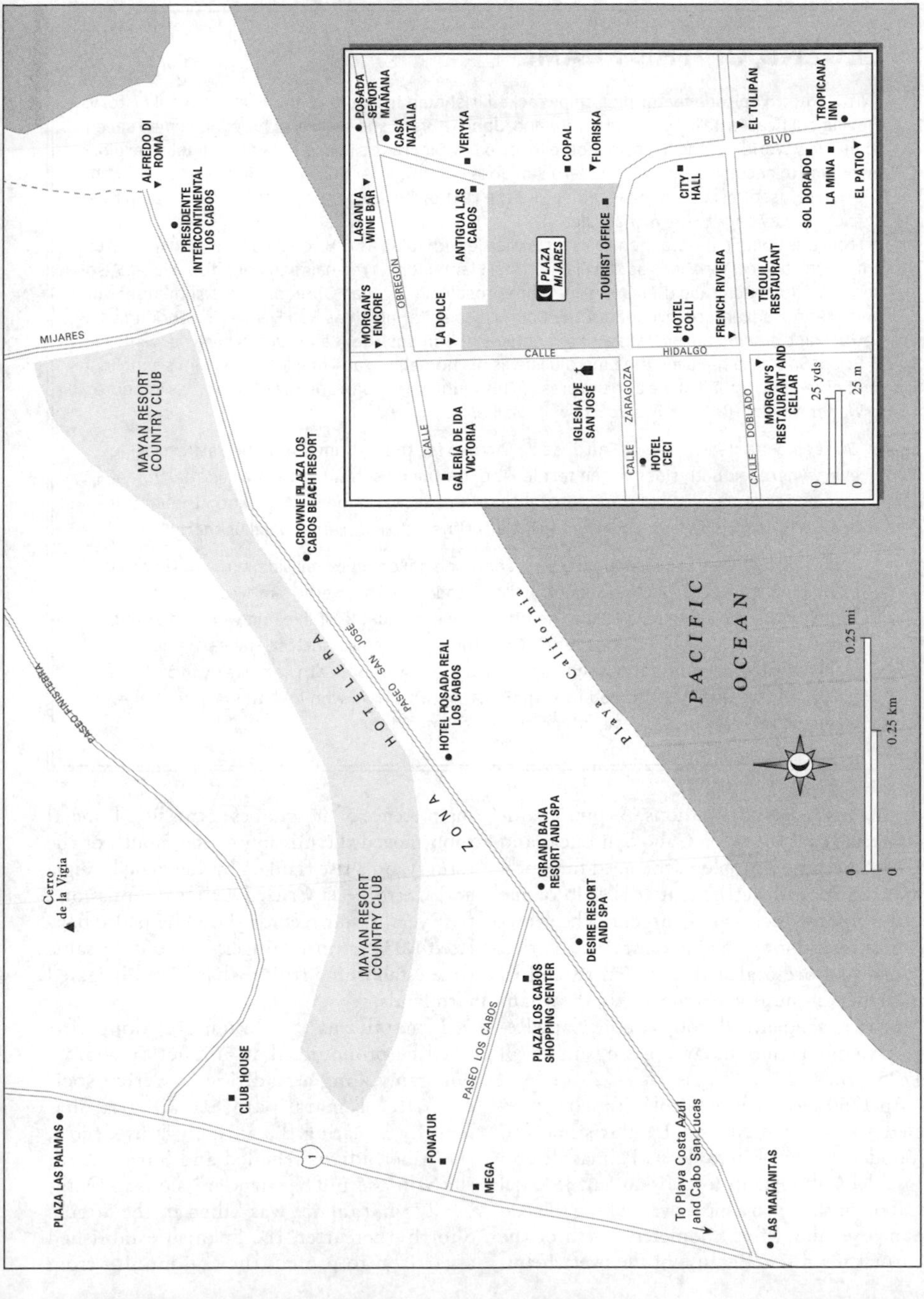
ALFREDO DI ROMA
PRESIDENTE INTERCONTINENTAL LOS CABOS
MIJARES
MAYAN RESORT COUNTRY CLUB
CROWNE PLAZA LOS CABOS BEACH RESORT
ZONA HOTELERA
PASEO SAN JOSÉ
PASEO FINISTERRA
HOTEL POSADA REAL LOS CABOS
Playa California
PACIFIC OCEAN
0.25 mi
0.25 km
0
0
Cerro de la Vigia
MAYAN RESORT COUNTRY CLUB
GRAND BAJA RESORT AND SPA
DESIRE RESORT AND SPA
PLAZA LOS CABOS SHOPPING CENTER
PASEO LOS CABOS
CLUB HOUSE
PLAZA LAS PALMAS
1
FONATUR
MEGA
To Playa Costa Azul and Cabo San Lucas
LAS MAÑANITAS
POSADA SEÑOR MAÑANA
CASA NATALIA
LASANTA WINE BAR
VERYKA
COPAL
FLORISKA
EL TULIPÁN
TROPICANA INN
BLVD
CITY HALL
SOL DORADO
LA MINA
EL PATIO
MORGAN'S ENCORE
OBREGÓN
ANTIGUA LAS CABOS
LA DOLCE
PLAZA MIJARES
TOURIST OFFICE
HOTEL COLLI
FRENCH RIVIERA
TEQUILA RESTAURANT
CALLE
HIDALGO
ZARAGOZA
IGLESIA DE SAN JOSÉ
MORGAN'S RESTAURANT AND CELLAR
DOBLADO
CALLE
GALERÍA DE IDA VICTORIA
CALLE
HOTEL CECI
CALLE
25 yds
25 m
0
0

LOS CABOS

© AVALON TRAVEL PUBLISHING, INC.

LEGEND OF THE FLAME

A little-known episode featuring a shipwrecked Irishman footnotes San José's colorful history. Fleeing political strife in 18th-century Ireland, John O'Brien and several of his countrymen sailed to the New World – along the same route followed by Sir Francis Drake and earlier English explorers – only to become stranded at Estero San José in 1795. After marrying a local Pericú woman, O'Brien refused rescue when his father and the rest of the Irish crew were later picked up by a ship on its way back to the British Isles.

From this point in the story onward, facts merge with fable as O'Brien gained legendary status among the *bajacalifornianos* as "La Flama" (The Flame) for his red hair and fiery disposition. Also known as Juan Colorado (Red John), or more prosaically as Juan Obregón, the Irishman set out on a lifetime adventure throughout the Californias as far north as San Francisco, working as a cowboy and singing the nostalgia-tinted praises of San José del Cabo everywhere he went. For O'Brien, San José replaced the Emerald Isle as his homeland, and one imagines him crying in a shot of tequila instead of ale as he expresses his longing for "San José del Arroyo," as imagined in Walter Nordhoff's book *The Journey of the Flame:*

> On seeing our dear Valley of San José del Arroyo for the last time, with the cattle grazing everywhere, on both sides of the fertile land, on the hillsides, I remembered the violent stampedes of the wild bulls and the delicious sips of warm milk I stole, and I thought: If heaven is like this valley, I can only repeat after the Indians, "Father, lead us there!"

> How many times, in subsequent years, someone galloping by my side in the desert has asked me, "Where are you from, countryman?" And when I answered him "From San José!" something crept into his voice that no other place is capable of evoking when he asked: "Would that be San José del Arroyo?" Then the horses could scatter, the cattle begin a stampede, the water be a thousand burning leagues away, or death lie close by in ambush for us, and nevertheless we had to stop. Because when two who love this Arroyo Valley meet and know each other, everything else loses importance.

during his coastal navigations. As pirate raids along the coast between Cabo San Lucas and La Paz became a problem, the need for a permanent Spanish settlement at the tip of the Cape became increasingly urgent. The growing unrest among the Guaicura and Pericú south of Loreto also threatened to engulf mission communities to the north; the Spanish had to send armed troops to the Cape Region to quell Amerindian uprisings in 1723, 1725, and 1729.

In 1730 Jesuit padre Nicolás Tamaral traveled south from Misión La Purísima and founded Misión Estero de las Palmas de San José del Cabo Añuiti (or Misión San José del Cabo, for short) on a mesa overlooking the Río San José, about five kilometers north of the current town site. Because of the overwhelm-ing presence of mosquitoes at this site, Tamaral soon moved the mission to the mouth of the estuary, on a rise flanked by Cerro de la Vigía and Cerro de la Cruz. During the mission's first year, Jesuit records show the padre baptized 1,036 *salvajes* (savages), while at the same time establishing fruit orchards and irrigated farmlands.

Tamaral and the Pericú got along fine until he pronounced an injunction against polygamy, long a tradition in Pericú society. After Tamaral punished a Pericú shaman for violating the antipolygamy decree, the Amerindians rebelled and burned both the San José and Santiago missions in October 1734. Tamaral was killed in the attack. Shortly thereafter, the Spanish established a garrison to protect the community from

© NIKKI GOTH ITOI

Plaza Mijares, San José's central plaza

insurgent natives and the estuary from English pirates.

By 1767, virtually all the Amerindians in the area had died either of European-borne diseases or in skirmishes with the Spanish. Surviving Pericú were moved to missions farther north, but San José del Cabo remained an important Spanish military outpost until the mid-19th century, when the presidio was turned over to Mexican nationals.

During the Mexican-American War (1846–1848), marines from the U.S. frigate *Portsmouth* briefly occupied the city. A bloody siege ensued, but the Mexicans prevailed under the leadership of Mexican naval officer José Antonio Mijares. Plaza Mijares, San José's town square, is named for him, as is Boulevard Mijares, the main avenue connecting the town center and the hotel zone. As mining in the Cape Region gave out during the late 19th and early 20th centuries, the population of San José and the rest of the region decreased. A few sugarcane farmers, cattle ranchers, and fishermen began trickling into the San José area in the 1930s, and in 1940 the church was rebuilt.

San José remained largely an agricultural backwater known for its avocados, mangoes, citrus, and other fruits until the Cape began attracting sportfishers and later the sun-and-sand set in the 1960s and 1970s. Since the late 1970s, Fonatur (the Mexican tourist bureau) has sponsored several tourist and residential development projects along San José's shoreline. Fortunately, the development has done little to change San José's Spanish-colonial character, and local residents take pride in restoring the town's 18th-century architecture and preserving its quiet, laid-back ambience.

SIGHTS
◖ Plaza Mijares

Most town festivals are centered at Plaza Mijares. The shady plaza, at the intersection of Boulevard Mijares and Calle Zaragoza (San José's two main streets), is a well-tended expanse of brick with benches and a gazebo. At the plaza's west end is the twin-towered **Iglesia San José,** built in 1940 on the site of the original 1730 Misión San José del Cabo. A mosaic over the main entrance depicts a scene from the infamous 1734 Pericú uprising, with Amerindians shown dragging Padre Tamaral toward a fire, presumably to be burned alive.

Estero San José

The freshwater Río San José meets the Pacific Ocean at this 50-hectare (125-acre) estuary just east of the Presidente InterContinental Los Cabos hotel. A sandbar at the mouth of the river forms a scenic lagoon surrounded by tall palms and marsh grasses—habitat for more than 200 species of birds, including brown pelicans, ring-necked ducks, common egrets, and herons. Bird connoisseurs should keep their eyes peeled for Belding's yellowthroat, also commonly seen here. You can rent canoes at Tío Sports, next to the Presidente, for paddling around the lagoon.

A public footpath, **Paseo del Estero,** follows the estuary and river through scenic fan palms, river cane, and tule—a perfect place for bird-watching. The path begins at the Presidente and comes out on Boulevard Mijares near a modern water-treatment plant. There is plenty of street parking near the hotel.

Zona Hotelera

Fonatur has developed 4,000 shoreline acres adjacent to San José into a hotel and recreation zone. Thus far, the zone contains several resort hotels, a golf course, shopping center, and several condo and housing developments. Between the Presidente InterContinental and Crowne Plaza resorts, the new Cabo Azul Resort & Spa, under construction by Pacific Monarch Resorts, will house 292 vacation villas. Mayan Resorts is also developing a new resort next door. Some of the nicest homes in the Fonatur zone are located along the north side of the golf course.

The wide, sandy beach here, known as either Playa Hotelera or Playa California, is perfect for sunbathing, but the undertow is strong.

La Playita and Pueblo La Playa

Just east of San José via Calle Juárez, adjacent to the village of Pueblo La Playa, is La Playita (Little Beach). An ocean beach away from the hotel zone, La Playita offers *pangas* for hire. Walk along the beach northeast of the Presidente InterContinental Los Cabos about a kilometer, or you can walk or drive a similar distance east along Calle Juárez from downtown. Continue along a dirt road through the middle of the village, past a radio tower, to reach the most secluded spots.

Along the dirt road from here to Pueblo La Playa and beyond to the East Cape are large banyan *(zalate)* and mango trees as well as wild sugarcane. Much of the Río San José valley was once planted in sugarcane.

Home development continues in the area. Fonatur has begun to develop a new tourist zone called Puerto Los Cabos (www.puertoloscabos) at La Playita. At last check, a four-lane boulevard with a landscaped median led the way through several traffic circles to the beach. Cranes were moving rocks one by one to

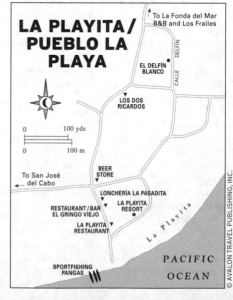

LA PLAYITA / PUEBLO LA PLAYA

To La Fonda del Mar B&B and Los Frailes

EL DELFÍN BLANCO

CALLE DELFÍN

LOS DOS RICARDOS

0   100 yds
0   100 m

To San José del Cabo

BEER STORE

LONCHERÍA LA PASADITA

RESTAURANT / BAR EL GRINGO VIEJO

LA PLAYITA RESORT

LA PLAYITA RESTAURANT

La Playita

SPORTFISHING PANGAS

PACIFIC OCEAN

© AVALON TRAVEL PUBLISHING, INC.

© NIKKI GOTH ITOI

dining under a *palapa* roof at Mariscos El Puerto, at La Playita

form a protected harbor around the sportfishing *pangas* that line the beach. When complete, the 2,000-acre development will include more five-star hotels and designer golf courses and a new marina that will allow large seagoing vessels to dock, ushering thousands of passengers into town.

Playa Costa Azul

Connecting San José to the Corridor, Plaza Costa Azul is gently washed by low breakers and often safe for swimming, except during the *chubasco* season (see *Surfing*). Several condo complexes line the beach. For travelers coming from San José, there is a new and unmarked exit ramp just after Havanas Restaurant and before the wide arroyo. Turn left off the ramp and park in the sandy lot that divides Mira Vista condos and Zippers Restaurant.

FISHING

Whether you're a seasoned veteran or you've never fished a day in your life, there are plenty of options near San José. For newbies, your captain and crew will find the right spot for the day, rig up the bait, and handle boating the fish. All you have to do is reel and smile for the picture. Later, top off the day by taking your fresh catch to a local restaurant to have it prepared to your liking.

Fishing boats for hire fall under two general categories: *pangas* and cruisers. Cruisers are the larger boats you'll see in the marina slips. They're often equipped with tuna-towers, enclosed cabins, bathroom, and other amenities. *Pangas* are the ubiquitous open launches, powered by outboard motor and sometimes featuring a sunshade and center console. If you see a *panga* with a newer four-stroke outboard, center console, sunshade, and mounted radio, jump in—you've got a winner. The fish don't care what kind of boat you're in, but the cruisers can handle the larger game fish and a nonfishing passenger in comfort.

Don't forget to pack a hat, sunglasses, sunscreen, water, food, waterproof camera, sandals/Tevas, and windbreaker. Take motion sickness medicine the night before and morning of the trip if you are prone to seasickness (or if you aren't sure).

All hotels in the *zona hotelera* can arrange guided fishing trips. Since San José has no harbor or marina (until the new one is completed in La Playita), all trips are in *pangas*. Well-known **Francisco's Fleet** (formerly Victor's Sportfishing, U.S. tel. 800/521-2281, www.jigstop.com) is based at Palmilla beach. A six-hour *panga* trip for 2–3 people costs US$190; bring your own food and drinks. An eight-hour trip aboard a 28- to 32-foot cabin cruiser can accommodate up to six anglers for US$395. **Gordo Banks Pangas** (tel./fax 624/142-1147, U.S. tel. 800/408-1199, www.gordobanks.com) launches out of La Playita and rents 22-foot *pangas* for US$200 (six hours, 1–3 anglers) or 23-foot super *pangas* for US$240 (six hours, 1–3 anglers), and cruisers for US$350–530.

There are a few extra costs to factor into the planning: Tips for the captain and fish-cleaning crew are the norm. Live bait is often not included in the cost of the *panga*, so expect to pay US$20 per boat. Fishing licenses cost US$11/day, US$23/week. You do not need a fishing license to fish from the shore. For details on fishing seasons and on-shore and inshore catches, see *Fishing* in the *Essentials* chapter.

Deportiva Piscis (tel. 624/142-0332, daily 8 A.M.–7 P.M.), on the south side of Calle Castro near the Mercado Municipal, sells fishing tackle as well as bait.

SNORKELING AND DIVING

San José visitors must head to the East Cape, the Corridor, or Cabo San Lucas for suitable snorkeling and diving sites. Expert divers who are comfortable in strong currents and choppy seas and interested in exploring the offshore Gorda Banks seamounts may be able to hire a *panga* from La Playita; however, be aware that even groups of experienced dive instructors have run into complications when attempting to turn a fisherman into a dive-boat captain for the day. The safer approach is to book a trip through one of the PADI-certified dive shops in Cabo San Lucas.

SURFING

Summer is the peak season for catching waves here, but good-sized swells occasionally roll through as late as mid-November. On the outskirts of San José, **Playa Costa Azul** (Blue Coast Beach) boasts two good summer breaks: a short fast inside known as Zippers, and a middle right point break called The Rock. Spectators watch the action below from a lookout at Km 28. At the next little bay south, almost invisible from the highway, **Playa Acapulquito** (Little Acapulco Beach, also known as Old Man's) gets an outside break that sometimes connects with the Costa Azul waves in larger summer swells. This spot is a popular choice for surf lessons. There are many lesser-known breaks along the Corridor that break on different sized swells (see *Surfing* under *The Corridor*).

Other options within an hour's drive of San José await along the East and West Cape shores. If you have a sturdy rental car or your own vehicle, you can drive northeast of San José along the coastal dirt road to several spots that break on south swells. Nine miles from San José, Shipwreck is a right point that tends to catch more of the south swell than the Corridor spots. There are several take-off zones from which to choose, and camping on the beach can be a relaxing way to escape the Corridor crowd. If you are going for the day, bring water, food, and shade.

Just up the road is Nine Palms. Waves here are a little softer than at Shipwreck and more popular with longboarders. When the waves get well overhead, the spot can transform into a high-performance, steeper wave that justifies its popularity. Don't bother counting the palms, as they've multiplied since the spot was named. The wreck at Shipwreck was also carried off by a storm long ago.

Equipment

Several shops near San José rent boards and other equipment. The **Cabo Surf Shop** (Km

28, tel. 624/178-6188, U.S. tel. 858/964-5117, www.cabosurfshop.com), located at the Cabo Surf Hotel, offers private or group instruction on Playa Acapulquito through the Mike Doyle Surf School (8 A.M.–8 P.M. daily, US$65/hr), as well as board rentals. Drop-ins are welcome. The **Costa Azul Surf Shop** (Km 28, Plaza Costa Azul, tel. 624/142-2771, www.costaazul.com, Mon.–Sat. 8 A.M.–7 P.M., Sun. 9 A.M.–5 P.M.) rents short boards, hybrids, and longboards to experienced surfers, as well as beginner boards with rubber fins, and offers lessons. Stop in for beach umbrellas, beach chairs, and snorkeling gear, too.

KAYAKING

Next to the Presidente InterContinental Resort, **Tío Sports** (tel. 624/142-4599, daily 8 A.M.–5:30 P.M.) rents sit-on-top kayaks for paddling the estuary.

MOUNTAIN BIKING

NaturAdventure (tel. 624/105-2050, www.naturadventure.com) leads half-day and full-day trail rides of varying levels around the Los Cabos area on Gary Fisher, Trek, and Specialized bikes. Destinations include Punta Gorda (US$65 pp), Cabo Pulmo (US$95 pp), and the Sierra de la Laguna (US$90 pp, US$75 half-day). Previous clients (only) can rent bikes for a self-guided tour (US$35–55 per day). MTB shoes and Shimano pedals are also available.

GOLF

The former Campo de San José got a makeover and new owner in 2006. The new **Mayan Resorts Country Club** (www.mayanresortsgolf.com) has an attractive, nine-hole, par-35 course surrounded by landscaped residential properties and has a sea view. Rates are US$130 for 18 holes, with considerable discounts for resort guests (US$89). Discounted twilight rates (US$69) begin at 2 P.M. An additional resort course designed by Jack Nicklaus and Greg Norman is scheduled to open in 2008. For other courses a short drive from town, see *Golf* under *The Corridor*.

YOGA

Yoga instructors Caryl Leffel and Victor Ramirez (tel. 624/105-2230) offer classes Monday–Saturday at 8:30 A.M. and 10 A.M. in a small chapel on El Encanto Suites property in downtown San José. They also teach evening classes Tuesday–Thursday at the Mayan Palace Gym at 7 P.M. and 8 P.M. They welcome all levels, with a maximum of 15 students per class (US$7 at the El Encanto).

SPA SERVICES

In addition to spa services at the resort hotels, **Equilibrium** (Plaza Catedral 8, tel. 624/128-7434, 10 A.M.–2 P.M. and 4 P.M.–9 P.M.) on Zaragoza at Plaza Mijares offers massages for US$38. Another option is a massage on the beach in front of the Coral Reef resort for US$40/hour or US$20/half hour.

ORGANIZED TOURS

Nomadas de Baja (Calle Zaragoza near the Pemex, tel./fax 624/146-9642, www.nomadasdebaja.com) organizes a full range of guided expeditions throughout southern Baja. You can choose from a desert hot springs walking tour (US$65), kayak adventures around Cabo Pulmo (nine hours, US$105), diving (two-tank dive, US$140), and mountain-bike tours (2.5–5 hours, US$85). Rates include a bilingual guide, all related gear, lunch and/or snacks, and beverages.

You can also tour the back roads of Baja in a fleet of Hummers with **Baja Outback** (tel. 624/142-9200, www.bajaoutback.com, US$165–220 pp). Single- and multi-day tours go to Todos Santos, Santiago, Rancho La Verdad, and Rancho Antares (between Cabo Pulmo and Los Frailes).

Located in front of the Presidente InterContinental hotel, **Baja's Activities** (tel. 624/142-2922, www.bajasactivities.com, 9 A.M.–6 P.M.) organizes horseback rides along the estuary and beach (US$35/1 hr, US$55/2 hrs), snorkeling tours to Santa María Bay (US$35 pp), and ATV tours of the East Cape (US$60/single, US$89/double). Credit cards are accepted. **Rancho Tours** (tel. 624/143-5464, www.ranchotours.com) leads walking tours of La Paz and Todo Santos for US$65 per person. Ecotourism specialist **Baja Wild Outfitters** (tel. 624/172-6300, www.bajawild.com) leads a variety of adventure trips, including kayaking, snorkeling, surfing, hiking, ATV, Jeep safaris, whale-watching, and turtle release programs. Half-day trips range US$60–98, and all-day trips are US$105–410, depending on the activity. Group and multisport packages are available.

ENTERTAINMENT AND EVENTS
Bars and Nightclubs

While San José doesn't offer as much of a nighttime party scene as Cabo San Lucas, neither does the town close down at sunset—although in low season it may seem that way.

Behind Plaza Mijares and close to El Encanto Suites, **LaSanta Wine Bar** (Obregón 1732 at Hidalgo, tel. 624/122-1898, www.lasanta.com.mx, Mon.–Thurs. 6 P.M.–1 A.M., Fri.–Sat. 6 P.M.–2 A.M.) opened in 2005 as a trendy bar and lounge featuring 27 wines by the glass (and 135 bottled labels) from California, Spain, and France, as well as some Baja labels, for US$6–24/glass. The atmosphere is historic Mexico meets Manhattan chic, complete with beamed ceilings, stone walls, red drapes, mood lighting, and contemporary suede sofas. To complement the wine, you can order oysters on the half shell, Spanish gazpacho with scallops, a charcuterie plate, risotto, foie gras, and salads for US$11–30. LaSanta plays live music every Wednesday and Thursday and has DJs on Saturdays.

The popular **Tropicana Bar and Grill** (Mijares 30, tel. 624/142-1580, Sun.–Thurs. 8 A.M.–midnight, Fri.–Sat. till 2 A.M.) features lounge-lizard folk music in the front room and canned music in the back. Both bars host a two-drinks-for-the-price-of-one happy hour in the late afternoon. Live Latin bands play on weekends from 10 P.M. on.

Morgan's Restaurant and Cellar (Hidalgo and Doblado, tel. 624/142-3825, morgans@prodigy.net.mx, daily 6–11 P.M.) often hosts live music, usually jazz, in the popular and comfy bar.

Shooters Bar & Grill (Doblado and Mijares, tel. 624/142-9900), above Tulipán Restaurant, is an open-air, rooftop bar with seating in plastic chairs and jazz music.

The nautical theme is a bit cheesy, and tunes are country oldies, but otherwise the **Cielito Lindo Sky Bar** (Paseo San José, tel. 624/142-9292, Tues.–Sun. 5 P.M.–midnight), in the lighthouse tower of the Crowne Plaza, is a great place to catch the sunset.

Behind the Mega shopping center, the **Rusty Putter Bar and Grille** (Hotelera Plaza Los Cabos, tel. 624/142-4546) is a sports bar/restaurant with some outdoor tables—the *palapa*-covered area is a great spot to catch an ocean breeze. Prices are reasonable considering the size of the portions (entrées start at US$6). The restaurant serves breakfast, lunch, and dinner daily from 8 A.M. till late, and the bar features live music on weekends. Satellite TV and an 18-hole miniature golf course provide additional entertainment.

Havana Supper Club (Km 29, tel. 624/142-2603, daily from breakfast till late night) perched on a rise overlooking Mexico 1 and Playa Costa Azul, hosts live jazz nightly. Nearby **Zippers** (Km 28.5, tel. 624/172-6162, daily 11 A.M.–10 P.M.), near Costa Azul, is a bar and grill with live "baby boomer music" Friday and Saturday nights.

Events

On most Saturday evenings during the December–March high tourist season, San José hosts a fiesta in Plaza Mijares. Although the fiestas are mostly held for the benefit of tourists, lots of locals attend as well. Typical events include folk dances, mariachi performances, cockfight demonstrations, and piñata-breaking. Numerous vendors sell arts and crafts and food; profits from food and beverage sales go to local charities and service clubs.

Many art galleries stay open late for weekly Art Walks on Thursday evenings.

San José's biggest annual festival is held March 19, the feast day of its patron saint. In

© NIKKI GOTH ITOI

Calle Zaragoza, opposite the plaza

addition to music, dancing, and food, celebratory activities include horse races and parades.

SHOPPING

From souvenirs to collectible furnishings, you can find a little of everything along the streets of San José. And unlike in Cabo San Lucas, here you can browse at a leisurely pace without worrying about aggressive shop owners encouraging you to make a purchase.

Arts, Crafts, and Souvenirs

Near the intersection of Boulevard Mijares and the road to Pueblo La Playa, about halfway between the *zona hotelera* and the plaza, is a large open-air market selling inexpensive Mexican handicrafts; it's generally open 11 A.M.–9 P.M.

Higher-quality, higher-priced arts and crafts are offered in shops along the east end of Calle Zaragoza and the north end of Boulevard Mijares. **Antigua Los Cabos** (Mijares 5, tel. 624/146-9933, antiguabcs@yahoo.com) has some antiques, as well as handmade rugs, folk art, ceramics, and tequilas. Across the street, **Veryka** (tel. 624/142-0575) and **Copal** (tel. 624/142-3070) both carry Mexican crafts. **Sol Dorado** (Mijares 33, across from the Tropicana, tel. 624/142-1950) is a multilevel store filled with ceramics, glassware, ironworks, mirrors, and furnishings. For large or fragile items, the store ships via DHL (fully insured). It will also deliver purchases to your hotel for US$10–85, depending on the location. The smaller **Mejicanisimo** (Zaragoza 8, tel. 624/142-3090, daily 9 A.M.–10 P.M.), next to the plaza, has much of the same.

Shop 12 Leather Factory, on the corner of Mijares and Coronado, has been in business since 1927 with a large selection of leather goods, including purses, shoes, belts, and even shotgun cases.

Jewelry

Several stores sell high-quality Mexican fire opals and other gemstones. Ask to see the opals in natural light—the more "fire," the higher the price. If you don't see what you want, ask to see individual stones. Most stores offer 24-hour turnaround for custom settings, but don't plan your pickup time to the minute, or you may be late to catch your flight home. Martha Rodriguez at **El Rincón del Ópalo** jewelry factory (Mijares 6, tel. 624/142-2566, beltran_018@hotmail.com, Mon.–Sat. 9 A.M.–9 P.M., Sun. till 2 P.M.) can help you choose a stone and setting in a pleasant gallery off the main plaza. **Jewelry Factory** (Mijares 5, tel. 624/142-6394) on the plaza next to Antigua Los Cabos, has some of the highest quality jewels in town, and service to match. **La Mina** (Mijares 33, tel. 624/142-3747, lamina788@hotmail.com) displays costume jewelry on the porous walls of a small cave and has a second location in Cabo San Lucas.

Fine Art Galleries

San José has a legitimate art district that is home to a number of first-rate galleries. Run by a graduate of the Parsons School of Design in New York City and a full-time Los Cabos resident, the three-story **Galería de Ida Victoria** (Guerrero 1128, tel. 624/142-5772, www.idavictoriaarts.com) has been recognized as one of the finest art galleries south of Los Angeles. State-of-the-art lighting and hanging systems were custom designed to showcase paintings, photography, sculpture, and other works of art. A fire in 2007 severely damaged the gallery, but the owner was planning to rebuild as quickly as possible.

The **Old Town Gallery** (Obregón 20, tel. 624/142-3662, www.oldtowngallery.net, Mon.–Sat. 10:30 A.M.–7:30 P.M., Thurs. till 9 P.M.) displays works by contemporary Mexican, American, and Canadian artists. **Galería Arenas** (Obregón 10, vicjorge71@hotmail.com, Mon.–Sat. 10 A.M.–2 P.M. and 4 P.M.–8 P.M.) has original Mexican pottery.

The eclectic **Pez Gordo Gallery** (Obregón 19, tel. 624/142-5788, www.pezgordogallery.com, Mon.–Sat. 10 A.M.–8 P.M.) represents more than 40 contemporary artists based in Baja and throughout Mexico. Works range from oil and acrylic to wax, collage, and photography.

Several galleries in this part of town stay open late on Thursday evenings (5–9 P.M.) for a weekly Art Walk that includes wine and food.

Home Decor

San José has amassed quite a collection of shops dealing in interior design products of all kinds. **Galería Los Cabos** (Hidalgo north of Obregón, tel. 624/142-0044) sells a unique assortment of antique and rattan furniture, stoneware, crafts, decorator items, and locally made barrel-back chairs. **Casa Paulina** (tel. 624/142-5555), on Obregón across from El Encanto Suites, sells high-quality, original home accessories and furniture in a two-level store—a perfect detour for anyone looking to furnish a vacation home. **Casa Maya** (Km 31.5, tel. 624/142-6611) displays handcrafted furnishings, fabrics, upholstery, bedding, and home accessories in a 15,000-square-foot showroom.

Sporting Goods

The **Big Tony** (tel. 624/142-0744) beachware store has locations in town on Zaragoza and next to Zippers Restaurant at Playa Costa Azul. Across the highway in a small shopping plaza, the **Costa Azul Surf Shop** (Km 28, tel. 624/142-2771, www.costa-azul.com.mx, Mon.–Sat. 8 A.M.–7 P.M., Sun. 9 A.M.–5 P.M.) has board rentals and surf and snorkel maps. You can also have your board repaired after a rough day in the water.

The **Cabo Surf Shop** (Km 28, tel. 624/178-6188, www.cabosurfshop.com, daily 8 A.M.–8 P.M.), located at the Cabo Surf Hotel, offers board rentals.

Deportiva Piscis (tel. 624/142-0332, daily 8 A.M.–7 P.M.), on the south side of Calle Castro near the Mercado Municipal, sells fishing tackle and bait *(carnada)* when it's available.

Bookstores

A branch of **Libros Libros/Books Books** (tel. 624/142-4433, daily 9 A.M.–7 P.M.), on the west side of Boulevard Mijares just north of Plaza José Green, carries one rack of English-language paperbacks, plus *USA Today* and a limited selection of maps and books about Baja.

ACCOMMODATIONS

Besides the major hotels and condotels in the *zona hotelera* along the beach, San José offers some smaller, reasonably priced inns in the town itself. A downtown location puts you close to shops and restaurants, with a short drive or long walk to the beach. Condos and hotels along Playa Azul are about a 5- to 10-minute drive from town, depending on traffic. Rates are given for double occupancy in the high season (holidays may be higher) and do not include 12 percent tax and 10 percent service, unless otherwise noted. Discounts may be available for stays of a week or longer.

Hotels in Town

Under US$50: The basic but clean **Hotel Ceci** (Calle Zaragoza 22 opposite the church, tel. 624/142-0051, US$34) contains 14 basic rooms with fans. Bathrooms are tiny and rather primitive, and at night, busy Calle Zaragoza might make this a noisy choice, but most of the noise subsides by 11 P.M. **Hotel Diana** (Zaragoza 30, tel. 624/142-0490, US$30), a bit west of the Hotel Ceci, has spartan rooms with air conditioning, TV, and hot water.

You'll find two **Posada Señor Mañana** lodging options in San José; more confusing, they sit side by side on Calle Obregón behind the plaza at the northeast edge of town, overlooking some *huertas*. A few years back, half of the original operation was bought out, including the name. The founder changed the original name for a couple of years but has reverted to the former appellation, thus the confusion. The original Posada Señor Mañana (Obregón 1A, tel./fax 624/142-0462, www.srmanana. net, US$40–67) is a rambling affair; rooms are clean and a variety of group sizes can be accommodated. Just to the east sits the other Posada Señor Mañana (tel./fax 624/142-1372, US$40–70). A small pool and open *palapa* sitting areas with hammocks are a bonus, as is the common kitchen area with individual locked pantry cabinets. Take a look at a few rooms here, as there is a variety.

Friendly and economical **⟨ Hotel Colli** (Hidalgo btw Zaragoza/Doblado, tel. 624/142-0725, US$49) offers 12 simple but clean and comfortable rooms in a family-run operation. This is the best deal in town under US$50. Some rooms have fans, others are air-conditioned, and all have a private bath.

US$50-150: The hospitable **Hotel Posada Terranova** (on Degollado just south of Zaragoza, tel. 624/142-0534, www.hterranova. com.mx, US$60) is a converted home that has been expanded to encompass 29 clean, air-conditioned rooms, each with satellite TV and two beds. Direct-dial phones are a plus (but make sure not to use the multiple-digit prefix option that allows use of a credit card, as this reaches one of the infamous price-gouging American phone companies). The inn also features a good Mexican restaurant (daily 7 A.M.–10 P.M., mains US$9–14) with an intimate dining room and an outdoor eating section, plus a bar.

The quiet, Mexican colonial–style **El Encanto Inn** (Morelos 133, tel. 624/142-0388, U.S. tel. 512/465-9751, www.elencantosuites.com, US$79–133) has expanded to two buildings, with the more upscale **⟨ El Encanto Suites** diagonally across from the original inn. Designed in grand hacienda style, the new, V-shaped building wraps 14 large, elegant suites around a small swimming pool and fountain. Fluffy towels, king-size beds, and remote-control air-conditioning are a few of the special touches. More economical standard and garden suites are located in the original inn. Rooms here are popular with travelers who plan a one-night stopover before heading to or from the East Cape. Yoga instructors Caryl Leffel and Victor Ramirez (tel. 624/105-2230) offer classes Monday–Saturday at 8:30 A.M. and 10 A.M. in a small chapel on the property. Wireless Internet works intermittently (15 minutes free, US$4 for 30 minutes, or US$10 for one hour), and there is an iMac for guest use in the lobby. A café near the pool serves breakfast and drinks, and you can park for free in a gated, but not guarded, lot across the street.

Behind the Tropicana Bar and Grill, **Tropicana Inn** (Mijares 30, tel. 624/142-1580,

THE PITCH

Few visitors board their flight to Los Cabos intending to buy a timeshare. Yet the timeshare market is booming as the destination evolves. Timeshares now command higher prices and higher occupancy rates than hotels. Nearly six million people now participate in fractional ownership vacation models (also called vacation clubs), and they spend US$1 billion a year on their condos and villas. How do so many travelers come to change their minds between arrival and departure?

LOS CABOS IS A BEAUTIFUL PLACE
It's a lot easier to pack up and head home when you know you can return again and again.

THE PITCH IS ALL AROUND
Timeshare salespeople disguise themselves as activities coordinators, concierges, restaurant hosts, and even grocery store staff. Europcar's Mexican office told at least one customer in early 2007 that they had to sign up for a timeshare presentation in order to get a rental car at the rate they had reserved. When the customer balked, the agent refused to give the customer a rental car. In another example, the Mayan Palace reportedly pays Mega thousands of dollars a month to have its reps roam the supermarket aisles. Their

goal is to draw unsuspecting visitors into a friendly conversation – *Is this your first time in Los Cabos? Where are you staying? Would you like to go whale-watching today? Can I help you find the sugar?* – and then invite them to a 90-minute presentation over breakfast in exchange for any number of giveaways. With prices ranging US$15,000–25,000, "owning" a timeshare in a world-class destination can be an attractive proposition. Why not hear what they have to say?

THE FREEBIES ARE ENTICING
Salespeople may offer US$200 in cash, free whale-watching or snorkeling tours, sunset horseback rides, restaurant coupons, and more. The deal gets better the longer you resist. Not a bad way to finance part of your trip if you don't mind giving up part of a day.

Everyone thinks they can work the system, and many who participate in a presentation do resist the temptation to buy. Some even sign up for a second pitch on their next visit. But here's the catch:

TIMESHARES ARE NOT REAL ESTATE
They are vacations. When you buy a timeshare, you prepay for vacations at a dis-

www.tropicanacabo.com, US$80–130) features 37 attractively decorated rooms around a tile-and-cobblestone fountain courtyard. Each room comes with air conditioning, satellite TV, coffeemaker, minibar, and direct-dial telephone; other amenities include a swimming pool and free transportation to La Playita and Playa Palmilla. A free continental breakfast is served in a gardenlike pool area.

Over US$250: The posh **Casa Natalia** (Mijares 4, tel. 624/142-5100 or 888/277-3814, www.casanatalia.com, US$295) is a contemporary European-style boutique hotel located right off the plaza with 14 deluxe rooms, two spa suites, and two connecting rooms, all individually decorated with authentic artwork

from San Miguel de Allende, Oaxaca, and Puebla. Besides the usual amenities found at accommodations in this price range, all rooms have small, private bougainvillea-covered terraces hung with hammocks. Other features include a heated pool, outdoor *palapa* bar, and in-room spa services. The attached Mi Cocina restaurant (daily 6:30–10 P.M., mains US$20 and up), run by owner Natalie Tenoux's husband, Loïc Tenoux, gets high marks for gourmet fare.

Beach Hotels
Occupancy rates for the hotels along Playa Hotelera have been climbing in recent years to match those of their busier Cabo San Lucas

counted rate. If you like the idea of returning to a familiar place in Los Cabos for one or two weeks each year, this model can make a lot of sense.

IT'S HARD TO SAY NO

Sales reps choreograph every aspect of the pitch, from the upbeat music to the champagne and cheers of congratulations echoing around the room. They face intense pressure to sell, so if the first approach doesn't win you over, there will be one or two more pitches as you attempt to leave the room. (Biannual weeks? Off-season weeks? Trial membership? Free Jet Ski tour? Take our survey before you go?) As prices come down, the deal gets sweeter, and suddenly you either begin to feel guilty for accepting all the freebies or you think you're crazy for not taking advantage now that you've negotiated the terms so low. Bottom line: That 90-minute breakfast presentation could result in a US$10,000 charge on your credit card.

YOU MAY NOT GET WHAT YOU PAID FOR

Timeshare developments typically begin selling when construction has just begun – sometimes they don't get finished, or when they do, they don't always shape up as promised. Stories abound of frustrated timeshare purchasers who don't get the weeks they originally bought, or whose reservations seem to get lost every time they book. Services may not be available as promised, and the quality of the accommodations may change as the years go by.

Also, because timeshare owners aren't year-round residents, they usually lack both a sense of community and a sense of responsibility toward the local environment. For the developer, timeshares mean huge profits, as the same space is sold repeatedly in one-week segments. Because land in Baja is relatively inexpensive, considering the charming scenery and climate, it seems to attract get-rich-quick developers who show a decided lack of respect for the fragile Baja environment.

PROCEED WITH CAUTION

Timeshares are not all bad, and attending a presentation may be a worthwhile experience for a variety of reasons. Just be sure you know what's coming before you give away any of your precious vacation time. And don't buy without considering all the options.

peers, though you may still be able to negotiate a deal during off-peak seasons. Whether you choose a hotel or condo, beware that demolitions, renovations, and new construction are in progress all over this area, even during the peak travel season. There's a good chance you'll end up next to, above, or below a noisy construction zone. The hammering, sawing, and drilling typically begins at 8:30 A.M. and lasts till 5:30 P.M. Do your homework before you book.

Over US$250: Although its brand name may conjure images of a business convention, the **Crowne Plaza Los Cabos Beach Resort** (tel. 624/142-9292, U.S. tel. 866/365-6932, www.cploscabos.com, US$250–400) is one of few resorts in Los Cabos where you can enjoy a stay free of condo sales pitches, as the property does not have timeshares onsite. Large guestroom terraces and a saltwater infinity pool are two more distinguishing features. Children four and up can play in the kids club while mom and dad relax by the pool. High-speed Internet access costs US$15 per day. All-inclusive meal plans are available.

Situated between the Desire and Posada Real resorts along the Zona Hotelera, **The Grand Baja Resort & Spa** (U.S. tel. 800/745-2226, www.grand-baja.com, US$265–390) has one-, two-, and three-bedroom suites and was transitioning to new owners in 2007. All-inclusive plans are no longer offered. A coffee shop/deli with Internet access is open all day Sunday, when most other cafés are closed, but the rates are the highest we found anywhere on the peninsula: US$8 per hour (prorated).

At the far northeastern end of the *zona hotelera*, next to the Estero San José, the 400-room **Presidente InterContinental Los Cabos Resort** (tel. 624/142-0211, U.S./Canada tel. 888/567-8725, www.ichotelsgroup. com, US$290–425) serves some of the best meals around for all-inclusive package guests. This resort in recent years completed a US$11 million expansion and renovation. The resort also maintains a playground and offers special children's activities. Tío Sports next to the hotel rents ATVs and sit-on-top kayaks.

All-Inclusive (Only) Resorts: The well-maintained **Hotel Posada Real Los Cabos** (tel. 624/142-0155, U.S. tel. 800/528-1234, www.posadareal.com.mx, US$130–195 pp) is a Best Western property with 156 rooms and suites that feature air conditioning, telephone, and satellite TV. Hotel facilities include a heated pool, swim-up pool bar, tennis courts, two seaside hot tubs, and restaurant. Most rooms offer ocean views. Rates cover meals, drinks, tips, and tax.

Next to the Crowne Plaza, the **Royal Solaris Los Cabos Hotel** (Lte. 10, Zona Hotelera, tel. 624/145-6800, U.S. tel. 866/289-8466, www. clubsolaris.com, US$125 pp) is targeting families with young children with a new water park. Most of its 389 rooms have ocean views. Entertainment options include a Tehuacan dinner theater show. A free snorkeling tour comes with a stay of six nights or more.

Clothing is optional at **Desire Resort & Spa Los Cabos** (formerly the Fiesta Inn, Blvd. Malecón Zona Hotelera, tel. 624/142-9300, U.S. tel. 888/201-7551, Canada tel. 800/655-9311, www.desireresorts.com, US$150–355 pp). Reactions ranged from shock to awe when this couples-only establishment opened in 2006, catering to upscale, "liberated" adults. A red and dark brown color scheme with hand-painted murals of scenes from the *Book of Kama Sutra* set the mood. A clothing-optional pool and jacuzzi, L'Alternative Disco, and Sen-

suous Playroom take it over the top. The resort's 150 rooms and suites have king-size beds and flatscreen TVs, among a complete list of standard amenities. From the beach, curious onlookers can recognize the resort by shoulder-height bamboo screens on the terraces that allow for private sunbathing.

Bed-and-Breakfasts

Next to the public golf course, **Casa del Jardín** (Paseo Finisterra 107, tel. 624/142-1964, www. casajardin.com, US$85–95) offers four rooms in a renovated former residence. Each room is named and decorated according to a different nature theme. All rooms have ceiling fans, air conditioning, and private balconies. The property is lushly planted with citrus trees, flowers, palms, and a large herb and vegetable garden. Guests have free run of the house (including an upstairs sitting room and downstairs living room, both equipped with TVs) as well as access to a telephone, fax, and computer. A full breakfast is served on a covered terrace overlooking the garden and swimming pool or in the formal dining room. Smoking is not permitted in the house.

Condominiums and Condotels

Condominium complexes are sprouting up on the outskirts of San José as fast as all-inclusive resorts. Las Olas (closest to the lookout point at Zippers surf break), El Zalate (next to the Coral Baja timeshare resort), and Sampiguita (closer to the hotel zone) are just a few of the newcomers. Owners rent vacant units to visitors for anywhere from US$120 a night for a studio or one-bedroom to around US$450 or more for a deluxe two- or three-bedroom unit. Rates can vary quite a bit even within the same complex, depending on location and views and how the unit is furnished. Be sure to inquire how close the unit is to the highway and whether there is construction underway inside the building. At Mykonos and other complexes nearby, the persistent sound of heavy traffic on Mexico 1 can drown out the sound of waves crashing onto the beach. Discounted weekly and monthly rates are sometimes available.

ALL-INCLUSIVE RESORTS

If making decisions about food adds stress to your vacation experience, look for a rate plan that includes meals, activities, and entertainment. The following resorts offer all-inclusive packages:

SAN JOSÉ DEL CABO

* Crowne Plaza Los Cabos Beach Resort (p. 345) – Business conventions

* Presidente InterContinental Los Cabos Resort (p. 346) – Good variety and quality of food

* Hotel Posada Real Los Cabos (p. 346) – Good deal for the money

* Royal Solaris Los Cabos Hotel (p. 346) – Families with young kids

* Desire Resort & Spa Los Cabos (p. 346) – Clothing optional

THE CORRIDOR

* Dreams Los Cabos (p. 362) – Weddings, honeymoons, anniversaries

* Meliá Cabo Real (p. 363) – Safe swimming beach

CABO SAN LUCAS

* Riu Palace (p. 389) – Largest of the all-inclusive set, with 642 guestrooms

* Tesoro Los Cabos Hotel (p. 391) – College students on spring break

Delfin Hotels & Resorts maintains a current list of all-inclusive resorts in the Los Cabos area at www.allinclusivescabo.com.

The payment process for a condo is different from reserving a hotel room: Property managers typically require a deposit of 50 percent of the rental fee by check or direct deposit to a U.S. bank account, and the remaining amount by cash upon arrival. Cleaning fees are often added to the rental fee. Sometimes full payment is required before arrival—all the more reason to get the information you need before committing to a particular unit.

Southwest of San José del Cabo proper, near Playa Costa Azul, **Mira Vista Beachfront Condos** (tel. 624/144-5049, US$110–160) rents one-bedroom condos by the week.

White-and-blue Mediterranean-style **Mykonos Bay Resort** (Km 29, tel. 624/142-3789, one bedroom US$130–290) rents one- and two-bedroom condos in three buildings, each with air conditioning, satellite TV, kitchen, and washer/dryer. Amenities include a basic gym and lighted tennis court. Buildings B and C have larger units and are closest to the beach and quieter than Building A, which has smaller units and picks up more noise from the highway.

Within walking distance of the Mega shopping plaza as well as the beach, the sprawling **Las Mañanitas** complex has some of the nicest condos around for US$225–475 per night. Next door, **Sampaguita Luxury Townhouse/Condominiums** is newer and smaller, with only 14 units in a quiet, gated complex that has a pool, hot tub, and tennis court. Two-bedrooms run about US$200–300/night.

Booking Services and Property Management Companies

Baja Properties (Doblado and Morelos, tel. 624/142-0988, U.S. tel. 877/462-2226, www.bajaproperties.com) manages one-, two-, and three-bedroom rentals in Las Mañanitas for US$225–475 per night, as well as a few less expensive locations. **Nash Group Properties** (Paseo Finisterra #107, www.bajaholidays.com), run by the owners of the Casa del Jardín B&B (see *Bed-and-Breakfasts*), manages several rental properties in Mykonos, Las Olas, and a few other complexes. **SeaSide Vacations** (tel. 624/142-3789, Canada tel. 604/484-8488, www.sea-side.com) has a variety of units in several buildings in the area, as does **Sunshine Services** (tel. 624/142-2212, U.S. tel. 888/545-4310, www.sunshineservices.com), with an office location next to the bus terminal.

LOS CABOS

La Playita

Under US$50: Northeast of San José, in the village of La Playita and within walking distance of the beach in Pueblo La Playa itself, cozy **El Delfín Blanco** (Delfínes, tel. 624/142-1212, tel./fax 624/142-1199, www.eldelfinblanco.net, US$39–50) offers simple cabañas facing the beach. Accommodations here are more traditionally Mexican style than resort-oriented. Some have private baths, others are shared.

US$50-100: Three miles past La Playita toward the East Cape, **La Fonda del Mar Bed and Breakfast** (U.S. tel. 951/303-9384, www.buzzardsbar.com, US$75–95) has three solar-powered *palapa* structures with comfortable beds and tile floors, all with private half-bath and shared shower, plus a suite with private bath. Breakfast for two at the adjacent Buzzards Bar & Grill is included.

A short walk from the sportfishing *pangas* on the beach, **La Playita Inn** (Pueblo La Playa, tel./fax 624/142-4166, www.laplayitahotel.com, US$69–109) offers well-tended rooms with air conditioning, ceiling fan, TV, and large shower. Standard rooms have two queen beds. A third-floor penthouse has one queen bed; another has two queens; and a third a kitchen and sitting area. Cash or travelers checks only.

Camping and RV Parks

Camping options are becoming increasingly limited in the wake of pervasive resort development. One of the last holdouts, Brisa del Mar RV Park, enjoyed its last winter season in 2006–2007. You can still camp for free on the beach at La Playita between San José and Pueblo La Playa, but that too may change as the Puerto Los Cabos project takes shape. For safe and secluded camping, best to head north along the East or West Cape Regions.

FOOD

Most of San José's growing number of fashionable restaurants are along Boulevard Mijares and Calle Zaragoza near the plaza. These eateries are for the most part geared to Mexican diners as well as foreigners—so far the town harbors no equivalents to Cabo San Lucas's Giggling Marlin or Squid Roe.

As a general rule, the closer a restaurant is to the plaza, the more expensive the menu. To save money and experience local flavor, seek out the spots where San José residents eat—most are in the western part of town toward Mexico 1.

Alta Cocina Mexicana

Restaurants specializing in Mexican foods prepared in the *alta cocina* ("high cuisine," or gourmet) style have proliferated in San José. **Tequila Restaurant** (Doblado 1011, tel. 624/142-1155, www.tequilarestaurant.com, daily for dinner, mains US$20 and up), in a restored classic adobe just west of Boulevard Mijares on the south side of Doblado, was the first of the high-class eateries to open. It looks small from the entryway but opens onto a sizable open-air, tree-shaded courtyard in back. In addition to a prime list of tequilas and a walk-in humidor, the restaurant blends Asian, Mexican, and Mediterranean flavors into a menu that highlights seafood cooked on the grill or baked in a wood-fired oven. Produce comes from its own organic farm, which also supplies some of the area's top resorts.

A member of the Slow Food movement emphasizing locally grown and prepared foods, **Don Emiliano** (Mijares 27, tel. 624/142-0266, daily 6–11 P.M., mains US$20–36) is run by a well-known chef from Mexico City, Margarita C. de Salinas. Try the six-course tasting menu (US$49) paired with Mexican wines (US$88) or order a la carte. At the upscale **Mi Cocina** (Mijares 4, tel. 624/146-7100, daily 6–11 P.M., mains US$20 and up), the husband of the owner of Casa Natalia serves nouvelle Mexican-Euro cuisine in a beautiful, contemporary outdoor setting.

Next to the plaza, **La Panga Antigua** (Zaragoza 20, tel. 624/142-4041, www.lapanga.com, daily for lunch and dinner, prix fixe US$18) is set in a colonial ambience, with a courtyard, lounge bar, and wine cellar. A menu of contemporary Mexican cuisine with a focus on

pizza on the plaza at La Dolce

seafood is prepared by a chef who is a graduate of the Culinary Institute of America. Credit cards are accepted.

Chilies in all their forms take center stage at **El Chilar** (1497 Juárez at Morelos, tel. 624/142-2544, Mon.–Sat. 3–10 P.M., mains US$10–30). A Oaxacan chef prepares an ever-changing menu of Mexican specialties at this small restaurant located near the Telmex tower. Cash only.

If you don't mind the strip-mall setting, **Habañeros Mexican Bistro** (Mijares in Plaza La Misión, tel. 624/142-2626, Mon.–Sat. 11 A.M.–10 P.M., lunch mains US$5–14, dinner mains US$9–18) doubles as an organic market. Dinner specials include roast pork tenderloin or surf and turf for US$20; Corona and Pacifico beers are only US$1.50.

Mexican

Restaurant Bar Jazmín (Zaragoza and Obregón, tel. 624/142-1760, daily 7 A.M.–10 P.M., mains US$13–40), just off Zaragoza on Morelos opposite the *nevería,* is a casual eatery

serving fresh juices and *licuados,* Mexican breakfasts, French toast and pancakes, *chilaquiles,* burgers, tortilla soup, *tortas,* tacos, tostadas, fajitas, and seafood—plus occasional live music. *Huachinango* (whole red snapper) and *carne asada a la tampiqueña* are served on sizzling hot platters. Credit cards, including American Express, are accepted.

Damiana (Mijares 8, tel. 624/142-0499, www.damiana.com.mx, daily 10:30 A.M.–10:30 P.M., dinner mains US$10–17), on the plaza, named for the Cape Region's legendary herbal aphrodisiac, is housed in a restored 18th-century townhouse and is one of the original romantic courtyard restaurants in Los Cabos. Rooms include a tastefully decorated bar, an indoor dining area, and a patio dining area—candlelit in the evening—surrounded by lush foliage. House specialties include cheese soup, shrimp, lobster, abalone, and steak. A free taste of *damiana* liqueur is served to guests upon request.

La Terraza Sidewalk Café (Mijares 30, tel. 624/142-1580, daily 8 A.M.–10:30 P.M., mains

US$10–15), at the Tropicana Bar and Grill, is a large, touristy restaurant/bar with outdoor patio, big-screen TV, and live music and dancing at night. The menu is basic Tourist Mex/Fake Caribbean, but the drinks are strong.

The family-run **Posada Terranova** (on Calle Degollado just south of Zaragoza, tel. 624/142-0534, daily 7 A.M.–10 P.M., mains US$5–18) features a small dining room and bar as well as outdoor seating. In addition to standard Mexican dishes, the menu offers a good variety of high-quality Mexican and American breakfasts.

(Mariscos Mazatlán II (Km 35, Mexico 1, tel. 624/143-8565, daily for lunch and dinner, mains US$10–14), near Soriana on the way to the airport, is a favorite among expats for fresh fish at reasonable prices in a nontouristy atmosphere. Look for a green *palapa*-roof building with outdoor seating on the west side of Mexico 1. There is also a sister location in Cabo San Lucas.

American and International

El Tulipán (The Tulip Tree, on Calle Doblado just off Mijares, tel. 624/146-9900, mains US$10–20), is a casual place open for lunch and dinner. The menu features hamburgers, rib-eye steak, veggie burgers, salads, stir-fries, and pastas—all served in large portions.

Baan Thai (Morelos and Comonfort, tel. 624/142-3344, daily noon–10:30 P.M., mains US$11–25) serves pad thai, wok-tossed salmon, and an assortment of curries, as well as a few other Pacific Rim dishes. Dining areas are nicely appointed with Asian furniture, and the food is light and tasty, a nice break from heavy Mexican fare.

Morgan's Restaurant and Cellar (Hidalgo and Doblado, tel. 624/143-3825, morgans@prodigy.net.mx, daily 6 P.M.–midnight, dinner till 10 P.M. only, closed Sept., mains US$20 and up) brings Mediterranean culinary influences to San José del Cabo. All breads and pastries are baked on the premises, and the wine list is stellar. The separate bar makes a favorite gathering place for residents and tourists alike. **Morgan's Encore** (Morelos and Obregón, tel.

624/142-4727, daily 6 P.M.–midnight, dinner till 10 P.M. only, closed Sept., mains US$20 and up), near the El Encanto Inn, is quieter, with a different menu and fewer tourists.

In a new plaza behind the Casa Paulina interior design store, **Voila! Bistro** (Plaza Paulina on Morelos and Comonfort, tel. 624/130-7569, www.voila-events.com, daily for lunch and dinner) serves a few wines by the glass, as well as soup, salads (US$9), and entrées like rib eye steak for US$28.

On Plaza Mijares, **La Dolce Ristorante Italiano & Pizzeria** (Hidalgo and Zaragoza, tel. 624/142-6621, daily 2 P.M.–11 P.M., mains US$7–14) serves pastas and pizzas, plus Italian starters and desserts. The upscale **Alfredo di Roma** (formerly Da Antonio, Mijares at the Presidente InterContinental Resort, tel. 624/142-1001, Tues.–Sat. 1–10:30 P.M., mains US$13–30), on the Estero San José, resembles an Italian trattoría. Outdoor tables have a pleasant view of the scenic estuary.

Pair the meat cut of your choice with one of four house sauces, add a side or two, and you have a fantastic meal at **La Bodega Steak and Wine House** (Zaragoza btw Guerrero/Morelos, tel. 624/142-6619, www.labodegadesanjose.com, Mon.–Sat. 6–11 P.M., mains US$17–29). Credit cards are accepted.

Antojitos and Fast Food

At the west end of Calle Doblado are several inexpensive taco stands and *fruterías*. The Mercado Municipal features a section of side-by-side, clean *loncherías* (Mon.–Sat. 6 A.M.–6 P.M., Sun. 6 A.M.–4 P.M.).

Restaurant El Descanso (daily 24 hours, mains US$5–10), an outdoor *palapa*-roofed place on Calle Castro diagonally opposite the Mercado Municipal, serves inexpensive *menudo, pozole, birria, barbacoa,* tamales, and other Mexican soul food 24 hours a day. Look for large vats on a wood fire. **Cafetería El Portón** (tel. 624/142-4115, Mon.–Sat. 8 A.M.–5:30 P.M., mains US$5–10), on the north side of Doblado east of Calle Muñoz, offers good basic Mexican fare in clean surroundings.

Restaurant Las Hornillas (daily noon–

© NIKKI GOTH ITOI

I scream, you scream; we all scream for *helado*.

9 P.M., mains US$5–10), toward the west end of Calle Doblado, specializes in inexpensive mesquite-grilled chicken, steaks, and burgers for a mostly local clientele. **Super Tacos de Baja California Hermanos Gonzales,** on the north side of Calle Doblado west of the Centro de Salud, is a branch of the famous taco stand of the same name in La Paz. Look for inexpensive fish, shrimp, and clam tacos (US$1–2), with a large selection of condiments.

Taquería Erika (daily for lunch and dinner), near Mexico 1 on the south side of the street, serves *tacos de carne asada* and *tripa,* as well as quesadillas. Two tacos al pastor cost about US$2.50.

Adventurous eaters should head to **Taquería El Ahorcado,** known among gringos as **The Hangman** (Pescadores and Marinos, tel. 624/172-2093, Tues.–Sun. 6 P.M.–midnight, mains US$5–10), in the Chamizal neighborhood across Mexico 1, for beef tongue tacos and other unusual fare. This funky, rustic outdoor place has a full selection of quesadillas (including *huitlacoche,* mushroom, squash-flower, and

cactus fillings), tacos, *frijoles charros, champurrado,* and *café de olla.* Bring your own beer and enjoy live music while you dine. In the same neighborhood, ◖ **Guacamaya** (open for dinner daily, mains US$8–12), off Calle Doblado, on the north side of Mexico 1, has become a local favorite for meat and fish tacos, including mouthwatering *tacos al pastor,* carved from a rotisserie spit and served with the signature toss of a pineapple slice. Huge stone bowls filled with flank steak and avocado are a super deal for US$7.

La Picazón (tel. 624/147-3857, Mon.–Sat. lunch and dinner, mains US$5–8), just east of the bus terminal on Calle González, serves good, basic *antojitos* at low prices in a pleasant outdoor *palapa* atmosphere. You can get *taquitos, tacones* (wraps), quesadillas, and even good burgers; more substantial fare includes chicken, lots of seafood, and steaks.

Good fish and shrimp tacos are available at **Cafetería El Recreo** (Hidalgo btw Zaragoza and Obregón, Wed.–Mon. 7 A.M.–9 P.M., mains US$5–10), a small stand with a few tables just north of the church on the Plaza Mijares. It's open for breakfast at 7 A.M., then 2–9 P.M. Wednesday–Monday for tacos.

Cafés

Enjoy coffee and pastries in air-conditioned comfort at **French Riviera** (corner of Hidalgo and Doblado, tel. 624/142-3350, www.frenchrivieraloscabos.com, daily 8 A.M.–11 P.M., breakfast mains US$5–10, lunch mains US$6–13). The menu offers a long list of hot and cold coffee drinks, chai, smoothies, Italian sodas, pies, cookies, and pastries along with cigars and liquors.

Sweets

For Mexican-style ice cream or fresh-fruit popsicles, try **Paletería y Nevería La Michoacana** on Calle Morelos near Zaragoza across from Restaurant Jazmín, or on Zaragoza across from the plaza. The *paletas de mango* (mango popsicles) are quite refreshing.

Dulcería Arco Iris, on the north side of Calle Doblado, west of Green, and **La Bonita del Señor San José,** on the south side of Doblado east of Morelos, both feature all types of Mexican candies.

Groceries

These days, the best place to stock up on food and other supplies is the **Mega** supermarket (tel. 624/142-4524), at the intersection of Paseo Los Cabos and Mexico 1. Choose from a full array of Mexican and American brands, decent produce, and a wide selection of cheeses and meats. There is a well-stocked pharmacy, and those traveling with youngsters will find all manner of supplies, from pacifiers to bouncy seats. The friendly "staff" wearing orange shirts and offering to help you find your groceries are actually timeshare reps. In the adjoining plaza are a Telcel store, surf shop, public restrooms, and numerous fast food options.

For a more authentic shopping experience, the **Mercado Municipal,** between Calles Castro and Coronado in the west part of town, provides fresh fruits and vegetables, fish, meats,

a *licuado* stand, and a cluster of *loncherías;* it's open from dawn to dusk daily.

On the east side of Mexico 1, just north of Calle Doblado, **Supermercado Grupo Castro** (tel. 624/143-0566) is larger than the other stores in town. A half kilometer north of town on the east side of Mexico 1, **Soriana** (tel. 624/142-6132) is a Walmart-style store with everything from beach towels to deli-meats. If you are heading directly to the East Cape, this is a good place to stock up on supplies for the week.

Tortillería Perla (diagonally opposite the Centro de Salud health center on Calle Doblado, tel. 624/142-0034, Mon.–Sat. 6 A.M.–1 P.M., Sun. 6 A.M.–3 P.M.) sells corn tortillas by the kilo. On the west side of Mexico 1, almost opposite the west end of Calle Doblado, **Tortillería de Harina** supplies flour tortillas during roughly the same hours.

The most convenient place in town to buy fresh seafood is **Pescadería San Marcos,** a small fish market near the Mercado Municipal on Calle Coronado.

On Calle Gonzalez, near the Corona supermarket and down the street from the bus terminal, **Panadería 1 de Mayo** has freshly baked breads and pastries with the usual tray-and-tong service.

La Playita and Pueblo La Playa

Just east of San José via Calle Juárez, **Los Dos Ricardos** (tel. 624/142-3068, Fri.–Wed. 9:30 A.M.–10:30 P.M., mains US$5–10) is a typical but out-of-the-way open-air seafood *palapa* on the road through Pueblo La Playa.

Palapa-roofed **La Playita** (daily for dinner, mains US$10–15), in Pueblo La Playa near the beach, has long held a good reputation for serving fresh seafood in a laid-back, beachy atmosphere. It changes management from time to time so it unfortunately lacks consistency, but it's worth a try in case it's going through a good phase. There's occasional live music.

La Playita Ali's International Place (mains US$5–10), the second thatched-roof building on the right as you enter La Playita proper, does fish tacos a little differently.

Instead of dunking the fillets in batter and deep-frying them, the cooks stir-fry unbattered fish in an onion and pepper sauce and serve it with large flour tortillas. Ali's will also be happy to cook (or smoke) any fish you may have caught.

Before you get to Tacos Ali and La Playita, look for **Mariscos El Puerto** (daily for lunch and dinner, mains US$4–7), which has about 10 tables with colorful checked tablecloths under a *palapa* roof and a menu of seafood cocktails, fish tacos that come with a tray of especially fresh condiments, and burgers.

Playa Costa Azul

Surfers, wannabes, and tourists head to **Zippers** (Km 28.5, tel. 624/172-6162, daily 11 A.M.–10 P.M., mains US$8–20), a round, *palapa*-topped beach restaurant at the southwest end of Playa Costa Azul. The menu offers tasty mesquite-grilled hamburgers, fish burgers, teriyaki chicken sandwiches, chili, chiles rellenos, and quesadillas. Indoor seating areas feature air conditioning, while the large outdoor patio offers a great ocean view. Enjoy live music on weekends during the tourist season.

INFORMATION AND SERVICES
Tourist Assistance

The Baja Sur **state tourism office** (tel. 624/146-9628, www.loscabos.gob.mx) is located at Boulevard Mauricio Castro, Plaza San José, Locales 3&4.

Money-Changing

There are now ATMs aplenty in San José, and several banks in town can still change dollars to pesos, for a fee. They are generally open Monday–Friday 8:30–11:30 A.M. **Santander Serfín,** two blocks west of Bancomer on Calle Zaragoza, usually has shorter lines. **HSBC,** in a small, relatively new shopping center on Boulevard Mijares just south of Calle Misiones, also offers exchange services. Another money exchange service is located in the Mega shopping plaza at the intersection of Mexico 1 and Paseo Los Cabos.

Major hotels will gladly take your dollars at a lower exchange rate. Use your credit card and ATM machines as much as possible to get the most pesos for your dollar.

Post and Telephone

San José's **post and telegraph office**, on Boulevard Mijares, is open Monday–Friday 8 A.M.–5 P.M. Next to the post office, the Telecomm office sends and receives Western Union telegrams.

Mail Boxes Etc. maintains an outlet at Plaza Las Palmas (Km 31, tel. 624/142-4355, fax 624/142-4360). MBE carries mailing supplies, postage stamps, and magazines and rents mailboxes.

The **public telephone office** on Calle Doblado, opposite the hospital, offers direct-dial long-distance phone service. Ladatel booths, the most convenient public phones for making international calls, can be found at Calles Doblado and Muñoz and on Calle Hidalgo between Obregón and Comonfort. The pharmacy counter of the Mega supermarket sells Ladatel phone cards, as does Havana's Restaurant near Plaza Costa Azul.

Internet Access

One of the best-operated Internet centers in town, **Trazzo Digital Internet** (Zaragoza 24 btw Hidalgo/Morelos, tel. 624/142-0303, www.trazzodigital.com, Mon.–Fri. 8 A.M.–9 P.M., Sat. 9 A.M.–7 P.M.) was also the fastest when we last checked. Trazzo has 15 comfortable workstations with wireless mice for US$1 up to 10 minutes, US$2.50 for 30 minutes, and US$0.30 for each additional 5 minutes. It also offers copies, printing, and scanning. Credit cards, including American Express, are accepted. **Ciber Espacio** (Mon.–Fri. 8 A.M.–9 P.M., Sat. 9 A.M.–9 P.M., US$2/hour) has 10 computer stations in an air-conditioned space near the school. There is also wireless access at the airport.

Medical Services

For medical assistance, visit the **Walk-in MediClinic** (Km 28, tel. 624/130-7011) in the El Zalate Plaza on Mexico 1. The facility has an

LOS CABOS

SAN JOSÉ DEL CABO PHONE NUMBERS

San José del Cabo area code: 624
General Hospital: 142-2770
Highway Patrol: 146-0573
Police, Fire Department, Red Cross (emergency): 066
Police (nonemergency): 142-2835
Tourism Office: 142-2960, ext. 150

emergency room, lab, pharmacy, and ambulance. Another option is **Médica Los Cabos** (Zaragoza 128, tel. 624/142-2770), near the Pemex station. Both will respond to emergencies 24/7.

Laundry

Lavandería Vera (tel. 624/124-1013) and **Lavamática San José** (tel. 624/142-4150), both on Calle González east of the bus terminal, offer washing, drying, and folding services Monday–Saturday 8 A.M.–8 P.M. **Eco Lavandería,** on Calle Obregón near Morgan's Encore, is a full-service laundry open Monday–Saturday 8 A.M.–9 P.M. and Sunday 8 A.M.–3 P.M. A small load costs about US$5.

RV Service and Supplies

Wahoo RV Center, near the CFE electric utility office in Colonia Chula Vista, off Mexico 1 (turn west between the Super Pollo and the turnoff for the Pemex station, tel./fax 624/142-3792, Mon.–Fri. 8 A.M.–1 P.M.), sells RV parts and accessories and does maintenance and repairs—including air conditioning and refrigeration—for trailers and motor homes, and it offers the use of a dump station.

Los Cabos Mini and RV Storage (Km 37 Mexico 1, tel. 624/142-0976, cell 624/147-3117, bombardelli@prodigy.net.mx) offers locked, garage-style storage units within a fenced and lighted complex with 24-hour security. One of the few services of its kind anywhere in southern Baja, the storage facility is

located about five kilometers from Los Cabos International Airport.

Canadian Consulate

The office of the Canadian consulate is on the second floor of Plaza José Green (Blvd. Mijares, tel. 624/142-4333, www.loscabos@canada.org.mx, Mon.–Fri. 9 A.M.–1 P.M.).

GETTING AROUND

Detailed information on how to get to Los Cabos is given at the beginning of this chapter. Once you've arrived, you can get around by foot, bike, bus, rental car, taxi, or shuttle.

By Bus

From San José's main bus station on Calle González (tel. 624/142-1100), Águila/ABC runs 15 buses a day to La Paz (US$17), with four buses a day from 7 A.M. and 3 P.M. continuing to Pichilingue for the ferry and six buses to Cabo San Lucas (US$3). The last bus to Cabo San Lucas leaves around 7 P.M. There is also hourly bus service between Cabo San Lucas and San José via the Flecha Verde and Estrella de Oro bus lines. The blue-and-orange Subur Cabo buses run between the two towns for US$2. It's easy to pick them up anywhere along Mexico 1. Officially, they're supposed to run till around 10 P.M.

By Car

You can do without a car if you plan to stay at an all-inclusive resort or a downtown hotel. Rent a car if you want the convenience of being able to drive yourself into town from a more remote location, or if you plan to take a day trip to the East Cape or Todos Santos. Most of the big auto rental agencies have desks at Los Cabos International Airport, as well as offices in or near town. Note: When renting in Mexico, you must buy Mexican liability insurance (typically about US$25/day). For details, see *Getting Around* in the *Essentials* chapter. The sidebar *Where to Rent a Car,* also in the *Essentials* chapter, has specific agency locations and contact information.

By Taxi and Shuttle

Visitors staying in town or at the beach are able to see most of what San José has to offer on foot. If you tire of walking, cabs are available; typical taxi fares are US$5 from the *zona hotelera* to the plaza downtown or from downtown to Pueblo La Playa, US$35 from town to Los Cabos airport or to Cabo San Lucas. Taxis congregate in front of the bus station, the beach hotels, and along Boulevard Mijares toward the plaza. Look for a taxi stand signed Sitio San José on Boulevard Mijares, just south of Plaza José Green. Call 624/142-0401 or 624/142-0105 for pickups.

The Corridor

This 29-kilometer (18-mi) section of Mexico 1, connecting San José del Cabo and Cabo San Lucas, represents one of Mexico's finest nontoll routes and passes by secluded beaches, rocky points, and tidal pools. It's known officially as the Corredor Náutico (Nautical Corridor), or more commonly in English simply as "the Corridor."

This section of Mexico 1, four lanes all the way, represents one of Mexico's finest nontoll routes. However, most of the roads branching south of the highway are unpaved. Almost all can be negotiated by ordinary passenger vehicles, though the overall number of public access roads continues to decline because of private development. Although it's illegal for any hotel or other private development to block all access to any beach along the Corridor, guarded gateways may dissuade all but the very bold. In some cases it's necessary to park along the highway or in a nearby hotel parking lot and walk down to the beach.

There aren't really separate towns along the Corridor; instead, the area is divided into

© PAUL ITOI

LOS CABOS

several *fraccionamientos*, or districts for development, each containing several resorts, golf courses, spas, and the like. At Km 19.5, the Cabo Real development presides over scenic Bahía El Bledito and comprises the Marquis Los Cabos, Meliá Cabo Real Convention Center Beach and Golf Resort, Hotel Casa del Mar, and Casa del Mar Condos, as well as the renowned Cabo Real Golf Course and the Jack Nicklaus–designed El Dorado Golf Course (see *Golf*). Stretching between Km 10 and Km 20, Cabo del Sol consists of the Sheraton and Fiesta America resorts and the Cabo del Sol golf course.

BEACHES

One after another, beautiful beaches and coves hug the coastline between San José and Cabo San Lucas. Some are hidden from highway view by bluffs, and others are marked by resort development, of which increasingly restricted access is an unfortunate side effect. To find the beaches that are still open, follow the blue-and-white signs along Mexico 1, sometimes labeled *Acceso a Playa* but more often than not simply bearing a simple outline of a snorkel mask or swimmer. Strong undertows and rocks make many of these beaches unsafe for swimming. Playas Chileno and Santa María are two exceptions. The sidebar *Beaches Along the Corridor* lists all beaches accessible from the highway.

Playa Palmilla

Playa Palmilla at Km 26 is a decent swimming beach—local kids dive here for golf balls that have dropped into Neptune's realm from the Palmilla Golf Club Ocean Course links. **Restaurant-Bar Pepe's** (Km 27, tel. 624/144-5040) will cook your catch for a few dollars, or you can rely on the restaurant's own dependable source of seafood (see *Food*).

Playa El Mirador/Playa Bledito

Farther southwest, a breakwater has tamed the waters along Playa El Mirador, a lengthy stretch of beach north of the Hotel Meliá Cabo Real and part of Bahía El Bledito. Look for an access road just north of Km 20. As the Cabo Real development expands, public access may change.

(Playas Chileno and Santa María

A little more than halfway to Cabo San Lucas, the wide crescents of sand rimming Bahía Chileno and Bahía Santa María constitute two of the Corridor's most popular and accessible swimming beaches. At Playa Chileno, visitors walk through a gate in the chain-link fence protecting the beach from vehicles and follow a path through a grove of fan palms to reach the beach itself. The palms provide natural shade, a component lacking at most other Corridor beaches. Beneath the houses perched on headlands at either end of the bay are rocky areas with good snorkeling. Once run-down, primitive restrooms were refurbished in 2006.

Though picturesque and suitable for swimming, Playa Santa María offers a smaller beach without shade; it's best enjoyed by snorkelers and divers rather than swimmers, and there are now snorkeling equipment and beach umbrellas for rent. Both of these beaches can get crowded with shoulder-to-shoulder snorkelers when the tour boats come in mid-morning to mid-afternoon. Best to get an early start if you'd like to have the bay to yourself.

Playa Las Viudas

Playa Las Viudas (Widows Beach), more commonly known as Twin Dolphin Beach, is reached via a rough sand turnoff at Km 11–12 next to the private entrance to the former Hotel Twin Dolphin. Vehicles with high road clearance will fare better than ordinary sedans. The tan-colored beach—actually several scalloped beaches separated by small rocky points—tends to be on the pebbly side, though the swimming is usually excellent.

Northeast of Cabo San Lucas at Km 4, little-known and uncrowded **Playa Cemeterio** offers calm swimming and white sands.

La Concha Beach Club

Just northeast of the Meliá Cabo Real at Km

BEACHES ALONG THE CORRIDOR

BEACH	NEAREST KM MARKER	DISTANCE WEST OF KM MARKER (IN METERS)
Costa Azul	29	500
Acapulquito	27	800
Playa Palmilla	26	400
Punta Bella	24	400
Buenos Aires	22	400
El Mirador	20	–
San Carlos	19	–
El Zalate	17	500
Costa Brava	17	100
Cantamar	16	700
Del Tule	15	400
Punta Chileno	14	–
Santa María	12	200
Las Viudas (Twin Dolphin)	12	500
Barco Varado (Shipwreck)	9-10	–
Cabo Bello	5-6	200
Cemeterio	4	–

19.5 is the upscale La Concha Beach Club and Restaurant (tel. 624/144-0102, daily 10 A.M.–10 P.M.). This beautiful secluded spot consists of three small, curving, sand-fringed bays. The club offers a splash pool, showers, beach umbrellas, and beach chairs and rents towels and snorkeling equipment. The restaurant serves international cuisine and is open for lunch and dinner daily 11 A.M.–10 P.M. Instead of an entrance fee, there's a reasonable food-and-drink minimum purchase requirement (easily achieved in the club's well-run open-air dining areas). No pets, ice chests, or food from the outside.

SURFING

Although Los Cabos is less famous than Baja's northern and central Pacific coast for surf, the summer southwest swell brings consistent wave action to the tip of the peninsula, when most of the west coast points are flat. The surf reaches peak height during the *chubasco* season, late summer to early fall. The most dependable surfing area between San José and Cabo

San Lucas is **Playa Costa Azul,** at Km 29–28, where a grinding shore-breaker called Zippers is sometimes backed by Hawaii-style outside breaks in heavy swell.

Punta Palmilla, below the One&Only Palmilla at Km 28–27, whips out a sometimes large right point break, while the bay to the point's immediate north, **Playa Acapulquito,** between Costa Azul and Palmilla, offers a good reef break in heavy swell.

Reef breaks sometimes occur at **Playa Buenos Aires,** Km 22 (beware strong rips), and at **Playa Cabo Real,** Km 20; then there's a gap until **Playa Cantamar** at Km 16 and **Punta Chileno** at Km 14, both offering workable point breaks. To reach Cantamar—which is often confused with **Playa El Tule** (also known as Puente del Tule)—you need eagle eyes. Coming from Cabo San Lucas in your own vehicle (the turnoff is accessible only from this side of the highway), cross Arroyo El Tule and then immediately turn right off the highway as the road begins to rise toward the Solidaridad monument. Here look for a small dirt road through a gate in a barbed-wire fence (usually open), after which a sand road leads around to the northeast end of Puente El Tule, a good spot to park and camp.

In summer, a good-sized, nicely shaped right point break sometimes forms off **Playa Barco Varado,** at Km 9—access comes just northeast of the turnoff for the Cabo del Sol golf course/ hotel complex.

Playa Cabo Bello, between Km 6 and Km 5, is known for a consistent left point break nicknamed Monuments for the H-shaped concrete monument that used to stand next to the highway near here. Northwest swell refracted off Cabo San Lucas fuels this band easternmost break for winter surfing. During heavier swell, it may be joined by an outer reef break. The spot seems to amplify the available swell and is one of the few left point breaks along the Corridor. Be prepared to wait your turn at the takeoff spot and keep an eye out for rocks and urchins.

Most of these beaches now feature some sort of condo or resort development in prog-

ress, but there's always a way to drive through or around them; it's illegal to restrict public beach access.

DIVING

Several beaches along the Corridor feature rock reefs suitable for snorkeling and scuba diving, particularly **Playa Santa María** (Km 12), **Playa Chileno** (Km 14), and **Playa Barco Varado** (Shipwreck Beach, Km 9–10). Santa María offers rock reefs at either end of a protected cove at depths of 13 meters (40 ft) or less. The north point displays sea fans and gorgonians, along with the usual assortment of tropical fish. The south end has sea caves, coral outcroppings, and large rocky areas inhabited by reef fish and lobster.

The remains of the Japanese tuna boat *Inari Maru No. 10,* stranded on rocky shoals in 1966, is the main diving destination at Shipwreck Beach. A local story says that when Cabo *pescadores* noticed the Japanese vessel fishing illegally, they extinguished the nearest lighthouse beacon and rigged a light of their own that lured the boat onto the shoals after nightfall. The hull and other wreckage lie 2–26 meters (6.5–85 ft) underwater, near scenic rock reefs. Tidal pools along Shipwreck Beach support starfish and sea urchins.

GOLF

Golf is king in the Corridor, which is home to three Jack Nicklaus–designed golf courses (the 27-hole Palmilla, 18-hole El Dorado at Cabo Real, and the 18-hole Cabo del Sol), the 18-hole Robert Trent Jones II–designed Cabo Real course, the Tom Fazio–designed 18-hole Querencia, and the 18-hole Tom Weiskopf addition to Cabo del Sol. The Cabo San Lucas Country Club, formerly known as the Raven Golf Club, was designed by Roy Dye. Keeping all of those fairways groomed and green in a desert environment doesn't come cheap: Greens fees average US$250. Discounted twilight rates begin at 2 P.M. Rates may vary according to the travel season and day of the week.

These courses boast landscapes and playing terrain comparable to those found in many Arizona and California desert courses, the main difference being the visual addition of the sparkling Sea of Cortez.

Palmilla

Opened in 1992, the Jack Nicklaus–designed 27-hole golf course at the One&Only Palmilla (Km 26, tel. 624/144-5250) is divided into arroyo, mountain, and ocean courses, splendid by all accounts. Nearly every hole has a view of the Sea of Cortez in the distance. This course hosted the 1997 PGA Senior Slam, 1997 Taylor Made Pro-Am, and 1998 World Pro-Am tournaments. Nicklaus himself, though admitting his bias as the designer (this was his first course in Latin America), claims the 17th and 18th holes are the best finishing holes in the world. The course's signature hole is the 440-yard, par-4 Mountain Five, which necessitates a long drive across two desert arroyos. Gray water irrigates the fairways and greens, easing the strain on the Los Cabos water supply. The public pays US$209–269 per 18 holes. Fees include golf cart, practice balls, bottled water, and use of the driving range. Callaway clubs rent for US$50 plus tax. The golf course serves as the centerpiece of a 384-hectare (950-acre) development surrounding the original hotel with fairway homes, a network of paved roads, a clubhouse, and a tennis complex.

Cabo Real

The Cabo Real complex at Km 19.5 boasts two world-class golf courses. The 18-hole, par-72 **Cabo Real Golf Course** (tel. 624/144-0040, U.S. tel. 800/393-0400, reservations@caboreal.com) stretches over more than 7,000 yards of verdant landscape with three ocean holes. There are five sets of tees from which to choose. The course is open to the general public for US$260–280 for 18 holes (9 holes US$180), including tax, golf cart, practice facilities, club service, and bottled water. Hotel guests staying at the Westin Los Cabos, Meliá Cabo Real, and Casa del Mar receive a 10 percent discount. King Cobra brand golf club rentals are US$50.

The Jack Nicklaus–designed **El Dorado Golf Club** (Km 10, tel. 624/144-5450) is the second championship course in the Cabo Real development. The 18-hole, par-72 course features six oceanfront holes; the rest are carved out of two picturesque canyons surrounded by trees, cacti, and rock formations. Six holes come into play beside four lakes. This 7,050-yard course has been called the finest course in Mexico and one of the best in the world. Greens fees run US$260–280 and include tax, golf cart with laser range finder, practice facilities, club service, and bottled water. The clubhouse and restaurant afford views of the Sea of Cortez and the 9th and 18th holes.

Cabo del Sol

Jack Nicklaus designed his second set of Mexican fairways on 730 hectares (1,800 acres) of land between Playa Barco Varado and Cabo Bello. Cabo del Sol (Km 10.5, tel. 624/145-8200, U.S. tel. 877/703-4394) is Los Cabos's highest-rated golf course so far. *Golf Digest* has rated it as one of the top 10 public golf courses anywhere; Nicklaus himself insists that it includes some of the greatest ocean holes in the world. Seven of the course's holes feature dramatic oceanfront play along the shore of Bahía de Ballenas. The front nine is 3,597 yards, par 36, while the back nine extends 3,440 yards, also par 36.

A newer desert course, a 7,100-yard, par-72 piece of eye-candy designed by PGA great Tom Weiskopf (his first golf course in Mexico), spreads across 57 hectares (140 acres) of desert landscape. A third 18-hole course for Cabo del Sol is still in the planning stages.

Fees start at US$350 for 18 holes on the ocean course (taco lunch included), or US$220 on the desert course, which includes tax, a golf cart, practice facilities, club service, and bottled water. Guests of the Fiesta Americana and Sheraton resorts receive a 10 percent discount. Callaway clubs rent for US$55.

Cabo San Lucas Country Club

This Roy Dye–designed, 300-hectare (745-acre), 18-hole course (501 Palo Blanco, tel.

COURTESY OF WESTIN LOS CABOS

seaside massage at the Westin Los Cabos

LOS CABOS

624/143-4653/4, U.S. tel. 888/328-8501) lies just one kilometer northeast of Cabo San Lucas, on sloping terrain facing the sea, with views of Land's End and Bahía San Lucas from each fairway and five tees for each hole (back, championship, member, forward, and front). At 610 yards (par 5), the seventh hole is said to be the longest in Mexico. The front nine is 3,651 yards (par 36), the back nine is 3,569 yards (par 36). Greens fees are among the lowest in the area, US$95–169 for 18 holes for nonmembers, including cart. Taylor-Made clubs rent for US$49. To avoid drawing excessively from the Cape's precious aquifer, gray water from the resort spends a month cycling through a series of duckweed ponds until the fast-growing plant renders the water safe for irrigation. Along with fairway homes, the resort features tennis, swimming, and fitness clubs.

SPA SERVICES

Most of the resorts listed in this chapter have their own spa facilities, with a menu of treatments from body wraps and massages to facials and pedicures. Services are typically offered inside or under a tent on the beach. Some of the standouts include heavenly body wraps at **The Spa at the Westin Los Cabos** (Km 22.5, tel. 624/142-9000, U.S. tel. 800/598-1864, www.westinloscabos.com), and indoor steam caves and waterfalls, plus holistic treatments using local fruits and vegetation at **Esperanza Resort** (Km 7, Punta Ballena, tel. 624/145-6400, U.S. tel. 866/311-2226, www.esperanzaresort.com), where 90-minute treatments cost US$198. The **Marquis Los Cabos** (Km 21.5, tel. 624/144-2000, U.S. tel. 877/238-9399, www.marquisloscabos.com) also boasts a gorgeous 10,000-square-foot spa with six additional massage tents on the beach. A 50-minute facial runs US$100–115; deep-tissue, Shiatsu, Thai, or sports massage services are US$115–125 for 50 minutes; mud therapy treatments are US$115 for 50 minutes; and body scrubs are US$79 for 25 minutes. Nonguests can use the spa facilities (steam room, whirlpool tubs, and spa swimming pool) without reserving a treatment for US$25. At the Palmilla exit (Km 27.5), **Hive Day Spa** (tel. 624/144-6123, U.S. tel. 312/602-9556, www.hivespa.com, Mon.–Fri. 10 A.M.–9 P.M.) offers 90-minute treatments for US$125–145. Credit cards are accepted.

SHOPPING

For jewelry, clothing, antiques, and home furnishings, look for an upscale shopping plaza called **Tiendas de Palmilla** (Km 27.5, Palmilla, 624/144-6999, www.lastiendasdepalmilla.com) on the north side of Mexico 1 at the Palmilla Resort exit. Among other boutiques, the eclectic **Pez Gordo Gallery** (tel. 624/144-5292) has opened a second location here. **Artesania Mágica** (tel 624/144-6046, www.artesania-magica.com, daily 10 A.M.–8 P.M.) has a selection of upscale Mexican handicrafts. Cabo San Lucas's outstanding sushi restaurant, **Nick-San** (tel. 624/144-6262, www.nicksan.com, Tues.–Sun. 12:30–10:30 P.M.) has opened a second location here.

ACCOMMODATIONS

The priciest and best-situated hotels in Los Cabos grace the coast along the Corridor. Designed to appeal to the well-heeled hedonist seeking a degree of privacy and seclusion not found in Mexican beach resorts such as Puerto Vallarta, Cancún, Mazatlán, or Acapulco (and avoiding the hot, rainy summers elsewhere in coastal Mexico), these resorts take full advantage of their desert remoteness. *Conde Nast Traveler* magazine named five of the Los Cabos resorts to its Gold List 2007, an annual ranking of the best places to stay worldwide: Las Ventanas, Esperanza, the Hilton, One&Only Palmilla, and Fiesta Americana Grand.

Prices for these resorts begin around US$300–400 for the Sheraton and Hilton, climb to US$500 for the Westin and Marquis, and top out at US$700–1,000 per night or more for the Palmilla, Esperanza, and Las Ventanas. The lowest rates at each resort typically require full payment at the time of booking, and cancellation fees apply.

Travel club memberships such as AAA can yield a discount of US$100 or more per night. The standard rates do not include 12 percent tax and 15 percent service, unless otherwise noted. Even if you have no plans to stay in the area, the hotel restaurants or bars are well worth a visit for a meal or drink and the ocean view.

Cabo Surf Hotel

Hidden away below Mexico 1, just two kilometers southwest of San José, Cabo Surf Hotel (Carr. Transp. Km 28, tel. 624/142-2676, www.cabosurfhotel.com, US$250–355) offers a small cluster of 10 remodeled comfortable apartments and villas overlooking Playa Acapulquito. All units come with a minibar, coffeemaker, satellite TV, and seaview terraces. Kitchenettes and kitchens are available. The grounds include a large barbecue area, restaurant/bar, hot tub, swimming pool, and plunge pool. Its **7 Seas** (www.7seasrestaurant.com, daily 7 A.M.–10 P.M., lunch mains US$7–13, dinner mains US$18–28) serves Mexican, Mediterranean, and seafood entrées under an open-air *palapa*.

Sheraton Hacienda del Mar

You won't have to get up at the crack of dawn to reserve a chaise lounge at the Sheraton (Km 10.5, Cabo del Sol, tel. 624/145-8000 or 800/903-2500, U.S. tel. 888/625-5144, www.sheratonhaciendadelmar.com, from US$400)—an abundance of patio furniture was part of the resort design. Even better, a poolside concierge helps guests plan the day's activities without having to leave the pool.

Part of the Cabo del Sol development, the Sheraton is a plush Mediterranean-style resort with 270 rooms and 31 suites; the latter were renovated in late 2006. Some rooms also contain hot tubs. Other amenities include a three-tier pool, two outdoor whirlpool tubs facing the ocean, a gym, spa, and tropical gardens.

The hotel boasts five bars and five restaurants, including the renowned **Pitahayas** (tel. 624/145-8010, daily for breakfast, lunch, and

LOS CABOS

TYING THE KNOT

Destination weddings are becoming big business in Los Cabos. Inviting your friends and family to a seaside marriage ceremony and wedding reception will create memories to last a lifetime. But the choices can be overwhelming, and there seems to be no upper limit on what you can spend. Consider these tips before you start planning the big day:

HIRE A WEDDING COORDINATOR

Different legal system, languages, and event business norms can make for a difficult planning process. Do yourself a favor and get help early. Dozens of wedding specialists operate from the area and can advise on reception sites, flowers, music, and food. Some are affiliated with a particular resort; others work independently. Booking service Earth, Sea, & Sky Vacations (www.cabovillas.com/weddings.asp) works with a professional coordinator to plan weddings in the area. Baja Weddings (www.bajawedding.com) is another reputable service.

CHOOSE YOUR PRIORITIES

When planning from afar, you won't be able to oversee every last detail of the event in person. Decide in advance what matters most and focus your attention there. Leave the other details in the hands of an experienced wedding coordinator.

FIND THE RIGHT SETTING FOR YOU AND YOUR GUESTS

An all-inclusive resort may simplify the logistics for some couples; others will prefer to select food, music, cake, photography, and flowers à la carte.

SET A BUDGET AND STICK TO IT

You may fall in love with the gourmet lunch at the One&Only Palmilla, but it may not be the place to host your 100-person event.

READ THE FINE PRINT BEFORE YOU BOOK

Are you committing to rent all the rooms in the inn? Make sure you know the terms of the deal before you pay a deposit.

DIG FOR DEALS

Join an online forum, such as CaboWeddings on Yahoo Groups (http://groups.yahoo.com/group/CaboWeddings), to learn from the experience of others. Brides report finding bands and vendors for as low as half the cost of vendors their coordinator recommended. The Los Cabos Guide keeps an online list of local wedding service providers (www.loscabosguide.com/services/weddings.htm).

dinner, mains US$15–40), which offers a creative menu of Pacific Rim cuisine. Dine inside or out at the more casual **Tomates** (tel. 624/145-8000, daily for breakfast, lunch, and dinner, mains US$10–15), serving a fusion of Mexican and international dishes. Look for the beautifully landscaped Cabo del Sol exit ramp near Km 10.

Dreams Los Cabos Suites Golf Resort & Spa

A favorite among wedding parties, honeymooners, and anniversary celebrants, Dreams Los Cabos (Km 18.5, Cabo Real, tel. 624/145-7600, U.S. tel. 866/237-3267 www.dreamsresorts.com, from US$600)

has 308 large and private luxury suites and all the amenities of a full-service resort. Its honeymoon packages include a champagne breakfast in bed. Book ahead if you have your heart set on a stay at Dreams; this popular resort has one of the highest occupancy rates in Los Cabos.

Hilton Los Cabos Beach & Golf Resort

Next door, the Hilton (Km 19.5, Cabo Real, tel. 624/145-6500, from US$400) features Mediterranean architecture, a beautiful infinity pool, and a complete list of luxury-style amenities, plus a favorable location near Playa Bledito. Rooms were recently renovated by designer Paul

Duesing and have large baths with soaking tubs, separate showers, and L'Occitane products.

Meliá Cabo Real

The Meliá Cabo Real (Km 19.5, tel. 624/142-2222, www.solmelia.com, from US$388) offers 305 well-appointed rooms plus several suites, almost all with ocean views—laid out like a squared-off horseshoe around a huge glass-and-onyx, pyramid-topped, open-air lobby. Guests can swim at the beach (tamed by the addition of a rock jetty) or in the hotel's freeform pool. On the beach, Tío Sports rents sports equipment and organizes scuba tours and instruction. Three restaurants prepare meals, although recent visitors have expressed disappointment in food quality and service. All-inclusive rates available.

Casa del Mar Golf Resort and Spa

The Casa del Mar (Km 19.5, tel. 624/145-7700, U.S. tel. 800/227-9621, www.casadelmarmexico.com, US$415–450) is a smaller place containing 24 oceanview rooms plus 32 deluxe one-bedroom suites with spacious bathrooms and complete kitchenettes. The premises also hold a full-service European-style spa, six pools, four tennis courts, the adjacent Cabo Real Golf Club, three bars, and a restaurant called **El Tapanco** (daily 5–10:30 P.M., mains US$10–20), serving Nuevo Mexican cuisine.

Fiesta Americana Grand Los Cabos

Adjacent to the Cabo del Sol golf course is the family-oriented Fiesta Americana Grand Los Cabos (Km 10.3, Cabo del Sol, tel. 624/145-6200, U.S. tel. 800/343-7821, www.fiestaamericana.com, US$476–662), with 250 oceanview guestrooms and suites and a secluded beach in front. Rooms are spread across six floors and feature private balconies. The resort's restaurant, **Rosato,** serves northern Italian cuisine.

Westin Resort & Spa Los Cabos

If you've been doing some research on resorts in Los Cabos, you've likely seen pictures of a dramatic architectural interpretation of the arch at Land's End. This is the Westin Los Cabos (Km. 22.5, tel. 624/142-9000, U.S. tel. 800/598-1864, www.westinloscabos.com, US$379–705), designed by renowned Mexican architect Javier Sordo Magdaleno, who endowed the bold curvilinear design with a bright palette of colors abstracted from the surrounding geological, floral, and marine environment. A Zenlike rock-and-cactus garden on a hillside overlooks a dramatic seaside pool fed by a sophisticated water-recycling system. A nine-hole putting green with its own shaded outdoor bar provides added entertainment. On the opposite hillside to the immediate north of the hotel stand numerous pastel timeshare and residential units managed by the hotel.

The chain's signature Heavenly Beds are reason enough to stay here. Separate tubs and showers in large marble bathrooms add even more of a distinctive touch. Flatscreen TVs, initially in premier World Club rooms, are in the plans for all guestrooms.

Several restaurants on-site provide a variety of dining experiences; they include eclectic **Arrecifes** and **La Cascada,** which serves *tapas* from around the world.

A state-of-the-art European spa offers body wraps, mud baths, and massage treatments inside or on the beach. Guests have golf privileges at the Cabo Real golf course, about 2.5 kilometers southwest.

Marquis Los Cabos

From the inlaid turquoise stones that accent resort corridors to perfectly filtered light in the spa rooms, meticulous attention to detail and contemporary Mexican decor set the tone for a stay at the Marquis Los Cabos (Km 21.5, tel. 624/144-2000, U.S. tel. 877/238-9399, www.marquisloscabos.com, US$445–700). Opened in 2003, the Mexican-owned resort was designed to reveal ocean views from every angle. Guests can move from their room to a restaurant, the spa, or the gym without losing sight of the sea. The Marquis' 237 rooms have soaking tubs and showers, Bulgary bath fixtures, mahogany woodwork, flatscreen TVs, and

LOS CABOS

Marquis Los Cabos

exquisite linens. Each morning, hotel staff delivers breakfast to guests through a private pass-through alcove. In addition, rooms and common areas showcase contemporary Mexican paintings and sculpture. And if you fall in love with the eclectic furnishings, as many guests apparently have, you'll soon be able to buy your own from a furniture store on the premises. Twenty-eight *casitas* have their own swimming pools. A 10,000-square-foot spa and an award-winning, 21-seat French restaurant, **Canto del Mar** (dinner only, prix fixe US$60 pp), set the hotel apart. Close proximity to the highway and small balconies are the only obvious disadvantages at this resort. A service charge of US$35 per day applies.

Las Ventanas al Paraíso

Romance defines the experience at Las Ventanas (tel. 624/144-0300, U.S. tel. 888/767-3966, www.lasventanas.com, junior suites US$650–1,350), just northeast of Km 20, which celebrated its 10th anniversary in 2007. Accordingly, one of your first choices upon arrival here will be selecting bed linens from the sheet menu. Under the auspices of Rosewood Hotels and Resorts, Las Ventanas was designed using an innovative combination of Mexican-Mediterranean architecture and interior design. Unlike the bright primary colors favored by many Mexican beach resorts, here pastels and earth tones are emphasized. Underground tunnels hide many of the day-to-day guest service activities to keep aboveground architecture to a minimum, adding to the overall sense of intimacy.

Guest suites average 90 square meters (960 sq ft)—among the largest standard room sizes in Mexico. Highlights include custom-made furniture, inlaid stone-and-tile floors, an adobe fireplace, private furnished patio with individual splash pool/hot tub, computerized telescope aimed at the sea (for viewing the whales offshore), freshly cut blooms, and a huge bathroom. Each room also comes with a small bottle of high-end tequila. Three spa suites have space for in-room treatments, as well as rooftop terraces with outdoor hot tubs.

Guests have free use of a full-service spa and fitness center. The beach in front of the resort, Playa Costa Brava, is a little too *brava* for most swimmers, but overlooking the beach is a large freeform horizon pool with "high tech" pebbles that change color according to the color of the sky and sea. The resort's restaurant, simply called **The Restaurant** (daily for breakfast, lunch, and dinner), has been managed by a new chef since 2005. Other dining options include a less formal restaurant and a tequila- and ceviche-tasting bar. Friday evening Tequila Nights, open to guests and nonguests, are run as tasting classes. Private movie nights on the beach, complete with wine and gourmet Mexican *botanas,* are another signature Las Ventanas diversion. Multiday spa and meal packages are available. For guests who want to venture away from the resort, Mini Cooper S convertibles, BMW motorcycles, and off-road Hummers are available for rent.

Esperanza Resort

By many accounts, Esperanza (Km 7, Punta

Esperanza Resort

Ballena, tel. 624/145-6400, U.S. tel. 866/311-2226, www.esperanzaresort.com, US$675–1,325) leads the pack for outstanding guest service. Located close to Cabo San Lucas, its 50 *casitas* and six suites feature original Mexican artwork and hand-crafted furnishings. A signature spa has indoor steam caves and waterfalls, with treatments that incorporate local fruits and vegetation. And the oceanfront Mediterranean restaurant, the **Signature Restaurant at Esperanza,** completes the picture; it's open for breakfast, lunch, and dinner. Esperanza also has its own art gallery with works by contemporary Mexican painters and sculptors for sale. A four-night minimum stay is required for all weekend bookings January–April except February and March, when a seven-night stay is required.

One&Only Palmilla

Today, the oldest resort in Los Cabos is also one of the destination's most expensive—and most popular—places to stay. The former Hotel Palmilla Resort received an $80 million makeover and opened as the One&Only Palmilla (Km 27, tel. 624/146-7000, U.S. tel. 866/829-2977, www.oneandonlyresorts.com, US$550–775) in early 2004. Covering 384 hectares (950 acres) of Punta Palmilla near Km 27, the resort was the Cape's first major resort; it was built in 1956 by "Rod" Rodríguez, son of former Mexican president Abelardo Luis Rodríguez. Coconut palms, clouds of hibiscus, and sweeping seaviews dominate the grounds. Facilities at the resort's latest incarnation include two infinity-edge pools and a children's pool; fitness center, yoga garden, and spa with 13 private treatment villas; and a rustic chapel used for weddings. All 172 rooms and suites feature flatscreen satellite TV with DVD and CD player with Bose system surround-sound, state-of-the-art voice and data lines, and separate sitting area. Rates include personal butler service, twice-daily maid service, daily fruit delivery, and an aromatherapy menu. The One&Only Palmilla maintains a sportfishing fleet and offers *panga* fishing trips, scuba diving, and snorkeling. Palmilla also boasts a world-class golf course (see *Golf*).

Guests enjoy 24-hour room service from the resort's two restaurants: **Restaurant C,** created by Charlie Trotter of Chicago restaurant fame, and the *palapa*-style **Agua Restaurant,** which offers a Mediterranean menu.

FOOD

Most restaurants along the Corridor are tucked inside full-service resorts (see *Accommodations*). Expect to pay at least US$100 for two (without drinks) at most of the restaurants in this section. Here are a few stand-alone eateries and some of the resort standouts.

Seafood and International

Restaurant-Bar Pepe's (Km 27, tel. 624/144-5040), on Playa Palmilla, will cook your catch for a few dollars, or you can rely on the restaurant's own dependable source of seafood.

Pecan-encrusted sea bass, mesquite grilled prawns, and live lobster anchor the menu at **Pitahayas** (Km 10, Cabo del Sol, tel. 624/145-8010, daily 5:30–10:30 P.M., mains US$15–40), at the Sheraton Hacienda del Mar, a large open-air restaurant with an impressive underground wine cellar, serves an innovative menu of Pacific Rim cuisine focusing on fresh seafood and a mesquite grill. Formal resort attire is required.

At the Cabo Surf Hotel, **7 Seas** (Km 28, tel. 624/142-2676, www.7seasrestaurant.com, daily 7 A.M.–10 P.M., lunch mains US$7–13, dinner mains US$18–28) serves breakfast, lunch, and dinner under an open-air *palapa*. The dinner menu features Mexican, Mediterranean, and seafood entrées with a decent wine list. Seafood-stuffed poblano peppers are one of the more unusual dishes.

At the Westin Los Cabos, **Arrecifes** (Km. 22.5, tel. 624/142-9000) commands a view of the wave-battered beach below and offers an eclectic menu emphasizing seafood and standout desserts; **La Cascada** underwent a US$900,000 renovation in 2006 featuring illuminated onyx cube tables, a new fire pit lounge, and a menu of creative *tapas del mundo,* or small plates from around the world paired with wines that match the flavors of the food.

And at the One&Only Palmilla, diners can choose between the *palapa*-style **Agua Restaurant,** featuring Mediterranean cuisine and a view of the sea, and Charlie Trotter's first overseas restaurant, called **Restaurant C** (Km 7.5, tel. 624/146-7000, www.charlietrotters. com, mains US$20 and up). Representative entrées at C include rockfish with ratatouille, quinoa, and a black olive–caper vinaigrette and steamed and spit-roasted duck with spiced carrots, parsnips, and a tangerine-merlot reduction. Both restaurants are open for breakfast, lunch, and dinner.

Italian and Continental

In the Misiones del Cabo complex, **Sunset da Mona Lisa** (formerly Da Giorgio, Km 5.5, tel. 624/145-8160, www.sunsetmonalisa.com, daily 8:30 A.M.–11 P.M., mains US$18–35) draws a crowd for sunset views and Italian fare. A multilevel patio overlooks the bay and Cabo San Lucas. Credit cards are accepted.

Dinner at the award-winning French restaurant **Canto del Mar** (tel. 624/144-2000, dinner only, prix fixe US$60 pp), inside the Marquis Los Cabos resort, is an Old World affair, complete with acoustic guitar music and a collection of masks from Florence on the walls. There are just 21 seats in the house for the nightly six-course tasting menu. An adjoining cigar room has a hardwood floor and ornate upholstered armchairs.

American and Eclectic

The Mediterranean-inspired **French Riviera** in San José and Cabo San Lucas has a third location between Cabo Bello and Misiones del Cabo (Km 6.3, tel. 624/104-3124, www.frenchrivieraloscabos.com, daily noon–11 P.M., mains US$33).

Mexican

Close to Cabo San Lucas, **Puerta Vieja** (Km 6.3, tel. 624/104-3252, www.puertavieja. com, mains US$13–23) offers a fantastic view and hearty fare like Sonora beef and fresh shellfish, prepared with Asian accents and offered at incredibly reasonable prices—a rare find along the Corridor. One more kilometer east, the same owners run the popular **Villa Serena Restaurant** (Km 7.5, tel. 624/145-8244, daily 7 A.M.–10 P.M., mains US$12–25) next to the Villa Serena RV Park. Tasty seafood platters or beef and chicken dishes are a great deal.

Groceries and Supplies

La Europea (Km 6.7, tel. 624/145-8755, Mon.–Fri. 9 A.M.–8 P.M., Sat. 9 A.M.–9 P.M.) stocks a wide variety of international gourmet foods, from prosciutto to wasabi, as well as an impressive selection of fine wines and liquor. Look for the main store at the first stoplight as you enter Cabo from the east. Smaller, satellite stores are located at the marina level of the Puerto Paraíso plaza in Cabo San Lucas and on the south side of Mexico 1, east of the Mega plaza in San José. Credit cards are accepted. **Costco** (Km 4.5, tel. 624/146-7180, daily 9 A.M.–9 P.M.) and **Home Depot** (Km 6.5, tel. 624/105-8600) have also opened stores close to Cabo San Lucas.

INFORMATION AND SERVICES

Pemex stations are located at Km 5 just outside of Cabo San Lucas and near the Westin between Km 24 and Km 25. Most of the resorts offer Internet access and phone services for guests. For medical needs, see *Information and Services* in the *San José del Cabo* and *Cabo San Lucas* sections.

GETTING AROUND

Resorts along the Corridor are a 30- to 60-minute drive from the airport. Many, including the Westin, offer shuttles to San José del Cabo and Cabo San Lucas for guests who want to see a little more than their hotel grounds. Car rental agencies have offices at many of the larger resorts. (See the sidebar *Where to Rent a Car in Baja* in the *Essentials* chapter.) For advice on how to get to Los Cabos from the United States, see *Getting There* at the beginning of this chapter.

Cabo San Lucas

Cabo San Lucas has a tourist-to-resident ratio higher than elsewhere in the Cape Region, especially during the peak November–March tourist season. Several cruise lines also feature Cabo San Lucas on their itineraries. Yet in spite of all the visitors—most of whom confine themselves to the waterfront—Cabo manages to retain something of a funky, small-town feel. Away from Boulevard Marina, many of the unpaved, sand streets are lined with the *tortillerías,* hardware shops, and markets typically found in any small coastal Mexican town.

Named for the slender cape extending eastward from Baja California's southernmost tip, Cabo San Lucas is the only city in Mexico with a marine preserve within its city limits. Created in 1973, the protected 36-square-kilometer (14-sq-mi) patch of sea and shore designates special boat lanes, boating speed limits, and restricted fishing and recreation craft areas, all under the watchful eye of Grupo Ecológico de Cabo San Lucas. Nowhere else among Mexico's top-drawing seaside resorts will you find such pristine beaches within so short a distance (5–10 minutes by boat taxi) of the town center.

Outside this area, however, hotel and condo development marches ahead full steam. Pedregal—a fashionable hillside district to the west—the marina, and Playa El Médano to the east are all chockablock with condos and villas. Next to undergo development will probably be the large section of unused harborfront property near the inner harbor entrance, where an old cannery and ferry pier sit abandoned.

While yachting and sportfishing bring an older, early-to-bed crowd to Cabo, the town's nightlife attracts an energetic youth market, creating a more vibrant ambience than at relatively staid San José del Cabo, 29 kilometers (18 mi) northeast. As the last stop on the 1,700-kilometer (1,000-mi) Transpeninsular Baja road trip, Cabo also acts as a receptacle for old Baja hands looking for a few days or weeks of R&R before beginning the long return drive across relatively unpopulated desert landscapes.

Thus, as residents and repeat visitors will point out, you never know who you'll run into in Cabo; yachties on their way to and from exotic South Pacific ports, cops on a fishing vacation, Baja road warriors, honeymoon couples, Mexico City denizens cleaning out their lead-filled lungs, rockers resting up after a continental tour, or Montana cowboys escaping the snow—they've all set themselves temporarily adrift in the Pacific.

HISTORY
The Pericú and the English

In pre-Cortesian times, the only humans enjoying Cabo San Lucas were the Pericú, one of the nomadic Guaycura Amerindian groups that inhabited the Cape Region for hundreds if not thousands of years. Standard anthropology says that, like other Amerindians in North and South America, the Pericú were descendants of Asian groups who traversed the prehistoric land bridge between the Eurasian and

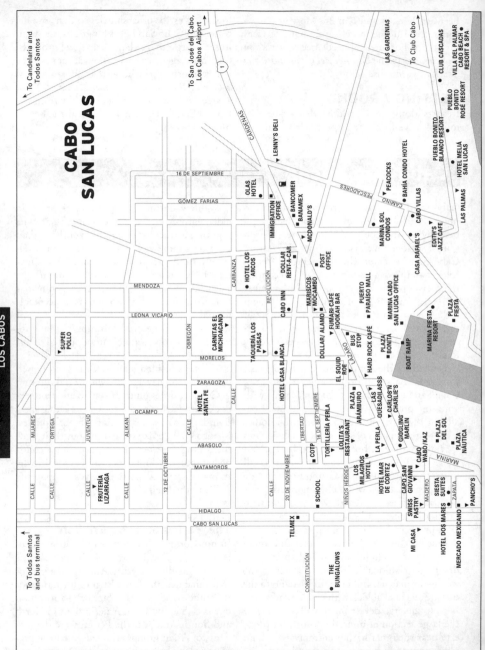

CABO
SAN LUCAS

To Candelaria and
Todos Santos

To San José del Cabo,
Los Cabos Airport

LAS GARDENIAS

To Club Cabo

CLUB CASCADAS

VILLA DEL PALMAR
CABO BEACH
RESORT & SPA

PUEBLO
BONITO
ROSÉ RESORT

PUEBLO BONITO
BLANCO RESORT

HOTEL MELIA
SAN LUCAS

LAS PALMAS

CABO VILLAS

BAHÍA CONDO HOTEL

PEACOCKS

CAMINO PESCADORES

CARDENAS

LENNY'S DELI

16 DE SEPTIEMBRE

GÓMEZ FARIAS

OLAS
HOTEL

BANCOMER

BANAMEX

MCDONALD'S

IMMIGRATION
OFFICE

MARINA SOL
CONDOS

EDITH'S
JAZZ CAFÉ

CASA RAFAEL'S

CARRANZA

HOTEL LOS
ARCOS

DOLLAR
RENT-A-CAR

POST
OFFICE

REVOLUCIÓN

MENDOZA

LEONA VICARIO

CABO INN

MARISCOS
MOCAMBO

FUMARI CAFÉ
HOOKAH BAR

PUERTO
PARAÍSO MALL

MARINA CABO
SAN LUCAS OFFICE

PLAZA
FIESTA

MARINA FIESTA
RESORT

OBREGON

SUPER
POLLO

CARNITAS EL
MICHOACANO

TAQUERÍA LOS
PAISAS

MORELOS

HOTEL CASA BLANCA

HARD ROCK CAFÉ

BUS
STOP

LÁZARO

PLAZA
BONITA

EL SQUID
ROE

BOAT RAMP

ZARAGOZA

HOTEL
SANTA FE

CALLE

CALLE

OCAMPO

MIJARES

ORTEGA

JUVENTUD

ALIKAN

CALLE

PLAZA
ARAMBURO

LAS
QUESADILLAS

CARLON'S

GIGGLING
CHARLIE'S

PLAZA
DEL SOL

PLAZA
NÁUTICA

LIBERTAD

16 DE SEPTIEMBRE

ABASOLO

FRUTERÍA
LIZARRAGA

12 DE OCTUBRE

CALLE

COTP

TORTILLERÍA PERLA

LOLITA'S
RESTAURANT

LA PERLA

CABO
WABO/KAZ

MATAMOROS

SCHOOL

20 DE NOVIEMBRE

NIÑOS HÉROES

LOS
MILAGROS
HOTEL

HOTEL MAR
DE CORTEZ

CAPO SAN
GIOVANNI

SWISS
PASTRY

MADERO

SIESTA
SUITES

ZAPATA

PANCHO'S

MARINA

HIDALGO

CALLE

CABO SAN LUCAS

TELMEX

MI CASA

HOTEL DOS MARES

MERCADO MEXICANO

CONSTITUCIÓN

THE
BUNGALOWS

To Todos Santos
and bus terminal

LOS CABOS

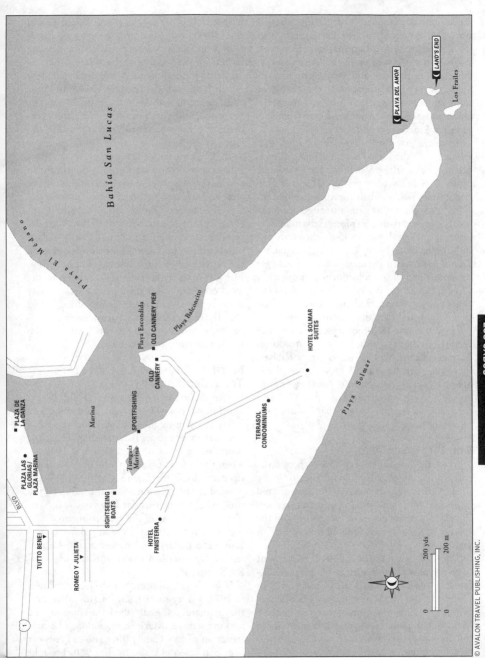

PLAYA DEL AMOR

LAND'S END

Los Frailes

Bahía San Lucas

Playa El Médano

Playa Escondida

OLD CANNERY PIER

Playa Balconcito

OLD CANNERY

SPORTFISHING

HOTEL SOLMAR SUITES

Marina

Playa Solmar

PLAZA DE LA DANZA

Tianguis Marina

TERRASOL CONDOMINIUMS

PLAZA LAS GLORIAS / PLAZA MARINA

BLVD

SIGHTSEEING BOATS

TUTTO BENE!

HOTEL FINISTERRA

ROMEO Y JULIETA

1

200 yds

200 m

0

0

LOS CABOS

American continents. One fringe theory, however, suggests that the Pericú may have descended from Tahitian mariners blown off course on their way to Hawaii. English accounts from the 17th and early 18th centuries lend at least partial credence to this theory by pointing out how much the physical and social characteristics of the Pericú differed from that of other Amerindians of the same era.

Spaniard Juan Rodríguez Cabrillo made first contact with the Pericú here in 1542 while exploring the coastline. Sir Francis Drake stopped off in 1578, followed by privateer Thomas Cavendish in 1587. English pirating exploits inspired the Spanish to gain a stronger foothold on the Cape. Spanish explorer Sebastián Vizcaíno spent a week here in 1596, then returned in 1602 to map the region with cartographer Gerónimo Martín Palacios. Vizcaíno strongly recommended the establishment of a colony at Cabo San Lucas; Loreto, farther north on the Sea of Cortez, was selected instead, leaving Cabo to the English for another hundred years.

Until the mid-18th century, English pirates used the harbor as a hiding place for attacks on Manila galleons. Woodes Rogers anchored here in 1709, when he and his crew captured the Spanish galleon *Encarnación*. Another English corsair, George Shelcocke, landed in 1721 and carried out a regional survey that included extensive drawings of the Pericú.

The First Settlers

During the remainder of the Spanish colonial era, Cabo's natural harbor was periodically used by passing galleons, but since it offered no source of freshwater and scant protection from late-summer *chubascos* rolling in from the southeast, it was largely ignored in favor of San José del Cabo.

The Mexican independence movement largely bypassed San Lucas, although the Chilean ship *Independence* visited Cabo in 1822 in support of the Mexican struggle. The visit accomplished little as a military exercise because Mexico had gained independence from Spain the previous year, but it may have sparked renewed interest in San Lucas as a convenient

harbor in this part of the world. By the end of the 19th century, an enterprising group of *bajacalifornianos* began processing and shipping bark from the local *palo blanco* tree, a key ingredient in leather tanning. The principal route for the bark trade ran between Cabo San Lucas and San Francisco. Shipping traffic gradually increased, and port authorities built the lighthouse now known as Faro Viejo at nearby Cabo Falso in 1890.

In 1917, an American company floated a tuna cannery from San Diego to San Lucas to take advantage of the abundance of tuna in the area. As San Lucas gathered a small population, a roadbed to San José del Cabo, the nearest federal government seat, was laid in the 1920s. By the 1930s, a cannery and a small fishing village inhabited by around 400 hardy souls occupied the north end of the Cabo San Lucas harbor. Fish-canning remained the backbone of the local economy until the cannery was heavily damaged by a hurricane in 1941. During World War II, the area was all but abandoned as Japanese submarines cruised the Pacific coast; Cabo seemed destined for obscurity.

Marlin Alley and La Carretera Transpeninsular

Fortunately for *sanluqueños* (residents of San Lucas), post–World War II leisure travel brought fly-in anglers, who spread the word that Cabo was a game fish paradise. The Cape sportfishing craze of the 1950s and 1960s—when the waters off the peninsula's southern tip earned the nickname Marlin Alley—expanded the population to around 1,500 by the time the Transpeninsular Highway was completed in 1973. After the establishment of the highway link between the United States and Cabo San Lucas, the town was transformed from a fly-in/sail-in resort into an auto-and-RV destination.

When Baja California Sur received statehood in 1974, a ferry route from Puerto Vallarta on the mainland was established, thus opening the area to increased Mexican migration. The construction of Los Cabos International Airport near San José del Cabo in the 1980s brought

© JOE CUMMINGS

LOS CABOS

El Arco

Cabo within reach of vacationers who didn't have the time for a six-day drive from border to Cape and back. The establishment of a water pipeline between San José and San Lucas further loosened the limits on development.

Today the local economy rests on the provision of tourism services and a booming construction industry, which supplies the growing need for leisure, residential, and business structures throughout the lower Cape Region.

◖ LAND'S END

You know you've reached the end of the road in Baja when the towering rock formations and signature arch at Land's End come into view. Forming the coccyx of a rocky spine that reaches northward all the way to Alaska's Aleutian Islands, the formations are collectively known as **Finisterra,** or Land's End. Take a water taxi beyond the harbor to get a closer look at the cliffs and watch sea lions play in the surge.

El Arco, a rock outcropping at the tip of Land's End, has become Cabo San Lucas's most immediately recognizable symbol. During low tide you can walk along Playa del Amor to the 62-meter (200-ft) rock formation, which features an eroded passage through the middle. El Arco is also known as the Arch of Poseidon since it marks the entrance to a precipitous submarine canyon—the perfect throne room for the King of the Seas—just offshore. Running northwest from El Arco and Playa del Amor are several more unnamed rock formations, including two large granite clusters as tall or taller than El Arco.

Just offshore stand **Los Frailes** (The Friars), two rock islets shaped like clusters of hooded monks and frequented by sea lions. A smaller, bird-limed rock pinnacle off the northeast side of the Cape, **Roca Pelícanos** (Pelican Rock), serves as a crowded pelican roost. The base of the pinnacle, about six meters (20 ft) down, is richly endowed with marinelife, including coral, sea fans, gorgonians, sea urchins, and numerous tropical fish. Recent reports from divers say visibility at the rock is declining,

© PAUL ITOI

Land's End

however, because of discharge from cruise ships moored in the outer harbor.

Cerro La Vigía, rising 150 meters (500 ft) above the harbor, once served as a lookout point for English pirates awaiting Manila galleons to plunder. Today it's still an excellent vantage point for viewing Land's End, the town, the marina, Playa Solmar (the beach next to the Hotel Solmar), and Cabo Falso. A steep trail begins just behind the old cannery on the harbor and leads to La Vigía's summit, which is marked by a crucifix.

BEACHES

Beachgoers can choose among five beaches close to the downtown area and a string of beaches and coves along the San José del Cabo to Cabo San Lucas Corridor.

Playa El Médano

The most popular and easily accessible local beach, Playa El Médano (Dune Beach) extends several kilometers along Bahía San Lucas northeast from the inner harbor's en-

trance channel. Baja's most heavily used beach is packed with swimmers and sunbathers during peak vacation periods—and is one of the few local beaches where swimming is safe year-round. Beach vendors rent *pangas,* personal watercraft, inflatable rafts, windsurfing and snorkeling equipment, kayaks, volleyball equipment, *palapas,* and beach furniture. Several *palapa* bars and restaurants scattered along the beach offer cold beverages, as well as burgers, seafood, and Mexican fare.

Minor annoyances at Playa El Médano include the many vendors who plod up and down the beach hawking jewelry, rugs, hammocks, hand-painted plates, and the like (they won't persist if you show no interest) and the sprawling condo developments in the background that mar the view of the Sierra de la Laguna foothills.

(Playa del Amor

Cabo's next most popular beach can be reached only by boat or by a difficult climb over two rock headlands along the ocean. Playa del Amor (Love Beach), also known as Playa del Amante (Lover's

Beach), lies near the tip of Cabo San Lucas—the cape itself, not the town—just northwest of the famous arch-shaped rock formation featured in virtually every Los Cabos advertisement. The wide, sandy, pristine beach extends across the cape behind the arch to the other side, forming two beachfronts—one on Bahía San Lucas and one on the Pacific. The latter is sometimes whimsically called "Divorce Beach."

Only the beachfront facing the bay is generally safe for swimming. The beach is supposed to be free of vendors and commercial enterprises; however, vendors do occasionally sell cold drinks out of a cooler. Unless you have a portable beach umbrella, go early in the day to command one of the shady rock overhangs. The southeast end of the bay features a series of coral-encrusted rocks suitable for snorkeling; a deep submarine canyon lying only 50 meters (164 ft) offshore is a popular scuba diving site.

You can reach Playa del Amor by water taxi from the marina, or take a glass-bottomed boat tour (US$10 round-trip for either option) and arrange a drop-off at the beach. Ask to see the boat before you pay, as some are in much better shape than others. Should the engine fail and cut your trip short, the person you paid will likely be nowhere in sight. Any tour boat in the vicinity should give you a ride back to the marina upon presentation of your ticket stub; the last tour boat leaves the marina around 3 P.M. In calm seas, you can also rent a kayak (US$10 pp/hr) on Playa El Médano and paddle across the inner harbor entrance to the beach. It's best to go in the morning, when the water is calm; the paddle takes about 40 minutes one-way.

Those skilled at bouldering can reach the south side of the beach by climbing from the east end of Playa Solmar (in front of the Hotel Solmar) over two rocky points that separate the two beaches. The climb is best attempted during low tide, when the cove between the rock formations reveals a sandy beach useful as a midway rest stop. The second set of rocks, to the east, is more difficult than those to the west; turn back after the first set if you've reached the limit of your climbing skills.

Playa El Médano

Playa Solmar

This very wide, very long beach running along the southwestern edge of the Cape is accessible via the road to Hotel Solmar. The strong undertow and heavy surf make it suitable for sunbathing and wading only. Solmar's biggest advantage is its lack of people, even during peak tourist seasons.

Cannery Beaches

Next to the abandoned Planta Empacadora (the old tuna cannery on the south side of the inner harbor entrance) are two small public beaches virtually ignored by most Cabo visitors. The first, **Playa Escondida** (Hidden Beach), lies next to the cannery pier and is easily reached by walking along the west bank of the marina and alongside the main cannery building. The sand extends only around 50 meters (164 ft), less in high tide, but it's popular with local Mexican families because Dad can fish from the pier while the kids play in the calm water. **Playa Balconcito** (Little Balcony Beach), a bit larger than Playa Escondida, lies beyond the pier on the other side of the cannery toward the sea. You must walk along a stone ledge—part of the cannery foundation—to get there.

Corridor Beaches

Northeast of Cabo San Lucas—on the way to San José del Cabo—a number of uncrowded, relatively pristine beaches are suitable for swimming, fishing, camping, snorkeling, and scuba diving (see *Beaches* in *The Corridor* section).

FISHING

Other than swimming and lying on the beach, sportfishing is Cabo's number-one outdoor activity. Tens of thousands of billfish are hooked off the Cape each year. The biggest trophy of all, the *marlín azul* (blue marlin), can reach five meters (16 ft) in length and weigh close to a ton. In the Cape area, it's not unusual to hook 200- to 400-kilogram (440- to 880-lb) blues. A smaller species, the *marlín rayado* (striped marlin), grows to more than 270 kilograms (600 lbs), while the *marlín negro* (black marlin) is almost as big as the blue.

yellowfin tuna

© JOE CUMMINGS

To catch a glimpse of these huge game fish, stop by the sportfishing dock on the marina's west side around 3–4 P.M., when sportfishing boats return with their catches. Note the flags flown over the boats: A triangular blue flag means a billfish has been bagged, while a red flag with a T means one has been tagged and released. All Cabo sportfishing outfits request that anglers release billfish to fight another day; some even require it. Instead of skinning and mounting these beautiful fish, they recommend bringing a video camera along to record the catch from start to finish. Even where customers demand to keep a billfish, the Sportfishing Association of Los Cabos stipulates that only one billfish per boat may be killed (you can catch and release as many as you like).

Good marlin-fishing spots include **Banco San Jaime,** 29 kilometers (18 mi) southwest of Cabo Falso, and **Banco Golden Gate,** 31 kilometers (19 mi) west of Cabo Falso. Dorado and wahoo are also common in those areas. Sportfishing cruisers—powerboats equipped with electronic fish-finders, sophisticated tackle,

FISH TRANSLATOR

Mexican guides who lead sportfishing trips often use the local terms for game fish; when they don't, the English terms they use aren't always correct. This works the other way, too – many gringos use incorrect Spanish names for Baja fish, which can cause confusion when asking about local fishing conditions. Here is a key to some of the more common translations:

albacore tuna – *albacora*
barracuda – *picuda*
black sea bass – *mero prieto*
bluefin tuna – *atún de aleta azul*
blue marlin – *marlín azul*
dolphinfish (mahimahi) – *dorado*
grouper (generic) – *garropa*
halibut – *lenguado*
hammerhead shark – *cornuda*
jack crevalle – *toro*
ladyfish – *sabalo*
mackerel – *sierra, makerela*
manta ray – *manta*
marbled scorpionfish – *cabezón*
octopus – *pulpo*
Pacific amberjack – *pez fuerte*
perch (generic) – *mojarra*
pompano – *palometa*
puffer (generic) – *bolete*
red snapper – *huachinango*

roosterfish – *papagallo, pez gallo*
sailfish – *pez vela*
seabass (cabrilla) – *cabrilla*
shark (generic) – *tiburón*
small shark – *cazón*
squid – *calamar*
stingray (generic) – *raya*
striped marlin – *marlín rayado*
swordfish – *pez espada*
triggerfish – *cochi*
wahoo – *sierra wahoo, peto*
whale shark – *pez sapo*
white seabass – *corvina blanca*
yellowfin tuna – *atún de aleta; amarilla*
yellowtail – *jurel*

Pez is the generic word for fish. Once fish has been caught and is ready for cooking (or has been cooked), it's called *pescado*.

fighting chairs and harnesses, and wells for keeping live bait—are the angler's best chance for landing large game fish.

Almost unbelievably, marlin are also somewhat common just beyond the steep drop-offs between Los Frailes and Cabo Falso, an area easily reached by *panga* or skiff. Without the technology of a fishing cruiser, *panga* marlin-fishing becomes the most macho hook-and-line challenge of all—the resulting fish stories reach *Old Man and the Sea* proportions. For anglers with more humble ambitions, black sea bass, cabrilla, sierra, and grouper are found in inshore waters; surfcasters can take corvina, ladyfish, sierra, and *pargo*.

Guided Sportfishing
Several outfitters arrange sportfishing trips aboard cruisers and *pangas*. Rates aver-

age US$350 a day on a four-angler, 28-foot cruiser and US$550 a day for a six-person, 36-foot fishing cruiser. Charter boats generally hold 4–6 anglers; rates usually include tax, license, gear, and ice. **Pisces Fleet** (Blvd. Marina at Madero, tel. 624/143-1288, www.piscessportfishing.com) is one of the more reliable independent outfitters. Bareboat rates are US$355 and US$450 for 28- and 31-foot boats (US$500/630 all-inclusive), US$850–1,650 for 35- to 42-foot boats. The fleet tops out with a 111-foot yacht that accommodates 12 anglers for US$9,500. Half-day rates are available.

Dream Maker Sportfishing (Locale 20, Hotel Tesoro complex, tel. 624/143-7266, www.dreammakercharter.com) leads five-hour and eight-hour trips with a fleet of nine boats that includes everything from a 22-foot *panga* (US$175/5 hrs) to a

WORLD FISHING RECORDS SET IN BAJA

The nonprofit International Game Fish Association (IGFA) tracks world records set for each species of game fish according to weight, weight/test ratio (fish weight to line test), place where the catch was made, and other significant record details. World-record catches achieved by Baja anglers for specific line classes include those for the following fish: Pacific blue marlin, striped marlin, Pacific sailfish, swordfish, roosterfish, dolphinfish (dorado), gulf grouper, California yellowtail, Pacific bonito, bigeye trevally, spotted cabrilla, spearfish, giant sea bass, white sea bass, California halibut, Pacific jack crevalle, black skipjack, yellowfin tuna, Pacific bigeye tuna, and chub mackerel.

Baja anglers hold all-tackle records – highest weight of any fish species regardless of line test – for gulf grouper, olive grouper, roosterfish, Pacific amberjack, white sea bass, spotted cabrilla, rainbow runner, black skipjack, yellowfin tuna, Pacific jack crevalle, chub mackerel, and California yellowtail.

For information on IGFA membership and record entries, contact IGFA (300 Gulf Stream Way, Dania Beach, FL 33004, igfahq@aol.com, www.igfa.org). Membership includes a copy of the IGFA's annual *World Record Game Fishes Book*, which contains a list of all current fishing records, as well as the bimonthly *International Angler* newsletter. IGFA members are also eligible for discounts on fishing charters offered by several sportfishing outfitters in Cabo San Lucas.

42-foot sportfisher (US$1,250 all-inclusive or US$1,050 boat only).

Located at the Bahia Hotel, **Gaviota Sportfishing** (U.S. tel. 800/932-5599, www.grupobahia.com) has experienced captains and 11 boats ranging from 26- to 36-foot cruisers. All-inclusive packages for four (US$755 including tax or US$595 boat charter only) come with tackle, bait, lunch, and a case of beer, soda, or bottled water. The same package for two aboard a 26-foot cruiser is US$440 (US$360 boat charter only). Boats leave at 7 A.M. and return at 3 P.M.

Guided cruiser trips are also easy to arrange through any major Cabo hotel. Solmar, Finisterra, and Meliá Cabo Real all have their own fleets, while other hotels typically use local brokers.

Whomever you go with, be sure to get a breakdown of exactly what to expect on any guided trip. One reader wrote to us and complained that he paid for eight hours of marlin fishing but got two hours of marlin fishing, three hours of bottom fishing, one hour waiting to buy bait, and two hours of idle boating. If you know that you're expected to provide your own bait, shop ahead. And expect that the farther out you go, the more time you'll spend in transit to and from your intended fishing destination.

Panga Trips

The least expensive fishing trips of all are those arranged directly with local *pangeros,* the men who own and operate single fishing *pangas.* Such *pangas* are sometimes available in Cabo San Lucas, but most *panga*-fishing trips operate out of La Playita near San José del Cabo. The typical *panga* trip costs US$175 for five hours in a three-person, 22-foot boat. *Panga* rates usually don't include rental gear or fishing licenses. When inquiring about rates—*panga* or cruiser—ask whether the quote includes filleting of edible game fish. The better outfits include fish preparation and packing among their services at no extra charge.

Surf Casting

Cheaper yet is to forgo boating altogether and drop a line from the beach. The best surf casting in the immediate area is at **Playa Solmar,** but watch the surf closely, as large waves sometimes seem to arrive out of nowhere. You can also fish from the old pier extending from the abandoned tuna cannery at the entrance to the harbor, where the water is relatively calm. On **Playa El Médano,** you can fish only at the far northeastern end of the beach.

Bait, Tackle, and Fish Processing

Minerva's Baja Tackle (on Blvd. Marina at Madero, tel. 624/143-1282, Mon.–Sat. 9 A.M.–7 P.M.), next door to Pisces Fleet, is well stocked with lures and other tackle designed specifically for Cabo sportfishing. Minerva's is also the area's official International Game Fish Association (IGFA) representative.

Buy fresh bait at the San Lucas harbor docks for a few dollars. Locals here will also clean and fillet your catch on the spot for tips. You can arrange to have fish cleaned, processed, vacuum-packed, and frozen through **Gricelda's Smoke House** (Loc 19 & 20 in the Tesoro Hotel complex, tel. 624/143-7266, www .dreammakercharter.com) on the marina.

DIVING AND SNORKELING

Cabo is a unique diving destination because it's in the middle of a transition zone between tropical and temperate waters. Strikingly large fish such as amberjack, hammerheads, and manta rays—which are partial to temperate waters—mix with the smaller, more colorful species typical of tropical waters. It's also unique in that some of the best snorkeling and scuba sites are only a 5- to 25-minute boat ride from the marina (compared to boat rides of 1–2 hours to the islands off La Paz).

Snorkelers explore the base of the cliffs on each side of **Playa del Amor,** about three meters (10 ft) deep, for coral and tropical fish. Nearby Pelican Rock, some six meters (20 ft) deep, is a bit more challenging. Strong swimmers, on calm days, can swim south around the arch to the sea lion colony at Los Frailes and frolic with the creatures. Several spots along the Corridor between San Lucas and San José feature good snorkeling, including **Playa Chileno** and **Playa Santa María** (see *Diving and Snorkeling* in *The Corridor* section).

Guided scuba dives tour many of the same sites as snorkelers, making it convenient to ac-

commodate mixed groups (but also making it more crowded, both above and below the surface). Also, given the proximity of these dive sites to the harbor, the loud and constant rumble of boat traffic overhead makes for an annoying distraction.

The most popular dive sites in the Cabo Marine Preserve include Pelican Rock, Neptune's Finger, and the point at Land's End. Pelican Rock and Neptune's Finger begin at shallow depth (20–25 ft), and then descend over boulders or along a wall into a vast submarine canyon, as diver skill, air consumption, and visibility allow.

Part of a national marine preserve, the canyon begins just 50 meters (164 ft) off Playa del Amor and is famous for its "sandfalls"—streams of sand tumbling over the canyon rim at a depth of around 30 meters and forming sand rivers between rock outcroppings. At a depth of around 40 meters (130 ft), the outcroppings give way to sheer granite walls, where the sand rivers drop vertically for more than two kilometers (to a depth of around 2,750 m/9,000 ft). The phenomenon was first documented by a Scripps Institute of Oceanography expedition in 1960 and later made famous in one of Jacques Cousteau's television documentaries. The size of the sandfalls and sand rivers depends to a large extent on climatic conditions; during long spells of calm weather they may even come to a halt. But there is plenty to see, whether or not the rivers are running. The edges of the canyon walls are layered with colorful coral, sea fans, and other marinelife. These in turn attract schools of tropical fish, including many open-ocean species not ordinarily seen this close to shore. Graceful eagle rays, good-sized grouper, and tiny zebra eels are just a few of the sightings divers may experience on these dives.

The Land's End dive begins in the surge under a sea lion colony on the Sea of Cortez side of the point and ends with an underwater swim around to the Pacific side, covering varied underwater topography along the way. Guitar fish, schooling amber jacks, green sea turtles, and countless other species are likely to make an appearance on this dive.

HOW MUCH DOES IT COST?

GUIDED DIVE AND SNORKEL TOURS
Discounts apply for multiday dives.

Snorkel tour (equipment included)	US$25-45
One-tank boat dive	US$45-65
Two-tank boat dive	US$70-85
Night dive	US$50-65
Cabo Pulmo day trip	US$120-155
Gorda Banks day trip	US$120-185
Nondiver passenger	US$10-15

SCUBA INSTRUCTION

Open Water referral (4 dives, for students who have completed classroom and pool work prior to arrival)	US$210-250
Open water certification (classroom and dives)	US$375-430
Discover Scuba/resort course (introduction to scuba)	US$90-100
Refresher dive	US$100
Advanced certification	US$280-330
Rescue diver course	US$300

EQUIPMENT RENTAL

Snorkel gear (usually included with tour)	US$4-12
Scuba package with dives (discounts for multiday dives)	US$20-25/day
Weight belt and weights	US$8
Regulator	US$12
Tanks	US$12
BCD	US$12
Wet suit	US$8
Airfills	US$45

Cabo San Lucas dive shops can also arrange trips to **Cabo Pulmo** for reef dives in a protected marine park (see *East Cape* in the *East and Central Cape* chapter) and the Gorda Banks, where advanced divers with experience in strong currents can explore seamounts at a depth of around 41 meters (135 ft) that are famous for sightings of hammerhead sharks, whale sharks (the world's largest fish), huge tuna, amberjack, grouper, and manta rays.

Dive Guides and Outfitters

Many Cabo hotels can arrange guided dive trips and equipment rentals. Some have their own shops onsite, while others book through one of the many independent shops in town. Dive operators typically organize two outings per day, weather permitting. Morning boats leave the harbor around 9 A.M., and the afternoon shift departs around 1 P.M. Mornings tend to be less crowded above and below the surface. In the afternoon, the wind kicks up and boat traffic increases, making water entries and exits a little trickier.

Manta (tel. 624/144-3871, www.caboscuba. com) is a professionally-run PADI shop conveniently located at Playa El Médano. Its custom-designed 35-foot boat holds 15 divers comfortably; additional 28-foot and 26-foot boats accommodate up to 10 divers each. All three boats are equipped with radios, first aid kits, and oxygen. For local dives in the Cabo Marine Preserve, advanced and novice divers often share the same boat, but have separate dive guides, since easy and advanced dives start at the same points. (Experienced divers go deeper and stay under longer than beginner groups.) Knowledgable boat captains and a friendly international guide staff make for a safe and enjoyable dive experience. An earlier morning start (8:30 A.M.) helps avoid the crowds. Rental gear is in good shape, with Sherwood regs, Aqualung and Genesis BCDs, and Akona, Body Glove, and Scuba Pro wetsuits. In addition to standard 80 cft tanks, smaller (63 cft) and larger (100 cft) sizes are available.

Underwater Diversions (tel. 624/143-4004, U.S. tel. 949/226-8987, www.divecabo. com) is another reputable shop in the Plaza Marina. **Blue Adventures** (tel. 624/144-4680, www.aventurasazul.com), also in the Plaza Marina, takes divers to sites in the Cabo Marine Preserve and along the Corridor. Longer trips to Gorda Banks and Cabo Pulmo are also possible. Nondivers can ride along for US$10 with a reservation. **Amigos del Mar** (tel. 624/143-0505, U.S./Canada tel. 800/344-3349, fax 624/143-0887) is next to Solmar Fleet on the west side of the harbor; and **Tío Watersports** (tel. 624/143-2986, daily 8 A.M.–5:30 P.M.) has facilities at the Meliá San Lucas, Meliá Cabo Real, and Marina Fiesta hotels.

See the sidebar *How Much Does It Cost?* for costs of guided tours, instruction, and equipment rental. During the slower summer season, some dive shops offer certification courses at heavily discounted rates; since underwater visibility is at its best during these months, this is a real bargain.

Liveaboards

Amigos del Mar (tel. 624/143-0505, U.S./Canada tel. 800/344-3349, fax 624/143-0887), next to Solmar Fleet on the west side of the harbor, arranges luxury liveaboard dive trips to the Socorro Islands, Guadalupe Island, Gorda Banks, Los Frailes, El Bajo, Cabo Pulmo, and other more remote sites aboard the 112-foot *Solmar V* (www.solmarv.com). The wood-and-brass-fitted boat features two onboard air compressors and a dive platform for easy exits. Prices run around US$2,100 for eight-day Sea of Cortez trips, including all land transfers, food and beverages, accommodations in air-conditioned staterooms, and up to three guided dives per day. Longer nine-day trips to the remote Socorro Islands run around US$3,000. The boat holds a maximum of 22 divers and 10 staff members.

Blue Adventure (tel. 624/144-4680, www. aventurasazul.com) also runs custom multiday trips to La Paz, Cabo Pulmo, and Gorda Banks for US$385 per person per day.

Snorkel Tours

Pez Gato (Camino Del Cerro 215, El Pedregal, tel. 624/143-3797, www.pezgatocabo. com, Mon.–Sat., US$45), offers four-hour sail and snorkeling tours to Bahía Santa María along the Corridor, aboard one of three catamarans. The tour includes two hours of swimming and snorkeling at Santa María, plus ceviche, tuna salad, guacamole, salsa and chips, open bar, bottled water, sodas, and cold beer on the way back. The boat departs at 10 A.M. and returns around 2 P.M. Monday–Thursday and Saturday; departure and return times are an hour later on Friday. Kids under 12 are free.

SunRider Adventure (tel. 624/143-2252, www.sunridertours.com) has a 60-foot vessel with a restaurant onboard. A snorkeling lunch tour to Playa Santa María for US$45 per person includes a Mexican buffet and open bar. Cash only.

Equipment

Most dive shops rent snorkel and dive equipment in packages or à la carte, so if you forget your fins or your mask strap breaks, you'll be able to borrow a replacement for the day. Repairs are a different story, however. If you're bringing your own gear, have it serviced before you leave home; check your computer batteries, and bring spare parts. Despite the number of dive shops, replacement parts are difficult, if not impossible, to come by in Baja.

Recompression

Clínica de Especialidades (Lopez Mateos btw Morelos/Vicario, tel. 624/143-3914 or 143-2919) maintains a hyperbaric recompression chamber that is available to recreational divers for emergencies.

SURFING

The nearest surfable waves occur well outside the city limits at **Playa Cabo Bello,** between Km 5 and Km 6 (see *Surfing* in *The Corridor* section). Well-known Monuments, a left point break at Misiones del Cabo, is another option close to town. Most good surf occurs here only during summer and early fall. Cabo Bello, recipient of a winter northwestern swell, is the one exception. The Pacific coast near Todos Santos is the place to head for waves in winter. If you need equipment or ding repair in Cabo San Lucas, try the **Cabo San Lucas Surf Shop** at the Plaza Marina.

PADDLING, SAILING, AND WINDSURFING

The onshore surf at Playa El Médano is mild enough for launching wind- and paddle-powered craft easily, and you can rent from a number of vendors along the beach. Kayaks cost US$10 per person/hour or US$50 for a half-day.

The water is calmest in the morning, and it takes about 40 minutes to get to Playa del Amor, so it's best to get an early start. Tell the vendors where you plan to take the craft; they'll know the conditions and advise accordingly. Watch out for powerboats, yachts, and cruise ships; larger craft have the de facto right of way. Novices should stick close to Playa El Médano, no matter what the conditions.

BOATING

With thousands of yacht arrivals per year, Cabo San Lucas is a major Baja California boating center. Even though harbor size and marine-repair facilities don't match those of La Paz, the greater variety of other services, nightlife, shopping, and dining venues more than compensates.

The outer harbor anchorages are mostly occupied by sportfishing cruisers; recreational boaters can moor off Playa El Médano to the northeast. Ringing the inner harbor, first dredged in the early 1970s, is **Marina Cabo San Lucas** (Lote A-18 De la Darsena, tel. 624/143-1251, U.S. tel. 310/541-3830, www. cabomarina.com.mx). Facilities include hot showers, restrooms, a pool, snack bar, laundry, dry storage and personal storage facilities, a chandlery, fuel (both diesel and gas), water, and 380 slips (20–416 ft) complete with electricity, telephone hookups, and satellite TV. Also available are a 75-ton lift and full-ser-

© PAUL ITOI

Cabo San Lucas marina

vice boatyard. Permanent and monthly renters at Marina Cabo San Lucas have priority over short-term visiting boaters; daily rentals are available on a first-come, first-served basis. Visiting boaters should contact the marina 15 days before arrival to check on the availability of slips. The Marina Cabo San Lucas office is open Monday–Saturday 9 A.M.–5 P.M., Sunday 10 A.M.–3 P.M. The marina's condos are occasionally available as rentals, and the adjacent Marina Fiesta Resort usually has vacant rooms. A convenience store and wireless Internet are also open Monday–Saturday 6 A.M.–7 P.M. and Sunday 6 A.M.–6 P.M.

Also in the inner harbor are two boat ramps, one near the old ferry pier and one at the northeast end of the harbor near the Tesoro Hotel. A fuel dock is between the old ferry pier and the abandoned cannery, just inside the entrance to the inner harbor. Cabo San Lucas is an official Mexican port of entry; the **COTP** office is on Calle Matamoros at 16 de Septiembre.

Cape Marine (Plaza Marina, Local J2-3, tel. 624/143-4970, Mon.–Sat. 8 A.M.–6 P.M.) carries hardware, apparel, yachting supplies and tools, and fishing equipment. Credit cards are accepted.

CRUISES

An abundance of glass-bottomed tour boats depart frequently from the marina and from Playa El Médano 9 A.M.–4 P.M. each day. The standard 45-minute tour costs US$8–12 per person and covers Pelican Rock, the famous Land's End arch, and the sea lion colony. For no extra charge, the crew will let passengers off at Playa del Amor near the arch; you can flag down any passing boat from the same fleet and catch a ride back to the marina later in the day. Be sure to see the boat you will board before you pay, as engines can be old and unreliable, and you may not get your money back if the trip is aborted due to engine failure. **Dos Mares** (tel. 624/143-4339) is one of the oldest fleet operators; **Esperanza's Fleet** (tel. 624/144-4666, www.esperanzas-fleet.com, US$12 or US$22 with snorkeling gear rental) is another option. Simpler launches without glass bottoms will do the same trip, including beach drop-off and pickup, for slightly less.

Sunset cruises with all the beer and margaritas you can drink are also popular and usually last around two hours and 15 minutes. You can make reservations at the marina or at most hotels; tickets cost US$25–50 per person depending on whether dinner is included. **Pez Gato** (Camino Del Cerro 215, El Pedregal, tel. 624/143-3797, www.pezgatocabo.com, Mon.–Sat.) offers an all-the-margaritas-you-can-drink sunset cruise that leaves from the main dock at 6 P.M. and returns at 8 P.M. for US$35 per person. (Book through any hotel or online.) **Jungle Cruise Tours** (tel. 624/143-7530, www.cabobooze-cruise.com) does an adults-only catamaran cruise that leaves from the marina at 6 P.M. in spring and summer and 5 P.M. in fall and winter for US$35 per person. A couple of similar boats operate sunset cruises from the west side of the harbor near the Tesoro Hotel. During high season these companies may offer sunset cruises on two separate boats simultaneously—a "romantic" cruise oriented toward couples, and a "booze cruise" for young singles.

A larger cruise ship, **Caborey** (tel. 624/143-8269, www.caborey.com) runs a dinner cruise for US$74 per person and a margarita cruise with appetizers for US$49.

Whale-Watching

Whales pass within a few hundred meters of Cabo San Lucas throughout the year, but the most activity occurs during gray whale migration season, January–March. The **Dos Mares** tour-boat fleet operates whale-watching trips from the marina during the migration season for US$35 per person. With binoculars you can also see passing whales from the Hotel Finisterra's Whale Watcher's Bar.

Swimming with Dolphins

At **Cabo Dolphins** (tel. 624/173-9500, www.cabodolphins.com, Mon.–Fri. 10 A.M., noon, 3 P.M., and 5 P.M., Sat.–Sun. 10 A.M. and noon), you can spend a half hour swimming

alongside playful bottlenose dolphins for US$165 per person. Children under 10 must be accompanied by a paying adult.

ATVS AND WAVERUNNERS

The sandy beaches and dunes in the Cabo San Lucas area are open to all-terrain vehicles (ATVs), as long as they're kept away from swimming areas (Playa El Médano) or turtle-nesting areas (Cabo Falso). Any of the hotels in town can arrange tours for around US$60 per person single/US$80 double. The basic route visits sand dunes, the ruins of El Faro Viejo, and a 1912 shipwreck; the six-hour tour adds La Candelaria, an inland village known for its pottery (see the *West Cape and Todos Santos* chapter). All-day trip rates include a box lunch and refreshments. Vendors along Boulevard Marina also book these trips. **Baja's Activities** (tel. 624/143-2050, www.bajasactivities.com), with locations at many local hotels and beaches, allows two riders per ATV at a discounted rate.

On a calm day, a WaveRunner can be a fast and fun way to explore the bay and Playa del Amor, and you don't have to be a speed demon to enjoy the ride. A number of vendors along Playa El Médano offer rentals for around US$70/hour.

MOUNTAIN BIKING

NaturAdventure (tel. 624/105-2050, www.naturadventure.com) leads half-day and full-day trail rides of varying levels around the Los Cabos area on Gary Fisher, Trek, and Specialized bikes. Destinations include Punta Gorda (US$65 pp), Cabo Pulmo (US$95 pp), and the Sierra de la Laguna (US$90 pp, US$75 half-day). Previous clients (only) can rent bikes for a self-guided tour (US$35–55 per day). MTB shoes and Shimano pedals available.

HORSEBACK RIDING

Red Rose (La Rosa) Riding Stables (Km 4, across from Cabo San Lucas Country Club, tel. 624/143-4826) appears to be the area's most serious saddle outfit. Choose Western or English tack. A one-hour ride along Playa El Médano costs about US$30; a two-hour mountain ride is US$45. Custom horseback trips and riding lessons are also available.

Rancho Collins (Camino Viejo a San José, tel. 624/143-3652, daily 8 A.M.–6 P.M.), across from Club Cascadas, offers 60-, 90-, and 120-minute horseback riding tours of nearby beaches and desert for US$30 per person/hour. Plan your ride in the morning or at sunset for maximum scenic effect. Its 45 horses are healthy and in good shape. Look for a pretty palomino near the road.

La Sanluqueña Bullring (tel. 624/143-8144), at the junction of Mexico 1 and Mexico 19, offers well-fed, well-trained horses for private trail rides or for rides along Playa El Médano. Horses are available for beginners as well as experts. A 75-minute ride runs about US$30.

SKYDIVING AND PARASAILING

Look for **Skydive El Sol** (tel. 624/129-7173, www.skydiveelsol.com, open daily year-round), a relative newcomer to Cabo San Lucas, near Club Cascadas on Playa El Médano, where the going rate is US$200 for a tandem jump that includes one minute of freefall time. Plan on a two-hour outing, from start to finish. For an additional US$90, you can return home with a DVD of the entire experience. Skydive El Sol needs at least two jumpers to book a trip.

The **Caborey** luxury cruise ship (tel. 624/143-8260, www.caborey.com) offers parasailing trips at a rate of US$35 for an eight- to ten-minute ride.

GOLF

About one kilometer north of the Cabo city limits, the 300-hectare (746-acre) **Cabo San Lucas Country Club** (tel. 624/143-4654, U.S. tel. 888/328-8501) offers a Roy Dye–designed course with views of Land's End and Bahía San Lucas from each fairway.

YOGA

Cabo Mind Body Fitness offers pilates and Bikram-method yoga sessions in the privacy of your own villa, but prices are correspondingly steep: Pilates sessions run US$158–190 per person/hour, down to US$50 per person/ hour for groups of seven or more. Yoga classes cost US$139 per person/hour, down to US$38 for groups of 11 or more. Discounts apply for pairs and triples too, so it pays to buddy up. Visit www.cabovillas.com for details.

SPA SERVICES

Most of the larger Cabo resorts have their own spas onsite. For example, **Armonia Spa** (tel. 624/142-9797, www.pueblobonito .com) opened in 2005 at the Pueblo Bonito Pacifica resort and offers 50-minute massage treatments for US$100. Choices include hot stone, Shiatsu, four hands, deep tissue, Swedish, and pregnancy massage. **Nahui Beauty & Day Spa** (tel. 624/143-7066, www.nahuibeautyspa.com, Mon.–Sat. 10 A.M.–8 P.M.) at the Marina Sol Resort, one block off Playa Médano, offers a full menu of massage therapy, including deep tissue, reflexology, and aromatherapy (US$49–59 for 50 minutes), plus facials, manicures, and pedicures.

ENTERTAINMENT AND EVENTS

With an emphasis on booze and music, Cabo nightlife begins early and ends late. The action starts in the bars downtown near the marina and after midnight moves to the discos, which stay open till 3 or 4 A.M.

Bars

Tourists bent on getting well-primed for the evening pack **Giggling Marlin** (Matamoros at Blvd. Marina, tel. 624/100-6956, www.gigglingmarlin.com). Among the row of bars and restaurants along the marina in Plaza Bonita, **The Nowhere Bar** (tel. 624/143-4493, www.nowherebar.com, daily 11 A.M.–1 A.M., margaritas US$5) is a popular stop, especially during March madness NCAA basketball championships, with a happy hour 5–9 P.M.); you'll get two drinks (served in glasses, not plastic) for the price of one, whether you need them or not.

For a taste of Manhattan, **Red** (Zaragoza, around the corner from Squid Roe, tel. 624/143-5645, Mon.–Sat. 6 P.M.–3 A.M.) is an open-air wine and martini lounge. The quirky **Latitude 22+ Roadhouse** (Km 4.5, tel. 624/143-1516, www.lat22nobaddays.com, Wed.–Mon. 8 A.M.–11 P.M.) attracts Corridor residents and Baja old-timers with ocean views, reasonably priced cocktails, and giant flatscreen TVs and offers a Croatian-influenced menu. Formerly a downtown hangout, "Lat 22" is now located next to Costco and behind the power plant. Credit cards are accepted.

At **Hemingway's** (Guerrero btw Cardenas/Madero, tel. 624/143-9845, www.jnjhabanos.com), you can order a US$150 sip of tequila (the bottle costs more than US$1,000). Or the knowledgeable bartenders can help you taste a variety of high-end tequilas in the range of US$7–10 per taste. There are more than 345 tequilas from which to choose. The immense walk-in humidor has a full selection of Cuban cigars from Cohiba, Montecristo, and Partagas. A cigar roller, or *torcedor,* rolls well-made cigars for US$11–15.

If wine is your beverage of choice, **Sancho Panza** (tel. 624/143-3212) off Blvd. Marina in the Tesoro Hotel complex, offers the best wine list in southern Baja. This is the perfect place for a quiet drink, and the tapas menu is tops.

Fumari Café Hookah Bar (Lázaro Cárdenas across from the Paraíso mall, Mon.–Thurs. 4–11 P.M., Fri.–Sat. 4 P.M.–2 A.M., drinks US$2–4) is a cozy second-story café with several tables inside and a large roof deck outside. Curl up on a sofa and play a game of chess while you smoke a flavored hookah (US$13) or sip a chai tea.

Friday is tango night at super chic **Barometro** (tel. 624/143-1466, 10 P.M.–2 A.M.) on the Plaza Marina.

The **Whale Watcher Bar** (tel. 624/143-3333) at the Hotel Finisterra has a more sedate but popular 3:30–5:30 P.M. happy hour. The bar hosts an excellent mariachi group Thursday–Sunday and offers great Pacific views any day of the week.

Edith's (tel. 624/143-0801, www.edithscabo.com, daily 6 P.M.–1 A.M.), near Playa El Médano on the west side of the Camino de los Pescadores, presents live and recorded jazz (mostly 1940s and 1950s vintage).

Hard Rock Café (Blvd. Marina, Plaza Bonito, tel. 624/143-3779, daily 11 A.M.–2 A.M.), marked by a pink vintage Cadillac protruding from the front of the building at Plaza Bonita, is a lively place featuring sports-oriented TV rather than music videos, the entertainment staple of HRCs elsewhere. The Hard Rock hosts occasional live rock bands from La Paz and the mainland.

Dance Clubs

Cabo's discos begin filling up around 11 P.M., but the crowd doesn't really break a sweat till around midnight or later. A perennial favorite is the two-story dance floor at **El Squid Roe** (Lázaro Cárdenas at Zaragoza, tel. 624/143-0655), where bleacher-balconies offer a bird's-eye view of the swirling masses below. Balloons and confetti falling from the sky, table dancing, centipedes, and two-for-one drinks are all part of the experience. The Squid may stay open as late as 3 A.M., depending on the crowd.

Californians are partial to **Cabo Wabo** (Guerrero btw Madero/Lázaro Cárdenas, tel. 624/143-1188, www.cabowabo.com, 7 P.M.–2 A.M.), a dance club/restaurant owned by California rock 'n' roller Sammy Hagar. The music

---

WABORITA

The signature Cabo Wabo drink looks like a tropical fish, blue on the bottom and green on top. Here's how to make one when you get home:

1 oz tequila
½ oz Damiana liquor
½ oz orange liquor
½ oz lime juice
Shake and serve straight up with a dash of blue curaçao.

here alternates between a recorded mix (with video) and live bands. Cabo Wabo was built in 1989 and named for a Van Halen song describing the "wobble" exhibited by tourists walking around town after a night of club-hopping. Sammy and his band play at the club at least twice a year (on the club's April anniversary and again for the Red Rocker's birthday in October) and occasionally more often—Christmas and New Year's are good bets.

Among the newer clubs targeting a younger crowd is **Zoo Bar & Dance** (Blvd. Marina across from Plaza Bonita, tel. 624/143-5500, 9 P.M.–4 A.M.). Ladies drink free Thursdays 9 P.M.–midnight.

Cinema

On the second floor of Puerto Paraíso mall, **Cinema Paraíso** (tel. 624/143-1515) shows first-run Mexican, American, and international films.

Charreada

Despite the name, **La Sanluqueña Bullring** (tel. 624/143-8144), a small wooden stadium at the northeast corner of Mexico 19 and Mexico 1, actually hosts horseback-riding shows rather than bullfights. One of the performances, here billed as "Ladies on Horseback Ballet"—is *escaramuza,* a female equestrian event from the traditional *charreada.* The facility also rents horses for private rides.

Race and Sports Book

Casino Real Casino Sports Bar (tel. 624/143-1934, daily 9 A.M.–11 P.M.), in Plaza Náutica near the marina, features a full-service bar and restaurant, and a bank of closed-circuit television screens tuned to various sporting events.

Also in Plaza Náutica next to Baskin-Robbins is **Caliente Race and Sports Book** (tel. 624/143-1934), where customers can place bets based on Las Vegas odds. Satellite-linked TV monitors show thoroughbred and greyhound races, as well as American football, basketball, baseball, and other games.

Events

Bike races, fishing tournaments, music festivals, and national holidays are just a few of the gatherings that take place in Cabo San Lucas each year. The Los Cabos Guide (www.loscabosguide.com) has the most up-to-date listing of events online. The largest of the fishing tournaments is **Bisbee's Black and Blue Marlin Jackpot Tournament** (tel. 624/143-1622, www.bisbees.com), held for three days each October. The purse for the contest has approached US$5 million in recent years, making it the world's richest billfish tournament. Proceeds go to local charities.

Another notable yearly event falls around the Festival of San Lucas on October 18; look for a week of music, dancing, and feasting in the Mexican tradition.

SHOPPING

The streets of Cabo are filled with souvenir shops, street vendors, clothing boutiques, and galleries—probably more shops of this type per capita than anywhere else in Baja. A number of new, upscale shops now line the Plaza Fiesta, near the Marina Fiesta hotel.

Arts, Crafts, and Souvenirs

For inexpensive handicrafts—rugs, blankets, baskets, leatherwork—from all over Mexico, try the outdoor **Mercado Mexicano** on Hidalgo at Obregón; for the best prices, you'll have to bargain. Get good deals on Talavera ceramics at the **Mexican Pottery Factory Outlet** (Madero btw Guerrero/Hidalgo, tel. 624/105-0046).

Taxco (Guerrero and Blvd. Marina, tel. 624/143-0551) has the best selection of silver jewelry in town. **Joyería Albert,** on Matamoros between Niños Héroes and Lázaro Cárdenas, is a branch of the reputable Puerto Vallarta jeweler.

The newer shopping centers are all along the marina side of Boulevard Marina. **Plaza Bonita** has **Dos Lunas** (tel. 624/143-1969, www.doslunas.com), which offers hand-painted clothing, with a second location in

Puerto Paraíso; and **Cartes** (tel. 624/143-1770, Mon.–Sat. 9 A.M.–9 P.M., Sun. 9 A.M.–4 P.M.), with rustic colonial furniture, Talavera pottery, arts and crafts, and classy home-decor accessories. The presence of a **Sergio Bustamante** gallery (Loc. 25 and 27, tel. 624/144-4894, daily 9 A.M.–9 P.M.) here (and second location in Puerto Paraíso) shows that Cabo San Lucas has attained a market rank similar to that of Cancún and Puerto Vallarta. People tend either to love or to hate Bustamante's whimsical but costly ceramic sculptures, with their angelic faces and otherworldly, Peter Max–like themes.

Across from Mi Mariscos restaurant at the corner of Paseo a la Marina and Camino Viejo a San José, **Chile & Anis** (tel. 624/143-7454, Mon.–Sat. 9 A.M.–8 P.M.) is a Baja arts and crafts store with silver jewelry, wood crafts, mirrors, and ceramics for sale. Upscale crafts line the shelves of **Mi Mexico Magico** (Loc. 52, tel. 624/143-5153, daily 8 A.M.–9 P.M.) in the Marina Fiesta plaza.

local pottery

© JOE CUMMINGS

Puerto Paraíso

The first enclosed shopping mall in Los Cabos, the glitzy Puerto Paraíso (tel. 624/144-3000), adjoining the marina, is Cabo's most upscale shopping and entertainment plaza. So far what you'll find for the most part are three levels of art galleries and international fashion franchises such as Quicksilver, Nautica, Mossimo, Guess, and Harley-Davidson, and even a Curves exercise center. American restaurants and food outlets include Ruth's Chris Steak House, Häagen-Dazs, Houlihan's, and Johnny Rockets. There is also a bowling alley on the third level. When finished, the mall will contain more pricey shops, a convention center, two hotels, condo units, and a spa. Clean public restrooms and free parking are added conveniences.

Fine Art Galleries

In the lobby of the Tesoro Los Cabos Hotel, a photography gallery displays prints by **Tomas Spangler,** whose work depicts images and scenes unique to the Baja peninsula. A rep-

resentative is available Monday–Saturday 10 A.M.–2 P.M. (www.fotomas.com).

Golden Cactus Gallery (Guerrero and Madero, tel./fax 624/143-6399, www.golden-cactusgallery.com) features the works of artist Chris MacClure in a second-story studio. MacClure's work captures local Baja imagery, and he has created commissioned paintings of yachts, airplanes, and the like for celebrity clients including John Travolta.

Home Decor

San José and the Corridor have a higher concentration of home furnishing stores, but there are a few in Cabo San Lucas as well. **Decor America Interiors** (Mendoza and Obregón, tel./fax 624/143-0575, www.decoramericainteriors.com, Mon.–Fri. 9:30 A.M.–6 P.M., Sat. 9:30 A.M.–1 P.M.) is a full-service interior design shop offering a wide selection of furniture, custom upholstery, and accessories.

Northeast of town, **Artesano Mexicano** (Km 2.5, tel. 624/143-7161, daily 9 A.M.–1 P.M. and 3 P.M.–8 P.M.) is a large shop selling rustic furniture, hand-painted Mexican tiles, colorful ceramic sinks, terra-cotta wall sconces, glassware, pewter, and many other ceramic and iron decorating accessories, all at low (for Cabo) prices.

Cigars

Many stores sell Cuban cigars in Los Cabos, but fakes are rampant. Buy from a reputable merchant if you want the real thing. And remember, Cubans never go on sale. **La Casa del Habano** (formerly J&J Habanos, Blvd. Marina near Madero, tel. 624/143-6160 or 877/305-6242, www.jnjhabanos.com) has a walk-in humidor and a few tables inside. Prices are steep, but you can be confident that you're getting what you pay for. The owners have also opened a new cigar bar called **Hemingway's,** across from the entrance to Cabo Wabo (see *Bars*).

Wine

La Europea (tel. 624/145-8755, Mon.–Fri. 9 A.M.–8 P.M., Sat. 9 A.M.–9 P.M.) has opened a small street-level store in the Puerto Paraíso complex. This satellite of the larger, main store on the Corridor features a good selection of discounted wines, including some California labels, plus just about every other type of booze and upscale deli items such as balsamic vinegar, crackers, olives, cheeses, rose petal marmalade, and fresh baguettes. Credit cards are accepted.

Sporting Goods

Cabo Sports Center (Plaza Náutica, tel. 624/143-4272, daily 9 A.M.–7 P.M.) sells beach supplies, sports sandals, and varied equipment for golf, swimming, surfing, snorkeling, boogie-boarding, and mountain biking. **Minerva's Baja Tackle** (on Blvd. Marina at Madero, tel. 624/143-1282, Mon.–Sat. 9 A.M.–7 P.M.), next door to Pisces Fleet, is well stocked with lures and other tackle designed specifically for Cabo sportfishing.

Books and Magazines

Libros Libros/Books Books (Plaza de La Danza, tel. 624/143-3172, daily 9 A.M.–9 P.M.) stocks a few English-language paperbacks, magazines, maps, books on Baja, children's books, and U.S. newspapers. A second, larger branch in Plaza Náutica, next to Dairy Queen, had no English titles at last check.

ACCOMMODATIONS

Cabo San Lucas offers a greater number and variety of hotels than neighboring San José. Most are in the US$50–150 range, although the high-end resorts cost well over US$250 in winter and early spring.

Unless otherwise noted, rate ranges quoted below are for double rooms, peak season, usually November–May. Some hotels may offer a 15–20 percent discount March–October and a discount for stays longer than a week. Add 12 percent tax to all rates; some hotels may charge an additional 10–15 percent service charge.

Downtown Hotels

Although Cabo's beaches are the average visitor's preferred address, you can save considerably by staying downtown and walking or driving to the beach.

Under US$50: A bit off the beaten track (and close to the bus terminal), **Hotel Casa Blanca** (on Calle Revolución a half block east of Morelos, tel. 624/143-5360, US$45–50), offers 20 newly renovated rooms with king-size beds and air conditioning. In the same vicinity, **Olas Hotel** (Revolución at Gómez Farías, tel. 624/143-1780, fax 624/143-1380, US$45) feels more like a hostel, with 28 rooms (some with one king-size bed, others with two single beds). Amenities include cable TV, fan, fridge, microwave, and patio. Budget travelers might also check out relative newcomer **Hotel Oasis,** across from the CCC (Centro Comercial California) on the west side of Mexico 19 just north of the junction with Mexico 1, where the going rate is US$35–45. The friendly **Hotel Dos Mares** (Zapata, tel. 624/143-0330, hoteldosmares@cabotel.com. mx, US$40–90) rents 37 quite adequate, air-conditioned rooms with TV and phone. A small pool is on the premises.

US$50-100: Cabo Inn Hotel (20 de Noviembre btw Vicario/Mendoza, tel./fax 624/143-0819, US$58) is a cash-only place with nice courtyard areas downstairs and small, clean rooms with air conditioning, ceiling fans, and tiny bathrooms. A shared TV is usually on in the downstairs lobby, though it's turned off at a reasonable hour. The roof patio has a seating area furnished with a sofa, chairs, and a cabinet full of books, as well as a "social pool." One *palapa* unit features a whirlpool and another can sleep up to six people.

One of the best values downtown is the friendly and efficient **Siesta Suites Hotel** (Zapata btw Guerrero/Hidalgo, tel./fax 624/143-2773, U.S. tel. 866/271-0952, www.cabosiestasuites.com, US$59), near the better downtown restaurants and one block from the marina. All 15 suites and five hotel-style rooms are clean and quiet. Suites come with a kitchen and separate bedroom. All rooms have air conditioning, cable TV, and telephone (local calls are free). The hotel also features a sundeck, barbecue area, and secured parking. Because of price and location, Siesta Suites is a popular (and somewhat noisy) spot; reservations are recommended, even in summer—ask for the highest floor available to minimize the noise. Credit cards are accepted.

The **El Dorado** (Morelos btw Obregón/Carranza, tel. 624/143-2810, US$55) offers basic rooms. The **Hotel Los Arcos** (Vicario and Revolución, tel. 624/143-0702, US$55) opened in December 2005 with 32 clean rooms in a two-story building with cable TV and air conditioning.

Three blocks back from the marina, old gringo standby **Hotel Mar de Cortez** (Blvd. Lázaro Cárdenas at Guerrero, tel. 624/143-0032, U.S./Canada tel. 800/347-8821, www.mardecortez.com, US$50–67) stays full virtually all season. Its clean, air-conditioned rooms surround a small pool and patio area planted with date palms; some of the rooms have small patios attached. Facilities include a restaurant and outdoor bar area.

A large arched metal door leads to the attractive walled courtyard of the **Los Milagros Hotel** (Matamoros 116, tel. 624/143-4566, U.S. tel. 718/928-6647, info@losmilagros.com. mx, US$75–115). The 12 spacious rooms—some with kitchenettes—are well appointed. An inviting splash pool/hot tub and free Wi-Fi are added conveniences.

Now owned by The Villa Group, **Hotel Santa Fe** (southwest corner of Zaragoza and Obregón, tel. 624/143-4401, U.S. tel. 877/845-5247, gerenciasantafe@prodigy.net. mx, US$74–95) is a tidy, Mexican-style compound containing 46 studios set around a pool. Each studio has a sliding glass door, recently renovated bath, kitchenette, new furnishings, air conditioning, satellite TV, and phone. Amenities include wireless Internet, offstreet parking, 24-hour security, a small counter restaurant with outdoor seating (daily 7 A.M.–7 P.M.), laundry, and a mini super (daily 7 A.M.–7 P.M.). A free beach shuttle was in the works for 2007.

One block off the marina on the second floor of Plaza de la Danza, **Viva Cabo Hotel** (Blvd. Marina, Plaza La Danza, tel./fax 624/143-5810, US$89–100) has eight studios with kitchens, air conditioning, satellite TV, and sitting areas. Amenities include a restaurant and bar, with a pool and fitness center next door.

Playa El Médano Hotels

The preponderance of Cabo's beach hotels are along this long strip of sand southeast of the town center.

US$50-100: East along Playa El Médano, behind San Vicente and Vagabundos RV Parks, **Club Cabo Hotel and Campground Resort** (tel./fax 624/143-3348, www.clubcaboinn. com, US$65–95) rents several suites and bungalows with air conditioning, verandas, and king-size beds. Other amenities include laundry facilities, wireless Internet access, table tennis, swimming pool, hot tub, large refrigerator for storing your catch, and shuttle to town. English, Spanish, and Dutch are spoken. Club Cabo is also an RV park (see *Camping and RV Parks*). It's a 15–20 minute walk from the park to the marina/downtown and a short walk to the beach, which is separated from the park by a dirt road and one of the last stands of natural thorn forest in the Cabo area—a good birding site.

Not on the beach, but close to it, is the 10-room **Casa Rafael's** (Pescador at El Médano, tel. 624/143-0739, www.casarafaels.com, US$75–100), tastefully decorated in Mexican-colonial style. Rooms with access for people with disabilities are available; some rooms have hot tubs and some have ocean views. The premises are planted in banana and papaya and feature exotic caged birds, a pool, hot tub, small gym, piano bar, cigar lounge, and a restaurant with a good wine collection (mains US$16–35). Credit cards are accepted.

US$150-250: Families particularly like **Villa del Palmar Cabo Beach Resort & Spa** (Km 0.5, tel. 624/145-7000, U.S. tel. 877/845-5247, www.villadelpalmarloscabos.com, junior suites US$200–400), which stands along a secluded area of El Médano and offers 458 suites, including junior suites and one- to three-bedroom oceanview deluxe suites, all with kitchens, marble bathrooms, and furnished balconies. Other amenities include two pools (one with poolside bar), two lighted tennis courts, a fitness center, a water-sports facility, and rooftop and beachside restaurants. Some units are available only by the week. The onsite Spa at Villa del Palmar offers individual and package treatments in a 10,000 square-foot European-style spa. Prices include tax; three-night minimum.

Over US$250: Next door to the Villa del Palmar, **Villa La Estancia** (Km 0.5 Camino Viejo a San José, tel. 624/143-8121, U.S. tel. 619/683-7883, www.villalaestancia.com) has 158 units ranging in size from one bedroom (US$550–650) to three bedrooms, as well as standard guestrooms (US$301–370) and junior suites. Still under construction at press time, **Villas del Arco** (tel. 624/145-7000, U.S. tel. 888/880-8512, www.villadelarcocabo.com) was to have three buildings when complete, with junior suites for around US$300, as well

as one- and two-bedroom units. Prices at both of these resorts include tax, and there is a three-night minimum.

The **ME Cabo** resort (Playa El Médano, tel. 624/145-7800, U.S. tel. 800/336-3542, www.solmelia.com, US$335–796) is a Spanish-owned Sol Meliá property with 108 recently remodeled rooms and suites built in a horseshoe shape around a large pool and patio area. Distinctive touches include an adults-only floor, free preloaded iPods, and home theaters. Most rooms have ocean views.

A couple hundred meters northeast along the beach is the striking **Pueblo Bonito Los Cabos** (tel. 624/142-9797, U.S. tel. 800/990-8250, www.pueblobonito.com, US$378–550), a white, five-story Mediterranean-style building topped by blue-tiled domes and arrayed in a horseshoe around gardens and a freeform pool with a waterfall. Purified water throughout the resort makes teeth-brushing less of an ordeal. The 148 junior and luxury suites come with kitchenettes and ocean views.

Farther northeast is another Pueblo Bonito resort, the **Pueblo Bonito Rosé** (tel. 624/142-9898, U.S. tel. 800/990-8250, www.pueblobonito.com, suites US$340–995). The 260 suites are situated on 2.2 hectares (5.5 acres). Not-especially-new rooms feature comfortable beds, private balconies, ocean views, hand-painted terra-cotta floors, kitchens, and original artwork. One of the hotel's finest features is its lavish lobby, which is decorated with velvet draperies, a 17th-century Flemish tapestry, and fountains surrounded by 16th-century Italian baroque cherubs.

Three miles east of Cabo San Lucas, beachfront **Riu Palace** (Km 5.5, Camino Viejo a San José, tel. 624/146-7160, U.S. tel. 888/666-8816, www.riu.com, US$248–310) comprises a town unto itself, with 642 guestrooms—that are booked almost all of the time, according to travel agents—and all-inclusive (only) meal plans. Part of a large international hotel chain, the lively Riu has so many dining and entertainment options that many guests never leave the resort during their visit. Rates include taxes. Riding the success of its first Los Cabos property, the company is reportedly building another resort next door.

Pacific Beach Hotels

Two of Cabo's most distinguished hotels are secluded from the rest of town by the rocky ridge leading to Land's End.

US$150-250: Impressively constructed high on the ridge itself, overlooking the beach and Pacific Ocean, is the 1971-vintage, 287-room ◖ **Hotel Finisterra** (tel. 624/143-3333, U.S. tel. 800/347-2252, www.finisterra.com, US$175–225). A newer tower wing, known as the Palapa Beach Club, offers spacious suites with ocean views and extends from the beach below all the way to the original hotel and lobby area, to which it is connected by a bridge. A gorgeous business center makes for a comfortable office away from home. It is equipped with leather chairs, five flatscreen TVs, and several Dell computer stations. Wireless Internet costs US$10/day. A 1,040-square-meter (11,200-sq-ft) swimming pool with whirlpools and swim-up bar sits on the beach at the foot of the Palapa Beach Club. Beds are on the firm side, and some of the rooms and suites in the original Finisterra section feature city, marina, or garden views rather than bay views. Amenities include lighted tennis courts, sauna, pool, massage service, and wedding chapel.

The sleek, V-shaped **Hotel Solmar Suites** (tel. 624/143-3535, U.S. tel. 310/459-9861 or 800/344-3349, www.solmar.com, US$170–330) features 180 rooms and suites built right on the beach directly into the rocks that form Land's End, plus additional timeshare/condo units overlooking the beach. Some of the suites have a private hot tub on the terrace. An older section of units directly on the beach has lower ceilings and less natural light; newer units are set back from the sand but have high ceilings, better lighting and newer furnishings. Down at the original beach wing are tennis courts, an aquatic center, an indoor-outdoor restaurant that cooks your fish anyway you like it (mains US$6–15), and two heated pools with swim-up *palapa* bars and hot tubs. The Solmar

is renowned for its fishing fleet; all-inclusive fishing packages are popular during the late-summer fishing season. The hotel's liveaboard dive boat, the *Solmar V* (www.solmarv.com) is one of the finest in Baja.

Over US$250: Open since 2002, the **Pueblo Bonito at Sunset Beach** (Cabo Pacifica, tel. 624/142-9999, U.S. tel. 800/990-8250, www.pueblobonito.com, US$394–550) has 327 suites on a 50-acre hillside overlooking the Pacific, behind the Pedregal development. Amenities include a hilltop "sky pool," a main pool that overlooks the beach, tennis courts, and a free shuttle into town (drop off at the Pueblo Bonito Blanco on Playa Medano). Fitness facilities cost extra (US$15/day) and massages run a steep US$130 at the Spa at Sunset Beach (daily 8 A.M.–7 P.M.). Two-for-one happy hour lasts exactly one hour, so best to load up on beverages during that time. Eat tacos and chicken sandwiches and the like poolside, or enjoy sushi in the bistro.

In the vicinity, the newest Pueblo Bonito property, **Pueblo Bonito Pacifica** (Cabo Pacifica, tel. 624/142-9696, U.S. tel. 800/990-8250, www.pueblobonito.com, US$400–494), opened in 2005. Couples in search of a romantic getaway like the no-kids factor at this boutique-style resort. Its 154 rooms, including 14 suites, are appointed in minimalist fashion, with a sand and ivory color scheme. Those who want a little more nightlife find the location a bit too remote. Strolling along the beach is discouraged due to heavy surf; you can, however, rent a bed on the beach for US$20 an hour. There is a free shuttle to town, or cabs for US$10 one-way. Meals at **Siempre,** the resort's main restaurant, are pricey, and food quality gets mixed reviews. The onsite **Armonia Spa** offers a variety of massage treatments, including hot stone, Shiatsu, four hands, deep tissue, Swedish, and pregnancy massage (US$100 for 50 minutes).

Marina Hotels

US$50-100: Overlooking the east side of the marina, the **Marina Cabo Plaza** (tel. 624/143-1833, US$100/day or US$700/week) has 63 rooms with a pool and location adjacent to a shopping center with restaurants, stores, and a private mail center. Playa El Médano is a 10-minute walk away. Kitchenettes are available.

US$150-250: Largest of the marina hotels, and the most basic all-inclusive resort in Los Cabos, the **Tesoro Los Cabos Hotel** (tel. 624/173-9300 or 800/716-8770, U.S. tel. 800/543-7556, www.tesororesorts.com, US$165–176 EP or US$183–194 AI)—formerly the Costa Real, and before that, the Hotel Plaza Las Glorias—is nicknamed "Cabo Jail" because it takes so long to walk from one end to the other. All rooms come with air conditioning, telephones, refrigerators, and in-room safety box. Facilities include a beach club at Playa El Médano. All-inclusive (AI) and European (EP) rate plans are available.

Next to Plaza Fiesta, near the Marina Cabo San Lucas office, stands the **Marina Fiesta Resort & Hotel** (tel. 624/145-6020, U.S. tel. 877/243-4880, www.marinafiestaresort.com, US$202–299). The hotel's well-designed, comfortable suites come with kitchenettes. Among the facilities are a sundeck and solarium (both with hot tubs), a massage and therapy room, 24-hour supermarket, drugstore, children's playground, and a freeform heated pool with a swim-up *palapa* bar.

Bed-and-Breakfasts

US$50-100: A few blocks from the town center, **Casa Pablito Bed and Breakfast Hotel** (Hidalgo and Ortega, tel. 624/143-1971, U.S. tel. 866/444-1139, www.casapablitoloscabos.com, US$90) is a new property opened by the owner of Club Cascadas. Originally built to house employees of the condo resort, the building has been converted into a traditional Mexican hacienda-style inn with 14 suites set around a pool and *palapa*-shaded breakfast area. Rooms have either one queen or two twin beds, plus kitchenettes, air conditioning, and cable TV.

US$100-150: Off Calle Constitución in the residential western part of town, **The Bungalows Breakfast Inn** (Dorado and Lienzo Charro, tel. 624/143-5035, U.S. tel. 888/424-2226,

www.cabobungalows.com, US$135–185) offers eight well-decorated one-bedroom suites, each with ceiling fan, air conditioning, fridge, stove, and TV; one larger, deluxe one-bedroom suite; one honeymoon suite with a private veranda and view of town; and six two-bedroom bungalows, each sleeping 4–6 guests. Smoking isn't permitted anywhere on the premises, inside or out. The small but well-landscaped grounds also contain a heated swimming pool, hot tub, and outdoor barbecue, plus a small gift shop selling many of the Mexican decor accessories seen in the guestrooms. A Mexican cook and pastry chef prepare the full breakfast.

US$150-250: One mile east of Cabo San Lucas and a half mile above Mexico 1, **Casa Contenta** (tel. 624/143-6038, www.cabocasacontenta.com, US$160–195/day or US$1,050–1,300/week) has five air-conditioned rooms with private baths in a three-story home with a swimming pool and wireless Internet throughout. Take a yoga class, book a spa treatment, or simply enjoy the view of Land's End on the rooftop terrace. There's a three-night minimum.

Condominiums and Condotels

Some of the best deals for families or small groups are rental condos, which usually sleep up to four for US$120–250 per night. Some condos take reservations directly, while others have booking services (some do both). And many different property management companies may have listings in the same complex. Rates do not include tax and service unless otherwise noted.

US$100-150: Well-managed, four-story **Bahía Condo Hotel** (tel. 624/143-1888, U.S. tel. 800/932-5599, www.grupobahia.com, US$129–149), just off Camino de los Pescadores above Playa El Médano, rents simple, clean, air-conditioned units, some with ocean views, all with minimally equipped kitchenettes, satellite TV, and direct-dial phones. Giant sculpted concrete shells frame the beds as headboards, and bamboo doors enclose the bathroom and closet. Faucets and tiling have aged a bit. The property includes laundry facilities, a decent restaurant, pool with hot tub and swim-up *palapa* bar, and free parking. Its studios feel more like basic hotel rooms than condos, but for the price, you can't beat the location and friendly service. Rates here include tax. Construction in front of the hotel detracts somewhat from the view, and like many affordable downtown locations, the place is overrun with college students on spring break during the month of March.

Close to downtown but also within easy walking distance of El Médano, **Marina Sol Condominiums** (tel. 624/143-3231, U.S. tel. 877/255-1721, www.marinasolresort.com) features simple one- and two-bedroom condos built around a garden courtyard with a pool. A room accessible to the disabled is available. The complex also has a hot tub, swim-up bar, and small gym. An independently operated grocery store, spa, and laundry service are located in the lobby.

US$150-250: Club Cascadas (Camino Viejo a San José, tel. 624/143-1882, U.S. tel. 800/365-9190 ext. 400, www.clubcascadasdebaja.com, one bedroom US$199–335), at the east end of El Médano, is a nicely designed timeshare complex with 110 interconnected villas, two pools, and tennis courts.

Near Casa Rafael's off Camino de los Pescadores, a short walk from Playa El Médano, stand the two round, whitewashed towers of **Cabo Villas** (tel. 624/143-9166, fax 624/143-2558, cabovillasresort@prodigy.net.mx). One-bedroom, one-bath units and two-bedroom, two-bath units are available.

The **Hotel Solmar Suites** (tel. 624/143-3535, U.S. tel. 310/459-9861 or 800/344-3349, www.solmar.com) rents a number of timeshare/condo units on the hill overlooking Playa Solmar. Next door, **Terrasol Condominiums** (tel. 624/143-1803, U.S. tel. 800/524-5104, www.terrasolcabo.com, one bedroom US$130–250) consists of studio, one-bedroom, and two-bedroom units, all with kitchens, ocean views, and wireless Internet access. On the premises are two pools, a tennis court, swim-up *palapa* bar, and snack bar. You can walk to the beach from both the Solmar and Terrasol.

Timeshares and Villas

As the new Pedregal develoment takes shape on the west side of town, a number of large, luxury beach homes have come on the rental market in Cabo San Lucas. Ranging in size from two to five or more bedrooms, these townhouses or private homes accommodate small groups with a creative list of in-villa services. For an extra fee, the property manager will stock your villa prior to your arrival with the foods and supplies you request. (You can also head to Costco and buy what you want when you get there.) Guests may schedule pilates or yoga classes, spa treatments, and chef services (one special meal or three meals daily). Prices start at about US$1,500 per night for a three-bedroom villa.

Booking Services and Property Management Companies

Delfin Hotels & Resorts (U.S. tel. 800/524-5104), described at the beginning of this chapter in the *Choosing an Accommodation* section, has Cabo San Lucas condos in the Terrasol complex. It also books for Casa Contenta B&B and most of the all-inclusive resorts. **Cabo Villa Rentals** (U.S. tel. 877/473-1946, www.cabovillarentals.com, 8:30 A.M.–5 P.M.) manages condos in the Terrasol and Villa La Estancia complexes and three- to five-bedroom villas in the Pedregal development. **Earth, Sea, and Sky Vacations** (U.S. tel. 800/745-2226, www.cabovillas.com), also described earlier, represents 90 luxury villa rentals, ranging from two- to nine-bedroom units with a starting pricepoint of US$1,500 per night, as well as 30 resorts. **Pedregal Escapes** (Camino de La Plaza 145, Fraccionamiento Pedregal, tel. 624/144-3222, www.pedregalescapes.com) is the vacation rental division of the company that developed the Pedregal gated community on the west side of Cabo San Lucas. It manages two- to five-bedroom villas, plus even a few larger homes. Prices start at about US$450 per night, and some properties require a security deposit.

Camping and RV Parks

Three kilometers northeast of Cabo San Lucas off Mexico 1, the **Vagabundos del Mar RV**

Park (Km 3, tel. 624/143-0290, www.vagabundosrv.com) has 52 slots with full hookups for US$20/day or US$120/week; discounts are available for members of the Vagabundos del Mar travel club (see *Travel Clubs* in the *Essentials* chapter). November–June, this park is usually booked up for weeks or months at a time, so be sure to make contact well in advance if you want to park here. Caravans are not accepted. Facilities include a restaurant, bar, flush toilets, *palapas,* showers, a pool, and laundry.

Behind the Vagabundos RV Park and Playa El Médano is the rustic **Club Cabo Hotel and Campground Resort** (tel./fax 624/143-3348, www.clubcaboinn.com, US$20). To get there, turn east off Mexico 1 onto the road to Club Cascada, then turn onto the first dirt road on your left and follow the signs. This small campground offers 10 tent sites and 10 slots for smaller RVs—some shaded, some not, all for US$20 per site. Facilities include well-kept toilets, hot showers, a hot tub, hammock lounge area, table tennis, trampoline, pool, wireless Internet and secure parking. Club Cabo also rents eight suites with kitchens (see *Playa El Médano Hotels*).

Nowadays Club Cabo is more likely to have a vacancy than Vagabundos; it is also closer to the beach than the others. The proprietor, an accomplished pilot, can arrange ultralight flights and instruction in the area. Visiting pilots may receive discounts on accommodations. Inquire about kayaking, sailing, horseback riding, and mountain biking. The adjacent natural thorn forest is a habitat for many resident and migratory bird species.

Villa Serena RV Park (Km 7.5, U.S. tel. 800/932-5599, www.grupobahia.com, US$21/day, US$112/week, US$391/month) has 54 spaces with full hookups but no shade, as well as a laundry room and bathroom with hot showers. In the adjacent *palapa* restaurant, a La Paz native serves delicious food (coconut shrimp, whole *huachinango*/red snappper) at reasonable prices (tel. 624/145-8244, daily 7 A.M.–10 P.M., mains US$12–25).

You can camp on the beaches farther northeast along Mexico 1 (see *The Corridor*) or northwest along Mexico 19.

FOOD

Downtown Cabo San Lucas is riddled with restaurants and bars, most of open-air design. Menus usually attempt to cover the main bases demanded by any Mexican resort area—seafood, Italian, Mexican, and steak. Because Cabo is Baja's number-one resort town, prices are higher than what you'd find in La Paz, Ensenada, Tijuana, or other tourist areas: Dinners run north of US$100 for two. Quality is also generally high since Cabo attracts chefs from all over Mexico and beyond. One complaint: Cabo restaurants sometimes hold back on the chilies in Mexican dishes and table salsas; hence *picante*-lovers may be forced to request extra chilies or fresh *salsa cruda* to bring things up to the proper level of heat.

Mexican

Mi Casa (Calle Cabo San Lucas opposite the plaza, tel. 624/143-1933, dinner daily 5:30–10:30 P.M., lunch Mon.–Sat. noon–3 P.M., mains US$13–30) is often cited as the most authentic Mexican restaurant in Cabo. The tastefully designed, half-*palapa,* half-open-air dining room is encircled by pastel murals intended to look like a small Central Mexican village. The menu lists dishes from all over Mexico, including fajitas, *mole verde, mole poblano, pipián, carne asada a la tampiqueña, pollo borracho,* and *cochinita pibil.* The food is good but doesn't always match the menu descriptions.

Just to the northeast of Plaza Náutica, in Plaza del Sol, **O Mole Mío** (tel. 624/143-7577, daily 11:30 A.M.–11:30 P.M., mains US$10–20) features original Mexican recipes such as El Solo Mío (grilled red snapper seasoned with Cajun spices and served with mango salsa) or Camarones Frida y Omar (shrimp baked in a tequila sauce and topped with julienned potatoes). The interior, decorated with unusual custom-designed wicker-and-iron furniture, is as interesting as the menu. The bar section is a fun place for drinks and *botanas.*

For authentic Mexican dishes that won't cost a lot, try **La Perla** (Blvd. Lázaro Cárdenas at Guerrero, Mon.–Sat. 9 A.M.–4:30 P.M.,

LOS CABOS

© PAUL ITOI

restaurants along the Cabo San Lucas marina

mains US$4–5), a simple Mexican eatery supported by a mainly local clientele. The menu features inexpensive *desayuno, tortas, molletes, tingas,* tacos, burritos, quesadillas, and *licuados*. **Lolita's Restaurant** (Niños Héroes near Matamoros, Mon.–Sat. 7 A.M.– 7:30 P.M., mains US$7–13) serves authentic *antojitos mexicanos* (*huachinango,* crab, fish filet), plus *champurrado* (hot chocolate made with cornstarch).

Among the best nontourist Mexican eateries in town is ❰ **Las Gardenias** (mains US$6– 12), a family-owned spot on the road to Playa El Médano. It's divided into two sections, the right side serving tacos of various kinds and the left side a changing menu that includes dishes such as chiles rellenos, *cochinita pibil, nopales,* and *chicharrón*.

Back in gringolandia, **Pancho's** (Hidalgo off Blvd. Marina, tel. 624/143-0973, daily 7 A.M.–11 P.M., dinner mains US$18–40) serves huge Mexican platters with somewhat inflated prices, plus tasty Mexican breakfasts and more than 190 varieties of tequila. All the

waiters speak English, and there is pleasant outdoor seating.

Carlos'n Charlie's (Blvd. Marina, tel. 624/143-1280, daily 11 A.M.–midnight, mains US$10–20) functions primarily as a place for tourists to drink themselves silly. But this Grupo Anderson restaurant serves good Mexican food. **El Squid Roe** (Blvd. Lázaro Cárdenas at Zaragoza, tel. 624/143-0655, daily noon–3 A.M., mains US$10–20) is one of the many Grupo Anderson restaurant/bars in Mexico that combine zany, tourist-on-the-loose fun with tried-and-true menus based on regional cuisine. Drinks are served in plastic cups.

Casa Rafael's (Pescador and Médano, tel. 624/143-0739, Mon.–Sat. 6–10 P.M., mains US$20 and up) is a small hotel with an elegant dining room specializing in nouvelle Mexican cuisine—served à la carte or as a seven-course, fixed-price meal. The changing menu also features international dishes and seafood. The wine list is impressive, and there is live music nightly. Reservations are suggested.

Cilantro's Bar & Grill (tel. 624/143-2900, daily 11 A.M.–11 P.M., mains US$10–20) at the Pueblo Bonito Resort on Playa El Médano, is one of Cabo's better hotel-oriented Mexican restaurants, featuring mesquite-grilled seafood and homemade tortillas. For a casual lunch or dinner at the beach, **Cascadas Beach & Grill** (Playa El Médano, tel. 624/143-0307, daily 7 A.M.–11 P.M., mains US$8–13) has reasonably priced Mexican plates.

Amber glassware and a free pomegranate tequila aperitif are nice touches at **Los Garcia** (mains US$8–15), one of the newer restaurants located at the street level of the Puerto Paraíso mall, serving upscale tacos, barbecued ribs, lobster salad, and other Mexican fare.

Tequila shrimp, made with the restaurant's own label, and lobster burritos are standout entrées at Sammy Hagar's **Cabo Wabo Restaurant** (Guerrero btw. Madero/Lázaro Cárdenas, tel. 624/143-1188, www.cabowabo.com, daily 11 A.M.–11 P.M., mains US$17–28). Try the Waborita cocktail to start the meal off right. Downstairs, the Cabo Wabo Cantina serves a more casual menu.

Seafood

Mocambo de Los Cabos (Vicario and 20 de Noviembre, tel. 624/143-6070, daily noon–10 P.M.; mains US$10–20) is a casual, local-style place with a huge seafood menu. Equally fresh but more creative and more expensive, **Fish House** (Plaza La Danza, upstairs from Nick-San and KFC, tel. 624/144-4501, daily noon–10 P.M., mains US$14–24) specializes in fresh clams and oysters, salmon pasta, and live Maine lobster. Despite the name, steak also holds a place of honor here, and the wine selection is good.

Try the *pescado zarandeado* (red snapper served whole in a tomato-based broth) or grilled fish *meniore* style (in a sauce of garlic, butter, white wine, and capers) at **Mariscos Mazatlán** (Mendoza and 16 de Septiembre, tel. 624/143-8565, mains US$10–14). The menu also includes 12 different preparations of shrimp. This restaurant has a second, less touristy location in San José del Cabo, on the West side of Mexico 1 on the way to the airport. Near the Ace Hardware store at the corner of Camino Real and Paseo de la Marina, **Mi Casa de Mariscos** (tel. 624/143-6898, micasa@cabonet.net.mx, daily 1 P.M.–10:30 P.M., mains US$13–29) has a raw bar with shrimp, scallops, oysters; "barely touched" dishes like ceviche and seared fresh catch; and fully cooked entrées like *huachinango frito a la talla* (fried whole red snapper).

El Shrimp Bucket (in the Plaza Fiesta shopping center on the marina, tel. 624/143-2598, daily 6 A.M.–11 P.M., mains US$10–20), near Marina Fiesta Resort, is a transplant from Mazatlán and the best of the several restaurants in town with the word "shrimp" in the name. The pink crustaceans are served in every conceivable fashion, including the ever-popular fried shrimp served in a terra-cotta bucket. Breakfasts are also good. At **The Shrimp Factory** (Blvd. Marina at Guerrero, tel. 624/143-5066, daily noon–11 P.M., mains US$10–20), order shrimp or lobster by the kilo (US$20–30 per half kilo), served with bread, salad, and crackers, and go to town.

Las Palmas (tel. 624/143-0447, daily 10 A.M.–11 P.M., mains US$10–15), on Playa El Médano, was the first *palapa* restaurant on Médano, and most residents agree it's still the best, in spite of the ugly concrete addition. The grilled seafood is always a good choice.

Another perennial favorite at the marina, **Solomon's Landing** (tel. 624/143-305, daily 7 A.M.–11 P.M., mains US$10–30), behind the Tesoro Hotel, specializes in lobster and shrimp dishes. Credit cards are accepted.

Italian and Continental

Capo San Giovanni (Guerrero at Madero, tel. 624/143-0593, Tues.–Sun. 5–11 P.M., mains US$13–32), just across the road and south of Cabo Wabo, has a spacious courtyard out back and an inventive southern Italian menu of seafood combos and pasta dishes.

Romeo & Julieta (Camino al Pedregal, tel. 624/143-0225, daily 4–11 P.M., mains US$10–20), near the Hotel Finisterra, offers a popular Italian menu featuring fresh pasta and wood-fired pizzas. In the plaza below the Puerto Paraíso mall, **Amarone** (Store #107, tel. 624/105-1035) prepares starters like antipasti or proscuito and melon for US$12 and lobster or veal filet for US$38. Also downtown, **La Dolce Italian Restaurant & Pizzeria** (Hidalgo and Zapata, tel. 624/143-4122, daily 6–11 P.M., mains US$10–20) serves a full menu of pastas and pizzas, plus Italian starters and desserts.

A German chef presides over a highly regarded kitchen at 【 **Peacocks Restaurant and Bar** (Camino de los Pescadores, tel. 624/143-1858, daily 6–10 P.M., mains US$15 and up), next to the driveway of Hotel Meliá San Lucas. The changing menu at this large, *palapa*-roofed, open-air restaurant is diverse and creative, and the wine list is extensive.

American and Eclectic

Popular with Corridor residents and Baja old-timers, **Latitude 22+ Roadhouse** (Km 4.5, tel. 624/143-1516, www.lat22nobaddays.com, Wed.–Mon. 8 A.M.–11 P.M., mains US$10–20) prepares a Croatian-influenced menu of slow-roasted prime rib, steak, burgers, ribs, shrimp, fish, chicken fried steak, and pastas. Ocean views, reasonably priced cocktails, and giant flatscreen TVs add to the dining experience. Formerly a downtown hangout, "Lat 22" is now located next Costco and behind the power plant. Credit cards are accepted.

In the Tesoro Hotel complex overlooking the marina, **Café Canela** (tel. 624/143-3435, daily 6 A.M.–5 P.M., mains US$6–10) has sandwiches, soups, salads, fresh-squeezed juices, and Mexican dishes with a twist, such as blue cheese quesadillas with smoked tuna. Canela also offers box lunches.

Olé Olé (Plaza Bonita Loc. 3A, tel. 624/143-0633, daily 7 A.M.–11 P.M., mains US$13–32) faces the marina at Plaza Bonita. The large outdoor tapas bar features Spanish cuisine and dinner combos such as *gazpacho andaluz, tortilla española,* and *jamón serrano* (Spanish-style cured ham). Try the *gambas a la ajo,* a plate of shrimp in garlic sauce, also available

in an octopus version. Paella is served from 1 P.M. only on Sunday (and sometimes on Friday, US$22).

Cozy 【 **Sancho Panza Wine Bistro and Jazz Club Restaurant** (Locales D19-22, Plaza Tesoro Hotel, tel. 624/143-3212, www.sanchopanza.com, daily 4 P.M.–11 P.M., mains US$10–20) is one of the best establishments of its kind in the entire Cape region. To find it, walk under the pedestrian bridge that connects the wings of the Tesoro Hotel Plaza and look for it on your right. Aided by an artistic and colorful Miró-esque decor, the proprietors have created a first-class wine bar that stocks such hard-to-find, top-of-the-line Baja labels as Monte Xanic and Chateau de Camou along with more than 150 other wines. The short menu offers delicious "new world tapas" that mix New American, Mediterranean, and Latin American influences with outstanding results.

Ruth's Chris Steak House (Puerto Paraíso, tel. 624/144-3232, daily 1 P.M.–11:30 P.M., mains US$20 and up), a branch of the U.S. chain of the same name, serves its trademark fresh broiled beef on an open-air patio with a marina view.

Giggling Marlin (Matamoros near Blvd. Marina, tel. 624/143-0606, www.gigglingmarlin. com, daily 8 A.M.–2 A.M., mains US$10–20) is better for appetizers and booze than entrées. Most tourists come here to snap photos of themselves hanging upside down—like landed marlins—from the restaurant's block-and-tackle rig. Others come for the big-screen satellite TV.

Serious carnivores should head to **Brasil Steakhouse** (Zapata at Hidalgo, tel. 624/143-8343, www.brasilcabo.com, daily 5 P.M.–11 P.M., US$28 pp) for an all-you-can-eat feast of top sirloin, New York strip, *arranchera,* sausage, ribs, and more. The chef slices meats from a serving skewer at the table, while the waitstaff delivers fresh salads and vegetables. The chicken wings that come as an appetizer rival the best you can find in the United States. Try the *carperinia* cocktail to start—essentially a mojito without the mint. **French Riviera** (Plaza del Rey btw Misiones/Cabo Bello, tel. 624/142-3350, www.frenchrivieraloscabos.

com, daily noon–11 P.M., mains US$33), an extension of the popular San José bakery, prepares Mediterranean specialties.

The English-speaking staff at the **Stop Light Bar and Grill** (Lazaro Cárdenas and Morelos, tel. 624/143-4740, mains US$6–19) serves a decent breakfast of eggs, pancakes, or *chilaquiles.* Portions are large, and cocktails are served in glasses, not plastic. Dinner fare includes ceviche, snails, sandwiches, salads, and enchiladas, as well as lobster, steak, and pasta.

Enjoy a sunset meal at the aptly named **Sunset Grill** (tel. 624/143-9199) atop the Cabo Villas complex at Playa El Médano. The restaurant serves breakfast (mains US$5–10), lunch (mains US$5–9), and dinner (mains US$13–22) daily. Empanada appetizers come with a side of guacamole; fish ceviche goes well with a martini. Cash only.

At **Edith's** (tel. 624/143-0801, www.edithscabo.com, daily 6 P.M.–1 A.M., mains US$10–20), near Playa El Médano on the west side of the Camino de los Pescadores, enjoy views of Bahía Cabo San Lucas and Land's End as long as the sun's up, and a hearty dinner of prime rib, rack of lamb, or any number of regional specialties through the evening hours.

Asian

€ **Nick-San Restaurant** (Lte. 10, Blvd. Marina, tel. 624/143-4484, www.nicksan.com, Tues.–Sun. 11:30 A.M.–10:30 P.M., mains US$20 and up) is centrally located along the main strip and serves excellent Japanese barbecue, seafood, and sushi. This is probably the most reliably high-quality restaurant in San Lucas, regardless of cuisine. Don't miss the sashimi salad.

Tacos and Fast Food

The local fast-food scene is concentrated along Calle Morelos, where you'll find a string of stands offering tacos, carne asada, and *mariscos* at the lowest prices in town. The taquerías seem to change owners and names every other year or so but rarely close down completely. A cluster of inexpensive restaurants serve seafood cocktails, chicken, and

tortas at the south end of Calle Ocampo where it meets Boulevard Lázaro Cárdenas. At the corner of Revolución and Morelos, **Tacos Condi** draws a crowd for *asada cabeza* and other tacos. North of Hemingway's on Guerrero, **Cheto Tacos** serves dependable fish tacos and licuados.

Las Quesadillasss (Blvd. Marina at Lázaro Cardénas, tel. 624/143-1373, daily 7 A.M.– 2 A.M., mains US$6–13), opposite Arámburo Plaza, is a good bet for late-night dining. Enjoy tacos, quesadillas, grilled lobster, steak, French dessert crepes, coffee drinks, and beer in a little two-story outdoor spot under a *palapa* roof.

A string of inexpensive Mexican restaurants lies along Calle Leona Vicario, north of Revolución. One is **Taquería los Paisas** serving tacos and stuffed potatoes (with two other locations—another along Leona Vicario and one opposite Hotel Casa Blanca). A bit farther north past Carranza is **Carnitas El Michoacano** (tel. 624/105-0713), where you can order carnitas by the kilo.

In the plaza below Cabo Wabo, **Taco Loco** serves bean, chicken, pork, and shrimp tacos for US$1 each. **La Luna** (tel. 624/105-0132, Tues.–Sat. noon–10 P.M., Sun. noon–6 P.M.), behind the Pueblo Bonito Rosé resort, serves wraps, burgers, and tacos.

Delicatessens

"Almost-kosher" **Lenny's Deli** (tel. 624/143-8380, daily 7 A.M.–4 P.M.), just east of Camino Pescadores and south off Lázaro Cárdenas, sells fresh-baked breads, imported cheeses, and cold cuts. You can also order sandwiches at **La Europea** (mains US$5–12) just outside the Puerto Paraíso mall. There are a few tables out front, overlooking the marina. Air-conditioned booths are a comfortable place to grab a sandwich (and check your email with free Wi-Fi) at **Señor Greenberg's Mexicatessen** (Plaza Náutica, tel. 624/143-5630, daily 24 hours, mains US$5–12), which has several locations, including a new deli next to Johnny Rockets in the Puerto Paraíso mall.

Cafés

Theory Café (tel. 624/143-5518, daily from 10 A.M., mains US$3–7) in the center of Plaza Bonita serves lattes, mochas, and frappucinos, and plays music like the Red Hot Chili Peppers. Use your laptop or theirs for wireless Internet. **Cabo Coffee Company** (tel. 624/105-1130) has expanded to a new Internet café with high-speed wireless connections on the corner of Hidalgo and Madero, across from its original roasting facility. A satellite location is also available outside the Giggling Marlin. **San Francisco Coffee Company** (Blvd. Marina 38, tel. 624/144-4387, www.sanfranciscocoffeecompany.com) brews hot and cold espresso drinks (US$2.50–5.50) and blends smoothies (US$4.50–5.50). It also has wireless Internet (US$2 for up to 15 minutes), DVD rentals, and English-language books.

Among the many dockside restaurants by the marina, **Baja Cantina** (Dock L–M, tel. 624/143-1591, mains US$7–15) serves tasty jalapeño poppers, artichoke and spinach dip, and other starters for US$5–8, as well as fish, burgers, and Mexican plates for dinner. Wireless Internet is a plus. Look for a second location at Playa El Médano (tel. 624/143-9773).

Palapa Restaurants

Several *palapa* bars and restaurants scattered along Playa El Médano—including **Billygan's Island** (tel. 624/143-0402), **The Office** (tel. 624/143-3464), and **Las Palmas** (tel. 624/143-0447)—offer cold beverages, as well as burgers, seafood, and Mexican plates (lunch mains US$8–15; dinner menus are more expensive).

Groceries

Cabo's several supermarkets stock Mexican and U.S. foodstuffs—from fresh Mexican cheeses to Sara Lee frozen cheesecake—plus cooking and cleaning supplies and even auto parts. Varying from small to huge, they include **Almacenes Grupo Castro** (southwest corner of Morelos and Revolución, tel. 624/143-0566), **Supermercado Sánliz** (three locations: Blvd. Marina at Madero,

Ocampo at Matamoros, and Vicario at López Mateos), and **Supermercado Arámburo** (at Arámburo Plaza, Lázaro Cárdenas at Zaragoza, tel. 624/143-1450). Supermercado Arámburo stocks a large selection of both domestic and imported foods, as does the **CCC** (Centro Comercial California, tel. 624/146-7200) on the east side of Mexico 19 just north of the junction with Mexico 1. A few hundred yards farther toward Todos Santos is **Soriana** (Carr. Todos Santos and Calle Guajitos, tel. 624/105-1290, www.soriana.com), a Walmart-esque superstore. On the other side of town, the same outfit runs warehouse-style **City Club** (Blvd. Lázaro Cárdenas at Paseo del Pescador, tel. 624/143-9492, www.soriana.com), with groceries, produce, and baked goods.

Pescadería El Dorado (tel. 624/143-2820), on the south side of 5 de Febrero between Abasolo and Ocampo, stocks a large selection of fresh finfish and shellfish. The most convenient place to buy fresh tortillas is **Tortillería Perla** (on Morelos btw Hidalgo/Matamoros, tel. 624/143-1381).

Panaficadora la Moderna, on Calle Leona Vicario across from Mariscos Mocambo, is a small bakery with a decent selection of Mexican baked goods.

La Baguette (tel. 624/142-1125, Mon.–Sat. 8:30 A.M.–7:30 P.M.), on Boulevard Lázaro Cárdenas next to the entrance for Pedregal, carries European and American-style baked goods including pastries, bagels, and breads. **Swiss Pastry** (Hidalgo at Lázaro Cárdenas across from the plaza, tel. 624/143-3494, Mon.–Sat. 7 A.M.–4 P.M.) serves chicken potpie, sandwiches, fresh bagels, and other pastries, as well as coffee. It has a few tables in front as well as inside.

Frutería Lizarraga (Matamoros at Av. de la Juventud, tel. 624/143-1215) stocks a good selection of fruits and vegetables; several local hotel and restaurant chefs shop here.

Tutto Bene! (Blvd. Marina opposite the Tesoro Hotel, daily 9:30 A.M.–9 P.M.), near the traffic circle, stocks an impressive selection of organic foods and imported wines.

The best shopping area for beer and liquor is the string of *subagencias* and *licores* along Calle Matamoros.

INFORMATION AND SERVICES

Tourist Assistance

The nearest Baja Sur state tourism office is located in San José del Cabo (Blvd. Mauricio Castro, Plaza San José, Locales 3&4, San José del Cabo, tel. 624/146-9628, www.loscabos.gob.mx). **Fonatur** (tel. 624/142-0146, www.fonatur.gob.mx) maintains an office on the marina. Its representatives are always interested in speaking with potential investors, but they don't distribute general tourist information.

Money-Changing

American dollars are readily accepted throughout Cabo, but you'll save money if you pay in pesos. Foreign-currency exchange service is available Monday–Saturday 8:30 A.M.–noon at **Bancomer** (Hidalgo at Guerrero), **Banamex** (Hidalgo at Lázaro Cárdenas), and **Santander Serfín** (in Arámburo Plaza). All three banks have ATMs. Hotel cashiers also gladly change dollars for pesos, albeit at a lower rate than at the banks.

There's a full-service **American Express office** in town near the marina in Plaza Bonita (tel. 624/143-5766, fax 624/143-5988, Mon.–Fri. 9 A.M.–6 P.M., Sat. 9 A.M.–1 P.M.). It offers emergency check cashing, cardmember services, foreign exchange, and tours.

Except in emergencies, stay away from Cabo's money changers, which charge high commissions or sell currency at low exchange rates.

Post and Telephone

Cabo's **post office**, on Boulevard Lázaro Cárdenas near 16 de Septiembre, is open Monday–Friday 8 A.M.–4 P.M., Saturday 9 A.M.–noon. Public telephone booths are at various locations throughout town, including the main plaza and Arámburo Plaza.

Mail Boxes Etc. (Blvd. Marina 39-F, Plaza Fiesta, tel. 624/143-3033, fax 624/143-3031) carries mailing supplies, postage stamps, and magazines and rents mailboxes.

CABO SAN LUCAS PHONE NUMBERS

Cabo San Lucas area code: 624
Cabo San Lucas Hospital: 144-3434
COTP (Captain of the Port): 143-0048
Hyperbaric chamber: 143-3666
Immigration: 143-0135
Police, Fire Department, Red Cross (emergency): 066
Police (nonemergency): 143-3977, 143-5123
Red Cross (nonemergency): 143-3300
U.S. Consulate: 143-3566

Internet Access

Cabo San Lucas has experienced a proliferation of Internet cafés, although they seem to come, change hands, and go as fast as taco stands. Coffee shops and real estate offices are good places to check. Prices have come down quite a bit in recent years, settling at about US$2–6 per hour. A few places are beginning to offer Internet phone services as well. The following list is by no means exhaustive.

BajaTech (tel. 624/143-4240), on Boulevard Lázaro Cárdenas across from the Pemex, sells computer time for email and Web surfing in a comfortable café/bar atmosphere. Free parking. A more expensive option is **Internet Café Cabomail** in Arámburo Plaza (tel. 624/143-7797, Mon.–Fri. 9 A.M.–9 P.M., Sat. 9 A.M.–6 P.M., Sun. noon–6 P.M.), which offers Internet calls to the United States for US$2 per 10 minutes. At **Cabo Clipper Internet & Computers Business Center** (Level 3 Puerto Paraíso Plaza, tel. 624/105-0482, caboclipper@gmail.com, daily 10 A.M.–10 P.M.), you'll pay US$2 for up to 15 minutes or US$6 for one hour. There was no wireless access last we checked, and you'll pay the same prices if you bring your own laptop. Credit cards are accepted.

A minimarket in the lobby of the Marina del Sol condo complex has three ancient PCs

LOS CABOS

connected to the Internet. Better yet, the onsite **Oasis Bar and Grill** (tel. 624/143-6285, www.marinasolresort.com, Thurs.–Tues. 9 A.M.–10:30 P.M.) now has wireless Internet. The lobby of the Siesta Suites Hotel also has three fast PCs (with USB ports) for US$3/hour.

There are several places in town where you can enjoy a latte or cappucino while you check your email: **Theory Café** (tel. 624/143-5518), in the center of Plaza Bonita, opens at 10 A.M. daily. **Cabo Coffee Company** (tel. 624/105-1130, www.cabocoffee.com) has expanded to a new Internet café with high-speed wireless connections on the corner of Hidalgo and Madero, across from its original roasting facility. A satellite location is also available outside the Giggling Marlin. **San Francisco Coffee Company** (38 Blvd. Marina, tel. 624/144-4387, www .sanfranciscocoffeecompany.com) has wireless Internet for US$2 up to 15 minutes. **Baja Cantina** (Dock L–M, tel. 624/143-1591) offers wireless Internet along with a full lunch and dinner menu.

Laundry

Cabo has a number of self-serve and full-service laundry facilities scattered about town. One of the most reputable is **Lavandería Evelyn** (tel. 624/143-0920, daily 7 A.M.– 7 P.M.), opposite El Faro Viejo Trailer Park on Calle Matamoros, with banks of washing machines for self-service laundry; ask the attendants to start the machines for you. Or you can pay (by weight) to have the washing, drying, and ironing done by the staff—one-day service is the norm.

Magazines and Newspapers

The annual magazine **Los Cabos Guide** (www.loscabosguide.com) contains a number of features, ads, annotated lists, and announcements concerning hotels, restaurants, clubs, and recreational events, as well as local social and business news. Its online listings are fairly complete, though some pages are more up to date than others. Pop into any real estate office for a free copy. Another handy re-

source is the **Gringo Pages of Los Cabos** (cell tel. 624/141-6471, http://worlddirectories@ sbcglobal.net), an annual yellow pages listing covering the entire Los Cabos Region, with some listings for Todos Santos and the East Cape as well.

The local Spanish-language newspaper is *El Heraldo de los Cabos. Gringo Gazette,* a tourist newspaper written and edited locally but printed in the United States, carries whimsical local news stories and events listings. Another tourist rag, *Destino,* contains less news and more ads. The bi-lingual *Los Cabos News* reports on happenings from Cabo San Lucas to San José.

USA Today and *The News* (from Mexico City) are usually available at **Supermercado Sánliz** (Blvd. Marina at Madero), as well as at other larger grocery stores catering to gringos. **Libros Libros/Books Books** in Plaza de la Danza carries *The News, USA Today,* and the *Los Angeles Times.*

Medical Services

Dial 066 for emergency situations. English-speaking doctors advertise in Los Cabos media and a couple of clinics specialize in gringo care. **AmeriMed,** in the Pioneros Building along Lázaro Cárdenas (Loc. 1, tel. 624/143-9670), is a 24-hour clinic with bilingual staff who specialize in urgent and emergency services, along with OB/GYN care, family practice, and more. Most insurance programs are accepted.

Immigration

Cabo's *migración* office is on Boulevard Lázaro Cárdenas between Gómez Farías and 16 de Septiembre.

U.S. Consular Agent

A U.S. consular agent in Cabo, under the auspices of the U.S. consul general in Tijuana, maintains a small office at Plaza Naútica (C-4, Blvd. Marina, tel. 624/143-3566, usconsulcabo@hotmail.com, Mon.–Fri. 10 A.M.– 1 P.M.). The consular agent can assist U.S. citizens with lost or stolen passports and other emergency situations.

panga at Playa del Amor

GETTING AROUND

In Cabo itself, you can easily get around on foot, bicycle, or scooter, though car taxis are available for around US$5–10 a trip. **Checker Cabo** is a fleet of mountain bikes welded to two-wheeled carts to produce Asian-style pedicabs.

You can hire **harbor skiffs** from the marina in front of the Tesoro Hotel to Playa El Médano and Playa del Amor (US$10 round-trip only). In the reverse direction, skiffs are plentiful at El Médano, but for Playa del Amor, arrangements for a pickup are necessary.

Vendors along Boulevard Marina rent mopeds, ATVs, and—less often—motorcycles. These are hard to come by without going on a three-hour, US$60 tour of some sort, usually to the Old Lighthouse. If you can find them by the hour, typical prices are US$20 per hour, US$60 for a half day, US$80 for a full day.

WEST CAPE AND TODOS SANTOS

A few hundred meters past the modern Soriana shopping complex in Cabo San Lucas, the urban sprawl abruptly ends, cows reclaim the road, and the Pacific Ocean eventually pops into view. A lone trailer or two has set up camp along the shore, but you can't quite tell which dirt road they drove to get there. If it's late fall or early winter, wildflowers may still dot the landscape with a splash of color.

Don't get too lost in the scenery, however, or the Águila bus driver tailgating from behind might very well decide to pass on a blind turn just as an 18-wheeler approaches from the opposite direction. Welcome to the West Cape, the least developed coastal stretch on the lower part of the Baja Peninsula. Although a paved, two-lane highway (Mexico 19) extends the full 76 kilometers (47 mi) between Cabo San Lucas

and Todos Santos (and beyond all the way to La Paz), housing developments are still few and far between. Several large real estate projects are in the early stages near the farming community of El Pescadero and close to Cabo San Lucas, leaving the middle stretch to the pelicans, rancheros, fishermen, and the occasional ATV tour.

Once considered a stopover on the drive from La Paz to Cabo San Lucas, bohemian Todos Santos has become a destination in its own right. Surfers, artists, retirees, exotic bird rescuers, and yoga students all cross paths here, and at least several hundred of them are permanent expat residents. At press time, Todos Santos was basking in the attention of its recent designation as a Pueblo Mágico—one of only 23 small towns in Mexico given government funding to make their culture and history more accessible

HIGHLIGHTS

◖ La Candelaria: Experience the rancho way of life in this rural village set in the foothills of the lower Sierra de la Laguna. Plan a day hike or a scenic drive from Cabo San Lucas on the way to Todos Santos (page 406).

◖ Playa Los Cerritos: Popular with novice surfers, swimmers, and sunbathers, this gently sloped beach lies comfortably protected from winter's northwest swell. Eagle rays, puffer fish, and other marinelife await discovery just below the surface (page 408).

◖ Playa San Pedrito (Playa Las Palmas): Rock cliffs at either end of the beach frame your view of the Pacific at this beach near Todos Santos. Bring a picnic and enjoy the secluded setting (page 410).

◖ Todos Santos Historic District: The most memorable postcards of Todos Santos depict rows of colorful, century-old facades with the signature large windows and doors of the Andalusian architecture style. Spend an afternoon exploring the town's galleries, shops, and restaurants on foot (page 417).

◖ Playa Las Pocitas (La Poza de Lobos): A small, freshwater lagoon within walking distance of Todos Santos is home to many types of waterfowl, as well as the area's finest boutique hotel, Posada La Poza (page 420).

LOOK FOR ◖ TO FIND RECOMMENDED SIGHTS, ACTIVITIES, DINING, AND LODGING.

to tourists and travelers. Gringo and Mexican locals alike were optimistic that the town would be able to preserve its artsy character even as the number of visitors increased.

PLANNING YOUR TIME

The drive from Cabo San Lucas to Todos Santos via Mexico 19 and the West Cape takes approximately one hour—making it an easy day trip for visitors who are staying in the Los Cabos area, or a slightly longer drive (90 minutes) directly from the airport.

You can take in most of what Todos Santos has to offer in a full day of sightseeing, cov-

ering the historic buildings and galleries in town and a beach or two along the coast. But as with most other towns in Baja, you'll enjoy the West Cape infinitely more if you stay long enough to wander miles of virgin, as-yet-undeveloped beaches stretching north and south from Todos Santos along the Pacific, explore the steep western escarpment of the Sierra de la Laguna, or simply hang out and soak up the small-town ambience.

Backpackers often plan multiday trips into the Sierra from the West Cape. If that sounds too challenging, guides also run half-day hikes as well as trail rides on ATVs. A day of

WEST CAPE

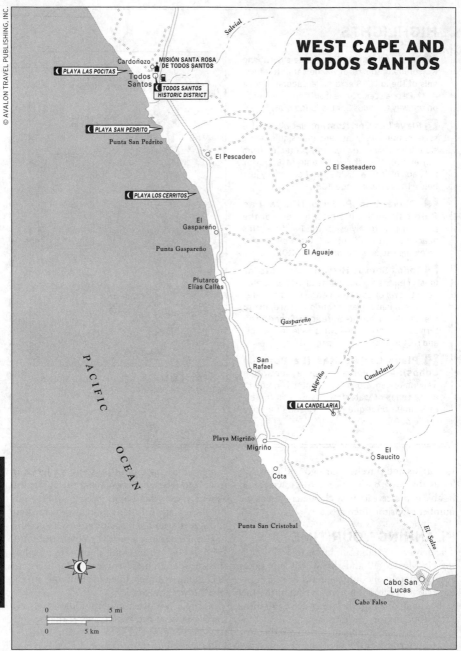

WEST CAPE AND TODOS SANTOS

Salvial

Cardoñozo

PLAYA LAS POCITAS

Todos
Santos

MISIÓN SANTA ROSA
DE TODOS SANTOS

TODOS SANTOS
HISTORIC DISTRICT

PLAYA SAN PEDRITO

Punta San Pedrito

El Pescadero

El Sesteadero

PLAYA LOS CERRITOS

El
G123pareño

Punta Gaspareño

El Aguaje

Plutarco
Elías Calles

Gaspareño

PACIFIC

San
Rafael

Migriño

Candelaria

LA CANDELARIA

OCEAN

Playa Migriño
Migriño

El
Saucito

Cota

Punta San Cristobal

El Salto

Cabo San
Lucas

Cabo Falso

0   5 mi

0   5 km

fishing or surfing could also lengthen your stay. Of course, if you're into these activities, a day probably isn't enough. Surfers can easily spend a week or a month trying to master the winter breaks here. And the fishing—whether by boat, surf rod, or hand line—is just as addictive.

GETTING THERE AND AROUND
By Air
Todos Santos is more or less equidistant from the Los Cabos and La Paz airports. A shuttle from Los Cabos costs approximately US$150, while a shuttle from La Paz runs US$200–300.

By Car
Though not essential, most travelers will want to have a car while staying in the West Cape and Todos Santos, as the beaches and sights are spread out from the two small towns. If you don't rent a car at the airport or drive your own from the States, you can rent one in Todos Santos. **Budget Car Rental** (Márquez de León 4, tel. 612/145-0062, egarcia@budgetbaja.com) has opened an office in Todos Santos next to the church and main plaza, and a second location inside the Milagro Real Estate office on Juárez.

Mexico 19 connects Todos Santos to Cabo San Lucas to the south and La Paz to the north. From the Los Cabos airport, follow the Transpeninsular Highway (Mexico 1) toward Cabo San Lucas, and take the turn-off for Todos Santos/Mexico 19. From La Paz, follow Mexico 1 south to the turnoff for Mexico 19. There are numerous Pemex stations in La Paz, Todos Santos, Pescadero, and Cabo San Lucas. If you need a car mechanic during your visit, there are a couple of options in Todos Santos, but you may have to head south to Cabo San Lucas for complicated transmission work.

By Taxi
As an alternative, a small fleet of blue vans parked next to the park in Todos Santos can provide taxi service around town for US$2 a trip. A van all the way to Los Cabos International Airport will cost around US$150; vans can hold 8–15 people with luggage. Call 612/145-0063 for more information.

By Bus
Nine Águila buses a day run between Todos Santos and La Paz to the north and Cabo San Lucas to the south. The La Paz and Cabo San Lucas bus trips take about two hours and cost about US$7 per person; a bus through to San José del Cabo costs US$10. In Pescadero, buses stop across the street from the Pemex. Tickets are sold on the buses, which arrive at and depart from Colegio Militar and Zaragoza (for San José del Cabo and Cabo San Lucas), or in front of Karla's Lonchería (for La Paz).

West Cape

Mexico 19 heads west out of Cabo San Lucas toward Cabo Falso before making a long, lazy arc to the north. An alternate route heads due north out of San Lucas, following unpaved ranch roads to the picturesque foothills village of La Candelaria. From there, those with four-wheel drive can follow a sandy arroyo road west, rejoining Mexico 19 near Playa Migriño. Those without four-wheel drive will find a visit to La Candelaria worthwhile but will have to return to Cabo San Lucas the way they came, then head north up Mexico 19. Both routes are covered in detail below.

CABO FALSO TO PLAYA MIGRIÑO

About three kilometers west of the Cabo San Lucas city limits is Cabo Falso, once incorrectly thought to be Baja California's southernmost point. Because the wide beach along Cabo Falso is protected as a nesting ground for sea turtles, visitors aren't permitted within 50 meters (165 ft) of the surf line. The dunes behind the beach, however, are a popular destination for rented ATVs from Cabo San Lucas. The abandoned lighthouse, **El Faro Viejo,** signaled ships 1895–1961; the original lens is now installed in a newer lighthouse higher on the beach. Surrounded by loose sand for at least a half mile, the old lighthouse can be approached only on foot, ATV, or horse.

Past Cabo Falso the highway begins climbing over the southwestern foothills and coastal plateaus of the Sierra de la Laguna to reach the small ranching settlement of Migriño after about 21 kilometers (13 mi). Playa Migriño, with access at Km 94 or 97, is a long section of beach next to Estero Migriño, a small estuary linked with Río Candelaria. In winter, surfers can catch a point break at the north end of the beach. Different sections of Playa Migriño are accessible via a network of sandy roads; several spots are suitable for camping.

☾ LA CANDELARIA

Palapa-roofed adobe and block homes, a small church, a school, split-rail and *carrizal* fences, and saddled burros tethered to paloverde and mesquite trees set the scene at this small village in the foothills of the lower Sierra de la Laguna. A palm oasis in a shallow canyon on the northwest edge of the quiet village holds an un-

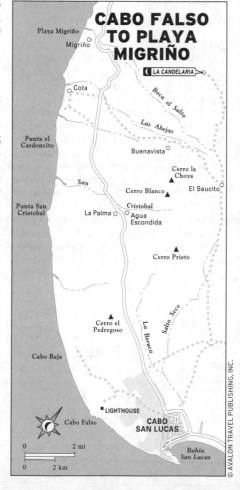

CABO FALSO TO PLAYA MIGRIÑO

CLAYWARE OF CANDELARIA

Candelaria is widely known in the Cape Region for its rustic clay pottery, known as *trastes de barro* locally or, among foreign collectors, as "ranchware." No one's sure how or when the pottery tradition arrived here, but one theory speculates that when the southern Baja missions were secularized in the 19th century, many mestizos who had worked for the mission system chose to establish ranches farther into the sierra, where water was more abundant and the land more fertile. They may have brought with them the simple pottery techniques that were eventually lost to the cities that grew up along the coast.

Earth for Candelaria ranchware is dug from local hillsides, traditionally during the two weeks between the full and new moons (because of a belief that earth collected during this time makes better potting material). After grinding and sifting the earth by hand, potters add water and knead it into clay, which is then pinched, pulled, and punched into the desired pot shape. Some coiling techniques – rolling clay into ropelike lengths, then coiling them in layers along the rim – may be used near the tops of the vessels.

When the basic shape is finished, the potter smoothes the vessel's surfaces using a cow's rib, a thick piece of leather, or a dried corncob. The pot is left to dry for 12 hours, then polished by troweling the surface with stones and water. Cycles of drying and polishing continue until the artisan is satisfied with the overall aesthetic result, and then, after a final drying, the pots are taken out of the sun in late afternoon and warmed on a stove until they are too hot to touch. Pots are then placed on a grate and individually covered with "cow chips" (dried cow dung), which are carefully ignited.

The burning fuel functions as a natural kiln, firing the pots without benefit of an oven or other exterior structure. Potters tend the fire to make sure it burns evenly and steadily, all the while checking between layers of chips to see how the pot is progressing; when the entire pot glows red (usually this takes about one hour), it is fired. Pots created this way have a smooth, burnished terra-cotta appearance. Chips that touch the pot's surface during firing create blurred black "fire clouds," considered an error in the world of refined kiln techniques but valued by ranchware collectors.

Trastes de barro come in all shapes and sizes, from teacups to *frijoles* bowls to the rare *porrón*, a very large jar used for grain or water storage. The larger the piece, the more difficult it is to make and the more expensive it is to buy. *Tinajas*, medium-sized water jars, are easier to find and very functional. The slightly porous surfaces allow a little water to leak out and evaporate, thus keeping the vessel and its contents cooler than the ambient air temperature – call it ranch refrigeration.

derground stream, which has been dammed to irrigate mangoes, citrus, guavas, avocados, papayas, corn, and bamboo. Pigs wander in and out of the canyon, seeking cool mud around the pump house. Around 80 people live in the village full time; the population swells during school sessions when children from ranchos deeper in the sierra board here to attend the local school.

The area's hilly, tropical-arid thorn forest makes for good hiking. Bring plenty of water, even in winter, as the sun bakes everything unprotected by shade. At the edge of town near an old cane mill is a hill surmounted by a cemetery that can be reached on foot. Look for the headstone of Rafael Salvatierra, whose engraved dates of birth and death indicate he lived to the age of 130; opinions are divided as to whether the dates are accurate, although several generations ago residents in this area often passed the century mark.

Getting There

From Playa Migriño: The quickest way to La Candelaria is via a 9.1-kilometer (5.6-mi) sandy arroyo road that turns inland off Mexico 19 near Playa Migriño (just on the north side of Río Candelaria). The unsigned turnoff lies three kilometers (1.9 mi) south of the Km 94 marker, or about a half kilometer (0.3 mile) north of the main Playa Migriño turnoff. This road, suitable for four-wheel-drive vehicles only, parallels the deep, wide Río Candelaria arroyo. It's sandy and narrow in spots, so drivers must take care not to stray off the track into sand traps. And since the road runs across the bottom of the arroyo at one point, it would be risky during or after a hard rain. If you're two-wheeling it, stick to the San Lucas road both ways.

From Cabo San Lucas: This route is longer and more scenic than the road from Playa Migriño. From downtown Cabo San Lucas, begin driving toward San José along Boulevard Lázaro Cárdenas, then turn left at a sign marked La Paz Via Corta, directly opposite the entrance to Club Cascada. You are now heading northwest toward Todos Santos and La Paz. After passing a soccer field on the left, look for a power plant on your right and turn onto the wide dirt road near the plant (1.7 km/1.1 mi from the Via Corta intersection).

From this intersection, La Candelaria is 27.7 kilometers (17.2 mi) away (the highway sign says 23 km). Make another right 4.3 kilometers (2.7 mi) from the highway at a road signed La Candelaria and Los Pozos; you'll pass through a fence and cattle guard here. A military checkpoint has on occasion been set up near this gate.

As you ascend the sierra foothills into a relatively dense thorn forest (green in early fall) and stands of *cardón* and *pitahaya,* it's not unusual to see cattle or burros in the road, so drive slowly. The road forks about 12 kilometers (7.5 mi) from the highway; don't take the right fork signed for San Felipe and El Sauzal but rather the left one, which leads to the charming *ranchitos* and adobe ruins of Los Pozos. Pass a small chapel at 14 kilometers (8.9 mi) and follow signs for La Candelaria and La Trinidad. Stay with the main road and ignore any smaller forks from this point.

The road begins climbing, and 18.5 kilometers (11.5 mi) from the highway you'll see the Pacific Ocean to the west. Around 21 kilometers (13 mi) from the highway you pass a signed turnoff for Rancho San Ramón, and at 24 kilometers (15 mi) you come to a relatively major fork. The right branch is more direct to La Candelaria, though the left curves around to a *ranchito* and eventually cuts back onto the same road. About 800 meters (half a mile) farther (following the right branch), the road crosses an arroyo that could be problematic in heavy rain. Ignore a right turn to La Trinidad at 26.4 kilometers (16.4 mi). Less than 1.6 kilometers (1 mi) later you'll arrive at La Candelaria.

Note: Almost any type of vehicle can safely navigate the Cabo San Lucas–Candelaria road in dry weather. Low-lying Los Pozos—almost halfway to La Candelaria—may flood in heavy rains, so if it begins raining during the first half of the drive, turn back. Once you're past Los Pozos, keep going! Becoming stranded in La Candelaria would beat getting mired in Los Pozos.

Another way to visit La Candelaria is by guided ATV tour. Contact **Baja's Activities** (Km 104–105, tel. 624/143-2050, www.bajasactivities.com).

PESCADERO AND VICINITY
Playa Las Cabrillas

Of the many deserted beaches strung out along the Pacific coast between Playa Migriño and Todos Santos, one of the easiest to reach is **Playa Las Cabrillas,** south of El Pescadero (turnoff at Km 81). Flat and sandy, the beach was named for the plentiful sea bass that can be caught from shore. Grass-tufted dunes provide partial windscreens for beach camping, which is free.

◖ Playa Los Cerritos

A new official road sign points the way to Playa Los Cerritos at Km 64 (12.8 km/8 mi south of Todos Santos). From the turn, follow a good dirt road 2.7 kilometers (1.7 mi) southwest until you reach the sandy parking area. Sheltered by Punta Pescadero at its north end, the beach is usually safe for swimming. Throw on a pair of goggles and you may even catch a glimpse of a spotted eagle ray gliding

PESCADERO TO TODOS SANTOS

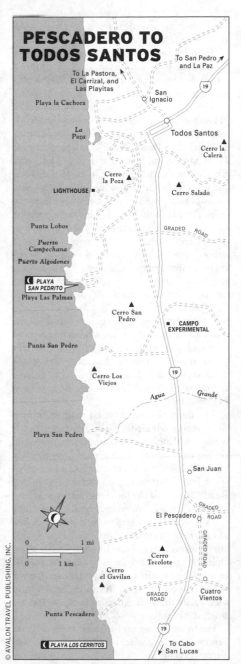

To San Pedro and La Paz

To La Pastora, El Carrizal, and Las Playitas

San Ignacio

19

Playa la Cachora

La Poza

Todos Santos

▲ Cerro la Calera

Cerro la Poza ▲

■ LIGHTHOUSE

▲ Cerro Salado

Punta Lobos

GRADED ROAD

Puerto Campechana

Puerto Algodones

◖ PLAYA SAN PEDRITO

Playa Las Palmas

▲ Cerro San Pedro

■ CAMPO EXPERIMENTAL

Punta San Pedro

▲ Cerro Los Viejos

19

Agua   Grande

Playa San Pedro

○ San Juan

GRADED ROAD

El Pescadero ○

0   1 mi

0   1 km

▲ Cerro Tecolote

GRADED ROAD

▲ Cerro el Gavilan

○ Cuatro Vientos

GRADED ROAD

Punta Pescadero

19

◖ PLAYA LOS CERRITOS

To Cabo San Lucas

© AVALON TRAVEL PUBLISHING, INC.

by just offshore. Boogie boarding is another popular activity.

During the winter, the northwest swell tips a surfable point break, and during the summer, a mushy beach break sometimes occurs. Because wave size rarely intimidates, Cerritos is popular with novice surfers. The **Los Cerritos Surf Shop** (Degollado and Rangel, a half block up the hill from Miguel's) rents boards at the beach dawn till dusk.

Campers note: Change is afoot at this much-loved beach. Having received its title to the land, the local *ejido* has been selling property near the beach. Campers and RVers who set up camp were asked to leave in late 2006, and the **Los Cerritos Club** bar and beach restaurant opened in 2007 (see *Food*).

Three miles south near Km 75, a new real estate development, **Tortuga del Sol** (www.tortugadelsol.net) is taking shape with 123 home sites.

El Pescadero

As you approach El Pescadero from the south (Km 62), hilly terrain gives way on the west side of Mexico 19 to a series of flat, cultivated fields, most of which are bordered by a single row of tall corn stalks. Between fields of cherry tomatoes and basil, a number of palm-lined dirt roads meander to the water's edge. Though still much smaller and more spread out than its neighbor to the north, Pescadero has evolved in recent years from a cluster of simple *tiendas* and *loncherías* into a more developed business center with its own Pemex and Oxxo convenience store. The first major real estate development underway in the area is the 50-acre gated community of **Playa Agave Azul**. A tequila distillery and restaurant were in the plans, as well as a bar and restaurant at nearby Playa Los Cerritos (see *Food*).

Local expat residents here are getting involved with turtle conservation efforts, through egg collection and baby turtle release programs, as well as the building of an educational amphitheatre, designed in the shape of a turtle, to promote ecological awareness. Visit www.bajaturtle.com for more information.

WEST CAPE

Dirt roads heading to the beach can be a bit tricky to navigate. There are no street names or signs, and many roads dead-end at someone's driveway. The easiest way to find most of Pescadero's waterfront attractions is to follow a wide dirt road with a row of palms in the median that meets Mexico 19 just across from the Sandbar restaurant. If you've rented a place along this stretch of coast, be sure to get specific directions to find it.

Playa San Pedro

Just south of Punta San Pedro begins the long Playa San Pedro (7.4 km/4.6 mi south of the Todos Santos town limits), which is stony at the north end but sandy for a long stretch south. The beach's south end, toward Punta Pescadero, is sometimes called Playa Pescadero. Surfing toward the north end can be good, and it's a lot easier to find than Playa San Pedrito; the 3.1-kilometer (1.9-mi) access road west from Km 59 is clearly marked.

During the winter surfing season, the local *ejido* sometimes collects a nominal parking fee for vehicles parked in the small area at the end of the road near Punta San Pedro.

◖ Playa San Pedrito (Playa Las Palmas)

Just north of Pescadero between Km 56 and 57 is an unsigned, 2.5-kilometer (1.5-mi) dirt road west to Playa San Pedrito, called "Palm Beach" or Playa Las Palmas by local *norteamericanos*. Stretched between two rocky points and backed by Mexican fan palms and a salt marsh, this scenic beach offers good fishing and the occasional mushy beach break for surfing or body-boarding. For swimming, the middle 200 meters or so in the center of the cove is usually safest. Toward the north and south ends, the water looks deceptively shallow and inviting, but riptides have been known to carry swimmers out of the cove into open ocean or onto the rocks.

The best thing about San Pedrito/Las Palmas is that there is no easy vehicle access, so the sand isn't crisscrossed with vehicle tracks like many other beaches along the West Cape. However, the beach sand is often streaked with black volcanic sediment from Puerto Algodones a little farther north.

Trails lead across the headlands at either end of the cove to beach vistas. In back of Punta San Pedro, the slopes of **Cerro Los Viejos** offer a rough but scenic hike.

This beach is sometimes incorrectly called "Playa San Pedro." Mexican topographic surveys confirm its original name as Playa San Pedrito, or "Little San Pedro Beach"—it's smaller than Playa San Pedro, immediately south of Punta San Pedro. Further proof can be found inside the Casa de la Cultura museum in Todos Santos, where a photo of this beach is clearly labeled Playa de San Pedrito. This same museum contains a historical photo of the Hacienda de San Pedrito—the hacienda now standing in ruins at the back of Playa San Pedrito. Nonetheless, most gringos and some locals confuse the names, chiefly because for years, a former campground on Playa San Pedro called itself San Pedrito.

Camping is no longer permitted in the palm grove or in the ruined hacienda behind it. Beach camping on the sand west of the palm grove is allowed, but don't leave any rubbish behind. Water is available from a spring at the south end of the beach; treat before drinking.

The more commonly used road to San Pedrito leaves Mexico 19 almost opposite the white buildings of the Campo Experimental on the east side of the highway between Km 56 and 57. A more direct road just a bit farther south is sometimes marked with a sign reading Road Closed; all the local residents use it anyway. Both roads intersect several other sandy tracks; when you see a ruined mansion just ahead, make sure you take the left fork that curves around to the south end of the palm orchard. If you head straight toward the middle or north end of the orchard you'll run into the salt marsh and have to hike a couple of hundred yards through tall salt grass and mud to reach the beach.

For information on beaches north of Playa San Pedrito, see *Sights* and *Beaches* in the *Todos Santos* section.

Exploring the Sierra

East of Pescadero, you can follow a network of dirt roads up into the sierra foothills to palm-filled arroyos, remote ranches, thick *cardonales* (*cardón* stands), and other delights. If you decide to explore the area, you should do so only in a high-clearance vehicle, preferably with four-wheel drive; better yet, park in the foothills and hike in. It's easy to become lost here, so you may be better off hiring a guide in Pescadero or in Todos Santos. Some of the best spots, such as **Cascada del Refugio,** a sparkling, palm-shaded waterfall, can be reached only by hiking across private land, for which you'll need permission—best arranged by someone local. At Rancho Pilar (Km 73, ranchopilar@yahoo.com), artisan and amateur naturalist Cuco Moyron can arrange mule trips into the Sierra de la Laguna and is a good source of information about sierra flora. He'll need about a week to make the arrangements. In Todos Santos, **Todos Santos Eco Adventures** (Juárez and Topete, tel. 612/145-0780, www.tosea.net) arranges one-day and multiday hikes.

One road leading southeast from south of town near Playa Los Cerritos continues approximately 56 kilometers (35 mi) across the Sierra de la Laguna to Mexico 1 between Santa Anita and Caduaño, about 16 kilometers (10 mi) south of Miraflores (see *Sierra de la Laguna* in the *East Cape and the Sierra de la Laguna* chapter). Parts of this road—properly called Ramal Los Naranjos but known by many Anglophone residents as the "Naranjas road"—are graded, but the middle section is passable only by sturdy four-wheel drive.

SURFING

Experienced surfers have several good options for waves along the West Cape. Playa Migriño offers an exposed right point and hollow beach break. Punta Gaspareño, around Km 73, catches a sandy right point break. Punta San Pedro (Km 59, site of the former San Pedrito RV park) offers consistent right reef and beach breaks; paddle out from the beach to avoid urchins on the reef. A little farther north, Playa San Pedrito has another beach break, best enjoyed during a west or north swell. Popular with novice surfers, Playa Los Cerritos has several left and right beach breaks. Experienced surfers will enjoy the right break off the point on larger northwest and south swells. Vacation rentals in the Pescadero area are popular with some surfers, while others prefer to camp north of Todos Santos. The **Pescadero Surf Camp** (Km 64, www.pescaderosurf.com) offers cabanas, camp sites, board rentals, and instruction.

SWIMMING

Most of the beaches along the West Cape are exposed to heavy surf; however, on calm days Playa Los Cerritos and Playa Las Palmas offer sheltered conditions for an ocean swim. At Las Palmas, the middle 200 meters or so in the center of the cove is usually safest. Toward the north and south ends, the water looks deceptively shallow and inviting, but riptides have been known to carry swimmers out of the cove into open ocean or onto the rocks.

SPA SERVICES

In a brick building three rows in from the beach, **Los Bules Day Spa** (Playa Congrejos, El Pescadero, tel. 612/108-4134, www.pescadise.com) offers deep tissue, hot stone, or Swedish massage (US$50), body wraps (US$45), and facials (US$40–70)—plus a native American *temazcal,* or sweat lodge (US$20). The proprietor, Maria, is also a gourd artist. Her gallery on the property contains pitchers, bowls, animals, candles, and teacups—all crafted from hard-shelled bottle gourds.

ENTERTAINMENT

These days, when Todos Santos residents want to go out for a night on the town, they head to Pescadero. Todos Santos may have more shops and restaurants, but Pescadero has the **Sandbar** (Km 63, tel. 612/130-3209, Mon.–Sat. 3 P.M. till late, Sun. 1–10 P.M.)—with a pool table, live music, and daily happy hour specials, as well as occasional cook-your-own kebab dinners.

SHOPPING

A string of *artesanías* selling such items as colorful Mexican blankets, hammocks, and pottery lines the highway in the Pescadero area.

Local artisans in Candelaria produce rustic ranchware pots, cane baskets, and *palo escopeta* chairs with palm-fiber bottoms. Look for a sign reading Pottery in the village if you're interested in buying these crafts. Candelaria resident Lorena Hankins sometimes leads pottery workshops; check with Lorena in La Candelaria, or inquire at Todos Santos Eco Adventures. At Km 80, **The Blanket Factory** is a popular stop for organized tours. Shop here for handmade rugs, blankets, clothing, and hammocks—or request a custom design.

Rancho Pilar

A sandy road near Km 73 leads to a trailer homestead where La Paz native Cuco Moyron (ranchopilar@yahoo.com) makes custom-fitted *bajacaliforniano*-style leather sandals with recycled tire-rubber soles for US$25–30 a pair. He can take your measurements one day and have the sandals ready the next. Cuco also makes clay pottery, and his wife, Pilar, makes beach rock and wire jewelry, as well as grass-woven hats. An amateur naturalist, Cuco can arrange mule trips into the Sierra de la Laguna and is a good source of information about sierra flora. He'll need about a week to make the arrangements. To find Rancho Pilar, follow the dirt road off Mexico 19 till it ends, then turn left and continue straight till you reach his gate; park outside the gate and walk in.

ACCOMMODATIONS

Several longtime Pescadero inns have changed hands in recent years, and new places are opening with each season. A number of private homes are also coming on the market as vacation rental properties.

US$50-100

On the beach in Pescadero, 3.5 kilometers from the wide dirt road that leaves Mexico 19

across from the Sandbar, the **San Pedrito Surf Hotel** (www.sanpedritosurf.com, US$65–150) is a remodel of the former Casa Cyrene. Now owned by two families from Hawaii, the property has five *casitas*. The surf bunkhouse has been converted into a two-bedroom family *casita*. All have full kitchens and king-size beds. Other amenities include bottled water, basic cooking utensils and spices, and linens. There is a washer/dryer on the property.

Right on the beach just south of the San Pedrito Surf Hotel, **Casa Simpatica** (http://todossantos.cc/casasimpatica.html, US$65) features three clean *casitas,* each with queen bed and private bath; amenities include a communal outdoor cooking area and Internet access. There's a three-night minimum.

At the San Pedrito surf break, **Las Palmas Tropicales** (www.tropicalcasitas.com, US$75–140) has four *palapa*-roof *casitas* (three with kitchens) with tiled baths and wireless Internet. Also close to the San Pedrito surf break, a couple from Santa Cruz, California own **Sierra de la Costa** (rcliv2surf@aol.com, US$70, three-night minimum), beach bungalow rentals with queen-size beds, tiled baths, private patios, and gas barbecues.

A little farther away from the beach and the surf breaks, **Rancho de Las Olas** (tel. 612/111-7121, ranchodelasolas@yahoo.com, www.bajacasitas.com, US$65–75) has three minimally furnished *casitas.* One is a stand-alone unit, while the others are second-story apartments. Weekly rates and longer-term discounts are available.

US$100-150

Near the San Pedrito Surf Hotel, **El Pozo Hondo** (pozohondobcs@yahoo.com, US$100–110) is a bed-and-breakfast with two *palapa*-roof bungalows surrounded by mango, avocado, and citrus trees.

US$150-250

Marble floors, robes, Egyptian cotton sheets, and fluffy towels are just a few of the luxury amenities at **La Alianza** (tel. 612/108-0436, www.bajaturtle.com, US$130–240), a five-room property near San Pedrito point. Guests share a third-floor *palapa*-roof deck and common kitchen. A separate, two-bedroom *casita* has two bedrooms, one bath, and a kitchen for US$150. Commissioned works from local artisan Cuco Moyron (see *Shopping*) add an authentic Baja twist to the grounds and home. This is the place to stay if you want privacy and that extra special touch. Owner Deborah McIntire is involved with local sea turtle conservation activities to protect the leatherbacks and olive ridleys that nest on the beach in Pescadero. Inquire about participating in a baby turtle release August–December.

Vacation Rentals

The Todos Santos community website, www.todossantos.cc, keeps a list of vacation rentals in the area. Here are a few of the most popular homes: For kids (and the young at heart), the highlight of a stay at **Villa del Faro** (U.S. tel. 707/468-0876, www.villadelfarobaja.com, US$3,000/week) is the curved waterslide that deposits swimmers into a 37-foot saltwater pool rimmed with fluorescent lights that glow after dark. Located at the south end of Pescadero Beach, the villa was built to handle a crowd, with three kitchens, five bedrooms, and a hot tub, plus massage, maid services, and catering available by request.

As the name implies, the **Beachfront Family Hacienda** (US$250/night or US$1,500/week), near the San Pedrito surf break, is a family-friendly 3,000-square-foot redbrick building with three bedrooms, two indoor baths, an outdoor shower, and a full kitchen. This home also comes with a washing machine and dishwasher, swing set, and beach gear.

Between the Los Cerritos and San Pedrito surf breaks, **Alhaja de Baja** is a recently remodeled two-bedroom house with king-size beds (www.alhajadebaja.com, US$990/week). **The Great Escape Ranch** at Los Cerritos (Km 66–67, US$125/night or US$700/week) has three rustically furnished bedrooms in a solar-powered home. Amenities include laundry, Internet, and satellite TV.

For luxury accommodations in a more remote location, **Noche de las Estrellas** (www.

nochedelasestrellas.com, US$350/night or US$5,000/week) sits on a bluff overlooking a sand beach at Elias Calles, 10 miles south of Pescadero. Four suites have private sitting areas, granite baths, and guest robes (for walking to the pool and hot tub). A shared living room has satellite TV and Wi-Fi, and the tiled kitchen has granite counters, an island and window bar with stools, and a table that seats eight. An outdoor kitchen is available for grilling.

Also in the Elias Calles area, **Casa Aqua Brillante** (Km 82, www.todossantos.cc/casaaquabrillante.html, US$3,500/week) is a luxury villa that sleeps six in three suites. Liberal use of marble, onyx, and granite set the stage. A 10-person dining table has ocean views. A fully equipped kitchen, satellite TV, and Wi-Fi complete the experience. The villa is off the grid, using solar power and propane for power and heat. Daily maid service is included in the rate. Inquire about food-stocking service and airport shuttles.

Surf and Fitness Camps

On the east side of the highway at Km 64, **Pescadero Surf Camp** (tel. 612/134-0480, www.pescaderosurf.com, US$60) is a good place for diehard surfers to meet kindred spirits. Besides tent and *palapa* camping, you can rent a cabaña that sleeps six and is equipped with kitchen and bath. Daily or weekly rates are available. Pescadero Surf Camp also offers campsites with shade *palapas* for US$7–10 per person per night. Amenities include water, electricity, bathrooms with hot showers, a pool with a swim-up bar, and a cooking area. The camp rents tents, as well as surfboards and boogie boards by the hour or day. Instruction is offered at all levels; guided "surfaris" are also available.

A raw-food diet and plenty of exercise define the detox experience at **Baja Life Camp** (Km 64, Barrio Las Palmitas, tel. 624/155-7057, U.S. tel. 858/764-4106, www.bajalifecamp.com). Run by a former NFL athlete, the camp has eight simple *palapa* structures set deep in the Pescadero *huerta*. Guests begin the day at sunrise with a warm-up and cardio workout and then relax for an afternoon siesta. Rates of US$1,000 per week for single occupancy in a private *casita* and US$800 per person double occupancy include meals, fitness instruction, lodging, airport transfer, and laundry.

Camping and RV Parks
RV Park Baja Serena (tel. 612/130-3006, US$20) in Pescadero offers eight spaces with water and sewer hookups (no electricity) that can be rented by the day, week, or month. The entrance is on Mexico 19 just south of Mini Super Los Arcos, which is where you check in.

Though the highway sign still stands, the popular **San Pedrito RV Park** was destroyed in 2003 by a hurricane. The property changed hands several times in 2006 and is likely to be developed soon.

Campers and trailers were asked to leave the former **Los Cerritos Trailer Park** in 2006–2007, as developers began work on a new oceanfront resort.

Free beach campsites along Mexico 19 can be found at the ends of dirt roads branching off Mexico 19 at Km 89–90, Km 86, Km 75, and Km 70–71.

FOOD
Simple **Restaurant Migriño,** on the ocean side of Mexico 19, just south of Km 102, serves *antojitos* and cold beer.

Lonchería Rosita (tel. 612/130-3094, daily 8 A.M.–8 P.M.), on the east side of Mexico 19 near the Pemex, is a small *palapa*-roofed place. Specialties include *pescado empanizado, tamales de puerco,* quesadillas, enchiladas, chicken and *machaca* burritos, and soft drinks.

Popular with locals and expats alike for its casual fare, **Felipe's Restaurant** (Km 61, mains around US$4) specializes in tasty Mexican dishes and seafood at nongringo prices for breakfast, lunch, and dinner.

Grill your own kebabs at the **Sandbar** (Km 63, tel. 612/130-3209, Mon.–Sat. 3 P.M. till late, Sun. 1–10 P.M.), or just pop in for daily happy hour specials, as well as weekly all-you-can-eat pizza.

The **Los Cerritos Club** (Km 66–67) at Playa Los Cerritos opened with multiple large-screen TVs just in time to host a Superbowl party in 2007. The preliminary menu included tacos, salads, and burgers.

Regulars praise **Art & Beer** (Km 69) for large signature cocktails—creative variations of the Bloody Mary, which comes generously garnished with all manner of shellfish. You must agree to buy a drink or a meal in order to view the art on display. When it's time to go, your eccentric hosts, Alfredo and Lourdes, may offer up a beer for the road.

Groceries
Mini Super Los Arcos is a *tienda* on Mexico 19 that carries a good selection of gringo items such as American cheese, nonfat milk, whole turkeys, yogurt, tofu, feta cheese, and balsamic vinegar. Special orders are welcomed.

Mini Super Los Cerritos (Km 63 Mexico 19) sells cold beer and ice, as well as some arts and crafts.

INFORMATION AND SERVICES
Pescadero has the only Pemex between Cabo San Lucas and Todos Santos, as well as an Oxxo convenience store. For emergencies, call 612/145-0445, or head to Todos Santos or the Los Cabos area for medical services. Buses en route to La Paz and Cabo San Lucas stop across from the Pemex. Many places in the Pescadero area now have wireless Internet, and a few of the networks were open at last check, but the closest Internet cafés were in Todos Santos.

Todos Santos

One of the more lushly vegetated arroyo settlements in the Cape Region, Todos Santos (pop. 5,000–7,000, depending on the season) sits on a *meseta* (low plateau) buttressing the sierra foothills. Looming over Todos Santos to the east, the sierra provides an underground stream that irrigates dozens of orchards laden with mangoes, avocados, guavas, papayas, citrus, coconuts, and other fruits. Most of these are cultivated along wide Arroyo de la Reforma to the town's immediate north, in an area commonly known as **La Huerta** or "The Orchard." At the west end toward the beach is **La Poza,** a small freshwater lagoon favored by resident and migrating waterfowl. North of town, amid a dense palm grove, is another natural pool where local children go swimming.

Beneath the town's sleepy surface, behind the century-old brick and adobe facades, lives a growing community of mostly American artists—with a few surfers and organic farmers mixed in—all of whom have found Todos Santos the ideal place to follow their independent pursuits. And discerning buyers say the art scene has come of age in Todos Santos in recent years, clearly setting itself apart from the typical retiree/artist community.

As a newly designated Pueblo Mágico, Todos Santos has received access to government funding for improving infrastructure and developing cultural tourism. To date, the money has been used to remodel the park and repair the auditorium. Next on the project list: burying wires and cables in the town center, repairing the theater, and protecting the oasis and lagoon.

In 2007, the town was also abuzz with talk of real estate development. One project near La Poza had run into problems with water and sewer rights; another at the San Pedrito surf break had changed hands three times in less than a year. There was talk of a fishing village at Punta Lobos. And new homes were popping up at the other end of town, along Playa Las Tunas, as power and water infrastructure crept northward. Locals remained optimistic

that Todos Santos would retain its bohemian character, even in the wake of increased development—with Carmel and Santa Fe as the model, rather than Los Cabos or Cancun.

HISTORY

The earliest traces of human habitation in the Todos Santos area date back 3,000 years to "Matancita Man," the defleshed and painted remains (thus indicating a second burial) of a tall male who lived to at least 75 years on a vegetable and animal-protein diet. The first Spaniard to sight the oasis, Jesuit padre Jaime Bravo, found nomadic Guaicura availing themselves of the inland water source and collecting shellfish along the coast.

Padre Bravo established a farm community and a *misión de visita* (visiting mission) called Todos Santos here in 1724, to supply the water-poor mission community at La Paz with fruits, vegetables, wine, and sugarcane. By 1731 Todos Santos was producing 200 burro-loads of *panocha* (raw brown sugar) annually, along with figs, pomegranates, citrus, and grapes. Two years later, deeming the local Guaicura amenable to missionization, Padre Sigismundo Taraval founded Misión Santa Rosa de las Palmas at the upper end of the arroyo about two kilometers inland from the Pacific. Taraval fled to Isla Espíritu Santo near La Paz after a 1734 native rebellion, and the mission returned to visiting-chapel status the following year.

The local Guaicura population was soon wiped out by smallpox, and Pericú were brought in to work the fields. Reinstated as a *misión de visita* in 1735, Todos Santos outgrew La Paz by the mid-18th century; from 1737 until 1748, Padre Bernardo Zumziel actually spent more time in Todos Santos than at the mission in La Paz. Renamed Nuestra Señora del Pilar de Todos Santos in 1749, the town served as Spanish military headquarters for La Escuadra del Sur, the southern detachment of the Loreto presidio. This enabled the community to weather the Pericú rebellions

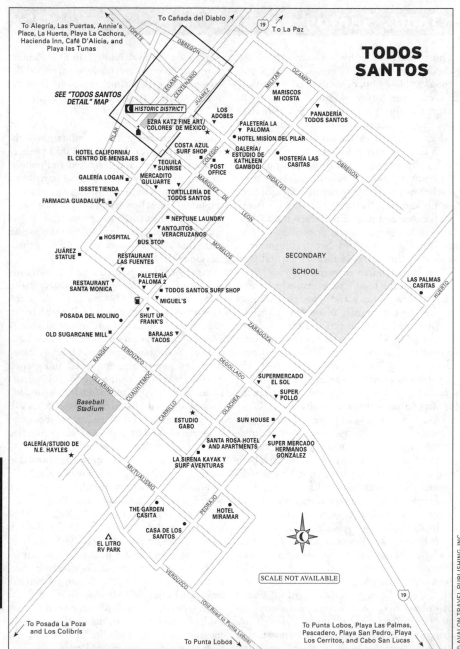

TODOS SANTOS

To Cañada del Diablo

19 To La Paz

To Alegría, Las Puertas, Annie's Place, La Huerta, Playa La Cachora, Hacienda Inn, Café D'Alicia, and Playa las Tunas

TOPETE
OBREGÓN
LEGASPI
CENTENARIO
JUÁREZ
PILAR

SEE "TODOS SANTOS DETAIL" MAP

HISTORIC DISTRICT

EZRA KATZ FINE ART/ COLORES DE MÉXICO

LOS ADOBES

MARISCOS MI COSTA

MILITAR
OCAMPO

PANADERÍA TODOS SANTOS

PALETERÍA LA PALOMA

HOTEL MISÍON DEL PILAR

COSTA AZUL SURF SHOP

HOTEL CALIFORNIA/ EL CENTRO DE MENSAJES

TEQUILA SUNRISE

GALERÍA/ ESTUDIO DE KATHLEEN GAMBOGI

HOSTERÍA LAS CASITAS

OBREGÓN

COLEGIO
POST OFFICE

GALERÍA LOGAN

MERCADITO GULUARTE

MÁRQUEZ DE
HIDALGO

ISSSTE TIENDA

TORTILLERÍA DE TODOS SANTOS

FARMACIA GUADALUPE

NEPTUNE LAUNDRY

LEÓN

ANTOJITOS VERACRUZANOS

HOSPITAL

BUS STOP

MORELOS

SECONDARY SCHOOL

JUÁREZ STATUE

RESTAURANT LAS FUENTES

LAS PALMAS CASITAS

RESTAURANT SANTA MONICA

PALETERÍA PALOMA 2

HUERTO

TODOS SANTOS SURF SHOP

MIGUEL'S

POSADA DEL MOLINO

SHUT UP FRANK'S

ZARAGOZA

OLD SUGARCANE MILL

BARAJAS TACOS

RANGEL
VERDUZCO
VILLARINO
CUAUHTEMOC

DEGOLLADO

SUPERMERCADO EL SOL

Baseball Stadium

SUPER POLLO

CARRILLO
OLACHEA

GALERÍA/STUDIO DE N.E. HAYLES

ESTUDIO GABO

SUN HOUSE

SANTA ROSA HOTEL AND APARTMENTS

SUPER MERCADO HERMANOS GONZÁLEZ

LA SIRENA KAYAK Y SURF AVENTURAS

MUTUALISMO

THE GARDEN CASITA

PEDRAJO

HOTEL MIRAMAR

CASA DE LOS SANTOS

EL LITRO RV PARK

SCALE NOT AVAILABLE

To Posada La Poza and Los Colibrís

VERDUZCO

Old Road to Punta Lobos

To Punta Lobos

To Punta Lobos, Playa Las Palmas, Pescadero, Playa San Pedro, Playa Los Cerritos, and Cabo San Lucas

19

WEST CAPE

© PAUL ITOI

side street in Todos Santos

to the southwest in Santiago and San José del Cabo, although 49 Todos Santos inhabitants were killed defending the town in one related skirmish. Polish Jesuit padre Carlos Neumayer presided over the mission from 1752 until his death in Todos Santos in 1764. Todos Santos remained an important mission settlement until secularization in 1840.

When Governor Luis del Castillo Negrete ordered the distribution of church lands to the local community in 1841, he was contested by Padre Gabriel González, a local priest and former president of the mission who had used mission property for his own farming and ranching, becoming a powerful local trader in the process. González's armed rebellion was put down in 1842; the priest and his followers fled to Mazatlán.

Anglo whalers visiting Todos Santos in 1849 praised the town as "an oasis" with "friendly and intelligent people." In the post-mission era, Todos Santos thrived as Baja's sugarcane capital, supporting eight sugar mills by the late 19th century. While carrying out a survey of Cape Region flora for the California Academy of Sciences in 1890, botanist T. S. Brandegee commented on the area's beauty and bounty. During this period handsome hotels, theaters, municipal offices, and homes for painters and sculptors were built.

Sugar prices dropped precipitously after World War II, and all but one mill closed when the most abundant freshwater spring dried up in 1950. The remaining mill closed in 1965, though smaller household operations continued into the early 1970s. The town faded into near obscurity.

Around 1981 the spring came back to life, and the arroyo once again began producing a large variety and quantity of fruits and vegetables. Three years later, Mexico 19 was paved between San Pedro and Cabo San Lucas, opening Todos Santos to tourists and expatriates for the first time.

SIGHTS
⟨ Historic District

Although Todos Santos has been inhabited continually since 1731, the oldest standing structures date back only 100–150 years. The town's most historic buildings—a mixture

WEST CAPE

of one- and two-story affairs, all with court-yards—can be seen along the streets nearest the plaza, particularly along Pilar, Centenario, Legaspi, Topete, and Obregón. Most are constructed of fired Mexican brick laid in double or sometimes triple courses (some walls are plastered, some not) topped by flat parapet roofs. A few feature palm-thatched roofs. Large windows and doors bounded by *pilastres* in the classic Andalusian style (favored in provincial Mexico from the time of the Spanish until the middle of the 20th century) predominate in this area. The large building housing Café Santa Fé on Calle Centenario, facing the plaza, is one of the only substantial adobe structures downtown. Many of the buildings in this area are owned or occupied by foreigners. And the facades are likely to look more homogenous in coming years, as a uniform appearance is one of the contingencies of funding made available through the Pueblo Mágico program. Check *El Calendario* for the timing of the annual historic home tour, when owners open their doors to visitors.

On the hill overlooking town (off Mexico 19 on the way out of town toward La Paz) stand a few older adobe ruins. The newer eastern half of Todos Santos holds many small residences built of adobe brick or *chiname*—mud plastered over woven *palo de arco* (trumpetbush) branches. Brick ruins of several of the old sugar mills can be seen around town.

TODOS SANTOS DETAIL

© AVALON TRAVEL PUBLISHING, INC.

Iglesia Nuestra Señora del Pilar

Although the structure itself is rather plain, this church facing the southwest edge of the main plaza contains an important orange- and blue-garbed figure of the Virgin of Pilar, the focus of the town's biggest festival each year in October. In August, the famous Virgin of Loreto—considered the "mother" of all Baja churches founded by the Jesuits—is brought to the church from Loreto.

Centro Cultural Profesor Nestor Agúndez Martínez

Housed in a restored U-shaped brick building on Avenida Juárez at Obregón, the Cen-tro Cultural (Mon.–Fri. 8 A.M.–5 P.M., Sat.–Sun. 9 A.M.–1 P.M., free admission) displays a modest collection of artifacts evoking the anthropology, ethnography, history, and natural history of the region, along with small displays of modern art and handicrafts. Named in honor of a venerated local high school teacher, the museum's pottery collection includes classic local ranchware, as well as older ceramics produced by the now-extinct Pericú. Some rare painted Amerindian skulls are also on display. One of the five exhibit rooms contains paintings by local artists, including a set of pastels of historic structures in Zacatecas.

BEACHES

None of the roads leading from Todos Santos to the beach are paved or even marked. To find them, you'll need good directions and a little patience for those inevitable moments when you realize you've taken a wrong turn and need to retrace your steps. The following list starts south of Todos Santos and proceeds north.

Punta Lobos

About two kilometers (1.2 mi) south of the town limits via Mexico 19, a signed, unpaved access road suitable for most vehicles leads 2.4 kilometers (1.5 mi) to Punta Lobos, a rocky point at the south end of a sandy cove. The point is named for a resident colony of sea lions. The surf here is usually okay for swimming, but take a good look at the currents before leaping in. This cove is used as a launching point for the local fishermen, so there's always a small fleet of *pangas* toward the point. The *pangas* usually bring the catch in after 3 P.M.; watching the pilots time the waves so that they can safely run the boats onto the beach is a treat. Sometimes fresh fish can be bought directly from the *pangeros*.

The ruins of an old stone-walled cannery lie at the side of the access road toward the beach; north along the beach stands a lighthouse. Swimming in the lighthouse area is not recommended because of strong currents. If you continue walking past the lighthouse you'll eventually reach Playa Las Pocitas and Playa La Cachora (described later in this section).

A small spring-fed lagoon lies behind the south end of the beach, marked by a large Virgin shrine. A narrow trail leads up and over the 215-meter (700-ft) headland to a panoramic view of the beach and sea below. On the other side of the headland you can see sandy **Puerto Campechano** and, farther south, Puerto Algodones.

Punta Lobos can be reached on foot from town by following Calle Pedrajo southwest one long block till you meet a wide dirt road. Turn left and follow the road until you can see the lighthouse on the right; take the next wide dirt road heading in that direction till you reach

WATER WARNINGS

While walking close to the surfline along any of the beaches north of Punta Lobos, watch out for "sneaker" waves that rise up seemingly out of nowhere to engulf the beach. Though rare, accidental drownings have occurred on these beaches.

Also beware – during the late *chubasco* season, especially September – of the small blue jellyfish, called *aguas malas*, that are commonly encountered in inshore waters.

Punta Lobos. This walk takes 20–30 minutes each way.

Hidden away two headlands south of Punta Lobos and almost surrounded by steep cliffs, this deep and secluded cove can be reached via a very rough, winding, and sometimes steep dirt and stone road that runs southwest off the Punta Lobos access road. According to local history, **Puerto Algodones** was used for the shipping of tomatoes, sugarcane, and canned fish from the 1930s through the 1950s, when a stone-block road was laid between the cannery and the bay. How it got the name "Algodones" (cotton) is a mystery; cotton was never cultivated in the Cape Region.

Along the north side of the U-shaped cove stands a tall pier made of rough-hewn stone blocks. The sure-footed can hike along a narrow trail at the bottom of a cliff and reach the rock pier—worth the effort for the view back into the bay. Smaller animal paths lead up a steep slope above the pier for more panoramic views. If you've got all day you could probably hike to Puerto Campechano and back from here.

A black-hued beach of rounded volcanic stones rims the middle reach of the bay, where the waves are sometimes suitable for bodysurfing. To reach the beach you can hike down a cliff or follow the old road. Snorkeling is good at the rocky headlands at each end of the bay, but currents and tidal surges can be too strong for some swimmers. Sea lions are sometimes seen along the rocks.

The old road to Algodones starts just east of the cannery ruins near Punta Lobos and climbs along the eastern rim of a large arroyo. You can hike to the bay from the cannery area in about 45 minutes at a steady pace, an hour if you take it slow. Start in the early morning and plan to spend the day there so that you can hike back in late afternoon, thus avoiding the hottest part of the day. If you have a sturdy off-highway vehicle that can take soft sand, you can drive about a fourth or a third of the way before the road becomes too rocky for anything but tractor tires.

For information on beaches south of Punta Lobos and Puerto Algodones, see *Pescadero and Vicinity*.

Playa La Cachora

Playa La Cachora is a broad swath of sand backed by verbena-trimmed dunes, a good spot for strolling and sunset-watching. From the Galería de Todos Santos, follow Calle Topete across the palm-filled arroyo known as La Huerta; the first sand road on the other side (turn left just before the low rock wall; if you start going uphill, you've gone too far) leads west to the beach after curving through a quiet residential section perched on a *meseta* above the northwest corner of the arroyo.

❰ Playa Las Pocitas (La Poza de Lobos)

If you walk south along Playa La Cachora, you'll come to scenic Las Pocitas, also known as La Poza de Lobos and a gold mine for bird-watchers. Along the back edge of the beach is a freshwater lagoon (La Poza), and toward the south end a rocky ridge heads inland. It's possible to walk back to town via a trail running along the base of the north side (the La Huerta side) of this ridge.

The undertow and shore break along La Cachora and Las Pocitas are usually too heavy for swimming, except during the summer when there are occasional long periods of relative calm.

La Poza de Lobos

WEST CAPE

COURTESY OF POSADA LA POZA, TODOS SANTOS

Playa La Pastora

A wider network of sand roads crosses the arroyo and runs north parallel to the beach for some 26 kilometers (16 mi). The roads pass small coconut and papaya orchards and larger farms at Las Playitas and El Carrizal, then head inland to join Mexico 19. Several sandy tracks branch west off this road to a lengthy succession of dune-lined beaches perfect for secluded sunbathing and beachcombing.

For much of the year the surfline here is too precipitous for swimming, though surfers can ride the waves at a break called La Pastora, named for a meadow some distance away. In winter, La Pastora offers a right point break in a northwest swell; in summer you'll find an occasional beach break in a southern swell, or a point break in a southwestern swell.

La Pastora is about 5.6 kilometers (3.5 mi) northwest of La Huerta via the only coastal road north; just past a wide arroyo that runs right up to the beach, look for a large, lone *palapa* next to a long, low stone wall.

Farther North

Beyond El Carrizal, a rough dirt road snakes north along and away from the coast 57 kilometers (36 mi) to a cluster of Ranchos—Los Inocentes, El Rosario, El Tepetate, and El Tomate—where another dirt road leads northeast 29 kilometers (18 mi) to meet Mexico 1. Sand beach lines the entire coastline here all the way north to **Punta Marqués** (about 24 km/15 mi north of Rancho El Tomate) and **Punta Conejo** (18 km/11 mi north of Punta Marqués). Both points offer excellent surfing and windsurfing in the winter and early spring. And surfable reef and point breaks can form in many other spots along the 58-kilometer (36-mi) stretch of sand extending south of Punta Marqués; check out **La Bocana,** an arroyo mouth near Los Inocentes. Self-contained beach camping is permitted anywhere along the shore.

FISHING

Many of the same game fish commonly found from Cabo San Lucas to La Paz can be caught offshore here. If you speak Spanish, you can go to Punta Lobos and ask the fishermen there about hiring *pangas* and fishing guides. The asking price is usually around US$30 per hour with a three-hour minimum. See *Organized Tours* for guided trips.

Surf casting, though possible at any of the Todos Santos area beaches, is safest and easiest at Playa San Pedrito (Palm Beach), Playa San Pedro, and Playa Los Cerritos (see *Pescadero and Vicinity*).

Ferreteria Oasis de Todos Santos (Rangel at Zaragoza, tel. 612/145-0754, Mon.–Fri. 8 A.M.–3 P.M. and 4–7 P.M., Sat. 8 A.M.– 4 P.M.) carries some fishing supplies. You can buy live bait from the local fishermen at Punta Lobos.

WHALE-WATCHING

Although you won't see as many whales close to shore here as farther north in Bahía Magdalena (an important calving bay for the Pacific gray whale), newborn calves and their mothers do swim by on their "trial run" to the Sea of Cortez before beginning the long migration back to the Arctic Circle. The best months for spotting grays are December–April.

With a pair of binoculars and some luck, you can stand on any beach in the vicinity and spot grays (and other whales) spouting offshore. One of the best places to see them is near the rocky ridge at Playa Las Pocitas. For a much better view from shore, climb Punta Lobos (see *Beaches*). *Pangeros* at Punta Lobos will take up to five passengers out to see the whales for about US$25 an hour; inquire at the beach or at any of the hotels in town (see *Organized Tours*).

SURFING AND KAYAKING

Most of the Pacific breaks near Todos Santos hit their peak during the northwest swell, December–March. Experienced surfers who paddle around the larger points at Punta Lobos and Punta San Pedro during the late summer southern swell will sometimes turn up a nice break, although the usual summer custom is to head for the Corridor between Cabo San Lucas

surf casting near Todos Santos

and San José del Cabo, or to lesser known spots around the east side of the Cape.

You may see auto window stickers bearing the label "Todos Santos Surfboards," but don't go looking for them—it's a small made-in-California brand. The **Todos Santos Surf Shop** (Degollado/Mexico 19 and Rangel, tel. 612/145-0882, mariosurfing@hotmail.com, daily 9 A.M.–5 P.M.) offers lessons, accessories, and ding repair; a satellite location at Playa Los Cerritos has rentals (open daily dawn till dusk). The newer **Costa Azul Surf Shop** on Juárez is an extension of same store at Playa Costa Azul in San Jose del Cabo.

La Sirena Kayak y Surf Aventuras (Olachea off Degollado, tel. 612/145-0353, www.lasirenakayaksurf.com) rents surfing equipment and supplies, offers surfing instruction (US$50/hour), and leads local kayak tours (US$50).

HIKING
Arrange guided day or overnight hikes into the Sierra de la Laguna at **Todos Santos Eco Adventures** (Juárez and Topete, tel. 612/145-0780, www.tosea.net) or **La Sirena Kayak y Surf Aventuras** (Olachea off Degollado, tel. 612/145-0353, www.lasirenakayaksurf.com).

YOGA, MEDITATION, AND MARTIAL ARTS
Hatha and Ashtanga yoga classes meet several times a week at the La Arca building on Topete (US$4 per class). In the same location, **El Dharma de Todos Santos** (tel. 612/145-0676, www.eldharma.com) offers dharma talks and *vipassana* meditation classes 10–11:30 A.M. each Sunday. And Carlos Martinez Hererra offers Aikido classes to beginners and experienced students (cell 612/018-1052, ranchaiki@aikifarms.com, US$4 per class).

Tai chi chuan instruction is available at the Centro Cultural Monday and Friday October–June, for a fee of around US$6. Hours vary with the season.

The Elephant Tree (Obregón btw Centenario/Juárez, tel. 612/145-0299) is an inner-resource community center holding a variety of workshops including yoga, tarot, and writing.

SPA SERVICES

Kathleen Nelson offers massage treatments through **Todos Santos Oasis** (19 Legaspi at Hidalgo, tel. 612/145-0545, US$35/hr).

ORGANIZED TOURS

Todos Santos Eco Adventures (Juárez and Topete, tel. 612/145-0780, www.tosea.net) leads half-day outings to nearby waterfalls, cliff walks, and La Candelaria for US$55, as well as overnight trips to the Sierra Laguna, fishing trips (US$275 per boat for up to 6 hrs), and horseback riding (US$45/hr). A 90-minute walking tour of historic sites in Todos Santos is US$15 per person. The Eco Adventures office is also a friendly source of tourist information.

La Sirena Kayak y Surf Aventuras (Olachea off Degollado, tel. 612/145-0353, www. lasirenakayaksurf.com) leads similar trips, including whale-watching (US$35 pp for two hours), fishing (US$50/hour), and waterfall hikes (US$40 pp).

SHOPPING

Although Todos Santos hardly compares with Cabo San Lucas or San José del Cabo when it comes to variety and quantity, several interesting, high-quality shops have opened here, most of them clustered around the historic district near the plaza.

Home Furnishings and Gifts

Sun House (Pedrajo just off Mexico 19, tel. 612/145-0355) sells unique home furnishings and gifts produced by local artists.

In the same building as El Tecolote, **Fénix de Todos Santos** (Juárez at Hidalgo, tel./ fax 612/145-0666) specializes in handcrafted Mexican art. Jewelry, rugs, leather bags, handwoven fabrics, *equipal* furniture, rugs, and decorative tinware are on display, as well as resortwear from Puerto Vallarta. In the same commercial center, **Tzintzuntzan** (Place of the Hummingbirds) is a small shop featuring un-

usual handcrafted *artesanías* and ornaments from Michoacán.

Emporio Hotel California (Juárez btw Morelos/Márquez de León, tel. 612/145-0525), attached to Hotel California, features an eclectic selection of decorative items, clothing, and jewelry.

In a refurbished historical building on Centenario opposite the Charles Stewart Gallery is **Mangos** (tel. 612/145-0451, Mon.–Sat. 10 A.M.–5 P.M.), a beautiful gift shop featuring Mexican folk art, ceramics, pewter ware, metal sculptures, silver jewelry, and beautiful Guatemalan textiles, rugs, and wood carvings.

On the opposite side of Centenario from El Perico Azul, **Manos Mexicanas** carries rustic Mexican furniture and an interesting selection of decorative accessories and unique jewelry, plus pottery made by Ruben Gutierrez.

Jewelry

El Filon de Taxco, opposite the Hotel California on Calle Juárez near Morelos, features a large selection of quality silver jewelry.

In the green building next to Mangos, **Arte Cactus** (Centenario, tel. 612/145-0773) offers a good selection of Mexican folk art and jewelry. Next door, check out **Joyería Brilantl** (Centenario near Topete, tel./fax 612/145-0726, www. brilanti.com) for good-quality silver jewelry. Brilanti has a second location nearby on the same street, next to El Perico Azul.

Clothing

El Perico Azul (Topete at Centenario, tel. 612/145-0222, Mon.–Sat. 11 A.M.–5 P.M., Sun. 11 A.M.–4 P.M.), opposite Caffé Todos Santos, features women's and men's clothing made from the best of Mexican textiles, handwoven and minimally processed. The shop also offers a few clothing items from Bali and India, local crafts, jewelry, and some leather pieces.

Beachwear and T-shirts, as well as imported perfumes, are sold at **Sisy's Boutique** (Hidalgo and Colegio Militar).

Books

In the Plaza de los Cardones commercial center,

El Tecolote Books/Libros (Juárez and Hidalgo, tel. 612/145-0295, fax 612/145-0288) carries a good selection of foreign and Mexican magazines (including surf magazines), new and used paperbacks (trades welcome), maps, and a large number of hardcover and softcover books on Mexican arts, architecture, and culture, as well as a good selection of books on tape and movies for sale or rent. The store also stocks art supplies such as paintbrushes and watercolor, acrylic, and oil paints. In a room in the back of El Tecolote is **Traditions,** a small shop featuring gifts, cards, and holiday decorations.

Arts and Crafts

Several shops in Todos Santos, all featuring typical Mexican art and crafts, seem to open in a new location with each successive season. Ones that have lasted longer than most are **La Iguana** and **Artesanías El Cardón,** *palapa-*roofed *artesanías* on the northwest corner of Márquez de León and Juárez opposite the church. They sell Mexican crafts, blankets, T-shirts, sterling silver, quartz, and onyx. Next door is **Bazar Agua y Sol** (tel. 612/145-0537) featuring exclusive jewelry designs, sculptures, pottery, and paintings. Credit cards are accepted here.

Artist Studios and Galleries

The art scene in Todos Santos has come of age in recent years, with more than a dozen galleries representing internationally-known artists from the United States and Mexico. One of the first artist arrivals was Charles Stewart, who has a home gallery, the **Charles Stewart Gallery & Studio** (Centenario and Obregón, tel./fax 612/145-0265, www.charlescstewart.com, Mon.–Sat. 11 A.M.–4 P.M.), usually referred to as "Stewart House." You can't miss this 1810-vintage, French-designed house smothered in foliage and enlivened by caged singing birds. Formerly of Taos, New Mexico, Stewart produces watercolor and oil paintings, wooden sculptures, and hand-carved doors; among his works are small *retablo-*style pieces that feature colorful *bajacaliforniano* pictograph motifs on salvaged wood. His home studio is open to the public daily 11 A.M.–4 P.M.

Newcomer **Galería On cé** (Hidalgo 11, tel. 612/145-0550) opened in November 2006 to showcase the photography of Howard Ekman and Jack Hamilton.

Galería de Todos Santos (Legaspi 33 at Topete, tel. 612/145-0500, www.galeriatodossantos.com, Mon.–Sat. 10 A.M.–4 P.M.), in the same building as the Todos Santos Inn, is owned by American artist Michael Cope and his wife, Pat. The high-ceilinged gallery focuses on the work of artists who live in Baja California. Look for pieces by Walker and Derek Buckner, Gloria Marie V., Carlos Uroz, Margaret Torres, Erick Ochoa, Anibal Angulo, Jack Smith, and Angelina Cimino. The works displayed are fine art and dimensional pieces, and the collection changes every six weeks or so. Michael and Pat have a second gallery at the site of a historic building at the corner of Centenario and Hidalgo that was formerly the town billiards hall; it once appeared in a Chris Isaak music video. This gallery features abstract pieces, while the original gallery displays more representational works of art.

A brightly hued house at Juárez and Morelos contains **Galería Logan** (tel. 612/145-0151, www.jilllogan.com, Mon.–Sat. 11 A.M.–4 P.M., Sun. by appointment), focusing on the work of artist Jill Logan, who creates dramatically colored landscapes, still lifes, and portraits in oil and acrylic.

La Paz native Ezra Katz, known for murals and etchings featured in a number of Cabo San Lucas restaurants and hotels, has opened **Ezra Katz Fine Art** (Juárez at Hidalgo, tel. 612/137-3473, Mon.–Sat. 10 A.M.–5 P.M., or by appt.), featuring John Comer, Lindy Duncan, Lesley Rich, and others, in addition to his own artwork.

Galería/Estudio de Kathleen Gambogi (Hidalgo btw Colegio Militar/Rangel, tel. 612/145-0460), near the Maria Bonita Hotel, features colorful paintings depicting Mexican scenes and still lifes by artist Kathleen Gambogi.

Galería/Studio de N. E. Hayles (Cuauhtémoc, tel./fax 612/145-0183, www.mexonline.com/hayles.htm, Mon.–Sat. 11 A.M.–4 P.M.) displays unique paper-tile mosaics, multimedia art, and tables fashioned by the artist/owner. **Galería Wall** (Juárez 4, tel. 612/145-0527, www.catherinewallart.com, Mon.–Sat. 11 A.M.–4 P.M.) shows Mexican-themed original oils by artist Catherine Wall.

Estudio Gabo (Verduzco 7 btw Olachea/Carrillo, tel. 612/145-0505, Mon.–Sat. 10 A.M.–4 P.M.) features paintings by La Paz native Gabo, whose work is inspired by Baja's colors and textures. His work can be found at Estudio Gabo and at the small **Gabo Galería** on Centenario near Topete.

Colores de México (Juárez at Hidalgo, tel. 612/145-0106, omommag@aol.com), opposite Los Adobes, is a photographic gallery featuring beautiful images by local residents Pat Gerhardt and Suzanne Hill. They specialize in photos of Mexico printed on watercolor paper in large format, suitable for framing.

ENTERTAINMENT AND EVENTS
Bars and Dancing

In 2007, **La Iguana Disco Bar** (Zaragoza and Rangel) opened after a period of closure, with live reggae and rock bands. The only real cantina in town is **Cañada del Diablo** (tel. 612/145-0022), a large, round, *palapa*-roofed place a little out of town at the northeastern end of Calle Centenario. Cañada del Diablo offers a fully stocked bar, including a few choice tequilas, and free popcorn. On occasion, local residents will hire a live *norteña* ensemble to play for a party here. Women and families, as well as men, patronize this bar, whose management is good about not letting the rare *borracho* get out of hand.

Near the Pemex station on Degollado, **Shut Up Frank's** (tel. 612/145-0707) is an expat bar featuring satellite broadcasts of sporting events. Happy hour is Monday–Friday 3–6 P.M.

In the gardens of the Todos Santos Inn, **La Copa** (Legaspi 33, tel. 612/145-0040, Tues.–Sat. 5–9 P.M.) is an upscale wine bar with a

cozy romantic ambience. Owner Michael Cope has added a tapas menu Wednesday–Friday evenings (US$10/plate). The entrance is on Calle Topete.

The bar in Hotel California's uniquely decorated **La Coronela** (Juárez btw Morelos/Márquez de León, tel. 612/145-0525), frequented by local expats as well as the hotel's guests, is a fun place to have a few drinks. Live music on Saturday evenings.

Theater

The nicely restored **Teatro Márquez de León** (Calle Legaspi at Márquez de León) hosts musical and folkloric dance performances from time to time, especially during the annual October fiesta. Before the Teatro de la Ciudad in La Paz was built, this was the only proper theater in the state of Baja California Sur.

Simple outdoor cinemas—featuring grade-C Mexican films with the usual *ranchero/narcotraficante* themes—are sometimes set up next to the soccer field near La Huerta.

Events

Fiesta Todos Santos is held around the feast day of the town's patron saint, Virgen del Pilar, on October 12. For four days beginning the second Saturday of the month, residents enjoy dances, soccer and basketball games, fishing tournaments, cockfights, horse races, theater performances, amusement-park rides, and other merriment centered around the church and town plaza.

For 12 days beginning on the **Día de Guadalupe** (December 12), Todos Santos Catholics participate in nightly candlelight processions to the plaza church. The celebrations culminate in a midnight Mass on **Christmas Eve.**

In late January or early February, the government-funded **Todos Santos Art Festival** features sculptures, paintings, ceramics, and other visual works by local artists, as well as dancing, music, and other performing arts from out of town. Then, in early March, the **Todos Santos Latin Film Festival** comes to town.

Also once a year, usually in February or

WEST CAPE

March, historic homes in Todos Santos open to the public. Check *El Calendario* (www.todossantos-baja.com) for more information.

ACCOMMODATIONS

Overnight guests in Todos Santos can choose from a variety of modest hotels, bed-and-breakfast inns, and private vacation rentals. As more visitors arrive each year, new properties are opening, old ones are renovating, and others are just raising prices without making significant improvements. Many properties are now up for sale, and if water and sewer rights are worked out, several large resorts may be coming to the area in the not-too-distant future.

There are three accommodations in town with "Todos Santos" in their name: The Hacienda Todos Los Santos is located in the palm grove at the end of Avenida Juárez; the Todos Santos Inn is on Calle Topete, with its own wine bar; and the Hacienda Inn Todos Santos is north of town. Details for each are given below.

Hotels, Inns, and Bed-and-Breakfasts

Under US$50: In a dusty but quiet neighborhood in the town's southwestern quarter stands **Hotel Miramar** (Mutualismo at Pedrajo, tel. 612/145-0341, US$30). The two-story L-shaped motel contains 10 clean, small rooms, each with two twin beds. On the premises are a pool, small restaurant, and laundry. It's about a 20-minute walk from the beach via the dirt road to Punta Lobos. Off-street parking is available.

US$50-100: The former Hotel Misión del Pilar got a fresh coat of paint inside and out in 2006 and has opened under new ownership as the (**Maria Bonita Hotel** (Colegio Militar at Hidalgo, tel. 612/145-0114, US$50–60). The office and 12 guestrooms are all on the second floor, above the popular Café Brown. Though rooms are plain, clean off-white walls, new curtains and bedspreads, and comfortable mattresses make for a pleasant stay. Small but clean bathrooms have shower stalls with glass

doors and hot water aplenty. Free and reliable wireless Internet will seal the deal for those who need to get online. A great value, this hotel is a wise choice for budget travelers who need a place to crash for the night. Through-traffic on Mexico 19 passes right by the hotel entrance, so expect to hear trucks and car radios unless you crank the fan on the air conditioner. Rates include tax.

On the road to La Pastora, the **Hacienda Inn Todos Santos** (tel./fax 612/145-0002, US$65–110) is about 2 kilometers from the center of town—a bit inconvenient for those without their own transportation. Amenities include a pool and restaurant/bar. The 14 rooms and suites come with cable TV, air conditioning, and bathrobes. Rates include continental breakfast. Turn right at the El Sol II grocery store to find the inn.

At **Hostería Las Casitas** (Rangel btw Obregón/Hidalgo, tel./fax 612/145-0255, www.lascasitasbandb.com, US$55–90), Canadian artist Wendy Faith has lovingly restored four *chiname* adobe cottages and one four-person suite over the last decade. Set among lush landscaping, rooms are small with low ceilings, one bed, and brightly colored walls and ceilings. Accommodations here are basic but artsy, with hand-painted murals in some rooms and the artist's own glasswork in others. Breakfast includes the B&B's own blend of coffee. An authentic *palo de arco casita* houses the owner's studio. This property was up for sale at last check.

The decade-old **Hotel Santa Rosa** (tel. 612/145-0394, www.hotelsantarosa.com.mx, US$60), on Calle Olachea near the south entrance to town, offers eight large, fairly well-maintained studio units with kitchenettes. Facilities include a good pool, laundry, and enclosed parking. Small discounts are available for long-term stays. The signed turnoff for the Santa Rosa is three blocks south of the Pemex station, after which it's another two blocks west to the hotel. Discounted monthly rates are available.

US$100-150: Set among towering palm, mango, and banana trees, **Jardín de Pilar**

(Pilar btw Topete/Hidalgo, tel. 612/145-0386, www.jardindepilar.com, US$105–120) has two beautifully appointed *casitas* for rent. Details include colorful high-end linens and bamboo accents, as well as wireless Internet.

Behind wrought-iron gates in a palm oasis at the south end of Juárez is **Hacienda Todos Los Santos** (Juárez, tel. 612/145-0547, www. mexonline.com/haciendatodoslossantos.htm). Operated as a hotel with daily housekeeping service, Hacienda Todos Los Santos has expanded to include eight rooms in four guesthouses. The original three guesthouses each have private terrace, fully equipped kitchen, and use of a swimming pool. Choose from Casa Santa Luz (US$185), with an air-conditioned bedroom with a queen-sized bed, TV, VCR, dining/day room with fireplace, living room with fireplace, and spacious bathroom; Casa del Palmar (US$165), a studio suite surrounded by terraces, with a king-sized bed, living area, spacious bathroom with shower and bathtub, and a TV/VCR; or Casita del Encanto (US$125), a studio suite with a queen-sized bed, wet bar, seating area, two patios, and a large bathroom. Access to a kitchen is available when Casita del Encanto is rented together with Casa del Palmar. A new four-bedroom/six-bath house, **Casa de Los Santos,** opened in 2007, has one room (US$125) and three suites (US$225–250), and the whole house rents for US$850/night. The upstairs suites have great views of the surrounding farmland. Owner Karen Rodriguez also rents a two-bedroom brick house with a *palapa* roof, called **Casa San Vicente,** on the corner of Pedrajo and Mutualismo.

US$150-250: The elegant 🇨 **Todos Santos Inn** (Legaspi 33 at Topete, tel./fax 612/145-0040, www.todossantosinn.com, US$125–225) occupies a well-restored, 1880-vintage brick building. The original owner was said to have thrown his cashbox down the hole of an outhouse to keep it from marauding revolutionaries in 1910. Since then the building has served as a school, cantina, and movie house; the faded mural in the foyer dates to the 1930s. Large rooms with high adobe-brick ceilings and private baths are tastefully decorated with Mexican furniture, Saltillo tile, oriental rugs, mosquito nets, and ceiling fans. Larger suites offer sitting areas, private patios, and air conditioning. Common areas include an inviting pool and cozy wine bar called La Copa. Spanish-language instruction is available, either separately or as a package with accommodations (10 hours for US$200).

Before it closed in January 1999, the run-down, two-story **Hotel California** (Juárez btw Morelos/Márquez de León, tel. 612/145-0525, hotelcaliforniareservations@hotmail.com, US$125–200) was the most popular place to stay in Todos Santos for first-time visitors, some of whom mistakenly believed the hotel had some connection with the Eagles' song of the same name. Reopened in 2003, the hotel was beautifully renovated by new owners. It features 11 suites, a pool and garden, restaurant/bar **La Coronela** (see *Food*), and **Emporio Hotel California** (see *Shopping*).

A large outdoor patio set around a lagoon and saltwater swimming pool is the highlight of a stay at the smoke-free **Alegría Inn** (tel. 612/145-0700, www.alegriainn.net, US$125–185). Part bed and breakfast, part camp lodge, the inn is located north of town in a former private residence on the north side of the road leading to Playa La Cachora, off Calle Topete, past the Huerta. The layout works best for guests who like to spend more time outside than in their rooms. Quality sheets and towels, comfortable mattresses, and good lighting compensate for the small size of standard rooms, painted concrete shower stalls, and hard-to-clean fieldstone floors. Rooms are tastefully furnished with rustic Mexican pieces, and a hot breakfast is included in the price. Although the inn itself is quiet and secluded, this is not the place for privacy, as most rooms are steps away from the common kitchen and living room. Sound carries from inside out and outside in. There is a TV in the living room, and wireless Internet was installed but not working at last check. The Todos Santos Inn is a better value at this pricepoint.

Guests of Todos Santos' finest boutique hotel

COURTESY OF POSADA LA POZA, TODOS SANTOS

Posada La Poza

receive a pair of binoculars and field guide to North American birds at check-in. Situated on the shore of a small lagoon, and set in a tropical desert garden, **☎ Posada La Poza** (tel. 612/145-0400, www.lapoza.com) blends the relaxed pace of life in Baja with a Swiss sensibility for quality and efficiency. Hosts Jörg and Libusche Wiesendanger opened the hotel in 2002. Guests stay in one of four garden suites (US$180), two junior suites with private hot tubs (US$240), or the honeymoon suite (US$440). All suites have ocean and lagoon views, air conditioning, and CD player, as well as Swiss linens and hypoallergenic blankets and pillows. Guestrooms and common areas also feature Libusche's oil and acrylic paintings. Splash around in a large saltwater swimming pool, watch for whales from the deck, or borrow a bicycle for a ride into town. And when you've had your fill of the great outdoors, you might give yourself an aromatherapy treatment in the onsite sweat lodge, which is filled with heated lava rocks topped with eucalyptus leaves, rosemary, or other herbs. Internet ac-

cess is available for travelers who can't entirely disconnect from the real world. Rates include continental breakfast; guests of the honeymoon suite also receive a fruit basket and bottle of champagne. The elegant **El Gusto!** restaurant serves hearty Mexican and international dishes like pork loin, rib eye, and lobster (see *Food*). The road to La Poza is well marked: Turn southwest off Degollado (Mexico 19) onto Calle Olachea or Calle Carrillo and follow the blue-and-white signs.

Guesthouses and Vacation Rentals

Several homes in town, most of them owned by American or Canadian expatriates, offer lodgings in cottages adjacent to, in back of, or attached to the principal house. Often the owners are happy to supply information about things to see and do in Todos Santos and environs. Price range US$65–225 for a one bedroom and US$200–400 for two bedrooms.

US$50-100: In a residential section of unpaved streets south of Mexico 19, **The Garden**

Casita (Olachea and Mutualismo, tel./fax 612/145-0129, www.todossantos-baja.com/gardencasita.htm, US$85/395 day/week) is an owner-designed *palapa*-roofed guesthouse with a living area, dining area, kitchenette, bedroom, and patio surrounded by an enclosed courtyard. Wireless Internet as well as weekly and monthly rates are available. Long-term rates include weekly maid service.

In roughly the same neighborhood, **Las Flores Posada** (formerly Jane's Place, Pedrajo and Villarino, tel. 612/145-0216, www.todossantos.cc/lasfloresposada.html, US$55), offers four clean and comfortable apartments on a large, landscaped lot surrounded by a security wall. Three units come with kitchenettes and full-sized refrigerators. Pleasant indoor and outdoor sitting areas are found throughout.

Three blocks from the center of town, north of Mexico 19, **Las Palmas Casitas** (Hidalgo and Huerto, tel./fax 612/145-0213, janeLB3@yahoo.com, US$65–95) consists of two one-bedroom *casitas* and one two-bedroom, two-story *casita,* each with *palapa* roof. All *casitas* are smoke-free. All come with a kitchen, covered patio, tropical gardens, modern amenities, and secure parking.

Across the *huerta,* north of town near Café D'Licia, a fun-loving retired Italian couple, Sandra and Enrico Ugolini, have built several charming one-bedroom *casitas* with separate kitchens, beautiful landscaping, and fabulous ocean views. Gourmet potluck dinners are a tradition for guests and friends alike.

Behind the Pemex, near the sugarcane mill ruins, the **Posada del Molino** (off Rangel, tel. 612/145-0233, www.todossantos.cc/PosadaDelMolino.html, US$75–90) was for sale at last check. The property has four comfortable, air-conditioned studios facing a swimming pool. Each studio sleeps two, and comes with satellite TV, CD player, and fully equipped kitchenettes. Maid service is included, and there are coin-operated laundry facilities on the grounds.

US$100-150: At **Los Colibrís** (tel. 612/145-0780, www.loscolibris.com, US$125), the proprietors of family-run Todos Santos

Eco Adventures have built three guest *casitas* on their hillside property, with stunning ocean views overlooking the freshwater estuary and Posada la Poza resort. Two twin beds in each *casita* can be arranged as a king. Meticulously tiled baths have rain showers and sculpted concrete countertops. Lampposts made of decorative tree trunks, colorful linens, and hummingbird feeders are few of the special touches. Rooms have ceiling fans (no air conditioner), bottled water, and CD players. Outdoor space is limited given the steep incline of the property, but the upper unit has its own balcony, and two others share a furnished patio. Two generations of the Jáuregui family attend to guest needs. (They also run Todos Santos Eco Adventures and manage Casa Colina, a separate stand-alone house with two bedrooms and a kitchen.) Breakfast room service and afternoon margaritas available upon request. The same family has also built **Casa Colina** (tel. 612/145-0780, www.casacolina-ts.com, US$150/890 night/week), a two-story, two-bedroom home located below Los Colibris *casitas* and above Posada la Poza. Large picture windows in the bedrooms and kitchen open to ocean views, while balconies on both bedrooms face the mountains. Each bedroom has a king-size bed with luxury linens, ceiling fan, and its own bath. The casa also has a fully equipped kitchen.

Another longtime Todos Santos property now up for sale, **Annie's Place** (tel. 612/145-0385, anniesplacebaja@yahoo.com, US$100–150/day, US$600–900/week, 3-night min) is north of town, on the north side of the road leading to Playa La Cachora. Casa de Arbol is a unique three-level "tree house" surrounded by coconut palms and mango trees. A perfect retreat for artists and writers, the tree house features a kitchen, sitting area, bathroom, and two patios on the first level. A light, airy bedroom fills the second level, while the third-level open deck boasts views of the ocean and mountains. Long-term stays are encouraged. Casa Amplia is a spacious two-bedroom *palapa*-roofed house with one and a half baths and a great room with fully equipped kitchen and a fireplace. Large covered patios extend the living space into true indoor/outdoor living.

Across the wide arroyo north of town, on the south side of the road leading to Playa La Cachora, the new owners of **Las Puertas** (tel./fax 612/145-0373, www.alaspuertas.com, US$135–175) are continuing to rent several *casitas:* a large two-bedroom, two-bath guesthouse with a fireplace; a smaller one-bedroom guesthouse; and an oceanview suite with a fireplace, all with thick adobe walls, *palapa* roofs, sunny patios, and custom, Baja-style furniture. Surrounded by mango and other fruit trees, all units have gourmet kitchens; one guesthouse comes with a separate, full kitchen while the other two have attached kitchens. Daily maid service is a plus. The beach is a five-minute walk away.

Property Managers

A number of part-time Todos Santos residents rent their houses by the day, week, or month. For current listings and availability, check with **El Centro de Mensajes** (The Message Center), in Hotel California (Avenida Juárez, tel. 612/145-0525, fax 612/145-0288, messagecenter1@yahoo.com); **Su Casa** (Degollado btw Pedrajo/Olachea, cell 612/157-5519, www.sucasa.cc); or **Como El Sol** (11 Hidalgo, tel./fax 612/145-0485, comoelsol@prodigy.net.mx, Mon.–Fri. 10 A.M.–2 P.M.) in the back of Colores de México.

Monthly rentals in town range from around US$400–700 a month for small, local-style cottages with few amenities to US$1,000–3,000 a month for larger, better-furnished houses.

Camping and RV Parks

El Litro RV Park (tel. 612/145-0389), a big dirt lot with 15 RV sites surrounded by palm trees, south of Mexico 19 at the end of Calle Olachea, invites campers and RVers to park alongside full hookups for US$12 a night or US$250 a month—the use of hot showers and clean bathrooms is included. The park also has 30 tent sites (US$8 per night) in an orchard camping area. From El Litro, it's a 15-minute walk to the beach. A washer and dryer were in

the plans at press time. The owners can store your rig for US$40/month.

North of town a maze of sandy roads leads to a string of undeveloped beaches suitable for camping (see *Sights* and *Beaches*). Camping, both free and fee, is also available at several of the beaches south of Todos Santos (see *Pescadero and Vicinity*).

FOOD

For a small town, Todos Santos has a surprising number of places to eat at every budget, though some seem to flourish and die with each successive tourist season.

Alta Cocina Mexicana

On the back patio of a beautifully restored adobe house, **Los Adobes** (Hidalgo btw Juárez/Colegio Militar, tel. 612/145-0203, www.losadobesdetodossantos.com, dail 11:30 A.M.–9 P.M., mains US$15–22), features upscale Mexican cuisine with prices to match. Under new ownership as of 2006, the menu includes grilled fish entrées, chicken mole, and steak fajitas. Visa and MasterCard are accepted.

Posada La Poza on Playa La Cachora features the elegant **El Gusto!** restaurant (tel. 612/145-0453, Fri.–Wed. 11:30 A.M.–4 P.M. and 6–9 P.M.), specializing in Mexican gourmet cuisine. The changing menu features a selection of delicious vegetarian dishes, as well as creative meat and seafood choices; all the produce used is organic and locally grown. Seating is available inside or out, with breathtaking views of the lagoon and ocean. The bar terrace and whale-watching deck are great spots for a sunset cocktail, and service is attentive. Tapas are available most days on the bar terrace.

Mexican

Made famous by a *New York Times* write-up several years ago, **Miguel's** (corner of Degollado and Rangel, daily 8 A.M.–9 P.M., mains US$6–10) has become known for lightly battered chiles rellenos smothered in sautéed tomatoes and onions. A dozen tables

© PAUL ITOI

Todos Santos *tortillería*

are arranged on a sand floor under a *palapa* roof. The garrulous proprietor, Miguel, speaks excellent English and usually takes time to chat with repeat and first-time visitors. The menu also features enchiladas, burritos, and cheeseburgers.

You'll be hard pressed to find anything on the menu over US$6 at **Restaurant La Ramada** (Militar and Obregón, mains US$3–6). This relative newcomer serves tacos, tostadas, and the like in a clean kitchen with friendly service; it's open for breakfast, lunch, and dinner.

On Avenida Juárez opposite Hotel California, **Tequila Sunrise Bar & Grill** (daily 10 A.M.–9 P.M.) is a colorfully decorated, tourist-oriented restaurant featuring home-style Mexican food.

Pancho Banano (Hidalgo 11, tel. 612/145-0885, daily for breakfast, lunch, and dinner, mains US$6–10) across from Los Adobes on Hidalgo, offers standard Mexican food—and real estate pitches—to a mostly gringo clientele.

Seafood

The friendly **Mariscos Mi Costa** (Colegio Militar at Ocampo, daily 10 A.M.–8 P.M., mains US$8–15) is a casual seafood place with a raked sand-floor. The *sopa de mariscos* and *camarón al ajo* are particularly recommended.

Nestled in an alley on Juárez between Topete and Hidalgo is **Fonda El Zaguán,** a popular place specializing in fish tacos, vegetarian tacos, seafood soups, organic salads, and delicious Mexican seafood dishes. Daily specials are shown on a chalkboard out in front. The smoked marlin salad is popular. Closed Sunday.

Open since 1973, the old standby **Restaurant Santa Monica** (tel. 612/145-0204, daily 8 A.M.–9 P.M.), just north of the Pemex station on Mexico 19 (Calle Degollado), serves tasty shrimp, lobster, and carne asada dinners at reasonable prices. Service can be slow, but everything is made from scratch. One of the house specialties is *pollo estilo Santa Monica,* a quarter chicken braised in something akin to barbecue sauce.

WEST CAPE

Popular among locals as well as visitors for fresh seafood, tasty Mexican dishes, and cold beer served in frosted mugs is **Restaurant Las Fuentes** (at Calles Degollado and Colegio Militar, tel. 612/145-0257, Tues.–Sun. 7:30 A.M.–9:30 P.M.). The house specialty is *pescado empapelado,* fish baked in paper with tomatoes, mild chilies, and various other condiments, and the chiles rellenos are the best. This restaurant also offers a full bar. You can dine in the well-lighted indoor seating area or out on the *palapa*-roofed patio, surrounded by three fountains, bougainvillea, and palms. Service is friendly and efficient. Visa and MasterCard are accepted here.

International

Hotel California on Calle Juárez boasts the atmospheric **La Coronela** restaurant/bar (Juárez btw Morelos/Márquez de León, tel. 612/145-0525, daily 7 A.M.–1 A.M., dinner mains US$8–20). Prepared by a Belgian chef, the international menu has some creative dishes, such as almond crusted Pacific oyster tacos and yellowtail in an opal basil ginger coconut sauce. Visa and MasterCard are accepted.

One block south of the park, **Ana San Sushi Bar** (tel. 612/137-9856, Tues.–Sat. 1–9 P.M.) prepares sushi, sashimi, soups, and salads.

Café Luna (Hidalgo and Juárez, Thurs.–Tues. 11 A.M.–3 P.M. and 6–10 P.M.) offers a choice of secluded patio dining as well as indoor seating. The international menu lists tapas such as tomato and goat cheese tarts, Aztec soup, and gazpacho. Entrées include seafood dishes, pasta, chicken stuffed with goat cheese and mushrooms, filet mignon, and beef medallions with peanut sauce. Open in December only, **Suki's** (Hidalgo btw Rangel/Cuauhtemoc, generally Tues.–Sat. 5–9 P.M.) prepares a moderately priced menu of pan-Asian cuisine, with pad Thai, teriyaki, and Korean specialties.

American

Shut Up Frank's (tel. 612/145-0707, www.shutupfranks.com, Mon.–Sat. 10 A.M.–10 P.M., Sun. 10 A.M.–8 P.M.), on Degollado, is a sports bar and grill offering decent American-style dinners such as steak and lobster and a variety of burgers (even veggie), as well as burritos and other Mexican fare.

A little out of town at the northeastern end of Calle Centenario, **Cañada del Diablo** hosts cook-your-own T-bone steak night with all the trimmings (US$14) on Thursdays starting at 5 P.M., and fish-and-chips night (US$7) on Sundays also starting at 5 P.M.

Italian

Housed in a 150-year-old *casona* with 46-centimeter-thick (18-in-thick) adobe walls, the atmospheric **Café Santa Fé** (Centenario 4, tel./fax 612/145-0340, Wed.–Mon. noon–9 P.M.), on Calle Centenario off Márquez de León facing the plaza, is still *the* place to eat and be seen during the December–April high tourist season. The changing, mostly Italian menu emphasizes the use of fresh, local ingredients (including organic vegetables) to produce wood-fired pizza, ravioli (a shrimp and lobster version is the house specialty), pasta primavera, lasagna, fresh seafood, octopus salad, and the occasional rabbit. Complementing the menu are espresso drinks, a full wine list, tiramisu, and fresh fruits. Choose between interior tables or courtyard dining amid palm greenery. Prices match the café's aristocratic flair, starting at US$18 and going all the way up to US$40 for rabbit, which you must order four days in advance. The Santa Fé often closes in October during the town fiesta.

Around the corner from Todos Santos Eco Adventures, **Tres Gallines** (Topete and Juárez, tel. 612/145-0274, Mon.–Sat. noon–10 P.M.) serves northern Italian fare, including homemade pasta and imported espresso, at more reasonable prices. New in 2007, **Buena Vida,** in a historical brick building on Calle Centenario next to Mangos, opened to rave reviews for its dinner menu of pizzas (US$8), salads, and wines. Another popular newcomer is **Il Giardino** (Degollado btw Olochea/Carrillo, Tues.–Sun. 1–10 P.M.), serving wood-fired thin crust pizza (US$10) and other casual Italian fare.

Antojitos and Fast Food

Several vendors in town offer inexpensive but tasty fish tacos—usually either shark or dorado—and shrimp tacos. **Tres Hermanos** vendor stand at the corner of Márquez de León and Juárez is among the best. Tres Hermanos sells especially good fish, shrimp, and clam tacos 8 A.M.–2 P.M. most days, sometimes longer depending on the season.

Just outside of town, heading north toward La Paz is the friendly **Antojitos Veracruzanos,** featuring Veracruz-style *antojitos* such as chicken or beef *empanadas* (turnovers), *sopes, gorditas,* and tamales.

Near the southwest corner of Juárez and Hidalgo in the center of town, **Tacos Chilakos** (Mon.–Sat. 9 A.M.–9 P.M., mains US$4–6) serves dependable carne asada, tacos, quesadillas, *machaca* burritos, and coffee at a few outdoor tables on the sidewalk. *Papas rellenas* (stuffed potatoes) are available in the evening.

Local Mexican residents praise (**Barajas Tacos** (Wed.–Mon. 8 A.M.–11 P.M.), on Degollado (Mexico 19) toward the south edge of town, for serving authentic *carnitas* and *tacos de pescado y camarones* during the day and *tacos de carne asada* and *papas rellenas* at night.

At least three or four hot dog vendor carts roll out in the evening—usually one each on Juárez, Colegio Militar, and Degollado. Most sell only turkey dogs—often wrapped in bacon (ask for *sin tocino* if you don't want the bacon wrap).

Cafés

Attention to detail and a love of improvisation set (**Café Brown** (Hidalgo and Militar, tel. 612/145-0813, Tues.–Sun. 7:30 A.M.–9 P.M., mains US$4–9) apart from your average small-town café. Enjoy a limited menu of home-style cooking made from quality ingredients (Sonora beef, breads from a bakery in La Paz) while you check your email on the fastest wireless connection in town (US$2/hr). Friendly and attentive service sets the tone; good music completes the experience. Art that doesn't have permanent gallery space often finds a home here. And from informal cooking classes and independent films to percussion instruction and

salsa dancing, owners Ekerd and his wife love to throw a good party. Look for Café Brown in the back of the Maria Bonita Hotel (formerly Hotel Misión del Pilar) complex.

Above the Costa Azul Surf Shop, **Vonn Café** (Juárez near Hidalgo, mains US$4–6) is a second-story café with a small patio overlooking the busy street below. Tasty sandwiches come on soft, lightly toasted rolls with crispy lettuce and fresh tomato. Salads and smoothies are other options.

The smell of homemade bread wafts out of **Caffé Todos Santos** (Centenario 33, tel. 612/145-0300, Mon. 7 A.M.–2 P.M., Tues.–Sun. 7 A.M.–9 P.M., mains US$6–12) in the morning. Housed in a historic building on Centenario between Topete and Obregón, the café offers indoor seating, on chairs painted by local artists, or outdoor dining, either in the garden area out back or on the shaded veranda in front. The café offers excellent cappuccino and other coffee drinks, hot chocolate, fresh pastries, waffles, omelets, deli sandwiches (smoked turkey is a specialty), vegetarian sandwiches, ice cream, bagels, granola, fruit shakes (made with produce from the owner's farm), fresh-baked bread, salads, and other snacks. Delicious cheesy pizzas are available 5–9 P.M. on Friday only. Prices are a little high by local standards, but so is the quality of the food, and portions are large.

On the plaza next to Café Santa Fé, the **Santa Fé Deli** (tel./fax 612/145-0301, Wed.–Mon. 8 A.M.–3 P.M., mains US$4–9) serves waffles for breakfast, cobb salad, soup, and other light fare for lunch. The deli gourmet market stays open till 6 P.M. Walk through the Galería Santa Fe to get to the deli.

Worth a two-kilometer drive to *el otro lado,* the other side of town, (**Café D'licia** (tel. 612/145-0862, Thurs.–Sun. 8:30 A.M.–2:30 P.M., mains US$5–12) in the Las Brisas area off Calle Topete, serves the best homemade cinnamon rolls and sticky buns on the peninsula, plus a full menu of breakfast and lunch specials, from eggs and pancakes to enchiladas and chiles rellenos. Drinks include smoothies, espresso, and fresh-squeezed juice.

Breads, salsas, and sauces are all homemade. This is a great place to bring young kids who like animals, as the owners rescue exotic birds, some of which have learned to speak a few words of Spanish. To find D'licia, follow Calle Topete past the Todos Santos Inn, across the lush *huerte,* past the primary school and into the dirt road that leads to Playa La Pastora. After the El Sol II market, look for a sign and driveway on the left.

If all you need is a cup of coffee, look for **Café Combate** on Juárez (Mexico 19) on the way to La Paz.

En Route to La Paz

If you're heading to La Paz along Mexico 19 and need a cup of java or a bite to eat, consider stopping off at **Lonchería La Garita** (daily 6 A.M.–6 P.M.), near Km 29, about 22.5 kilometers (14 mi) northeast of Todos Santos. With its large *palapa* roof and open-front *carrizo* eating area, it looks much like any other Baja highway truck stop. But the family operating La Garita seems to have a special flair for preparing humble but high-quality fare. The fresh ranch cheese and the bean or *machaca* burritos with *panela* are superb here, as are empanadas filled with slightly sweet, cinnamon-spiced *frijolitos.* Yet another major draw is the coffee, made from fresh-roasted and fresh-ground Chiapas beans; many people buy bags of coffee beans from La Garita.

Groceries

The usual assortment of staples can be bought at any of several markets in town, which include: **Mercadito Guluarte** (next to Hotel Guluarte), **Tienda Disconsa** (Calle Colegio Militar), **Super Mercado Hermanos González** (Calle Pedrajo), and **Supermercado El Sol** (Calle Degollado).

The friendly **Super Mercado Hermanos González,** off Mexico 19 at the south end of town on Calle Pedrajo, has the usual *tienda* items but also caters to the northern population by stocking such items as nonfat milk, bagels, yogurt, ricotta cheese, and balsamic vinegar, to name a few. Special orders are welcome. The larger **Supermercado El Sol** also stocks gringo items and is open until 10 P.M. A second El Sol is on the road to Playa La Pastora one block west of Hacienda Inn Todos Santos.

La Siempre Viva, at Calles Juárez and Márquez de León, opens around 7 A.M., which is an hour or two earlier than the others. La Siempre Viva stocks household wares and a few ranch supplies as well as groceries; the meats, cheeses, produce, and honey sold here come from local farms and ranches.

The government-subsidized **ISSSTE Tienda** (Juárez btw Zaragoza/Morelos) offers an ever-changing selection of inexpensive groceries and holds a fairly well-stocked pharmacy.

Panadería Todos Santos (Mon.–Sat. 2–8 P.M. or until sold out) sells *bolillos, pan dulce, coyotes, arepas,* and other Mexican-style baked goods cooked in the wood-fired oven, as well as *pan salado,* an Italian-style loaf. The bakery operates from an unsigned two-story brick building at the north end of Calle Rangel near Ocampo.

You can buy fresh and inexpensive corn tortillas for about US$0.50 per kilo at the **Tortillería de Todos Santos** (Colegio Militar btw Morelos/Márquez de León). Fresh seafood can often be purchased from the *pangeros* at Punta Lobos, south of town.

All the various *tiendas* mentioned here sell purified water in *garafónes,* 20-liter returnable containers, as well as the usual smaller-sized bottles. Beer is available from any market in town or from the *depositos* on Calle Colegio Militar adjacent to the post office; on Calle Degollado near the gas station; and also on Calle Degollado next to Super Pollo. Ice is available at most *tiendas,* as well as at the ice plant on Mexico 19 on the southern outskirts of town, and at beer *depositos.*

Fresh tropical fruits—mangoes, guavas, figs—are most abundantly available during the July–September rainy season, although certain fruits, such as papaya, are available year-round. Fresh vegetables peak in January and February. **Huerta Tropical,** on Colegio Militar across the street from Paletería la Paloma, sells locally grown produce in season.

Homemade ice cream can be found at **Paletería la Paloma** (daily 8 A.M.–9 P.M.), on Colegio Militar next to Hotel Maria Bonita, along with refreshing fresh-fruit *paletas* (popsicles). You may see pushcart vendors selling the *paletas* around town. A second location, **Paletería la Paloma 2,** is opposite the Pemex. **Nevería Rocco** (Hidalgo btw Centenario/Juárez), a small shop in a pink house, sells Carnation ice cream and *paletas.*

Just north of town on the way to La Paz, along the east side of Mexico 19, vendors sell candies and pastries made from local produce. Among the goodies available are tasty empanadas made from mango, guava, and *cajete* (goat milk caramel); *panocha* (brown-cane-sugar cakes); lemon peel and coconut candies; wild honey; and refreshing sugarcane juice.

INFORMATION AND SERVICES
Tourist Assistance

Although Todos Santos has no tourist office as such, you can usually find someone to answer your questions at El Tecolote Libros, El Centro de Mensajes, Eco Adventures, or Caffé Todos Santos. If you speak Spanish and seek information on the sierra backcountry, try La Siempre Viva at Calles Juárez and Márquez de León; this is where sierra ranchers traditionally come to supplement foods they produce at home.

The locally produced *El Calendario de Todos Santos* (www.todossantos-baja.com), issued monthly, is an excellent source of current events and short articles on regional culture; it's distributed free at El Centro de Mensajes, El Tecolote Libros, and many other establishments in town. *El Mirador* is a smaller, bilingual publication (tel. 612/145-0559, www.elmirador.tv) with much of the same, plus an online phone directory.

The Todos Santos Book, written by local residents Lee Moore and Janet Howe and available at El Tecolote Books, contains lots of information on things to see and do in the area.

Medical Services

The local emergency number for police, fire, and Red Cross is tel. 612/145-0445. The Centro de Salud (tel. 612/145-0095) is located on Mexico 19, at the corner of Juárez and Degollado.

Pharmacies

Farmacia Guadalupe (Av. Juárez, tel. 612/145-0300) can fill prescriptions any time of day or night. Other pharmacies in town include **Farmacia Hipocrates,** on Morelos opposite Mercado Guluarte, and **Farmacia Similares,** in the Hotel Maria Bonita complex, which offers discounted generic versions of most prescriptions.

Money-Changing

BANORTE, on Calles Juárez at Obregón, is open Monday–Friday 9 A.M.–2 P.M. To cash travelers checks or exchange dollars here you need to show your passport. A 24-hour *cajero* (ATM) is available outside the bank. Instructions are in English and Spanish, but the machine dispenses only pesos.

Post and Telephone

The post office in Todos Santos is literally a one-man operation. Located on Colegio Militar (Mexico 19) between Hidalgo and Márquez de León, it's supposed to open Monday–Friday 8 A.M.–1 P.M. and 3–5 P.M., but the hours can be erratic, since the manager is often out delivering mail.

Long-distance phone calls can be made from several Ladatel phones around town, including one on Hidalgo near Tecolote Books. **El Centro de Mensajes Todos Santos (The Message Center),** Juárez in the lobby of Hotel California (Apdo. Postal 48, Todos Santos, BCS 23305, tel. 612/145-0033, fax 612/145-0288, messagecenter1@yahoo.com, Mon.–Fri. 8 A.M.–3 P.M., Saturday 8 A.M.–2 P.M.), can give you a quick and honest rate comparison between TelMex, AT&T, MCI, and other telephone companies. The office charges a reasonable surcharge over whichever long-distance service you choose. In addition to long-distance calling, this office offers fax, DHL courier, mail forwarding, reservations, travel agency, and answering services.

For mobile phone needs, two Telcel stores are located on Militar, between Hidalgo and Degollado.

Internet Access

Many Todos Santos guesthouses and hotels now have wireless Internet service. In addition, **Café Brown** (Hidalgo and Militar, tel. 612/145-0813, Tues.–Sun 7:30 A.M.–9 P.M.) in the Hotel Maria Bonita complex has high speed access on its own PC or via a wireless connection. The **Todos Santos Internet Café** (Juárez at Topete, tel. 612/145-0219, Mon.–Sat. 9 A.M.–5 P.M.), in the Milagro Real Estate office, has five desktop stations and two Ethernet connections for laptops.

Pemex

There is a Pemex in town located at the intersection of Militar and Degollado (Mexico 19), and a new one at Km 50–51 on the way north to La Paz.

Laundry

The *lavandería* (tel. 612/145-0006, daily 8 A.M.–6 P.M.) on Juárez in the Hotel Guluarte, offers wash-and-dry service for about US$4 per load; for US$0.50 less you can do it yourself. Hot water and soap are available. **Neptune Laundry** on Colegio Militar, is similar.

Language Courses

Guillermo Bueron (tel. 612/145-0119, g_bueron@yahoo.com) offers one-hour **Spanish, English,** and **French lessons** at the Centro Cultural. Guillermo uses the Berlitz total-immersion method of instruction. Group and individual classes are available at all levels.

Hardware Store

Ferre Todos Santos (Zaragoza at Rangel, tel. 612/145-0565, Mon.–Sat. 8 A.M.–2 P.M. and 3–6:30 P.M.) has employees who speak English, and stocks a decent selection of hardware goods. **Ferreteria Oasis de Todos Santos** (Rangel at Zaragoza, tel. 612/145-0754, Mon.–Fri. 8 A.M.–3 P.M. and 4–7 P.M., Sat. 8 A.M.–4 P.M.) has fishing supplies, as well as plumbing and electric parts.

BACKGROUND

The Land

BIRTH OF A PENINSULA

Baja California is the world's fourth-longest peninsula after the Kamchatka, Malay, and Antarctic. Today the peninsula is separated from mainland Mexico by roughly 250 kilometers (155 mi) of ocean at the widest gap, but it wasn't always so. At one time its entire length was attached to a broad tropical plain along Mexico's Pacific coast; about two-thirds of the area lay beneath the ocean. The 23-ton duck-billed hadrosaur roamed the region (its fossilized bones have been found near El Rosario), as did the mammoth, bison, hyracotherium (a small, primitive horse), and camel. The peninsula's eventual divergence from the mainland came about as a result of the continual shifting of massive sections of the earth's surface, a process known as plate tectonics.

Like much of coastal California to the north, Baja California is part of the North Pacific Plate, while the rest of the North American continent belongs to the North American Plate. The boundary line between these two plates is the San Andreas Fault, which extends northward through the center of Mexico's Sea of Cortez and into California, where it parallels the coast on a southeast-northwest axis before veering off into the Pacific Ocean near San Francisco. The North Pacific and North American Plates have shifted along this gap for

© PAUL ITOI

millions of years, with the Pacific Plate moving in a northwesterly direction at a current rate of about 2–5 centimeters (1–2 in) a year.

This movement eventually tore basins in the earth's crust that allowed the Sea of Cortez to form, thus separating the land area west of the fault zone from land to the east. At one time the Sea of Cortez extended as far north as Palm Springs, California; the sea would have continued moving northward at a gradual pace had it not met with the Colorado River. Silting in the Colorado River delta reversed the northward movement of the basins, holding the northern limit of the Sea of Cortez at a point well below what is now the U.S.–Mexico border. Cut off by delta sedimentation, California's Salton Sea is a remnant of the northernmost extension of the Sea of Cortez.

As the peninsula moved slowly northwestward (257 km from the mainland by the time the Sea of Cortez became a stable feature—about five million years ago), the coastal plains tipped toward the west, creating a series of faultblock mountain ranges that now form one of Baja California's most outstanding topographic features. Volcanism further contributed to the peninsular and island geography, as seen in the massive lava flows east of San Ignacio (where the Tres Vírgenes volcanoes erupted as recently as 1746), the basaltic geology south of Bahía de los Ángeles, the various cinder cones near San Quintín, and the volcanic islands of Isla Raza, Isla Guadalupe, and Isla San Luis. At Laguna de los Volcanes in northeastern Baja, boiling mud pits and steam vents are the most visible signs of recent volcanic activity.

A third topographical contributor, sedimentation, has created the salient features of Baja's larger valleys and southwestern coastal plains. Prehistoric Mexican rivers, cut off from their mainland sources upon the creation of the Sea of Cortez, deposited sediments west of Mexicali to form the vast Laguna Salada. The fertile Valle de Mexicali, like California's Imperial Valley, holds silt from the Colorado River—much of it composed of earth and rock once contained in the Grand Canyon. The low coastal plain that forms the western portion of the Vizcaíno Desert region features sedimentary deposits up to 16 kilometers (10 mi) thick, a combination of sierra river deposits and material left over from the period 15 million years ago when this area lay beneath the Pacific Ocean.

GEOGRAPHY
Size and Area
Baja California extends 1,300 kilometers (806 mi) from the U.S.–Mexico border to the peninsula's southernmost tip—a hundred miles longer than Italy and twice the length of Florida. If the coastline could be straightened, it would span a distance equivalent to that between Tijuana and Juneau, Alaska. Its widest girth, measured across land only, is at the 193-kilometer (120-mi) border. Measuring across land and water to include Bahía de Sebastián Vizcaíno, the widest point is about 230 kilometers (143 mi), from Punta Eugenio on the west coast to Punta San Francisquito on the east. The peninsula reaches its narrowest point at a section 161 kilometers (100 mi) above the southern tip, where it's only 45 kilometers (28 mi) between the Pacific Ocean and Bahía de la Paz.

The total land area of the states of Baja California (or Baja California Norte) and Baja California Sur is about 144,000 square kilometers (55,600 sq mi)—add another 2,460 square kilometers (950 sq mi) for the dozens of islands and islets nearby. The coastline created by the Pacific Ocean, the Sea of Cortez, and the dozens of bays, lagoons, coves, and inlets totals about 4,800 shore kilometers (3,000 mi).

Mountains
Baja's most striking geographical feature is the spine of mountain ranges, or sierras, that runs down its center from northwest to southeast. For the most part, Baja's sierras are a continuation of a mountain system that stretches southward from Alaska's Aleutian Islands to the spectacular rock formations at Cabo San Lucas. The peninsula holds 23 named ranges in all; most are of fault-block origin, but a scattered few are volcanic.

Because of the way the underground fault blocks tipped to create these sierras, the moun-

MAJOR BAJA CALIFORNIA MOUNTAIN RANGES

RANGE	HIGHEST PEAK	SUMMIT ELEVATION
Sierra de San Pedro Mártir	Picacho del Diablo	3,095 meters (10,154 ft)
Sierra de la Laguna	Picacho de la Laguna	2,161 meters (7,090 ft)
Sierra de San Francisco	Pico Santa Monica	2,104 meters (6,904 ft)
Sierra San Borja	Pico Echeverría	1,907 meters (6,258 ft)
Sierra Juárez	Cerro Torre Blanco	1,800 meters (5,904 ft)
Sierra de la Giganta	Cerro La Giganta	1,765 meters (5,792 ft)
Sierra de la Asamblea	Cerro Dos Picachos	1,658 meters (5,438 ft)
Sierra de Guadalupe	Monte Thetis	1,640 meters (5,380 ft)

tains tend to slope gradually toward the west and fall off dramatically toward the east (the Cape Region's Sierra de la Laguna is the one major exception). Like California's Sierra Nevada, Baja's high sierras typically feature granitic peaks topped by conifer forests. The eastern escarpment, facing the Sea of Cortez, is dissected by stream-eroded canyons and usually dry arroyos.

Baja's four most substantial mountain ranges are the **Sierra Juárez** and **Sierra de San Pedro Mártir** in the north, the volcanic **Sierra de la Giganta** in the upper south, and the **Sierra de la Laguna** in the center of the southern Cape. Baja's highest peak, **Picacho del Diablo** (3,095 m/10,154 ft), lies in the Sierra de San Pedro Mártir; during the winter its snowcapped peak can be seen from the Mexican mainland 225 kilometers (140 mi) away.

Deserts

About 65 percent of Baja California's total land area can be classified as desert; these portions receive an average of less than 25 centimeters (10 in) of rain per year. From a botanical perspective, Baja's desert lands belong to the Sonoran Desert, which extends across northwestern Mexico into parts of southeastern California and southern Arizona. However, Baja's portion supports so many endemic plant species that it probably deserves a classification all its own.

Any visitor who has previously traveled in the Sonoran Desert areas of Northern Mexico, southeastern California, or southern Arizona will note many subtle differences in Baja. Because of the peninsula's numerous sierras and its location between two large bodies of water, aridity varies considerably along the peninsula. As a result, Baja's deserts can be divided into four subregions, each distinguished by its own unique geography and dominant flora.

San Felipe Desert: This southwestern extension of California's Colorado Desert is wedged between the eastern escarpment of the northern sierras and the coastal plains of the Sea of Cortez. The peninsula's driest desert, it averages only five centimeters (2 in) of rainfall a year. Most of the topography is a mixture of salt flats, rocky plains, sand dunes, arroyos, and extinct volcanic craters.

The Valle de Mexicali is part of the San Felipe Desert, but it is made productive by an irrigation system fed by the Colorado River. The large Isla Ángel de la Guarda and nearby islands also belong to this region. The dominant plant species throughout the sparsely vegetated area are bursage (*huizapol*) and creosote bush (*hediondilla*), along with a variety of succulents and hardy trees.

Gulf Coast Desert: This narrow subregion stretches along the Sea of Cortez from just below Bahía de los Ángeles to the tip of the peninsula near San José del Cabo. On average, the elevation is substantially higher here (with peaks up to 1,500 m/5,000 ft) than in the San Felipe Desert to the north, and the terrain is marked by several broken sierras of granitic and volcanic rock. These sierras contain numerous arroyos and a few perennial streams that allow for pockets of subsistence farming. The underground stream at Mulegé supports intensive cultivation in the surrounding valley.

The southern reaches of the Gulf Coast Desert receive a bit of extra precipitation from the occasional tropical storm that blows in from the south. As a result of the added moisture and elevation, many more trees and flowering cacti are found here than in the San Felipe Desert, including *torote, palo blanco, paloverde, palo adán,* and *palo de arco.* Sea of Cortez islands to the east feature similar terrain, although the endemic vegetation varies from island to island.

Vizcaíno Desert: After a worldwide search for the perfect desert habitat, the designers of **Biosphere II,** an ecological research laboratory in Arizona, modeled their dome's desert biome on the Vizcaíno Desert. Baja's largest desert area, this subregion lies along the Pacific coast from a point just north of El Rosario to the Magdalena Plains some 1,000 kilometers (600 mi) south. Its eastern boundary is the eastern escarpment of the central sierras. This positioning places it just out of reach of the northwestern rains, so important to coastal California and northwestern Baja, as well as the southern tropical storms that bring water to the Cape Region and lower Gulf Coast Desert. In 1988 a large portion of the Vizcaíno Desert was declared a Biosphere Reserve under the United Nations' Man and the Biosphere program.

In spite of the lack of measurable precipitation, desert plants proliferate here. The entire region is sparsely populated because of the lack of dependable water sources, but the desert vegetation, especially yucca, thrives on night and morning fog from the Pacific Ocean. The whimsical-looking *cirio* (called "boojum tree" by many Californians) is another dominant succulent in the Vizcaíno Desert; toward the Pacific coast it's often draped with ball moss. Other common species here include agave, mesquite, cholla, prickly pear, and *pitahaya.*

The major coastal feature in this subregion is Laguna Ojo de Liebre, also called Scammon's Lagoon, one of several bays favored by wintering gray whales. The most substantial inland water source is the Río San Ignacio, which flows westward from a large date palm oasis in the heart of the peninsula into the open desert near the coast.

Magdalena Plains (Llano Magdalena): Beginning below the Vizcaíno Desert and bounded by the Pacific coast on the west and by the central and southern sierras on the east, the Magdalena Plains extend southward until they come to an abrupt halt at the northwestern escarpment of the Sierra de la Laguna. The main feature of the Pacific side is Bahía Magdalena, Baja's largest bay, which is sheltered by the huge, L-shaped Isla Magdalena to the northwest and the equally large Isla Santa Margarita to the southwest. The Canal Gaviota connects Bahía Magdalena with Bahía Almejas to the immediate south. Other saltwater bays and lagoons along the Pacific coast include Bahía de Ballenas and Laguna San Ignacio; all are used as calving areas by migrating whales.

Other coastal features include mangrove swamps, dunes, and small sandbar islands. The only inland waterway of note is the Río La Purísima, which drops westward from the Sierra de la Giganta to Punta San Gregorio on the Pacific coast. Large underground aquifers in the vicinity of Ciudad Constitución support intensive area agriculture. The aquifer is becoming increasingly saline, however, as freshwater is pumped out faster than it's replenished. Arroyos on the west side of the Sierra de la Giganta supply water to the area when rainfall is sufficient.

Cactus varieties are abundant throughout the Magdalena Plains. Stands of date palm, paloverde, *torote,* mesquite, and palo blanco line the riverine corridors and upland arroyos.

The Vizcaíno Desert and the Magdalena Plains are sometimes referred to as one entity, the **Central Desert.**

Californian Region

Most of northwestern Baja California features the same topography, climate, and ecosystems as southwestern California. These conditions extend almost as far south as El Rosario, near the Pacific coast, and eastward to the eastern escarpment of the Sierra Juárez and Sierra de San Pedro Mártir. Within this region are four subregions, for the most part defined by changes in elevation from the coast to the highest mountain peaks in the center of the peninsula.

Conifer Forests: This subregion begins at an elevation of about 1,500 meters (5,000 ft) in the Sierra Juárez and from about 2,400 meters (8,000 ft) in the Sierra de San Pedro Mártir. The granitic substrata of these faultblock mountains becomes more apparent the higher you go, as rocky ledges poke through soil and sediment accumulated over the eons. Abundant precipitation supports lush forests and meadows along the flats, ridges, and plateaus of both ranges. In winter, snow is the most common source of moisture in the higher elevations; peaks are often snowcapped.

Dominant trees in the Sierra Juárez include the canyon live oak, juniper, piñon pine, and Jeffrey pine. The forests of the Sierra de San Pedro Mártir also feature incense cedar, white fir, and sugar pine, and at least three tree types not found in either the Sierra Juárez or San Diego County, California: quaking aspen, lodgepole pine, and the endemic San Pedro Mártir cypress. Along the streams and meadows at slightly lower elevations are manzanita, Indian paintbrush, hedgehog cactus, snowberry, and other flowering plants.

Pine-Juniper-Oak Woodlands: On the intermediate slopes of the two sierras, at elevations of about 900–1,500 meters (3,000–5,000 ft), are stands of pine, oak, and juniper. The lower southern reaches of the Sierra de San Pedro Mártir offer a Darwinian salad of conifer, chaparral, and desert species, mixing pines and juniper with blue fan palm, Mojave yucca, palmita, sagebrush, sand verbena, and barrel cactus.

Chaparral: At just below 900 meters (3,000 ft) on either side of the mountain ranges, the woodlands give way to chaparral, a dense shrub community that supports sagebrush, scrub oak, wild lilac, manzanita, coast live oak, chaparral ash, and other hardy species with deep-branching root systems. Interspersed with the chaparral are boulders of varying size; some of the larger are used as billboards by *bajacalifornianos,* who paint them with political slogans, declarations of love, and religious messages.

Palm Canyons: These lie at chaparral elevation on the eastern slopes, but because of abundant water year-round they feature unique terrain. Eroded by mountain streams that terminate in the San Felipe Desert, these canyons and steep-walled arroyos shelter picturesque groves of California fan palm and endemic blue fan palm. Volcanic activity on the peninsula's eastern side has resulted in underground geothermal reservoirs; hot springs are found in some of the canyons.

Coastal Sage Scrub: On the Sea of Cortez side of the northern mountain ranges, the chaparral subregion gives way to the arid San Felipe Desert. On the Pacific side, chaparral fades into the rolling hills of the coastal plains. The terrain is rocky, with a blend of chaparral vegetation and the low-lying shrubs that dominate the coastal sage-scrub biome. Common species include chamiso, barrel cactus, agave, ash, cholla, flat-top buckwheat, hedgehog cactus, jimsonweed, margarita, buckeye, jojoba, saltbush, and a variety of grasses.

Cape Region

In many ways, Baja California's Cape Region has the most distinctive geography on the peninsula. The Sierra de la Laguna, in the center of the Cape, runs north to south rather than northwest to southeast. And unlike other ranges in the southern half of the peninsula, it's granitic rather than volcanic. Yet in contrast to the granitic, fault-block ranges of northern Baja, it tips eastward so that its steepest slopes face west. It's also more lushly vegetated than the northern sierras. Arroyos on the eastern slopes of the Sierra de la Laguna are filled with water much of the year, enabling this area to support fruit and vegetable farming.

The entire region receives substantially more rainfall than any other part of Baja, save the Californian Region in the northwest. Most of the rain falls in the highland areas, however, leaving the coastal lowlands fairly dry for beach-going tourists. About a fourth of the Cape Region falls below the Tropic of Cancer; the combination of dry coastal areas, moist uplands, and tropical latitudes has created two unique subregions.

Cape Oak-Piñon Woodlands: The Sierra de la Laguna has been called an "island in the sky" because of its remarkable isolation from the Central Desert to the north and the Gulf Coast Desert to the east. The peaks receive up to 100 centimeters (40 in) of annual rainfall; extensive stands of Mexican piñon pine, *madroño,* and *palmita* grow at higher elevations. Oaks are also found on the higher slopes of the Sierra de la Giganta to the north, which also falls within the Cape Region.

Cape Arid Tropical Forest: The coastal areas of the Cape Region as well as the lower slopes of the region's sierras share characteristics typical of both tropical and arid biomes, hence the seemingly oxymoronic term "arid tropical forest." Like tropical forests worldwide, the lower Cape forests hold trees, shrubs, and undergrowth of varying heights that create a canopied effect. Mixed with this tangled growth is a profusion of succulents more associated with arid climes, including the *cardón-barbón,* a shorter cousin of the towering *cardón* found throughout Baja's deserts.

Much of the vegetation in the Cape Arid Tropical Forest is normally associated with the tropical thornforests of coastal Colima and Guerrero on the Mexican mainland. Prominent marker plants unique to the Cape subregion include the native Tlaco palm, wild fig *(zalate), mauto,* and the alleged aphrodisiac herb damiana.

Coastal Wetlands Region

Wetland pockets exist in numerous spots along the peninsular coast; they lie in shallow areas along bays and lagoons and aren't limited to any particular longitude or latitude. In Baja, these wetlands usually consist of salt marshes (which contain high concentrations of salt-tolerant plants such as cordgrass, eelgrass, saltwort, and salt cedar) or mangrove *(mangle)* communities containing one or more of the five species common in Baja—black mangrove, white mangrove, red mangrove, buttonwood mangrove, and sweet mangrove. Within any given wetland, salinity, temperature, and wetness can vary considerably; hence, an extensive variety of plants and animals can adapt to wetland areas. Because of this environmental variation, salt marshes and mangrove wetlands support the highest biomass concentrations on the planet. For most visitors, the main attraction of the wetlands is the abundance of waterfowl.

Areas with substantial wetlands include Bahía San Quintín (salt marshes), Laguna Ojo de Liebre (saltwater estuarine marshes), Laguna San Ignacio (salt marshes, mangrove forests), Bahía Magdalena (salt marshes, mangrove forests), Bahía de la Paz (mangrove forests), Río Mulegé (mixed saltwater/freshwater estuarine marshes), Estero San Bruno (mangrove forests), Bahía de los Ángeles (salt marshes, some mangrove), and Bahía San Luis Gonzaga (salt marshes).

Islands

More than a hundred islands and islets surround the Baja peninsula, with the great preponderance on the Sea of Cortez side. Accounting for more than half of Mexico's island territory, the Sea of Cortez islands comprise one of the most ecologically intact archipelagos in the world. Many of them were created as the peninsula broke away from mainland Mexico and hence are "land-bridge" or "continental" islands rather than true oceanic islands. Because of their low elevation, these islands don't snag much of the rain that moves up from the south in summer. As a result, they're arid, although the larger islands harbor a number of endemic plant and animal species. Among the largest of these islands are Isla Ángel de la Guarda, Isla Espíritu Santo, and Isla Cerralvo. The smaller Isla San Luis and Isla Raza are of volcanic origin. Isla Raza is one of the most important bird rookeries in Mexico and has been a national reserve since 1964.

On the Pacific side, Baja's islands tend to feature semimoist Californian Region climates on their northwestern (windward) shores and desert conditions on their southeastern (leeward) shores. Isla Guadalupe, about 250 kilometers (155 mi) west of the Pacific coast, is one of the few islands of volcanic (therefore, oceanic) origin. It's rarely visited by cruising boats because of its steep (up to 450 meters) shores but is an important habitat for the endemic Guadalupe fur seal and northern elephant seal, as well as various species of endemic pine, cypress, and palm.

Other Pacific islands of note are the Islas de Todos Santos, just 16 kilometers (10 mi) southwest of Ensenada. These twin isles are well known among surfers for having the highest surf—up to nine meters (30 ft) high in winter—on the entire North American west coast. The state of Baja California has five inhabited islands, while Baja California Sur counts six. The most populated are Isla San Marcos in the Sea of Cortez—where gypsum mining and fishing support a population of around 590—and Isla Cedros, north of the Vizcaíno Peninsula in the Pacific, where a transshipment port for salt from the huge Guerrero evaporative saltworks employs many of the island's nearly 3,000 inhabitants.

THE SEA OF CORTEZ

The Sea of Cortez was apparently named by Spanish sea captain Francisco de Ulloa after he sailed the entire perimeter of this body of water in 1539 and 1540 at the command of the most famous of all Spanish conquistadors, Hernán Cortés. Four years previously Cortés himself had sailed the sea in an aborted attempt to colonize the peninsula. The name Mar de Cortés henceforth appeared intermittently on maps of the region, alternating with Mar Vermejo (Vermillion Sea, in reference to the color reflected

from huge numbers of pelagic crabs) until the Mexican government officially renamed it the Gulf of California (Golfo de California) early in the 20th century. Sailors, writers, and other assorted romantics, however, have continued to call it by its older name.

The sea is roughly 1,125 kilometers (700 mi) long, with an average width of 150 kilometers (93 mi). Oceanographers have divided it into four regions based on the prominent characteristics—depth, bottom contours, and marine productivity—of each zone. The northern quarter of the gulf, between the Colorado River delta and the Midriff Islands, is shallow in relation to the zones farther south because of silt deposited by the Colorado River. The silt has also rounded the bottom contours. The tidal range in this zone is up to 10 vertical meters (33 vertical ft), and the seawater is highly saline due to evaporation. Before the damming of the Colorado River, the bore created when the seaward river currents met the incoming tide was powerful enough to sink ships.

The next zone farther south encompasses the Midriff Islands, where basins reach depths of 820 meters (2,700 ft) and strong currents bring nutrients up from the bottom while aerating the water. This leads to an unusually high level of biological productivity, otherwise known as "good fishin'."

From the Midriff Islands to La Paz, basin depth doubles, silting is minimal, and water temperatures begin decreasing dramatically.

The final sea zone below La Paz is oceanic, with trenches and submarine canyons more than 3,650 meters (12,000 ft) deep. Around the tip of the Cape, the Sea of Cortez meets the Pacific Ocean and their respective currents battle, producing some wicked riptides. This means that although the tip of the Cape is the warmest area on the peninsula during the winter months, beach swimming can be treacherous.

Of the 25 named islands in the Sea of Cortez, the largest is Isla Tiburón (Shark Island), a geological remnant of the mainland with an area of around 1,000 square kilometers (386 sq mi). Because of their isolation, the Cortez islands feature a high number of endemic natural species; at least half of the 120 cactus varieties found on the islands are endemic.

The Sea of Cortez is biologically the richest body of water on the planet, supporting more than 900 species of marine vertebrates and more than 2,000 invertebrates at last count. The reported number rises with the publication of each new marine study. Scripps Institution of Oceanography in San Diego, California, has pronounced the Cortez "one of the most productive and diverse marine nurseries on Earth," while at the same time recognizing that greedy commercial interests may be devastating the natural balance in the Cortez through overfishing.

ENVIRONMENTAL ISSUES

The rapid growth of tourism and real estate development, especially in the Los Cabos area, has strained fragile ecosystems up and down the Baja Peninsula. Coastal development threatens mangrove habitat on the Mogote Peninsula near La Paz and the Estero San José. The delicate coral reef offshore from Cabo Pulmo could deteriorate rapidly if the water gets polluted from ongoing beachfront development. Even the pristine islands offshore from La Paz are showing early signs of stress from the increase in camping and organized trips.

On both sides of the peninsula, endangered sea turtles face poaching and loss of habitat for laying eggs. Commercial fishing has taken a toll on other species as well, with prize billfish reportedly now much smaller in size than in the early years of Baja's fishing camps.

Long-term, the scarcity of freshwater and

ECOTOURISM

In recent years, the number of low-impact activities and accommodations throughout the peninsula has increased, giving travelers a way to experience Baja without wreaking havoc on its fragile desert and marine ecosystems. From Bahía de los Ángeles to Loreto to Cabo Pulmo, you'll find solar-powered *casitas*, organic produce, self-sufficient resorts, and proprietors who put the environment first. Bird-watching near San Ignacio, whale-watching in Bahía Magdalena, and sea turtle conservation efforts at Bahía de los Ángeles and around the Cape Region are just a few of the ways to get involved.

ability of municipalities to keep up with water and sewage treatment needs pose another concern. The *Escalera Náutica* project, through which the Mexican government plans to build a network of 10 new ports and expand a dozen existing ports may further disrupt ecosystems and local communities.

Residents and visitors, both Mexican and foreign, are getting involved to help conserve the environment for years to come. For example, Grupo Tortuguero (www.grupotortuguero .org) runs a turtle conservation program in Baja, and Pro Peninsula (www.propeninsula .org) publishes an informative website and quarterly newsletter about Baja's environmental concerns.

Climate

In satellite photographs of the North American continent snapped a hundred miles above the earth, Baja California invariably jumps off the plate. The rest of the continent north and east may be obscured by whorls of clouds while the shores, plains, and mountains of Baja are carved into the photographic image, remarkably clear. According to truth-in-travel magazine *Condé Nast Traveler,* Baja California is the best dollar value per hour of sunshine for any North American area west of Denver; the chances of a day without rain in the winter are 95 percent in Baja, beating out Hawaii's 84 percent and Florida's 87 percent.

How does Baja California get so much sunshine? The simple answer is that it's almost out of reach of the major weather systems that influence climate in western North America. Northwesterly storms from Eurasia and the Arctic bring rain and snow to the American Northwest and Midwest all winter long, while tropical storms roll across the South Pacific from Asia, dumping loads of rainfall along the lower Mexican coast and Central America in summer.

Baja is only slightly affected by the outer edges of these systems. Anchored between the warm, fish-filled waters of the Sea of Cortez and the heaving Pacific Ocean, bisected by plains and cordilleras, the peninsula's isolated ecosystems range in climate from Mediterranean to desert to tropical. In some areas, overlapping microclimates defy classification, combining elements of semiarid, arid, subtropical, and tropical climes.

HOT AND COLD

Three variables influence temperatures at any given Baja California location: elevation, latitude, and longitude. In plain talk, that means the higher you climb, the cooler it gets; the farther south you go, the warmer it gets; and it's usually cooler on the Pacific side of the peninsula and warmer on the Sea of Cortez side.

Pacific Coast

Because of prevailing ocean currents, the Pacific coast shows the least overall variation in temperature, staying relatively cool year-round. From March to July, the California Current flows southward along the coast, bringing cooler temperatures from the north that moderate seasonal atmospheric warming, while in December and January the coast is warmed by the northward movement of the Davidson Current. These seasonal currents stabilize the air temperatures so that Ensenada, for example, averages 12°C (54°F) in January and 20°C (68°F) in August, a range of only 8°C (14°F). Along much of the central Pacific coast during the summer, the cool air brought by the California Current meets warm air from the interior of the peninsula, resulting in fog masses that can sweep as far inland as 32 kilometers (20 mi).

In winter, the southern Pacific coast from Bahía Magdalena to Cabo San Lucas usually enjoys the warmest temperatures of any coastal region on the peninsula because of its relative protection from cool northern winds.

Sea of Cortez

The Sea of Cortez has its own set of currents—sometimes lumped together as the Gulf Current—that are fed by tropical waters of the South Pacific. The waters travel counterclockwise north along the mainland's upper Pacific coast and then south along the peninsular coast. As a result, the Sea of Cortez enjoys an average annual surface temperature of 24°C (75°F), significantly warmer than the Pacific's 18°C (64°F). The high rate of evaporation at the north end of the sea also contributes to warmer air temperatures; this combination of warm air and water temperatures means the Sea of Cortez can be classified as tropical over its entire length.

Temperature differences between winter and summer, however, are more extreme than along the Pacific coast. The weather along the Cortez coast is mild and sunny all winter long with average January temperatures ranging from 13°C (55°F) in San Felipe to 18°C (64°F) in Loreto. Summer temperatures leap up the thermometer. In August, average temperatures are 28°C (82°F) in San Felipe and 31°C (88°F) in Loreto, although daily high figures in the summer, at either locale, can easily reach 38°C (100°F) or more. La Paz is usually warmer than San Felipe but cooler than Loreto.

Winters on the Sea of Cortez coast can be cooler than you might suspect, due to the coastline's relatively open exposure to northeastern winds. In Mulegé and Loreto, for example, it's not unusual for nighttime temperatures in January and February to drop as low as 14°C (57°F). At the same time, the Pacific coastline directly opposite may be as much as 5°C (10°F) warmer, especially along the southern Pacific coast. Cabo San Lucas has the warmest overall winter temperatures of any coastal location in Baja.

Chubascos, Cordonazos, and Coromuels

Monthly average wind velocities for Baja California as a whole are moderate. Mid-May–mid-November, however, tropical storms from the south or east, known as *chubascos,* can bring high winds and rain to the coasts of the Cape Region. Although they usually blow over quickly, local mythology has it that if a *chubasco* lasts more than three hours, it will last a day; if it lasts more than a day, it will last three days; and if more than three days, it'll be a five-day blow.

Occasionally these storms escalate into hurricanes, which are much less frequent here than in the Gulf of Mexico and the Caribbean. In 1997 two such storms passed near the west coast of Baja, neither doing much damage (that same year the Gulf of Mexico saw around a dozen hurricanes), and in 2001 a hurricane hit the Cape, causing some flood damage. Back in 1993 a *chubasco* caused major damage and loss of life along the Sea of Cortez coast between Cabo San Lucas and San José del Cabo (the area of the Cape Region most exposed to tropical storms).

Another Sea of Cortez weather pattern is the *cordonazo,* a small but fierce summer storm that originates locally and is usually spent within a few hours. A more welcome weather phenomenon is the *coromuel* of Bahía de la Paz, a stiff afternoon breeze that blows from offshore during the hot summer and early fall months. This wind was named for English Lord Protector Oliver Cromwell, identified with English pirates who took advantage of the wind's regular occurrence for the plunder of ships trapped in the bay.

WET AND DRY

The Land of Little Rain, as Baja has been called, isn't unique in its aridity, since most of the earth's desert areas are found between 15° and 30° latitude either north or south of the equator; Baja is positioned roughly between 23° N and 31° N. Global convection currents in the atmosphere create a more or less permanent high-pressure shield over these zones, insulating them from the low-pressure fronts that bring rain clouds.

Only about two-thirds of Baja California can be classified as true desert (less than 25 cm/10 in of annual precipitation), and even the driest areas receive occasional rain. In the peninsula's Central Desert this may be as little as 2.5 centimeters (1 in) a year, while in the interior of the Cape Region's Sierra de la Laguna annual rainfall may approach 100 centimeters (40 in). Since mountain peaks trap rain clouds, Baja's higher elevations invariably receive more rain than the low-lying coastal zones.

Variation in rainfall also occurs on a seasonal basis. For the northwestern peninsula, the wettest months are December–April (with about 7.5 centimeters/3 in per month in Ensenada, more in the mountains), while in the Cape Region rain usually arrives August–November (an average of 5.8 cm/2.3 in in September for Cabo San Lucas and La Paz). The central peninsula, including both coasts, is relatively dry all year long, receiving only brief spurts of rain from the north in the winter or from the south in the late summer and early fall.

The driest coastal area in all of Baja lies along the northwestern shores of the Sea of Cortez. San Felipe records an average annual precipitation of only five centimeters, with no measurable rainfall most months. At the other extreme, the peaks of the Sierra de San Pedro Mártir are often covered with a one-meter snowpack during the winter.

Flora

A thorough examination of all the plants and creatures of interest in Baja California would take volumes. The following sections cover only a few of either the most remarkable or most common forms of Baja plant life. The complex interconnecting ecosystems of the peninsula and its islands hold a high number of unique species and remain relatively unexplored by biologists. Several botanists, marine biologists, zoologists, and paleontologists have undertaken solo research in the area, but only in the last five years has the first interdisciplinary team, sponsored by a Canadian university, begun studying the region.

In many ways, these researchers are heir to the Spanish fortune-seeker tradition of nearly five centuries ago. As George Lindsay, director of the California Academy of Sciences, has said, "For the scientist, Baja California is a treasure chest, just barely opened." Botanists estimate that more than 4,000 varieties of plants make Baja California their home. The most complete reference available on Baja vegetation, Dr. Ira L. Wiggins's *Flora of Baja California,* lists 2,958 species among 155 families and 884 genera. Another good source of information is Norman C. Roberts's *Baja California Plant Field Guide,* which covers more than 550 notable species and provides excellent photos of about half of these.

CACTI

Many visitors find the desert plants of Baja the most exciting simply because they're often the most exotic-appearing forms of life in the region. Like Alice in *Through the Looking Glass,* they find that the farther they travel into the interior, the "curiouser and curiouser" the landscape becomes. The seemingly bizarre ap-

pearance of many succulents is due to the evolutionary gymnastics they've had to perform to adapt themselves to an environment where water is scarce.

Around 120 species of cactus have been identified on the peninsula and its surrounding islands, more than anywhere else on the planet. Almost three-fourths are unique to Baja.

Cardón

One of the most common cacti throughout Baja is the towering *cardón (Pachycereus pringlei),* the world's tallest species of cactus. Individuals can reach as high as 18 meters (60 ft) or more and weigh 12 tons, not counting the root system, which can spread up to 50 meters (165 ft) in diameter. More commonly they top out at 7–9 meters (23–30 ft). The giant, pale-green trunks feature 11–17 vertical ribs and may measure one meter thick. Some live more than 400 years.

The *cardón* is often confused with the smaller saguaro cactus of Sonora and Arizona; one major difference is that the branches of the *cardón* tend to be more vertical than those of the saguaro.

The *cardón* is near-endemic to Baja California, found throughout the peninsula—except in the Californian Region—and islands, and also along the coast of Sonora. The hardwood cores of *cardón* columns have been used by *bajacalifornianos* for centuries as building beams and fence posts. Among Baja residents, a *cardón* forest is called a *cardonal.* The state of Baja California Norte sent a 13-meter (43-ft) *cardón* as a gift to the recent Seville World Fair.

Biznaga

Another extremely common and highly visible cactus is the *biznaga,* or barrel cactus (genus

Ferocactus). There are at least 15 species in Baja, most endemic. The cactus's English name refers to its shape, which is short and squat like a barrel. Most common varieties reach about waist-high. One variety, however, *Ferocactus diguettii,* easily reaches four meters (13 ft) in height and a meter (3 ft) in diameter. It grows only on a few Sea of Cortez islands, sporting red-tinged spines and, in spring, gorgeous yellow to red flowers.

The indigenous Amerindians of Baja reportedly used hollowed-out *biznagas* as Dutch ovens, inserting food into the cavity along with heated stones, then sealing off the cactus till the food was cooked. The sturdy, curved spines also served as fishhooks on native fishing expeditions.

Pitahaya

Among Baja's original populations, another important cactus was the *pitahaya dulce,* known among Anglos as organ pipe cactus. It has slender, vertical ribs that grow in clusters, and its spiny, orange-size fruit contains a sweet, juicy, pleasant-tasting pulp the color of red watermelon. According to accounts of Spanish missionaries, the Pericú Amerindians based their yearly calendar on the harvest of the ripe fruit in late summer and early fall. During this season, the Amerindians engaged in a veritable fruit orgy, gorging themselves on the pulp until they fell asleep, then waking to begin eating again. The early Spanish explorers took the fruit along on long sea journeys—its vitamin C content helped to prevent scurvy.

The *pitahaya dulce* is commonly found on the peninsula south of the Sierra de San Borja and on several Sea of Cortez islands. A similar species, *pitahaya agria* (*agria* means sour in Spanish; *dulce* is sweet), branches more densely and lower to the ground, hence its English name, galloping cactus. It grows throughout the peninsula and on most Sea of Cortez islands. The fruit of the *pitahaya agria* is similar in appearance to that of the *pitahaya dulce,* but, as implied by the Spanish name, it's less sweet, more acidic. Both types of *pitahaya* fruit remain popular among Baja residents and travelers; the sweet ones ripen in July.

Opuntia

Another cactus variety well represented throughout Baja is the genus *Opuntia,* which includes all types known as **cholla,** as well as the **nopal,** or prickly pear. Chollas are a bane to Baja hikers because they're so prolific and densely covered with spines. A typical branch looks somewhat like braided or twisted rope. The cholla historically has had few domestic uses, although a tea made from the roots of the fuzzy-looking **teddy-bear cholla** (also called "jumping cholla" for its propensity to cling to the legs of hikers), found along the east coast of the peninsula, is reportedly used by the Seri Amerindians as a diuretic.

In contrast, the much-loved prickly pear has broad, flat stems and branches and a sparser distribution of spines. In Northern Mexico and Baja its fleshy pads are a dietary staple. The most highly prized parts of the nopal are the young stem shoots, called *nopalitos,* and the ripe fruits, dubbed *tuna.* The flavor of the pads is a bit bland, like a cross between bell pepper and okra. The fruit, on the other hand, is juicy and sweet, available in season in many Baja markets. If you want to taste it in the wild, remove the *tunas* carefully, cut them lengthwise with a sharp knife, and scoop out the insides with a spoon. Nine species of nopal are found in Baja, including the endemic *tuna tapona* found south of Loreto.

AGAVES

Nineteen species of the sizable agave family grow in Baja; 11 are native. All have long, spine-edged leaves, as well as flowers that bloom on tall stalks.

Yucca

One of the most common and striking desert plants is the yucca, which appears in several varieties throughout Baja. The largest is the **tree yucca,** called *datilillo* or "little date" for its resemblance to a date palm. *Datilillos* grow in clusters 3–7 meters (10–23 ft) tall, their daggerlike blades supported by long woody trunks. This endemic is found throughout the desert plains and chaparral subregions of the peninsula—just about anywhere except in the mountains. The best place to view it in numbers is on the Pacific side of the Vizcaíno Desert, where it's the dominant plant.

Yuccas are extremely useful plants for rural *bajacalifornianos*. The fruit and flowers are edible (a candy called *colache* is made from the cooked flower buds), the roots can be boiled to make soap or leather softener, and the tough leaf fibers are used to make cordage, sandals, baskets, and mats. In some parts of central Baja you may see fences made from packed-together *datilillo* stalks, which often take root and produce a living fence.

Maguey

Also common in Baja are the many varieties of maguey, or century plant. The maguey has broad, closely clustered leaves that grow at ground level without a visible trunk. In most species, the plant flowers only once in its lifetime, sending up a tall, slender stalk after maturation—typically at 5–20 years, depending on variety and locale. Early Anglo settlers in the southwestern U.S. spread the myth that magueys bloomed only once in a hundred years, hence the fanciful name "century plant."

The maguey was an important food source for certain aboriginal populations, who harvested the plant just before it bloomed (when it's full of concentrated nutrients). Trimmed of its leaves, the heart of the plant was baked in an underground pit for 1–3 days, then eaten or stored. Some ranchers still prepare it in this manner. As with *datilillo,* the leaf fibers are used as cordage for weaving various household goods.

Sotol

Sotol is similar to yucca, but its leaves are narrower and softer. Some sotols produce long flower stalks like those of the century plant, though the flower buds occur along the stalk's entire length instead of only at the top.

One spectacular variety of sotol in Baja is the endemic *Nolina beldingii,* sometimes called *palmita* because of its resemblance to a small palm tree. *Palmitas,* which can reach seven meters (23 ft) in height, grow clusters of thick leaves branching from their short, woody trunks. They're most commonly found at higher elevations in the Cape Region; isolated stands also exist in mountain areas northwest of Mulegé, north of Bahía de los Ángeles, and on Volcán Las Tres Vírgenes.

FOUQUIERIACEAE
Cirio

The Fouquieria family of succulents contains what many travelers consider to be the plant most symbolic of Baja—the *cirio,* or "boojum tree." Most naturalists describe the *cirio* by likening it to an inverted carrot, since the plant's tall stalk is thickest near the ground and gradually tapers along its height until it reaches a skinny point at the top. The Spanish name *cirio* (candle) seems far more evocative when one compares the plant to the slender wax tapers typically found on mission altars. In times of abundant rain, the *cirio* even puts forth at its tip a golden bloom resembling a flaring candle flame.

In height, the *cirio* is second only to Baja's *cardón* cactus, with mature plants extending 12–15 meters (40–50 ft) high from a base 30 centimeters (12 in) or so in diameter. Since a *cirio* on average grows only three centimeters a year (or a foot every 10 years), a 15-meter individual is around 500 years old.

The whimsical name "boojum" was bestowed ad hoc upon the *cirio* by Arizona botanist Godfrey Sykes during a 1922 expedition to Baja. Sykes had apparently been reading Lewis Carroll's *Hunting of the Snark,* a tale that mentioned an imaginary boojum without describing it except to say it inhabited "distant shores." In this sense Sykes's spontaneous epithet was indeed descriptive since the *cirio* grows only in a relatively narrow, 320-kilometer-wide (200-mi-wide) band between the 30th and 27th parallels on the Baja peninsula; the exception is a small *cirio* colony near La Libertad in Sonora, at the same latitude. Although the *cirio* is abundant within this area, the area itself is distant from the "tourist shores" of northwestern Baja, Loreto, and Los Cabos.

Because of its uniqueness, some botanists award the *cirio* with its own genus, *Idria,* within the Fouquieria family, so the Latin name can appear as either *Fouquieria columnaris* or *Idria columnaris.* Like all plants in this family, the white-barked *cirio* sprouts tiny leaves over the entire plant surface when there's sufficient rainfall. During long periods of dry weather, the leaves drop off to conserve the internal water supply.

Ocotillo and *Palo Adán*

Much more common throughout Baja's desert lands are two other members of the Fouquieria family, the **ocotillo** and *palo adán* (Adam's tree). The ocotillo features long, whiplike branches that radiate directly from the ground in a shape comparable to an exploding shell. In the southwestern United States, it's sometimes known as a "coachwhip." As with the *cirio,* tiny leaves come and go on ocotillo stems according to changing weather conditions. After a good rainfall, a mature (2 m or more) plant puts forth droopy red blossoms at the end of each branch.

Ocotillo grows profusely in all the desert regions of Baja north of the 28th parallel and as far northeast as New Mexico and Texas, occasionally appearing as far south as Bahía Concepción. A rare endemic species, *Fouquieria burragei (ocotillo de flor),* is distinguished by its salmon-pink flowers and grows between Bahía Concepción and La Paz and on a few Sea of Cortez islands. Rancheros use ocotillo branches for fencing, shade ramadas, and as bracing in adobe construction.

At about the point on the peninsula where ocotillo begins fading, its cousin the *palo adán* begins making an appearance. Looking like a larger ocotillo, the Adam's tree has considerably thicker branches radiating from a short, woody trunk. The leaves, when present, are slightly larger than the ocotillo's, while the flowers are smaller. In the Bahía de los Ángeles area, ocotillo and Adam's tree often grow side by side. The latter is also popular as a fencing material and makes excellent firewood when dry.

TREES
Palms

Seven varieties of palm grow wild in Baja California; four are native to the peninsula and islands while three are introduced species. Palms are important to the local economy of the peninsula's southern half, where they're most common. The long, straight trunks are used as roof beams, the leaves are used in basketry and for roof and wall thatching, and the fruits provide nutrition.

Among the most handsome Baja palm trees is the endemic **blue fan palm,** or *palma azul,* which reaches up to 24 meters (79 ft) tall and sports bluish, fan-shaped leaves at its crown. The 4.5-meter (15-ft) flower stalks, which usually appear February–March, often extend well below the shag, or thatch of dead leaves below the crown. The blue fan palm typically grows in the canyons and arroyos of the Sierra Juárez and in similar locales as far south as San Ignacio.

Another native variety, the **Tlaco palm** (also called "taco palm," *palma palmía,* and *palma colorado),* is common in the canyons and arroyos of the Cape Region sierras below Loreto. The smooth, slender trunks, crowned by stiff, fan-shaped leaves, stand up to 20 meters (65 ft) tall. Its durable trunks have long been valued for house construction in Baja California Sur's Cape Region. A closely related species, the **Guadalupe Island palm,** is native to Isla Guadalupe; its self-shedding trunk leaves little or no shag, which has made the tree popular as a cultivated palm.

Baja's tallest palm variety is the endemic **Mexican fan palm** (also known as Baja California fan palm, skyduster, or *palma blanca),* which reaches heights of 27–30 meters (90–100 ft). As the name implies, its leaves are fan-shaped. Although it's not as durable as the Tlaco palm, the long trunk makes the tree useful for local construction. The fan palm's native habitats include the Sierra de la Giganta and Isla Ángel de la Guarda, but it has also spread west of Cataviña and reached southern California as an ornamental import. More common in the northern peninsula is the similar, nonendemic **California fan palm,** which is a bit shorter than its Mexican cousin.

Two palm varieties were imported to Baja for their fruit value. The **date palm** was introduced to Baja by Jesuit missionaries and is now common near former mission sites, including Loreto, Comondú, Mulegé, San Ignacio, and San José del Cabo. The tree typically reaches 15–20 meters (50–65 ft) tall at maturity; its oblong fruit grows beneath feather-shaped leaves in large clusters, turning from pale yellow to dark brown as it ripens. Baja dates are eaten locally and shipped to mainland Mexico but are generally not considered of high enough quality for export. The 30-meter (100-ft), feather-leafed **coconut palm** commonly grows along coastal areas of the Cape Region as far north as Mulegé and is an important local food source.

Elephant Trees

At least two different species from completely different plant families have received the name "elephant tree." The first, which some Baja experts claim is the only "true" elephant tree, is the sumac family's *Pachycormus discolor,* called either *copalquín* or *torote blanco.* The English name refers to the thick, gray, gnarled-looking trunks and branches. Travelers to East Africa may note a resemblance to the baobab tree.

The papery bark of the elephant tree continually peels off in sheets to reveal the dark green, spongy inner trunk. Drought-deciduous leaves form on the branches when rainfall is sufficient; between May and September small pink flowers may bloom for a few weeks, casting a pink glow over the whole. This endemic species is often seen in the same central desert areas that feature *cirios.* It's particularly prolific in volcanic soils and lava flows.

The second elephant tree, similar in appearance to the *Pachycormus* but belonging to the torchwood family, is the *Bursera odorata.* Like the other elephant tree, the *Bursera* has thick, gnarled trunks and branches; the thin bark also peels off in papery sheets. The inner trunk is yellow, however, rather than dark green. This one grows south of Bahía Concepción and

on the Mexican mainland only. The Spanish name for the tree is the same as for the "true" elephant tree, *torote blanco.* A close relative, the *torote colorado* (another *Bursera*), has a reddish bark. It's found throughout the deserts of Baja and on many Sea of Cortez islands, as well as in California's Anza-Borrego Desert (in the United States).

Conifers

The high sierras of Baja support a surprising number and variety of conifers, including species of cypress, cedar, juniper, fir, and pine. Among the most interesting, because of its relative confinement to the Baja region, is the **Tecate cypress,** found on the western slopes of the Sierra Juárez and in the Valle San Vicente, as well as in southern California as far north as Orange County. Likewise, the **San Pedro Mártir cypress** is confined to the eastern escarpment of the Sierra de San Pedro Mártir, the **Cedros Island pine** is found only on Isla Cedros, and the **Guadalupe Island pine** grows only on Isla Guadalupe.

Other, more common conifer varieties found at higher elevations include incense cedar, Mormon tea, white fir, piñon pine, Jeffrey pine, sugar pine, bishop pine, and lodgepole pine.

Oaks

Varieties of oak *(encino)* abound along the Pacific slopes of the northern sierras and in the canyons, arroyos, and meadows of the two Cape Region sierras. Of the many species found in Baja, four are endemic: the **cape oak,** found in the canyons and arroyos of the Cape Region sierras; **black oak,** confined to the lower slopes of the Cape Region; **Cedros Island oak,** on Isla Cedros and from San Vicente south to Sierra San Borja; and **peninsular oak,** on the lower slopes of the northern and central sierras. Other common oaks are coast live oak, canyon live oak, white oak, scrub oak, mesa blue oak, and Palmer oak.

Mimosas

This subfamily of the Leguminosae, or pea family, includes dozens of genera common to arid and semiarid zones worldwide. Characterized by linear seedpods and double rows of tiny leaves, common mimosa varieties in Baja include the **mesquite** and various endemic kinds of **acacia.**

Amerindians have long used the trunk, roots, leaves, beans, and bark of the mesquite tree for a variety of purposes, from lumber to medicine. Ground mesquite leaves mixed with water form a balm for sore eyes, a remedy still used by *curanderos* (healers) in rural Mexico today. Chewing the leaves relieves toothache. And mesquite gum has been used as a balm for wounds, a ceramic glue, dye, and digestive.

Mesquite beans are a good source of nutrition—a ripe bean pod, growing as long as 23 centimeters (9 in), contains roughly 30 percent glucose and is high in protein. Many animals and birds savor the beans; horses will eat them until they're sick. Rural Mexicans grind the dried pods into a flour, with which they make bread and a kind of beer. The Seri Amerindians, who live along the Sonoran coast of the Sea of Cortez, have separate names for eight different stages of the bean pod's development.

One of the prettiest endemic mimosas is the **palo blanco,** which has a tall, slender trunk with silver-white bark and a feathery crown that produces small, white, fragrant blossoms March–May. This tree is found the length of the peninsula although it's most easily seen in the Sierra de la Giganta and in the vicinity of Loreto.

Wild Figs

Three types of wild fig trees *(zalates),* one endemic, are common in peninsular Baja. Most are found in rocky areas of the Cape Region. In the village of Pueblo La Playa, east of San José del Cabo, stands a venerable collection of *zalates* of impressive stature.

Cottonwoods and Willows

Various cottonwoods *(alamos)* and willows *(sauces)* grow at higher elevations throughout the peninsula. The **huerivo,** or **güeribo** *(Populus brandegeei),* is a beautiful endemic cottonwood found in the canyons and arroyos of the Cape Region sierras. Its tall, straight trunk reaches heights of 30 meters (100 ft) and is a highly valued source of lumber for building construction and furniture-making.

An unlikely Baja find is the **quaking aspen,** which grows in high mountain meadows of the Sierra de San Pedro Mártir and nowhere else in Baja. The name derives from the fluttering of the small leaves as they turn yellow in the fall and shimmer against the white bark of the tree. In Spanish this tree is called *alamillo,* or "little cottonwood."

HERBS

Most herbs—those shrubs with culinary, medicinal, or religious value—thrive in arid climates, and in Baja California they grow in some abundance. To get an idea of the variety, visit any peninsula *botánica* (herb shop) and ask to see *yerbas indígenas.* Most likely your query will turn up the following herbs, plus a dozen others.

One of the most common plants in northern Baja is **Great Basin sagebrush,** named for the area of the western United States where it's a dominant species. In Baja it's called *chamizo blanco* and is found in chaparral and piñon-juniper zones throughout the foothills of the northern sierras. Despite its name, the bluish evergreen shrub isn't a true sage but a member of the mayweed tribe. Like sage, however, its leaves are sometimes used by Mexican herbalists in medicinal teas.

True sages, or *salvia,* belong to the mint family and are readily identified by the savory aroma of their crushed leaves. **White sage** proliferates on rocky hillsides from southern California to as far south as Punta Prieta. The grayish-green shrub grows up to three meters tall and between March and July produces pale lavender flowers along its stalks. Several varieties of white sage are endemic to the peninsula and islands. Sage tea will mitigate the symptoms of a sore throat; the crushed leaves are also used to flavor cooked meats.

The much sought-after *chia* is a species of sage that grows only in the desert areas of Baja, Sonora, and the southwestern United States.

The plant produces sizable rose-colored flowers and 2.5-centimeter-wide (1-in-wide) nutlets containing seeds valued for their stimulant properties.

Another psychoactive plant found in Baja is **datura,** or **jimsonweed** *(toloache).* A member of the potato family—a group that also includes nightshade and tobacco—jimsonweed produces large, fragrant, trumpet-shaped flowers that open in the evening and close by noon the following day. According to one folk remedy, the flowers will relieve insomnia if placed beside the pillow at night. All parts of the plant are considered toxic; in certain Yaqui Amerindian ceremonies, the seeds are eaten for their hallucinatory effect. Datura grows in abundance on rocky and sandy soils below 800 meters (2,600 ft) throughout the peninsula and on some Sea of Cortez islands.

More docile but also widespread in dry, lower elevations is the **creosote bush** *(gobernadora),* also found in the deserts of Northern Mexico, Utah, and Texas. This venerable shrub originated near the lower Colorado River and has been around at least 17,000 years, cloning itself in rings that widen with time. It's a fairly inconspicuous plant, with sparse evergreen branches that reach a maximum height of about 3.5 meters (11 ft). The English name derives from the creosote-like odor the shrub exudes after rainfall. Dubbed "the smell of the desert" by admirers, this redolence is caused by the reaction of rainwater with a resin on the plant's outer skin. In periods of drought the resin protects the plant from dehydration.

The indigenous peoples of Baja California and Northern Mexico have known about the medicinal properties of *gobernadora* for ages. A tea made from the leaves relieves indigestion, coughs, and colds; a root tea is used to treat ulcers; a root poultice eases arthritis. Rancheros wash their feet in a root solution to prevent foot odor. Pharmacologists are now experimenting with several different chemical components of the plant shown to possess analgesic, diuretic, antihistaminic, expectorant, and antibacterial properties.

The homely **oregano** plant belongs to the same botanical family (Verbenaceae) as the creosote bush. The crushed leaves of this herb are used mainly in Mexico as a flavoring for stews and tomato sauces; oregano tea is also used by some women to relieve menstrual pain. The small evergreen shrub is found on Isla Magdalena, along the peninsula near Bahía Magdalena, and on many Sea of Cortez islands.

Probably the most well-known herb native to Baja is **damiana** *(Turnera diffusa),* a small shrub with bright, five-petaled yellow or golden flowers. The plant's aphrodisiac properties are its main claim to fame; these are often derided as nonsense by self-appointed Baja analysts. But according to botanist Norman C. Roberts, damiana "stimulates the genito-urinary tract and is used in the treatment of sexual problems such as impotence, frigidity, sterility, and sexual exhaustion." Other benefits ascribed to the herb include use as a sedative and diuretic.

Damiana grows most commonly in rocky areas of the Cape Region but is also found as far away as Sonora, Texas, and in the West Indies. The two most common ways of ingesting the herb are in sweetened tea made from the leaves or in a liqueur containing damiana extract. In resort areas, a "Baja margarita" substitutes damiana liqueur for triple sec.

Fauna

LAND MAMMALS

Had Charles Darwin happened to explore the peninsula and islands of Baja California instead of Ecuador's Galapagos Islands, he might well have arrived at the same conclusions about evolution. Baja's unique environment—an arid-to-tropical slice of mountains and plains isolated between two large bodies of water—has led to superlative endemism, or what one naturalist called "a nice degree of freakishness," among its plant and animal species.

Of the hundred or so species of mammals found in Baja California, around 28 are endemic.

Carnivores

One of the most widespread carnivores on the peninsula as well as on some Sea of Cortez islands is the **coyote,** which seems to adapt itself equally well to mountain, desert, and coastal terrain. Anyone venturing into the interior of the peninsula is virtually guaranteed to spot at least one. In some areas they don't seem particularly afraid of humans, although they always maintain a distance of at least 15 meters (50 ft) between themselves and larger mammals. A coyote will sometimes fish for crab, placing a furry tail in the water, waiting for a crab to grab on, then, with a flick of the tail, tossing the crab onto the beach. Before the crustacean can recover from the shock, the coyote is enjoying a fine crab feast.

Rarely sighted is the **mountain lion**—also called cougar, panther, or puma—which, like all cats, is mostly nocturnal. These beautiful creatures occasionally attack humans, so those hiking in the sierras should avoid hiking at night. If you do meet up with a lion, wildlife experts suggest you convince the beast you are not prey and may be dangerous yourself. Don't run from the animal, as this is an invitation to chase. Instead, shout, wave your hands, and, if the lion acts aggressively, throw stones at it. If you're carrying a backpack, raise it above your shoulders so that you appear larger. One or more of these actions is virtually guaranteed to frighten the lion away. If not, grab the biggest, heaviest stick you can find and fight it out to avoid becoming cat food.

Smaller, less intimidating carnivores commonly encountered in Baja include the kit fox, gray fox, northern fox, ringtail, bobcat, lynx, skunk, raccoon, and badger. Although there haven't been any recent sightings, the **gray wolf** may still exist in small numbers in the central sierras. Until the middle of this century the gray wolf was fairly common in Baja, but farmers and ranchers made an unfortunate tradition of killing them on sight.

Ungulates

One of the largest hoofed beasts still roaming wild in Baja is the **mule deer,** of which there is an endemic peninsular variety. Mule deer are most commonly seen on mountain slopes below 1,500 meters (5,000 ft). Lesser numbers of **white-tailed deer** inhabit higher elevations. Deer are a popular source of meat for ranchers living in the sierras, who also use deerskin to make soft, homemade boots called *teguas.*

At one time herds of **desert bighorn sheep** *(borrego cimarrón)* lived throughout the peninsular deserts. Big-game hunting in the 1920s and 1930s as well as overgrazing of domestic livestock reduced their numbers to an estimated 4,500–7,500 individuals. An adult ram measures 81–124 centimeters (32–48 in) high at the shoulder and may weigh around 73 kilograms (160 lbs).

Rams rut in summer, the only time dominant rams mingle with ewes; the rest of the year they roam only with other rams. During mating season, butting matches between bighorn rams are common.

The elegant but endangered **peninsular pronghorn** *(berrendo),* often mistakenly referred to as an antelope, was once found from San Felipe south to Bahía Magdalena. Until recently it was thought that fewer than 100 pronghorns were hanging on in the Vizcaíno

THE BURRO

Long-eared, slow-plodding, dim-witted, the quintessential beast of burden: This is the city person's image of *Equus asinus*. But to rural Mexicans, the donkey, or *burro*, is a beast of strength and surefootedness. Compared to its taller, more graceful-appearing cousin the horse, the burro is a far more useful animal in mountainous or arid domains. On slopes, rocky surfaces, and sand, the burro moves with great agility while balancing any load – whether human or inanimate. Standing only about a meter high at the shoulder, burros can also cover greater distances than horses on less water and food; they actually seem to prefer rough forage such as dead cactus or thorny paloverde over nutrient-rich – and, in Baja, scarce – grasses.

Although a burro's coloring may vary from light to dark brown, its withers are almost always marked with a cross of darker hair. Mexican mythology explains this cross as a symbol of divine protection – the burro's reward for carrying Mary and the infant Christ from Egypt to the Holy Land. The burro's legendary stubbornness can often be attributed to mistreatment by its owner; an animal well cared for is usually quite loyal.

Wild burros roam the peninsula's interior, particularly in the area between the Sierra de la Asamblea and Sierra San Borja. Ranchers, or *campesinos*, occasionally capture a wild burro for domestic use – they're fairly easy to tame. The wild male burro, or "jack," is considered the best stud for producing a mule, so ranchers occasionally turn mares loose to breed with them. Mules produced from such a union are especially hardy.

Mountain trekkers occasionally hire burros or mules as pack animals in Baja's sierras. For long forays, it's sometimes cheaper to purchase a burro rather than pay a daily hire rate; prices range from around US$40 for a poor animal to around US$80 for an exemplary burro – if you can find a rancher willing to sell one. If the price doesn't include an *aparejo* (or *burriqueta*), a saddlelike wooden frame for carrying cargo, you'll have to buy one or have one made. The best are made from the wood of the *zacate* (wildfig) tree and sheathed in hand-tooled leather. If possible, have a veterinarian inspect the animal for diseases before agreeing on a purchase.

Desert, but recent aerial surveys have concluded there are around 200 *berrendo*, all of which are under the official protection of the Mexican government. Like many life forms on the Vizcaíno Peninsula, pronghorns draw moisture from dew left behind by Pacific fogs. The penalties for killing a pronghorn include a large fine plus three years in prison.

In the central Baja sierras roam a smattering of wild horses and many wild cattle. Every five years or so local vaqueros gather in the El Arco area to round up wild, unbranded cattle.

Rabbits

At least four varieties of rabbit hop around Baja: the brush rabbit, desert cottontail, black-tailed jackrabbit, and the rare, endemic black jackrabbit. Each is especially adapted to its particular habitat. The long, upright ears of the **black-tailed jackrabbit,** for example, enable it to hear sounds from a long distance, a necessity for an animal that is prey for practically every larger animal in Baja. The more delicate ears of the **desert cottontail** act as radiators on hot desert days, allowing it to release excess body heat into the air.

The **black jackrabbit** *(Lepus insularis)* is found only on Isla Espíritu Santo. Zoologists haven't yet been able to explain why the fur of this rabbit is mostly black, or why a cinnamon-red coloring appears along the ears and underparts.

Rodents

The Californian Region and the sierras of Baja support a wide variety of common and not-so-common rodents—the white-tailed antelope squirrel, marsh rice rat, Botta's pocket gopher, and piñon mouse, to name a few. What may surprise some travelers is how many varieties manage to survive in the desert. Among these are the desert pocket mouse, cactus mouse, desert wood rat, and five endemic species of kangaroo rat.

The **kangaroo rat,** which you may see hopping in front of your headlights at night—its long tail acts as a powerful spring—is built so it doesn't need to drink water, ever. It derives moisture from seeds, from the air deep inside its burrows where the relative humidity is 30–50 percent, and from condensation in its nasal passages (its nostrils are much cooler than the rest of its body). The creature's efficient kidneys excrete uric acid in a concentrated paste, rather than in liquid form. Because its body is so full of moisture, it's prized quarry for larger desert mammals and birds of prey. Backcountry rancheros occasionally trap kangaroo rats for fiesta food.

GRAY WHALES

The marine mammal usually of most interest to Baja travelers is the gray whale, which migrates some 19,300 kilometers (12,000 mi) a year between its feeding grounds above the Arctic Circle and its calving grounds in the Pacific lagoons of southern Baja California. The gray is the easiest of the whales to view since it frequents shallow coastal waters.

Physiology and Behavior

The *Eschrichtius robustus,* or gray whale, often called the California gray whale, reaches 10–15 meters (35–50 ft) in length at maturity (the average length is 13 meters (43 ft) for males, slightly longer for females) and weighs 20–40 tons. Its skin is almost black at birth, but mottling caused by barnacles and barnacle scars imparts an overall gray tone to the portion of the animal exposed when it breathes. Bite scars on flukes and flippers from orca (killer whale) attacks are common—at least 20 percent of all grays are attacked at one time or another. Most survive; juveniles are the most common fatalities.

Unlike many other whale species that feed on plankton, the gray whale feeds mainly on amphipods, small crustaceans that live on the ocean floor. To get at them, the gray dives to the bottom, scoops water and sand into its mouth cavity, then expels the water through its baleen (a whalebone "sieve" in the mouth), filtering out the amphipods. In spite of an esophagus that's only about 10 centimeters (4 in) wide, one whale can ingest up to a ton of food per day.

Although gray whales may engage in mating behavior at any point along their migration route, females conceive only while at the north end, in the vicinity of the Bering Strait, and give birth at or near the southern end, in Baja's Pacific lagoons. In a remarkable display of tribal rhythm, 90 percent of all gray whale conceptions take place within three weeks of December 5. Hence it's incorrect to say the whales "breed" in Baja lagoons, since the females cannot conceive at that point in the calendar. The female grays give birth after a gestation period of about 13 months, by which time the whales have arrived at the lagoons and are well on their way.

The females usually calve in water 3–15 meters (10–50 ft) deep, which is remarkably shallow considering newborn grays are four to five meters long (13–16 ft) and weigh up to 1.5 tons. Following birth, the newborns are exercised and fattened up so they'll be strong enough for the migration north. A female gray has recessed nipples on her underside, but the calf doesn't actually suck the milk from the mammaries like other mammals; instead the calf takes the nipple in its mouth, and, after a watertight seal has formed, the mother discharges a stream of milk into the calf's throat.

Since whale milk is about 800 percent richer in fat than human milk, the calves gain weight rapidly. By the time the return migration begins, roughly three months after birth, the young whales average six meters (20 ft) long and weigh about 2.5 tons.

Migration

At one time the gray whale swam the Atlantic Ocean, Baltic Sea, and North Sea as well as the

Pacific. It was wiped out by Dutch, British, and American whalers in the North Atlantic by the beginning of the 19th century and now survives only in the Arctic–Pacific corridor. In the 1930s, its numbers were estimated at just 250 worldwide. After passage of the U.S. Marine Mammal Protection Act of 1972, grays rebounded and now number around 21,000. They spend their summers feeding in the Bering, Chukchi, and Beaufort Seas in the vicinity of Alaska and Siberia, where the long Arctic days result in highly productive marine growth.

The gray's primary feeding grounds lie in the Chirikof Basin, where they begin their annual migration south in mid- to late fall. Swimming at an average of four knots, the whales cover the 9,600-kilometer (6,000-mile) journey to the southern Baja lagoons in about two months. Traveling in pods of three or four whales, they typically rest for a few hours each night. When there's a full moon, they swim all night.

On their way southward the grays follow the North American shoreline closely, taking the outside coast of major islands. Like many two-legged mammals, gray whales prefer to spend their winters south of the border, and by early January they begin arriving at protected bays and lagoons on the Pacific side of Baja, primarily Laguna Ojo de Liebre, Laguna San Ignacio, and Bahía Magdalena. The grays used to winter farther north in California's San Diego Bay, but heavy sea traffic now forces them to stay south.

During the grays' winter sojourn in Baja, the females calve and nurse their young in the interiors of the lagoons, while the males tend to loiter at or near the lagoon entrances. Since female grays are fertile every other year, each available female—those not calving or nursing—has an average of two suitors at each lagoon entry at any given time. When not actively mating, males watch their rivals coupling or seek out other females. Fighting for access to a female is not a known whale behavior.

Calving season runs December–April, but because of individual differences in pacing, some whales begin migrating north as early as February while others may linger in the lagoons until June. The entire 19,000-kilometer (12,000-mi) migration, the longest of any mammal on the planet, occurs within a period of 7–8 months. Apparently, adult whales don't eat during this interval.

The Rise and Fall of Pacific Whaling

The Amerindians of Alta and Baja California as well as the Inuit of Alaska were known to hunt whales for tribal consumption. But whaling as an industry didn't begin along the Pacific coast until the 19th century, when American whaleboats from New England and Hawaii began cruising Pacific waters in significant numbers. At first gray whales were left alone; because they're fiercely defensive when under attack, grays are difficult to kill using traditional harpooning techniques. Often they would destroy attacking whaleboats.

The gray's destiny was altered in 1857 when Boston whaler Charles Melville Scammon followed a pod into Baja's Laguna Ojo de Liebre. Taking advantage of the local geography, Scammon figured out how to bomb the trapped whales with explosive harpoons while his whaleboats remained safely anchored in the shallows, where larger whales couldn't reach them. Scores of whalers followed his example, and within less than 20 years an estimated 10,000 gray whales had been killed.

The slaughter quickened in the 20th century with the introduction of factory boats, which meant whales could be processed on site. By the 1930s the estimated number of grays was down to 250 from a pre-1850s population of 25,000. International fishing agreements signed in 1937 and 1946 forbade the killing of gray whales, but American whalers didn't comply until the U.S. government enacted the Marine Mammal Protection Act of 1972, by which time the gray whale was thought to be extinct. The animal's remarkable comeback over the last 30 years has been one of the greatest successes of the environmental movement.

In an ironic historical footnote, whaler Charles Melville Scammon later became a naturalist of some note, and his book, *The Marine Mammals of the Northwestern Coast of North America*, is considered a classic of amateur zoology. It remains one of the most important reference works on whales and the whaling industry.

OTHER MARINE MAMMALS
Cetaceans

The protected lagoons of Baja California's Pacific coast and the warm waters of the Sea of Cortez are practically made for whales and dolphins. Twenty-five species of cetaceans—about a third of all world species—frequent Baja waters, from the **blue whale,** the largest mammal on earth, to the **common dolphin** *(Delphinus delphis),* which is sometimes seen in the Sea of Cortez in pods as large as 10,000.

In addition to the gray whale (discussed at length earlier), whale species known to visit Baja or make it their year-round habitat include minke, fin, Sei, Bryde's, humpback, goose-beaked, sperm, dwarf sperm, false killer, killer, and pilot. Commonly seen dolphins include the Pacific white-sided, bottle-nosed, spotted, Risso's, spinner, and striped. The **vaquita,** a rare type of harbor porpoise, is endemic to the northern Sea of Cortez.

Seals and Sea Lions

Various seals and sea lions flourish along Baja's coasts, including two species, the **elephant seal** (or sea elephant) and the **Guadalupe fur seal,** that have only recently come back from the brink of extinction. Both are native to the volcanic Isla Guadalupe and were heavily hunted in the 19th century, the elephant seal for its oil and the Guadalupe fur seal for its furry skin.

The elephant seal is the largest seal on the planet. Males reach five meters (16 ft) or more and weigh up to two tons, while females are typically around three meters and about half a ton. The male's thick, flexible proboscis resembles a bobbed elephant's trunk. To scare off rivals in breeding season (December–February), the male places the tip of his trunk into his mouth and blows, producing a roaring snort. If the rival doesn't flee, a bloody fight ensues until one bull surrenders.

Lumbering on land but amazingly graceful in water, elephant seals can dive 1,490 meters (4,900 ft) below the sea's surface—deeper than any other seal—to feed on squid, their favorite source of nourishment.

When the seal-hunting era began in the early 19th century, the elephant seal's range extended all the way north to California's Point Reyes, near San Francisco. By 1911 seal hunters had wiped out every elephant seal in California waters and reduced the elephant's numbers on Isla Guadalupe to 125. After the Mexican government enacted a ban on seal hunting in 1922, the seals began repopulating Isla Guadalupe and nearby islands. The current population is estimated at around 80,000, most living on Pacific islands of Baja California. The elephant seal is gradually working its way back up the California coast as well.

The smaller Guadalupe fur seal had a more difficult time recovering from the seal-hunting era. It was believed to be extinct by the end of the 19th century, but in 1926 a small herd of around 60 living on Isla Guadalupe was discovered by American angler William Clover. Clover captured a pair of the seals and sold them to the San Diego Zoo, but, following a quarrel with the zoo's director, he returned to the island and attempted to kill and skin the entire remaining population. After selling the skins in Panama he met his demise in a barroom brawl. Fortunately he missed some of the seals in his massacre, and the current population on the island is estimated at around 500.

California sea lions, or *lobos marinas,* number some 145,000, 62 percent of which live in the Sea of Cortez—principally around the islands of San Esteban, San Jorge, Ángel de la Guarda, San Pedro Mártir, and Espíritu Santo.

FISH

The seas surrounding Baja California contain an amazing variety of marinelife. In the Sea of Cortez alone, around 900 varieties of fish have been identified. Marine biologists estimate around 3,000 species, including invertebrates, between the Golfo de Santa Clara at the north end of the sea and the southern tip of Cabo San Lucas. This would make the area the richest sea, or gulf, in the world. The wide spectrum of aquatic environments along both coasts is largely responsible for this abundance and has led to Baja's reputation as a mecca for seafood aficionados and fishing and diving enthusiasts.

About 90 percent of all known Baja fish varieties are found close to the shores of the peninsula or its satellite islands. The Midriff Islands area in the center of the Sea of Cortez is especially rich—tidal surges aerate the water and stir up nutrients, supporting a thick food chain from plankton to fish to birds and sea lions. The Cortez, in fact, has acted as a giant fish trap, collecting an assortment of marine species over thousands of years from the nearby Pacific, the more distant equatorial zones of South America, and even the Caribbean, through a water link that once existed between the two seas.

A brief guide to Baja's fish is provided below. Habitats are described as being onshore, inshore, or offshore. Onshore fish frequent the edge of the tidal zone and can be caught by casting from shore; inshore fish inhabit shallow waters accessible by small boat; and offshore fish lurk in the deep waters of the open Pacific or the southern Sea of Cortez. (See also *Sports and Recreation* in the *Essentials* chapter.)

Billfish

Baja is the world capital of sailfish and marlin fishing; serious saltwater anglers from across the globe make the pilgrimage to La Paz or Cabo San Lucas in hopes of landing a swordfish, sailfish, or striped, blue, or black marlin. The sailfish and striped marlin are generally the most acrobatic, but all billfish are strong fighters. They inhabit a wide range of offshore waters in the Pacific and in the Sea of Cortez south of Bahía Magdalena and the Midriff Islands; the swordfish is found mostly on the Pacific side.

Corvinas and Croakers

About 30 species in Baja belong to this group of small- to medium-size fish that make croaking sounds. Among the largest is the **totuava,** formerly one of the most famous game fish in the upper Sea of Cortez. Overfishing has led to a scarcity of these silvery 35- to 250-pounders (15–115 kg), and it's now illegal to take or possess them in Mexico. The totuava is reportedly one of best tasting of all game fish; others in this category, found inshore to onshore in a variety of coastal waters, include white sea bass, Gulf corvina, orangemouth corvina, California corvina, yellowfin croaker, and spotfin croaker.

Jack

Popular jacks include yellowtail (one of the most popular fish for use in *tacos de pescado*), Pacific amberjack, various pompanos, jack crevalle, and the strong-fighting roosterfish, named for its tall dorsal comb. These fish are most prevalent in inshore to onshore areas in the Sea of Cortez and in the Pacific south of Magdalena.

Dorado, Mackerel, and Tuna

Among the more sought-after food fish, found offshore to inshore throughout parts of both seas, are: dorado, sometimes called dolphinfish (though it isn't related to mammalian dolphins or porpoises) or mahimahi (its Hawaiian name); sierra, especially good in ceviche; the knife-shaped wahoo, one of the fastest of all fish, reaching speeds of 50 knots; Pacific bonito; and three kinds of tuna—the bluefin, albacore, and highly prized yellowfin. Yellowfins can weigh up to 180 kilograms (400 lbs) and are among the best tasting of all tunas.

Bass

Sea bass are an inshore fish; different species dominate different Baja waters, and all commonly find their way into Mexican seafood restaurants. The larger bass are *garropa* (groupers), the smaller *cabrilla*. Popular varieties are the leopard grouper, found in the Sea of Cortez near San Felipe; the gulf grouper, which weighs up to 90 kilograms (200 lbs) and inhabits waters off San Felipe to the Midriff Islands; giant sea bass, ranging from San Quintín to above the Midriff Islands; spotted cabrilla, Isla Cedros to the upper Sea of Cortez; flag cabrilla, lower Sea of Cortez; kelp bass, northwest Pacific coast;

and spotted sand bass, Pacific coast north of Magdalena and the upper Sea of Cortez.

Bottomfish

These smaller (13 kg/29 lbs or less) bottom-feeding fish favor the inshore Pacific above Magdalena and include the lingcod, sculpin, and rockfish.

Surf Fish

Most of the 25 or so species of surf fish weigh less than two kilograms (4.5 lbs) and are found along the Pacific coast, since there's no surf to speak of in the Sea of Cortez. Popular catches among gringos—this isn't a popular fish with Mexican anglers—are barred surfperch, rubberlip surfperch, and sargo. The sargo also frequents the upper Sea of Cortez coast.

Flatfish

These include flounder and halibut, usually called *lenguado* in Spanish. The most common variety on the Pacific side is California halibut; on the gulf side it's Cortez halibut. Both make good eating and are often used in tourist areas for *tacos de pescado.*

Snapper

Generally found south of Magdalena and round the Cape as far north as the upper Sea of Cortez, locally popular snappers include red snapper, yellow snapper, barred pargo, and dog snapper. All snappers are called *pargo* in Spanish, except for the red snapper, which is *huachinango*. All are common food fish.

Sharks, Rays, and Squid

Of the more than 60 species of sharks found in Baja waters, some are rare and most stay clear of humans. The more common species are found offshore to inshore from Magdalena to the Midriff, and include the smooth hammerhead; common thresher; bonito (mako); sand; blue; blacktip; and the whale shark, the world's largest fish, which reaches 18 meters (59 ft) and 3,600 kilograms (almost 4 tons). Shark-fishing is an important activity in Baja, supplying much of the seafood eaten locally.

Hammerhead, thresher, bonito, and leopard shark fillets are all tasty.

Rays are common in warmer offshore-to-inshore waters throughout Baja. Many varieties have barbed tail spines that can inflict a painful wound. Contrary to myth, the barb is not actually venomous, although a ray "sting" can be extremely painful and easily becomes infected. Experienced beachgoers perform the "stingray shuffle" when walking on sandy bottoms: if you bump into a ray resting on the bottom, it will usually swim away; if you step on one, it's likely to give you a flick of the barb.

Common smaller rays found inshore include the butterfly ray and the aptly named shovelnose guitarfish, a ray with a thick tail and a flat head. Two species of rays—the mobula and the huge Pacific manta ray—are sometimes called "devilfish" because of their hornlike pectoral fins. The Pacific manta possesses a "wingspan" of up to seven meters (23 ft) and can weigh nearly two tons. Pacific mantas have become rare due to overfishing. Another fairly large ray, the bat ray, is sometimes confused with the manta, though it doesn't have the characteristic pectoral fins. A friendly manta will allow scuba divers to hitch rides by hanging on to the base of the pectorals, although most divemasters now discourage such activity.

Squids of various species and sizes, most under 30 centimeters (1 ft) in length, are found throughout the Pacific Ocean and Sea of Cortez. In deeper Pacific waters off the west coast glides the enormous Humboldt squid, which reaches lengths of 4.5 meters (15 ft) and may weigh as much as 150 kilograms (330 lbs). In the Cape Region, squid (*calamar* in Spanish) is popularly eaten in *cocteles* or used as sportfishing bait.

Elongated Fish

These varieties share the characteristics of long, slender bodies and beaklike jaws. The sharp-toothed California barracuda swims in the Pacific from the border down to Cabo San Lucas, while a smaller, more edible variety is found in the Sea of Cortez. In spite of their somewhat frightful appearance, barracudas rarely attack humans.

The silvery flying fish can be seen leaping above offshore waters throughout the Pacific and lower Sea of Cortez. It is not generally considered a food fish. The most edible of the elongated fish is probably the acrobatic Mexican needlefish, or *agujón,* which reaches two meters (6.5 ft) in length and has green bones.

Shellfish

Baja's shores abound with deep-water and shallow-water shellfish species, including around 75 varieties of clams, oysters, mussels, scallops, and shrimp, many of which have disappeared from coastal California in the United States. Baja's most famous shellfish is undoubtedly the spiny lobster, which appears on virtually every *mariscos* menu on the peninsula.

BIRDS

Hosting around 300 known species of birds (one of the highest concentrations in North America), the peninsula and islands of Baja California provide undisturbed avian habitat par excellence. Ornithological research is incomplete, however, and reference materials are difficult to come by; one of the most up-to-date works available is Ernest Preston Edwards's *The Birds of Mexico and Adjacent Areas,* published in 1998 (see *Suggested Reading* in *Resources*).

Coastal and Pelagic Species

The vast majority of Baja's native and migrating species are either coastal or open-sea (pelagic) birds. The Sea of Cortez islands are particularly rich in bird life; the Mexican government has designated 49 of the Midriff Islands as wildlife refuges to protect the many rare and endangered species there. The most famous of these islands among birders is Isla San Pedro Mártir, home to the rare and clownish **blue-footed booby** and its more common cousins, the **brown booby** and the **masked booby.**

Isla de Raza, a tiny guano-covered Midriff island of only 100 hectares (250 acres), is another birding mecca. Every April this island is the site of territorial "wars" between **Heermann's gulls** and **elegant terns.**

Common throughout the coastal areas of southern Baja is the **magnificent frigate,** called *tijera* (scissors) in Mexico because of its scissors-shaped tail. In spite of their seafood diet, frigates can't swim or even submerge their heads to catch fish—instead they glide high in the air on boomerang-shaped wings, swooping down to steal fish from other birds, especially slow-witted boobies.

Among the more commonly seen birds along the Sea of Cortez coast is the **brown pelican,** which in global terms is not so common. The pelican species go back 30 million years; paleontologists use the modern pelican as a model for creating visual representations of the pteranodon, an extinct flying reptile with an eight-meter wingspan. Brown pelicans, the only truly marine species among the world's seven pelican species, dive 10–30 meters (30–100 ft) underwater to catch fish. Other pelicans only dip their beaks beneath the surface and tend to frequent inland waterways rather than marine habitats. Browns have disappeared almost entirely from the U.S. shores of the Gulf of Mexico and are declining in the coastal islands of California—apparently due to the pesticide content of the Pacific Ocean. Baja's Cortez and Pacific coasts are among the last habitats where the brown pelican thrives.

Another noteworthy bird along the coast is the **fisher eagle,** which, as its name implies, catches and eats fish. The fisher eagle is also occasionally seen along freshwater rivers and around the Pacific lagoons.

Other coastal birds of Baja include two species of cormorant, the long-billed curlew, four species of egret, four species of grebe, 10 species of gull, three species of heron, the belted kingbird, two species of ibis, three species of loon, the osprey, the American oystercatcher, six species of plover, six species of sandpiper, the tundra swan, and seven species of tern.

Certain fish-eating birds are usually seen only by boaters since they tend to fly over open ocean. These pelagics include two species of albatross, the black-legged kittiwake, the red phalarope, three species of shearwater, the surf scoter, the south polar skua, five species of storm petrel, the black tern, and the red-billed tropic bird.

Estuarine and Inland Species

Another group of waterfowl in Baja frequents only freshwater ponds, *tinajas* (springs), lakes, streams, and marshes. These birds include two species of bittern, the American coot, two species of duck, the snow goose, the northern harrier, six species of heron, the white-faced ibis, the common moorhen, two species of rail, five species of sandpiper, the lesser scaup, the shoveler, the common snipe, the sora, the roseate spoonbill, the wood stork, three species of teal, the northern waterthrush, and the American wigeon. Some of these birds are native; others only winter over.

In Baja's sierras dwell the golden eagle, the western flycatcher, the lesser goldfinch, the black-headed grosbeak, the red-tailed hawk, two species of hummingbird, the pheasant, the yellow-eyed junco, the white-breasted nuthatch, the mountain plover, four species of vireo, eight species of warbler, the acorn woodpecker, and the canyon wren.

Common in the desert and other open country are three species of falcon (peregrine, prairie, and Cooper's), three species of flycatcher, six species of hawk, the black-fronted hummingbird, the American kestrel, the merlin, two species of owl, the greater roadrunner, eight species of sparrow, two species of thrasher, the vernon, the turkey vulture, the ladder-backed woodpecker, and the cactus wren.

Once common throughout Baja California, the **California condor** *(Gymnogyps californianus)* is now an endangered species, with just over 150 individuals alive in the world. Weighing up to 11 kilograms (24 lbs), with a wingspan of nearly 3.6 meters (12 ft), California condors are the largest North American bird, and the second largest bird in the world after the Andean condor of South America. Captive breeding at zoos in Los Angeles and San Diego has met limited success, but subsequent release programs in the Grand Canyon and southern California have not been successful. A group of U.S. and Mexican scientists has plans to try releasing condors in Baja's Sierra de San Pedro Mártir, in hopes that the more limited human presence will permit the bird to survive in the wild.

REPTILES AND AMPHIBIANS

Among the slippery, slimy, scaly, crawly things that live in Baja California are around 30 species of lizards, including two endemics; five species of frogs and toads; six species of turtles; and around 35 different kinds of snakes, including the endemic rattleless rattlesnake.

Lizards

One four-legged reptilian of note is the **chuckwalla,** which is found on certain islands in the Sea of Cortez; it sometimes grows to nearly a meter in length. The chuckwalla drinks fresh water when available, storing it in sacs that gurgle when it walks; when a freshwater source is not available, the lizard imbibes saltwater, which it processes through a sort of internal desalinator. Another good-sized Baja lizard is the **desert iguana,** found throughout the Gulf Coast Desert and possibly farther north. Larger iguanas are sometimes eaten in ranchero stews and are said to taste better than chicken. The **coast horned lizard,** similar to the horny toad of the American Southwest, is another Baja endemic.

Turtles

Of the six turtle varieties present in Baja, five are sea turtles: the leatherback, green, hawksbill, western ridley, and loggerhead. The **loggerhead** migrates back and forth between the Japanese island of Kyushu and the Sea of Cortez, a distance of 10,460 kilometers (6,500 mi). Because their eggs, meat, and shells are highly valued among coastal Mexican populations, all sea turtles are on the endangered species list. The Mexican government has declared turtle hunting and turtle egg collecting illegal; the devastation of the turtles has slowed considerably but hasn't yet stopped. *Bajacalifornianos* say they're upholding the laws while anglers along the mainland coast of the Sea of Cortez still take sea turtles.

turtle nest

The main culprit has apparently been Japan, which is the world's largest importer of sea turtles—including the endangered ridley and hawksbill. The Japanese use the turtles for meat, turtle leather, and turtle-shell fashion accessories. In 1991, the Japanese government announced a ban on the importation of sea turtles, so perhaps the Sea of Cortez populations will eventually make a comeback.

Snakes

The rocky desert lands and chaparrals of Baja are perfect snake country. The bad news is that about half the known species are venomous; the good news is they rarely come into contact with humans. Scorpion stings far outnumber snakebites in Baja.

Harmless species include the western blind snake, rosy boa, Baja California rat snake, spotted leaf-nosed snake, western patch-nosed snake, bull snake, coachwhip, king snake, Baja sand snake, and California lyre snake.

The venomous kinds fall into two categories, one of which contains only a single snake species, the **yellow-bellied sea snake.** Sea snakes usually flee the vicinity when they sense human presence, but as a general precaution don't grab anything in the water that looks like a floating stick—that's how sea snakes deceive their prey.

The other venomous category comprises the rattlesnakes, of which there are supposedly 18 species stretched out along Baja California. The most common species is the near-endemic **Baja California rattler,** whose range includes the lower three-fourths of the peninsula. Look for scaly mounds over the eyes if you care to make an identification. The **red diamondback** frequents the northern deserts and chaparral and is also fairly common. The most dangerous of Baja rattlers is the **Western diamondback;** it's the largest and therefore has the greatest potential to deliver fatal or near-fatal doses of venom. Fortunately, the diamondback is mostly confined to the canyons of the northern sierras.

All other rattlesnakes in Baja are more a nuisance than an actual threat since they overwhelmingly tend toward the injection of nonfatal doses of venom. For Graham Mackintosh, the Briton who hiked almost the entire perimeter of the Baja peninsula and wrote a book about his experiences *(Into a Desert Place),* rattlesnake became a welcome part of his desert diet.

The only rattler fully endemic to Baja is also the strangest. The **rattleless rattlesnake** *(Crotalus catalinensis)* was first discovered in 1952 on Isla Santa Catalina, a small mountainous Sea of Cortez island south of Loreto. Fortunately, Santa Catalina is the only habitat for this snake; its lack of a warning signal might otherwise keep most of us away from the peninsular deserts forever.

The general all-inclusive Spanish term for snake is *serpiente;* a nonvenomous snake is referred to as *culebra,* the venomous sort *víbora.* A rattlesnake is *un serpiente de cascabel* or simply *un cascabel.* For tips on how to avoid snakebite, see the sidebar *Snakebite Prevention and Treatment* in the *Essentials* chapter. An encouraging factoid: According to Spanish records, no missionary ever died of snakebite during the 300-year period of Spanish colonization of the New World.

History

PRE-CORTESIAN HISTORY

Because Baja California lacks spectacular archaeological remains, such as the Mayan and Aztec ruins in the southern reaches of mainland Mexico, it has largely been ignored by archaeologists. It is highly likely, however, that the Baja California peninsula was inhabited by human populations well before the rest of Mexico. Baja was the logical termination for the coastal migration route followed by Asian groups who crossed the Bering Strait land bridge between Asia and North America beginning around 50,000 B.C.

San Dieguito and La Jolla Cultures

The earliest known Baja inhabitants were members of the San Dieguito culture who migrated south into northern Baja approximately 7,000 years ago. Evidence of their presence in California dates back 9,000 years. The San Dieguito people spent much of the year wandering in small migratory bands of 15–20, guided by freshwater sources and the availability of game. Their simple economy was based on hunting, fishing, and the gathering of edible wild plants. Archaeological remains include circles of stones, stone tools—choppers, raspers, knives, spear points, axe heads, mortars *(metates)*—and simple pottery.

Evidence suggests the San Dieguitos coexisted, at least for a time, with the Jollanos (or La Jolla culture), about whom little is known except that they lived by gathering fish and shellfish, seeds, roots, and wild vegetables.

The Yumanos

The San Dieguito culture either developed into or was superseded by that of the Yumanos, whose archaeological signature of rock paintings and petroglyphs indicates their presence on the peninsula around 2,500 years ago. The Yumanos made use of more sophisticated hunting equipment as well as fishing nets; they also seem to have developed ceramics well before their counterparts in the American Southwest. Upon the arrival of the Spanish in the 16th century, some Yumano groups were practicing cultivation in the Río Colorado floodplains of northern Baja. These groups included the Cucapá, Tipai, Paipai (or Pa'ipai), Kumyai, and Kiliwa.

Like many of the less aggressive Amerindians throughout Mexico and Mesoamerica, the Yumano tribes didn't last long after missionization. Those who weren't killed by European-borne diseases or executed for rebelling against the padres were assimilated. All that is left of the Yumano culture today is scattered galleries of petroglyphs and rock paintings.

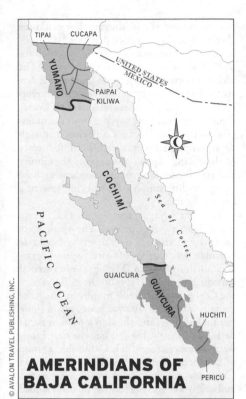

AMERINDIANS OF BAJA CALIFORNIA

A Yumano rock painting near La Rumorosa depicts a winter solstice celebration, suggesting a rudimentary knowledge of astronomy. One of the figures in the painting, a 30-centimeter (12-inch) red human caricature that may represent a shaman, catches light only on December 21, for about 20 minutes beginning at sunrise.

The Cochimís and Guaycuras

Amerindian groups living in the central and southern reaches of the peninsula when the Spanish arrived were apparently much less advanced technologically than the Yumanos. Because of the lack of archaeological research in these areas, the only record we have of these cultures consists of Spanish accounts, which were undoubtedly biased in light of their mis-

sion to subordinate the peoples of the New World. Mission histories are full of lurid tales of Amerindian customs, many probably written to convince the Spanish crown of the desperate need to convert the natives. Nevertheless, the Amerindians of central and southern Baja appear to have been among the more "primitive" of the tribes encountered by the Spanish in Mexico or Mesoamerica. In modern archaeological terms, they hadn't progressed beyond the Paleolithic epoch (the early Stone Age).

According to these accounts, the Cochimís inhabited the central peninsula and Comonú while Guaycuras—divided into the Pericú, Huchiti, and Guaicura tribes—occupied the Cape Region. One fringe anthropological view has suggested that a portion of the Guaycura tribes may have descended from Tahitian seafarers who were blown off course on their way to Hawaii. Whatever their place of origin, they spent most of their daylight hours searching for food; the men hunted small game or gathered shellfish while the women gathered fruit, seeds, and roots. If game was scarce, the people subsisted on insects and would even eat dried animal skins, including, according to reports, the leather boots of the conquistadors.

The southern Amerindians generally lived in the open and sought shelter only in the severest weather. Men wore little or no clothing, while women wore leather or yucca-fiber thongs around the waist with woven grasses or twigs suspended from the front and animal skins in the back. These garments were sometimes painted with bright colors. The tips of arrows and spears were generally of sharpened hardwood only, though chipped stone points were occasionally used. The Guaycuras also used reed blowguns. The most important time of year among these Amerindians was when the fruit of the *pitahaya* cactus ripened; the fruit was then so abundant the Amerindians allegedly abandoned all activities save sleeping and eating.

Neither the Guaycuras nor the Cochimís apparently left behind any artwork. This has been attributed to their harsh living environment; they had little time or energy for artistic pursuits. However, in the inland areas of the peninsula once inhabited by the Guaycura and Cochimí tribes, numerous spectacular rock-art sites have been discovered. The Cochimís told the Spanish this rock art was created by a race of giants who'd preceded them. Almost nothing is known about this lost Amerindian culture, a people Baja rock-art expert Harry Crosby has dubbed "the Painters."

THE SPANISH CONQUEST OF MEXICO

Following 700 years of conflict with the Moors over control of the Iberian peninsula, Spain in the 15th century emerged as the most powerful nation in Europe. Convinced that a Roman Catholic God was destined to rule the world with Spain as his emissary, the Spanish monarchy sent Christopher Columbus in search of a new route to the Far East. His mission was to establish contact with a mythical "Great Khan" to develop an alternate trade route with the Orient, since Arabs controlled the overland route through the Middle East. Along the way as many pagans as possible would be converted to Christianity. Once the Arab trade monopoly was broken, the Holy Land would be returned to Christian control.

Columbus's landing in the West Indies in 1492 was followed by Pope Alexander VI's historic 1493 decree, which gave the Spanish rights to any new land discovered west of the Azores, as long as the Spanish made "God's name known there." Hence, the Spanish conquest of the New World started as a roundabout extension of the Holy Crusades.

A succession of Spanish expeditions into the Caribbean and Gulf of Mexico rapidly achieved the conquest of Mexico and Central America. Conquistador Hernán Cortés subdued the Valley of Mexico Aztecs in three years (1519–1521), and the allegiance—or decimation—of other Aztecs and Mayans followed quickly.

Early Explorations

When the Spanish conquistadors came to the western edge of mainland Mexico and looked beyond toward the landforms they could see above the sea, they concluded that Baja California was a huge island and that the as-yet-unnamed Sea of Cortez led to the Atlantic. The idea of a northwest passage to the Atlantic persisted for years, even among seasoned explorers like Cabrillo, Drake, and Vizcaíno. Cortés himself directed four voyages from the mainland to the island of La California, although he accompanied only the third. The history of these early expeditions exposes the enmity and extreme sense of competition among those conquistadors supposedly working toward a common cause.

The first voyage, launched in 1532, never made it to the peninsula. The ships were captured in the Sea of Cortez by Nuño de Guzmán, an archrival of Cortés operating farther north in Mexico. The next year a second expedition, under Captain Diego Becerra of the *Concepción,* suffered a mutiny in which the captain was killed. Basque pilot Fortún Jiménez took charge, and the ship landed in Bahía de la Paz in early 1534. Thus the first European visitors to reach Baja California, a group of mutineers, arrived there just 42 years after Columbus touched down in the West Indies and nearly a century before the Pilgrims landed at Plymouth Rock.

Before they had much of a chance to explore, Jiménez and 22 of his crew were killed by Amerindians while filling their water casks at a spring. The survivors managed to sail the *Concepción* back to the mainland, where most were promptly captured by Guzmán. One of the escapees managed to reach Cortés with tales of rich caches of black pearls on a huge island with "cliffs and headlands and rocky coasts," as in the California of popular myth.

Cortés, inspired by these stories, organized and led a third expedition, partially financed by his own personal wealth. His party consisted of three ships and a group of 500 Spanish colonists that included women and children. They landed at the northeast end of Bahía de la Paz—which Cortés named Santa Cruz—in May of 1535, the same year New Spain was officially established. Although Cortés apparently found pearls in abundance, his attempt to colonize the peninsula lasted only two years, by which time disease, hostile Amerindians, and *chubascos* had driven the colonists back to the mainland.

The fourth attempt by Cortés to establish a Spanish foothold on Baja was led by the highly competent Captain Francisco de Ulloa, who'd accompanied Cortés on the failed Santa Cruz expedition. Cortés stayed behind on this one, hoping Ulloa's expedition would be able to find a more hospitable Baja beachhead. Ulloa set sail from Acapulco with two ships in July 1539, and over the next eight months he managed to explore the entire perimeter of the Sea of Cortez, reaching the mouth of the Río Colorado and rounding the Cape along the Pacific coast as far north as Isla Cedros.

Upon reaching Isla Cedros, Ulloa reportedly sent one ship back to Acapulco for supplies; it isn't known for certain what happened to the other vessel. According to some historical accounts, Ulloa found his way back to the mainland and was murdered by one of his own crew near Guadalajara; other accounts say he disappeared north of Isla Cedros. At any rate, his written report of the voyage—which indicated Baja was not an island but a peninsula—didn't surface until a hundred years later. His biggest contribution to the geography of the times was the naming of the Mar de Cortés, now the Sea of Cortez or Gulf of California.

After squandering most of his wealth in futile attempts to explore Baja, Cortés was recalled to Spain in 1541, never to return to Mexican shores. In his place, Spain dispatched experienced Portuguese navigator Juan Rodríguez Cabrillo in 1542 with orders to explore the Pacific coast. Starting from the southern tip of the peninsula, his expedition made it as far north as the Oregon coast and mapped several major bays along the way, including those of San Diego and Monterey. Cabrillo himself never made it past California's Santa Barbara Islands, where he died following a mysterious fall.

Manila Galleons and Privateers

On the other side of the globe, events were unfolding that would influence Baja California's history for the next 250 years. Although Portuguese navigator Ferdinand Magellan reached the Philippines in 1521, it wasn't until 1565 that López de Legaspi defeated the archipelago's native defenders. Immediately thereafter, Esteban Rodríguez and Padre Andrés de Urdaneta pioneered a ship route from Manila to the New World that took advantage of the 14,500-kilometer (9,000-mi) Japanese Current across the northern Pacific, thus establishing a trade connection between the Orient and New Spain.

The ships making the annual roundtrip voyages between Manila and Acapulco beginning in 1566 came to be called "Manila galleons." The lengthy sea journey was difficult, however, because of the lack of fresh water during the final weeks of the five- to seven-month eastward crossing. This provided further impetus for establishing some sort of settlement in Baja where ships could put in for water and supplies.

A Baja California landfall became even more desirable when in 1572 the Manila galleons started carrying shipments of gold, silks, and spices to New Spain. Laden with Asian exports, these ships were so heavy they became easy prey for faster pirate vessels. By 1580, England's Sir Francis Drake had entered the Pacific via the Straits of Magellan and circumnavigated the globe, thus ending Spanish dominion over the seas. Drake plundered Spanish ships with regularity, and as news of the treasure-laden ships spread, other English as well as Dutch privateers were lured into the Pacific.

Their raids on Spanish ships became an embarrassment to the crown and a drain on Spanish wealth, so the Spaniards were forced to seek out harbors in Baja's Cape Region where they could hide. Since the first land sighting on the east Pacific leg of the Manila–Acapulco voyage was below the peninsula's midpoint, the Cape Region was the logical choice for a landing. Following much experimentation, Bahía San Lucas and Bahía de la Paz became the two harbors most frequently used.

Eventually, however, the keen privateers figured out how to trap Spanish ships in the bays their crews sought for protection. Thomas Cavendish plundered the Manila galleon *Santa Ana* at Cabo San Lucas in 1587, and so many ships were captured in Bahía de la Paz that the landfall there, originally called Santa Cruz by Cortés, eventually earned the name Pichilingue, a Spanish mispronunciation of Vlissingen, the provenance of most of the Dutch pirates.

Pirating continued off the Baja coast throughout the entire 250-year history of the Manila–Acapulco voyages. One of the more celebrated English privateers in later years was Woodes Rogers, who arrived in the Pacific in 1709 and captured the Manila galleon *Encarnación* off Cabo San Lucas. On his way to Baja California that same year Rogers rescued Alexander Selkirk, a sailor marooned on an island off the coast of Chile for four years. Selkirk served as shipmaster on Rogers's vessel and later became the inspiration for Daniel Defoe's 1719 novel *Robinson Crusoe*.

Further Exploration and Colonization Attempts

As the Spaniards' need for a permanent settlement in California grew more dire, coastal explorations were resumed after a hiatus of more than 50 years. Cabrillo was succeeded by merchant-turned-admiral Sebastián Vizcaíno, who in 1596 landed at the same bay on the southeast coast chosen by his predecessors, Jiménez and Cortés. This time, however, the natives were friendly (perhaps because it was *pitahaya* fruit season when they arrived) and Vizcaíno named the site La Paz (Peace). After loading up on *pitahaya* fruit—effective for preventing scurvy—and pearls, Vizcaíno continued north along the Sea of Cortez coast, stopping to gather more pearls before returning to the mainland.

In 1602 Vizcaíno commanded a second, more ambitious expedition that sailed along the Pacific coast to near present-day Mendocino, California. His names for various points and bays along the coasts of both Californias superseded most of those bestowed by Cabrillo and Cortés.

Upon his return Vizcaíno told his superiors that the Monterey Bay area of California was well suited to colonization. However, because he was no longer in favor with New Spain's

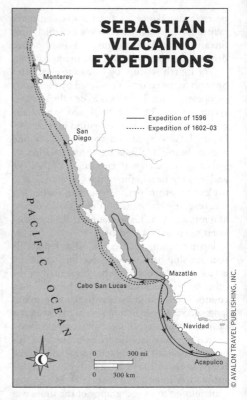

SEBASTIÁN VIZCAÍNO EXPEDITIONS

——— Expedition of 1596
------- Expedition of 1602–03

Monterey

San Diego

PACIFIC OCEAN

Mazatlán

Cabo San Lucas

Navidad

0   300 mi

0   300 km

Acapulco

© AVALON TRAVEL PUBLISHING, INC.

fickle viceroys, no one paid much attention to his findings and he was reassigned to an obscure Sinaloa port. The cartographer for the voyage, Gerónimo Martínez, was beheaded for forgery, although his maps of the California coast and Baja remained the best available for more than 200 years.

This neglect of California's potential enabled an Englishman to put first claim to the territory. Sir Francis Drake, who landed at what is now Drake's Bay in northern California during his 1578–1780 voyage, christened the land New Albion on behalf of the English crown. Like the Spanish maps of the time, his maps depicted California and Baja as an island.

For a time Spain left both Californias unexplored. In 1615 Captain Juan de Iturbi obtained the first official concession for peninsular pearl diving, but no land settlement was established. After two of his ships were captured by Dutch privateers off Cabo San Lucas, de Iturbi sailed his remaining vessel northward in the Sea of Cortez as far as the 28th parallel, harvesting pearls along the way. Because of dwindling provisions, the expedition was forced to turn back to the mainland after only a few months.

The peninsula remained unconquered by the Spanish for another 80 years. In 1683, Spain's Royal Council for the Indies authorized an expedition under Admiral Isidor Atondo y Antillón and Padre Eusebio Francisco Kino, which managed to occupy an area of La Paz for three and a months before being driven back to the mainland by dwindling provisions and hostile natives. After two months of rest and provisioning on the mainland, they crossed the Sea of Cortez again, this time establishing a mission and presidio just above the 26th parallel at a place they named San Bruno. Supported by a friendly Amerindian population, the mission lasted 19 months. Lack of water and food—they had to rely on supply ships from the mainland—forced Kino and Atondo back to the mainland.

Kino never returned to Baja California but later became famous for his missionary efforts in northwestern Mexico and Arizona, where he is said to have converted thousands of Amerindians to Roman Catholicism. In 1701 he accompanied an expedition from the northwest of Sonora to the mouth of the Río Colorado that confirmed Ulloa's claim that Baja California was a peninsula. He died in Sonora in 1711.

THE MISSION PERIOD
The Founding of the Jesuit Missions

Padre Juan María Salvatierra finally succeeded in giving Spain and the church what they wanted: a permanent Spanish settlement on the Baja California peninsula. Backed by the mainland missionary system, a 30,000-peso annual subsidy from the Royal Council of the Indies, and a contingent of Spanish soldiers, Salvatierra landed in San Bruno in October 1697, located a better water source 24

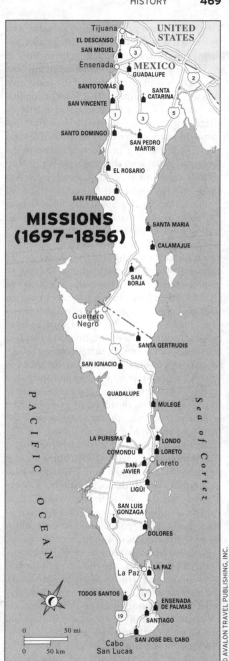

MISSIONS (1697-1856)

kilometers south of the original presidio, and proceeded to establish the mother of all California missions, Nuestra Señora de Loreto.

The founding of the Loreto mission initiated what Baja historians usually call the Jesuit missionary period, lasting 1697–1767. During this interval, the Jesuits established 20 missions, stretching from the southern tip of the peninsula to near present-day Cataviña in central Baja. That wasn't a spectacular accomplishment compared with the progress of mainland colonization, but Baja was a much more difficult area to colonize. It had taken 167 years from the time the first Spaniard had set foot on the shore until the first successful settlement was established on Baja California soil.

The Spanish mission system basically worked like this: The padres, always in the company of armed escorts, approached groups of natives and offered them the protection of the church and the Spanish crown in return for a willingness to undergo religious instruction. Those natives who agreed were congregated at a suitable spot and directed to build a mission. The mission in turn became a refuge for the Amerindians and a place for them to learn European farming techniques and other trades, as well as Catholic ways. Once pacification was complete, the mission became a secularized church community *(pueblo),* and the missionaries moved on to new areas.

The system worked well with the docile Amerindians of Central Mexico but was often unsuccessful among the nomadic, fiercely independent Amerindians of Northern Mexico and Baja. Elsewhere in Mexico and Latin America, the norm was to secularize after 10 years; in Baja, the Spanish church never voluntarily secularized its missions.

Amateur historians like to say Baja was missionized by the cross, not the sword. This was actually no more true in Baja than it was on the mainland. The military presence here was indeed less, but only because the Jesuits were given greater administrative power in Baja and had to finance themselves, and their militia, through church funds. The conversion techniques were the same: natives who obeyed the padres were rewarded with land and protection, those who rebelled were punished, and those who organized rebellions were executed. Apologists claim the padres never endorsed violence, but if this were true, they wouldn't have brought along the militia in the first place.

Of the 21 principal Jesuit padres who missionized Baja, only four came from Spain. The other 17 hailed from Italy, Germany, Honduras, Bohemia, Austria, and France. Unlike their counterparts on the mainland, who managed to publish 11 grammars analyzing the Uto–Aztecan languages of northwestern Mexico, none of these Jesuit priests ever published a text describing any of the Baja languages.

A contemporary report of the founding of Misión San Juan Bautista describes how Padres Salvatierra and Pedro de Ugarte approached the natives of Liguí in 1703:

> The two Padres, the soldier who accompanied them, and two Christian Indians were given a real fright by a large band of Indians who fired a shower of arrows toward them, but after the soldier...discharged his musket into the air the Indians threw down their weapons and prostrated themselves on the earth, presently sitting up to await the coming of the Padres. Through an interpreter, Padre Salvatierra explained to them the purpose of their visit and distributed among them some small gifts, expressing the hope that Padre Pedro de Ugarte might return later and be welcomed by them. Before leaving they brought 48 Indian children for baptism.

Amerindian Revolts, Disease, and the Decline of the Jesuits

Several times during the Jesuit period, groups of Amerindians revolted against missionization. The most significant rebellion occurred in 1734–1736 among the Pericú of the southern peninsula. Apparently the revolt was triggered by Padre Nicolás Tamaral's injunction against polygamy—long a practice among the Pericú and Guaicura, tribes in which women outnumbered men. The punishment of a Pericú shaman under the injunction doubled the perceived assault on native culture, and a group of disaffected Amerindians organized themselves against the entire mission structure.

In October 1734, the Pericú attacked and burned the missions at Santiago and San José del Cabo, killing Padre Tamaral and his counterpart at Santiago; they also set fire to the mission in La Paz although the padre there escaped unharmed and was able to send to the mainland for assistance. In Todos Santos, the rebels killed 49 Amerindian inhabitants who tried to defend their pueblo. The provincial governor of Sinaloa, after receiving letters from Loreto describing the uprising, dispatched a ship from the mainland with 60 Yaqui warriors and a number of Spanish soldiers. The troops marched from mission to mission, meeting little resistance from the poorly equipped Pericú.

Unrest among the Pericú continued for another two years, a situation that led to the founding of a large garrison at San José del Cabo. As a further precaution, the garrisons at every mission in the south were expanded by 10 soldiers each. Besides reinforcing the missions, this increased military presence encouraged Manila galleons to make Cabo San Lucas a regular stop on their return voyages from the Orient.

In the years to follow, epidemics of smallpox and measles—diseases borne by Europeans for which Amerindians had no natural immunity—devastated the Amerindian population. In 1738, Padre Jacobo Baegert of Misión San Luis Gonzaga estimated Baja California's Amerindian population at about 50,000. In three outbreaks of smallpox in 1742, 1744, and 1748, an estimated 42,000 Amerindians—84 percent of the native population—perished. Gathering the natives into mission settlements only hastened their demise, intensifying the spread of contagions. A significant number of Amerindians also lost their lives in continued rebellions against the padres. The La Paz mission was abandoned in 1748; by 1767, only one member of the entire Huchiti branch of the Guaycura nation survived.

As the southern Amerindians died out, the missionaries moved quickly northward, seeking new sheep for their flocks. The last four missions established by the Jesuits—Santa Gertrudis (1752), San Borja (1762), Calamajué (1766), and Santa María (1767)—were scattered widely in northern Baja in an obvious push toward California.

In 1767, King Charles III ordered the expulsion of the Jesuit Order from all Spanish dominions, including Baja California. Accounts of the expulsion disagree as to the reasons behind his action. According to crown representatives, the Jesuits were too power-hungry and would no longer be held accountable for their actions. The Jesuits themselves claimed persecution because they'd dared criticize corruption among the nobility and royalty of Europe. Whatever the reason, in 1768 the 16 Jesuit padres of Baja found themselves herded onto a ship bound for the mainland port of San Blas, where the same ship received a contingent of Franciscan padres sent to replace them.

The Franciscans and Dominicans

The 14 Franciscan padres who arrived in Loreto in 1768 included Padre Junípero Serra, often dubbed the Father of California. That title really belongs to Italian Padre Salvatierra, who established the first mission in Baja California 72 years prior to Serra's arrival at San Diego.

To counter the flow of non-Spanish Europeans toward California—the English across the south and middle of today's United States, the French across Canada, and the Russians south from Alaska along the coast—Serra was under orders to establish missions and presidios as quickly as possible in a northward direction.

Serra and the Franciscans only established one mission in Baja before moving on to California. This was San Fernando Velicatá, founded in 1769 about 64 kilometers southeast of today's El Rosario. The Velicatá mission was primarily used as a staging area for expeditions to California. There were two initial expeditions, one by sea from La Paz and one by land from Velicatá; both would rendezvous in San

Diego Bay. Padre Serra accompanied the land expedition, led by Captain Gaspár de Portolá, and established California's first mission at San Diego, the first in a chain of 20 missions that stretched along the upper California coast as far as Sonoma, north of San Francisco.

The ambitious Serra, realizing that the arid, underpopulated peninsula did not offer the empire-building potential of California, sent to Mexico City a proposal that the administration of the Baja California missions be released to the Dominican Order, who'd been clamoring for a place in California/Baja missionary action. The viceroy approved Serra's request in 1772, and the first Dominican priests arrived on the peninsula in 1773 under the direction of Padre Vicente Mora.

The first new Dominican mission, Nuestra Señora del Rosario Viñaraco, was founded in the valley now known as Arroyo del Rosario in 1774. Eight more missions and one visiting chapel were established by the Dominicans between 1774 and 1834, all north of El Rosario. The northernmost was Misión El Descanso, located between modern-day Ensenada and Rosarito and built on the edge of Arroyo del Descanso, the official boundary line separating the respective domains of the Dominican order to the south and the Franciscan order to the north. This boundary also served to separate the New Spain provinces of Alta and Baja California, as officially designated in 1777. The current border between Baja California and the U.S. state of California was created by the Treaty of Hidalgo at the end of the Mexican-American War in 1848.

By the end of the 18th century it was clear that Spain and the church could no longer afford to support the Baja missions. The peninsula's Amerindian population had dwindled to less than 5,000 by 1800, and without an abundance of free native labor, maintaining a colony wasn't an easy task. The California missions to the north seemed much more promising—water was more available and the Amerindian labor force was more docile and plentiful. The growing unrest in Mexico placed the peninsula even lower on Spain's list of priorities.

INDEPENDENCE FROM SPAIN

The Catholic Church in Mexico had amassed huge amounts of wealth by the beginning of the 19th century and had become a lender to the colony's growing entrepreneurial class. At the other end of the economic spectrum, the increasing numbers of mestizos—Mexican-born residents of mixed Spanish and Amerindian ancestry—were denied land ownership and other rights and were generally treated as second-class citizens.

Fearing the church was becoming too powerful, King Charles III of Spain decreed in 1804 that all church funds be turned over to the royal coffers. As padres all over Mexico were forced to comply with the decree, calling back large sums of money lent out to entrepreneurs, economic chaos ensued. Mexicans blamed their economic and social problems on Spain's remote rule; when Napoleon invaded Spain in 1808, limiting authority to Spanish loyalists in Mexico City, the disaffected clergy began planning a revolt.

Mexico's struggle for independence from Spain began on September 16, 1810, a date celebrated annually as Día de la Independencia, or Mexican Independence Day. Padre Miguel Hidalgo y Costilla issued a call for independence today known as the Grito de Dolores (Dolores Cry) from the mainland city of Dolores, Guanajuato. Although the rebels who gathered around Hidalgo soon captured Zacatecas, Valladolid, and San Luis Potosí, Mexico wasn't completely free of Spanish rule for another 11 years. When Hidalgo was captured and executed by loyalists, another padre took his place, and the fighting continued until Mexico City acceded to the demands of the rebels in 1821.

The 1821 Plan de Iguala treaty between Spain and Mexico guaranteed three political underpinnings of the new regime: the religious dominance of the Catholic Church, a constitutional monarchy, and equal rights for mestizos as well as Mexican-born Spaniards. Former viceroy Agustín de Iturbide was appointed emperor of the new republic, but his reign lasted only two years before he was overthrown by another junta that established a short-lived federal republic called Los Estados Unidos de México—the United States of Mexico—in 1824.

Over the next six years the Mexican republic endured two more coups; it wasn't until 1829 that all Spanish troops were expelled from Mexico. In 1832 all non-Dominican missions in Baja were secularized and converted to parish churches. The Dominican missions of the northern peninsula were allowed to remain because they were considered the only outposts of civilization north of La Paz and Loreto and as such were important links with prospering Alta California. Another change in policy involved the encouragement of Anglo-American immigration to the northeastern Mexican state of Coahuila y Texas—a policy that would have profound implications later on.

The Mexican-American War

In 1833 Antonio López de Santa Anna, a megalomaniac general in charge of enforcing the expulsion of Spanish troops, seized power and revoked the Constitution of 1824, thus initiating a series of events that eventually led to a war with the United States and the resultant loss of huge amounts of territory. During the first 30 years of Mexican independence, Mexico changed governments 50 times; Santa Anna—who called himself the Napoleon of the West—headed 11 of these regimes.

Mexican citizens everywhere were angry at the revocation of their republican constitution by a self-appointed dictator. But none were more frustrated than the Anglo-American immigrants who had voluntarily abandoned their U.S. citizenship to take Mexican citizenship under the Constitution of 1824 and live in the northern half of Coahuila y Texas. In 1836 the "Texicans" declared an independent Republic of Texas, fought and lost San Antonio's famous Battle of the Alamo, then routed Santa Anna's defending troops in San Jacinto, Texas.

Defeated and captured, Santa Anna signed the Velasco Agreement, which guaranteed Texas independence and recognized the Rio Grande as the border between Mexico and the new Texan republic. There matters lay until the United States granted statehood to the near-bankrupt republic in 1845. Santa Anna's government refused to recognize the Velasco Agreement, claiming Texas only extended as far south as the Nueces River, about 160 kilometers north of the Rio Grande at the widest gap. When the U.S. Army moved into the area south of the Nueces, Santa Anna retaliated by sending troops across the Rio Grande, thus initiating the Mexican-American War.

After a series of skirmishes along the Rio Grande, U.S. president James Polk ordered the army to invade Mexico. In Baja California, Mexican and American forces engaged at Santo Tomás, Mulegé, La Paz, and San José del Cabo. Mexico City finally fell to U.S. troops in March 1847, and Santa Anna signed the Treaty of Guadalupe Hidalgo in 1848. In the treaty, Mexico conceded not only the Rio Grande area of Texas but part of New Mexico and all of California for a payment of US$25 million and the cancellation of all Mexican debt.

In retrospect, it is likely the annexation of Texas was part of a U.S. plan to provoke Mexico into declaring war so the United States could gain more of the Southwest. The war so damaged Mexico's already weakened economy that in 1853 Santa Anna sold Arizona and southern New Mexico to the United States for another US$10 million. During that same year, American freebooter William Walker sailed to La Paz and declared himself President of Lower California. He and his mercenary troops fled upon hearing that Mexican forces were on the way. He was later tried—and acquitted—in the United States for violation of neutrality laws. Walker was executed after a similar escapade in Nicaragua two years later.

For the Mexican population, already strongly dissatisfied with Santa Anna, these losses of territory became the final straw; in 1855 Santa Anna was overthrown by populist Benito Juárez.

Depopulation of the Peninsula, Civil War, and Reform

The second half of the 19th century was even more turbulent for Mexico than the first. At the end of the Mexican-American War, the

California Gold Rush of 1849 lured many Mexicans and Amerindians away from the peninsula to seek their fortunes in California, reducing Baja's already scant population even further and transforming it into a haven for bandits, pirates, and an assortment of other outlaws and misfits. Only six Dominican padres remained on the peninsula by the 1880s.

Meanwhile, back on the mainland, a civil war (called the War of Reform in Mexico) erupted in 1858 following the removal of Santa Anna; self-appointed governments in Mexico City and Veracruz vied for national authority. Once again, church wealth was the principal issue. The liberals, under Zapotec lawyer Benito Juárez, had promulgated a new constitution in 1857 and passed a law further restricting the financial powers of the church; all church property save for church buildings themselves had to be sold or otherwise relinquished. A reactionary opposition group took control of Mexico City, and fighting continued until 1861, when the liberals won and Juárez was elected president.

Juárez immediately had to deal with the 1862 French invasion of Mexico, which came in response to Mexico's nonpayment of debts to France. Napoleon III's first invading force was defeated at Puebla near the Gulf of Mexico coast, but the following year the French captured the city and continued onward to take Mexico City, where they installed Austrian Ferdinand Maximilian as emperor of Mexico. Under U.S. pressure, the French gradually withdrew from Mexico, and Juárez was back in power by 1867.

Over the next four years Juárez initiated many economic and educational reforms. Upon his death in 1872, political opponent Porfirio Díaz took over and continued reforms begun by Juárez, albeit in a more authoritarian manner. Díaz and/or his cronies ruled for the next 28 years, suspending political freedoms but modernizing the country's education and transportation systems.

Foreign Investment in Baja California

In Baja, Díaz and the "Porfiriato" encouraged foreign investment on a large scale, and in the 1880s vast land tracts were sold to American or European mining, farming, manufacturing, and railway concessions. All but the mining concessions met failure within a few years, mainly because the investors weren't prepared to deal with the peninsula's demanding climate and lack of transportation. A Connecticut company invested US$5 million as a down payment on US$16 million for extensive land holdings in Ensenada and San Quintín. There it planned to develop farmlands, railways, and seaports. When the first wheat crop succumbed to lack of rain, the company sold out to a similar English development syndicate, which also failed.

Mineral excavation in late-19th-century Baja enjoyed a boom—gold, silver, copper, and gypsum were the main finds, along with graphite, mercury, nickel, and sulfur. One of the most successful mining endeavors was that of Compañía del Boleo, a French mining syndicate in Santa Rosalía that for many years was the largest copper-mining and smelting operation in Mexico.

THE 20TH CENTURY
The Mexican Revolution

By the early 20th century, it was obvious that the gap between rich and poor was increasing, caused by the extreme procapitalist policies of the Díaz regime and the lack of a political voice for workers and peasants. In response to the situation, a liberal opposition group, using Texas as a base, formed in exile, organizing strikes throughout the country. This forced Díaz to announce an election in 1910; his opponent was Francisco Madero, a liberal from Coahuila. As it became clear that Madero was garnering mass support, Díaz imprisoned him on trumped-up charges.

Upon his release, Madero fled to Texas and began organizing the overthrow of the Díaz government. The rebels, with the assistance of colorful bandit-turned-revolutionary Pancho Villa and peasant-hero Emiliano Zapata, managed to gain control of the Northern Mexico states of Sonora and Chihuahua. Unable to contain the revolution, Díaz resigned in May 1910, and Madero was elected president. His one-time allies, however, broke into several factions—the Zapatistas, Reyistas, Vasquistas, and Felicistas, named for the leaders of each movement—and Madero was executed in 1913. Baja California had its own faction, the Magonistas, who briefly held Tijuana in 1911.

For the next six years the various factions played musical chairs with national leadership; Mexico remained extremely unstable until revolutionary leader Venustiano Carranza emerged as president. Carranza held a historic convention that resulted in the Constitution of 1917, the current Mexican constitution. This document established the *ejido* program to return lands traditionally cultivated by the Amerindian peasantry, but taken away by rich ranch and plantation owners under Díaz, to local communities throughout Mexico. Three years later opponent Álvaro Obregón and his supporters overthrew Carranza.

Obregón managed to hang onto the office for four years, establishing important educational reforms; he was followed in 1924 by Plutarco Elías Calles. Calles instituted wide-reaching agrarian reforms, including the redistribution of three million hectares of land. He also participated in the establishment of the National Revolutionary Party (PNR), the forerunner of the Institutional Revolutionary Party (PRI), which remained Mexico's dominant party until the National Action Party (PAN) won the presidency in 2000.

U.S. Prohibition

In the same year that Obregón took power in Mexico City, the U.S. government amended its own constitution to make the consumption, manufacture, and sale of alcoholic beverages a federal offense. This proved to be a disastrous experiment for the United States, ushering in an era of organized crime, but was a boon to Baja California development. Americans began rushing across the border to buy booze from the restaurants, cantinas, and liquor stores of Northern Mexico.

Border towns added casinos and brothels to the assortment of liquor venues and became so prosperous that the municipal leadership

was able to lobby successfully for the division of Baja California into northern and southern territories. On the negative side, Tijuana and Mexicali became renowned as world sleaze capitals. Their reputations persisted long after Prohibition ended in 1933 and the Mexican government outlawed gambling—prostitution remained legal—in 1938. The cities wisely channeled much of their unexpected revenue into manufacturing, agriculture, and other non-tourist-related development.

Nationalist Reforms and World War II

The year 1938 proved a turning point in modern Mexican history as PNR candidate Lázaro Cárdenas ascended to the presidency. Cárdenas, a mestizo with Tarascan Amerindian heritage, instituted the most sweeping social reforms of any national leader to date, effecting significant changes in education, labor, agriculture, and commerce.

His land reforms included the redistribution of 18.6 million hectares (46 million acres) among newly created *ejidos*—a legacy that is as hot a topic for debate today as it was then. Foreign-owned oil interests were expropriated, and a national oil company, Petróleos Mexicanos (Pemex), was established. Even though foreign investors were compensated for expropriations at fair market value (under a treaty signed by both the United States and Mexico), these reforms frightened off foreign investors for many years, and it has been only recently that Mexico has re-attracted foreign capital. Cárdenas also reorganized the PNR as the Mexican Revolution Party (PRM—Partido de la Revolución Mexicana), which soon changed its name to the Institutional Revolutionary Party (PRI—Partido Revolucionario Institucional).

Between the Cárdenas period and the 2000 presidential election, Mexican political history was characterized by comparatively subtle shifts. Mexican leadership succession also had stabilized, a process often referred to as the oxymoronic "institutionalization of the revolution" (meaning the PRI had won every national election in that period).

During World War II, Mexican troops fought in the Pacific on the Allied side. The Mexican economy grew with the increased demand for materials and labor in the United States; the scarcity of imported goods in Mexico forced the nation to increase domestic production. In 1942 the United States instituted the Bracero Program, which permitted Mexicans to work north of the border for short periods of time; the program lasted until 1962 and had a profound effect on urban development along the U.S.–Mexico border.

Baja Statehood and the Transpeninsular Highway

After the war Mexico continued to industrialize, and the economy remained relatively stable under one PRI president after another. In 1952, the Territory of (Northern) Baja California was declared Mexico's 29th state as its population moved past the 80,000 required for statehood. Northern Baja was, in fact, better off economically than most of the rest of the country. The boomtowns of Tijuana and Mexicali were servicing a fast-growing border economy, and Valle de Mexicali farming competed well with California's Imperial Valley. In 1958 it was determined that Baja was second only to Mexico City in the number of automobiles per capita.

Throughout the 1960s, most of Baja south of Ensenada remained benevolently neglected, which led travel writers of the time to employ the famous catchphrase, "the forgotten peninsula." The population of the Territory of Southern Baja California was stagnating, perhaps even decreasing; except for La Paz, it was limited to tiny collections of hardy souls here and there who scratched for cash as rancheros or *pescadores* (fishermen). Even La Paz was just a step above a sleepy backwater port, although its status as a duty-free port was beginning to attract a steady trickle of mainland Mexicans.

By the 1970s, it was obvious that southern Baja wasn't going to catch up with northern Baja unless transportation between the south, north, and mainland improved. Travel between Tijuana and La Paz took up to 10 days

via rough dirt tracks. Construction of the Transpeninsular Highway (Mexico 1) was finally completed in 1973, connecting Tijuana with Cabo San Lucas for the first time. In less than a year, the population of Baja California Sur passed the 80,000 mark, and the territory became Mexico's 30th state.

The 1,700-kilometer-long (1,054-mi-long) Trans-peninsular Highway has greatly contributed to the modernization of one of Mexico's last frontiers. Fishing and agricultural cooperatives can now transport their products to the border or to the ports of Santa Rosalía, Guerrero Negro, and La Paz. The highway has brought Americans, Canadians, and Europeans deep into the peninsula in greater numbers than ever before, and the revenue from their visits provides another means of livelihood for the people of Baja.

Another boost to peninsular political and economic development came along in the 1980s when former president Miguel de la Madrid proclaimed a new era of modernization and plupartyism—equivalent in word if not in deed to Gorbachev's perestroika/glasnost proclamation. Already-modernizing Baja California Norte, partial stronghold of the PAN (Partido Acción Nacional, the nation's conservative opposition party) particularly benefited from a relaxation of PRI's hold. The era of optimism was extended by Mexican president Carlos Salinas de Gortari, who was a strong supporter of the much-debated North American Free Trade Agreement (NAFTA); see *Government and Economy*, later in this chapter, for more information on the treaty.

The Crisis of 1994-1995

Although the Mexican economy went for a roller-coaster ride in the 1970s and early 1980s when the government nationalized banks and devalued the peso, things brightened considerably in the late 1980s and early 1990s under Salinas's market modernization. Then, in 1994, everything seemed to go awry on the mainland.

On January 1, 1994, the day NAFTA took effect, a group of several hundred armed Lacandón Amerindians under the leadership of a masked, pipe-smoking mestizo who dubbed himself "Subcommandante Marcos" dramatically seized four towns in the state of Chiapas in a series of well-coordinated attacks. The group retreated swiftly in the face of overwhelming Mexican armed force but not before 145 people were killed in armed skirmishes. The Zapatista National Liberation Army (EZLN), as the guerrilla group called itself, was not only protesting NAFTA—which the EZLN believed would have negative effects on the rural southern Mexican economy—but was also airing traditional grievances regarding fraudulent regional elections and land seizure from Lacandón peasants.

While the EZLN and Mexican government were negotiating in Chiapas, another event unfolded to create even more difficulties for the Salinas government. Luis Donaldo Colosio, the PRI's prime presidential candidate groomed to take Salinas's place, was shot to death by a factory worker while campaigning in Tijuana on March 23, 1994. In the ensuing federal investigation the deputy attorney general, Mario Ruiz Massieu, and Salinas's brother, Raúl, were implicated in the suspected assassination plot.

Meanwhile, Colosio's campaign manager, Yale University graduate Ernesto Zedillo, was elected to the presidency in an August 1994 election widely considered the cleanest in Mexico's history. The decisive PRI victory was little cause for optimism, however; Mexico City politics unraveled further when investigators uncovered a trail of corruption that threatened to implicate Mexico's former wunderkind, Carlos Salinas. To avoid testifying against his own brother—or perhaps to protect himself—Carlos fled the country (Salinas now resides in Dublin, Ireland).

Raúl Salinas was subsequently found to have amassed a US$24 million fortune through illicit means. In May 1994, the government seized 117 kilograms of cocaine base during a raid on a ranch in Quintana Roo owned by a PRI senator, and around the same time a senior Ministry of Tourism official involved in deciding whether to legalize gambling casinos was arrested and charged with illegal enrichment.

By the end of 1994 the events in Chiapas, the Colosio assassination, and glimpses into high-level Mexican corruption had resulted in an extreme loss of investor confidence in Mexico, leading in turn to a stock sell-off and a domestic run on the U.S. dollar. To protect draining reserves, Mexico City responded by allowing the peso to float, sending the currency into a deflationary tailspin at the beginning of 1995.

Over the months of January and February 1995 the peso dropped from an exchange rate of N$3 per U.S. dollar to around N$8. The worst recession the country had seen in 60 years ensued. The Clinton administration, along with the International Monetary Fund (IMF), bailed out the government with loans to pay off international debt, but Mexicans of all economic classes—especially those involved with international business—suffered heavy losses and a substantial drop in standard of living.

In Baja California Norte, home base for the notorious Arellano Félix drug cartel, seven federal agents and a state prosecutor involved in antinarcotics efforts were assassinated in 1996. Such assassinations may be seen as a tribute to the integrity of the agents, for whom the only real choice when confronting powerful *narcotraficantes* may be to accept bribes or be assassinated.

INTO THE 21ST CENTURY

In his first state-of-the-nation address, President Zedillo acknowledged that corruption was deeply rooted in Mexican institutions and in the general social conduct of the nation. He confirmed the determination of his administration to confront official corruption and to encourage the creation of a new culture of respect for law, beginning with the behavior of public officials. Zedillo also signed the Organization of American States (OAS) Corruption Convention, which was ratified unanimously by the Mexican Senate. Whether any of this will make a difference is difficult to tell; virtually every president who has taken office in Mexico during the last 25 years has vowed to fight corruption. Antonio Lozano Gracia, Mexico's first attorney general ever appointed from an opposition party, dismissed more than 1,250 officials for incompetence or corruption and completely revamped hiring, training, and internal accountability.

Shortly thereafter, the attorney general himself was forced to resign for alleged corruption. Once again mass firings of state and local police took place, this time for dereliction of duty. Often these positions were taken over by military officers, who are presumed to be less corruptible than civilian law-enforcement agents. In Baja California, all 87 *judiciales,* or federal agents, involved in narcotics interdiction were replaced by members of the Mexican military in 1996. Mexico's increasing militarization is itself cause for concern, as there is no evidence whatsoever that members of the military, with less training in law enforcement than their police counterparts, will be any less corrupt than the police. The army general put in charge of the national counternarcotics effort quickly succumbed to cartel bribes and was forced to resign that same year. Most observers agree they have only so far seen gradual success at the lower levels of government and law enforcement.

Baja, because of its ties to the U.S. economy and access to the U.S. dollar, weathered "the crisis" much better than most parts of Mexico. By 2000 most sectors of the Mexican economy showed signs of recovery, though foreign investor confidence remained shaky as scandals in law enforcement, the military, and the drug arena continued to surface on an almost weekly basis. Many observers, both Mexican and international, now see the rosy Salinas years as an elaborate setup of smoke and mirrors that masked the overvaluation of the peso, corruption, and other economic and political ills that had just begun to be addressed by the sober Zedillo administration. In Baja, people just shake their heads and blame it all on the *chilangos* (Mexico City residents).

Most *bajacalifornianos* are facing the new millennium with the same self-reliance and flexibility that have enabled them to cope with the two political systems, two economies, and singular isolation that have helped forge their unique destiny.

Government

POLITICAL BOUNDARIES
The 28th parallel divides the peninsula into two states, officially named Baja California (abbreviated BC) above the parallel and Baja California Sur (BCS) below. Unofficially, the northern state is often called Baja California Norte (BCN); a debate continually simmers as to whether or not to make this version official. In this book, BCN is used so as not to confuse the northern state with the whole peninsula.

Mexicali is BCN's state capital, which governs five *municipios* that are similar to U.S. counties: Tijuana, Rosarito, Ensenada, Mexicali, and Tecate. Besides its southern border with BCS, BCN shares a northern border with the United States and an eastern border, formed above the Sea of Cortez by the Colorado River, with the Mexican state of Sonora.

Baja California Sur is likewise divided into five *municipios:* La Paz, Cabo San Lucas, Mulegé, Loreto, and Comondú. La Paz is the state capital.

POLITICAL SYSTEM
As Mexican states, BCN and BCS are part of Mexico's federal system (Estados Unidos Mexicanos, or United Mexican States), which allows for some degree of autonomous rule by state governors and their legislatures. Both states are considered among the nation's most socially progressive. More than half of Mexico's orphanages, for example, are in Baja. In 1989, BCN became the first state in Mexico to vote in an opposition party when citizens elected a PAN (Partido Acción Nacional, or National Action Party) state government—most other

states in Mexico have been ruled by the PRI (Partido Revolucionario Institucional) since the Mexican Revolution. PAN is usually described as a conservative party because it favors private over government ownership, yet in the context of Mexican politics it's more reform-minded than PRI. As elsewhere in the world, political labels and their meanings shift with time. Baja California has tended to follow the example of other wealthier northern Mexican states by keeping PAN administrations in office.

Meanwhile, the residents of Baja California Sur most recently voted in a leftist coalition party consisting of the PRD (Partido Revolucionario Democrático, or Democratic Revolutionary Party) and the PT (Partido Trabajadores, or Workers Party). Many were surprised to see that the state containing Baja's most extensive resort area (Los Cabos) elected a PRD/PT candidate. However, these parties are well organized in southern Baja, whose residents are generally more agrarian and poorer than their neighbors to the immediate north.

PAN and PRD/PT victories in BCN and BCS are considered by some as watersheds in Mexican political affairs, which have been notorious for election fraud since adopting the republican system in 1917. Hard-boiled cynics insist all high political offices are part of a ruling dynasty extending outward from the presidency in Mexico City; even municipal mayors in Mexico are called *el presidente,* and the local seat of government is the *palacio municipal.* Wags point out other symbolic evidence—the president wears an imperial sash and sits upon a throne when making official proclamations—and note that political candidates endorsed by the incumbents always win succeeding elections.

The PRI won every presidential election, held every six years, for more than 70 years until the 2000 runoff installed, for the first time in Mexican history, an opposition president—Vicente Fox.

In July 2006, Felipe Calderón (PAN) was elected President of Mexico in a contentious election by a margin of only 0.56 percent over López Obrador (PRD). Amidst allegations of voting irregularities by the losing party, the initial election results were challenged. The ghosts of Mexico's past civil unrest hung in the air during the months it took to confirm the initial results.

Since taking office, Calderón has taken on the drug cartels and corruption at the city level. Most notably, the Tijuana city police force had its guns confiscated and officers temporarily armed themselves with sling shots.

Economy

INCOME AND EMPLOYMENT

Agriculture, fishing, and tourism are Baja's main revenue-earners, followed by manufacturing and services in the border area. Per-capita income figures for BCN and BCS are well above the Mexican national average and second within the nation only to that of Mexico's D.F. (Distrito Federal) and neighboring states in the Valle de México. Both states of Baja register the lowest unemployment in the country; of the new jobs created in Mexico these days, more are on the peninsula than in any other part of the country.

Most large-scale farming is centered in the Río Colorado delta (Valle de Mexicali), Valle de Guadalupe, Valle de San Quintín, and the Plano de Magdalena surrounding Ciudad Constitución. Fishing boats work both coasts, but the Sea of Cortez produces the largest catch, and La Paz is the main fishing center. Tourism is for the most part concentrated in Tijuana, Rosarito-Ensenada, Mulegé-Loreto, La Paz, and Los Cabos (San José del Cabo and Cabo San Lucas).

Despite NAFTA, the stars of the manufacturing sector remain the *maquiladoras,* or in-bond industries, which combine developing-world labor costs with industrialized-world capital and management. These are predominantly located in special export-processing zones in the Tijuana area, although nearby Tecate and Mexicali also feature industrial parks. While wages at the *maquiladoras* are far below comparable wages in the United States, on average they're about twice Mexico's current minimum daily wage of US$5 a day and in many cases up to four times higher.

Border Economy

The border is also the focus of a mostly undocumented shadow economy supported by both legal and illegal migrant Mexican labor in the United States. Mexican labor migration has become so integrated into the regional economy that it is now considered largely responsible for the competitive and stable pricing of U.S. consumer goods.

That Mexican labor is essential to U.S. production is also indicated by the cyclical nature of immigration statistics relative to upturns and downturns in the U.S. economy. Intertwined with the shadow economy, Baja's border economy tends to move with the U.S. economic tide.

Ejidos

One of the unique features of the Mexican economy is the *ejido* institution, which has its roots in the Spanish *reconquista* (when Spanish Christians retook the Iberian Peninsula from the Moors during the late 15th century). The Spanish crown honored Spanish nobles who had fought in the conflict by granting them land tracts confiscated from the Moors. In Nueva España, the Spanish monarchy continued the tradition by offering communal land to conquistadors in return for dominating the Amerindian inhabitants. In his reforms of 1863 and 1867, Benito Juárez, Mexico's first president, converted church and *ejido* lands into individually owned plots in Mexico's first attempt to give peasants land rights.

Following the Mexican Revolution the *ejido* concept became a way of restoring lands that had been taken (usually legally purchased) from peasants by rich *hacendados* (big ranchers and plantation owners) during Spanish colonization and early Mexican independence. Considered a mainstay of PRI policy, nowadays in Mexico an *ejido* is a land tract held in common by a peasant community. It usually includes not only cultivated fields but also school properties, urban zones, water and forest resources, and any other facilities or resources either native to the land or produced by collective efforts. *Ejidos* are granted to *ejidatarios* by the government without rents or fees of any kind. They were originally nontransferable, nonattachable, and inalienable, i.e., *ejido* lands couldn't be sold, used as loan collateral, or taken away by local, regional, or national legal bodies.

According to Mexican law, *ejidos* are considered neither state property nor private property but are entities of the "social interest sector." How they are used is solely the concern of the peasant communities that hold them, but around 95 percent of them are "individual" *ejidos* in which the common holdings are divided into individual plots and cultivated by individual *ejidatarios* and their families. The remaining 5 percent are "collective" *ejidos* that pool all land resources for collective production. The number and total acreage of Mexico's *ejidos* is not well documented, but by 1970 they were estimated to encompass around 46 percent of national farmlands. According to every survey ever conducted nationwide, *ejido* lands are the least productive of all agricultural lands in Mexico.

Various bits of *ejido* legislation enacted since the Revolution have alternately strengthened and weakened the program. In the 1980s laws were passed that allowed *ejidatarios* to lease their lands to neighboring private estates for agricultural or livestock purposes. In the 1990s the government established regulations that now permit the sale of *ejido* lands. Thus for the first time ever individuals living in *ejidos* have property rights.

Has the *ejido* program been successful? On the one hand, it has kept hereditary lands in the hands of peasant communities who have worked them for hundreds of years—without them, many *ejidatarios* would probably become landless migrant workers. On the other hand, because *ejido* production is notoriously low (as are fixed prices for agricultural products), the need for cash to survive in Mexico's cash economy has forced many *ejidatarios* to work as laborers on private neighboring lands. As a result, it has been estimated that *ejidatarios* are among the poorest and most exploited of Mexico's rural workers.

The selling of *ejido* lands, as is now permitted, may gradually erode the *ejido* system, although it will certainly enrich many *ejidatarios* in the short term. Without the opportunity to buy, sell, and trade their lands, however, *ejidatarios* live entirely without true ownership rights, and their lands remain the Mexican equivalent of U.S. Amerindian reservations.

RECENT ECONOMIC CONDITIONS

On a macroeconomic level, Baja finds itself caught between two economic systems. Because it's so isolated from the rest of Mexico, the regional economy tends to be U.S.-influenced yet subject to the same economic vicissitudes as the rest of the country, most notably a weak currency and high inflation. Although the country's current account balance rose from a deficit of US$6.2 billion in 1982 to a surplus of US$4 billion in 1987, the inflation rate that same year hit 146 percent. Because of its regional ties to the United States, particularly California, the Baja economy weathered this period better than many areas of Mexico. A similar phenomenon occurred during the 1994–1995 period, when a negative balance reappeared.

Since Mexico's 1994 economic meltdown and another recession in 2000–2001, Mexico has recovered to become the 13th largest economy in the world as a measure of GDP. Mexico has the highest per capita income in Latin America. And tourism is the third largest contributor to the economy.

On a microeconomic level, the national minimum wage hovers at US$5 per day, attractive to foreign manufacturers looking for cheap labor but just barely enough for survival in today's Mexico.

People and Culture

The people of Baja California are in many ways a breed apart from their compatriots on the mainland. As Mexico's last frontier, the peninsula continues to attract residents seeking something they haven't been able to find elsewhere, whether it's the rugged, independent life of the interior deserts and sierras, the tropical ambience of La Paz or Cabo San Lucas, or the promising multicultural world in Tijuana and Mexicali, where California and Baja California meet.

For the rest of Mexico, Baja California occupies a place in the national psyche somewhat analogous to that of Hawaii for many Americans. It's seen as a place that's part of the nation yet almost out of reach—an exotic destination that most of the population will never have an opportunity to see. Hence, mainlanders typically regard *bajacalifornianos* as somehow different from themselves.

POPULATION

The current population of the entire peninsula is approximately 2.5 million, about 85 percent of whom live above the 28th parallel in Baja California Norte. Well over half the people on the peninsula live in Mexicali and Tijuana, with an additional 13 percent in Ensenada. Obviously, most of the peninsula is sparsely populated—the average density, even if these and all other Baja cities are included in the estimate, is only 1.5 persons per square kilometer (about 4 persons per sq mi). Outside the three most populated cities, it's less than one person per 26 square kilometer (one body per 10 sq mi).

Mexico's population growth rate is estimated at 1.16 percent per annum for 2006. The average for Baja California is probably somewhat higher than the national average because of immigration. Baja California Sur is Mexico's least populated state.

ORIGINS

Bajacalifornianos (sometimes called *bajacalifornios*) are an unusually varied lot. Elsewhere in Mexico, the average citizen is a mix of Spanish and Amerindian bloodlines. In Baja, the mix is typically more complicated, mainly because the peninsula remained a frontier much longer than most of the mainland, attracting people who arrived in the New World long after the Spanish colonized the Mexican mainland. It was 167 years after the conquest of Mexico before the Spanish were able to maintain a permanent settlement on the peninsula; by this time, tales of the Californias were on the tongues of adventurers throughout the world.

By the end of the 19th century the peninsula had become a favorite spot for sea-weary sailors to jump ship. The eastern shores of the peninsula were placid, and there was little chance deserters would be rounded up and incarcerated by local militia, who were scarce then and remain so today. Most of the ex-sailors who retired to Baja in this manner were English, but during World War I a few Germans and other Europeans came ashore. Their ship captains might have considered them cowardly deserters, but survival in Baja in the 19th and early 20th centuries was possible only for the brave, hardy, and resourceful.

Other immigrants who pioneered the Baja frontier included Chinese workers who came via the Mexican mainland and eventually flourished in the Mexicali area, Russian viticulturists who settled the Valle de Guadalupe, French miners in Santa Rosalía and Mulegé, and Mexican intellectuals and dissidents fleeing political oppression on the mainland and gravitating toward La Paz, Ensenada, and Tijuana. Many of these newcomers intermarried, and their descendants have greatly contributed to the peninsula's multicultural spirit.

Since in a very real sense much of Baja is still a frontier area—with more immigrants wandering in year by year—Baja's demographics have yet to solidify into recognizable pie-graph proportions. About two percent of the residents aren't even Mexican citizens; many are American, Canadian, or European retirees, and a lesser number are gringos who've simply dropped out of the rat race. With the current relaxation of investment and trade laws, a growing number of foreigners are also setting up businesses on the peninsula.

Bajacalifornianos

If there's a personality trait common to all true *bajacalifornianos,* it's a do-or-die spirit that says, "I belong here because my family was tough enough to survive in Baja back when this was the toughest place in Mexico to survive." While opinions vary, the popular definition of a "true" *bajacaliforniano* is someone whose forebears came to and stayed on the peninsula sometime before World War II.

A self-adopted nickname for *bajacalifornianos,* particularly popular in northern Baja, is *cachanilla* (sometimes spelled *cachanía*), the name of a hardy desert plant (arrowweed) that produces rose-colored flowers under even the harshest conditions.

Bajacalifornianos love to rant about how the peninsula was neglected by the mainland for centuries, how they cultivated Baja for themselves, without any help from Mexico City. Now that the Transpeninsular Highway is complete and the economic infrastructure is expanding, the *bajacalifornianos* complain that weak mainlanders are coming to harvest the fruits of Baja's development. A special scorn is reserved for *chilangos,* a derogatory term used by *bajacalifornianos* for Mexico City politicians or businesspeople who come to Baja and tell the *cachanillas* how to run things.

Amerindians

Of the estimated 50,000 Amerindians who inhabited the peninsula when the Spanish established their first Baja mission of any duration in 1697, at least 80 percent were wiped out by disease or colonial violence within 100 years. None of the Guaycura tribes of the south—Guaicura, Pericú, Huchiti—survived the Spanish occupation, but small numbers of the central and northern Cochimí and Yumano tribes still reside in the valleys and sierras of BCN.

According to Mexico's most recent census (1995), the Paipai (Pa'ipai, or "Clever People") are the largest surviving native tribe, numbering around 300; most are concentrated in the vicinity of Santa Catarina and San Isidoro. About 165 Kumyai live in Valle de Guadalupe and Juntas de Neji, 200 Cochimí in Valle Ojos Negros and San Antonio Necua, 200 Kiliwa (Quilihua) in Ejido Tribu Quilihua, and about 200 Cucapá in Cucapá El Mayor in the Río Colorado delta.

The Mexican government has set aside tracts of BCN land for each tribe; the Paipai, for example, own 160,000 acres from the Alamo plain eastward. For the most part, Baja's native tribespeople work on small ranches and farms; the livestock trade in particular has been a primary source of income ever since the Amerindians acquired horses, burros, cattle, goats, and sheep from Spanish missionaries. It is not known how many *indígenas* preserve tribal traditions, since, as in the American Southwest, many customs and ceremonies have gone underground due to a deep and understandable suspicion of outsiders. The Cucapá, who call themselves Koi'Pat (Those Who Come and Go), appear to live the most traditional lifestyle of the Yumano groups, preferring a seminomadic existence dependent on hunting, gathering, and fishing; in winter they live in semi-subterranean shelters and in summer under thatched-roof ramadas. The Kiliwa of the northern Sierra de San Pedro Mártir also maintain a hunter-gatherer culture. The Cucapá and the Kiliwa together comprise the last surviving cultures of this kind left along the entire North American Pacific coast. Most other groups may marry along tribal lines but in most other respects appear to lead the sedentary existence of the average rural Mexican peasant.

Outnumbering the Amerindians native to Baja are the thousands of Amerindians from Sonora, Oaxaca, and Chiapas who've come to Baja to work as migrant laborers, mirroring the transmigration of mestizo laborers north into the United States. Most numerous in the Valle de San Quintín, they're also commonly found in the Ensenada and Ciudad Constitución areas. Migrant Amerindians unable to find agricultural jobs are often seen hawking blankets and other handicrafts on the streets of the tourist districts in Tijuana, Ensenada, and Cabo San Lucas.

RELIGION

The original inhabitants of Mexico were indoctrinated in the ways of Roman Catholicism by Spanish missionaries between the 16th and 19th centuries. That Catholicism is now the majority religion in Mexico (around 90 percent) is an amazing achievement considering that it was laid over a vast variety of native belief systems in existence for perhaps thousands of years, and considering that the Mexicans eventually forcefully expelled the Spanish.

Mexican Catholics tend to be devout practitioners of their faith. Mexican Catholicism, however, has its own variations that distinguish the religion from its European predecessors. Some of these variations can be traced to preexisting Amerindian spiritual traditions that were absorbed by the Catholic faith and are localized according to tribe.

One variation common to all of Mexican Catholicism is the Virgin of Guadalupe cult, which began in 1531 when a dark-skinned Virgin Mary appeared before Amerindian peasant Juan Diego (1474–1548) in a series of three visions at Tepeyac, near Mexico City—which was, coincidentally, a sacred Aztec site dedicated to the goddess Tonantzin. According to legend, in the third vision the Virgin commanded Diego to gather roses and present them to the local bishop, requesting that a church be built in her honor. When the devout Diego unfolded his rose-filled cloak on December 12, 1531, both he and the bishop beheld an image of the dark-skinned Virgin imprinted on the garment. This was deemed a miracle, and church construction commenced at once. The Vatican beatified Juan Diego in 1990 and is considering full canonization, which would add the peasant to the Catholic pantheon of saints.

Today, many Mexican churches are named for Our Lady of Guadalupe, who has become so fused with Mexican identity that the slogan *¡Viva Guadalupe!* is commonly used at political rallies. The affectionate Mexican nickname for Guadalupe is La Morenita, "Little Darkling." She has become, as Mexican-American cultural commentator Richard Rodriguez puts it, the "official private flag of Mexico" and symbolizes one way in which Catholicism has been absorbed by indigenous cultures rather than vice versa. The official feast day for Guadalupe, December 12, is fervently celebrated throughout the country.

At one time the entire peninsula was under the ecclesiastical jurisdiction of the Guadalajara diocese; now there are regional dioceses centered in Tijuana, Mexicali, and La Paz. Since Baja has fewer churches per capita than the mainland, a church *(iglesia)* will sometimes hold as many as 18 masses a day. In southern Baja it isn't uncommon for a parish priest to hail from abroad—usually Italy—since native priests are in short supply on the peninsula.

Roadside Religion

Along Baja's roadways you'll occasionally see small roadside crosses (sometimes in clusters) or shrines. Often placed at fatal accident sites, each cross marks a soul's point of departure from this world. Larger shrines containing Christ or Virgin figures are erected to confer blessings or protection on passing motorists. These can vary from simple enclosures made of vegetable-oil cans to elaborate sculptural designs.

LANGUAGE

As in the rest of Mexico, Spanish is the primary language in Baja California. English is widely spoken by merchants, hotel staff, and travel agents in Tijuana, Mexicali, Ensenada, Loreto, La Paz, San José del Cabo, and Cabo San Lucas. Even in these cities, however, you can't count on finding English-speaking Mexicans outside the tourist districts. Hence it's incumbent upon the non-Spanish-speaking visitor to learn at least enough Spanish to cope with everyday transactions. Knowing a little Spanish will not only mitigate communication problems, it will also bring you more respect among

the local Mexicans, who quite naturally resent foreign visitors who expect Mexicans to abandon their mother tongue whenever a gringo approaches. A popular sign seen in tourist restaurants reads "We promise not to laugh at your broken Spanish if you won't laugh at our broken English." Out of courtesy, you should at least attempt to communicate in Spanish whenever possible.

The type of Spanish spoken in Mexico is usually referred to as Latin-American Spanish, in contrast to the Castilian Spanish spoken in Spain. Still, the Spanish here differs significantly from that of even other Spanish-speaking countries in the Western Hemisphere. In Baja California especially, many Anglicisms have crept into the language. For example, the common Latin-American Spanish term for "car" is *coche,* but in Baja you'll more often hear *carro.* Signs at automotive stores may read *auto partes* rather than *refacciones; yonke* or *yunque* (junk) is also commonly seen, and refers to new and used auto parts rather than junked cars.

Dictionaries and Phrasebooks

The *Glossary* and *Spanish Phrasebook* at the back of this book will get you started on a basic vocabulary in *español.* For further study, you'll want a dictionary and a larger phrasebook. One of the best portable dictionaries for the Spanish student is the paperback *University of Chicago Spanish-English, English-Spanish Dictionary,* which emphasizes New World usages and contains useful sections on grammar and pronunciation. If even this small volume is too large for your backpack, the *Collins Gem Dictionary: Spanish-English, English-Spanish* comes in a tiny 4-by-3.5-by-1-inch edition with a sturdy plastic cover and more than 40,000 entries.

Berlitz's *Latin-American Spanish for Travellers* is a small phrasebook divided by topics and situations (e.g., grammar, hotel, eating out, post office). Not all the phrases and terms it contains are used in Baja, but it's better than nothing.

One of the best references for off-the-road adventurers is Burleson and Riskind's *Backcountry Mexico: A Traveler's Guide and Phrase Book* (University of Texas Press). Although it's rather bulky for carrying in a backpack and is oriented toward travel in northern mainland Mexico, it contains many words and phrases of value to Baja hikers and campers.

Advanced Spanish students can improve their command of idiomatic Spanish with Frances de Talavera Berger's *¡Mierda!* (Plume, New York). Subtitled *The Real Spanish You Were Never Taught in School,* the book's copious *vulgarismos,* or slang expressions, have a decidedly scatological slant and should probably be aired in public only after practice with a trusted native speaker.

Language Schools in Baja

Those who plan to spend an extended period of time in Baja should seriously consider enrolling in an intensive Spanish course. Night classes at an adult community school or summer university courses are a fine introduction, but the most time- and cost-effective study programs are those that immerse you in the language and culture of the country. Mainland Mexico holds several Spanish language schools, but if Baja is your travel focus, it would be prudent to investigate schools on the peninsula. At the moment only two cities offer regularly scheduled instruction: Ensenada and La Paz.

Ensenada has three well-established schools, the Colegio de Idiomas de Baja California (Baja California Language College, www.bajacal.com), the International Spanish Institute of Ensenada, and the Center of Languages and Latin American Studies, while La Paz offers the relatively new Centro de Idiomas, Cultura y Comunicación (CICC) and Se Habla . . . La Paz—see the *Ensenada* and *La Paz* sections for more information.

ESSENTIALS

Getting There

BY AIR
International Flights

Baja's most commonly used air gateway for flights from the United States (the only country with direct international flights to Baja) is Los Cabos (SJD), a modern airport about 15 kilometers (9 mi) north of San José del Cabo. Daily direct flights to Los Cabos originate in Atlanta, Chicago, Dallas, Denver, Houston, Los Angeles, New York, Oakland, Phoenix, San Diego, San Francisco, and San Jose. Many other cities in the United States post flights to Los Cabos with one or more stopovers along the way, usually Mexico City or Monterrey. Los Cabos is well connected by air with mainland Mexico.

International flights to La Paz (LAP) arrive from El Paso, Los Angeles, Phoenix, San Antonio, and Tucson—all but Los Angeles flights require stops along the way. La Paz is well connected with mainland Mexico, however.

Loreto (LTO) also fields regularly scheduled flights from the United States, but via Los Angeles only. Nondirect, connecting flights from Tucson and San Diego are also available. Aerolitoral provides service from mainland Mexico.

The small airport at San Felipe has received on-and-off service from various airlines based in Los Angeles or San Diego, but at the moment all services have been discontinued.

Tijuana International Airport (TIJ) fields

© NIKKI GOTH ITOI

one direct flight weekly from Los Angeles and is well linked with La Paz, Los Cabos, and the Mexican mainland. Depending on the travel season and the dollar–peso exchange rate, it may be less expensive to fly from Tijuana to Los Cabos than from San Diego to Los Cabos. When this is the case, Cabo-bound San Diego residents counting pennies should consider taking a bus or taxi across the border to Tijuana and using Mexican air services.

Santa Rosalía has an airport reportedly equipped to handle international service, but so far the only way to fly there is by chartered plane.

Air/Hotel Packages

Airlines serving Baja often offer package deals that include airfare, hotel, and airport transfers at money-saving prices. A typical package includes three nights' hotel accommodations, airfare, and airport transfers for about the same as airfare alone. Contact the airlines directly to inquire about such packages, or check with a good travel agent. Newspaper travel sections often carry advertisements for air/hotel deals in Los Cabos.

Private Planes

Baja is a popular destination among North American light-aircraft pilots. Entry procedures are minimal, air traffic over the peninsula light, and nearly 200 airstrips take pilots and their passengers in a matter of hours to corners of Baja usually accessible only by days of driving. Most of these airstrips are unpaved and unstaffed.

Flight plans must be filed in advance with US Flight service to a Mexican airport of entry. Landing fees at airports of entry will vary US$7–20 for most private planes. Southbound, pilots must clear immigration and customs at the Mexican airport of entry; northbound, a stop on either side of the border is required for pilots and passengers to satisfy both Mexican and U.S. border formalities. Mandatory paperwork includes your aircraft registration, pilot's license, medical certificate, Mexican liability aircraft insurance, and proof of citizenship for each passenger (see *Visas and Officialdom*).

Fees and taxes for flying private aircraft into Mexico currently total around US$50 per craft along with the usual US$18 per person tourist fee. Other landing fees and taxes may be charged locally, typically US$8 for single-engine craft, US$12 for twin. Many airports in Baja are undergoing privatization, which means that new fees and policies may come into effect in the future.

For further information on flying regulations in Baja, contact a Mexican consulate or **Baja Bush Pilots** (U.S. tel. 480/730-3250, www.bajabushpilots.com). For more information on flying conditions in Baja, see *Getting Around*.

BY BUS
To San Diego or Los Angeles

Whether they reach the U.S.–Baja California border by train, bus, or trolley, most visitors using public transportation first pass through San Diego. From there they can choose from several options for traveling to Tijuana or Mexicali. San Diego is connected to other points in the United States by frequent long-distance bus and rail service. From both Los Angeles and San Diego, there are frequent buses to Tijuana and Mexicali.

Intercity buses generally depart more frequently and are less expensive than trains. Greyhound Bus Lines is the major carrier into San Diego. If you're busing a long distance to San Diego, a bus pass may be more economical than single-journey tickets. A **Greyhound Discover Pass** allows unlimited bus travel within the United States and includes cross-border bus trips to Tijuana. It's valid between specified dates and may be purchased directly from Greyhound or from a travel agent.

San Diego to Tijuana

Greyhound Bus Lines (U.S. tel. 619/239-3266, www.greyhound.com) operates around 16 buses a day from the San Diego bus terminal (120 W. Broadway) to Tijuana's downtown bus terminal for US$12 one-way (approx. 1 hr) or US$24 round-trip. Greyhound also runs a number of buses daily to Tijuana's Central de Autobuses—where you'll find the greatest selection of buses heading to Baja California Sur—for about the same fare.

The cheapest bus to the border from San Diego is the Metropolitan Transit System's (www.sdcommute.com) city bus no. 932, which travels from the downtown area (Centre City) to San Ysidro every 30 minutes from around 5:40 A.M. to 10:52 P.M. (6:12 A.M.–10:52 P.M. weekends and holidays) for just US$2.25. Because it makes several stops along the way, the city bus takes 80 minutes to reach San Ysidro. For automated schedule information, call U.S. tel. 619/685-4900.

The San Diego Metropolitan Transit System's trolley line to San Ysidro, nicknamed the **Tijuana Trolley,** is probably the easiest form of public transportation to the border. San Ysidro–bound trains leave every 15 minutes 5 A.M.–1 A.M. from downtown San Diego (plus Sat. "night owl" service 2–5 A.M.). Tickets cost US$1–2.50, depending on the distance traveled. Like the city bus, the trolley makes numerous stops along the way to San Ysidro—figure on about an hour from downtown. Bicycles may be taken on the trolley. Call tel. 619/685-4900 for general MTS information and 619/233-3004 for information on scheduling and stops.

Bright red, comfortable **Mexicoach** buses (tel. 664/685-1470, U.S. tel. 619/428-9517) leave every 30 minutes 9 A.M.–9 P.M. from the San Ysidro border gateway for the Terminal Turística Tijuana on Avenida Revolución between Calles 6 and 7, in the middle of the tourist district. Drivers will also stop at the Tijuana Cultural Center on request. The fare is US$5 each way.

All of the border shuttles, including Mexicoach, leave from a spot in San Ysidro next to the Tijuana Trolley terminus, so a connection between the two is easy.

Los Angeles to Tijuana
Greyhound Bus Lines (1716 E. 7th St., U.S. tel. 213/629-8401) in Los Angeles operates more than 12 buses a day, nearly round the clock, from Los Angeles to Tijuana's downtown terminal. The fare is US$23 one-way.

Travel time is around four hours. Mexican Customs doesn't make everyone get off the bus at the border; U.S. Customs does. Boxed bicycles may accompany paying passengers at no extra charge.

Buses to Mexicali and Calexico
Greyhound (Mex. tel. 800/710-8819, www.greyhound.com.mx), along with its Mexican partner Crucero, operates several buses daily to Mexicali from Los Angeles (US$36) and San Ysidro (US$31). The Calexico Greyhound terminal is on 1st Street; from there it's a short walk through the immigration and customs checkpoint into downtown Mexicali.

Buses from Mainland Mexico
Transportes Norte de Sonora (TNS, tel. 664/688-1979) and **Autotransportes Estrellas del Pacífico** (tel. 664/683-5022) operate long-distance express buses to Mexicali and Tijuana from various towns in Guanajuato, Nayarit, Sonora, Chihuahua, Michoacán, Jalisco, Sinaloa, Zacatecas, Querétaro, and Mexico City.

Green Tortoise
To those who have never traveled by Green Tortoise (U.S. tel. 415/956-7500 or 800/867-8647, www.greentortoise.com), it's difficult to describe the experience. Imagine a sort of youth hostel on wheels, with a bit of a '60s spirit, and you'll begin to get the idea. The buses are refurbished Greyhounds with convertible beds and tables, comfortable but a bit of a tight squeeze at night when everyone's lying down. That's also when the bus travels. It's a great way to meet people.

Green Tortoise operates nine-day (from US$441) and 15-day (US$649) trips to Baja November–April that begin in San Francisco (pickups in L.A. and San Diego are possible) and range as far south as La Paz. Prices are reasonable and include transportation and lodging on the bus, plus guided hikes and side trips to remote Baja beaches. The food fund adds another US$9–10 per day to the trip; communal meals cover about 70 percent of the meals—

some meals are left to the participants. The trips include an optional windsurfing and sailing program available for an additional fee. All things considered, it's a travel bargain and a novel introduction to Baja.

BY RAIL
Getting to San Diego
The only long-distance passenger rail line to San Diego is **Amtrak**'s San Diegan, which rolls between Los Angeles and San Diego 10 times daily. Other Amtrak lines serve Los Angeles from points north and east. Amtrak offers special one-way, round-trip, or excursion fares on occasion; always ask before booking.

Outside the United States, some travel agencies sell a **USA Railpass** allowing unlimited rail travel within specified dates. For schedule information or bookings inside the U.S., call 800/872-7245 or visit www.amtrak.com.

BY CAR
Driving into Baja
The red tape for driving into Baja is minimal. No vehicle permits of any kind are required, no matter how long you stay in Baja, unless you plan to cross to the mainland by road (via San Luis Río Colorado) or ferry (Santa Rosalía or La Paz). For stays of less than 72 hours no farther south than Ensenada, U.S. and Canadian citizens don't even need a tourist permit, just identification.

More people drive private vehicles across the U.S.–Mexico border at Tijuana than at any other point along its 1,600-kilometer (1,000-mi) length—nearly 20 million per year on average. If you find the traffic daunting, you can avoid Tijuana altogether by choosing any of four other Baja border crossings.

Mexican Auto Insurance
There is a lot of confusion and misinformation in travel circles about why and how to insure your vehicle when driving in Mexico. Whether you are driving your own vehicle into Mexico, renting a car to drive over the border, or renting within Mexico, read this section carefully: *Before driving into Baja, all drivers should arrange for Mexican vehicle insurance.* Why? Mexican law requires drivers to have proof of financial liability (a minimum of US$50,000 worth) for any property damage or bodily injury they cause to other parties in an accident. Unless you have a bond with a Mexican bank or cash in hand at the time of an accident, the only practical way to comply with the law is to purchase an insurance policy underwritten by a Mexican company. Without it, a minor traffic accident can turn into a nightmare, involving jail time and steep financial penalties. *No matter what your own insurance company may tell you, Mexican authorities do not recognize foreign insurance policies for private vehicles in Mexico.*

If you are planning to drive your own vehicle, you can purchase short-term insurance—as little as one day's worth—from one of 20 or so online vendors of Mexican Tourist Auto Insurance. Simply request a quote, complete an application, pay by credit card, and print a certificate from home before you leave for your trip. (You can purchase a policy in advance, and set it to begin on the day you plan to cross the border.) Policy terms and quality of service vary significantly, so be sure you are dealing with a reputable broker before you buy. A good way to tell is to call and speak to a live person, then complete the process online.

If you're not the plan-ahead type, or you prefer to deal in person, you can stop in several agencies found in nearly every border town between the Pacific Ocean and the Gulf of Mexico. Again, read the terms carefully before paying.

The first decision you'll need to make is between a liability-only policy (to comply with the law) or full coverage (to protect your vehicle). Liability-only policies typically cover third-party liability from a minimum of US$50,000, up to US$300,000; plus legal expenses (levels range widely from US$500 to US$30,000), medical payments for you and your passengers (US$2,000–5,000 per person; US$19,000–25,000 per accident), and some form of roadside assistance. Higher-end policies may include medical evacuation and

MEXICAN AUTO INSURANCE POLICY CHECKLIST

Consider the following criteria before buying Mexican insurance for your private vehicle:

- Look for a U.S.-based claims office.

- Deductibles should be clearly stated, typically a minimum of $500 or 2 percent of the value of the vehicle.

- The better policies include legal coverage, roadside assistance, plane tickets home if your car cannot be driven, and medical evacuation.

- Some premium policies include extra coverage for uninsured drivers.

- Policies with a "combined single limit" (CSL) for bodily and property damage are preferred over "split limits," which are less flexible.

- The policy should allow you to handle repairs in the United States or Canada.

- The policy should clearly state an hourly labor rate high enough to cover the cost of repairs in the United States (the US$15/hour standard in Mexico will not be sufficient).

- Keep one copy of your policy in the glove box and another in your wallet (in case the car is stolen).

- Call your claims number when you cross into Mexico to verify that it works.

- If you have a claim, report it before you leave Mexico within the time limit specified in your policy; some companies will not honor the policy once you have left the country.

- Claims adjusters can reach most parts of Baja within two hours.

- Driving on the beach is considered a non-conventional road: If you get stuck and the tide comes in and floods your car, it's probably not going to be covered.

- Any roads that require four-wheel drive are probably not covered.

When shopping online:

- Websites should display an insurance license logo.

- Check that the site is secure before you transmit personal data.

- When in doubt, call the vendor to verify services.

---

a flight home if your car is stolen or not drivable. Standard deductibles begin at US$500 and scale to 2–10 percent of the value of the vehicle; a flat US$5,000 for motorcycles.

Full coverage adds physical damage and theft coverage to the list above. Since the cost of upgrading from liability-only to full coverage amounts to a few dollars more per day, it usually makes sense to add the theft coverage and enjoy the peace of mind. Theft coverage typically carries a higher deductible than just liability. See the sidebar *Mexican Auto Insurance Policy Checklist* for more on the fine print.

In business since 2001, Santa Cruz, California–based **Adventure Mexican Insurance** (U.S. tel. 831/477-9208 or 800/485-4075, www.mexadventure.com) provides daily, monthly, and annual Mexican auto insurance to individual travelers, as well as travel organizations. The company's website clearly explains Mexican insurance options and allows you to compare various policies from its three underwriters; well armed with information, you can then purchase online in a matter of minutes. For a long weekend trip to Baja, you'll pay around US$30 for liability only, and US$40 for full coverage (both at the minimum liability level of US$50,000). Full coverage monthly rates range US$150–250, depending on the value of the vehicle. Its policies cover repairs in the United States and include a bundled travel assistance package for medical evacuation of up to four passengers and plane tickets home if your vehicle is undrivable. Call toll-free for detailed information about insuring an RV, trailer, or other special circumstances. Short-term policies cover travel in all of Mexico, but for long-term policies, customers have the option of a regional North West policy covering Baja as well as the mainland states of Sonora, Chihuahua, and Sinaloa, at a reduced rate.

Several travel clubs offer discounted rates to members: For example, **Discover Baja Travel Club** (U.S. tel. 800/727-2252, www.discoverbaja.com) offers liability insurance for only US$75 per year and full coverage starting at US$122. AAA members can purchase Mexican auto insurance through the travel club website (www.aaa.com) or by phone.

If you forget to purchase insurance before you leave or prefer to purchase your policy in person, try **Instant Mexico Insurance Services** (223 Via de San Ysidro, U.S. tel. 619/428-4714, or 800/345-4701, www.instant-mex-auto-insur.com, open 24 hrs daily) at the last exit before the San Ysidro/Tijuana border crossing. You can also purchase tourist cards, fishing and boating permits, maps, guidebooks, and other Baja requisites here.

Whichever policy you choose, always make photocopies of it and keep originals and copies in separate, safe places. It's also a good idea to carry a photocopy of the first page—the "declaration" or "renewal of declaration" sheet—of your home country policy, as Mexican law requires that you cross the border with at least six months' worth of home country insurance.

Temporary Vehicle Import Permits

If you're only driving in the states of Baja California and Baja California Sur, you won't need one of these. However, if you plan to take a vehicle aboard a ferry bound for the mainland from Santa Rosalía or La Paz, you need a temporary vehicle import permit before you'll be allowed to book a ferry ticket. To receive this permit, simply drive your vehicle to a Mexican customs office (this can be done at any official border crossing or in La Paz) and present the following: a valid state

registration for the vehicle (or similar document certifying legal ownership), a driver's license, and a credit card (Visa, MasterCard, American Express, or Diner's Club) issued outside Mexico.

If you are leasing or renting the vehicle, you'll also have to present a leasing or rental contract made out to the person bringing the vehicle into Mexico. If the vehicle belongs to someone else (e.g., a friend or relative), you must present a notarized letter from the owner giving you permission to take the vehicle to Mexico. Contrary to rumor, you aren't required to present the "pink slip" or ownership certificate unless the state registration certificate is for some reason unavailable.

Once Mexican customs officials have approved your documents, you'll proceed to a Banjército (Banco del Ejército or Military Bank) office attached to the customs facilities, and your credit card account will be charged US$17 for the permit fee. This fee must be paid by credit card; cash is not accepted. If you don't have a credit card, you'll have to post a bond (1–2 percent of the vehicle's blue-book value) issued by an authorized Mexican bond company, a time-consuming and expensive procedure. Banjército is the bank used for all Mexican customs charges; the operating hours for each module are the same as for the border crossing at which it's located.

Once the fee has been charged to your credit card, the permit is issued, with a validity period equal to that shown on your tourist card or visa. You may drive back and forth across the border—at any crossing—as many times as you wish during the permit's validity. You are supposed to surrender the permit at the border when your trip is over, however.

In the United States, further information on temporary vehicle importation can be obtained by calling 800/922-8228. Under an agreement between the American Automobile Association (AAA) and the Mexican government, U.S. motorists with credit cards are able to obtain both tourist cards and auto permits from AAA offices in Texas, New Mexico, Arizona, and California. In reality, all AAA does is fill out the papers for you—you still have to stop at the border, walk into the customs office, and get the papers validated. When we tried doing this with AAA forms, Mexican customs rejected them because AAA had translated some of the forms into English, and this was deemed unacceptable. In addition, the AAA office we used in California filled the forms in incorrectly, writing in the section marked "For Official Use Only." We had to start from scratch, so the trip to AAA was wasted time.

If you're renting a car with Mexican license tags, none of the above is necessary, of course.

Parking in San Ysidro

Another alternative is to drive to San Ysidro, park your vehicle in one of the guarded fee lots, and walk across the border at Tijuana or take a Mexicoach bus. San Ysidro parking lots charge US$6–10 per day or any portion thereof. To use one these lots, take the exit off I-5 reading Last U.S. Exit. **Five-Star Parking** is a good choice if you want to shuttle across the border; Mexicoach stops there.

BY FERRY FROM MAINLAND MEXICO

Private passenger and vehicle ferry services connecting southern Baja with the Pacific Coast of mainland Mexico allow anyone driving in the Mazatlán area to reach La Paz without a time-consuming trip all the way around the Sea of Cortez. Many drivers from the American West Coast use Baja ferry services as an alternative way of reaching the mainland, since it allows them to avoid traffic-heavy Mexico 15 (or its expensive toll equivalent, Mexico 15-D) on the way to Mazatlán and points farther south. The ferries are comfortable and efficient in all classes. In heavy seas, you may want to consider taking motion sickness tablets before boarding.

The ferry services seem to change routes and schedules frequently, so check websites or visit offices at least a week before you plan to cross. At last check, **Baja Ferries** (Pichilinque Terminal, tel. 612/125-6324, U.S. tel. 915/833-3107, www.bajaferries.com, daily 8 A.M.–5 P.M.) was servicing two routes: A modern ship makes the crossing from La Paz to Topolobampo/Los Mochis daily in six hours each way. This ferry has space for 1,000 passengers, including a choice of seats or cabins with 2–4 berths and attached bath. A seat on the ferry costs US$68. If you want a cabin berth, add US$76 to this fare. You can take a car or pickup truck along for US$100 (US$600 for an RV up to 10 meters). Baja Ferries has added a second route from La Paz to Mazatlán (Tues., Thurs., Sat., with return trips on Mon., Wed., Fri., US$77 one-way) in a ship that holds 600 passengers in bus-style seats or cabins. Cars cost US$200 one-way (US$1,200 for an RV up to 10 meters). All rates include tax. Pets are not allowed. Baja Ferries has a ticket office in downtown La Paz (at Calle Isabel la Católica and Navarro, tel. 612/125-7443 or 800/122-1414). If you're starting from Topolobampo, the local number is 668/862-1003.

Transportación Marítima de California (TMC) (La Paz office tel. 800/744-5050, Mazatlán office tel. 800/700-0433, www.ferry tmc.com) also runs a car ferry between La Paz and Mazatlán (15.5 hrs). A car and driver cost US$237; RVs up to 10 meters cost US$600.

The Santa Rosalia ferry (tel. 615/152-0013, www.ferrysantarosalia.com) is now running several times a week, leaving Santa Rosalía in the evening and returning from Guaymas in the morning.

To book vehicle passage, you must hold a valid temporary vehicle import permit (see *Temproary Vehicle Import Permits* earlier in this chapter). Show up three hours before the scheduled departure. You must drive the vehicle into the cargo hold yourself; this is usually the most unpleasant part of the journey, as most of the vehicles crossing are Mexican 18-wheeled trucks; the diesel fumes that accumulate in the hold while everyone gets in position (as directed by the ferry crew) can be intense. Soldiers or federal police are present on the piers at both ends of the journey, searching for arms and illegal drugs with the help of trained dogs.

Getting Around

Many visitors to Baja travel the peninsula with their own vehicles—cars, trucks, campers, RVs, or motorcycles. Alternative transportation includes domestic airlines, rented cars, public buses, bicycles, and hitchhiking.

BY AIR

Domestic air travel in Baja is generally less expensive than international flights of comparable distances from the United States to Baja. It's cheaper to fly from Tijuana to La Paz or Los Cabos than from San Diego to La Paz or Los Cabos, for example. Hence, especially for San Diego residents, the minor inconvenience of flying out of Tijuana could result in a considerable savings—if your destination is either La Paz or Los Cabos.

Charter Flights

Companies that can arrange small-plane charters to almost any legally open airfield in Baja from Southern California include: **AeroCargo in Los Angeles** (800/428-2163); **California Jet LLC** (8721 Santa Monica Blvd. #150, Los Angeles, CA 90069, 302/744-9273, www.californiajetcharter.com); and **West Coast Charters** (19711 Campus Dr. Suite 200, Santa Ana, CA 92707, 800/352-6153, www.westcoastcharters.com).

Private Flights

With a pilot's license and a plane, you can fly to any of Baja's nearly 200 airstrips. Air traffic over Baja is light, and the paperwork for crossing the border is minimal. See *Private Planes* under *Getting There* for a summary of landing taxes and fees charged to foreign pilots flying into Mexico.

Note that it is illegal to fly at any height over two bays in the Vizcaíno Biosphere Reserve— Laguna de Ojo de Liebre (Scammon's Lagoon) and Laguna San Ignacio—during the period January 1–June 30 every year. This law has been enacted, and is strictly enforced, to protect the large numbers of gray whales calving

in the lagoons in the winter and the thousands of migratory birds feeding and nesting on the islands and along the shores of these lagoons throughout the winter and extending into the summer months.

Baja Bush Pilots publishes a 384-page guide, *Airports of Baja and Northwest Mexico.* Now in its 20th edition, the book contains aerial photos, sketch maps, and descriptions of virtually every landing strip in Baja. Few pilots fly to Baja without this book, which is available through pilot supply sources for around US$70, or you can order the book directly from Baja Bush Pilots (www.bajabushpilots.com). BBP also maintains a membership organization of the same name. For an annual US$50 membership fee, you'll receive quarterly updates to the airport guide, the quarterly *Baja Bush Pilots Journal,* discounts at Baja hotels and resorts, and discounted Mexican insurance rates.

Planes that fly into Mexico are required to carry Mexican liability insurance. Baja Bush Pilots offers inexpensive annual **aircraft insurance** policies. Current rates are posted at www.bajabushpilots.com. Every pilot must show a valid insurance policy at the border to clear customs. In addition, U.S. Customs requires an annual inspection for planes flying into the United States, whether U.S.- or foreign-owned.

BY BUS
Intercity Bus Service

Baja's reliable intercity bus transportation covers the peninsula from Tijuana to Cabo San Lucas. The longest direct ride available is the Tijuana–Cabo San Lucas route (about 30–32 hours), operated once daily by **Autotransportes águila** (tel. 612/122-4270). Many people break up the bus trip with an overnight stop in La Paz (25–28 hours from Tijuana) and change to one of the many La Paz–Cabo San Lucas buses the following day. **Transportes Norte de Sonora** (TNS, tel.

664/688-1979) operates buses between Tijuana, Tecate, Mexicali, and points farther west, including destinations on the Mexican mainland as far away as Mexico City.

Special express buses with hostess service and air conditioning are used on long-distance trips. Shorter trips may or may not have air conditioning, but the buses are always tolerably comfortable. Schedules aren't always precise, but even smaller bus terminals may feature public phones, restrooms, and cafés. The infamous "chicken buses" of southern Mexico and Central America don't exist in Baja.

Bus fares are moderate. A Tijuana–La Paz ticket on a *primera,* or first-class bus, for example, costs about US$134. Second class costs about half that (although to travel second class all the way from Tijuana to La Paz would necessitate changing buses along the way). Reservations for bus travel aren't usually necessary and for shorter distances aren't accepted. On longer trips, such as Tijuana–La Paz or Mexicali–Guerrero Negro, buses may depart only once daily, so it's a good idea to drop by the terminal a day in advance to ensure seat availability.

All the Spanish you need for riding a bus is *boleto* (ticket), the name of your destination (have a map handy just in case), and a reasonable command of spoken Spanish numbers for quoted fares (although the fare is always posted somewhere on the ticket office wall).

City Buses and *Colectivos*
Tijuana, Ensenada, Mexicali, San Quintín, and La Paz offer comprehensive city bus systems with fares averaging less than US$1, payable in pesos only. City buses come in a variety of sizes and shapes, from 12-passenger vans called *colectivos* to huge modern vessels with automatic doors. In Mexicali, painted school buses are the norm. The destination or general route—typically a street name—is usually painted somewhere on the front of the bus or displayed on a marquee over the front windshield.

Printed bus schedules are either hard to come by or nonexistent. If you can't figure out which bus to take by comparing the destination sign with a map, just ask other waiting bus passengers or, if your Spanish isn't up to that, make inquiries at the tourist office.

BY TAXI
Route Taxis
Tijuana, Rosarito, Ensenada, and Mexicali feature *taxis de ruta,* specially licensed cars that follow set routes similar to and often paralleling the bus routes. These vehicles are usually large American station wagons that hold up to 12 passengers. Unlike city buses, you can flag them down anywhere along the route. The destination is usually painted in whitewash on the windshield, but locals often distinguish the route by the taxis' two-tone color scheme. A *roja y crema* may run from the central bus station to a market on the outskirts of town while a *negro y azul* may travel from the cathedral to the main shopping district. Other than the terminating points of the route at either end, there are no predetermined taxi stops; passengers must let the driver know where they want off. As on city buses, route taxi fares are the same no matter where you disembark. Usually they're only a bit higher than bus fares.

Hire Taxis
Regular-hire taxis congregate at hotels and designated taxi stands in most towns of any size. Sometimes fares are posted at the hotel or taxi stand, but often you must ask for a fare quote. If possible, try to find out the fare from hotel staff or a friendly resident before approaching a taxi driver—you'll feel more secure about not getting ripped off. If the quoted fare doesn't match what you've been told in advance, you can negotiate or try another driver. Fortunately, most *bajacaliforniano* city taxi drivers quote the correct fare immediately.

In smaller towns with no buses or route taxis you may sometimes find a few regular-hire taxis hanging out by the town plaza. They're generally used for reaching out-of-town destinations, since any place in Baja without a city bus system is small enough to wander around on foot. Although the locals pay a set fare based on distance, gringos are sometimes quoted a much higher fare. Dig in and negotiate until it's reasonable. Even if you can afford the higher fare, you owe it to other foreign visitors not to encourage price gouging.

BY CAR

For the most part, the 1973 completion of the Transpeninsular Highway opened Baja travel to ordinary folks driving ordinary passenger cars, as long as they employ a little common sense. For the adventurer, there remain miles of unpaved roads that will take you as far from civilization as anyone would care to go.

Baja Highways

The Transpeninsular Highway is somewhat akin to two-lane driving in some of the less populated areas of the American Southwest, with two main differences: The road conditions vary more (sometimes a lot) from one section of highway to another, and once you're well into the center of the peninsula, you're farther from any significant population centers than on any comparable section of U.S. highway—hence accidents or errors of judgment can have serious ramifications. Drivers from western Canada may feel more at home than Americans on desolate sections of Baja highway—except that the terrain is completely different from anything in Canada.

Six paved national highways grace the Baja California peninsula: Mexico 1 (the Transpeninsular, from Tijuana to Cabo San Lucas), Mexico 2 (from Tijuana to Sonora), Mexico 3 (Tecate to El Sauzal, near Ensenada, and east to Crucero La Trinidad at Mexico 5), Mexico 5 (Mexicali to San Felipe), Mexico 19 (between Cabo San Lucas and San Pedro, via Todos Santos), and Mexico 22 (Ciudad Constitución to San Carlos). The only state highways are a small cluster of relatively short blacktops in the northeast corner above the Sea of Cortez (BCN 1, 2, 3, 4, and 8, which link farm communities in the Valle de Mexicali with Mexicali and the state of Sonora), BCN 23 (linking Mexico 1 with Punta Banda), and the solitary BCS 286 in the south between La Paz and San Juan de los Planes.

In addition, Mexico 1 features two alternate routings, a four-lane toll road between Tijuana and Ensenada and a two-lane digression to Bahía de los Ángeles on the Sea of Cortez coast. Work was underway in 2007 to pave several dirt roads connecting inland communities such as San Javier, near Loreto and Los Planes, near La Paz, to the Transpensular Highway. But aside from those developments, all other roads in Baja are gravel, dirt, or some combination thereof.

HOW MUCH FARTHER?

Distances from Tijuana, along the Transpeninsular Highway, using the Tijuana-Ensenada toll road:

Ensenada:	109 km (68 mi)	**Guerrero Negro:**	714 km (443 mi)
San Quintín:	301 km (187 mi)	**San Ignacio:**	856 km (531 mi)
El Rosario:	359 km (226 mi)	**Santa Rosalía:**	928 km (575 mi)
Cataviña:	481 km (298 mi)	**Mulegé:**	990 km (614 mi)
Punta Prieta:	599 km (371 mi)	**Loreto:**	1,125 km (698 mi)
Bahía de los Ángeles:	654 km (405 mi)	**Ciudad Constitución:**	1,268 km (786 mi)
		La Paz:	1,483 km (919 mi)
		Cabo San Lucas:	1,704 km (1,056 mi)

Off-Highway Travel

Like the highways, Baja's unpaved roads vary considerably, from rutted jeep tracks to elevated, graded, gravel boulevards. The trouble with the graded unpaved roads is that they tend to degenerate quickly between gradings into washboard surfaces impossible to drive at anything but low speeds (8–16 kph/5–10 mph)—unless you want to risk crushed vertebrae and a dropped transmission.

The effect of these unpaved roads on you and your vehicle depends a lot on what you're driving. Some off-highway Baja navigators drive pickups with customized shocks and suspension that enable a driver to float over the worst washboard surfaces. Other drivers—like many of the local residents, who can't afford heavy-duty, customized rigs—learn to drive slowly and appreciate the scenery.

The best unpaved roads are probably those that have evolved more or less naturally, with little or no grading. When the weather's dry, some of these roads ride better than the Transpeninsular. Of course, unpaved roads may sometimes start out nicely but get increasingly worse with each passing mile, to the point where even the most intrepid explorers are forced to turn around. At other times, a road will suddenly improve after a long stretch of cavernous potholes and caved-in sides. Weather is a big determining factor; even the best ungraded, unpaved roads are often impassable during or following a hard rain.

How do you know when to turn around? There's always an element of risk when driving down a dirt road for the first—or even the hundredth—time, but it helps to ask around before embarking on a road that doesn't see much traffic. A good road map can also assist with such decisions. The AAA map (see *Information and Services*) classifies unpaved roads into four categories: gravel, graded, dirt, and poor. The annotated ITM map uses a similar but more specific fourfold system: gravel, graded, unimproved dirt, and vehicular track. Although neither of these maps is entirely up-to-date nor 100 percent accurate, using one or both in conjunction with local input will greatly improve your decision-making. A topographical map could be of considerable value to a four-wheel-drive navigator as well, since sometimes it's the steep canyon grades that spell defeat.

Even with the best planning there's always the possibility of getting stuck in muddy or sandy areas. Anyone engaging in serious off-highway driving should carry along a sturdy shovel for digging out mired wheels. The folding trench shovels sold at army surplus stores pack well and may even fit beneath the passenger seat in some vehicles. Some four-wheelers carry lengths of heavy rippled plastic—the kind used for "hall runners" to protect carpet in tacky home decor—to place between the front and back wheels when mired in soft sand; these can easily be rolled up and stored when not needed. Another handy trick for negotiating soft ground is to let the air out of your tires to a pressure of around 12–15 psi. This really works, but you should also carry along a 12-volt air compressor, one that will plug into the cigarette lighter, for pumping the tires back up after you're on firm ground again.

A nylon web towing strap—rather than chains, rope, or steel cable—is the best towing medium.

Driving Precautions

The first rule of Baja driving, no matter what kind of road you're on, is *never* take the road for granted. Any highway in Baja, including the Transpeninsular, can serve up 100 meters of smooth, seamless blacktop followed immediately by 100 meters of contiguous potholes or large patches of missing asphalt. A cow, horse, or burro could be right around the next curve, or a large dog could leap out in front of your vehicle just as you fasten your eyes on a turkey vulture drying its wings on top of a tall *cardón*.

The speed limits set by the Mexican government—80 kph (48 mph) on most highways, 110 kph (66 mph) on the Ensenada toll road—are reasonable for Baja's highway conditions. Obey them and you'll be much safer than if you try to keep the speedometer needle in the spot you're accustomed to. Wandering livestock, relatively narrow highways widths

(6–8 m/19–25 ft max), and inconsistent highway maintenance mean you simply can't drive at U.S./Canada speeds.

Most Baja roadways also suffer from a conspicuous lack of shoulders. This doesn't mean you won't find any places to pull off, as some Baja writers have implied—gravel turnouts appear fairly regularly, and in many areas you can drive directly onto the roadside from the highway. It just means you can't count on a safe margin in an emergency situation. At the very least, an emergency turnout will raise a lot of rocks and dirt—small dangers in themselves—and in some spots, like the sierras on Mexico 3, leaving the highway can launch you and your vehicle into a thousand-foot freefall. Guardrails are often flimsy or nonexistent.

Yet another reason not to take the road for granted is the high frequency of sometimes unmarked blind curves and blind hilltops. Never assume a clear path around a curve or over a hilltop—potential obstructions include an oblivious 18-wheeler or bus passing in the opposite direction, wandering livestock, rock slides, or road washouts. To be on the safe side, keep toward the outside edge of your own lane. Commercial truck drivers in Baja roar down the road as if they're exempt from all speed limits, almost always flying at least 40 kph over the posted limit.

Rule number two: Never drive the highways at night. Except along portions of the Ensenada toll road and along the Corridor Highway that runs between San José del Cabo and Cabo San Lucas, Baja highways have no lighting. In addition, reflectors and even painted lines are absent from many highway sections; even if no other vehicles besides your own were on the road at night, you could easily overshoot an unexpected curve. Add to this the fact that many poorly maintained local vehicles have nonfunctioning headlights, taillights, or brake lights, and it should be obvious that trying to make highway miles after sundown is crazy. Some *bajacalifornianos* may do it, but they're used to local conditions and know the roads relatively well. A high proportion of car accidents in Baja—around 80 percent according to insurance companies—occur at night.

When you see road signs marked **Vado** or **Zona de Vados,** slow down. The word *vado* is most often translated as "dip," but in Baja it usually means more than a slight depression in the road—it's any place where the road intersects an arroyo, or dry stream wash. The danger lies not only in the sudden grade drop but in the potential for running into a recently accumulated body of water. Some *vados* feature measuring sticks marked in meters; when water is present, you'll know roughly how deep it is. If you come to a *vado* full of water with no measuring stick, get out of your vehicle and measure the depth yourself using an ocotillo branch or other suitable object.

Vados aren't always signposted, so stay alert—they appear even on relatively flat terrain. Some *vados* are relatively mild road dips, while others are particularly treacherous, even in dry weather. The *vados* south of San Felipe on the road to Puertecitos are deadly—crossing them at a high rate of speed can severely damage the undercarriage of a passenger car.

Also watch out for sand drifts, which often aren't visible until it's almost too late to avoid them. They're most common in the San Felipe area but can occur anywhere in Baja where a road runs through sandy terrain.

In cities, pueblos, *ejidos,* or anywhere else people live in Baja, you'll encounter *topes* (speed bumps). Often unpainted and unsignposted, they can really sneak up on you. Some *topes* are real industrial-strength tire-poppers, so always take it slow when traversing them.

Highway Signs

One of the pleasures of driving in Baja is the relative absence of signs cluttering the roadside. Billboards, in fact, are virtually nonexistent in most areas. The Mexican government does have a system of highway signs, however, based on common international sign conventions followed throughout most of the world; these can be helpful as long as you know what they mean. Most display self-explanatory symbols (e.g., a silhouette of a person holding a shovel means "road crew working").

Along the Transpeninsular Highway as well

as on many secondary roads, you can measure driving progress with the assistance of regularly spaced kilometer markers, usually black lettering on a reflective white background. In northern Baja these markers start at zero (K0) in Tijuana and ascend in number as you proceed southward. Starting at *paralelo* 28, the state borderline between Baja California Norte and Baja California Sur (BCN and BCS) the markers descend as you move southward, beginning with K220 in Guerrero Negro. These contrary directions can be traced to the original construction of the Transpeninsular, which started at either end of the peninsula and met in the middle. To further add to the confusion, sometimes the numbers run only as far as the next town, then start over. Still, the markers can be a significant navigational aid, especially when you want to take note of a remote off-highway spot for a future trip.

Cautionary sign captions are especially helpful, including *Curva Peligrosa* (Dangerous Curve), *Despacio* (Slow), and *Zona de Vados* (Dip Zone). Other common highway signs include *Desviación* (Detour), *No Tire Basura* (Don't Throw Trash), *Conserve Su Derecha* (Keep to the Right), *Conceda Cambio de Luces* (Dim Your Lights), *No Rebase* (No Passing), and *No Hay Paso* (Road Closed).

If you're having tire trouble, look for homemade signs reading *Llantera, Desponchadora,* or *Vulcanizadora,* all of which indicate tire repair shops. Our favorite Mexican traffic sign is *No Maltrate las Señales*—Don't Mistreat the Signs.

Traffic Offenses

Although Mexican traffic police don't go out of their way to persecute foreign drivers, it may seem that way when you're the foreigner who's stopped. The more cautiously you drive, the less likely you'll inadvertently transgress local traffic codes. This would seem like obvious advice, but for some reason many visiting motorists in Baja drive as if they think there are no traffic laws in Mexico. Most of these people seem to have California plates.

If you're stopped by a *tránsito* (traffic cop), the first rule is to behave in a patient, civil manner. The officer might then let you off with just

a warning. If the officer decides to make a case of it, you'll be asked to proceed to the nearest police post or station, where a fine will be assessed and collected. This is a perfectly legal request. But if the cop suggests or even hints at being paid on the spot, you're being hit up for *la mordida,* the minor bribe.

In Baja, requests for *mordida* from foreigners—for traffic offenses, at least—have become increasingly rare (except in Tijuana and Rosarito, where the problem persists), and the government is making admirable progress toward stamping out the practice altogether. If confronted with such a situation, you have two choices. Mexico's Attorney General for the Protection of Tourists recommends you insist on going to the nearest station to pay the fine, and that as you pay you request a receipt. Such a request may result in all charges being dropped. If you don't feel like taking the time for a trip to the station, you can choose to negotiate the "fine" on the spot. Doing so, however, won't contribute to the shrinking of the *mordida* phenomenon.

Along Mexico 1-D, the toll highway between Tijuana and Ensenada, the federal highway police claim to be using radar speed detectors nowadays. Fines are assessed at a day's Mexican minimum wage (currently about US$5) for each kilometer over the speed limit. The fine is the same for foreigners as for Mexican nationals. The offender's driving license is attached to the citation and delivered to the nearest Baja *tránsito* station, or to another Baja station chosen by the offender, where the license is returned upon payment of the assessed fine. If you're cited just outside Tijuana, for example, you can elect to settle your citation in Ensenada.

Aside from speeding on Mexico 1-D, driving the wrong direction on one-way streets and running stop signs are the two most common traffic violations among foreign drivers in Baja. In Ensenada, for example, the stop (Alto) signs seem almost intentionally hidden in places; also, several intersections display no vertical signs at all, only broad stripes painted on the pavement indicating where vehicles are supposed to stop. The best practice is to assume you're supposed to stop at every single intersection in the city, which is pretty close to the truth. This can be generalized to include most other urban areas on the peninsula.

In Mulegé, only two streets in town are open to two-way traffic; all the others are supposed to be one-way, although they're not signposted at every intersection. Always look carefully at the cars driving or parked on a street to determine which direction is legal before turning.

Note to patriotic visitors: In Mexico, it's illegal to display any foreign national flag except over an embassy or consulate. A miniature flag flying from a vehicle's radio antenna provides Mexican police with a valid excuse to pull you over. It may also invite vandalism—Mexicans are extremely nationalistic. This is rarely a problem, but don't say you weren't warned.

Mexican Auto Insurance

It's extremely important to carry a Mexican liability insurance policy on your vehicle while driving in Baja. In case of an accident, such a policy could keep you from going to jail. (For details, see *Mexican Auto Insurance* under *Getting There,* earlier in this chapter.)

Fuel

The only automotive fuel commercially available in Mexico is sold at government-owned Pemex stations. The total number of Pemex stations in Baja varies from year to year, but they're always scarce outside the large cities. It's best to top off your tank whenever it reaches the half-empty mark and there's a Pemex station at hand.

Three kinds of fuel are available: an unleaded fuel with an octane rating of 87 (Magna Sin); a high-test unleaded rated at 89 (Premium), and diesel. All three are priced by Pemex according to standard rates and shouldn't vary from station to station. Because Pemex is government-owned, you don't see the week-to-week price fluctuations common in countries where oil companies are privately owned and rates influenced by small changes in international oil prices. All are roughly equivalent in price to their U.S. or Canadian counterparts. The price should always be marked in pesos on the pump. Nearly all Pemex pumps in Baja now give readouts calibrated for the new peso, and they zero out automatically when the fuel nozzle is lifted from the pump.

AUTOMOTIVE EQUIPMENT

Although plenty of visitors drive the length of the Baja peninsula and back without so much as a spare tire, anyone driving long distances in Baja should consider bringing the following extras, regardless of the type of vehicle:

- air filters
- battery cables
- brake, clutch, steering, and transmission fluids
- eight-meter (25-foot) tow rope
- emergency flares
- fan belts
- fire extinguisher
- fuel filters
- fuses
- lug wrench and jack
- one five-gallon water container
- one or two five-gallon gas cans
- radiator hoses
- spare tire
- spark plugs
- tire gauge
- tube-repair kit (if appropriate)
- 12-volt air compressor

Most Pemex stations are full-serve (though Los Cabos now has the first self-serve station on the peninsula), and a visit begins with two questions: How much and what type of gas do you want? *"Lleno con premio/magna, por favor"* is the usual answer. It's customary to leave a small tip (up to US$1) for window washing or other extra services.

An early 2007 National Public Radio segment in the United States reported that Mexican authorities had determined that 9 out of 10 gas stations in the country were rigging their pumps, costing drivers some US$1 billion per year. Pay attention at the pump, but don't assume every attendant intends to rip you off.

Check to make sure the pump is zeroed before the attendant starts pumping your gasoline/diesel. If the nozzle hasn't been returned to the pump since the last sale, you could find your fuel total added to the previous customer's. This seems to be less of a problem than in previous years; stations in the border towns are still the most likely places to overcharge. It helps to get out of your vehicle to keep an eye on the pumping procedures. If you're confused by the pump readout, currency conversion, or price per liter, carry a handheld calculator to make sure it all adds up; a calculator held in clear view deters most potential cheaters. As more new pumps are added they will be calibrated to read in new pesos to conform to the currency. This should make calculations considerably easier. A new scam (to us) for gas overcharging at modern, auto-zeroing pumps is to use a gas hose that comes from an open pump on the opposite side, so you can't see whether the readout starts at zero.

Fuel must be paid for in cash, and you should count your change, especially when paying with large, 500-peso bills. Be sure to carry plenty of pesos for fuel purchases. Mexican currency is the overwhelming preference of most Pemex stations; some stations near the U.S.–Mexico border take U.S. dollars, but the rate is always rounded down.

Rumors about the quality of Pemex fuels sometimes suggest an extra fuel filter or additive are necessary. This may have been the case 15 or more years ago, but nowadays Pemex fuel seems to perform well with all types of vehicles.

The main problem with Pemex fuel remains its availability, although in recent years the situation has improved considerably. Gas is delivered to Baja from the mainland via the ferry service, so when the seas are rough, the gas doesn't always arrive on time. To notify customers, the hose is usually draped over the top of a pump when it's empty.

Liquefied petroleum gas (LPG) is available in Baja. The price per liter is about the same as for Magna Sin when bought for vehicular purposes. LPG sold for heating and cooking is subsidized and costs less than in the United States or Canada. The difficulty is finding it. Look for signs reading Butano.

Oil

Motor oil is widely available at *tiendas* and Pemex stations throughout Baja. If your vehicle takes anything lower (thinner) than 30-weight, however, you'd better bring along your own; most places stock only 30- or 40-weight oil.

Parts and Repairs

Good auto shops and mechanics are available in Tijuana, Mexicali, Ensenada, La Paz, San José del Cabo, and, to a lesser extent, San Quintín, El Rosario, Mulegé, Loreto, and Cabo San Lucas. Elsewhere in Baja, if you have a breakdown, it's either do it yourself or rely on the mercy of passing drivers. In areas where you can find a mechanic, the following makes can usually be serviced: Chevrolet, Dodge, Ford, Nissan, Toyota, and Volkswagen. For anything else, you should carry spare filters, plugs, points, hoses, belts, and gaskets—even for the shortest of trips.

Green Angels (Roadside Assistance)

The Secretaría de Turismo operates a fleet of green trucks called **Ángeles Verdes** (Green Angels) that patrol Baja's highways and offer professional assistance to anyone with automotive problems. Founded in 1960, this is the only such highway-assistance program in the world.

Each truck carries a first-aid kit, a short-wave radio, gasoline, and a variety of common auto parts. They're usually staffed by two uniformed employees, one of whom may speak some English. The drivers will perform minor repairs for the cost of the parts and can provide towing for distances up to 24 kilometers (15 mi). If they can't remedy the problem or tow your vehicle to a nearby mechanic, they'll give you a lift or arrange for other assistance. They can also radio for emergency medical assistance if necessary.

The trucks supposedly patrol assigned highway sections at least twice a day; the authors' experience is that the Green Angels are much more commonly seen south of Santa Rosalía, where they're most needed due to the longer distances between towns.

Mexico's federal highway department maintains 29 **roadside call boxes** at approximate three-kilometer intervals along the Tijuana–Ensenada toll road. Calls are free and bilingual operators are on duty 24 hours a day to help arrange emergency medical or automotive assistance.

Trailers and RVs

Baja is a popular destination for RVers. Not only are there plenty of RV parks with services, but you can pull off the road and camp just about anywhere outside the cities, with few restrictions. The restrictions are largely physical; numerous places simply can't accommodate a wide trailer or motor home because of narrow roadways, steep grades, or sharp curves. Even the Transpeninsular is tight in some places. In fact, you shouldn't even attempt a Baja trip in any rig wider than three meters (10 ft).

Caravans: An RV caravan, in which a number of individual RV owners travel as an organized group with a caravan leader, is one way to accomplish an RV trip to Baja. Average costs run about US$100 a day, not including food and gasoline. In theory, RV caravans are a great introduction to Baja for RVers apprehensive about going it alone. The reality, however, is that everyone else on the road will hate an RV caravan if its members cause traffic jams—especially on winding, mountainous roads—or suck the Pemex stations dry. Those traveling to Baja in RV caravans must therefore carefully monitor their own behavior to ensure they do not become a menace or trial to others on the road. Caravans limited to no more than two or three vehicles are probably best. Keep in mind, though, that it's much cheaper to do it on your own—for US$100 a day you could be driving a more manageable sedan and staying in hotels.

The type of rig most suited to Baja travel is probably a well-equipped camper or van. With a bed, two 20-liter (five-gallon) water containers, a small propane stove and refrigerator, and a portable toilet, you can travel just as independently as someone driving a 12-meter (40-ft) motor home. Add a deep-cycle RV battery under the hood and you can run a variety of electrical appliances for at least a week without turning over your engine. For extra power, mount a solar panel on top of the cab or camper.

When tricking out your rig, consider oversized tires for more traction and road clearance, overload shocks to protect your vehicle and its contents on rough roads, and a rollbar over the front seats. Whether or not you have high clearance, skid plates under your fuel tank, engine, and transmission are a good idea if you plan any off-highway driving.

What's the perfect Baja rig? Such a beast doesn't really exist, of course, because we all have individual needs. (How about a kayak with wings?) Probably a near-perfect rig would combine features of the self-sufficient camper as described above with those of a rugged four-wheel-drive vehicle featuring a turning circle of six meters (20 ft) or less. Ambitious Baja hands have successfully tried everything from jeeps to three-ton diesel cabs as bases for custom-built campers. **Callen Camper** (125 S. Marshall Ave., El Cajon, CA, tel. 619/442-3305, www.callencamper.com) specializes in custom-outfitting Baja camper rigs.

For four-wheel-drive truckers expecting to travel off-highway, **Four Wheel Pop-Up Camper** (1460 Churchill Downs Ave., Woodland, CA 95776, tel. 800/242-1442,

WHERE TO RENT A CAR IN BAJA

More than a dozen international brands and independent agencies rent vehicles for self-guided exploration of the Baja Peninsula. The major chains are listed below.

AGENCY	CONTACT	LOCATIONS
Advantage Rent a Car	tel. 624/143-0466	Cabo San Lucas (Ave. Lázaro Cardénas)
	www.arac.com	
Alamo	tel. 800/849-8001	San José del Sabo (Blvd. Castro)
	reservaciones@ alamorentacar.com.mx	Los Cabos Intl Airport
	www.alamorentacar.com	
Avis	tel. 624/146-0201	Los Cabos Intl Airport (SJD)
	U.S. tel. 800/331-2112	Cabo San Lucas Airport
	www.avis.com	Cabo San Lucas (Ave. Lázaro Cardénas)
		Pueblo Bonito Sunset Beach (Los Cabos)
		Grand Baja Resort (Los Cabos)
		Hotel Pueblo Bonito Rose (Los Cabos)
		Pueblo Bonito Pacifica (Los Cabos)
		La Paz Intl Airport (LAP)
		La Paz (Obregón)
		Tijuana Intl Airport
		Tijuana (Zona Rio)
Budget	tel. 624/146-5333	La Paz Intl Airport (LAP)
	U.S. tel. 800/527-0700	Los Cabos Intl Airport
	www.budget.com	Loreto Intl Airport
	loscabos@budgetbaja.com	Marquis Hotel (Los Cabos)
		Mexicali Airport
		Tijuana Airport
		Todos Santos (Márquez de León 4)
Dollar Rent A Car	tel. 624/142-0100	La Paz Intl Airport (LAP)
	U.S. tel. 866/434-2226	La Paz (Obregón)
	www.dollar.com	Los Arcos Hotel (La Paz)
	www.dollarloscabos.com	Los Cabos Intl Airport (SJD)
		Hote Meliá Cabo Real (Los Cabos)

		Hotel Presidente (Los Cabos)
		San José del Cabo (Blvd. Castro)
		Cabo San Lucas (Blvd. Marina)
		Club Cascadas (Los Cabos)
		Mexicali (Blvd. Benito Juárez)
Europcar	tel. 612/124-7011	La Paz Intl Airport
	U.S. tel. 877/940-6900	La Paz (Obregón)
	www.europcar.com	Loreto Airport
		Loreto
		Los Cabos Intl Airport
Hertz	tel. 624/146-1803	Cabo San Lucas (Ave. Lázaro Cardénas 6)
	U.S. tel. 800/654-3001	Ensenada (Ave. Alvarrado 143)
	www.hertz.com	La Paz Intl Airport (LAP)
		La Paz (Obregón 2130-D)
		Marina Costa Baja (Km 61 Carr. A Pichilingue)
		Loreto Airport (Km 5, Mexico 1)
		Loreto (Calle Romanita)
		Mexicali Hotel Araiza Inn
		Mexicali Intl Airport
		Mexicali (Blvd. Benito Juárez)
		Los Cabos Intl Airport
		Westin Resort Los Cabos
		Tijuana Intl Airport (TIJ)
		Camino Real (Tijuana)
		Grand Hotel Tijuana
		Hotel Pueblo Amigo (Tijuana)
		Tijuana (Zona Rio 9575)
National	tel. 624/146-5021	Cabo San Lucas (Ave. Lázaro Cardénas)
	U.S. tel. 800/227-7368	Hotel Casa del Mar (Los Cabos)
	www.nationalcar.com	Riu Palace (Los Cabos)
		Hilton Los Cabos

(continued on next page)

WHERE TO RENT A CAR IN BAJA (continued)

National *(continued)*		Posada Real Los Cabos
		One&Only Palmilla (Los Cabos)
		Sheraton Hacienda del Mar (Los Cabos)
		Los Cabos Intl Airport
		La Paz Intl Airport
		La Paz (Obregón)
		Los Barriles (20 de Noviembre)
		Tijuana Intl Airport
		Tijuana (Ave. Nezahuatcoyotl 1640)
Payless Car Rental	tel. 624/146-5290	Cabo San Lucas (Camino Viejo a San José)
	www.paylesscarrental.com	Los Cabos Intl Airport (SJD)
	sanJosedelcabomexico@ paylesscarrental.net	San José del Cabo (Paseo San José)
Thrifty Car Rental	tel. 624/146-5030 or 800/021-2277	Cabo San Lucas (Blvd. Marina)
		La Paz Intl Airport
	www.thrifty.com	Westin Los Cabos
	gerencia.loscabos@ thrifty.com.mx	Crown Plaza Hotel (Los Cabos)
		Dreams Los Cabos
		San Felipe Airport
		San José del Cabo (Blvd. San José 20000A)
		Tijuana Intl Airport (TIJ)

www.fourwheelcampers.com) offers a compact, stable solution. The camper's low-profile design produces less wind drag than conventional cab-over campers and helps maintain a lower center of gravity. The roof lifts to provide a stand-up camper when parked.

Car Rental

You can rent cars in Tijuana, Rosarito, Mexicali, Ensenada, Loreto, La Paz, Los Barriles, Todos Santos, San José del Cabo, and Cabo San Lucas. In general, Tijuana, Cabo San Lucas, and San José del Cabo offer the least-expensive rentals, while the smaller town agencies are the most expensive. Most of the international chains offer economy/compact cars for around US$30–45/day with unlimited miles or US$60–75 for an SUV or jeep. Rates in La Paz are slightly lower than in Los Cabos. Mexican liability insurance costs an additional US$25/day with these companies, and deductibles are often high (US$1,000 and up). It pays to shop around. Book ahead online, or comparison shop when you arrive.

Online discount car rental services, such as Hotwire (www.hotwire.com), offer substantially lower rates than the major brands by selling excess inventory for their partner companies. Rentals through Hotwire come from names like Avis, Hertz, or Budget, but you won't know which company until you agree to purchase the rental. The other difference is that you prepay for the rental at the time of reservation, so you won't be able to change your mind once you get to Baja.

Independent agencies are another option, sometimes at lower cost but often with per-kilometer charges in addition to the daily rate.

Rentals out of San Diego are sometimes a bit cheaper, but most agencies that allow their cars into Mexico won't allow them any farther south than Guerrero Negro. Some only allow travel 25 miles into Baja. If you drive beyond these limits, you won't be covered. They often add mandatory collision damage waivers to the cost as well. If you're planning to rent in San Diego, note that even though Avis and other companies allow you to drive across the border, Hotwire's contracts with its partners stipulate no cross-border travel. Go directly to the rental car provider if you want to rent from San Diego.

California Baja Rent-A-Car (9245 Jamacha Blvd., Spring Valley, CA 91977, U.S. tel. 619/470-7368 or 888/470-7368, www.cabaja.com) specializes in vehicle rentals for all-Baja driving. California Baja offers Jeep Cherokees, Jeep Wranglers, GMC Suburbans, Ford Explorers, Ford 4x4 pickups, plus various passenger cars, vans, and convertibles. Internet discount rates start at about US$60 a day plus US$0.32 per mile beyond 100 miles per day for a subcompact. A Wrangler rents for US$120 a day plus US$0.32 per mile (100 free miles per day), while a Landrover Discovery II 4X4 costs US$140 daily plus US$0.38 per mile (100 free miles per day). Mexican insurance is included in these discounted rates. Drop-offs in Cabo San Lucas can be arranged for an extra charge. Optional accessories include satellite phones, Sirius satellite radio, and coolers. Note: This agency is located about 20 minutes from the San Diego airport, and did not have a shuttle at press time, so customers need to take a US$40–45 cab to the pickup location.

Insuring Your Rental Car

The Mexican proof of financial responsibility law (See *Driving into Baja* under *Getting There*) applies to drivers of rental cars in Mexico, except in this case, you don't get to choose a specific policy—rather, you agree to pay an additional US$25–40 per day for whatever coverage the rental car company provides. The exact amount depends on the size of the rental car and how far into Baja you drive it (if you rent from San Diego). Terms and coverage limits vary among the various agencies, and they don't make it easy to see the fine print before you arrive at the counter. To learn about the policy before you agree to rent the car, call the local office for the company you are considering. Read the contract carefully at the rental car counter, and be sure you understand the terms. If you drive farther than the contract permits, fail to report an accident within the time specified, or violate other clauses, your coverage may be nullified.

Avis (U.S. tel. 619/231-7171 or 800/852-4617) allows renters to drive 450 miles south of the border to Guerrero Negro. **Hertz** (U.S. tel. 619/767-5700) allows customers to drive a rental car from the San Diego airport location only into Baja. Mexican insurance costs US$25/day for an economy- to regular-size car, US$35/day for a premium car or minivan, up to 25 miles south into Mexico (which won't get you very far); and US$35/40 a day for travel between 26–250 miles south of the border. Coverage limits are US$25,000 for collision, US$25,000 for theft, US$50,000 for liability; legal and medical are not specified.

Deductibles at Thrifty were reportedly as high as US$2,500 at last check.

BY MOTORCYCLE

Much of Baja is excellent motorcycle country. The winding sierra roads are especially challenging, and since traffic is generally light you can really let it rip. Another advantage of motorcycle travel in Baja is that if your bike gets mired in soft ground, you can almost always extricate it without assistance.

As with automotive travel in Baja, pre-departure planning is important. You should be able to carry enough gear in two panniers and a backpack (tied down on the rear) for a trip all the way down the peninsula.

Motorcycle mechanics in Baja are few and far between—you must be entirely self-reliant to make this trip safely and successfully. Besides the usual camping and first-aid gear, bikers should carry all tools needed for routine maintenance, spare brake shoes, a tire repair kit, spare levers, an extra battery, a clutch cable, spare light bulbs, a four-liter reserve gas can, and a spare helmet visor.

For a Transpeninsular trip, any bike smaller than 600cc is too small. A four-stroke gets better mileage than a two-stroke, an important consideration given the Baja gas station situation. Experienced Baja bikers replace standard fuel tanks with larger 20-liter tanks to extend their fuel range.

The same driving precautions that apply to four-wheel driving should be followed by bikers as well. Special care should be taken when negotiating blind curves because buses and trucks in Baja aren't used to seeing motorcycles on the highway. As with bicycle touring, motorcyclists may find that an 11 A.M.–3 P.M. siesta is necessary to avoid the sun's worst rays.

Several small tour operators have tried to offer motorcycling programs in Baja, but so far only two have lasted more than a couple of years. **Chris Haines Motorcycle Adventure** (P.O. Box 966, Trabuco Canyon, CA 92678, U.S. tel. 866/262-8635, www.bajaoffroadtours.com) operates four-day rides from Ensenada to Mike's Sky Ranch for US$2,050 and seven-day rides from Ensenada to Cabo San Lucas for US$4,500, inclusive of all equipment and road support. Custom itineraries are also available. The company uses Honda XR series off-road bikes, ranging from 200cc–650cc. **Baja Off-Road Adventures** (www.bajaoffroad.com) is similar.

BY BICYCLE

Among cyclists, Baja is the most popular area in all of Mexico. Traffic is relatively light, the scenery is striking, and cyclists can pull over and camp just about anywhere.

Touring or mountain bike? If you're only heading straight down the peninsula and back on the Transpeninsular, or doing the northern loop on Mexico 2, 3, and 5, a touring bike would be the best choice, as it's lighter and faster than a mountain bike. On the other hand, the Baja peninsula offers so many great off-road rides that anyone who really wants to see Baja—and has the time—should consider a mountain bike. Off-road riding requires a stronger frame, higher clearance, and wider tires.

Many interesting trail rides lie within 95 kilometers (60 mi) of the U.S.–Mexico border. Parque Nacional Constitución de 1857—less than 80 kilometers (50 mi) southwest of Mexicali—has been called "fat-tire heaven" by cycling editors at *Outside* magazine, offering rides through startling pine forests and subalpine meadows. The Cataviña Boulder Field in the Central Desert also features some excellent trails; don't forget the antipuncture booting on that one. For coastal routes, Baja's best overall rides are in Baja California Sur, particularly the unpaved Camino Rural Costero between San José del Cabo and Cabo Pulmo and the unnamed, unpaved road between Los Barriles and Bahía de los Muertos. The unpaved road network along the coast between San José and La Paz will astound even the most jaded dirt bikers as it takes them past deserted white-sand coves with coral reefs, over jagged desert peaks, and then down into lush San Juan de los Planes.

Popular paved touring routes include Tecate to Ensenada (116 km/72 mi) and Ensenada to San Felipe (236 km/146 mi), both on scenic Mexico 3, as well as the Cape loop on Mexico 1 and Mexico 19 (La Paz–Cabo San Lucas–Todos Santos–La Paz).

Because the sun can be particularly strong when you're on paved surfaces, which both reflect and radiate heat, you may find an 11 A.M.–3 P.M. siesta necessary no matter what time of year you ride. Don't forget to bring sunglasses and plenty of high-SPF sunscreen.

Equipment and Repairs

Whether you're riding a mountain or touring bike, you'll need the same basic essentials to handle long-distance Baja riding. If you plan to camp along the way, you'll need the usual camping and first-aid gear, selected to fit your panniers. Camping is often your only choice, even on Transpeninsular trips, because some cyclists simply can't make the mileage from hotel to hotel in central Baja.

Helmets are particularly important; a head injury is even more serious when you're in the middle of nowhere. A helmet also keeps direct sun off the top of your skull. A rearview mirror is a must for keeping an eye on motorists coming from behind on narrow roads. A locking cable is preferable to a clunky U-lock for long-distance trips because it weighs less, although bicycle theft isn't much of a problem in Baja. The only other security you might need is a removable handlebar bag for carrying your camera and valuables; you can take the bag with you when stopping at restaurants or *tiendas* and fill it with snacks for eating on the fly.

Water is the uppermost consideration on overnight trips. No matter what the time of year, cyclists should carry four one-liter bottles of water per day. The one-liter bottles used for cycling are more puncture-resistant than water containers designed for camping. Punctures are always a concern in Baja because of all the trees and plants bearing spines.

The puncture threat means you should outfit your bike with heavy-duty tires and tubes. Bring along two or three spare tubes, one spare tire, a tire gauge, and a complete tire repair kit. You should also carry duct tape and moleskin—or commercial plastic booting—to use as booting material against sidewall cuts caused by sharp rocks or cactus.

Check the nuts and bolts on your rack daily and retighten as necessary. Applying Locktite should lessen the need for retightening—carry a small supply along with extra nuts and bolts. Baling wire can be used for improvised repairs; carry two or three meters along with wire cutters.

Bike shops operate in Tijuana, Ensenada, San Quintín, Ciudad Constitución, La Paz,

and Cabo San Lucas. Although the Mexicans who run these shops can sometimes perform miraculous repairs using nothing resembling a bike's original parts, it's safer to come prepared with spares, especially for parts that aren't easily jury-rigged. At a minimum, carry a spare freewheel, a rear derailleur, and all the wrenches and screwdrivers necessary to work on your bike. If in addition you bring along several extra spokes, cables, and a spare chain, you'll be ready for just about any repair scenario.

Bicycle Transportation

You can take bikes on the **Tijuana Trolley** (U.S. tel. 619/233-3004) to San Ysidro and then walk over the border (see *Getting There*).

Mexicoach and **Greyhound** will transport bikes of paying passengers in bus luggage compartments for no additional cost, but bikes should be boxed. For return trips from Baja, you should be able to pick up a box from bicycle shops in Tijuana or Ensenada or build your own from discarded cardboard boxes.

Guided Bicycle Trips

If you're unsure of your off-road cycling skills, you might want to tackle Baja with an experienced cycle guide. Several tour operators now run cycling programs in Baja.

One of our favorites is **Pedaling South** (U.S. tel. 707/942-4450 or 800/398-6200, www.tourbaja.com), which runs the following multiday cycling tours: Sierra Ridge Ride (nine days for US$795 pp), San Javier Singletrack (eight days, US$795), Oasis Bases (seven days or eight days, US$695), and Cross Baja/Whale Watch (nine days, US$995). Combo sea kayak/mountain bike trips are also available at US$795 for seven days. If you bring your own bike, Pedaling South deducts US$95 from the tour rates. Included in the price are accommodations, ground transport, meals on tour days, camping gear, tents, guides, tracking vehicles, and first aid.

Visas and Officialdom

ENTRY REGULATIONS
Passports and Tourist Permits
Under the Western Hemisphere Travel Initiative, as of January 2007, anyone traveling by air between the United States, Canada, Mexico, Central and South America, the Caribbean, and Bermuda is required to present a valid passport. The same applies to anyone traveling by land or sea as of January 2008.

Citizens of the United States or Canada (or of 42 other designated countries in Europe and Latin America, plus Singapore) visiting Mexico solely for tourism are not required to obtain a visa. Instead they must carry validated "tourist cards" (*formas migratorias turistas,* or FMTs), which aren't actually cards but slips of paper. These are available free at any Mexican consulate or Mexican tourist office, from many travel agencies, on flights to Mexico, or at the border. The tourist card is valid for stays of up to 180 days and must be used within 90 days of issue. Your card becomes invalid once you exit the country—you're supposed to surrender it at the border—even if your 180 days hasn't expired. If you'll be entering and leaving Mexico more than once during your trip, you should request a multiple-entry tourist card, available from Mexican consulates only.

To obtain the FMT you need proof of citizenship—a birth certificate (or certified copy), voter's registration card, certificate of naturalization, or passport. A driver's license doesn't qualify.

Once you cross the border (or land at an airport on an international flight), your tourist card must be **validated** by a Mexican immigration officer. You can arrange this at any *migración* office in Baja (many *municipio* seats have them), but it's accomplished most conveniently at the border crossing itself or at the immigration office in Ensenada (right around the corner from the tourist information booth on Boulevard Costero). Note: FMTs are also inspected at the army checkpoint at the north end of Guerrero Negro, so you'd best have your papers in order before entering Baja California Sur.

At airports you pass through immigration, where an officer stamps your paperwork with the date of entry and the number of days you're permitted to stay in Mexico.

Make sure you receive enough days to cover your visit. Some immigration officers, especially those at airports near tourist resorts, may fill in your FMT for 30 days, figuring that's sufficient for most holidays. If you want more than 30 days, it's best to mention it to the officer in advance.

In mid-1999, the Mexican government began collecting a tourist fee (currently around US$22) from all tourists entering the country. If you fly in, this fee is tacked on to your airfare. If you arrive by land, you can pay this fee at any bank in Mexico. The bank will issue a receipt, which you must show when you leave the country. *If you're going no farther south than Ensenada or San Felipe, you do not have to pay this fee.*

Before 1991, Mexican regulations required **children under the age of 18** crossing the border without one or both parents to carry a notarized letter granting permission from the absent parent, or both parents if both were absent. This regulation is no longer in effect, but we've heard that some Mexican border officers, as well as airline check-in crews, are still asking for the letter, apparently unaware the regulation has been rescinded. Hence, unaccompanied minors or minors traveling with only one parent should be prepared for all situations with notarized letters. In cases of divorce, separation, or death, the minor should carry notarized papers documenting the situation.

In reality, minors with tourist cards are rarely asked for these documents. Children under 15 may be included on their parents' tourist card, but this means that neither the child nor the parents can legally exit Mexico without the other.

Tourist Visas
Tourists from countries other than the 45 countries for which no visa is necessary must

obtain tourist visas before arriving in Mexico. You must apply for your visa in person at a Mexican consulate; you usually can obtain a tourist visa within two weeks of filing an application. The Mexican Consulate General in San Diego can usually issue tourist visas on the day of application. Requirements include a valid passport, valid U.S. visa for multiple entries, form I-94, proof of economic solvency (such as an international credit card), a round-trip air ticket to Mexico, and a visa fee of around US$40.

Foreign visitors who are legal permanent residents of the United States do not need visas to visit Mexico for tourism. A free tourist card can be obtained by presenting your passport and U.S. residence card to any travel agency or at the airport or border crossing.

Business Travel

Citizens of Mexico's NAFTA (North American Free Trade Agreement) partners, the United States and Canada, are not required to obtain a visa to visit Mexico for business purposes. Instead, you receive a free NAFTA business permit (*forma migratoria nafta,* or FMN), similar to a tourist card, at the point of entry (border crossing or airport); it's valid for 30 days. At the port of entry you must present proof of nationality (valid passport or original birth certificate plus a photo identification or voter's registration card) and proof that you are traveling for "international business activities," usually interpreted to mean a letter from the company you represent, even if it's your own enterprise.

Those who arrive with the FMN and wish to stay longer than the authorized period of 30 days must replace their FMN with an FM-3 form at an immigration office in Mexico. The FM-3 is valid for up to one year, for multiple entries, and may be extended. Note that the FMN is not valid for persons who will be earning a salary during their stay in Mexico.

Citizens of other countries visiting for business purposes must obtain an FM-3 visa endorsed for business travel, which is valid for one year.

Overstays

If you overstay your visa and are caught, the usual penalty is a fine of around US$45 for overstays up to a month. After that the penalties become more severe. It's rare that a Mexican border official asks to see your FMT or visa when you're leaving the country. Your main risk comes if you get into trouble with the police somewhere in Mexico and they ask to see your immigration documents. Having expired papers only complicates your situation, so the best policy is to stay up-to-date in spite of the apparent laxity of enforcement.

Pets

Dogs and cats may be brought into Mexico if each is accompanied by a **vaccination certificate** that proves the animal has been vaccinated or treated for rabies, hepatitis, pip, and leptospirosis. You'll also need a **health certificate** issued no more than 72 hours before entry and signed by a registered veterinarian.

Since 1992 the requirement that the health certificate be stamped with a visa at a port of entry or at a Mexican consulate has been repealed. The certificate is still necessary; the visa isn't.

Upon recrossing the border into the United States, the U.S. Customs Service will ask to see the vaccination certificate.

Visitante Rentista and *Inmigrante Rentista* Visas

FM-3 visas may be issued to foreigners who choose to live in Mexico on a "permanent income" basis. This most often applies to foreigners who decide to retire in Mexico, though it is also used by artists, writers, and other self-employed foreign residents. With this visa you're allowed to import one motor vehicle as well as your household belongings into Mexico tax-free.

The basic requirements for this visa are that applicants must forgo any kind of employment while living in Mexico and must show proof (bank statements) that they have a regular source of foreign-earned income amounting to at least US$1,000 per month (plus half that for each dependent over the age of 15, e.g.,

US$1,500 for a couple). A pile of paperwork, including a "letter of good conduct" from the applicant's local police department, must accompany the initial application, along with an immigration tax payment and various application fees totaling about US$135.

The visa must be renewed annually, but the renewal can be accomplished at any immigration office in Mexico. After five years in Mexico, you have to start over or move up to the FM-2 or *inmigrante rentista* visa, which has higher income requirements and signifies an intent to stay longer. After five years on an FM-2, an *inmigrante rentista* is eligible to apply for *inmigrado* status, which confers all the rights of citizenship (including employment in Mexico), save the rights to vote and hold public office.

Many foreigners who have retired in Mexico manage to do so on the regular 180-day tourist visa; every six months they dash across the border and return with a new tourist card (issued at the border) on the same day. This method bypasses all the red tape and income requirements of the retirement visa. If you own a home in Baja, however, some local immigration officials may interpret the law to mean that you must have an FM-2 or FM-3 visa—not an FMT or tourist visa—to be able to stay in that home for any period of time whatsoever. Although it's clear from a straight reading that Mexico's immigration laws do not require any special visas for home ownership (just as you don't need a particular visa to own property in the United States or Canada), each immigration district behaves like an individual fiefdom at the mercy of the local immigration chief.

Monthly income requirements for both *rentista* visas are keyed to the Mexican daily minimum wage (400 times minimum wage for the FM-2, 250 times for the FM-3), hence figures may vary according to the current dollar–peso exchange rate.

Reentering the United States

Overseas visitors need a passport and visa to enter the United States. Except for diplomats, students, or refugees, this means a nonimmigrant visitor's visa, which must be obtained in advance at a U.S. consulate or embassy abroad. Residents of Western European and Commonwealth countries are usually issued these readily; residents of other countries may have to provide the consulate with proof of "sufficient personal funds" before the visa is issued.

Upon arrival in the United States, an immigration inspector decides how long the visa will be valid—the maximum for a temporary visitor's visa (B-1 or B-2) is six months. If you visit Mexico from California (or from anywhere else in the United States) for stays of 30 days or less, you can reenter the United States with the same visa, provided the visa is still valid, by presenting your stamped arrival/departure card (INS form I-94) and passport to a U.S. immigration inspector. If your U.S. visa has expired, you can still enter the country for a stay of 29 days or less on a transit visa—issued at the border—but you may be required to show proof of onward travel, such as an air ticket or ship travel voucher.

BORDER CROSSINGS

Baja California's U.S.–Mexico border has six official border crossings: San Ysidro/Tijuana (24 hrs), Otay Mesa (24 hrs), Tecate (5 A.M.–11 P.M.), Calexico East and West/Mexicali (24 hrs), and Los Algodones (6 A.M.–10 P.M.). Tijuana is the largest and also the most heavily used, connecting Baja with U.S. Interstate 5, which extends all the way up the U.S. west coast to the Canadian border.

At any of the border crossings, you'll find the shortest waits (15–30 minutes at Tijuana) are 10 A.M.–3:30 P.M. or after 7 or 8 P.M. on weekdays. Weekends are the worst days in either direction, except late at night or before dawn, when traffic is light. If you're on your way out of Baja and find yourself near the border during rush hours, it might be best to find a restaurant and wait it out. A Saturday or Sunday morning wait at the Tijuana crossing can be as long as two hours in either direction; it's always longer going north.

If you're on foot, crossing is usually a breeze. Public and chartered buses also get through more quickly, utilizing special traffic lanes.

UNITED STATES-MEXICO BORDER CROSSINGS

CROSSING	HOURS
Calexico (Mexicali) East	24 hrs/day
Calexico (Mexicali) West	24 hrs/day
Los Algodones	6 A.M.-10 P.M.
Otay Mesa (Tijuana)	24 hrs/day
San Ysidro (Tijuana)	24 hrs/day
Tecate	5 A.M.-11 P.M.

Visit the U.S. Customs Border Protection website at http://apps.cbp.gov/bwt/index.asp to check border wait times before you cross.

Mexican Consulate in San Diego

San Diego's Mexican Consulate General (1549 India St., San Diego, CA 92101, U.S. tel. 619/231-8414, www.consulmexsd.org, Mon.–Fri. 8 A.M.–1:30 P.M.) is relatively close to the Tijuana border crossing, about 30–45 minutes by car. The staff can assist with visas, immigration problems, special-import permits, and questions concerning Mexican customs regulations.

CUSTOMS
Entering Mexico

Officially, tourists are supposed to bring only those items into Mexico that will be of use during their trip. This means you can bring in practically anything as long as it doesn't appear in large enough quantities to qualify for resale. Firearms and ammunition, as well as boats, require special permits (see *Sports and Recreation*).

Technically speaking, you're allowed to import one still camera and one video camera, up to 12 rolls of unused film or blank videocassettes for each, and used or developed film. Anything more is supposed to require permission from a Mexican consulate. In everyday practice, however, Mexican customs officials rarely blink at more film or an extra camera or two. Professional photographers and others who would like to bring more cameras and film into Mexico can apply for dispensation through a Mexican consulate abroad. Regarding audio equipment, you're limited to one CD player and one audio-cassette player (or combo), five laser discs, five DVDs, and up to 20 CDs or recording cassettes. Other per-person limitations include one typewriter, a cellular phone and a pager, a new or used laptop computer, a musical instrument, two used personal sports gear items, one tent and accompanying camping gear, one set of fishing gear, a pair of skis, a pair of binoculars, two tennis rackets, five "toys," and one sailboard.

Other limits include three liters of liquor, beer, or wine and two cartons (20 packs) of cigarettes or 25 cigars or 200 grams of tobacco.

Other than the above, you're permitted to bring in no more than US$300 worth of other articles if arriving by air, US$50 if you arriving by land. You will be subject to duty on personal possessions worth more than US$300 (or US$50), to a maximum of US$1,000 (except for new computer equipment, which is exempt up to US$4,000).

Foreign-registered motor vehicles—cars,

trucks, RVs, motorcycles, etc.—do not require permits for travel anywhere on the Baja California peninsula. However, if you plan to take a vehicle registered outside Mexico onto one of the vehicle ferries that sail from Baja to the mainland, or if you plan to drive farther east than San Luis Río Colorado in Sonora, you must obtain an auto permit. These are available from any Mexican consulate abroad, or at the border, or from the ferry office in La Paz.

If you're bringing a vehicle across the border, you need Mexican auto insurance. For further information on vehicle permits and insurance, see the *Getting There* and *Getting Around* sections.

Returning to the United States

Visitors returning to the United States from Mexico may have their luggage inspected by U.S. Customs officials. The hassle can be minimized by giving brief, straight answers to their questions (e.g., "How long have you been in Mexico?" "Do you have anything to declare?") and by cooperating with their requests to open your luggage, vehicle storage compartments, and anything else they want opened. Sometimes the officers use dogs to sniff luggage and/or vehicles for contraband and illegal aliens.

Nearly 3,000 items—including all handicrafts—made in Mexico are exempt from any U.S. Customs duties. Adults over 21 are allowed one liter (33.8 fluid ounces) of alcoholic beverages and 200 cigarettes (or 100 cigars) per person. Note that Cuban cigars may not be imported into the United States and will be confiscated at the border if discovered. Since an estimated 9 out of 10 cigars sold as Cubans in Mexico are reportedly fake, it's not worth the hassle, especially since a good hand-rolled cigar from Veracruz can challenge most Cubans. All other purchases or gifts up to a total value of US$400 within any 31-day period can be brought into the United States duty-free.

The following **fruits and vegetables** cannot be brought into the United States from Mexico: oranges, grapefruits, mangoes, avocados (unless the pit is removed), and potatoes (including yams and sweet potatoes). All other

fruits are permitted (including bananas, dates, pineapples, cactus fruits, grapes, and berries of all types).

Other prohibited plant materials are straw (including packing materials and items stuffed with straw), hay, unprocessed cotton, sugarcane, and any plants in soil (this includes houseplants).

Animals and animal products that cannot be imported include wild and domesticated birds (including poultry, unless cooked), pork or pork products (including sausage, ham, and other cured pork), and eggs. Beef, mutton, venison, and other meats are permitted at up to 23 kilograms (50 lbs) per person.

Customs regulations can change at any time, so if you want to verify the regulations on a purchase before risking duties or confiscation at the border, check with a U.S. consulate in Baja before crossing or visit www.cbp.gov.

Returning to Canada

Duty-frees include 200 cigarettes (or 50 cigars or 200 grams of tobacco) and one bottle (1.1 liters) of booze or wine, 24 cans or bottles (355 ml) of beer or ale, and gifts to the value of C$60 per gift (other than alcohol or tobacco). Exemptions run from C$50 to C$750 depending on how long you've been outside Canada. To reach the maximum exemption of C$750 you must be gone at least one week. Because Canada is also signatory to NAFTA, customs legalities will change over the next decade.

LEGAL MATTERS

All foreign visitors in Mexico are subject to Mexican legal codes, which are based on Roman and Napoleonic law updated with U.S. constitutional theory and civil law. The most distinctive features of the Mexican judiciary system, compared to Anglo-American systems, are that the system doesn't provide for trials by jury (the judge decides) nor writs of habeas corpus (though you must be charged within 72 hours of incarceration or else released). Furthermore, bail is rarely granted to an arrested foreigner—for many offenses, not even Mexican nationals are allowed bail. Hence, once arrested and jailed for a serious offense, it can be difficult to arrange release. The lesson here is: Don't get involved in matters that might result in your arrest. This primarily means anything having to do with drugs or guns.

The oft-repeated saw that in Mexico an arrested person is considered guilty until proven innocent is no more true south of the border than north. As in Canada, the United States, or western Europe, an arrested person is considered a criminal *suspect* until the courts confirm or deny guilt. You have the right to notify your consulate if detained.

Mexican federal police *(federales* and *judiciales)*, as well as the Mexican army, mostly under pressure from the United States, occasionally set up roadblocks to conduct searches for drugs and for arms. Such roadblocks used to be rare in Baja but have recently increased in number. On recent Transpeninsular drives we've been stopped at six or seven different military checkpoints *(puestos de control)* between Tijuana and Cabo San Lucas. In each case, the soldiers were courteous and the vehicle searches were brief and cursory. If your vehicle is stopped at a *puesto de control,* be as cooperative as possible. If there are any irregularities or if you object to the way in which the procedure is carried out, make note of the incident, including whatever badge numbers, names, or license numbers you can obtain discreetly, and later file a report with the Mexican Attorney General for Tourist Protection. So far we've not heard of any problems encountered by foreign visitors, although a couple of Americans were arrested for carrying unregistered firearms—a serious federal offense in Mexico—in 1996.

La Mordida

In the past, Mexican police had a reputation for hassling foreigners, especially those who drove their own vehicles in Mexico. Tales of the legendary *mordida* (literally, "bite"), or minor bribe, supposedly a necessary part of navigating one's way around Mexico, swelled way out of proportion to reality but were nonetheless based on real incidents.

For several years now, the Mexican police have for the most part ceased singling out foreigners for arrest (except in Tijuana and Ro-

sarito, where the problem persists), partly as a result of anticorruption efforts by the federal government but more importantly because of a conscious effort to attract more tourists. Most foreign visitors who drive in Baja these days complete their trips without any police hassles. (See *Getting Around* for tips on traffic laws and dealing with traffic police.)

Military

In recent years, the Mexican government has replaced many federal police officers around the country with active-duty army officers in an effort to clean up corruption among nonmilitary law enforcement agencies. In Baja, all 84 *judiciales* involved in antidrug operations were replaced with army officers in 1996. Opinions are sharply divided as to whether this is having a net positive or negative effect on law enforcement, but it's a fact that you can see more military around the country than at any time in Mexico's history since 1920. Roadblock inspection points, or *puestos de control,* along major and minor highways have become increasingly common. All manner of vehicles—buses, trucks, private autos—may be stopped and searched at such inspection points; if you get stopped at one, the best thing to do is simply be patient till it's over, usually in five minutes or less. For the most part, soldiers stationed at these checkpoints perform their duties in a serious but respectful manner. Typically they speak very little English; this usually works in favor of the non-Spanish-speaking foreign visitor because it means they can't ask many questions.

In Case of Arrest

If you get into trouble with Mexican law, for whatever reason, you should try to contact your nearest consulate in Baja. Embassies and consulates for each town are listed under the respective destination chapters. You can also contact the local state tourism offices—see the sections on each town for phone numbers and addresses. These agencies routinely handle emergency legal matters involving visiting foreigners; you stand a much better chance of resolving legal difficulties with their assistance.

Sports and Recreation

Baja California's major attractions largely fall under this heading—from trekking in the Sierra de San Pedro Mártir to scuba diving off Cabo Pulmo. An added bonus is that, for the most part, you can enjoy Baja outdoor recreation at little or no cost. User demand is low, and when fees are involved they're usually reasonable.

HIKING AND BACKPACKING
National Parks, Natural Areas, and Wildlife Preserves

Baja has two national parks (Parque Nacional Sierra San Pedro Mártir and Parque Nacional Constitución de 1857), three natural parks (Parque Natural del Desierto Central de Baja California, Parque Natural Isla Ángel de la Guarda, and Parque Natural de la Ballena Gris), two wildlife sanctuaries (Isla Guadalupe and the Midriff Islands), two underwater marine parks (Arrecife Pulmo and Bahía Cabo San Lucas), and one regular marine park (Bahía de Loreto). At the two national parks, public facilities are few and rudimentary; in the other government-protected areas they're virtually nonexistent. In 1975 the islands of the Sea of Cortez were declared a Zona de Reserva y Refugio de Aves Migratorias y de la Fauna Silvestre (Migratory Bird Reserve and Wildlife Refuge), a status somewhat strengthened in 1995 with the formation of the Secretaría de Medio Ambiente y Recursos Naturales (SEMARNAT, the Secretariat of the Environment and Natural Resources).

In addition, Baja boasts one UNESCO Biosphere Reserve, the Desierto del Vizcaíno.

Trails

Hiking trails are plentiful in the northern sierras, from wide, 150-year-old paths created by Amerindians or shepherds to smaller, more recent trails worn by hikers. In the smaller central sierras, which are more arid, trails are scarce—it's a good idea to scout an area first and ask questions locally about the best way to get from point A to point B. Although it's sometimes tempting to venture off established trails, that's a good way to get lost; you might also contribute to the destruction of delicate ecosystems. Light trails that don't seem to go anywhere may be cattle or coyote trails that connect surface water sources.

Maps

Topographic maps, which chart trails and elevation differentials, are essential for extended hiking and backpacking. **Map Link** (U.S. tel. 805/692-6777 or 800/962-1394, www.maplink.com) and **Map Centre** (U.S. tel. 619/291-3830 or 888/849-6277, www.mapcentre.com) carry a complete line of Baja topo maps in three scales (1:1,000,000, 1:250,000, and 1:50,000), sold separately according to region. The maps cost around US$13–15 each. **Mexico Maps** (U.S. tel. 805/687-1011, www.mexicomaps.com) offers GPS maps and digital maps, for some areas, as well as printed topo maps.

These same topographic maps are also available in Baja from the **Instituto Nacional de Estadística, Geografía e Informática (INEGI)** office in La Paz (Plaza Cuatro Molinos, Calle Altamirano 2790, Col. Centro, tel. 612/123-1545 or 612/122-4146, www.inegi.gob.mx) for about US$4 per sheet. Some topos may be out of print, in which case you can usually obtain a photocopy of archival prints from an INEGI office for US$6. These maps show not only trails and contour lines, but villages not normally marked on other maps.

Although you won't need a great deal of Spanish to read the INEGI maps, you might need to know the following translations for the map legend:

- *brecha*—gravel road

- *vereda*—path

- *terracería transitable en todo tiempo*—all-weather dirt road

- *terracería transitable en tiempo de secas*—dirt road passable only in dry weather

- *carretera pavimentada*—paved highway

- *carretera de más de dos carriles, caseta de pago*—toll highway of more than two lanes

INEGI (www.inegi.gob.mx) has three offices in Baja where maps are distributed: in Mexicali (at the Palacio Federal, 3rd floor, Centro Cívico, tel. 686/557-3914 or 686/556-0932); in Tijuana (at Avenida Revolución 1041, Col. Centro, tel. 664/638-7938); and in La Paz (at Plaza Cuatro Molinos, Calle Altamirano 2790, Col. Centro, tel. 612/123-1545 or 612/122-4146).

What to Bring

For a hike of a day or less, all you need is sturdy footwear (light, high-topped hiking boots are preferable to sneakers in rocky terrain) and whatever food or water you plan to consume for the day. Count on at least two liters of water per person for chaparral or lower sierra hiking, more if the weather is hot.

Longer hikes obviously require more preparation and equipment. Whether in the desert or the mountains, bring clothing that allows you to remain comfortable at both ends of the temperature spectrum; throughout the peninsula days tend to be warm, nights chilly. A light sleeping bag, for temperatures down to -4°C (25°F) in the high sierras, and a backpacking tent with plenty of ventilation for camping at lower elevations are necessities for coping with potentially harsh environments.

Good hiking boots are essential. Thick lug soles with steel shanks are preferable, as they provide protection from sharp rocks and desert plants. Bring along a first-aid kit that includes an elastic bandage for sprains, snakebite treatment, as well as a pair of tweezers for removing thorns and cactus spines. Also pack a flashlight, compass, waterproof matches, knife, extra batteries, foul-weather gear, and a signal device (mirror or whistle). A handy addition, if you're hiking near Baja's shoreline, is a telescoping fishing rod with light tackle, as surf fish are usually plentiful.

Always carry plenty of water: a minimum of five liters per person per full day of walk-

ing during hot weather, two liters in winter. Although springs and *tinajas* exist in the sierras, the water level varies considerably, and you shouldn't count on finding water sources along the way. If you need drinking water from one of these sources, always boil it first for at least 10 minutes or treat it with iodine or a water filter designed to remove impurities. Bring enough food for the duration of your hike (count on about 1.5 pounds of dry food per person per day), plus an extra one or two days' worth. One to three nestable pans will suffice for up to six hikers, along with a spoon, small plastic bowl, and cup for each person.

Camping Tips

In addition to all the usual rules for choosing campsites, don't camp beneath coconut palms (a falling coconut could knock down your tent or fracture your skull) or in arroyos (danger of flash floods).

Open fires are permitted just about anywhere in Baja except within city limits. Even in the desert, fuel is plentiful, as dried ocotillo and cactus skeletons make excellent fuels. Imitate the locals and keep your fires small. Never leave hot coals or ashes behind; smother with sand—or water, if you can spare it—till cool to the touch.

Pack out all trash that won't burn, including cigarette butts; they take 10–12 years to decompose. Bury human waste six inches down, and don't use soap in streams or springs.

Desert Hiking

For hikes in Baja's desert lands, special precautions are appropriate. Water is the most important concern; desert hiking requires at least five liters of water per day per person. Some people recommend at least eight liters per day for hikes that span the midday hours. On extended excursions of more than a night or two, the weight of anything beyond eight liters—water weighs about one kilogram per liter—is prohibitive; you'll need to learn in advance where to obtain water from reliable local sources. While hiking, keep your mouth closed and breathe through your nose to keep the mouth and throat from drying out. This will keep you cooler, as the nasal cavities are designed to moderate outside air temperature as air passes into your lungs.

Sun protection is especially essential in the desert. Wear long-sleeved clothing in light, reflective colors (white is best), sunglasses, a wide-brimmed hat, and sunscreen. It's best to take shelter from the sun 11 A.M.–3 P.M., especially during the hotter months. Most of Baja's deserts offer plenty of shade in the form of mesquite trees, overhanging cliffs, or leaning boulders. But it's also a good idea to carry your own shade—a light, opaque tarp. A poncho can double as tarp and rain protection; yes, it does occasionally rain in the desert. The Desierto del Vizcaíno is the most barren of the peninsular deserts, but also the coolest because of the tendency for fog to form when the hot desert air meets cool Pacific breezes.

Anyone contemplating an extended desert hike for the first time might consider reading at least one of the books on desert travel listed in this tome's *Suggested Reading* section. These contain important information on desert survival topics, from how to test the edibility of plants to making your own water with an improvised solar still.

Organized Trips

Few outfitters have attempted to lead hiking or backpacking trips in Baja. **Baja Motion Tours** (U.S. tel. 800/511-4848, www.2gobaja.com) offers a few interesting land-only itineraries in northern Baja at reasonable prices.

FISHING

Baja's reputation as one of the world's best sportfishing regions is well deserved. Nowhere else will you find as many varieties of fish in an area as compact and accessible as the waters of Baja. Although it's most famous for acrobatic billfish—marlin, sailfish, and swordfish—and other deep-sea fishing, Baja also offers opportunities for surf casters, small-boaters, and sport divers, as well as folks who don't yet know a rod from a reel. The bible of Baja fishing continues to be *Baja Catch,* now in its 3rd edition

by Neil Kelly and Gene Kira. Look for it in bookstores or www.bajabooksandmaps.com.

Onshore Fishing

Most accessible to travelers, since it doesn't require a boat, is onshore or surf fishing, which you can enjoy anywhere along the coast where you can get a line into the water. In Baja, Prohibido Pescar (Fishing Prohibited) signs are vary rare. Fishing from shore does not required a Mexican fishing license, but you may be asked to show proof that you acquired the fish legally if you plan on bringing your fish back to the United States.

Surf fishing is best along the Pacific coast between El Rosario and Bahía Magdalena, and on the Sea of Cortez between San José del Cabo and La Paz, but fish can be taken just about anywhere along Baja's 4,800-kilometer (3,000-mi) shoreline. Common onshore fish include surfperch, *cabezón,* sand bass, ladyfish, halibut, corvina, opaleye, leopard shark, triggerfish, and croakers. Submarine canyons along the shore of the East Cape can yield onshore catches of roosterfish, California yellowtail, and yellowfin tuna for anglers using the right tackle; shore-caught dorado (dolphinfish) and even marlin are not unknown. All of these except the marlin are considered excellent food fish, and even the marlin is edible when smoked.

One fish commonly caught onshore, the puffer, is *not* a good food fish; the meat is toxic to humans and can cause poisoning. The two puffer species common to Baja are easily identified, as their bodies expand like balloons when they're disturbed. Further identifiers: The bull's-eye puffer features a brownish body with black spots; depending on its stage of maturity, the golden puffer is either all golden or a dark purple-black with white spots and white fin trim. In Mexico, this fish is called *bolete.*

Inshore Fishing

Anyone with access to a small boat, either a skiff trailered in or a rented *panga* (an open fiberglass skiff that's usually 5–6 meters long and powered by a 40–60 hp outboard motor), can enjoy inshore fishing at depths of around 50–100 meters (165–330 ft). Common inshore catches include many of the surf fishes mentioned above, plus various kinds of groupers, sea bass, bonito shark, sculpin (scorpionfish), barracuda, rockfish, lingcod, sierra, pompano, amberjack, red and yellow snapper, pargo, and cabrilla. Cabrilla, however, must be released when caught.

Larger game fish occasionally taken inshore are the bluefin and yellowfin tuna, yellowtail, dorado, jack crevalle, and roosterfish. Again, all fish mentioned make good eating.

Offshore Fishing

The bigger game fish are found in deeper waters—over 200 meters (650 ft)—and require bigger tackle and more technique, including specialized trolling methods prescribed for each type of fish. Larger boats—fishing cruisers—are usually necessary simply because of the distance from shore to the fishing area. In the Cape Region, however, you can reach depths of over 200 meters less than 1.5 kilometers (1 mi) offshore. These areas are accessible by skiff or *panga,* though strong seasonal currents are sometimes a problem, requiring a larger outboard motor. Contrary to the popular image of Cabo San Lucas sportfishing, it isn't necessary to use a boat equipped with fighting chairs to catch the big ones, although it's undoubtedly more comfortable.

Because of the special tackle and techniques involved in offshore fishing, many Baja visitors hire local fishing guides, who usually provide boats and tackle, to transport them to offshore fishing grounds. A sometimes less expensive alternative involves signing up for fishing cruises, which take groups of tourist anglers out on big powerboats.

Most offshore anglers go after striped, blue, or black marlin, sailfish, swordfish, wahoo, dorado, roosterfish, yellowtail, and tuna. These fish are large, powerful fighters, requiring skill in handling rod and line. The billfish are the most acrobatic, performing high leaps and pirouettes when hooked; wahoo and roosterfish will also "greyhound," performing a series of long, low jumps while swimming rapidly in one direction.

Of the billfish, only the swordfish is considered good eating. The rest are traditionally regarded as trophy fish, meant to be stuffed and mounted in the den or living room. To their credit, an increasing number of anglers these days release billfish after catch; many outfitters discourage or even forbid the taking of these beautiful creatures unless the fish has been badly damaged in the fight.

The wahoo, dorado, roosterfish, yellowtail, and various tunas all make excellent eating.

Fishing Seasons

Baja presents a complex set of fishing conditions that vary from month to month and year to year. Fish are biting somewhere in Baja waters year-round, but water temperature, ocean currents, weather patterns, fish migrations, and other variables mean you usually won't find the same type of fish in the same spot in, say, December as in July. An unusually dry year in the American Southwest, for example, lessens the outflow of nutrients from the Colorado River into the Sea of Cortez, diminishing the store of plankton and other small marine creatures at the bottom of the Cortez food chain. This in turn affects populations of larger fish, from sea bass to whale sharks.

Because of the numerous variables, all the fishing calendars can serve only as guidelines. But some calendars are more accurate than others. The best is the set devised by the late Tom Miller in his *Angler's Guide to Baja California,* which divides the Baja coast into 10 fishing zones, with a calendar for each zone. Even with detailed calendars in hand, it's wise to seek the counsel of local fishing guides or other anglers on the scene before investing time and money in trying to catch a particular fish in a particular area.

A few generalizations are possible. The greatest variety and number of game fish swim the widest range of Baja waters April–October, when the water temperatures are relatively warm. In winter, many species migrate south and are available only off the Cape. Fortunately for winter anglers farther north, exceptions abound. The widely distributed California yellowtail, for example, is present year-round, migrating up and down the Sea of Cortez— La Paz and the East Cape in winter, central to northern Cortez in summer—as well as the lower Pacific coast. Barred perch and rock cod are present year-round on the northern Pacific coast. Sierra peak season is winter, when they're found in abundance near Bahía Magdalena. Wahoo generally spend December–April at the Cape, moving up toward Bahía Magdalena and the southern Cortez in the warmer months.

If your trip occurs December–April, head for the Cape; May–November you can angle anywhere along a horseshoe-shaped loop extending from Bahía Magdalena on the Pacific side to Mulegé on the Cortez. You can, if you wish, fish farther north on both coasts, especially in the summer, but if sportfishing is your reason for traveling to Baja, you're more likely to be satisfied by heading to the other areas.

As a final caveat, remember that an unusually warm winter means better fishing all over Baja; likewise a particularly cold winter forces many fish far south, making even Cabo San Lucas, the "fisherman's paradise," less productive.

Tackle

Although bait and tackle are available at shops in Ensenada, San Felipe, Loreto, Mulegé, La Paz, and Cabo San Lucas, supplies are variable, and you can't count on finding exactly what you want. Therefore, you ought to have your gear assembled before arriving in Baja.

A full fishing kit containing tackle for every conceivable Baja sportfishing possibility would probably weigh in excess of 70 kilograms (150 lbs). Seasoned Baja anglers claim you can get by in just about any situation with four basic rigs: two trolling rods with appropriate reels and 50- to 80-pound-test monofilament line for offshore fishing; one medium-duty eight- or nine-foot rod and spinner with 30-pound mono for surf casting and onshore fishing; and a six-foot light spinning rig loaded with four- to eight-pound line for bait fishing, freshwater fishing, or light surf casting. Two trolling rigs

are recommended because these are the rods used against fish most likely to yank your outfit into the sea; it's always best to have a spare.

No matter how many rods you bring into Mexico, you're legally permitted to fish with only one at a time. Electric reels are permitted for use by handicapped persons only.

Bait

What a fish will take at any given moment is highly variable, hence the properly equipped angler comes prepared with an array of natural and artificial bait. Live or frozen bait—including everything from squid to mackerel to clams—is usually available near the more frequented fishing areas; you can also catch your own bait easily with a light rig. A cooler is necessary for keeping bait fresh; hired boats will usually supply them. Among the vast selection of artificial lures available, the most reliable seem to be those perennials that imitate live bait, such as spoons, leadheads, candybars, swimmers, and, for offshore fishing, trolling heads. Bring along a few of each in different colors and sizes. You can purchase a few highly specialized lures, such as marlin heads and wahoo specials, in Loreto and Cabo San Lucas.

Tide Tables

Serious onshore-inshore anglers should bring along a set of current tide tables so they can decide what time to wake up in the morning.

Fishing Licenses

The red tape surrounding fishing in Mexico is minimal. The basic requirement is that anyone over 16 who intends to fish must possess a Mexican fishing license; technically, this includes all persons aboard boats equipped with fishing tackle, whether they plan to fish or not. This is important to remember for anyone going along on fishing trips as a spectator.

A single license is valid for all types of fishing, anywhere in Mexico, and is issued for periods of one day, one week, one month, or one year. A license is usually included in the price of sportfishing cruises, but not necessarily on *panga* trips—if you don't have a license, be sure to ask if one is provided before embarking on a guided trip. The cost of a Mexican license has risen steadily over the last few years but remains less expensive than most fishing licenses in the United States or Canada. Last time we checked the cost was US$11.00 for a day, US$22.90 for a week, US$32.80 for a month, and US$42.70 for an annual license.

Fishing licenses are available from a number of sources, including tackle shops and Mexican insurance companies near the U.S.–Mexico border. They can be obtained by mail from the **Mexico Department of Fisheries (PESCA)** (2550 Fifth Ave., Suite 101, San Diego, CA 92103-6622, U.S. tel. 619/233-4324), or from California branches of the **American Automobile Association** (AAA, www.aaa.com) and **Discover Baja Travel Club** (3089 Clairemont Dr., San Diego, CA 92117, U.S. tel. 619/275-1836 or 800/727-2252, www.discoverbaja.com).

Mexican Regulations

The general daily bag limit is 10 fish per person, including no more than five of any one species. Certain fish varieties are further protected as follows (per-day limits): one full-grown marlin, sailfish, or swordfish; two dorado, roosterfish, halibut, tarpon, or shark. Extended sportfishing by boat is limited to three consecutive days if the daily bag limit is reached each of the three days.

Bag limits are the same for free divers as for rod-and-reelers. Only handheld spears and band-powered spearguns—no gas guns or powerheads—are permitted, and no tanks or compressors may be used. A further weight limitation permits no more than 25 kilograms (55 lbs) of fish in a day's catch of five specimens, or one specimen of unlimited weight. Gillnets, purse nets, and every other kind of net except for handling nets are prohibited for use by nonresident aliens, as are traps, explosives, and poisons.

The taking of shellfish—clams, oysters, abalone, shrimp, and lobster—by nonresident aliens is officially prohibited. However, taking a reasonable amount—no more than can be eaten in a meal or two—is customarily permitted. This regulation is in place to protect Mexican fishing unions; even buying shellfish from local sources is prohibited unless you purchase from a public market or *cooperativa*. Obtain a receipt in case of inspection.

Totuava, sea turtles, and cabrilla are protected species that cannot be taken by anyone. Nor can any fish be caught for "ornamental purposes" (i.e., for aquarium use). Mexican fishing regulations are subject to change; check with the Mexico Department of Fisheries for the latest version before embarking on a fishing expedition.

Two areas off limits to all fishing are Bahía Cabo San Lucas harbor and Pulmo Reef, the only official fish sanctuaries along the peninsular coast. Many other areas probably ought to be protected for educational and recreational purposes, since the government-regulated bag limits help to preserve fish species but not fish habitats. Fishing, boating, diving, and other aquatic activities can wreak havoc on lagoons and delicate reef systems; use special care when traversing these areas. Never drop an anchor or a fishing line on a coral reef; such contact can cause irreversible damage to reef systems.

U.S. Customs and California State Regulations

Once you've obeyed Mexican fishing regulations and bagged a load of fish, you still have to conform to U.S. Customs regulations if you wish to enter the United States with your catch. Fortunately, U.S. regulations conform with Mexican bag limits, so whatever you've legally caught south of the border can be transported north.

The U.S. state of California further requires anyone transporting fish into the state to present a completed California Declaration of Entry form, available at the border or at any international airport in California. To facilitate identification of the transported fish, some part of each fish—head, tail, or skin—must be left intact. In other words, you can't just show up at the customs station with a cooler full of anonymous fish fillets. You may also be asked to show a valid Mexican fishing license or a PESCA form confirming legal purchase of fish or shellfish. For more information, contact the California Department of Fish and Game (1416 9th St., Sacramento, CA 95814, U.S. tel. 916/445-0411, www.dfg.ca.gov).

HUNTING

The Mexican government allows licensed hunting in season, as regulated by the Secretaría de Medio Ambiente y Recursos Naturales (SEMARNAT). Hunting has long been popular in Baja among foreigners and Mexicans alike but is for the most part restricted to various species of rabbit, quail, dove, pheasant, and waterfowl (ducks, widgeons, and geese). White-tailed deer and mule deer are also hunted, but permits are limited in number and quite expensive by international standards. Occasionally the government sponsors a special hunt (in southern Baja only) for the rare desert bighorn sheep *(borrego cimarrón);* bighorn permits cost a rich US$30,000 and aren't usually issued to foreigners. Early in the 20th century bighorn hunting by foreigners nearly wiped out the entire population.

Permits come in six types: Type I, waterfowl; Type II, doves; Type III, other birds; Type IV, small mammals; Type V, limited; and Type VI, special. Hunting regulations, which include bag limits (size and number), are strictly enforced. Signs that say Prohibido Cazar mean Hunting Prohibited. To apply directly to the Mexican government for a permit, contact **SEMARNAT** (Av. Francisco I. Madero #537, Col. Centro, Mexicali, BCN, 686/551-8700); or in La Paz (Calle Ocampo 1045 btw Rubio/ Ortiz de Domínguez, 612/122-4414). The offices are open Monday–Friday 9 A.M.–2 P.M. You can also check SEMARNAT's website at www.semarnat.gob.mx or email contactodgeia@semarnat.gob.mx.

In addition to the SEMARNAT hunting permit, foreign hunters need a consular certificate, special visa, and military gun permit. You can obtain the consular certificate from any Mexican consulate upon presentation of a letter from your local law enforcement agency verifying you have no criminal record. This certificate is also necessary for obtaining the military gun permit, issued by the army garrison in Tijuana or Mexicali. Proof of U.S. citizenship is required, plus eight passport-sized pictures for each gun permit and hunting license. The hunting license costs about US$450 and includes the gun permit. Once you possess the consular certificate, gun permit, and hunting permit, you can bring your guns across the border, where you'll receive a special hunter's visa. A maximum of two rifles per hunter is allowed, along with 50 American cartridges per gun. With the proper hunting permit, additional shells may be purchased in Mexico through the specially licensed sporting goods dealers. Only .22-caliber bullets or 12-, 16-, 20-, and 40-gauge shotgun cartridges are legally available. *Do not attempt to bring either guns or ammo into Mexico without a permit; penalties for either offense are severe.*

A newer regulation requires that all foreign hunters be accompanied by a licensed Mexican hunting guide. If this whole process sounds daunting (it is actually time-consuming, even if you speak perfect Spanish), you'd be much better off arranging the guide and all the necessary paperwork through a U.S. broker or Mexican hunting outfitter; a list of outfitters can be requested from any Mexican consulate. This costs considerably more than applying directly through SEMARNAT because you have to pay either membership dues or a surcharge, but the procedure is guaranteed to be much smoother and quicker.

BOATING

Recreational boating along Baja's peninsular and island coastlines has been popular since the 1950s. In the days before the Transpeninsular Highway, it was one of the safest, if slowest, ways of traveling from California to the southern peninsula. Despite recent improvements in highway travel, interest in navigating Baja waters has only increased. The main difference now is that smaller vessels can be trailered or cartopped down the peninsula, saving days and weeks that might otherwise be spent just reaching your cruising destination.

© NIKKI GOTH ITOI

the *panga* lineup at Cabo Pulmo

An extremely wide range of pleasure boats plies Baja waters, from sea kayaks to huge motor yachts. The most heavily navigated areas lie along the northwest coast between San Diego and Ensenada and in the Cabo San Lucas to La Paz corridor, but even these waters are relatively uncrowded compared to the marinas and bays of California. Cabo San Lucas, the most popular southern Baja harbor, checks in only around 2,000 foreign-owned vessels per year, an average of less than six arrivals per day.

The Pacific vs. the Sea of Cortez

Although some visitors circumnavigate the entire Baja peninsula, most boaters select one area for cruising and transport their crafts to that area by land. Because of the relative safety of Sea of Cortez boating, it's the most popular coast, particularly for smaller craft—kayaks, skiffs, and motor- or sail-powered vessels under 10 meters (35 ft). Cortez waters are relatively calm most of the time; late summer and early fall are the exceptions, when *chubascos* or hur-

ricanes can whip up sizable and sometimes treacherous swells. The Pacific coast is prone to high winds and challenging swells throughout the year.

The major difference between the two coasts is the number of available, safe anchorages. The Pacific side offers about 30 anchorages along the peninsula as well as island shorelines that provide protection when northwest winds prevail; this number is reduced to approximately 12 anchorages during prevailing southwesterlies, common July–September. Over on the Cortez side lie more than 60 protected anchorages—roughly 35 along the peninsula and 30 more on islands just off the coast. The Sea of Cortez offers not only safer waters but a wider selection of places to drop anchor.

Open-ocean Pacific sailing is not for the novice and shouldn't be attempted along Baja's Pacific coast without plenty of prior experience. The relative absence of assistance and boat-repair facilities makes Pacific boating south of Ensenada an especially risky venture.

If they wish, boaters may navigate from

ports in California, British Columbia, or Alaska to the Ensenada marina and then arrange for overland transportation of their boats on hired trailers from Ensenada to San Felipe on the Cortez side. Contact the **Ensenada Tourist Office** (Blvd. Costero at Calle Las Rocas, Ensenada, BCN, tel. 646/172-3022) for details on this service.

Cartopping

The most popular boats for short-range cruising, fishing, and diving are those that can be transported on top of a car, RV, or truck—aluminum skiffs in the four- to five-meter (12- to 15-ft) range. This type of boat can be launched just about anywhere; larger, trailered boats are restricted to boat launches with trailer access. The most appropriate outboard motor size for a boat this size is 15–20 hp; larger motors are generally too heavy to carry separately from the boat, a necessity for cartopping.

If you decide to transport a skiff or sea kayak on top of your vehicle, be sure to use a sturdy, reliable rack or loader with a bow line to the front bumper and plenty of tie-downs. The rough road surfaces typical of even Baja's best highways can make it difficult to keep a boat in place; crosswinds are also a problem in many areas. Frequent load checks are necessary. If you're shopping around for a rack, the type that bolts to the vehicle roof will hold up better than the kind that clamps to the roof gutters or door edges.

Inflatables

Rigid inflatable boats (RIBs), such as those manufactured by Achilles or Zodiac, are also well suited to Baja travel as they allow easy, stable beach landings. You can carry them on top or even in the cargo area of a large car or truck and inflate them with a foot pump or compressor as needed. A small 24-hp outboard motor is the best source of power.

NavTec Expeditions (321 N. Main St., Moab, UT 84532, U.S. tel. 800/833-1278, www.navtec .com) organizes guided kayaking trips with RIB support boats in the Sea of Cortez along the coast of Baja California Sur for US$1,195

per person for seven nights/eight days. NavTec also offers three-day trips from Loreto to offshore islands for US$595 per person.

Trailering

Larger boats that require trailering because of their weight, and which then must be floated from the trailer at a launch site, are much less versatile than cartop boats. On the entire peninsula fewer than 20 launches—five or six on the Pacific side, the remainder on the Sea of Cortez—offer trailer access. Another disadvantage to boat trailering is that Baja road conditions make towing a slow, unpleasant task. On the other hand, if one of these spots happens to be your destination and you plan to stay awhile, the added cruising range of a larger vessel might be worthwhile.

Ocean Cruising

The typical ocean cruiser on Baja's Pacific side is a 12- to 24-meter (40- to 80-ft) powerboat; on the Cortez side, 10- to 18-meter (35- to 60-ft) sailboats are popular. Properly equipped and crewed, these boats can navigate long distances and serve as homes away from home. Smaller motor-powered vessels are usually prevented from ocean cruising simply because of the lack of available fueling stations—their smaller fuel capacities greatly diminish cruising range. Sailboats smaller than nine meters (30 ft) have a similar problem because of the lack of storage space for food and water.

If you want to try your hand at ocean cruising, contact **Cortez Yacht Charters** (U.S. tel. 619/469-4255, www.cortezcharters.com), or **Baja SeaFaris** (933 Márquez de León, La Paz, tel. 612/125-9765, www.bajaseafaris.com).

Charts

The best nautical charts for Baja waters are those compiled by the U.S. government. They come in two series: the Coastal Series, which covers the entire Pacific and Cortez coastlines in three large charts (numbers 21008, 21014, and 21017) with a scale of around 1:650,000 each; and the Golfo de California Series, which offers much more detailed maps—in scales from 1:30,000 for La Paz to 1:290,610 for the entire Cape Region—of selected areas along the Cortez coast and around the Cape. Both series are based on nautical surveys conducted 1873–1901, so many of the place-names are out of date.

You can purchase these charts individually from the **Defense Mapping Agency (DMA)** (Washington, DC 20315-0010, 301/227-2000). Two of the Coastal Series are out of print, however, and others may eventually drop from sight as well. A much better and less expensive source of these charts is *Charlie's Charts: The Western Coast of Mexico (Including Baja),* which is a compilation of all U.S. nautical charts from San Diego to Guatemala, including those currently unavailable from the DMA. The charts have been extensively updated from the DMA originals, with more recent markings for anchorages, boat ramps, hazards, and fishing and diving spots. The spiral-bound volume, 7th edition, is available from **Charles E. Wood** (Box 1244, Station A, Surrey, BC, Canada V3W 1G0). It's also available in many California marine supply stores and from www.amazon.com.

Waterproof, tear-resistant double-sided plastic charts published by **Fish-n-Map** (U.S. tel. 303/421-5994, www.fishnmap.com) are available in four sheets: Sea of Cortez North Chart (San Felipe to Mulegé, with inset maps of Bahía de los ángeles, Las Islas Encantadas, Bahía San Francisquito, Puerto Refugio, and Guaymas); Sea of Cortez South Chart (Loreto to Cabo San Lucas, with inset maps of Loreto south to Bahía Agua Verde, Bahía de la Paz, Isla Espírito Santo, and Cabo San Lucas); the Baja California Chart North Pacific (Tijuana to Bahía Tortugas, with inset maps of the Coronado Islands, San Quintín area, Isla San Benito, and Isla Guadalupe); and Baja California Chart South Pacific (Punta Eugenia to Cabo San Lucas). Each of these measures 60 by 90 centimeters (24 by 36 in), or 10 by 22.5 centimeters (4 by 9 in) folded, costs US$7, and is available wherever Baja maps are sold.

Gerry Cruising Charts (U.S. tel. 520/394-2393, www.gerrycruise.com) produces 15 navigation charts for the entire Sea of Cortez (including the mainland Mexico side), plus a packet of charts for the Pacific side of Baja, costing US$21–45 depending on the number of charts per packet. Gerry Cunningham, who compiled these charts, also wrote *The Complete Guide to the Sea of Cortez,* which comes in three volumes and costs US$29–42 per volume or US$95 for the whole set. Also available on CD-ROM for US$95, the set contains 360 color photos.

Tide Tables

Tide tables are published annually; to cover the entire Baja coastline you'll need two sets: one that pertains to the Pacific tides and one for the Sea of Cortez tides. Both are available from **Map Link** (U.S. tel. 805/692-6777 or 800/962-1394, www.maplink.com), **Gerry Cruising Charts** (see *Charts*); or marine supply stores. You can also order Sea of Cortez tide tables from the **University of Arizona** (Printing and Graphics Services, 102 W. Stadium, Tucson, AZ 85721, tel. 520/621-2571, fax 520/621-6478).

Boat Permits

Any nonresident foreigner operating a boat in Mexican waters who intends to fish from that boat is required to carry a Mexican boat permit as well as a fishing permit. Even if you transport a boat to Baja with no fishing tackle and no plans to fish, it's a good idea to obtain a boat permit; first, because you might change your mind when you see all the fish everyone else is pulling in, and second, because you never know when you might end up carrying a passenger with fishing tackle. *All* boats used for fishing require a permit, whether cartopped, trailered, carried inside a motor vehicle, or sailed on the open seas.

Permits are available by mail from the Mexico Department of Fisheries (2550 5th Ave., Suite 101, San Diego, CA 92103-6622, tel. 619/233-6956, fax 619/233-0344), or from the Discover Baja Travel Club (3089 Clairemont Dr., San Diego, CA 92117, U.S. tel. 619/275-1836 or 800/727-2252, www.discoverbaja.com). A boat permit is valid for 12 months; fees vary according to the length of the craft.

Temporary Import Permits

These aren't necessary for Baja but are required if you plan to take a boat to mainland Mexico, whether by land or water. You can obtain the permit from offices in La Paz or Santa Rosalía or from a Registro Federal de Vehículos office in Tijuana, Mexicali, Ensenada, or La Paz.

Port Check-Ins

If you launch a boat at a Mexican port, specifically within the jurisdiction of a captain of the port (COTP), you must comply with official check-in procedures. This simply involves reporting to the COTP office and completing some forms. The only time it's a hassle is when the captain isn't present; you may have to wait around a few hours. Some ports charge filing fees of up to US$15.

Anytime you enter another COTP's jurisdiction, you're required to check in. Checking out is not required except when you leave the port of origin—i.e., the port at which you first launched. Currently, COTPs in Baja are found at Ensenada, Guerrero Negro, Bahía Magdalena (San Carlos), Cabo San Lucas, San José del Cabo, La Paz, Puerto Escondido, Loreto, Mulegé, Santa Rosalía, Bahía de los Ángeles, and San Felipe.

Fuel, Parts, and Repairs

At present only seven permanent marinas offer fuel year-round: one each in Ensenada, Cabo San Lucas, Puerto Escondido, and Santa Rosalía, and three in La Paz. Elsewhere, you must count on your own reserves or try your luck at canneries, boatyards, and fish camps, where prices will probably exceed official Pemex rates. At places other than marinas, you'll often have to go ashore and haul your own fuel back to the boat; come prepared with as many extra fuel containers as you can manage.

Obtaining marine supplies and repairs in Baja is more challenging than finding fuel. Ensenada, Cabo San Lucas, and La Paz are the best locales for both—there's usually someone

around who can work minor miracles. To a limited extent, parts—but not necessarily competent repair work—are also available for established-brand outboard motors in San Felipe, Santa Rosalía, Loreto, and Mulegé. As with all other motorized conveyances in Baja, it's best to bring along plenty of spare parts, especially props, filters, water pumps, shear pins, hoses, and belts. Don't forget to bring at least one life jacket per person—statistics show that in 80 percent of all boating fatalities, the victims weren't wearing them.

Emergencies

The U.S. Coast Guard monitors VHF radio channel 16 and can pick up transmissions from as far south as Ensenada. Elsewhere along the Baja coastline, this channel is monitored by Mexican agencies (including the Mexican Navy and all COTPs), ferry vessels, and commercial ships.

Citizens-band (CB) radio is commonly used as a substitute for a telephone system in the peninsula's remote areas; it's also heavily used by RVers, the Green Angels, CB clubs, and other boaters and is a quick way to get attention. As in the United States and Canada, channel 9 is the most used, but channels 1, 3, 4, 7, and 10 are also monitored. Special radio permits for foreign visitors are no longer required for CB radios with a transmission power of five watts or less.

SEA KAYAKING

Kayaking is one of the best ways to experience coastal Baja. Coves, inlets, water caves, and beaches inaccessible to skiffs or four-wheel-drive vehicles are easily approached in a kayak, especially on the Sea of Cortez. The Cortez is truly a world-class kayaking environment, as more and more kayakers discover each year. It's also an excellent place to learn sea kayaking skills, because seas are generally calm compared to the Pacific side.

The most popular kayaking areas on the Cortez coast lie between Mulegé and Loreto and between Puerto Escondido and La Paz. Bahía Concepción, protected by land on three sides, is a favorite among novice kayakers. Bahía de los Ángeles, with its many islets and islands, is good for kayakers of all levels, though the strong channel currents require some caution.

Wherever you go in the Sea of Cortez, the Gulf Current, which runs counterclockwise around the Cortez, favors trips planned in a north–south direction, with pickup arranged at the south end. A few intrepid, experienced kayakers have completed voyages across the currents from Bahía de los Ángeles to the Mexican mainland by using the "Stepping Stones" route from island to island. Seri Amerindians once followed the same route in reed canoes. Extended Cortez trips are fairly easy when the weather's good, since campsites are available at a huge selection of beaches and coves. If you bring along some light fishing gear, you'll never go without food.

Kayaking on the Pacific side is for the experienced paddler only. Punta Banda, an inlet-scalloped cape near Ensenada, is the most popular Pacific Baja kayaking area because of its proximity to San Diego. Bahía Magdalena, a large, protected bay in southern Baja, also attracts many kayakers with more time; whale-watching is a big attraction here. Gray whales sometimes use their enormous tails to toss kayaks around, however, so your first Magdalena Bay outing in whale season should be in the company of someone who understands whale behavior. Rule one: Never paddle directly toward a nearby whale; instead, run parallel to the whale's course. Also, never paddle between a cow and her calf.

Elsewhere on the Pacific coast, high surf and strong currents require equal quantities of strength and expertise. Finding a beach campsite isn't too difficult, but reaching it through the surf might be.

Types of Kayaks

Sea-touring kayaks come in four basic types, each with several variations. All fall in the 4.2- to 6.4-meter (14- to 21-ft) range necessary for extended paddling. The traditional closed-cockpit, hardshell boat comes in single (one-person) and double (two-person) models and is made of either molded polyethylene plastic or fiberglass. A "glass" boat is lighter and faster; a polyethylene boat, though heavier and slower, holds up on Baja's rocky beaches much better. This type of kayak is easily cartopped, but a sturdy, secure rack is necessary on Baja's rough roads. Touring models can carry up to 115 kilograms (250 lbs) of gear in built-in hatches, an attribute that makes them a good choice for extended overnight kayaking. Because of the sealed cockpits, they're also good in the colder waters of the Pacific and the northern Cortez.

Folding kayaks are much easier to transport and are popular among kayakers who fly to their destinations or who want to keep boats inside their vehicles rather than on top. The disadvantages are that a folding kayak costs more and is a bit slower because of a wider beam, up to 86 centimeters (34 in) compared with a 60-centimeter (24-in) beam on a hardshell boat. The hull is usually hypalon, a synthetic rubber, stretched over aluminum tubing—assembly and disassembly is not as easy as the sales representative claims. For carrying convenience, however, it can't be beat. The wider beam also means the craft will carry up to twice the payload of a hardshell.

Gaining popularity in recent years, especially in Baja, are open-cockpit kayaks. The advantage to these is that the paddler sits on top of the deck rather than underneath it, which makes it much easier to exit and thus somewhat safer overall. Like the closed-cockpit variety, some models feature hatched stowage compartments that carry up to 115 kilograms. Open-cockpit kayaks are easier to paddle and more stable than traditional kayaks; just about anyone can paddle one with little or no practice. An open-cockpit model is also a bit slower because of a wider beam and higher center of gravity. An open-cockpit kayak costs several hundred dollars less than the closed-deck version, making it the ideal kayak for the Baja visitor for whom kayaking is just one among several recreational activities; it also makes an excellent dive station for short scuba or free diving trips. A few models, such as the Aquaterra Kahuna or Scupper Scrambler, are designed specifically to carry scuba gear. As with other hardshell kayaks, they're easily cartopped.

Inflatables are the lightest of the touring kayaks, which makes them even easier to transport than folding kayaks. However, inflation requires an air compressor or electric air pump because the craft's rigidity depends on air pressure of 2–4 pounds per square inch. Like the folding kayak, an inflatable's main advantage is ease of storage and transport.

Accessories
Paddle styles are very much a matter of personal choice; as a general rule, Aleuts or asymmetrical paddles are useful on the windy Pacific side, traditional shapes on the Cortez. Whatever you bring, bring a spare. Other essentials include a paddle leash, a 15-meter (50-ft) parachute-cord towline, a waterproof flashlight, and, in winter, a wetsuit. A detachable two-wheel cart or "skate" for the stern is helpful for transporting a kayak short distances on land; you can easily store it in one of the hatches.

Foot-controlled rudders are not necessary for Sea of Cortez kayaking for much of the year because winds and currents are usually moderate. The exception is November–March when wind and swells are up. Parts and service for a broken rudder are virtually nonexistent. On the Pacific side, or if you're going to attempt a cross-Cortez route to the mainland, a foot-controlled rudder is a good idea. Bring spare parts.

If you can manage the extra weight, include a kayak sail rig to give your arms a rest during a good breeze—common in the Cortez as well as the Pacific.

Equipment Sales and Rentals
If you're on your way to Baja by vehicle and need kayaking equipment or supplies, a convenient stop is **Southwind Kayak Center** (17855-A Sky Park Circle, Irvine, CA 92614, tel. 949/261-0200 or 800/768-8494, www.southwindkayaks.com). They offer classes and rentals as well as sales.

Maps and Tide Tables
Nautical charts are of little use for kayak navigation. A better choice is 1:50,000-scale topo maps, available from Map Link, Map Centre, or Gerry Cruising Charts (see *Boating*). Tide tables are also invaluable.

Organized Kayak Trips
A great way to learn sea kayaking in Baja is to join an organized trip led by experienced kayakers. Based in Loreto part of the year, **Paddling South** (U.S. tel. 707/942-4550 or 800/398-6200, www.tourbaja.com) leads multiday trips (see *Loreto and Vicintiy* in the *Central Baja* chapter). **Baja Expeditions** (U.S. tel. 858/581-3311 or 800/843-6967, www.bajaex.com) offers kayaking trips to Bahía Magdalena and to the Midriff Islands in the winter (see *Puerto San Carlos* in the *Central Baja* chapter).

Outside Mexico, one of the most established outfitters is **Sea Trek** (U.S. tel. 415/488-1000, www.seatrekkayak.com, US$1,150/8 days).

Another good source of information on organized kayak trips and on Baja kayaking in general is **California Kayak Friends** (www.ckf.org).

KITEBOARDING AND WINDSURFING
From November through March, the Sea of Cortez is a windsurfing and kiteboarding paradise, particularly from the central coast southward. Bahía de los Ángeles and Bahía Concepción are perfect for beginning and intermediate board-sailors, while the high winds of the East Cape will delight those in the advanced class. Any of the channels between the peninsula's east coast and the larger offshore islands—Canal de Cerralvo, Canal San José, Canal de Ballenas—usually offer good sideshore wind action, although sometimes with strong currents. If you don't see other sailboards out, try to find someone who knows the currents before launching.

La Paz is also a good area, even in summer, when a strong breeze called *el coromuel* comes in just about every afternoon. The best spots here lie along the mostly deserted beaches of the peninsula northeast of town—Punta Balandra to Punta Coyote. When nothing's blowing in the Bahía de la Paz vicinity, dedicated windsurfers can shuttle west across the peninsula to check out the action at Punta Márquez on the Pacific side, only 72 kilometers (45 mi) away.

Los Barriles on Bahía de Palmas, along the East Cape, is one of the more accessible windsurfing areas in southern Baja. The wind blows a steady 18–30 knots all winter long, and wavesailing is possible in some spots. During the season, uphauling (pulling mast and sail up from the water) is usually out of the question due to chop and high winds, so the ability to waterstart (mount and launch a sailboard from deep water) is a prerequisite for board-sailing in this area.

Los Barriles is also home to **Vela Windsurf Resorts** (U.S./Canada tel. 800/223-5443, www .velawindsurf.com), which offers highly rated instruction and package deals mid-November– early March. Even if you're not a participant in one of its windsurfing vacations, you may be able to arrange for service and parts.

The Pacific side of Baja generally demands a more experienced board-sailor. Those who can handle high surf and strong winds will love it. Novices and intermediate windsurfers will enjoy the larger bays of Bahía de San Quintín, Bahía Magdalena, and Bahía Almejas, all protected from major swells in all but the worst weather. Board-sailors with sturdy transport—four-wheel-drive or high-clearance trucks—can choose from dozens of smaller bays connected to Mexico Highway 1 by dirt roads of varying quality.

SURFING

At even the most remote spots in Baja, the chances you're the first one to surf a break are low, but with an empty lineup and not a building in sight, you can get the full surf pioneer experience within a few hours of the California border.

The variety of surf experiences you can have in Baja runs the entire spectrum. You can ride your first wave on a longboard with the Pescadero Surf Camp or you can win US$50,000

for charging down a 60-foot face at Isla Todos Santos. The saturated breaks along the northern beaches from Rosarito to Ensenada can feel like extensions of the localized and agro scene in Southern California. For those willing the walk to the next point, or drive a little farther, you can quickly fall off the known surf map and find your own mecca. Perhaps the biggest threat to Baja surfing isn't the fleets of Honda Elements or the longboarders poaching waves on the outside, but the accelerating development along the coastline and the drive to close off beach access along the Baja coastline.

You'll find the Pacific south to Punta Abreojos slightly warmer than in Southern California, and south of Abreojos the water starts becoming noticeably warmer. Around the Cape Region you can wear shorties all year— or no wetsuit at all May–October.

From the border all the way down to Cabo, most of the good surf areas lie below *puntas* (points) that offer right point breaks stoked by a northwest windswell all year-round and by a stronger west-northwest groundswell October–May. The latter usually comes without the heavy weather associated with the westnorthwest groundswell in central and northern California, hence you can expect cleaner surf conditions in Baja than farther north. This time of year, even without any advance tips, a surfer need only drive down the Transpeninsular with a good road map in hand, turning west wherever the map shows a side road leading off to "Punta X." As with all other coastal recreation, more places are accessible to those with high-clearance vehicles or four-wheel drive, although many good surf spots lie within range of ordinary passenger cars as well.

In the summer, the surf's mostly small to flat in northern Baja, except when a tropical storm comes up from the south. When this happens, there's usually high surf at the southern end of many offshore Pacific islands, the most notorious being Isla Natividad and Islas de Todos Santos. In southern Baja—particularly in the area curving around the Cape from Todos Santos (not the islands, the town) to San José del Cabo—a seasonal southeast-to-southwest groundswell forms good beach breaks March–November. Stronger southwest-southeast hurricane swells usually arrive July–November and can extend along the entire Pacific coast of Baja.

Surf Locations

The number of surfers diminishes as you proceed south of Ensenada or north of Cabo San Lucas; any point between involves some serious road travel. In fact, even when the surf's really pumping in this middle zone, you stand a good chance of sharing monster breaks with only a handful of others—or even having them all to yourself—since there are no "surf hotlines" for central and southern Baja. This means serendipity is a major element in Baja surfing safaris—those who have the most time to scout the coastline will find the best wave action.

In the Ensenada area, the hot spot is San Miguel (also known as Rincón), a small bay just south of the last tollgate on the Tijuana–Ensenada toll road. A number of surfers live here year-round, and others make weekend trips from Southern California, so at times it's a bit on the crowded side. The fast right point break here is usually reliable in the winter, pumping for weeks at a time. And when the surf's too small onshore, you can always climb in a *panga* and cruise 20 kilometers (12 mi) out to Islas de Todos Santos, home of the biggest breaks on the entire west coast of North America. When San Miguel's nearly flat, Todos Santos waves may hit 3–4 meters (10–12 ft); when San Miguel's ripping at 2.5–3.5 meters (8–10 ft), the pros will be out at northern Todos on their nine-foot guns, tearing down 10-meter (30-ft) Waimea-style walls. The southern island of the twin Islas de Todos Santos produces a good left break during summer swells.

Several spots can also be found between Ensenada and the border in and around La Fonda, La Misión, and Rosarito, especially Punta Descanso, Punta Mesquite, and Punta Salsipuedes. South of Ensenada to the Cape are dozens of places with intermittent point breaks, but the most reputable for accessibility and steady surf are at Punta San José, Punta

Baja, Punta Santa Rosalillita, Punta Abreojos, Punta El Conejo, and beaches in the vicinity of Todos Santos (the Baja California Sur town, not the islands).

Visit www.surfline.com for up-to-date info on conditions, and for additional reports on individual sites. The US$70 annual fee includes long-term forecasts, which can help you to change your itinerary according to the swell. Keep in mind that surf breaks do change over time due to erosion and other factors.

Cape Region surfers are blessed; they can enjoy both winter and summer wave action within a radius of roughly 100 kilometers (62 mi). In winter, a west-northwest groundswell combines with the year-round northwest windswell to stoke point breaks along the Pacific shore from Punta Márquez all the way to Migriño.

During summer's southern swell, the place to be is the Corridor between Cabo San Lucas and San José del Cabo, where beach breaks predominate at dependable spots such as Costa Azul (Zipper's). When the southern swell is really happening, surfable waves wrap right around San José del Cabo as far north up the Sea of Cortez as Los Barriles.

There are more than 25 known point, reef, and beach breaks around the cape. Stop by the **Costa Azul Surf Shop** along the Corridor at Playa Costa Azul or in Todos Santos for a map with descriptions of the breaks, or buy a copy of the incredibly detailed *Surfer's Guide to Baja California,* by Mike Parise.

Equipment

For any extended trip down the coast, carry both a short and a long board—or a gun for the northwest shores of Isla Natividad or Islas de Todos Santos in winter. Longboards aren't used much in the Cape Region, however. Besides wax and a cooler, about the only other items you need to bring are a fiberglass-patching kit for bad dings and a first-aid kit for routine surf injuries. Most surf spots are far from medical assistance—don't forget butterfly bandages. Boards can be repaired at just about any boatyard on the coast, since most Mexican *pangas* are made of fiberglass and require a lot of patching.

Several surf shops in San José del Cabo and Cabo San Lucas sell boards, apparel, and accessories.

Airlines have made it more expensive these days to fly with your quiver; check the going rate before you head for the airport. Renting a board sounds pretty good when checking it costs US$100 each way. For longer trips, buying and reselling a board while you're there is another option.

Tide charts come in handy for predicting low and high tides; a pocket-sized tide calendar available from **Tidelines** (U.S. tel. 800/345-8524, www.tidelines.com) charts daily tide changes from Crescent City, California, to Manzanillo, Mexico, with +/- corrections from a Los Angeles baseline.

Organized Trips

Baja Surf Adventures (BSA, U.S. tel. 800/428-7873, www.bajasurfadventures.com) maintains a "surf resort" in northern Baja that accepts novice as well as experienced surfers. The beach features a long right point break, and that six other prime breaks lie within driving distance. The resort offers four separate sleeping quarters, men's and women's bathrooms, hot showers, a raised sundeck, three *palapas* with hammocks, a kitchen and mess hall, and on-demand electricity. Leisure activities other than surfing include fishing, kayaking, snorkeling, diving, horseshoes, darts, ping-pong, beach volleyball, basketball, and mountain biking. Two nights/three days at the resort costs US$375 per person, while six nights/seven days is US$750. Prices include all meals plus transport to and from San Diego. A special instruction package for beginners goes for US$515/925 (3/7 days) and includes two hours of training each day.

BSA also operates surf trips to central and southern Baja for advanced surfers only. Surfers aren't usually big on organized travel, but for one destination in Baja, Isla Natividad, some make an exception. Getting to Natividad ordinarily involves driving to Punta Eugenia on the Vizcaíno Peninsula, an ordeal in itself, and then chartering a boat to the island. BSA offers a special concession for the famous Open Doors break at Isla Natividad. It leads three- to five-day package surf trips to the island July–September—peak time for the south swell—that include round-trip airfare from Ensenada, lodging on Natividad, and two meals per day. Tours are limited to 12 people.

Mag Bay Tours (tel. 949/650-2775 or 800/599-8676, www.magbaytours.com) operates two surf camps at opposite ends of Bahía Santa María, part of the Bahía de Magdalena (Mag Bay in gringo-speak) on the Pacific coast of southern Baja. From June to mid-October, during the southern swell, the camp at the north end of the bay is open; during the November–April northern swell, the fun switches to the southern camp. Eight-day trips at Mag Bay start at US$1,100, not including airfare.

SCUBA DIVING AND SNORKELING

The semitropical Sea of Cortez coral reefs at the southern tip of the Cape Region are among the most well-known dive locations in Baja, simply because they're so close to shore. But many spots of interest along much of the coastline are accessible to divers with good boat transportation and the necessary diving skills. For the most part, Pacific diving is for experienced offshore scuba divers only, while the Cortez coast and islands are excellent for inshore novice divers as well as snorkelers.

Marinelife in Baja is concentrated among three types of environments: kelp fields, reefs (both rock and hard coral), and shipwrecks. The wrecks develop into artificial reefs with time and are particularly plentiful in Baja waters. Some of the sunken vessels available for exploration are Liberty ships, junks, steamers, tuna clippers, submarines, yachts, ferryboats, tugs, and full-rigged barques.

Pacific Diving

The most popular diving areas are those in the northwest—Islas Todos Santos and Islas Coronados—accessible to day-tripping Southern Californians. As at most of Baja's Pacific islands, the west and southwest sides tend to offer the greatest proliferation of sea life, including kelp beds, rock reefs, and encrusted sea pinnacles amid scenic sandflats. Both the Todos Santos and Coronado Islands are popular among spearfishing enthusiasts because of the large yellowtail populations that feed in the vicinity (but remember that use of spears or spearguns while wearing scuba equipment is illegal). Halibut, various sea bass, and bonito are also common, as is lobster. The cold, fast-running currents mean visibility is usually good in offshore areas.

Farther south at Bahía del Rosario, off the coast near the town of El Rosario, are large kelp beds and the Arrecife Sacramento (Sacramento Reef). Along with an abundance of marinelife, this four-kilometer-long (2.5-mi-long) reef features so many shipwrecks it's dubbed the "Graveyard of the Pacific." The reef—named for the paddlewheeler *Sacramento,* which ran aground here in 1872—is also home to a population of large lobsters referred to locally as *burros* (donkeys) or *caballos* (horses). Isla San Gerónimo, 2.5 kilometers (1.5 mi) northwest of the reef, is known as an excellent spearfishing location.

The next diving area south lies off the tip of the Vizcaíno Peninsula at Isla Cedros, Isla Natividad, and Islas San Benito. These islands feature kelp beds, sea pinnacles, shoals, and rock reefs. Bahía Magdalena, much farther south, is of interest for its shallows teeming with sea life, including sea turtles, sharks, manta rays, seals, and whales. Heavy swells and surging along the Pacific coast mean that it should only be tackled by experienced scuba divers or with an experienced underwater guide. Ensenada has three dive shops; southward along the Pacific coast there are none before Cabo San Lucas.

Sea of Cortez Diving

The Sea of Cortez offers one of the world's richest marine ecosystems, and the underwater scenery is especially vivid and varied. Sea lions, numerous whale and dolphin varieties, colorful tropical species, manta rays, and schooling hammerhead sharks are all part of a thick food chain stimulated by cold-water upwellings amid the more than 100 islands and islets that dot the Cortez. The largest proportion of Cortez sea life consists of species of tropical Pan-American origins that have found their way north from Central and South American waters.

Most divers avoid the northern Cortez because of strong tidal surges, speedy currents, and overall lack of underwater marine variety relative to the central and southern Cortez. In general, the northernmost diving area is Bahía de los Ángeles, where tidal conditions and visibility are suitable for recreational diving. The offshore islands are the main attractions here; a few small hotels service divers and arrange guided trips (see *Bahía de los Ángeles* in *Central Baja*).

Next south are the Midriff Islands, which require long-range boats and an experienced appraisal of local currents and tidal changes. Rock reefs are abundant throughout these islands. Below the Midriffs, tidal conditions calm down considerably, and the water is generally warmer. Marinelife is plentiful and varied, and spearfishing is excellent in many areas.

In the central Cortez, **Cortez Explorers** (Moctezuma 75A, Mulegé, tel./fax 615/153-0500, www.cortez-explorers.com) has air, equipment, and boat charters. Many of the nearby islands, bays, and points are suitable for snorkeling as well as scuba diving; Isla San Marcos, Punta Chivato, Islas Santa Inés, and Bahía Concepción are among the best-known areas. Loreto, a bit farther south, also offers dive services and several popular nearby diving areas, including Isla Coronado, Punta Coyote, Isla del Carmen, and Isla Danzante; rock reefs, boulders, volcanic ridges, and sandflats are common throughout. Farther east in the Cortez lie vast submarine canyons as well as more remote volcanic and continental islands best left to experienced scuba divers.

From La Paz south, onshore water temperatures usually hover between 21°C (70°F) and 29°C (85°F) year-round, making the southern Cortez the most popular diving destination on this side of Baja. The area is known for Pulmo Reef, the only hard-coral reef in the Sea of Cortez and the northernmost tropical reef in the Americas, and for the islands and seamounts offshore from La Paz. Water visibility is best July–October, when it exceeds 30 meters (100 ft); this is also when the air temperature is warmest, often reaching well over 32°C (90°F).

Several coves along the coast toward Cabo San Lucas make good snorkeling sites. Bahía Cabo San Lucas itself is a protected marine park; the rocks and points along the bayshore are suitable for snorkelers and novice scuba divers while the deep submarine canyon just 45 meters (150 ft) offshore attracts experienced thrill-seekers. This canyon is known for its intriguing "sandfalls," streams of falling sand channeled between rocks along the canyon walls. Nearby Playa Santa María and Playa Chileno, on the way east toward San José del Cabo, are popular snorkeling areas with soft corals at either end of a large cove.

Equipment

Except in the Cape Region, divers shouldn't count on finding the equipment they need in Baja, even in resort areas. Since most equipment sold or rented in Baja dive shops is imported from the United States, stocks vary from season to season. Purchase prices are also generally higher in Mexico than north of the border.

For Pacific diving south to Punta Abreojos, a full quarter-inch wetsuit is recommended year-round; from Punta Abreojos south lighter suits are sufficient in the summer. At Cabo San Lucas and around the Cape as far north as the central Cortez, a light suit may be necessary late November–April; shorties or ordinary swimsuits will suffice the rest of the year. From the Midriff Islands north in the Sea of Cortez, heavier suits are necessary December–early April. In summer, many Sea of Cortez divers wear Lycra skins to protect against jellyfish stings.

Because divers and anglers occasionally frequent the same areas, a good diving knife is essential for dealing with wayward fishing line. Bring two knives, so you'll have a spare. Include extra CO_2 cartridges (for flotation vests), O-rings, and a wetsuit patching kit.

Air

Dependable air for scuba tanks is usually available in Ensenada, Mulegé, Loreto, La Paz, Cabo Pulmo, and Cabo San Lucas. Always check the compressor first, however, to make sure it's well maintained and running clean. Divers with extensive Baja experience usually carry a portable compressor not only to avoid contaminated air but to use in areas where tank refills aren't available.

Recompression Chambers

Buceo Medico Mexicano (tel. 624/143-3666) operates a **hyperbaric decompression chamber** in Cabo San Lucas at Plaza Marina (next to the Hotel Tesoro). The facility is equipped with two compressors, an oxygen analyzer, closed-circuit TV, and a hotline to Divers Alert Network (DAN). In La Paz, **Baja Diving and Service** (tel. 612/122-7010, www.clubcantamar.com) also operates a recompression chamber on the Pichilingue Peninsula.

In the north, the nearest full-time, dependable recompression facility is the **Hyperbaric Medicine Center** at the University of California Medical Center in San Diego (619/543-6222, Mon.–Fri. 7:30 A.M.–4:30 P.M. and for emergencies). For emergency air transportation to the facility contact one of the air-evacuation organizations servicing Baja (see *Emergency Evacuation*, later in this chapter). In Playas de Tijuana, **Centro Hosp. Internacional Pacifico** (CHIP, tel. 664/685-2566) also has a recompression chamber.

Organized Diving Trips

Divers will find skilled guides in Ensenada, Bahía de los Ángeles, Mulegé, Loreto, La Paz, Cabo Pulmo, and Cabo San Lucas. Most of the Baja dive outfits also offer instruction and scuba certification at reasonable rates. Note, for the protected marine parks, diving with a guide is required by law. For this reason, shops in Cabo Pulmo do not offer airfills to independent divers.

Several San Diego–based businesses offer prebooked dive trips along the Pacific coast:

Horizon Charters (U.S. tel. 858/277-7823, www.horizoncharters.com) and **Lois Ann Dive Charters** (U.S. tel. 800/201-4381, www.loisann.com) are two of the best.

Over on the Sea of Cortez side, **Baja Expeditions** (U.S. tel. 858/581-3311 or 800/943-6967, www.bajaex.com) leads both day and liveaboard scuba diving excursions in the La Paz area.

RACE AND SPORTS BETTING

During the U.S. Prohibition era of the 1920s, casinos were a major part of Baja high life in Tijuana, Mexicali, the Coronado Islands, and Ensenada. Although the Mexican government outlawed casino gambling in the 1930s, it allows race and sports books in both states of Baja California—a significant source of revenue for the state, from betting locals as well as foreigners.

The heir to Tijuana's lavish El Casino de Agua Caliente is the **Caliente Race and Sports Book** (www.caliente.com.mx), with locations at the famed Caliente Greyhound Track in Tijuana as well as in Los Algodones, Ensenada, Rosarito, Tecate, Mexicali, San Felipe, La Paz, and Cabo San Lucas. The Caliente Greyhound Track hosts weekly greyhound racing, and at all Caliente Race and Sports Book locations you can bet on basketball, football, baseball, and other sports. The Caliente betting lounges also feature bars and restaurants; betting is not required if patrons just want a drink or a meal while watching sports events on multiple screens. The Caliente in Cabo San Lucas even shows free American movies.

Entertainment

Most visitors to Baja California come for the beaches, mountains, deserts, fishing, or water sports, not for what would normally be considered "entertainment." Nonetheless, it's not necessarily bedtime when the sun goes down, except in the most remote areas. The larger cities—Tijuana, Mexicali, Rosarito, Ensenada, La Paz, and Cabo San Lucas—offer museums, theaters, cinemas, concert halls, bars, and discos. For specific recommendations regarding these types of entertainment venues, see the destination sections of this book.

MUSIC

When most Americans think of Mexican music they think of brass-and-violins mariachi music, a style from the state of Jalisco on the Mexican mainland. In Baja, mariachi music is generally reserved for weddings and tourists, as is the music of the so-called Baja Marimba Band. (Marimba music also hails from elsewhere in Mexico.) The most commonly heard music on the peninsula is *la música norteña,* a style that's representative of ranchero life yet has a wide appeal throughout Northern Mexico and beyond, including as far north as Chicago and as far south as Colombia and Venezuela.

Norteña and *Grupera*

Norteña music shares common roots with Tex-Mex *(tejano)* or *conjunto* music enjoyed in Texas and New Mexico and made famous by Flaco Jiménez, Ramón Ayala, Los Tigres del Norte, Los Lobos, and the Grammy-winning Texas Tornados. It's typically played by an ensemble led by an accordion and *bajo sexto,* a large Mexican 12-string guitar. Originally, these two instruments were supported by a string bass and sometimes a trap drum set; later, electric bass and guitar were occasionally added, along with alto sax and keyboards. Still, most *norteña* bands maintain the traditional accordion, *bajo sexto,* and acoustic bass lineup. The music itself encompasses an exciting mix of Latinized polkas and waltzes, *rancheras* (similar to American country and western), and *corridos* (Mexican ballads), as well as modern Latin forms like *cumbias* and salsa.

In Mexico, *norteña* has evolved into a more popular subgenre known as *grupera,* because it's almost always performed by groups rather than solo artists. *Grupera* blends the *ranchera*-and-polka *música norteña* with Sinaloan *perrada* or *tambora sinaloense*. The most popular *grupera* bands among *bajacalifornianos* are Los Tigres del Norte and Banda El Recodo, both bands with *superestrella* (superstar) status throughout Mexico. The lyrics of *norteña/grupera* reflect the daily lives and sentiments of Northern Mexican peasants, often with a political edge. In Mexico, *norteña* lyrics often chronicle the tragedies and triumphs of *mota* (marijuana) smugglers and other *narcotraficantes* on the run from law enforcement. Some of the songs recorded by Los Tigres and other *norteña* groups are banned by the Mexican government and can only be heard on bootleg tapes that circulate at cantinas or local fiestas. A Los Tigres album, *Jefe de Jefes,* contains two overtly political *corridos* (ballads), one chronicling the short career of Mexico's former antinarcotics czar, General Jesús Gutiérrez Rebollo, arrested in 1997 for allegedly taking bribes from Sinaloa drug kingpin Amado Carillo, and another about the 1994 assassination of presidential candidate Luis Donaldo Colosio.

Borrowing from the *antillana* or Afro-Caribbean songbook, many *grupera* tunes nowadays are based on *cumbia* rhythms.

Live *norteña* music is often heard at fiestas throughout Baja and in Mexican bars and cantinas in larger towns and cities. Strolling *trovadores,* for example, wander most evenings from bar to bar playing *norteña* music along Calle Ruiz in Ensenada. It's not the nicest area of town, but it's a place for the musically curious to hear the local sounds.

In more upscale *norteña* clubs in Tijuana, Ensenada, and Mexicali, you can still see the biggest dance craze to sweep Baja and Northern Mexico in the 1990s: the *caballito* (little horse). Danced to up-tempo *rancheras,* the dance utilizes a set of fancy equestrian-type maneuvers, including a step in which the female dancer briefly mounts the upper leg of the male dancer. *Bajacalifornianos* have developed their own variation of this dance called the *quebradita* (little break), which adds a steep bobbing of the head from side to side. Spear-headed by the popularity of Selena, the late Texan singing sensation, *tejano* (an updated, urbanized version of Tex-Mex music) has made serious inroads into the Mexican music scene in certain cities, including Tijuana.

Banda

Also *muy popular* in Baja is brassy *banda,* a style that originated in late-19th-century Sinaloa and is currently undergoing a big resurgence throughout Mexico. *Banda* ensembles consist mostly of brass instruments and drums that play loud instrumental march music against the familiar two-step or waltz rhythms found in *norteña* music. La Banda Sinaloense carries the banner for this style (lots of bands manage to work "Sinaloa" or "Sinaloense" into their names). A permutation known as *tecnobanda* adds or substitutes electronic keyboards and may add vocals as well.

Rock en Español/La Onda Nueva/ Guacarock

Although lyrically descended from Latin American *nuevo canto* folk/rock music, *rock en español* (rock in Spanish, i.e., rock music with Spanish lyrics) takes its majo r musical inspiration from Anglo-American rock and Anglo-Jamaican ska. Starting with Mexico City the premier center for the movement, this international genre has spread all over Latin America, particularly to Argentina and Brazil. Also known as La Nueva Onda (The New Wave), the music began reaching critical popular mass in the mid-1980s. In the late 1980s, Botellita de Jeréz (Little Bottle of Sherry) and Maldita Vecindad (Cursed Neighborhood) began blending ska, punk, rock, jazz, and traditional Mexican elements as part of a movement within *La Onda Nueva* known by the descriptive *guacarock,* a reference to the mix of influences that are blended together like the ingredients in the Mexican avocado dip, guacamole. Maldita Vecindad's first major hit was "Mojado" ("Wetback"), a tribute to transborder Mexican workers. Botellita has since disbanded, but Maldita Vecindad still flourishes at the center of the *guacarock* movement.

Also popular are rock fusion/art groups Los

Jaguares and Café Tacuba, bands that mix alternative rock sounds with some Amerindian instrumentation and wild live performances in the *guacarock* tradition. Santa Sabina adds a hint of Latin jazz improvisation to the mix. All the major groups working in this medium come from D.F. or the state of México except for ¡Tijuana No!, possibly the most political of all the current bands (the name signifies a plea not to flee Tijuana for the United States).

Other seminal groups working in this genre include La CuCa, Maná (with a lead vocalist who sounds exactly like Sting), Acido Verde, Plexo Solar, La Castañeda, La Barranca, El Sr. Gonzalez, Garigoles, Caifanes, La Lupita, El Tri, Amantes de Lola, and Fobia. You may also come across bands who sing in Spanish but cleave more closely to Anglo styles, such as the glam/metal/goth Víctimas del Doctor Cerebro and Plastilina Mosh, or the punk/metal/rap sounds of Mauricio Garces. None of these bands was the first in Mexico to play rock music; Los Apson and Los Locos del Ritmo created Spanish versions of Chuck Berry and Bill Haley in the 1950s, and 1960s indie garage rock produced sufficient output to fill two current CD compilations available in the United States, *Mexican Rock and Roll Rumble* and *Psych-Out South of the Border.*

To get an idea of what young Mexicans are listening to, watch MTV Latino (formerly MTV Internacional), the Spanish version of America's MTV music channel available via cable or satellite throughout Mexico and in selected markets throughout the Americas, including the United States. The selections present a balance of English-language performances by groups from the United States or the United Kingdom, Mexican performances in Spanish, and a good dose of Spanish-language videos from Spain and Latin America.

BULLFIGHTS

One type of entertainment you won't find north of the border is the bullfight. Variously called *la corrida de toros* (the running of bulls), *la fiesta brava* (the brave festival), *la lidia de toros* (the fighting of bulls), and *sombra y sol*

(shade and sun), the bullfight can be perceived as sport, art, or gory spectacle, depending on the social conditioning of the observer.

To the aficionado, the *lidia* is a ritual drama that rolls courage, fate, pathos, and death together into a symbolic event. No matter how one may feel toward the bullfight, it is undeniably an integral part of Mexican history and culture. Every town of any size has at least one *plaza de toros* or bullring; in Baja California you'll find one major stadium in Mexicali and two in Tijuana, including the second-largest ring in the world. Occasionally, a small bullring is improvised for a rural fiesta.

History

Ritualistic encounters with bulls have been traced as far back as 3000 B.C., when the Minoans on the Greek island of Crete performed ritual dives over the horns of attacking wild bulls. A closer antecedent developed around 2000 B.C. on the Iberian peninsula, where a breed of fierce, wild bulls roamed the plains. Iberian hunters—ancestors of the Spanish and Portuguese—figured out how to evade the dangerous bull at close quarters while delivering a fatal blow with an axe or spear. When the Romans heard about this practice they began importing wild Spanish bulls and accomplished bullfighters for their coliseum games—possibly the first public bullfights.

During the Middle Ages, bullfighting became a royal sport practiced on horseback by both the Spanish and the occupying Moors, who used lances to dispatch the wild bulls. As the *toreros* (bullfighters) began dismounting and confronting the bulls on the ground, the game eventually evolved into the current *corrida* as performed in Spain, Portugal, Mexico, and throughout much of Latin America.

In the early years the only payment the *torero* received was the bull's carcass. Nowadays bullfighters receive performance fees that vary according to their status within the profession.

El Toro

The bulls used in the ring, *toros de lidia* (fighting bulls), are descendants of wild Iberian bulls that have been specially bred for over four centuries for their combative spirit. They're not trained in any way for the ring, nor goaded into viciousness, but as a breed are naturally quick to anger. The fighting bull's neck muscles are much larger than those of any other cattle breed, making the animal capable of tossing a *torero* and his horse into the air with one upward sweep.

Bulls who show an acceptable degree of bravery by the age of two are let loose in huge pastures—averaging 10,000 acres per animal—to live as wild beasts until they reach four years, the age of combat. By the time *el toro* enters the ring, he stands around 125 centimeters (4 ft) high at the withers and weighs 450 kilograms (a half ton) or more.

The carcass of a bull killed in the ring does not go to waste, at least not from a meat eater's perspective. Immediately after it's taken from the ring, it's butchered and dressed, and the meat is sold to the public.

El Torero

The bullfighter is rated by his agility, control, and compassion. The *torero* who teases a bull or who is unable to kill it quickly when the moment of truth arrives is considered a cruel brute. To be judged a worthy competitor by the spectators, *el torero* must excel in three areas: *parar,* or standing still as the bull charges, with only the cape and the torero's upper body moving; *templar,* or timing and grace, the movements smooth, well timed, and of the right proportion; and *mandar,* or command, the degree to which the *torero* masters the entire *lidia* through his bravery, technique, and understanding of the bull, neither intimidating the animal nor being intimidated by it.

Standard equipment for the torero is the *capote de brega,* the large cape used in the first two-thirds of the *lidia;* the *muleta,* a smaller cape used during the final third; the *estoque,* or matador's sword; and the *traje de luces* (suit of lights), the colorful torero's costume originally designed by the Spanish artist Goya.

Although it's usually the bull who dies in a *lidia, toreros* are also at great risk. Over half of all professional matadors on record worldwide during the last 250 years have been gored to death in the ring.

La Lidia

The regulated procedures *(suertes)* followed in a bullfight date from 18th-century Spain. Anywhere from four to eight bulls (typically six) may appear in a *corrida,* with one *torero* on hand for every two bulls scheduled. The order of appearance for the *toreros* is based on seniority. *Toreros* who've proven their skills in several bullfighting seasons as *novilleros* (novice fighters) are called *matadores de toros* (bull killers). Ordinarily each *torero* fights two bulls; if one is gored or otherwise put out of action, another *torero* takes his place, even if it means facing more than his allotment of bulls.

Each *lidia* is divided into *tercios* (thirds). In *el tercio de varas,* the bull enters the ring and the matador performs *capeos* (cape maneuvers that don't expose the matador's body to the bull's horns, meant to test the bull or lead it to another spot in the ring) and *lances* (cape maneuvers that expose the matador's body to the horns and bring the bull closer to him). Meanwhile, two horsemen receive the bull's charge with eight-foot *varas,* or lances. The *varas* have short, pyramid-shaped points, which are aimed at the bull's neck muscle and do not penetrate deeply on contact.

The purpose of the encounter is to force the bull to lower his horns and to give him the confidence of meeting something solid so he won't be frustrated by the emptiness of the cape as the *lidia* proceeds. Usually only two *vara* blows are administered, but more are permitted if necessary to produce the intended effect: the lowering of the head. The crowd protests, however, when more than two are applied, as they want the matador to face a strong bull.

In *el tercio de banderillas,* the bull's shoulders receive the *banderillas,* 26-inch wooden sticks decorated with colored paper frills, each tipped with a small, sharp, iron barb. They can be placed by the matador himself or more often by hired assistant *toreros,* called *banderilleros* when performing this function. The purpose of *banderilla* placement is to "correct" the bull's posture; the added punishment also makes the bull craftier in his charges. Placed in pairs, up to six *banderillas* may be applied to the bull, varying in number and position according to the reactions of the individual animal.

At the end of the *tercio de banderillas,* signaled by a bugle fanfare, the matador takes up his *muleta* and sword and walks before the box of the *juez* (judge) presiding over the *lidia.* He looks to the *juez* for permission to proceed with the killing of the bull and, after receiving a nod, offers his *brindis* (dedication). The *brindis* may go to an individual spectator, a section of the plaza, or the entire audience. If the dedication is to an individual, he presents his *montera* (matador's hat) to that person, who will return it, with a present inside, to the matador after the *lidia.* Otherwise, he waves his hat at the crowd and then tosses it onto the sand; he remains hatless for the final *tercio,* a gesture of respect for the bull.

The final round of the *lidia* is called *el tercio de muerte* (the third of death). The main activity of this *tercio* is *la faena* (literally, "the work") involving cape and sword, during which a special set of passes leads to the killing of the bull. The first two *tercios* have no time limit; for the last, however, the matador has only 15 minutes to kill the bull, or else he is considered defeated and the bull is led from the ring, where it is killed immediately by the plaza butcher.

In a good *faena,* a matador tempts fate over and over again, bringing the bull's horns close to his own heart. The time for the kill arrives when the bull is so tired from the *faena* that he stands still, forelegs squared as if ready to receive the sword. Then, with his cape, the matador must draw the bull into a final charge while he himself moves forward, bringing the sword out from under the cape, sighting down the blade, and driving the blade over the horns and between the animal's shoulders. A perfect sword thrust severs the aorta, resulting in instant death. If the thrust is off, the matador must try again until the bull dies from one of the thrusts.

It is not necessary to kill the bull in one stroke, which is quite an extraordinary accomplishment; the matador's honor is preserved as long as he goes in over the horns, thus risking his own life, every time. If the bull falls to his knees but isn't dead, another *torero* immediately comes forward and thrusts a dagger *(puntilla)* behind the base of the skull to sever the spinal cord and put the beast out of his misery. When the bull is dead, the *lidia* is over. If the matador has shown bravery and artistry, the crowd rewards him with applause; an unusually dramatic performance results in hats and flowers thrown into the ring. In cases of outstanding technique or bravado, the *juez* awards the bull's ears or tail to the matador.

Practicalities

It's usually a good idea to buy tickets for a *corrida* in advance; it's not unusual for an event to sell out. Check with the local tourist office to determine if any seats are available. In the event of a sellout, you may still be able to buy a ticket—at a higher price—from a scalper, or *revendedor.* In a large stadium, the spectator sections are divided into *sol* (sunny side) and *sombra* (shaded side), then subdivided according to how close the seats are to the bullring itself. Since the *corrida* doesn't usually begin until around 4 P.M., the *sol* tickets aren't bad, as long as you bring a hat, sunglasses, and sunscreen, plus plenty of pesos to buy beverages. Tequila and beer are usually available, along with soft drinks.

CHARREADAS

Decreed the national sport of Mexico in a 1933 presidential edict, the *charreada,* or Mexican-style rodeo, can be seen in Baja only in Tijuana, Rosarito, and Mexicali. *Charreadas* are held in skillet-shaped *lienzos charros* or *charro* rings by private *charro* associations. Much like its U.S. counterpart (which was inspired by the Mexican version), *charreada* is a contest of equestrian and ranching skills. Though open to everyone, *charrería* (the *charro* art) is an expensive pastime requiring the maintenance of trained horses and elaborate clothing—somewhat analogous to polo in the Anglo world.

Unlike in American and Canadian rodeo, *charros* and *charras* (gentleman and lady riders) compete for team, not individual, awards. Each team fields six to eight persons, who singly or in combination perform a series of nine *suertes* (maneuvers or events); upon completion of all *suertes,* the team with the most points wins. Another difference is that *charreada* points are usually scored for style rather than speed. Live mariachi music adds drama and romance to the events.

One of the more thrilling *suertes* is the *paso de la muerte,* in which a *charro* leaps from the back of a horse onto the back of an unbroken mare—while both horses are at full gallop! In the *coleadero,* a *charro* leans down from his horse and throws a steer by catching its tail with his leg. For a *terna en el ruedo,* three mounted *charros* rope a wild bull and bring it to the ground within 10 minutes or three casts of *la reata* (origin of the English word "lariat"); points are scored for the complexity and style of the rope work, not speed.

Also striking is the *escaramuza charra,* a women's event featuring rapid, precision-timed, and carefully choreographed and executed equestrian moves by a group of 6–10 riders. This extremely colorful and popular event owes its name to the Italian *scaramuccia,* a 16th-century cavalry maneuver.

In the bull-riding event, or *jinete de toro,* the rider must stay atop the bull until it stops bucking, then dismount with the cinch in hand, landing on both feet simultaneously. By contrast, the American rodeo counterpart to this event requires a cowboy to stay mounted for only eight seconds.

A serious *charreada* regular maintains four *charro* suits: the *traje de faena,* or plain working outfit; the *traje de media gala,* a semiformal suit with embroidery; and two *trajes de gala*—the silver-buttoned *traje de etiqueta* (dress suit) and the *traje de ceremonia,* an elegant tuxedo outfit for special ceremonies. Each *traje* consists of a broad-brimmed sombrero, tight-fitting trousers of cloth or leather, a short-waisted jacket, boots, and—when the *charro* is mounted—deerskin *chaparreras* (chaps). *Charras* generally dress in *coronela* or *china poblana* outfits, late 19th-century styles featuring full, embroidered blouses and long, billowing, brightly colored skirts with layers of lace and petticoats.

HOLIDAYS, FESTIVALS, AND EVENTS

Mexicans love a fiesta, and *bajacalifornianos* are no exception. Any occasion will suffice as an excuse to hold a celebration, from a birthday to a lobster harvest. Add to all the civic possibilities the vast number of Mexican Catholic religious holidays, and there's potential for some kind of public fiesta at least every week of the year, if not all 365 days. Besides the national religious holidays, Mexico has feast days for 115 Catholic saints per year, 9 or 10 each month. Any town, pueblo, *ejido,* or *colonia* named for a saint will usually hold a fiesta on the feast day of its namesake. Individuals named for saints often host parties on their *día de santo* (saint's day), too.

The primary requisites of a fiesta are plenty of food (especially tamales, considered a festive dish), beer and liquor, music, and dancing. More elaborate celebrations include parades, exhibitions, *charreadas* (Mexican rodeos), and occasional fireworks.

Some of the more memorable yearly events and public holidays observed throughout Baja are highlighted below by month. Smaller festivals and events held locally are mentioned earlier in the text. Actual dates can vary from year to year, so be sure to check with the appropriate tourist office in advance.

Government offices and some businesses close on national holidays. These closings are not always mentioned in the text; you may want to call ahead to find out.

January
New Year's Day, January 1, is an official holiday.

Día de los Santos Reyes is January 6. See Las Posadas under *December.*

February
Constitution Day, February 5, is an official holiday.

The pre-Lenten **Carnaval** festival is held in late February or early March as a last celebration of the carnal pleasures Catholics must forgo during the 40-day Lent season preceding Easter. The fiesta's name derives from the Italian *carne vale*, "flesh taken away." In Mexico, Carnaval is traditionally observed only in port towns; in Baja, the festival is celebrated most grandly in La Paz and Ensenada. Like New Orleans's Mardi Gras, Carnaval features lots of music, dancing, costumes, parades, and high-spirited revelry. See *Ensenada and Vicinity* for more information.

Flag Day, February 24, is an official holiday.

March

Birthday of Benito Juárez, March 21, is an official holiday.

Spring Break is not a Mexican holiday at all, but an annual ritual for American college and university students—mostly Southern Californians and Arizonans—who go on the rampage in Rosarito, Ensenada, San Felipe, and Los Cabos. The spring break season usually straddles late March and early April. Unless you're one of the revelers, these towns should be avoided during this period.

April

Semana Santa—"Holy Week," or Easter Week (the third week in April)—is second only to Christmas as the most important holiday period of the year. One of the most prominent Semana Santa customs is breaking *cascarones,* colored eggs stuffed with confetti, over the heads of friends and family. Besides attending mass on Good Friday and Easter Sunday, many Mexicans take this opportunity to go on vacations. Baja resorts—particularly Rosarito, Ensenada, San Felipe, and Los Cabos—can be overcrowded this week because the peninsula receives a large influx of both Mexican mainlanders and gringos.

The Rosarito-Ensenada 50-Mile Bicycle Ride takes place on a Saturday in April and attracts as many as 10,000 participants, making it one of the world's largest cycling events. The route follows the coast, with an elevation differential of around 300 meters (1,000 ft). The same ride is repeated in fall. Sponsored by **Bicycling West** (P.O. Box 15128, San Diego, CA 92175-5128, 619/424-6084). To register online, go to www.rosaritoensenada.com.

The Newport-Ensenada Yacht Race, reportedly the world's largest international yachting regatta, is held the last weekend in April. Boats race from Newport Beach, California, to Ensenada. Sponsored by the Newport Ocean Sailing Association (949/644-1023, www.nosa.org).

May

International Workers' Day, May 1, is an official holiday.

Cinco de Mayo: Held on May 5, this festival commemorates the defeat of an attempted French invasion at Puebla de los Ángeles, on Mexico's Gulf of Mexico coast, in 1862. Features music, dance, food, and other cultural events.

Mother's Day (Día de las Madres) is observed on May 10.

Fiesta de Corpus Christi is a religious holiday celebrated 60 days after Easter to honor the Body of Christ and the Eucharist. Corn-husk figurines and miniature mules are displayed in stores and homes.

June

Navy Day, June 1, is an official holiday.

September

Día de Nuestra Señora de Loreto is held in Loreto on September 8 to commemorate the founding of the first mission in the Californias. Special masses, processions, music, dancing, and food.

Mexican Independence Day (Fiesta Patria de la Independencia), also called Diez y Seis, since it falls on September 16, celebrates the country's independence from Spain, as announced in 1821 in the town of Dolores. Festivities begin on the 15th and last for two days. The biggest celebrations are centered in Mexicali and La Paz and include fireworks, parades, *charreadas,* music, and folk-dance performances.

The **Rosarito-Ensenada 50-Mile Bicycle Ride** is held on the last Saturday in September; see description under *April.*

October

Día de la Raza, celebrated as Columbus Day north of the border, October 12 in Mexico, commemorates the founding of the Mexican race as heralded by the arrival of Columbus in the New World.

November

Día de los Muertos, the "Day of the Dead," is Mexico's third most important holiday, corresponding to Europe's All Saints Day except that it's celebrated November 1 and 2 instead of only November 1. Some of the festivities are held in cemeteries where children clean the headstones and crucifixes of their deceased relatives *(los difuntos)* and play games unique to this fiesta. Roadside shrines throughout Baja are laid with fresh flowers and other tributes to the dead. Offerings of *pan de los muertos* (bread of the dead) and food and liquor are placed before family altars on behalf of deceased family members, along with papier-mâché skulls and skeletons.

In the second or third week of November, North America's most famous desert race, the **Baja 1000,** draws a dedicated crowd of off-road fanatics and automotive manufacturers hoping to gain advertising copy like "Baja 1000 Winner" or at least "Baja 1000-Tested." These days, the course follows established auto trails to avoid further damage to Baja's fragile desert lands; the course alternates from year to year between a full 1,000-mile (1,600-km) race between Ensenada and La Paz and a 1,000-kilometer (621-mi) race that loops through the northern state only. The race runs in several classes from dirt bikes to four-wheel-drive trucks; about 400 drivers compete. Sponsored by SCORE International (tel. 818/225-8402, www.score-international.com).

Anniversary of the 1910 Revolution, November 20, is an official holiday.

December

Día de Nuestra Señora de Guadalupe, the feast day of the Virgin of Guadalupe, Mexico's patron saint, is December 12; special masses are held that day throughout Mexico. The nearest Sunday to the 12th also features special events such as mariachi masses, food booths, and games. The celebrations at the border town of Tecate are particularly well attended.

Beginning on December 16, Mexicans hold nightly *posadas*—candlelight processions terminating at elaborate, community-built nativity scenes—in commemoration of the Holy Family's search for lodging. The processions continue for nine consecutive nights. Other activities include piñata parties where children shatter hanging papier-mâché figures filled with small gifts and candy. Churches large and small hold continuous Christmas masses beginning at midnight on the 25th (Día de la Navidad).

Las Posadas culminates on January 6, which is Día de los Santos Reyes—literally, Day of the King-Saints, referring to the story of the Three Wise Men. On this day Mexican children receive their Christmas gifts, and family and friends gather to eat a wreath-shaped fruitcake called *rosca de reyes* (wreath of the kings), baked especially for this occasion. Hidden inside each *rosca* is a small clay figurine *(muñeco)* that represents the infant Jesus. While sharing the *rosca* on this day, the person whose slice contains the *muñeco* is obliged to host a *candelaria,* or Candlemas party, on February 2 for everyone present.

At the *candelaria*—which commemorates the day the newborn Jesus was first presented at the Temple in Jerusalem—the host traditionally displays a larger Christ-infant figure and serves tamales and *atole,* a thick, hot grain drink flavored with fruit or chocolate.

Accommodations

Places to stay in Baja run the gamut from free campgrounds and budget motels to quaint bed-and-breakfast inns and plush resort hotels. Camping spots are more numerous than hotels or motels, so visitors who bring along camping gear have a greater range of options at any given location. Larger cities—Tijuana, Ensenada, Mexicali, La Paz, and Cabo San Lucas—have dozens of hotels to choose from.

HOTELS AND MOTELS
Rates

At many hotels and motels, midweek rates are lower than weekend rates. In northern Baja, some places charge high-season rates May–October. In southern Baja, it's generally the opposite; i.e., winter rates are highest. To save money on accommodations, try traveling in the off-season for each region; except for the inland deserts, most of the peninsula is livable year-round.

Whatever the rack rate (the main listed room rate), you can usually get the price down by bargaining, except during the peak period of Christmas, spring break, and Easter. When checking in, be sure to clarify whether the room rate includes meals—occasionally it does. Asking for a room without meals *(sin comidas)* is an easy way to bring the rate down, or simply ask if there's anything cheaper *(¿Hay algo más barato?)*.

Large tourist hotels may add a 12 percent hotel tax to quoted rates. Some also add a 10 percent service charge. When quoted a room rate, be sure to ask whether it includes tax and service to avoid a 22 percent surprise over posted rates when you check out.

Unless otherwise specified, the price ranges quoted in this book are based on double-occupancy, high-season rates. Single-occupancy prices may be lower, and suites may be available at higher rates. All rates are per room, per night. Many properties offer discounts for long-term stays.

While hotels and motels in Baja tend to be

palapa-roofed *casita*

© NIKKI GOTH ITOI

less expensive than their counterparts in the United States, Canada, or Europe, they're also usually more expensive than equivalent accommodations in mainland Mexico.

Under US$50

The largest number of hotels and motels in Baja fall into this price range; most everything in this price range comes with heating and air conditioning. Lodging under US$25 per night is rare unless you stay at a youth hostel, *casa de huéspedes,* or *pensión,* where bathrooms are usually shared. The term *baño colectivo* indicates shared bathroom facilities. Soap, towels, toilet paper, and purified drinking water are usually provided; in some places you may have to ask. Rooms in this price range don't offer air conditioners or heaters. In northern Baja, you can often obtain a *calentador,* or space heater, on request for especially cool nights.

US$50-100

In this range is the **Desert Inn** (formerly La Pinta Hotel) chain, with locations in Ensenada, San Quintín, Cataviña, Guerrero Negro, San Ignacio, and Loreto. Several of its properties, most recently, San Ignacio and San Quintín, have been renovated in recent years.

Desert Inn/La Pinta hotels are similar in appearance and facilities; the Las Cazuelas restaurant at each features the same menu, though the food quality varies according to the talents of the local kitchen staff. Room rates are similar throughout the chain, around US$65–80, not including 12 percent tax. La Pinta hotels in Loreto and Ensenada fall at the lower end of this rate spectrum but are also the least well maintained. These prices assume you're paying in pesos—if you pay in dollars, the low exchange rate will cost you extra. Between Ensenada and Loreto, these are virtually the only hotels that accept credit cards for room and meal charges.

Members of the Discover Baja Travel Club receive a card entitling the bearer to a 20 percent discount on all La Pinta stays. If you stay at two or more branches of La Pinta during a single Baja visit, your Discover Baja membership will have paid for itself.

Reservations for any La Pinta hotel can be made by calling 800/800-9632 in the United States and Canada, or at www.lapinta hotels.com.

US$100-150

Higher-end places are found in or near Tijuana, Rosarito, Ensenada, San Felipe, La Paz, San José del Cabo, and Cabo San Lucas. Prices in Baja for "international-class accommodations" average around US$100–150. Many bed-and-breakfast inns are priced in this range as well. Some of these places are good values, while others are definitely overpriced. When in doubt, stick to the less-expensive hotels, or ask about "specials."

US$150-250

A number of boutique hotels and luxury vacation rentals fall into this range; mostly in the Los Cabos area, as well as Todos Santos, La Paz, and Loreto. In the north, some of the newer Valle de Guadalupe wine country accommodations are opening in this range.

Over US$250

The most luxurious hotels in all of Baja—indeed among the best in all of Mexico—are found along the coast between San José del Cabo and Cabo San Lucas, in an area known as The Corridor. Beach frontage, huge pools, spas, world-class restaurants, and golf course privileges are all part of the experience at these resorts. Prices start around US$250 a night for the Sheraton and soar to more than US$1,000 a night for the region's top three: Las Ventanas al Paraíso, Esperanza, and the One&Only Palmilla.

Hotel Reservation Services

Most of the hotels and motels mentioned in this guidebook take advance reservations directly by phone, mail, or website. Some visitors may find it more convenient to use a reservation service such as **Baja California Tours** (U.S. tel. 800/336-5454, www.bajaspecials.com). Occasionally these agencies can arrange lower room rates or special packages not offered directly by the hotels themselves. Note that the lives of these kinds of booking agencies tend to be

BOUTIQUE HOTELS AND GOURMET EATS

Once confined to the Los Cabos area of the peninsula, boutique hotels and gourmet restaurants are popping up from Ensenada to El Pescadero. Here are some of the highlights:

BAJA'S BOUTIQUE HOTELS

La Villa del Valle (Valle de Guadalupe, p. 104)
Tuscan-style accommodations atop a hill on 70 acres with sweeping views of surrounding vineyards, orchards, and gardens.

Casa Natalie (Ensenada, p. 94)
Five suites and three newer rooms, all furnished to a level rarely seen in Baja. The ideal home base for a weekend of wine-tasting in the Guadalupe Valley.

Clementine's Inn (Mulegé, p. 204)
The most comfortable beds in Baja in a moderate price range. The owners made a speedy recovery after the flood of September 2006 and bought all new beds, linens, appliances, and artwork for their guest accommodations.

Posada de las Flores (Punta Chivato, p. 209; Loreto, p. 226; La Paz, p. 273)
Among the most charming properties found in Baja. Rustic Mexican furniture and tile are used throughout, and all-marble bathrooms feature large bathtubs and extra-thick towels.

Posada La Poza (Todos Santos, p. 428)
Enjoy the relaxed pace of life in Baja with a Swiss sensibility for quality and efficiency.

La Alianza (El Pescadero, p. 412)
Marble floors, robes, Egyptian cotton sheets, and fluffy towels in a five-room property near San Pedrito point.

Casa Natalia (San José del Cabo, p. 344)
A contemporary European-style boutique hotel with rooms set around a small pool and individually decorated with authentic artwork from San Miguel de Allende, Oaxaca, and Puebla.

---

short. Your local travel agent may also be able to book lodging in Baja.

ALTERNATIVES TO HOTELS AND MOTELS
Casas de Huéspedes and Pensiones

Aside from free or basic campgrounds, *casas de huéspedes* (guesthouses) and *pensiones* (boardinghouses) are the cheapest places to stay in Baja. Unfortunately for budgeteers, they aren't plentiful. They're most numerous in Baja California Sur towns, especially Mulegé and La Paz. The typical *casa de huéspedes* offers rooms with shared bath *(baño colectivo)* for US$10–15; US$15–20 with private bath. A *pensión* costs about the same but may include meals. At either, most lodgers are staying for a week or more, but the proprietors are usually happy to accept guests by the night.

The main difference between these and budget hotels/motels—besides rates—is that they're usually in old houses or other buildings (e.g., convents) that have been converted for guesthouse use. Soap, towels, toilet paper, and drinking water are usually provided, but you may have to ask.

Youth Hostels

Baja has one youth hostel (*villa deportiva juvenil,* or youth sports villa) each in Mexicali, La Paz, Punta Colonet, Rosarito (not recommended), and El Sauzal. They feature shared dormitory-style rooms where each guest is assigned a bed and a locker. Bathing facilities are always com-

BAJA'S GOURMET RESTAURANTS

La Diferencia (Tijuana, p. 47)
Seasonally available *chile en nogada* or duck with a hibiscus flower-based sauce stand out on an all-around excellent menu. Attentive service and a contemporary setting make the meal.

El Taco de Huitzilopochtli (Ensenada, p. 96)
No other restaurant in the area serves more authentic central Mexican food.

Restaurant Laja (Valle de Guadalupe, p. 105)
The brainchild of former Four Seasons chef Jair Téllez prepares farm-fresh cuisine on par with California's celebrated Chez Panisse and French Laundry restaurants.

Art & Beer (West Cape, p. 414)
Large signature cocktails are a meal in a glass, generously garnished with all manner of shellfish.

Sancho Panza (Cabo San Lucas, p. 396)
The best wine list in southern Baja. This is the perfect place for a quiet drink, and the tapas menu is tops.

Nick-San Restaurant (Cabo San Lucas, p. 397)
This is probably the most reliably high-quality restaurant in San Lucas, regardless of cuisine. Don't miss the sashimi salad.

Don Emiliano (San José del Cabo, p. 348)
A member of the Slow Food movement and run by a well-known chef from Mexico City, Margarita C. de Salinas.

Las Tres Virgenes (La Paz, p. 275)
Local expats are calling it the best meal they've had in La Paz, period.

---

munal, and guests must supply their own soap and towels. Rates are US$10–15 per night.

Staying at these hostels is a great way to meet young Mexicans and improve your Spanish; English is rarely spoken. About the only drawback is that some hostels are inconveniently located some distance from the center of town, so transportation can be a problem. For the fitness-oriented, they're ideal; sports facilities usually include a gym, swimming pool, and courts for basketball, volleyball, and tennis.

House Rentals and House-Sitting

For long-term stays of a month or more—and occasionally for stays of as short as a week—house rental may be significantly less expensive and more convenient than staying at a hotel or motel. Rents vary wildly according to facilities, neighborhood, and general location in Baja. The most expensive rentals are those in beach areas along the Tijuana–Ensenada corridor, followed by those in Los Cabos. Expect to pay a minimum of US$500 a month in these beach areas (in some instances you could easily pay that for a weekend), more typically US$1,000–1,500 a month for something quite simple.

Some of the best deals on beach houses can be found in Los Barriles, Buena Vista, and Todos Santos, all in Baja California Sur. At any of these places, you can rent a furnished one- or two-bedroom with kitchen starting at around US$400–700 a month. In the Tijuana–Ensenada corridor of Baja California Norte, expect to pay about twice that. Property management services and real estate companies in these areas can help locate something in your price range—see the appropriate destination chapters for contact information.

In smaller Baja, towns you'll be hard-pressed to find any real estate or property-management companies, so the best thing to do is just ask the locals. In interior towns like San Ignacio, even San Quintín, livable houses can be rented for as low as US$300 a month. Farther off the beaten track in such relatively remote oases as La Purísima, Comondú, or San Javier, rents may be even lower—if you can find someone with a place to rent.

CAMPING AND RV PARKS
Both states of Baja California boast more campgrounds, RV parks, and wilderness camping areas than any other state in Mexico. Because the peninsula's population density is so dramatically low, it's easy to find hidden campsites offering idyllic settings and precious solitude, often for free. For travelers who like the outdoors, camping is also an excellent way to slash accommodations costs.

The Baja peninsula offers roughly 100 campgrounds—perhaps 125 if you count Sea of Cortez fish camps—that charge fees ranging from around US$3 for a place with virtually zero facilities to as high as US$30 for a developed RV park with full water, electrical, and sewage hookups plus recreation facilities. Most campgrounds charge around US$5–15 for tent camping, US$12–20 for full hookups.

If you can forgo permanent toilet and bathing facilities, you won't have to pay anything to camp, since there's a virtually limitless selection of free camping spots, from beaches to deserts to mountain slopes. You won't necessarily need four-wheel drive to reach these potential campsites, as plenty of turnouts and graded dirt *ramales* (branch roads) off the main highways can be negotiated by just about any type of vehicle.

Food and Drink

Much of what *bajacalifornianos* eat can be considered Northern Mexican cuisine. Because Northern Mexico is generally better suited to ranching than farming, ranch-style cooking tends to prevail in rural areas, which means that ranch products—beef, poultry, and dairy foods—are highly favored.

Unlike the northern mainland, however, just about any point in Baja is only a couple of hours' drive from the seashore, so seafood predominates here more than anywhere else in Mexico. In most places on the peninsula, seafood is more common than meat or poultry. If there's anything unique about Baja cuisine, it's the blending of ranch cooking with coastal culture, which has resulted in such distinctive Baja creations as the *taco de pescado* (fish taco).

WHERE TO EAT
Your selection of eating venues in Baja depends largely on where you are on the peninsula at any given moment. The most populated areas lie at either end of the peninsula, where you'll find the greatest range of places to eat. Baja's larger towns and cities—Tijuana, Mexicali, Ensenada, La Paz, and Cabo San Lucas—offer everything from humble sidewalk taco stands to *gran turismo* hotel restaurants.

Between Ensenada and La Paz the choices are fewer and more basic. Along certain lengthy stretches of the Transpeninsular Highway in central Baja, about the only places to eat are ranchos that serve whatever's on the stone hearth that day. Usually, ranchos that take paying diners hang a sign out front or post an arrow along the highway that says Lonchería, Café, Comedor, Comida, Eat, or Food. A few post no signs and are known only by word of mouth.

Small towns might have only two or three restaurants *(restaurantes)* serving basic Mexican dishes or, if near the coast, *mariscos* (seafood). Most hotels in Baja have restaurants; in small towns they may be among the best choices. While the Desert Inn/La Pinta Hotel chain's res-

COOKING METHODS

Entrées, whether meat, poultry, or seafood, are most commonly prepared in one of the following styles:

adobo, adobada – marinated or stewed in a sauce of vinegar, chilies, and spices
a la parrilla – broiled or grilled
a la veracruzana – seafood, often *al carbón* (charcoal-grilled)
albóndigas – meatballs
al mojo de ajo – in a garlic sauce
al pastor – slowly roasted on a vertical spit
al vapor – steamed
asado/asada – grilled
barbacoa – pit-roasted
con arroz – steamed with rice
empanizada – breaded
encebollado – cooked with onions
entomado – cooked with tomatoes
frito – fried
guisado – in a spicy stew
machaca – dried and shredded

antojitos (snacks or one-plate dishes). Some *loncherías* offer *comida corrida,* a daily fixed-price meal that includes a beverage, an entrée or two, side dishes, and possibly dessert.

A *comedor* is a more basic version of a *lonchería;* they aren't as common in Baja as on the mainland but are seen occasionally. Cafés or *cafeterías* are similar to *loncherías* except that they may open earlier and serve *desayuno* (breakfast) in addition to other meals.

A *cenaduría* is yet another simple, café-style restaurant, this time concentrating on *la cena,* the evening meal. Often the menu will be similar to that of a *lonchería*—mostly *antojitos*—but the hours are later, typically 5–10 P.M.

Ordering and Paying
You really don't need much Spanish to get by in a restaurant. Stating what you want, plus *por favor* (please), will usually do the trick (e.g., *"dos cervezas, por favor,"* "two beers, please"). Don't forget to say *"gracias"* ("thank you"). The menu is called *el menú* or, much less commonly in Baja, *la carta.*

La cuenta is the bill. A tip *(la propina)* of 10–15 percent is expected at any restaurant with table service; look to see if it's already been added to the bill before placing a tip on the table.

Costs
In this guidebook, we've tried to give some guidance as to the approximate meal cost at most sit-down restaurants. At inexpensive places, you can count on spending less than US$7 for an entrée (or for a *comida corrida,* where available—see *Comida* later in this section), while a moderate meal will cost up to US$15, and an expensive one more than US$15.

WHAT TO EAT
Breakfasts
Menus at tourist restaurants are often confusing because some of the same "breakfast" dishes may end up on more than one section of the menu. Mexicans have two kinds of breakfasts, an early one, called *desayuno,* eaten shortly after rising, and a second one, called *almuerzo,* that's usually taken around 11 A.M. To further confuse the issue, Spanish-English dictionaries usually

taurants are not known for their culinary excellence, in the desert pit stop of Cataviña, the one is about the only place you can get a full meal. Sometimes the best meals on the road come from what you improvise yourself after a visit to a local *tienda de abarrotes* (grocery store).

Back in the city, one of the main nonrestaurant choices is the taquería, a small, inexpensive diner where tacos are assembled before your eyes—sort of the Mexican equivalent of the old-fashioned American hamburger stand. Taquerías tend to be in areas with lots of foot traffic—near bus terminals, for example. The good ones are packed with diners in the early evening.

Another economical choice is anything called a *lonchería,* which is a small, café-style place that usually serves *almuerzo* (late breakfast/early lunch) and *comida* (the main, midday meal). *Lonchería* hours are typically 11 A.M.–5 P.M. Municipal markets in Baja often feature rows of *loncherías* serving inexpensive basic meals and

translate *almuerzo* as "lunch," while bilingual menus often read "breakfast."

The most common Baja *desayuno* is simply *pan dulce* (sweet pastry) or *bolillos* (torpedo-shaped, European-style rolls) with coffee or milk. Cereal is also sometimes eaten for *desayuno;* e.g., *avena* (oatmeal), *crema de trigo* (cream of wheat), or *hojuelas de maíz* (corn flakes).

The heavier eggs-and-frijoles dishes known widely as "Mexican breakfasts" in the United States and Canada are usually taken as *almuerzo,* the late breakfast, which is most typically reserved for weekends and holidays. Eggs come in a variety of ways, including *huevos revueltos* (scrambled eggs), *huevos duros* (hard-boiled eggs), *huevos escafaldos* (soft-boiled eggs), *huevos estrellados* (eggs fried sunny side up), *huevos a la mexicana* (also *huevos mexicanos,* eggs scrambled with chopped tomato, onion, and chilies), *huevos rancheros* (fried eggs served on a tortilla), and *huevos divorciados,* two *huevos estrellados* separated by beans, each egg usually topped with a different salsa.

Eggs also come *con chorizo* (with ground sausage), *con machaca* (with dried, shredded meat), *con tocino* (with bacon), or *con jamón* (with ham). All egg dishes usually come with frijoles and tortillas. The biggest *almuerzo* package on the menu is typically called *almuerzo albañil* (brickmason's *almuerzo*) or *huevos albañil* (brickmason's eggs); this means eggs with one or more varieties of meat on the side.

One of the cheapest and tastiest *almuerzos* is *chilaquiles,* tortilla chips in a chili gravy with crumbled cheese on top. Eggs and/or chicken can be added to *chilaquiles.* Another economical choice is *molletes,* which consists of a split *bolillo* spread with mashed beans and melted cheese, served with salsa on the side.

Comida

Bajacalifornianos typically eat the main meal of the day, *comida,* sometime between 2 and 5 P.M. While *desayuno* (breakfast) may consist of nothing more than a roll and coffee, and *cena* (the evening meal) not much more, *comida* is where Mexicans pack on most of the calories they take in during a day's eating. Whether eaten at home or in a *lonchería,* restaurant, or bar, this meal usually consists of several different dishes, including rice, soup, and a *plato fuerte* (main dish).

Many restaurants offer a *comida corrida* or *comida del día,* a special fixed-price, multi-course menu costing US$2.50–5. The typical *comida corrida* includes soup, a plate of flavored rice (served as an appetizer), a main dish, one or two side dishes, dessert, and a nonalcoholic beverage (often an *agua fresca*).

Cena

The large afternoon *comida* sustains most Mexicans till at least 8 P.M. or so, when it's time for *cena,* a light evening meal usually consisting of *pan dulce* (Mexican pastries) with herb tea or coffee. A larger repast taken in a restaurant may be called *merienda.*

Tortillas

A Mexican meal is not a meal without tortillas, the round, flat, pancakelike disks eaten with nearly any nondessert dish, including salads, meats, seafood, beans, and vegetables. Both wheat-flour and cornmeal tortillas are commonly consumed throughout Baja, although flour tortillas *(tortillas de harina)* are the clear favorite. Corn tortillas *(tortillas de maíz)* are more common in southern Mexico, where Amerindian populations (the first corn cultivators) are larger, while flour tortillas are more popular in the ranching areas of northern Mexico. Among northern Mexicans, it is said that meat and poultry dishes taste best with flour tortillas while vegetable dishes go best with corn. Most restaurants offer a choice. If you order tortillas without specifying, you may get *"¿de harina o de maíz?"* as a response.

Although prepackaged tortillas are available in *supermercados* (supermarkets), most *bajacalifornianos* buy them fresh from neighborhood *tortillerías* or make them at home. Many restaurants and cafés in Baja, and virtually all *loncherías* and taquerías, serve fresh tortillas.

Incidentally, a tortilla has two sides, an inside and an outside, that dictate which direction the tortilla is best folded when wrapping it around food. The side with the thinner layer—sometimes called the *pancita,* or belly—should face the inside when folding the tortilla. If you notice the outside of your tortilla cracking, with pieces peeling off onto the table, you've probably folded it with the *pancita* outside instead of inside.

Antojitos and Main Dishes

Antojitos literally means "little whims," thus implying snacks to many people. However, the word also refers to any food that can be ordered, served, and eaten quickly—in other words, Mexican fast food. Typical *antojitos* include tamales, enchiladas, burritos, flautas, chiles rellenos, chalupas, *picadillo,* quesadillas, *tortas,* and tacos.

Visitors who identify these terms with dishes at Mexican restaurants in their home countries are sometimes confused by the different shapes and forms they may take in Mexico. Tacos can be rolled as well as folded, and enchiladas can be folded or stacked as well as rolled; shape is irrelevant. An enchilada (literally "chilied") is any *antojito* made with a tortilla dipped or cooked in a chili sauce; an *entomada* (or *entomatada*) is the equivalent made with tomatoes, while the *enfrijolada* is the same made with a thin bean sauce.

A taco is any type of plain tortilla surrounding other ingredients. In some eateries you can order tacos either *suave*—heated, soft tortillas stuffed with meat and vegetable fillings—or *dorado* (golden)—thin corn tortillas stuffed

---

ANTOJITOS

No trip to Cabo would be complete without a sampling of traditional Mexican fast-food dishes.

birria – lamb or goat stew in a sauce spiced with cinnamon, cloves, cumin, and oregano

burrito – a flour tortilla rolled around meat, beans, or seafood fillings; Baja's lobster burritos are legendary

chalupa – a crisp, whole tortilla topped with beans, meat, etc. (also known as a tostada)

chile relleno – a mild poblano chili stuffed with cheese, deep-fried in egg batter, and served with a ranchero sauce (tomatoes, onions, and chilies)

enchilada – a corn tortilla dipped in chili sauce, then folded or rolled around a filling of meat, chicken, seafood, or cheese and baked in an oven

enfrijolada – same as enchilada except dipped in a sauce of thinned refried beans instead of chili sauce

entomatada – same as enchilada except dipped in a tomato sauce instead of chili sauce

flauta – a small corn tortilla roll, usually stuffed with beef or chicken and fried

gordita – a small, thick, corn tortilla stuffed with a spicy meat mixture

huarache – literally, "sandal"; a large, flat, thick, oval-shaped tortilla topped with fried meat and chilies

menudo – a thick soup made with cows' feet and stomachs (and less commonly, intestines) and seasoned with *chiles de árbol,* oregano, and fresh chopped onion; reputedly a sure hangover cure

pozole – hominy stew made with pork or chicken and garnished with radishes, oregano, onions, chili powder, salt, and lime

picadillo – a spicy salad of chopped or ground meat with chilies and onions (also known as *salpicón*)

quesadilla – a flour tortilla folded over sliced cheese and grilled; ask the cook to add *chiles rajas* (pepper strips) for extra flavor

sope – a small, thick, round corn cake with dimpled edges, topped with a spicy meat mixture and crumbled cheese

taco – a corn tortilla folded or rolled around anything and eaten with the hands; *tacos de pescado,* or "fish tacos," are a Baja specialty

tamal – plural *tamales;* cornmeal (*masa*) dough wrapped in a corn husk and steamed; sometimes stuffed with corn, olives, pork, or turkey

torta – a sandwich made with a Mexican-style roll (*bolillo/birote* or the larger *pan telera*); one of the most popular is the *torta de milanesa,* made with breaded, deep-fried veal or pork

tightly with meat, then deep-fried whole and served with lettuce and grated cheese.

The main dish, or *el plato fuerte*, of any meal can be a grander version of an *antojito*, a regional specialty (*mole poblano*, for example), or something the *cocineros* (cooks) dream up themselves. Typical entrées are centered around meats, seafood, or poultry.

Meats

Common meats include *carne de res* (beef), *puerco* (pork), and *cabrito* (kid goat). *Jamón* (ham), chorizo (sausage), and *tocino* (bacon) are usually reserved for *almuerzo*. Steak may appear on menus as *bistec, bistek, biftec,* or "steak." *Venado* (deer meat or venison) and *conejo* (rabbit) are commonly served on ranchos. Poultry dishes include *pollo* (chicken), *pavo* (turkey), and, less frequently, *pato* (duck) and *codorniz* (quail).

Carnitas: This dish from the state of Michoacán belongs in a category all its own and is usually sold only at butcher shops or at restaurants specializing in it. The usual method for producing *carnitas* is to slowly braise an entire pig in a huge cauldron, along with a variety of flavorings that are a closely guarded secret among *carnitas* purveyors. The results are chopped into thin slices and eaten with stacks of tortillas, pickled vegetables and chilies, guacamole, and various salsas.

Carnitas are almost always sold by weight. You can order by the *kilo* (1 kg, about 2.2 lb), *medio* (half kilo), *cuarto* (quarter kilo), or sometimes in 100-gram increments (*cien gramos*). Figure on a quarter kilo (about a half pound) per hungry person and you won't have much left over. One of the best places to eat *carnitas* in all Baja is La Flor de Michoacán in Rosarito.

Seafood

Pescado (fish) entrées on the menu are often seasonal or dependent on the "catch of the day." Often just the word *pescado* and the method of cooking will appear (e.g., *pescado al mojo de ajo*). If you need to know exactly what kind of fish, just ask "*¿Hay qué tipo de pescado?*"—although in some cases the only response you get is something generic, like "*pescado blanco*" ("white

fish"). For specific fish names, see the sidebar *Fish Translators* in the *Los Cabos* chapter.

Baja's number-one seafood specialty is the *taco de pescado* (fish taco). If you've never tried one, you're most likely wondering "What's the big deal—a fish taco?" Eat one, though, and you're hooked for life. Short, tender, fresh fish fillets are dipped in batter and fried quickly, then folded into a steaming corn tortilla with a variety of condiments, including *salsa fresca* (chopped tomatoes, onions, chilies, and lime juice), marinated cabbage (similar to coleslaw in the United States), guacamole (a savory avocado paste), and sometimes a squirt of mayonnaise or *crema* (fresh Mexican cream). *¡La última!* Any kind of white-fleshed fish can be used—the best fish tacos are those made from yellowtail (*jurel*), halibut (*lenguado*), or mahimahi (*dorado*).

Shellfish dishes (*mariscos*) popular on Baja menus include *ostiones* (oysters), *almejas* (clams), *callos* (scallops), *jaibas* (small crabs), *cangrejos* (large crabs), *camarones* (shrimp), *langosta* (lobster), *langostina* (crayfish, also called *cucarachas*), and *abulón* (abalone). They can be ordered as *cocteles* (cocktails—steamed or boiled and served with lime and salsa), *en sus conchas* (in the shell), or in many other ways.

Beans

The beans (*frijoles*) preferred in Baja, as on the northern mainland, are pinto beans, usually dried beans boiled until soft, then mashed and fried with lard or vegetable oil (usually the former). Often this preparation is called *frijoles refritos* (refried beans), although they're not really refried except when reheated. Sometimes the beans are served whole, in their own broth, as *frijoles de olla* (boiled beans), or with bits of roast pork as *frijoles a la charra* (ranch-style beans). Frijoles can be served with any meal of the day, including breakfast.

Cheese

Even the most remote rancho usually has some cheese (*queso*) around, so if your appetite isn't stimulated by the *iguana guisada* simmering on the hearth, you can usually ask for chiles rellenos (mild poblano chilies stuffed with cheese and fried in an egg batter) or quesadillas (cheese melted in folded flour tortillas). A meal of beans, tortillas, and cheese provides a complete source of protein for travelers who choose to avoid meat, poultry, or seafood for health, economic, or moral reasons.

Among the most commonly used are *queso cotijo* (also called *queso añejo*), *queso chihuahuense* (called *queso menonita* in the state of Chihuahua), *queso manchego*, *queso oaxaqueño*, and *queso asadero*.

Queso menonita or *queso chihuahuense* (Mennonite or Chihuahuan cheese) is a mild, white cheddar produced in wheels by Mennonite colonists in Chihuahua and Durango. Spanish import (though also made in Mexico) *queso manchego* is similar but usually softer. *Queso asadero* (griller cheese) is a braided cheese somewhat similar to Armenian string cheese, made by combining sour milk with fresh milk. *Chihuahuense* is a common ingredient in dishes stuffed with cheese, such as enchiladas or chiles rellenos, which won't receive high, direct heat. *Asadero* melts well at high temperatures, without burning or separating, and as such is well suited to *chile con queso* (hot, blended chili-cheese dip), *queso fundido* (hot melted cheese topped with chorizo or mushrooms), and other dishes in which the cheese is directly exposed to high heat. *Queso oaxaqueño*, also called *quesillo*, is a lump-style cheese similar to *asadero* but a little softer—close to mozzarella. It's popular in *tortas*, or Mexican-style sandwiches.

Cotijo or *añejo* is a crumbly aged cheese that resists melting and is commonly used as a topping for enchiladas and beans; the flavor and texture is somewhat like a cross between feta and Parmesan.

Many ranchos produce their own *queso fresco* (fresh cheese) from raw cow's, goat's, or sheep's milk. To make *queso fresco*, the rancheros first cure the milk with homemade rennet (from a calf's fourth stomach) until the milk separates, then press the curds with weights (sometimes under flat rocks lined with cloth) to remove excess moisture. In more elaborate operations, the initial pressing is then ground up and repressed into small round cakes. If you want to buy some *queso fresco*, look for Hay Queso signs as you pass ranchos. If you're fortunate, you might even come across *panela*, an extra-rich cheese made from heavy cream.

Vegetables and Vegetarian Food

Although vegetables are sometimes served as side dishes with *comidas corridas*, with restaurant entrées, or in salads *(ensaladas)*, they're seldom listed separately on the menu. When they do appear on menus, it's usually at restaurants in towns near farming areas in northern Baja or else in the La Paz–Los Cabos area, where many vegetables come over by boat from the mainland. The best place to add vegetables to your diet is at a market or grocery store.

It's difficult but not impossible to practice a vegetarian regime in Baja. Vegetarians can eat quesadillas (ask for corn tortillas, which unlike most flour tortillas do not contain lard) or *enchiladas de queso* (cheese enchiladas). With some luck, you'll stumble across restaurants that can prepare a variety of interesting cheese dishes, including *queso fundido con champiñones* (melted cheese with mushrooms, eaten with tortillas) and quesadillas made with *flor de calabeza* (squash flower). Some places make beans without lard *(sin manteca)*, but you'll have to ask to find out. Many larger towns have at least one vegetarian/health food store (usually called *tienda naturista*) with a small dining section as well as bulk foods.

Vegans, for the most part, will do best to prepare their own food. Look for shops with signs reading *semillas* (seeds) to pin down a good selection of nuts and dried beans. You'll find plenty of fresh fruits and vegetables in markets and grocery stores.

Soup

The general menu term for soup is *sopa*, although a thick soup with lots of ingredients is usually a *caldo* or *caldillo*. *Menudo* is a soup of hominy *(nixtamal)* and cow's feet and stomach (or, less commonly, intestine) in a savory, reddish-brown broth, served with chopped onions, chilies, and crumbled oregano. It's seen throughout Mexico and is highly prized as a hangover remedy. *Pozole* is a similar soup with a much lighter-colored broth; some varieties of *pozole* are made with chicken instead of tripe.

Other tasty soups include *sopa de tortillas, sopa azteca,* and *sopa tlapeño,* all variations of artfully seasoned chicken broth garnished with *totopos* (tortilla wedges) and sliced avocado.

Bread and *Pan Dulce*

Bread *(pan)* arrived in Mexico not with the Spanish but during the brief era of French rule in the late 19th century. The most common bread is the *bolillo* (little ball), a small torpedo-shaped roll, usually rather hard on the outside. *Pan telera* ("scissor bread," so named for the two clefts on top) rolls resemble *bolillos* but are larger and flatter; they're mainly used for making *tortas,* the ubiquitous Mexican sandwich. *Pan de barra,* American-style sliced bread, is also occasionally available but never measures up to crusty *bolillos* or *teleras.*

Sweetened breads or pastries are known as *pan dulce* (sweet bread). Common *pan dulce* varieties include *buñuelos* (crisp, round, flat pastries fried and coated with cinnamon sugar), *campechanas* (flaky, sugar-glazed puff pastries), *canastas* (thick, round, fruit-filled cookies), *capirotada* (bread pudding), *cortadillos* (cake squares topped with jelly and finely shredded coconut), *cuernitos* (small crescent rolls rolled in cinnamon sugar), *galletas* (cookies), *palmitas* (flat, fan-shaped, crispy pastries), *pan de huevos* (spongy yeast bread with patterned sugar toppings), and *polvorones* (small shortbread cookies).

Salsas and Condiments

Any restaurant, café, taquería, *lonchería,* or *comedor* offers a variety of salsas. Sometimes only certain salsas are served with certain dishes, while at other times one, two, or even three salsas are stationed on every table. Often each place has its own unique salsa recipes—canned or bottled salsas are rarely used. The one ingredient common to all salsas is chili peppers, though these vary in heat from mild to incendiary.

There are as many types of salsas as there are Mexican dishes—red, green, yellow, brown, hot, mild, salty, sweet, thick, thin, blended,

and chunky. The most typical is the *salsa casera* (house salsa), a simple, fresh concoction of chopped chilies, onions, and tomatoes mixed with salt, lime juice, and cilantro. This is what you usually get with the complimentary basket of *totopos* (tortilla chips) served at the beginning of every Mexican meal. Another common offering is *salsa verde* (green sauce), made with a base of tomatillos (small, tart, green, tomato-like vegetables). Some salsas are *picante,* or spicy hot (also *picosa*), so it's always a good idea to test a bit before pouring the stuff over everything on your plate.

Whole pickled chilies are sometimes served on the side as a condiment, especially with tacos and *carnitas.* Salt *(sal)* is usually on the table, although it's rarely needed since Mexican dishes tend to be prepared with plenty of it. Black pepper is *pimiento negro,* and if it's not on the table it's normally available for the asking. Butter is *mantequilla,* sometimes served with flour tortillas.

In taquerías, guacamole (mashed avocado blended with onions, chilies, salt, and sometimes other ingredients) is always served as a condiment. In restaurants it may be served as a salad or with tortilla chips.

Desserts and Sweets

The most popular of Mexican desserts, or *postres,* is a delicious egg custard called flan. It's listed on virtually every tourist restaurant menu, along with *helado* (ice cream). Other sweet alternatives include pastries found in *panaderías* (bakeries) and the frosty offerings at the ubiquitous *paleterías.* Strictly speaking, a *paletería* serves only *paletas,* flavored ice on sticks (like American popsicles but with a much wider range of flavors), but many also serve *nieve,* literally "snow," which is flavored grated ice served like ice cream in bowls or cones.

Another common street vendor food is *churros,* sweet fried pastries something like donut sticks sprinkled with sugar. One of the best places to sample *churros* is at La Bufadora at Punta Banda, just south of Ensenada. Nowhere else in Baja will you find so many *churro* vendors in one place.

Dulcerías, or candy shops, sell a huge variety of sticky Mexican sweets, usually wrapped individually. Often brightly decorated, *dulcerías* are oriented toward children and sometimes carry inexpensive toys as well as sweets. The larger ones sell piñatas, colorful papier-mâché figures filled with candy and small gifts and hung at parties (where children are allowed to break them with sticks, releasing all the goodies inside). Traditionally, piñatas are crafted to resemble common animals, but these days you'll see all kinds of shapes, including Pokémon, Santa Claus, and Batman.

Fruits

A large variety of delicious fruits are available in local markets and grocery stores. Most common are mango *(mango),* banana *(plátano),* guava *(guayaba),* papaya *(papaya),* grapes *(uvas),* pineapple *(piña),* and apple *(manzana),* but you may occasionally see more exotic fruits from the mainland.

BUYING GROCERIES

The cheapest way to feed yourself while traveling in Baja is the same way you save money at home: Buy groceries at the store and prepare meals on your own. Even the smallest towns in Baja have a little grocery store or corner market. A ripe avocado, a chunk of *queso fresco,* and a couple of *bolillos* can make a fine, easy-to-fix meal.

The humblest type of store is the small family-owned *tienda de abarrotes,* usually recognizable by the single word *abarrotes* (groceries) printed somewhere on the outside *(tienda* means "store"). These stock the basics—tortillas, dried beans, flour, herbs and spices, bottled water, a few vegetables, possibly *bolillos* and *queso fresco*—as well as limited household goods like soap and laundry detergent. As at convenience stores back home, the food at the average *tienda de abarrotes* is not particularly inexpensive. Cheaper, when you can find them, are government-sponsored Diconsa (Distribuidora Conasupo), *tienda rural,* and ISSSTE (Instituto de Seguridad y Servicios Sociales para Trabajadores del Estado) markets.

Privately run supermarkets are found in larger towns. Like their American counterparts, they're usually well stocked with a wide variety of meats, baked goods, vegetables, household goods, and beer and liquor. Supermarket prices are often lower than those of smaller grocery stores.

Several towns and cities in Baja feature *mercados municipales* (municipal markets), large warehouse-type structures where meat, fruit, and vegetable producers sell their goods directly to the public. Prices are often good at these markets, but it helps if you know how to bargain.

Another common *tienda* is the *ultramarinos,* which is primarily a place to buy beer and liquor, along with a few food items.

Panaderías

Although you can often buy a few bakery items at the aforementioned stores, the best place to buy them is at their source—a *panadería* (literally, "breadery," i.e., bakery). Many of the *panaderías* in Baja still use wood-fired *hornos* (ovens), which make the *bolillos* (Mexican rolls), *pasteles* (cakes), and *pan dulce* (cookies and sweet pastries) especially tasty. *Pan de barra,* American-style sliced bread, is also occasionally available. To select bakery items from the shelves of a *panadería,* simply imitate the other customers—pick up a pair of tongs and a tray from the counter near the cash register and help yourself, cafeteria-style.

Tortillerías

Unless you make them yourself, the best tortillas are found where they make them fresh every day. The automated process at a *tortillería* uses giant electric grinders and conveyor belts to transform whole corn into fresh tortillas, which you purchase by weight, not number. A kilo yields about 40 average, 12-centimeter (5-in) tortillas; you may be able to order by the *cuarto* or *medio* (quarter or half kilo). The government-subsidized prices are low. Restaurants, *tiendas,* and home cooks purchase tortillas from the local *tortillería* to avoid spending hours at a *metate* (grinder) and *comal* (griddle).

THE LIQUID HEART OF MEXICO

Tequila is a pallid flame that passes through walls and soars over tile roofs to allay despair.

Álvaro Mútis, *Tequila: Panegyric and Emblem*

Mexico's national drink has been in production, in prototypical form, since at least the time of the Aztecs. The Aztecs, in fact, called themselves Mexicas in direct reference to the special spiritual role mescal – tequila's forerunner – played in their culture via Mextli, the god of agave (the desert plant from which *pulque*, mescal, and tequila are derived). These names, as interpreted by the Spanish, eventually yielded "Mexico."

The Spaniards levied a tax on tequila as early as 1608, and in 1795, King Carlos IV granted the first legal concession to produce tequila to Don José María Guadalupe Cuervo. The liquor's name was taken from the Ticuila Amerindians of Jalisco, who mastered baking the heart of the *Agave tequiliana weber*, or blue agave, and extracting its juice, a process employed by tequila distilleries today. Native to Jalisco, this succulent is the only agave that produces true tequila as certified by the Mexican government. Contrary to the myth that all true tequila must come from Tequila, Jalisco, Mexican law enumerates specific districts in five Mexican states where tequila may be legally produced, including as far away as Tamaulipas on the U.S.-Mexico border.

All liquors labeled "tequila" must contain at least 51 percent blue agave distillates. Sugarcane juice or extracts from other agaves usually make up the rest. Many tequila aficionados will caution you to look for the initials NOM – for Norma Oficial Mexicana – on the label to be sure it's "real" tequila, but we've never seen a bottle of tequila sold in Mexico that didn't bear those letters.

Despite the fact that tequila sales are booming today, much of the tequila-making process is still carried out *a mano* (by hand). In the traditional method, the mature heart of the tequila agave, which looks like a huge pineapple and weighs 18-56 kilograms (50-150 lbs), is roasted in pits for 24 hours, then shredded and ground by mule- or horse-powered mills. After the juice is extracted from the pulp and fermented in ceramic pots, it's distilled in copper stills to produce the basic tequila, which is always clear and colorless, with an alcohol content of 38-40 percent.

True "gold" tequilas are produced by aging the tequila in imported oak barrels to achieve a slightly mellowed flavor. The *reposado*, or "rested," type is oak-aged for at least two months, while *añejo*, or "aged," tequila must stay in barrels at least a year. Inferior "gold" tequilas may be nothing more than the silver stuff mixed with caramel coloring – always look for *reposado* or *añejo* on the label if you want the true gold.

José Cuervo, Sauza, and Herradura are well-established, inexpensive to medium-priced tequila labels with international notoriety. Of these three, Herradura is said to employ the most traditional methods; tequila connoisseurs generally prefer it over the other two. In 1983 Chinaco, based in the state of Tamaulipas, became the first label to produce a tequila made from 100 percent blue agave, a formula now considered standard for all high-end tequilas. Many tasters claim a label called Reserva del Patrón (sold simply as "Patrón" north of the Mexican border)

NONALCOHOLIC BEVERAGES
Water

Bottled drinking water is usually available at every *tienda de abarrotes* or supermarket throughout Baja. If you're car camping, renting a house, or staying in one place for a long time, it may be more convenient to use the 20-liter (roughly five-gallon) reusable plastic containers called *garafónes* available in most Mexican towns. These typically cost around US$6 for the first bottle of water and bottle deposit, then US$1.60 for each 20-liter refill. This is much cheaper than buying individual liter or half-liter bottles, which can cost as much as US$2 apiece, and you won't be throwing away

is the finest and smoothest tequila tipple of them all. Other very fine *tequilas reposadas* include Don Eduardo, Ecuario Gonzales, La Perseverancia, Don Felipe, and our personal favorite for flavor and price, Las Trancas. To emphasize the limited production nature of these private reserve distillations, these brands are usually sold in numbered bottles with fancy labels. Less expensive but also very good are the Jimador, Centenario, and Orendain labels. As with wine, it's all a matter of personal preference; try a few *probaditos* ("little tastes," or shots) for yourself to determine which brand best tickles your palate. The fancier tequilas may be served in brandy snifters instead of the traditional tall, narrow shot glass *(caballito)*.

MESCAL AND THE WORM

The distillate of other agave plants – also known as magueys or century plants – is called mescal (sometimes spelled "mezcal"), not to be confused with the nondistilled mescal – *pulque* – prepared in pre-Hispanic Mexico. The same roasting and distilling process is used for today's mescal as for tequila. Actually, tequila is a mescal, but no drinker calls it that, just as no one in a United States bar orders "whiskey" when they mean to specify scotch or bourbon. Although many states in Mexico produce mescal, the best is often said to come from the state of Oaxaca.

The caterpillar-like grub, or *gusano de maguey* (maguey worm), floating at the bottom of a bottle of mescal lives on the maguey plant itself. They're safe to eat – just about anything pickled in mescal would be – but not particularly appetizing. By the time you hit the bottom of the bottle, though, who cares? Maguey worms are often fried and eaten with fresh corn tortillas and salsa – a delicious appetizer.

TEQUILA DRINKS

The usual way to drink tequila is straight up, followed by a water or beer chaser. Licking a few grains of salt before taking a shot and sucking a lime wedge afterward make it go down smoother. The salt raises a protective coating of saliva on the tongue while the lime juice scours the tongue of salt and tequila residues.

Tequila con sangrita, in which a shot of tequila is chased with a shot of *sangrita* (not to be confused with *sangría*, the wine-and-fruit punch), is a slightly more elegant method of consumption. *Sangrita* is a bright red mix of orange juice, lime juice, grenadine, red chile powder, and salt.

An old tequila standby is the much-abused margarita, a tart Tex-Mex cocktail made with tequila, lime juice, and Cointreau (usually "Controy" or triple sec in Mexico) served in a salt-rimmed glass. A true margarita is shaken and served on the rocks (crushed or blended ice tends to kill the flavor) or strained, but just about every other gringo in Baja seems to drink "frozen" margaritas, in which the ice is mixed in a blender with the other ingredients.

If you detect a noticeable difference between the taste of margaritas north or south of the border, it may be because bartenders in the United States and Canada tend to use bigger and less flavorful Persian limes *(Citrus latifolia)*, while in Mexico they use the smaller, sweeter key or Mexican lime *(Citrus aurantifolia swingle)*. A "Baja margarita" substitutes Baja's own damiana liqueur for the triple sec. The damiana herb is said to be an aphrodisiac.

---

so much plastic. The water will be easier to dispense if you also buy a *sifón* (siphon) designed for that purpose. These are available for around US$2.50 at many grocery stores.

The water and ice served in restaurants in Baja is always purified—it's not necessary to order *agua mineral* (mineral water) unless you need the minerals. Likewise, the water used as an ingredient in "handmade" drinks, e.g., *licuados* or *aguas frescas,* also comes from purified sources.

Soft Drinks

Licuados are similar to American "smoothies"—fruit blended with water, ice, honey or sugar, and sometimes milk or raw eggs to produce something like a fruit shake. In Baja, *tuna* (not the fish but the fruit of the prickly pear cactus) *licuados* are particularly delicious. Any place that makes *licuados* will also make orange juice *(jugo de naranja)*. Orange juice is popular in Baja; you'll often see street vendors who sell nothing but fresh-squeezed OJ.

Aguas frescas are colorful beverages sold from huge glass jars on the streets of larger cities or at carnivals, usually during warm weather. They're made by boiling the pulp of various fruits, grains, or seeds with water, then straining it and adding sugar and large chunks of ice. *Arroz* (rice) and *horchata* (melon-seed), both usually spiced with cinnamon and vanilla, are two of the tastiest *aguas*.

American soft drinks *(refrescos)* such as 7UP, Coke, and Pepsi are common; their Mexican equivalents are just as good. An apple-flavored soft drink called Manzanita is popular.

Hot Drinks

Coffee is served in a variety of ways. The best, when you can find it, is traditional Mexican-style coffee (ranchos sometimes serve it), which is made by filtering near-boiling water through fine-ground coffee in a slender cloth sack. Instant coffee *(nescafé)* is often served at small restaurants and cafés; a jar of instant coffee may be sitting on the table for you to add to hot water. When there's a choice, a request for *café de olla* (pot coffee) should bring you real brewed coffee. When you order coffee in a Mexican restaurant, some servers will ask *"¿de grano o de agua?"* (literally "grain or water?"), meaning "brewed or instant?" One of the better Mexican brands found in supermarkets is Café Combate. If you'd like a darker roast than normally available, buy a bag of green coffee beans (available at most supermarkets) and roast your own in a dry iron skillet.

Café con leche is the Mexican version of café au lait, i.e., coffee and hot milk mixed in near-equal proportions. *Café con crema* (coffee with cream) is not as available; when it is, it usually means a cup of coffee with a packet of non-dairy creamer on the side.

Hot chocolate *(chocolate)* is fairly common on Baja menus. It's usually served sweet and may contain cinnamon, ground almonds, and other flavorings. A thicker version made with cornmeal—almost a chocolate pudding—is called *champurrado* or *atole*.

Black tea *(té negro)* is not popular among *bajacalifornianos,* although you may see it on tourist menus. Ask for *té helado* or *té frío* if you want iced tea. At home many Mexicans drink *té de manzanilla* (chamomile tea), *té de yerba buena* (mint tea), or *té de canela* (cinnamon tea) in the evenings.

ALCOHOLIC BEVERAGES

Drinking laws in Mexico are quite minimal. The legal drinking age in Mexico is 18 years. It's illegal to carry open containers of alcoholic beverages in a vehicle. Booze of every kind is widely available in bars, restaurants, grocery stores, and *licorerías* (liquor stores). *Borracho* means both "drunk" (as an adjective) and "drunkard."

Cerveza

The most popular and available beer brand in northern Baja is Tecate, brewed in Tecate, while in the south it's Pacífico, from Mazatlán, just across the Sea of Cortez from Cabo San Lucas. Both are good-tasting, light- to medium-weight brews, with Tecate holding a slight edge (more hops) over Pacífico. You can't compare either of these with their export equivalents in the United States, because Mexican breweries produce separate brews for American consumption that are lighter in taste and lower in alcohol content. It's always better in Mexico.

Other major Mexican brands such as Corona Extra (the number-one-selling beer in mainland Mexico and number-one-selling imported beer in the United States), Dos Equis (XX), Superior, Carta Blanca, Bohemia, and Negra Modelo are available in tourist restaurants, but you'll notice the locals stick pretty

BAR LINGO

Do you want to order your margarita on the rocks? Wondering how to treat a hangover? Use this cheat-sheet to find your way around Baja's bar scene.

botanas – snacks
cantinero/cantinera – bartender
casco – empty bottle
cerveza – beer
envase, botella – bottle
con hielo – with ice
con sal – with salt
la cruda – hangover
lo mismo – the same
rocas – on the rocks
sin hielo – without ice
una copita, uno tragito – a drink
una mas – one more
una fría – a cold one
vaso, copa – glass

donnay, chenin blanc, pinot noir, barbera, zinfandel, nebbiolo, and tempranillo. These and other grapes are also blended to produce cheaper *vino tinto* (red wine) and *vino blanco* (white wine). Better vintages may be labeled *reserva privada* (private reserve). When ordering wine in Spanish at a bar, you may want to specify *vino de uva* (grape wine), as *vino* alone can refer to distilled liquors as well as wine. *Vino blanco,* in fact, can be interpreted as cheap tequila.

Two of the more reliable and reasonably priced labels are L. A. Cetto and Santo Tomás, both produced in northern Baja. Domecq also produces a good medium-priced series of wines under the Domecq XA label. Better but more expensive—and hard to find—are Baja California's Monte Xanic and Château Camou. Monte Xanic's Cabernet y Merlot is considered one of the finest wines ever produced in Mexico. Camou makes an excellent *coupage* of cabernet franc, cabernet sauvignon, and merlot, labeled Gran Vino de Château Camou.

much to Tecate and Pacífico, perhaps out of regional loyalty.

The cheapest sources for beer are the brewery's agents or distributors (look for signs saying Agencia, Subagencia, Cervecería, or Depósito), where you can return deposit bottles for cash or credit. You can buy beer by the bottle *(envase),* can *(bote),* six-pack *(canastilla),* or 20-bottle case *(cartón).* A *cartón* of Pacífico or Tecate costs US$11.50, not counting the refundable bottle deposit. Most Pacífico *agencias* also sell Corona Extra for the same price. Large, liter-size bottles are called *ballenas* (whales) or *caguamas* (sea turtles) and are quite popular. When buying beer at an *agencia* or *depósito,* specify *fría* if you want cold beer, otherwise you'll get beer *al tiempo* (at room temperature). Many *depósitos* offer free ice with the purchase of a case of beer.

Wine
Baja is one of Mexico's major wine-production areas, and Baja wines are commonly served in restaurants. A broad selection of varietals is available, including cabernet sauvignon, char-

Liquor
Tequila is Mexico's national drink and also the most popular distilled liquor in Baja. The second most popular is brandy, followed closely by *ron* (rum), both produced in Mexico for export as well as domestic consumption. A favorite rum drink in Baja is the *cuba libre* (free Cuba), called *cuba* for short—a mix of rum, Coke, and lime juice over ice. Similar is the *cuba de uva,* which substitutes brandy for rum. Other hard liquors—gin, vodka, scotch—may be available only at hotel bars and tourist restaurants.

CANTINAS AND BARS
Traditionally, a cantina is a Mexican-style drinking venue for males only, but in modern urban Mexico the distinction between a bar and a cantina is becoming increasingly blurred. Is Hussong's Cantina in Ensenada a true cantina? Plenty of women are present each evening holding their own with the best of the machos, yet among locals it still has the reputation of a place where "nice" Mexican girls don't go. On the other hand, La Cañada del Diablo in Todos Santos is a perfect example

of a *cantina familiar* (family cantina), where everyone is welcome.

A more typical Baja cantina is the kind of place you'll occasionally stumble upon in a small town—usually on the outskirts—where blinking Christmas lights festoon a *palapa* roof and palm-thatch or ocotillo walls. Inside are a few tables and chairs and a handful of *borrachos;* if any women are present, they're either serving the booze or serving as hired "dates." Unlike their counterparts in mainland Mexican cities, most Baja cantinas do not serve food. The only drink choices will be beer, Mexican brandy, and cheap tequila or *aguardiente*—moonshine. Often when you order tequila in a place like this, you'll be served a large glass of *aguardiente,* considered an acceptable substitute.

Bars, on the other hand, are found only in hotels and in the larger cities or resort areas, i.e., Tijuana, Mexicali, Ensenada, San Felipe, La Paz, San José del Cabo, and Cabo San Lucas. They've developed largely as social venues for tourists or for a younger generation of Mexicans for whom the cantina is passé. A bar, in contrast to a cantina, offers a variety of beer, wine, and distilled liquor. By Mexican standards, bars are considered upmarket places to hang out, so they aren't extremely popular—many young Mexicans would rather drink at a disco where they can dance, too.

Incidentally, a sign outside a bar reading Ladies Bar almost always means the bar provides ladies for male entertainment, not that it admits women, although it may.

Conduct and Customs

TIME AND APPOINTMENTS

Of the many stereotypes about Mexican culture, the one about the Mexican sense of time being highly flexible is probably the most accurate. The whys and wherefores are too numerous and complex for the context of this book; read Octavio Paz's *The Labyrinth of Solitude* for a glimpse of an explanation. However, it's important to realize that the so-called *mañana* attitude is a generalization; in many cases Mexican individuals are punctual—especially when it comes to doing business with Americans. Furthermore, *bajacalifornianos,* it is said, tend to be more punctual than their mainland counterparts.

If you make an appointment with a *bajacaliforniano* for dinner, a party, or some other social engagement, you should figure the actual meeting time will occur two hours later than verbally scheduled. As with business engagements, if the person involved has dealt frequently with Americans, this might not always be the case. Also, Mexicans will typically accept an invitation rather than say no, even if they don't plan to attend the scheduled event. This is because, within the Mexican social context, it is usually worse to refuse an invitation than to not show up. To avoid disappointment, prepare yourself for any of these scenarios.

When hiring a fishing boat or any sort of guide in Baja, you can expect a modicum of punctuality—most Mexicans in the tourist industry have adapted themselves to the expectations of gringo tourists. Again, note the difference between business and social appointments.

SIESTA

The stereotypical afternoon siesta, when everyone goes off to sleep for a couple of hours, is fast becoming history throughout Mexico. Nevertheless, a vestige of the siesta lingers in the hours kept by offices and small businesses, which are typically closed 2–4 P.M. or 3–5 P.M. The first hour is reserved for *comida,* the midday meal, while the second hour is for relaxing or taking care of personal business. This long lunch hour is usually offset by longer evening hours; most Mexican offices and businesses stay open until 7–8 P.M.

No matter what hours are posted for small businesses, the actual opening and closing times may vary with the whims of the propri-

WHAT'S A GRINGO?

The Latin-American Spanish word "gringo," reportedly a corruption of the Spanish word *greigo*, or "Greek," has different meanings in different parts of Latin America. In Argentina and Uruguay, for example, it is used to refer to anyone of Italian descent. In Mexico and Central America, it's almost always reserved for people of northern European descent, especially Canadians and Americans. In spite of everyday linguistic evidence to the contrary, many non-Spanish speakers insist that only Americans are gringos. The Mexicans, however, have a more precise epithet for Americans: *yanquis*, or "Yankees."

Is "gringo" a derogatory term? It can certainly be used that way. Most of the time, however, it's simply an unconscious racial identification of neutral value. Educated Mexicans tend not to use it; instead they typically say *norteamericano* or *americano* for Americans. Some Mexicans insist on the former even though the term is a slight to Canadians and Mexicans, who, after all, are North Americans, too. *Canadiense* is used for Canadians, *alemán* for Germans, and so forth. A more precise term for U.S. citizens is *estadounidense*.

etors. This is also true for tourist information offices. Banks, on the other hand, usually follow their posted hours to the minute.

MEAL TIMES

If you'll be meeting Mexican acquaintances for meals, whether at a restaurant or in their homes, be aware that customary eating times differ from those north of the border.

The first meal of the day, *desayuno* (breakfast), is usually taken at about the same time as the average American breakfast, say 6–8 A.M. Around 11 A.M., another breakfast/early lunch, called *almuerzo*, is sometimes eaten; on weekdays it's light, on weekends and holidays it may be more substantial. Around 2 or 3 P.M. comes the *comida*, the largest meal of the day. In small towns, workers often go home for this meal, not returning to the workplace until around 4 or 5 P.M.

After work, at anywhere from around 8 to 10 P.M., *la cena*, the final meal of the day, is eaten. *Cenas* are usually as light and informal as *desayunos*, so it's not often that guests are invited to a home for this meal. On weekends and holidays, the *cena* can become a grander occasion.

TERMS OF ADDRESS

Mexicans frequently use titles of respect when addressing one another. At a minimum, *señor* will do for men, *señora* for married women, and *señorita* for unmarried women or girls. When in doubt about a woman's marital status, *señorita* can be used.

Professional titles can also be used for variety and to show additional respect. *Maestro* (master) or *maestra* (mistress) are common and can be used to address skilled workers (cobblers, auto mechanics, seamstresses, etc.) and any teacher except those at secondary schools and colleges or universities (who are *profesores*).

College graduates are *licenciado* (men) or *licenciada* (women), while doctors are *doctor* or *doctora*. Some other professional titles include *arquitecto* (architect), *abogado* (attorney), *ingeniero* (engineer), and *químico* (chemist).

BODY LANGUAGE

Mexicans tend to use their arms and hands a lot during verbal communication. Learning to "read" the more common gestures can greatly enhance your comprehension of everyday conversations, even when you don't understand every word being spoken.

One of the more confusing gestures for Americans is the way Mexicans beckon to other persons by holding the hand out, palm down, and waving in a downward motion. This looks similar to a farewell gesture in the United States and Canada but means "come here" in Mexico. Holding the palm upward and crooking the fingers toward the body, the typical American gesture for "come here," is a vaguely obscene gesture in Mexico.

Extending the thumb and forefinger from a closed hand and holding them about a half-inch apart means "a little bit" in America but in Mexico usually means "just a moment" or "wait a minute," and is often accompanied by the utterance *"momentito"* or *"poquito."*

The wagging of an upright forefinger means "no" or "don't do that." This is a good gesture to use when children hanging around at stoplights or gasoline pumps begin wiping your windshield and you don't want them to. Don't overdo it, though—they only need to see a few seconds of the wagging finger—otherwise you'll look out of control.

Mexicans commonly greet one another with handshakes, which are used universally, including between the sexes and among children and adults. Mexican males who are friends will sometimes greet one another with an *abrazo* (embrace), and urban women may kiss one another on the left cheek. Foreigners should stick to the handshake until they establish more intimate relationships with *bajacalifornianos*. Handshakes are also used upon parting.

DRESS

Compared to their mainland counterparts, who tend to be more conservative, *bajaca-lifornianos* are relatively tolerant about the way visitors dress. Nonetheless, invisible lines exist that, out of respect for Mexican custom, shouldn't be crossed.

Number one is that beachwear is not considered suitable dress for town visits. Rosarito, Cabo San Lucas, and San Felipe are the most obvious exceptions to this general rule since during peak tourist seasons visitors outnumber residents in these towns, so the locals are used to gringo immodesty. In Ensenada, however, beachwear will result in indignant stares if you wander far from the Avenida López Mateos tourist strip. In La Paz and other Baja towns, you're disrespecting local custom if you wear a bathing suit anywhere other than the beaches.

Upon entering a church or chapel in Baja, men are expected to remove their hats. Many Mexican males will also remove their hats when passing in front of a church. More tradition-minded *bajacaliforniano* women will cover their heads when inside a church, but younger women usually don't and foreign females aren't expected to. Shorts, sleeveless shirts/blouses, sandals, and bare feet are considered improper dress (for both men and women) in churches, even for brief sightseeing visits.

Health and Safety

By and large, Baja California is a healthy place. Sanitation standards are relatively high compared to many other parts of Mexico, and the tap water quality in some areas is superior to that of many places in California. The visitor's main health concerns are not food or water sources but avoiding mishaps while driving, boating, diving, surfing, or otherwise enjoying Baja's great outdoor life. Health issues directly concerned with these activities are covered under the relevant sections in this book.

FOOD AND WATER

Visitors who use common sense will probably never come down with food- or water-related illnesses while traveling in Baja. The first rule is not to overdo it during the first few days of your trip—eat and drink in moderation. Shoveling down huge amounts of tasty, often heavy Mexican foods along with pitchers of margaritas or strong Mexican beer is liable to make anyone sick from pure overindulgence. If you're not used to the spices and different ways of cooking, it's best to ingest small amounts at first.

Second, take it easy with foods offered by street vendors, since this is where you're most likely to suffer from unsanitary conditions. Eat only foods that have been thoroughly cooked and are served either stove-hot or refrigerator-cold. Many gringos eat street food without any problems whatsoever, but it pays to be cautious, especially if it's your first time in Mexico. Concerned with the risk of cholera, the Baja California Sur state government in July 1992 banned the sale of ice cream and ceviche (raw seafood salad) by street vendors.

Doctors usually recommend you avoid eating peeled, raw fruits and vegetables in Baja. Once the peel has been removed, it is virtually impossible to disinfect produce. Unpeeled fruits and vegetables washed in purified water and dried with a clean cloth are usually okay. After all, plenty of Mexican fruit is consumed daily in Canada and the United States.

Hotels and restaurants serve only purified drinking water and ice, so there's no need to ask for mineral water or refuse ice. Tap water, however, should not be consumed except in hotels where the water system is purified (look for a notice over the washbasin in your room). Most grocery stores sell bottled purified water. Water purification tablets, iodine crystals, water filters, and the like aren't necessary for Baja travel unless you plan on backpacking.

Turista

People who've never traveled to a foreign country may undergo a period of adjustment to the new gastrointestinal flora that comes with new territory. There's really no way to avoid the differences wrought by sheer distance. Unfortunately, the adjustment is sometimes unpleasant.

Mexican doctors call gastrointestinal upset of this sort "turista," because it affects tourists but not the local population. The usual symptoms of turista—also known by the gringo tags "Montezuma's Revenge" and "the Aztec Two-Step"—are nausea and diarrhea, sometimes with stomach cramps and a low fever. Again, eating and drinking only in moderation will help prevent the worst of the symptoms, which rarely persist more than a day or two. And if it's any consolation, Mexicans often get sick the first time they go to the United States or Canada.

Many Mexico travelers swear by a **preventive regimen** of Pepto-Bismol begun the day before arrival in country. Opinions vary as to how much of the pink stuff is necessary to ward off or tame the foreign flora, but a person probably shouldn't exceed the recommended daily dose. Taper off after four days or so until you stop using it altogether.

Another regimen that seems to be effective is a daily tablet of 100-milligram doxycycline (sold as Vibramycin in the United States), a low-grade antibiotic that requires a prescription in most countries. It works by killing all the bacteria in your intestinal tract—including the ones that reside there naturally and help protect your bowels. It's available without a prescription in Mexican *farmacias,* but you should check with your doctor first to make sure you're not sensitive to it—some people have problems with sunlight while taking doxycycline. Consume with plenty of food and water. Some physicians believe when you stop taking the drug you're particularly susceptible to intestinal upset because there are no protective bacteria left to fight off infections.

Neither Pepto nor Vibramycin is recommended for travelers planning trips of three weeks or longer.

If you come down with a case of turista, the best thing to do is drink plenty of fluids. Adults should drink at least three liters a day, a child under 37 kilograms (80 lbs) at least a liter a day. Lay off tea, coffee, milk, fruit juices, and booze. Eat only bland foods—nothing spicy, fatty, or fried—and take it easy. Pepto-Bismol or similar pectin-based remedies usually help. Some people like to mask the symptoms with a strong over-the-counter medication like Imodium AD (loperamide is the active ingredient), but though this can be effective, it isn't a cure. Only time will cure traveler's diarrhea.

If the symptoms are unusually severe (especially if there's blood in the stools or a high fever) or persist more than one or two days, see a doctor. Most hotels can arrange a doctor's visit, or you can contact a Mexican tourist office, U.S. consulate, or Canadian consulate for recommendations.

SUNBURN AND DEHYDRATION

Sunburn probably afflicts more Baja visitors than all other illnesses and injuries combined. The sunlight in Baja can be exceptionally strong, especially in the center of the peninsula and along the Sea of Cortez coast. For outdoor forays, sun protection is a must, whatever the activity. The longer you're in the sun, the more protection you'll need.

A hat, sunglasses, and plenty of sunscreen or sunblock make a good start. Bring along a sunscreen with a sun protection factor (SPF) of at least 25, even if you don't plan on using it all the time. Apply it to *all* exposed parts of your body—don't forget the hands, top of the feet, and neck. Men should remember to cover thinned-out or bald areas on the scalp. Sunscreen must be reapplied after swimming or after periods of heavy perspiration.

If you're going boating, don't leave shore with just a bathing suit. Bring along an opaque shirt—preferably with long sleeves—and a pair of long pants. Since you can never know for certain whether your boat might get stranded or lost at sea for a period of time (if, for example, the motor conks out and you get caught in an offshore current), you shouldn't be without extra clothing for emergencies.

It's also important to drink plenty of water or nonalcoholic, noncaffeinated fluids to avoid dehydration. Alcohol and caffeine—including the caffeine in iced tea and cola—increase your potential for dehydration. Symptoms of dehydration include darker-than-usual urine or inability to urinate, flushed face, profuse sweating or an unusual lack thereof, and sometimes headache, dizziness, and general feeling of malaise. Extreme cases of dehydration can lead to heat exhaustion or even heatstroke, in which the victim may become delirious or convulse. If either condition is suspected, get the victim out of the sun immediately, cover with a wet sheet or towel, and administer a rehydration fluid that replaces lost water and salts. If you can get the victim to a doctor, all the better—heatstroke can be serious.

If Gatorade ·or a similar **rehydration fluid** isn't available, you can mix your own by combining the following ingredients: one liter purified water or diluted fruit juice; two tablespoons sugar or honey; one-quarter teaspoon salt; and one-quarter teaspoon baking soda. If soda isn't available, use another quarter teaspoon salt. The victim should drink this mixture at regular intervals until symptoms subside substantially. Four or more liters may be necessary in moderate cases, more in severe cases.

MOTION SICKNESS

Visitors with little or no boating experience who join fishing cruises in Baja, especially on the Pacific side, sometimes experience motion sickness caused by the movement of a boat over ocean swells. The repeated pitching and rolling affects a person's sense of equilibrium to the point of nausea. *Mareo* (seasickness) can be a unpleasant experience not only for those green at the gills but for fellow passengers anxious lest the victim spew on them.

The best way to prevent motion sickness is to take one of the preventives commonly available from a pharmacist: promethazine (sold as Phenergan in the United States), dimenhydrinate (Dramamine), or scopolamine (Transderm Scop). The latter is available as an adhesive patch worn behind the ear—the time-release action is allegedly more effective than tablets. These medications should be consumed *before* boarding the vessel, not after the onset of symptoms. It's also not a good idea to eat a large meal before getting on a boat.

If you start to feel seasick while out on the bounding main, certain actions can lessen the likelihood that it will get worse. First, do not lie down. Often the first symptom of motion sickness is drowsiness, and if you give in to the impulse you'll almost certainly guarantee a worsening of the condition. Second, stay in the open air rather than below deck—fresh air usually helps. Finally, fix your gaze on the horizon; this helps steady your disturbed inner ear, the proximate cause of motion sickness.

BITES AND STINGS
Mosquitoes and Jejenes

Mosquitoes breed in standing water. Since standing water isn't that common in arid Baja, neither are mosquitoes. Exceptions include palm oases, estuaries, and marshes when there isn't a strong breeze around to keep mosquitoes at bay. The easiest way to avoid mosquito bites is to apply insect repellent to exposed areas of the skin and clothing whenever the mossies are out and biting. For most species, this means between dusk and dawn.

The most effective repellents are those containing a high concentration of DEET (N,N-diethyl-metatoluamide). People with an aversion to applying synthetics to the skin can try citronella (lemongrass oil), which is also effective but requires more frequent application.

More common in Baja than mosquitoes are *jejenes*, tiny flying insects known as "no-see-ums" among Americans—you almost never see them while they're biting. The same repellents effective for mosquitoes usually do the trick with *jejenes*.

For relief from the itchiness of mosquito bites, try rubbing a bit of hand soap on the affected areas. For some people this works, for others it doesn't do a thing. Andantol, available in many Mexican pharmacies, is a German-made cream that relieves itchy insect bites. *Jejene* bites usually stop itching in less than 10 minutes if you refrain from scratching them. Excessive scratching of either type of bite can lead to infection, so be mindful of what your fingers are up to.

In spite of the presence of the occasional mosquito, the U.S. Centers for Disease Control has declared all of Baja California malaria-free.

Wasps, Bees, and Hornets

Although stings from these flying insects can be painful, they aren't of mortal danger to most people. If you're allergic to such stings and plan to travel in remote areas of Baja, consider obtaining antiallergy medication from your doctor before leaving home. At the very least, carry a supply of Benadryl or similar over-the-counter antihistamine. Dramamine

(dimenhydrinate) also usually helps mitigate allergic reactions.

For relief from a wasp/bee/hornet sting, apply a paste of baking soda and water to the affected area. Liquids containing ammonia, including urine, also help relieve pain. If a stinger is visible, remove it—by scraping if possible, or with tweezers—before applying any remedies. If a stung limb becomes unusually swollen or if the victim exhibits symptoms of a severe allergic reaction—difficulty breathing, agitation, hives—seek medical assistance.

Ticks

If you find a tick embedded in your skin, don't try to pull it out—this may leave the head and pincers under your skin and lead to infection. Covering the tick with petroleum jelly, mineral oil, gasoline, kerosene, or alcohol usually causes the tick to release its hold to avoid suffocation.

Burning the tick with a cigarette butt or hot match usually succeeds only in killing it—when you pull it out, the head and pincers may not come with it. Stick with the suffocation method, and if the beast still doesn't come out, use tweezers.

Scorpions

The venom of the scorpion *(alacrán)* varies in strength from individual to individual and species to species, but the sting is rarely dangerous to adults. It can be painful, however, resulting in partial numbness and swelling that lasts several days. In Baja, the small yellow scorpions inflict more-painful stings than the larger, dark-colored ones.

The best treatment begins with persuading the victim to lie down and relax to slow the spread of the venom. Keep the affected area below the level of the heart. Ice packs on the sting may relieve pain and mitigate swelling; aspirin also helps.

Children who weigh less than about 13 kilograms (30 lbs) should receive medical attention if stung by a scorpion. Doctors in Baja usually have ready access to scorpion antivenin

SNAKEBITE PREVENTION AND TREATMENT

The overall risk of being bitten by a rattlesnake while hiking in Baja California is quite low, mainly because the snake avoids contact with all large mammals, including humans. Most of the unfortunate few who are bitten by snakes in Baja are local ranchers who spend a great deal of time in snake habitats, or small children who may not know to retreat from a coiled rattler.

Nonetheless, anyone spending time in the Baja outback, including campers and hikers, should follow a few simple precautions.

PREVENTION

First of all, use caution when placing hands or feet in areas where snakes may lie. These include rocky ledges, holes, and fallen logs. Always look first, and if you must move a rock or log, use a long stick or other instrument. Wear sturdy footwear when walking in possible snake habitat; high-top leather shoes or boots are best. Rancheros wear thick leather leggings called *polainas* when working in known snake territory; these are sometimes sold at *zapaterías* (shoe stores) or leather and saddle shops.

Most snakes strike only when threatened. Naturally, if you step on or next to a snake, it's likely to strike. If you see or hear a rattlesnake, remain still until the snake moves away. If it doesn't leave, simply back away slowly and cautiously. Sudden movements may cause a snake to strike; rattlers rarely strike a stationary target. A rattler can't strike a target that is farther away than three-fourths of its body length; use this rough measure to judge when it may be safe to move away. Leave plenty of room for error.

Don't attempt to kill a rattler unless you have a genuine need to use it as food (or unless you've been bitten; see below). As nasty as they may seem, snakes are as important to the desert ecosystem as the most beautiful flowering cactus.

TREATMENT

When bitten by a rattler or other poisonous snake, it's important to remain calm in order to slow the spread of venom, and to follow the necessary steps for treatment in a cool-headed manner. Don't panic – remember that few rattlesnake bites are fatal, even when untreated.

First, immediately following the bite, try to identify the snake. At the very least, memorize the markings and physical characteristics so a physician can administer the most appropriate antivenin. If you can kill the snake and bring it to the nearest treatment center, do it. Just

---

(anti-alacrán), but it should be administered only under qualified medical supervision.

Scorpions prefer damp, dark, warm places—dead brush, rock piles, fallen logs—so exercise particular caution when placing your hands in or near such areas. Hands are the scorpion's most common targets on the human body; campers should wear gloves when handling firewood in Baja.

Other favorite spots for scorpions are crumpled clothing and bedding. In desert areas of Baja, always check your bed sheets or sleeping bag for scorpions before climbing in. In the same environments, shake out your shoes and clothing before putting them on. Lots of palm trees around a house or hotel mean there's a

good chance scorpions will find their way to your room—they're nonaggressive creatures, so just keep an eye out for them.

Poisonous Sea Creatures

Various marine animals can inflict painful stings on humans. In Baja, such creatures include jellyfish, Portuguese men-of-war, cone shells, stingrays, sea urchins, and various fish with poisonous spines.

The best way to avoid jellyfish and Portuguese men-of-war is to scope out the water and the beach before going in—if you see any nasties floating around or washed up on the sand, try another beach. You can avoid stingrays by shuffling your feet in the sand as you walk in

remember that this could expose you or your fellow hikers to the risk of another bite.

Second, examine the bite for teeth marks. A successful bite by a poisonous pit viper will leave one or two large fang punctures in addition to smaller teeth marks; a bite by a nonpoisonous snake will not feature fang punctures. In general, nonpoisonous bites cause relatively small, shallow marks or scratches.

If you suspect the snake inflicting the bite was poisonous, immobilize the affected limb and wrap it tightly in an elastic bandage. This slows the spread of venom through the lymph system and mitigates swelling. Be careful that the bandage isn't wrapped so tightly that it cuts off circulation – you should be able to insert a finger under it without difficulty. Keep the limb below the level of the heart. Avoid all physical activity, since increased circulation accelerates the absorption of the venom. For this same reason, avoid aspirin, sedatives, and alcohol. Do not apply cold therapy – ice packs, cold compresses, and so on – to the bite area or to any other part of the victim's body. The old "slice and suck" method of snakebite treatment has likewise been discredited.

Get the victim to a hospital or physician if possible. Where feasible, carry the victim to restrict physical exertion. Even when wrapping the limb appears successful in preventing symptoms, the bite needs medical attention, and a physician may decide antivenin treatment is necessary. The general all-inclusive Spanish terms for snake are *serpiente* and *culebra*. A rattlesnake is *un serpiente de cascabel* or simply *un cascabel*.

It's possible for a poisonous snake to bite without injecting any venom; up to 20 percent of all reported bites are "dry bites."

Snakebite victims who require antivenin treatment usually receive the broad-spectrum North American Antisnakebite Serum for pit viper poisoning, which is available only in larger cities like Tijuana, Mexicali, La Paz, and Cabo San Lucas. Your home physician may be able to provide a prescription for the serum in advance of your trip if convinced you'll visit areas where antivenin is unavailable or medical treatment inaccessible.

In cases where it's been determined a bite is venomous and serum unavailable, the best you can do is follow the treatment outlined above and keep the victim immobile and cool until the symptoms – pain in the affected limb, abdominal cramps, headache – have subsided. For some bites, wrapping the limb in an elastic bandage will avoid all or most of the worst symptoms. The victim should drink plenty of water.

shallow surf, which usually causes rays resting in the sand to swim away.

To avoid cone shell and sea urchin stings, wear shoes in the water; several sport shoe manufacturers now produce specialized water shoes, e.g., Nike's Aqua Socks. You can also often spot cones and urchins in clear water, especially when wearing a diving mask. Anglers should take care when handling landed fish to avoid poisonous spines.

The treatment for stings from all of the above is the same: remove all tentacles, barbs, or spines from the affected area; wash the area with rubbing alcohol or diluted ammonia (urine will do in a pinch) to remove as much venom as possible; and wrap the area in cloth to reduce the flow of oxygen to the wound until pain subsides. If an acute allergic reaction occurs, get the victim to a doctor or clinic as quickly as possible.

Painful stingray wounds may require the famous hot-water treatment. If pain persists after thoroughly cleaning the wound, soak the affected limb in the hottest water the victim can stand. Continue soaking till the pain subsides—this can sometimes take up to an hour. The local folk remedy in Baja is to treat the wound with the sap of the *garambullo* cactus, often available from *botánicas* if not from a nearby patch of desert. Some stingray wounds may require medical treatment, even stitches.

MEDICAL ASSISTANCE

The quality of basic medical treatment, including dentistry, is relatively high in Baja's cities and larger towns; ask at a tourist office or at your consulate for recommendations. Hospitals can be found in Tijuana, Mexicali, Ensenada, Guerrero Negro, Ciudad Constitución, San José del Cabo, and La Paz; there are public IMSS clinics or Red Cross (Cruz Roja) stations in nearly every other town. In many areas the Red Cross can be reached by dialing 066 (toll-free) from any pay phone.

Emergency Evacuation

Over the years, several American companies have offered emergency 24-hour airlift service (accompanied by licensed physicians and nurses) from anywhere in Mexico to U.S. hospitals. Few have lasted more than a year or two. One of the longer-running operations is **Aeromedevac** (U.S. tel. 619/284-7910 or tel. 800/462-0911, Mexico tel. 800/832-5087, www.aeromedevac.com). Aeromedevac accepts collect calls. Payment for the service can be made with a credit card or through your health insurance company.

Other companies with similar services include **Air Evac Services, Inc.** (U.S. tel. 602/273-9348 or 800/421-6111, www.airevac.com) and **Advanced Aeromedical Air Ambulance Service** (U.S./Canada tel. 800/346-3556, www.aeromedic.com).

For information on other air evacuation services, contact the **Association of Air Medical Services** (526 King St. #415, Alexandria, VA 22314-3143, 703/836-8732, www.aams.org).

SAFETY

Statistics clearly show that violent crime is overall less common in Mexico than anywhere in the United States. In Baja California, crime statistics are many times lower than the U.S. national average. Yet Americans seem to be the most paranoid of all visitors to Mexico.

Historical reasons, to a large degree, account for this paranoia. Chief among them is the general border lawlessness that was the norm in the early 20th century—an era of border disputes

and common banditry on both sides of the border. Americans living in these areas came to fear *bandidos* who stole livestock and occasionally robbed the Anglo ranchers themselves, while the Mexicans in turn feared American cattle rustlers, horse thieves, gunslingers, and the infamous Texas Rangers, a private militia whose conduct at the time fell somewhere between that of the Hell's Angels motorcycle gang and the Los Angeles Police Department.

Soon after this era had begun to wane, as politics on both sides of the border stabilized, the U.S. Prohibition experiment sent millions of Americans scrambling into Mexican border towns for booze. In the illicit atmosphere, boozers were soon rubbing elbows with gamblers and pimps, and it wasn't long before Mexican border towns gained an even more unsavory reputation.

Once Prohibition was lifted, Americans no longer had reason to come to Mexico solely for drinking, and the border towns began cleaning up their acts. Among the uninformed and inexperienced, however, the border-town image remains, sadly mixing with the equally outdated *bandido* tales to prevent many Americans from enjoying the pleasures of life south of the border.

Precautions

Visitors to Baja should take the same precautions they would when traveling anywhere in their own countries or abroad. Keep money and valuables secured, either in a hotel safe or safety deposit box, or in a money belt or other hard-to-reach place on your person. Keep an eye on cameras, purses, and wallets to make sure you don't leave them behind in restaurants, hotels, or campgrounds. At night, lock the doors to your hotel room and vehicle.

Private campgrounds usually have some kind of security, if only a night watchman, to keep out intruders. Secluded beach campsites seem to be safe due to their isolation—in Baja, it's rare for crime to occur in such areas. Nonetheless, don't leave items of value lying around outside your tent, camper, or RV at night. Over the last five years or so, we've heard

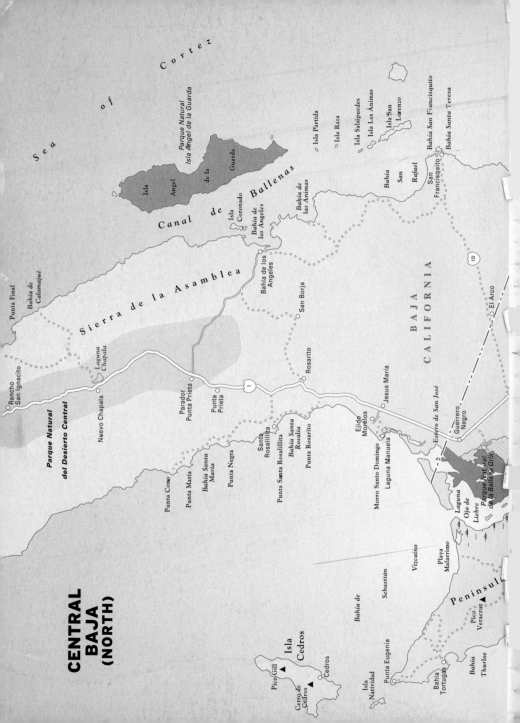

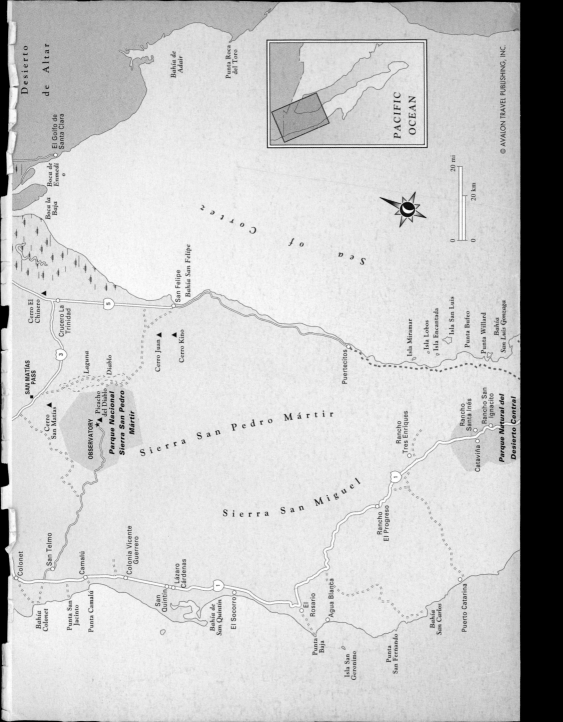

Desierto de Altar

Bahía de Adair

Punta Roca del Toro

PACIFIC OCEAN

El Golfo de Santa Clara

Boca de Enmedio

Boca la Baja

20 mi

20 km

0

0

Sea of Cortez

San Felipe

Bahía San Felipe

Cerro El Chinero

Crucero La Trinidad

5

Cerro Juan

Cerro Kino

Isla Miramar

Isla Lobos

Isla Encantada

Isla San Luis

Punta Bufeo

Punta Willard

Bahía San Luis Gonzaga

Puertecitos

SAN MATÍAS PASS

3

Laguna Diablo

Cerro San Matías

Picacho del Diablo

Parque Nacional Sierra San Pedro Mártir

OBSERVATORY

Sierra San Pedro Mártir

Rancho Santa Inés

Rancho San Ignacito

Parque Natural del Desierto Central

Cataviña

Rancho Tres Enriques

Sierra San Miguel

1

Colonet

San Telmo

Camalú

Colonia Vicente Guerrero

Lázaro Cárdenas

Rancho El Progreso

1

Bahía Colonet

Punta San Jacinto

Punta Camalú

San Quintín

Bahía de San Quintín

El Socorro

El Rosario

Agua Blanca

Bahía San Carlos

Puerto Catarina

Punta Baja

Isla San Gerónimo

Punta San Fernando

tales of campers getting robbed at certain beaches in northern Baja. The places with the worst reputations appear to be the beaches at or near Baja Malibu (between Tijuana and Rosarito) and at San Quintín. If you plan to camp at or near either of the latter, you'd be much safer to pay to camp at a private campground rather than to "boondock" for free.

SECTUR (the State Secretary of Tourism) maintains a 24-hour travelers' aid hotline for emergencies of all kinds: 55/5250-0123 or 01 800/903-9200.

Money

CURRENCY

The unit of exchange in Mexico is the **peso,** which comes in paper denominations of Mex$20, Mex$50, Mex$100, Mex$200, and Mex$500. Coins come in denominations of 5, 10, 20, and 50 centavos, and Mex$1, Mex$2, Mex$5, Mex$10, Mex$20, and Mex$100.

Prices

While it's highly unlikely you'll ever confuse dollar and peso prices because of the differing values, you should ask when in doubt, as they both use the same $ symbol. Sometimes the abbreviation *m.n.* will appear next to a price—this means *moneda nacional* (national money) and also refers to pesos. Coins smaller than one peso are often scarce, so payments often must be rounded off to the nearest peso or at least to the nearest 50 centavos.

Dollars vs. Pesos

Most places on the Cape will take U.S. dollars as well as pesos. Paying with pesos, however, usually means a better deal when the price is fixed in pesos; if you pay in dollars, the vendor can determine the exchange rate. If a can of motor oil, for example, is marked at Mex$18, and the bank rate is Mex$9 per dollar, you'll pay US$2 for the oil with pesos changed at the bank. However, if you ask to pay in dollars, the vendor may charge US$2.50 since vendors have the right—by custom rather than law—to charge whatever exchange rate they wish. If you're bargaining for price, it really doesn't matter what currency you use.

Some stores in smaller towns prefer not to take dollars since this means keeping track of two currencies and makes banking more complicated. Pemex stations sometimes refuse dollars—attendants are usually too busy to stop and calculate rates.

For anything larger than a Mex$100 note, getting change can sometimes be a problem in small towns, so try to carry plenty of notes and coins in denominations of Mex$50 or smaller. Small change is commonly called *morraya*.

CHANGING MONEY

The best way to obtain local currency is to withdraw cash from an ATM machine using your debit card from home, or pay with a credit card whenever possible (mainly at larger stores and moderate to upscale establishments in Los Cabos and La Paz). In some cases, however, you may need to exchange U.S. dollars or other currency for pesos. Several alternatives are discussed below.

Debit Cards and ATM Cards

Most Mexican ATMs (automatic teller machines) accept MasterCard or Visa debit cards as well as ATM cards on the Plus or Cirrus systems. Using an ATM card to obtain pesos from ATMs in Mexico is much more convenient than cashing travelers checks. Most Mexican banks now charge nominal fees for withdrawing cash from their ATMs with cards from other banks. ATMs are called *cajeros automáticos* (automatic cashiers) in Mexico.

At this time the most reliable machines seem to be those operated by **Banamex, Bancomer, HSBC, Banorte,** and **Banca Serfín,** whose ATMs accept cards coded for the Visa, MasterCard, Cirrus, and Plus systems.

Credit Cards

Visa and MasterCard are widely accepted in the Cape region at large hotels, at restaurants catering to tourists or businesspeople, at car rental agencies (you can't rent a car without a credit card), and at shops in tourist centers or large cities. If in doubt, flash your card and ask *"¿Se aceptan tarjetas de crédito?"* A reply containing *"solo efectivo"* means "only cash."

It's important to keep in mind that many shops and some hotels add a 3–6 percent surcharge to bills paid with a credit card. Credit cards are not accepted at Pemex stations in Baja.

Cash advances on credit card accounts—a useful service for emergencies—are available at many Mexican banks.

Banks

Banks offer the best exchange rate for buying pesos, and they all offer the same rate, set by the Bank of Mexico. This rate is usually posted behind the counter where foreign exchange is handled. Banks also accept a wide range of foreign currencies, including euros, British pounds, Japanese yen, and Canadian dollars. Cash and travelers checks are accepted. The main drawbacks with banks are the long lines and short hours (Mon.–Fri. or Sat. 9 or 10 A.M.–1:30 or 3 P.M.); the foreign-exchange service usually closes at noon or 12:30 P.M.

Money Changers

The second best rate, generally speaking, is found at the *casa de cambio*, or private money-changing office. The *casa de cambio* (also called *servicio de cambio*) either knocks a few centavos off the going bank rate or charges a percentage commission. It pays to shop around for the best *casa de cambio* rates since some places charge considerably more than others. Rates are usually posted; *compra*, always the lower figure, refers to the buying rate for US$ (how many pesos you'll receive per dollar), while *vende* is the selling rate (how many pesos you must pay to receive a dollar).

Money changers are usually open much later than banks; some even work evening hours, which makes them immeasurably more convenient than banks. U.S. dollars are generally preferred, though many *casas* also accept Canadian dollars. However, Canadians should keep a reserve supply of U.S. dollars for instances when Canadian currency isn't accepted. Money changers usually accept travelers checks; some border-town *casas*, however, take only cash. The latter often offer the best exchange rates.

Only the larger towns and tourist centers offer money-changing offices. In smaller towns, you'll have to resort to a bank or local merchant. Many storekeepers are happy to buy dollars at a highly variable and sometimes negotiable rate. Few take traveler's checks, however, unless you make a purchase.

Money changers at Mexican airports offer notoriously low rates. Try to buy pesos in advance if arriving by air, or pay with dollars until you can get to a bank or *casa de cambio*.

Hotels

Hotels, motels, *pensiones,* and other lodgings generally offer the lowest exchange rates. If you're trying to save money, avoid changing currency where you stay. Pay for your room in pesos if possible, since the same low rate often applies to room charges paid in dollars.

MONEY MANAGEMENT
Estimating Costs

Inflation in Mexico runs high. This means that when estimating travel costs based on prices quoted in this book, some allowance must be made for inflation.

Because of fluctuations in the peso–dollar ratio, and in an effort to keep prices up to date, all prices in this book are quoted in U.S. dollars. This doesn't mean, however, that there won't be any increase in prices by the time you arrive. A couple of phone calls to hotels for price quotes should give you an idea of how much rates have increased, if at all; this difference can be applied as a percentage to all other prices for a rough estimate of costs.

Tipping

A tip of 10–15 percent is customary at restaurants with table service unless a service charge is added to the bill. Luggage handling at hotels or airports warrants a tip of US$0.50 per bag. A few hotels maintain a no-tipping policy; details will be posted in your room. The tipping of chambermaids is optional—some guests tip and some don't. Remember that these folks typically earn minimum wage; even a small tip may mean a lot to them.

You don't need to tip Pemex station attendants unless they wash your windows, check the oil, or perform other extra services beyond pumping gas. The equivalent of US$0.50–1 in pesos is sufficient. When the change due on a gasoline purchase is less than Mex$1, it's customary to let the attendant keep the change.

Taxes
The Mexican government collects an *impuesta al valor agregado* (IVA) or "value-added tax" (VAT) of 10 percent on all goods and services in Baja, including hotel and restaurant bills and international phone calls. On the mainland, the same tax is 15 percent, so Baja is a bargain in this respect. Although by American standards this may seem high, the tax is lower than the rate in other countries that employ value-added taxes, such as France, where the VAT runs more than 20 percent.

Hotels add a further 2 percent lodging tax. Many, but not all, hotel rate quotes include taxes, but to make sure, you might ask *"¿Se incluyen los impuestos?"*

Information and Services

BUSINESS HOURS
The typical small business is open Monday–Friday 9 A.M.–2 P.M., closed until 4 or 5 P.M., then open again until 7 or 8 P.M. Retail businesses are usually open on Saturday as well. Official government offices typically maintain an 8:30 A.M.–3:30 P.M. schedule, although Secretary of Tourism offices usually open again 5–7 P.M.

Bank hours vary. Most are open Monday–Friday 8:30 A.M.–3 P.M., though some banks in larger towns are open on Saturday. The foreign exchange service usually closes around noon—probably to lock in the exchange rate before afternoon adjustments.

TRAVEL SERVICES
Tourist Information
Mexico's federal tourist bureau, the Secretaría de Turismo (SECTUR), has an office in La Paz that stocks free brochures, maps, hotel and restaurant lists, and information on local activities (Km 5–6 Mexico 1 or Av. Abasolo, tel. 612/124-0100, turismo@correro.gbcs.gob.mx).

To contact the national office directly, call or write the **Secretaría de Turismo de México** (Presidente Mazaryk 172, 11587 México, D.F.,

tel. 55/3002-6300). Or call these toll-free information lines: SECTUR, Mex. tel. 800/903-9200, U.S. tel. 800/482-9832, www.sectur.gob.mx/wb2.

Outside Mexico, SECTUR operates Mexican Tourism Board (www.visitmexico.com) offices to handle requests for tourist information; several are in the United States.

Travel Clubs
Baja's popularity as a boating and RV destination has spawned California-based travel clubs that specialize in recreational travel on the peninsula. Membership benefits include discounts (usually 10–20 percent) at various hotels, restaurants, and other tourist-oriented establishments in Mexico; discounted group auto and boat insurance; the opportunity to participate in such club events as tours and fiestas; and subscriptions to newsletters containing tips from other club members, short travel features, and the latest information on road conditions and Mexican tourism policy. The clubs can also arrange tourist cards, boat permits, and fishing licenses by mail.

Such clubs come and go, some lasting only a year or two. **Discover Baja Travel Club**

(3089 Clairemont Dr., San Diego, CA 92117, U.S. tel. 619/275-1836 or 800/727-2252, www.discoverbaja.com, US$39/yr), the largest and most successful club of this nature, invites members or potential members to visit its San Diego area office on the way to Baja for up-to-date road and weather information. DB publishes an online newsletter and printed color magazine, both packed with information on road travel, sightseeing, and new developments in Baja travel.

Vagabundos del Mar (190 Main St., Rio Vista, CA 94571, U.S. tel. 707/374-5511 or 800/474-2252, www.vagabundos.com, US$35/yr), the older of the two clubs, is oriented toward boaters and RVers and publishes its newsletter, *Chubasco,* every two months. Its 13,000 members enjoy reduced rates for Mexican insurance, organized trips and events, online discussion boards, and good prices on charts, maps, and books.

MAPS

For general road travel in the Cape Region, the maps in this guidebook should suffice. If you're planning to drive farther north than La Paz, pick up one of the many Baja California maps available to visitors. Two maps are particularly well suited to general-purpose Baja road travel. One is published by the Automobile Club of Southern California and is available from most AAA offices; maps are free to AAA members, or available online for about US$5 through Baja Books and Maps (www.bajabooksandmaps.com) and other sellers. This map is easy to read, accurate, and detailed enough for any border-to-Cape auto trip. Its excellent graphics include topographic shading. At last check, the most recent edition had been published in 2004.

International Travel Maps and Books (ITM or ITMB) publishes a well-researched map (last updated 2003) that's a bit harder to find. Ashland, Oregon–based Travel Essentials stocks it for purchase online (US$8,

www.travelessentials.com), or it can be ordered from ITM (345 W. Broadway, Vancouver, BC V5Y 1P8, Canada). In spite of its smaller scale (1:650,000), the ITM map is far more detailed than the AAA map, and all distances are entered in kilometers as well as miles. Many dirt roads, trails, and destinations unmarked on the AAA map appear on the ITM map. In addition, the map features contour lines in 200-meter intervals and is annotated with useful historical and sightseeing information. The main drawback is that it's so detailed it's difficult to read. In addition, the map's graphics scheme uses far too much red, a color particularly difficult to read in low light (e.g., under a car dome light). A waterproof version with inset maps of Tijuana, Mexicali, and La Paz was revised in 2006; available from Amazon.com.

For getting around La Paz, **Guia Roji** (www.guiaroji.com.mx), the largest map publisher in Mexico, publishes a detailed city map (scale 1:20,000) with street index. Guia Roji also publishes state maps to Baja California Sur (scale 1:350,000; including a La Paz city map) and Baja California Norte (scale 1:1,000,000; include Tijuana and Mexicali city maps)—last updated in 2004 and both available from Amazon.com for US$7 each. The complete Mexico atlas is invaluable for extended trips that will include the mainland.

Topographical Maps

Because differences in elevation often determine backcountry route selection, hikers, kayakers, mountain bikers, and off-road drivers should consider obtaining topographical maps before arriving in the Cape Region (see *Sports and Recreation*). Topo maps are difficult to come by in the Cape Region; in La Paz, try the Instituto Nacional de Estadística Geografía e Informática (INEGI, in Plaza Cuatro Molinos at Calle Altamirano 2790, Col. Centro, tel. 612/123-1545 or 612/122-4146, www.inegi .gob.mx). INEGI sells topo maps for Baja California Sur at around US$4 a sheet.

Communications and Media

TELEPHONE SERVICES

The national telephone company, TelMex, privatized in 1990 and has improved its services considerably in the last decade or so. Local phone calls are relatively cheap—a two-peso coin pays for a phone-booth call—as are long-distance calls *within* Mexico. If you can find a working phone (many public phones seem permanently "out of order") connections are usually good, though you may have to wait a while to get through to the operator during busy periods such as Sundays and holidays.

If you don't want to use a phone booth or a hotel phone (hotels usually add their own surcharges to both local and long-distance calls), you can make a call during business hours from a TelMex office. Only large towns offer TelMex offices with public telecommunications facilities; a small town may offer a private telephone office (usually called *caseta de teléfono* or *caseta de larga distancia*), often set up in the corner of a local shop, where you can make calls. Like hotels, private telephone offices add surcharges to calls, but rates are usually reasonable.

A public pay phone service called Ladatel (acronym for "Larga Distancia Teléfono") offers phone booths where you can pay for local or long-distance calls with a *tarjeta de teléfono* (phone card) issued by TelMex. You can buy debit cards in denominations of Mex$20, Mex$30, Mex$50, and Mex$100 at many pharmacies, convenience stores, supermarkets, bus terminals, and airports.

Area Codes and Local Numbers

All area codes in Mexico now have three digits, except for Mexico City (area code 55). You may occasionally see phone numbers written using older numbering systems. The number

---

TELEPHONE CODES

Mastering telephone dialing codes in a foreign country can confuse even the most technically proficient traveler. Here's a list of the most frequently used access codes, emergency numbers, and area codes.

USEFUL NUMBERS

Long-distance operator (national): 020
Time: 030
Directory assistance (local): 040
Mexico City area code: 55
Police, Red Cross, fire: 060
Emergency response: 066
Spanish-English emergency info: 07
International operator: 090

BAJA CALIFORNIA AREA CODES

Ciudad Constitución/Puerto San Carlos: 613
Ensenada: 646
Guerrero Negro/San Ignacio/Mulegé: 615
La Paz/Todos Santos: 612
Loreto: 613
Mexicali: 686
Rosarito: 661
San Felipe: 686
San José del Cabo/Cabo San Lucas: 624
San Quintín/El Rosario: 616
Tecate: 665
Tijuana: 664

CALLING MEXICO FROM ABROAD

Mexico's country code is 52. To call Mexico direct from outside the country, dial your international access code + 52 + area code + number. For example, to call the number 684-0461 in Tijuana from the United States, dial 011 (international access code) + 52 (Mexico country code) + 664 (Tijuana area code) + 684-0461. To dial a Mexican cell phone number from abroad, add a 1 before the area code, and omit the prefix 044 (used only when calling within Mexico).

612/142-4274 in La Paz, for example, appeared as 1/142-4274 in 2000, and as 114/2-4274 before that year.

As of November 2001, all telephone numbers in both states of Baja California, and most phone numbers elsewhere in Mexico, consist of seven digits. This means if you are in La Paz and intend to call what would formerly have been written as 114/2-4274 or 1/142-4274 under one of the earlier systems, you must now dial 612/142-4274.

There's no standard way of hyphenating the numbers in Mexico. You may see the number in our La Paz example written as 1424274, 14-24274, 14-24-274, and so on.

Long-Distance Domestic Calls

To make a long-distance call within Mexico, dial 01 plus the area code and number.

If you have a calling-card number for Sprint, AT&T, MCI, Bell Canada, or British Telecom, you can use it to make long-distance calls. Each has its own access code for direct dialing.

Mobile Phones

Most of the Cape Region now enjoys reliable mobile phone access through two competing companies: Telcel and Moviestar. Telcel has better coverage and lower rates. For extended stays in Baja, during which you plan to make a number of local calls, buying a low cost GSM phone and prepaid cards can make sense. Using it to call the United States will cost a fortune, unless you are a Cingular/AT&T customer in the United States.

Two U.S. carriers offer North America plans that include calling to/from Mexico and the United States: Cingular (www.cingular.com/mexico) charges US$4.99/month and US$0.59/minute for roaming in Mexico. Verizon (www.verizonwireless.com/international) partners with Moviestar to offer North America calling for US$60/month for 450 minutes, and US$0.45/minute after the monthly allowance. International roaming on a standard U.S. plan through Verizon costs US$0.69/minute. Text messaging is not supported.

In 2007, rates for calling a Mexican cell phone from the United States jumped about US$0.17 cents a minute, due to changes in the Mexican government's regulation of the telephone industry. Also, a caller-pays policy began in 2006. When calling a Mexican cell phone number from the United States, it's now necessary to add a 1 after the country code: 52 1 612/xxx-xxxx. Within Mexico, you need to add 044 before the area code: 044 612/xxx-xxxx.

International Calls

To direct dial an international call to the United States or Canada via TelMex, dial 001 plus the area code and number for a station-to-station call. For international calls to other countries, dial 00 plus the country code, area code, and number. For operator-assisted calls, dial 09 plus the country code, area code, and number. Long-distance international calls are heavily taxed and cost more than equivalent international calls from the United States or Canada.

To reach toll-free 800 numbers in Mexico, dial 01 first. Dial 001 first for numbers in the United States, or 091 for Canada.

Internet Phones

In areas with Internet access, voice-over-IP (VoIP) calling is fast replacing the need for satellite phones and Ladatel cards. Skype (www.skype.com), Gizmo VoIP (www.gizmovoip.com), and Crystal Voice (www.crystalvoice.com) are three of many service providers out there. Rates are about US$0.01é0.03 per minute, plus an account setup fee of around US$10. Some companies include a free U.S. number for family and friends back home to dial while you are on the road.

Long Distance the Old-Fashioned Way

If you don't have access to the Internet, you can dial access numbers to reach operators from AT&T, MCI, or Sprint for calling-card or credit card calls. For Canada Direct, dial 01 800/010-1990, and for BT Direct dial *791 (see the sidebar *Telephone Codes*).

The appropriate long-distance operator can

then place a collect call on your behalf or charge the call to your account if you have a calling card for that service. If you try these numbers from a hotel phone, be sure the hotel operator realizes the call is toll-free; some hotel operators use their own timers to assess phone charges. *Warning:* Since the deregulation of Mexican telephone service, several unscrupulous U.S.-based long-distance phone companies have set up shop in Mexico to take advantage of undiscerning tourists. The English-language signs next to the phone usually read "Call the U.S. or Canada Collect or With a Credit Card" or "Just Dial Zero to Reach the U.S. or Canada." Another clue is that the name of the company is not posted on the sign. If you try asking the operators on the line who they represent, you'll find the same company often operates under several different names in the same area, charging at least 50 percent more per international call than TelMex, AT&T, MCI, or Sprint—or even many times more, as much as US$10–20 for the first minute, plus US$4 each additional minute, even on weekends. A percentage of these charges usually goes to the hotel or private phone office offering the service. At most private phone offices, it's cheaper to use TelMex, even if you have to pay a service charge on top of TelMex rates, than to use these price-gouging U.S. companies. Or use MCI, Sprint, AT&T, or one of the other more well-known international companies, which charge around US$0.15–0.35/minute. Unless you're independently wealthy, always ask which company is being used before you arrange an international call through a hotel or private phone office. Some Mexican hotels are now cooperating with these cutthroat American companies—the tip-off is a card next to the phone that says you can use credit cards to make a call to the United States or Canada.

Collect Calls

For international service, calling collect often saves hassles. In Spanish, the magic words are *por cobrar* (collect), prefaced by the name of the place you're calling (e.g., *"a los Estados Unidos, por favor—por cobrar"*). This connects you to an English-speaking international operator. For best results, speak slowly and clearly. You may reach an international operator directly by dialing 090.

Satellite Phone

For the many areas of Baja where there are no regular telephone lines, no radio phones, no Internet, and no cellular phone service, the only solution is satellite phone—assuming you *have* to stay in phone contact at all times. California Baja Rent-a-Car rents GPS-satellite phones, as does Discover Baja Travel Club (3089 Clairemont Dr., San Diego, CA 92117, U.S. tel. 619/275-1836 or 800/727-2252, www.discoverbaja.com).

EMAIL AND INTERNET ACCESS

To the surprise of many first-time visitors, high-speed Internet access is almost ubiquitous in the Cape Region these days. Hundreds of miles of fibre-optic cable were buried alongside the Transpeninsular Highway in 2002–2003, replacing the need for slow dial-up connections in most towns, and connecting Baja residents and visitors to computers and websites around the world.

Reliability is another matter, however. Even the most well-equipped business centers have trouble keeping their connections up 24/7. If all you need to do is check your email now and then, this won't be a problem. But if you intend to run business processes remotely while on the road, it may be difficult to find a good setup.

Five-star resorts, espresso bars, marinas, and RV parks all have set wireless antennas for guests who travel with their own laptop or other Internet-enabled device. Some charge extra by the hour or day; others throw it in for the price of a latte. In the larger condo complexes, you may be able to find an open (unsecured) Wi-Fi network to use. And for those traveling sans computer, there are dozens of Internet cafés in hotels, real estate offices, and business centers with desktop machines, as well as printers, copiers, and scanners for imaging needs.

Rates vary widely, from free with a food or

beverage purchase to US$8/hour at one of the hotels in San José.

In more remote areas of the peninsula, some residents and RV owners have costly satellite Internet service through providers like HughesNet (formerly Direcway) and Starband.

POSTAL SERVICES

The Mexican postal service, though reliable, is relatively slow. Average delivery time between Mexico and the United States or Canada is about 10 days, while to Europe you must figure two weeks. Mail sent to Mexico from outside the country generally reaches its destination more quickly.

Most towns in the Cape Region have a post office *(correo)* where you can receive general-delivery mail. Have correspondents address mail in your name (last name capitalized), followed by a/c Lista de Correos, Correo Central, the town name, the state, and the country; e.g., John SMITH, a/c Lista de Correos, Correo Central, La Paz, Baja California Sur, Mexico. Mail sent this way is usually held 10 days. If you want your mail held up to 30 days, substitute the words "Poste Restante" for Lista de Correos in the address. If you have the postal code for the town or city, insert it just after the state name. Since delivery time is highly variable, it's best to use *poste restante* just to be safe.

Many foreigners who are seasonal Cape residents have their mail sent in care of a hotel or RV park. You can rent boxes at larger Mexican post offices, but the initial application process often takes several weeks. Todos Santos, Cabo San Lucas, and La Paz have private mail companies that also rent boxes with minimal red tape.

The Mexican post office offers an express mail service (EMS) called Mexpost. International rates are relatively high; a Mexpost express letter to the United States or Canada, for example, costs US$15, to Europe US$18. Mexpost claims to deliver almost anywhere in Mexico within 48 hours, to major cities around the world within 72 hours.

UPS, Airborne Express, DHL, FedEx, and other courier services operate in La Paz and Cabo San Lucas. So far DHL and UPS seem to offer the lowest prices and best services. Local companies such as Estafeta and Aeroflash are also available, but reliability does not appear to match that of the international services.

MEDIA
Newspapers

Several Spanish-language newspapers are published in Baja; *El Mexicano,* published daily in Tijuana, has the highest circulation, closely followed by Mexicali's *La Voz de la Frontera* (Voice of the Border). Also of considerable interest is the progressive *Zeta* (Z), in Tijuana. *El Sudcaliforniano,* out of La Paz, covers Baja California Sur news but is not a good newspaper overall.

A few English-language newspapers are published monthly in Baja, all heavily oriented toward tourists. Although not exactly pillars of journalism, they nonetheless contain much information of value to the visitor, including up-to-date sketch maps. Typical features include restaurant reviews, cultural primers on upcoming festivals, Spanish language lessons, seasonal fishing recommendations, and the occasional editorial on national or local tourism policies. The content of each is oriented toward the town in which it is published.

In southern Baja, several papers focusing on Los Cabos have come and gone over the years. *Gringo Gazette* contains the most useful information overall, even if the paper's reporting on Mexican affairs on occasion reveals a seemingly intentional lack of cultural comprehension. *El Calendario de Todos Santos,* based in Todos Santos, does a wonderful job of covering the West Cape.

In tourist hotels you'll often see day-old copies of *The San Diego Union-Tribune, Los Angeles Times,* or *USA Today.*

Radio and Television

In the border area of northern Baja, radios and TVs pick up a mix of broadcasts from Tijuana and San Diego. Farther south the San Diego stations first begin to fade, then the Tijuana stations. South of Ensenada you need shortwave radio to receive anything until you arrive in La Paz or Los Cabos, where TV and radio reception begin again.

Because of the lack of TV and radio reception in most of Baja, it would be pointless to pack an AM/FM radio or portable TV. An audiocassette or portable CD player makes more sense. Many towns in Baja have shops selling tapes and CDs, for prices generally less expensive than in the United States or Canada. U.S., Canadian, and European releases—in addition to Latino recordings—often appear on Mexican labels.

Measurements and Standards

WEIGHTS AND MEASURES

Mexico uses the metric system as the official system of weights and measures. This means the distance between Maneadero and San Quintín is measured in kilometers, cheese is weighed in grams or kilograms, a hot day in San Felipe is 32°C, gasoline is sold by the liter, and a big fish is two meters long. A chart at the end of this book converts pounds, gallons, and miles to kilograms, liters, and kilometers.

Bajacalifornianos used to dealing with American tourists often use the Anglo-American and metric systems interchangeably. Even rancheros in remote areas occasionally use *millas* (miles) as a measure.

In this book, distances are rendered in kilometers, often followed by miles in parentheses. All road markers in Baja employ the metric system. Dimensions and weights are usually quoted using the metric system, but boat lengths and fishing line tests are quoted in feet and pounds (due to the influence of American boaters and anglers).

TIME

Baja California Norte lies in the Pacific time zone, Baja California Sur in the mountain time zone. This means you should set your timepieces an hour ahead when crossing the BCS state line going south and back an hour when crossing north. Baja observes daylight saving time from the first Sunday in April to the last Sunday in October.

Time in Mexico is often expressed according to the 24-hour clock, from 0001 to 2359 (one minute past midnight to 11:59 P.M.). A restaurant posting hours of 1100–2200, for example, is open 11 A.M.–10 P.M.

ELECTRICITY

Mexico's electrical system is the same as that in the United States and Canada: 110 volts, 60 cycles, alternating current (AC). Electrical outlets are of the North American type, designed to work with appliances that have standard double-bladed plugs.

574

RESOURCES

Glossary

abarrotes groceries

aduana customs service

alta cocina mexicana Mexican food prepared in a "high cuisine," or gourmet, style

antojitos literally "little whims," quick Mexican dishes like tacos and enchiladas

aparejo burro saddle

bahía bay

basura trash or rubbish; a sign saying No Tire Basura means Don't Throw Trash.

BCD buoyancy compensation device

BCN the state of Baja California Norte, more properly called just Baja California

BCS the state of Baja California Sur

boca literally "mouth," a geographic term describing a break in a barrier island or peninsula where sea meets lagoon

calle street

callejón alley or lane

cañon canyon

cardón Pachycereus pringlei, the world's tallest cactus

casa de huéspedes guesthouse

cerro mountain peak

cerveza beer

charreada Mexican-style rodeo

charro/charra horseman/horsewoman

colectivo van or taxi that picks up several passengers at a time for a standard per-person fare, much like a bus

correo post office

corrida de toros "running of the bulls" or bullfight

COTP captain of the port, *capitanía del puerto* in Spanish

curandero traditional healer

Diconsa Distribuidora Conasupo, S.A., a government-subsidized food distributor

efectivo cash payment

ejido collectively owned agricultural lands

ensenada cove or small bay

Fonatur Fondo Nacional de Fomento del Turismo (National Foundation for Tourism Development)

Gral. abbreviation for General (rank)

hostería hostelry, inn

IMSS Instituto Mexicano del Seguro Social (Mexican Social Security Institute)

INAH Instituto Nacional de Antropología e Historia (National Institute of Anthropology and History)

indios Mexicans of predominantly Amerindian descent; *indígenas* (indigenes) is the less common, but more politically correct, term

INEGI Instituto Nacional de Estadística, Geografía e Informática (National Institute of Statistics, Geography, and Information)

ISSSTE Instituto de Seguridad y Servicios Sociales para Trabajadores del Estado (Security and Social Services Institute for Government Workers)

laguna lagoon, lake, or bay

llano plains

lleno full

malecón waterfront promenade

maquiladora (maquila) a "twin-bond" or "in-plant" manufacturing enterprise where foreign components may be imported and assembled, then exported to a foreign country, free of customs duties in each direction; now that NAFTA has been enacted, the maquiladora may become extinct

mariscos literally "shellfish," but often used as a generic term for seafood

mercado market

mochila knapsack or backpack

mochilero backpacker

nopalitos strips of cooked or pickled prickly-pear cactus

PADI Professional Association of Dive Instructors

palacio municipal literally "municipal palace," equivalent to city or county hall in the United States

palapa thatched, umbrella-like shade shelter or roof

PAN Partido Acción Nacional

panadería bakery

parrada bus stop

Pemex Petroleos Mexicanos (Mexican Petroleum)

pensión boardinghouse

playa beach

plazuela smaller plaza

PRD Partido Revolucionario Democrático

pre-Cortesian a reference to Mexican history before the arrival of Spanish conquistador Hernán Cortés, i.e., before 1518; other terms with the same meaning include pre-Columbian (before Columbus's arrival) and pre-Hispanic (before the arrival of the Spanish)

PRI Partido Revolucionario Institucional

punta point

ramal branch road

ranchería a collection of small ranching households, most often inhabited by *indios*

ranchito small ranch

SECTUR Secretaría de Turismo (Secretariat of Tourism)

SEDESOL Secretaría de Desarrollo Social (Secretariat of Social Development)

SEMARNAT Secretaría de Medio Ambiente y Recursos Naturales (Secretariat of the Environment and Natural Resources)

tienda store

tinaja pool or spring

topes speed bumps

ultramarinos minimarket/delicatessen

ABBREVIATIONS

Av. Avenida

Calz. Calzada

Col. Colonia (neighborhood)

nte. *norte* (north)

ote. *oriente* (east)

pte. *poniente* (west)

s/n *sin número* ("without number," used for street addresses without building numbers)

Spanish Phrasebook

Your Mexico adventure will be more fun if you use a little Spanish. Mexican folks, although they may smile at your funny accent, will appreciate your halting efforts to break the ice and transform yourself from a foreigner to a potential friend.

Spanish commonly uses 30 letters – the familiar English 26, plus four straightforward additions: ch, ll, ñ, and rr, which are explained in "Consonants," below.

PRONUNCIATION

Once you learn them, Spanish pronunciation rules – in contrast to English – don't change. Spanish vowels generally sound softer than in English. (*Note:* The capitalized syllables below receive stronger accents.)

Vowels

a like ah, as in "hah": *agua* AH-gooah (water), *pan* PAHN (bread), and *casa* CAH-sah (house)

e like ay, as in "may:" *mesa* MAY-sah (table), *tela* TAY-lah (cloth), and *de* DAY (of, from)

i like ee, as in "need": *diez* dee-AYZ (ten), *comida* ko-MEE-dah (meal), and *fin* FEEN (end)

o like oh, as in "go": *peso* PAY-soh (weight), *ocho* OH-choh (eight), and *poco* POH-koh (a bit)

u like oo, as in "cool": *uno* OO-noh (one), *cuarto* KOOAHR-toh (room), and *usted* oos-TAYD (you); when it follows a "q" the **u** is silent; when it follows an "h" or has an umlaut, it's pronounced like "w"

Consonants

**b, d, f, k, l, m, n, p, q, s,
t, v, w, x, y, z, and ch**
pronounced almost as in English; **h** occurs, but is silent – not pronounced at all.

c like k as in "keep": *cuarto* KOOAR-toh (room), Tepic tay-PEEK (capital of Nayarit state); when it precedes "e" or "i," pronounce **c** like s, as in "sit": *cerveza* sayr-VAY-sah (beer), *encima* ayn-SEE-mah (atop).

g like g as in "gift" when it precedes "a," "o," "u," or a consonant: *gato* GAH-toh (cat), *hago* AH-goh (I do, make); otherwise, pronounce **g** like h as in "hat": *giro* HEE-roh (money order), *gente* HAYN-tay (people)

j like h, as in "has": *Jueves* HOOAY-vays (Thursday), *mejor* may-HOR (better)

ll like y, as in "yes": *toalla* toh-AH-yah (towel), *ellos* AY-yohs (they, them)

ñ like ny, as in "canyon": *año* AH-nyo (year), *señor* SAY-nyor (Mr., sir)

r is lightly trilled, with tongue at the roof of your mouth like a very light English d, as in "ready": *pero* PAY-doh (but), *tres* TDAYS (three), *cuatro* KOOAH-tdoh (four).

rr like a Spanish r, but with much more emphasis and trill. Let your tongue flap. Practice with *burro* (donkey), *carretera* (highway), and Carrillo (proper name), then really let go with *ferrocarril* (railroad).

Note: The single small but common exception to all of the above is the pronunciation of Spanish **y** when it's being used as the Spanish word for "and," as in "Ron y Kathy." In such case, pronounce it like the English ee, as in "keep": Ron "ee" Kathy (Ron and Kathy).

Accent

The rule for accent, the relative stress given to syllables within a given word, is straightforward. If a word ends in a vowel, an n, or an s, accent the next-to-last syllable; if not, accent the last syllable.

Pronounce *gracias* GRAH-seeahs (thank you), *orden* OHR-dayn (order), and *carretera* kah-ray-TAY-rah (highway) with stress on the next-to-last syllable.

Otherwise, accent the last syllable: *venir* vay-NEER (to come), *ferrocarril* fay-roh-cah-REEL (railroad), and *edad* ay-DAHD (age).

Exceptions to the accent rule are always marked with an accent sign: (á, é, í, ó, or ú), such as *teléfono* tay-LAY-foh-noh (telephone), *jabón* hah-BON (soap), and *rápido* RAH-pee-doh (rapid).

BASIC AND COURTEOUS EXPRESSIONS

Most Spanish-speaking people consider formalities important. Whenever approaching anyone for information or some other reason, do not forget the appropriate salutation – good morning, good evening, etc. Standing alone, the greeting *hola* (hello) can sound brusque.

Hello. *Hola.*
Good morning. *Buenos días.*
Good afternoon. *Buenas tardes.*
Good evening. *Buenas noches.*
How are you? *¿Cómo está usted?*
Very well, thank you. *Muy bien, gracias.*
Okay; good. *Bien.*
Not okay; bad. *Mal or feo.*
So-so. *Más o menos.*
And you? *¿Y usted?*
Thank you. *Gracias.*
Thank you very much. *Muchas gracias.*
You're very kind. *Muy amable.*
You're welcome. *De nada.*
Goodbye. *Adios.*
See you later. *Hasta luego.*
please *por favor*
yes *sí*
no *no*
I don't know. *No sé.*
Just a moment, please. *Momentito, por favor.*
Excuse me, please (when you're trying to get attention). *Disculpe or Con permiso.*
Excuse me (when you've made an error). *Lo siento.*
Pleased to meet you. *Mucho gusto.*
How do you say . . . in Spanish? *¿Cómo se dice . . . en español?*
What is your name? *¿Cómo se llama usted?*
Do you speak English? *¿Habla usted inglés?*
Is English spoken here? (Does anyone here speak English?) *¿Se habla inglés?*
I don't speak Spanish well. *No hablo bien el español.*
I don't understand. *No entiendo.*
How do you say . . . in Spanish? *¿Cómo se dice . . . en español?*
My name is . . . *Me llamo . . .*
Would you like . . . *¿Quisiera usted . . .*

Let's go to . . . *Vamos a . . .*

TERMS OF ADDRESS

When in doubt, use the formal *usted* (you) as a form of address.

I *yo*
you (formal) *usted*
you (familiar) *tu*
he/him *él*
she/her *ella*
we/us *nosotros*
you (plural) *ustedes*
they/them *ellos* (all males or mixed gender); *ellas* (all females)
Mr., sir *señor*
Mrs., madam *señora*
miss, young lady *señorita*
wife *esposa*
husband *esposo*
friend *amigo* (male); *amiga* (female)
sweetheart *novio* (male); *novia* (female)
son; daughter *hijo; hija*
brother; sister *hermano; hermana*
father; mother *padre; madre*
grandfather; grandmother *abuelo; abuela*

TRANSPORTATION

Where is . . . ? *¿Dónde está . . . ?*
How far is it to . . . ? *¿A cuánto está . . . ?*
from . . . to . . . *de . . . a . . .*
How many blocks? *¿Cuántas cuadras?*
Where (Which) is the way to . . . ? *¿Dónde está el camino a . . . ?*
the bus station *la terminal de autobuses*
the bus stop *la parada de autobuses*
Where is this bus going? *¿Adónde va este autobús?*
the taxi stand *la parada de taxis*
the train station *la estación de ferrocarril*
the boat *el barco*
the launch *lancha; tiburonera*
the dock *el muelle*
the airport *el aeropuerto*
I'd like a ticket to . . . *Quisiera un boleto a . . .*
first (second) class *primera (segunda) clase*
roundtrip *ida y vuelta*
reservation *reservación*

baggage *equipaje*
Stop here, please. *Pare aquí, por favor.*
the entrance *la entrada*
the exit *la salida*
the ticket office *la oficina de boletos*
(very) near; far *(muy) cerca; lejos*
to; toward *a*
by; through *por*
from *de*
the right *la derecha*
the left *la izquierda*
straight ahead *derecho; directo*
in front *en frente*
beside *al lado*
behind *atrás*
the corner *la esquina*
the stoplight *la semáforo*
a turn *una vuelta*
right here *aquí*
somewhere around here *por acá*
right there *allí*
somewhere around there *por allá*
road *el camino*
street; boulevard *calle; bulevar*
block *la cuadra*
highway *carretera*
kilometer *kilómetro*
bridge; toll *puente; cuota*
address *dirección*
north; south *norte; sur*
east; west *oriente (este); poniente (oeste)*

ACCOMMODATIONS

hotel *hotel*
Is there a room? *¿Hay cuarto?*
May I (may we) see it? *¿Puedo (podemos) verlo?*
What is the rate? *¿Cuál es el precio?*
Is that your best rate? *¿Es su mejor precio?*
Is there something cheaper? *¿Hay algo más económico?*
a single room *un cuarto sencillo*
a double room *un cuarto doble*
double bed *cama matrimonial*
twin beds *camas gemelas*
with private bath *con baño*
hot water *agua caliente*
shower *ducha*

towels *toallas*
soap *jabón*
toilet paper *papel higiénico*
blanket *frazada; manta*
sheets *sábanas*
air-conditioned *aire acondicionado*
fan *abanico; ventilador*
key *llave*
manager *gerente*

FOOD

I'm hungry *Tengo hambre.*
I'm thirsty. *Tengo sed.*
menu *carta; menú*
order *orden*
glass *vaso*
fork *tenedor*
knife *cuchillo*
spoon *cuchara*
napkin *servilleta*
soft drink *refresco*
coffee *café*
tea *té*
drinking water *agua pura; agua potable*
bottled carbonated water *agua mineral*
bottled uncarbonated water *agua sin gas*
beer *cerveza*
wine *vino*
milk *leche*
juice *jugo*
cream *crema*
sugar *azúcar*
cheese *queso*
snack *antojo; botana*
breakfast *desayuno*
lunch *almuerzo*
daily lunch special *comida corrida (or el menú del día depending on region)*
dinner *comida (often eaten in late afternoon); cena (a late-night snack)*
the check *la cuenta*
eggs *huevos*
bread *pan*
salad *ensalada*
fruit *fruta*
mango *mango*
watermelon *sandía*
papaya *papaya*

banana *plátano*
apple *manzana*
orange *naranja*
lime *limón*
fish *pescado*
shellfish *mariscos*
shrimp *camarones*
meat (without) *(sin) carne*
chicken *pollo*
pork *puerco*
beef; steak *res; bistec*
bacon; ham *tocino; jamón*
fried *frito*
roasted *asada*
barbecue; barbecued *barbacoa; al carbón*

SHOPPING

money *dinero*
money-exchange bureau *casa de cambio*
I would like to exchange traveler's
   checks. *Quisiera cambiar cheques de*
   viajero.
What is the exchange rate? *¿Cuál es el tipo*
   de cambio?
How much is the commission? *¿Cuánto*
   cuesta la comisión?
Do you accept credit cards? *¿Aceptan*
   tarjetas de crédito?
money order *giro*
How much does it cost? *¿Cuánto cuesta?*
What is your final price? *¿Cuál es su último*
   precio?
expensive *caro*
cheap *barato; económico*
more *más*
less *menos*
a little *un poco*
too much *demasiado*

HEALTH

Help me please. *Ayúdeme por favor.*
I am ill. *Estoy enfermo.*
Call a doctor. *Llame un doctor.*
Take me to . . . *Lléveme a . . .*
hospital *hospital; sanatorio*
drugstore *farmacia*
pain *dolor*
fever *fiebre*

headache *dolor de cabeza*
stomach ache *dolor de estómago*
burn *quemadura*
cramp *calambre*
nausea *náusea*
vomiting *vomitar*
medicine *medicina*
antibiotic *antibiótico*
pill; tablet *pastilla*
aspirin *aspirina*
ointment; cream *pomada; crema*
bandage *venda*
cotton *algodón*
sanitary napkins *use brand name, e.g., Kotex*
birth control pills *pastillas anticonceptivas*
contraceptive foam *espuma anticonceptiva*
condoms *preservativos; condones*
toothbrush *cepilla dental*
dental floss *hilo dental*
toothpaste *crema dental*
dentist *dentista*
toothache *dolor de muelas*

POST OFFICE AND COMMUNICATIONS

long-distance telephone *teléfono larga*
   distancia
I would like to call . . . *Quisiera llamar a . . .*
collect *por cobrar*
station to station *a quien contesta*
person to person *persona a persona*
credit card *tarjeta de crédito*
post office *correo*
general delivery *lista de correo*
letter *carta*
stamp *estampilla, timbre*
postcard *tarjeta*
aerogram *aerograma*
air mail *correo aereo*
registered *registrado*
money order *giro*
package; box *paquete; caja*
string; tape *cuerda; cinta*

AT THE BORDER

border *frontera*
customs *aduana*
immigration *migración*

tourist card *tarjeta de turista*
inspection *inspección; revisión*
passport *pasaporte*
profession *profesión*
marital status *estado civil*
single *soltero*
married; divorced *casado; divorciado*
widowed *viudado*
insurance *seguros*
title *título*
driver's license *licencia de manejar*

AT THE GAS STATION

gas station *gasolinera*
gasoline *gasolina*
unleaded *sin plomo*
full, please *lleno, por favor*
tire *llanta*
tire repair shop *vulcanizadora*
air *aire*
water *agua*
oil (change) *aceite (cambio)*
grease *grasa*
My . . . doesn't work. *Mi . . . no sirve.*
battery *batería*
radiator *radiador*
alternator *alternador*
generator *generador*
tow truck *grúa*
repair shop *taller mecánico*
tune-up *afinación*
auto parts store *refaccionería*

VERBS

Verbs are the key to getting along in Spanish. They employ mostly predictable forms and come in three classes, which end in *ar, er,* and *ir,* respectively:

to buy *comprar*
I buy, you (he, she, it) buys *compro, compra*
we buy, you (they) buy *compramos, compran*

to eat *comer*
I eat, you (he, she, it) eats *como, come*
we eat, you (they) eat *comemos, comen*

to climb *subir*

I climb, you (he, she, it) climbs *subo, sube*
we climb, you (they) climb *subimos, suben*

Here are more (with irregularities indicated):
to do or make *hacer* (regular except for *hago,* I do or make)
to go *ir* (very irregular: *voy, va, vamos, van*)
to go (walk) *andar*
to love *amar*
to work *trabajar*
to want *desear, querer*
to need *necesitar*
to read *leer*
to write *escribir*
to repair *reparar*
to stop *parar*
to get off (the bus) *bajar*
to arrive *llegar*
to stay (remain) *quedar*
to stay (lodge) *hospedar*
to leave *salir* (regular except for *salgo,* I leave)
to look at *mirar*
to look for *buscar*
to give *dar* (regular except for *doy,* I give)
to carry *llevar*
to have *tener* (irregular but important: *tengo, tiene, tenemos, tienen*)
to come *venir* (similarly irregular: *vengo, viene, venimos, vienen*)

Spanish has two forms of "to be":
to be *estar* (regular except for *estoy,* I am)
to be *ser* (very irregular: *soy, es, somos, son*)
Use *estar* when speaking of location or a temporary state of being: "I am at home." "*Estoy en casa.*" "I'm sick." "*Estoy enfermo.*" Use *ser* for a permanent state of being: "I am a doctor." "*Soy doctora.*"

NUMBERS

zero *cero*
one *uno*
two *dos*
three *tres*
four *cuatro*
five *cinco*
six *seis*

seven *siete*
eight *ocho*
nine *nueve*
10 *diez*
11 *once*
12 *doce*
13 *trece*
14 *catorce*
15 *quince*
16 *dieciseis*
17 *diecisiete*
18 *dieciocho*
19 *diecinueve*
20 *veinte*
21 *veinte y uno* or *veintiuno*
30 *treinta*
40 *cuarenta*
50 *cincuenta*
60 *sesenta*
70 *setenta*
80 *ochenta*
90 *noventa*
100 *ciento*
101 *ciento y uno* or *cientiuno*
200 *doscientos*
500 *quinientos*
1,000 *mil*
10,000 *diez mil*
100,000 *cien mil*
1,000,000 *millón*
one half *medio*
one third *un tercio*
one fourth *un cuarto*

TIME
What time is it? *¿Qué hora es?*
It's one o'clock. *Es la una.*
It's three in the afternoon. *Son las tres de la tarde.*

It's 4 A.M. *Son las cuatro de la mañana.*
six-thirty *seis y media*
a quarter till eleven *un cuarto para las once*
a quarter past five *las cinco y cuarto*
an hour *una hora*

DAYS AND MONTHS
Monday *lunes*
Tuesday *martes*
Wednesday *miércoles*
Thursday *jueves*
Friday *viernes*
Saturday *sábado*
Sunday *domingo*
today *hoy*
tomorrow *mañana*
yesterday *ayer*
January *enero*
February *febrero*
March *marzo*
April *abril*
May *mayo*
June *junio*
July *julio*
August *agosto*
September *septiembre*
October *octubre*
November *noviembre*
December *diciembre*
a week *una semana*
a month *un mes*
after *después*
before *antes*

(Courtesy of Bruce Whipperman, author of *Moon Pacific Mexico*.)

Suggested Reading

TRAVELOGUES

Amey, Ralph. *Wines of Baja California: Touring and Tasting Mexico's Undiscovered Treasures.* South San Francisco: The Wine Appreciation Guild, 2003. For those who plan to explore the Valle de Guadalupe, this small book gives a good overview of the wineries, with some history, as well as background on grapes and vintages.

Berger, Bruce. *Almost an Island: Travels in Baja California.* Tucson: University of Arizona Press, 1998. Berger, a pianist, poet, desert aficionado, and keen observer of human behavior, surveys Baja's social landscape, with a special focus on La Paz.

Burleson, Bob, and David H. Riskind. *Backcountry Mexico: A Traveler's Guide and Phrase Book.* Austin, TX: University of Texas Press, 1986. Part guidebook, part anthropological study covering Northern Mexico, with some relevance to Baja California backcountry travel.

Cudahy, John. *Mañanaland: Adventuring with Camera and Rifle Through California in Mexico.* New York: Duffie and Co., 1928. This hard-to-find text provides an interesting glimpse of pre–World War II Baja, but no outstanding revelations. Out of print.

Mackintosh, Graham. *Into a Desert Place.* New York: W. W. Norton & Co., 1994. A thoroughly engaging report of Mackintosh's walk around the entire coastline of Baja California during the course of two years. A classic of gringo-in-Baja travel literature for its refreshingly honest style and insights into Baja fishcamp and village life.

Mayo, C. M. *Miraculous Air: Journey of a Thousand Miles through Baja California, the Other Mexico.* University of Utah Press, 2002. Poignant, contemporary memoir by a fiction writer, Spanish/English translator, and editor, who lives in Mexico City.

Miller, Max. *Land Where Time Stands Still.* New York: Dodd, Mead, and Co., 1943. A classic travelogue that chronicles Baja life during World War II, when Mexicans alternately fell prey to German and American propaganda. Out of print.

Salvadori, Clement. *Motorcycle Journeys Through California and Baja,* 2nd Ed. North Conway, NH: Whitehorse Press, 2007. Having written more than 1,000 articles for dozens of motorcycle magazines in his 30-year career, this author does an admirable job of digesting the peninsula for other motorcyclists who might want to tackle the Holy Grail of North American road trips. Contains lots of invaluable tips.

Steinbeck, John. *The Log from the Sea of Cortez.* New York: Penguin USA, Viking, 1951. This chronicle of the author's Baja research voyage with marine biologist Ed Ricketts (the inspiration for *Cannery Row* protagonist "Doc") reveals Steinbeck as a bit of a scientist himself. Annotated with Latin, the book is full of insights into Pacific and Sea of Cortez marinelife as well as coastal *bajacaliforniano* society. Sprinkled throughout are expositions of Steinbeck's personal philosophy, implicit in his novels but fully articulated here. Also reveals the source for his novella *The Pearl.*

HISTORY AND CULTURE

Crosby, Harry. *Antigua California: Mission and Colony on the Peninsular Frontier, 1697–1768.* Albuquerque: University of New Mexico Press, 1994. This well-researched and detailed history covers the Jesuit period in Baja, from the mission planning stages in Sonora and Sinaloa through the expulsion from New Spain.

Francez, James Donald. *The Lost Treasures of Baja*

California. Chula Vista, CA: Black Forest Press, 1997. A slim, hardbound volume containing chronicles of 19 Jesuit missions, in Spanish and English. Notable for its identification of some of the more obscure saints and iconographic elements in the mission sanctuaries and the inclusion of photos of models constructed by the author depicting missions—such as Comondú—that no longer exist.

Niemann, Greg. *Baja Legends.* San Diego, CA: Sunbelt Publications, 2002. A colorful gringo account of the people, events, and locations that shaped Baja California into the travel destination it is today.

Paz, Octavio. *The Labyrinth of Solitude: Life and Thought in Mexico.* New York: Grove/Atlantic Inc., Grove Press, 1961. Paz has no peer when it comes to expositions of the Mexican psyche, and this is his best work. Out of print.

Robertson, Tomás. *Baja California and Its Missions.* Glendale, CA: La Siesta Press, 1978. Robertson was the patriarch of an old Baja California–Sinaloa family of northern European extraction as well as a patron of Baja mission restoration. His useful amateur work synthesizes Baja mission history from several sources; like its sources, the book contains a few minor contradictions and muddy areas. Out of print.

NATURAL HISTORY AND FIELD GUIDES

Case, T. J., and M. L. Cody, eds. *A New Island Biogeography in the Sea of Cortez,* 2nd Ed. Oxford University Press, 2002. An updated and revised (from the 1983 original) collection of essays on the geography and wildlife of various Cortez islands.

Edwards, Ernest Preston. *The Birds of Mexico and Adjacent Areas.* Austin: University of Texas Press, 1998. A field guide to birds of Mexico, Belize, Guatemala, and El Salvador, with excellent illustrations and detailed descriptions for easy identification of all of Mexico's regular species.

Gotshall, Daniell W. *Sea of Cortez Marine Animals: A Guide to the Common Fishes and Invertebrates Baja California to Panama.* Sea Challengers, 1998. A good reference guide to divers, sailors, and snorkelers.

Krutch, Joseph Wood. *The Forgotten Peninsula: A Naturalist in Baja California.* Tucson: University of Arizona Press, 1986 (reprint from 1961). Combines natural history and a curmudgeonly travelogue style to paint a romantic portrait of pre–Transpeninsular Highway Baja.

Leatherwood, S., and R. R. Reeves. *The Sierra Club Handbook of Whales and Dolphins.* San Francisco: Sierra Club Books, 1983. A useful field guide for identifying cetaceans in Baja seas.

Nickerson, Roy. *The Friendly Whales: A Whalewatcher's Guide to the Gray Whales of Baja California.* San Francisco: Chronicle Books, 1987. A light study, with photographs, of the friendly whale phenomenon in Laguna San Ignacio, where gray whales often initiate contact with humans. Out of print.

Peterson, R. T., and E. L. Chaliff. *A Field Guide to Mexican Birds.* Boston: Houghton Mifflin Co., 1999. Although it may be a little weak on birds found in Baja, this updated edition is still one of the best handbooks for identifying Mexican bird life.

Roberts, Norman C. *Baja California Plant Field Guide.* Natural History Publishing Co., 1989. Contains concise descriptions of more than 550 species of Baja flora, more than half illustrated by color photos.

Scammon, Charles Melville. *The Marine Mammals of the Northwestern Coast of America.* Mineola, NY: Dover Publications reprint, 1968. Originally published in the 19th century by the whaler who almost brought about the gray whale's complete demise, this is *the* classic, pioneering work on Pacific cetaceans, including the gray whale. Out of print.

Thomson, Donald A. and Lloyd T. Findley, Alex N. Kerstitch. *Reef Fishes of the Sea of Cortez: The Rocky-Shore Fishes of the Gulf of California. Revised Edition.* University of Texas Press, 2000. Produced by an ecologist, a taxonomist, and an artist-photographer, the new version of this 1979 reference guide gives Spanish (and English) names for fish.

Wiggins, Ira L. *Flora of Baja California.* Stanford, CA: Stanford University Press, 1980. This weighty work, with listings of more than 2,900 species, is a must for the serious botanist. But for the average layperson with an interest in Baja vegetation, Norman Roberts's *Baja California Plant Field Guide* (see above) will more than suffice.

Zwinger, Ann Raymond. *A Desert Country near the Sea.* New York: Penguin USA, Truman M. Talley Books, 1983. A collection of poetic essays centered around Baja natural history (including a rare passage on the Sierra de La Laguna), with sketches by the author and an appendix with Latin names for flora and fauna. Out of print.

SPORTS AND RECREATION

Fons, Valerie. *Keep It Moving: Baja by Canoe.* Seattle: The Mountaineers, 1986. Well-written account of a canoe trip along the Baja California coastline; recommended reading for sea kayakers as well as canoeists. Out of print.

Kelly, Neil, and Gene Kira. *The Baja Catch: A Fishing, Travel & Remote Camping Manual for Baja California,* 3rd Ed. Valley Center, CA: Apples and Oranges, 1997. Contains extensive discussions of lures and tackle, expert fishing techniques, and detailed directions to productive fisheries, plus numerous maps.

Lehman, Charles. *Desert Survival Handbook,* Revised Ed. Phoenix: Primer Publishers, 1998. A no-nonsense guide to desert survival

techniques; should be included in every pilot's or coastal navigator's kit.

Parise, Mike. *The Surfer's Guide to Baja.* Surfpress Publishing, 2001. A must-have resource for Baja-bound surfers, the guide includes detailed directions to more than 75 breaks along the peninsula, plus maps and wave height charts.

Romano-Lax, Andromeda. *Sea Kayaking in Baja.* Berkeley, CA: Wilderness Press, 1993. This inspiring 153-page guide to Baja kayaking contains 15 one- to five-day paddling routes along the Baja coastline, plus many helpful hints on kayak camping. Each route is accompanied by a map; although these maps are too sketchy to be used for navigation, a list of Mexican topographic map numbers is provided so that readers can go out and obtain more accurate material. Out of print.

Tsegeletos, George. *Under the Sea of Cortez (Early Underwater Exploration and Spearfishing).* Chapel Hill, NC: Professional Press, 1998. Early in this case means starting in 1962, and the accounts make for fascinating, if a bit sorrowful (knowing how much marinelife has been lost in just 40 years), reading. Out of print.

Williams, Jack. *Baja Boater's Guide, Vols. I and II.* Sausalito, CA: H. J. Williams Publications, 2001 (Vol. I, 3rd Ed.) and 2003 (Vol. II, 4th Ed.). These ambitious guides, one each on the Pacific Ocean and the Sea of Cortez, contain useful aerial photos and sketch maps of Baja's continental islands and coastline.

Wong, Bonnie. *Bicycling Baja.* El Cajon, CA: Sunbelt Publications, 1988. Written by an experienced leader of Baja cycling tours, this book includes helpful suggestions on trip preparation, equipment, and riding techniques, as well as road logs for 17 different cycling routes throughout the peninsula. Out of print.

Wyatt, Michael. *The Basic Essentials of Sea Kayaking,* 3rd Ed. Falcon, 2005. A good introduction to sea kayaking, with tips on buying gear, paddling techniques, and safety.

REAL ESTATE AND LIVING ABROAD

Luboff, Ken. *Living Abroad in Mexico.* Emeryville, CA: Avalon Travel Publishing, 2005. This resource gives advice and tips for Americans thinking of moving to Mexico.

Peyton, Dennis John. *How to Buy Real Estate in Mexico.* San Diego: Law Mexico Publishing, 2006. The most thorough and in-depth reference available in English on buying Mexican property. Anyone considering real estate investments in Mexico should read this book before making any decisions.

Internet Resources

Most of the travel information you find on the Web today is clearly tailored to selling a tourism product—hotel, condo, restaurant, sports activity—without offering related information of much use. And many of these sites were designed in the mid-1990s and haven't been redesigned since. Forums, in which impassioned participants voice their many opinions, are a notable exception.

Baja.com
www.baja.com
One of the earliest Baja-focused online communities still ranks among the highest in traffic.

Baja Books and Maps
www.bajabooksandmaps.com
Online bookstore with an impressive collection of Baja-related titles.

Baja Bush Pilots
www.bajabushpilots.com
A must-read for pilots interested in flying a private aircraft to Baja.

Baja Nomad
www.bajanomad.com
Still the best all-around Baja site for hard information that doesn't appear to have been paid for, with more nitty-gritty information than any rival. Great links page, copious information on hotels and restaurants, plus continually updated Baja news and essays.

BajaQuest
www.bajaquest.com
Mainly classified listings, with several active discussion boards.

Baja Travel Guide
www.bajatravel.com
An advertiser-driven site covering all of Baja, with telephone listings, maps, and calendar of events.

Cruise the Sea of Cortez
www.cruisecortez.com
A site for people who sail or who would like to sail the Cortez. Although the home page says the site was last updated in 2003, the message-board has a number of current posts.

In Search of the Blue Agave
www.ianchadwick.com/tequila
An excellent website devoted to tequila connoisseurship, though it hasn't been updated in several years.

Instituto Nacional de Estadística, Geografía e Informática
www.inegi.gob.mx
This Mexican government agency publishes statistics on population and economics for all of Mexico, as well as complete topographical maps. Spanish only.

iWindsurf.com and iKitesurf.com
www.iwindsurf.com
www.ikitesurf.com
Daily Baja wind forecast and reports for

windsurfers, plus a whole range of consumer weather delivery services, from the parent company WeatherFlow.

Los Cabos Guide
www.loscabosguide.com

Relatively up-to-date, advertiser-driven listings of hospitality and tourism businesses in the Los Cabos area, with some coverage of the East Cape and Todos Santos.

Mexico Online
www.mexonline.com/baja.htm

Advertiser-driven site that hosts home pages for many Baja businesses.

Mr.News.Mx
www.mrnewsmx.com

A news digest for Mexico news in English from many sources.

NaftaNet
www.nafta-sec-alena.org

Information pertinent to the North American Free Trade Agreement.

Olsen Currency Converter
www.oanda.com/converter/travel

For fast quotes on exchange rates for all international currencies, including the Mexican peso. Print out a "cheat sheet" to make easy conversions without having to do any math.

Sunbelt Publications
www.sunbeltpub.com

This book publisher specializing in upper and lower California has an online catalog of its Baja titles.

U.S. Embassy
http://mexico.usembassy.gov

Contains the home page for the U.S. Embassy in Mexico City, with information on consular services to U.S. citizens as well as State Department warnings.

Index

M

Acknowledgments

Besides our own adventures, family, friends, and kindred spirits contributed their many travel experiences to shape this edition of *Moon Baja*. Adrienne Mohadjerin and Kristina Curtis accompanied us to Cabo San Lucas for their first spring break and lived to tell the tale. Susan Harper came along for a fun-filled week in San José del Cabo. Sandra and Vinny Creta abandoned family in Phoenix to spend Thanksgiving in Los Cabos—and got the lowdown on Mexican fire opals.

Hally and Greg Bayer recalled details of their first Cape Region tour and reported on a New Year's trip to Rosarito. Judy and Kellen Glinder contributed photos from Todos Santos. Kristi Kull sent notes from a first trip to Los Cabos, while newlywed Jennifer Librach shared advice on planning a Los Cabos destination wedding.

Photographer Tomas Spangler lent the use of his beautiful Baja images and also reported from the road. Steve Dryden filled us in on new the latest happenings in the Valle de Guadalupe, and Jeff Nordahl helped us understand the ins and outs of Mexican car insurance.

Many Baja residents helped us separate fact from fiction this time around. Cecilia Moller told us about the hot new places in La Paz, while Nancy Delerey enlightened us on the current real estate climate there. Tim Hatler sent detailed notes from nearby La Ventana. And we commiserated with Los Barriles retiree Lon Fitter while stuck in traffic outside Los Barriles during the weekend of the Baja 1000.

Over the past couple of years, we've enjoyed several chances to socialize with new friends in Cabo Pulmo, Marly Rickers and Clint Fultz, as well as dive instructors Carmel Lamar and Pablo Nobili. In Loreto, Jeannine Perez clued us in to new hotels and restaurants while we browsed her wonderful collection of books about Baja.

Alessandra and Enrico Ugolini introduced us to Todos Santos years ago, inviting us to sample produce from their garden and teaching us how to fish from the beach. On our most recent visit, Don Mitchell and Alicia Dufaux filled us in on recent developments in town and gave us sweets for the road. Lynne Cummings and Howard Ekman generously helped complete our coverage of the area.

Special thanks to Joe Cummings for the many years of research and on-the-ground reporting that have made *Moon Baja* the comprehensive and authoritative guide it is today. It is going to be a tough act to follow. The friendly and capable team at Avalon, led by editor Kathryn Ettinger, helped transform raw text files into a printable manuscript.

On a personal note, Paul Itoi shouldered much of the weight of the project, logging thousands of miles behind the wheel as we ventured up and down the peninsula—and later, hours in front of the computer as we worked our way through maps and manuscript. His passion for outdoor adventure prompted our first trip to Baja California nearly a decade ago and has shaped our coverage of sports and recreation in this edition.

Baby Emmett Itoi completed his first international road trip at the age of five months. He let us dip his feet in the Pacific at Playa Los Cerritos, rode patiently in the backpack while we walked through towns, and made friends at just about every stop. We could not have imagined a more perfect travel companion.

www.moon.com

For helpful advice on planning a trip, visit www.moon.com for the **TRAVEL PLANNER** and get access to useful travel strategies and valuable information about great places to visit. When you travel with Moon, expect an experience that is uncommon and truly unique.

HANDBOOKS | METRO | OUTDOORS | LIVING ABROAD

MAP SYMBOLS

≈≈≈ Expressway	**◖** Highlight	✗ Airfield	⚲ Golf Course
— Primary Road	○ City/Town	✈ Airport	**P** Parking Area
⋯ Secondary Road	◉ State Capital	▲ Mountain	⬟ Archaeological Site
‑ ‑ ‑ Unpaved Road	⊛ National Capital	✦ Unique Natural Feature	⛪ Church
‑ ‑ ‑ Trail	★ Point of Interest		⛽ Gas Station
⋯⋯ Ferry	• Accommodation	🦋 Waterfall	Glacier
┼┼┼ Railroad	▼ Restaurant/Bar	⚑ Park	Mangrove
▰▰▰ Pedestrian Walkway	▪ Other Location	⬛ Trailhead	Reef
⬛⬛⬛ Stairs	△ Campground	⛷ Skiing Area	Swamp

CONVERSION TABLES

$$°C = (°F - 32) / 1.8$$
$$°F = (°C \times 1.8) + 32$$
1 inch = 2.54 centimeters (cm)
1 foot = 0.304 meters (m)
1 yard = 0.914 meters
1 mile = 1.6093 kilometers (km)
1 km = 0.6214 miles
1 fathom = 1.8288 m
1 chain = 20.1168 m
1 furlong = 201.168 m
1 acre = 0.4047 hectares
1 sq km = 100 hectares
1 sq mile = 2.59 square km
1 ounce = 28.35 grams
1 pound = 0.4536 kilograms
1 short ton = 0.90718 metric ton
1 short ton = 2,000 pounds
1 long ton = 1.016 metric tons
1 long ton = 2,240 pounds
1 metric ton = 1,000 kilograms
1 quart = 0.94635 liters
1 US gallon = 3.7854 liters
1 Imperial gallon = 4.5459 liters
1 nautical mile = 1.852 km

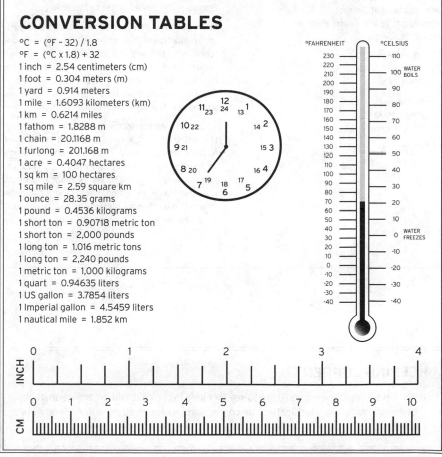

MOON BAJA

Avalon Travel Publishing
a member of the Perseus Books Group
1400 65th Street, Suite 250
Emeryville, CA 94608, USA
www.moon.com

Editor and Series Manager: Kathryn Ettinger
Copy Editor: Kay Elliott
Graphics Coordinator: Stefano Boni
Production Coordinator: Tabitha Lahr
Cover Designer: Stefano Boni
Cartography Director: Mike Morgenfeld
Map Editor: Albert Angulo
Cartographer: Kat Bennett
Proofreader: Valerie Sellers Blanton
Indexer: Judy Hunt

ISBN-10: 1-56691-800-6
ISBN-13: 978-1-56691-800-8
ISSN: 1098-6685

Printing History
1st Edition – 1992
7th Edition – October 2007
5 4 3 2 1

Text © 2007 by Joe Cummings and Avalon Travel
Publishing, Inc.
Maps © 2007 by Avalon Travel Publishing, Inc.
All rights reserved.

Some photos and illustrations are used by permission
and are the property of the original copyright
owners.

Front cover photo: © Mike Brinson/Getty Images
Title page photo: © Tomas Spangler Photography
Interior photos: page 8, © Nikki Goth Itoi; page 9, 10
© Paul Itoi; page 11, © HowardEkmanPhotography
.com; page 12, © JimCline.com

Printed in the United States by Worzalla

KEEPING CURRENT

If you have a favorite gem you'd like to see included in the next edition, or see anything that needs updating, clarification, or correction, please drop us a line. Send your comments via email to feedback@moon.com, or use the address above.